Psychology

MYERS IN MODULES

Psychology
MYERS IN MODULES

SIXTH EDITION

DAVID G. MYERS

HOPE COLLEGE
HOLLAND, MICHIGAN

WORTH PUBLISHERS

To Catherine Woods

whose bold, warm, and creative
support enabled this book

Psychology, Myers in Modules, sixth edition

Copyright © 2001 by Worth Publishers
All rights reserved.
Printed in the United States of America.
ISBN: 1-57259-980-4
Printing: 5 4 3 2
Year: 04 03 02 01

Publisher: Catherine Woods
Development Editors: Christine Brune, Nancy Fleming
Senior Marketing Manager: Renée Altier
Associate Managing Editor: Tracey Kuehn
Project Editor: Margaret Comaskey
Production Manager: Barbara Anne Seixas
Art Director, Text and Cover Design: Barbara Reingold
Assistant Designer and Layout: Lee Ann Mahler
Photo Researcher: Tobi Zausner
Illustration Coordinator: Lou Capaldo
Cover and Chapter Opener Illustrations: John Collier © 2000
Illustrations: Alan Reingold, B. K. Taylor, Shawn Kenny, Bonnie Hofkin, and
    Demetrios Zangos
Composition: TSI Graphics, Inc.
Printing and Binding: Courier Kendallville, Inc.

Illustration and photo credits begin on page IC-1 and constitute an extension of the copyright page.

All royalties from the sale of this book are assigned to the David and Carol Myers Foundation, which
exists to receive and distribute funds to other charitable organizations.

Library of Congress Cataloging-in-Publication Data
Myers, David G.
    Psychology / David G. Myers.—6th ed., in modules.
      p. cm.
    Includes bibliographical references and indexes.
    ISBN 1-57259-980-4
      1. Psychology.   I. Title.
    BF121 .M94 2000b
    150—dc21   99-087967

Worth Publishers
41 Madison Avenue
New York, NY 10010
www.worthpublishers.com

About the Author

David G. Myers
is professor of psychology at Michigan's Hope College, where he has spent his career and been voted "outstanding professor" by students. His writings have appeared in five dozen journals and magazines, from *Science* to *Scientific American*, and in a dozen books. For more information on Myers and his writings, visit www.davidmyers.org.

Contents in Brief

Contents

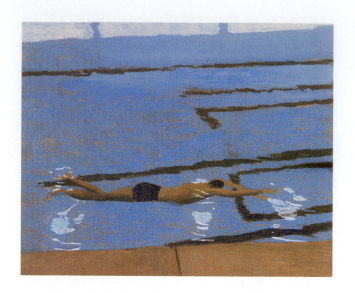

Preface

Why Modular?

This new, 55-module version of my *Psychology,* sixth edition, is a longtime wish come true. It breaks out of the box by restructuring the text into a buffet of (a) short, digestible chapters (called modules), that (b) can be selected and assigned in any order.

Have we not all heard the familiar student complaint: "The chapters are too long!" Our typical 30- to 50-page chapters cannot be read in a single sitting before the eyes grow weary and the mind wanders. So why not parse the material into readable units? Ask your students whether they would prefer a 700-page book to be organized as fourteen 50-page chapters or as fifty 14-page chapters. You may be surprised at their overwhelming support for shorter chapters. Indeed, students digest material better when they process in smaller chunks—as "spaced" rather than massed practice.

I have equally often heard from instructors bemoaning the fact that they "just can't get to everything" in the book. Sometimes professors want to cover certain sections in a traditional, long chapter but not others. For example, in the typical States of Consciousness chapter, someone may want to cover Sleep and Hypnosis but not Drugs. In *Myers in Modules,* instructors could easily choose to cover Module 17, Waking and Sleeping Rhythms, and Module 18, Hypnosis, but not Module 19, Drugs and Consciousness.

How Is This Different from *Psychology,* Sixth Edition?

So, what are the primary differences between this book and *Psychology,* sixth edition? They are organization, independence of the modules, and pedagogy.

Organization

Myers in Modules really IS *Psychology,* sixth edition—just in a different format. So, *Myers in Modules* contains all the updated research and innovative new coverage from *Psychology,* sixth edition. A very few sections have moved around to accommodate the modular structure. For example, "Rates of Psychological Disorders" is a separate section at the end of the Psychological Disorders chapter in *Psychology,* sixth edition, but it is covered in the first of the Psychological Disorders modules in *Myers in Modules.* And "Selective Attention" is covered at the beginning of the Perception chapter in *Psychology,* sixth edition, but is covered at the beginning of the Sensation/Perception group of modules for *Myers in Modules* (in Module 11, Introduction to Sensation and Perception).

The Modules Are Independent

Each module in this book is now self-standing rather than dependent upon the others. Cross references to other modules have been replaced with brief explanations. In some cases, illustrations or key terms are repeated to avoid possible confusion. No assumptions are made about what students have read prior to each module. This independence gives instructors ultimate flexibility in deciding which modules to use, and in what order.

Table 1 Coverage of Evolution and Behavior Genetics

In addition to the coverage found in new Modules 5 and 6, the **evolutionary perspective** is covered on the following pages; module number is in parentheses.

Aging, pp. 153–154 (10)

Anxiety disorders, pp. 560–562 (44)

Attraction, p. 712 (55)

Biological predispositions in learning, pp. 295–297 (20), 311 (21)

Charles Darwin, p. 2 (1)

Electromagnetic spectrum, sensitivity to, pp. 178–179 (12)

Emotional expression, p. 172 (11)

Evolutionary perspective, defined, p. 6 (1)

Fear, p. 491 (38)

Hearing, p. 190 (13)

Instincts, p. 436 (33)

Intelligence, pp. 427–429 (32)

Language, pp. 383–386 (29)

Love, p. 162 (10)

Need to belong, p. 460 (35)

Overconfidence, pp. 373–375 (28)

Sensation, p. 170 (11), p. 199–200 (14)

Sensory adaptation, p. 174 (11)

Signal detection theory, p. 171 (11)

Sleep, pp. 250–253 (17)

Stress and the immune system, pp. 646–647 (52)

In addition to the coverage found in new Modules 5 and 6, **behavior genetics** is covered on the following pages; module number is in parentheses.

Abuse, intergenerational transmission of, p. 317 (22)

Aggression, p. 699 (55)

Biomedical therapies, pp. 619–624 (50)

Body type, p. 517 (40)

Depth perception, pp. 213–214 (15)

Drives and incentives, p. 437 (33)

Drug use, pp. 280–284 (19)

Emotion and cognition, pp. 477–478 (37)

Fear, pp. 490–492 (38)

Happiness, pp. 498–499 (38)

Intelligence, pp. 416–418 (31), p. 422–424 (32)

Learning, pp. 295–297 (20), 311 (21)

Obesity and weight control, pp. 665–666 (52)

Perception, pp. 224–231 (16)

Personality traits, pp. 518–520 (40)

Psychological disorders:

anxiety disorders, pp. 560, 562 (44)

bio-psycho-social perspective, p. 550 (43)

depression, pp. 572–573 (47)

personality disorders, pp. 566–567 (45)

schizophrenia, pp. 584–585 (47)

Romantic love, pp. 162–163 (10)

Sexuality, pp. 448–455 (35)

Sexual orientation, p. 458 (35)

Smell, pp. 204–206 (14)

Stress, personality, and illness, pp. 640–648 (52)

New SQ3R Pedagogy

Myers in Modules also includes helpful SQ3R pedagogy. Clearly hierarchical headings allow students to scan ahead to *survey* what's to come. Each main section of text starts with a Preview *Question* that alerts students to the key concepts to focus on while *reading* that section. The "Review and Reflect" sections at the end of each module contain five parts that encourage *rehearsing* and *reviewing* concepts learned: First, the Preview Questions are repeated and then answered in paragraph form as a review of the module. Second, all key terms from that module are listed in order of appearance with page references. Third, several Test Yourself questions in multiple-choice format help students determine whether they have learned the concepts from that module. Fourth, at least one Review question tests students on the take-home message(s) from that module. Fifth, at least one Reflect question gets students to apply what they're learning to their own lives, with the idea that making the concepts personally meaningful will make them memorable for students. Answers to the Test Yourself and Review questions can be found at the end of the book.

What's New Since *Psychology,* Fifth Edition?

This new edition retains its predecessor's voice and much of its content and organization. Yet change is reflected on every page. In addition to the 800 new references in this edition and updates on every page, I have introduced the following major changes to this sixth edition.

NEW: Two Modules Cover the Nature and Nurture of Behavior

Introducing psychology in the new millennium calls for an understanding of the relative effects of nature and nurture on so many of our behaviors. These new modules: 5, Genetic Influences on Behavior, and 6, Environmental Influences on Behavior, in-

Table 2 Coverage of the Psychology of Men and Women

Coverage of the psychology of women and men can be found on the following pages; module number is in parentheses.

Arousal in REM sleep, p. 249 (17)

Behavioral effects of gender, p. 38 (2)

Biological sex/gender, pp. 109–110 (6)

Body image, pp. 444–447 (34)

Depression, p. 571 (47)

Dieting, p. 667 (52)

Dream content, p. 255 (17)

Eating disorders, pp. 444–447 (34)

Emotional expression, pp. 482–483 (38)

Empty nest, p. 163 (10)

Freud's views, p. 507 (39)

Gender and childrearing, p. 112 (6)

Gender roles, pp. 110–111 (6)

Generic pronoun "he," pp. 390–392 (29)

Happiness, p. 499 (38)

Heart disease, p. 636 (51)

Help-receiving, p. 717 (55)

Hormones and

aggression, p. 700 (55)

sexual behavior, pp. 450–451 (35)

sexual development, pp. 118 (7), 142–143 (9)

Immune system, p. 638 (51)

Intelligence, pp. 429–431 (32)

Leadership, p. 469 (36)

Life expectancy, p. 154 (10)

Maturation, pp. 142–143 (9)

Menarche, p. 143 (9)

Menopause, pp. 152–153 (10)

Midlife crisis, p. 161 (10)

Pornography, p. 451 (35)

Psychological disorders, rates of, pp. 553, 555 (43)

Rape, pp. 300 (20), 704–707 (55)

Sexual disorders, p. 452 (35)

Sexual fantasies, p. 242 (17)

Sexuality, pp. 451–455 (35)

Sexual orientation, pp. 455–459 (35)

Smoking, p. 659 (52)

Social connectedness, pp. 148–149 (9)

Stereotyping, pp. 230–231 (16)

Suicide, p. 574 (46)

Weight discrimination, pp. 662–663 (52)

Women and work, pp. 163–164 (10)

Women in psychology, p. 9 (1)

Table 3 Coverage of Culture and Multicultural Experience

Coverage of culture and multicultural experience permeates the book in the following discussions; module number is in parentheses.

Aggression, p. 702 (55)

Aging population, p. 154 (10)

Alcoholism, p. 553 (43)

Anger, pp. 492–493 (38)

Attractiveness, p. 712 (55)

Behavioral effects of culture, pp. 37–38 (2)

Conformity, p. 684 (54)

Corporal punishment practices, pp. 307–309 (21)

Culture context effects, pp. 230–231 (16)

Culture shock, p. 533 (41), 540 (42)

Deaf culture, pp. 75 (4), 195–197 (13), 383, 388, 390, 391 (29)

Depression, pp. 571–572 (47)

Development:

adolescence, pp. 141–150 (9)

attachment, pp. 136–137 (8)

child-rearing, p. 108 (6)

cognitive development, pp. 143–144 (9)

developmental similarities, p. 109 (6)

fetal alcohol syndrome, p. 120 (7)

moral development, pp. 144–146 (9)

motor development, p. 124 (8)

social development, p. 131 (8)

Dieting, p. 667 (52)

Drugs, psychological effects of, p. 274 (19)

Emotion:

experiencing, p. 490 (38)

expressing, pp. 487–488 (38)

Human diversity/kinship, pp. 37–38 (2)

Hunger, p. 444 (34)

Individualism/collectivism, pp. 533–535 (41)

Intelligence, pp. 412–413 (31), 427–429 (32)

Language, pp. 383–384, 390–392 (29)

Life expectancy, p. 154 (10)

Management styles, pp. 469–470 (36)

Marriage, pp. 162–163 (10)

Obesity, pp. 662–663 (52)

Participative management, pp. 469–470 (36)

People with disabilities, pp. 494, 498 (38)

Perception, pp. 220–221 (15), 231 (16)

Personal space, p. 107 (6)

Prejudice prototypes, pp. 366–367 (28)

Psychological disorders, pp. 550, 553 (43)

dissociative identity disorder, p. 565 (45)

eating disorders, pp. 444–447 (34)

schizophrenia, pp. 583–584 (47)

Psychotherapy, p. 617 (49)

Self-esteem, p. 530 (41)

Self-serving bias, pp. 531–533 (41)

Sensory restriction, pp. 225–226 (16)

Sexual orientation, pp. 455–456 (35)

Sexual standards, pp. 453–455 (35)

Size-distance relationship, pp. 220–222 (15)

Smoking, pp. 658–659 (52)

Social clock, p. 161 (10)

Social-cultural perspective, p. 6 (1)

Suicide, p. 574 (46)

Teen sexuality, pp. 453–455 (35)

Testing bias, pp. 431–432 (32)

Work-related values, p. 161 (10)

See also Modules 53–55 on Social Psychology

troduce students to the nature and nurture concepts that they will encounter throughout psychology. I have taken a developmental approach, attempting to weave new thinking and research—from evolutionary psychology and behavior genetics on the "nature" side, and gender and cultural influences on the "nurture" side—into a coherent story of the origins of our human kinship and our human diversity. Later modules will apply these concepts when considering topics such as the evolutionary psychology of sleep, the genetics of altruism, gender and intelligence domains, and culture and physique. For a complete list of integrated coverage of these issues, see Table 1, Table 2, and Table 3.

Increasingly Global Perspective on Psychology

For this and succeeding editions I also am working to offer a world-based psychology for our worldwide student readership. Thus, I continually search the world for research findings and text and photo examples, conscious that readers may be in Melbourne, Sheffield, Vancouver, or Nairobi. North American and European examples come easily, given that I reside in the United States, maintain contact with friends and colleagues in Canada, subscribe to several European periodicals, and live periodically in the United Kingdom. But this edition also offers 56 mentions of Australia and New Zealand. We are all citizens of a shrinking world, thanks to increased migration and the growing global economy. Thus, American students, too, benefit from information and examples that internationalize their awareness. And if psychology seeks to explain *human* behavior (not just American or Canadian or Australian behavior), the broader the scope of studies presented, the more accurate is our picture of this world's people. My aim is to expose all students to the world beyond their own country. Thus, I continue to welcome input and suggestions from all readers.

Enhanced Critical Thinking Coverage

I introduce students to critical thinking in a very natural way throughout the book, with even more in this edition to encourage active learning of critical thinking principles.

+ *Module 2 takes a unique, critical thinking approach to introducing students to psychology's research methods,* emphasizing the fallacies of our everyday intuition and common sense and, thus, the need for psychological science. Critical thinking is introduced as a key term in this module (p. 16). New to this module is a section titled "Statistical Reasoning," which encourages students to "focus on thinking smarter by applying simple statistical principles to everyday reasoning" (pp. 30–33).

+ *Thinking Critically About . . ." boxes* are found throughout the book, modeling for students a critical approach to some key issues in psychology. For example, see "Thinking Critically About: The Death Penalty—When Beliefs Collide With Psychological Science" (p. 43) or "Thinking Critically About: Do Video Games Teach or Release Violence?" (which is new to this edition) p. 705. The book's table of contents provides a complete list of these boxes.

+ *Detective-style stories* throughout the narrative get students thinking critically about psychology's key research questions.

+ *"Apply this" style questions and activities* and *"Think about it" style discussions* keep students active in their study of each module.

+ *Critical examinations of pop psychology* spark interest and provide important lessons in thinking critically about everyday topics.

    See Table 4 for a complete list of this text's coverage of critical thinking topics.

Statistical Methods Now Covered in Module 2

In an effort to complete Module 2's story of Research Strategies: How Psychologists Ask and Answer Questions, I have incorporated a concise version of the previous edition's Statistics Appendix. This new coverage explains what psychologists *do* with data after collecting it—how we interpret data with statistics—and why statistical reasoning is so important in everyday life. Now a friendly introduction to statistical methods is available to students right up front—where they need to know it.

Table 4 Critical Thinking Topics

Critical thinking coverage can be found on the following pages; module number is in parentheses.

Thinking Critically About . . . boxes:

Hot and Cold Streaks in Basketball and the Stock Market, p. 27 (2)

The Death Penalty—When Beliefs Collide with Psychological Science, p. 43 (2)

Left Brain/Right Brain, pp. 78–79 (4)

Mind Over Matter: Firewalking, p. 201 (14)

PMS, p. 244 (17)

Hypnotic Age Regression: A True Story, p. 264 (18)

Risks—When Statistics Clash with Heuristics, p. 372 (28)

Lie Detection, p. 484 (38)

How to Be a "Successful" Astrologer or Palm Reader, p. 522 (40)

Insanity and Responsibility, p. 554 (43)

"Regressing" from Unusual to Usual, p. 608 (49)

Alternative Medicine: New Ways to Health or Old Snake Oil?, pp. 652–663 (52)

Do Video Games Teach or Release Violence?, p. 705 (55)

Critical Examinations of Pop Psychology:

Perceiving order in random events, pp. 24–26 (2)

Can subliminal tapes improve your life?, pp. 29–30 (2), p. 172 (11)

Do we use only 10 percent of our brains?, p. 69 (4)

Critiquing the evolutionary explanation, pp. 91–92 (5)

How great is the power of parenting?, pp. 105–106 (6)

Sensory restriction, pp. 225–226 (16)

Is there extrasensory perception?, pp. 231–236 (16)

Can hypnosis enhance recall? Coerce action? Be therapeutic? Alleviate pain?, pp. 260–266 (18)

Has the concept of "addiction" been stretched too far?, pp. 270–272 (19)

Near-death experiences, p. 278 (19)

Discerning true and false memories, pp. 355–360 (27)

Do animals exhibit language?, pp. 395–398 (29)

Is repression a myth?, pp. 512–513 (39)

How valid is the Rorschach test?, pp. 509–510 (39)

Is Freud credible?, pp. 514–515 (39)

The Wounds of War: Post-traumatic stress disorder, p. 561 (44)

Is psychotherapy effective?, pp. 606–607 (49)

Evaluating alternative therapies, pp. 611–613 (49)

Is aerobic exercise therapeutic?, pp. 644–646 (52)

Spirituality and faith communities, pp. 651, 654–655 (52)

Thinking Critically with Psychological Science (the entirety of Module 2):

The limits of intuition and common sense, p. 12

"Critical thinking" introduced as a key term, p. 16

The scientific attitude, pp. 15–16

The scientific method, pp. 16–17

Correlation and causation, p. 23

Illusory correlation, pp. 23–24

Statistical reasoning, pp. 30–33

Evaluating therapies, pp. 28–29

Making inferences, pp. 32–33

Scientific Detective Stories:

Language in the brain, pp. 70–71 (4)

Our divided brains, pp. 72–76 (4)

The case of the disappearing southpaws, pp. 77–79 (4)

The twin and adoption studies, pp. 92–96 (5)

How a child's mind develops, pp. 125–131 (8)

Aging and intelligence, pp. 158–160 (10)

Parallel processing, pp. 184–186 (12)

How do we see in color? pp. 186–188 (12)

The puzzles of perceptual illusions, pp. 208–210 (15)

Why do we sleep?, pp. 250–253 (17)

Why do we dream?, pp. 256–257 (17)

Is hypnosis an altered state of consciousness?, pp. 266–268 (18)

How do we store memories in our brains?, pp. 336–341 (25)

Memory construction, pp. 352–360 (27)

Do animals exhibit language?, pp. 395–398 (29)

Is intelligence neurologically measurable?, pp. 405–406 (30)

Why do we feel hunger?, pp. 440–443 (34)

What determines sexual orientation?, pp. 456–459 (35)

The pursuit of happiness: Who is happy, and why?, pp. 493–499 (38)

Self-esteem versus self-serving bias, pp. 529–533 (41)

What causes mood disorders?, pp. 571–578 (46)

Do prenatal viral infections increase risk of schizophrenia?, pp. 583–584 (47)

Is psychotherapy effective?, pp. 606–610 (49)

Why—and in whom—does stress contribute to heart disease?, pp. 635–637 (51)

How and why is social support linked with health?, pp. 648–651 (52)

Why do people fail to help in emergencies?, pp. 716–717 (55)

New, Comprehensive Online Teaching and Learning Resources

Wonderful new online resources authored by Thomas Ludwig (Hope College) and a team of contributors are keyed to the organization and coverage of *Myers in Modules: Psychology,* sixth edition. With PsychOnline, you pick and choose from a buffet of resources that can be used as a complete online course or a component of a more traditional lecture-based course.

Choose from over 100 **interactive Tutorials**, which review the key concepts in each module. Dozens of **Demonstrations, Simulations, Critical Thinking Activities**, and data-collecting **Research Projects** give students an opportunity to learn the core concepts hands-on (Figure 1). Students have many opportunities for review. PsychOnline includes hundreds of periodic **Concept Checks** within the Tutorials, a **Practice Quiz** at the end of each Tutorial, key concept **Flashcards**, and drag-and-drop—style **labeling** of anatomical and other art.

PsychOnline includes an **Instructor's Resource Library**, with numerous illustrations available in an easy-to-pick-up format for lecture presentations, and the complete *Myers in Modules: Psychology,* sixth edition, Test Bank.

Additional resources within PsychOnline include

+ **Psychology in the News**—summaries of general news and journal news about human behavior,

+ **Psychology in Everyday Life**—stories, jokes, and anecdotes related to teaching and learning specific, important topics in the introductory course,

+ **Psychology Around the Globe**—cross-cultural and international applications,

+ **Psychology on the Web**—carefully selected, informative sites keyed to important topics in the Myers book,

FIGURE 1 PsychOnline Sample Screens

The video in the screen at left (from the "Cognitive Development in Infancy and Childhood" tutorial) allows students to watch a baby displaying the beginnings of object permanence. At right (from a Demonstration activity in the "Color Vision" tutorial), students can interact with wavelength, cone response, and experienced hue until they understand how and why they affect each other. Note in both screens that there is always just enough text to put the images and interactions into a meaningful context for students.

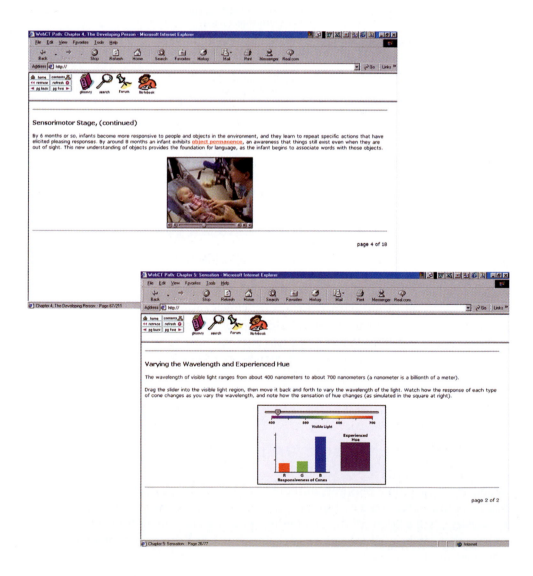

+ the **Psychology Testing Center**—making it easy for instructors to create and administer secure quizzes and exams over the Web on the material in *Myers in Modules: Psychology,* sixth edition, and

+ the **Psychology Forum**—with discussion topics, organized by text module, designed to encourage student participation.

Trademark Features

As a reporter, there is no beat I'd rather cover than psychology. Week by week, new information surprises us with discoveries about how the brain's chemical messengers control moods, about animal abilities, about unconscious ("automatic") thinking, about the roots and fruits of happiness, about the effects of stress on our capacity to fight disease. Indeed, this book, following the field, has changed dramatically since I set to work on the first edition nearly 20 years ago. Today's psychological science is more attuned to the relative effects of nature and nurture, to gender and cultural diversity, and to the neuroscience revolution. We today can also harness new ways to present information, both in books and via electronic media. These changes are exhilarating! Keeping up with new discoveries and technologies fills each day and connects me with many colleagues and friends.

The thousands of instructors and millions of students across the globe who have studied this book have contributed immensely to its development. Much of this has occurred spontaneously, through correspondence and conversations. For this edition, we also welcomed extensive input on design and pedagogy from twelve instructors and their students, and we solicited nearly six dozen other content reviews from teaching psychologists and researchers around the world. I look forward to continuing feedback as we strive, over future editions, to create an ever better book.

Throughout its many editions, however, my vision for *Psychology* has not wavered: *to merge rigorous science with a broad human perspective in a book that engages both mind and heart.* My aim has been to create a state-of-the-art introduction to psychology, written with sensitivity to students' needs and interests. I aspire to help students understand and appreciate the wonder of important phenomena in their lives. I also want to convey the inquisitive, caring spirit in which psychologists *do* psychology. The study of psychology, I believe, enhances our abilities to restrain intuition with critical thinking, judgmentalism with compassion, and illusion with understanding.

Believing with Thoreau that "Anything living is easily and naturally expressed in popular language," I seek to communicate psychology's scholarship with crisp narrative and vivid storytelling. Writing as a solo author, I hope to tell psychology's story in a way that is warmly personal as well as rigorously scientific. I love to reflect on connections between psychology and other realms, such as literature, philosophy, history, sports, religion, politics, and popular culture. And I love to provoke thought, to play with words, and to laugh.

Throughout this revision, I have steadfastly followed eight principles:

1. ***To exemplify the process of inquiry***   I strive to show students not just the outcome of research, but how the research process works. Throughout, the book tries to excite the reader's curiosity. It invites readers to imagine themselves as participants in classic experiments. Several modules introduce research stories as mysteries that progressively unravel as one clue after another falls into place. (See, for example, the historical story of research on the brain's processing of language—pages 70–71.)

2. ***To teach critical thinking*** By presenting research as intellectual detective work, I exemplify an inquiring, analytical mind-set. Whether students are studying development, cognition, or statistics, they will become involved in, and see the rewards of, critical reasoning. Moreover, they will discover how an empirical approach can help them evaluate competing ideas and claims for highly publicized phenomena—ranging from subliminal persuasion, ESP, and facilitated communication to astrology, basketball streak-shooting, and repressed and recovered memories.

3. ***To put facts in the service of concepts*** My intention is not to fill students' intellectual file drawers with facts, but to reveal psychology's major concepts—to teach students how to think, and to offer psychological ideas worth thinking about. In each chapter I place emphasis on those concepts I hope students will carry with them long after they complete the course. Always, I try to follow Albert Einstein's dictum that "everything should be made as simple as possible, but not simpler."

4. ***To be as up-to-date as possible*** Few things dampen students' interests as quickly as the sense that they are reading stale news. While retaining psychology's classic studies and concepts, I also present the discipline's most important recent developments. Nearly 600 references in this edition are dated 1998 to 2000.

5. ***To integrate principles and applications*** Throughout—by means of anecdotes, case histories, and the posing of hypothetical situations—I relate the findings of basic research to their applications and implications. Where psychology can illuminate pressing human issues—be they racism and sexism, health and happiness, or violence and war—I have not hesitated to shine its light.

6. ***To enhance comprehension by providing continuity*** Because the book has a single author, many significant issues—such as behavior genetics, cultural diversity, the bold thinking of intellectual pioneers, human rationality and irrationality, empathy for and understanding of troubled lives—weave throughout many modules, and students hear a consistent voice. "The uniformity of a work," observed Edward Gibbon, "denotes the hand of a single artist."

7. ***To reinforce learning at every step*** Everyday examples and rhetorical questions encourage students to process the material actively. Concepts are presented and then frequently applied to reinforce learning. A marginal glossary and end-of-module key terms list help students master important terminology. Major sections begin with Preview Questions, and modules end with Review and Reflect sections that highlight the organization and key concepts.

8. ***To convey respect for human unity and diversity*** Time and again, readers will see evidence of our human kinship—our shared biological heritage, our common mechanisms of seeing and learning, hungering and feeling, loving and hating. They will also better understand the dimensions of our diversity—our *individual* diversity in development and aptitudes, temperament and personality, and disorder and health; and our *cultural* diversity in attitudes and expressive styles, childrearing and care for the elderly, and life priorities.

The Multimedia Supplements Package

Worth Publishers has outdone itself with this edition. *Myers in Modules: Psychology,* sixth edition, boasts a host of new electronic and print supplements titles, making this package the most impressive thus far in a history of impressive ancillary packages.

NEW! PsychOnline offers comprehensive resources for the introductory course. This impressive new project is detailed on pages xix–xx.

NEW! A *Scientific American Reader* includes 12 articles I hand-selected from recent issues of *Scientific American*. I have written introductions for each article to tie them specifically into the text.

NEW! The **Expanded Myers Psychology Web Companion (http://www. worthpublishers.com/myers)** provides an even wider variety of activities and study aids. Features include Overviews, Thinking Critically Exercises, Psychology in the News, Web links, Close Up sections (providing the author's perspective on significant research that emerged after this book went to press), interactive animations, simulations and demonstrations, online quizzes, and flashcards.

NEW! Thomas Ludwig's (Hope College) award-winning programs, *PsychQuest* and *PsychSim* are now available online. They are also available on CD-ROM.

NEW! Student Activity CD-ROM is designed for students with limited Internet access or for lab settings. The student CD provides all of the multimedia content from the Myers Web site, including Thinking Critically Exercises, animations, simulations, demonstrations, flashcards, drag-and drop-exercises, and complete versions of *PsychQuest* and *PsychSim* 4.0.

NEW! Image and Lecture Gallery (http://www.worthpublishers.com/ ILG) is Worth's convenient way to access electronic versions of lecture materials. Registered users can browse, search, and download illustrations from Worth titles and pre-built PowerPoint presentation files for specific chapters. Instructors can also create personal folders on a personalized home page for easy organization of the materials.

NEW! PowerPoint Slides are now available. They can be used as is, or customized to fit your needs. We also have available an enhanced version of Harvey Shulman's (Ohio State University) **PowerPoint Presentation Slides.** These slides focus on key topics in introductory psychology, and feature PowerPoint-designed tables, graphs, and figures.

NEW! Presentation Manager Pro 2.0 is an easy-to-operate CD-ROM that is compatible with most commercially available presentation software, such as PowerPoint. With Presentation Manager Pro, instructors can build classroom presentations using graphic material from the book and CD, and their own digital material (including video) imported from the Internet or other sources.

NEW! WebCT is available to all adopters. With WebCT, instructors can create a course Web site and/or online course with content, threaded discussions, quizzing, an online grade book, a course calendar and more! *Myers in Modules: Psychology,* sixth edition's graphic and media content is available in the WebCT format.

NEW! Online Testing is now available with Diploma from the Brownstone Research Group. Instructors can now create and administer secure exams over a network and over the Internet with questions that incorporate multimedia and interactive exercises. The program includes impressive security features and grade book and result-analysis features.

Scientific American Frontiers Video Collection in a **NEW Second Edition** is a renowned series hosted by Alan Alda. These 10–12-minute modules provide an excellent way to show how psychological research is actually conducted, focusing on the work of Steve Sumi, Renee Baillargeon, Carl Rosengren, Laura Pettito, Steven Pinker, Barbara Rothbaum, Bob Stickgold, Irene Pepperberg, Marc Hauser, Linda Bartoshuk, and Michael Gazzaniga.

The Mind **Video Teaching Modules** in a **NEW Second Edition** offers 35 brief, engaging video clips to enhance and illustrate lecture topics.

The Brain **Video Teaching Modules** in a **NEW Second Edition** offers more engaging video clips to help you teach.

In addition to all these fabulous new resources, *Myers in Modules: Psychology,* sixth edition, is accompanied by smartly updated versions of the widely acclaimed print supplements package.

The updated and better-than-ever **Instructor's Resources** by Martin Bolt (Calvin College) has been hailed as the finest set of psychology teaching resources ever assembled, including ready-to-use demonstration handouts, detailed lecture/discussion ideas, student projects, classroom exercises, and video and film suggestions.

The **Student Study Guide** by Richard O. Straub (University of Michigan, Dearborn) follows the text's content and offers the following for every major section in the text: a new "Stepping Through the Section" feature, Self Tests, and "Web Sightings"—Internet activities. The **Guide** also includes Cornelius Rea's (Douglas College, British Columbia) helpful "Focus on Vocabulary and Language" feature, designed to help clarify idioms and other phrases potentially unfamiliar to students for whom English is a second language.

The **Test Bank** by John Brink (Calvin College) is broken down into two banks, providing over 4000 multiple-choice factual/definitional and conceptual questions, plus essay questions. Each question is page-referenced to the textbook and Instructor's Resources and rated for level of difficulty. The second Test Bank includes optional questions on *PsychQuest* and *PsychSim* computer simulations and *The Brain* and *The Mind* videos.

The Critical Thinking Companion by Jane Halonen (James Madison University) and Cynthia Gray (Alverno College) is now available in a NEW second edition. This collection of engaging, challenging, and fun critical-thinking exercises is tied to the main topics in *Myers in Modules: Psychology,* sixth edition.

Our **Psychology Videodisc** will help you bring to life for your students all of the major topics in *Myers in Modules: Psychology,* sixth edition, combining brief, exciting video clips and animated segments with a library of stills. This videodisc is accompanied by an extensive *Instructor's Guide,* by Martin Bolt and Richard O. Straub, and an accompanying presentation software package by Thomas Ludwig.

In Appreciation

If it is true that "whoever walks with the wise becomes wise," then I am wiser for all the wisdom and advice received from expert colleagues. Aided by several hundred consultants and reviewers over the last decade, this has become a better, more accurate book than one author alone (this author, at least) could write. My indebtedness continues to each of the teacher-scholars whose influence I acknowledged in the five previous editions.

My gratitude now extends to the colleagues who contributed criticism, corrections, and creative ideas related to the content of this new edition. For their expertise and encouragement, I thank the following reviewers:

Gregory Aarons,
Child and Family Research Group, San Diego

Larry Anderson,
Kwantlen University College, Surrey

Lamia Barakat,
Drexel University

Jackson Beatty,
University of California, Los Angeles

James D. Becker,
Kapi'olani Community College

Nancy S. Breland,
The College of New Jersey

Charles L. Brewer,
Furman University

Frederick M. Brown,
Penn State University

Danuta Bukatko,
Holy Cross College

Jim Calhoun,
University of Georgia

Tricia Callahan,
University of Louisville

Dennis Cogan,
Texas Tech University

Deborah Corbett,
Raritan Valley Community College

Thaddeus Cowan,
Kansas State University

Donald Cronkite,
Hope College

Maria K. Crothers,
University of Wisconsin, Eau Claire

Douglas Detterman,
Case Western Reserve University

Jill Francis,
La Trobe University, Bendigo (Australia)

Larry Fujinaka,
Leeward Community College

Wendy Gardner,
Northwestern University

Ken Gray,
College of DuPage

Richard Griggs,
University of Florida

Beth Halpern,
Long Island University

O. Joseph Harm,
University of South Carolina, Aiken

Bryan Hendricks,
University of Wisconsin, Marathon Center

Robert Hines,
University of Arkansas, Little Rock

Carl A. Kallgren,
Penn State Erie, The Behrend College

Matt Kaplan,
Hawaii Pacific University

Lynda LaBounty,
Macalester College

Fred Leavitt,
California State University, Hayward

Mike Maratsos,
University of Minnesota

Jerry Marshall,
Green River Community College

Donald McBurney,
University of Pittsburgh

Roger Mellgren,
University of Texas, Arlington

Joyann Montgomery,
Spokane Community College

Kevin Moore,
Lincoln University (New Zealand)

Paul Nesselroade,
Simpson College

Michael Nietzel,
University of Kentucky

David Payne,
Binghamton University, SUNY

Paul Pintrich,
University of Michigan

Robert Plomin,
Institute of Psychiatry, London

Robert D. Ridge,
Brigham Young University

Robert A. Rosenberg,
Community College of Philadelphia

Harvey Schiffman,
Rutgers University

A. René Schmauder,
University of South Carolina

Frank Sjursen,
Shoreline Community College

Keith Stanovich,
University of Toronto

Thomas Swan,
Siena College

Lynda Szymanski,
The College of St. Catherine, St. Paul

Christopher Taylor,
University of Arizona

David Uttal,
Northwestern University

Frank Vattano,
Colorado State University

Darren Walton,
The Open Polytechnic of New Zealand

Dennis Wanamaker,
Bellevue Community College

W. Jeffrey Wilson,
Indiana University Purdue University, Fort Wayne

Charlotte vanOyen Witvliet,
Hope College

I thank the following colleagues and students for their extensive input on design and pedagogy for this edition:

Kathy Bell,
University of North Carolina, Greensboro

Justin Boyce *(student),*
Raritan Valley Community College

Charles L. Brewer,
Furman University

Dennis Cogan,
Texas Tech University

Deborah Corbett,
Raritan Valley Community College

Robert Davidson *(student),*
Raritan Valley Community College

Jennifer Detelich *(student),*
Penn State Erie, The Behrend College

Julie L. Earles,
Florida Atlantic University

April Foreman, and other students,
Texas Tech University

Michelle Glitter (*student*),
University of North Carolina, Greensboro

Richard Griggs and his students,
University of Florida

Laura Hunt (*student*),
University of North Carolina, Greensboro

Julia Zuwerink Jacks,
University of North Carolina, Greensboro

Carl A. Kallgren,
Penn State Erie, The Behrend College

Charles T. Lo Presto and his students,
Loyola College, Maryland

Thomas Ludwig,
Hope College

James Maas,
Cornell University

Julie Meredith (*student*),
University of North Carolina, Greensboro

Sharon Micke (*student*),
Colorado State University

Kristen Potter (*student*),
Cornell University

Rachel Reese (*student*),
Penn State Erie, The Behrend College

Cindy Stettner (*student*),
Raritan Valley Community College

Frank Vattano,
Colorado State University

Julian Wilson (*student*),
University of North Carolina, Greensboro

Several other colleagues helped define priorities as special consultants in the planning of this new edition, including:

Renee L. Babcock,
Central Michigan University

Martin Bolt,
Calvin College

Charles L. Brewer,
Furman University

John Brink,
Calvin College

Richard Griggs,
University of Florida

Jim Howell,
Portland Community College

Richard A. Lambe,
Providence College

Ted Lewandowski,
Delaware County Community College

Thomas Ludwig,
Hope College

James Maas,
Cornell University

Marta Meana,
University of Nevada, Las Vegas

Lee Osterhout,
University of Washington

Richard O. Straub,
University of Michigan, Dearborn

Frank Vattano,
Colorado State University

Al Witkofsky,
Salisbury State University

Lee Woodson,
Kwantlen University College, Surrey

In addition, Jean Alvers, Roberta Eveslage, Richard Gist, Toby Klinger, Michelle Moriarty, Peter Peterson, and Brad Redburn at Johnson County Community College have been helpful consultants for this and previous editions of *Psychology.* Nancy S. Breland (The College of New Jersey) also reviewed every graph and chart in the book for effective pedagogy, and the result is an even more effective art program.

At Worth Publishers a host of people played key roles in creating this book. Editors Christine Brune and Nancy Fleming offered just the right mix of encouragement, gentle admonition, attention to detail, and passion for excellence. An author could not ask for more. Christine and Nancy also guided the development of the new *PsychOnline* resources.

Chief Operating Officer Susan Driscoll and Publisher Catherine Woods helped construct and execute the plan for this new book. Catherine was also a trusted sounding board as we faced the myriad discrete decisions along the way. Media and Supplements Editor Graig Donini coordinated production of the huge supplements package. Betty Probert efficiently edited and produced the print supplements. Editorial Assistant Lawrence Guerra and Assistant Editor Miriam Beyer provided invaluable support in commissioning reviews, mailing information to professors, and numerous other daily tasks related to the book's development and production. Lee Mahler did a splendid job of laying out each page. Lou Capaldo effectively coordinated the complex process of creating and assembling artistic elements, much of it created by Alan Reingold. Jennifer MacMillan and Toby Zausner worked together to locate the myriad photographic illustrations.

Associate Managing Editor Tracey Kuehn and Project Editor Margaret Comaskey displayed tenacity, commitment, and impressive organization in leading Worth's gifted artistic production team and coordinating editorial input throughout the production process. Production Manager Barbara Seixas masterfully kept the book to its tight schedule, and Barbara Reingold skillfully directed creation of the distinctive design and art program. Supplements Production Manager Stacey Alexander did her usual excellent work of producing the many supplements.

At Hope College, the supporting team members for this edition included Kathryn Brownson, who researched countless bits of information and proofed hundreds of pages. Typesetters Phyllis and Richard Vandervelde worked faithfully and joyfully to enter or revise every one of the more than 400,000 words, and finally to code them for electronic delivery.

Again, I gratefully acknowledge the influence and editing assistance of my writing coach, poet Jack Ridl, whose influence resides in the voice you will be hearing in the pages that follow. He more than anyone cultivated my delight in dancing with the language, and taught me to approach writing as a craft that shades into art.

After hearing countless dozens of people say that this book's supplements have taken their teaching to a new level, I reflect on how fortunate I am to be a part of a team on which everyone has produced on-time work marked by the highest professional standards. For their remarkable talents, their long-term dedication, and their friendship, I thank Martin Bolt, John Brink, Thomas Ludwig, and Richard Straub.

Finally, my gratitude extends to the many students and instructors who have written to offer suggestions, or just an encouraging word. It is for them, and those about to begin their study of psychology, that I have done my best to introduce the field I love.

When those who paint the Golden Gate Bridge finish, it is time to start over again. So with this book. The ink is barely dry before one begins envisioning the next edition. By the time you read this, I will be gathering information for the seventh edition. Your input will again influence how this book continues to evolve. So, please, do share your thoughts.

David Myers

Hope College
Holland, Michigan 49422-9000
USA
Web site: www.davidmyers.org

Introduction to the History and Science of Psychology

People occasionally ask my wife, "What's it like being married to a psychologist? Does he use his psychology on you?"

"So, does your dad, like, analyze you?" my children have been asked hundreds of times by friends.

"What do you think of me?" asked one barber, hoping for an instant personality analysis after learning that I was a psychologist.

For these questioners, as for most people whose exposure to psychology comes from popular books, magazines, and TV, psychologists analyze personality, offer counseling, and dispense child-rearing advice.

Do they? Yes, and much more. Consider some of psychology's questions that from time to time you may wonder about:

Have you ever found yourself reacting to something just as one of your parents would—perhaps in a way you vowed you never would—and then wondered how much of your personality you inherited? To what degree are you really like your mother or your father? *To what extent is your parents' influence transmitted through their genes, to what extent through the home and neighborhood environments they gave you?*

Have you ever played peekaboo with a 6-month-old infant and wondered why the baby finds the game so delightful? The baby reacts as though, when you momentarily move behind a door, you actually disappear—only to reappear later out of thin air. *What do babies actually perceive and think?*

Have you ever awakened from a nightmare and, with a wave of relief, wondered why you had such a crazy dream? *How often, and why, do we dream?*

Have you ever wondered what leads to school and work success? Are some people just born smarter? *Does sheer intelligence explain why some people get richer, think more creatively, or relate more sensitively?*

Do you ever get depressed or anxious and wonder whether you'll ever feel "normal"? *What triggers our bad moods—and our good ones?*

Have you ever worried about how to act among people of a different culture, race, or gender? *In what ways are we alike as members of the human family? How do we differ?*

Such questions provide grist for psychology's mill (Module 1) because psychology is a science (Module 2) that seeks to answer all sorts of questions about us all: how we think, feel, and act.

1

The History and Scope of Psychology

Psychology's Roots

Preview Question: How did psychology develop?

To be human is to be curious about ourselves and the world around us. Psychology's ancestors therefore date to the world's early writings. Before 300 B.C., the Greek naturalist and philosopher Aristotle theorized about learning and memory, motivation and emotion, perception and personality. Today we chuckle at some of his guesses, like his suggestion that a meal makes us sleepy by causing gas and heat to collect around the source of our personality, the heart. But credit Aristotle with asking the right questions.

Philosophers' thinking about thinking continued until the birth of psychology as we know it, on a December day in 1879. In a small room on the third floor of a shabby building at Germany's University of Leipzig, two young men were helping a long-faced, austere, middle-age professor, Wilhelm Wundt, create an experimental apparatus. Their machine measured the time lag between people's hearing a ball hit a platform and their pressing a telegraph key (Hunt, 1993). Later, the researchers compared this lag to the time required for slightly more complex tasks. Wundt was seeking to measure the "atoms of the mind"—the fastest and simplest mental processes. Thus began what many consider psychology's first experiment, launching the first psychological institute, staffed by Wundt and psychology's first graduate students.

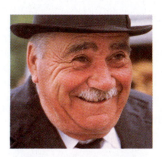

A smile is a smile the world around Psychology studies not only our cultural and gender diversity but also the similarities that define our shared human nature. Men and women in different cultures show differences in when and how often they smile, but a smile *means* the same thing anywhere in the world.

The young science of psychology evolved from the more established fields of philosophy and biology. Wundt was both a philosopher and a physiologist. Charles Darwin, who proposed evolutionary psychology, was an English naturalist. Ivan Pavlov, who pioneered the study of learning, was a Russian physiologist. Sigmund Freud, renowned personality theorist, was an Austrian physician. Jean Piaget, the twentieth century's most influential observer of children, was a Swiss biologist. William James, author of an important 1890 psychology textbook, was an American philosopher. This list of pioneering psychologists—"Magellans of the mind," as Morton Hunt (1993) has called them—illustrates that psychology has its origins in many countries and disciplines (**FIGURE 1.1**).

So what is psychology? With activities ranging from psychotherapy to the study of nerve cell activity, psychology is not easily defined. Psychology began as the science of mental life. Wundt's basic research tool became introspection—self-examination of one's own emotional states and mental processes. Wundt focused on *inner* sensations, feelings, and images. Thus, until the 1920s, psychology was defined as "the science of mental life."

FIGURE 1.1

A timeline of psychology's pioneers, 1879–1913

Hermann Ebbinghaus in Germany reports the first experiments on memory (1885).

Alfred Binet (shown) and **Theodore Simon** publish the first intelligence test for use with Parisian schoolchildren (1905).

Wilhelm Wundt establishes the first psychology laboratory at the University of Leipzig, Germany (1879).

Edward L. Thorndike in the United States conducts the first experiments on animal learning (1898).

Margaret Floy Washburn, the first woman to receive a Ph.D. in psychology, synthesizes research on animal behavior in *The Animal Mind* (1908).

American Psychological Association is founded (1892).

1875 1880 1885 1890 1895 1900 1905 1910 1915

G. Stanley Hall, a student of Wundt's, establishes what many consider the first American psychology laboratory at Johns Hopkins University (1883).

Sigmund Freud in Austria introduces his psychoanalytic theory in *The Interpretation of Dreams* (1900).

John B. Watson in the United States champions psychology as the science of behavior (1913).

William James publishes the widely used *Principles of Psychology* in the United States (1890).

Mary Whiton Calkins creates paired-associates technique for studying memory; becomes president of American Psychological Association (1905).

Ivan Pavlov in Russia begins to publish his classic studies of animal learning (1906).

■ **psychology** the science of behavior and mental processes.

Throughout this book, important concepts are **bold faced.** As you study, you can find these terms with their definitions in a nearby margin. They are also listed at the end of each module and defined in the Glossary at the end of the book.

"Once expanded to the dimensions of a larger idea, [the mind] never returns to its original size."

Oliver Wendell Holmes, 1809–1894

From the 1920s into the 1960s, American psychologists, initially led by flamboyant and provocative John B. Watson, dismissed introspection and redefined psychology as "the science of observable behavior." After all, said these *behaviorists*, science is rooted in observation. You cannot observe a sensation, a feeling, or a thought, but you *can* observe people's *behavior* as they respond to different situations.

In the 1960s, psychology began to recapture its initial interest in mental processes through studies of how our minds process and retain information. To encompass psychology's concern both with observable behavior and with inner thoughts and feelings, **psychology** has become *the science of behavior and mental processes.*

Let's unpack this definition. *Behavior* is anything an organism *does*—any action we can observe and record. Yelling, smiling, blinking, sweating, talking, and questionnaire-marking are all observable behaviors. *Mental processes* are the internal subjective experiences we infer from behavior—sensations, perceptions, dreams, thoughts, beliefs, and feelings.

For many psychologists, the key word in psychology's definition is *science*. Psychology, as I will emphasize throughout this book, is less a set of findings than a way of asking and answering questions. As a science, psychology attempts to sift opinions and evaluate ideas with careful observation and rigorous analysis. In its quest to describe and explain nature (human nature included), psychological science welcomes hunches and plausible-sounding theories. And it puts them to the test. If a theory works—if the data support its predictions—so much the better for that theory. If the predictions fail, the theory will be revised or rejected.

My aim in this text, then, is not merely to report results but also to show you how psychologists play the game. How do researchers sift contesting opinions and ideas? And how might all of us, whether scientists or simply curious people, think smarter when describing and explaining the events of our lives?

Of course, psychology also has content: Its scientific sifting of ideas has produced a smorgasbord of concepts and findings, from which we can only sample the fare. Once aware of psychology's well-researched ideas—about how body and mind connect, how a child's mind grows, how we construct our perceptions, how we remember (and misremember) our experiences, how people across the world differ (and are alike)—your mind may never again be quite the same.

Psychology's Big Issues

Preview Question: What are the recurring issues that cut across psychology?

During its short history, which we will explore in more detail as we move through the pages of this book, psychology has wrestled with some issues that will reappear in many different contexts. One such issue concerns *stability versus change*. Do our individual traits persist as we age? Do we become older versions of our same old selves? Does a reactive infant become a volatile adult? Or do people change? Can shy preschoolers become teenage class clowns? Can troubled teens become mature executives? Do our personalities change in different situations?

Another issue concerns human *rationality versus irrationality*. How deserving are we of our name *homo sapiens*—wise humans? We will see that in some ways—recognizing patterns, handling language, processing abstract ideas—we outstrip the smartest computers. The simple act of perceiving this book involves disassembling visual stimuli into millions of nerve impulses, distributing them for processing in different brain regions, and then, in an imperceptible instant, reassembling the information into a colorful image. As human observers, we all have an urge to explain behavior, to attribute it to some cause. Indeed, using certain rules of thumb, we make snap judgments with amazing efficiency and sufficient rationality. "How noble in reason!" declared Shakespeare's Hamlet.

But we are prone to err. We sometimes shoehorn reality into our preconceptions. Our memories err. We overestimate our judgments. We are often swayed more by compelling anecdotes than by statistical reality. We "see" causes and associations that don't exist. We treat others in ways that lead them to confirm our mistaken ideas about them. These limits to human rationality—also spelled out in the pages to come—caused philosopher Bertrand Russell to lament that "most people would sooner die than think; in fact, they do so."

The biggest and most persistent issue, however concerns *the relative contributions of biology and experience*. This **nature-nurture** debate is longstanding. Do our human traits develop through experience, or do we come equipped with them? The Greek philosopher Plato assumed that character and intelligence are largely inherited and that certain ideas are inborn. Aristotle replied that there is nothing in the mind that does not first come in from the external world through the senses. In the 1600s, philosophers rekindled the debate. John Locke also rejected the notion of inborn ideas, saying that at birth, the mind is but a *tabula rasa*—a blank tablet—upon which experience writes. René Descartes disagreed, believing that some ideas are innate.

Two centuries later, Descartes' views gained support from a curious naturalist. In 1831, an indifferent student but ardent collector of beetles, mollusks, and shells set sail on what was to prove a historic round-the-world journey. The 22-year-old voyager was Charles Darwin, and for some time afterward, he pondered the incredible species variation he had encountered, including tortoises on one island that differed from those on other islands of the region. Darwin's 1859 *Origin of Species* explained this diversity of life by proposing an evolutionary process. From among chance variations in organisms, he believed, nature selects those that best enable an organism to survive and reproduce in a particular environment. Darwin's big idea— "the single best idea anyone has ever had," says philosopher Daniel Dennett (1996)—is called **natural selection**, and it is still with us more than 140 years later, having become an organizing principle of biology. Evolution also has become an important principle for psychology. This would surely have pleased Darwin, for he believed his theory explains not only animal structures (such as why polar bear coats are white) but also animal behaviors (such as the emotional expressions associated with lust and rage).

The nature-nurture debate weaves a thread from the distant past to our time. Today's psychologists have continued the debate by asking these and other questions:

+ Are differences in intelligence, personality, and psychological disorders more influenced by heredity or by environment?
+ Is children's grammar innate or formed by experience?
+ Are eating and sexual behavior more "pushed" by inner biology or "pulled" by external incentives?
+ Is depression a brain disorder or a thought disorder?
+ How are humans alike (because of their common biology) and different (because of their differing cultures)?
+ Are gender differences biologically predisposed or socially constructed?

The debate continues. Yet over and over again we will see the nature-nurture tension dissolve: *Nurture works on what nature endows.* Our species is biologically endowed with an enormous capacity to learn and adapt. Moreover, every psychological event (every thought, every emotion) is simultaneously a biological event. Thus depression can be *both* a thought disorder and a brain disorder.

■ **nature-nurture issue** the long-standing controversy over the relative contributions that genes and experience make to the development of psychological traits and behaviors.

■ **natural selection** the principle that, among the range of inherited trait variations, those contributing to reproduction and survival will most likely be passed on to succeeding generations.

Like peas in a pod
Because identical twins have the same genes, they are ideal participants in studies designed to shed light on hereditary and environmental influences on temperament, intelligence, and other traits. Studies of identical and fraternal twins provide a rich array of findings—described throughout this text—that underscore the importance of both nature and nurture.

Psychology's Perspectives

Preview Question: What theoretical perspectives do psychologists take?

We can simultaneously view any psychological event from several perspectives (Table 1.1). Let's consider anger, for example.

+ Someone working from a *neuroscience perspective* might study the brain circuits that trigger the physical state of being "red in the face" and "hot under the collar."
+ Someone working from an *evolutionary perspective* might analyze how anger facilitated the survival of our ancestors' genes.
+ Someone working from a *behavior genetics* perspective might study how heredity and experience influence our individual differences in temperament.
+ Someone working from a *psychodynamic perspective* might view an outburst as an outlet for unconscious hostility.
+ Someone working from a *behavioral perspective* might study the facial expressions and body gestures that accompany anger, or might attempt to determine which external stimuli result in angry responses or aggressive acts.
+ Someone working from a *cognitive perspective* might study how our interpretation of a situation affects our anger and how our anger affects our thinking.
+ Someone working from a *social-cultural perspective* might explore which situations produce the most anger, and how expressions of anger vary across cultural contexts.

Views of anger
How would each of psychology's perspectives explain what's going on here?

Information sources are cited in parentheses, with name and date, then provided fully in the References section at the book's end.

Such perspectives needn't contradict one another. Rather, they are complementary outlooks on the same biological state. It's like explaining why grizzly bears hibernate. Is it because hibernation enhanced their ancestors' survival and reproduction? Because their inner physiology drives them to do so? Because cold environments hinder food gathering during winter? Such perspectives are complementary, because "everything is related to everything else" (Brewer, 1996).

This important point—that different perspectives on the big issues can complement one another—is also true of the different academic disciplines. Each provides a particular perspective on nature and our place in it. The basic sciences investigate nature's building blocks, seeking principles based on objective observation. The humanities (including literature and philosophy) address questions of

TABLE 1.1

PSYCHOLOGY'S CURRENT PERSPECTIVES

Perspective	Focus	Sample Questions
Neuroscience	How the body and brain create emotions, memories, and sensory experiences	How are messages transmitted within the body? How is blood chemistry linked with moods and motives?
Evolutionary	How nature selects traits that promote the perpetuation of one's genes	How does evolution influence behavior tendencies?
Behavior genetics	How much our genes, and our environment, influence our individual differences	To what extent are psychological traits such as intelligence, personality, sexual orientation, and vulnerability to depression attributable to our genes? To our environment?
Psychodynamic	How behavior springs from unconscious drives and conflicts	How can someone's personality traits and disorders be explained in terms of sexual and aggressive drives or as the disguised effects of unfulfilled wishes and childhood traumas?
Behavioral	How we learn observable responses	How do we learn to fear particular objects or situations? What is the most effective way to alter our behavior, say, to lose weight or stop smoking?
Cognitive	How we encode, process, store, and retrieve information	How do we use information in remembering? Reasoning? Solving problems?
Social-cultural	How behavior and thinking vary across situations and cultures	How are we—as Africans, Asians, Australians, or North Americans—alike as members of one human family? As products of different environmental contexts, how do we differ?

life's meaning and value, using more subjective methods. Psychology lies near the middle of this continuum; it uses scientific methods to explore our thoughts, feelings, and actions.

Each perspective has its questions and its limits. Differing perspectives are like different two-dimensional views of a three-dimensional object (FIGURE **1.2**). Each two-dimensional perspective is helpful, but by itself fails to reveal the whole picture.

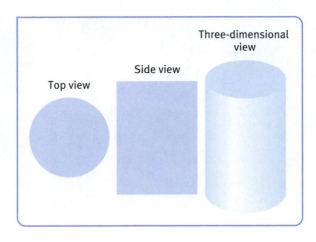

FIGURE 1.2
Complementary perspectives
What is this object? One person, looking down from the top, sees a disk. Another, looking at it from the side, sees a rectangle. Their differing perspectives seem contradictory. In fact, they are complementary, for we can assemble these images into a three-dimensional view of the object, a cylinder. The views offered by psychology's different perspectives are often like this: A lot depends on your point of view.

So bear in mind psychology's limits. Don't expect it to answer the ultimate questions posed by Russian novelist Leo Tolstoy (1904): "Why should I live? Why should I do anything? Is there in life any purpose which the inevitable death that awaits me does not undo and destroy?" Instead, expect that psychology will help you understand why people think, feel, and act as they do. Then you should find the study of psychology both fascinating and useful.

Psychology's Subfields

Preview Question: What are psychology's specialized subfields?

Picturing a chemist at work, you probably envision a white-coated scientist surrounded by glassware and high-tech equipment. Picture a psychologist at work and you would be right to envision

+ a white-coated scientist probing a rat's brain.
+ an intelligence researcher measuring how quickly an infant becomes bored with (looks away from) a familiar picture.
+ an executive proposing a new "healthy life-styles" training program for employees.
+ someone at a computer keyboard analyzing data on whether adopted teens' temperaments more closely resemble those of their adoptive parents or their biological parents.
+ a therapist listening carefully to a client's depressed thoughts.
+ a traveler en route to another culture to collect data on variations in human values and behaviors.
+ a teacher or writer sharing the joy of psychology with others.

The cluster of subfields that we call psychology has less unity than most other sciences. But there is a payoff: Psychology is a meeting ground for different disciplines and is thus a perfect home for those with wide-ranging interests. In their diverse activities, from biological experimentation to cultural comparisons, psychologists share a common quest: describing and explaining behavior and the mental processes that underlie it.

Some psychologists conduct **basic research** that builds psychology's knowledge base. In the pages to follow we will meet a wide variety of such researchers:

+ *Biological psychologists* exploring the links between brain and mind
+ *Developmental psychologists* studying our changing abilities from womb to tomb
+ *Cognitive psychologists* experimenting with how we perceive, think, and solve problems
+ *Personality psychologists* investigating our inner traits
+ *Social psychologists* exploring how we view and affect one another

"I'm a social scientist, Michael. That means I can't explain electricity or anything like that, but if you ever want to know about people I'm your man."

■ **basic research** pure science that aims to increase the scientific knowledge base.

Psychology: A science and a profession

In their laboratories and consulting rooms, psychologists study and treat a wide range of human conditions. Here you see a face-to-face encounter typical of psychotherapy, a researcher introducing a participant to a laboratory experiment designed to test social judgment, and a psychologist testing a child.

Other psychologists conduct **applied research** that tackles practical problems. For example, *industrial/organizational psychologists* study and advise on behavior in the workplace. They use psychology's concepts and methods to help organizations and companies to select and train employees more effectively, to boost morale and productivity, to design products, and to implement systems.

Although most psychology textbooks focus on the methods and results of psychological science, psychology is also a helping profession devoted to such practical issues as how to have a happy marriage, how to overcome anxiety or depression, and how to raise thriving children. **Clinical psychologists** study, assess, and treat troubled people. After graduate school training, they administer and interpret tests, provide psychotherapy, manage mental health programs, and conduct research. By contrast, **psychiatrists**, who also often provide psychotherapy, are medical doctors licensed to prescribe drugs and otherwise treat physical causes of psychological disorders.

I see you!

A biological psychologist might view this child's delighted response as evidence for brain maturation. A cognitive psychologist might see it as a demonstration of the baby's growing knowledge of his surroundings. For a cross-cultural psychologist, the role of grandparents in different societies might be the issue of interest. These and other perspectives offer complementary views of behavior.

With perspectives ranging from the biological to the social, and with settings from the laboratory to the clinic, psychology relates to many disciplines. More and more, psychology connects with fields ranging from mathematics and biology to sociology and philosophy. And more and more, psychology's methods and findings aid other disciplines. Psychologists teach in medical schools, law schools, and theological seminaries, and they work in hospitals, factories, and corporate offices. They engage in interdisciplinary studies, such as psychohistory (the psychological analysis of histo-rical characters), psycholinguistics (the study of language and thinking), and psycho-ceramics (the study of crackpots).[1]

Today, psychology's researchers and students, like its historic pioneers, are citizens of many lands, from Australia to Western Europe to the developing nations. Worldwide, the number of psychologists—now well over 500,000—has doubled since 1980 (Rosenzweig, 1992). British Psychological Society membership quadrupled between 1980 and 2000. In China, five universities had psychology departments in 1985; in 1999, there were 50 (Jing, 1999). Sixty-four nations, from Argentina to Zimbabwe, participate in the International Union of Scientific Psychology (Rosenzweig, 1999).

---

[1] I wrote the last part of this sentence on April Fools' Day.

Thanks to the tripling of psychologists in the work force and to women's increased professionalism, psychology now includes increasing numbers of women. In Britain, 51 percent of recent doctorates have gone to women, as have 69 percent in the United States (APA Research Office, 1997; Cantor, 1995; Colley, 1995; NRC, 1995). In both countries, women earn more than 7 in 10 undergraduate psychology degrees. In Canada, 69 percent of students receiving professional training in psychology during the mid-1990s were women, as were 70 percent in The Netherlands, 73 percent in Denmark, and 89 percent in Spain (Adair & others, 1996; Foltved, 1996; Sanchez & others, 1996; van Drunen, 1996). Between 1996 and 1999, all four elected American Psychological Society presidents were women. What a change from the turn of the twentieth century, when—because she was a woman—Harvard University denied Mary Whiton Calkins the Ph.D. she had earned. (Calkins refused Harvard's offer of a doctorate from its undergraduate sister school for women, and she went on to become the American Psychological Association's first female president.)

Psychology's influence also penetrates into modern culture. Knowledge transforms us. Learning to read, to understand the solar system, and to comprehend the germ theory of disease alters the way people think and act. Learning psychology's findings also changes people: They less often judge psychological disorders as a moral failing, treatable by punishment and ostracism. They less often regard and treat women as men's mental inferiors. They less often view and rear children as ignorant willful beasts in need of taming. "In each case," notes Morton Hunt (1990, p. 206), "knowledge has modified attitudes, and, through them, behavior."

Studying Psychology

Preview Question: Do psychology's findings offer any hints that can help you study effectively and boost your performance in this course and other courses?

The investment you are making in studying psychology should enrich your life and enlarge your vision. Although many of life's significant questions are beyond psychology, some very important ones are illuminated by even a first psychology course. Through painstaking research, psychologists have gained insights into brain and mind, depression and joy, dreams and memories. Even the unanswered questions can enrich us, by renewing our sense of mystery about "things too wonderful" for us yet to understand. What is more, your study of psychology can help teach you *how to ask and answer important questions*—how to think critically as you evaluate competing ideas and claims.

Having your life enriched and your vision enlarged (and getting a decent grade, too) requires effective study. To master information you must *actively process it.* Your mind is not like your stomach, something to be filled passively; it is more like a muscle that grows stronger with exercise. Countless experiments reveal that people learn and remember material best when they put it in their own words, rehearse it, and then review and rehearse it again.

A simple study method incorporates these principles. You can remember it as PRTR: *P*review, *R*ead, *T*hink critically, and *R*eview.

First, *preview* what you're about to read. Each module's headings and Preview Questions provide a framework on which you can hang the information to come. We tend to remember organized information and to forget disorganized facts.

Second, *read* the module. Unlike most psychology texts (including others that I have written) this book is organized by *short* chapters (modules) of readable length.

Third, *think actively and critically.* Ask questions and answer the Preview Question. Make notes. Reflect on implications: How does what you've read support or challenge your assumptions? How convincing is the evidence? How does it relate to your own life? (The Test Yourself, Review, and Reflect questions at the end of each module should help to stimulate your active thinking.)

- **applied research** scientific study that aims to solve practical problems.
- **clinical psychology** a branch of psychology that studies, assesses, and treats people with psychological disorders.
- **psychiatry** a branch of medicine dealing with psychological disorders; practiced by physicians who sometimes provide medical (for example, drug) treatments as well as psychological therapy.

Fourth, *review*. To drive a section's organization more deeply into your memory, rescan the section and the marginal definitions of key terms, or read its Review paragraphs. Glance over your notes or highlighting. Then stop and let it all sink in. Better yet, summarize the material for a friend or lecture about it to an imaginary audience.

Preview, read, think, review. I have organized this book to facilitate your using the PRTR study method. Each module begins with an outline that helps you preview what's upcoming, and most begin with a Preview Question that can help you read and think actively. The Review and Reflect sections summarize the module's essentials and the "Test Yourself" quizzes help you check your mastery of important concepts. Preview, read, think, review.

Four additional study hints may further boost your learning:

1. **Distribute your study time.** One of psychology's oldest findings is that spaced practice promotes better retention than massed practice. You'll remember material better if you space your time over several study periods—perhaps one hour a day, six days a week—rather than cram it into one long study blitz. Spacing your study sessions requires a disciplined approach to managing your time. (Richard O. Straub explains time management in the study guide that accompanies this text.) For example, rather than trying to read several modules in a single sitting, read just one and then turn to something else.

2. **In class, listen actively.** As psychologist William James urged some 100 years ago, *"No reception without reaction, no impression without . . . expression."* Listen for the main idea and subideas in lectures. *Write them down.* Ask questions during and after class. In class, as in your private study, process the information actively and you will understand and retain it better.

3. **Overlearn.** Psychology tells us that "overlearning improves retention." The more often students read the current assignment and the fewer classes they miss, the better their exam scores are (Woehr & Cavell, 1993). Students frequently stop short of overlearning and overestimate how much they know. Really *learning* something requires more than momentarily understanding it. You may understand a module as you read it, but if you devote extra study time to rereading, to testing yourself, and to reviewing what you think you know, you will actually *learn* the material and retain your new knowledge longer.

4. **Be a smart test-taker.** If a test contains both multiple-choice questions and an essay question, turn first to the essay. Read the question carefully, noting exactly what the instructor is asking. On the back of a page, pencil in a list of points you'd like to make, and then organize them. Before writing, put the essay aside and work through the multiple-choice questions. (As you do so, you may continue to mull over the essay question. Sometimes the objective questions will bring pertinent thoughts to mind.) Then reread the essay question, rethink your answer, and start writing. When you finish, proofread your work to eliminate spelling and grammatical errors that make you look less competent than you are.

   When reading multiple-choice questions, don't confuse yourself by trying to imagine how each choice might be the right one. Try instead to answer the question as if it were a fill-in-the-blank. First, cover the answers, recall what you know, and complete the sentence in your mind. Then read the answers on the test and find the alternative that best matches your own answer.

As you read psychology, you will learn much more than effective study techniques. Psychology teaches us how to ask important questions—how to think critically as we evaluate competing ideas and popular claims. It deepens our appreciation for how we humans perceive, think, feel, and act. By so doing, it can enrich our lives and enlarge our vision. Through this book I hope to help guide you toward that end. As educator Charles Eliot said a century ago, "Books are the quietest and most constant of friends, and the most patient of teachers."

REVIEW AND REFLECT:

The History and Scope of Psychology

How did psychology develop ?

Psychology has roots in several countries and mother disciplines, including philosophy, biology, and medicine. After beginning as a "science of mental life," psychology evolved into a "science of observable behavior," and finally to today's "science of behavior and mental processes."

What are the recurring issues that cut across psychology?

Psychologists wrestle with several recurring issues. These include how consistently stable and rational we are over time. But the biggest and most enduring issue concerns the roles of nature (genes) and nurture (all other influences, from womb to tomb).

What theoretical perspectives do psychologists take?

Psychologists view behavior and mental processes from various perspectives. These currently include the neuroscience, evolutionary, behavior genetics, psychodynamic, behavioral, cognitive, and social-cultural perspectives. Each of them provides useful insights.

What are psychology's specialized subfields?

Psychology's subfields encompass basic research (often done by biological, developmental, cognitive, personality, and social psychologists), applied research (sometimes conducted by organizational/industrial psychologists), and clinical applications.

Do psychology's findings offer any hints that can help you study effectively and boost your performance in this course and other courses?

Mastering psychology requires active study. A *preview, read, think, review* study method, combined with distributing your study time, listening actively, overlearning, and being a smart test-taker, should boost your learning and performance.

Terms and Concepts to Remember

psychology, p. 4
nature-nurture issue, p. 5
natural selection, p. 5
basic research, p. 7

applied research, p. 8
clinical psychology, p. 8
psychiatry, p. 8

Test Yourself

1.1. Psychology is the science of behavior and mental processes. The perspective in psychology that focuses on how behavior and thought differ from situation to situation and from culture to culture is the
   a. cognitive perspective.
   b. behavioral perspective.
   c. social-cultural perspective.
   d. neuroscience perspective.

1.2. In the history of psychology, one of the main debates has been over the nature-nurture issue. Nature is to nurture as
   a. personality is to intelligence.
   b. biology is to experience.
   c. intelligence is to biology.
   d. psychological traits are to behaviors.

1.3. The behavioral perspective in psychology emphasizes observable responses and how the are acquired and modified. A behavioral psychologist would be most likely to study
   a. the effect of school uniforms on classroom behaviors.
   b. the hidden meaning in children's themes and drawings.
   c. the age at which children can learn algebra.
   d. whether certain mathematical abilities appear to be inherited.

1.4. A psychologist who treats emotionally troubled adolescents at the local mental health agency is most likely to be a/an
   a. research psychologist.
   b. psychiatrist.
   c. industrial/organizational psychologist.
   d. clinical psychologist.

1.5. A psychologist who conducts basic research to expand psychology's knowledge base would be most likely to
   a. design a computer screen with limited glare and assess the effect on computer operators' eyes after a day's work.
   b. treat older people who are overcome by depression.
   c. observe 3- and 6-year-old children solving puzzles and analyze differences in their abilities.
   d. interview children with behavioral problems and suggest treatments.

Review: What is behavior, and what are mental processes?

Reflect: When you signed up for this course, what did you think psychology would be all about?

Answers to the Test Yourself and Review questions can be found in the green appendix at the end of the book.

Each Review and Reflect section will end with some important questions. The Test Yourself and Review questions offer you a handy self-test on the material you have just read. Answers are provided in the Answers Appendix at the end of the book. The Reflect Questions will help you connect the key issues to your own life. Making these issues personally meaningful will make them *memorable*.

2 Research Strategies: How Psychologists Ask and Answer Questions

Hoping to satisfy their curiosity about people and to remedy their own woes, millions turn to "psychology." They listen to over-the-air counseling on talk shows, read articles on harnessing psychic powers, attend seminars on how to stop smoking through hypnosis, and absorb self-help books on the meaning of dreams, the secrets of ecstatic love, the roots of personal happiness.

Others, intrigued by claims of psychological truth, wonder: Do mothers and infants bond in the first hours after birth? Should we trust people's memories of childhood sexual abuse "recovered" in adulthood—and prosecute the alleged predators? Are first-born children more driven to achieve? Does handwriting offer clues to personality? Does psychotherapy heal?

In working with such questions, how can we separate uninformed opinions from examined conclusions? *How can we best use psychology to understand why people think, feel, and act as they do?*

> What good fortune for those in power that people do not think.
>
> Adolph Hitler, 1889–1945

Thinking Critically With Psychological Science

Preview Questions: Why are the answers that flow from the scientific approach more reliable than those based on intuition and common sense? How do psychologists use the scientific method to construct theories?

The Limits of Intuition and Common Sense

In sifting reality from illusion, won't intuition and plain common sense suffice for everyday life? Some say psychology merely documents what people already know and dresses it in jargon: "So what else is new—you get paid for using fancy methods to prove what my grandmother knew?"

Others scorn a scientific approach because of their faith in human intuition. Advocates of "intuitive management" urge us to distrust statistical predictors and tune into our hunches when hiring, firing, and investing. Like *Star Wars'* Luke Skywalker, we should trust the force within.

> "The naked intellect is an extraordinarily inaccurate instrument."
>
> Madeleine L'Engle, "A Wind in the Door," 1973.

The limits of intuition
Personnel interviewers tend to be overconfident of their gut feelings about job applicants. Their confidence stems partly from their recalling cases where their favorable impression proved right, and from their ignorance about rejected applicants who succeeded elsewhere.

Actually, our intuition can lead us astray. Consider two examples:

+ Imagine (or ask someone to imagine) folding a sheet of paper on itself 100 times. Roughly how thick would it then be?

+ Given our year with 365 days, a group needs 366 people to ensure that at least two people share the same birthday; how big should a group be to have a 50 percent chance of finding a birthday match? (See page 15 for the answers.)

Our notions of common sense similarly err. We're all after-the-fact pundits, presuming we could have foreseen what we know happened.

Did We Know It All Along? The Hindsight Bias

How easy it is to seem astute when drawing the bull's eye after the arrow has struck. *After* each stock market downswing, for example, investment gurus say "the market was obviously overdue for a correction." And physicians given case information plus an autopsy report may find a cause of death obvious—something they easily could have foreseen, knowing the symptoms. But it is not so obvious to doctors told the same symptoms without the autopsy report (Dawson & others, 1988). Finding out that something has happened makes it seem inevitable. Psychologists call this 20/20 hindsight vision the **hindsight bias**, also known as the *I-knew-it-all-along phenomenon.*

Psychologists Paul Slovic and Baruch Fischhoff (1977) and Gordon Wood (1979) have shown how unanticipated scientific results and historical happenings can indeed *seem* like obvious common sense. This phenomenon is easy to demonstrate by giving half the members of a group some purported psychological finding, and the other half an opposite result. If you were in the first group, you might read, "Psychologists have found that separation weakens romantic attraction. As the saying goes, 'Out of sight, out of mind.'" Could you imagine why this might be true? Most people can, and nearly all will then regard this true finding as unsurprising.

But what if you had read the opposite: "Psychologists have found that separation strengthens romantic attraction. As the saying goes, 'Absence makes the heart grow fonder.'" People given this result can also easily explain it, and they overwhelmingly see it as unsurprising common sense. Obviously, when both a supposed finding and its opposite seem like common sense, there is a problem.

Consider hindsight bias in a judicial context. When viewing a police lineup, eyewitnesses often feel uncertain: "I'm not sure. . . . I think it's one of those two, maybe the shorter guy on the left." If told they have chosen the actual suspect, they may later, when testifying in court, recall easily identifying the person. "There was no maybe about it," recalled one formerly uncertain eyewitness. Gary Wells and Amy Bradfield (1998) demonstrated this I-knew-it-all-along effect after showing 352 Iowa State University students a grainy security video of a man entering a store just before murdering a security guard. When shown a photospread from the actual case, minus the actual gunman's photo, all 352 students made a false identification. Those told "Good. You identified the actual suspect" were now understandably more confident in their identification—but were also *four times* more likely to recall having felt great confidence when earlier making their identification. Were they aware of how the experimenter's off-hand comment had influenced their recollections? No, most denied being influenced by the casual feedback, yet they were just as influenced as the minority who acknowledged that the feedback might have colored their memory.

Such errors in our recollections and explanations show why we need psychological research. Just asking people how and why they felt or acted as they did sometimes can be misleading—*not* because common sense is usually wrong, but because it is after the fact. Common sense describes what has happened more easily than it predicts what will happen. As Dr. Watson said to Sherlock Holmes, "Anything seems commonplace, once explained."

Nevertheless, Grandmother is often right. As Yogi Berra once said, "You can observe a lot by watching." (We have Berra to thank for other gems, such as "Nobody ever comes here—it's too crowded," and "If the people don't want to come out to the ballpark, nobody's gonna stop 'em.") Because we're all behavior-watchers, it would be surprising if many of psychology's findings had *not* been foreseen. Many people believe that love breeds happiness, and they are right, according to researchers who have found that we humans have a deep "need to belong" to others.

But some research findings *do* jolt our common sense. Sometimes Grandmother's intuition has it wrong. Informed by countless casual observations, our intuition may tell us that familiarity breeds contempt, that dreams predict the future, and that emotional reactions coincide with menstrual phase. The available evidence

■ **hindsight bias** the tendency to believe, after learning an outcome, that one would have foreseen it. (Also known as the *I-knew-it-all-along phenomenon.*)

"Life is lived forwards, but understood backwards."

Søren Kierkegaard, 1813–1855

"There are three things extremely hard, Steel, a Diamond, and to know one's self."

Benjamin Franklin, 1706–1790

suggests that these common sense ideas are wrong, wrong, and wrong. Throughout this book we will see how research has both inspired and overturned popular ideas—about aging, about sleep and dreams, about personality. And we will also see how it has surprised us with discoveries about how the brain's chemical messengers control our moods and memories, about animal abilities, and about the effects of stress on our capacity to fight disease.

Overconfidence

Our everyday thinking is limited not only by our after-the-fact common sense but also by our human tendency toward overconfidence. We tend to think we know more than we do. Asked how sure we are of our answers to factual questions (is Boston north or south of Paris?), we tend to be more confident than correct.[1] Or consider these three anagrams, which Richard Goranson (1978) asked people to unscramble.

WREAT → WATER
ETRYN → ENTRY
GRABE → BARGE

Reflect for a moment: About how many seconds do you think it would have taken you to unscramble each of these?

Once people know the target word, hindsight makes it seem obvious—so much so that they become overconfident. They think they would have seen the solution in only 10 seconds or so, when in reality the average subject spent 3 minutes, as you also might, given a similar anagram without the solution: OCHSA (see page 19 to check your answer).

Are we any better at predicting our social behavior? To find out, Robert Vallone and his associates (1990) had students predict at the beginning of the school year whether they would drop a course, vote in an upcoming election, call their parents more than twice a month, and so forth. On average, the students felt 84 percent confident in making these self-predictions. Later quizzes about their actual behavior showed their predictions were correct only 71 percent of the time. Even when they were 100 percent sure of themselves, their self-predictions erred 15 percent of the time.

Or consider the confidence of new collegians about their college future: As they begin college, only 2 percent of American students say there is a very good chance they will drop out permanently or temporarily (Sax & others, 1996). But the optimism of the other 98 percent is often unrealistic. Nearly half of the students entering a four-year college or university do not earn a degree within five years.

It's not just collegians. For a dozen years, Ohio State University psychologist Philip Tetlock (1998) has been collecting experts' predictions of political, economic, and military situations. In the late 1980s, for example, he invited expert professors, think tank analysts, government experts, and journalists to project the governance of the Soviet Union or of South Africa five years later, and to rate how confident they felt. Others did the same for the future of Canada in 1992. After the five years had elapsed (and communism had collapsed in the Soviet Union, South Africa had become a multiracial democracy, and the Canadian constitution continued), Tetlock invited the experts to recall and reflect on their predictions—which, as in laboratory studies, were far more confident than correct. Experts who had felt more than 80 percent confident were right less than 40 percent of the time.

Despite their lackluster predictions, those who erred were nearly as likely as those who got it right to convince themselves that their initial analysis was *still basically right*. I was "almost right," many of them felt. "The hardliners almost succeeded in their coup attempt against Gorbachev." "The Quebecois separatists almost won

> "It ain't so much the things we don't know that get us into trouble. It's the things we know that just ain't so."
>
> **Artemus Ward, 1834–1867**

> "We don't like their sound. Groups of guitars are on their way out."
>
> **Decca Records, in turning down a recording contract with the Beatles in 1962**

> "Computers in the future may weigh no more than 1.5 tons."
>
> ***Popular Mechanics*, 1949**

> "The telephone may be appropriate for our American cousins, but not here, because we have an adequate supply of messenger boys."
>
> **British expert group evaluating the invention of the telephone**

> "They couldn't hit an elephant at this dist—."
>
> **General John Sedgwick's last words, uttered during a U.S. Civil War Battle, 1864**

[1]Boston is south of Paris.

the secessionist referendum." "But for the coincidence of de Klerk and Mandela, the transition to black majority rule in South Africa would have been a lot bloodier." The overconfidence of political experts (and stock market forecasters and sports prognosticators) is therefore hard to dislodge, no matter what the outcome.

The Scientific Attitude

Underlying all science is a hard-headed *curiosity*, a passion to explore and understand without misleading or being misled. Some questions (Is there life after death?) are beyond science. To answer them in any way requires a leap of faith. With many other ideas (Can some people demonstrate ESP?), the proof is in the pudding. No matter how sensible or crazy-sounding an idea, the hard-headed question is, Does it work? When put to the test, can its predictions be confirmed?

This scientific approach has a long history. As ancient a figure as Moses used such an approach. How do you evaluate a self-proclaimed prophet? His answer: Put the prophet to the test. If the predicted event "does not take place or prove true," then so much the worse for the prophet (*Deuteronomy* 18:22). Magician James Randi uses Moses' approach when testing those claiming to see auras around people's bodies:

Randi: Do you see an aura around my head?
Aura-seer: Yes, indeed.
Randi: Can you still see the aura if I put this magazine in front of my face?
Aura-seer: Of course.
Randi: Then if I were to step behind a wall barely taller than I am, you could determine my location from the aura visible above my head, right?

Randi tells me that no aura-seer has yet agreed to take this simple test.

When subjected to such scrutiny, crazy-sounding ideas sometimes find support. During the 1700s, scientists scoffed at the notion that meteorites had extraterrestrial origins. When two Yale scientists dared to deviate from the conventional opinion, Thomas Jefferson jeered, "Gentlemen, I would rather believe that those two Yankee Professors would lie than to believe that stones fell from heaven." Sometimes scientific inquiry refutes skeptics.

More often, it relegates crazy-sounding ideas to the mountain of forgotten claims of perpetual motion machines, miracle cancer cures, and out-of-body travels into centuries past. To sift reality from fantasy, sense from nonsense, therefore, requires a scientific attitude: being skeptical but not cynical, open but not gullible.

As scientists, psychologists approach the world of behavior with a curious *skepticism*. They persistently ask two questions: What do you mean? How do you know? Consider some familiar claims: that theater owners can make you hungry by flashing an imperceptibly brief message—EAT POPCORN; that lie detectors tell the truth; that astrologers can analyze your character and predict your future based on the position of the planets at your birth. As you will see in the pages that follow, we can test such claims. In the arena of competing ideas, skeptical testing can reveal which ones best match the facts. "To believe with certainty," says a Polish proverb, "we must begin by doubting."

Putting a scientific attitude into practice requires not only skepticism but also *humility* because we may have to reject our own ideas. In the last analysis, what matters is not my opinion or yours, but the truths nature reveals in response to our questioning. If people don't behave as our ideas predict, then so much the worse for our ideas. This is the humble attitude expressed in one of psychology's early mottos: "The rat is always right."

Historians of science tell us that these attitudes of curiosity, skepticism, and humility helped make modern science possible. Many of its founders were people whose religious convictions made them humble before nature and skeptical of any human authority (Hooykaas, 1972; Merton, 1938). Of course, scientists, like anyone else,

Answers to questions on page 12: Given a 0.1-millimeter-thick sheet, the thickness after 100 folds would be 800 trillion times the distance between the Earth and the Sun (Gilovich, 1991). Only 23 people are needed to give better than even odds of any two people having the same birthday.

"The scientist . . . must be free to ask any question, to doubt any assertion, to seek for any evidence, to correct any errors."

Physicist J. Robert Oppenheimer, *Life*, October 10, 1949

The amazing Randi
The magician James Randi exemplifies skepticism. He has tested and debunked a variety of psychic phenomena.

"A skeptic is one who is willing to question any truth claim, asking for clarity in definition, consistency in logic, and adequacy of evidence."

Philosopher Paul Kurtz, *The Skeptical Inquirer*, 1994

"My deeply held belief is that if a god anything like the traditional sort exists, our curiosity and intelligence are provided by such a god. We would be unappreciative of those gifts . . . if we suppressed our passion to explore the universe and ourselves."

Carl Sagan (1979a)

"The real purpose of the scientific method is to make sure Nature hasn't misled you into thinking you know something you don't actually know."

Robert M. Pirsig, *Zen and the Art of Motorcycle Maintenance*, 1974

can have big egos and may cling to their preconceptions. We all view nature through the spectacles of our preconceived ideas. Still, the ideal that unifies psychologists with all scientists is the skeptical yet humble scrutiny of competing ideas. As a community, scientists check and recheck one another's findings and conclusions.

This scientific attitude, with its principles for sifting reality from illusion, prepares us to think smarter. Smart thinking, called **critical thinking**, examines assumptions, discerns hidden values, evaluates evidence, and assesses conclusions. Whether reading a news report or listening to a conversation, critical thinkers ask questions. They wonder, How do they know that? What's this person's agenda? Is the conclusion based on anecdote and gut feelings, or on evidence? Does the evidence justify a cause-effect conclusion? What alternative explanations are possible? Carried to an extreme, healthy skepticism can degenerate into a negative cynicism that scorns any unproven idea. But a critical attitude can also produce humility—an awareness of our own vulnerability to error and an openness to surprises and new perspectives.

Has psychology's own critical inquiry indeed been open to surprising findings? The answer is plainly yes. Believe it or not . . .

+ massive losses of brain tissue early in life may have minimal long-term effects.
+ within days, newborns can recognize their mother's odor and voice.
+ prolonged stress hinders the body's disease-fighting immune system, making people more vulnerable to physical illness.
+ diverse groups—men and women, old and young, rich and working class, those with disabilities and without—report roughly comparable levels of personal happiness.
+ electroconvulsive ("shock") therapy is often a very effective treatment for severe depression.

And has critical inquiry convincingly debunked popular presumptions? The answer is again yes. The available evidence indicates that . . .

+ as part of their passage to middle adulthood, men in their early forties do *not* typically undergo a midlife crisis, and most mothers are *not* depressed for a time after their children grow up and leave home.
+ sleepwalkers are *not* acting out their dreams; sleeptalkers are *not* verbalizing their dreams.
+ our past experiences are *not* all recorded verbatim in our brains; with brain stimulation or hypnosis, one *cannot* simply "play the tape" and relive long-buried or repressed memories.
+ most people do *not* suffer from unrealistically low self-esteem.
+ opposites do *not* generally attract.

The Scientific Method

Psychologists arm their scientific attitude with the *scientific method*: They make observations, form theories, and then refine their theories in the light of new observations. In everyday conversation, we tend to use "theory" to mean "mere hunch." In science, "theory" is linked with observation. A scientific **theory** *explains* through an integrated set of principles that *organizes* and *predicts* observable behaviors or events. By organizing isolated facts, a theory simplifies things. Psychologists now know so many facts about behavior that we could never hope to remember them all. By linking such observations and bridging them to deeper principles, a theory offers a useful summary. By connecting the observed dots, theories reveal a coherent picture.

A good theory of depression, for example, will first help us organize countless observations concerning depression into a much shorter list of principles. Say we observe over and over that people with depression describe themselves—their past, pre-

■ **critical thinking** thinking that does not blindly accept arguments and conclusions. Rather, it examines assumptions, discerns hidden values, evaluates evidence, and assesses conclusions.

sent, and future—in gloomy terms. We might therefore theorize that low self-esteem contributes to depression. So far so good: Our self-esteem principle neatly summarizes a long list of facts about people with depression.

Yet no matter how reasonable a theory may sound—and low self-esteem certainly seems a reasonable explanation of depression—we must put it to the test. A good theory doesn't just sound appealing. It must imply testable predictions, called **hypotheses**. By enabling us to test and reject or revise the theory, such predictions give direction to research. They specify in advance what results would support the theory and what results would disconfirm it. To test our self-esteem theory of depression, we might give people a test of self-esteem on which they respond to statements such as "I have good ideas." Then we could see whether, as we hypothesized, people who report poorer self-images are indeed more depressed (**FIGURE 2.1**).

In testing our theory, we should be aware that it can bias our observations. Having theorized that depression springs from low self-esteem, we may see what we expect to see. We may be tempted to perceive depressed people's comments as self-disparaging.

As one check on their biases, psychologists report their research precisely enough—with clear **operational definitions** of concepts—to allow others to **replicate** (repeat) their observations. If other researchers re-create the essence of a study with different participants and materials and get similar results, then our confidence in the reliability of the finding grows. The first study of hindsight bias aroused psychologists' curiosity. Now, after many successful replications with different people and questions, we feel quite sure of the phenomenon's power.

In the end, our theory will be useful if it (1) effectively *organizes* a range of self-reports and observations and (2) implies clear *predictions* that anyone can use to check the theory or to derive practical applications. (If we boost people's self-esteem, will their depression lift?) Eventually, our research will probably lead to a revised theory that better organizes and predicts what we know about depression.

Our research strategies include descriptive, correlational, and experimental methods. We test hypotheses and refine our theories by making *observations* that *describe* behavior, detecting *correlations* that help *predict* behavior, and doing *experiments* that help *explain* behavior. To think critically about popularized psychology claims, we need to recognize these designs and to know how we can use them to sharpen our everyday thinking.

- **theory** an explanation using an integrated set of principles that organizes and predicts observations.

- **hypothesis** a testable prediction, often implied by a theory.

- **operational definition** a statement of the procedures (operations) used to define research variables. For example, *intelligence* may be operationally defined as what an intelligence test measures.

- **replication** repeating the essence of a research study, usually with different participants in different situations, to see whether the basic finding generalizes to other participants and circumstances.

Good theories explain by
1. organizing and linking observed facts.
2. implying hypotheses that offer testable predictions and, sometimes, practical applications.

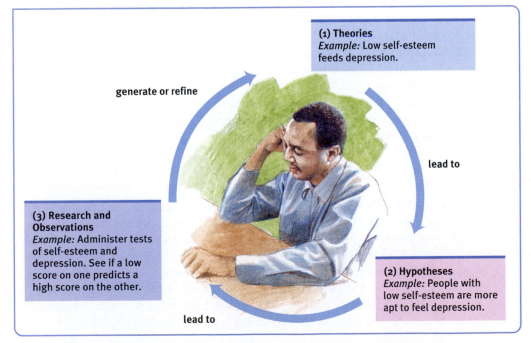

(1) Theories
Example: Low self-esteem feeds depression.

generate or refine

lead to

(3) Research and Observations
Example: Administer tests of self-esteem and depression. See if a low score on one predicts a high score on the other.

(2) Hypotheses
Example: People with low self-esteem are more apt to feel depression.

lead to

FIGURE 2.1
The scientific method
A self-correcting process for asking questions and observing nature's answer.

Description

Preview Question: How do psychologists observe and describe behavior?

The starting point of any science is description. In everyday life, all of us observe and describe people, often drawing conclusions about why they behave as they do. Professional psychologists do much the same, only more objectively and systematically.

The Case Study

Among the oldest research methods is the **case study**, in which psychologists study one or more individuals in great depth in the hope of revealing things true of us all. Some examples: Much of our early knowledge about the brain came from case studies of individuals who suffered a particular impairment after damage to a certain brain region. Sigmund Freud constructed his theory of personality from a handful of case studies. Developmental psychologist Jean Piaget taught us about children's thinking after carefully observing and questioning but a few children. Studies of only a few chimpanzees have revealed their capacity for understanding and language. Intensive case studies are sometimes very revealing.

Although case studies can also suggest hypotheses for further study, they sometimes mislead us: Any given individual may be atypical. Unrepresentative information can lead to mistaken judgments and false conclusions. Indeed, anytime a researcher mentions a finding ("Smokers die younger: 95 percent of men over 85 are nonsmokers") someone is sure to offer a contradictory case ("Well, I have an uncle who smoked two packs a day and lived to be 89"). Anecdotal cases—dramatic stories, personal experiences, even psychological case examples—have a way of overwhelming general truths. Numbers can be numbing (in one study of 1300 dream reports concerning a kidnapped child, only 5 percent correctly envisioned the child as dead). Anecdotes can be alarming ("But I know a man who dreamed his sister was in a car accident, and two days later she was badly injured").

After 12-year-old Polly Klaas was kidnapped from her California bedroom and murdered, after 2-year-old James Bulger was abducted from a Liverpool shopping mall and bludgeoned to death, and again after a murderous rampage at Colorado's Columbine High School, children and parents in both countries became noticeably "scared" (as a *Newsweek* cover story put it)—much more scared than they were of car accidents or cancer, which cause child deaths many hundreds of times more often than kidnapping and school assassinations do. The brutal kidnappings were impressed on people's memories, and people intuitively judge various risks based on how easily they remember examples of them. As psychologist Gordon Allport said, "Given a thimbleful of [dramatic] facts we rush to make generalizations as large as a tub."

So, individual cases can suggest fruitful ideas. What's true of all of us can be glimpsed in any one of us. But to discern the general truths that cover individual cases, we must answer questions with other methods.

The Survey

The **survey** method, commonly used in both descriptive and correlational studies, looks at many cases in less depth. A survey asks people to report their behavior or opinions. Questions about everything from sexual practices to political opinions get put to the public. It's hard to think of a significant question that survey researchers have not asked. For example, recent Harris and Gallup polls have revealed that 72 percent of Americans think there is too much TV violence, 84 percent favor equal job opportunities for homosexual people, 89 percent say they face high stress, 95 percent believe in God, and 96 percent would like to change something about their appearance.

"'Well my dear,' said Miss Marple, 'human nature is very much the same everywhere, and of course, one has opportunities of observing it at closer quarters in a village.'"

Agatha Christie, *The Tuesday Club Murders*, 1933

The case of the conversational chimpanzee
In intensive case studies of chimpanzees, psychologists have explored the intriguing question of whether language is uniquely human. Here the late Nim Chimpsky signs "hug" as his trainer, psychologist Herbert Terrace, shows him the puppet Ernie. But are chimps really capable of using language? Cognitive psychologists continue to debate this issue.

Wording Effects

Asking questions is tricky. Even subtle changes in the order or wording of questions can have major effects. Should cigarette ads or pornography be allowed on television? People are much more likely to approve "not allowing" such things than "forbidding" or "censoring" them. In a recent national survey, only 27 percent of Americans approved of "government censorship" of media sex and violence, though 66 percent approved of "more restrictions on what is shown on television" (Lacayo, 1995). People are similarly much more approving of "aid to the needy" than of "welfare," of "affirmative action" than of "preferential treatment," and of "revenue enhancers" than of "taxes." Because wording questions is such a delicate matter, critical thinkers will reflect on how the phrasing of a question might have affected the opinions respondents expressed.

Sampling

In our everyday experience we spend most of our time with a biased sample of people—mostly those who share our attitudes and habits. Thus, when we wonder how many people hold a particular belief, those who think as we do come to mind most readily. This tendency to overestimate others' agreement with us is the **false consensus effect** (Ross & others, 1977). Vegetarians will think more people are vegetarians than will meat-eaters, and conservatives will perceive more support for conservative views than will liberals. To restrain this bias, researchers aim to gather a representative sample of people.

Most surveys sample a target group. If you wished to survey the students at your college or university you could question them all, but probably there are too many to do so. Instead, you could survey a representative sample of the total student **population**—the whole group you wanted to study and describe. How could you make your sample representative of this population? By making it a **random sample**, one in which every person in the entire group has an equal chance of participating.

To sample the students at your institution randomly, you would *not* send them all a questionnaire. (The conscientious people who return it would not be a random sample.) Rather, you would aim for a representative sample by, say, using a table of random numbers to pick participants from a student listing and then making sure you involve as many as possible. Large representative samples are better than small ones, but a small representative sample of 100 is better than an unrepresentative sample of 500.

The point to remember: Before believing survey findings, think critically: Consider the sample. You cannot compensate for an unrepresentative sample by simply adding more people.

You can forecast the weather by taking an arbitrary sample—by looking at the clouds and holding your finger in the wind—or you can look at weather maps based on comprehensive reporting. You can describe human experience using common sense, dramatic anecdotes, personal experience, and arbitrary samples. But for an accurate picture of the experiences and attitudes of a whole population, there's only one game in town—the representative sample.

We can extend this point to everyday thinking, as we generalize from samples we observe. We meet a few students and attend a few classes during a visit to a college and infer from those instances how friendly the campus is and how good the teaching is. We observe the weather during a three-day visit to Copenhagen and then tell our friends about the climate there.

Overgeneralizing from such select samples is tempting, especially when they are vivid cases. Given (a) a statistical summary of a professor's student evaluations and (b) the vivid comments of two irate students, an administrator's impression of the professor may be influenced as much by the two unhappy students as by the many favorable evaluations in the statistical summary. Standing in the checkout line at the supermarket, George sees the woman in front of him pay with government-provided food stamps and then watches with dismay as she drives away in a fancy car. In both situations, the temptation to generalize from a few vivid but unrepresentative cases is nearly irresistible.

- **case study** an observation technique in which one person is studied in depth in the hope of revealing universal principles.

- **survey** a technique for ascertaining the self-reported attitudes or behaviors of people, usually by questioning a representative, random sample of them.

- **false consensus effect** the tendency to overestimate the extent to which others share our beliefs and behaviors.

- **population** all the cases in a group, from which samples may be drawn for a study.

- **random sample** a sample that fairly represents a population because each member has an equal chance of inclusion.

With very large samples, estimates become quite reliable. *E* is estimated to represent 12.7 percent of the letters in written English. *E*, in fact, is 12.3 percent of the 925,141 letters in Melville's *Moby Dick*, 12.4 percent of the 586,747 letters in Dickens' *A Tale of Two Cities*, and 12.1 percent of the 3,901,021 letters in 12 of Mark Twain's works (*Chance News*, 1997).

Solution to anagram on page 14: CHAOS.

This Modern World by Tom Tomorrow © 1991.

FIGURE 2.2
World in a jar

If marbles of two colors are mixed well in the large jar, the fastest way to know their ratio is to blindly transfer a few into a smaller one and count them. This approach is called random sampling.

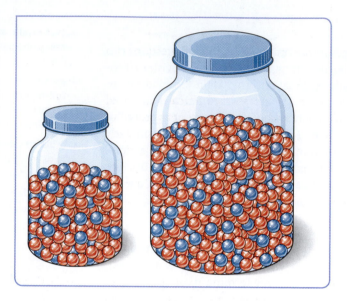

The point to remember: The best basis for generalizing is not from the exceptional cases one finds at the extremes, but from a representative sample of cases.

The random-sampling principle also works in national surveys. Imagine that you had a giant barrel containing 60 million white beans mixed with 40 million red beans. A scoop that randomly sampled 1500 of them would contain about 60 percent white and 40 percent red beans, give or take 2 or 3 percent. Sampling voters in a national election survey is like sampling the beans; 1500 randomly sampled people, drawn from all areas of a country, provide a remarkably accurate snapshot of the opinions of a nation (**FIGURE 2.2**).

Because gathering a random sample can be a huge task, some don't make the effort. Shere Hite's book *Women and Love* reported survey findings based on only a 4.5 percent response rate from mailings to an unrepresentative sample of 100,000 women. The response was doubly unrepresentative because not only did she have a modest, self-selected return, but the women initially contacted were members of women's organizations. Nonetheless, "It's 4500 people. That's enough for me," reported Hite. And it was apparently enough for *Time* magazine, which made a cover story of her findings—that 70 percent of women married five or more years were having affairs, and that 95 percent of women felt emotionally harassed by the men they love (Wallis, 1987). Evidently it didn't matter that on less publicized surveys, *randomly* sampled American women expressed much higher levels of satisfaction: And only 1 in 7 reported having had an affair during their current marriage—a level of faithfulness replicated in British, French, and Danish surveys (Greeley, 1991, 1994). Without random sampling, large samples like Hite's—including call-in phone samples—merely give better estimates of a misleading number.

"How would you like me to answer that question? As a member of my ethnic group, educational class, income group, or religious category?"

Naturalistic Observation

A third descriptive research method involves watching and recording the behavior of organisms in their natural environment and is known as **naturalistic observation**.

Naturalistic observations range from watching chimpanzee societies in the jungle, to unobtrusive measures of parent-child interactions in different cultures, to recording students' self-seating patterns in the lunchrooms of multiracial schools.

Like the case study and survey methods, naturalistic observation does not *explain* behavior. It *describes* it. Nevertheless, description can be revealing. We once thought, for example, that only humans use tools. Then naturalistic observation revealed that chimpanzees sometimes insert a stick in a termite mound and withdraw it, eating the stick's load of termites. Such naturalistic observations, recalls chimpanzee observer Jane Goodall (1998), paved the way for later studies of animal thinking, language, and emotion. "Observations, made in the natural habitat, helped to show that the societies and behavior of animals are far more complex than previously supposed," thus expanding our understanding of our fellow animals. We later learned that chimps and baboons also use deception to achieve their aims.

Naturalistic observation

Some psychologists study human and animal behavior in natural environments. As University of St. Andrews psychologist Richard Byrne observes an adult gorilla, recording its behavior on a hand-held computer, a curious infant approaches and investigates his camera lens cap.

Psychologists Andrew Whiten and Richard Byrne (1988) repeatedly saw one young baboon pretending to have been attacked by another as a tactic to get its mother to drive the other baboon away from its food.

Naturalistic observation also enabled Robert Levine and Ara Norenzayan (1999) to compare the pace of life in 31 countries. By operationally defining *pace of life* as walking speed, the speed with which postal clerks completed a simple request, and the accuracy of public clocks, they concluded that life is fastest-paced in Japan and Western Europe, and slower paced in economically less developed countries. People in colder climates also live at a faster pace (and are more prone to die from heart disease). Naturalistic observation is often used to describe behavior. But this study, correlating pace of life with culture and climate, illustrates how it can also be used with correlational (and experimental) research.

Correlation

Preview Questions: What does it mean when we say two things are correlated? Why do correlations permit prediction but not explanation?

Describing behavior is a first step toward predicting it. When surveys and naturalistic observations reveal that one trait or behavior accompanies another, we say the two correlate. The **correlation coefficient** is a statistical measure of relationship (**FIGURE 2.3**): It reveals how closely two things vary together and thus how well either one *predicts* the other. Knowing how much aptitude test scores *correlate* with school success tells us how well the scores *predict* school success.

Throughout this book we will often ask how much two things relate: How closely related are the personality scores of identical twins? How well do intelligence test scores predict achievement? How often does stress lead to disease?

FIGURE 2.4 illustrates perfect positive and negative correlations, which rarely occur in the "real world." These graphs are called **scatterplots**, because each point *plots* the value of two variables. A correlation's being negative has nothing to do with its strength or weakness; a negative correlation means two things relate inversely (one set of scores goes up precisely as the other goes down). A weak correlation, indicating little or no relationship, is one that has a coefficient near zero. A positive correlation means that one set of scores increases in direct proportion to the other set of scores' increase.

- **naturalistic observation** observing and recording behavior in naturally occurring situations without trying to manipulate and control the situation.
- **correlation coefficient** a statistical measure of the extent to which two factors vary together, and thus of how well either factor predicts the other.
- **scatterplot** a graphed cluster of dots, each of which represents the values of two variables. The slope of the points suggests the direction of the relationship between the two variables. The amount of scatter suggests the strength of the correlation (little scatter indicates high correlation). (Also called a *scattergram* or *scatter diagram*.)

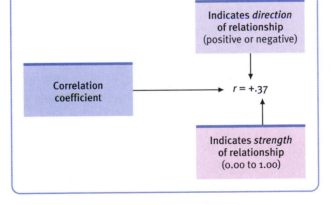

FIGURE 2.3
How to read a correlation coefficient
Correlations can range from +1.00 (one score increases in direct proportion to the other) to −1.00 (one set of scores goes up precisely as the other goes down).

FIGURE 2.4 **Perfect correlations**

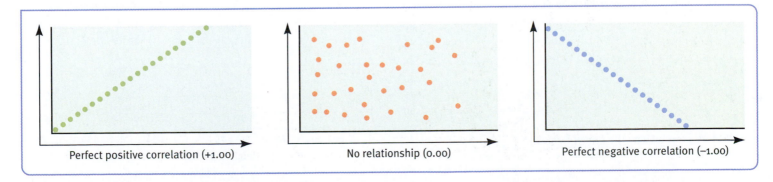

Perfect positive correlation (+1.00)   No relationship (0.00)   Perfect negative correlation (−1.00)

TABLE 2.1

HEIGHT AND TEMPERAMENT OF 20 MEN

Subject	Height in Inches	Temperament
1	80	75
2	63	66
3	61	60
4	79	90
5	74	60
6	69	42
7	62	42
8	75	60
9	77	81
10	60	39
11	64	48
12	76	69
13	71	72
14	66	57
15	73	63
16	70	75
17	63	30
18	71	57
19	68	84
20	70	39

Statistics can help us see what the naked eye sometimes misses. To demonstrate this for yourself, try an imaginary project to discern what relationship, if any, exists between two sets of scores: men's heights and men's temperaments. Assume you have measured the heights of 20 men, have had someone else independently assess their temperaments (from zero for extremely calm to 100 for highly reactive), and have obtained the data in Table 2.1.

With all the relevant data right in front of you, can you tell whether there is (1) a positive correlation between height and reactive temperament, (2) very little or no correlation, or (3) a negative correlation?

Comparing the columns in Table 2.1, most people detect very little relationship between height and temperament. In fact, the correlation in this imaginary example is moderately positive, +0.63, as we can see if we display the data as a scatterplot. In **FIGURE 2.5** the upward, oval-shaped slope of the cluster of points as one moves to the right shows that the two sets of scores (height and reactivity) tend to rise together.

If we fail to see a relationship when data are presented as systematically as in Table 2.1, how much less likely are we to notice them in everyday life? To see what is right in front of us, we sometimes need statistical illumination. We can easily see evidence of gender discrimination when given statistically summarized information about job level, seniority, performance, gender, and salary. But we often see no discrimination when the same information dribbles in, case by case (Twiss & others, 1989).

Though informative, psychology's correlations usually leave most of the variation among individuals unpredicted. As we will see, there is a correlation between parents' abusiveness and their children's later abusiveness when they become parents. But this does not mean that most abused children become abusive. The correlation simply indicates a statistical relationship: Although most abused children do not grow into abusers, nonabused children are even less likely to become abusive.

Likewise, early crime correlates with later crime. Boys arrested by age 14 are eighteen times more likely to become chronic offenders than are boys who have not been arrested by that age, and chronic offenders are fourteen times more likely to commit violent offenses. Yet two-thirds of boys arrested only once do *not* go on to commit violent crime (Forgatch, 1995). Correlations point us toward predictions, but usually imperfect ones.

The point to remember: Although the correlation coefficient tells us nothing about cause and effect, it *can* help us see the world more clearly by revealing the actual extent to which two things relate.

FIGURE 2.5

Scatterplot for height and temperament

This display of data from the 20 imagined people of Table 2.1 (each represented by a data point) reveals an upward slope, indicating a positive correlation. The considerable scatter of the data indicates the correlation is much lower than +1.0.

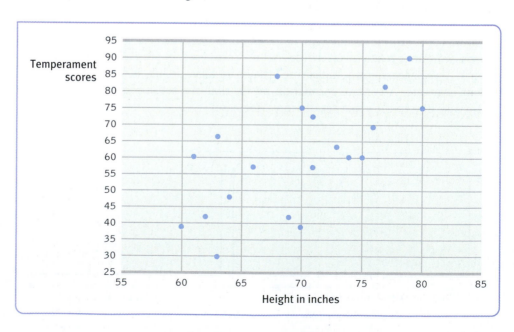

■ **illusory correlation** the perception of a relationship where none exists.

Correlation and Causation

We have seen that correlations, however imperfect, do help us predict and restrain the illusions of our flawed intuition. Watching violence correlates with (and therefore predicts) aggression. But does that mean it *causes* aggression? Does low self-esteem *cause* depression? If, based on the correlational evidence, you assume that they do, you have much company. Among the most irresistible thinking errors made both by laypeople and by professional psychologists is assuming that correlation proves causation. And yet, no matter how strong the relationship, it does not! If watching TV violence correlates positively with aggressiveness, does this mean that watching TV violence influences aggressive behavior? Perhaps. But perhaps it means that aggressive people prefer violent programs. Or perhaps both are true.

And what about the negative correlation between self-esteem and depression? Perhaps low self-esteem does cause depression. But as **FIGURE 2.6** suggests, we'd get the same coincidence of low self-esteem and depression if depression caused people to be down on themselves or if something else—a third factor such as heredity or brain chemistry—caused both low self-esteem and depression. Among men, length of marriage correlates positively with hair loss—because both are associated with a third factor, age. And people who wear hats are *more* likely to suffer skin cancer—because both are associated with fair-skinned people (who are vulnerable to skin cancer and more likely to wear protective hats).

This point is so important—so basic to thinking smarter with psychology—that it merits one more example, from a survey of 12,118 adolescents: The more teens feel loved by their parents, the less likely they are to behave in unhealthy ways—having early sex, smoking, abusing alcohol and drugs, exhibiting violence (Resnick & others, 1997). "Adults have a powerful effect on their children's behavior right through the high school years," gushed an Associated Press story on the study. But the correlation comes with no built-in cause-effect arrow. Thus, the AP could as well have said, "Well-behaved teens feel their parents' love and approval; out-of-bounds teens more often think their parents are disapproving jerks."

The point to remember: Correlation indicates the *possibility* of a cause-effect relationship, *but it does not prove causation.* Knowing that two events are correlated need not tell us anything about causation. Remember this principle and you will be wiser as you see reports of scientific studies in the news and in this book.

Illusory Correlations

Correlations make visible the relationships that we might otherwise miss. They also restrain our "seeing" relationships that actually don't exist. A perceived correlation that does not really exist is an **illusory correlation**. When we *believe* there is a relationship between two things, we are likely to *notice* and *recall* instances that confirm our belief (Troilier & Hamilton, 1986).

Illusory correlations help explain many a superstitious belief, such as the presumption that more babies are born when the moon is full or that infertile couples who adopt become more likely to conceive (Gilovich, 1991). Those who conceive after adopting capture our attention. We're less likely to notice those who adopt and never conceive, or those who conceive without adopting. In other words, illusory correlations occur when we over-rely on the top left cell of **FIGURE 2.7**, ignoring equally essential information in the other cells.

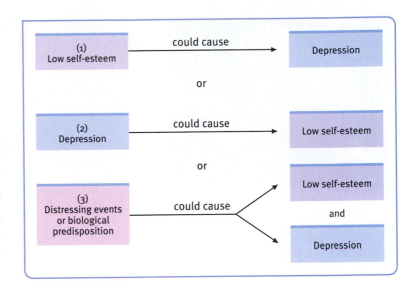

FIGURE 2.6

Three possible cause-effect relationships

People low in self-esteem are more likely to report depression than are those high in self-esteem. One possible explanation of this negative correlation is that a bad self-image causes depressed feelings. But, as the diagram indicates, other cause-effect relationships are possible.

FIGURE 2.7

Illusory correlation in everyday life

Many people believe infertile couples become more likely to conceive a child after adopting a baby. Their belief arises from their attention being drawn to such cases. The many couples who adopt without conceiving or conceive without adopting grab less attention. To determine whether there actually is a correlation between adoption and conception we need data from all four cells in this figure. (From Gilovich, 1991.)

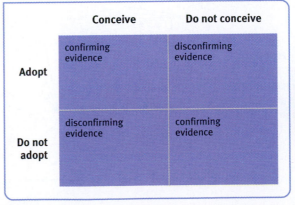

Correlation need not mean causation

Length of marriage correlates with hair loss in men. Does this mean that marriage causes men to lose their hair (or that balding men make better husbands)? In this case, as in many others, a third factor obviously explains the correlation: Golden anniversaries and baldness both accompany aging.

Such illusory thinking helps explain why for so many years people believed (and many still do) that sugar made children hyperactive, that getting cold and wet caused one to catch a cold, and that weather changes trigger arthritis pain. Physician Donald Redelmeier, working with Amos Tversky (1996; Kolata, 1996), a psychologist who specialized in "debugging human intuition," followed 18 arthritis patients for 15 months. The researchers recorded both the patients' pain reports and the daily temperature, humidity, and barometric pressure. Despite patients' beliefs, the weather was uncorrelated with their discomfort, either on the same day or up to two days earlier or later. Shown columns of random numbers labeled "arthritis pain" and "barometric pressure," even college students saw a correlation where there was none. We are, it seems, very, very good at detecting patterns, whether they're there or not, and not so good at testing our hypotheses.

Because we are sensitive to dramatic or unusual events, we are especially likely to notice and remember the occurrence of two such events in sequence—say, a premonition of an unlikely phone call followed by the call. When the call does not follow the premonition, we are less likely to note and remember the nonevent.

Likewise, instances of positive-thinking people being cured of cancer impress those who believe that positive attitudes counter disease. But to assess whether positive thinking actually affects cancer, we need three more types of information. First, we need an estimate of how many positive thinkers were *not* cured. Then we need to know how many people with cancer were and were not cured among those not using positive thinking. Without these comparison figures, the positive examples of a few tell us nothing about the actual correlation between attitudes and disease.

The point to remember: When we notice random coincidences, we may forget that they are random and instead see them as correlated. Thus, we can easily deceive ourselves by seeing what is not there.

Perceiving Order in Random Events

Illusory correlations arise from our natural eagerness to make sense of our world—what poet Wallace Stevens called our "rage for order." Given even random data, we look for order, for meaningful patterns. And we usually find such, because *random sequences often don't look random.* Consider a random coin flip: If someone flipped a coin six times, which of the following sequences of heads (H) and tails (T) would be most likely: HHHTTT or HTTHTH or HHHHHH?

Daniel Kahneman and Amos Tversky (1972) found that most people believe HTTHTH would be the most likely random sequence. Actually, all are equally likely (or, you might say, equally unlikely) to occur. A bridge or poker hand of 10 through Ace, all of hearts, would seem extraordinary; actually, it would be no more or less likely than any other specific hand of cards (**FIGURE 2.8**).

Psychologists Thomas Holtgraves and James Skeel (1992) exposed people's perceptions of randomness in their bets placed in Indiana's Pick-3 Lottery. You can play, too: Pick any three-digit number from 0 to 999.

Did your number have a repeated digit (as in 525)? Probably not. Only 14 percent of 2.24 million number strings chosen in July 1991 had a repeated digit. Although repeated digits actually occur in 28 percent of the available numbers, such numbers *look* less random (and people prefer to bet random-looking series). In actual random sequences, seeming patterns and streaks (such as repeating digits) occur more often than people expect. Thus, shown random data, scientists and

FIGURE 2.8
Two random sequences
Your chances of being dealt either of these hands is precisely the same: 1 in 2,598,960.

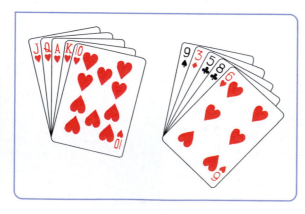

psychics alike can often "see" an interesting pattern (Guion, 1992). To demonstrate this phenomenon for myself (as you can do), I flipped a coin 51 times, with these results:

1. H	10. T	19. H	28. T	37. T	46. H
2. T	11. T	20. H	29. H	38. T	47. H
3. T	12. H	21. T	30. T	39. H	48. T
4. T	13. H	22. T	31. T	40. T	49. T
5. H	14. T	23. H	32. T	41. H	50. T
6. H	15. T	24. T	33. T	42. H	51. T
7. H	16. H	25. T	34. T	43. H	
8. T	17. T	26. T	35. T	44. H	
9. T	18. T	27. H	36. H	45. T	

Bizarre-looking, perhaps. But actually no more unlikely than any other number sequence.

Looking over the sequence, patterns jump out: Tosses 10 to 22 provided an almost perfect pattern of pairs of tails followed by pairs of heads. On tosses 30 to 38 I had a "cold hand," with only one head in eight tosses. But my fortunes immediately reversed with a "hot hand"—seven heads out of the next nine tosses.

What explains these patterns? Was I exercising some sort of paranormal control over my coin? Did I snap out of my tails funk and get in a heads groove? No such explanations are needed, for these are the sorts of streaks found in any random data. Comparing each toss to the next, 24 of the 50 comparisons yielded a changed result—just the sort of near 50-50 result we expect from coin tossing. Despite the seeming patterns in these data, the outcome of one toss gives no clue to the outcome of the next toss.

Failing to recognize random occurrences for what they are can predispose people to seek extraordinary explanations for ordinary events. Imagine that on one warm spring day 4000 college students gather for a coin-tossing contest. Their task is to flip heads. On the first toss, 2000 students do so and remain standing for a second round. As you might expect, about 1000 of these progress to a third round, 500 to a fourth, 250 to a fifth, 125 to a sixth, 62 to a seventh, 31 to an eighth, 15 to a ninth, and 8 amazing individuals, having flipped heads nine times in a row with ever-increasing displays of concentration and effort, remain standing for the tenth round.

By now, the crowd of losers is in awestruck silence as these expert coin tossers prepare to display their amazing ability yet again. The proceedings are temporarily halted. A panel of impartial scientists assembles to observe and document the incredible achievement of these gifted and talented individuals. Alas, on each succeeding toss half of those remaining flip a tail, until all have sat down. "Oh! Of course," their admirers say, "coin tossing is after all a highly sensitive skill. The tense, pressured atmosphere created by the scientists' scrutiny has disturbed their fragile gift."

However, some happenings seem so extraordinary that we struggle to conceive an ordinary, chance-related explanation (as applies to our coin-tosses). In such cases, statisticians often are less mystified. When Evelyn Marie Adams won the New Jersey lottery *twice*, newspapers reported the odds of her feat as 1 in 17 trillion. Bizarre? Actually, 1 in 17 trillion are the odds that a given person who buys a single ticket for two New Jersey lotteries will win both times. But statisticians Stephen Samuels and George McCabe (1989) report that, given the millions of people who buy U.S. state lottery tickets, it was "practically a sure thing" that someday, somewhere, someone would hit a state jackpot twice. Indeed, say fellow statisticians Persi Diaconis and Frederick Mosteller (1989), "with a large enough sample, any outrageous thing is likely to happen."

We all experience events that make us feel astonished now and then. One day when my daughter bought two pairs of shoes, we later were astounded to discover that the two brand names were her first and last names. Checking out a photocopy counter from our library, I confused the clerk when giving him my six-digit department charge number—which just happened at that moment to be identical to the counter's one-in-a-million number on which the last user had finished. Ron Vachon was astounded while sitting among thousands of fans at a September 1990 baseball game in Boston. Oakland A's outfielder Rickey Henderson hit two foul balls right to

Given enough random events, something weird will happen
Evelyn Marie Adams was the beneficiary of one of those extraordinary, chance events when she won the New Jersey lottery a second time.

On March 11, 1998, Utah's Ernie and Lynn Carey gained three new grandchildren when three of their daughters gave birth—on the same day (*Los Angeles Times*, 1998).

him, on successive pitches. That something like that should have happened to Va-chon (who dropped them both) was incredibly unlikely. That it sometime would happen to someone was not. An event that happens to but one in 1 billion people every day occurs about six times a day, 2000 times a year. (For two provocative instances of random sequences that don't look random, see Thinking Critically About Hot and Cold Streaks in Basketball and the Stock Market.)

Experimentation

Preview Questions: How do experiments clarify or reveal cause-and-effect relationships? What is random assignment, and why is it important?

Happy are they "who have been able to perceive the causes of things," remarked the Roman poet Virgil. We endlessly wonder and debate why we act as we do. Why do people smoke? Have babies while they are still children? Do stupid things when drunk? Become troubled teens and open fire on their classmates? Though psychology cannot answer these questions directly, it has helped us to understand what influences drug use, sexual behaviors, thinking when drinking, and aggression.

Many factors influence our everyday behavior. To isolate cause and effect—say, in looking for possible causes of depression—psychologists sometimes try to statistically control for other factors and study the sequence of events. For example, the Internet-use researchers found that people who felt lonely and depressed at the start of their study were not more likely to use the Internet. But two years later, those who had spent the most hours in cyberspace had become more lonely and depressed (Kraut & others, 1998).

The clearest and cleanest way to isolate cause and effect is, however, to **experiment**. Experiments enable a researcher to focus on the possible effects of one or more factors by (1) *manipulating the factors of interest* and (2) *holding constant ("controlling") other factors*. Imagine some researchers studying the effect of alcohol consumption on thinking ability. Before giving a thinking test, they would *manipulate* alcohol consumption (by giving some people a strong-tasting drink mixed with alcohol, others a drink that contained no alcohol but tasted the same). By randomly assigning people to the two conditions, which otherwise were similar, the researchers would hold all other factors constant. This would eliminate alternative explanations for why thinking might vary with drinking.

If behavior changes when we vary an experimental factor, such as alcohol, then we know that the factor is having an effect. *The important point to remember:* Unlike correlational studies, which uncover naturally occurring relationships, an experiment manipulates a factor to determine its effect.

Evaluating Therapies

Our tendencies to seek new remedies when we are ill or emotionally down can produce misleading testimonies. When our health or emotions return to normal, we attribute the return to something we have done. If three days into a cold we start taking vitamin C tablets and find our cold symptoms lessening, the pills may seem more potent than they are (an illusion of control). If, after nearly failing the first exam, we listen to a "peak learning" subliminal tape and then improve on the next exam, we may credit the tape rather than conclude that our performance has returned to our average. In the 1700s, blood-letting *seemed* effective. Sometimes people improved after the treatment; when they didn't, the practitioner inferred the disease was too far advanced to be reversed. So, whether or not a remedy is truly effective, enthusiastic users will probably endorse it. To find out whether it actually is effective, we must experiment.

And that is precisely how new drug treatments and new methods of psychological therapy are evaluated. In many of these studies, the participants are *blind* (uninformed) about what treatment, if any, they are receiving. One group receives the treatment. Others receive a pseudotreatment—an inert **placebo** (perhaps a pill with no drug in it).

■ **experiment** a research method in which an investigator manipulates one or more factors (independent variables) to observe the effect on some behavior or mental process (the dependent variable). By random assignment of participants the experimenter controls other relevant factors.

■ **placebo** [pluh-SEE-bo; Latin for "I shall please"] an inert substance or condition that may be administered instead of a presumed active agent, such as a drug, to see if it triggers the effects believed to characterize the active agent.

THINKING CRITICALLY ABOUT :

HOT AND COLD STREAKS IN BASKETBALL AND THE STOCK MARKET

Misinterpreting random sequences is common in sports and investing. In both arenas, the statistical facts collide with common-sense intuition.

Basketball Players' "Hot Hands"

Every basketball player and every fan intuitively "knows" that players have hot and cold streaks. Players who have "hot hands" can't seem to miss. Those who have "cold" ones can't find the center of the hoop. When Thomas Gilovich, Robert Vallone, and Amos Tversky (1985) interviewed Philadelphia 76ers, the players estimated they were about 25 percent more likely to make a shot after they had just made one than after a miss. In one survey, 9 in 10 basketball fans agreed that a player "has a better chance of making a shot after having just *made* his last two or three shots than he does after having just *missed* his last two or three shots." Believing in shooting streaks, players will feed the ball to a teammate who has just made two or three shots in a row. Many coaches will bench the player who has just missed three in a row.

The only trouble is (believe it or not), it isn't true! When Gilovich and his collaborators studied detailed individual shooting records, they found that the 76ers—and the Boston Celtics, the New Jersey Nets, the New York Knicks, and Cornell University's men's and women's basketball players—were equally likely to score after a miss and after a basket. A typical 50 percent shooter averages 50 percent after just missing three shots, and 50 percent after just making three shots. It works with free throws, too. Celtics star Larry Bird made 88 percent of his free throws after making a free throw and 91 percent after missing. (Did this reduce Larry Bird to a mere puppet, manipulated by statistical laws? No, his skill was reflected in his 90 percent average.)

Why, then, do players and fans alike believe that players are more likely to score after scoring and to miss after missing? It's because streaks do occur, more than people expect in random sequences. In any series of 20 shots by a 50 percent shooter (or 20 flips of a coin), there is a 50-50 chance of four baskets (or heads) in a row, and it is quite possible that one person out of five will have a streak of 5 or 6. Players and fans notice these random streaks and so form the errant conclusion that "when you're hot, you're hot" (FIGURE 2.9).

Mutual Funds: Does Past Performance Predict Future Returns?

The same misinterpretation of random sequences occurs when investors believe that a mutual fund that has had a string of good years will likely outperform one that has had a string of bad years. Based on that assumption, investment magazines report mutual funds' performance. But, as economist Burton Malkiel (1989, 1995) documents, past performances of mutual funds do *not* predict their future performance. If on January 1 of each year since 1980 we had bought the previous year's top-performing funds, our hot funds would not have beaten the next year's market average. If we had put our money instead on the *Forbes* "Honor Roll" of funds each year for the two decades following 1975, we would have pulled in an annual return of 13.5 percent (compared with the market's overall 14.9 percent annual return). Of the top 81 Canadian funds during 1994, 40 performed above average and 41 below average during 1995 (Chalmers, 1995).

When funds have streaks of several good or bad years, we may nevertheless think that past success predicts future success. "Randomness is a difficult notion for people to accept," notes Malkiel. "When events come in clusters and streaks, people look for explanations and patterns. They refuse to believe that such patterns—which frequently occur in random data—could equally well be derived from tossing a coin. So it is in the stock market as well."

The point to remember: When watching basketball, choosing stocks, or flipping coins, remember that our intuition often misleads us. Random sequences frequently don't look random. Expect streaks. ■

Throughout this book, you will encounter "Thinking Critically About . . ." boxes. Each highlights careful thinking about some interesting or important issue using key methodology tools.

FIGURE **2.9** Who is the chance shooter?
Here are 21 consecutive shots, each scoring either a basket or a miss, by two players who each make 11. Within this sample of shots, which player's sequence looks more like what we would expect in a random sequence? (See page 29; adapted from Barry Ross, *Discover*, 1987.)

double-blind procedure an experimental procedure in which both the research participants and the research staff are ignorant (blind) about whether the research participants have received the treatment or a placebo. Commonly used in drug-evaluation studies.

placebo effect any effect on behavior caused by a placebo.

experimental condition the condition of an experiment that exposes participants to the treatment, that is, to one version of the independent variable.

control condition the condition of an experiment that contrasts with the experimental condition and serves as a comparison for evaluating the effect of the treatment.

random assignment assigning participants to experimental and control conditions by chance, thus minimizing preexisting differences between those assigned to the different groups.

independent variable the experimental factor that is manipulated; the variable whose effect is being studied.

dependent variable the experimental factor—in psychology, the behavior or mental process—that is being measured; the variable that may change in response to manipulations of the independent variable.

Often neither the participant nor the research assistant collecting the data knows whether the participant's group is receiving the treatment. This **double-blind procedure** enables researchers to check a treatment's actual effects apart from the research participants' (and their own) enthusiasm for it and from the healing power of belief. The **placebo effect** is well documented (Kirsch & Sapirstein, 1998). Just *thinking* one is getting a treatment can boost one's spirits, relax one's body, and lead to symptom relief.

The double-blind procedure creates an **experimental condition** in which people receive the treatment and a contrasting **control condition** without the treatment. By **randomly assigning** people to these conditions the two groups should otherwise be identical. Random assignment roughly equalizes the two groups in age, attitudes, and every other characteristic. With random assignment, we can know that any later differences between people in the experimental and control conditions must be the result of the treatment.

A potent example: The drug Viagra was approved for use after 21 clinical trials, including an experiment in which researchers randomly assigned 329 men with impotence to either an experimental condition (Viagra) or a control condition (a placebo). Neither the men nor the person who gave them the pills knew which drug they were receiving. The result: At peak doses, 69 percent of Viagra-assisted attempts at intercourse were successful, compared with 22 percent for men receiving the placebo (Goldstein & others, 1998). Viagra worked.

This simple experiment manipulated just one drug factor. We call this experimental factor the **independent variable** because we can vary it independently of other factors, such as the men's age, weight, and personality (which random assignment controls). Experiments examine the effect of one or more independent variables on some measurable behavior, called the **dependent variable** because it can vary *depending* on what takes place during the experiment. Both variables are given precise operational definitions, which specify the procedures that manipulate the independent variable (the precise drug dosage and timing in this study) or measure the dependent variable (the questions that assessed the men's responses). Thus they answer the "What do you mean?" question with a level of precision that enables others to repeat the study.

Let's recap. An experiment has at least two different conditions: a comparison or control condition and an experimental condition. Random assignment equates the conditions before any treatment effects. In this way, an experiment tests the effect of at least one independent variable (the experimental factor) on at least one dependent variable (the measured response). Table 2.2 compares the features of psychology's research methods.

TABLE 2.2

COMPARING RESEARCH METHODS

Research Method	Basic Purpose	How Conducted	What Is Manipulated
Descriptive	To observe and record behavior	Case studies, surveys, and naturalistic observations	Nothing
Correlational	To detect naturally occurring relationships; to assess how well one variable predicts another	Computing statistical association, sometimes among survey responses	Nothing
Experimental	To explore cause and effect	Manipulating one or more factors and using random assignment to eliminate preexisting differences among subjects	The independent variable(s)

These concepts—experimental and control conditions, independent and dependent variables, random assignment—are important, yet easily confused. So let's put them to work with another intriguing set of experiments.

Can Subliminal Tapes Improve Your Life?

A new generation of entrepreneurs would have you believe so. We are bombarded by mail-order catalogs, cable television ads, and bookstores offering tapes whose imperceptibly faint messages supposedly "reprogram your unconscious mind for success and happiness." While struggling students listen to soothing music, subliminal messages (those below one's hearing threshold) are said to persuade the unconscious that "I am a good student. I love learning." Procrastinators can be similarly reprogrammed: "I set my priorities. I get things done ahead of time!"

Is there anything to these claims? Could positive subliminal messages help us, even a little? Subliminal sensation is real. We, in fact, do process much information without conscious awareness. And under certain conditions, a stimulus too weak to recognize can affect us, *briefly*.

But does this subtle, fleeting effect extend to the powerful, enduring influence claimed by the subliminal tape merchants? Anthony Greenwald and his colleagues (1991) wanted to find out, so they randomly assigned university students to listen daily for five weeks to commercial subliminal tapes claiming to improve either self-esteem or memory. Then the researchers manipulated an experimental factor. On half the tapes they switched the labels. Some students *thought* they were receiving affirmations of self-esteem when they actually were hearing the memory enhancement tape. Others got the self-esteem tape but *thought* their memory was being recharged (**FIGURE 2.10**).

Were the tapes effective? Their scores on tests for both self-esteem and memory, taken before and after the five weeks, revealed zilch. No effects. None. And yet, those who *thought* they had heard a memory tape *believed* their memories had improved. A similar result occurred for those who thought they had heard a self-esteem tape. The tapes had no effects, yet the students *perceived* themselves receiving the benefits they *expected*. When reading this research, you can hear echoes of the testimonies that ooze from the mail-order tape catalogs. Many customers, having bought what is not supposed to be heard, and having indeed not heard it, actually write things like, "I really know that your tapes were invaluable in reprogramming my mind." Greenwald conducted 16 double-blind experiments evaluating subliminal self-help tapes over one 10-year period. His results were uniform: Not one had any therapeutic effect (Greenwald, 1992).

Unfortunately, the general public is surprisingly uninformed about the importance of controlled experiments such as this. One science literacy survey asked people to imagine testing a new drug to combat high blood pressure (Miller & Pifer, 1996). The survey asked whether it would make more sense to give the drug to 1000 individuals and see what happened, or to give it to half of them and compare their reactions to those who got no drug. One-third said it would make more sense to give the drug to all 1000 people, reasoning that the greater the number tested, the more reliable the finding. Among those who selected the option with the control group, 30 percent did so simply to save lives, saying "If the drug kills people, it kills only half as many." Again, remember: Psychology's most powerful tool for sorting reality from wishful thinking and for evaluating cause and effect is the control group.

Experiments can also help us evaluate social programs. Do early childhood education programs boost impoverished children's chances for success? What are the effects of different antismoking campaigns? Does school sex education reduce teen pregnancies? To answer these questions, we can use experiments: If an intervention is

Note the distinction between random sampling in surveys and random *assignment* in experiments. Random sampling helps us generalize to a larger population. Random assignment controls extraneous influences, which helps us infer cause and effect.

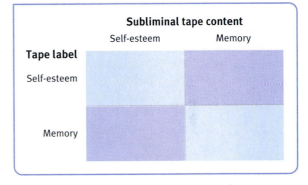

FIGURE 2.10 Design of the subliminal tapes experiment
Students' self-esteem and memory abilities were assessed before and after listening to subliminal tapes purporting to increase either self-esteem or memory. Half the students, however, received deliberately mislabeled tapes.

In this experiment, what was the independent variable? The dependent variable? (See page 30.)

Answer to question in Figure 2.9 (page 27): Player B, whose outcomes may look more random, actually has fewer streaks than would be expected by chance. Chance shooting, like chance coin tossing, should produce a change in outcome about 50 percent of the time. But 70 percent of the time (14 times out of 20) Player B's outcome changes on successive shots. Player A's sequence is changing more as we would expect from a 50 percent shooter; 10 times out of 20, Player A's next outcome differs from the last.

Answer to question on page 29: In the subliminal tapes experiment, the primary independent variable was the type of subliminal message, self-esteem versus memory. (This experiment actually had a second independent variable as well: people's beliefs about which tape they received.) The primary dependent variable was improvement on the self-esteem and memory measures.

welcomed but resources are scarce, we could use a lottery to randomly assign some people (or regions) to experience the new program and others to a control condition. If later the two groups differ, there will be less to argue about (Passell, 1993).

Statistical Reasoning

Preview Question: How can statistics help us to organize, summarize, and make inferences from the data we have gathered?

Off-the-top-of-the-head estimates often misread reality and then mislead the public. Someone throws out a big round number. Others echo it and before long the big round number becomes public misinformation. A few examples:

+ *One percent of Americans (2.6 million) are homeless.* Or is it 300,000, an earlier estimate by the federal government? Or 600,000, the estimate by the Urban Institute (Crossen, 1994)?
+ *Ten percent of people are lesbians or gay men.* Or is it 2 to 3 percent, as suggested by various national surveys?
+ *We ordinarily use but 10 percent of our brain.* Or is it closer to 100 percent? (Which 90 percent, or even 10 percent, would you be willing to sacrifice?)

   The point to remember: Doubt big, round, undocumented numbers. Rather than swallow top-of-the-head estimates, focus on thinking smarter by applying simple statistical principles to everyday reasoning.

Describing Data

Once researchers have gathered their raw data, their first task is to *organize* it. One way is to use a simple *bar graph,* as in **FIGURE 2.11**, which displays a distribution of trucks of different brands still on the road after a decade.

   When reading statistical graphs such as this, take care, however. Depending on what people want to emphasize, they can design the graph to make a difference look small or big. *The point to remember:* Think smart when viewing figures in magazines and on television—read the scale labels and note their range.

FIGURE 2.11
Read the scale labels
An American truck manufacturer offered a graph (a)—with actual brand names included—to suggest the much greater durability of its trucks. Note, however, how the apparent difference shrinks as the vertical scale changes (graph b).

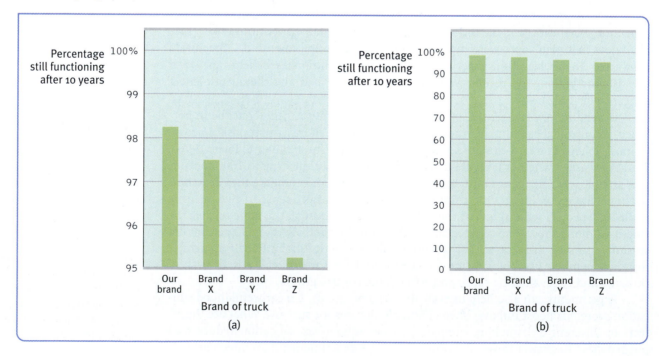

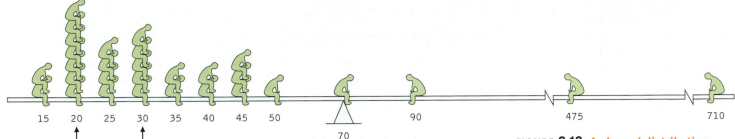

15   20   25   30   35   40   45   50   70   90   475   710

Mode   **Median**   **Mean**

One family   Income per family in thousands of dollars

Drawing by Mirachi; © 1988 The New Yorker Magazine, Inc.

FIGURE 2.12 A skewed distribution
This graphic representation of the distribution of incomes illustrates the three measures of central tendency—mode, median, and mean. Note how just a few high incomes make the mean—the fulcrum point that balances the incomes above and below—deceptively high.

Measures of Central Tendency

The next step is to summarize the data using the three measures of *central tendency*. The simplest measure is called the **mode**, the most frequently occurring score. The most commonly reported is the **mean**, or arithmetic average—the total sum of all the scores divided by the number of scores. The **median** is the middle score—the 50th percentile; if you arrange all the scores in order from the highest to the lowest, half will be above the median and half will be below it.

Measures of central tendency neatly summarize data. But consider what happens to the mean when a distribution is lopsided or *skewed*. With income data, for example, the mode, median, and mean often tell very different stories (**FIGURE 2.12**). This is because the mean is biased by a few extreme scores. If Microsoft founder Bill Gates were to move to a town with 52,000 penniless people, his June, 2000, net worth of $52 billion would instantly make its average (mean) resident a millionaire. Understanding this, you can see how a British newspaper could accurately run the headline "Income for 62% Is Below Average" (Waterhouse, 1993). Because the bottom *half* of British income earners receive only a *quarter* of the national income cake, most British people, like most people everywhere, make less than the mean. Professional athletes' incomes also form skewed distributions. In 1998, 66 percent of the National Basketball Association's 411 players made less than the average (mean) player salary (DuPree, 1998). The average ($2.24 million) was, of course, inflated by a few superstar salaries, led by Michael Jordan's $33.14 million.

The point to remember: Always note which measure of central tendency is reported. Then, if it is a mean, consider whether a few atypical scores could be distorting it.

"The poor are getting poorer, but with the rich getting richer it all averages out in the long run."

The average adult has one ovary and one testicle.

Measures of Variation

Knowing the value of an appropriate measure of central tendency can tell us a great deal. But it also helps to know something about the amount of *variation* in the data— how similar or diverse the scores are. Averages derived from scores with low variability are more reliable than averages based on scores with high variability. Consider a basketball player who scored between 13 and 17 points in each of her first 10 games in a season. Knowing this, we would be more confident that she would score near 15 points in her next game than if her scores had varied from 5 to 25 points.

The **range** of scores—the gap between the lowest and highest scores—provides only a crude estimate of variation because a couple of extreme scores in an otherwise uniform group, such as the $475,000 and $710,000 in Figure 2.12, will create a deceptively large range.

The more standard measure of how much scores deviate from one another is the **standard deviation**. It better gauges whether scores are packed together or dispersed, because it uses information from each score. (The computation assembles information about how much individual scores differ from the mean.)

- **mode** the most frequently occurring score in a distribution.
- **mean** the arithmetic average of a distribution, obtained by adding the scores and then dividing by the number of scores.
- **median** the middle score in a distribution; half the scores are above it and half are below it.
- **range** the difference between the highest and lowest scores in a distribution.
- **standard deviation** a computed measure of how much scores vary around the mean score.

Making Inferences

Data are "noisy." One group's average score (women's salaries) could conceivably differ from another's (men's salaries) not because of any real difference but merely due to chance fluctuation in the people sampled. How confidently, then, can we infer that an observed difference accurately estimates the true difference?

When Is a Difference Reliable?

In deciding when it is safe to generalize from a sample, three principles are worth keeping in mind. Let's look at each in turn.

1. **Representative samples are better than biased samples.** As we have noted, the best basis for generalizing is not from the exceptional and memorable cases one finds at the extremes but from a representative sample of cases. No research involves a representative sample of the whole human population. Thus, it pays to keep in mind what population a study has sampled.

2. **Less-variable observations are more reliable than those that are more variable.** As we noted in the example of the basketball player whose scores were consistent, an average is more reliable when it comes from scores with low variability.

3. **More cases are better than fewer.** An eager prospective university student visits two college campuses, each for a day. At the first, the student randomly attends two classes and discovers both instructors to be witty and engaging. At the next campus, the two sampled instructors seem dull and uninspiring. Returning home, the student tells friends about the "great teachers" at the first school, and the "bores" at the second. Again, we know it but we ignore it: Small samples provide less reliable estimates of the average than do large samples. The proportion of heads in samples of 10 coin tosses varies more than in samples of 100 tosses. Said differently, *averages based on many cases are more reliable* (less variable) than averages based on only a few cases.

   The point to remember: Don't be overly impressed by a few anecdotes. Generalizations based on a few unrepresentative cases are unreliable.

When Is a Difference Significant?

We can justifiably have the most confidence when we generalize from samples that (1) are representative of the population we wish to study, (2) give us consistent rather than highly variable data, and (3) are large rather than small. These principles extend to the inferences we make about differences between groups—as when we generalize from a gender difference in grades in our sample to the whole campus population.

Statistical tests help us decide significance by indicating the reliability of differences. Here is the logic behind them: When *averages* from two samples are each *reliable* measures of their respective populations (as when each is based on many observations that have small variability), then their difference (sometimes even a very small difference) is likely to be reliable as well. But when the *difference* between the sample averages is *large*, we have even more confidence that the difference between them reflects a real difference in their populations.

In short, *when the sample averages are reliable and the difference between them is relatively large*, we say the difference has **statistical significance**. This simply means that the difference we observed is probably not due to chance variation between the samples. In judging statistical significance, psychologists are conservative. They are like juries who must presume innocence until guilt is proven. Statistical significance provides a criterion for rejecting the presumption of innocence (no difference between the groups). But caution is advised until further studies replicate the difference.

■ **statistical significance** a statistical criterion for rejecting the assumption of no differences in a particular study.

When reading about research, you should remember that, given large enough or homogeneous enough samples, a difference between them may be "statistically significant" yet have little practical significance. For example, comparisons of intelligence test scores among several hundred-thousand first-born and later-born individuals indicate that there is a highly significant tendency for first-born individuals within a family to have higher average scores than their later-born siblings (Zajonc & Markus, 1975). But because the scores differ by only one or two points, the difference has little practical importance. Such findings have caused some psychologists to advocate alternatives to significance testing (Hunter, 1997). Better, they say, to use other ways to express a finding's magnitude and reliability.

The point to remember: Statistical significance indicates the *likelihood* that a result will happen by chance. It does not indicate the *importance* of the result.

Using the principles discussed in this module will help us to think critically—to see more clearly what we might otherwise miss or misinterpret and to generalize more accurately from our observations. We do think smarter when we understand and use the principles of research methods and statistics (Fong & others, 1986; Lehman & others, 1988; VanderStoep & Shaughnessy, 1997). It requires training and practice, but developing clear and critical thinking abilities is part of your becoming an educated person. An Association of American Colleges' report eloquently asserts why there are few higher priorities in a college education:

> If anything is paid attention to in our colleges and universities, thinking must be it. Unfortunately, thinking can be lazy. It can be sloppy. . . . It can be fooled, misled, bullied. . . . Students possess great untrained and untapped capacities for logical thinking, critical analysis, and inquiry, but these are capacities that are not spontaneous: They grow out of wide instruction, experience, encouragement, correction, and constant use. (Project on Redefining the Meaning and Purpose of Baccalaureate Degrees, 1985)

REVIEW AND REFLECT:

Research Strategies: How Psychologists Ask and Answer Questions

Why are the answers that flow from the scientific approach more reliable than those based on intuition and common sense?

Although limited by the testable questions it can address, a scientific approach helps us sift reality from illusion, taking us beyond the limits of our intuition and common sense. Without scientific inquiry and critical thinking we readily succumb to *hindsight bias,* also called the I-knew-it-all-along phenomenon. Learning the outcome of a study (or of an everyday happening) can make it seem like obvious common sense. We also are routinely *overconfident* of our judgments, thanks partly to our bias to seek information that confirms them. Science, with its procedures for gathering and sifting evidence, restrains error.

Scientific inquiry begins with an attitude—a curious eagerness to skeptically scrutinize competing ideas and an open-minded humility before nature. Putting ideas, even crazy-sounding ideas, to the test helps us winnow sense from nonsense. The curiosity that drives us to test ideas and to expose their underlying assumptions carries into everyday life as *critical thinking.*

How do psychologists use the scientific method to construct theories?

Research stimulates the construction of *theories,* which organize *observations* and imply predictive *hypotheses.* These hypotheses (predictions) are then tested to validate and refine the theory and to suggest practical applications. Precise operational definitions enable other researchers to replicate (repeat) observations.

How do psychologists observe and describe behavior?

Through individual case studies, surveys among random samples of a population, and naturalistic observations, psychologists observe and describe behavior and mental processes. In generalizing from observations, remember: Representative samples are a better guide than vivid examples.

What does it mean when we say two things are correlated?

The strength of the relationship between one factor and another is expressed in their *correlation.* Correlations help us to see relationships that the naked eye might miss and to discount illusory correlations and random events that might otherwise look significant.

Why do correlations permit prediction but not explanation?

Knowing how closely two things are positively or negatively correlated tells us how much one predicts the other. But it is crucial to remember that correlation is a measure of relationship; it does not reveal cause and effect.

How do experiments clarify or reveal cause-and-effect relationships?

To discover cause-and-effect relationships, psychologists conduct *experiments.* By constructing a controlled reality, experimenters can manipulate one or more factors and discover how these independent variables affect a particular behavior, the dependent variable.

What is random assignment, and why is it important?

In many experiments, control is achieved by assigning people by chance either to the experimental condition, the group exposed to the treatment, or to a control condition (a group that experiences no treatment or a different version of the treatment). Random assignment minimizes preexisting differences among the group conditions.

How can statistics help us to organize, summarize, and make inferences from the data we have gathered?

To be an educated person today is to be able to apply simple statistical principles to everyday reasoning. One needn't remember complicated formulas to think more clearly and critically about data.

From this section's consideration of how we can organize, summarize, and make inferences from data—by constructing distributions and computing measures of central tendency, variation, and statistical significance—we derived five points to remember:

1. Doubt big, round, undocumented numbers.
2. When looking at statistical graphs in books and magazines and on television ads and news broadcasts, think critically: Always read the scale labels and note their range.
3. Always note which measure of central tendency is reported. Then, if it is a mean, consider whether a few atypical scores could be distorting it.
4. Don't be overly impressed by a few anecdotes. Generalizations based on only a few cases are unreliable.
5. Statistical significance indicates the *likelihood* that a result will occur by chance. It does not indicate the importance of the result.

Terms and Concepts to Remember

hindsight bias, p. 13	experiment, p. 26
critical thinking, p. 16	placebo [pluh-SEE-bo], p. 26
theory, p. 16	double-blind procedure, p. 28
hypothesis, p. 17	placebo effect, p. 28
operational definition, p. 17	experimental condition, p. 28
replication, p. 17	control condition, p. 28
case study, p. 18	random assignment, p. 28
survey, p. 18	independent variable, p. 28
false consensus effect, p. 19	dependent variable, p. 28
population, p. 19	mode, p. 31
random sample, p. 19	mean, p. 31
naturalistic observation, p. 20	median, p. 31
correlation coefficient, p. 21	range, p. 31
scatterplot, p. 21	standard deviation, p. 31
illusory correlation, p. 23	statistical significance, p. 32

Test Yourself

2.1. As scientists, psychologists view theories with skepticism and humility. This means that they
   a. approach research with a negative cynicism.
   b. assume that an article published in a reputable journal must be true.
   c. realize that some issues should not be studied.
   d. persistently ask questions and are willing to reject ideas that cannot be verified by research.

2.2. A newspaper article describes how a "cure for cancer has been found." A critical thinker probably will
   a. immediately dismiss the article as untrue because there is no evidence to back up the facts.
   b. accept the information as a wonderful breakthrough.
   c. question the article, evaluate the evidence, and assess the conclusions.
   d. question the article but quickly accept it as true due to the author's excellent reputation.

2.3. Psychology tells us what we already know from common sense, say some skeptics. Hindsight bias refers to our tendency to
   a. perceive events as obvious or inevitable after the fact.
   b. assume that two events happened because we wished them to happen.
   c. overestimate our abilities to predict the future.
   d. make judgments that fly in the face of common sense.

2.4. In psychology a good theory implies hypotheses, or predictions that can be tested. When hypotheses are tested, the result is typically
   a. increased skepticism.
   b. rejection of the merely theoretical.
   c. confirmation or revision of the theory.
   d. personal bias on the part of the investigator.

2.5. Psychology's basic *research strategies* are description, correlation, and experimentation. Which of the following would you use in an attempt to predict college grades from high school grades?
   a. A case study
   b. Naturalistic observation
   c. Correlational research
   d. Experimental research

2.6. You wish to take an accurate poll in a certain country by questioning people who truly represent the country's adult population. Therefore, you need to make sure the people are
   a. at least 30 percent urban dwellers.
   b. registered voters.
   c. a very large sample of the population.
   d. a random sample of the population.

2.7. Suppose a psychologist finds that the *more* natural childbirth training classes a woman attends, the *less* pain medication she requires during childbirth. The relationship between the number of training sessions and the amount of pain medication required is a
   a. positive correlation (direct relationship).
   b. negative correlation (inverse relationship).
   c. cause-effect relationship.
   d. controlled experiment.

2.8. Some people wrongly perceive that their dreams predict future events. This is an example of a/an
   a. negative correlation.
   b. positive correlation.
   c. illusory correlation.
   d. naturalistic correlation.

2.9. Knowing that two events are correlated does not tell us what is the cause and what is the effect. However, it does provide
   a. a basis for prediction.
   b. an explanation of events.
   c. proof that as one increases, the other also increases.
   d. an indication that an underlying third factor is at work.

2.10. A researcher wants to determine whether noise level affects the blood pressure of elderly subjects. In one group she varies the level of noise in the environment and records blood pressures. In this experiment the level of noise is the
   a. control condition.
   b. dependent variable (the factor being measured).
   c. independent variable (the factor being manipulated).
   d. cause of any blood pressure variations.

2.11. To test the effect of a new drug on depression, we randomly assign subjects to control and experimental conditions. Those in the experimental condition take a pink pill containing the new medication; the control group takes a pink pill that contains no medication. Which statement is true?
   a. The medication is the dependent variable.
   b. Depression is the independent variable.
   c. The subjects in the control group take a placebo.
   d. Neither the experimental nor the control group is told the purpose of the experiment.

2.12. To eliminate the biasing effect of a researcher's positive expectations on the outcome of a health clinic's research experiment
   a. subjects are randomly assigned to the control and experimental groups (random assignment).
   b. neither the subjects nor the researcher will know whether a given subject has been assigned to the experimental or control condition (double-blind procedure).

Continued

  c. the experimental subjects are carefully matched for age, sex, income, and level of education with subjects in the control group (controlled selection).

  d. experimental subjects are chosen by selecting every tenth person in an alphabetical listing of all the clinic's patients (random selection).

2.13. Psychology's most powerful tool for evaluating cause and effect is the control group. A researcher who remembered this would randomly assign a new drug to be tested to _____ percent of the participants in a large group in order to _____.

  a. 100; maximize the chance of seeing what happens
  b. 10; minimize the risk of adverse reactions in the control group
  c. 50; compare reactions between a control group and an experimental group
  d. 50; increase the reliability of the control group

2.14. The three measures of central tendency are the mode, the mean, and the median. Which of these three measures is most easily distorted by a few very large or very small scores?

  a. The mode
  b. The mean
  c. The median
  d. They are equally vulnerable to distortion from atypical scores.

2.15. When sample averages are _____ and the difference between them is _____ , we can say the difference has statistical significance.

  a. reliable; large
  b. reliable; small
  c. due to chance; large
  d. due to chance; small

Review

• What are the strengths and weaknesses of the three different methods psychologists use to describe behavior—case studies, surveys, and naturalistic observation?

• Here are some recently reported correlations, with the interpretations drawn by journalists noted in the parentheses.

Further research, often including experiments, has clarified cause and effect in each case. Knowing just these correlations, can you come up with other possible explanations for each of these?

  a. Alcohol use is associated with violence. (Interpretation: Drinking triggers or unleashes aggressive behavior.)
  b. Educated people live longer, on average, than less-educated people. (Interpretation: Education lengthens life and enhances health.)
  c. People who spend long hours on the Internet are somewhat less engaged with family and are lonelier and more depressed. (Interpretation: By isolating people from face-to-face contact, Internet absorption can be depressing.)

• Consider a question posed by Christopher Jepson, David Krantz, and Richard Nisbett (1983) to University of Michigan introductory psychology students:

  The registrar's office at the University of Michigan has found that usually about 100 students in Arts and Sciences have perfect marks at the end of their first term at the University. However, only about 10 to 15 students graduate with perfect marks. What do you think is the most likely explanation for the fact that there are more perfect marks after one term than at graduation?

Reflect

• Your friend Jason wants to buy a new car. He decides to buy a car he has seen in TV ads. How might he instead have used principles of *critical thinking* to make his choice?

• Does sleep deprivation erode people's mental quickness? Design an experiment that could help answer that question.

• Find a graph in a popular magazine ad. How has the advertiser used (or abused) statistics to make a point?

Answers to the Test Yourself and Review questions can be found in the green appendix at the end of the book.

Reflections on Some Frequently Asked Questions About Psychology

We have seen how case studies, surveys, and naturalistic observations help us describe behavior. We have also noted that correlational studies, assessing the relationship between two factors, can indicate how, knowing one thing, we can predict another. We have examined the logic that underlies experiments, which use control conditions and random assignment of subjects to isolate the effects of an independent variable on a dependent variable. We have reflected on how a scientific approach, aided by statistics, can restrain biases.

You are now prepared to understand what lies ahead and to think critically about psychological matters. Yet, even knowing this much, you may still be approaching psychology with a mixture of curiosity and apprehension. So before we plunge in, let's confront some questions and concerns.

Can Laboratory Experiments Illuminate Everyday Life?

When you see or hear about psychological research, do you ever wonder whether people's behavior in the lab will predict their behavior in real life? For example, does detecting the blink of a faint red light in a dark room have anything useful to say about flying a plane at night? Does our tendency to remember best the first and last items in a list of unrelated words tell us anything about why we remember the names of certain people we meet at a party? After viewing a violent, sexually explicit film, does an aroused man's increased willingness to push buttons that he thinks will electrically shock a woman really say anything about whether violent pornography makes a man more likely to abuse a woman?

Before you answer, consider: The experimenter *intends* the laboratory environment to be a simplified reality—one in which important features of everyday life can be simulated and controlled. Just as an aeronautical wind tunnel enables an engineer to re-create atmospheric forces under controlled conditions, a laboratory experiment enables a psychologist to re-create psychological forces under controlled conditions.

Obviously, deciding whether or not to push a button that delivers a shock is not literally the same as slapping someone in the face. However, the principle is the same. The experiment's purpose, notes Douglas Mook (1983), is not to re-create the exact behaviors of everyday life but to test theoretical principles. *It is the resulting principles—not the specific findings—that help explain everyday behaviors.* When psychologists apply laboratory research on aggression to actual violence, they are applying theoretical *principles* of aggressive behavior, principles they have refined through many experiments. Similarly, it is the principles of the visual system, developed from experiments in artificial settings (such as looking at red lights in the dark), that we apply to more complex behaviors such as night flying. And many investigations show that principles derived in the laboratory *do* typically generalize to the everyday world (Anderson & others, 1999).

The point to remember: As psychologists, our concerns lie less with particular behaviors than with the general principles that help explain many behaviors.

Does Behavior Depend on One's Culture?

If culture shapes behavior, what can psychological studies done in one culture, often with white North Americans, really tell us about people in general? As we will see time and again, *culture*—shared ideas and behaviors that one generation passes

A cultured greeting

Because culture shapes people's understanding of social behavior, actions that seem ordinary to us may seem quite odd to visitors from far away. Yet underlying these differences are powerful similarities. Schoolchildren everywhere greet their teachers with respect, although not necessarily with the formality of this young Japanese schoolchild.

on to the next—matters. Our culture influences our standards of promptness and frankness, our attitudes toward premarital sex and varying body shapes, our tendencies to be casual or formal, and much, much more. Being aware of such differences, we can restrain our assumptions that others will—or necessarily should—think and act as we do. Given the growing mixing and clashing of cultures, our need for such awareness is urgent.

Our shared biological heritage does, however, unite us as a universal human family. The same underlying processes guide people everywhere. Variation in languages—spoken and gestured—may impede communication across cultures, yet all languages share deep principles of grammar, and people from opposite hemispheres can communicate with a smile or a frown. People in different cultures do vary in feelings of loneliness, but across cultures shyness and low self-esteem magnify loneliness (Jones & others, 1985). Japanese prefer their fish raw and North Americans prefer theirs cooked, but the same principles of hunger and taste influence both when they sit down to a meal. We are each in certain respects like all others, like some others, and like no other. Studying people of all races and cultures helps us discern our similarities and our differences.

The point to remember: Even when specific attitudes and behaviors vary across cultures, as they often do, the underlying processes are much the same.

"All people are the same; only their habits differ."

Confucius, 551–479 B.C.

Does Behavior Vary With Gender?

At your birth, friends and family immediately wondered which of the two human types you were: male or female. Given how important our gender is to our identity and to others' perceptions of us, do we need a different psychology for women and for men?

You will see throughout this book that gender issues do indeed permeate psychology. Researchers report gender differences in what we dream, in how we express and detect emotions, and in our risk of alcoholism, depression, and eating disorders. Not only is studying such differences interesting, it is also potentially beneficial. For example, many researchers believe that women carry on conversations more readily to build relationships; men usually talk to give information and advice (Tannen, 1990). Knowing this difference can help us prevent conflicts and misunderstandings in everyday relationships.

Nevertheless, it's important to remember that psychologically as well as biologically, women and men are overwhelmingly similar. Whether female or male, we learn to walk at about the same age; experience the same sensations of light and sound; feel the same pangs of hunger, desire, and fear; and exhibit similar overall intelligence and well-being. We also tend to exhibit and perceive the very behaviors our culture expects of males and females.

So, gender matters. Biology determines our sex, and then culture further bends the genders. But viewing life through the lens of gender can exaggerate differences. The lesson of research embedded throughout this book is expressed by a children's song: "We're all the same and different."

Why Do Psychologists Study Animals?

Many psychologists study animals because they find them fascinating. They want to understand how different species learn, think, and behave. Psychologists also study animals to learn about people, by doing experiments that are permissible only with animals. Because human physiology resembles that of many other animals, animal experiments have led to treatments for human diseases—insulin for diabetes, vaccines to prevent polio and rabies, transplants to replace defective organs.

Likewise, the same processes by which humans see, exhibit emotion, and become obese are present in rats and monkeys. To discover more about the basics of human learning, researchers even study sea slugs. To understand how a combustion engine works, you would do better to study the engine of a lawn mower than that of a Mercedes. Humans, like Mercedes, are complex. But it is precisely the simplicity of the sea slug's nervous system that makes it so revealing of the neural mechanisms of learning.

Is It Ethical to Experiment on Animals?

If we share important similarities with other animals, then should we not respect them? "We cannot defend our scientific work with animals on the basis of the similarities between them and ourselves and then defend it morally on the basis of differences," notes Roger Ulrich (1991). The animal protection movement protests the use of animals in psychological, biological, and medical research—some 20 million U.S. animals annually, according to the National Academy of Sciences (1991), plus 3 million British and 2 million Canadian animals (Mukerjee, 1997). Researchers remind us that these 25 million animals are less than 1 percent of the 6 billion animals killed annually in these countries as a source of food (which means the average person eats 20 animals a year). While researchers each year conduct experiments on some 200,000 dogs and cats cared for under humane regulations, humane animal shelters are forced to kill 50 times that many.

Mobilization for Animals, a network of animal protection organizations, has nevertheless been concerned. It has declared that animals used in psychological experiments are shocked "until they lose the ability to even scream in pain, . . . [are] deprived of food and water to suffer and die slowly from hunger and thirst, . . . [are] put in total isolation chambers until they are driven insane or even die from despair and terror," and are made "the victims of extreme pain and stress, inflicted upon them out of idle curiosity." However, when psychologists Caroline Coile and Neal Miller (1984) analyzed every animal research article published in the American Psychological Association's journals during the preceding five years, they found no study in which any of these allegations was true. Even when researchers used shock, it was usually of a mild intensity, one that humans can easily endure on their fingers. Only 7 percent of psychology's studies involved animals, 95 percent of which were rats, mice, rabbits, or birds. About 10 percent of these animal studies involved electric shock (Coile & Miller, 1984; Gallup & Suarez, 1985). In British psychology departments, where animal use dropped by two-thirds in the dozen years after 1977, electric shock had been used in only 4 percent of animal studies. All involved rats (Thomas & Blackman, 1991).

Animal protection organizations, such as Psychologists for the Ethical Treatment of Animals, advocate naturalistic observation of animals rather than laboratory manipulation. However, many researchers say this is not the morality of good versus evil but of compassion (for animals) versus compassion (for people). How many of us would have attacked Pasteur's experiments with rabies, which in causing some dogs to suffer led to a vaccine that spared millions of people, and dogs, from agonizing death? And would we really wish to have deprived ourselves of the animal research that led to effective methods of training children with mental disorders; of

"I believe that to prevent, cripple, or needlessly complicate the research that can relieve animal and human suffering is profoundly inhuman, cruel, and immoral."

Psychologist Neal Miller (1983)

Justifiable experimentation?
Is it right to use animals to advance our understanding of humans? For animal rights activists, no purpose justifies hurting, frightening, or (as here) manipulating an animal. For most psychologists and medical researchers, animal research is ethically justified as long as researchers observe strict standards and inflict no unnecessary pain.

"Please do not forget those of us who suffer from incurable diseases or disabilities who hope for a cure through research that requires the use of animals."

Psychologist Dennis Feeney (1987)

understanding aging; of relieving fears and depression; of controlling obesity, alcoholism, and stress-related pain and disease?

Out of this heated debate, two issues emerge. The basic one is whether it is right to place the well-being of humans above that of animals. In experiments on stress and cancer, is it right that mice get tumors in hopes that people might not? Should some monkeys be exposed to an HIV-like virus in the search for developing an AIDS vaccine? Is our use of other animals as natural as the behavior of carnivorous hawks, cats, and whales? (Animals themselves do not assign rights to other animals lower on the food chain.) Defenders of research on animals argue that anyone who has eaten a hamburger, worn leather shoes, tolerated hunting and fishing, or supported the extermination of crop-destroying or plague-carrying pests has already agreed that, yes, it is sometimes permissible to sacrifice animals for the sake of human well-being.

Scott Plous (1993) notes that our compassion for animals varies, as does our compassion for people, based on their perceived similarity to us. Few people equate all animals, as did Ingrid Newkirk, the director of People for the Ethical Treatment of Animals: "A rat is a pig is a dog is a boy" (quoted by Baldwin, 1993). Research in social psychology shows that we feel more attraction, give more help, and act less aggressively toward similar others. Likewise, we value animals according to their perceived kinship with us. Thus, primates and companion pets get top priority. (Western people raise or trap mink and foxes for their fur, but not dogs or cats.) Other mammals occupy the second rung on the privilege ladder, followed by birds, fish, and reptiles on the third rung, with insects at the bottom. In human-animal relations, a cockroach is not a crow is not a cow is not a collie is not a chimpanzee. In deciding which animals have rights, we draw a cut-off line somewhere across the animal kingdom.

If we give human life first priority, the second issue is the priority given the well-being of animals. What safeguards should protect animals? Most researchers today feel ethically obligated to enhance the well-being of captive animals and protect them from needless suffering. Humane care also leads to more effective science, because pain and stress would distort the animals' behavior during experiments. Thus, researchers welcomed the national animal protection legislation updated by the United States in 1985 and by Britain in 1986, and they supported the accompanying regulations and laboratory inspections (Cherfas, 1990; Johnson, 1990).

Animals have themselves benefited from animal research. Studies have helped improve their care and management not only in laboratories and zoos but even in

"The righteous know the needs of their animals."

Proverbs 12:10

their natural habitats. By revealing our behavioral kinship with animals and the remarkable intelligence of some animals, experiments have also led to an increase in our empathy with them. At its best, a psychology concerned for humans and sensitive to animals serves the welfare of both.

Is It Ethical to Experiment on People?

If the image of animals or people receiving supposed electric shocks troubles you, you may find it a relief that most psychological research involves no such stress. Blinking lights, flashing words, and pleasant social interactions are the rule.

Occasionally, though, researchers do temporarily stress or deceive people, but only when they believe it is essential to a justifiable end, such as understanding and controlling violent behavior or studying mood swings. Such experiments wouldn't work if the participants knew all there was to know about the experiment beforehand. Either the procedures would be ineffective or the participants, wanting to be helpful, might try to confirm the researchers' predictions.

Ethical principles developed by the American Psychological Association (1992) and the British Psychological Society (1993) urge investigators to (1) obtain the informed consent of potential participants, (2) protect them from harm and discomfort, (3) treat information about individual participants confidentially, and (4) fully explain the research afterward. Moreover, most universities today screen research proposals through an ethics committee that safeguards the well-being of every participant.

Much research, however, occurs outside of university laboratories, in places where there often are no ethics committees. For example, companies routinely survey people, photograph their purchasing behavior, track their buying patterns, and test the effectiveness of advertising. Curiously, however, such research attracts less attention than is given to scientific research done to advance human understanding.

Is Psychology Free of Value Judgments?

Psychology is definitely not value-free. Values affect what we study, how we study it, and how we interpret results. Consider: Researchers' values influence their choice of research topics—whether to study worker productivity or worker morale, sex discrimination or gender differences, conformity or independence. Values can even color "the facts." Our preconceptions can bias our observations and interpretations; sometimes we see what we want or expect to see (**FIGURE 1**). Even the words we use to describe a phenomenon can reflect our values. Labeling the sex acts we do not practice as "perversions" or as "sexual variations" conveys a value judgment. The same holds true in everyday speech, when one person's "terrorists" are another's "freedom fighters," or one person's "faith" is another's "fanaticism." Our labeling someone as "firm" or "stubborn," "careful" or "picky," "discreet" or "secretive" reveals our feelings. Both in and out of psychology, labels describe and labels evaluate.

Popular applications of psychology also contain hidden values. If you defer to "professional" guidance about how to live—how to raise children, how to achieve self-fulfillment, what to do with sexual feelings, how to get ahead at work—you are accepting value-laden advice. A science of behavior and mental processes can certainly help us reach our goals, but it cannot decide them. (See "Thinking Critically About the Death Penalty" on page 43.)

> "The greatness of a nation can be judged by the way its animals are treated."
>
> **Mahatma Gandhi, 1869–1948**

FIGURE 1 What do you see?
People interpret ambiguous information to fit their preconceptions. Did you see a duck or a rabbit? Before showing some friends this image, ask them if they can see the duck lying on its back (or the bunny in the grass). (From Shepard, 1990.)

"It is doubtless impossible to approach any human problem with a mind free from bias."

Simone de Beauvoir, *The Second Sex*, 1953

Is Psychology Potentially Dangerous?

If some people see psychology as merely common sense, others have a different concern—that it is becoming dangerously powerful. Is it an accident, someone once wondered, that astronomy is the oldest science and psychology the youngest? Exploring the external universe is one thing, but exploring our own inner universe seems even more dangerous and threatening. Won't psychology be used to manipulate people?

Knowledge, like all powers, can be used for good or evil. Nuclear power has been used to light up cities—and to demolish them. Persuasive power has been used to educate people—and to deceive them. The power of mind-altering drugs has been used to restore sanity—and to destroy it.

Although psychology does indeed have the power to deceive, its purpose is to enlighten. Psychologists every day are exploring ways to enhance learning, creativity, and compassion. Psychology also speaks to many of our world's great problems—war, overpopulation, prejudice, family dysfunction, crime—all of which involve attitudes and behaviors. And psychology speaks to our deepest longings—for nourishment, for love, for happiness. True, psychology cannot address all of life's great questions, but it speaks to some mighty important ones.

THINKING CRITICALLY ABOUT :

THE DEATH PENALTY—WHEN BELIEFS COLLIDE WITH PSYCHOLOGICAL SCIENCE

An influential modern viewpoint, ironically called *postmodernism*, questions scientific objectivity. Rather than mirroring the real world, say postmodernists, scientific concepts are socially constructed fictions. Like all knowledge, they reflect the culture that formed them. "Intelligence," for instance, is a concept we cre-ated and defined. Because personal values guide theory and research, truth is actually personal and subjective. (What behaviors shall we call "intelligent"?) In our quest for truth, we cannot help following our hunches, our biases, our cultural bent.

Psychological scientists agree that many important questions lie beyond the reach of science. And they agree that personal beliefs often shape perceptions. But they also believe that there is a real world out there, and that we advance truth by checking our hunches against it. Madame Curie did not just construct the concept of radium, she *discovered* radium. It really exists. In the social sciences, pure objectivity, like pure love, may be unattainable. Yet most would argue that it is better to humble ourselves before reliable evidence than to cling to untested presumptions.

Letting go of presumptions is what the U.S. Supreme Court justices did. After considering pertinent social science evidence, they decided to disallow five-member juries and to end school desegregation. These very decisions helped inspire hundreds more studies that researchers hoped would inform future judicial decisions. Recently, however, the Court has joined postmodernists in discounting social science research. In deciding whether the death penalty falls under the Constitution's ban on "cruel and unusual punishment," the Court wrestled with whether society defines execu-

tion as cruel and unusual, whether courts inflict the penalty arbitrarily, whether they apply it with racial bias, and whether execution deters crime more than all other available punishments. The social science answers to each of these questions, note psychologists Mark Costanzo (1997) and Craig Haney and Deana Logan (1994), could hardly be clearer. And yet, on two of these issues—the fairness of the death penalty and its effectiveness—the Court has disregarded social science research.

Is the Death Penalty Fair?

Should it be permissible to execute a person with mental retardation—someone having the mental age of a $6\frac{1}{2}$-year-old, as in one case? Attitudes toward capital punishment tend to follow a nation's legal practice. It is therefore mostly favored by Americans and opposed by those in many other nations (as readers in Canada, Western Europe, Australia, New Zealand, and most of South America will recognize). Nevertheless, public opinion surveys show Americans are overwhelmingly opposed to executing people with mental retardation. Some justices have dismissed such surveys, preferring instead to trust state legislation and jury decisions as indicators of public attitudes. However, studies show that those eligible to serve as jurors in capital punishment cases—those who accept the death penalty—do not represent the greater population. Compared with people excluded by virtue of their qualms about capital punishment, those chosen are less likely to be minorities and women. They are also more likely to believe the prosecution's arguments, and they are more conviction-prone.

The Court has accepted social science evidence that a 15-year-old is too immature emotionally and too vulnerable to peer pressure for the death penalty to be appropriate. Yet, without explanation, it ignored the very same body of evidence when it decided that a 16-year-old, and even someone with the mental ability of a $6\frac{1}{2}$-year-old, could be executed.

Does the Death Penalty Work—Does It Deter Crime?

The evidence is consistent: States with a death penalty do not have lower homicide rates. After instituting the death penalty, their rates have not dropped. And homicide has not risen when states abandoned the death penalty. A person committing a crime of passion does not pause to calculate the consequences (and, if she or he did, would likely consider life in a prison cell an ample deterrent).

Still, the Court persists in deciding that 16-year-olds and adults with the mental abilities of $6\frac{1}{2}$-year-olds have sufficient judgment and perspective to be executable, that admitting only jurors who accept the death penalty provides a fair and representative jury of one's peers, and that "the death penalty undoubtedly is a significant deterrent."

It is clear that beliefs *do* guide perceptions. And that, say psychological scientists responding to postmodernists, is why we *need* to think smarter—to restrain our hunches, our biases, and our cultural leanings by checking them against available evidence. Why not put our testable beliefs to the test? If they find support, so much the better for them. If they collide against a wall of observation, so much the worse for them. These ideals of skeptical scrutiny and humility fuel all scientific endeavor.

Neuroscience and Behavior

No principle is more central to today's psychology, or to this book, than this: *Everything psychological is simultaneously biological.* Your every idea, every mood, every urge is a biological happening. You think, feel, and act with your body. You relate to the world through your body. (Try laughing, crying, or loving without it.) Without your body—your genes, your brain, your body chemistry, your inner organs, your appearance—you are, indeed, nobody. Although we find it convenient to talk separately of biological and psychological influences on behavior, we need to remember: To think, feel, or act without a body is as plausible as running without legs.

As we enter the new century, science is riveted on the most amazing parts of our body—our brain, its component neural systems, and their genetic blueprints. The brain's ultimate challenge? To understand itself. How does our brain organize and communicate with itself? How does our heredity prewire the brain and our experience modify it? How does the brain process the information we need to shoot a basketball? To delight in the nuances of a pianist's notes? To remember our first kiss?

Our understanding of how the brain enables the mind has come a long way. Although the ancient philosopher Plato correctly located the mind in the spherical head—his idea of the perfect form—Aristotle believed the mind was in the heart, which pumps warmth and vitality to the body. The heart remains our symbol for love, but science has long overtaken philosophy on this issue. It's your brain, not your heart, that falls in love.

On the timescale of human existence, the last 150 years are but a few ticks of the clock. Yet that's how recently a scientific understanding of the brain-mind connection began to emerge. We have come far since the early 1800s, when the German physician Franz Gall invented *phrenology*, an ill-fated theory that claimed bumps on the skull could reveal our mental abilities and our character traits. At one point, Britain had 29 phrenological societies, and phrenologists traveled North America giving skull readings (Hunt, 1993).

Phrenology did, however, correctly focus attention on the idea that various brain regions have particular functions. Within little more than the last century, we have realized, as we will see in Module 3, that the body is composed of cells and that among these are nerve cells that conduct electricity and "talk" to one another by sending chemical messages across a tiny gap that separates them. We have also learned, as we will see in Module 4, that specific brain systems serve specific functions (though not the functions Gall supposed) and that from the information processed in these different brain systems, we construct our experience of sights and sounds, meanings and memories, pain and passion. You and I are privileged to live in a time when discoveries about the interplay of our biology and behavior are occurring at an exhilarating pace.

A wrongheaded theory
Despite initial acceptance of Gall's speculations, bumps on the skull tell us nothing about how the brain works. Nevertheless, some of his assumptions have held true: Different parts of the brain do control different aspects of behavior.

3 Neural and Hormonal Systems

We are each a system composed of subsystems that are in turn composed of even smaller subsystems. Tiny cells organize to form our body organs such as our stomach, heart, and brain. These organs in turn form larger systems for digestion, circulation, and information processing. And those systems are part of an even larger system—you, who in turn are a part of your family, community, and culture. We are *bio-psycho-social* systems, so to more deeply understand our behavior, we need to study how biological, psychological, and social systems work and interact.

Throughout this book you will find examples of how our biology underlies our behavior and mental processes. By studying the links between biological activity and psychological events, **biological psychologists** are gaining a better understanding of sleep and dreams, depression and schizophrenia, hunger and sex, stress and disease. We therefore begin our study of psychology with a look at its biological roots. We will start small and build—from neurons in this module and on to the environmental and cultural influences that interact with our biology in later modules. At all levels, psychologists examine how we process information—how we take in information; how we organize, interpret, and store it; and how we use it. For scientists, it is a fortunate fact of nature that the information systems of humans and other animals operate similarly—so similarly, in fact, that you could not distinguish between small samples of brain tissue from a human and a monkey. This similarity allows researchers to study relatively simple animals, such as squids and sea slugs, to discover how our neural systems operate, and to study mammals' brains to understand the organization of our own. Though human brains are more complex, they follow principles that govern all of the animal world.

Neurons and Neural Impulses

Preview Question: What are neurons, and how do they transmit information?

Our body's neural information system is complexity built from simplicity. Its building blocks are **neurons**, or nerve cells. There are many different types of neurons, but they are all variations on the same theme (**FIGURE 3.1**). Each consists of a cell body and its branching fibers. The fibers are of two types: The bushy **dendrites** receive information, and the **axons** pass it along to other neurons or to muscles or glands. Unlike the short dendrites, axons are sometimes very long, projecting several feet through the body. A neuron carrying orders to a leg muscle has a cell body and axon roughly on the scale of a basketball attached to a rope 4 miles long. A layer of fatty tissue, called the **myelin sheath**, insulates the axons of some neurons and helps speed their impulses. Evidence for the myelin sheath's importance appears in multiple sclerosis, a disease in which the myelin sheath degenerates. The result is a slowing of all communication to muscles and the eventual loss of muscle control.

Depending on the type of fiber, the neural impulse travels at speeds ranging from a sluggish 2 miles per hour to, in some myelinated fibers, a breakneck 200 or more miles per hour. But even this top speed is 3 million times slower than that of electricity through a wire. We measure brain activity in milliseconds (thousandths of a second) and computer activity in nanoseconds (billionths of a second). That helps to explain why, unlike the nearly instantaneous reactions of a high-speed computer, your reaction to a sudden event, such as a child darting in front of your car, may take a quarter-second or more.

- **biological psychology** a branch of psychology concerned with the links between biology and behavior. (Some biological psychologists call themselves *behavioral neuroscientists, neuropsychologists, behavior geneticists, physiological psychologists,* or *biopsychologists.*)

- **neuron** a nerve cell; the basic building block of the nervous system.

- **dendrite** the bushy, branching extensions of a neuron that receive messages and conduct impulses toward the cell body.

- **axon** the extension of a neuron, ending in branching terminal fibers, through which messages are sent to other neurons or to muscles or glands.

- **myelin [MY-uh-lin] sheath** a layer of fatty tissue segmentally encasing the fibers of many neurons; enables vastly greater transmission speed of neural impulses as the impulse hops from one node to the next.

- **action potential** a neural impulse; a brief electrical charge that travels down an axon. The action potential is generated by the movement of positively charged atoms in and out of channels in the axon's membrane.

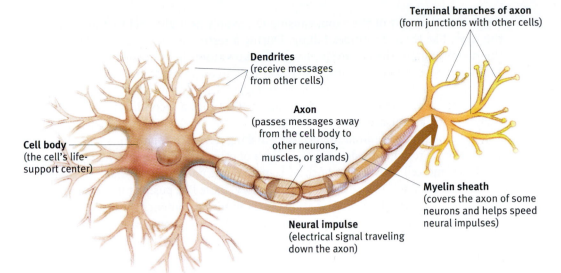

Terminal branches of axon
(form junctions with other cells)

FIGURE **3.1** A motor neuron

Dendrites
(receive messages
from other cells)

Axon
(passes messages away
from the cell body to
other neurons,
muscles, or glands)

Cell body
(the cell's life-
support center)

Myelin sheath
(covers the axon of some
neurons and helps speed
neural impulses)

Neural impulse
(electrical signal traveling
down the axon)

A neuron fires an impulse when it receives signals from sense receptors stimulated by pressure, heat, or light, or when it is stimulated by chemical messages from adjacent neurons. The impulse, called the **action potential**, is a brief electrical charge that travels down the axon, rather like a line of dominoes falling, each one tripping the next. This is real electricity. A handful of neurons together produce enough power to light up a flashlight bulb.

Neurons, like batteries, generate electricity from chemical events. The chemistry-to-electricity process involves the exchange of electrically charged atoms, called *ions*. The fluid interior of a resting axon has an excess of negatively charged ions, while the fluid outside the axon membrane has more positively charged ions. This positive-outside/negative-inside polarization, called the *resting potential*, occurs because an unmyelinated axon's membrane is selectively permeable—it has gates that the positive sodium ions cannot pass through. When a neuron fires, the first bit of the axon opens its gates, rather like a manhole cover flipping open, and the positively charged sodium ions flood through the channel (**FIGURE 3.2**). This

2. This depolarization produces another action potential a little farther along the axon. Gates in this neighboring area now open, and more positively charged atoms rush in, while the positively charged atoms in the previous section of axon exit.

FIGURE **3.2** Action potential

3. As the action potential continues speedily down the axon, the first section has now completely recharged.

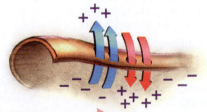

Cell body end of axon

1. Neuron stimulation causes a brief change in electrical charge. If strong enough, this produces depolarization and an action potential.

Direction of neural impulse: toward axon terminals

depolarizes that part of the axon, causing the axon's next channel to open, and then the next, like those dominoes falling. During a resting pause (the *refractory period*), the neuron pumps the positively charged sodium atoms back outside. Then it can fire again. (In myelinated neurons, the action potential speeds up by hopping from one myelin "sausage" to the next, as shown in Figure 3.1.) The mind boggles when imagining this electrochemical process repeating 100 times a second. But this is just the first of many astonishments.

The neuron is a miniature decision-making device that performs some complex calculations. From hundreds, even thousands of other neurons, it receives signals on its dendrites and cell body. Some of these signals are *excitatory*, somewhat like pushing a neuron's accelerator. Other signals are *inhibitory*, more like pushing its brake. If excitatory signals minus inhibitory signals exceed a minimum intensity, called the **threshold**, the combined signals trigger an impulse. (Think of it this way: If the excitatory party animals outvote the inhibitory party poopers, the party's on.) The electrical impulse (the action potential) transmits down the axon, which branches into junctions with hundreds or thousands of other neurons and with the body's muscles and glands.

Increasing the stimulus above the threshold, however, will not increase the impulse's intensity. (The neuron's reaction is an *all-or-none response*; like guns, neurons either fire or they don't.) Nor does the strength of the stimulus affect the impulse's speed.

How then do we detect the intensity of a stimulus? How do we distinguish a gentle touch from a big hug? A strong stimulus cannot trigger a stronger or faster impulse in a neuron—squeezing a trigger harder won't make a bullet go faster. But a strong stimulus can trigger more neurons to fire, and to fire more often.

Neural Communication

Preview Question: How does a neuron communicate with other cells to influence our behavior?

Neurons interweave so intricately that even with a microscope it is hard to see where one neuron ends and another begins. Scientists once believed that the branching axon of one cell fused with the dendrites of another in an uninterrupted fabric. Then a Spanish anatomist, Santiago Ramon y Cajal (1852–1934), described gaps between individual nerve cells and concluded that the individual neurons must function as independent agents within the nervous system. At the same time, the British physiologist Sir Charles Sherrington (1857–1952) noticed that neural impulses were taking an unexpectedly long time to travel a neural pathway. Sherrington inferred there must be a brief interruption in the transmission.

We now know that the axon terminal of one neuron is in fact separated from the receiving neuron by a gap less than a millionth of an inch wide. Sherrington called this junction the **synapse**, and the gap is called the *synaptic gap* or *cleft*. To Cajal, these near-unions of neurons—"protoplasmic kisses," he called them—were another of nature's marvels. How does the nerve impulse execute the protoplasmic kiss? How does it cross the tiny synaptic gap? The answer, it turns out, is one of the important scientific discoveries of our age.

When the action potential reaches the knoblike terminals at an axon's end, it triggers the release of chemical messengers, called **neurotransmitters** (FIGURE 3.3). Within 1/10,000th of a second, the neurotransmitter molecules cross the synaptic gap and bind to receptor sites on the receiving neuron—as precisely as a key fits a lock. For an instant, the neurotransmitter unlocks tiny channels at the receiving site. This allows ions to enter the receiving neuron, thereby either exciting or inhibiting its readiness to fire. Excess neurotransmitters are reabsorbed by the sending neuron in a process called *reuptake*. Many drugs increase the availability of selected neurotransmitters by blocking their reuptake.

- **threshold** the level of stimulation required to trigger a neural impulse.

- **synapse [SIN-aps]** the junction between the axon tip of the sending neuron and the dendrite or cell body of the receiving neuron. The tiny gap at this junction is called the *synaptic gap* or *cleft*.

- **neurotransmitters** chemical messengers that traverse the synaptic gaps between neurons. When released by the sending neuron, neurotransmitters travel across the synapse and bind to receptor sites on the receiving neuron, thereby influencing whether it will generate a neural impulse.

1. Electrical impulses (action potentials) travel from one neuron to another across a tiny junction known as a synapse.

FIGURE 3.3
How neurons communicate

Sending neuron

Receiving neuron

Action potential

Sending neuron

Action potential

Vesicle containing neurotransmitters

Axon terminal

Synaptic gap

Receptor sites on receiving neuron

Neurotransmitter

Reuptake

2. When an action potential reaches an axon terminal, it stimulates the release of neurotransmitter molecules from sacs called vesicles. These molecules cross the synaptic gap and bind to receptor sites on the receiving neuron. This allows electrically charged atoms (not pictured here) to enter the receiving neuron and excite or inhibit a new action potential.

3. The sending neuron normally reabsorbs excess neurotransmitter molecules, a process called reuptake.

Most neurons have a resting rate of random firing that either increases or decreases with input from other neurons and from chemicals that affect their sensitivity. Roughly speaking, the neuron is democratic: If it receives many more excitatory than inhibitory messages, the cell fires often. More electrical impulses flash down its axon, releasing more packets of neurotransmitters, which diffuse across their synaptic gaps to other neurons.

As researchers discovered dozens of different neurotransmitters, they also encountered new questions: Are certain neurotransmitters found only in specific places? What are their effects? Can we boost or diminish these effects through drugs or diet? Could such changes affect our moods, memories, or mental abilities?

Later in this text we examine the role of neurotransmitters in depression and euphoria, hunger and thinking, addictions and therapy. For now, let's glimpse how neurotransmitters influence our motions and our emotions. We now know that a particular neural pathway in the brain may use only one or two neurotransmitters (**FIGURE 3.4**), and that particular neurotransmitters may have particular effects on behavior and emotions. Some examples:

+ *Dopamine* influences movement, learning, attention, and emotion. Excess activity at dopamine receptors has been linked with schizophrenia.
+ *Serotonin* affects mood, hunger, sleep, and arousal. Prozac and similar antidepressant drugs raise serotonin levels.

FIGURE 3.4 Neurotransmitter pathways
Each of the brain's differing chemical messengers has designated pathways where it operates, as shown here for dopamine and serotonin (Carter, 1998).

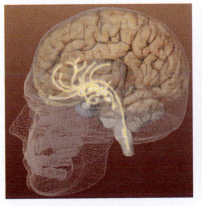
Dopamine pathways

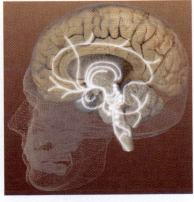
Serotonin pathways

"When it comes to the brain, if you want to see the action, follow the neurotransmitters."

Neuroscientist Floyd Bloom (1993)

+ *Norepinephrine* helps control alertness and arousal.
+ *Gamma-aminobutyric acid* (GABA) serves inhibitory functions and is sometimes implicated in eating and sleep disorders.
+ *Acetylcholine* works on neurons involved in muscle action, learning, and memory. The neurons that produce this vital chemical messenger deteriorate when a person has Alzheimer's disease.

Acetylcholine (ACh) is one of the best-understood neurotransmitters. In addition to its vital role in learning and memory, ACh is the messenger at every junction between a motor neuron and skeletal muscle. Using powerful electron microscopes, neurobiologists can magnify thinly sliced specimens of tissue enough to see the sacs that store and release ACh molecules. When ACh is released to our muscle cells, the muscle contracts.

If the transmission of ACh is blocked, our muscles cannot contract. Curare, a poison that certain South American Indians have put on the tips of their hunting darts, occupies and blocks ACh receptor sites, leaving the neurotransmitter unable to affect the muscles. Struck by one of these darts, an animal becomes paralyzed. Botulin, a poison that can form in improperly canned food, causes paralysis by blocking ACh release from the sending neuron. By contrast, the venom of the black widow spider causes a synaptic flood of ACh. The result? Violent muscle contractions, convulsions, and possible death.

Molecules and muscles
When your body moves, a flood of acetylcholine molecules triggers the muscle action.

The Endorphins

An exciting discovery about neurotransmitters occurred when Candace Pert and Solomon Snyder (1973) attached a radioactive tracer to morphine, allowing them to see exactly where in an animal's brain it was taken up. Pert and Snyder discovered that the morphine, an opiate drug that elevates mood and eases pain, was taken up by receptors in areas linked with mood and pain sensations.

It was hard to imagine why the brain would contain these "opiate receptors" unless it had its own naturally occurring opiates. Why would the brain have a chemical lock, unless it also had a corresponding key? Researchers soon confirmed that the brain does indeed contain several types of neurotransmitter molecules similar to morphine. Named **endorphins** (short for *endo*genous [produced within] m*orphine*), these natural opiates are released in response to pain and vigorous exercise (Farrell & others, 1982; Lagerweij & others, 1984). They may therefore help explain all sorts of good feelings, such as the "runner's high," the painkilling effects of acupuncture, and the indifference to pain in some severely injured people, such as David Livingstone reported in his 1857 *Missionary Travels*:

Physician Lewis Thomas, on the endorphins:
"There it is, a biologically universal act of mercy. I cannot explain it, except to say that I would have put it in had I been around at the very beginning, sitting as a member of a planning committee."

The Youngest Science, 1983

> I heard a shout. Starting, and looking half round, I saw the lion just in the act of springing upon me. I was upon a little height, he caught my shoulder as he sprang, and we both came to the ground below together. Growling horribly close to my ear, he shook me as a terrier does a rat. The shock produced a stupor similar to that which seems to be felt by a mouse after the first shake of the cat. It caused a sort of dreaminess in which there was no sense of pain nor feeling of terror, though [I was] quite conscious of all that was happening. . . . This peculiar state is probably produced in all animals killed by the carnivora; and if so, is a merciful provision by our benevolent Creator for lessening the pain of death.

How Drugs and Other Chemicals Alter Neurotransmission

If indeed the endorphins lessen pain and boost mood, why not flood the brain with artificial opiates, thereby intensifying the brain's own "feel-good" chemistry? One problem is that when flooded with opiate drugs such as heroin and morphine, the brain may stop producing its own natural opiates. When the drug is withdrawn, the brain may therefore be deprived of any form of opiate. For a drug addict, the result is agony that persists until the brain resumes production of its natural opiates or receives more artificial opiates. Mood-altering drugs, from alcohol to nicotine to heroin, share a common effect: They trigger unpleasant, lingering aftereffects. For suppressing the body's own neurotransmitter production, nature charges a price.

Drugs affect communication at the synapse, often by exciting or inhibiting neuron firing. *Agonists* excite by mimicking a particular neurotransmitter or blocking its reuptake (**FIGURE 3.5**). An agonist can be a drug molecule that is similar enough to the neurotransmitter to mimic its effects. Some opiate drugs, for example, produce a temporary "high" by amplifying normal sensations of arousal or pleasure. *Antagonists* inhibit by blocking neurotransmitters or by diminishing their release. An antagonist can be a drug molecule that is enough like the natural neurotransmitter to occupy its receptor site and block its effect but not similar enough to stimulate the receptor, rather like foreign coins that fit into, but won't operate, a soda or candy machine. As noted earlier, botulin poison causes paralysis by blocking acetylcholine receptors that produce muscle movement.

- **acetylcholine [ah-seat-el-KO-leen] (ACh)** a neurotransmitter that, among its functions, triggers muscle contraction.
- **endorphins [en-DOR-fins]** "morphine within"—natural, opiatelike neurotransmitters linked to pain control and to pleasure.

FIGURE 3.5
Agonists and antagonists

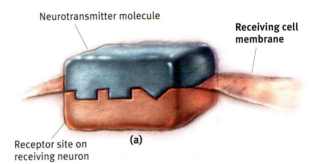
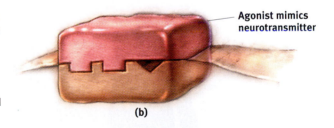
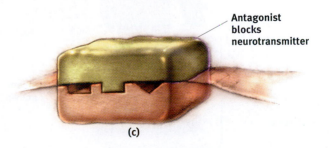
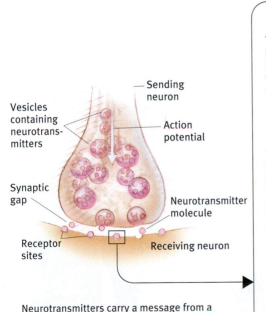

Vesicles containing neurotransmitters — Sending neuron — Action potential — Synaptic gap — Neurotransmitter molecule — Receptor sites — Receiving neuron

Neurotransmitters carry a message from a sending neuron across a synapse to receptor sites on a receiving neuron.

This neurotransmitter molecule has a molecular structure that precisely fits the receptor site on the receiving neuron, much as a key fits a lock.

This agonist molecule excites. It is similar enough in structure to the neurotransmitter molecule that it mimics its effects on the receiving neuron. Morphine, for instance, mimics the action of endorphins by stimulating receptors in brain areas involved in mood and pain sensations.

This antagonist molecule inhibits. It has a structure similar enough to the neurotransmitter to occupy its receptor site and block its action, but not similar enough to stimulate the receptor. Botulin poisoning paralyzes its victims by blocking ACh receptors involved in muscle movement.

Neurotransmitter molecule — Receiving cell membrane — Receptor site on receiving neuron — (a) — Agonist mimics neurotransmitter — (b) — Antagonist blocks neurotransmitter — (c)

- **nervous system** the body's speedy, electrochemical communication system, consisting of all the nerve cells of the peripheral and central nervous systems.

- **central nervous system (CNS)** the brain and spinal cord.

- **peripheral nervous system (PNS)** the sensory and motor neurons that connect the central nervous system (CNS) to the rest of the body.

- **nerves** neural "cables" containing many axons. These bundled axons, which are part of the peripheral nervous system, connect the central nervous system with muscles, glands, and sense organs.

- **sensory neurons** neurons that carry incoming information from the sense receptors to the central nervous system.

- **interneurons** central nervous system neurons that internally communicate and intervene between the sensory inputs and motor outputs.

- **motor neurons** the neurons that carry outgoing information from the central nervous system to the muscles and glands.

Neurotransmitter research is enabling the creation of new therapeutic drugs such as those used to alleviate depression and schizophrenia. But designing a drug can be harder than it sounds. A *blood-brain barrier* enables the brain to fence out unwanted chemicals circulating in the blood, and some chemicals don't have the right shape to slither through this barrier. Scientists know, for example, that the tremors of Parkinson's disease result from the death of nerve cells that produce the neurotransmitter dopamine. Giving the patient dopamine as a drug doesn't help, though, because dopamine cannot cross the blood-brain barrier. But L-dopa, a raw material the brain can convert to dopamine, can sneak through. Given L-dopa, many patients gain better muscular control.

The Nervous System

Preview Question: What are the elementary components of our nervous system, and what are the functional divisions of that system?

Neurons communicating with other neurons form our body's primary information system, the **nervous system** (FIGURE 3.6). The brain and spinal cord form the **central nervous system (CNS)**. The **peripheral nervous system (PNS)** links the central nervous system with the body's sense receptors, muscles, and glands. The sensory and motor axons carrying this PNS information are bundled into the electrical cables that we know as **nerves**. The optic nerve, for example, bundles nearly a million axon fibers into a single cable carrying the information that each eye sends to the brain.

Information travels in the nervous system through three types of neurons. The **sensory neurons** send information from the body's tissues and sensory organs inward to the brain and spinal cord, which process the information. This processing involves a second class of neurons, the central nervous system's own **interneurons**, which enable its internal communication. The central nervous system then sends instructions out to the body's tissues via the **motor neurons**. Our complexity, though, resides mostly in our interneuron systems. Our nervous system has a few million sensory neurons, a few million motor neurons, but billions and billions of interneurons.

FIGURE 3.6
The functional divisions of the human nervous system

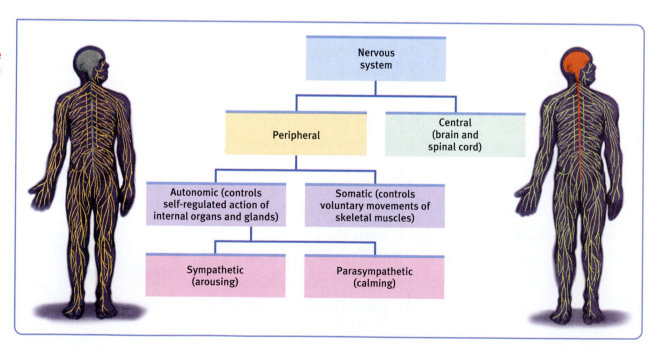

The Peripheral Nervous System

Our peripheral nervous system has two components—somatic and autonomic. The **somatic nervous system** controls the movements of our skeletal muscles. As you reach the bottom of this page, the skeletal nervous system will report to your brain the current state of your skeletal muscles and carry instructions back, triggering your hand to turn the page.

Our **autonomic nervous system** controls the glands and the muscles of our internal organs. Like an automatic pilot, it may sometimes be consciously overridden. But usually it operates on its own to influence our internal functioning, including our heartbeat, digestion, and glandular activity. (*Autonomic* means "self-regulating.")

The autonomic nervous system is a dual system (**FIGURE 3.7**). The **sympathetic nervous system** arouses us for defensive action. If something alarms or enrages you, the sympathetic system will accelerate your heartbeat, slow your digestion, raise your blood sugar, dilate your arteries, and cool you with perspiration, making you alert and ready for action. When the stress subsides, the **parasympathetic nervous system** produces opposite effects. It conserves energy as it calms you by decreasing your heartbeat, lowering your blood sugar, and so forth. In everyday situations, the sympathetic and parasympathetic nervous systems work together to keep us in a steady internal state.

- **somatic nervous system** the division of the peripheral nervous system that controls the body's skeletal muscles. Also called the *skeletal nervous system*.
- **autonomic [aw-tuh-NAHM-ik] nervous system** the part of the peripheral nervous system that controls the glands and the muscles of the internal organs (such as the heart). Its sympathetic division arouses; its parasympathetic division calms.
- **sympathetic nervous system** the division of the autonomic nervous system that arouses the body, mobilizing its energy in stressful situations.
- **parasympathetic nervous system** the division of the autonomic nervous system that calms the body, conserving its energy.

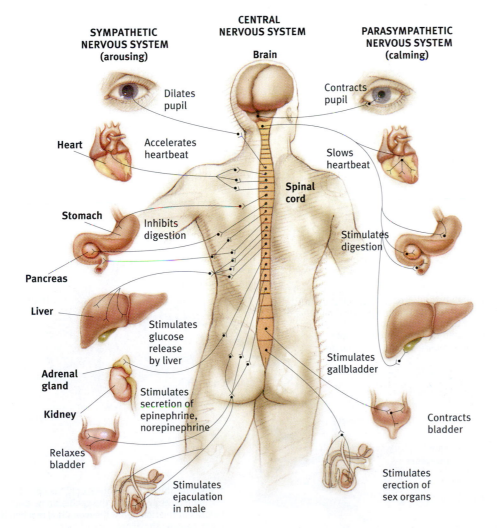

SYMPATHETIC NERVOUS SYSTEM (arousing)

CENTRAL NERVOUS SYSTEM

PARASYMPATHETIC NERVOUS SYSTEM (calming)

Brain

Dilates pupil

Contracts pupil

Heart — Accelerates heartbeat

Slows heartbeat

Spinal cord

Stomach — Inhibits digestion

Stimulates digestion

Pancreas

Liver — Stimulates glucose release by liver

Stimulates gallbladder

Adrenal gland — Stimulates secretion of epinephrine, norepinephrine

Kidney

Relaxes bladder

Contracts bladder

Stimulates ejaculation in male

Stimulates erection of sex organs

FIGURE 3.7

The dual functions of the autonomic nervous system

The autonomic nervous system controls the more autonomous (or self-regulating) internal functions. Its sympathetic division arouses and expends energy. Its parasympathetic division calms and conserves energy, allowing routine maintenance activity. For example, sympathetic stimulation accelerates heartbeat, while parasympathetic stimulation slows it.

The Central Nervous System

From the simplicity of neurons "talking" to other neurons arises the complexity of the central nervous system that enables our humanity—our thinking, feeling, and acting. Tens of billions of neurons, each communicating with thousands of other neurons, yield an ever-changing wiring diagram that dwarfs a powerful computer. One of the great remaining mysteries is how this neural machinery organizes itself into complex circuits capable of learning, feeling, and thinking.

Spinal Cord and Brain

The central nervous system's spinal cord is an information highway connecting the peripheral nervous system to the brain. Ascending neural tracts send up sensory information, and descending tracts send back motor-control information.

The neural pathways governing our **reflexes**, our automatic responses to stimuli, illustrate the spinal cord's work. A simple spinal reflex pathway is composed of a single sensory neuron and a single motor neuron. These often communicate through an interneuron. The knee-jerk response, for example, involves one such simple pathway; a headless warm body could do it.

Another such pathway enables the pain reflex (**FIGURE 3.8**). When your fingers touch a flame, neural activity excited by the heat travels via sensory neurons to interneurons in your spinal cord. These interneurons respond by activating motor neurons to the muscles in your arm. That's why it feels as if your hand jerks away not by your choice, but on its own.

Because the simple pain reflex pathway runs through the spinal cord and out, your hand jerks from the candle's flame *before* your brain receives and responds to the information that causes you to feel pain. Information travels to and from the brain by way of the spinal cord. Were the top of your spinal cord severed, you would not feel such pain. Nor would you feel pleasure. Your brain would literally be out of touch with your body. You would lose all sensation and voluntary movement in body regions whose sensory and motor neurons connect with the spinal cord below its point of injury. Men paralyzed below the waist are usually capable of an erection (a simple reflex) if their genitals are stimulated. Females similarly paralyzed respond with vaginal lubrication. But, depending on where and how completely the spinal

> "If the nervous system be cut off between the brain and other parts, the experiences of those other parts are nonexistent for the mind. The eye is blind, the ear deaf, the hand insensible and motionless."
>
> **William James,** *Principles of Psychology,* **1890**

FIGURE **3.8 A simple reflex**   1. In this simple hand-withdrawal reflex, information is carried from skin receptors along a sensory neuron to the spinal cord (shown by the red arrows). From here it is passed via interneurons to motor neurons that lead to muscles in the hand and arm (blue arrows).

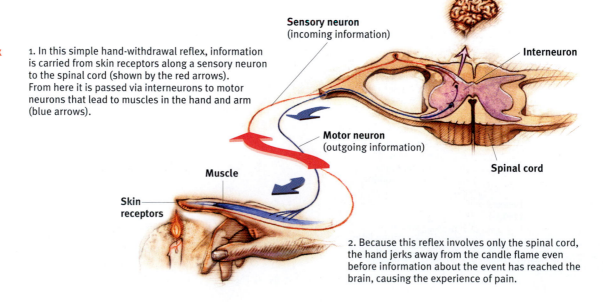

2. Because this reflex involves only the spinal cord, the hand jerks away from the candle flame even before information about the event has reached the brain, causing the experience of pain.

cord is severed, they may be genitally unresponsive to erotic images and have no genital feeling (Kennedy & Over, 1990; Sipski & others, 1999). To produce bodily pain or pleasure, the sensory information must reach the brain.

Neural Networks

The other part of your central nervous system, your brain, receives information, interprets it, and decides responses. In doing so, the brain functions rather like a computing machine. It receives slightly differing images of an object from the two eyes, computes their difference, and instantly infers how far away the object must be to project such a difference. As Michael Jordan shot a falling-away jump shot, his agile brain performed an incredible number of instant computations, adjusting for body position and movement, distance, and angle.

How did Jordan's brain perform such computations? First, each neuron connects with thousands of others. To get a feel for the complexity of these interconnections, consider that you could join two 8-studded Lego bricks 24 ways, and six bricks nearly 103 million ways. With some 30 billion neurons, each having roughly 10,000 contacts with other neurons, we end up with something like 300 trillion cortical synaptic connections. Being human takes a lot of nerve.

Neurons cluster into work groups called **neural networks**. To understand why neurons tend to connect with nearby neurons, Stephen Kosslyn and Olivier Koenig (1992, p. 12) invite us to "think about why cities exist; why don't people distribute themselves more evenly across the countryside?" Like people networking with people, neurons network with nearby neurons with which they can have short, fast connections. As in **FIGURE 3.9**, the cells in each layer of a neural network connect with various cells in the next layer. Learning occurs as feedback strengthens connections that produce certain results. New computer models simulate neural networks, complete with excitatory and inhibitory connections that gain strength with experience—and mimic the brain's capacity for learning.

Of course, the system inside each of us is more complicated than the networks depicted in Figure 3.9. In our brains, one neural network is interconnected with other networks that do different things. There are no arrows to tell us where one network ends and the next begins; what distinguishes them is their specific functions. Each is a subnetwork, contributing its little bit of information to the whole information-processing system that we call the brain.

- **reflex** a simple, automatic, inborn response to a sensory stimulus, such as the knee-jerk response.

- **neural networks** interconnected neural cells. With experience, networks can learn, as feedback strengthens or inhibits connections that produce certain results. Computer simulations of neural networks show analogous learning.

- **endocrine [EN-duh-krin] system** the body's "slow" chemical communication system; a set of glands that secrete hormones into the bloodstream.

- **hormones** chemical messengers, mostly those manufactured by the endocrine glands, that are produced in one tissue and affect another.

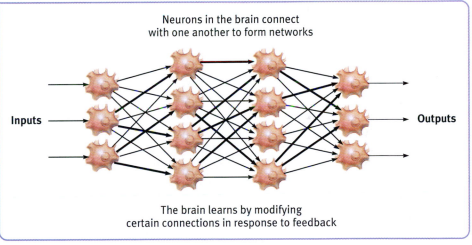

Neurons in the brain connect
with one another to form networks

Inputs → → Outputs

The brain learns by modifying
certain connections in response to feedback

FIGURE 3.9

A simplified neural network

Neurons network with nearby neurons. Given feedback, the network can strengthen connections that produce a given output in response to a given pattern of inputs.

The Endocrine System

Preview Question: How does the endocrine system—the body's slower information system—deliver its messages?

Interconnected with the nervous system is the second of the body's communication systems, the **endocrine system** (**FIGURE 3.10**, page 56). The endocrine system's glands secrete another form of chemical messengers, **hormones**. Hormones originate in one tissue, travel through the bloodstream, and affect other tissues, including the brain. When they act on the brain, they influence our interest in sex, food, and aggression.

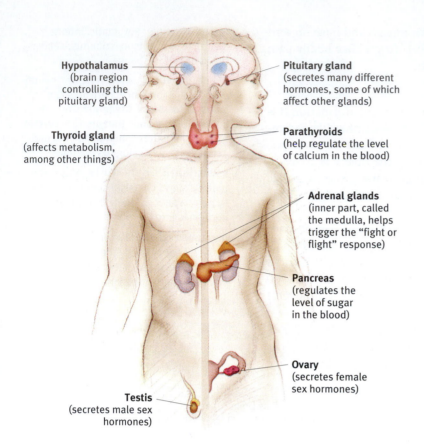

Hypothalamus
(brain region
controlling the
pituitary gland)

Pituitary gland
(secretes many different
hormones, some of which
affect other glands)

Thyroid gland
(affects metabolism,
among other things)

Parathyroids
(help regulate the level
of calcium in the blood)

Adrenal glands
(inner part, called
the medulla, helps
trigger the "fight or
flight" response)

Pancreas
(regulates the
level of sugar
in the blood)

Ovary
(secretes female
sex hormones)

Testis
(secretes male sex
hormones)

FIGURE 3.10
The body's major endocrine glands

■ **adrenal [ah-DREEN-el] glands** a pair
of endocrine glands just above the
kidneys. The adrenals secrete the
hormones epinephrine (adrenaline) and
norepinephrine (noradrenaline), which
help to arouse the body in times of stress.

■ **pituitary gland** the endocrine system's
most influential gland. Under the
influence of the hypothalamus, the
pituitary regulates growth and controls
other endocrine glands.

Some hormones are chemically identical to neurotransmitters (those chemical messengers that diffuse across a synapse and excite or inhibit an adjacent neuron). The endocrine system and the nervous system are therefore kindred systems: Both secrete molecules that activate receptors elsewhere. But unlike the speedy nervous system, zipping messages from eyes to brain to hand in a fraction of a second, endocrine messages trudge along. If the nervous system's communication delivers messages rather like e-mail, the endocrine system is the body's snail mail. Several seconds or more may elapse before the bloodstream carries a hormone from an endocrine gland to its target tissue. But these endocrine messages are often worth the wait because their effects usually last longer than the effects of a neural message.

The endocrine system's hormones influence many aspects of our lives—growth, reproduction, metabolism, mood—working to keep everything in balance while we respond to stress, exertion, and our own thoughts. In a moment of danger, for example, the autonomic nervous system orders the **adrenal glands** on top of the kidneys to release *epinephrine* and *norepinephrine* (also called *adrenaline* and *noradrenaline*). These hormones increase heart rate, blood pressure, and blood sugar, providing us with a surge of energy. When the emergency passes, the hormones—and the feelings of excitement—linger a while.

The most influential endocrine gland is the **pituitary gland**, a pea-sized structure located in the base of the brain, where it is controlled by an adjacent brain area called the hypothalamus. The pituitary releases hormones that influence growth, and its secretions also influence the release of hormones by other endocrine glands. The pituitary then is really a sort of master gland (whose own master is the hypothalamus). For example, under the brain's influence, the pituitary triggers your sex glands to release sex hormones. These may in turn influence your brain and behavior.

This feedback system (brain → pituitary → other glands → hormones → brain) reveals the intimate connection of the nervous and endocrine systems: the nervous system directing endocrine secretions, which then affect the nervous system. In fact, the two systems are so closely connected that the distinction between them sometimes blurs. Researchers have discovered that neurotransmitters can drift in the brain's fluid to nerve receptors at distant sites, thereby affecting overall alertness or mood (Agnati & others, 1992; Pert, 1986). In such cases, the distinction between certain neurotransmitters and their chemical twins—which are called hormones when released by glands—is no longer so clear. Conducting and coordinating this whole electrochemical orchestra is that maestro we call the brain.

REVIEW AND REFLECT:

Neural and Hormonal Systems

What are neurons, and how do they transmit information?

The body's circuitry, the nervous system, consists of billions of individual cells called *neurons*. A neuron receives signals from other neurons through its branching dendrites and cell body, combines these signals in the cell body, and transmits an electrical impulse (the action potential) down its axon.

How does a neuron communicate with other cells to influence our behavior?

When electrical signals reach the end of the axon, they stimulate the release of chemical messengers called *neurotransmitters*. These molecules pass on their excitatory or inhibitory messages as they traverse the synaptic gap between neurons and combine with receptor sites on neighboring neurons.

Researchers are studying neurotransmitters to discern their role in behavior and emotion. They have discovered dozens of different neurotransmitters, and the functions of some, such as acetylcholine (ACh), are now well understood. Learning about endorphins, the feel-good neurotransmitters, has helped us understand how drugs affect our brain chemistry. Some drugs (agonists) excite by mimicking particular neurotransmitters or blocking their reuptake; others (antagonists) inhibit by blocking neurotransmitters.

What are the elementary components of our nervous system, and what are the functional divisions of that system?

Neurons are the elementary components of our nervous system, our body's speedy electrochemical information system. The two main divisions of the nervous system are the central nervous system and the peripheral nervous system. The central nervous system's neurons in the brain and spinal cord communicate with the peripheral nervous system's sensory and motor neurons. The peripheral nervous system also has two main divisions. The somatic nervous system directs voluntary movements and reflexes. The autonomic nervous system, through its sympathetic and parasympathetic divisions, controls our involuntary muscles and glands.

How does the endocrine system—the body's slower communication system—deliver its messages?

Hormones released by the glands of the endocrine system travel through the bloodstream and affect other tissues, including the brain. The endocrine system's master gland, the pituitary, influences hormone release by other glands. The adrenal glands are activated in stressful times by the autonomic nervous system.

Terms and Concepts to Remember

biological psychology, p. 46
neuron, p. 46
dendrite, p. 46
axon, p. 46
myelin [MY-uh-lin] sheath, p. 46
action potential, p. 47
threshold, p. 48
synapse [SIN-aps], p. 48
neurotransmitters, p. 48
acetylcholine [ah-seat-el-KO-leen] (ACh), p. 50
endorphins [en-DOR-fins], p. 50
nervous system, p. 52
central nervous system (CNS), p. 52
peripheral nervous system (PNS), p. 52
nerves, p. 52
sensory neurons, p. 52
interneurons, p. 52
motor neurons, p. 52
somatic nervous system, p. 53
autonomic [aw-tuh-NAHM-ik] nervous system, p. 53
sympathetic nervous system, p. 53
parasympathetic nervous p. 53
reflex, p. 54
neural networks, p. 55
endocrine [EN-duh-krin] system, p. 55
hormones, p. 55
adrenal [ah-DREEN-el] glands, p. 56
pituitary gland, p. 56

Test Yourself

3.1. The neuron fiber that carries messages to other neurons is the

a. dendrite.　　　　c. cell body.

b. axon.　　　　　d. myelin.

3.2. The neuron's response to stimulation is an *all-or-none* response, meaning that the intensity of the stimulus determines

a. whether or not an impulse is generated.

b. how fast an impulse is transmitted.

c. how intense an impulse will be.

d. whether the stimulus is excitatory or inhibitory.

3.3. There is a minuscule space between the axon of a sending neuron and the dendrite or cell body of a receiving neuron. This small space is called the

a. axon terminal.　　　　c. synaptic gap.

b. sac or vesicle.　　　　d. threshold.

3.4. When the action potential reaches the axon terminal of a neuron, it triggers the release of chemical messengers called

a. ions.　　　　　c. neural impulses.

b. synapses.　　　　d. neurotransmitters.

3.5. When the transmission of acetylcholine (ACh) is blocked,

a. death from convulsions may result.

b. the brain is flooded with substitute excitatory neurotransmitters, causing a brief "rush."

c. paralysis may result.

d. the brain starts producing antagonists, resulting in depression.

Continued

3.6. Endorphins are released in the brain in response to
a. morphine or heroin.
b. pain or vigorous exercise.
c. antagonists.
d. all of the above.

3.7. Information travels to and from the brain mostly by way of the spinal cord. The neurons of the spinal cord are called
a. motor neurons.
b. sensory neurons.
c. sending neurons.
d. interneurons.

3.8. The autonomic nervous system controls internal functions, such as heart rate and glandular activity. The word *autonomic* means
a. peripheral.
b. voluntary.
c. self-regulating.
d. arousing.

3.9. Usually, the sympathetic nervous system arouses us for action, and the parasympathetic nervous system calms us down. Together the two systems make up the
a. autonomic nervous system.
b. somatic nervous system.
c. central nervous system.
d. peripheral nervous system.

3.10. The neurons of the spinal cord are part of the
a. somatic nervous system.
b. central nervous system.
c. autonomic nervous system.
d. peripheral nervous system.

3.11. The endocrine system, the second and slower bodily communication system, produces chemical messengers that travel through the bloodstream and affect other tissues. These chemical substances are
a. hormones.
b. neurotransmitters.
c. endorphins.
d. glands.

3.12. The pituitary gland releases hormones that influence growth and the activity of other glands. The pituitary gland is part of the
a. endocrine system.
b. peripheral nervous system.
c. sympathetic nervous system.
d. central nervous system.

Review

- How does information flow through your nervous system as you pick up a fork? Can you summarize this process?

Reflect

- Does our nervous system's design—with its synaptic gaps that chemical messenger molecules leap in an imperceptibly brief instant—surprise you? Would you have designed yourself differently?

- Can you recall a time when the endorphin response may have protected you from feeling extreme pain?

Answers to the Test Yourself and Review questions can be found in the green appendix at the end of the book.

The Brain

In a jar on a display shelf in Cornell University's psychology department resides the well-preserved brain of Edward Bradford Titchener, a great turn-of-the-century experimental psychologist and proponent of the study of consciousness. Imagine yourself gazing at that wrinkled mass of grayish tissue, wondering if in any sense Titchener is still in there?[1]

You might answer that, without the living whir of electrochemical activity, there could be nothing of Titchener in his preserved brain. Consider then an experiment about which the inquisitive Titchener himself might have daydreamed. Imagine that just moments before his death, someone removed Titchener's brain from his body and kept it alive by pumping enriched blood through it as it floated in a tank of cerebral fluid. Would Titchener now still be in there? Further imagine, to carry our fantasy to its limit, that someone transplanted the still-living brain into the body of a person with severe brain damage. To whose home should the recovered patient return?

That we can imagine such questions illustrates how convinced we are that we live in our heads. And for good reason: The brain enables the mind: seeing, hearing, remembering, thinking, feeling, speaking, dreaming. Indeed, say neuroscientists, the *mind is what the brain does*. But precisely where and how are the mind's functions tied to the brain? To see how scientists explore such questions, see the Close-Up on The Tools of Discovery on pages 60 and 61.

"I am a brain, Watson. The rest of me is a mere appendix."

Sherlock Holmes, in Arthur Conan Doyle's "The Adventure of the Mazarin Stone"

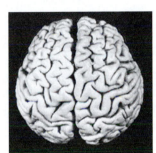

Einstein's brain
For you and me, as well as for Albert Einstein (whose brain is shown here), this small wrinkled organ is far more complex than the most sophisticated computer. What you see here is only a portion of the brain's outer layer. Most of its surface lies hidden within its convoluted folds.

Lower-Level Brain Structures

Preview Question: What are the lower-level brain structures, and what are their functions?

If you could open the skull and look inside, the first thing you might note is the brain's size. In dinosaurs, the brain represents 1/100,000th of the body's weight, in whales 1/10,000th, in elephants 1/600th, in humans 1/45th. It looks as though a principle is emerging. But keep on. In mice the brain is 1/40th the body's weight, and in marmosets 1/25th. So there are exceptions to the rule of thumb that the ratio of brain to body weight provides a clue to a species' intelligence.

More useful clues to an animal's capacities come from the brain's structures. In primitive vertebrate (backboned) animals, such as sharks, the brain primarily regulates basic survival functions: breathing, resting, and feeding. In lower mammals, such as rodents, a more complex brain enables emotion and greater memory. In advanced mammals, such as humans, the brain processes more information, enabling us to act with foresight.

Biological history has not greatly altered the basic mechanisms for survival. Rather, as the English neurologist John Hughlings Jackson recognized a century ago, species have elaborated new brain systems on top of the old, much as the Earth's landscape covers the old with the new. Digging down, one discovers the fossil remnants of the past—brainstem components still performing much as they did for our distant ancestors. Starting with the brainstem and working up, let's now explore the brain.

[1] Carl Sagan's *Broca's Brain* (1979a) inspired this question.

THE TOOLS OF DISCOVERY

It is exciting to consider how fast and how far the neurosciences have progressed within a lifetime. For centuries, the human brain lay largely beyond the reach of science. The neuron was too small to study with the naked eye, its impulses too faint to record with ordinary electrodes. We were able to feel bumps on the skull, dissect and analyze lifeless brains, and observe the effects of specific brain diseases and injuries. But there were no tools high-powered yet gentle enough to explore the living brain. Now, that has changed. Whether in the interests of science or medicine, we can selectively **lesion** tiny clusters of normal or defective brain cells, leaving their surroundings unharmed. We can probe the brain with tiny electrical pulses. We can snoop on the messages of individual neurons and on the mass action of billions of neurons. We can see color representations of the brain's energy-consuming activity. These new tools and techniques have enabled a neuroscientific revolution.

Clinical Observations

The oldest method of studying brain-mind connections is to observe the effects of brain diseases and injuries. Such observations were first recorded some 5000 years ago. But it was not until the last two centuries that physicians began systematically recording the results of damage to specific brain areas. Some noted that damage to one side of the brain often caused numbness or paralysis on the body's opposite side, suggesting that the right side of the body is wired to the brain's left side, and vice versa. Others noticed that damage to the back of the brain disrupted vision, and that damage to the left-front part of the brain produced speech difficulties. Gradually, the brain was being mapped. Today, records of more than 1500 brain-injured patients have been assembled by University of Iowa researchers into the largest-ever brain-damage registry.

THE FAR SIDE

"That's a lie, Morty! . . . Mom says you might have got the brains in the family, but I got the looks!"

Manipulating the Brain

Today's scientists, however, do not need to await brain injuries. They can electrically, chemically, or magnetically *stimulate* various parts of the brain and note the effects. They can also surgically lesion (destroy) tissue in specific brain areas in animals. For example, a lesion in one area of the hypothalamus in a rat's brain reduces eating, causing the rat to starve unless force-fed. A lesion in another area produces *over*eating.

Recording the Brain's Electrical Activity

Right now, your mental activity is giving off telltale electrical, metabolic, and magnetic signals that would enable neuroscientists to eavesdrop on your brain with increasing precision. The tips of modern microelectrodes are so small they can detect the electrical pulse in a single neuron, making possible some astonishingly precise findings. For example, we can now detect exactly where the information goes after someone strokes a cat's whisker.

Electrical activity in the brain's billions of neurons sweeps in regular waves across its surface. The **electroencephalogram (EEG)** is an amplified tracing of such waves by an instrument called an *electroencephalograph*. Studying an EEG of the gross activity of the whole brain is like studying the activity of a car engine by listening to the hum of its motor. However, by presenting a stimulus repeatedly and having a computer filter out brain activity unrelated to the stimulus, one can identify the electrical wave evoked by the stimulus (**FIGURE 4.1**).

Neuroimaging Techniques

Other new windows into the brain give us a Supermanlike ability to see inside the brain without lesioning it. For example, the **CT (computed tomography) scan** examines the brain by taking x-ray photographs that can reveal brain damage. Even more dramatic is the **PET (positron emission tomography) scan** (**FIGURE 4.2**), which depicts brain activity by showing each brain area's consumption of its chemical fuel, the sugar glucose (see illustration, page 71). Active neurons are glucose hogs. A person is given a temporarily radioactive form of glucose, and the PET scan locates and measures the radioactivity, thereby detecting where this "food for thought" goes. In this way, researchers can see which brain areas are most active as the person performs mathematical calculations, listens to music, or daydreams.

FIGURE 4.1 An electroencephalograph providing amplified tracings of waves of electrical activity in the brain Here it is detecting brain response to sound, making possible an early evaluation of what may be a hearing impairment.

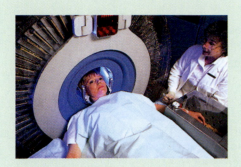

FIGURE 4.2 The PET scan
To obtain a PET scan, researchers inject volunteers with a low and harmless dose of a short-lived radioactive sugar. Detectors around the subject's head pick up the release of gamma rays from the sugar, which has concentrated in active brain areas. A computer then processes and translates these signals into a map of the brain at work.

Another new way of looking into the living brain exploits the fact that the centers of atoms, including those in our brains, spin like tops. In **MRI (magnetic resonance imaging)** scans, the head is put in a strong magnetic field, which aligns the spinning atoms. Then a brief pulse of radio waves disorients the atoms momentarily. When the atoms return to their normal spin, they release detectable signals, which become computer-generated images of their concentrations. The result is a detailed picture of the brain's soft tissues. For example, MRI scans reveal enlarged fluid-filled brain areas in some patients who have schizophrenia, a disabling psychological disorder (**FIGURE 4.3**).

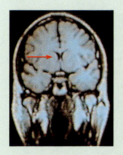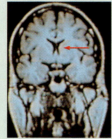

FIGURE 4.3
MRI scan of a healthy individual (left) and a person with schizophrenia (right)
Note the enlarged fluid-filled brain region in the image on the right.

By taking pictures less than a second apart, MRI scans can now show the brain lighting up (with increased oxygen-laden bloodflow) as a research participant performs different mental functions. As the person looks at a face, a *functional MRI* machine detects blood rushing to the back of the brain, which processes visual information (Figure 4.11, page 68). Ask the participant to solve a verbal analogy problem, and the part of the brain's left side near the front will light up. Such snapshots of the brain's activity provide new insights into how and where the brain divides its labor. They also reveal *when* things happen, how brain areas *change* with experience, and what brain areas work together. For example, imaging research reveals that similar brain areas are involved in reading and remembering words—a finding that informs memory theory (Posner & Raichle, 1998).

These new brain-imaging instruments are doing for psychological science what the microscope did for biology and the telescope for astronomy. To be learning about the neurosciences now is like studying world geography while Magellan was exploring the seas. Every year the explorers announce new discoveries, which also generate new interpretations of old discoveries. Here is a small sampling of new revelations:

+ PET scans show that the brain areas that light up when people silently say the name of an animal differ from those that light up when they say the name of a tool (Martin & others, 1996).
+ MRI scans reveal a larger-than-average neural area in the left brain of musicians who display perfect pitch (Schlaug & others, 1995).
+ MRI scans of bilingual people's brains reveal that second languages are represented in the same area as the first if learned early, and in differing areas if learned late (Kim & others, 1997).
+ Functional MRI scans reveal that, during a rhyming task, men's brains have a distinctively active left brain area, whereas women's brains are active on both sides (Shawitz & others, 1995).

Data from different brain-imaging techniques are appearing faster than anyone can read and remember them. One recent Society for Neuroscience meeting offered the 23,000 attendees 12,000 scientific presentations. Researchers are assembling this information in computer databases. This brain cartography will give all researchers instant access through electronic networks to PET or MRI studies that reveal activity in a particular brain area while a person, for example, solves math problems. Clearly, this is the golden age of brain science.

■ **lesion [LEE-zhuhn]** tissue destruction. A brain lesion is a naturally or experimentally caused destruction of brain tissue.

■ **electroencephalogram (EEG)** an amplified recording of the waves of electrical activity that sweep across the brain's surface. These waves are measured by electrodes placed on the scalp.

■ **CT (computed tomography) scan** a series of x-ray photographs taken from different angles and combined by computer into a composite representation of a slice through the body. Also called *CAT scan*.

■ **PET (positron emission tomography) scan** a visual display of brain activity that detects where a radioactive form of glucose goes while the brain performs a given task.

■ **MRI (magnetic resonance imaging)** a technique that uses magnetic fields and radio waves to produce computer-generated images that distinguish among different types of soft tissue; allows us to see structures within the brain.

- **brainstem** the oldest part and central core of the brain, beginning where the spinal cord swells as it enters the skull; the brainstem is responsible for automatic survival functions.

- **medulla [muh-DUL-uh]** the base of the brainstem; controls heartbeat and breathing.

- **reticular formation** a nerve network in the brainstem that plays an important role in controlling arousal.

- **thalamus [THAL-uh-muss]** the brain's sensory switchboard, located on top of the brainstem; it directs messages to the sensory receiving areas in the cortex and transmits replies to the cerebellum and medulla.

- **cerebellum [sehr-uh-BELL-um]** the "little brain" attached to the rear of the brainstem; it helps coordinate voluntary movement and balance.

- **limbic system** a doughnut-shaped system of neural structures at the border of the brainstem and cerebral hemispheres; associated with emotions such as fear and aggression and drives such as those for food and sex. Includes the hippocampus, amygdala, and hypothalamus.

- **amygdala [ah-MIG-dah-la]** two almond-shaped neural clusters that are components of the limbic system and are linked to emotion.

The Brainstem

The brain's basement—its oldest and innermost region—is the **brainstem**. It begins where the spinal cord enters the skull and swells slightly, forming the **medulla**. Here lie the controls for your heartbeat and breathing. If the top of a cat's brainstem is severed from the rest of the brain above it, the animal will still breathe and live—and even run, climb, and groom (Klemm, 1990). But cut off from the brain's higher region, it won't purposefully run or climb to get food.

The brainstem is also the crossover point, where most nerves to and from each side of the brain connect with the body's opposite side. This peculiar cross-wiring is but one of many surprises the brain has to offer.

Inside the brainstem, the **reticular** ("netlike") **formation**, a finger-shaped network of neurons, extends from the spinal cord right up to the thalamus (**FIGURE 4.4**). As the spinal cord's sensory input travels up to the thalamus, some of it branches off to the reticular formation, which filters incoming stimuli and relays important information to other areas of the brain. Among its other functions, the reticular formation helps control arousal.

In 1949, Giuseppe Moruzzi and Horace Magoun discovered that electrically stimulating the reticular formation of a sleeping cat almost instantly produced an awake, alert animal. Magoun also severed a cat's reticular formation from higher brain regions without damaging the nearby sensory pathways. The effect? The cat lapsed into a coma from which it never awakened. Magoun could clap his hands by the cat's ear, even pinch it; still, no response. The conclusion? The reticular formation was involved in arousal. Later researchers discovered that elsewhere in the brainstem are neurons whose activity is needed for sleep.

The Thalamus

Atop the brainstem sits the brain's sensory switchboard, a joined pair of egg-shaped structures called the **thalamus** (Figure 4.4). It receives information from all the senses except smell and routes it to the higher brain regions that deal with seeing, hearing, tasting, and touching. Think of the thalamus as being to sensory input what London is to England's trains: a hub through which traffic passes en route to various destinations. The thalamus also receives some of the higher brain's replies, which it then directs to the cerebellum and medulla.

FIGURE 4.4

The brainstem and thalamus
The brainstem, including the medulla, is an extension of the spinal cord. The thalamus is attached to its top. The reticular formation passes through both structures.

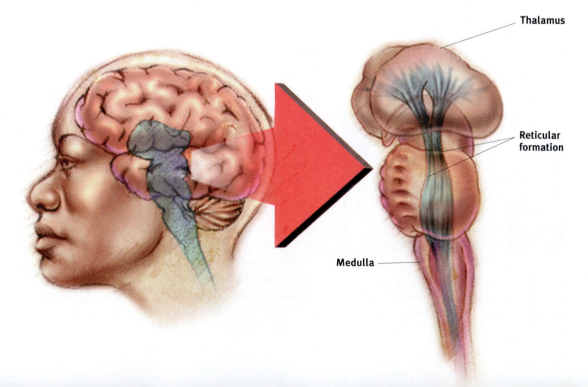

Thalamus

Reticular formation

Medulla

The Cerebellum

Extending from the rear of the brainstem is the **cerebellum**, meaning little brain, which is what its two wrinkled hemispheres rather look like (**FIGURE 4.5**). The cerebellum enables one type of nonverbal learning and memory, but its most obvious function is coordinating voluntary movement. When baseball great Sammy Sosa smacks a home run with a perfectly timed swing of the bat, give his cerebellum some credit. If you injured your cerebellum, you would likely have difficulty walking, keeping your balance, or shaking hands. Your movements would be jerky and exaggerated.

Note: These lower brain functions all occur without any conscious effort. This illustrates another of our recurring themes: *Our brain processes most information outside of our awareness*. We are aware of the *results* of our brain's labor (say, our current visual experience) but not of *how* we construct the visual image. Likewise, whether we are asleep or awake, our brainstem manages its life-sustaining functions, freeing our higher brain regions to dream or to think, talk, or savor a memory.

FIGURE 4.5 The cerebellum
Hanging at the back of the brain, this "little brain" coordinates our movements. The cerebellum helps soccer players such as Mia Hamm direct the ball precisely.

The Limbic System

At the border ("limbus") of the brain's older parts and the cerebral hemispheres is a doughnut-shaped neural system, the **limbic system** (**FIGURE 4.6**). One limbic system component, the *hippocampus*, is essential to memory processing. If animals or humans lose their hippocampus to surgery or injury, they become unable to lay down new memories of facts and episodes. The limbic system also has important links to emotions such as fear and anger, and to basic motives such as those for food and sex. The limbic system's influence on emotions and motives occurs partly through its control of the body's hormones.

The Amygdala

In the limbic system, two almond-shaped neural clusters, called the **amygdala**, influence aggression and fear. In 1939, psychologist Heinrich Klüver and neurosurgeon Paul Bucy surgically lesioned the part of a rhesus monkey's brain that included the amygdala. The result? The normally ill-tempered monkey turned into the most mellow of creatures. Poke it, pinch it, do virtually anything that normally would trigger a ferocious response, and still the animal remained placid. In later studies with other wild animals, including the lynx, wolverine, and wild rat, researchers noted the same effect. What then might happen if we electrically stimulated the amygdala in a normally placid domestic animal such as a cat? Do so in one spot and the cat prepares to attack, hissing with its back arched, its pupils dilated, its hair on end. Move the electrode only slightly within the amygdala, cage the cat with a small mouse, and now the cat cowers in terror.

These experiments affirm the amygdala's role in rage and fear, not to mention the perception of such emotions in others (Adolphs & others, 1994). Still, we must be careful not to think of the amygdala as *the* control center for aggression and fear. The brain is *not* neatly organized into structures that correspond to our categories of behavior. Actually, aggressive and fearful behavior both involve neural activity in all levels of the brain. Even within the limbic system, stimulating neural structures other than the amygdala can evoke such behavior. If you put a charge to your car's dead battery, you can activate your car's engine. That does not mean that the battery runs the car by itself. It is merely one link in an integrated system.

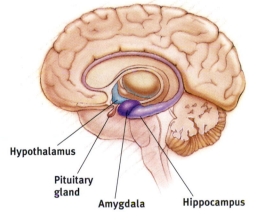

Hypothalamus

Pituitary gland

Amygdala

Hippocampus

FIGURE 4.6 The limbic system
Limbic structures form a doughnut-shaped neural system between the brain's older parts and its cerebral hemispheres. Although part of the hormonal (endocrine) system, not the brain, the pituitary gland is controlled by the limbic system's hypothalamus, just above it.

Aggression as a brain state
Back arched and fur fluffed, this fierce cat is ready to attack. Electrical stimulation of a cat's amygdala provokes reactions such as the ones shown here, suggesting its role in emotions like rage. Which division of the autonomic nervous system is activated by such stimulation? (See page 68.)

Given that amygdala lesions can transform violent monkeys into mellow ones, might such lesions do the same in violent humans? You might think so. But such *psychosurgery* has produced varied results (Mark & Ervin, 1970; Valenstein, 1986). In a few cases involving patients who suffered brain abnormalities, it reduced fits of rage, though sometimes with devastating side effects on the patient's everyday functioning. For ethical reasons, and because of the uncertainties involved, drastic psychosurgery is highly controversial and seldom used. Perhaps, though, as we learn more about how the brain controls behavior, we will learn to alleviate brain disorders without creating new ones.

The Hypothalamus

Another of the limbic system's fascinating structures lies just below (*hypo*) the thalamus, and so is called the **hypothalamus**. Neuroscientists, by lesioning or stimulating different areas in the hypothalamus, have isolated within it neural networks that perform specific maintenance duties for the body. Some neural clusters influence hunger; still others regulate thirst, body temperature, and sexual behavior.

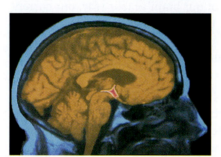

The hypothalamus
This small but important structure, colored red in this MRI brain scan photograph, helps keep the body's internal environment in a steady state by regulating thirst, hunger, and body temperature. Its activity also influences experiences of pleasureful reward.

The hypothalamus both monitors blood chemistry and takes orders from other parts of the brain. For example, thinking about sex (in your brain's cerebral cortex) can stimulate your hypothalamus to secrete hormones. Through these hormones, the hypothalamus controls the adjacent "master gland," the pituitary (Figure 4.6), which in turn influences hormone release by other glands, which the hypothalamus monitors. (Note the interplay between the nervous and hormone systems: The brain influences the hormone system, which in turn influences the brain.) The powerful little hypothalamus also exerts control by triggering autonomic nervous system activity.

The story of a remarkable discovery about the hypothalamus illustrates how progress in scientific research often occurs—when curious, open-minded investigators make an unexpected observation. Two young McGill University neuropsychologists, James Olds and Peter Milner (1954), were trying to implant electrodes in the reticular formations of white rats when they made a magnificent mistake. In one rat, they incorrectly placed an electrode in what was later discovered to be a region of the hypothalamus (Olds, 1975). Curiously, the rat kept returning to the place on its tabletop enclosure where it had been stimulated by this misplaced electrode, as if seeking more stimulation. Upon discovering their mistake, they alertly recognized that they had stumbled upon a brain center that provides a pleasurable reward.

FIGURE 4.7
Rat with an implanted electrode
With an electrode implanted in a reward center of its hypothalamus, the rat readily crosses an electrified grid, accepting the painful shocks, to press a lever that sends electrical impulses to its "pleasure centers."

In a meticulous series of experiments, Olds (1958) went on to locate other "pleasure centers," as he called them. (What the rats actually experience only they know. And they aren't telling. Today's scientists do not want to attribute human feelings to rats, so they refer to reward centers, not "pleasure centers.") When Olds allowed rats to trigger their own stimulation in these areas by pressing a pedal, he noticed that they would sometimes do so at a feverish pace—up to 7000 times per hour—until they dropped from exhaustion. Moreover, they would do anything to get this stimulation, even cross an electrified floor that a starving rat would not cross even to reach food (**FIGURE 4.7**).

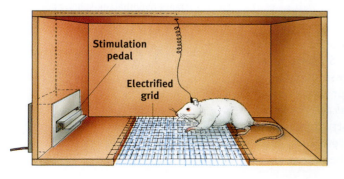

Stimulation pedal

Electrified grid

Similar reward centers in or near the hypothalamus were later discovered in many other species, including goldfish, dolphins, and monkeys. In fact, animal research has revealed both a general reward system that triggers the release of the neurotransmitter dopamine and specific centers associated with the pleasures of eating, drinking, and sex. Animals, it seems, come equipped with built-in systems that reward activities essential to survival.

These were dramatic findings. They led people to wonder whether humans, too, might have limbic centers for pleasure. Indeed we do. One neurosurgeon has used electrodes to calm violent patients. Stimulated patients reported mild pleasure; however, unlike rats, they were not driven to a frenzy by it (Deutsch, 1972; Hooper & Teresi, 1986). Some researchers believe that addictive disorders, such as alcoholism, drug abuse, and food binging, may stem from a *reward deficiency syndrome*—a genetically disposed deficiency in the natural brain systems for pleasure and well-being that leads people to crave whatever provides that missing pleasure or relieves negative feelings (Blum & others, 1996).

The Cerebral Cortex

Preview Question: How do the neural networks within the cerebral cortex enable our perceiving, thinking, and speaking?

The **cerebral cortex** is an intricate covering of interconnected neural cells that, like bark on a tree, forms a thin surface layer on the cerebral hemispheres. It is our body's ultimate control and information-processing center.

With the elaboration of the cerebral cortex, tight genetic controls relax and the organism's adaptability increases. Frogs and other amphibians have a small cortex and operate extensively on preprogrammed genetic instructions; the larger cortex of mammals offers increased capacities for learning and thinking, enabling them to be more adaptable. What makes us distinctively human mostly arises from the complex functions of our highly developed cerebral cortex.

Structure of the Cortex

If you opened a human skull, exposing the brain, you would see a wrinkled organ, shaped somewhat like the meat of an oversized walnut. Eighty percent of the brain's weight lies in the ballooning left and right cerebral hemispheres, which are mostly filled with axon connections between the brain's surface and its other regions. The thin surface layer of the cerebral hemispheres is the cerebral cortex, a sheet of cells that is one-eighth of an inch thick and contains some 30 billion nerve cells—an estimate projected from a square millimeter speck of cortical tissue packed with nearly 150,000 neurons (Ornstein, 1991). Supporting these billions of nerve cells are nine times as many **glial cells**—"glue cells" that guide neural connections, provide nutrients and insulating myelin, and mop up ions and neurotransmitters. Some researchers believe that glial cells are more than neural nannies. By "chatting" with neurons they may also participate in information transmission and memory (Travis, 1994).

Looking at the brain, the first thing you would notice about the cerebral cortex is its wrinkled surface, only about one-third of which would be visible. These folds greatly increase the brain's surface area. If flattened, the brain's surface would be roughly the size of a large pizza. (To fit a thin pizza crust inside a skull, we would need to crumple it up.) In rats and other lower mammals, the surface of the cortex is much smoother, which means there is less of this neural fabric (**FIGURE 4.8**, page 66).

"If you were designing a robot vehicle to walk into the future and survive, . . . you'd wire it up so that behavior that ensured the survival of the self or the species—like sex and eating—would be naturally reinforcing."

Candace Pert (1986)

The people who first dissected and labeled the brain used the language of scholars—Latin and Greek. Their words are actually attempts at graphic description: For example, *cortex* means "bark," *cerebellum* is "little brain," and *thalamus* is "inner chamber."

■ **hypothalamus [hi-po-THAL-uh-muss]** a neural structure lying below (*hypo*) the thalamus; it directs several maintenance activities (eating, drinking, body temperature), helps govern the endocrine system via the pituitary gland, and is linked to emotion.

■ **cerebral [seh-REE-bruhl] cortex** the intricate fabric of interconnected neural cells that covers the cerebral hemispheres; the body's ultimate control and information-processing center.

■ **glial cells** cells in the nervous system that are not neurons but that support, nourish, and protect neurons.

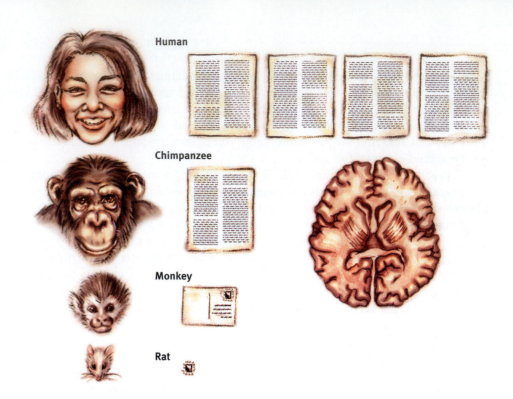

FIGURE 4.8 The cerebral cortex
If flattened, a human cortex would cover about four pages of this book. A chimpanzee's would cover one page, a monkey's a postcard, and a rat's a postage stamp. (From *Scientific American*, October 1994, p. 102.)

Human

Chimpanzee

Monkey

Rat

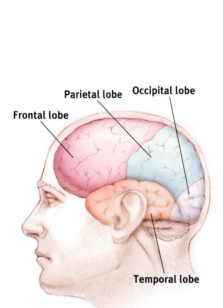

Parietal lobe   Occipital lobe

Frontal lobe

Temporal lobe

FIGURE 4.9
The basic subdivisions of the cortex

Singing in the brain
An activity as seemingly simple as listening to a song involves multiple brain areas, including independent processing of the lyrics and the tune.

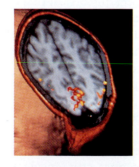

■ **frontal lobes** the portion of the cerebral cortex lying just behind the forehead; involved in speaking and muscle movements and in making plans and judgments.

Each brain hemisphere is divided into four regions, or *lobes*. Starting at the front of your brain and going around over the top, there are the **frontal lobes** (behind your forehead), the **parietal lobes** (at the top and to the rear), the **occipital lobes** (at the back of your head), and the **temporal lobes** (just above your ears). These lobes are convenient geographic subdivisions separated by prominent folds (**FIGURE 4.9**). Each lobe carries out many functions. Some functions require the interplay of several lobes.

Functions of the Cortex

More than a century ago, autopsies of people partially paralyzed or speechless revealed specific cortex areas that had been damaged. But this rather crude evidence did not convince researchers that specific parts of the cortex perform specific functions. After all, if control of speech and movement were diffused across the cortex, damage to almost any area might produce the same effect. A television would go dead with its power cord cut, but we would be deluding ourselves if we were to think we had "localized" the source of the picture in the cord.

This analogy reminds us how easy it is to err when trying to localize brain functions. We cannot draw lines around brain areas as in a meat market's beef chart; complex activities such as speaking, drawing, and shooting pool involve many brain areas. For example, our experience of listening to vocal music integrates brain activity in areas involved in speech and music processing. Mereille Besson and colleagues (1998) discovered this when recording electrical activity in the brains of French musicians listening to operatic solos sung a cappella (unaccompanied). The musicians' brains processed the lyrics and tunes in separate brain areas en route to their experiencing "the exquisite unity of vocal music."

Motor Functions

Scientists have, however, localized simpler brain functions. For example, in 1870, when German physicians Gustav Fritsch and Eduard Hitzig applied mild electrical stimulation to the cortexes of dogs, they made an important discovery: They could make different body parts move. The effects were selective: Stimulation caused movement only when applied to an arch-shaped region at the back of the frontal lobe, running roughly from ear to ear across the top of the brain. This arch we now call the **motor cortex** (FIGURE **4.10**). Moreover, when the researchers stimulated specific parts of this region in the left or right hemisphere, specific body parts moved on the *opposite* side of the body.

A half-century ago, neurosurgeons Otfrid Foerster in Germany and Wilder Penfield in Montreal mapped the motor cortex in hundreds of wide-awake patients. Before putting the knife to the brain, the surgeons needed to know the possible side effects of removing different parts of the cortex. They painlessly (the brain has no sensory receptors) stimulated different cortical areas and noted the body responses. Like Fritsch and Hitzig, they found that when they stimulated different areas of the motor cortex at the back of the frontal lobe, different body parts moved. They were now able to map the motor cortex according to the body parts it controlled (Figure 4.10). Interestingly, those areas of the body requiring precise control, such as the fingers and mouth, occupied the greatest amount of cortical space.

Neuroscientist José Delgado demonstrated the mechanics of motor behavior. In one monkey, he evoked a smiling response over 400,000 times. In a human patient, he stimulated a spot on the left motor cortex that triggered the right hand to make a fist. Asked to keep the fingers open during the next stimulation, the patient, whose fingers closed despite his best efforts, remarked, "I guess, Doctor, that your electricity is stronger than my will" (Delgado, 1969, p. 114). More recently, scientists have been able to predict a monkey's arm motion a tenth of a second before it does—by repeatedly measuring motor cortex activity preceding specific arm movements (Gibbs, 1996).

As interesting as the early brain stimulation studies were, more recent research has revealed that the precise muscle-to-brain connections are not so simple as the early work suggested. In one recent study, researchers examined these connections

■ **parietal [puh-RYE-uh-tuhl] lobes** the portion of the cerebral cortex lying at the top of the head and toward the rear; includes the sensory cortex.

■ **occipital [ahk-SIP-uh-tuhl] lobes** the portion of the cerebral cortex lying at the back of the head; includes the visual areas, which receive visual information from the opposite visual field.

■ **temporal lobes** the portion of the cerebral cortex lying roughly above the ears; includes the auditory areas, each of which receives auditory information primarily from the opposite ear.

■ **motor cortex** an area at the rear of the frontal lobes that controls voluntary movements.

FIGURE 4.10 Left-hemisphere tissue devoted to each body part in the motor cortex and the sensory cortex
As you can see, the amount of cortex devoted to a body part is not proportional to that part's size. Rather, the brain devotes more tissue to sensitive areas and to areas requiring precise control. Thus, the fingers have a greater representation in the cortex than does the upper arm. However, the neural wiring is complex. Individual muscles are linked with multiple neural clusters, which in turn may also link with other muscles.

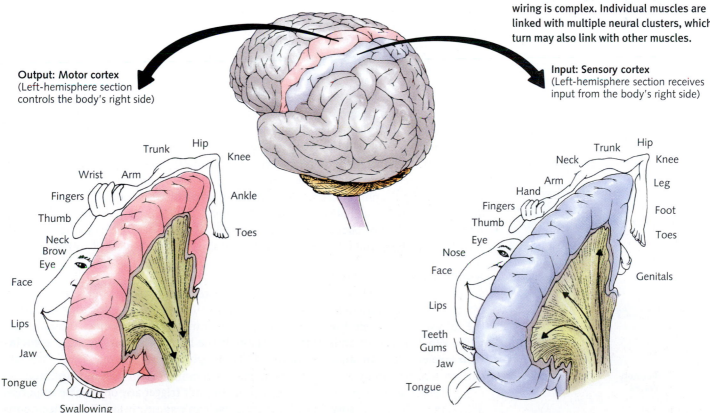

Output: Motor cortex
(Left-hemisphere section controls the body's right side)

Input: Sensory cortex
(Left-hemisphere section receives input from the body's right side)

Trunk Hip Knee Arm Wrist Ankle Fingers Thumb Toes Neck Brow Eye Face Lips Jaw Tongue Swallowing

Neck Trunk Hip Knee Arm Leg Hand Foot Fingers Thumb Toes Eye Nose Face Genitals Lips Teeth Gums Jaw Tongue

■ **sensory cortex** the area at the front of the parietal lobes that registers and processes body sensations.

■ **association areas** areas of the cerebral cortex that are not involved in primary motor or sensory functions; rather, they are involved in higher mental functions such as learning, remembering, thinking, and speaking.

The cat on page 64 is aroused via its sympathetic nervous system.

using functional MRI scans to observe where the brain lights up when specific muscles are moved (Sanes & others, 1995). They found that a given finger or wrist movement, for example, would activate multiple and overlapping sites. Although it's true that certain areas of the cortex control certain areas of the body and that some areas require more brain tissue than others, the wiring pattern is complex—complex enough to enable the many different muscle combinations needed to produce specific gestures.

Sensory Functions

If the motor cortex sends messages out to the body, where are *incoming* messages received in the cortex? Penfield identified a cortical area that specializes in receiving information from the skin senses and from the movement of body parts. This area, parallel to the motor cortex and just behind it at the front of the parietal lobes, we now call the **sensory cortex** (Figure 4.10). Stimulate a point on the top of this band of tissue, and a person may report being touched on the shoulder; stimulate some point on the side, and the person may feel something on the face.

The more sensitive a body region, the greater the area of the sensory cortex devoted to it; your supersensitive lips project to a larger brain area than do your toes (Figure 4.10). (That's one reason we kiss with our lips rather than our toes.) Similarly, rats have a large area of the brain devoted to their whisker sensations, owls to their hearing sensations, and so forth. If a monkey or a human loses a finger, the region of the sensory cortex devoted to receiving input from that finger branches to receive sensory input from the adjacent fingers. They then become more sensitive (Fox, 1984). MRI scans show that well-practiced pianists likewise have a larger-than-usual auditory cor-

FIGURE 4.11 New technology shows the brain in action
This functional MRI scan shows the visual cortex—the occipital lobes—activated (color representation of increased bloodflow) as the subject looks at faces. When the person stops looking at faces, the region instantly calms down.

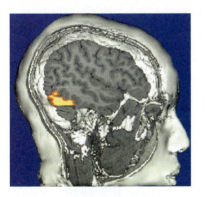

tex area that encodes piano sounds (Pantev & others, 1998). The brain is sculpted not only by our genes but also by our experience.

Scientists explored further and identified areas where the cortex receives input from the other senses. At this moment you are receiving visual information in the occipital lobes at the very back of your brain (**FIGURE 4.11**). A bad enough bash there and you would go blind. Stimulated there, you might see flashes of light or dashes of color. In a sense, we *do* have eyes in the back of our head! From your occipital lobes, the visual information you are now processing goes to other areas that specialize in tasks such as identifying words, detecting emotions, and recognizing faces.

Any sound you are now hearing you processed with the auditory areas in your temporal lobes (**FIGURE 4.12**). Most of this auditory information travels a circuitous route from one ear to the auditory receiving area above your opposite ear. If you were stimulated there, you might hear a sound. The sound needn't be real. MRI scans of people with schizophrenia reveal that auditory areas of the temporal lobe are active during auditory hallucinations (Lennox & others, 1999). Even the phantom ringing sound experienced by people with hearing loss is—if heard in one ear—associated with activity in the temporal lobe on the brain's opposite side (Muhlnickel & others, 1998).

Association Functions

So far, we have pointed out small areas of the cortex that either receive sensory information or direct muscular responses. In humans, that leaves a full three-fourths of the thin wrinkled layer, the cerebral cortex, uncommitted to sensory or muscular activity. What then goes on in this vast region of the brain? Neurons in these **association areas** (the tan areas in **FIGURE 4.13**) integrate information. They associate various sensory inputs with stored memories—a very important part of thinking.

Electrically probing the association areas doesn't trigger any observable response. So, unlike with the sensory and motor areas, we can't so neatly specify the functions

FIGURE 4.12
The visual cortex and auditory cortex
The occipital lobes at the rear of the brain receive input from the eyes. An auditory area of the temporal lobes receives information from the ears.

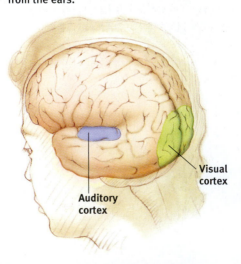

Visual cortex

Auditory cortex

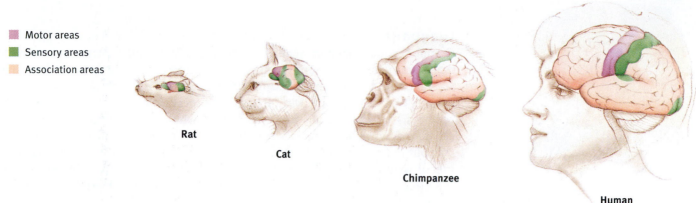

Motor areas
Sensory areas
Association areas

Rat

Cat

Chimpanzee

Human

of the association areas. Their silence seems to be what someone had in mind when formulating one of pop psychology's most widespread falsehoods: that we ordinarily use only 10 percent of our brains. This fabrication—"one of the hardiest weeds in the garden of psychology," writes Donald McBurney (1996, p. 44)—implies that if we could activate our whole brain, we would be far smarter than those who drudge along on 10 percent brain power. But from observing surgically lesioned animals and brain-damaged humans, we know that the association areas are in fact not dormant. (The brain has no appendix—no apparently purposeless tissue.) Rather, the association areas interpret, integrate, and act on information processed by the sensory areas.

Our association areas in the frontal lobes enable us to judge, plan, and process new memories. People with damaged frontal lobes may have intact memories, score high on intelligence tests, and be able to bake a cake—yet be unable to plan ahead to *begin* baking the cake for the birthday party. After the sister of famed neurosurgeon Wilder Penfield suffered frontal lobe damage, she was unable to prepare the simplest of meals. She retained her knowledge of recipes, measurements, and techniques, but she could not decipher the order of steps in preparing the meal (Kimberg & others, 1998).

Frontal lobe damage also can alter personality, removing a person's inhibitions. Consider the classic case of railroad worker Phineas Gage. One afternoon in 1848, Gage, then 25 years old, was packing gunpowder into a rock with a tamping iron. A spark ignited the gunpowder, shooting the rod up through his left cheek and out the top of his skull, leaving his frontal lobes massively damaged. To everyone's amazement, Gage was immediately able to sit up and speak, and after the wound healed he returned to work. Although his mental abilities and memories were intact, his personality was not. The affable, soft-spoken Phineas Gage was now irritable, profane, and dishonest. He eventually lost his job and ended up earning his living as a fairground exhibit. This person, said his friends, was "no longer Gage." With his frontal lobes ruptured, Gage's moral compass became disconnected from his behavior. The same loss of moral compass was recently discovered to be true of two people who as young children had experienced frontal lobe damage similar to Gage's. Both of these individuals recovered, but they also matured as morally deficient—stealing, lying, and abusing and neglecting their out-of-wedlock children without remorse (Dolan, 1999). Although raised in good homes, they seemingly didn't know right from wrong.

The association areas of the other lobes also perform mental functions. For example, the parietal lobes, parts of which were large and unusually shaped in Einstein's normal-weight brain, are involved in mathematical and spatial reasoning (Witelson & others, 1999). An area on the underside of the right temporal lobe enables us to recognize faces. If a stroke or head injury destroyed this area of your brain, you would still be able to describe facial features and to recognize someone's gender and approximate age, yet be strangely unable to identify the person as, say, Nelson Mandela or your next-door neighbor or even your spouse. But by and large, complex mental functions such as learning and memory don't reside in any one place. There is no one spot in a rat's small association cortex that, when damaged, will obliterate its ability to learn or remember a maze. Such functions are spread throughout much of the cortex.

FIGURE 4.13

Areas of the cortex in four mammals
More intelligent animals have increased "uncommitted" or association areas of the cortex. These vast areas of the brain are responsible for integrating and acting on information received and processed by sensory areas. The frontal lobes are 4 percent of the brain surface in a cat, 17 percent in a chimp, and 29 percent in a human.

The "10 percent myth"—which many people presume true because they have so often heard it—presumes that brain functions are neatly localized. But don't bother to hope that a bullet about to enter your brain would harmlessly damage only the unused 90 percent (Radford, 1999).

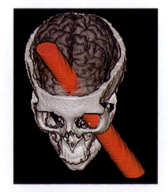

Phineas Gage reconsidered
Using measurements of his skull (which was kept as a medical record) and modern neuroimaging techniques, researcher Hanna Damasio and her colleagues (1994) have reconstructed the probable path of the rod through Gage's brain.

Language

Complex human abilities, such as language, result from the intricate coordination of many brain areas. For example, consider this curious finding: Damage to any one of several cortical areas can cause **aphasia**, an impaired use of language. It is even more curious that some people with aphasia can speak fluently but cannot read (despite good vision), while others can comprehend what they read but cannot speak. Still others can write but not read, read but not write, read numbers but not letters, or sing but not speak. This all is very puzzling. After all, we think of speaking and reading, or writing and reading, or singing and speaking as merely different examples of the same general ability. So, how did researchers solve this mystery? Consider these clues.

Clue 1 In 1865, French physician Paul Broca reported that after damage to a specific area of the left frontal lobe, later called **Broca's area,** a person would struggle to form words while still being able to sing familiar songs and comprehend speech.

Clue 2 In 1874, German investigator Carl Wernicke discovered that after damage to a specific area of the left temporal lobe **(Wernicke's area)** people could speak only meaningless words. Asked to describe a picture that showed two boys stealing cookies behind a woman's back, one patient responded: "Mother is away her working her work to get her better, but when she's looking the two boys looking the other part. She's working another time" (Geschwind, 1979).

Clue 3 It was later discovered that reading aloud involves a third brain area. The *angular gyrus* receives the visual information from the visual area and recodes it into the auditory form, which Wernicke's area uses to derive its meaning.

Clue 4 Nerve fibers interconnect these brain areas.

Norman Geschwind assembled these clues into an explanation of how we use language. When you read aloud, the words (1) register in the visual area, (2) are relayed to the angular gyrus that transforms the words into an auditory code that is (3) received and understood in the nearby Wernicke's area and (4) sent to Broca's area, which (5) controls the motor cortex, creating the pronounced word (**FIGURES 4.14** and **4.15**). Depending on which link in this chain is damaged, a different form of aphasia occurs. Damage to the angular gyrus leaves the person able to speak and understand but unable to read. Damage to Wernicke's area disrupts understanding. Damage to Broca's area disrupts speaking. The general principle bears repeating: Complex abilities result from the intricate coordination of many brain areas.

Said another way, the brain operates by dividing its mental functions—speaking, perceiving, thinking, remembering—into subfunctions. Our conscious experience *seems* indivisible. Right now you are experiencing a whole visual scene as if your eyes were video cameras projecting the scene into your brain. Actually, researchers have discovered that your brain breaks vision into specialized subtasks, such as discerning color, depth, movement, and form. (After a localized stroke that destroys one of these neural work teams, people may lose just one aspect of vision, such as the ability to perceive movement.) These specialized neural networks, each having simultaneously done its own thing, then feed their information to "higher-level" networks that combine the

FIGURE 4.14 Specialization and integration in language

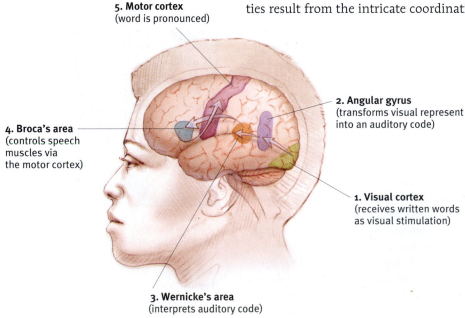

5. Motor cortex (word is pronounced)

4. Broca's area (controls speech muscles via the motor cortex)

2. Angular gyrus (transforms visual represent into an auditory code)

1. Visual cortex (receives written words as visual stimulation)

3. Wernicke's area (interprets auditory code)

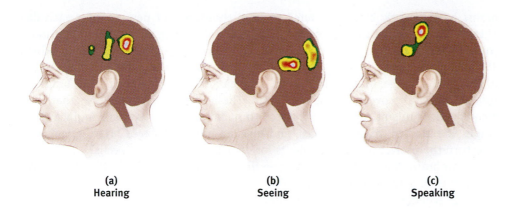

(a)
Hearing

(b)
Seeing

(c)
Speaking

FIGURE **4.15**
Brain activity when hearing, seeing, and speaking words
PET scans such as these detect the activity of different areas of the brain by measuring their relative consumption of a temporarily radioactive form of the brain's normal fuel, glucose. This series of PET scans shows levels of increased brain activity in specific areas: (a) when hearing a word—auditory cortex and Wernicke's area; (b) when seeing a word—visual cortex and angular gyrus; and (c) when repeating a word—Broca's area and the motor cortex. The red blotches show where the brain is rapidly consuming glucose.

atoms of experience and relay them to progressively higher-level association areas, enabling us to recognize a face as "Grandmother." The same is true of reading a word: The brain computes the word's form, sound, and meaning using different neural networks (Posner & Carr, 1992). Think about it: *What you experience as a continuous, indivisible stream of perception is actually but the visible tip of the information-processing iceberg, most of which lies beneath the surface of your conscious awareness.*

To sum up, the mind's subsystems are localized in particular brain regions, yet the brain acts as a unified whole. Moving your hand; recognizing faces; even perceiving color, motion, and depth all depend on specific neural networks. Yet complex functions such as language, learning, and loving involve the coordination of many brain areas. Both principles—specialization and integration—appear in research on the two brain hemispheres.

Brain Reorganization

Nurture's sculpting of the ever-changing brain is evident in studies of the brain's **plasticity**. Most severed neurons will not regenerate (if your spinal cord were severed, you likely would be permanently paralyzed). But neural tissue can *reorganize* in response to damage.

In one experiment, neuroscientists severed the neural pathways for incoming information from a monkey's arm. The area of the sensory cortex that formerly received this input gradually shifted its function and began to respond when researchers touched the animal's face (Pons & others, 1991). Similarly, if a laser beam damages a spot in a cat's eye, the brain area that received input from that spot will soon begin responding to stimulation from nearby areas in the cat's eye. If a blind person uses one finger to read Braille, the brain area dedicated to that finger expands (Barinaga, 1992a). The sense of touch invades the part of the brain that normally helps people see. PET scans also reveal activation of the *visual* cortex when blind people read Braille (Sadato & others, 1996). Among deaf people who communicate with sign language, it is the temporal lobe area normally dedicated to auditory information that waits in vain for stimulation. Finally, it looks for other signals to process, such as those from the visual system.

Thus, the brain may not be as "hard-wired" as once thought. Unlike fixed computer circuits, brain hardware changes with time. In response to changing stimulation, the brain can either rewire itself with new synapses or (according to another theory) select new uses for its prewired circuits (Gazzaniga, 1992; Kolb & Whishaw, 1998). When one brain area is damaged, other areas may in time reorganize and take over some of its functions. If neurons are destroyed, nearby neurons may partly compensate for the damage by making new connections that replace the lost ones. These new connections are one way the brain struggles to recover from a minor stroke.

New evidence reveals that, contrary to long-held belief, adult humans can also generate new brain cells (Kempermann & Gage, 1999). Moreover, monkey

■ **aphasia** impairment of language, usually caused by left-hemisphere damage either to Broca's area (impairing speaking) or to Wernicke's area (impairing understanding).

■ **Broca's area** an area of the frontal lobe, usually in the left hemisphere, that directs the muscle movements involved in speech.

■ **Wernicke's area** a brain area involved in language comprehension and expression; usually in the left temporal lobe.

■ **plasticity** the brain's capacity for modification, as evident in brain reorganization following damage (especially in children) and in experiments on the effects of experience on brain development.

Brain plasticity
Believe it or not, this 4-year-old is functioning with only half a brain. Her right hemisphere was surgically removed to eliminate seizures. Now neurons in her left hemisphere have made countless new connections to take over the tasks once performed by her right hemisphere.

brains have recently been discovered to form thousands of new neurons each day. These baby neurons originate deep in the brain and then migrate to the thinking frontal lobe and form connections with neighboring neurons (Gould & others, 1999). Such are the brain's ways of partially compensating for the gradual loss of neurons with age. Master "stem cells" that can develop into any type of brain cell have also been discovered in the fetal brain. These discoveries raise hopes that these recovery mechanisms might be enhanced to mend a disease-damaged brain. For example, if extracted, mass produced, and injected into a damaged brain, might stem cells turn themselves into replacements for damaged or dead brain cells?

Our brains are most plastic when we are young children (Kolb, 1989). Children are born with a surplus of neurons. If an injury destroys one part of a child's brain, the brain will compensate by putting other surplus areas to work. Thus, if the speech areas of an infant's left hemisphere are damaged, the right hemisphere will take over much of its language function.

As an extreme example of plasticity, consider a 5-year-old boy whose severe seizures, caused by a deteriorating left hemisphere, require removing the *entire* hemisphere. What hope for the future would such a child have? Is there any chance he might attend school and lead a normal life, or would he suffer permanent retardation?

Astonishingly, one such individual was at last report an executive. Half his skull is filled with nothing but cerebrospinal fluid—functionally it might as well be sawdust—yet he has scored well above average on intelligence tests, has completed college, and has attended graduate school (Smith & Sugar, 1975; A. Smith, 1987). Although paralyzed on the right side, this man (along with other such cases of "hemispherectomy") testifies to the brain's extraordinary powers of reorganization when damaged before it is fully developed. Indeed, one Johns Hopkins medical team, reflecting on the 58 child hemispherectomies they have performed, reports being "awed" by how well children retain their memory, personality, and humor after removal of either brain hemisphere (Vining & others, 1997).

Our Divided Brains

Preview Question: What is a split brain, and what does it reveal about brain functioning?

For more than a century, clinical evidence has shown that the brain's two sides serve differing functions. Accidents, strokes, and tumors in the left hemisphere generally impair reading, writing, speaking, arithmetic reasoning, and understanding. Similar lesions in the right hemisphere seldom have such dramatic effects.

It is small wonder that by 1960 the left hemisphere was well accepted as the "dominant" or "major" hemisphere, and its silent companion to the right as the "subordinate" or "minor" hemisphere. The left, verbal hemisphere is rather like the moon's facing side—the one easiest to observe and study. The other side is there, of course, but less visibly noticeable. (For some people, including one-fourth of all left-handers, speech is processed in the right hemisphere—see page 75.) But then researchers found that the "minor" right hemisphere was not so limited after all. The story of this discovery is a fascinating chapter in psychology's history.

Splitting the Brain

In 1961, two Los Angeles neurosurgeons, Philip Vogel and Joseph Bogen, speculated that major epileptic seizures were caused by an amplification of abnormal brain activity that reverberated between the two hemispheres. They therefore wondered whether they could reduce seizures in their patients with uncontrollable epilepsy by

■ **corpus callosum [KOR-pus kah-LOW-sum]** the large band of neural fibers connecting the two brain hemispheres and carrying messages between them.

■ **split brain** a condition in which the two hemispheres of the brain are isolated by cutting the connecting fibers (mainly those of the corpus callosum) between them.

cutting communication between the hemispheres. To do this, Vogel and Bogen knew they would have to sever the **corpus callosum**, the wide band of axon fibers connecting the two hemispheres (**FIGURE 4.16**).

The surgeons had reason to believe such an operation would not be incapacitating. Psychologists Roger Sperry, Ronald Myers, and Michael Gazzaniga had divided the brains of cats and monkeys in this manner with no serious ill effects. So Vogel and Bogen operated. The result? The seizures were all but eliminated and the patients with these **split brains** were surprisingly normal, their personalities and intellect hardly affected. Waking from the surgery, one patient even managed to quip that he had a "splitting headache" (Gazzaniga, 1967).

Only a decade earlier, neuropsychologist Karl Lashley had jested that maybe the corpus callosum served only "to keep the hemispheres from sagging." The ingenious experiments of Sperry and Gazzaniga revealed that this broad band of more than 200 million nerve fibers, capable of transferring more than a billion bits of information per second between the hemispheres, has a more significant purpose. Their work provided a key to understanding the two hemispheres' complementary functions.

Sperry and Ganzzaniga were not surprised that, after the split-brain operation, a patient could not identify an unseen object, such as a spoon, placed in his left hand. They knew that information travels from the left hand to the right hemisphere, and their animal split-brain experiments suggested that the right hemisphere would be unable to send this information to the left hemisphere (which in most humans controls speech). More extraordinary results came when Sperry and Gazzaniga conducted some perceptual tests.

Our eyes connect to our brains in such a way that, when we look straight ahead, the left half of our field of vision transmits through both eyes to our right hemisphere (**FIGURE 4.17**). Likewise, the right side of our field of vision transmits to our left hemisphere. In most of us with healthy, intact brains, information presented only to our right hemisphere is quickly sent to our left hemisphere, which names it. But what happens in a person whose corpus callosum has been severed? To find out, experimenters ask the person to look at a designated spot. Then they send information to either the left or right hemisphere (by flashing it to the spot's right or left). Finally, they quiz each hemisphere separately.

See if you can guess the results of an experiment using this procedure (Gazzaniga, 1967). While the patients stared at a dot, the word HEART was flashed across the visual field with HE in the left visual field and ART in the right. First, what did the patients *say* they saw? Second, asked to identify with their *left* hands what they had seen, did they *point* to HE or ART?

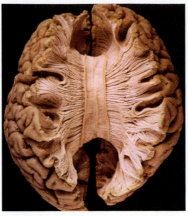

FIGURE 4.16 The corpus callosum
This large band of neural fibers connects the two brain hemispheres. In the top view at left, a surgeon has cut back brain tissue to expose the corpus callosum and bundles of fibers coming out from it. To photograph the half brain shown at right, the hemispheres were separated by cutting through the corpus callosum and lower brain regions.

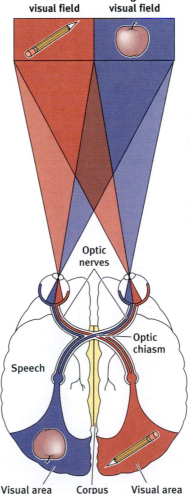

FIGURE 4.17

The information highway from eye to brain
Information from the left half of your field of vision goes to your right hemisphere, and information from the right half of your visual field goes to your left hemisphere, which usually controls speech. (Note, however, that each eye receives sensory information from both the right and left visual fields.) The data received by either hemisphere are quickly transmitted to the other across the corpus callosum. In a person with a severed corpus callosum, this information sharing does not take place.

As **FIGURE 4.18** shows, the patients *said* they saw ART and so were startled when their left hands *pointed* to HE. Given an opportunity to express itself, each hemisphere reports only what it has seen.

Similarly, when a picture of a spoon was flashed to their right hemisphere, the patients could not say what they saw. But when asked to identify what they had seen by feeling with their left hands an assortment of objects hidden behind a screen, they readily selected the spoon. If the experimenter said, "Right!" the patient might reply, "What? Right? How could I possibly pick out the right object when I don't know what I saw?" It is, of course, the left hemisphere doing the talking here, bewildered by what its nonverbal right hemisphere knows.

A few people who have had split-brain surgery have been for a time bothered by the unruly independence of their left hand, which might unbutton a shirt while the right hand buttoned it or put grocery store items back on the shelf after the right hand put them in the cart. It was as if each hemisphere was thinking "I've half a mind to wear my green (blue) shirt today." Indeed, said Sperry (1964), split-brain surgery leaves people "with two separate minds." (Reading these reports, I fantasize a split-brain person enjoying a solitary game of "rocks, paper, and scissors"—left versus right hand.)

When the "two minds" are at odds, the left hemisphere seems to act as the brain's press agent, doing mental gymnastics to rationalize reactions it does not understand. If a patient follows an order sent to the right hemisphere ("Walk"), the interpretive left hemisphere will offer a ready explanation ("I'm going into the house to get a Coke"). Thus, Michael Gazzaniga (1988) concludes that the left hemisphere is an "interpreter" that instantly constructs theories to explain our behavior.

These experiments demonstrate that the right hemisphere understands simple requests and easily perceives objects. In fact, the right hemisphere is superior to the left at copying drawings, recognizing faces, perceiving differences, perceiving emotion, and expressing emotion through the more expressive left side of the face (Hauser, 1993; Heller & others, 1998; Metcalfe & others, 1995; Skinner & Mullen, 1991). Most of the body's paired organs—kidneys, lungs, breasts—perform identical functions, providing a backup system should one side fail. Not so the brain's two halves. They are a biological odd couple, serving differing functions, each seemingly with a mind of its own.

> "Do not let your left hand know what your right hand is doing."
>
> Matthew 6:3

Question: If we flashed a red light to the right hemisphere of a split-brain patient and flashed a green light to the left hemisphere, would each observe its own color? Would the person be aware that the colors differ? What would the person verbally report seeing? (Answers on page 79.)

FIGURE 4.18

Testing the divided brain
When an experimenter flashes the word HEART across the visual field, the split-brain patient reports seeing the portion of the word transmitted to her left hemisphere. However, if asked to indicate with her left hand what she saw, she points to the portion of the word transmitted to her right hemisphere. (From Gazzaniga, 1983.)

"Look at the dot."

Two words separated by a dot are momentarily projected.

Art

"What word did you see?"

or

"Point with your left hand to the word you saw."

Studying Hemispheric Differences in the Intact Brain

What about the 99.99+ percent of us with undivided brains? Have scientists found our hemispheres to be similarly specialized? Yes they have, in several different types of studies. For example, when a person performs a *perceptual* task, brain waves, blood-flow, and glucose consumption reveal increased activity in the *right* hemisphere; when a person speaks or calculates, activity increases in the *left* hemisphere.

On occasion, hemispheric specialization has been even more dramatically shown by briefly sedating an entire hemisphere. To check for the locus of language before surgery, a physician may inject a sedative into the neck artery that feeds blood to the hemisphere on its side of the body. Before the drug is injected, the patient is lying down, arms in the air, conversing easily. You can likely predict what happens when the drug flows into the artery going to the left hemisphere: Within seconds, the person's right arm falls limp and, if the left hemisphere controls language, the subject becomes speechless until the drug wears off. When the drug goes into the artery to the right hemisphere, the *left* arm falls limp, but the person can still speak.

Other tests also confirm hemispheric specialization. For example, most people recognize a picture faster and more accurately when it is flashed to the right hemisphere. But they recognize a word faster and more accurately when it is flashed to the left hemisphere. If a word is flashed to your right hemisphere, perception takes a fraction of a second longer—the length of time it takes to send the information through the corpus callosum to the more verbal left-hemisphere.

Catherine Best and Robert Avery (1999) offer fresh evidence of the left hemisphere's contribution to speech perception. The Zulu language employs as consonants certain click sounds, such as the "tsk" sound made with the tip of the tongue. Zulu speakers' brains process these sounds as language. Best and Avery designed a study in which participants heard competing sounds in their right and left ears. Zulu speakers more accurately recognized the click sounds heard in the right ear, which projects mostly to the left hemisphere. English speakers, for whom the same clicks are nonspeech sounds, did not show this left-hemisphere advantage.

Which hemisphere would you suppose enables sign language among deaf people? The right, because of its visual-spatial superiority? Or the left, because of its preparedness to process language? Studies reveal that, just as hearing people use the left hemisphere to process speech, deaf people use the left hemisphere to read signs (Corina & others, 1992). A stroke in the left hemisphere will disrupt a deaf person's signing much as it would disrupt a hearing person's speaking. Broca's area is similarly involved in both spoken and signed speech production (Corina, 1998). To the brain, language is language, whether spoken or signed.

Although the left hemisphere is adept at making quick, literal interpretations of language, the right hemisphere excels in making subtle inferences (Beeman & Chiarello, 1998; Beeman & others, 1994; Bowden & Beeman, 1998). If "primed" with the flashed word *foot*, the left hemisphere will be especially quick to then recognize the closely associated word *heel*. But if primed with *foot*, *cry*, and *glass*, the right hemisphere will more quickly recognize another word that is distantly related to all three (*cut*). And if given an insightlike problem—what word goes with *high*, *district*, and *house?*—the right hemisphere has better access to the solution. (The right hemisphere more quickly than the left recognizes that the solution is *school*.) As one patient explained after suffering right-hemisphere stroke damage, "I understand words, but I'm missing the subtleties." Thus, the right hemisphere helps us modulate our speech to make meaning clear—as when we ask "What's that in the road ahead?" instead of "What's that in the road, a head?" (Heller, 1990).

From simply looking at the two hemispheres, which appear alike to the naked eye, who would suppose that they contribute so uniquely to the harmony of the whole? Yet a variety of observations—of people with split brains and people with normal brains—converge beautifully, leaving little doubt that we have unified brains with specialized parts.

Brain Organization and Handedness

About 90 percent of the human population is right-handed. The remaining 10 percent (somewhat more among males, somewhat less among females) is left-handed. Tests reveal that about 95 percent of right-handers process speech primarily in the left hemisphere (Springer & Deutsch, 1985). Left-handers are more diverse. More than half process speech in the left hemisphere, as right-handers do. About one-quarter process language in the right hemisphere; the other quarter use both hemispheres more or less equally.

Is Handedness Inherited?

Judging from cave drawings and the tools of prehistoric humans, this veer to the right occurred long ago in the development of our species. Right-handedness prevails in all human cultures (Corballis, 1989). Moreover, it appears prior to the impact of culture. Ultrasound observations of fetal thumb-sucking reveal that more than 9 in 10 fetuses suck the right hand's thumb (Hepper & others, 1990). This bias for the right hand is uniquely human; other primates are more ambidextrous.

If handedness is inherited, however, there is no simple genetic code for it. In fact, it is one of but a few traits that genetically identical twins aren't especially likely to share (Halpern & Coren, 1990). Nevertheless, observing 150 babies during the first 2 days after their birth, George Michel (1981) found that two-thirds consistently preferred to lie with their heads turned to the right. When he again studied a sample of these babies at age 5 months, almost all of the "head right" babies reached for things with their right hands, and almost all of the "head left" babies reached with their left hands. Such findings, along with the universal prevalence of right-handers, indicate that either genes or some prenatal factor influences handedness.

So, Is It All Right to Be Left-Handed?

Judging by our everyday conversation, left-handedness is not all right. To be "coming out of left field" or to offer a "left-handed compliment" is hardly better than to be "gauche" or "sinister" (words derived from the French and Latin for left). On the other hand, right-handedness is "right on," which any "righteous" "right-hand man" "in his right mind" usually is.

Lefties
Famous left-handers include Bill Clinton, Jimi Hendrix, and Monica Seles.

Left-handers are more numerous than usual among those with reading disabilities, allergies, and migraine headaches (Geschwind & Behan, 1984). But left-handedness is also more common among musicians, mathematicians, professional baseball and cricket players, architects, and artists, including such luminaries as Michelangelo, Leonardo da Vinci, and Picasso.[2] Although left-handers must tolerate elbow-jostling at dinner parties, right-handed desks, and awkward scissors, the pros and cons of being a lefty seem roughly equal. But researchers have turned up one con that deserves more attention: Left-handers seem to disappear with age!

[2] Strategic factors explain the higher-than-normal percentage of lefties in sports. For example, it helps a soccer team to have left-footed players play the left side of the field (Wood & Aggleton, 1989).

The Case of the Disappearing Southpaws

While studying handedness, psychologist Stanley Coren (1993) stumbled upon a rather stunning fact: With age, the percentage of left-handers declines dramatically. In his initial sample of 5147 people, he found that left-handers were 14.6 percent of 10-year-olds, 4.6 percent of 50-year-olds, and less than 1 percent of those over age 80 (**FIGURE 4.19**). Other researchers around the world have confirmed Coren's finding. Intrigued, Coren and fellow sleuth Diane Halpern (1991; Halpern & Coren, 1988, 1991, 1993) set out in search of an answer. (If you were they, what explanations might have come to mind?)

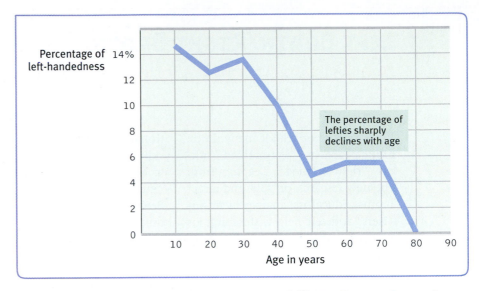

The percentage of lefties sharply declines with age

FIGURE **4.19** **The disappearing southpaws**
The percentage of left-handers decreases sharply in samples of older people. (Adapted from Coren, 1993.)

Perhaps, Coren and Halpern first thought, childhood coercion causes natural lefties to become right-handed as they age. (Many older people can recall having their left hands slapped, tied down, or even balled into a fist with surgical tape when they tried to use it.) If today's parents and teachers are more accepting of left-handedness than were those earlier, the result might be more young left-handers. But North American and European studies suggest that during the twentieth century, left-handers increased only from about 6 percent of the population to 10 percent (Porac & others, 1980), too little to explain the much greater percentage of left-handers among the very young. Coren and his colleagues found further support for the stability of left-handedness in art works dated from 15,400 to 3000 B.C., where 10 percent of the people were depicted as left-handed. In modern art works, 11 percent were left-handers.

Might simple learning explain the slow and gradual disappearance of left-handers? Might the world's being designed for right-handers make it easier for lefties to learn *gradually* to use their right hands? But again, no—preschoolers who switch handedness complete the process before adolescence. Handedness rarely switches after age 8 or 9, and even before then it occurs only for specific coerced actions (such as eating or writing).

What else remains? Coren and Halpern dared to think the unthinkable: that left-handers die younger. "That can't be true," skeptical colleagues replied when Coren first voiced the idea. "If true, surely someone would have noticed by now. Besides, my paternal grandmother was left-handed and lived to 91." As we have seen many times, vivid anecdotes ("I know a person who . . .") are no substitute for conclusions based on large and representative samples. Neither examples nor counter-examples prove a generality.

So Coren and Halpern decided to explore their morbid idea. They first reflected on the lefties' known health risks. Left-handers are more likely to have experienced birth stress, such as prematurity or the need for assisted respiration. They also endure more headaches, have more accidents (partly because of right-handed equipment), have more knee and joint problems, use more tobacco and alcohol, and suffer more immune system problems (including allergies such as asthma, eczema, and hay fever).

"Truth is arrived at by the painstaking process of eliminating the untrue. When you have eliminated the impossible, whatever remains, *however improbable*, must be the truth."

Sherlock Holmes in Arthur Conan Doyle's *The Sign of the Four*, 1890

The southpaw's hazardous life
In the book *The Left-Hander Syndrome*, Stanley Coren illustrates risks posed by a world made for right-handers. When left-handers use a drill press, their left arm may obscure their view.

Right-hander

Left-hander

THINKING CRITICALLY ABOUT :

LEFT BRAIN/RIGHT BRAIN

"Error flies from mouth to mouth, from pen to pen, and to destroy it takes ages."

—Voltaire, 1694–1778

You've heard or read it many times: Some people are "left-brained," others "right-brained." Leaping from the new research on split and intact brains, educators, management advisers, and self-help writers urge us to harness the undeveloped half of our brain. Do you want to develop your creativity, music appreciation, or emotional empathy? Well, get your brain in balance. Awaken your dormant right hemisphere. Advocate "whole brain" education in your schools. Unleash intuitive, right-brained management from the chains of cold logic and statistics. Try *Drawing on the Right Side of the Brain* (the title of a million-copy bestseller translated into 10 languages).

What should we make of all this? By calling my friend Elsie "right-brained" have I explained why she's such a zany free spirit? And why her "left-brained" husband Bill is so coolly analytical? We've seen that research does show that each hemisphere serves special functions. The left is more logical, verbal, and able to deal with things in sequence. The right is more emo-

tionally intuitive and expressive, skilled at spatial relations, and able to deal with things all at once. But neuroscientists raise a caution flag: Beware the fad of locating complex human abilities such as science or art in either hemisphere. "The left-right dichotomy in cognitive mode

is an idea with which it is very easy to run wild," warned Sperry (1982). Actually, such complex activities as doing science or creating art require the integration of both hemispheres. Even when reading a story, we use both hemispheres—the left processing the words and finding

Left brain/right brain Is the artist a "right-brained" person? Such notions distort scientific findings regarding the cerebral hemispheres. While some areas of each hemisphere specialize in different tasks, the brain's two sides cooperate to enable the person in whatever he or she does.

Long-lived left-handers:
- Benjamin Franklin (84)
- Charlie Chaplin (88)
- Pablo Picasso (92)

Short-lived left-handers:
- Babe Ruth (53)
- Marilyn Monroe (36)
- Alexander the Great (33)

These handedness differences aren't huge (individual differences are much greater). But might they, like sex differences in health risks, add up to differing life spans? When Coren and Halpern studied a random sample of recently deceased people of all ages they found that, on average, right-handers did live 8 or 9 years longer. This difference dwindled a bit when Coren, Halpern, and other researchers excluded children. By comparing left-handed and right-handed former baseball and cricket players, they found the life-span difference reduced—3 years, Coren now estimates— but still apparent (Aggleton & others, 1993; Rogerson, 1994; Seppa, 1997).

This stunning finding triggered an avalanche of publicity, much of it distorted, which in turn triggered nasty letters ("You have some gall to publicly ridicule people you have just condemned to an early death"), newspaper columns ("Dear professor . . . we strongly suggest that you beware of sinister lefties bearing grudges—and chain saws"), and phone messages ("You right-handers think that you'll live longer than left-handers but you won't if we kill you first" [Halpern &

meaning, the right appreciating humor, imagery, and emotional content (Hellige, 1993; Levy, 1985).

Why, then, do the popularizations of brain research so greatly exaggerate the findings? In *The Left-Hander Syndrome*, University of British Columbia psychologist Stanley Coren (1993) illustrates how journalism often oversimplifies and embellishes science. He recalls hearing a convention talk by Doreen Kimura, a psychologist at the University of Western Ontario in London, Ontario. Kimura reported that melodies fed to the left ear were more easily recognized than melodies fed to the right ear. Knowing that the left ear sends most of its information to the right hemisphere, she concluded that, among her right-handed student volunteers, the right brain was better at recognizing melodies.

A few days later, the *New York Times* reported that "Doreen Kimura, a psychologist from London, Ontario, has found that *musical ability* is controlled by the right side of the brain" (italics highlight the embellishment). Apparently drawing from the *Times* story, a syndicated newspaper story then reported that "London psychologist, Dr. Doreen Kimura,

claims that musicians are right-brained!" (But Kimura studied university students, not musicians.) Later, a follow-up newspaper article further distorted the study: "An English psychologist has finally explained why there are so many great left-handed musicians."

Knowing that Kimura is not English, did not study musicians, and did not study left-handers, Coren recalled the words of an American editor: "Everything you read in the newspaper is absolutely true, except for the rare story of which you happen to have first-hand knowledge."

What can happen is this: As information flows from scientist to reader, it gets simplified as well as embellished, much as gossip does in passing from one person to the next. A TV network picks up an interesting finding, then reduces it to a 30-second report with an 11-second sound bite from the researcher. This alerts a major newspaper to a story angle, which in turn gets picked up by popular science magazines and, eventually, by supermarket magazines and tabloids.

At each step, notes Coren, "Ideas become more speculative and more distant from the actual re-

search. . . . After a while, the neuropsychologist is no longer even visible in the communication chain." The rumors grow, accumulate, and evolve into scientific misinformation that becomes "'accepted truths,' which show up in conversation and writing in sentences that begin with, 'As everybody knows . . . ,' or 'Scientists have shown that . . . .'" In the end, sighs Coren, the public myth drowns out the voices of dissenting scientists.

The moral is not to discount everything you read. Surely Oscar Wilde was too cynical when expressing gratitude "for modern journalism. By giving us the opinions of the uneducated, it keeps us in touch with the ignorance of the community." (Some journalists check the accuracy of their draft articles with those they've interviewed.) The moral is to beware. Reporters want their stories to be newsworthy. When at their best, their ideal (and mine, in writing this book) is to extract the essence—to simplify without becoming simplistic. When at their worst, they distort a pretzel-shaped finding into a breadstick-shaped story: Some people are left-brained, others right-brained. . . . ■

others, 1996]). The finding also stimulated some follow-up research that produced no life-expectancy advantage for right-handers (Harris, 1993). One National Institute of Aging research team followed 3800 East Boston adults for 6 years and found that, at any age, left-handers were *not* more likely to die (Salive & others, 1993). Coren (1993) responded that 6 years is not long enough to catch a statistically significant handedness effect in a sample this small.

The unfinished case of the disappearing southpaws illustrates the very heart of science, how it dares to ask researchable questions, even those with unsettling implications. In the court of scientific judgment, researchers are welcome to state new ideas but they must expose themselves to counterexamination from opposing views and to heated debate. Over time, science has a way of unmasking error, taking us closer to factual truth, and often to an improved world. For example, as it explains the absence of elder left-handers, it may also point the way to safer, more comfortable environments for left-handed people.

Answers to questions on page 74: Yes. No. Green.

REVIEW AND REFLECT:

The Brain

What are lower-level brain structures, and what are their functions?

The brainstem begins where the spinal cord swells to form the medulla, which controls heartbeat and breathing. Within the brainstem, the reticular formation controls arousal. Atop the brainstem is the thalamus, the brain's sensory switchboard. The cerebellum, attached to the rear of the brainstem, coordinates muscle movement.

Between the brainstem and cerebral cortex is the limbic system, which is linked to memory, emotions, and drives. One of its neural centers, the amygdala, is involved in responses of aggression and fear. Another, the hypothalamus, is involved in various bodily maintenance functions, pleasurable rewards, and the control of the hormonal system.

Clinical observations have long revealed the general effects of damage to various areas of the brain. But CT and MRI scans now reveal brain structures, and EEG, PET, and functional MRI recordings reveal brain activity. By surgically lesioning or electrically stimulating specific brain areas, by recording the brain's surface electrical activity, and by displaying neural activity with computer-aided brain scans, neuroscientists explore the connections among brain, mind, and behavior.

How do the neural networks within the cerebral cortex enable our perceiving, thinking, and speaking?

Each hemisphere of the cerebral cortex—the neural fabric that covers the hemispheres—has four geographical areas: the frontal, parietal, occipital, and temporal lobes. Small, well-defined regions within these lobes control muscle movement and receive information from the body senses. However, most of the cortex—its association areas—is uncommitted to such functions and is therefore free to process other information.

Some brain regions serve specific functions (FIGURE 4.20). The brain divides its labor into specialized subtasks and then integrates the various outputs from its neural networks. Thus, our emotions, thoughts, and behaviors result from the intricate coordination of many brain areas. Language, for example, depends on a chain of events in several brain regions. If one hemisphere is damaged early in life, the other will pick up many of its functions, thus demonstrating the brain's plasticity. The brain becomes less plastic later in life. Frequently, however, nearby neurons can partially compensate for damaged ones, as when a person recovers from a stroke or brain injury.

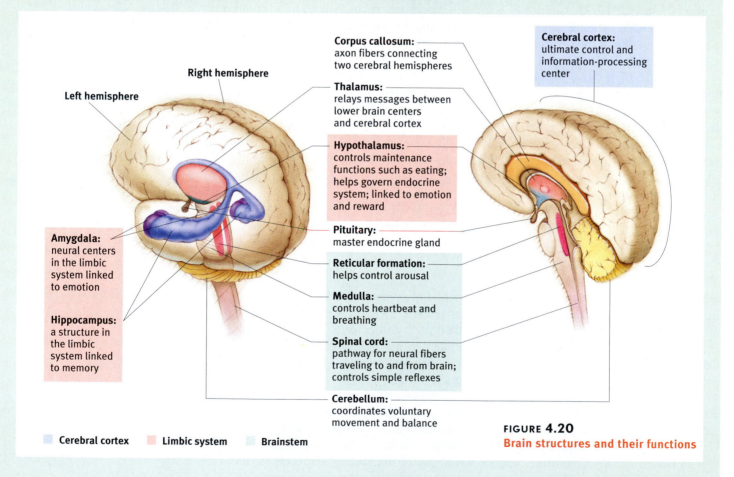

Corpus callosum: axon fibers connecting two cerebral hemispheres

Cerebral cortex: ultimate control and information-processing center

Right hemisphere

Left hemisphere

Thalamus: relays messages between lower brain centers and cerebral cortex

Hypothalamus: controls maintenance functions such as eating; helps govern endocrine system; linked to emotion and reward

Amygdala: neural centers in the limbic system linked to emotion

Pituitary: master endocrine gland

Reticular formation: helps control arousal

Medulla: controls heartbeat and breathing

Hippocampus: a structure in the limbic system linked to memory

Spinal cord: pathway for neural fibers traveling to and from brain; controls simple reflexes

Cerebellum: coordinates voluntary movement and balance

■ Cerebral cortex ■ Limbic system ■ Brainstem

FIGURE 4.20
Brain structures and their functions

Experiments on people with a severed corpus callosum have refined our knowledge of each hemisphere's special functions. Separately testing the two hemispheres, researchers have confirmed that in most people the left hemisphere is the more verbal, and that the right hemisphere excels in visual perception and the recognition of emotion. Studies of healthy people with intact brains confirm that each hemisphere makes unique contributions to the integrated functioning of the brain.

Terms and Concepts to Remember

lesion [LEE-zhuhn], p. 60
electroencephalogram (EEG), p. 60
CT (computed tomography)scan, p. 60
PET (positron emission tomography) scan, p. 60
MRI (magnetic resonance imaging), p. 61
brainstem, p. 62
medulla [muh-DUL-uh], p. 62
reticular formation, p. 62
thalamus [THAL-uh-muss], p. 62
cerebellum [sehr-uh-BELL-um], p. 63
limbic system, p. 63
amygdala [ah-MIG-dah-la], p. 63
hypothalamus [hi-po-THAL-uh-muss], p. 64

cerebral [seh-REE-bruhl] cortex, p. 65
glial cells, p.65
frontal lobes, p. 66
parietal [puh-RYE-uh-tuhl] lobes, p. 66
occipital [ahk-SIP-uh-tuhl] lobes, p. 66
temporal lobes, p. 66
motor cortex, p. 67
sensory cortex, p. 68
association areas, p. 68
aphasia, p. 70
Broca's area, p. 70
Wernicke's area, p. 70
plasticity, p. 71
corpus callosum [KOR-pus kah-LOW-sum], p. 73
split brain, p. 73

Test Yourself

4.1. The brainstem is the oldest and innermost region of the brain. The part of the brainstem that controls heartbeat and breathing is the
a. cerebellum.
b. medulla.
c. cortex.
d. thalamus.

4.2. The lower brain structure that governs arousal is the
a. spinal cord.
b. cerebellum.
c. reticular formation.
d. medulla.

4.3. The thalamus receives information from the sensory neurons and routes it to the higher brain regions that control the senses. The thalamus functions like a
a. memory bank.
b. pleasure center.
c. breathing regulator.
d. switchboard.

4.4. The part of the brain that coordinates voluntary movement is the
a. cerebellum.
b. medulla.
c. thalamus.
d. reticular formation.

4.5. The limbic system, a doughnut-shaped structure at the border of the brain's older parts and the cerebral hemispheres, is associated with basic motives, emotions, and memory functions. Two parts of the limbic system are the amygdala and the
a. reticular formation.
b. hippocampus.
c. thalamus.
d. medulla.

4.6. A ferocious response to electrical brain stimulation would lead you to suppose that the electrode had been touching the
a. medulla.
b. pituitary.
c. hippocampus.
d. amygdala.

4.7. The neural structure that most directly regulates eating, drinking, and body temperature is the
a. cerebellum.
b. hypothalamus.
c. thalamus.
d. amygdala.

4.8. The motor cortex is the brain region that controls voluntary muscle movement. If a neurosurgeon stimulated your right motor cortex, you would most likely
a. see light.
b. hear a sound.
c. feel a touch on the right arm.
d. move your left leg.

4.9. The sensory cortex registers and processes body sensations, with the more sensitive body regions having the greatest representation. Which of the following has the greatest representation?
a. knee
b. toes
c. fingers
d. thumb

Continued

4.10. About three-fourths of the cerebral cortex is not committed to any specific sensory or muscular function. The "uncommitted" areas are called
a. occipital lobes.
b. fissures.
c. association areas.
d. Wernicke's area.

4.11. Judging and planning are enabled by the
a. occipital lobes.
b. parietal lobes.
c. frontal lobes.
d. temporal lobes.

4.12. The area in the brain that, if damaged, might impair your ability to form words is
a. Wernicke's area.
b. Broca's area.
c. the left occipital lobe.
d. the angular gyrus.

4.13. Plasticity refers to the brain's ability to reorganize itself after damage. Especially plastic are the brains of
a. split-brain patients.
b. young adults.
c. young children.
d. right-handed people.

4.14. The brain structure that enables the right and left hemispheres to communicate is
a. the medulla.
b. Broca's area.
c. Wernicke's area.
d. the corpus callosum.

4.15. The study of split-brain patients has allowed us to observe the special functions of each hemisphere of the brain. The left hemisphere excels in
a. processing language.
b. visual perceptions.
c. recognition of emotion.
d. recognition of faces.

4.16. Damage to the brain's right hemisphere is most likely to reduce a person's ability to
a. recite the alphabet rapidly.
b. recognize a picture.
c. understand verbal instructions.
d. solve arithmetic problems.

Review: Within what brain region would damage be most likely to disrupt your ability to skip rope? Your ability to sense tastes or sounds? In what brain region would damage perhaps leave you in a coma? Without the very breath and heartbeat of life?

Reflect: How might you feel with two separate brain hemispheres, both of which controlled your thought and action but one of which dominated your consciousness and speech? How might that affect your sense of self, as one indivisible person?

Answers to Test Yourself and Review questions can be found in the green appendix at the end of the book.

Reflections on the Biological Revolution in Psychology

We have glimpsed the truth of our overriding principle: Everything psychological is simultaneously biological. Modules 3 and 4 have focused on how our thoughts, feelings, and actions arise from our specialized yet integrated brain. Later in this book we will further explore the significance of the biological revolution in psychology. We will see, for example, how

+ brain development underlies a child's mental development.
+ the brain compensates for brain damage that occurs early in life.
+ genes and experience jointly influence our personality, emotions, and intelligence.
+ our sense organs and our brain enable us to see and hear.
+ the brain records memories.
+ aberrant brain anatomy and chemistry influence depression and schizophrenia, and how biological treatments can alleviate these conditions.
+ our brain and body work to create our experiences of hunger and sexuality, anger and fear, sleep and dreams.
+ mind and body together influence our vulnerability to disease and our capacity for healing.
+ our species' evolutionary history may predispose us to hurt, help, or love certain others.

From nineteenth-century phrenology to today's neuroscience we have come a long way. Yet what is unknown still dwarfs what is known. We can describe the brain. We can learn the functions of its parts. We can study how the parts communicate. But how does the electrochemical whir in a hunk of tissue the size of a head of lettuce give rise to elation, a creative idea, or that memory of Grandmother?

Much as gas and air, above certain concentrations, give rise to something different—fire—so, believed Sperry, does the complex human brain give rise to something different: consciousness. The mind, he argued, emerges from the brain's dance of ions, yet is not reducible to it. Cells cannot be fully explained by the actions of atoms, nor minds by the activity of cells. It is true that psychology is rooted in biology which is rooted in chemistry which is rooted in physics. Yet psychology is more than applied physics. As Jerome Kagan (1998) reminds us, the meaning of the Gettysburg Address is not reducible to neural activity. Sexual love is more than blood flooding to the genitals. Morality and responsibility become possible when we understand the mind as a "holistic system property," said Sperry (1992). We are not mere jabbering robots.

The mind boggles both at what is known and what is not. Interviews with leading brain scientists reveal their own awe and wonder. Others ponder philosophical mysteries: How does the material brain give rise to consciousness? To what extent can a thing understand itself? The mind seeking to understand the brain—that is indeed among the ultimate scientific challenges.

> "If the human brain were so simple that we could understand it, we would be so simple that we couldn't."
>
> **Emerson M. Pugh, quoted by George E. Pugh,** *The Biological Origin of Human Values*, 1977

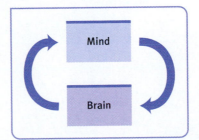

Mind and brain as holistic system
In Roger Sperry's view, the brain creates and controls the emergent mind, which in turn influences the brain. (Think vividly about biting into a lemon and you may salivate.)

The Nature and Nurture of Behavior

What makes you you? To answer, we must first understand how you come to be so much like everyone else. Whatever our differences, we are the leaves of one tree. Our human family shares not only a common biological heritage—cut us and we bleed—but also common behavioral tendencies. Our shared brain architecture predisposes us to sense the world, develop language, and feel hunger through identical mechanisms.

Whether we live in the Arctic or the tropics, we prefer sweet tastes to sour, we divide the color spectrum into similar colors, and we feel drawn to behaviors that produce and protect offspring. Regardless of our culture or our gender, we regard female features that signify youth and health—and reproductive potential—as attractive. Whether our last name is Wong, Nkomo, Smith, or Gonzales, at about eight months we start fearing strangers, and as adults we prefer the company of those whose attitudes and attributes are similar to our own. Coming from different parts of the globe, we know how to read one another's smiles and frowns. As members of one species, we affiliate, conform, reciprocate favors, punish offenses, organize hierarchies of status, and grieve a child's death. A visitor from outer space could drop in anywhere and find humans dancing and feasting, singing and worshiping, playing sports and games, laughing and crying, living in families, and forming groups. Taken together, such universal behaviors reveal our human nature.

Telling the story of you also requires explaining your individuality. Why are you more or less intelligent? Happy? Aggressive? Why is one person gay or lesbian while another is straight? Why is one person distressed by imagined voices while others are not? Why is one person unable to keep pounds off while another can't put them on? Also, what's the source of our *group* differences in whether we think plump is beautiful or unattractive, whether we hide or readily express anger, whether we tend to do our own thing or honor others' expectations?

Psychology's answer to these questions begins with a backward look at how our species developed the body-mind system—a system that enabled our distant ancestors to solve problems they faced while navigating their physical worlds, hunting, gathering food, encountering others, and reproducing. The story continues as we move forward to look at the genetic inheritance that designs each unique new body-mind system. Psychologists are exploring how—and how much—our individual heredity predisposes our differing personalities, preferences, and abilities. To what extent are we shaped by our heredity (our *nature*) and by our life history (including the *nurture* we have received since our conception)? Does our individual genetic makeup explain why one person is outgoing, another shy? Why one person is slow-witted and another quick? Or do we travel different developmental roads depending on our life experiences and our current environment?

The conclusions—that *nature* is crucially important (Module 5), and that *nurture* is crucially important (Module 6)—are central to today's psychology. Genes—and the rest of our bodies—matter. Culture—and everything we experience from womb to tomb—matters. Consider, then, how nature and nurture together shape us.

5 Genetic Influences on Behavior

Genes: Our Biological Blueprint

Preview Question: Our genes provide the blueprint for our biology; does this mean they determine our behaviors?

"Thanks for almost everything, Dad."

Behind the story of our body and our brain—surely the most awesome thing on our little planet—are the blueprints that design both our universal human attributes and our individual traits. Every cell nucleus in your body contains the genetic master code for the entire body. It's as if every room in the Tower of London had a bookcase containing the architect's plans for the entire building. These plans run to 46 books—23 donated by your mother (from her egg) and 23 by your father (from his sperm). These books, called **chromosomes**, are each composed of a coiled chain of the molecule **DNA (deoxyribonucleic acid)**. Small segments of the giant DNA molecules, called **genes**, form the words of these chromosome books (**FIGURE 5.1**). All told, each of us has some 100,000 of these gene words, give or take 40,000 (Wade, 1999). Each gene is a self-replicating unit capable of synthesizing proteins—the building blocks of our physical development.

Our genes are in turn defined by a four-letter alphabet of life, composed of biochemical letters called *nucleotides*. The smallest human chromosome (Y) has 50 million nucleotide "letters"; the largest has 250 million. Collectively, some 3 billion paired nucleotides define the genes that determine your individual biological development. To get a sense of the vast library of information contained in each of your cells consider this: At 2000 nucleotide "letters" to a page, the 46 chromosome "books" containing your complete genetic code would need to run more than 30,000 pages each.

The sequence of the four nucleotide letters—A, T, C, and G—is virtually the same in all humans; genetically speaking, every human being is close to being your identical twin. By 2003, the Human **Genome** Project will have discovered the common sequence of all 3 billion letters within human DNA. It is this shared genetic profile that makes us humans, rather than dogs or tulips.

Geneticists and psychologists are also interested in the occasional variations found at particular gene sites in the DNA—variations that in their many combina-

---

FIGURE 5.1

The genes: Their location and composition

Contained in the nucleus of each of the trillions of cells in your body are chromosomes. Each chromosome contains a coiled chain of the molecule DNA. Genes are DNA segments that form templates for the production of proteins. By directing the manufacture of proteins, the genes determine our individual biological development.

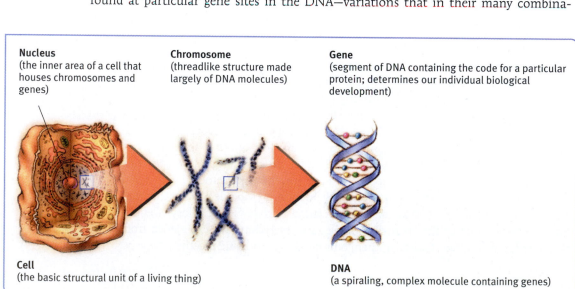

Nucleus (the inner area of a cell that houses chromosomes and genes)

Chromosome (threadlike structure made largely of DNA molecules)

Gene (segment of DNA containing the code for a particular protein; determines our individual biological development)

Cell (the basic structural unit of a living thing)

DNA (a spiraling, complex molecule containing genes)

tions define each person's uniqueness. The differences are few. More than 98 percent of our letter sequences match those of chimpanzees, and 99.9 percent match those of all other humans (Plomin & Crabbe, in press). But vive la différence! Slight person-to-person variations from the common pattern give clues to why one person has a disease that another does not, why one person is short and another tall, why one is happy and another depressed.

Most human traits are influenced by many genes acting in concert. How tall you are, for example, reflects the height of your face, the size of your vertebrae, the length of your leg bones, and so forth—each of which may be influenced by different genes. Ditto for complex human traits such as intelligence, happiness, and aggressiveness. Still, researchers have discovered that variations in a single gene are part of the recipe for certain forms of Alzheimer's disease, for alcoholism, for schizophrenia, for reading disabilities, and the list grows.

Our genetic predispositions help explain both our shared human nature and our individual differences. Evolutionary psychology sheds light on what's universal, and behavior genetics on our differences.

Evolutionary Psychology: Explaining Universal Behaviors

Preview Question: How do evolutionary psychologists use natural selection to explain behavioral tendencies?

A fox is a wild and wary animal, if ever there was one. "Sly as a fox" is a deserved image. If you capture a pair and try to befriend them or their offspring, be careful. Stick your hand in the cage and, if the timid fox can't flee, it probably will make a snack of your fingers. Working at the Russian Academy of Science's Institute of Cytology and Genetics, Dmitry Belyaev was wondering how our human ancestors had domesticated dogs from their wolf forebears. Might he, within a comparatively short stretch of time, accomplish a similar feat by evolving the fearful fox into a friendly fox?

To find out, Belyaev set to work with 30 male and 100 female foxes. From their offspring he selected and mated the tamest 5 percent of males and 20 percent of females, measuring tameness by the foxes' responses to attempts to feed, handle, and stroke them. Over more than 30 generations, Belyaev and his successor, Lyudmila Trut, repeated that simple procedure. Today, 40 years and 45,000 foxes later, they have a new breed of foxes that, in Trut's (1999) words, are "docile, eager to please and unmistakably domesticated. . . . Before our eyes, 'the Beast' has turned into 'beauty,' as the aggressive behavior of our herd's wild [ancestors] entirely disappeared." So friendly and eager for human contact are they, so inclined to whimper to attract attention and to lick people like affectionate cats, that the cash-strapped Institute has seized on a way to raise funds—by marketing its foxes to people as house pets.

As Belyaev and Trut demonstrated, when certain traits are *selected*—by conferring a reproductive advantage upon them—those traits, over time, come to prevail. Over many generations, wild wolves can become tame dogs, and wary foxes can have descendants who love to cuddle with us. Dog breeders, as Robert Plomin and his colleagues (1997) remind us, have given us sheepdogs that herd, retrievers that retrieve, trackers that track, and pointers that point. They also have given us placid clumber spaniels and aggressive pit bulls. Psychologists, too, have bred dogs, mice, and rats whose genes predispose them to be serene or reactive, quick learners or slow learners.

From beast to beauty
Forty years into the fox-breeding experiment, most of the offspring are devoted, affectionate, and capable of forming strong bonds with people.

- **chromosomes** threadlike structures made of DNA molecules that contain the genes.

- **DNA (deoxyribonucleic acid)** a complex molecule containing the genetic information that makes up the chromosomes. (A DNA molecule has two strands—forming a "double helix"—held together by bonds between pairs of nucleotides.)

- **genes** the biochemical units of heredity that make up the chromosomes; a segment of DNA capable of synthesizing a protein.

- **genome** the complete instructions for making an organism, consisting of all the genetic material in its chromosomes. The human genome has 3 billion weakly bonded pairs of nucleotides organized as coiled chains of DNA.

Natural Selection

In natural environments, a mutant shark with keener than normal smell would find more prey, enabling it to live longer and leave more offspring. As nature continued over countless generations to give an edge to sharks best suited to their ecological niche, an exquisitely effective predator came into being. Natural history has similarly favored bull moose with large antler racks, enabling them to prevail against rivals for access to females. But there are tradeoffs. Those with gargantuan antler racks become vulnerable when chased into trees by a wolf pack. (Imagine trying to run through a forest with thick tree branches sprouting from the sides of your head.) The antlers of today's bull moose represent the fittest compromise.

Does **natural selection** also explain our shared human traits? Extended over many thousands of years and feeding off new gene combinations and **mutations**—random errors in gene replication—has natural selection favored advantageous variations? Do we tend to fear snakes and heights because our ancestors who feared them more often survived to spread their genes?

Everyone agrees that the tight genetic leash that predisposes an ant's nest building, a dog's retrieving, or a cat's pouncing is looser on humans. Our genes provide more than a long leash; they endow us with a capacity to learn and therefore to adapt to life on the tundra or in the jungle. Yet in the big picture our lives are remarkably alike. Visit the international arrivals area at London's Heathrow Airport, a world hub where arriving passengers meet their excited loved ones. There you will see the same delighted joy in the faces of Kenyan grandmothers, Chinese children, and Canadian tourists. Although human differences grab our attention, our deep similarities also demand explanation.

These behavioral similarities arise from our biological similarity. Of our relatively few genetic differences, only 6 percent are differences among races. Only 8 percent are differences among groups within a race. The rest—over 85 percent—are individual variations within local groups. The typical genetic difference between two Icelandic villagers or between two Kenyans is much greater than the *average* difference between the two groups. Thus, notes geneticist Richard Lewontin (1982), if after a worldwide catastrophe only Icelanders or Kenyans survived, the human species would suffer only "a trivial reduction" in its genetic diversity.

Why are we all so much alike? Since the dawn of human history, our ancestors all faced certain questions: Who is my ally, who my foe? What food should I eat? With whom should I mate? Some individuals answered those questions more successfully than others. Those disposed to eat nourishing rather than poisonous food survived to contribute their genes to later generations. Similarly successful were those who mated with someone with whom they could produce and nurture offspring. The genes of individuals not so disposed tended, over generations, to be lost from the human gene pool. As further mutations occurred, genes providing an adaptive edge continued to be selected. "This process, say **evolutionary psychologists**, led not only to muscles and bone structures, but also to behavioral tendencies and ways of thinking that prepared our Stone Age ancestors to survive, reproduce, and send their genes into the future." Nature selected the fittest adaptations.

As inheritors of this prehistoric genetic legacy, we love the taste of sweets and fats, which once were hard to come by but which prepared our ancestors to survive famines. Ironically, with famine rare in Western cultures, and sweets and fats beckoning us from store shelves, fast-food outlets, and vending machines, obesity has become a growing problem. We are, in some ways, biologically prepared for a world that no longer exists.

Evolution has been an organizing principle for biology for a long time. But only recently, in "the second Darwinian revolution," have psychologists attempted to harness evolutionary principles. Charles Darwin (1859) anticipated this application of evolutionary principles to psychology. In concluding *The Origin of Species*, he foresaw "open fields for far more important researches. Psychology will be based on a new foundation" (p. 346).

Those who are troubled by an apparent conflict between scientific and religious accounts of human origins may find it helpful to recall that different perspectives of life can be complementary. For example, the scientific account attempts to tell us when and how; religious creation stories usually aim to tell about an ultimate who and why. As Galileo explained to the Grand Duchess Christina, "The Bible teaches how to go to heaven, not how the heavens go."

Psychologists, as we will see, are now using evolutionary principles to explore questions such as these:

+ Why do infants start to fear strangers about the time they become mobile?
+ Why do we so naturally divide people into categories—male and female, children and grown-ups, blacks and whites, geeks and studs?
+ Why are most parents so passionately devoted to their children?
+ Why do so many more people have phobias about spiders and snakes than about more dangerous guns and electricity?
+ Why do we display greater empathy and helpfulness toward those who look, think, and act as we do?
+ How and why do men and women differ? For example, why are men quicker than women to perceive friendliness as sexual interest, to initiate sexual relations, and to feel jealous rage over a mate's having sex with someone else?

To see how evolutionary psychologists think and reason, let's pause to explore this last question.

Sexuality

"With few exceptions anywhere in the world," report cross-cultural psychologist Marshall Segall and his colleagues (1990, p. 244), "males are more likely than females to initiate sexual activity." Across 177 studies of some 130,000 people, men are much more accepting of casual sex, and they report masturbating much more often (Oliver & Hyde, 1993). This is among the largest of **gender** differences. There are others:

+ In a Canadian survey, 80 percent of 2350 customers of adults-only video stores were males (although half claimed to engage a partner in watching the movies—Jenish, 1993). And if you guessed that most hard-core pornography readers are male and most romance novel readers are female, you would be right (Malamuth, 1996).
+ In a 1999 survey of 261,000 entering American college students, 53 percent of men but only 30 percent of women agreed that "if two people really like each other, it's all right for them to have sex even if they've known each other for a very short time" (Sax & others, 1999).
+ In a careful survey of 3432 U.S. 18- to 59-year-olds, 48 percent of the women but only 25 percent of the men cited affection as a reason for first intercourse. And how often do they think about sex? "Every day" or "several times a day," acknowledged 19 percent of the women and 54 percent of the men (Laumann & others, 1994).
+ Such gender differences characterize both heterosexual and homosexual people. Gay men report more interest in uncommitted sex, more responsiveness to visual sexual stimuli, and more concern with their partner's physical attractiveness than lesbians do (Bailey & others, 1994). (Aware of HIV risks, gay men were, however, having fewer partners in 1998 than in 1985 [Altman, 1999].)
+ Worldwide, men in survey after survey claim having much more sex with many more women than women acknowledge having with men. An example: Although most single Korean students (average age 19) in a recent survey were celibate, the males were more than twice as likely as their female counterparts to report having had intercourse. Moreover, among those who did so, two-thirds of the males but only one-third of the females reported more than one partner. All told, the men claimed five times as many sexual partners as did the women (Youn, 1996). Surveys in other countries have found that men report two or four times as many sex partners as do women. These conflicting recollections by men and women reflect the gender difference in sexual attitudes and fantasies (Wiederman, 1997).

Gender differences in attitudes extend to differences in behavior. Casual hit-and-run sex is most frequent among males with traditional masculine attitudes (Pleck & others, 1993). Russell Clark and Elaine Hatfield (1989) observed this striking gender

---

■ **natural selection** the principle that, among the range of inherited trait variations, those contributing to reproduction and survival will most likely be passed on to succeeding generations.

■ **mutations** random errors in gene replication that lead to a change in the sequence of *nucleotides*; the source of all genetic diversity.

■ **evolutionary psychology** the study of the evolution of behavior and the mind, using principles of natural selection. Natural selection is presumed to have favored genes that predisposed behavior tendencies and information-processing systems that solved adaptive problems faced by our ancestors, thus contributing to the survival and spread of their genes.

■ **gender** in psychology, the characteristics, whether biologically or socially influenced, by which people define male and female.

"It's not that gay men are oversexed; they are simply men whose male desires bounce off other male desires rather than off female desires."

Steven Pinker, *How the Mind Works*, 1997

difference in sexuality when in 1978 they sent some average-looking student research assistants strolling across the Florida State University quadrangle. Spotting an attractive person of the other sex, a researcher would approach and say, "I have been noticing you around campus and I find you to be very attractive. Would you go to bed with me tonight?" The women all declined, some obviously irritated ("What's wrong with you, creep! Leave me alone."). But 75 percent of the men readily agreed, often replying with comments such as "Why do we have to wait until tonight?" Somewhat astonished by their result, Clark and Hatfield repeated their study in 1982 and twice more during the late-1980s AIDS era (Clark, 1990). Each time, virtually no women, but half or more of the men, agreed to go to bed with a stranger.

Men also have a lower threshold for perceiving warm responses as a sexual come-on. In study after study, men more often than women attribute a woman's friendliness to sexual interest (Abbey, 1987; Johnson & others, 1991). Misattributing women's cordiality as a come-on helps explain men's greater sexual assertiveness (Kenrick & Trost, 1987). The unfortunate results can range from sexual harassment to date rape (Kanekar & Nazareth, 1988; Muehlenhard, 1988; Shotland, 1989).

An Evolutionary Explanation

Evolutionary psychologists have a ready explanation for women's more relational and men's more recreational approach to sex. It goes like this: Compared with eggs, sperm are cheap. Moreover, while a woman incubates and nurses one infant, a male can spread his genes by impregnating other females. Our natural yearnings, argue evolutionary psychologists, are our genes' way of reproducing themselves. In our ancestral history, women most often sent their genes into the future by pairing wisely, men by pairing widely. "Humans are living fossils—collections of mechanisms produced by prior selection pressures," says David Buss (1995).

And what do men and women find attractive in the other sex? Some aspects of attractiveness cross place and time. It comes as no surprise to evolutionary psychologists that men in 37 cultures, from Australia to Zambia, judge women as more attractive if they have a youthful appearance (FIGURE 5.2). Psychologists who view behavior from an evolutionary perspective say that men drawn to healthy, fertile-appearing women—women with smooth skin and a youthful shape suggesting many childbearing years to come—have stood a better chance of sending their genes into the future. From yesterday's Stone Age figurines to today's *Playboy* centerfolds and Miss America winners—and regardless of cultural variations in ideal weight—men feel most attracted to women whose waists are roughly a third narrower than their hips—a sign of youthful fertility (Singh, 1993).

© 1994 Ruben Bolling. Distributed by Quaternary Features.

FIGURE **5.2**
Worldwide mating preferences
David Buss and an international team of collaborators surveyed the mating preferences of 10,047 people in 37 countries depicted by the dots (from Buss, 1994b). Men everywhere preferred attractive physical features suggesting youth and health—and reproductive potential. Women everywhere preferred men with resources and social status. This gender difference, evolutionary psychologists believe, is the result of natural selection favoring those whose choices help perpetuate their genes.

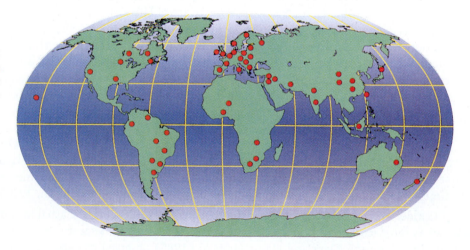

Women also feel attracted to healthy looking men, but especially to those who seem mature, dominant, and affluent (Singh, 1995a). Such attributes, say the evolutionary psychologists, connote a capacity to support and protect (Buss, 1996; Geary, 1998). Henry Kissinger, an adviser to U.S. presidents, had the same idea: "Power is the world's greatest aphrodisiac." Evolutionary psychologists also are unsurprised that each sex tends to advertise the qualities that maximize its odds of attracting desirable partners: women by spending time and money on appearance, men by trying to establish their status and dominance. In singles ads, for example, women tend to offer looks and seek status; men do the reverse (Rajecki & others, 1991). Why do even successful men lust after ever more money and power? Some evolutionary psychologists reason that such attributes are to men what antlers are to a stag or tail feathers to a male peacock. Men needn't consciously think, "I'm trying to outdo my male rivals in the competition for female attention." They're just hard-wired to want to outdo their rivals, because those who did so in the past put more of their genes into our human gene pool.

Women also prefer mates with the potential for long-term mating and investment in their joint offspring (Gangestad & Simpson, 2000). They prefer potential dads over likely cads. Thus, for men there are genetic tradeoffs between seeking to distribute one's genes widely and being willing to co-parent.

There is a principle at work here, say evolutionary psychologists: Nature selects behavioral tendencies that increase the likelihood of sending one's genes into the future. As mobile gene machines, we are predisposed to prefer whatever worked for our ancestors. They were predisposed to act in ways that would leave grandchildren—had they not been, we wouldn't be here—and as carriers of their genetic legacy, so are we.

Critiquing the Evolutionary Explanation

Without disputing nature's selection of traits that enhance gene survival, critics see problems with evolutionary psychology. It often, they say, starts with an effect (such as the gender sexuality difference) and works backward to propose an explanation. If men were uniformly loyal to their mates, might we not reason that the children of committed, supportive fathers more often survived to perpetuate their genes? Might not men also be better off bonded to one woman—both to increase the otherwise slim odds of impregnation and to keep her from the advances of competing men? Might not a ritualized bond—a marriage—also spare women from chronic male harrassment? (Such suggestions are, in fact, evolutionary explanations for why humans tend to pair off monogamously.) And what about those species, such as chimpanzees and bonobos, in which ardent females mate with numerous males? Is it so that the males, not knowing the true paternity of a female's offspring will join in tolerating or protecting them? One can hardly lose at hindsight explanation, which is, says paleontologist Stephen Jay Gould (1997), mere "speculation [and] guesswork in the cocktail party mode."

Moreover, says anthropologist Meredith Small (1999), evolutionary speculation about sex and gender "reinforces male-female stereotypes." Natalie Angier (1999) sees evolutionary psychology "glaring through an overwhelmingly masculinized lens. . . . Hard-core evolutionary psychology types go to extremes to argue in favor of the yawning chasm that separates the innate desires of women and men." But if women's sex drive is so much less wandering than men's, ask feminist researchers, then why must men go to such lengths to control women's sexuality? Why are women across the world beaten for promiscuity and adultery?

Critics also remind us that much of who we are is not hard-wired. Cultural expectations also bend the genders. For example, what's attractive varies somewhat with time and place. The voluptuous Marilyn Monroe ideal of the 1950s has been replaced by the turn-of-the-century leaner, athletic female image. Moreover, if socialized to value lifelong commitment, men may sexually bond with one partner; if socialized to accept casual sex, women may willingly have sex with many partners. Women's sexual variability is especially striking, notes Roy Baumeister (2000). Across

"I had a nice time, Steve. Would you like to come in, settle down, and raise a family?"

"I contend that nature has given males the heaviest burden of all: the burden of always having to Make the First Move, and thereby risk getting Shot Down. I don't know WHY males get stuck with this burden, but it's true throughout the animal kingdom. . . . It's always the male bird who does the courting dance, making a total moron of himself, while the female bird just stands there, looking aloof, thinking about what she's going to tell her girlfriends. ('And then he hopped around on one foot! Like I'm supposed to be impressed by THAT!')."

Dave Barry, *Miami Herald*, 1999

■ **behavior genetics** the study of the relative power and limits of genetic and environmental influences on behavior.

■ **environment** every nongenetic influence, from prenatal nutrition to the people and things around us.

■ **identical twins** twins who develop from a single fertilized egg that splits in two, creating two genetically identical organisms.

■ **fraternal twins** twins who develop from separate eggs. They are genetically no closer than brothers and sisters, but they share a fetal environment.

time, across cultures, across situations, and across differing levels of education, religiosity, and peer influence, adult women's sexual drive and interests are more flexible and varying than adult men's—a phenomenon Baumeister calls the gender difference in "erotic plasticity." Women, more than men, for example, prefer to alternate periods of high sexual activity with periods of almost none.

Some gender differences in mate preferences indeed seem universal across cultures. But again, critics question whether such gender differences may to some extent be by-products of a culture's social and family structures. Show Alice Eagly and Wendy Wood (1999) a culture with gender inequality—where men are providers and women are homemakers—and they will show you a culture where men strongly desire youth and domestic skill in their potential mates, and women seek status and earning potential in their mates. Show Eagly and Wood a culture with gender equality, and they will show you a culture with smaller gender differences in mate preferences. They draw their conclusions from an analysis of the same 37 cultures studied earlier by David Buss.

Evolutionary psychologists respond to such criticisms by acknowledging our great human capacity for learning. (We come equipped to adapt and survive, whether living in igloos or tree houses.) They also point to the coherence of evolutionary principles and their ability to unify science. And they offer testable predictions (for example, that we will favor others to the extent they share our genes or can later reciprocate our favors). Some have even gleaned predictions for business. For example, given that early human communities apparently banded together in groups no larger than about 150, organizations today may function best if organized into extended family-size groups within work units no bigger than 150 (Nicholson, 1998).

Behavior Genetics: Explaining Individual Differences

Preview Question: How do behavior geneticists explain individual differences?

While evolutionary psychologists apply Darwin's big idea in hopes of explaining our universal human tendencies, **behavior geneticists** explore our differences from one another. How much are our differences shaped by our differing genetic blueprints? By our upbringing? By our culture and current circumstances? By how our **environment**—every external influence, from maternal nutrition while in the womb to social support while nearing the tomb—reacts to our genetic traits?

To disentangle the threads of heredity and environment, behavior geneticists often use two sets of tweezers: twin studies and adoption studies.

The nurture of nature
Parents everywhere wonder: Will my baby grow up to be peaceful or aggressive? Homely or attractive? Successful or struggling at every step? What are children born with, and what is nurtured—and how?

Twin Studies

To tease apart environment and heredity, it would be nice if we could control the home environment while varying heredity. Happily for our purposes, nature has given us ready-made subjects for this experiment: identical versus fraternal twins. **Identical twins**, who develop from a single fertilized egg that splits in two, are *genetically* identical (**FIGURE 5.3**). They are—millions and millions of them—nature's own human clones. (The possibility of laboratory human cloning raises new ethical issues but hardly new psychological issues.)

Fraternal twins, who develop from separate eggs, are genetically no more similar than ordinary brothers and sisters. A person whose identical twin has Alzheimer's disease has a 60 percent risk of sharing the disease; if the affected twin is fraternal, the risk is only 30 percent (Plomin & others, 1997). Such a difference suggests a genetic influence.

Behavior geneticists ask: Are identical twins, being genetic clones of one another, behaviorally more similar than fraternal twins? Studies of nearly 13,000 pairs of Swedish twins, of 7000 Finnish twin pairs, and of 3810 Australian twin pairs provide a consistent answer: On both extraversion (outgoingness) and neuroticism (emotional instability), identical twins are much more similar than fraternal twins. In explaining individual differences, genes matter.

If genes influence traits such as emotional instability, might they also influence the social effects of such traits? To find out, Matt McGue and David Lykken (1992) studied divorce rates among 1500 same-sex, middle-age twin pairs. Their result: If you have a fraternal twin who has divorced, the odds of your divorcing go up 1.6 times (compared to those with a not-divorced twin). If you have an identical twin who has divorced, the odds of your divorcing go up 5.5 times. From such data McGue and Lykken estimated that people's differing divorce risks are about 50 percent attributable to genetic factors. Another study of 2315 twin pairs confirms that identical twins' recent troubles at home, work, and elsewhere are more alike than are those of fraternal twins' (Kendler & others, 1993).

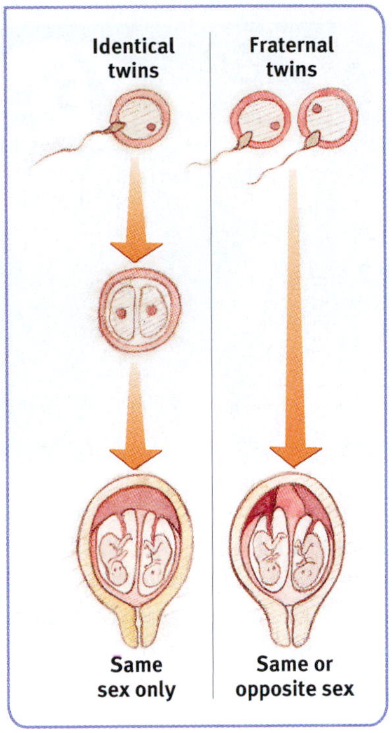

Other dimensions of personality and ability also reflect genetic influences. When John Loehlin and Robert Nichols (1976) gave a battery of questionnaires to 850 U.S. twin pairs, identical twins were much more similar than fraternals in many ways—in abilities, personality traits, even interests. However, the identical twins, more than fraternal twins, also reported being treated alike. So, did their experience rather than their genes account for their similarity? No, said Loehlin and Nichols. Identical twins whose parents treated them alike were *not* psychologically more alike than identical twins who were treated less similarly.

Separated Twins

Imagine the following science fiction experiment: A mad scientist decides to separate identical twins at birth, then rear them in differing environments. Better yet, consider a true story:

On a chilly Ohio Saturday morning in February 1979, some time after divorcing his first wife, Linda, Jim Lewis awoke in his modest, middle-class home next to his second wife, Betty. Jim—a romantic, affectionate type—was determined that this marriage would work and made a habit of leaving love notes to Betty around the house. As Jim lay in bed he thought about others he had loved, including his son, James Alan, and his faithful dog, Toy.

Having outfitted a workshop in a corner of his basement, he looked forward to spending some of the day's free time on his woodworking hobby. Jim had derived many hours of satisfaction from building furniture, picture frames, and an assortment of other items, including a circular white bench around a tree in his front yard. Jim also liked to spend free time driving his Chevy, watching stock-car racing, and drinking Miller Lite beer.

Jim was basically healthy. Having undergone a vasectomy, he was done having children. His blood pressure was a little high, perhaps related to his chain-smoking habit. He chewed his fingernails to the nub. And he suffered occasional half-day migraine headaches—"like somebody's hitting you with a two-by-four in the back of the neck." He had become overweight awhile back but had shed some of the pounds.

FIGURE 5.3
Same egg, same genes; different eggs, different genes
Identical twins develop from a single fertilized egg, fraternal twins from two.

Curiously, twinning rates vary by race. The rate among Caucasians is roughly twice that of Asians and half that of Africans. In Africa and Asia, most twins are identical. In Western countries, most twins are fraternal, and fraternal twins are increasing with the use of fertility drugs (Diamond, 1986; Brody, 1998).

Twins Lorraine and Levinia Christmas, driving to deliver presents to each other near Flitcham, England, collided (Shepherd, 1997).

Affable by nature?
Identical twins Gerald Levey and Mark Newman were separated at birth and raised in different homes. When reunited at age 31, they discovered that they both volunteered as firefighters. Research has shown remarkable similarities in the life choices of separated identical twins, lending support to the idea that genes influence personality.

What was most extraordinary about Jim Lewis, however, was that at that same moment (I am not making this up) there existed another man—also named Jim—for whom all these things (right down to the dog's name) were also true.[1] This other Jim—Jim Springer—just happened, 38 years earlier, to have been his womb mate. Thirty-seven days after their birth, these two genetically identical twins were separated, adopted by blue-collar families, and reared with no contact or knowledge of the other's whereabouts until one February day when Jim Lewis' phone rang. The caller was his genetic clone (who, having been told he had a twin, set about to find him).

One month after that fateful encounter, the brothers became the first twin pair tested by University of Minnesota psychologist Thomas Bouchard and his colleagues, thus beginning a study of separated twins that extends to the present (Holden, 1980a,b; Wright, 1998). When given tests measuring their intelligence, personality, heart rate, and brain waves, the Jim twins—despite 38 years of separation—were virtually as alike as the same person tested twice. Their voice intonations and inflections were so similar that, hearing a playback of an earlier interview, Jim Springer guessed "That's me." Wrong—it was his brother.

Identical twins Oskar Stohr and Jack Yufe presented equally striking similarities. One was raised by his grandmother in Germany as a Catholic and a Nazi, while the other was raised by his father in the Caribbean as a Jew. Nevertheless, they share traits and habits galore. They like spicy foods and sweet liqueurs, have a habit of falling asleep in front of the television, flush the toilet before using it, store rubber bands on their wrists, and dip buttered toast in their coffee. Stohr is domineering toward women and yells at his wife, as did Yufe before he and his wife separated.

Aided by publicity in magazine and newspaper stories, Bouchard and his colleagues (1990; DiLalla & others, in press; Segal, 1999) have located and studied more than 70 pairs of identical twins reared apart. They continue to find similarities not only of tastes and physical attributes but also of personality, abilities, attitudes, interests, and even fears.

In Sweden, which has a national registry of 25,000 pairs of adult twins, Nancy Pedersen and her co-workers (1988) identified 99 separated identical twin pairs and more than 200 separated fraternal twin pairs. Compared with equivalent samples of identical twins reared together, the separated identical twins had more dissimilar personalities. Still, separated twins were more alike when genetically identical than when fraternal. Separation shortly after birth (rather than, say, at age 8) didn't amplify their personality differences. And what about twins of parents who misidentify their similar-appearing fraternal siblings as identical twins, or who misperceive their identical twins as fraternal twins? In both cases, their tested similarities have reflected what they really were, not what their parents thought them to be (Kendler, 1983). Parental perceptions hardly mattered.

The startling twin similarity stories do not impress Bouchard's critics. They contend that if any two strangers of the same sex and age were to spend hours comparing their behaviors and life histories, they would probably discover many coincidental similarities (although Bouchard's fraternal twins did not exhibit

> "In some domains it looks as though our identical twins reared apart are . . . just as similar as identical twins reared together. Now that's an amazing finding and I can assure you none of us would have expected that degree of similarity."
>
> **Thomas Bouchard (1981)**

---

[1] Actually, this description of the two Jims errs in one respect: Jim Lewis named his son James Alan. Jim Springer named his James Allan.

comparable similarities). Even the more impressive data from the personality assessments are clouded by the reunion of many of the separated twins some years before they were tested.

Moreover, separated twins shared an environment for at least their first nine months. They share an appearance, and the responses it evokes. And adoption agencies tend to place separated twins in similar homes. When environments are similar, the impact of environment looks smaller relative to heredity. Nevertheless, the twin studies illustrate why scientific thinking has shifted toward a greater appreciation of genetic influences. Genes-R-Us.

Adoption Studies

Another real-life experiment, adoption, creates two groups of relatives: the adoptees' genetic relatives (biological parents and siblings) and environmental relatives (adoptive parents and siblings). For any given trait we can therefore ask whether adopted children are more like their adoptive parents, who contribute a home environment, or their biological parents, who contributed their genes. While sharing the same home environment, do adopted siblings come to share traits?

The stunning finding from studies of hundreds of adoptive families—toppling many of our cherished notions about parental influence—is that people who grow up together, whether biologically related or not, do not much resemble one another in personality (McGue & Bouchard, 1998; Plomin & others, 1998; Rowe, 1990). Adoptees' traits bear more similarities to their biological parents than to their caregiving adoptive parents.

If parental nurture mattered as much as most people suppose, then shouldn't people's personalities be more alike if they were reared in the same home? Shouldn't it matter whether the parents work or don't, fight or don't, drink or don't? Whether the house is a crowded apartment or a spacious estate? Whether the kitchen is stocked with green veggies or Twinkies, the family room with books or toy guns, the neighborhood school with computers or metal detectors? The finding is stunning enough to bear repeating: So far as personality development is concerned, environmental factors shared by a family's children have virtually no impact on their personalities. Two adopted children reared in the same home are no more likely to share personality traits with one another than with the child down the block.

What we have here is developmental psychology's biggest puzzle: Why are children in the same family so different? (Even nontwin biological brothers and sisters tend to be strikingly different.) Why do the shared genes and the shared family environment (the family's social class, the parents' personalities and marital status, day care versus home care, the neighborhood) have so little discernible effect on children's personalities? Is it because each sibling nevertheless has differing experiences—differing peer influences and life events (Dunn & Plomin, 1990; Hetherington & others, 1993)? Is it because siblings—despite sharing half their genes—have very different combinations of genes (Lykken & others, 1992)? Does parental influence therefore affect an easygoing child one way, an emotionally reactive child another? "Child-rearing is not something a parent does to a child," notes Judith Rich Harris (1998). "It is something the parent and the child do together. . . . I would have been pegged as a permissive parent with my first child, a bossy one with my second."

So, is adoptive parenting a fruitless venture? Adoption studies show that, although the personalities of adopted children do not much resemble those of their adoptive parents, adoption matters (Brodzinsky & Schechter, 1990). Although the genetic leash limits the family environment's influence on personality, parents do influence their children's attitudes, values, manners, faith, and politics. A pair of adopted children or identical twins *will* have more similar religious beliefs if reared in the same home (Kelley & De Graaf, 1997; Rohan & Zanna, 1996). Parenting matters!

Coincidences are not unique to twins. Patricia Kern of Colorado was born March 13, 1941, and named Patricia Ann Campbell. Patricia DiBiasi of Oregon also was born March 13, 1941, and named Patricia Ann Campbell. Both had fathers named Robert, worked as bookkeepers, and had children ages 21 and 19. Both studied cosmetology, enjoyed oil painting as a hobby, and married military men, within 11 days of each other. They are not genetically related (From an AP report, May 2, 1983).

Family ties
Studies of adoptive families have provided new clues to hereditary and environmental influences. How similar would you expect adopted children to be to their adoptive parents? To their biological parents?

"The same fire that tempers steel melts butter."

Anonymous

Moreover, in adoptive homes, child neglect and abuse and even parental divorce are rare. (Adoptive parents are carefully screened; natural parents are not.) So it is not surprising that, despite a somewhat greater risk of psychological disorder, most adopted children thrive, especially when adopted as infants (Benson & others, 1994; Wierzbicki, 1993). They score higher than their biological parents on intelligence tests. Seven in eight report feeling strongly attached to one or both adoptive parents. They generally become happier and more stable people than they would have been in a stressed or neglectful environment. And, typically as children of self-giving parents, they grow up to be more self-giving and altruistic than average (Sharma & others, 1998). In a Swedish study, infant adoptees grew up with fewer problems than were experienced by children whose biological mothers had initially registered them for adoption but then decided to raise the children themselves (Bohman & Sigvardsson, 1990). Clearly, to benefit from adoption, children need not have personalities that resemble those of their adoptive parents.

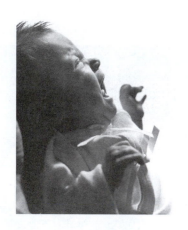

The greater uniformity of adoptive homes—mostly healthy, nurturing homes—helps explain the lack of striking differences when comparing child outcomes of different adoptive homes. (Stoolmiller, 1999)

Temperament Studies

As most parents will tell you after having their second child, babies differ even before gulping their first breath. Consider one quickly apparent aspect of personality. An infant's **temperament** includes inborn emotional excitability—whether reactive, intense, and fidgety, or easygoing, quiet, and placid. From the first weeks of life, "difficult" babies are more irritable, intense, and unpredictable. "Easy" babies are cheerful, relaxed, and predictable in feeding and sleeping (Chess & Thomas, 1987).

Temperament endures. Consider these findings:

+ The most emotionally reactive newborns tend also to be the most reactive 9-month-olds (Wilson & Matheny, 1986; Worobey & Blajda, 1989).
+ Four-month-olds who react to changing scenes with arched back, pumping legs, and crying are usually fearful and inhibited in their second year. Those who react with relaxed smiles are usually fearless and sociable in their second year (Kagan, 1990).
+ Exceptionally inhibited and fearful 2-year-olds often are still relatively shy as 8-year-olds; about half will become introverted adolescents (Kagan & others, 1992, 1994).
+ The most emotionally intense preschoolers tend to be relatively intense as young adults (Larsen & Diener, 1987).

In one study that is following more than 900 New Zealanders through time, emotionally reactive and impulsive 3-year-olds developed into somewhat more impulsive, aggressive, and conflict-prone 21-year-olds (Newman & others, 1997). Inhibited 3-year-olds still tended to be more cautious and unassertive 18 years later. Many shy, inhibited infants relax with age, but few fearless, spontaneous infants become shy.

Like human infants, infant monkeys vary in temperament. Some are timid and fearful, others more relaxed. Researcher Stephen Suomi (1987) placed infant monkeys that were genetically predisposed to be "uptight" or "easygoing" with foster mothers who were themselves uptight or easygoing. The result? Heredity overrode rearing. Compared with the easygoing monkeys, the uptight monkeys reacted more anxiously to stress, even when they were being raised by easygoing, nurturant foster mothers.

Heredity seems to predispose human temperament differences, too. Physiological tests reveal that anxious, high-strung

"Oh, he's cute, all right, but he's got the temperament of a car alarm."

human infants have high and variable heart rates and a reactive nervous system (Kagan & others, 1992). They become more physiologically aroused when facing new or strange situations. Compared with fraternal twins, twins who share identical genes are more likely to have similar temperaments (Emde & others, 1992; Gabbay, 1992; Robinson & others, 1992).

Genetic influences may also help explain why several studies find infants of Asian descent calmer, more placid, and less reactive than infants of European descent. That should not stun us, say Jerome Kagan and his colleagues (1994), because Europeans and Asians were "reproductively isolated for about 30,000 years, or about 1500 generations." There is a practical moral here, says Kagan (1995): We "should not automatically assume that every anxious child had an insensitive parent but should entertain the possibility that temperament" also makes the child.

Calm down!
Many Navajo babies have calmly accepted the cradleboard; Caucasian babies often protest vigorously (Freedman, 1979). Some psychologists take such findings to suggest that the rudiments of personality are to some extent genetically influenced.

Heritability

Using the twin and adoption methods, behavior geneticists can mathematically estimate the **heritability** of any trait—the extent to which variation among individuals is due to their differing genes. If the heritability of height is 90 percent, this does not mean that a 60-inch-tall woman can credit her genes for 54 inches and her environment for the other 6 inches. Rather, it means that we can attribute to genetic influence 50 percent of the observed height variation among people. The same logic applies to variations among people's intelligence or happiness or temperament. This point is so often misunderstood that I repeat: We can never say what percentage of an *individual's* personality or intelligence is inherited. Heritability refers instead to the extent to which *differences among people* are attributable to genes.

Even this conclusion must be qualified, because heritability can vary from study to study. If we were to follow humorist Mark Twain's (1835–1910) proposal to raise boys in barrels to age 12, feeding them through a hole, they would emerge with lower-than-normal intelligence scores. Yet, given their equal environments, their individual IQ score differences at age 12 could be explained only by their heredity. In other words, heritability for their differences would be near 100 percent. *As environments become more similar, heredity as a source of differences necessarily becomes more important.* If all schools were of uniform quality, all families equally loving, and all neighborhoods equally healthy, heritability—differences due to genes—would *increase* (because differences due to environment would decrease). At the other extreme, if all people had similar heredities but were raised in drastically different environments (barrels versus advantaged homes), heritability would be much lower.

Group Differences

If genetic influences help explain individual differences in traits such as aggressiveness, can the same be said of group differences between men and women, or between people of a different race? Not necessarily. Individual differences in height and weight are highly heritable. Yet nutritional rather than genetic influences explain

■ **temperament** a person's characteristic emotional reactivity and intensity.

■ **heritability** the proportion of variation among individuals that we can attribute to genes. The heritability of a trait may vary, depending on the range of populations and environments studied.

why, as a group, today's adults are taller and heavier than those of a century ago. The two groups differ, but not because human genes have changed in a mere century's eyeblink of time. As with height and weight, so with personality and intelligence scores: Heritable individual differences need not imply heritable group differences. If some individuals are genetically disposed to be more aggressive than others, that needn't explain why some groups are more aggressive than others. Putting people in a new social context changes their aggressiveness.

Nature Enables Nurture

Among our similarities, the most important—the behavioral hallmark of our species— is an enormous adaptive capacity. Some human traits, such as having two eyes, de- velop the same in virtually every environment. But most psychologically interesting traits are expressed in particular environments. We all are driven to eat, but depend- ing on our culturally learned tastes, we may have a yen for fish eyes, black bean salad, or chicken legs. Go barefoot for a summer and you will develop toughened, callused feet—a biological adaptation to friction. Meanwhile, your shoed neighbor will remain a tenderfoot. The difference between the two of you is, of course, an effect of envi- ronment. But it is also the product of a biological mechanism. Our shared biology en- ables our developed diversity (Buss, 1991).

An analogy may help: Genes and environment—nature and nurture—work to- gether like two hands clapping, with the environment reacting to and shaping what nature predisposes. Thus, asking whether your intelligence or personality is more a product of your genes or environment is like asking whether the area of a field is more the result of its length or width. We could, however, ask whether the *differing* areas of various fields are more the result of differences in their length or width. For psychological traits, human differences are nearly always the result of both genetic and environmental variations. Thus (to give a preview of coming attractions), eating disorders are genetically influenced: Some individuals are more at risk than others. But culture also bends the twig, for eating disorders are a contemporary Western cul- tural phenomenon. Likewise, criminal and aggressive tendencies are known to be ge- netically influenced. But genetic changes did not explain the explosion in juvenile violence during the 1980s and early 1990s.

Gene-Environment Interaction

To say that genes and experience are *both* important is true, but it is an oversimplifi- cation. More precisely, their effects intertwine. Imagine two babies, one genetically predisposed to be attractive, sociable, and easygoing, the other less so. Assume further that the first baby attracts more affectionate and stimulating care than the second and so develops into a warmer and more outgoing person. As the two children grow older, the more naturally outgoing one more often seeks activities and friends that encourage further social confidence.

What has caused their resulting personality differences? We can't say simply that individual personalities are *x* percent due to genes and *y* percent to experience, because neither heredity nor experience dances alone. Our genetically influenced traits *evoke* significant responses in others. Thus, an aggressive child may be yelled at by a teacher who talks warmly to the child's model classmates.

This helps explain why identical twins reared in different families recall their parents' warmth as remarkably similar—almost as similar as if they had had the same parents (Plomin & others, 1988, 1991, 1994). Fraternal twins recall their early family life more differently—even if reared in the same family! "Children experience us as different parents, depending on their own qualities," notes Scarr (1990). Moreover, as we grow older we also *select* environments well suited to our natures.

"To reveal and identify that which unites us rather than that which divides us [is] the principal challenge of the coming century and the coming millennium."

Vaclev Havel, *The Art of the Impossible,* **1997**

So, from conception onward, we are the product of a cascade of **interactions** between our genetic predispositions and our surrounding environments. Our genes affect how people react to and influence us. Biological appearances have social consequences. Asking whether genes or experiences are more important is therefore like asking whether an engine or a steering wheel is more important for driving a car. So, forget nature *versus* nurture; think nature *via* nurture.

The New Frontier: Molecular Genetics

Behavior geneticists have progressed from asking "Do genes influence behavior?" to asking "How much?" and "Which ones?" The new frontier of behavior-genetics research is the "bottom up" **molecular genetics** quest to identify the *specific genes* that influence behavior. As psychologist Robert Plomin (1997) observes, "The DNA train [is] pulling out of the station," and psychologists are climbing aboard.

It seems clear that most human traits are influenced by a combination of genes. For example, twin and adoption studies tell us that heredity influences body weight, but there is no single "obesity gene." More likely, some genes influence how quickly the stomach tells the brain "I'm full." Others might dictate how efficiently the body makes extra calories into fat, how much fuel the muscles need, and how many calories are burned off by fidgeting (Vogel, 1999). There surely are many genes that predict obesity. The goal of molecular behavior genetics is to find some of the many genes that contribute to a trait such as obesity, reading ability, or shyness.

In dozens of labs worldwide, molecular geneticists are teaming with psychologists in search of genes that put people at risk for genetically influenced disorders. In one notable example, a worldwide research effort is under way to sleuth the genes that make one vulnerable to the emotional swings of bipolar disorder (formerly known as manic-depressive disorder). To tease out the implicated genes, molecular geneticists seek links between certain genes or chromosome segments and specific disorders. First, they find families that have had the disorder across several generations. Then they draw blood from both affected and unaffected family members and examine their DNA, looking for differences. "The most powerful potential for DNA," note Robert Plomin and John Crabbe (2000), "is to predict risk so that steps can be taken to prevent problems before they happen."

"Heredity deals the cards; environment plays the hand."

Psychologist Charles L. Brewer, 1990

"We predict that DNA will revolutionize psychological research and treatment early in the twenty-first century."

Robert Plomin and John Crabbe (in press)

■ **interaction** the effect of one factor (such as environment) depends on another factor (such as heredity).

■ **molecular genetics** the subfield of biology that studies the molecular structure and function of genes.

"I thought that sperm-bank donors remained anonymous."

With this benefit come the risks of labeling people in ways that might lead to discrimination or self-fulfilling prophecies, as when a child is said to be at risk for learning disorders. Prenatal screening also poses significant ethical issues. Already it is easily possible for expectant parents to ascertain their offspring's sex. In China and India, where boys are highly valued, such testing has enabled sex-selective abortions that have resulted in millions—yes, millions—of "missing women." It also is becoming possible (by a new technique for sorting sperm carrying male or female chromosomes) to choose a child's sex before conception with reasonable chances of success. Genetic tests can now also reveal who is at risk for at least a dozen diseases. Before long, researchers may also identify genes that influence depression, schizophrenia, aggressiveness, reading disability, alcoholism, body weight, and sexual orientation. Aided by new techniques for scanning relevant DNA snips, medical personnel may soon be able to give would-be parents a read-out on how their fetus' genes differ from the normal pattern and what this might mean.

These blueprints for "designer babies" are, of course, constrained by the reality that it takes many genes to influence behavior in combination with complex environments. But assuming it were possible, should prospective parents take their eggs and sperm to a genetics lab for screening before combining them to produce an embryo? Before scoffing at this possibility, recall that two decades ago people were horrified at the prospect of in vitro fertilization ("test-tube" conception). Today, infertile couples demand it. A half-century ago, people worried about the kind of control that novelist Aldous Huxley imagined in his *Brave New World*, in which government social engineers bred hothouse babies genetically assigned to roles such as clever "alphas" and dim-witted "epsilons." In today's more plausible new world, notes Robert Wright (1999), millions of parents will freely select for health, and perhaps for brains, beauty, and athleticism. But as always, progress is a two-edged sword, raising both hopeful possibilities and difficult problems. By "selecting" out certain traits, we may deprive ourselves of future Handels and van Goghs, Churchills and Lincolns, Tolstoys and Dickinsons—troubled people all.

REVIEW AND REFLECT:

Genetic Influences on Behavior

Our genes provide the blueprint for our biology; does this mean they determine our behaviors?

Genes, segments of complex DNA molecules that form the chromosomes, are the biochemical units of heredity. They provide the blueprint for protein molecules, the building blocks of our physical and behavioral development. Our genetic predispositions help explain our behaviors, but they do not determine them.

How do evolutionary psychologists use natural selection to explain behavior tendencies?

Evolutionary psychologists study how natural selection has shaped our universal behavior tendencies. They reason that if organisms vary, if only some mature to produce surviving offspring, and if certain inherited behavior tendencies assist that survival, then nature must select those tendencies. Critics maintain that evolutionary psychologists make too many hindsight explanations.

How do behavior geneticists explain individual differences?

Behavior geneticists explore our individual differences using methods such as twin, adoption, and temperament studies. By such methods they identify the heritability of various traits and disorders.

Studies of the inheritance of temperament, and of twins and adopted children, provide scientific support for the idea that nature *and* nurture influence one's developing personality. Genes and environment, biological and social factors, direct our life courses as their effects intertwine.

Molecular geneticists are on a fast-moving frontier in their work to identify the specific genes that influence behaviors.

Terms and Concepts to Remember

chromosomes, p. 86
DNA (deoxyribonucleic acid), p. 86
genes, p. 86
genome, p. 86
natural selection, p. 88
mutations, p. 88
evolutionary psychology, p. 88
gender, p. 89

behavior genetics, p. 92
environment, p. 92
identical twins, p.92
fraternal twins, p. 92
temperament, p. 96
heritability, p. 97
interaction, p. 99
molecular genetics, p. 99

Test Yourself

5.1. If nucleotides are the "letters," and genes are the "words," _____ are the "books" that hold all this information.
 a. DNA
 b. nuclei
 c. chromosomes
 d. cells

5.2. When the egg and sperm unite, each contributes
 a. one chromosome pair.
 b. 23 chromosomes.
 c. 23 chromosome pairs.
 d. an *XY* chromosome.

5.3. Evolutionary psychologists focus on the
 a. ways in which we differ from one another.
 b. links between biology and behavior.
 c. natural selection of the fittest adaptations.
 d. random assignment of genes over several generations.

5.4. Fraternal twins result when
 a. a single egg is fertilized by a single sperm and then splits.
 b. a single egg is fertilized by two sperm and then splits.
 c. two eggs are fertilized by two sperm.
 d. two eggs are fertilized by a single sperm.

5.5. Adoption studies seek to reveal genetic influences on personality mainly by
 a. comparing adopted children with nonadopted children.
 b. evaluating whether adopted children more closely resemble their adoptive parents or their biological parents.
 c. studying the effect of prior neglect on adopted children.
 d. studying the effect of one's age at adoption.

5.6. Although development is lifelong, there is stability of personality over time. For example,
 a. most personality traits emerge in infancy and persist throughout life.
 b. temperament tends to remain stable throughout life.
 c. few people change significantly after adolescence.
 d. people tend to undergo greater personality changes as they age.

5.7. The heritability of a trait may vary, depending on the range of populations and environments studied. To say that the heritability of intelligence is 60 percent means that 60 percent of
 a. intelligence is due to genetic factors.
 b. the similarities among groups of people are attributable to genes.
 c. the *variation* in intelligence within a group of people is attributable to genetic factors.
 d. intelligence is due to the mother's genes and the rest is due to the father's genes.

5.8. Molecular geneticists are now working with psychologists to ask
 a. do genes influence behavior?
 b. which genes influence which behaviors?
 c. how does culture bend the genetic influence?
 d. how many genes are there?

Review

- Explain the relationship among chromosomes, DNA, genes, genome, and nucleotides.

- What is heritability?

Reflect

- Whose reasoning do you find most persuasive—that of evolutionary psychologists or their critics? Why?

- Would you want genetic tests on your unborn offspring, in the uterus? What would you do if you knew your child would have hemophilia? Schizophrenia? A learning disability? Would society benefit or lose if such embryos were aborted?

Answers to the Test Yourself and Review questions can be found in the green appendix at the end of the book.

6 Environmental Influences on Behavior

Preview Questions: To what extent are our lives shaped by parental nurture, prenatal nutrition, early stimulation, and peer influences? How do cultural norms and gender roles affect our behavior?

Genetic influences explain roughly 40 to 50 percent of our individual variations in many personality traits. When asked what accounts for the rest, many people presume it is parental nurture. Parental influence is "enormously powerful in determining what happens to a child," say Sylvia Ann Hewlett and Cornel West (1998, pp. 47–48). "Whether a child acquires discipline and self-esteem and becomes a well-adjusted, productive person is largely a function of parental input" plus communal support.

But Peter Neubauer and Alexander Neubauer (1990, pp. 20–21) illustrate how, with hindsight, we may inappropriately credit or blame our parents:

> Identical twin men, now age thirty, were separated at birth and raised in different countries by their respective adoptive parents. Both kept their lives neat—neat to the point of pathology. Their clothes were preened, appointments met precisely on time, hands scrubbed regularly to a raw, red color. When the first was asked why he felt the need to be so clean, his answer was plain.

> "My mother. When I was growing up she always kept the house perfectly ordered. She insisted on every little thing returned to its proper place, the clocks—we had dozens of clocks—each set to the same noonday chime. She insisted on this, you see. I learned from her. What else could I do?"

> The man's identical twin, just as much a perfectionist with soap and water, explained his own behavior this way: "The reason is quite simple. I'm reacting to my mother, who was an absolute slob."

How Much Credit (or Blame) Do Parents Deserve?

Parents typically feel enormous pride in their children's successes, and guilt or shame over their failures. They beam when folks offer congratulations for the child who wins an award. They wonder where they went wrong with the child repeatedly called into the principal's office. Freudian psychiatry and psychology have been among the sources of such ideas, by blaming problems from asthma to schizophrenia on "bad mothering." And society reinforces such parent-blaming: Believing that parents shape their children as a potter molds clay, people readily praise parents for their children's virtues and blame them for their children's vices. Popular culture of the 1990s endlessly proclaimed the psychological harm parents inflict on their fragile children. "The major source of human misery" is the "neglected, wounded child" within each of us, claimed author-lecturer John Bradshaw (1990, p. 7). Having survived our "toxic" parents, today's "adult children" have swarmed to "recovery groups."

But do parents really produce future adults with a wounded child within by being (take your pick from the toxic lists) overbearing—or uninvolved? Pushy—or ineffectual? Overprotective—or distant? Are children really so easily wounded by well-meaning but occasionally exhausted parents who don't always successfully cross the psychological tightrope? If so, should we then blame our parents for our failings, and ourselves for our

Even among chimpanzees, when one infant is hurt by another, the victim's mother will often attack the offender's mother (Goodall, 1968).

children's failings? Should we shame the parents of troubled children or pass city ordinances that punish them for their children's misdeeds? Does all the talk of wounding fragile children through normal parental mistakes trivialize the brutality of real abuse?

If parental handling shapes children's personalities, then children who share the same parents should be somewhat similar, yes? But as we have seen, behavior geneticists have repeatedly found this to be untrue. Shared environmental influences—including the home influences that siblings share—typically account for less than 10 percent of their personality differences (though it accounts for more of their beliefs and values). In the words of behavior geneticists Robert Plomin and Denise Daniels (1987), "Two children in the same family [are on average] as different from one another as are pairs of children selected randomly from the population." To developmental psychologist Sandra Scarr (1993), this implies that "parents should be given less credit for kids who turn out great and blamed less for kids who don't." Although environments matter, "extreme environmentalism is cruel," contends Michael Gazzaniga (1992, p. 202). Why? "Because it suggests to the parents that their child has been warped by something they did." It indeed may be scary to realize how risky it is to have and raise children. In procreation, a woman and a man shuffle their gene decks and deal a life-forming hand to their child-to-be, who is then subjected to countless influences beyond their control. Keeping in mind that lives are formed by influences beyond parents' control is another reason for caution in crediting parents for their children's achievements and blaming them for their children's troubling traits. And if our children are not formless blobs sculpted by parental nurture, then perhaps we parents can relax a bit more and love our children for who they are.

If parental influence on personality is more limited than popular psychology supposes, what aspects of the environment do matter? Psychologists searching for environmental influences they know exist are like astronomers seeking the hidden "dark" matter which they know the universe contains. It's there, somewhere, but where? We will glean answers throughout this book. Here, for starters, are five: prenatal environment, early learning experiences, peer influence, culture, and gender.

> "If you want to blame your parents for your own adult problems, you are entitled to blame the genes they gave you, but you are not entitled—by any facts I know—to blame the way they treated you. . . . We are not prisoners of our past."
>
> Martin Seligman, *What You Can Change and What You Can't*, 1994

Prenatal Environment

"Nurture" begins in the womb, as embryos receive differing nutrition and varying levels of exposure to toxic agents. Even identical twins may receive not-so-identical prenatal nurture. Some identical twins share the same placenta, and thus a more similar prenatal environment (though one might get a richer blood supply and may weigh more at birth). Other twins have separate placentas (**FIGURE 6.1**). In this arrangement, one placenta sometimes has a more advantageous placement that provides better nourishment and therefore a better placental barrier against viruses. Early indications are that, compared with same-placenta identical twins, those who develop with separate placentas are somewhat less similar in their psychological traits (Phelps & others, 1997).

FIGURE 6.1 Two placental arrangements in identical twins
Identical twins may (a) have separate placentas and blood sources, as do all fraternal twins. Or they may (b) share the same placental blood. Researchers are now studying how this variation predicts later differences between identical twins. (From Davis & others, 1995.)

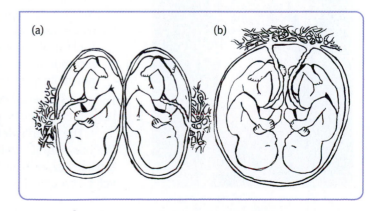

Experience and Brain Development

Experience helps develop the brain's neural connections. Even if forgotten, early learning helps prepare our brains for thought and language, and also for later experiences. But how do early experiences leave their "marks" in the brain? Mark Rosenzweig and David Krech reared some young rats in solitary confinement and others in a communal playground (**FIGURE 6.2**). When their brains were then analyzed, the rats who died with the most toys had won. Those living in the enriched environment, which simulated a natural environment, usually developed a heavier and thicker brain cortex. Rosenzweig (1984; Renner & Rosenzweig, 1987) was so surprised by this discovery that he repeated the experiment several times before publishing his findings. The effects are great enough that, shown brief video clips of rats, you could tell from their activity and curiosity whether their rearing was impoverished or enriched (Renner & Renner, 1993). Bryan Kolb and Ian Whishaw (1998) report that rats housed for 60 days in enriched environments showed brain weight increases of 7 to 10 percent, and the number of synapses mushroomed by about 20 percent—"an extraordinary change!" Such results have motivated improvements in the environments we provide for laboratory, farm, and zoo animals—and for children in institutions.

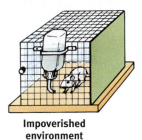

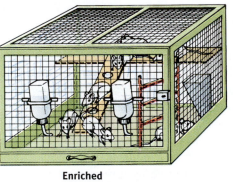

Impoverished environment — **Rat brain cell** — **Enriched environment** — **Rat brain cell**

Several research teams have found that the stimulation of touch or massage benefits infant rats and premature babies (Field, 1998; Meaney & others, 1988). "Handled" infants of both species gain weight more rapidly and develop faster neurologically. William Greenough and his University of Illinois colleagues (1987) further discovered that repeated experiences modify a rat's neural tissue—at the very spot in the brain that processes the experience. After brain maturation provides us with an abundance of neural connections, experience preserves our activated connections while allowing our unused connections to degenerate. The result by puberty is a massive loss of unemployed connections.

Here, then, at the juncture of nurture and nature, is where a child's environment normally activates and preserves connections that, given impoverished experiences, might have died off from disuse. There is a biological reality to early childhood education. Consider:

Stringing the circuits young
String musicians who started playing before age 12 have larger and more complex neuron circuits controlling the note-making left-hand fingers than do string musicians whose training started after age 13 (Elbert & others, 1995).

+ Children from impoverished environments score better on intelligence tests given at age 12, if given stimulating infant care (Ramey & Ramey, 1992).
+ During early childhood—while the excess connections are still on call—youngsters can most easily master the grammar and accent of another language. Lacking any exposure to language (written or signed) before adolescence, the person will never master any language.
+ Lacking visual experience during the early years, people whose vision is restored by cataract removal never achieve normal perceptions. The brain cells normally assigned to vision have died or been diverted to other uses.

For us to have optimum brain development, normal stimulation during the early years is critical. The maturing brain seems governed by a rule: Use it or lose it.

The brain's development does not, however, end with childhood. Throughout life our neural tissue is changing. Sights and smells, touches and tugs activate and strengthen some neural pathways while others weaken from disuse. Similar to pathways through a forest, less traveled paths gradually disappear, popular paths are broadened. Our genes dictate our overall brain architecture, but experience directs the details. If a monkey is trained to push a lever with a finger several thousand times a day, the brain tissue that controls the finger changes to reflect the experience. Human brains work similarly. The wiring of Eric Clapton's brain reflects the thousands of hours he has spent playing the guitar. Similarly, while learning to keyboard or rollerblade or perform a laboratory task, we perform with increasing skill as our brain incorporates the learning (**FIGURE 6.3**). Experience nurtures nature.

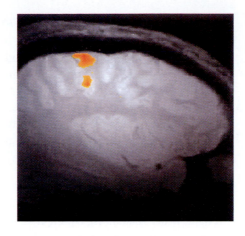
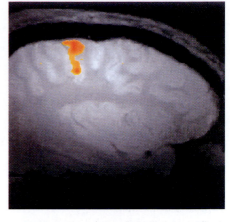

FIGURE 6.3 A trained brain
A well-learned finger-tapping task activates more motor cortex neurons (orange area, right) than were active in the same brain before training (left).

Peer Influence

As children develop, experience sculpts their brains. But what types of experience are potent? Experiences with peers powerfully socialize children and youth, notes Judith Harris (1998). Consider:

+ Preschoolers who disdain a certain food despite parents' urgings often will eat the food if put at a table with a group of children who like it.
+ A child who hears English spoken with one accent at home and another in the neighborhood and at school will invariably adopt the accent of the peers, not the parents. Moreover, immigrant children who are placed in peer groups of nonimmigrants quickly lose their parents' culture. "When in Rome, they become Romans," notes Harris. "Even if their parents happen to be British or Chinese or Mesquakie."
+ Direct parental influences on smoking are less important than many people suppose. Rather, teens who start smoking typically have *friends* who model smoking, who suggest its pleasures, and who offer cigarettes (Rose & others, 1999).

Part of the similarity to peers may result from a "selection effect," as kids seek out peers with similar attitudes and interests. Those who smoke (or don't) may select as friends those who also smoke (or don't). But our sensitivity to peers makes biological sense, suggests Harris (1998). Parental nurture is essential to our early survival, and parental influence is especially discernible while children are in the home. But in the long run, we are destined to play with, work with, and mate with peers. Small wonder that nature predisposes us to be acutely sensitive to their styles and opinions (another example of how our evolved nature *enables* our cultural nurture). That being so, intervention programs for youth had best be aimed at a whole school or neighborhood and not just at isolated individuals. If the vapors of a toxic climate are seeping into a child's life, that climate—not just the child—needs reforming.

Predictably, other psychologists remind us that there is some power to parenting (Eisenberg & others, 1998a,b). The power of parenting to shape our differences is clearest at the extremes—the abused who become abusive, the neglected who become neglectful, the loved but firmly handled children who become self-confident and socially competent. The power of the family environment also shows up in the remarkable academic and vocational successes of children of the refugee Asian boat people—successes attributed to close-knit, supportive, even demanding families (Caplan & others, 1992).

Parental nurture is like nutrition. It may not matter much whether we get our protein from eating chicken or beans and rice, but we must have food. Likewise, it may not matter whether we grew up with parents who toilet trained us early or late, but it sure helps to have someone we belong to and who cares about us.

Peer power
As we develop we must play, work, mate, and partner with peers. No wonder children and youth are so sensitive and responsive to peer influences.

Howard Gardner (1998) concludes that parents and peers are complementary:

Parents are more important when it comes to education, discipline, responsibility, orderliness, charitableness, and ways of interacting with authority figures. Peers are more important for learning cooperation, for finding the road to popularity, for inventing styles of interaction among people of the same age. Youngsters may find their peers more interesting, but they will look to their parents when contemplating their own futures. Moreover, parents choose the neighborhoods and schools that supply the peers.

Culture

Compared with the narrow path taken by flies, fish, and foxes, nature has built for us a longer, wider road along which environment drives us. The mark of our species—nature's great gift to us—is our ability to learn and adapt. We come equipped with a huge cerebral hard drive ready to receive many gigabytes of cultural software.

Culture is the behaviors, ideas, attitudes, and traditions shared by a large group of people and transmitted from one generation to the next (Brislin, 1988). If we all lived in homogeneous ethnic groups in separate regions of the world, as some people still do, cultural diversity would be less relevant. In Japan, 99 percent of the country's 126 million people are Japanese. Internal cultural differences are therefore minimal compared with those found in Los Angeles, where the public schools recently taught 82 different languages, or in Toronto or Vancouver, where minorities are one-third the population and many are immigrants (as are 17 percent of Canadians) (Iyer, 1993; Statistics Canada, 1999). I am ever mindful that the readers of this book are culturally diverse. You reach from Australia to Africa, from Singapore to Sweden.

Variation Across Cultures

We see our adaptability in cultural variations among our beliefs and our values, in how we raise our children and bury our dead, in what we wear (or whether we wear anything at all). Riding along with a unified culture is like riding a bike with the wind: As it carries us along, we hardly notice it is there. When we try riding *against* the wind we feel its force. Face to face with a different culture, we become aware of the cultural winds. Visiting Europe, most North Americans are struck by the smaller cars, the left-handed use of the fork, the uninhibited attire on the beaches. Stationed in Saudi Arabia, European and American soldiers alike realized how liberal their home cultures were. Arriving in North America, visitors from some cultures struggle to understand why many people wear their dirty *street* shoes in the house, or why people find it fun to eat a picnic lunch out in the woods amid flies and ants.

Each cultural group evolves its own **norms**—the rules for accepted and expected behavior. Muslims, for example, use only the right hand's fingers for eating. The Japanese have norms for taking off street shoes, and the British have a norm for orderly waiting in line. Sometimes social expectations seem oppressive: "Why should it matter how I dress?" Yet, norms grease the social machinery. Prescribed, well-learned behaviors free us from self-preoccupation. When we know when to clap or bow, which fork to pick up first at the dinner party, and what sorts of gestures and compliments are appropriate, we can relax and enjoy one another without fear of embarrassment or insult. Likewise, having a well-understood norm for greeting people in one's culture—by shaking hands or kissing each cheek—precludes awkward moments of indecision about whether to lead with one's hand or cheek.

Uniform requirements
People in individualist Western cultures sometimes see traditional Japanese culture as confining. But from the Japanese perspective the same tradition expresses a "serenity that comes to people who know exactly what to expect from each other" (Weiss & others, 1984).

When cultures collide, their differing norms often befuddle. For example, if someone invades our **personal space**—the portable buffer zone we like to maintain around our bodies—we feel uncomfortable. Scandinavians, North Americans, and the British prefer more personal space than do Latin Americans, Arabs, and the French (Sommer, 1969). At a social gathering, a Mexican seeking a comfortable conversation distance may end up walking around a room with a backpedaling American. (You can experience this at a party by playing Space Invader as you talk with someone.) To the American, the Mexican may seem intrusive; to the Mexican, the American may seem cold and standoffish.

Cultures also vary in their expressiveness. Those whose roots are in northern European culture often perceive people from Mediterranean cultures as warm and charming, but inefficient. The Mediterraneans, in turn, see northern Europeans as efficient, but cold and preoccupied with punctuality (Triandis, 1981). When cultures mix, misunderstandings are commonplace. This was disastrously apparent after Iraqi representatives met U.S. Secretary of State James Baker in Geneva on January 9, 1991, in a last-minute effort to avert war. Baker clearly warned that the United States would attack Iraq if it did not leave Kuwait. But he said it so calmly that Saddam Hussein's half-brother reported, "The Americans will not attack. . . . They are calm. They are not angry." The Iraqi style, by contrast, was expressive to the point of exaggeration: "If you attack you will face the mother of all battles!" Cross-cultural expert Harry Triandis (1994) speculates that had Baker communicated in a traditional (rather than Westernized) Iraqi style—by banging the table, looking ferocious, and snarling, "We are going to make hamburgers out of you," his message would have been read correctly.

Cultures vary in their pace of life, too. A British businessperson may feel frustrated by a Latin American client who arrives 30 minutes after the time set for lunch. People from time-conscious Japan—where bank clocks keep exact time, pedestrians walk briskly, and postal clerks fill requests speedily—may find themselves growing impatient when visiting Indonesia, where clocks keep less accurate time and the pace of life is more leisurely (Levine & Norenzayan, 1999). In adjusting to their host countries, U.S. Peace Corps volunteers reported that two of their greatest culture shocks, after the language difference, were the differing pace of life and the people's differing sense of punctuality (Spradley & Phillips, 1972).

Variation Over Time

Consider, too, how rapidly cultures may change over time. English poet Geoffrey Chaucer (1342–1400) is separated from a modern Britisher by only 20 generations, but the two would converse with great difficulty. In the thinner slice of history since 1960, most Western cultures have changed with remarkable speed. Middle-class people fly to places they once only read about, e-mail those they once snail-mailed, and work in air-conditioned comfort where they once sweltered. They enjoy the convenience of on-line holiday shopping, make and take calls on cell phones anywhere, and—enriched by doubled per-person real income—eat out two and a half times as often as did their parents back in the culture of 1960. With greater economic independence, today's women are more likely to marry for love and less likely to endure abusive relationships out of economic need. Various minorities enjoy expanded human rights.

But some changes seem not so wonderfully positive. Had you fallen asleep in the United States in 1960 and awakened at the end of the millennium, you would have opened your eyes to a culture with a doubled rate of divorce, a tripled rate of teen suicide, a quadrupled rate of reported juvenile violent crime, a quintupled prison population, and escalating depression (Myers, 2000). Americans also are spending more hours at work, fewer hours sleeping, and fewer hours with friends and family

Culture influences personal space
Behavior that is seen as appropriate in one culture may violate the norms of another group. In Arab countries, such as Morocco, people typically require less personal space than do members of some European and North American groups.

Cross-cultural communication can also suffer in translation, as in these signs for English-speaking tourists (Lederer, 1987; Triandis, 1994):

- *In a Greek tailor shop:* "Because of a big rush, we will execute customers in strict rotation."
- *An Italian laundry:* "Ladies, leave your clothes here and spend the afternoon having a good time."
- *A Danish airline:* "We take your bags and send them in all directions."
- *A Moscow hotel room:* "If this is your first visit to the USSR, you are welcome to it."
- *A detour sign in Japan:* "Stop: Drive Sideways."

■ **culture** the enduring behaviors, ideas, attitudes, and traditions shared by a large group of people and transmitted from one generation to the next.

■ **norm** an understood rule for accepted and expected behavior. Norms prescribe "proper" behavior.

■ **personal space** the buffer zone we like to maintain around our bodies.

■ **memes** self-replicating ideas, fashions, and innovations passed from person to person.

(Frank, 1999; Putnam, 2000). Similar cultural transformations have occurred in Canada, Britain, the European continent, Australia, and New Zealand.

Whether we love or loathe these changes, we cannot fail to be impressed by their breathtaking speed. And we cannot explain them by changes in the human gene pool, which evolves far too slowly to account for high-speed cultural transformations. Cultures vary, cultures change, and cultures shape our lives.

So rapidly can cultural fashions, ideas, inventions, and habits change that evolutionary psychologists have coined a term—**memes**—for these self-replicating cultural mutations. Memes, like genes, compete to get copied, not into our cells but into our memories and media. As genes create bodies, so memes create our minds and our cultures, notes Susan Blackmore (1999). Memes may be true or uplifting (arithmetic, Bach's music), neutral (new pronunciations), or false (alien abduction reports). Ironically, the fast-spreading concept of "meme" is itself a meme, an idea passed from person to person.

Culture and Child-Rearing

Child-rearing practices are not immune to the variations in cultural values from one time and place to another. Do you prefer children who are independent or children who comply with what others think?

If you live in a Westernized culture, the odds are you prefer the former. Westernized countries derived from northern Europe are noted for their *individualism* (giving priority to group goals and identity). Most parents in these societies want their children to think for themselves. "You are responsible for yourself," Western families and schools tell their children. "Follow your conscience. Be true to yourself. Discover your gifts. Think through your personal needs." But these cultural values represent change over time. A half-century ago, Western parents placed greater priority on obedience, respect, and sensitivity to others (Alwin, 1990; Remley, 1988). "Be true to your traditions," they taught their children. "Be loyal to your heritage and country. Show respect toward your parents and other superiors."

Unlike most Westerners, who now raise their children to be independent, many Asians and Africans favor *collectivism* (giving priority to group goals and identity). They tend to live in communal cultures, cultures that focus on cultivating emotional closeness. Rather than being given their own bedrooms and entrusted to day care, infants and toddlers typically sleep with their mothers and spend their days close to a family member (Morelli & others, 1992; Whiting & Edwards, 1988). Children of communal cultures grow up with a stronger sense of "family self"—a feeling that what shames the child shames the family, and what brings honor to the family, brings honor to the self. Compared with Westerners, people in Japanese and Chinese cultures, for example, exhibit greater shyness toward strangers and greater concern for social harmony and loyalty (Bond, 1988; Cheek & Melchior, 1990; Triandis, 1994). "My parents will be disappointed in me" is a concern of 7 percent of American and Italian teenagers and 14 percent of Australian teens, but nearly 25 percent of teens in Taiwan and Japan (Atkinson, 1988).

Children across place and time have thrived under various child-rearing systems. Upper-class British parents traditionally handed off routine caregiving to nannies, then sent their children off to boarding school at about age 11 or 12. Their children generally grew up to be pillars of British society, just like their parents and their boarding-school peers. In the African Gusii society, babies nurse freely but spend most of the day on their mother's back—with lots of body contact but little face-to-face and language interaction. When the mother becomes pregnant, the toddler is weaned and handed over to someone else, often an older sibling. Westerners may wonder about the negative effects of this lack of verbal interaction, but then the African Gusii would in turn wonder about Western mothers pushing their babies around in strollers and leaving them in playpens and car seats (Small, 1997). Such diversity in child-rearing cautions us against presuming that our culture's way is the only way to rear children successfully.

Parental involvement promotes development
Parents in every culture facilitate their children's discovery of their world, but cultures differ in what they deem important. Asian cultures place more emphasis on school and hard work than does North American culture. This may help explain why Japanese and Taiwanese children get higher scores on mathematics achievement tests.

Developmental Similarities Across Groups

Because we are so mindful of how others differ from us, we often fail to notice the similarities predisposed by our shared biology. Cross-cultural research can help us by leading us to appreciate both our cultural diversity *and* our human kinship. Compared with the person-to-person differences within groups, the differences between groups are small. Regardless of our culture, we humans share the same life cycle. We all speak to our infants in similar ways and respond similarly to their coos and cries (Bornstein & others, 1992a,b). All over the world, the children of parents who are warm and supportive feel better about themselves and are less hostile than are the children of parents who are punitive and rejecting (Rohner, 1986; Scott & others, 1991).

Within a larger culture, ethnic subgroups may differ in their behavior and yet be influenced by the same underlying processes. Differences sometimes attributed to race may therefore actually result from other factors. David Rowe and his colleagues (1994, 1995) illustrate this with an analogy: Black men tend to have higher blood pressure than white men. Suppose that (1) in both groups salt consumption correlates with blood pressure, and (2) salt consumption is higher among black men than among white men. What then might we expect? A blood pressure "race difference" that may actually be a *diet* difference.

And that, say Rowe and his colleagues, parallels psychological findings: Behavior differences, like blood pressure differences, can result from differing inputs to the same process. Or so they concluded after distilling data from six major investigations of ethnic differences in behavior. Although American Hispanic, Asian, black, and white ethnic groups differed in levels of school achievement and delinquency, the differences were "no more than skin deep." The factors that influenced adolescent behavior in different ethnic groups were "statistically indistinguishable." To the extent that variables such as family structure, peer influences, and parental education predicted behavior in one ethnic group, they did so for other groups as well.

The available data so far have come mostly from the United States. But "it bodes well," say the researchers, "that developmental processes are alike in many subgroups of *Homo sapiens*." In surface ways we may differ, but as members together of one species we seem subject to the same psychological forces. As members of different ethnic and cultural groups, our languages vary, yet they reflect universal principles of grammar. Our tastes vary, yet they reflect common principles of hunger. Our social behaviors vary, but they reflect pervasive principles of human influence.

Gender

The shaping of gender illustrates that nature and nurture together predispose our behavior. Genes and hormones help define gender, but environment plays a key role, too. Cultural variations in gender roles demonstrate our capacity for learning and adapting.

The Nature of Gender

In domains where men and women have faced similar challenges—regulating heat with sweat, developing tastes that nourish, growing callouses where the skin meets friction—the sexes are similar. Even when describing the ideal mate, both men and women put traits such as "kind," "honest," and "intelligent" at the top of their lists. But in some domains pertinent to mating, evolutionary psychologists contend, guys act like guys whether they are elephants or elephant seals, rural peasants or corporate presidents. Such differences between the sexes arise, genetically, from their differing sex chromosomes and, physiologically, from their differing concentrations of sex hormones.

"When someone has discovered why men on Bond Street wear black hats he will at the same moment have discovered why men in Timbuctoo wear red feathers."

G. K. Chesterton, 1874–1936

Courtesy of Nick Downes.

■ **X chromosome** the sex chromosome found in both men and women. Females have two X chromosomes; males have one. An X chromosome from each parent produces a female.

■ **Y chromosome** the sex chromosome found only in males. When paired with an X sex chromosome from the mother, it produces a male child.

■ **testosterone** the most important of the male sex hormones. Both males and females have it, but the additional testosterone in males stimulates the growth of the male sex organs in the fetus and the development of the male sex characteristics during puberty.

■ **role** a set of expectations (norms) about a social position, defining how those in the position ought to behave.

■ **gender role** a set of expected behaviors for males and for females.

"Genes, by themselves, are like seeds dropped onto pavement: powerless to produce anything."

Primatologist Frans B. M. de Waal (1999)

Males and females are variations on a single form. Seven weeks after conception, you were anatomically indistinguishable from someone of the other sex. Then your genes activated your biological sex. Your sex is determined by your twenty-third pair of chromosomes, the sex chromosomes. The member of the pair that came from your mother was an **X chromosome**. From your father, you received the one chromosome out of 46 that is not unisex. This was either an X chromosome, making you a girl, or a **Y chromosome**, making you a boy. The Y chromosome contains a single gene that throws a master switch triggering the testes to develop and produce the principal male hormone, **testosterone**, which about the seventh week starts the development of external male sex organs. Another key period for sexual differentiation falls during the fourth and fifth prenatal months, when different brain-wiring patterns for males and females develop under the influence of testosterone and the female's ovarian hormones (Fitch & Dennenberg, 1998).

What do you suppose happens when glandular malfunction or hormone injections expose a female embryo to excess testosterone? These genetically female infants are born with masculine-appearing genitals, which can be corrected surgically. Until puberty, such females tend to act in more aggressive "tomboyish" ways than do most girls, and they dress and play in ways more typical of boys than of girls (Berenbaum & Hines, 1992; Ehrhardt, 1987). Given a choice of toys, they (like boys) are more likely to play with cars and guns than with dolls and crayons. Some develop into lesbians, but most—like nearly all girls with traditionally feminine interests—become heterosexual.

Is the behavior of these girls due to the prenatal hormones? If so, may we conclude that biological sex differences produce behavioral gender differences? Experiments with many species, from rats to monkeys, confirm that female embryos given male hormones will later exhibit atypically masculine appearance and more aggressive behavior (Hines & Green, 1991). Among humans, such girls frequently *look* masculine and are known to be "different," so perhaps people also treat them more like boys. Early exposure to sex hormones thus affects us both directly, in our biological appearance, and indirectly, by influencing social experiences that shape us. Like a sculptor's two hands shaping a lump of clay, nature and nurture work together.

The Nurture of Gender

Although biologically influenced, gender is also socially constructed. What biology initiates, culture accentuates.

Gender Roles

In psychology, as in the theater, a **role** refers to a cluster of prescribed actions—the behaviors we expect of those who occupy a particular social position. One set of norms defines our culture's **gender roles**—our expectations about the way men and women behave. Traditionally, men have initiated dates, driven the car, and picked up the check; women have decorated the house, bought and cared for the children's clothes, and selected the wedding gifts. In the United States, for example, married mothers do 90 percent of the laundry and 13 percent of the car maintenance (Acock & Demo, 1994). And, I do not have to tell you which parent, about 90 percent of the time in two-parent families, stays home with a sick child, arranges for the baby-sitter, or calls the doctor (Maccoby, 1995). Such formulas can smooth social relations, saving awkward decisions about who does what. But they often do so at a cost: If we deviate from such conventions, we may feel anxious.

Perhaps evolution predisposes men everywhere to be aggressive and tough in order to serve their reproductive goals, and predisposes women to the interpersonal skills that serve their reproductive goals (Archer, 1996). But we know that

"How is it gendered?"

gender roles are not rigidly fixed by evolution, because they vary across cultures. In nomadic societies of food-gathering people, there is minimal division of labor by sex. Boys and girls receive much the same upbringing. However, in agricultural societies, women remain close to home, working in the fields and staying with the children; men often roam more freely, herding cattle or sheep. Such societies typically socialize their children into distinct gender roles (Segall & others, 1990; Van Leeuwen, 1978).

Gender roles everywhere have tended to limit women's rights and power. "There are no human societies in which women dominate men," notes Felicia Pratto (1996). In 1997, women were 11.7 percent of the world's national legislators (Briscoe, 1997). They were only 3 percent of United Nations ambassadors, less than 1 percent of the presidents and prime ministers of the world's countries, and 0 percent of the Nobel awardees in economics since the prize began in 1901 (Sivard, 1995). Even in Israel's communal farms, the kibbutzim, where children have been reared together—dressed, bathed, and given toys without regard to gender—boys have grown up to do mostly masculine things and to dominate the leadership roles. Girls, although legally equal, play more with dolls and in adulthood seek more contact with children (Wilson, 1993).

Among the industrialized countries, gender roles vary widely. Women recently filled 48 percent of managerial positions in Switzerland, 28 percent in Austria, 17 percent in the United States, 3 percent in Ghana, and 2 percent in South Korea (Triandis, 1994). In North America, medicine and dentistry have been predominantly male occupations; in Russia, most medical doctors are women, as are most dentists in Denmark.

Gender roles vary over time as well as across cultures:

+ As we began the last century only one country—New Zealand—granted women the right to vote. As we ended it, only one democracy—Kuwait—did not (Briscoe, 1995).
+ With the flick of an apron, the number of U.S. college women hoping to be full-time homemakers plunged during the late 1960s and early 1970s (**FIGURE 6.4**).
+ In developing countries, too, gender roles are changing. Between 1970 and 1992, girls' enrollment in schools rose from 38 to 68 percent, shrinking the gender gap (UNICEF, 1996).

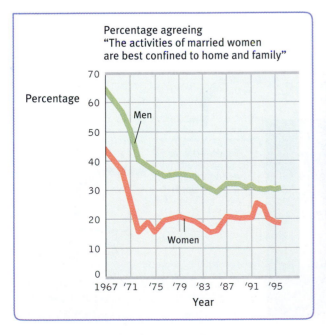

Gender roles have changed, but not every male has changed with them.

FIGURE 6.4 Changing attitudes about gender roles
U.S. college students' endorsement of the traditional view of women's roles has declined dramatically. Men's and women's attitudes have also converged. (From Dey & others, 1991; Sax & others, 1999.)

- **gender identity** one's sense of being male or female.

- **gender-typing** the acquisition of a traditional masculine or feminine role.

- **social learning theory** the theory that we learn social behavior by observing and imitating and by being rewarded or punished.

- **gender schema theory** the theory that children learn from their cultures a concept of what it means to be male and female and that they adjust their behavior accordingly.

Gender and Child-Rearing

Society assigns each of us—even those few whose biological sex is ambiguous at birth—to a *gender*, the social category of male or female. The inevitable result is our strong **gender identity**, our sense of being male or female. To varying extents, we also become **gender-typed**. That is, some boys more than others exhibit traditionally masculine traits and interests, and some girls more than others become distinctly feminine.

Social learning theory assumes that children learn gender-linked behaviors by observing and imitating and by being rewarded or punished. "Nicole, you're such a good mommy to your dolls"; "Big boys don't cry, Alex." But modeling and rewarding is not done by parents alone, because the differences in the way parents rear boys and girls aren't enough to explain gender-typing (Lytton & Romney, 1991). In fact, even when their families discourage traditional gender-typing, children organize themselves into "boy worlds" and "girl worlds," each guided by rules for what boys and girls do.

Gender schema theory combines social learning theory with cognition: Out of your struggles to comprehend the world came concepts, or *schemas*, including a schema for your own gender (Bem, 1987, 1993). Gender became a lens (a schema) through which you view your experiences (**FIGURE 6.5**). By age 3, language forces chil-dren to begin organizing their worlds on the basis of gender. English, for example, uses the pronouns *he* and *she*; other languages classify objects as masculine ("*le* train") or feminine ("*la* table"). Through language, dress, toys, and songs, social learning shapes gender schemas. Children then compare themselves with their concept of gender ("I am male—thus, masculine, strong, aggressive," or "I am female—therefore, feminine, sweet, and helpful") and adjust their behavior accordingly.

Gender-typing

Popular culture, from children's movies to professional wrestling, often appeals to boys' and girls' eagerness to categorize the world by gender, with images of macho men and coy, helpless women.

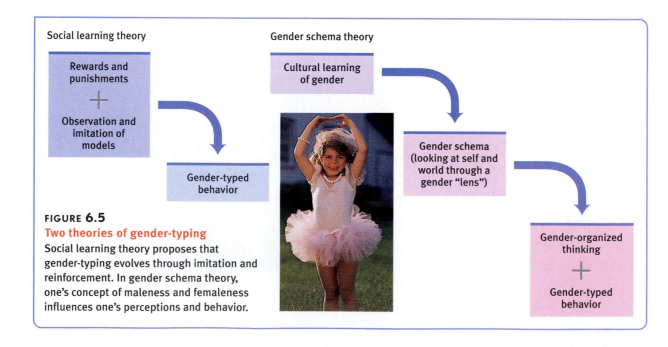

FIGURE 6.5

Two theories of gender-typing

Social learning theory proposes that gender-typing evolves through imitation and reinforcement. In gender schema theory, one's concept of maleness and femaleness influences one's perceptions and behavior.

Social learning theory

Rewards and punishments
+
Observation and imitation of models

→

Gender-typed behavior

Gender schema theory

Cultural learning of gender

→

Gender schema (looking at self and world through a gender "lens")

→

Gender-organized thinking
+
Gender-typed behavior

REVIEW AND REFLECT:

Environmental Influences on Behavior

To what extent are our lives shaped by parental nurture, prenatal nutrition, early stimulation, and peer influences?

Genetic influences are pervasive, but so are prenatal environments, early experiences, peer influences, and cultures. Sculpted by experience, neural interconnections multiply rapidly after birth.

How do cultural norms and gender roles affect our behavior?

Human variations across cultures and over time show how differing norms, or expectations, guide behavior. Cultures differ in their norms for personal space, expressiveness, and pace of life.

Gender illustrates the interaction between nature and nurture. Although males and females share similarly adaptive bodily procedures, differing sex chromosomes and differing concentrations of sex hormones lead to significant physiological sex differences. Yet gender differences vary widely depending upon cultural socialization through social learning and gender schemas.

Terms and Concepts to Remember

culture, p. 106	role, p. 110
norm, p. 106	gender role, p. 110
personal space, p. 107	gender identity, p. 112
memes, p. 108	gender-typing, p. 112
X chromosome, p. 110	social learning theory, p. 112
Y chromosome, p. 110	gender schema theory, p. 112
testosterone, p. 110	

Test Yourself

6.1. Normal levels of stimulation are important during infancy and early childhood because during these years,
   a. a rich environment can override a child's genetic limits.
   b. experience activates and preserves neural connections that might otherwise die off from disuse.
   c. experience stimulates the growth of new brain cells.
   d. experience triggers the production of human growth hormones.

6.2. Children and youth are particularly responsive to influences of their
   a. peers.   c. teachers and caretakers.
   b. fathers.   d. mothers.

6.3. In psychology, *personal space* refers to the portable buffer zone we like to maintain around our bodies. This space varies according to cultural norms. Which of the following prefer *less* personal space than the others?
   a. Americans   c. Arabs
   b. British   d. Scandinavians

6.4. Cultural values vary over time and place. Western cultures are to _____ as Asian and African cultures are to _____ .
   a. obedience; social harmony
   b. independence; emotional closeness
   c. loyalty; interdependence
   d. respect; morality

6.5. Human developmental processes tend to _____ from one group to another because we are members of _____ .
   a. be the same; the same ethnic group
   b. be the same; the same species
   c. differ; different species
   d. differ; different ethnic groups

6.6. The fertilized egg will develop into a boy if it receives
   a. an X chromosome from its mother.
   b. an X chromosome from its father.
   c. a Y chromosome from its mother.
   d. a Y chromosome from its father.

6.7. Gender roles vary across cultures and over time. "Gender role" refers to our
   a. sense of being male or female.
   b. expectations about the way men and women behave.
   c. biological sex.
   d. beliefs about how men and women should earn a living.

6.8. Psychologists differentiate between our biological sex and our gender. As a consequence of the gender assigned to us by society, we develop a gender identity, which means that we
   a. exhibit traditional masculine or feminine roles.
   b. are socially categorized as male or female.
   c. have a sense of being male or female.
   d. have an ambiguous biological sex.

Review

- Many researchers have recently concluded that the shared home environment has less effect on children's development than is often supposed, and that peer influences matter more than we realized. What evidence supports that conclusion?

- What are gender roles, and what do their variations tell us about our human capacity for learning and adaptation?

Reflect

- To what extent, and in what ways, have your peers and your parents helped shape who you are?

- Do you consider yourself strongly gender-typed or *not* strongly gender-typed? What factors do you think have contributed to your feelings of masculinity or femininity?

Answers to the Test Yourself and Review questions can be found in the green appendix at the end of the book.

Postscript: Reflections on Nature and Nurture

"There are trivial truths and great truths," reflected the physicist Niels Bohr on some of the paradoxes of modern science. "The opposite of a trivial truth is plainly false. The opposite of a great truth is also true." It appears true that our ancestral history helped form us as a species. Where there is variation, natural selection, and heredity, there will be, on some scale, evolution. The unique gene combination created when our mother's egg engulfed our father's sperm also helped form us, as individuals. Genes predispose both our shared humanity and our individual differences. This is a great truth about human nature. Genes form us.

But it also is true that our experiences help form us. In the womb, in our families, and in our other social relationships, we learn ways of thinking and acting. Even differences initiated by our nature may be amplified by our nurture. If our genes and resulting brain organization and hormone mix predispose males to be more physically aggressive than females, culture may magnify this gender difference through norms that encourage males to be macho and females to be the kinder, gentler sex. If men are inclined to roles that demand physical power, and women to more nurturing roles, each may then exhibit the actions expected of those who fill such roles and find themselves shaped accordingly. Presidents in time become more presidential, servants more servile. In such ways, our life experiences in local environments and surrounding cultures help form us. This, too, is a great truth about human nurture. Our genes and our experience together form who we are.

* * *

If nature and nurture jointly form us, are we "nothing but" the product of nature and nurture?

We *are* the product of nature and nurture, but we are also an open system. Genes, for example, are all-pervasive but not all-powerful. Constrained by the dictates of their DNA, organisms construct themselves in particular places and times. Sometimes people defy their genetic bent to reproduce, by electing celibacy. Culture, too, is all-pervasive but not all-powerful. Sometimes people defy peer pressures, by asserting their freedom and doing the opposite. To excuse our failings by entirely blaming our nature and nurture is what philosopher-novelist Jean-Paul Sartre called "bad faith"—evading responsibility by blaming bad genes or bad influences for one's fate.

In reality, we are both the creatures and the creators of our worlds. We are—it is a great truth—the products of our genes and environments. Nevertheless—another great truth—the stream of causation that shapes the future runs through our present choices. Our decisions today design our environments tomorrow. The human environment is not like the weather—something that just happens. We are its architects. And that is what enables cultures to vary and to change so quickly.

* * *

I know from my mail and from public opinion surveys that some readers feel troubled by the naturalism and evolutionism of contemporary science. They worry that a science of behavior (and evolutionary science in particular) will destroy our sense of the beauty, mystery, and spiritual significance of the human creature. For those concerned, I offer some reassuring thoughts.

When Isaac Newton explained the rainbow in terms of light of differing wavelengths, the poet Keats feared that Newton had destroyed the rainbow's mysterious beauty. Yet, notes Richard Dawkins (1998) in *Unweaving the Rainbow,* Newton's

"The causes of life's history [cannot] resolve the riddle of life's meaning."

Stephen Jay Gould, *Rocks of Ages: Science and Religion in the Fullness of Life,* 1999

"Let's hope that it's not true; but if it is true, let's hope that it doesn't become widely known."

Lady Ashley, commenting on Darwin's big idea

analysis led to Maxwell's theory of electromagnetism and onward to an even deeper mystery—Einstein's theory of special relativity. Moreover, nothing about Newton's optics need diminish our appreciation for the dramatic elegance of a rainbow arching across a rain-darkened sky.

When Galileo assembled evidence that the Earth revolved around the Sun, not vice versa, he did not offer irrefutable proof for his theory. Rather he offered a coherent explanation for a variety of observations, such as the changing shadows cast by the Moon's mountains. His explanation eventually won the day because it described and explained things in a way that made sense, that hung together. Darwin's big idea likewise is a coherent view of natural history. It offers an organizing principle that unifies various observations.

Although some people of faith find the scientific idea of human origins troubling, many others find it congenial with their spirituality. In the fifth century, St. Augustine (quoted by Wilford, 1999) wrote, "The universe was brought into being in a less than fully formed state, but was gifted with the capacity to transform itself from unformed matter into a truly marvelous array of structures and life forms." Some 1600 years later, Pope John Paul II in 1996 welcomed science-religion dialogue, finding it noteworthy that evolutionary theory "has been progressively accepted by researchers, following a series of discoveries in various fields of knowledge." Evolution, he concluded, is "more than just a theory."

Meanwhile, many people of science are awestruck at the emerging understanding of the universe and the human creature. It boggles the mind—the entire universe popping out of a point some 14 billion years ago and instantly inflating to cosmological size. Had the energy of this Big Bang been the tiniest bit less, the universe would have collapsed back on itself. Had it been the tiniest bit more, the result would have been a soup too thin to support life.

What caused this fine-tuned universe? Why is there something rather than nothing? What made it—like Baby Bear's porridge—"just right"? How did it come to be, in the words of Harvard-Smithsonian astrophysicist Owen Gingerich (1999), "so extraordinarily right, that it seemed the universe had been expressly designed to produce intelligent, sentient beings"? Is there a benevolent superintelligence behind it all? Or have there actually been an infinite number of universes born and we just happen to be the lucky inhabitants of one that, by chance, was exquisitely fine-tuned to give birth to us? On most of these questions, science is silent.

Rather than fearing or restraining science, we can welcome its enlarging our understanding and awakening our sense of awe. In *The Fragile Species*, Lewis Thomas (1992) described his utter amazement that the Earth in time gave rise to bacteria and eventually to Bach's Mass in B-Minor. In a short 4 billion years, life has come from nothing to structures as complex as a 6-billion-unit strand of DNA and the incomprehensible intricacy of the human brain. Nature, says cosmologist Paul Davies (1992, 1999), seems cunningly devised to produce extraordinary, self-replicating, information-processing systems—us. Although we appear to have been created from dust, over eons of time, the end result is a priceless creature, one rich with potentials beyond our imagining.

"Is it not stirring to understand how the world actually works—that white light is made of colors, that color measures light waves, that transparent air reflects light . . . ? It does no harm to the romance of the sunset to know a little about it."

Carl Sagan, *Skies of Other Worlds*, 1988

"The fairest thing we can experience is the mysterious. It is the fundamental emotion which stands at the cradle of true art and true science."

Albert Einstein, *The World as I See It*, 1949

"The larger the island of knowledge, the longer the shoreline of wonder."

Ralph W. Sockman

The Developing Person

In mid-1978, the newest astonishment in medicine . . . was the birth of an English baby nine months after conception in a dish. The older surprise, which should still be fazing us all, is that a solitary sperm and a single egg can fuse and become a human being. . . . This has been going on under our eyes for so long a time that we've gotten used to it; hence the outcries of amazement at this really minor technical modification of the general procedure—nothing much, really, beyond relocating the beginning of the process from the fallopian tube to a plastic container.

Lewis Thomas, *The Medusa and the Snail*, 1979

The developing person is no less a wonder after birth than in the womb. As we journey through life from womb to tomb, when and how do we change? We invariably notice how we differ. However, to *developmental psychologists*, who study physical, mental, and social changes throughout the human life cycle, discerning our commonalities is just as important. Virtually all of us began walking around age 1 and talking by age 2. As children, we each engaged in social play in preparation for life's work. As adults, we all smile and cry, love and loathe, and occasionally ponder the fact that someday we will die. Psychology's developmental perspective examines how people are continually developing, from infancy through old age. Much of its research centers on three major issues:

1. *Nature/nurture:* How much do genetic inheritance (our *nature*) and experience (the *nurture* we receive) influence our development? We engaged this issue in depth in Modules 5 and 6.
2. *Continuity/stages:* Is development a gradual, continuous process like riding an escalator, or does it proceed through a sequence of separate stages, like climbing rungs on a ladder? Generally speaking, researchers who emphasize experience and learning see development as a slow, continuous shaping process of gradual, cumulative growth. Those who emphasize biological maturation tend to see development as a sequence of genetically predetermined stages or steps; although progress through the various stages may be quick or slow, everyone passes through the stages in the same order.
3. *Stability/change:* Do our early personality traits persist through life, or do we become different persons as we age? If reunited with a long-lost grade school friend, would you instantly recognize that "it's the same old Andy"? Or does a person at one period of life seem like a different person at a later period?

In Modules 5 and 6 we engaged the nature/nurture issue. In Modules 7, 8, 9, and 10 we will reflect on the continuity and stability issues throughout the lifespan. In the Reflections section after Module 10 we will assess what we have learned about our shared journey from womb to tomb.

"Nature is all that a man brings with him into the world; nurture is every influence that affects him after his birth."

Francis Galton, *English Men of Science*, 1874

7 Prenatal Development and the Newborn

Preview Questions: How does life develop before birth? What abilities do newborns bring with them at birth that help ensure their survival?

From the union of sperm and egg to birth of the newborn, development progresses in an orderly, though fragile, sequence. By birth, infants are equipped with perceptual and behavioral abilities that facilitate their survival. We begin with a look at what developmental biologists have learned about life before birth, and we then turn to some of the findings of **developmental psychology** about the newborn.

Conception

Nothing is more natural than a species reproducing itself. Yet nothing is more wondrous. Consider human reproduction. The process starts when a woman's ovary releases a mature egg, a cell roughly the size of the period at the end of this sentence, and when the 200 million or more sperm deposited during intercourse begin their race upstream toward it. The woman was born with all the immature eggs she would ever have, although only 1 in 5000 will ever mature and be released. A man, in contrast, begins producing sperm cells at puberty. The manufacturing process continues 24 hours a day for the rest of his life, although the rate of production—more than 1000 sperm during the second it takes to read this phrase—does slow down with age.

Like space voyagers approaching a huge planet, the sperm approach a cell 85,000 times their own size. The relatively few that make it to the egg release digestive enzymes that eat away the egg's protective coating, allowing a sperm to penetrate (**FIGURE 7.1**). But the egg is hardly passive. As soon as one sperm begins to penetrate, the egg's surface blocks out the others. Meanwhile, fingerlike projections sprout around the successful sperm and pull it in. Before half a day elapses, the egg nucleus and the sperm nucleus fuse. The two have become one. Consider it your luckiest of moments. Among 200 million sperm, the one needed to make you, in combination with that one particular egg, won the race.

- **developmental psychology** a branch of psychology that studies physical, cognitive, and social change throughout the life span.

- **zygote** the fertilized egg; it enters a 2-week period of rapid cell division and develops into an embryo.

- **embryo** the developing human organism from about 2 weeks after fertilization through the second month.

- **fetus** the developing human organism from 9 weeks after conception to birth.

- **teratogens** agents, such as chemicals and viruses, that can reach the embryo or fetus during prenatal development and cause harm.

 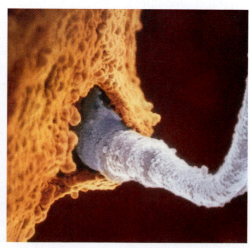

FIGURE 7.1
The union of egg and sperm
(a) A hoard of sperm cells surrounds an ovum. (b) As one sperm penetrates the egg's jellylike outer coating, a series of chemical events begins that will cause sperm and egg to fuse into a single cell. If all goes well, that cell will subdivide again and again to emerge 9 months later as a 100-trillion-cell human being.

(a)   (b)

Prenatal Development

Fewer than half of all fertilized eggs, called **zygotes**, survive beyond the first 2 weeks (Grobstein, 1979). But for you and me, good fortune prevailed. Beginning as one cell, each of us became 2 cells, then 4—each cell just like the first. Then, within the first week, when this cell division had produced a zygote of some 100 cells, the cells began to *differentiate*—to specialize in structure and function. How identical cells do this—as if one decides "I'll become a brain, you become intestines!"—is a scientific puzzle that developmental biologists are just beginning to solve.

About 10 days after conception, the increasingly diverse cells attach to the mother's uterine wall, beginning approximately 37 weeks of the closest human relationship. The zygote's outer part attaches to the uterine wall, forming the placenta, through which nourishment passes. The inner cells become the **embryo** (FIGURE 7.2). Over the next 6 weeks, organs begin to form and function. The heart begins to beat and the liver begins to make red blood cells.

By 9 weeks after conception, the embryo looks unmistakably human. It is now a **fetus**. By the end of the sixth month, organs such as the stomach are sufficiently formed and functional to allow a prematurely born fetus a chance of survival. At this point, the fetus is also responsive to sound. Microphone readings taken inside the uterus have revealed that the fetus is exposed to the sound of its mother's muffled voice (Ecklund-Flores, 1992). Immediately after birth, infants prefer this voice to another woman's voice or their father's (Busnel & others, 1992; DeCasper & others, 1984, 1986, 1994). Even while in the womb, they prefer (as shown by decreased heart rate) a rhyme that their mother has read daily from the thirty-third to thirty-seventh week.

At each prenatal stage, genetic *and* environmental factors affect our development. The placenta carries nutrients and oxygen from mother to fetus, while screening out many potentially harmful substances. But some substances slip by. The placental screen can admit **teratogens**—harmful agents such as particular viruses and drugs. If she is a heroin addict, her baby will be born a heroin addict. If she carries the AIDS virus, her baby may also. A pregnant woman never smokes alone; she and her fetus both experience reduced blood oxygen and a shot of nicotine. If she is a heavy smoker, her fetus may receive fewer nutrients and be born underweight. Heavy maternal smoking may also affect the fetal brain. And that could help explain why a recent correlational study of 4169 Danish men found markedly increased violent crime rates among men whose mothers smoked heavily during pregnancy—even after statistically controlling for other factors such as economic status and father criminality (Brennan & others, 1999).

> "From the very moment that the sperm hits the egg, a precarious trip on the thin edge of biological extinction has begun."
>
> Ralph Blair, *Nevertheless Joy!* 1989

Prenatal development

zygote:	conception to 2 weeks
embryo:	2 weeks through 8 weeks
fetus:	9 weeks to birth

FIGURE 7.2 Prenatal development
(a) The embryo grows and develops rapidly. At 40 days, the spine is visible and the arms and legs are beginning to grow. (b) Five days later, the inch-long embryo's proportions have begun to change. The rest of the body is now bigger than the head, and the arms and legs have grown noticeably. (c) By the end of the second month, when the fetal period begins, facial features, hands, and feet have formed. (d) As the fetus enters the fourth month, its 3 ounces could fit in the palm of your hand.

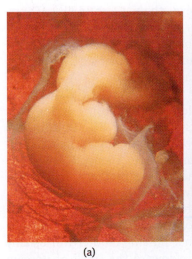
(a)

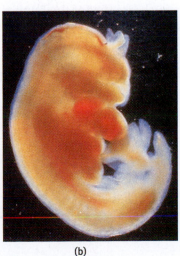
(b)

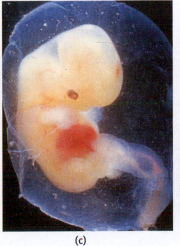
(c)

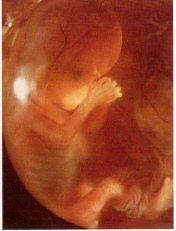
(d)

■ **fetal alcohol syndrome (FAS)** physical and cognitive abnormalities in children caused by a pregnant woman's heavy drinking. In severe cases, symptoms include noticeable facial misproportions.

■ **rooting reflex** a baby's tendency, when touched on the cheek, to open the mouth and search for the nipple.

"You shall conceive and bear a son. So then drink no wine or strong drink."

Judges 13:7

"The first lecture on psychology I ever heard was the first I ever gave."

William James, American psychologist (1842–1910)

There is no known safe amount of alcohol for a pregnant woman—even moderate drinking can affect the fetal brain (Braun, 1996). Alcohol enters the woman's bloodstream—and her fetus'—and depresses activity in both their central nervous systems. If she drinks heavily, her baby will be at risk for birth defects and mental retardation. For 1 in 750 infants, the effects are visible as **fetal alcohol syndrome (FAS)**, marked by a small, misproportioned head and lifelong brain abnormalities. FAS is now the leading cause of mental retardation (Niccols, 1994; Streissguth & others, 1991). More children suffer from it where maternal drinking is commonplace (Dorozyaski, 1993; Dorris, 1989). Children of alcoholic mothers are especially at risk. About 4 in 10 alcoholic mothers who drink during pregnancy have babies with FAS. "If women didn't drink during pregnancy," notes researcher Ann Streissguth (1993), "there would *never* be another baby born with fetal alcohol syndrome."

The Competent Newborn

Having survived prenatal hazards, we as newborns come equipped with reflexes ideally suited for our survival. We withdraw a limb to escape pain. If a cloth over our face interferes with our breathing, we turn our head from side to side and swipe at it. New parents are often in awe of the coordinated sequence of reflexes by which their baby gets food. The **rooting reflex** illustrates this: When something touches their cheek, babies open their mouth and vigorously "root" for a nipple. Finding one, they automatically close on it and begin sucking—which itself requires a coordinated sequence of tonguing, swallowing, and breathing. Failing to find satisfaction, the hungry baby may cry—a behavior parents are predisposed to find highly unpleasant and very rewarding to relieve.

The pioneering American psychologist William James presumed that the newborn experiences a "blooming, buzzing confusion." Until the 1960s, few people disagreed. It was said that, apart from a blur of meaningless light and dark shades, newborns could not see. Then, just as new technology led to progress in neuroscience, so, too, did new investigative techniques enhance infant studies. Scientists discovered that babies can tell you a lot—if you know how to ask. To ask, you must capitalize on what the baby can do—gaze, suck, turn her head. So, equipped with eye-tracking machines and pacifiers wired to electronic gear, researchers set out to answer parents' age-old questions: What can my baby see, hear, smell, and think?

What they discovered was fascinating. We are born preferring sights and sounds that facilitate social responsiveness. As newborns, we turn our heads in the direction of human voices. We gaze longer at a drawing of a facelike image (**FIGURE 7.3**) than at a bull's-eye pattern; yet we gaze more at a bull's-eye pattern—which has contrasts much like that of the human eye—than at a solid disk (Fantz, 1961). We prefer to look at objects 8 to 12 inches away, which, wonder of wonders, just happens to be the approximate distance between a nursing infant's eyes and its mother's (Maurer & Maurer, 1988).

Our perceptual abilities develop continuously during the first months of life. Within days of birth, our brain's neural networks were stamped with the smell of our mother's body. Thus, a week-old nursing baby, placed between a gauze pad from its mother's bra and one from another nursing mother will usually turn toward the smell of its own

FIGURE 7.3
Newborns' preference for faces
When shown these two stimuli with the same elements, Italian newborns spent nearly twice as many seconds looking at the facelike image (Johnson & Morton, 1991). Canadian newborns—average age 53 minutes in one study—displayed the same apparently inborn preference to look toward faces (Mondloch & others, 1999).

CLOSE-UP:

RESEARCH STRATEGIES FOR UNDERSTANDING INFANTS' THINKING

Can a newborn see well enough to distinguish shapes? Can a 3-month-old recognize faces? Does a 5-month-old have a concept of number? If babies could talk, we would ask them. But they can't, so psychologists let behavior do the talking. Developmental researchers, for example, exploit a simple form of learning called **habituation**—a decrease in responding with repeated stimulation. A novel stimulus gets attention when first presented. But the more it is presented, the weaker the response becomes. This seeming boredom with familiar stimuli gives us a way to ask infants what they see and remember.

Alan Slater and his University of Exeter colleagues (1988) illustrated this strategy when they asked newborns as young as 7 hours old what they could see. When first shown a stimulus like the one within **FIGURE 7.4**, the newborns gazed intently for an average 41 seconds. With repeated presentations, their interest soon waned.

What if the figure were rotated 90 degrees? Could the infants remember the initial stimulus and perceive the new one as different? As **FIGURE 7.5** indicates, they could indeed. Shown a stimulus with lines oriented as already seen, plus another stimulus with the novel, rotated orientation, the infants looked three times longer at the new one. Their behavior indicated they could remember and discriminate between differing visual stimuli. Other researchers using the habituation phenomenon report that infants can also discriminate colors, shapes, and sounds and can understand some basic concepts of numbers and physics (for example, that two solid objects cannot occupy the same space). In all these studies, researchers assume that infants' greater attention to some stimuli reveals their ability to distinguish different stimuli.

Why have such elegantly simple studies been done only recently? Researcher Slater (1994) explains: To recognize a new stimulus as different, an infant must remember the initial stimulus. Until the early 1980s, researchers assumed a newborn's brain was too immature to enable such memory. Then, as their appreciation for a newborn's abilities grew, they devised new ways to test the scope of infant cognition.

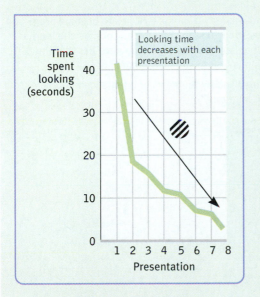

FIGURE 7.4 Habituation
Newborns become bored with (look less at) a repeatedly presented visual stimulus. (Data from Slater & others, 1988.)

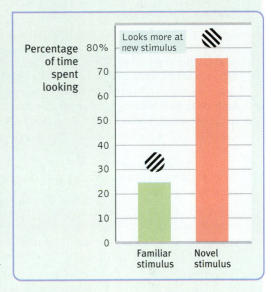

FIGURE 7.5 Novelty preference
Having habituated to the old stimulus, newborns preferred gazing at a new one. Their renewed attention to a slightly different stimulus reveals their visual ability. (Data from Slater & others, 1988.)

- **habituation** decreasing responsiveness with repeated stimulation. As infants gain familiarity with repeated exposure to a visual stimulus, their interest wanes and they look away sooner.

mother's pad (MacFarlane, 1978). At 3 weeks, if given a pacifier that sometimes turns on recordings of its mother's voice and sometimes that of a female stranger's, an infant will suck more vigorously when it hears its now-familiar mother's voice (Mills & Melhuish, 1974). Newborns can also learn to turn their heads to the left or right to receive a sugar solution when their forehead is stroked (Lancioni, 1980). So not only can we as young infants see what we need to see, and smell and hear well, but we are already using our sensory equipment to learn.

REVIEW AND REFLECT:

Prenatal Development and the Newborn

How does life develop before birth?

By studying the human life span from conception to death, developmental psychologists examine how we develop physically, cognitively, and socially. The life cycle begins when one sperm cell, out of the some 200 million ejaculated, unites with an egg to form a zygote. Attached to the uterine wall, the developing embryo begins to form body organs. By two months, the fetus becomes recognizably human. Along with nutrients, teratogens ingested by the mother can reach the developing child and place it at risk.

What abilities do newborns bring with them at birth that help ensure their survival?

Using new methods, researchers have discovered that newborns are born with sensory equipment and reflexes that facilitate their interacting with adults and securing nourishment. For example, they quickly learn to discriminate the smell and sound of their mothers.

Terms and Concepts to Remember

developmental psychology,
  p. 118
zygote, p. 119
embryo, p. 119
fetus, p. 119

teratogens, p. 119
fetal alcohol syndrome
  (FAS), p. 120
rooting reflex, p. 120
habituation, p. 121

Test Yourself

7.1. The 9 months of prenatal development prepare the individual for survival outside the womb. The body organs first begin to form and function during the period of the ————; within 6 months, during the period of the ————, the organs are sufficiently functional to allow a chance of survival.

    a. zygote; embryo   c. embryo; fetus
    b. zygote; fetus   d. placenta; fetus

7.2. Teratogens are chemicals that pass through the placenta's screen and may harm an embryo or fetus. Which of the following is *not* a teratogen?

    a. oxygen   c. alcohol
    b. heroin   d. nicotine

7.3. Stroke a newborn's cheek and he or she will root for a nipple. This illustrates

    a. a reflex.   c. perceptual ability.
    b. sensorimotor learning.   d. a gender difference.

7.4. In the past two decades, developmental researchers have designed tests of infant cognition by exploiting a simple form of learning called

    a. continuity.   c. the rooting reflex.
    b. nurturing.   d. habituation.

Review: Your friend—a heavy smoker—hopes to become pregnant soon. She says she will stop smoking as soon as she learns she is pregnant. What can you tell her to convince her that the time to stop smoking is before she is pregnant?

Reflect: Are you surprised by the news of infants' competencies? Or did you "know it all along"?

Answers to the Test Yourself and Review questions can be found in the green appendix at the end of the book.

Infancy and Childhood

8

During infancy, a baby grows from newborn to toddler, and during childhood from toddler to teenager. We will see how we all travel this path and develop physically, cognitively, and socially. From infancy on, brain and mind, neural hardware and cognitive software, develop together. The association areas of the cortex—those linked with thinking, memory, and language—are the last brain areas to develop. As they do, the child's mental abilities surge ahead (Chugani & Phelps, 1986; Thatcher & others, 1987).

Physical Development

Preview Question: How do brain and motor skills develop during infancy and childhood?

> "It is a rare privilege to watch the birth, growth, and first feeble struggles of a living human mind."
>
> Annie Sullivan, in Helen Keller's *The Story of My Life*, 1903

Brain Development

While you resided in your mother's womb, your body was forming nerve cells at the rate of nearly one-quarter million per *minute*. On the day you were born, you had most of the brain cells you would ever have. However, at birth your nervous system was immature: After birth, the neural networks that eventually enabled you to walk, talk, and remember had a wild growth spurt (**FIGURE 8.1**). Fiber pathways supporting language and agility continue developing into adolescence (Paus & others, 1999).

A flower unfolds in accord with its genetic blueprint. So do we, experiencing an orderly sequence of genetically designed biological growth processes called **maturation**. Maturation decrees many of our commonalities—from standing before walking, to using nouns before adjectives. Severe deprivation or abuse will retard development, and ample experiences with parents who talk and read to the child will help sculpt those important early neural connections. Yet the genetic growth tendencies are inborn. Maturation sets the basic course of development; experience adjusts it.

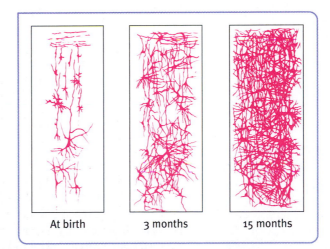

At birth — 3 months — 15 months

FIGURE 8.1

Drawings of human cerebral cortex sections

In humans, the brain is immature at birth. As the child matures, the neural networks grow increasingly more complex.

Maturation and Infant Memory

The lack of neural connections helps explain why our earliest memories seldom predate our third birthdays (Howe & Courage, 1993; Nelson, 1993). We see this in the memories of a group of preschoolers who experienced an emergency fire evacuation caused by a burning popcorn maker. Seven years later they were able to recall the alarm and what caused it—*if* they were 4 to 5 years old at the time. Those who experienced the event as 3-year-olds could not remember the cause and usually misrecalled being already outside when the alarm sounded (Pillemer, 1995).

For parents, this blank memory for our infancy can be disconcerting. After all, we spend countless hours with our babies—frolicking on the rug, diapering, feeding, and rocking them to sleep. But what will they consciously remember of us if we die before they reach age 3? Virtually nothing!

■ **maturation** biological growth processes that enable orderly changes in behavior, relatively uninfluenced by experience.

FIGURE 8.2 Infant at work
Babies only 3 months old can learn that kicking moves a mobile—and can retain that learning for a month. (From Rovee-Collier, 1989, 1997.)

Because we organize our memories differently after age 5, most of us have few memories of our preschool years. Trying to access such memories, note Elizabeth Loftus and Leah Kaufman (1992), is like trying to read a document that was formatted by an earlier version of a computer operating system.

Although little is consciously recalled from before age 3 or 4, some memories exist, at least for a time. Consider:

+ Given occasional reminders, 3-month-old infants who learn that moving their leg propels a mobile will remember the association for at least a month (**FIGURE 8.2**).
+ Eleven-month-olds who observe a researcher making a rattle by putting a button in a box will imitate the act if given the objects a day or even three months later (Mandler & McDonough, 1995).
+ Shown an out-of-focus picture, 3-year-olds will more quickly recognize it if they saw a clear version of the picture three months earlier—despite having no conscious recall of seeing it before (Drummey & Newcombe, 1995).
+ Shown photos of former classmates whom they had not seen since preschool, 10-year-olds recognize (amid other photos of preschoolers) only 1 in 5 of their onetime compatriots. Yet their physiological responding (measured as skin perspiration) is greater to their former classmates, whether consciously recognized or not (Newcombe & Fox, 1994). What the conscious mind did not know and could not express in words, the nervous system somehow remembered.

Motor Development

The developing brain also enables physical coordination. As an infant's muscles and nervous system mature, more complicated skills emerge. With minor exceptions, the sequence of physical (motor) development is universal. Babies roll over before they sit unsupported, and they creep on all fours before they walk. These behaviors reflect not imitation but a maturing nervous system; blind children, too, crawl and walk.

There are, however, individual differences in the timing of this sequence. In the United States, for example, 25 percent of all babies walk by age 11 months, 50 percent within a week after their first birthday, and 90 percent by age 15 months (Frankenburg & others, 1992).

There are also cultural differences in timing. Ugandan babies, for example, usually walk by 10 months. Unlike babies from other cultures who spend much of the day lying in a crib, Ugandan babies experience more intimate and rhythmic physical contact (Bril, 1986). Although such differences could be genetic, experiments reveal that experience does predict motor behavior. Two-week-old babies wave their arms more if they can see them, suggesting that they are learning to visually control their movements (van der Meer & others, 1995). And in 3-month-old infants, who still cannot efficiently reach and grab something, seemingly spontaneous kicking movements become more purposeful and coordinated when they activate a mobile (Thelen, 1994, 1995).

Nature (genes) plays a major role, too. Identical twins typically begin sitting up and walking on nearly the same day (Wilson, 1979). Biological maturation—including the rapid development of the cerebellum at the back of the brain—creates our readiness to learn walking at about age 1. Experience before that time has a limited effect. This is true for other physical skills, including bowel and bladder control. Before necessary muscular and neural maturation, no pleading, harassment, or punishment will produce successful toilet training.

Triumphant toddlers
Roll, crawl, walk, run—the sequence of these motor development milestones is the same the world around, though babies reach them at varying ages.

Cognitive Development

Preview Questions: How did Piaget view the development of a child's mind, and what are current researchers' views?

■ **schema** a concept or framework that organizes and interprets information.

"Who knows the thoughts of a child?" wondered poet Nora Perry. As much as anyone of his generation, developmental psychologist Jean Piaget (pronounced Pee-ah-ZHAY) knew. His interest began in 1920, when he was working in Paris to develop questions for children's intelligence tests. While administering tests to find out at what age children could answer certain questions correctly, Piaget became intrigued by children's *wrong* answers. Where others saw childish mistakes, Piaget saw intelligence at work. The errors made by children of a given age, he noted, were often strikingly similar.

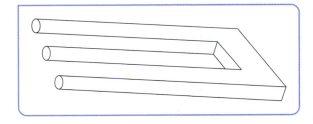

An impossible object
Look carefully at the "devil's tuning fork" at left. Now look away—no, better first study it some more—and then look away and draw it.... Not so easy, is it? Because this tuning fork is an impossible object, you have no schema for such an image.

A half century spent with children convinced Piaget that a child's mind is not a miniature model of an adult's. And, just as Copernicus revolutionized our understanding of the solar system, Piaget revolutionized our understanding of children's minds, suggests William Damon (1995). Until Piaget, most people—forgetting their own preschool days—assumed children "simply knew less, not *differently*, than adults" (p. 100). Thanks partly to his work, we now understand that "children reason in wildly illogical ways about problems whose solutions are self-evident to adults" (Brainerd, 1996).

Piaget further believed that a child's mind develops through a series of stages, in an upward march from the newborn's simple reflexes to the adult's abstract reasoning power. An 8-year-old child therefore comprehends things that a 3-year-old cannot. An 8-year-old might grasp the analogy "getting an idea is like having a light turn on in your head." Trying to teach the same analogy to a 3-year-old would be fruitless. Our adult minds likewise engage in moral reasoning uncomprehended by 8-year-olds.

"Childhood has its own way of seeing, thinking, and feeling, and there is nothing more foolish than the attempt to put ours in its place."

Philosopher Jean Jacques Rousseau, 1798

Piaget felt that the driving force behind this intellectual progression is our unceasing struggle to make sense of our experience. His core idea is that "children are active thinkers, constantly trying to construct more advanced understandings of the world" (Siegler & Ellis, 1996). To this end, the maturing brain builds concepts, which Piaget called **schemas**. Schemas (or schemes) are pliable mental molds into which we pour our experience. By adulthood we have built countless schemas ranging from knowing how to tie a knot to a concept of love.

Pouring experience into mental molds
We use our existing schemas to assimilate new experiences. But sometimes we need to accommodate (adjust) our schemas to include new experiences.

Two-year-old Gabriella has learned the schema for "cow" from her picture books.

Gabriella sees a moose and calls it a "cow." She is trying to assimilate this new animal into an existing schema. Her mother tells her, "No, it's a moose."

Gabriella accommodates her schema for large, shaggy animals and continues to modify that schema to include "mommy moose," "baby moose," etc.

■ **assimilation**   interpreting one's new experience in terms of one's existing schemas.

■ **accommodation**   adapting one's current understandings (schemas) to incorporate new information.

■ **cognition**   all the mental activities associated with thinking, knowing, and remembering.

■ **sensorimotor stage**   in Piaget's theory, the stage (from birth to about 2 years of age) during which infants know the world mostly in terms of their sensory impressions and motor activities.

■ **object permanence**   the awareness that things continue to exist even when not perceived.

Jean Piaget
"If we examine the intellectual development of the individual or of the whole of humanity, we shall find that the human spirit goes through a certain number of stages, each different from the other" (1930).

To explain how we use and adjust our schemas, Piaget proposed two concepts. First, we **assimilate** new experiences—we interpret them in terms of our current understandings (schemas). Given a simple schema for *dog*, for example, a toddler may call all four-legged animals *doggies*. But we also adjust, or **accommodate**, our schemas to fit the particulars of new experiences. The child soon learns that the original *doggie* schema is too broad and accommodates by refining the category. As children interact with the world, they construct and modify their understandings.

Piaget's Theory and Current Thinking

Cognition refers to all the mental activities associated with thinking, knowing, remembering, and communicating. Piaget described cognitive development in four stages—sensorimotor, preoperational, concrete operational, and formal operational (Table 8.1). He believed that children experience spurts of change followed by greater stability as they move from one developmental plateau to the next. Each plateau has distinctive characteristics that permit specific kinds of thinking. To appreciate how a child's mind grows, let's look at Piaget's stages in the light of our current thinking about cognitive development.

Sensorimotor Stage

During Piaget's **sensorimotor stage**, from birth to nearly age 2, babies take in the world through their sensory and motor interactions with objects—through looking, hearing, touching, mouthing, and grasping.

Very young babies seem to live in the present: What is out of sight is out of mind. In one of his tests, Piaget would show an infant an appealing toy and then flop his beret over it to see whether the infant searched for the toy. Before the age of 6 months, the infant did not. Young infants lack **object permanence**—the awareness that objects continue to exist when not perceived. By 8 months, infants begin exhibiting memory for things no longer seen. If you hide a toy, the infant will momentarily look for it. Within another month or two, the infant will look for it even after being restrained for several seconds.

But do children's cognitive abilities really grow through distinct stages? Does object permanence in fact blossom by 8 months, much as tulips blossom in spring? Today's researchers see development as more continuous. For example, they now view object permanence as unfolding gradually, as when young infants look for a toy where they saw it hidden a second before.

TABLE 8.1

PIAGET'S STAGES OF COGNITIVE DEVELOPMENT

Typical Age Range	Description of Stage	Developmental Phenomena
Birth to nearly 2 years	*Sensorimotor* Experiencing the world through senses and actions (looking, touching, mouthing, and grasping)	• Object permanence • Stranger anxiety
About 2 to 6 years	*Preoperational* Representing things with words and images but lacking logical reasoning	• Pretend play • Egocentrism • Language development
About 7 to 11 years	*Concrete operational* Thinking logically about concrete events; grasping concrete analogies and performing arithmetic operations	• Conservation • Mathematical transformations
About 12 through adulthood	*Formal operational* Abstract reasoning	• Abstract logic • Potential for mature moral reasoning

Researchers believe that Piaget and his followers underestimated young children's competence. Piaget assumed that before age 2, infants cannot think. They can recognize things, smile at them, crawl to them, manipulate them. But they have no abstract concepts or ideas. Theirs is a life lived, but not thought about.

Consider, however, some simple experiments on baby logic:

+ Andrew Meltzoff and Richard Borton gave 1-month-old babies one of two pacifiers to suck on without letting them see the objects (**FIGURE 8.3**). When they were later shown both pacifiers, the infants *looked* mostly at the nipple they had *felt* in their mouth. Follow-up studies revealed the same amazing result with infants 12 hours old (Kaye & Bower, 1994).

+ Like adults staring in disbelief at a magic trick, infants look longer at an unexpected scene of a car seeming to pass through a solid object, a ball stopping in midair, or an object violating object permanence by magically disappearing (Baillargeon, 1995, 1998; Wellman & Gelman, 1992). Babies seem to have a more intuitive grasp of simple laws of physics than Piaget realized.

+ Babies also have a head for numbers. Karen Wynn (1992, 1998) showed 5-month-old infants one or two objects. Then she hid the objects behind a screen, sometimes removing or adding one through a trap door (**FIGURE 8.4**). When she lifted the screen, the infants sometimes did a double take, staring longer when shown a wrong number of objects. But were they just responding to a greater or smaller mass of objects, rather than a change in number? Later experiments showed that babies' number sense extends to such things as drumbeats and motions. If accustomed to a Daffy Duck puppet jumping three times on stage, they show surprise if it jumps only twice. Clearly, infants are smarter than Piaget appreciated.

Object permanence
Infants younger than 6 months do not understand that things continue to exist when they are out of sight. But for this infant, out of sight is definitely not out of mind.

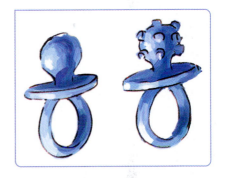

FIGURE 8.3 Infants can think
After sucking on one of these two pacifiers, babies looked longer at the nipple they had felt in their mouth. (From Meltzoff & Borton, 1979.)

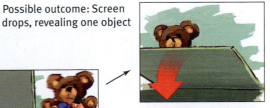

4. Possible outcome: Screen drops, revealing one object

1. Objects placed in case.

2. Screen comes up.

3. Infant watches as one object is removed.

4. Impossible outcome: Screen drops, revealing two objects.

FIGURE 8.4
Baby mathematics
Shown a numerically impossible outcome, infants stare longer. (From Wynn, 1992.)

■ **preoperational stage** in Piaget's theory, the stage (from about 2 to 6 or 7 years of age) during which a child learns to use language but does not yet comprehend the mental operations of concrete logic.

■ **conservation** the principle (which Piaget believed to be a part of concrete operational reasoning) that properties such as mass, volume, and number remain the same despite changes in the forms of objects.

■ **egocentrism** in Piaget's theory, the inability of the preoperational child to take another's point of view.

Question: If most 2½-year-olds do not understand how miniature dolls and toys can symbolize real objects, should anatomically correct dolls be used when questioning such children about alleged physical or sexual abuse? Judy DeLoache (1995) reports that "very young children do not find it natural or easy to use a doll as a representation of themselves."

Preoperational Stage

Piaget believed that during the preschool period and up to about age 6 or 7, children are in a **preoperational stage**—too young to perform mental operations. For a 5-year-old, the quantity of milk that is "too much" in a tall, narrow glass may become an acceptable amount if poured into a short, wide glass. This is because the child focuses only on the height dimension and is incapable of performing the *operation* of mentally pouring it back. A child lacks the concept of **conservation**—the principle that quantity remains the same despite changes in shape.

Piaget did not view the stage transitions as abrupt. Even so, symbolic thinking appears at an earlier age than he supposed. Judy DeLoache (1987) discovered this when she showed children a model of a room and hid a model toy in it (a miniature stuffed dog behind a miniature couch). The 2½-year-olds easily remembered where to find the miniature toy, but they could not use the model to locate an actual stuffed dog behind a couch in a real room. Three-year-olds—only 6 months older—usually went right to the actual stuffed animal in the real room, showing that they *could* think of the model as a symbol for the room. Piaget probably would have been surprised.

EGOCENTRISM   Seen through the eyes of Piaget, preschool children are aware of themselves, of time, and of the permanence of objects. Yet they are **egocentric**: They cannot perceive things from another's point of view. They may think the Sun and Moon follow them around. Asked to "show Mommy your picture," 2-year-old Gabriella holds the picture up facing her own eyes. Three-year-old Rebecca hides under a table, assuming that if she can't see someone's eyes they can't see her. Children's conversations also reveal their egocentrism, as one young boy demonstrated (Phillips, 1969, p. 61):

> *"Do you have a brother?"*
> *"Yes."*
> *"What's his name?"*
> *"Jim."*
> *"Does Jim have a brother?"*
> *"No."*

TV-watching preschoolers who block your view of the television assume that you see what they see. Preschoolers who ask you a question while you are on the phone assume that you hear no more than they hear. When relating to a young child, remember that such behaviors reflect a cognitive limitation: The egocentric preschoolers are not intentionally "selfish" or "inconsiderate." They simply have not developed the ability to take another's viewpoint.

Parents who abuse their children generally have no understanding of these limits. They see their children as junior adults able to control their behavior (Larrance & Twentyman, 1983). Thus, they perceive a child who stands in the way, spills food, disobeys negative instructions, or cries as willfully malicious.

Piaget's test of conservation
This preoperational child does not yet understand the principle of conservation of substance. Closed beakers with identical volumes seem suddenly to hold different amounts after one is merely inverted.

THEORY OF MIND Although still ego-centric, preschoolers begin forming a **theory of mind**. Rather than think of people as breathing wind-up dolls, they come to realize that people have minds. When Little Red Riding Hood realizes her "grandmother" is really a wolf, she swiftly revises her ideas about the creature's intentions and races away.

As their ability to infer intentions and other mental states develops, children seek to understand what made a playmate angry, when a sibling will share, and what might make a parent buy a toy. The preschooler's growing ability to tease, empathize, and persuade stems from a growing ability to take another's perspective. Between 3 and 5, for example, children come to realize that others may hold false beliefs. Jennifer Jenkins and Janet Astington (1996) showed Toronto children a Band Aids (plasters) box and asked them what was inside. The children naturally expected Band Aids, and so were surprised to discover that the box actually contained pencils. Asked what a child who had never seen the box would think was inside, 3-year-olds typically answered "pencils." By age 4 to 5, the children's "theory of mind" had leapt forward, and they delighted in anticipating their friends' false belief that the box would hold Band Aids.

This is Sally   This is Anne

Sally puts her ball in the red cupboard

Sally goes away

Anne moves the ball to the blue cupboard

Where will Sally look for her ball?

Testing children's theory of mind
Children younger than age 4, and children with autism, often seem not to appreciate others' mental states—such as Sally's state of mind in this scenario (adapted from Baron-Cohen & others, 1985).

Autism, a disorder characterized by deficient communication and social interaction, is marked by an impaired theory of mind (Klein & Kihlstrom, 1998; Yirmiya & others, 1998). In one experiment, children see a doll named Sally leaving her ball in a red cupboard. Another doll, Anne, then moves the ball to another cupboard. A question is then posed: When Sally returns, where will she look for the ball? Children with autistic syndrome have difficulty understanding that Sally's state of mind differs from their own—that Sally, not knowing the ball has been moved, will return to the red cupboard. They also have difficulty reflecting on their own mental states. They are, for example, less likely to use the personal pronouns *I* and *me*. Deaf children who have hearing parents and minimal opportunities for communication have similar difficulty inferring others' states of mind (Peterson & Siegal, 1999).

Our abilities to perform mental operations, to think symbolically, and to take another's perspective are not absent in the preoperational stage, and then miraculously present later. Rather, these abilities begin early and develop gradually.

By age 7, children become more capable of verbal thinking and of using it to work out solutions to problems. They do this, noted the Russian psychologist Lev Vygotsky (1896–1934), by no longer thinking aloud. Instead they internalize their culture's language and rely on inner speech. Parents who say "no" when pulling a child's hand away from a cake are giving the child a self-control tool. When later needing to resist temptation the child may likewise say "no." Second-graders who mutter to

■ **theory of mind** people's ideas about their own and others' mental states—about their feelings, perceptions, and thoughts and the behavior these might predict.

Private speech

A badger starring in a series of children's books sings to herself—in this case, to help her cope with the jealousy she feels toward her younger sister, who is soon to celebrate a birthday. The commonality of private speech is illustrated in many children's books.

Everybody makes a fuss for birthday girls who are not us

DENNIS THE MENACE

"Cut it up into a LOT of slices, Mom. I'm really hungry!"

themselves while doing math problems grasp third-grade math better the following year (Berk, 1994). Whether out loud or inaudible, talking to themselves helps children control their behavior and emotions and master new skills.

Concrete Operational Stage

By the time children are about 6 or 7 years of age, said Piaget, they enter the **concrete operational stage**. Given concrete materials, they begin to grasp that change in shape does not mean change in quantity. They can mentally pour milk back and forth between glasses of different shapes. They enjoy jokes that allow them to use their new concepts, such as conservation:

Mr. Jones went into a restaurant and ordered a whole pizza for his dinner. When the waiter asked if he wanted it cut into 6 or 8 pieces, Mr. Jones said, "Oh, you'd better make it 6, I could never eat 8 pieces!" (McGhee, 1976)

During the concrete operational stage, said Piaget, children fully gain the mental ability to comprehend mathematical transformations and conservation. When my daughter Laura was 6, I was astonished at her inability to reverse arithmetic operations—until I considered Piaget's observation. Asked, "What is 8 plus 4?" she required 5 seconds to compute "12," and another 5 seconds to then compute 12 minus 4. By age 8, she could answer the second question instantly.

Formal Operational Stage

By age 12, our reasoning expands from the purely concrete (involving actual experience) to encompass abstract thinking (involving imagined realities and symbols). As children approach adolescence, said Piaget, many become capable of solving hypothetical propositions and deducing consequences: *If* this, *then* that. Systematic reasoning, what Piaget called **formal operational** thinking, is now within their grasp. Consider this simple problem:

If John is in school, then Mary is in school. John is in school. What can you say about Mary?

Formal operational thinkers have no trouble answering correctly; nor do most 7-year-olds (Suppes, 1982). This illustrates, once again, why critics say the rudiments of Piaget's cognitive stages begin earlier than he realized.

Reflecting on Piaget's Theory

Piaget's stage theory is controversial. For some things, it gets high marks. Studies around the globe, from aboriginal Australia to Algeria to North America, reveal that human cognition everywhere unfolds basically in the sequence he proposed (Segall & others, 1990). However, today's researchers see development as more continuous than did Piaget. By detecting the beginnings of each type of thinking at earlier ages, they have revealed conceptual abilities Piaget missed. Moreover, they see formal logic as a smaller part of cognition than he did.

What remains of Piaget's ideas about the child's mind? Plenty—enough to merit his being singled out in 1999 by *Time* magazine as one of the century's 20 most influential scientists and thinkers. Piaget identified significant cognitive milestones and stimulated worldwide interest in how the mind develops. His emphasis was less on the ages at which children typically reach specific milestones than on their sequence—a sequence that later research has shown is pretty much as he described (Lourenco & Machado, 1996). Piaget would not be surprised that today we are adapting his ideas to accommodate new findings—as part of our own cognitive development.

What are the implications of all this for parents and teachers? Piaget contended that children construct their understandings from their *interactions* with the world. This implies that children are not passive receptacles waiting to be filled with a teacher's knowledge. Teachers would do better to build on what children already know, engaging them in concrete demonstrations and stimulating them to think for themselves. Future parents and teachers, remember: Young children are incapable of adult logic. Realize that what is simple and obvious to you—that getting off a teeter-totter will cause their friend on the other end to crash—may be incomprehensible to a 3-year-old. And accept children's cognitive immaturity as adaptive—as nature's strategy for keeping children close to protective adults and providing time for learning and socialization (Bjorklund & Green, 1992).

> "Assessing the impact of Piaget on developmental psychology is like assessing the impact of Shakespeare in English literature."
>
> **Developmental psychologist Harry Beilin (1992)**

Social Development

Preview Questions: How do the bonds of attachment form between parents and infants, and what are their long-term effects? When and how does our sense of self develop?

From birth, babies are social creatures. In all cultures, infants develop an intense bond with those who care for them. Beginning with a newborn's attraction to humans in general, infants soon come to prefer familiar faces and voices, then to coo and gurgle when given their mother's or father's attention. Soon after object permanence emerges and children become mobile enough to crawl into danger, a curious thing happens: They develop a fear of strangers, called **stranger anxiety.** Beginning at about 8 months, they tend to greet strangers by crying and reaching for their familiar caregivers. "No! Don't leave me!" their distress seems to say. At about this age, children have schemas for familiar faces; when they cannot assimilate the new face into these remembered schemas, they become distressed (Kagan, 1984). This illustrates an important principle: The brain, mind, and social-emotional behavior develop together.

Stranger anxiety
A newly emerging ability to evaluate people as unfamiliar and possibly threatening helps protect babies 8 months and older.

At 12 months, many infants cling tightly to a parent when they are frightened or expect separation. Reunited, after being separated, they shower the parent with smiles and hugs. No social behavior is more striking than this intense and mutual infant-parent bond. Called **attachment**, it is a powerful survival impulse that keeps infants close to their caregivers.

Origins of Attachment

A number of elements work to create the parent-infant bond. Infants become attached to those—typically their parents—who are comfortable, familiar, and responsive to their needs.

- **concrete operational stage** in Piaget's theory, the stage of cognitive development (from about 6 or 7 to 11 years of age) during which children gain the mental operations that enable them to think logically about concrete events.

- **formal operational stage** in Piaget's theory, the stage of cognitive development (normally beginning about age 12) during which people begin to think logically about abstract concepts.

- **stranger anxiety** the fear of strangers that infants commonly display, beginning by about 8 months of age.

- **attachment** an emotional tie with another person; shown in young children by their seeking closeness to the caregiver and showing distress on separation.

FIGURE 8.5 Harlow's mothers
Psychologist Harry Harlow reared monkeys with two artificial mothers—one a bare wire cylinder with a wooden head and an attached feeding bottle, the other a cylinder with no bottle but covered with foam rubber and wrapped with terry cloth. Harlow's discovery surprised many psychologists: The monkeys much preferred contact with the comfortable cloth mother, even while feeding from the nourishing mother.

Lee Kirkpatrick (1999) reports that for some people a perceived relationship with God functions as do other attachments—by providing a secure base for exploration and a safe haven when threatened.

■ **critical period**   an optimal period shortly after birth when an organism's exposure to certain stimuli or experiences produces proper development.

■ **imprinting**   the process by which certain animals form attachments during a critical period very early in life.

Body Contact

For many years, developmental psychologists reasoned that infants became attached to those who satisfied their need for nourishment. It only made sense. But an accidental finding revealed that this explanation is actually incomplete. During the 1950s, University of Wisconsin psychologist Harry Harlow bred monkeys for his learning studies. To equalize the infant monkeys' experiences and to prevent the spread of disease, he separated the monkeys from their mothers shortly after birth and raised them in sanitary individual cages, which included a cheesecloth baby blanket (Harlow & others, 1971). Surprisingly, the infants became intensely attached to their blankets: When the blankets were taken to be laundered, the monkeys became distressed.

Harlow soon recognized that this attachment to the blanket contradicted the idea that attachment derives from an association with nourishment. But how could he show this more convincingly? To pit the drawing power of a food source against the contact comfort of the blanket, Harlow created two artificial mothers. One was a bare wire cylinder with a wooden head, the other a cylinder wrapped with terry cloth. By attaching a bottle he could associate either with nourishment.

When reared with both a nourishing wire mother and a nonnourishing cloth mother, the monkeys overwhelmingly preferred the cloth mother (**FIGURE 8.5**). Like human infants clinging to their mothers, the monkeys would cling to their cloth mothers when anxious. They also used her as a secure base from which to venture into the environment, as if attached to the mother by an invisible elastic band that stretched so far and then pulled the infant back. Further studies revealed other qualities—rocking, warmth, and feeding—that made the cloth mother even more appealing.

Human infants, too, become attached to parents who are soft and warm and who rock, feed, and pat. And human attachment also consists of one person providing another with a *safe haven* when distressed and a *secure base* from which to explore the world. As we mature, our secure base and safe haven shift—from parents to peers and partners (Cassidy & Shaver, 1999). But at all ages we are social creatures. We gain strength when someone says to us, by words and actions, "I am here. I will be here. I am interested in what you do and what you think and feel. I will actively support you" (Crowell & Waters, 1994). We are "happiest and able to deploy [our] talents to best advantage," said attachment researcher John Bowlby (1979), when we know that one or more trusted friends will stand behind us, come what may.

Familiarity

Contact is one key to attachment. Another is familiarity. We know that nature opens windows of opportunity for wiring the brain for vision and language, then slams them shut. In many animals, attachments based on familiarity likewise form during a sensitive **critical period**—an optimal period shortly after birth when certain events must take place to facilitate proper development (Bornstein, 1989). The first moving object a gosling, duckling, or chick sees during the hours shortly after hatching is normally its mother. From then on, the young fowl follows her, and her alone.

This rigid attachment process, called **imprinting**, was explored by Konrad Lorenz (1937). He wondered: What would ducklings do if *he* was the first moving creature they observed? What they did was follow him around: Everywhere that Konrad went, the ducks were sure to go. Further tests revealed that although baby birds imprint best to their own species, they also will imprint to a variety of moving objects—an animal of another species, a box on wheels, a bouncing ball (Colombo, 1982; Johnson, 1992). And, once formed, this attachment is difficult to reverse.

Proponents of a critical "bonding" period argue that for humans, too, contact during the first hours after birth boosts parent-infant attachment (Kennell & Klaus, 1982). Following this thinking, many hospitals introduced "bonding rooms" where staff members work to ensure that bonding occurs before the mother and infant leave.

Developmental psychologists are unconvinced that this very early contact is essential (Eyer, 1992). True, human infants do prefer familiar faces and objects, but there is no precise critical period for becoming attached. Psychologists certainly welcome and encourage the trend toward humanizing childbirth, but adoptive parents and others who must miss their child's birth need not feel deficient. Human attachment develops gradually. There is plenty of time for parents and their infants to come to know and love each other. Maternity ward cuddling is simply a beginning.

Children—unlike ducklings—do not imprint. However, they do become attached to what they've known. "Mere exposure" to people and things fosters fondness—children like to reread the same books, watch the same movies over again, reenact family traditions. They prefer to eat familiar foods, live in the same familiar neighborhood, attend school with the same old friends. Familiarity breeds content.

Responsive Parenting

In studies the world over, some babies seem more disposed to forming a secure attachment. Placed in a strange situation (usually a laboratory playroom), about 60 percent of infants display *secure attachment*. In their mother's presence they play comfortably, happily exploring their new environment. When she leaves, they are distressed; when she returns, they seek contact with her. Other infants show *insecure attachment*. They are less likely to explore their surroundings; they may even cling to their mother. When she leaves, they either cry loudly and remain upset or seem indifferent to their mother's going and returning (Ainsworth, 1973, 1989; Kagan, 1995; van IJzendoorn & Kroonenberg, 1988). What accounts for these differences?

One possible explanation is the mother's behavior. Female rats reared by relaxed, attentive adoptive mothers become more relaxed and attentive to their offspring than do those reared by stress-prone, inattentive adoptive mothers (Francis & others, 1999). Do human infants likewise pick up their mothers' tendencies?

Mary Ainsworth (1979) studied attachment differences by observing mother-infant pairs at home during their first six months. Later she observed the 1-year-old infants in a "strange situation" without their mothers—a strange little mini-drama that she and others came to believe gives insight into the child's emotional health and future relationships. Sensitive, responsive mothers—those who noticed what their babies were doing and responded appropriately—had infants who usually became securely attached. Insensitive, unresponsive mothers—mothers who attended to their babies when they felt like doing so but ignored them at other times—had infants who often became insecurely attached. Harlow's monkey studies, in which the artificial structures were certainly the ultimate unresponsive mothers, produced even more striking effects. When put in strange situations without their artificial mothers, the deprived infants were terrified (**FIGURE 8.6**).

Follow-up studies have confirmed that sensitive mothers—and fathers—tend to have securely attached infants (De Wolff & van Ijzendoorn, 1997). But is attachment style the result of parenting or of temperament, which, as research has shown, is genetically influenced? By neglecting heredity, these studies are like "comparing foxhounds reared in kennels with poodles reared in apartments," chides Judith Harris (1998). So, to separate nature and nurture, Dutch researcher Dymphna van den Boom (1990) varied parenting while controlling temperament. (Pause and think: If you were the researcher, how might you have done this?)

Van den Boom's solution was to randomly assign one hundred 6- to 9-month-old temperamentally difficult infants to either an experimental condition, in which mothers received personal training in sensitive responding, or to an untreated control condition in which they did not. At age one, 68 percent of the experimental-condition infants were rated securely attached; of the control-condition infants, only 28 percent were.

FIGURE 8.6

Social deprivation and fear
Monkeys raised by artificial mothers were terror-stricken when placed in strange situations without their surrogate mothers. (Today's climate of greater respect for animal welfare prevents such primate studies.)

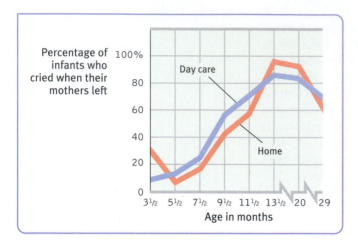

FIGURE 8.7 Infants' distress over separation from parents
In an experiment, groups of infants were left by their mothers in an unfamiliar room. In both groups, the percentage who cried when the mother left peaked at about 13 months. (From Kagan, 1976.) Whether the infant had experienced day care made little difference.

As these examples indicate, researchers have more often studied mother care than father care. Infants who lack a caring mother are said to suffer "maternal deprivation"; those lacking the care of a father are said merely to experience "father absence." "Fathering a child" has meant impregnating; "mothering" has meant nurturing. But evidence increasingly indicates that fathers are more than just mobile sperm banks. Paternal deprivation resulting from nonmarital childbearing, separation, and divorce puts children at increased risk for various psychological and social pathologies. This is true even after we control for income and educational differences between father-present and father-absent families (Myers, 2000).

Whether children are raised entirely at home or also in a day-care center, whether they live in North America, Guatemala, or the Kalahari Desert, anxiety over separation from parents peaks at around 13 months, then gradually declines (**FIGURE 8.7**). Does this mean our need for and love of others also fades away? Hardly. In fact, in other ways our capacity for love grows, and our pleasure in touching and holding those we love never ceases. The power of early attachment does nonetheless gradually relax, allowing us to move out into a wider range of situations and communicate with strangers more freely. One might even say that much of the life cycle story boils down to a poignant rhythm of attachment and separation—from the attachment of fetal life to the separation of birth, from infant attachment to adolescent separation, from the attachments of marriage and parenthood to the separation of death.

Effects of Attachment

Does a trusting, secure attachment have lasting benefits? And what are the long-term effects when attachment bonds are absent or severed?

Secure Attachment Predicts Social Competence

At the University of Minnesota, Alan Sroufe and his colleagues (1983) identified infants who were securely attached at 12 to 18 months of age. Sroufe restudied these infants as 2- to 3-year-olds, and saw them functioning more confidently than other toddlers. Given challenging tasks, they were more enthusiastic and persistent. With other children they were more outgoing and responsive.

Developmental theorist Erik Erikson (1902–1994), in collaboration with his wife, Joan Erikson, said that securely attached children approach life with a sense of **basic trust**—a sense that the world is predictable and reliable. Erikson attributed basic trust not to one's continuing positive environment or inborn temperament, but to early parenting. He theorized that infants blessed with sensitive, loving caregivers form a lifelong attitude of trust rather than fear. Erikson would not have been surprised that as adults, our styles of romantic love exhibit either secure, trusting attachment; insecure, anxious attachment; or the avoidance of attachment (Feeney & Noller, 1990; Shaver & Hazan, 1993; Simpson & others, 1992). Although debate continues, many researchers now believe that our early attachment experiences lay the foundation for our adult relationships.

Deprivation of Attachment

If secure attachment nurtures social competence, what happens when circumstances prevent a child's forming attachments? In all of psychology, there's no sadder research literature. Babies reared in institutions without the stimulation and attention of a regular caregiver, or locked away at home under conditions of abuse or extreme neglect, are often withdrawn, frightened, even speechless. Those abandoned in Ro-

"Out of the conflict between trust and mistrust, the infant develops hope, which is the earliest form of what gradually becomes faith in adults."

Erik Erikson, 1983

■ **basic trust** according to Erik Erikson, a sense that the world is predictable and trustworthy; said to be formed during infancy by appropriate experiences with responsive caregivers.

manian orphanages during the 1980s looked "frighteningly like Harlow's monkeys" (Carlson, 1995). If institutionalized more than 8 months, they often bore lasting scars (Chisholm, in press; Malinosky-Rummell & Hansen, 1993; Rutter & others, 1998).

Harlow's monkeys similarly bore scars if reared in total isolation, without even an artificial mother. As adults, when placed with other monkeys their age, they either cowered in fright or lashed out in aggression. When they reached sexual maturity, most were incapable of mating. If artificially impregnated, females often were neglectful, abusive, even murderous toward their first-born. In the wild, too, some monkey mothers neglect or abuse their infants (Maestripieri & Carroll, 1998).

In humans, too, the unloved often become the unloving. Most abusive parents report having been neglected or battered as children (Kempe & Kempe, 1978). Many condemned murderers report the same. One study of 14 young men awaiting execution for juvenile crimes found that all but two had histories of brutal physical abuse (Lewis & others, 1988).

But does this mean that today's victim is predictably tomorrow's victimizer? The answer is no. Though most abusers were indeed abused, most abused children do *not* later become violent criminals or abusive parents. Even after years of banishment to a speechless attic environment, some children have matured—after adoption into loving homes—into normal adults with careers and families (Clarke & Clarke, 1998). But many children are not so dramatically resilient, especially those who experience no sharp break from their abusive past. Some 30 percent of those abused do abuse their children—a rate four times higher than the national rate of child abuse (Kaufman & Zigler, 1987; Widom, 1989a,b). Moreover, young children terrorized through sexual abuse, physical abuse, or wartime atrocities (being beaten, witnessing torture, and living in constant fear) may suffer other lasting wounds—often nightmares, depression, and a troubled adolescence involving substance abuse, binge eating, or aggression (Kendall-Tackett & others, 1993; Polusny & Follette, 1995; Trickett & McBride-Chang, 1995).

Such experiences can leave footprints on the brain. When normally placid golden hamsters are repeatedly threatened and attacked while young, the effects linger into their adult lives. They grow up to be cowards when caged with same-sized hamsters or bullies when caged with weaker ones (Ferris, 1996). Such animals show changes in such brain chemicals as serotonin, which calms aggressive impulses. A similarly sluggish serotonin response has been found in abused children who become aggressive teens and adults.

Disruption of Attachment

What happens to an infant when attachment is disrupted? Separated from their families, both monkey and human infants become upset and, before long, withdrawn and even despairing (Bowlby, 1973; Mineka & Suomi, 1978). Fearing that such extreme stress might cause lasting damage (and when in doubt, acting to protect parents' rights), courts are usually reluctant to remove children from their homes.

If placed in a more positive and stable environment, most infants recover from the distress of separation. In studies of adopted children, Leon Yarrow and his co-workers (1973) found that when children between 6 and 16 months of age were removed from their foster mothers, they initially had difficulties eating, sleeping, and relating to their new mothers. But when these children were studied at age 10, little visible effect remained. Thus, they fared no worse than children placed before the age of 6 months (with little accompanying distress). Likewise, Romanian orphans adopted during infancy or childhood into a loving home usually progressed rapidly, especially in their cognitive development. Moreover, foster care that prevents attachment by moving a child through a series of foster families can be very disruptive. So can repeated and prolonged removals from a mother and reunions with her.

"What is learned in the cradle, lasts to the grave."

French proverb

Adults also suffer when attachment bonds are severed. Whether it occurs through death or separation, the break produces a predictable sequence of agitated preoccupation with the lost partner, followed by deep sadness and, eventually, the beginnings of emotional detachment and a return to normal living (Hazan & Shaver, 1994). Newly separated couples who have long ago ceased feeling affection are sometimes surprised at their desire to be near the former partner. Deep and long-standing attachments seldom break quickly. Detaching is a process, not an event.

Does Day Care Affect Attachment?

In the mid-twentieth century, when Mom-at-home was the social norm, researchers asked, "Is day care bad for children? Does it disrupt children's attachments to their parents?" For the high-quality day-care programs usually studied, the answer was no (Belsky, 1990). In *Mother Care/Other Care*, developmental psychologist Sandra Scarr (1986) explained that children are "biologically sturdy individuals . . . who can thrive in a wide variety of life situations." Scarr spoke for many developmental psychologists, whose research has uncovered no major impact of maternal employment on children's development (Hoffman, 1989; Mott, 1991).

Today's issues are different. Slightly more than half of all mothers of preschoolers are employed, and the proportion of American preschoolers in day care is up from 6 percent in 1965 to a current 31 percent. Research has shifted to the effects of different forms of day care on different types and ages of children (Scarr, 1998). Fortunately, we can now distinguish good day care from poor. Scarr (1997) explains: Around the world, "high-quality child care consists of warm, supportive interactions with adults in a safe, healthy, and stimulating environment. . . . Poor care is boring and unresponsive to children's needs." The ideal, then? A verbally stimulating environment in which any child can frequently talk with a familiar adult caregiver. In this regard, quality day care may offer a child a greater intellectual boost and opportunity for social development than does most home care with a sitter (Clarke-Stewart & others, 1994; Zaslow, 1991).

Such findings should encourage parents of children 2 years and older. But for infant day care the scientific jury is still out. Developmental psychologists Jay Belsky (1988, 1994) and Edward Zigler (1986) have expressed concern. In Belsky's words, "Children growing up in families using more than 20 hours per week of nonparental care in their first year of life are at heightened risk of seeming insecure as 1-year-olds and of being disobedient and aggressive at older ages." The risk appears greatest when such care is not only early but also extensive throughout the preschool years in centers with staff who are poorly trained, poorly paid, and frequently changed.

Many developmentalists believe that *quality* infant day care does not hinder secure attachment. They find support in two studies of enriched infant day care, one in Sweden and one in the United States (Andersson, 1989; Field, 1991). In both, schoolchildren who had experienced quality day care during their first 6 months were more outgoing, popular, and academically successful than those who had no similar experience. Even routine day care seems not harmful for the children of sensitive, responsive parents. That's the preliminary conclusion from an ongoing study of 1153 infants in 10 cities, following them from the age of 1 month to first grade. At the latest observation (age 3), children who had spent the most time in day care had slightly advanced mental development and slightly "less sensitive and engaged mother-child interactions" (NICHD, 1997a, 1999). But family qualities and the child's temperament mattered much more.

> "There is near consensus among developmental psychologists and early childhood experts that child care per se does not constitute a risk factor in children's lives; rather, poor quality care and poor family environments can conspire to produce poor developmental outcomes."
>
> Sandra Scarr, Deborah Phillips, and Kathleen McCartney (1990)

An example of high-quality day care
Forms of day care differ widely in philosophy and quality. Research has shown that in safe, stimulating environments like this day-care center, young children thrive both socially and intellectually. A ratio of about one caregiver for every three or four children is especially important in producing this outcome.

Children's ability to thrive under varied types of responsive caregiving should not surprise us, given how cultures vary in attachment patterns. Westernized attachment features one or two caregivers and their offspring. In other cultures, such as the Efe Pygmies of Zaire, multiple caregivers are the norm (Field, 1996). Even before the mother holds her newborn, the baby is passed among several women. In the weeks to come, the infant is constantly held and fed, often by other breast-feeding women. The result is multiple attachments. As the now-famous African proverb says, "It takes a village to raise a child."

There is little disagreement that the half million preschool children actually left *alone* for part of the time their parents are at work deserve better. So do the children who merely exist for 9 hours a day in minimally equipped, understaffed centers. What all children need is a consistent, warm relationship with people whom they can learn to trust.

Self-Concept

The number one social achievement of infancy is attachment. Childhood's major social achievement is a positive sense of self. By the end of childhood, at about age 12, most children have developed a **self-concept**—a sense of their own identity and personal worth. Parents often wonder when and how this sense of self develops. "Is my baby girl aware of herself—does she know she is a person distinct from everyone else?"

Of course we cannot ask the baby directly, but we can again capitalize on what she can do—letting her *behavior* provide clues to the beginnings of her self-awareness. In 1877, biologist Charles Darwin offered one idea: Self-awareness begins when we recognize ourselves in a mirror. By this indicator, self-recognition emerges gradually over about a year, starting in roughly the sixth month as the child reaches toward the mirror to touch her image as if it were another child (Damon & Hart, 1982, 1988).

But how can we know when the child recognizes that the girl in the mirror is indeed herself, not just an agreeable playmate? In a simple variation of the mirror procedure, researchers sneakily dabbed rouge on children's noses before placing them in front of the mirror. Beginning by 15 to 18 months, children will touch their own noses when they see the red spot in the mirror (Butterworth, 1992; Gallup & Suarez, 1986). Apparently, 18-month-olds have a schema of how their faces should look, and they wonder, "What is that spot doing on *my* face?"

Beginning with this simple self-recognition, the child's self-concept gradually strengthens. By school age, children start to describe themselves in terms of their gender, group memberships, and psychological traits, and they compare themselves with other children (Newman & Ruble, 1988; Stipek, 1992). They come to see themselves as good and skillful in some ways but not others. They form a concept of which traits, ideally, they would like to have. By age 8 or 10, their self-images are quite stable.

Children's views of themselves affect their actions. Children who form a positive self-concept are more confident, independent, optimistic, assertive, and sociable (Maccoby, 1980). This then raises important questions: How can parents encourage a positive self-concept? In what ways does parenting style affect children?

■ **self-concept** a sense of one's identity and personal worth.

After prolonged exposure to mirrors, four other species—chimpanzees, orangutans, gorillas, and dolphins—have similarly demonstrated self-recognition of their mirror image (Marino & others, 1994; Wright, 1996).

Self-awareness
Mirror images fascinate infants from the age of about 6 months. Only at about 18 months, however, does the child recognize that the image in the mirror is "me."

Child-Rearing Practices

Parenting styles vary. Some parents spank, some reason. Some are strict, some are lax. Some show little affection, some liberally hug and kiss. Do such differences affect children?

The most heavily researched aspect of parenting has been how, and to what extent, parents seek to control their children. Several investigators have identified three parenting styles:

1. *Authoritarian* parents impose rules and expect obedience: "Don't interrupt." "Do keep your room clean." "Don't stay out late or you'll be grounded." "Why? Because I said so."
2. *Permissive* parents submit to their children's desires, make few demands, and use little punishment.
3. *Authoritative* parents are both demanding and responsive. They exert control not only by setting rules and enforcing them but also by explaining the reasons and, especially with older children, encouraging open discussion and allowing exceptions when making the rules.

Too hard, too soft, and just right, these styles have been called. Studies by Stanley Coopersmith (1967), Diana Baumrind (1996), and John Buri and others (1988) reveal that children with the highest self-esteem, self-reliance, and social competence usually have warm, concerned, *authoritative* parents. Although the participants in most studies have been middle-class white families, studies with families of other races and in more than 200 cultures worldwide confirm the social and academic benefits of loving and authoritative parenting (Baumrind, 1991; Rohner, 1994).

What accounts for this finding? Research indicates that people given *control* over their lives become motivated and self-confident; those with little control tend to see themselves as helpless and incompetent. Moreover, children who sense enough control to attribute their behaviors to their choices ("I obey because I am good") internalize their behaviors. Coerced children ("I obey or I get in bad trouble") tend not to internalize their actions.

Of the three parenting styles, authoritative parenting provides children with the greatest sense of control. Authoritative parents openly discuss family rules by explaining them to younger children and reasoning about them with older children. When they feel that rules are more negotiated than imposed, older children feel more self-control (Baumrind, 1983; Lewis, 1981). And when parents enforce rules with consistent, predictable consequences, children feel they control the outcome.

But wait. Before jumping to conclusions about the results of different parenting styles, heed this caution: *Correlation is not causation.* The association between certain parenting styles (being firm but open) and certain childhood outcomes (social competence) is correlational. There are other possible explanations (**FIGURE 8.8**). Perhaps children's traits influence parenting more than vice versa. Parental warmth and control vary somewhat from child to child even in the same family (Holden & Miller, 1999). So perhaps socially mature, agreeable, easygoing children *elicit* greater trust and warmth from their parents, and less competent and less cooperative children elicit less. This possibility is supported by twin studies (Kendler, 1996).

Or there may be some underlying third factor. Consider this: Authoritative parents are more often well educated and less often stressed by poverty or a recent divorce, factors that can affect children's competence (Hetherington, 1979). Or this: Maybe competent parents and their competent children share genes that predispose social competence.

FIGURE 8.8 The correlation between authoritative parenting and social competence in children
Three possible explanations are (1) parenting may influence children's competence; (2) children's social competence may influence parenting; or (3) both may be influenced by an underlying third factor.

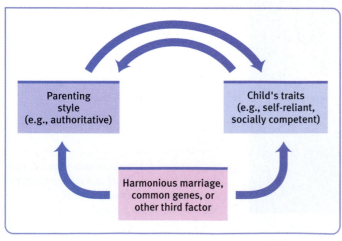

Parents struggling with conflicting advice and with the stresses of child-rearing should remember that *all advice reflects the advice-giver's values*. For those who prize unquestioning obedience from a child, an authoritarian style may have the desired effect. For those who value children's sociability and self-reliance, authoritative firm-but-open parenting is advisable.

The investment in raising a child buys many years not only of joy and love but of worry and irritation. Yet for most parents, a child is one's biological and social legacy—one's personal investment in the human future. To paraphrase psychiatrist Carl Jung, we reach backward into our parents and forward into our children, and through their children into a future we will never see, but about which we must therefore care.

REVIEW AND REFLECT:

Infancy and Childhood

How do brain and motor skills develop during infancy and childhood?

Within the brain, nerve cells form before birth. Sculpted by maturation and experience, their interconnections multiply rapidly after birth. The lack of neural connections in our earliest years helps explain why we lose conscious memories of experiences from those years. Experiments do, however, show that infants can retain learning over time. Infants' more complex physical skills—sitting, standing, walking—develop in a predictable sequence whose actual timing is a function of individual maturation rate and culture.

How did Piaget view the development of a child's mind, and what are current researchers' views?

Jean Piaget's observations of children convinced him—and almost everyone else—that the mind of the child is not that of a miniature adult. Piaget theorized that our mind develops by forming schemas that help us assimilate our experiences and that must occasionally be altered to accommodate new information. In this way, children progress from the sensorimotor simplicity of the first two years to more complex stages of thinking.

Piaget believed that preschool children, in the preoperational stage, are egocentric and unable to perform simple logical operations. At about age 6 or 7 they enter the concrete operational stage and can perform concrete operations, such as those required to comprehend the principle of conservation. Finally, at about age 12, children enter the formal operational stage, in which systematic reasoning is within their grasp.

Recent research indicates that human cognition, regardless of culture, tends to unfold basically in the sequence Piaget proposed. However, young children are more capable, and development more continuous, than Piaget believed. The cognitive abilities that emerge at each stage apparently begin developing in a rudimentary form in the previous stage.

How do the bonds of attachment form, and what are their long-term effects? When and how does our sense of self develop?

Infants become attached to their mothers and fathers not simply because mothers and fathers gratify biological needs but, more important, because they are comfortable, familiar, and responsive. If denied such care, both monkey and human infants may become pathetically withdrawn, anxious, and eventually abusive. Once an attachment forms, infants who are separated from their caregivers will, for a time, be distressed. Attachment style in infancy predicts later social development.

As with cognitive abilities, a self-concept develops gradually. By 18 months, infants recognize themselves in a mirror. By age 8 or 10, children's self-images are quite stable and are linked with their independence, optimism, and sociability. Children who develop a positive self-image and a happy, self-reliant manner tend to have been reared by parents who are neither permissive nor authoritarian, but authoritative while allowing their children a sense of control.

Terms and Concepts to Remember

maturation, p. 123
schema, p. 125
assimilation, p. 126
accommodation, p. 126
cognition, p. 126
sensorimotor stage, p. 126
object permanence, p. 126
preoperational stage, p. 128
conservation, p. 128
egocentrism, p. 128

theory of mind, p. 129
concrete operational stage, p. 130
formal operational stage, p. 130
stranger anxiety, p. 131
attachment, p. 131
critical period, p. 132
imprinting, p. 132
basic trust, p. 134
self-concept, p. 137

Test Yourself

8.1. The orderly sequence of biological growth is called maturation. Maturation explains why
   a. children differ greatly in temperament.
   b. most children have begun walking by 12 months.
   c. enriching experiences may affect brain tissue.
   d. differences between the sexes are minimal.

8.2. Most of us remember nothing before our third birthday because
   a. we are not born with enough brain cells to form memories.
   b. we were not given the extra "handling" and environmental stimulation we needed.
   c. the connections between our brain cells had not yet become complex enough to form permanent memories.
   d. we do not enter the memory stage until our third year.

Continued

8.3. As the infant's muscles and nervous system mature, more complicated skills emerge. Which of the following is true of motorskill development?

a. It is determined solely by genetic factors.

b. The sequence, but not the timing, is universal.

c. Maturation has a limited effect if the environment is not right.

d. Environment creates a readiness to learn.

8.4. A toddler who calls a cow "doggie" is _____ her new experience of seeing a cow into her current _____ for dogs.

a. accommodating; schema

b. assimilating; schema

c. intuiting; mental operation

d. shaping; mental operation

8.5 According to Piaget, the preoperational stage extends from about age 2 to 6. During this period the young child's thinking is

a. abstract.   c. conservative.

b. negative.   d. egocentric.

8.6. The principle of conservation explains why a pint of milk remains a pint, whether poured into a tall thin glass or a round goblet. Children acquire the mental operations necessary to understand conservation during

a. infancy.

b. the sensorimotor stage.

c. the preoperational stage.

d. the concrete operational stage.

8.7. Piaget's stage theory continues to inform our understanding of cognitive development in childhood. However, many researchers believe that

a. Piaget's "stages" begin earlier and development is more continuous than Piaget realized.

b. children do not progress as rapidly as Piaget predicted.

c. few children really progress to the concrete operational stage.

d. there is no way of testing much of Piaget's theoretical work.

8.8. After about 8 months of age, infants develop schemas for familiar objects. Faced with a new babysitter, they will show distress, a behavior referred to as

a. conservation.   c. imprinting.

b. stranger anxiety.   d. maturation.

8.9. Body contact facilitates attachment between infant and parent. In a series of experiments, Harry Harlow found that monkeys raised with artificial mothers tended when afraid to cling to

a. the wire mother.

b. the cloth mother.

c. whichever mother held the feeding bottle.

d. none of the artificial mothers.

8.10. Children who in infancy formed secure attachments to their parents

a. are likely to become good parents.

b. prefer the company of adults to that of their peers.

c. usually become socially competent youngsters.

d. have less stranger anxiety.

Review

- Researchers have presumed that Ugandan babies' earlier walking is a product of their nurture. Others might wonder if credit should instead go to their genetically predisposed nature. How might we test these alternative ideas?

- Use Piaget's first three stages of cognitive development to explain why young children are *not* just miniature adults in the way they think.

- Parents who spank tend to have more physically aggressive children. What might explain this correlation?

Reflect

- What is your earliest memory? Was that memory influenced by stories older siblings or parents may have told you or by photos you have seen?

- Can you recall a time when you have misheard some song lyrics, by *assimilating* them into your own *schema?* (For hundreds of examples of such, visit www.kissthisguy.com.)

- Which parental style feels right to you: permissive, authoritarian, or authoritative? Why?

Answers to the Test Yourself and Review questions can be found in the green appendix at the end of the book.

Adolescence

9

Among developmental psychologists, the view that childhood fixes our traits has given way to an awareness that as long as we live, we develop. At a five-year high school reunion, former soul mates may be surprised at the divergence of their paths; a decade later, they may have trouble keeping a conversation going.

As today's life-span perspective emerged, psychologists began to look at how maturation and experience shape us not only in infancy and childhood but also in adolescence and beyond. **Adolescence** is life between childhood and adulthood. It starts with the physical beginnings of sexual maturity and ends with the social achievement of independent adult status. In the Western world, this period now roughly corresponds to the teen years, but at earlier times—and in some developing countries today—adolescence was a brief interlude between the dependence of childhood and the responsibilities of adulthood (Baumeister & Tice, 1986). Shortly after sexual maturity, adult responsibilities and status were bestowed, often marked by an elaborate initiation. The new adult then worked, married, and had children.

Then, with improved nutrition, sexual maturity began to occur earlier in many countries. Both physically and socially, kids have been getting older younger. And influenced by compulsory schooling, adult independence began occurring later. As a result, the once brief interlude between biological maturity and social independence has widened (**FIGURE 9.1**). That gap—the years spent morphing from child to adult—is adolescence.

What are the teen years like? In Leo Tolstoy's *Anna Karenina*, the teen years were "that blissful time when childhood is just coming to an end, and out of that vast circle, happy and gay, a path takes shape." But in her diary, written when she and her family hid from the Nazis, teenager Anne Frank described tumultuous teen emotions:

> My treatment varies so much. One day Anne is so sensible and is allowed to know everything; and the next day I hear that Anne is just a silly little goat who doesn't know anything at all and imagines that she's learned a wonderful lot from books. . . . Oh, so many things bubble up inside me as I lie in bed, having to put up with people I'm fed up with, who always misinterpret my intentions.

■ **adolescence** the transition period from childhood to adulthood, extending from puberty to independence.

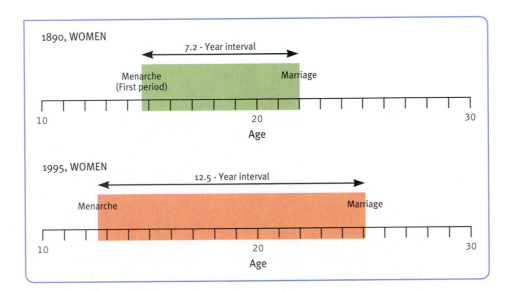

FIGURE 9.1 Adolescence is being stretched from both ends
In the 1890s the average interval between a woman's first menstrual period and marriage was about 7 years; today in industrialized countries it is nearly 12 years. (Guttmacher, 2000.)

Tweens: Eleven going on fifteen
Sexual maturity and interests emerge at younger ages than a half-century ago, as reflected in preteens' toys, music, and clothes. "The 12- to 14-year-olds of yesterday are the 10 to 12's of today," says Bruce Friend (1998), Nickelodeon vice-president.

To G. Stanley Hall (1904), one of the first psychologists to describe adolescence, the tension between biological maturity and social dependence created a period of "storm and stress." Indeed, after age 30, many who grow up in independence-fostering Western cultures look back on their teenage years as a time they would not want to relive, a time when their peers' social approval was imperative, their sense of direction in life was in flux, and their feeling of alienation from their parents was deepest (Arnett, 1999; Macfarlane, 1964). Humorist Dave Barry (1996) is one such person:

> When my dad pulled up, wearing his poodle hat and driving his Nash Metropolitan—a comically tiny vehicle resembling those cars outside supermarkets that go up and down when you put in a quarter, except the Metropolitan looked sillier and had a smaller motor—I was mortified. I might as well have been getting picked up by a flying saucer piloted by some bizarre multi-tentacled stalk-eyed slobber-mouthed alien being that had somehow got hold of a Russian hat. I was horrified at what my peers might think of my dad; it never occurred to me that my peers didn't even notice my dad, because they were too busy being mortified by THEIR parents.
>
> Of course eventually my father stopped being a hideous embarrassment to me, and I, grasping the Torch of Dorkhood, became a hideous embarrassment to my son.

How will you look back on your life 10 years from now? Are you making choices that someday you will recollect with satisfaction? In one survey, adults' most common regret was not having taken their education more seriously (Kinnier & Metha, 1989).

Embarrassment is just one of the many adolescent moods. Despite the mood swings, adolescence can also be as Tolstoy described it—a time of vitality without the cares of adulthood, a time of rewarding friendships, of heightened idealism and a growing sense of life's exciting possibilities (Coleman, 1980). Tolstoy would probably not have been surprised that 9 of 10 high school seniors agree with the statement, "On the whole, I'm satisfied with myself" (*Public Opinion*, 1987).

Physical Development

Preview Question: What major physical changes occur during adolescence?

Adolescence begins with **puberty**, the time when one is maturing sexually. Puberty follows a surge of hormones, which may intensify moods and which trigger a two-year period of rapid physical development, usually beginning at about age 11 in girls and at about age 13 in boys. About the time of puberty, boys' growth propels them to greater height than their female counterparts (**FIGURE 9.2**). During this growth spurt, the **primary sex characteristics**—the reproductive organs and external genitalia—develop dramatically. So do **secondary sex characteristics**, the nonreproductive traits such as breasts and hips in girls, facial hair and deepened voice in boys, pubic and underarm hair in both sexes (**FIGURE 9.3**). A year or two before puberty, however, boys and girls often feel the first stirrings of attraction toward those of the other (or their own) sex (McClintock & Herdat, 1996).

FIGURE 9.2 Height differences
Throughout childhood, boys and girls are similar in height. At puberty, girls surge ahead briefly, but then boys overtake them at about age 14. (Data from Tanner, 1978.)

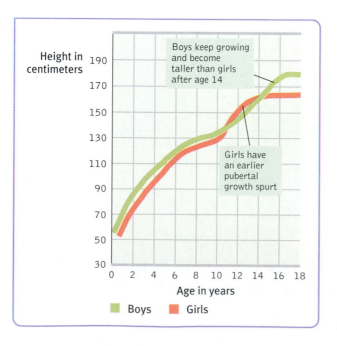

Height in centimeters

Boys keep growing and become taller than girls after age 14

Girls have an earlier pubertal growth spurt

Age in years

■ Boys ■ Girls

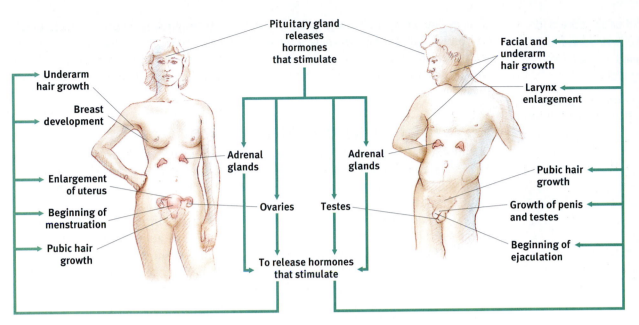

FIGURE **9.3 Body changes at puberty** At about age 11 in girls and age 13 in boys, a surge of hormones triggers a variety of physical changes.

In girls, puberty starts with breast development, which now often begins by age 10 (Brody, 1999). But puberty's landmarks are the first ejaculation in boys, usually by about age 14, and the first menstrual period in girls, by about age 13. The first menstrual period, called **menarche** (meh-NAR-key), is usually a memorable event. Nearly all adult women recall it and remember experiencing a mixture of feelings—pride, excitement, embarrassment, and apprehension (Greif & Ulman, 1982; Woods & others, 1983). For the first few months many keep it a secret from friends. While most discuss it with their mothers, very few discuss it with their fathers (Brooks-Gunn, 1989). Girls who have been prepared for menarche usually experience it as a positive life transition. Afterward, regardless of their age, girls increasingly see and present themselves as different from boys and function more independently of their parents (Golub, 1983). Most men similarly recall their first ejaculation, which usually occurs as a nocturnal emission (Fuller & Downs, 1990).

Just as in the earlier life stages, the *sequence* of physical changes in puberty (for example, breast buds and visible pubic hair before menarche) is far more predictable than their *timing*. Some girls start their growth spurt at 9, some boys as late as age 16. Though such variations have little effect on height at maturity, they may have psychological consequences. Early maturation pays dividends for boys. Boys, being stronger and more athletic during their early teen years, tend to be more popular, self-assured, and independent. But for girls, early maturation can be stressful (Caspi & Moffitt, 1991; Ellis & others, 1999; Stattin & Magnusson, 1990). If a young girl's body is out of sync with her emotional maturity and with what her friends are experiencing, she may begin associating with older adolescents or may suffer teasing. It's not only when we mature that counts, but how people react to our genetically influenced physical development. Remember: *Heredity and environment interact.*

Cognitive Development

Preview Question: How did Piaget and Kohlberg describe cognitive and moral development during adolescence?

Adolescents' developing ability to reason gives them a new level of social awareness and moral judgment. As young teenagers become capable of thinking about their thinking, and of thinking about other people's thinking, they begin imagining what

■ **puberty**   the period of sexual maturation, during which a person becomes capable of reproducing.

■ **primary sex characteristics**   the body structures (ovaries, testes, and external genitalia) that make sexual reproduction possible.

■ **secondary sex characteristics**   nonreproductive sexual characteristics, such as female breasts and hips, male voice quality, and body hair.

■ **menarche [meh-NAR-key]**   the first menstrual period.

"When the pilot told us to brace and grab our ankles, the first thing that went through my mind was that we must all look pretty stupid."

Jeremiah Rawlings, age 12, after a 1989 DC-10 crash in Sioux City, Iowa

"Ben is in his first year of high school, and he's questioning all the right things."

other people are thinking about *them*. (Adolescents might worry less about what others think of them if they knew how similarly self-preoccupied their peers are.) As their cognitive abilities mature, many adolescents start to think about what is ideally possible, and they begin to criticize their society, their parents, and even their own shortcomings.

Developing Reasoning Power

During the early teen years, reasoning is often self-focused. Adolescents may think their private experiences are unique. They may assume their parents just can't understand what it feels like to be dating or to hate school: "But, Mother, *you* don't really know how it feels to be in love" (Elkind, 1978).

Gradually, though, most achieve the intellectual summit that Piaget called *formal operations*. Preadolescents reason concretely, but adolescents become more capable of abstract logic: *If* this, *then* that. We can see this new abstract reasoning power as adolescents ponder and debate human nature, good and evil, truth and justice. Having perhaps envisioned God as an old man in the clouds when they were first capable of symbolic thinking in early childhood, they may now seek a deeper conception of God and existence (Elkind, 1970; Worthington, 1989). Adolescents' ability to reason hypothetically and deduce consequences also enables them to detect inconsistencies in others' reasoning and to spot hypocrisy. This can lead to heated debates with parents and silent vows never to lose sight of their own ideals (Peterson & others, 1986).

Demonstrating their reasoning ability

Although on opposite sides of the abortion debate, these teens demonstrate their newfound ability to think logically about abstract topics. According to Piaget, they are in the final cognitive stage, formal operations.

Developing Morality

A crucial task of childhood and adolescence is discerning right from wrong and developing character—the psychological muscles for controlling impulses. To be a moral person is to *think* morally and *act* accordingly. But as the German poet Goethe noted, "To put one's thoughts into action [is] the most difficult thing in the world."

"It is a delightful harmony when doing and saying go together."

Michel Eyquemde Montaigne (1533–1592)

Moral Thinking

Piaget (1932) believed that children's moral judgments build on their cognitive development. Agreeing with Piaget, Lawrence Kohlberg (1981, 1984) sought to describe the development of *moral reasoning*, the thinking that occurs as we consider right and wrong. Kohlberg posed moral dilemmas to children, adolescents, and adults, then analyzed their answers for evidence of stages of moral thinking. Consider his best-known dilemma:

In Europe, a woman was near death from a very bad disease, a special kind of cancer. There was one drug that the doctors thought might save her. It was a form of radium that a druggist in the same town had recently discovered. The drug was expensive to make, but the druggist was charging 10 times what the drug cost him to make. He paid $200 for the radium and charged $2000 for a small dose of the drug. The sick woman's husband, Heinz, went to everyone he knew to borrow the money, but he could get together only about $1000, which was half of what it cost. He told the druggist that his wife was dying and asked him to sell it cheaper or let him pay later. But the druggist said, "No, I discovered the drug and I'm going to make money from it." Heinz got desperate and broke into the man's store to steal the drug for his wife.

What do you think: Should Heinz have stolen the drug? Why was what he did right or wrong? Kohlberg would not have been interested in your judging Heinz's behavior as right or wrong—either answer could be justified—but rather in your reasoning. All of us are moral philosophers, Kohlberg proposed, and our moral reasoning helps guide our judgments and behavior.

Kohlberg argued that as we develop intellectually we pass through as many as six stages of moral thinking, moving from the simplistic and concrete toward the more abstract and principled. He clustered these six stages into three basic levels: preconventional, conventional, and postconventional.

+ **Preconventional morality** Before age 9, most children have a preconventional morality of self-interest: They obey either to avoid punishment ("If you let your wife die, you will get in trouble") or to gain concrete rewards ("If you save your wife, you will be a hero").

+ **Conventional morality** By early adolescence, morality usually evolves to a more conventional level that cares for others and upholds laws and social rules simply because they are the laws and rules. Being able to take others' perspectives, adolescents may approve actions that will gain social approval or that will help maintain the social order ("If you steal the drug, everyone will think you are a criminal").

+ **Postconventional morality** Some of those who develop the abstract reasoning of formal operational thought may come to a third level. Postconventional morality affirms people's agreed-upon rights ("People have a right to live") or follows what one personally perceives as basic ethical principles ("If you steal the drug, you won't have lived up to your own ideals").

Kohlberg's claim was that these levels form a moral ladder (**FIGURE 9.4**), from the bottom rung of a young child's immature, preconventional morality, to the top rung of an adult's self-defined ethical principles, which only some attain. As with all stage theories, the sequence is unvarying. We begin on the bottom rung and ascend to varying heights.

Research confirms that children in various cultures progress from the level Kohlberg called preconventional into the stages of his conventional level (Edwards, 1981, 1982; Snarey, 1985, 1987). And as our *thinking* matures, our *behavior* also becomes less selfish and more caring (Krebs & Van Hesteren, 1994; Miller & others, 1996). However, the postconventional level is more controversial. It appears mostly in

FIGURE 9.4

Kohlberg's moral ladder

Why is it wrong to steal or cheat on an exam? As moral development progresses, the focus of concern moves from the self to the wider social world. Kohlberg contended that postconventional moral thinking, embodied by Martin Luther King, Jr., may be rejected by those who do not comprehend it.

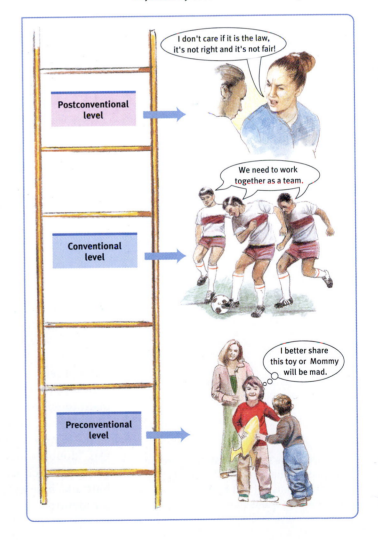

the European and North American educated middle class, which prizes *individualism*—giving priority to one's own goals rather than to group goals (Eckensberger, 1994; Miller & Bersoff, 1995). Critics therefore contend that the theory is biased against the moral reasoning of those in communal societies such as China and India—and also against Western women, whose morality may be based less on abstract, impersonal principles and more on caring relationships.

Moral Action

Our moral reasoning surely influences our moral talk. But sometimes talk is cheap. Morality is also *doing* the right thing, and what we do depends not only on our thinking but on social influences. As political theorist Hannah Arendt (1963) observed, many Nazi concentration camp guards during World War II were ordinary "moral" people who were corrupted by a powerfully evil situation.

Because of social influences, people's willingness to cheat, to discriminate racially, and to smoke marijuana are not neatly determined by their attitudes toward cheating, race, and drugs. The best predictor of whether a teenager smokes marijuana, for instance, is simply how many of the teen's friends smoke it (Oetting & Beauvais, 1987).

Because of the slack between thinking and acting, effective moral education must focus on both. We can stimulate children's moral reasoning through discussions of moral issues and their implications. We can teach children empathy for others' feelings. And we can teach them the self-discipline needed to restrain their impulses—to delay small gratifications now for the sake of bigger gratifications later. Those who do learn to delay gratification become more socially responsible, academically successful, and productive (Funder & Block, 1989; Mischel & others, 1988, 1989).

We can also model just and caring moral behavior. When parents practice what they preach, their moral principles have an impact. Such was true of the caring parents of those who courageously protected Jews in Nazi Europe (Oliner & Oliner, 1988). And when acted upon, moral ideas grow stronger. Our actions feed our attitudes. We are as likely to act ourselves into a way of thinking as to think ourselves into action. To stand up and be counted, to explain and defend our convictions, to commit money and energy is to believe our convictions even more strongly.

Social Development

Preview Question: What tasks and challenges do adolescents face en route to mature adulthood?

Theorist Erik Erikson (1963) contended that each stage of life has its own "psychosocial" task, a crisis that needs resolution. Young children wrestle with issues of *trust*, then *autonomy* (independence), then *initiative* (Table 9.1). School-age children strive for *competence*, the sense that they are able and productive human beings. In adolescence, the task is to synthesize past, present, and future possibilities into a clearer sense of self. Adolescents wonder "Who am I as an individual? What do I want to do with my life? What values should I live by? What do I believe in?" Erikson called this quest to refine one's sense of self the adolescent's "search for identity."

As sometimes happens in psychology, Erikson's interests were bred by his own life experience. As the son of a Jewish mother and a Danish father, Erikson was "doubly an outsider," reports Morton Hunt (1993, p. 391). He was "scorned as a Jew in school but mocked as a Gentile in the synagogue because of his blond hair and blue eyes." Such episodes fueled his interest in the adolescent struggle for identity.

"I am a bit suspicious of any theory that says that the highest moral stage is one in which people talk like college professors."

James Q. Wilson, *The Moral Sense*, 1993

"This might not be ethical. Is that a problem for anybody?"

■ **identity** one's sense of self; according to Erikson, the adolescent's task is to solidify a sense of self by testing and integrating various roles.

TABLE 9.1

ERIKSON'S STAGES OF PSYCHOSOCIAL DEVELOPMENT

Identity Stage (approximate age)	Issues	Description of Task
Infancy (to 1 year)	Trust vs. mistrust	If needs are dependably met, infants develop a sense of basic trust.
Toddlerhood (1 to 2 years)	Autonomy vs. shame and doubt	Toddlers learn to exercise will and do things for themselves, or they doubt their abilities.
Preschooler (3 to 5 years)	Initiative vs. guilt	Preschoolers learn to initiate tasks and carry out plans, or they feel guilty about efforts to be independent.
Elementary school (6 years to puberty)	Competence vs. inferiority	Children learn the pleasure of applying themselves to tasks, or they feel inferior.
Adolescence (teen years into 20s)	Identity vs. role confusion	Teenagers work at refining a sense of self by testing roles and then integrating them to form a single identity, or they become confused about who they are.
Young adulthood (20s to early 40s)	Intimacy vs. isolation	Young adults struggle to form close relationships and to gain the capacity for intimate love, or they feel socially isolated.
Middle adulthood (40s to 60s)	Generativity vs. stagnation	The middle-aged discover a sense of contributing to the world, usually through family and work, or they may feel a lack of purpose.
Late adulthood (late 60s and up)	Integrity vs. despair	When reflecting on his or her life, the older adult may feel a sense of satisfaction or failure.

Forming an Identity

To refine their sense of identity, adolescents in Western cultures usually try out different "selves" in different situations—perhaps acting out one self at home, another with friends, and still another at school and work. If two of these situations overlap—as when a teenager brings home friends with whom he is Joe Cool—the discomfort can be considerable. The teen asks, "Which self should I be? Which is the real me?" Often, this role confusion is resolved by the gradual reshaping of a self-definition that unifies the various selves into a consistent and comfortable sense of who one is—an **identity**.

But not always. Erikson noticed that some adolescents forge their identity early, simply by taking on their parents' values and expectations. (Traditional, less individualistic cultures inform adolescents who they are rather than leaving them to decide on their own.) Other adolescents may adopt a negative identity that defines itself in opposition to parents and society but in conformity with a particular peer group—the jocks, the preppies, the geeks, the goths. Still others never quite seem to find themselves or to develop strong commitments. For most, the identity question—Who am I?—continues past the teen years and reappears at turning points during adult life.

"I am becoming still more independent of my parents; young as I am, I face life with more courage than Mummy; my feeling for justice is immovable, and truer than hers. I know what I want, I have a goal, an opinion, I have a religion, and love. Let me be myself and then I am satisfied. I know that I'm a woman, a woman with inward strength and plenty of courage."

Anne Frank, *Diary of a Young Girl*, 1947

Who shall I be today?
By varying the way they look, adolescents try out different "selves." Although we eventually form a consistent and stable sense of identity, the "self" we present may change with the situation.

intimacy in Erikson's theory, the ability to form close, loving relationships; a primary developmental task in late adolescence and early adulthood.

The late teen years, when many people begin attending college or working full time, provide new opportunities for trying out possible roles. As seniors, many college students have achieved a clearer identity than they had as first-year students (Waterman, 1988). Their identity typically incorporates an increasingly positive self-concept. In several nationwide studies, researchers have given young Americans tests of self-esteem. (Sample item: "I am able to do things as well as most other people.") Between ages 13 and 23, the self-concept usually becomes more positive, especially among boys and among those who belong to a satisfying peer group. A clearer, more self-affirming identity is forming, and with it comes a greater sense of control over one's future (Baumgardner, 1990; O'Malley & Bachman, 1983; Strange & Forsyth, 1993).

Identity also becomes more personalized. Daniel Hart (1988) asked youths of various ages to imagine a machine that would clone (a) what you think and feel, (b) your appearance, or (c) your relationships with friends and family. When he then asked which clone would be "closest to being you?" three-fourths of the seventh-graders chose (c), the clone with the same social network. In contrast, three-fourths of the ninth-graders chose (a), the one with their individual thoughts and feelings.

Developing Intimacy

Erikson contended that the adolescent identity stage is followed in young adulthood by a developing capacity for **intimacy**, the ability to form emotionally close relationships. Once you have a clear and comfortable sense of who you are, said Erikson, you are ready for close relationships.

Gender and Social Connectedness

To Carol Gilligan and her colleagues (1982, 1990), the "normal" struggle to create one's separate identity describes individualist males more than relationship-oriented females. Gilligan believes females differ from males both in being less concerned with viewing themselves as separate individuals and in being more concerned with "making connections."

These gender differences surface early, in children's play. Boys typically play in large groups with an activity focus and little intimate discussion. Girls usually play in smaller groups, often with one friend. Their play is less competitive than boys' and more imitative of social relationships. Both in play and other settings, females are more open and responsive to feedback than are males (Maccoby, 1990; Roberts, 1991). As teens, girls spend more time with friends and less time alone (Wong & Csikszentmihalyi, 1991).

"What's the difference between a man and E.T.? E.T. phoned home."

Anonymous

The gender difference in connectedness carries into adulthood. Women, being more *interdependent*, use conversation to explore relationships; men use it to communicate solutions (Tannen, 1990). Asked difficult questions—"Do you have an idea why the sky is blue?" "Do you have any idea why shorter people live longer?"—men are more likely than women to hazard answers rather than admit they don't know, a phenomenon that Traci Giuliano and her colleagues (1998a,b) call the *male answer syndrome.*

Women emphasize caring and provide most of the care to the very young and the very old. Women purchase 85 percent of greeting cards (*Time*, 1997). Although 69 percent of people say they have a close relationship with their father, 90 percent feel close to their mother (Hugick, 1989). Men, like empowered people generally, emphasize freedom and self-reliance. (That helps explain why at all ages men assign less importance to religion and pray less often than their female counterparts [Benson, 1992].)

Bonds and feelings of support are also stronger among women than among men (Rossi & Rossi, 1993). Women's ties—as mothers, daughters, sisters, aunts, and grandmothers—bind families together. As friends, women are more intimate than men; they talk more often and more openly (Berndt, 1992; Dindia & Allen, 1992). Curiously, women's friends are less often friends with each other than are men's friends (Kashima & others, 1995).

In one survey of 4000 middle-aged twins, 78 percent of the women rated their "nurturance" above the men's average self-rating (Lykken, 1999), and both men and women report their friendships with women to be more intimate, enjoyable, and nurturing (Rubin, 1985; Sapadin, 1988). When wanting understanding and someone with whom to share worries and hurts, both men and women usually turn to women.

Gender differences in connectedness and other traits peak in late adolescence and early adulthood—the very years most commonly studied. As teenagers, girls become progressively less assertive and more flirtatious; boys become more domineering and unexpressive. But by age 50, these differences have diminished. Women become more assertive and self-confident and men more empathic and less domineering (Maccoby, 1998).

Some see biological wisdom in these changing gender roles. They speculate that, during courtship and early parenthood, social expectations lead both sexes to downplay traits that interfere with their roles. As long as men are expected to provide and protect, they forgo their more dependent and tender sides (Gutmann, 1977). As long as women are expected to nurture, they forgo their impulses to be assertive and independent. When they graduate from these early adult roles, men and women are freer to develop and express their previously inhibited tendencies.

> "In the long years liker must they grow; The man be more of woman, she of man."
>
> Alfred, Lord Tennyson, *The Princess*, 1847

Separating From Parents

As adolescents seek to form their own identities, they begin to separate themselves from their parents (Paikoff & Brooks-Gunn, 1991). The preschooler who can't be close enough to mother, who loves to touch and cling to her, becomes the 14-year-old who wouldn't be caught dead holding hands with mom. The transition occurs gradually (**FIGURE 9.5**). By adolescence, arguments occur more often, usually over mundane things—household chores, bed time, homework (Tesser & others, 1989). From early to late adolescence, parent-adolescent conflicts become less frequent but temporarily (during early adolescence) more intense (Laursen & others, 1998).

For a minority of parents and their adolescents, differences lead to estrangement. But for most, disagreement at the level of bickering is not destructive.

+ A study of 6000 adolescents in 10 countries, from Australia to Bangladesh to Turkey, found that most liked their parents (Offer & others, 1988). "We usually get along but . . .," adolescents often report (Galambos, 1992; Steinberg, 1987).

+ In one survey of 25,000 middle-class teens worldwide, more than 80 percent rated family relationships as an "important" guiding principle for their lives, and more than half said it was *most* important—more significant than their "relationship with friends," "having fun," or "making the world a better place" (Stepp, 1996).

+ A Gallup poll (1996) of American teens reported that 97 percent said they got along "fairly" or "very" well with their parents. Most, however, reported getting along better with Mom than with Dad. Positive relations with parents support positive peer relations. High school girls who have the most affectionate relationships with their mothers tend also to enjoy the most intimate friendships with girlfriends (Gold & Yanof, 1985). And teens who feel close to their parents tend to be healthy and happy and to do well in school (Resnick & others, 1997). Of course, we can state this correlation the other way: Misbehaving teens are more likely to have tense parental relationships and to say their parents are jerks.

FIGURE 9.5

The changing parent-child relationship
Interviews from a large, national study of Canadian families reveal that the typically close, warm relationships between parents and preschoolers loosen as children age. (Data from *Statistics Canada*, 1999.)

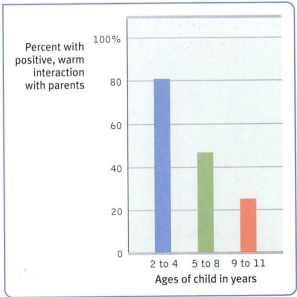

DOONESBURY

Parent–adolescent relations
For a relative few, adolescence means estrangement from parents.

In Western cultures, adolescence is typically a time of diminishing parental influence and growing peer influence. Asked in a survey if they had "ever had a serious talk" with their child about illegal drugs, 85 percent of American *parents* answered yes. But the teens sometimes tuned out this earnest advice, for only 45 percent could recall such a talk (or saw it as less serious [Morin & Brossard, 1997]). Instead, what their friends are—what "everybody's doing"—they often become.

Heredity does much of the heavy lifting in forming individual differences in character and personality, and peer influences do much of the rest. Teens are herd animals. They talk, dress, and act more like their peers than their parents. But peers see their parents as having more influence in other areas—in shaping their religious faith and practices, and in thinking about college and career choices, for example (*Emerging Trends*, 1997).

As people mature in young adulthood, the emotional ties between parents and children continue to loosen. During their early twenties, many still lean heavily on their parents. By their late twenties, most feel more comfortably independent of their parents and better able to empathize with them as fellow adults (Frank, 1988; White, 1983). As we enter the new millennium, this graduation from adolescence to adulthood is taking longer. From Europe to Australia, adolescents are taking more time to finish college, to leave the nest, to establish their careers. In the United States, for example, the average age at first marriage has increased nearly 4 years since 1960 (to 26 for men, 24 for women).

REVIEW AND REFLECT:

Adolescence

Due to earlier maturation and prolonged education, adolescence—the transition years between biological maturity and social independence—has lengthened in many countries.

What major physical changes occur during adolescence?

Adolescence begins with a growth spurt that heralds the period of sexual maturation we call puberty and ends with the achievement of adult independence. Depending on how other people react, early or late maturation can influence adjustment, again illustrating how our genes and our environment interact in shaping us.

How did Piaget and Kohlberg describe cognitive and moral development during adolescence?

Piaget theorized that adolescents develop the capacity for formal operations, which enables them to reason abstractly. However, some developmentalists believe that the development of formal logic depends on schooling as well, and that the rudiments of logic appear earlier than Piaget believed.

Following Piaget's lead, Lawrence Kohlberg contended that moral thinking likewise proceeds through a sequence of stages, from a preconventional morality of self-interest, to a conventional morality concerned with gaining others' approval or doing one's duty, to (in some people) a postconventional morality of agreed-upon rights or universal ethical principles. But morality also lies in actions, which are influenced by the social situation and inner attitudes as well as by moral reasoning. Moreover, say Kohlberg's critics, the postconventional level represents morality from the perspective of individualist, liberal-minded males.

What tasks and challenges do adolescents face en route to mature adulthood?

Erik Erikson theorized that a chief task of adolescence is solidifying one's sense of self—one's identity. For many people, this struggle continues into the adult years as new relationships emerge and new roles are assumed. Although adolescence has traditionally been viewed as a time of storm and stress, researchers have found that most teenagers relate to their parents reasonably well and generally affirm their parents' beliefs and attitudes.

Terms and Concepts to Remember

adolescence, p. 141
puberty, p. 142
primary sex characteristics,
   p. 142
  secondary sex characteristics,
    p. 142

menarche [meh-NAR-key],
   p. 143
identity, p. 147
intimacy, p. 148

Test Yourself

9.1. Adolescence is marked by the onset of
  a. an identity crisis.   c. separation anxiety.
  b. puberty.   d. parent-child conflict.

9.2. The adolescent growth spurt is marked by dramatic developments in the sex characteristics. Primary sex characteristics relate to _____; secondary sex characteristics refer to _____.
  a. ejaculation; menarche
  b. breasts and facial hair; ovaries and testes
  c. emotional maturity; hormone surges
  d. reproductive organs; nonreproductive traits

9.3. According to Piaget, the ability to think logically about abstractions indicates
  a. concrete operational thought.
  b. egocentrism.
  c. formal operational thought.
  d. conservation.

9.4. According to Kohlberg, preconventional morality focuses on _____; conventional morality is more concerned with _____.
  a. upholding laws and social rules; self-interest
  b. self-interest; basic ethical principles
  c. upholding laws and social rules; basic ethical principles
  d. self-interest; upholding laws and social rules

9.5. Erik Erikson contends that each stage of life has its own special psychosocial task or challenge. The primary task during adolescence is to
  a. attain formal operations.
  b. forge an identity.
  c. develop a sense of intimacy with another person.
  d. live independent of parents.

9.6. The differences among individuals of each sex are much greater than the differences between men and women. Nevertheless, women more than men exhibit a concern for
  a. independence and self-reliance.
  b. social connections.
  c. competitive achievement.
  d. social stereotyping.

9.7. Earlier maturation and prolonged education have tended to
  a. lengthen the period between biological maturity and social independence.
  b. shorten the period between biological maturity and social independence.
  c. magnify the effects of the biological differences between men and women.
  d. diminish the effects of the biological differences between men and women.

Review: To predict whether a teenager smokes marijuana, ask how many of the teen's friends smoke it. One explanation for this correlation is peer influence. What's another?

Reflect: What are the most positive and most negative things you remember about your own adolescence? And who do you credit or blame more—your parents or your peers?

Answers to Test Yourself and Review questions can be found in the green appendix at the end of the book.

10 Adulthood

At one time, psychologists viewed adulthood, especially the center-of-life years between adolescence and old age, as one long plateau. No longer. Those who follow the unfolding of people's adult lives now believe our development continues. Physically, cognitively, and especially socially, people at age 50 differ from their 25-year-old selves.

It is more difficult to generalize about adulthood stages than about life's early years. If you know that James is a 1-year-old and Jamal is a 10-year-old, you could say a great deal about each child. Not so with adults who differ by a similar number of years. The boss may be 30 or 60; the marathon runner may be 20 or 50; your classmates may be teenagers or grandparents. Likewise, a 19-year-old can be a parent who supports a child or a child who gets an allowance. Yet our life courses are in some ways similar. Our bodies, our minds, and our relationships undergo some changes in common with those of our childhood friends, who in other ways now seem so very different.

"I am still learning."

Michelangelo, 1560, at age 85

Physical Changes

Preview Questions: How do our bodies change in middle and late adulthood? What sensory and neural changes mark the aging process?

Our physical abilities—muscular strength, reaction time, sensory keenness, and cardiac output—all crest by the mid-twenties. Like the declining daylight after the summer solstice, declining physical prowess begins imperceptibly. Athletes are often the first to notice. World-class sprinters and swimmers peak in their teens or early twenties. Women, because they mature earlier than men, also peak earlier. But most of us—especially those of us whose daily lives do not require top physical performance—hardly perceive the early signs of decline.

Physical Changes in Middle Adulthood

Middle-aged athletes know all too well that physical decline gradually accelerates. As a 57-year-old who regularly plays basketball, I now find myself occasionally wondering whether my team really needs me down court. But even diminished vigor is sufficient for normal activities. Moreover, during early and middle adulthood, physical vigor has less to do with age than with a person's health and exercise habits. Many of today's physically fit 50-year-olds run 4 miles with ease, while sedentary 25-year-olds find themselves huffing and puffing up two flights of stairs. Even many 70-year-olds don't yet feel old.

How old does a person have to be before you think of him or her as old? The average 18- to 29-year-old says 67. The average person 60 and over says 76 (Yankelovich, 1995).

As in adolescence, the physical changes of adult life may trigger psychological responses, which vary depending on how one views growing older. In some Eastern cultures, where respect and power come with age, outward signs of advancing years are accepted and even welcomed. In Western cultures, where the perceived ideal is smooth skin and a slim torso, the wrinkles and bulges that frequently accompany middle age can threaten self-esteem. Millions therefore spend billions in hopes of slowing the process. But nature will not be denied; inevitably the lines appear and the youthful form begins to change its shape.

For women, the foremost biological sign of aging is **menopause**, the ending of the menstrual cycle, usually beginning within a few years of age 50. Menopause and its physical symptoms accompany a reduction in the hormone estrogen. For 4 or 5 in 10 Canadian and U.S. women, but only 1 in 7 Japanese women, these include occasional hot flashes (Goode, 1999; Lock, 1998). Like the stereotype of adolescent storm and stress, the image of menopausal emotionality and depression clashes with reality: Menopause usually does *not* create psychological problems for women. One survey of 2500 middle-aged Massachusetts women, another that followed 541 middle-aged Pennsylvania women for 3 years, and yet another that followed 3049 middle-aged women over 10 years all found them no more or less depressed if experiencing menopause (Busch & others, 1994; Matthews, 1992; McKinlay & others, 1987a,b).

A woman's expectations and attitudes influence the emotional impact of menopause. Does she see it as a sign that she is losing her femininity and sexual attractiveness and growing old? Or does she view it as liberation from menstrual periods, fears of pregnancy, and children's demands? To learn women's attitudes toward menopause, Bernice Neugarten and her colleagues (1963) did what, amazingly, no one had ever done: They questioned women whose experience of menopause had not led them to seek treatment. When asked whether it is true that after menopause "women generally feel better than they have for years," only one-fourth of the pre-menopausal women under age 45 guessed yes. Of the older women who had experienced menopause, two-thirds said yes. As one woman said, "I can remember my mother saying that after her menopause she really got her vigor, and I can say the same thing myself." In one MacArthur Foundation study of 3000 midlife adults, most postmenopausal women recalled "only relief" when their periods stopped; just 2 percent felt "only regret" (Goode, 1999).

Men experience no equivalent to menopause—no cessation of fertility, no sharp drop in sex hormones. They do experience a more gradual decline in sperm count, testosterone level, and speed of erection and ejaculation. If testosterone levels plummet too fast and far, the result may be depression, irritability, insomnia, impotence, or weakness, which can be treated by testosterone replacement therapy (Sternbach, 1998). Some may also experience psychological distress related to their perception of decreased virility and declining physical capacities. But most men age without such problems.

After middle age, most men and women remain capable of satisfying sexual activity. When people over 60 were surveyed by the National Council on Aging, 39 percent expressed satisfaction with the amount of sex they were having and 39 percent said they wished for sex more frequently (Leary, 1998).

Physical Changes in Later Life

Is old age "more to be feared than death" (Juvenal, *Satires*)? Or is life "most delightful when it is on the downward slope" (Seneca, *Epistulae ad Lucilium*)? What is it like to grow old? To gauge your own understanding, take the following true/false quiz:

1. By the year 2050, 1 in 10 people worldwide will be 65 or older (see page 154).
2. Older people become more susceptible to short-term illnesses (see page 155).
3. About one-fourth of people over age 65 live in nursing homes, hospitals, homes for the aged, or other institutions (see page 155).
4. During old age many of the brain's neurons die (see page 155).
5. If they live to be 90 or older, most elderly people eventually become senile (see page 156).
6. Recognition memory—the ability to identify things previously experienced—declines with age (see pages 157–158).
7. Life satisfaction peaks in the fifties and then gradually declines after age 65 (see pages 164–165).

menopause the time of natural cessation of menstruation; also refers to the biological changes a woman experiences as her ability to reproduce declines.

"If the truth were known, we'd have to diagnose [older women] as having P.M.F.—Post-Menstrual Freedom."

Social psychologist Jacqueline Goodchilds (1987)

"Happy fortieth. I'll take the muscle tone in your upper arms, the girlish timbre of your voice, your amazing tolerance for caffeine, and your ability to digest french fries. The rest of you can stay."

World record for longevity?
French woman Jeanne Calment, possibly the oldest human in history, died in 1998 at age 122. At age 100, she was still riding a bike. Sierra Leone has the world's shortest life expectancy (38 years). Japan has the longest (80 years).

After age 30, the risk of death doubles every 8 years. Although 48-year-olds' life expectancy is greater today than it was a century ago, their risk of dying is still twice as high as that of 40-year-olds (National Center for Health Statistics, 1992; Olshansky & others, 1993).

Most stairway falls taken by older persons occur on the top step, precisely where the person typically descends from a window-lit hallway into the darker stairwell (Fozard & Popkin, 1978). Our knowledge of aging could be used to design environments that would reduce such accidents (National Research Council, 1990).

Life Expectancy

The statements on page 153—all false—are among the misconceptions about aging exploded by recent research on the world's most rapidly growing population group. The post–65-year-old population rose from fewer than 1 in 100 in 1900 to 1 in 16 in 1992, en route to 1 in 5 by 2050 (Olshansky & others, 1993). Worldwide, life expectancy at birth increased from 49 years in 1950 to 67 in 1995—and to 75 in the more developed countries (PRB, 1998; Sivard, 1996). This increasing life expectancy combines with decreasing birthrates to make the elderly a bigger and bigger population segment. Clearly, countries that have depended on children to care for the aged are destined for major social changes.

Although 126 male embryos begin life for every 100 females who do so, males are more prone to dying (Strickland, 1992). By birth, the sex ratio is down to 105 males for every 100 females. During the first year, male infants' death rates exceed females' by one-fourth. Women outlive men by 4 years worldwide and by nearly 7 years in Canada, the United States, and Australia. (Rather than marrying a man older than themselves, 20-year-old women who want a husband who shares their life expectancy should wait for the 14-year-old boys to mature.) By age 100, females outnumber males 5 to 1.

But few of us live to 100. Even if no one died before age 50 and cancer, heart disease, and infectious illness were eliminated, average life expectancy would still increase only to about 85 or a few years beyond (Barinaga, 1991). The body ages. Its cells stop reproducing. It becomes frail. It becomes vulnerable to tiny insults—hot weather, a fall, a mild flu bug—that at age 20 would have been trivial.

Why do we eventually wear out? Why don't we, like the bristlecone pine trees, rockfish, and some social insect queens, grow older without withering? One theory, proposed by evolutionary biologists, speculates that the answer relates to our survival as a species: We pass on our genes most successfully when we raise our young and then stop consuming resources. Moreover, once we've fulfilled our gene-reproducing task, there are no natural selection pressures against genes that cause degeneration in later life (Olshansky & others, 1993; Sapolsky & Finch, 1991).

Sensory Abilities

As we have seen, physical decline begins in early adulthood, but we are not usually acutely aware of it until later life. Visual sharpness diminishes, and adaptation to changes in light level slows. Muscle strength, reaction time, and stamina also diminish noticeably, as do hearing, distance perception, and the sense of smell (**FIGURE 10.1**). In later life, the stairs get steeper, the newsprint gets smaller, and people seem to mumble more.

FIGURE **10.1**
The aging senses
Sight, smell, and hearing all decline after age 70. (From Doty & others, 1984.)

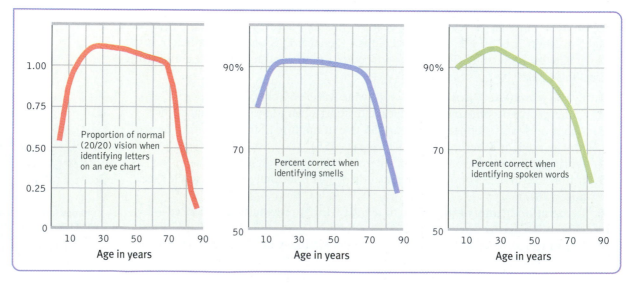

With age, the eye's pupil shrinks and its lens becomes less transparent, reducing the amount of light reaching the retina. In fact, a 65-year-old retina receives only about one-third as much light as its 20-year-old counterpart (Kline & Schieber, 1985). Thus, to see as well as a 20-year-old when reading or driving, a 65-year-old needs three times as much light—a reason for buying cars with untinted windshields. This also explains why older people sometimes ask younger people, "Don't you need better light for reading?"

Health

For those growing older, there is both bad and good news about health. The bad news: The body's disease-fighting immune system weakens, making the elderly more susceptible to life-threatening ailments such as cancer and pneumonia. The good news: Thanks partly to a lifetime's accumulation of antibodies, older people *less* often suffer short-term ailments, such as common flu and cold viruses. For example, those over 65 are half as likely as 20-year-olds and one-fifth as likely as preschoolers to suffer upper respiratory flu each year (National Center for Health Statistics, 1990). This is one reason why older workers have lower absenteeism rates (Rhodes, 1983).

One survey revealed that most elderly people believe the majority of their peers suffer serious health problems. But when asked about their own health, fewer than one in four reported that *they* have such a problem (National Council on the Aging, 1976). In Canada, only 8 percent of those over 75 describe their health as "poor" (*Statistics Canada*, 1999). So it shouldn't surprise us that only 5 percent of all those over 65 live in hospitals, nursing homes, and other such institutions.

Aging levies a tax on the brain by slowing our neural processing. Up to the teen years, we process information with greater and greater speed (Fry & Hale, 1996; Kail, 1991). But compared with teens and young adults, older people take a bit more time to react, to solve perceptual puzzles, even to remember names (Bashore & others, 1997; Verhaeghen & Salthouse, 1997). And, as **FIGURE 10.2** indicates, car accident rates per mile sharply increase after age 75. By age 75, they reach the relatively high teenage level (National Research Council, 1990). Speed slows especially when the task becomes complex (Cerella, 1985; Poon, 1987). At video games, most 70-year-olds are no match for a 20-year-old.

During aging, brain regions important to memory begin to atrophy (Schacter, 1996). In young adulthood, a small, gradual net loss of brain cells begins, contributing to a 5 percent or so reduction of brain weight by age 80. Aging may proceed more slowly in women. Not only do women worldwide live four years longer than men, their brains shrink slower than men's (Coffey & others, 1998).

> "For some reason, possibly to save ink, the restaurants had started printing their menus in letters the height of bacteria."
>
> Dave Barry, *Dave Barry Turns Fifty*, 1998

Keeping the biological clock running smoothly
How quickly people age depends in part on their health habits. As this cheerful group makes clear, the more active people remain, the more vigor they retain.

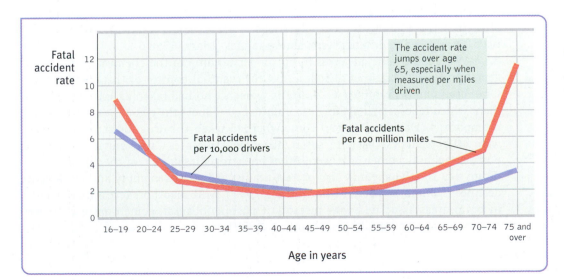

FIGURE 10.2
Age and fatal accidents
Slowing reactions contribute to increased accident risks among those 75 and older (Stock, 1995). Would you favor driver exams based on performance, not age, to screen out those whose slow reactions or sensory impairments indicate accident risk?

(Graph: Fatal accident rate vs. Age in years. Annotation: "The accident rate jumps over age 65, especially when measured per miles driven." Lines labeled "Fatal accidents per 10,000 drivers" and "Fatal accidents per 100 million miles." Age groups on x-axis: 16–19, 20–24, 25–29, 30–34, 35–39, 40–44, 45–49, 50–54, 55–59, 60–64, 65–69, 70–74, 75 and over.)

■ **Alzheimer's disease** a progressive and irreversible brain disorder characterized by gradual deterioration of memory, reasoning, language, and, finally, physical functioning.

The birth of new cells and the proliferation of neural connections, especially in those who remain active, helps compensate for the cell loss (Coleman & Flood, 1986). This helps explain the common finding that adults who remain active—physically, sexually, and mentally—retain more of their capacity for such activities in later years (Jarvik, 1975; Pfeiffer, 1977). Physical exercise enhances muscles, bones, and energy and helps prevent obesity and heart disease. It also, it now seems, stimulates brain cell development, thanks perhaps to increased oxygen and nutrient flow (Kempermann & others, 1998). And that may explain why sedentary older adults randomly assigned to a walking program exhibit enhanced memory and sharpened judgment (Kramer & others, 1999). We are more likely to rust from disuse than to wear out from overuse. "Use it or lose it" is sound advice.

Dementia and Alzheimer's Disease

Some adults do, unfortunately, suffer a substantial loss of brain cells. Up to age 95, the incidence of mental disintegration doubles roughly every 5 years (**FIGURE 10.3**).

A series of small strokes, a brain tumor, or alcoholism can progressively damage the brain, causing that mental erosion we call *dementia*. So, too, can the most feared of all brain ailments, **Alzheimer's disease**, which strikes 3 percent of the world's population by age 75. Alzheimer's symptoms are *not* the same as normal aging. (Occasionally forgetting where you laid the car keys is no cause for alarm; forgetting how to get home does suggest Alzheimer's.)

Alzheimer's destroys even the brightest of minds. First memory, then reasoning and language deteriorate. Robert Sayre (1979) recalls his father shouting at his afflicted mother to "think harder," while his mother, confused, embarrassed, on the verge of tears, randomly searched the house for lost objects. As Alzheimer's runs its course, after 5 to 20 years, the patient becomes emotionally flat, then disoriented, then incontinent, finally mentally vacant—a sort of living death, a mere body stripped of its humanity.

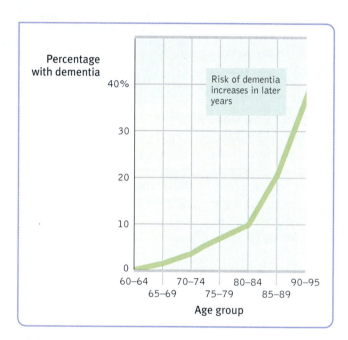

FIGURE 10.3 Incidence of dementia (mental disintegration) by age
Risk of mental loss due to Alzheimer's disease or a series of strokes doubles about every 5 years in later life. (From Jorm & others, 1987, based on 22 studies in industrial nations.)

Underlying the symptoms of Alzheimer's is a deterioration of neurons that produce the neurotransmitter acetylcholine. Deprived of this vital chemical messenger, memory and thinking suffer. An autopsy reveals two telltale abnormalities in these acetylcholine-producing neurons: shriveled protein filaments in the cell body and plaques (globs of degenerating tissue) at the tips of neuron branches. Different forms of Alzheimer's disease have been linked to different gene abnormalities (Marx, 1998).

With continuing advances in our understanding of the chemical, neural, and genetic roots of Alzheimer's, hopes grow for eventual control of this dread disease. One recent study examined 1124 elderly women who had taken an estrogen supplement which relieves menopause discomforts and reduces the risk of heart disease and osteoporosis (Davidson, 1996). Those who had taken the drug for at least a decade were 40 percent less likely to suffer Alzheimer's disease. Other studies comparing postmenopausal women who were either on estrogen replacement therapy or not indicate that the therapy may also protect against age-related memory and intelligence declines (Kimura, 1995; Resnick & others, 1997). MRI snapshots reveal more activity in brain areas associated with memory if postmenopausal women are on estrogen rather than a placebo (Shaywitz & others, 1999).

As it becomes possible to discern by brain scans or genetic testing those likely to suffer Alzheimer's disease, would you want to take the test? If so, at what age would you take it?

Cognitive Changes

Preview Question: In what ways do memory and intelligence change as we age?

Among the most controversial questions in the study of the human life span is whether adult cognitive abilities, such as memory, creativity, and intelligence, parallel the gradually accelerating decline of physical abilities. Employers, for example, may wonder whether they should encourage their senior workers to retire—or capitalize on their experience. Does the common perception that elderly people are generally less sharp (Kite & Johnson, 1988) lend truth to the proverb, "You can't teach an old dog new tricks"? Or does the evidence support another proverb: "You're never too old to learn"?

Aging and Memory

As we age, we remember some things well. Looking back in later life, people most vividly recall not only recent happenings but also their experiences in life's second two decades (Holmes & Conway, 1999; Rubin & others, 1998). Asked to recall the one or two most important events over the last half century, they tend to name events from their teens or twenties. Whatever one experienced around this stage of life—the Great Depression, World War II, the civil rights movement, the Vietnam war (or, for current twenty-somethings, perhaps the explosion of the Internet)—becomes pivotal (Pillemer, 1998; Schuman & Scott, 1989). Our teens and twenties are also the time when we experience so many of life's memorable "firsts"—first date, first job, first going to college, first meeting your parents-in-law.

Early adulthood is a peak time for some types of learning and remembering. In one experiment, Thomas Crook and Robin West (1990) invited 1205 people to learn some names. Fourteen videotaped people said their names, using a common format: "Hi, I'm Larry." Then the same individuals reappeared and said, for example, "I'm from Philadelphia"—thus providing a visual and voice cue for remembering the person's name. As **FIGURE 10.4** shows, everyone remembered more names after a second and third replay of the introductions, but younger adults consistently surpassed older adults in their name recall. Similar results appear in other studies. Within hours after Prime Minister Margaret Thatcher announced her resignation, young and old British people recalled how they heard the news. When asked again 11 months later, 90 percent of the younger group but only 42 percent of the older group told the same story (Cohen & others, 1994).

But consider another experiment. David Schonfield and Betty-Anne Robertson (1966) asked adults of various ages to learn a list of 24 words. Without giving any clues, the researchers asked some to recall as many words as they could from the list, and others simply to *recognize* words, using multiple-choice

If you are within five years of 20, what experiences from your last year will you likely never forget? If you are older, what do you remember most vividly from that era of your life?

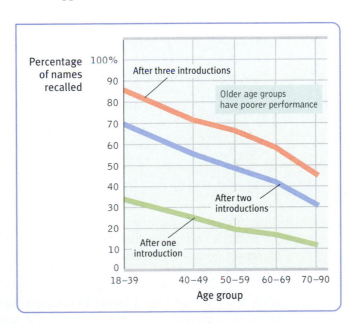

FIGURE 10.4 Tests of recall
Recalling new names introduced once, twice, or three times is easier for younger adults than for older ones. (Data from Crook & West, 1990.)

FIGURE 10.5 Recall and recognition in adulthood

In this experiment, the ability to *recall* new information declined during early and middle adulthood, but the ability to *recognize* new information did not. (From Schonfield & Robertson, 1966.)

Taking several pills several times each day provides many opportunities to become confused about whether one has taken the pills or only thought about doing so. The simple solution is an external aid: Put each week's pills into a box that has slots for all the days and times. (Pharmacies offer these.)

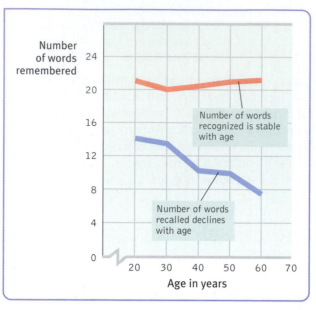

Number of words remembered

Number of words recognized is stable with age

Number of words recalled declines with age

Age in years

questions. As FIGURE 10.5 shows, younger adults had better recall, but researchers found no similar memory decline with age on the recognition tests. Tests also reveal that recognition memory is better for older adults early rather than late in the day (May & others, 1993). So, how well older people remember depends: Are they being asked simply to *recognize* what they have tried to memorize (minimal decline) or to *recall* it without clues (greater decline)?

Forgetting seems also to depend on the type of information we are trying to remember. If you are asked to recall meaningless information—nonsense syllables or unimportant events—then the older you are, the more errors you are likely to make. However, if the information is meaningful and you are older, your rich web of existing knowledge will help you to catch it. Older people's capacity to learn and remember skills and *meaningful* material shows less decline (Graf, 1990; Labouvie-Vief & Schell, 1982; Perlmutter, 1983).

Prospective memory—"Remember to pick up milk"—remains strong when events help trigger the memory. (We walk by a convenience store on the way home.) Time-based tasks ("Remember the 3:00 meeting") prove somewhat more challenging for the elderly. Habitual tasks, such as remembering to take medications three times daily, can be especially challenging for older people, report Gilles Einstein, Mark McDaniel, and their colleagues (1990, 1995, 1998).

Those who study our capacity to learn and remember are aware of one other important complication: Right through our later years, we continue to diverge. If you think 20-year-olds differ widely in their abilities to learn and remember, consider this: 70-year-olds differ much more. Some 70-year-olds perform below nearly all 20-year-olds; other 70-year-olds match or outdo the average 20-year-old. Neuropsychologist Michela Gallagher (1990) has found that aging rats, too, vary much more than do young rats. Some old rats are as quick-witted as the smartest of young rats; others, for reasons related to brain deterioration, show their age.

Adults' learning skills can be seen in classrooms. In recent years, more and more adults have turned to leisure education programs or returned to school (including many of you reading this book). Despite occasional difficulties in adjusting to the demands of course work and testing, most older students do better than the typical 18-year-old, perhaps because they have clearer goals (Badenhoop & Johansen, 1980).

Aging and Intelligence

What happens to our broader intellectual powers as we age? Do they gradually decline, as does our ability to recall new material? Or do they remain constant, as does our ability to recognize meaningful material? The evolving answer to this question makes an interesting research story, one that illustrates psychology's self-correcting process (Woodruff-Pak, 1989).

Phase I: Cross-Sectional Evidence for Intellectual Decline

In **cross-sectional studies**, researchers test and compare people of various ages. When giving intelligence tests to representative samples of people, researchers consistently find that older adults give fewer correct answers than do younger adults. David Wechsler (1972), creator of the most widely used adult intelligence test, therefore concluded that "the decline of mental ability with age is part of the general [aging] process of the organism as a whole."

For a long time, this rather dismal view of mental decline went unchallenged. Many corporations established mandatory retirement policies, assuming the companies would benefit by replacing aging workers with younger, presumably more capable, employees. As everyone "knew," you couldn't teach an old dog new tricks.

Phase II: Longitudinal Evidence for Intellectual Stability

After colleges began giving intelligence tests to entering students about 1920, several psychologists saw their chance to study intelligence **longitudinally**—retesting the same people over a period of years. What they expected to find was a decrease in intelligence after about age 30 (Schaie & Geiwitz, 1982). What they actually found was a surprise: Until late in life, intelligence remained stable (**FIGURE 10.6**). On some tests, it even increased.

How then are we to account for the findings from the cross-sectional studies? In retrospect, researchers saw the problem. When a cross-sectional study compares 70-year-olds and 30-year-olds, it compares people not only of two different ages but of two different eras. It compares generally less-educated people (born, say, in the early 1900s) with better-educated people (born after 1950), people raised in large families with people raised in smaller families, people growing up in less affluent families with people raised in more affluent families.

According to this more optimistic view, the myth that intelligence sharply declines with age is laid to rest. As everyone "knows," given good health you're never too old to learn. At age 70, John Rock developed the birth control pill. At age 78, Grandma Moses took up painting, and she was still painting after age 100. At age 81—and 17 years from the end of his college football coaching career—Amos Alonzo Stagg was named coach of the year. At age 89, architect Frank Lloyd Wright designed New York City's Guggenheim Museum. Moreover, when people have kept alive their expertise—typing, playing chess, playing the piano—their abilities often remain intact well into their eighties (Schaie, 1987).

Phase III: It All Depends

But the controversy continues. For one thing, longitudinal studies have their own pitfalls. Those who survive to the end of longitudinal studies may be bright, healthy people whose intelligence is least likely to decline. (Perhaps people who died younger and were removed from the study had declining intelligence.) Adjusting for the loss of subjects, as did a recent study following more than 2000 people over 75 in Cambridge, England, reveals a steeper intelligence decline. This is especially so as people age after 85 (Brayne & others, 1999).

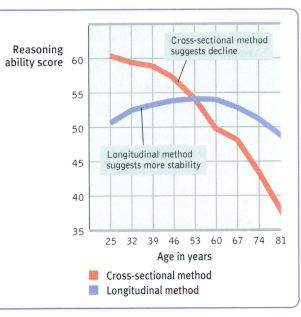

FIGURE 10.6

Cross-sectional versus longitudinal testing of intelligence at various ages
In this test of one type of verbal intelligence (inductive reasoning), the cross-sectional method produced declining scores with age. The longitudinal method (in which the same people were retested over a period of years) produced a slight *rise* in scores well into adulthood. (Adapted from Schail, 1994.)

■ **cross-sectional study** a study in which people of different ages are compared with one another.

■ **longitudinal study** research in which the same people are restudied and retested over a long period.

Research is further complicated by the finding that intelligence is not a single trait but rather a number of distinct skills and abilities. Intelligence tests that assess speed of thinking may place older adults at a disadvantage because of their slower neural mechanisms for processing information. Meeting old friends on the street, names rise to the mind's surface more slowly—"like air bubbles in molasses" says David Lykken (1999). But slower need not mean less intelligent. Given other tests that assess general vocabulary, knowledge, and ability to integrate information, older adults generally hold their own. Older Canadians surpass younger Canadians at answering questions such as, "Which province was once called New Caledonia?" (Told the right answer, young Canadians have the edge a week later at recalling these answers [Craik, 1986].)

German researcher Paul Baltes and his colleagues (1993, 1994, 1999) have developed "wisdom" tests that assess "expert knowledge about life in general and good judgment and advice about how to conduct oneself in the face of complex, uncertain circumstances." Their results suggest that older adults more than hold their own on such tests. Thus, despite 30-year-olds' quick-thinking smarts, we usually select older people to be president of the company, the college, or the country. Age is sage. To paraphrase one 60-year-old, "Forty years ago I had a great memory, but I was a fool."

So, whether intelligence increases or decreases with age depends on the type of intellectual performance we measure. **Crystallized intelligence**—one's accumulated knowledge as reflected in vocabulary and analogies tests—*increases* up to old age. **Fluid intelligence**—one's ability to reason speedily and abstractly, as when solving novel logic problems—*decreases* slowly up to age 75 or so, then more rapidly, especially after age 85 (Cattell, 1963; Horn, 1982). We can see this pattern in the intelligence scores of a national sample of adults. After adjustments for education, verbal scores (reflecting crystallized intelligence) held relatively steady from ages 20 to 74. Nonverbal, puzzle-solving intelligence declined (**FIGURE 10.7**).

These cognitive differences help explain why mathematicians and scientists produce much of their most creative work during their late twenties or early thirties, whereas those in literature, history, and philosophy tend to produce their best work in their forties, fifties, and beyond, after accumulating more knowledge (Simonton, 1988, 1990). For example, poets (who depend on fluid intelligence) reach their peak output earlier than prose authors (who need a deeper knowledge reservoir)—a finding observed in every major literary tradition, for both living and dead languages. So, whether intellectual performance increases or decreases with age depends on how we assess it and on what we assess.

"In youth we learn, in age we understand."

Marie Von Ebner-Eschenbach, *Aphorisms*, 1883

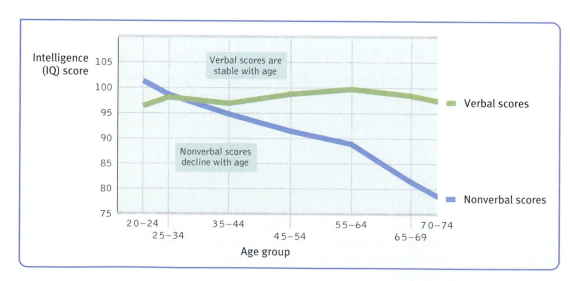

FIGURE 10.7

Intelligence and age

After adjustments for education, verbal intelligence scores hold steady with age, while nonverbal intelligence scores decline. (Intelligence scores from standardization sample of the Wechsler Adult Intelligence Scale, based on norms for 25- to 34-year-olds.) (Adapted from Kaufman & others, 1989.)

Social Changes

Preview Questions: Is the journey from adolescence to death marked by stages that serve as developmental milestones? What do psychologists view as the two primary commitments of adulthood?

Many of the differences between younger and older adults are created not by the physical and cognitive changes that accompany aging but by life events associated with family relationships and work. A new job means new relationships, new expectations, and new demands. Marriage brings the joy of intimacy and the stress of merging your life with another's. The birth of a child introduces responsibilities and significantly alters your life focus. The death of a loved one creates an irreplaceable loss and a need to reaffirm your own life. Do these normal events of adult life shape a predictable sequence of life changes?

Adulthood's Ages and Stages

Some psychologists have argued that as people enter their forties, they undergo a "midlife transition" to middle adulthood, which for many is a crisis, a time of great struggle, of regret, or even of feeling struck down by life. The popular image of the midlife crisis is a man who forsakes his family for a younger girlfriend and a hot sports car. But the fact—reported by large samples of people—is that unhappiness, job dissatisfaction, marital dissatisfaction, divorce, anxiety, and suicide do *not* surge during the early forties (Hunter & Sundel, 1989; Mroczek & Kolarz, 1998). Divorce, for example, is most common among those in their twenties, suicide among those in their seventies and eighties. One study of emotional instability in nearly 10,000 men and women found "not the slightest evidence" that distress peaks anywhere in the midlife age range (**FIGURE 10.8**).

There is another reason skeptics question age-linked stages such as "midlife crisis." The **social clock**—the cultural prescription of "the right time" to leave home, get a job, marry, have children, and retire—varies from culture to culture and era to era. In Jordan, 40 percent of brides are in their teens; in Hong Kong, only 3 percent are (United Nations, 1992). In Western Europe, fewer than 10 percent of men over 65 remain in the work force, as do 16 percent in the United States, 36 percent in Japan, and 69 percent in Mexico (Davies & others, 1991). And the once rigid sequence for Western women—of student to worker to wife to at-home mom to older worker—has loosened. Contemporary women occupy these roles in any order or all at once. Given variations in the social clock and individual experience, the critics of stage theory are suspicious of any neat timetable of adult stages with ages.

Life Events and Chance Encounters

More important than one's chronological age are life events. Marriage, parenthood, vocational changes, divorce, nest emptying, relocation, and retirement mark transitions to new life stages whenever they occur—and increasingly they are occurring at unpredictable ages. The social clock still ticks, but people feel freer about being out of sync with it.

Even chance events can have lasting significance because they often deflect us down one road rather than another (Bandura, 1982). Romantic attraction, for example, is often influenced by chance encounters. Consider one study of identical twins and their spouses. Twins, especially identical twins, make similar choices of friends, clothes, vacations, jobs, and so on. So, if your identical twin

- **crystallized intelligence** one's accumulated knowledge and verbal skills; tends to increase with age.

- **fluid intelligence** one's ability to reason speedily and abstractly; tends to decrease during late adulthood.

- **social clock** the culturally preferred timing of social events such as marriage, parenthood, and retirement.

"Midway in the journey of our life I found myself in a dark wood, for the straight way was lost."

Dante, *The Divine Comedy*, 1314

FIGURE 10.8

Early-forties midlife crises?
Among 10,000 people responding to a national health survey, there was no early-forties increase in emotional instability ("neuroticism") scores. (From McCrae & Costa, 1990.)

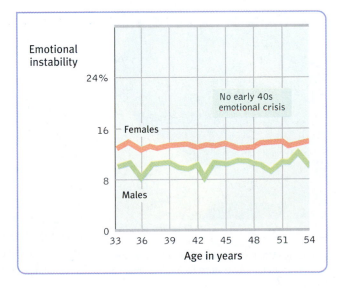

Resetting the social clock
The social clock once prescribed that university graduation should occur around age 22. For this proud graduate, "standard time" is no longer the only setting.

became engaged to someone, wouldn't you (being in so many ways the same as your twin) expect to also feel attracted to this person? Surprisingly, only half the identical twins recalled really liking their co-twin's selection, and only 5 percent said, "I could have fallen for my twin's fiancée." Researchers David Lykken and Auke Tellegen (1993) surmise that romantic love is rather like ducklings' imprinting: Given repeated exposure to someone after childhood, you may form a bond (infatuation) with almost any available person who has a roughly similar background and level of attractiveness and who reciprocates your affections.

Adulthood's Commitments

Two basic aspects of our lives do, however, dominate adulthood. Erik Erikson called them *intimacy* (forming close relationships) and *generativity* (being productive and supporting future generations). Researchers have chosen various terms—*affiliation* and *achievement*, *attachment* and *productivity*, *commitment* and *competence*. Sigmund Freud (1935) put it most simply: The healthy adult, he said, is one who can *love* and *work*. For most adults, love centers on family commitments toward partner, parents, and children. Work encompasses all our productive activities, whether for pay or not.

Love

"One can live magnificently in this world if one knows how to work and how to love."

Leo Tolstoy, 1856

Across time and place, human societies have nearly always included a relatively monogamous bond between men and women and a bond between parents and their children. We flirt, fall in love, and marry—one person at a time. "Pair-bonding is a trademark of the human animal," notes anthropologist Helen Fisher (1993). From an evolutionary perspective, the arrangement makes sense: Parents who cooperated to nurture their children to maturity were more likely to have their genes passed along to posterity than parents who didn't.

Research indicates that the bond of love is most satisfying and enduring when marked by a similarity of interests and values, a sharing of emotional and material support, and intimate self-disclosure. Women's marital satisfaction, even more than men's, is colored by their mate's social support (Acitelli & Antonucci, 1994). Happiness can occur in a relationship when one has a reassuring, respectful, caring, and mutually confiding partner.

Marriage bonds are more likely to last when couples marry after age 20 and are well educated. Compared with their counterparts of 40 years ago, people in Western countries *are* better educated and are marrying later. And yet, ironically, they are twice as likely to divorce than they would have been in 1960. This is in part because of rising expectations. We now not only hope for an enduring bond, but also for a mate who is a wage earner, caregiver, intimate friend, and warm and responsive lover. Women are also less dependent economically. To judge from the divorce rate—both Canada and the United States now have about one divorce for every two marriages—marriage has become a union that often defies management (Bureau of the Census, 1999). In Europe, divorce is only slightly less common.

Might test-driving life together in a "trial marriage" minimize divorce risk? It seems not. Ten studies in Europe, Canada, and the United States find a positive

Love
Intimacy, attachment, commitment—love by whatever name—is central to healthy and happy adulthood.

correlation between living together before marriage and risk of divorce after marriage. Compared with couples who do not cohabit with their spouses-to-be, those who do have markedly *higher* divorce rates (see Myers, 2000, for more information). This correlation doesn't prove that cohabitation *causes* divorce, but it hardly seems to prevent it.

Nonetheless, the institution of marriage endures. More than 9 in 10 heterosexual adults marry. Of those who divorce, 75 percent remarry—and their second marriages are virtually as happy as the average first marriage (Vemer & others, 1989). Although the relatively few people who feel trapped in an unhappy marriage typically feel miserable, most married Europeans and most North Americans of both sexes feel happier than those who are unmarried, especially when compared with others who are separated and divorced (Inglehart, 1990). For example, surveys of more than 32,000 Americans since 1972 reveal that 23 percent of unmarried adults and 40 percent of married adults report being "very happy" (Myers, 2000). Lesbian women in couples, too, report greater well-being than those who are alone (Wayment & Peplau, 1995).

Marriages that last are not always devoid of conflict. Some couples fight but also shower one another with affection. Other couples never raise their voices yet also seldom praise one another or nuzzle. Both styles can last. After observing the interactions of 2000 couples, John Gottman (1994) reported a better indicator of likely marital success: at least a five-to-one ratio of positive to negative interactions. Stable marriages provide five times more instances of smiling, touching, complimenting, and laughing than of sarcasm, criticism, and insults. So, if you want to predict which newlyweds will stay together, do not pay attention to how passionately they are in love. The couples who make it are more often those who restrain putting down their partners. Put downs, unchecked, can take over a relationship (Notarius & Markman, 1993). To prevent a cancerous negativity, successful couples learn to fight fair (to state feelings without insulting) and to steer conflict away from chaos with comments like "I know it's not your fault" or "I'll just be quiet for a moment and listen."

Often, love bears children. For most people, the most enduring of life changes, having a child, is a happy event. However, when children begin to absorb time, money, and emotional energy, satisfaction with the marriage itself may decline. This is especially likely among employed women who, more than they expected, carry the traditional burden of doing the chores at home (Belsky & others, 1986; Hackel & Ruble, 1992). The effort to create an equitable relationship can pay double dividends, making for a more satisfying marriage, which also breeds better parent-child relations (Erel & Burman, 1995).

Although love bears children, children eventually leave home. This departure is a significant event, but seven national surveys reveal that the empty nest is for most people a happy place (Adelmann & others, 1989; Glenn, 1975). Compared with middle-aged women who still have children at home, those whose nest has emptied report greater happiness and greater enjoyment of their marriage. Many parents experience what sociologists Lynn White and John Edwards (1990) call a "postlaunch honeymoon," especially if they maintain close relationships with their children.

Work

For many adults, the answer to "Who are you?" depends a great deal on the answer to "What do you do?" Was Freud right? Does work, including a career, indeed contribute to self-fulfillment and life satisfaction? One approach to answering this question has been to compare the roughly equal numbers of North American women who are or are not employed. From their studies at the Wellesley College Center for Research on Women, Grace Baruch and Rosaline Barnett (1986) conclude that what matters is not which roles a woman occupies—whether it be as paid worker, wife, and/or mother—but the quality of her experience in those roles.

What do you think? Does marriage correlate with happiness because marital support and intimacy breed happiness, because happy people more often marry and stay married, or both?

If you have left home, did your parents suffer the "empty nest syndrome"—a feeling of distress focusing on a loss of purpose and relationship? Did they mourn the lost joy of listening for you in the wee hours of Saturday morning? Or did they seem to discover a new freedom, relaxation, and (if still married) renewed satisfaction with their own relationship?

Job satisfaction and life satisfaction
Work can provide us with a sense of identity and competence and opportunities for accomplishment. Perhaps this is why challenging and interesting occupations enhance people's happiness.

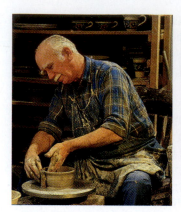  

For women and men, choosing a career path is difficult, especially in today's changing work environment. During the first two years of college or university, most students cannot predict their later careers. Most shift from their initially intended majors, many find their postcollege employment in fields not directly related to their majors, and most will change careers (Rothstein, 1980). In the end, happiness is about having work that fits your interests and provides you with a sense of competence and accomplishment. And for those who choose to marry, it is having a partner who is a close, supportive companion and who sees you as special, and/or having loving children whom you like and feel proud of.

Well-Being Across the Life Span

To live is to grow older. That means we all can look back with satisfaction or regret, and forward with hope or dread. When people are asked what they would have done differently if they could relive their lives, their most common answer is "taken my education more seriously and worked harder at it." Other regrets—"I should have told my father I loved him," "I regret that I never went to Europe"—also focus less on mistakes made than on the things one *failed* to do (Gilovich & Medvec, 1995).

In later life, income shrinks, work is taken away, the body deteriorates, recall fades, energy wanes, family members and friends die or move away, and the great enemy, death, looms ever closer. Small wonder that many presume the over-65 years to be the worst of times (Freedman, 1978). But they are not, as Ronald Inglehart (1990) discovered when he amassed interviews conducted during the 1980s with representative samples of nearly 170,000 people in 16 nations. As **FIGURE 10.9** illustrates, older people report as much happiness and satisfaction with life as younger people do. Given that growing older is one sure consequence of living, an outcome most of us prefer to its alternative, we can all take comfort in this finding.

The astonishing stability of well-being across the life span obscures some interesting age-related emotional differences. As the years go by, feelings mellow (Costa & others, 1987; Diener & others, 1986). Highs become less high, lows less low. Thus, although the *average* feeling level may remain stable, with age we find ourselves less often feeling excited, intensely proud, and on top of the world, but also less often depressed. Compliments provoke less elation and criticisms less despair, as both become merely additional feedback atop a mountain of accumulated praise and blame. Psychologists Mihaly Csikszentmihalyi (pronounced chick-SENT-me-hi) and Reed Larson (1984) mapped people's emotional terrain by periodically signaling them with electronic beepers to report their current activities and feelings. They found that teenagers typically come down from elation or up from gloom in less than an hour. Adult moods are less extreme but more enduring. For most people, old age offers less intense joy but greater contentment, especially for those who remain socially engaged (Harlow & Cantor, in press). As we age, life becomes less an emotional roller coaster, more like paddling a canoe.

Social engagement becomes progressively more focused throughout adulthood. While many a 20-year-old wonders where the party is, older adults prefer a smaller social network marked by emotionally meaningful relationships with relatively few close friends and with family (Carstensen & Charles, 1999).

Death and Dying

Most of us will suffer and cope with the deaths of relatives and friends. Usually, the most difficult separation is from one's spouse—a loss suffered by five times more women than men. Grief is especially severe when the death of a loved one comes suddenly and before its expected time on the social clock. The accidental death of a child or the sudden illness that claims a 45-year-old spouse may trigger a year or more of mourning flooded with memories, eventually subsiding to a mild depression that sometimes continues for several years (Lehman & others, 1987). AIDS, which so often strikes down people in midlife and younger, has left countless grief-stricken partners experiencing such bereavement, as well as 11 million orphaned (and mostly African) children (Folkman & others, 1996; *New York Times*, 1999). In 1999, the disease killed 2.6 million people worldwide. In the southern African nations of Botswana, Namibia, Swaziland, and Zimbabwe, where the United Nations reports more than a quarter of adults carry the AIDS virus, the resulting death and treatment needs are also sapping social resources (France-Presse, 1999).

The normal range of reactions to a loved one's death is wider than most suppose. Some cultures encourage public weeping and wailing; others hide grief. Within any culture some individuals grieve more intensely and openly; however, contrary to a popular misconception, those who express the strongest grief immediately do not purge their grief more quickly (Bonanno & Kaltman, 1999; Wortman & Silver, 1989). Research also discounts the popular idea that terminally ill and bereaved people go through predictable stages, such as denial, anger, and so forth (Nolen-Hoesksema & Larson, 1999). Given similar losses, some people grieve hard and long, others more lightly and briefly.

We can be grateful for the waning of death-denying attitudes. Facing death with dignity and openness helps people complete the life cycle with a sense of life's meaningfulness and unity—the sense that their existence has been good and that life and death are parts of an ongoing cycle. Although death may be unwelcome, life itself can be affirmed even at death. This is especially so for people who review their lives not with despair but with what Erik Erikson called a sense of *integrity*—a feeling that one's life has been meaningful and worthwhile.

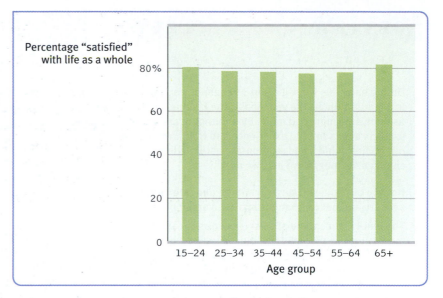

Percentage "satisfied" with life as a whole

FIGURE 10.9 Age and life satisfaction
With the tasks of early adulthood behind them, many older adults have more time to pursue personal interests. No wonder their satisfaction with life remains high, especially if they are healthy and active. As this graph based on multinational surveys shows, age differences in life satisfaction are trivial. (Data from Inglehart, 1990.)

"Do not go gentle into that good night, Old age should burn and rave at close of day; Rage, rage against the dying of the light."

Dylan Thomas, "Do not go gentle into that good night," 1952, poem written to his father as he lay dying peacefully

"Consider, friend, as you pass by, as you are now, so once was I. As I am now, you too shall be. Prepare, therefore, to follow me."

Scottish tombstone epitaph

REVIEW AND REFLECT:

Adulthood

During early life, we sail a narrow channel, constrained by biological maturation. As the years pass, the channel widens, allowing us to diverge more and more. By adulthood, age no longer neatly predicts a person's life experience and traits. Yet in some ways our bodies, minds, and relationships still undergo predictable changes. As long as we live, we adapt.

How do our bodies change in middle and late adulthood? What sensory and neural changes mark the aging process?

The barely perceptible physical declines of early adulthood begin to accelerate during middle adulthood. For women, a significant physical change is menopause, which generally seems to be a smooth rather than rough transition. After 65, perceptual acuity, strength, and stamina decline, but short-term ailments are fewer. Neural processes slow, and except for those who suffer brain disease, such as the progressive deterioration of Alzheimer's disease, the brain remains healthy.

In what ways do memory and intelligence change as we age?

As the years pass, recognition memory remains strong, although recall begins to decline, especially for meaningless information. Research on how intelligence changes with age has progressed through several phases: cross-sectional studies suggesting a steady intellectual decline after early adulthood; longitudinal studies suggesting intellectual stability until very late in life; and today's view that fluid intelligence declines in later life, but crystallized intelligence does not.

Is the journey from adolescence to death marked by stages that serve as developmental milestones? What do psychologists view as the two primary commitments of adulthood?

From close study of small samples of individuals, some theorists maintain that adults pass through an orderly sequence of life stages. Some theorists have contended that moving from one stage to the next entails recurring times of crisis, such as the transition to midlife during the early forties. But people are not so predictable. Although adulthood's two primary commitments—love and work—do help shape adult life, we are also influenced by chance occurrences. Since 1960, marriage has been in decline, as reflected in later marriages, increased cohabitation, and doubled divorce rates.

Few people grow old gratefully, but most age gracefully, retaining a sense of well-being throughout life. Those who live to old age must, however, cope with the deaths of friends and family members and with the prospect of their own deaths. Our experience with death is influenced by our experiences in life.

Terms and Concepts to Remember

menopause, p. 152
Alzheimer's disease, p. 156
cross-sectional study, p. 158
longitudinal study, p. 159

crystallized intelligence, p. 160
fluid intelligence, p. 160
social clock, p. 161

Test Yourself

10.1. By age 75, a person has experienced declining heart and muscular strength and losses in sight and hearing. However, this older adult is *less* likely than younger people to suffer from
a. Alzheimer's disease.
b. accidents and falls.
c. short-term illnesses such as the flu.
d. chronic illnesses such as diabetes.

10.2. Some types of learning and remembering peak in early adulthood. By age 65, a person would be most likely to experience a decline in the ability to
a. recall and list all the items in the chapter glossary.
b. select the correct definition in a multiple-choice question.
c. evaluate whether a statement is true or false.
d. exercise sound judgment in answering an essay question.

10.3. In longitudinal studies the same people are retested at different ages. Longitudinal research suggests that intelligence
a. steadily declines with age.
b. peaks at age 25.
c. generally increases in later life.
d. remains stable until very late in life.

10.4. Most middle-aged adults define themselves in terms of their career. Which of the following has research shown to be true of women and work?
a. Women who work for wages are happier than those who do not.
b. Women whose roles are wife and mother are happier than those who also work for wages.
c. The quality of a woman's experience in her role matters more than the role she occupies.
d. A woman's age determines which role makes her happier.

10.5. Freud defined the healthy adult as one who is able to love and work. Erikson agreed, observing that the adult struggles to attain intimacy and
a. affiliation.   c. competence.
b. identity.   d. generativity.

10.6. Contrary to what many people assume,
a. older people are much happier than adolescents.
b. men in their forties express much greater dissatisfaction with life than do women of the same age.
c. people of all ages report similar levels of happiness.
d. those whose children have recently left home—the empty nesters—have the lowest level of happness of all groups.

Review: Research has shown that living together before marriage predicts an increased likelihood of future divorce. Can you imagine two possible explanations for this correlation?

Reflect: As you reflect on your last four years—four formative years if you are a young adult—what do you most regret? What do you feel best about?

Answers to Test Yourself and Review questions can be found in the green appendix at the end of the book.

Reflections on Two Major Developmental Issues

We conclude our womb-to-tomb journey where we began, with two of developmental psychology's big questions: Does life unfold through predictable stages? And as we develop, do our traits typically change or remain consistent?

Continuity and Stages

Do adults differ from infants as a giant redwood differs from its seedling—a difference created by gradual, cumulative growth? Or do they differ as a butterfly differs from a caterpillar—a difference of distinct stages? Are there clear-cut stages of psychological development, as there are physical stages (crawling before walking)? We have considered the stage theories of Jean Piaget on cognitive development, Lawrence Kohlberg on moral development, and Erik Erikson on psychosocial development. And we have seen their stage theories criticized: Young children have some abilities that Piaget attributed to later stages. Kohlberg's work exhibited a worldview characteristic of educated males in individualistic cultures. Erikson's ideas are contradicted by research showing that adult life does not progress through fixed, predictable steps.

Although research casts doubt on the idea that life proceeds through neatly defined, age-linked stages, the concept of stage remains useful. There are spurts of brain growth during childhood and puberty that correspond roughly to Piaget's stages (Thatcher & others, 1987). And stage theories contribute a developmental perspective on the whole life span, by suggesting how people of one age think and act differently when they arrive at a later age.

Stability and Change

This leads us to the final question: Over time, are people's personalities consistent, or do they change? Researchers who follow lives through time have found evidence for both stability and change. There is continuity to personality and yet, happily for troubled youth, present struggles may lay a foundation for a happier tomorrow. More specifically, researchers generally agree on the following points:

1. The first two years of life provide a poor basis for predicting a person's eventual traits (Kagan, 1978, 1998). Even children and adolescents often change: Many confused and troubled children have blossomed into mature, successful adults (Macfarlane, 1964; Thomas & Chess, 1986). As people grow older, however, continuity of personality does gradually increase (Costa & McCrae, 1989; Klohnen & Bera, 1998; Stein & others, 1986).

2. Some characteristics, such as temperament, are more stable than others, such as social attitudes (Moss & Susman, 1980). But attitudes, too, become more stable with age (Krosnick & Alwin, 1989).

3. In some ways, we all change with age. Most shy, fearful toddlers begin opening up by age 4, and during adulthood most of us mellow. In the years after college, most people become calmer and more self-disciplined (McCrae & Costa, 1994). Many a 20-year-old goof-off has matured into a 40-year-old business or cultural leader. Such changes can occur without changing a person's position *relative* to others of the same age. The hard-driving young adult may mellow by later life yet still be a relatively hard-driving senior citizen.

Finally, we should remember that life contains *both* stability and change. Stability enables us to depend on others, motivates our concern for the healthy development of children, and provides our identity. Change motivates our concerns about present influences, sustains our hope for a brighter future, and enables us to adapt and grow with experience.

As adults grow older, there is continuity of personality.

"At 70, I would say the advantage is that you take life more calmly. You know that 'this, too, shall pass'!"

Eleanor Roosevelt, 1954

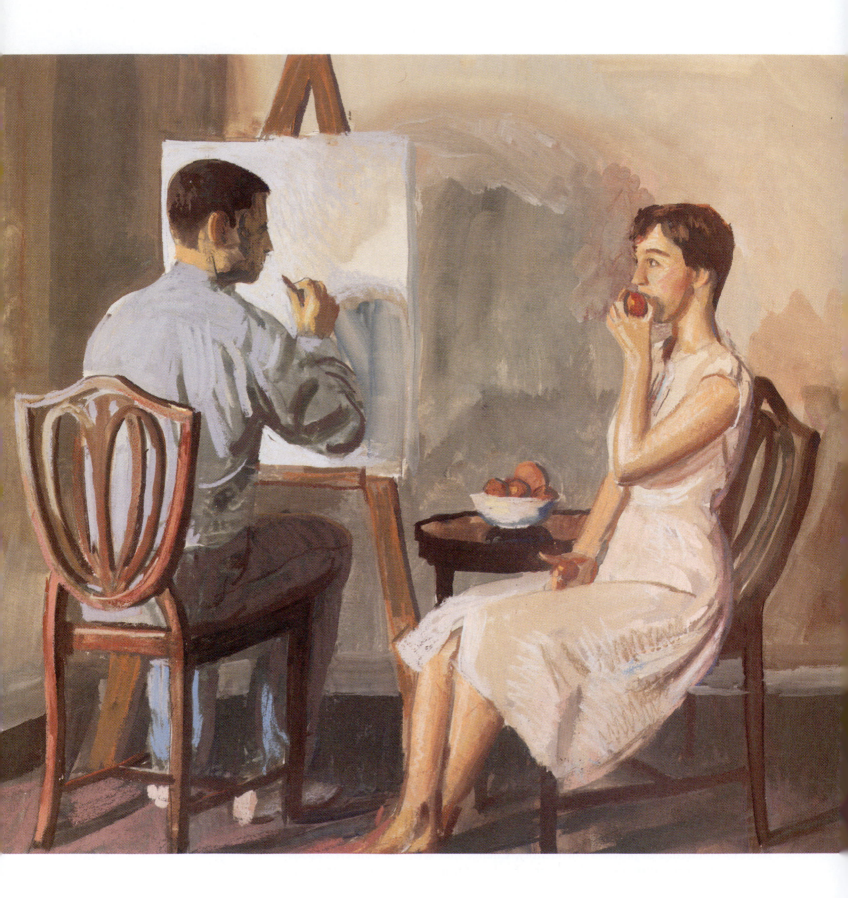

Sensation and Perception

Twenty-four hours a day stimuli from the outside world bombard your body. Meanwhile, in a silent, cushioned, inner world, your brain floats in utter darkness. This raises a question, one that predates psychology by thousands of years and helped inspire its beginnings a century ago: *How does the world out there get in?*

To modernize the question: How do we construct our representations of the external world? How do we represent a campfire's flicker, crackle, and smoky scent as patterns of active neural connections? And how, from this living neurochemistry, do we create our conscious experience of the fire's motion and temperature, its aroma and beauty?

To represent the world in our head, we must detect physical energy from the environment and encode it as neural signals, a process traditionally called *sensation*. And we must select, organize, and interpret our sensations, a process traditionally called *perception*. In our everyday experiences, sensation and perception blend into one continuous process. In Modules 11 through 16, we slow down that process to study its parts.

In Modules 11 through 14, we will start with the sensory receptors and work up to higher levels of processing. Psychologists refer to sensory analysis that starts at the entry level as *bottom-up processing*. Modules 15 and 16 will focus on how our minds interpret what our senses detect. We construct perceptions drawing both on sensations coming bottom-up to the brain, and on our experience and expectations, which psychologists call *top-down processing*.

Failures of perception may occur anywhere between sensory detection and perceptual interpretation. For example, after losing a temporal lobe area essential to recognizing faces, patient "E. H." suffers from a condition called *prosopagnosia*. She has complete sensation but incomplete perception. She can sense visual information—indeed may accurately report the features of a face—yet she is unable to recognize it. Shown an unfamiliar face, she does not react. Shown a familiar face, her autonomic nervous system responds with measurable perspiration. Still, she hasn't a clue who the person is. Shown her own face in a mirror, she is again stumped. Because of her brain damage, she cannot process top-down—she cannot relate her stored knowledge to the sensory input.

Introduction to Sensation and Perception

To construct the outside world inside our heads we must detect physical energy from the environment and then encode it as neural signals (a process traditionally called **sensation**). And we must also select, organize, and interpret our sensations (a process traditionally called **perception**). We not only sense raw sights and sounds, tastes and smells, we *perceive*. We hear not just a mix of pitches and rhythms but a child's cry of pain, the hum of distant traffic, a symphony. In short, we transform sensations into perceptions. We create meaning.

Our sensory and perceptual processes work together to help us sort out the complex images in the **FIGURE 11.1** painting. Through **bottom-up processing**, which begins with our sense receptors, we detect the lines, angles, and colors that form the horses, rider, and surroundings. But we also apply **top-down processing**, drawing on our experience and expectations, when we consider the painting's title, notice the apprehensive expressions, and then direct our attention to aspects of the painting that will give those observations meaning.

We begin our introduction to sensation and perception with a look at some basic principles by which we experience the world.

FIGURE 11.1

Top-down and Bottom-up processing: The Forest Has Eyes

(Detail, "The Forest Has Eyes" by Bev Doolittle © The Greenwich Workshop, Inc., Trumbull, CT.)

- **sensation** the process by which our sensory receptors and nervous system receive and represent stimulus energies from our environment.

- **perception** the process of organizing and interpreting sensory information, enabling us to recognize meaningful objects and events.

- **bottom-up processing** analysis that begins with the sense receptors and works up to the brain's integration of sensory information.

- **top-down processing** information processing guided by higher-level mental processes, as when we construct perceptions drawing on our experience and expectations.

- **psychophysics** the study of relationships between the physical characteristics of stimuli, such as their intensity, and our psychological experience of them.

Thresholds

Preview Questions: What stimuli cross our threshold for conscious awareness? Could we unknowingly be influenced by subliminal stimuli too weak to be perceived?

We exist in a sea of energy. At this moment, you and I are being struck by x-rays and radio waves, ultraviolet and infrared light, and sound waves of very high and very low frequencies. But to all of these we are blind and deaf. The shades on our senses are open just a crack, allowing us only a restricted awareness of this vast sea. **Psychophysics** is the study of how this physical energy relates to our psychological experience. What stimuli can we detect? At what intensity? How sensitive are we to changing stimulation?

Absolute Thresholds

To some kinds of stimuli we are exquisitely sensitive. Standing atop a mountain on an utterly dark, clear night, we can, given normal senses, see a candle flame atop another mountain 30 miles away. In a silent room, we can hear a watch ticking 20 feet away. We can feel the wing of a bee falling on our cheek. We can even smell a single drop of perfume in a three-room apartment (Galanter, 1962).

Our awareness of these faint stimuli illustrates our **absolute thresholds**—the minimum stimulation necessary to detect a particular stimulus (light, sound, pressure, taste, odor). Psychologists usually measure absolute threshold by recording the stimulation needed for us to pinpoint its appearance 50 percent of the time. To test your absolute threshold for sounds, a hearing specialist would expose each of your ears to varying sound levels. For each pitch, the hearing test defines where half the time you correctly detect the sound and half the time you do not. For each of the senses, that 50–50 point defines your absolute threshold.

Signal Detection

Sensory systems enable organisms to obtain needed information. And nature's sensory gifts suit each recipient's needs. Consider:

- A frog, which feeds on flying insects, has eyes with receptor cells that fire only in response to small, dark, moving objects. A frog could starve to death knee-deep in motionless flies. But let one zoom by and the frog's "bug detector" cells snap awake.
- A male silkworm moth has receptors so sensitive to the odor of the female sex-attractant that a single female silkworm moth need release only a billionth of an ounce per second to attract every male silkworm moth within a mile. That is why there continue to be silkworms.
- We are similarly designed to detect what are, for us, the important features of our environments. Our ears are most sensitive to sound frequencies that include human voice consonants and a baby's cry.

For people, detecting a weak stimulus, or signal, depends not only on the signal's strength (such as the tone on a hearing test), but also on our psychological state—our experience, expectations, motivation, and alertness. **Signal detection theory** predicts when we will detect weak signals, measured as our ratio of "hits" to "false alarms." Signal detection theorists have observed that absolute thresholds vary. Exhausted parents of a newborn will notice the faintest whimper from the cradle, while failing to notice louder, unimportant sounds. Responsiveness also increases in a horror-filled wartime situation, where the failure to detect an intruder may mean death. A sentry standing guard alone at night may therefore notice—and fire at—an almost imperceptible noise. With such heightened responsiveness come more false alarms. In peacetime, when survival is not threatened, the same sentry requires a stronger signal before sensing danger.

Signal detection theorists seek to understand why people respond differently to the same stimuli, and why the same person's reactions vary as circumstances change. Signal detection can have life-or-death consequences when people are responsible for detecting blips on a radar screen, watching for weapons at an airport security checkpoint, or monitoring equipment at an intensive care nursing station. Signal detection studies have shown, for example, that people's vigilance diminishes after about 30 minutes of judging when a faint signal appears. But this diminishing response depends on the task, on the time of day, and even on whether the participants periodically exercise (Warm & Dember, 1986).

Sensory limits

A mosquito's buzz can sound like a dive-bomber, thanks to our low threshold for sounds at its pitch. But a shrieking, dive-bombing bat will seem silent, its cries too high-pitched. Our ears are most sensitive to the pitch range of human speech.

Signal detection

How soon would you notice the radar blips of an approaching object? Fairly quickly if (1) you expect it, (2) it's important that you detect it, and (3) you are alert.

■ **absolute threshold** the minimum stimulation needed to detect a particular stimulus 50 percent of the time.

■ **signal detection theory** predicts how and when we detect the presence of a faint stimulus ("signal") amid background stimulation ("noise"). Assumes that there is no single absolute threshold and that detection depends partly on a person's experience, expectations, motivation, and level of fatigue.

Subliminal Stimulation

In 1956, controversy erupted over a false report that New Jersey movie audiences were unwittingly being influenced by imperceptible flashed messages to DRINK COCA-COLA and EAT POPCORN (Pratkanis, 1992).

Many years later, the controversy erupted anew. Advertisers were said to manipulate consumers by imperceptibly printing the word *sex* on crackers and by embedding erotic images in liquor ads. Rock recordings were said to contain "satanic messages" that could be heard if the recordings were played backward and that, even when played forward, could unconsciously persuade the unwitting listener. Hoping to trespass on our unconscious, entrepreneurs offer audiotapes to help us lose weight, stop smoking, or improve our memories. These tapes contain soothing ocean sounds that mask unheard messages such as, "I am thin," "Smoke tastes bad," or "I do well on tests. I have total recall of information." Claims like these make two assumptions: that unconsciously we can sense **subliminal** (literally, "below threshold") stimuli, and that, without our awareness, these stimuli have extraordinary suggestive powers. Can we? Do they?

Can we sense stimuli below our absolute thresholds? In one sense, the answer is clearly yes. Remember that the "absolute" threshold is merely the point at which we detect a stimulus half the time (**FIGURE 11.2**). At or slightly below this threshold we will still detect the stimulus some of the time. The answer is yes in another sense, too. People who plead total ignorance when asked to make some perceptual judgment—for example, when deciding which of two very similar weights is heavier—usually beat chance. Sometimes we know more than we think we do.

Can we be affected by stimuli so weak as to be unnoticed? Recent experiments hint that, under certain conditions, the answer may again be yes. One experiment subliminally flashed either emotionally positive scenes (such as kittens or a romantic couple) or negative scenes (such as a werewolf or a dead body) an instant before participants viewed slides of people (Krosnick & others, 1992). Although the participants consciously perceived only a flash of light, they gave more positive ratings to people whose photos had been associated with positive scenes. People somehow looked nicer if their photo immediately followed unperceived kittens rather than an unperceived werewolf. Chinese characters, too, seemed nicer if preceded by a flashed but unperceived smiling face rather than a scowling face (Murphy & Zajonc, 1993). And graduate students evaluate their research ideas more negatively shortly after viewing the unperceived scowling face of their adviser—as if a sense of the adviser's disapproval was lurking in the unconscious mind (Baldwin & others, 1991).

Consider, too, how an invisible image or word can briefly *prime* your response to a later question. In a typical experiment, the image or word is quickly flashed, then replaced by a "masking" stimulus that interrupts the brain's processing before conscious perception. For example, picture yourself in an experiment by Moshe Bar and Irving Biederman (1998). If you are like their University of Southern California students, the chances are less than 1 in 7 that you could name a simple image such

FIGURE 11.2
Absolute threshold

Do I smell it or not? When stimuli are detectable less than 50 percent of the time, they are "subliminal." Absolute threshold is the intensity at which we can detect a stimulus half the time.

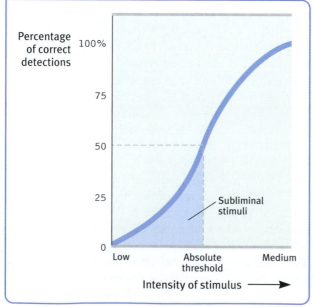

Percentage of correct detections

100%

75

50

25

0

Low · Absolute threshold · Medium

Subliminal stimuli

Intensity of stimulus ⟶

as a hammer after its presentation for 47 milliseconds. But what if you witness the image again in the same position as much as 15 minutes later and after 20 presentations of other images? The chances of your naming the hammer would now be better than 1 in 3. It is as if the second presentation, combined with the first presentation, sufficiently awakened the brain for some awareness. Similarly, if the imperceptible word *bread* were flashed and masked, you might then detect a related word such as *butter* faster than unrelated words such as *bottle* or *bubble* (Bornstein & Pittman, 1992; Carr & others, 1987; Marcel, 1983). The effect is intriguing: Sometimes we *feel* what we do not know and cannot describe.

Subliminal persuasion?
Although subliminally presented stimuli *can* subtly influence people, experiments discount attempts at subliminal advertising and self-improvement. (The playful message here is not, however, subliminal—because you can perceive it.)

So, we *can* process information without being aware of it. An imperceptibly brief stimulus evidently triggers a weak response that evokes a feeling, though not a conscious awareness of the stimulus. What the conscious mind can't recognize, the heart may know.

But does the fact of subliminal *sensation* verify entrepreneurial claims of subliminal *persuasion*? Can advertisers really manipulate us with "hidden persuasion"? The near-consensus among research psychologists is no. Their verdict is similar to that of astronomers who say of astrologers, yes, they are right that stars and planets are out there, but no, they don't directly affect us. The laboratory research reveals a *subtle, fleeting* effect on *thinking*, but the subliminal tape hucksters claim something different: a *powerful, enduring* effect on *behavior*. Experiments show that commercial subliminal tapes have no effect beyond that of a placebo—an effect of one's belief in them (Moore, 1988; Pratkanis & others, 1994; Smith & Rogers, 1994).

> "The heart has its reasons which reason does not know."
>
> Pascal, *Pensees*, 1670

For example, the Canadian Broadcasting Corporation used a popular Sunday night TV show to flash a subliminal message 352 times (*Advertising Age*, 1958). Asked to guess the message, not one of the almost 500 letter-writers did. Nearly half, however, reported feeling strangely hungry or thirsty during the show. But this was merely an effect of expectations. The actual message was TELEPHONE NOW. The effect of these 352 subliminal messages on Canadian telephone usage? Zilch. All the evidence considered, say researchers Anthony Pratkanis and Anthony Greenwald (1988), "Subliminal procedures offer little or nothing of value to the marketing practitioner."

Difference Thresholds

To function effectively, we need absolute thresholds low enough to allow us to detect important sights, sounds, textures, tastes, and smells. We also need to detect small differences among stimuli. A musician must detect minute discrepancies in an instrument's tuning. A wine taster must detect the slight flavor difference between two vintage wines. Parents must detect the sound of their own child's voice amid other children's voices.

The **difference threshold** (also called the *just noticeable difference*, or *jnd*) is the minimum difference a person can detect between any two stimuli. The difference threshold increases with the magnitude of the stimulus. Thus, if you add 10 grams to a 100-gram weight, you will detect the difference; add 10 grams to a

subliminal below one's absolute threshold for conscious awareness.

difference threshold the minimum difference that a person can detect between two stimuli. We experience the difference threshold as a just noticeable difference. (Also called *just noticeable difference* or *jnd*.)

The LORD is my shepherd;
    I shall not want.
He maketh me to lie down
        in green pastures:
    he leadeth me
        beside the still waters.
He restoreth my soul:
    he leadeth me
        in the paths of righteousness
        for his name's sake.
Yea, though I walk through the valley
    of the shadow of death,
    I will fear no evil:
for thou art with me;
    thy rod and thy staff
    they comfort me.
Thou preparest a table before me
    in the presence of mine enemies:
    thou anointest my head with oil,
        my cup runneth over.
Surely goodness and mercy
        shall follow me
    all the days of my life:
and I will dwell
    in the house of the LORD
        for ever.

The difference threshold
In this computer-generated copy of the Twenty-third Psalm, each line of the typeface changes imperceptibly. How many lines are required for you to experience a just noticeable difference?

"We need above all to know about changes; no one wants or needs to be reminded 16 hours a day that his shoes are on."

Neuroscientist David Hubel (1979)

For 9 in 10 people—but, curiously, for only 1 in 3 of those with schizophrenia—this eye flutter turns off when the eye is following a moving target (Holzman & Matthysse, 1990).

1-*kilogram* weight and you will not, because the difference threshold has increased. More than a century ago, Ernst Weber noted that regardless of their magnitude, two stimuli must differ by a constant proportion for their difference to be perceptible. This principle—that the difference threshold is not a constant amount but some constant *proportion* of the stimulus—is so simple and so widely applicable that we still refer to it as **Weber's law**. The exact proportion varies, depending on the stimulus. For the average person to perceive their differences, two lights must differ in intensity by 8 percent. Two objects must differ in weight by 2 percent. And two tones must differ in frequency by only 0.3 percent (Teghtsoonian, 1971).

Weber's law is a rough approximation. It works well for nonextreme sensory stimuli, and it parallels some of our life experiences. If the price of a 50-cent chocolate bar goes up by 5 cents, shoppers might notice the change; similarly, it might take a £4000 price hike in a £40,000 Mercedes to raise the eyebrows of its potential buyers. In both cases, the price went up by 10 percent. Weber's principle: Our thresholds for detecting differences are a roughly constant proportion of the size of the original stimulus.

Sensory Adaptation

Preview Question: Why are we unaware of unchanging stimuli, such as the watch pressing against our wrist?

Entering your neighbors' living room, you smell an unpleasant odor. You wonder how they can stand the stench, but within minutes you no longer notice it. Jumping into a swimming pool, you shiver and complain about how cold it is. A short while later a friend arrives and you exclaim, "C'mon in. Water's fine!" These examples illustrate **sensory adaptation**—our diminishing sensitivity to an unchanging stimulus. (To experience this phenomenon, move your watch up your wrist an inch: You will feel it—but only for a few moments.) After constant exposure to a stimulus, our nerve cells fire less frequently.

Why, then, if we stare at an object without flinching, does it not vanish from sight? Because, unnoticed by us, our eyes are always moving, quivering just enough to guarantee that retinal stimulation continually changes.

But what if we actually could stop our eyes from moving? Would sights seem to vanish, as odors do? To find out, psychologists have devised ingenious instruments for maintaining a constant image on the retina. Imagine that we fitted a volunteer, Mary, with one of these instruments—a miniature projector mounted on a contact lens (**FIGURE 11.3a**). When Mary's eye moves, the image from the projector moves as well. Thus, everywhere that Mary looks the scene is sure to go.

FIGURE 11.3
Now you see it, now you don't!
(a) A projector mounted on a contact lens makes the projected image move with the eye. (b) Initially the person sees the stabilized image, but soon she sees fragments fading and reappearing. (From "Stabilized images on the retina" by R. M. Pritchard. Copyright © 1961 Scientific American, Inc. All rights reserved.)

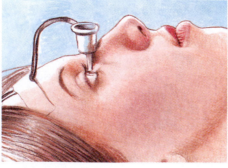

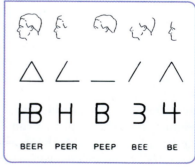

(a)   (b)

If we project the profile of a face through such an instrument, what will Mary see? At first, she will see the complete profile. But within a few seconds, as her sensory receptors begin to fatigue, things get weird. Bit by bit, the image vanishes, only later to reappear and then disappear—in recognizable fragments or as a whole (**FIGURE 11.3b**). Interestingly, the disappearance and reappearance of an image occurs in meaningful units. If a person is shown a word, it will disappear, and new words made up of parts of that word will appear and then vanish. This phenomenon illustrates one of psychology's major conclusions: Our perceptions are organized by the meanings that our minds impose.

Although sensory adaptation reduces our sensitivity, it offers an important benefit: It enables us to focus on *informative* changes in our environment without being distracted by the uninformative constant stimulation of garments, odors, and street noise. Our sensory receptors are alert to novelty; bore them with repetition and they free our attention for more important things. This reinforces a fundamental lesson: We perceive the world not exactly as it is, but as it is useful for us to perceive it.

> "My suspicion is that the universe is not only queerer than we suppose, but queerer than we can suppose."
>
> J. B. S. Haldane, *Possible Worlds*, 1927

Selective Attention

Preview Question: How does our ability to focus on a limited aspect of our experience help us transform sensations into meaningful perceptions?

Perceptions come to us moment by moment, one perception vanishing as the next appears. Note how **FIGURE 11.4** evokes more than one perception. The circles can be organized into several coherent images, each equally plausible, and your mind switches back and forth from one to the next. You *know* that alternative interpretations of this Necker cube are possible, but you can consciously experience only one at any moment. This illustrates an important principle: *Our conscious attention is selective.*

Selective attention means that at any moment we focus our awareness on only a limited aspect of all that we are capable of experiencing. Until reading this sentence, you have been unaware that your shoes are pressing against your feet or that your nose is in your line of vision. Now, suddenly, your attentional spotlight shifts. Your feet feel encased, your nose stubbornly intrudes on the page before you. While attending to these words, you've also been blocking from awareness information coming from your peripheral vision. But you can change that. While staring at the X below, notice what surrounds the book (the edges of the page, your desk top, and so forth).

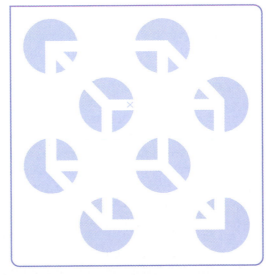

FIGURE 11.4
Selective attention
What do you see: circles with white lines, or a cube? If you stare at the cube, you may notice that it reverses location, moving the tiny X in the center from the front edge to the back. At times the cube may seem to float in front of the page, with circles behind it; other times the circles may become holes in the page through which the cube appears, as though it were floating behind the page. Because attention is selective, you see only one interpretation at a time. (From Bradley & others, 1976.)

X

Another example of selective attention, the *cocktail party effect*, is the ability to attend selectively to only one voice among many. Imagine hearing two conversations over a headset, one in each ear, and being asked to repeat the message in your left ear while it is spoken. When paying attention to what is being said in your left ear, you won't perceive what is said in your right. If you are asked later what language your right ear heard, you may draw a blank (though you could report the speaker's gender and loudness). At the level of conscious awareness, whatever has your attention pretty much has your undivided attention.

■ **Weber's law** the principle that, to perceive their difference, two stimuli must differ by a constant minimum percentage (rather than a constant amount).

■ **sensory adaptation** diminished sensitivity as a consequence of constant stimulation.

■ **selective attention** the focusing of conscious awareness on a particular stimulus, as in the cocktail party effect.

FIGURE **11.5**
Testing selective attention
In this experiment, viewers who were attending to basketball tosses among the black-shirted players usually failed to notice the umbrella-toting woman sauntering across the screen. (From Neisser, 1979.)

It is true of the other senses, too. From the immense array of visual stimuli constantly before us, we select just a few to process. Ulric Neisser (1979) and Robert Becklen and Daniel Cervone (1983) demonstrated this dramatically. They showed people a one-minute videotape in which the images of three men in black shirts tossing a basketball were superimposed over the images of three men in white shirts doing the same thing. They asked the viewers to press a key every time the black-shirted players passed the ball. Midway through the tape, a young woman carrying an umbrella sauntered across the screen (**FIGURE 11.5**). Most viewers had focused their attention so completely on the black-shirted players that they failed to notice the woman. When the researchers replayed the tape for them, they were astonished to see her.

Can stimuli that we do not notice affect us? Indeed yes. In one experiment, women students listened through headphones as a prose passage played in one ear. Their task was to repeat its words out loud and to check them against a written transcript (Wilson, 1979). Meanwhile, some simple, novel tunes played in the other ear. The tunes were not subliminal—the women could hear them easily. But with their attention selectively focused on the passage, the women were no more aware of the tunes than you normally are of your shoes. Thus, when they later heard these tunes interspersed among new ones, they could not recognize them (just as we cannot recall a conversation to which we paid no attention). Nevertheless, when asked to rate how much they liked each tune, they *preferred* the ones previously played. Their preferences revealed what their conscious memories could not.

In other experiments, listeners attend to an ambiguous message piped into one ear (such as, "We stood by the bank"). When a pertinent word (*river* or *money*) is simultaneously sent to the other ear—the unattended one—the listeners do not consciously perceive it. Yet the word influences their interpretation of the ambiguous sentence (Baars & McGovern, 1994). Although perception requires attention, even unattended stimuli sometimes have subtle effects. Moreover, if someone at a loud party audibly speaks your name, your attuned perceptual system may bring the voice to consciousness.

Introduction to Sensation and Perception

To study sensation and perception is to study an ageless question: How does the world out there get represented in here, inside our heads? Put another way, how are the external stimuli that strike our bodies transformed into messages that our brains comprehend and interpret?

What stimuli cross our threshold for conscious awareness? Could we unknowingly be influenced by subliminal stimuli too weak to be perceived?

Each species comes equipped with sensitivities that enable it to survive and thrive. We sense only a portion of the sea of energy that surrounds us, but to this portion we are exquisitely sensitive. Our absolute threshold for any stimulus is the minimum stimulation necessary for us to detect it 50 percent of the time. Signal detection researchers report that our individual absolute thresholds vary with our psychological state.

Experiments reveal that we *can* process some information from stimuli too weak to recognize. But the restricted conditions under which this occurs would not enable unscrupulous opportunists to exploit us with subliminal messages.

To survive and thrive, an organism must have difference thresholds low enough to detect minute changes in important stimuli. In humans, a difference threshold (also called a *just noticeable difference*, or *jnd*) increases in proportion to the size of the stimulus—a principle known as Weber's law.

Why are we unaware of unchanging stimuli, such as the watch pressing against our wrist?

The phenomenon of sensory adaptation focuses our attention on informative changes in stimulation by diminishing our sensitivity to constant or routine odors, sounds, and touches.

How does our ability to focus on a limited aspect of our experience help us transform sensations into meaningful perceptions?

At any moment we are conscious of a very limited amount of all that we are capable of experiencing. One example of this selective attention is the cocktail party effect—attending to only one voice among many.

Terms and Concepts to Remember

sensation, p. 170
perception, p. 170
bottom-up processing, p. 170
top-down processing, p. 170
psychophysics, p. 170
absolute threshold, p. 171

signal detection theory, p. 171
subliminal, p. 172
difference threshold, p. 173
Weber's law, p. 174
sensory adaptation, p. 174
selective attention, p. 175

Test Yourself

11.1. To construct meaning out of our external environment, we select, organize, and interpret sensory information. This is the process of
   a. sensation.
   b. persuasion.
   c. encoding.
   d. perception.

11.2. Sensation is to _____ as perception is to _____.
   a. absolute threshold; difference threshold
   b. bottom-up processing; top-down processing
   c. interpretation; detection
   d. conscious awareness; persuasion

11.3. The absolute threshold is the minimum stimulation that a person can detect 50 percent of the time. Knowing your absolute threshold for sound tells you

   a. the smallest difference you can detect between two sounds.
   b. how likely you are to hear a particular faint sound.
   c. why you become used to background noise.
   d. whether you are being affected by subliminal stimulation.

11.4. People wonder whether subliminal stimuli, such as undetectably faint sights or sounds, influence us. Subliminal stimuli are
   a. too weak to be processed by the brain in any way.
   b. consciously perceived only 50 percent of the time.
   c. strong enough to affect our behavior.
   d. below the absolute threshold for conscious awareness.

11.5. To be perceived as different, two lights must differ in intensity by at least 8 percent. This illustrates a general principle called Weber's law, which states that for a difference to be perceived, two stimuli must differ by
   a. a fixed or constant amount.
   b. a constant minimum percentage.
   c. a constantly changing amount.
   d. more than 7 percent.

11.6. Confronted with an unchanging stimulus, we experience sensory adaptation. Sensory adaptation explains why we
   a. perceive subliminal stimuli.
   b. notice only large differences between two stimuli.
   c. soon get used to an unpleasant smell.
   d. have difficulty keeping our eyes completely still when staring at an object.

11.7. Sensory adaptation reduces our sensitivity to some stimuli in the environment. However, sensory adaptation has survival benefits. It helps us focus on
   a. the world as it really is.
   b. underlying phenomena and stimuli.
   c. constant features of the environment.
   d. important changes in the environment.

11.8. Selective attention is the focusing of conscious awareness on a particular stimulus. An example of selective attention is the "cocktail party effect," which is the ability to
   a. drink without becoming intoxicated.
   b. follow many voices simultaneously.
   c. attend to but one voice among many other voices.
   d. be affected by unnoticed stimuli.

Review

- What is the rough distinction between sensation and perception?

- Your friend insists that he *did* call you to dinner as you intently watched TV. Was your not perceiving him a likely instance of subliminal stimulation?

Reflect

- What are some types of sensory adaptation that you have experienced in just the last day?

- Can you recall a recent time when, your attention focused on one thing, you were oblivious to something else (perhaps to pain, to someone's approach, or to the background music)?

Answers to the Test Yourself and Review questions can be found in the green appendix at the end of the book.

12 Vision

P art of our genius is our body's ability to convert one sort of energy to another. Sensory **transduction** is the process by which our sensory systems convert stimulus energy into neural messages. Your eyes, for example, receive light energy and manage an amazing feat: They transduce (transform) the energy into neural messages that the brain then processes into what you consciously see. How does such a remarkable thing happen?

Differing eyes

When it comes to vision, humans and bees are on different wavelengths. Compare the way a flower is registered by a human and a bee's eye. The bee detects reflected ultraviolet wavelengths, enabling it to see the pollen landing field. The differing ecological niches occupied by different species demand sensitivity to different stimuli.

Human eye

Bee's eye

- **transduction** conversion of one form of energy into another. In sensation, the transforming of stimulus energies into neural impulses.

- **wavelength** the distance from the peak of one light or sound wave to the peak of the next. Electromagnetic wavelengths vary from the short blips of cosmic rays to the long pulses of radio transmission.

- **hue** the dimension of color that is determined by the wavelength of light; what we know as the color names *blue*, *green*, and so forth.

- **intensity** the amount of energy in a light or sound wave, which we perceive as brightness or loudness, as determined by the wave's amplitude.

- **pupil** the adjustable opening in the center of the eye through which light enters.

- **iris** a ring of muscle tissue that forms the colored portion of the eye around the pupil and controls the size of the pupil opening.

The Stimulus Input: Light Energy

Preview Question: What are the characteristics of the wavelengths that we see as visible light?

Scientifically speaking, what strikes our eyes is not color but pulses of electromagnetic energy that our visual system experiences as color. What we see as visible light is but a thin slice of the whole spectrum of electromagnetic radiation. As **FIGURE 12.1** illustrates, this *electromagnetic spectrum* ranges from imperceptibly short pulses or waves of gamma rays, to the narrow band that we see as visible light, to the long waves of radio transmission. Other organisms are sensitive to differing portions of the spectrum. For instance, bees cannot see red but can see ultraviolet light (see photos above).

Two physical characteristics of light and sound help determine our sensory experience of them. Light's **wavelength**—the distance from one wave peak to the next (**FIGURE 12.2a**)—determines its **hue** (the color we experience, such as blue or green). **Intensity**, the amount of energy in light waves (determined by a wave's *amplitude*, or height), influences brightness (**FIGURE 12.2b**). To understand *how* we transform physical energy into a sensation of color, we first need to understand our mind's window, the eye.

The Eye

Preview Question: How does the eye transform particles of light energy into neural messages?

Light enters the eye through the *cornea*, a transparent protector, then passes through the **pupil**, a small adjustable opening (**FIGURE 12.3**). The pupil's size, and therefore the amount of light entering the eye, is regulated by the **iris**, a colored

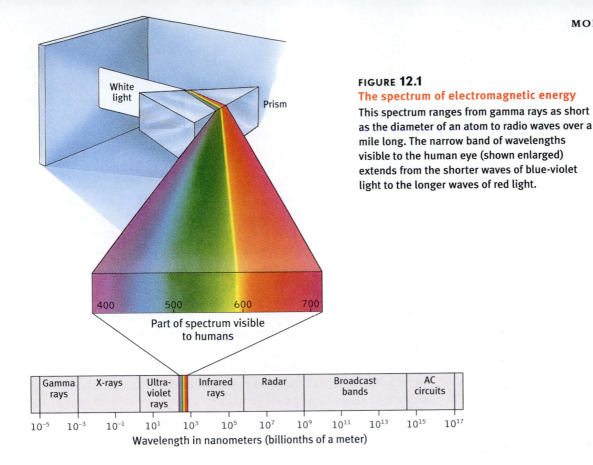

FIGURE 12.1

The spectrum of electromagnetic energy
This spectrum ranges from gamma rays as short as the diameter of an atom to radio waves over a mile long. The narrow band of wavelengths visible to the human eye (shown enlarged) extends from the shorter waves of blue-violet light to the longer waves of red light.

FIGURE 12.2

The physical properties of waves
(a) Waves vary in wavelength, the distance between successive peaks. Frequency, the number of complete wavelengths that can pass a point in a given time, depends on the wavelength. The shorter the wavelength, the higher the frequency. (b) Waves also vary in amplitude, the height from peak to trough. Wave amplitude determines the intensity of colors and sounds.

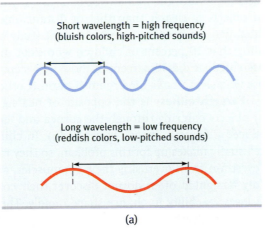

(a)

(b)

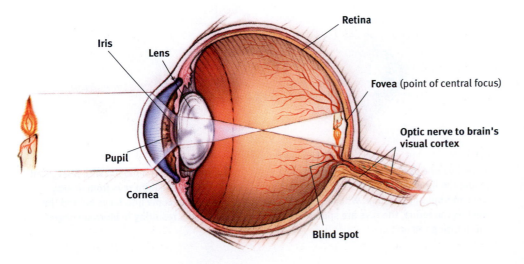

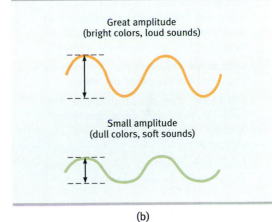

FIGURE 12.3

The eye
Light rays reflected from the candle pass through the cornea, pupil, and lens. The curvature and thickness of the lens change to bring either nearby or distant objects into focus on the retina. Light rays travel in straight lines. So rays from the top of the candle strike the bottom of the retina and those from the left side of the candle strike the right side of the retina. The candle's retinal image is thus upside-down and reversed.

lens the transparent structure behind the pupil that changes shape to focus images on the retina.

accommodation the process by which the eye's lens changes shape to focus the image of near objects on the retina.

retina the light-sensitive inner surface of the eye, containing the receptor rods and cones plus layers of neurons that begin the processing of visual information.

acuity the sharpness of vision.

nearsightedness a condition in which nearby objects are seen more clearly than distant objects because the lens focuses the image of distant objects in front of the retina.

farsightedness a condition in which faraway objects are seen more clearly than near objects because the image of near objects is focused behind the retina.

rods retinal receptors that detect black, white, and gray; necessary for peripheral and twilight vision, when cones don't respond.

cones receptor cells that are concentrated near the center of the retina and that function in daylight or in well-lit conditions. The cones detect fine detail and give rise to color sensations.

optic nerve the nerve that carries neural impulses from the eye to the brain.

blind spot the point at which the optic nerve leaves the eye, creating a "blind" spot because no receptor cells are located there.

fovea the central focal point in the retina, around which the eye's cones cluster.

muscle surrounding the pupil. The iris has a remarkable ability to adjust light intake by dilating and constricting in response to light intensity and even to inner emotions. When we're feeling amorous, our telltale dilated pupils subtly signal our interest. Behind the pupil is a **lens** that focuses the incoming rays into an image on the light-sensitive back surface. It does so by changing its curvature in a process called **accommodation**. The eyeball's light-sensitive surface on which the rays focus is a multilayered tissue, the **retina**.

For centuries, scientists have known that when the image of a candle passes through a small opening, its mirror image appears inverted on a dark wall behind (as in Figure 12.3). This fact was baffling. If the retina receives an upside-down image, how can we see the world right side up? One idea was that the eye's sensing device is the lens. Realizing this wasn't so, the ever-curious Leonardo da Vinci had another idea: Perhaps the eye's watery fluids bent the light rays, reinverting the image to the upright position as it reached the retina. But then in 1604, the astronomer and optics expert Johannes Kepler showed that the retina did receive upside-down images of the world (Crombie, 1964). And how could we understand such a world? "I leave it," said the befuddled Kepler, "to natural philosophers."

The "natural philosophers" eventually included research psychologists who discovered that the retina doesn't read the image as a whole. Rather, its millions of receptor cells convert light energy into neural impulses. These impulses are sent to the brain and constructed *there* into a perceived, upright-seeming image.

Acuity, or sharpness of vision, can be affected by small distortions in the shape of the eye. Normally the lens focuses the image of any object on the retina (**FIGURE 12.4a**). In **nearsightedness**, the misshapen eyeball focuses the light rays from distant objects in front of the retina (**FIGURE 12.4b**). If you are nearsighted, your perception of near objects is clearer than that of distant objects, but if you are extremely nearsighted you see nothing clearly. A recent study of 479 children revealed the curious finding that 10 percent of children who slept in the dark before age 2 later became nearsighted, as did 34 percent of those who slept with a night light and 55 percent of those who slept in a lighted room (Quinn & others, 1999).

Farsightedness is the opposite of nearsightedness. Here, the light rays from near objects entering through the cornea and lens reach the retina before they have produced a focused image (**FIGURE 12.4c**). In children, the eye's ability to accommodate usually makes up for this problem, so they rarely need glasses—but they may suffer eyestrain from overusing their eye muscles, and some get headaches. People only mildly farsighted often do not discover their condition until middle age, when the lens loses its ability to change shape rapidly. They then begin to have trouble seeing near objects clearly.

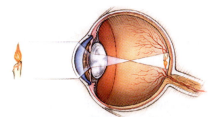

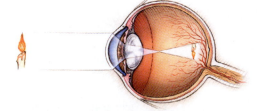

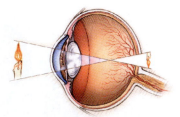

FIGURE 12.4 (a) Normal vision
Rays of light converge on the retina of a normal eye. This occurs for both nearby objects and, with appropriate readjustments in the curvature of the lens, for objects far away.

(b) Nearsighted vision
In the eye of a person with nearsighted vision, the light rays from distant objects focus in front of the retina. When their image reaches the retina, the rays are spreading out, blurring the image.

(c) Farsighted vision
In the eye of a person with farsighted vision, the light rays from nearby objects come into focus behind the retina, resulting in blurred images.

The Retina

If you followed a single particle of light energy into your eye, you would see that it first makes its way through the retina's outer layer of cells to its buried receptor cells, the **rods** and **cones** (FIGURE **12.5**). Light energy striking the rods and cones produces chemical changes that generate neural signals. These signals activate the neighboring *bipolar cells*, which in turn activate the neighboring *ganglion cells*. The axons from the network of ganglion cells converge like the strands of a rope to form an **optic nerve** that carries information to your brain. Nearly a million messages can be sent by the optic nerve at once, through nearly 1 million ganglion fibers. (The auditory nerve, which enables hearing, carries much less information through its mere 30,000 fibers.) Where the optic nerve leaves the eye there are no receptor cells—creating a **blind spot** (FIGURE **12.6**).

Cones are clustered around the **fovea**, the retina's area of central focus (Figure 12.3, page 179). In fact, the fovea contains only cones, no rods. Unlike rods, many cones have their own bipolar cells to help relay their individual messages to the cortex, which devotes a large amount of its area to impulses from the fovea. This preserves the cones' precise information, making them better able to detect fine detail. (Rods have no such hotline to the brain; they share bipolar cells with other rods, so their individual messages get combined.) To illustrate, if you pick a word in this sentence and stare directly at

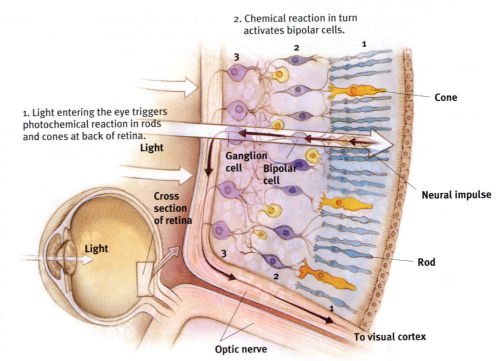

2. Chemical reaction in turn activates bipolar cells.

1. Light entering the eye triggers photochemical reaction in rods and cones at back of retina.

Light

Ganglion cell

Bipolar cell

Cone

Neural impulse

Rod

Cross section of retina

Light

To visual cortex

Optic nerve

3. Bipolar cells then activate the ganglion cells, the axons of which converge to form the optic nerve. This nerve transmits information to the visual cortex in the brain's occipital lobe.

FIGURE **12.5**
The retina's reaction to light

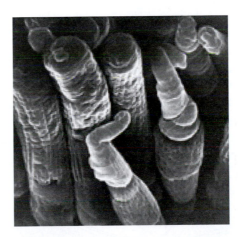

Rod-shaped rods and cone-shaped cones

As this scanning electron microscope shows, rods and cones are well-named. The rods are more sensitive to light than are the color-sensitive cones, which is why the world looks colorless at night. Some nocturnal animals, such as toads, mice, rats, and bats, have retinas made up almost entirely of rods, allowing them to function well in dim light. These creatures probably have very poor color vision.

FIGURE **12.6 The blind spot**
Where the optic nerve leaves the eye (Figure 12.5), there are no receptor cells. This creates a blind spot in our vision. To demonstrate, close your left eye, look at the spot, and move the page to a distance from your face (about a foot) at which the car disappears. In everyday vision the blind spot doesn't impair your vision because your eyes are moving and because one eye catches what the other misses.

TABLE **12.1**

RECEPTORS IN THE HUMAN EYE

	Cones	Rods
Number	6 million	120 million
Location in retina	Center	Periphery
Sensitivity in dim light	Low	High
Color sensitive?	Yes	No
Detail sensitive?	Yes	No

When viewing an eye chart, people with normal 20/20 vision can read material of a certain size from a distance of 20 feet. If you're standing 20 feet away and can discriminate only what people with normal vision can see at 50 feet, then you have 20/50 vision.

it, focusing its image on the cones in your fovea, you will see that words a few inches off to the side appear blurred. This is because their image strikes the more peripheral region of your retina, where the rods predominate (Table 12.1).

Rods enable black-and-white vision; cones enable you to see color. If illumination diminishes, the cones become ineffectual. The rods, however, remain sensitive in dim light, because several rods will funnel their faint energy from dim light onto a single bipolar cell. That is why you do not see colors in dim light. Thus, cones and rods each provide a special sensitivity—cones to detail and rods to faint light.

When you enter a darkened theater or turn off the light at night, your pupils dilate to allow more light to reach the rods in the retina's periphery. It typically takes 20 minutes or more before our eyes fully adapt. You can demonstrate dark adaptation by closing or covering one eye for up to 20 minutes. Then make the light in the room not quite bright enough to read this book with your open eye. Now open the dark-adapted eye and read (easily). This period of dark adaptation is yet another instance of the remarkable adaptiveness of our sensory systems, for it parallels the average natural twilight transition between the sun's setting and darkness.

Knowing just this much about the eye, can you imagine why a cat sees so much better at night than you do? There are at least two reasons: A cat's pupils can open much wider than yours, letting in more light; and a cat has a higher proportion of light-sensitive rods (Moser, 1987). But there is a trade-off: With fewer cones, a cat sees neither details nor color as well as you do.

Visual Information Processing

Preview Question: How is visual information processed in the brain?

Visual information percolates through progressively more abstract levels. At the entry level, the retina—which is actually a piece of the brain that migrates to the eye during early fetal development—processes information before routing it to the cortex. The retina's neural layers are not just passing along electrical impulses; they also help to encode and analyze the sensory information. The third neural layer in a frog's eye, for example, contains the "bug detector" cells that fire only in response to flylike stimuli.

FIGURE 12.7 Pathway from the eyes to the visual cortex

The visual cortex receives information from the eyes by way of optic nerves, which come together at the optic chiasm. From here neural messages are transmitted to the thalamus and onto the visual cortex.

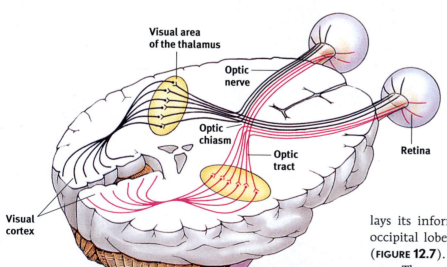

Visual area of the thalamus

Optic nerve

Optic chiasm

Optic tract

Retina

Visual cortex

In human eyes, the information from the retina's nearly 130 million receptor rods and cones is received and transmitted by the million or so ganglion cells, whose fibers make up the optic nerve. A typical ganglion cell responds to light/dark contrasts revealed by its receptor cells. This helps the brain detect edges and other important features of the visual world. But most information processing occurs in the brain. Any given area of the retina relays its information to a corresponding location in the occipital lobe—the visual cortex at the back of the brain (**FIGURE 12.7**).

The same sensitivity that enables retinal cells to fire messages can lead them to misfire as well. Turn your eyes to the left, close them, and then gently rub the right side of your right eyelid with your fingertip. Note the patch of light to the left, moving as your finger moves. Why do you see light? Why at the left?

Your retinal cells are so responsive that even pressure triggers them. But your brain interprets their firing as light. Moreover, it interprets the light as coming from the left—the direction light normally comes from when it activates the right side of the retina.

Feature Detection

When individual ganglion cells register information in their region of the visual field, they send signals to the visual cortex. Nobel prize winners David Hubel and Torsten Wiesel (1979) demonstrated that when certain cortical neurons, called **feature detectors**, receive this information, they respond to specific features of a scene—to particular edges, lines, angles, and movements. From these elements the brain assembles the perceived image.

For example, Hubel and Wiesel report that a given brain cell might respond maximally to a bar flashed at a 2 o'clock tilt (**FIGURE 12.8**). If the bar is tilted further—say, to a 3 o'clock or 1 o'clock position—the cell quiets down. Thus, the feature detection cells record amazingly specific features taken in by the eye. Feature detection cells pass this information to other cells that respond only to more complex patterns. The basic idea is that perceptions arise from the interaction of many neuron systems, each performing a simple task.

■ **feature detectors** nerve cells in the brain that respond to specific features of the stimulus, such as shape, angle, or movement.

Going left or right?

In the semifinal game of the 1996 European Cup, German goalie Andreas Kopke anticipates the direction of Gareth Southgate's tiebreaker kick for England. Before Southgate's foot connects with the ball, Kopke's visual system has processed information from Southgate's eyes, posture, and movement, activating "going right" supercells. Kopke blocks the kick and Germany wins.

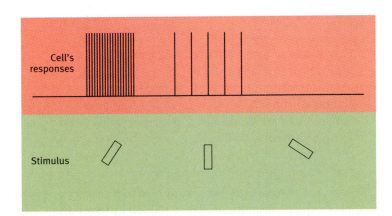

FIGURE 12.8

Electrodes record how individual cells in this monkey's visual cortex respond to different visual stimuli

Hubel and Wiesel won the Nobel prize for their discovery that most cells in the visual cortex respond only to particular features—for example, to the edge of a surface or to a bar at a 30-degree angle in the upper right part of the field of vision. More complex features trigger higher-level detector cells, which integrate information from these simpler ones.

The visual cortex passes this information along to the temporal and parietal cortex, which includes higher-level brain cells that respond to specific visual scenes, such as a face or an arm movement in a particular direction. Psychologist David Perrett and his colleagues (1988, 1992, 1994) report that for biologically important objects and events, monkey brains (and surely ours as well) have a "vast visual encyclopedia" distributed as cells that respond to one stimulus but not to others. Perrett has identified nerve cells that specialize in responding to a specific gaze, head angle, posture, or body movement. Other supercell clusters integrate this information and fire only when the cues collectively indicate the direction of someone's attention and approach. This instant analysis, which aided our ancestors' survival, also helps a soccer goalie anticipate the direction of an impending kick and a pedestrian anticipate another pedestrian's next movement.

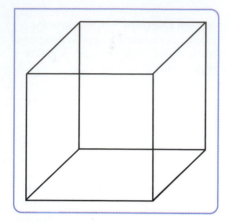

FIGURE 12.9 How the brain perceives
As you stare at this Necker cube, providing fairly constant stimulation to your retina, your perception—and accompanying neural activity in your brain—will change every couple of seconds.

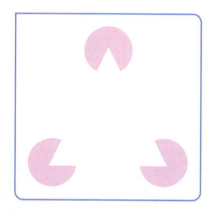

FIGURE 12.10
An example of the brain's virtual reality: Illusory contours
Simulated neural networks respond to the illusory triangle as humans do—as if it were a real triangle, and not just three Pac-Man faces.

As your perception of the Necker cube in **FIGURE 12.9** shifts every few seconds, so it seems does neural activity in your visual cortex. Although the same image continues to strike the retina, the brain constructs varying perceptions. Researchers also have identified nerve cells that activate or not, depending on how a monkey *perceives* a given image, as reported by the monkey's up or down eye movements (Barinaga, 1997; Logothetis & Schall, 1989). Such studies remind us that our visual system works both bottom-up and top-down. Although our visual pathway faithfully represents retinal stimulation, our brain's representation also incorporates our assumptions, interests, and expectations (Maunsell, 1995). The higher-level brain activity that underlies perception combines sensory input and cognition.

Researchers continue to debate the precise nature of the features and patterns that brain cells detect. Recent research suggests that any image, such as a face, can be broken down into patterns of changing light intensity that can be described mathematically. Thus, in seeing, the brain may actually be processing mathematical-like codes that represent a perceived image (Kosslyn & Koenig, 1992; Marr, 1982). Neuroscientists working with computer experts are simulating the activity of the brain's interconnected, multilevel neural networks. Their goal is to build artificial vision systems that respond in the ways our own visual system responds. For example, their simulated neural networks respond as humans do to the illusory image of a triangle like that in **FIGURE 12.10**, as if they were reacting to a real triangle (Finkel & Sajda, 1994).

Parallel Processing

Consider some actual cases of peculiar visual disabilities produced by peculiar brain damage (from Hoffman, 1998).

+ Looking at an American flag, Ms. W is able to see lines and stars. But "it's like you have one part here and one part there, and you put them together to see what they make."
+ Mr. I, an artist until suffering a concussion at age 65, no longer perceives colors, only shades of gray. Tomatoes look black, flowers an assortment of grays. Even his once vivid imagination of colors is now gone.
+ Ms. M, having suffered stroke damage near the rear of both sides of her brain, can no longer perceive movement. People moving about a room seem "suddenly here or there but I have not seen them moving." It's a challenge to pour tea into a cup because the fluid appears frozen and she cannot perceive the rising in the cup. (You could experience this same loss of motion if given disruptive magnetic stimulation to the corresponding neural area in your brain.)

These and other cases suggest that, unlike most computers, which do step-by-step serial processing, our brains engage in **parallel processing**. That means we can do several things at once. We construct our perceptions by integrating the work of different visual teams, working in parallel. Destroy or disable the neural workstation for a visual subtask and something peculiar results.

Parallel processing
Studies of brain-damaged patients suggest that the brain delegates the work of processing color, motion, form, and depth to different areas. After taking a scene apart, how does the brain integrate these subdimensions into the perceived image? The answer to this question is the Holy Grail of vision research.

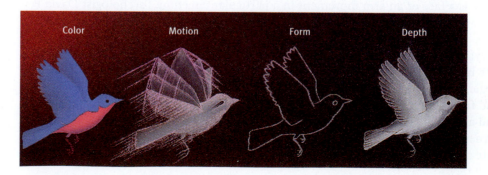

The brain divides a visual scene into subdimensions such as color, depth, movement, and form and works on each aspect simultaneously (Livingstone & Hubel, 1988). As David Rumelhart (1989) explains, this division of labor to specialized but overlapping neural networks more than makes up for the brain's slowness:

> Although the brain has *slow* components, it has *very many* of them. The human brain contains billions of such processing elements. Rather than organize computation with many, many serial steps, as we do with [computer] systems whose steps are very fast, the brain must deploy many, many processing elements cooperatively and in parallel to carry out its activities.

Thus the retina projects not just to one visual cortex area but to several areas, each of which becomes active in response to retinal stimulation. When the brain integrates this visual information, further processing in another cortex area, the temporal lobe, enables us to recognize an image as, say, Whoopi Goldberg. The whole process of facial recognition requires tremendous brain power—30 percent of the cortex, 10 times the area the brain devotes to hearing. And the computations required for sensorimotor coordination dwarf even those involved in reasoning. We now have computers that can play chess with champion Garry Kasparov, but we're a long way from computer-driven robots that can play tennis with Venus Williams, much less dust the house. Such observations reveal the remarkable powers of our human visual intelligence. Neural impulses travel a million times slower than a computer's internal messages, yet our brains humble any computer by recognizing a familiar face instantly. "You can buy a chess machine that beats a master," notes Donald Hoffman (1998, p. xiii), "but can't yet buy a vision machine that beats a toddler's vision."

The distribution of visual tasks to different neural work teams explains the peculiar cases. After her stroke damage, for example, Ms. M lost just one aspect of vision and was unable to perceive movement. When something moved, it disappeared until it stopped. Other brain-damaged patients can tell you all about the subdimensions of an object or person (a rose's color or a woman's height) but cannot name the object or the person.

Still others have lost a neural area involved in consciously perceiving some aspect of their field of vision. One such woman was shown two drawings of a house—identical except that the house's left side was on fire in one drawing. Asked to select the house she would prefer to live in, she thought the question silly, "because they're the same." Yet she consistently chose the house that was not burning (Marshall & Halligan, 1988; Milner, 1995). This uncanny ability to respond to something not consciously perceived, called *blindsight*, reminds us once again of the startling truth: Our brains do many things at once, automatically and without our awareness.

Senses other than vision also process information with similar speed and intricacy. Opening the back door, you recognize the aroma wafting from the kitchen even before you step inside. Answering the phone, you recognize the friend calling from the moment she says "Hi." Within a fraction of a second after such events stimulate the senses, millions of neurons have simultaneously coordinated in extracting the essential features, comparing them with past experience, and identifying the stimulus (Freeman, 1991).

At the instant your brain pulls all this information together, enabling you to recognize your sister in a sea of faces, distant clusters of brain neurons momentarily synchronize their activity. With distributed parts of the brain having done their processing, EEG recordings reveal their integration: For about a fourth of a second thousands of neurons emit equivalent signals 40 times a second, creating gamma waves (Rodriguez & others, 1999). For this fleeting moment, distant brain areas collaborate and the result is something no single neural cluster could achieve: a conscious recognition (**FIGURE 12.11**).

■ **parallel processing** the processing of several aspects of a problem simultaneously; the brain's natural mode of information processing for many functions, including vision. Contrasts with the step-by-step (serial) processing of most computers and of conscious problem solving.

FIGURE 12.11
The shadow of a perception
Shortly after seeing a face, brain waves detected by various scalp electrodes become momentarily synchronized. Green lines between electrode points indicate increased synchrony. (From Rodriguez & others, 1999.)

Perception   No perception

FIGURE **12.12**
A simplified summary of visual information processing

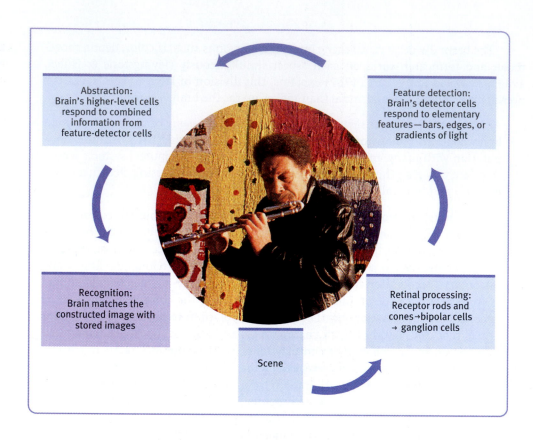

This scientific understanding of sensory information processing is illustrated by neuropsychologist Roger Sperry's (1985) reflection: The "insights of science give added, not lessened, reasons for awe, respect, and reverence." Think about it: As you look at someone, the visual information is sent to your brain as millions of neural impulses, then constructed into its component features, and finally, in some as yet mysterious way, composed into a meaningful perceived image, which is then compared with previously stored images and recognized as, for example, your grandmother. The whole process (**FIGURE 12.12**) is more complex than taking a car apart, piece by piece, transporting it to a different location, then having specialized workers reconstruct it. That all of this happens instantly, effortlessly, and continuously is indeed awesome.

Color Vision

Preview Question: What theories contribute to our understanding of color vision, and how are we affected by color constancy?

We talk as though objects possess color. We say, "A tomato is red." Perhaps you have pondered the old question, "If a tree falls in the forest and no one hears it, does it make a sound?" We can ask the same of color: If no one sees the tomato, is it red?

The answer is no. First, the tomato is everything *but* red, because it *rejects* (reflects) the long wavelengths of red. Second, the tomato's color is our mental construction. As Isaac Newton (1704) noted, "The [light] rays are not coloured." Color, like all aspects of vision, resides not in the object but in the theater of our brains. Even while dreaming, we may perceive things in color.

In the study of vision, one of the most basic and intriguing mysteries is how we see the world in color. How, from the light energy striking the retina, does the brain manufacture our experience of color—and of such a multitude of colors? Our difference threshold for colors is so low that we can discriminate some 7 million different color variations (Geldard, 1972).

"I am fearfully and wonderfully made."

King David, *Psalms* 139:14

"Only mind has sight and hearing; all things else are deaf and blind."

Epicharmus, *Fragments*, 550 B.C.

At least most of us can. For about 1 person in 50, vision is color-deficient—and that person is usually male, because the defect is genetically sex-linked. To understand why some people's vision is color-deficient, it will help to first understand how normal color vision works.

Modern detective work on the mystery of color vision began in the nineteenth century when Hermann von Helmholtz built on the insights of an English physicist, Thomas Young. Young and Helmholtz knew that any color can be created by combining the light waves of three primary colors—red, green, and blue. So, they inferred that the eye must have three types of receptors, one for each primary color of light.

Years later, researchers measured the response of various cones to different color stimuli and confirmed the **Young-Helmholtz trichromatic (three-color) theory**, which simply states that the retina has three types of color receptors, each especially sensitive to one of three colors. And surprise! Those colors are, indeed, red, green, or blue. When we stimulate combinations of these cones, we see other colors. For example, there are no receptors especially sensitive to yellow. Yet when both red- and green-sensitive cones are stimulated, we see yellow.

If you are trying to make sense of all this by thinking back to mixing paints, you had better think again. Mixing paints is *subtractive color mixing* because it *subtracts* wavelengths from the reflected light. The more colors you mix in, the fewer wavelengths can be reflected back. So, mixing blue and yellow paint leaves only green to be reflected back. Combining red, blue, and yellow means no light waves will be reflected and you will see brown or black. But mixing *lights*, as Young and Helmholtz did, is *additive color mixing*, because the process adds wavelengths and thus *increases* light—combining red, blue, and green lights makes white light (**FIGURE 12.13**).

Most color-deficient people are not actually "colorblind." They simply lack functioning red- or green-sensitive cones. Their vision is dichromatic (two-color) instead of trichromatic, making it difficult to distinguish red and green, as in **FIGURE 12.14** (Boynton, 1979). Dogs, too, lack receptors for the wavelengths of red, giving them only limited, dichromatic color vision (Neitz & others, 1989).

Soon after Young and Helmholtz proposed the trichromatic theory, physiologist Ewald Hering pointed out that other parts of the color vision mystery remained unsolved. For example, we see yellow when mixing red and green light. But how is it that those blind to red and green can often still see yellow? And why does yellow appear to be a pure color and not a mixture of red and green, the way purple is of red and blue?

Hering found a clue in the well-known occurrence of *afterimages*. When you stare at a green square for a while and then look at a white sheet of paper, you see red, green's *opponent*

■ **Young-Helmholtz trichromatic (three-color) theory** the theory that the retina contains three different color receptors—one most sensitive to red, one to green, one to blue—which when stimulated in combination can produce the perception of any color.

Additive color mixing

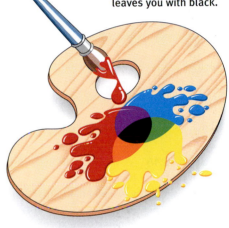

FIGURE 12.13
Additive and subtractive color mixing
Mixing lights is additive, because wavelengths from each light in the mix reach the eye, and mixing all three primary light colors creates white. Mixing paint colors subtracts wavelengths. Mixing all three primary colors leaves you with black.

Subtractive color mixing

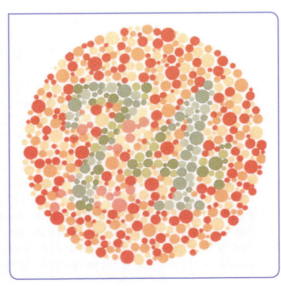

FIGURE 12.14
Color-deficient vision
People who suffer red-green deficiency have trouble perceiving the number within the design.

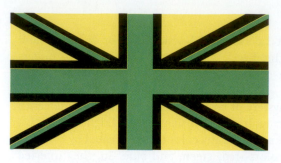

FIGURE 12.15 Afterimage effect
Stare at the center of the flag for a minute and then shift your eyes to the dot in the white space beside it. What do you see? (After tiring your neural response to black, green, and yellow, you should see their opponent colors.) Stare at a white wall and note how the size of the flag grows with the projection distance!

FIGURE 12.16
Color depends on context
In this painting by Joseph Albers (1975), the unchanging line seems to vary from gray to yellow as its surrounding context changes.

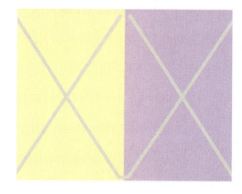

■ **opponent-process theory** the theory that opposing retinal processes (red-green, yellow-blue, white-black) enable color vision. For example, some cells are stimulated by green and inhibited by red; others are stimulated by red and inhibited by green.

■ **color constancy** perceiving familiar objects as having consistent color, even if changing illumination alters the wavelengths reflected by the object.

color. Stare at a yellow square and you will later see its opponent color, blue, on the white paper (as in the flag demonstration in **FIGURE 12.15**). Hering surmised that there were two additional color processes, one responsible for red versus green perception, and one for blue versus yellow.

A century later, researchers confirmed Hering's **opponent-process theory**. *After* leaving the receptor cells, visual information is analyzed in terms of the opponent colors red and green, blue and yellow, and also black and white. In the retina and in the thalamus (where impulses from the retina are relayed en route to the visual cortex) some neurons are turned "on" by red but turned "off" by green. Others are turned on by green but off by red (DeValois & DeValois, 1975). So if you detect one of these colors at a particular point on the retina, you cannot simultaneously detect the opposing color at the same point; you therefore cannot see a greenish red.

Opponent processes explain afterimages, such as in the flag demonstration, in which we tire our green response by staring at green. When we then stare at white (which contains all colors, including red), only the red part of the green/red pairing will fire normally.

The present solution to the mystery of color vision is therefore roughly this: Color processing occurs in two stages. The retina's red, green, and blue cones respond in varying degrees to different color stimuli, as the Young-Helmholtz trichromatic theory suggested. Their signals are then processed by the nervous system's opponent-process cells, en route to the visual cortex.

Color Constancy

Our experience of color depends on something more than the wavelength information received by our trichromatic cones and transmitted through the opponent-process cells.

That something more is the surrounding *context*. If you view only part of a tomato, its color will seem to change as the light changes. But if you see the whole tomato as one item in a bowl of fresh vegetables, its color will remain roughly constant as the lighting and wavelengths shift—a phenomenon known as **color constancy**. Dorothea Jameson (1985) notes that a chip colored blue under indoor lighting matches the wavelengths reflected by a gold chip in the sunlight. Yet bring a bluebird indoors and it won't look like a goldfinch. Likewise, a green leaf hanging from a brown branch may, when the illumination changes, reflect the same light energy that formerly came from the brown branch. Yet to us the leaf stays greenish and the branch stays brownish. Put on yellow-tinted ski goggles and the snow, after a second, looks as white as before.

Though we take this color constancy for granted, the phenomenon is truly remarkable. It demonstrates that our experience of color comes not just from the object—the color is not in the isolated leaf—but from everything around it as well. You and I see color thanks to our brains' computations of the light reflected by any object *relative to its surrounding objects.*

In a context that does not vary, we maintain color constancy. But what if we change the context? Because the brain computes the color of an object relative to its context, the perceived color changes (as is dramatically apparent in **FIGURE 12.16**). This principle—that we perceive objects not in isolation but in their environmental context—is especially significant for artists, interior decorators, and clothing designers. Our perception of the color of a wall or of a swatch of paint on a canvas is determined not just by the paint in the can but by the surrounding colors.

REVIEW AND REFLECT:

Vision

Each sense receives stimulation, transduces it into neural signals, and sends these neural messages to the brain. We have glimpsed how this happens with vision.

What are the characteristics of the wavelengths that we see as visible light?

The energies we experience as visible light are a thin slice from the broad spectrum of electromagnetic radiation. The hue and brightness we perceive in a light depend on the wavelength and intensity.

How does the eye transform particles of light energy into neural messages?

After entering the eye and being focused by a cameralike lens, light waves strike the retina. The retina's light-sensitive rods and color-sensitive cones convert the light energy into neural impulses, which are coded by the retina before traveling along the optic nerve to the brain.

How is visual information processed in the brain?

In the cortex, individual neurons, called feature detectors, respond to specific features of a visual stimulus, and their information is pooled for interpretation by higher-level brain cells. Subdimensions of vision (color, movement, depth, and form) are processed separately and simultaneously, illustrating the brain's capacity for parallel processing. The visual pathway faithfully represents retinal stimulation, but the brain's representation incorporates our assumptions, interests, and expectations.

What theories contribute to our understanding of color vision, and how are we affected by color constancy?

Research on how we see color supports two nineteenth-century theories. First, as the Young-Helmholtz trichromatic (three-color) theory suggests, the retina contains three types of cones. Each is most sensitive to the wavelengths of one of the three primary colors of light (red, green, or blue). Second, as opponent-process theory maintains, the nervous system codes the color-related information from the cones into pairs of opponent colors, as demonstrated by the phenomenon of afterimages and as confirmed by measuring opponent processes within visual neurons of the thalamus. The phenomenon of color constancy under varying illumination shows that our brains construct our experience of color.

Terms and Concepts to Remember

transduction, p. 178
wavelength, p. 178
hue, p. 178
intensity, p. 178
pupil, p. 178
iris, p. 178
lens, p. 180
accommodation, p. 180
retina, p. 180
acuity, p. 180
nearsightedness, p. 180
farsightedness, p. 180

rods, p. 181
cones, p. 181
optic nerve, p. 181
blind spot, p. 181
fovea, p. 181
feature detectors, p. 183
parallel processing, p. 184
Young-Helmholtz trichromatic (three-color) theory, p. 187
opponent-process theory, p. 188
color constancy, p. 188

Test Yourself

12.1. Two physical characteristics of light help determine our sensory experience of it. The characteristic that determines the color we experience is
a. intensity.
c. amplitude.
b. wavelength.
d. hue.

12.2. The blind spot is located in the area of the retina in which
a. there are rods but no cones.
b. there are cones but no rods.
c. the optic nerve leaves the eye.
d. the bipolar cells meet the ganglion cells.

12.3. Rods and cones are the eye's receptor cells. Cones are especially sensitive to _____ light and are responsible for our _____ vision.
a. bright; black-and-white
c. bright; color
b. dim; color
d. dim; black-and-white

12.4. According to Hubel and Wiesel, the brain includes cells that respond maximally to certain bars, edges, and movements. These cells are called
a. rods and cones.
c. bug detectors.
b. feature detector cells.
d. ganglion cells

12.5. Unlike most computers, the brain is capable of simultaneously processing separate aspects of an object or problem. We call this ability
a. parallel processing.
c. recognition.
b. feature detection.
d. accommodation.

12.6. Researchers today believe that the Young-Helmholtz and Hering theories together account for color vision. The Young-Helmholtz theory shows that the eye contains _____ and the Hering theory accounts for the brain having _____.
a. opposing retinal processes; three pairs of color receptors
b. opponent-process cells; three types of color receptors
c. three pairs of color receptors; opposing retinal processes
d. three types of color receptors; opponent-process cells

12.7. We perceive tomatoes and stringbeans as consistently red and green, respectively, even though shifting illumination may alter their reflective wavelengths. This demonstrates the phenomenon of
a. afterimages.
c. trichromatic vision.
b. color constancy.
d. color processing.

Review: Retrace the rapid sequence of events involved in seeing and recognizing someone you know.

Reflect: If you were forced to give up one sense, which would it be? Why?

Answers to the Test Yourself and Review questions can be found in the green appendix at the end of the book.

Hearing

ike our other senses, our hearing, or **audition**, is highly adaptive. We hear a wide range of sounds, but we hear best those sounds having frequencies within a range that corresponds to the range of the human voice. And we are remarkably sensitive to faint sounds, an obvious boon to our ancestors' survival when hunting or being hunted or detecting a child's whimper. (If our ears were much more sensitive, we would hear a constant hiss from the movement of air molecules.) We are also acutely sensitive to differences in sounds. We easily detect differences among thousands of human voices, helping us to recognize immediately the voice of almost anyone we know.

For hearing as for seeing, one fundamental question remains—How do we do it?

The sounds of music

A violin's short, fast waves create a high pitch, an accordion's longer, slower waves a low pitch. Differences in the waves' height or amplitude also create differing degrees of loudness.

The Stimulus Input: Sound Waves

Preview Question: What are the characteristics of the air pressure waves that we hear as meaningful sounds?

Hit a piano key and the resulting stimulus energy is sound waves—jostling molecules of air, each bumping into the next, like a shove being transmitted through a concert hall's crowded exit tunnel. The resulting waves of compressed and expanded air are like the ripples on a pond circling out from where a stone has been tossed. As we swim in our ocean of moving air molecules, our ears detect these brief air pressure changes. They then transform them into nerve impulses, which our brain decodes as sounds. The strength, or amplitude, of sound waves determines their *loudness*. Waves also vary in length, and therefore in **frequency** (**FIGURE 13.1**). Their frequency determines their **pitch**: The longer the waves (the lower their frequency), the lower the pitch; the shorter the waves (the higher their frequency), the higher the pitch. A piccolo produces much shorter sound waves than does a tuba.

FIGURE 13.1 The physical properties of waves

(a) Waves vary in wavelength, the distance between successive peaks. Frequency, the number of complete wavelengths that can pass a point in a given time, depends on the wavelength. The shorter the wavelength, the higher the frequency. (b) Waves also vary in amplitude, the height from peak to trough. Wave amplitude determines the intensity of colors and sounds.

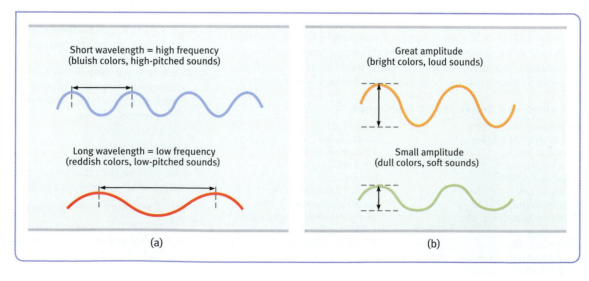

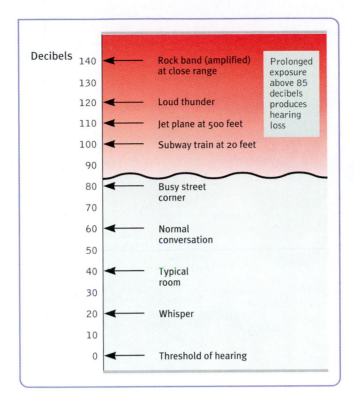

Decibels

140	← Rock band (amplified) at close range
130	
120	← Loud thunder
110	← Jet plane at 500 feet
100	← Subway train at 20 feet
90	
80	← Busy street corner
70	
60	← Normal conversation
50	
40	← Typical room
30	
20	← Whisper
10	
0	← Threshold of hearing

Prolonged exposure above 85 decibels produces hearing loss

FIGURE 13.2
The intensity of some common sounds
At close range, the thunder that follows lightning has 120-decibel intensity.

Decibels are the measuring unit for sound energy. The absolute threshold for hearing is arbitrarily defined as 0 decibels. Every 10 decibels correspond to a tenfold increase in sound. Thus, normal conversation (60 decibels) is 10,000 times louder than a 20-decibel whisper. And a tolerable 100-decibel passing subway train is 10 billion times louder than the faintest detectable sound. (For light we can tolerate a stimulus a trillion times more intense than a barely noticeable glimmer.) When prolonged, however, exposure to sounds above 85 decibels can produce hearing loss (**FIGURE 13.2**).

The Ear

Preview Questions: How does the ear transform sound energy into neural messages that the brain interprets as a particular sound? How do we localize sounds as coming from a particular place?

To hear, we must somehow convert sound waves into neural activity. But how? The human ear accomplishes this feat through an intricate mechanical chain reaction (**FIGURE 13.3**, page 192). First, the visible outer ear channels the sound waves through the auditory canal to the *eardrum*, a tight membrane that vibrates with the waves. The **middle ear** then transmits the eardrum's vibrations through a piston made of three tiny bones (the *hammer, anvil,* and *stirrup*) to a snail-shaped tube in the **inner ear** called the **cochlea** (KOHK-lee-uh). The incoming vibrations cause the cochlea's membrane (the *oval window*) to vibrate the fluid that fills the tube. This motion causes ripples in the *basilar membrane*, which is lined with *hair cells*, so named because of their tiny hairlike projections. At the end of this sequence, the rippling of the basilar membrane bends these hair cells, not unlike the wind bending a wheat field. The movement of the hair cells triggers impulses in the adjacent nerve fibers, which in turn converge to form the auditory nerve. By means of this mechanical chain of events, sound waves cause the hair cells of the inner ear to send neural messages up

- **audition** the sense of hearing.
- **frequency** the number of complete wavelengths that pass a point in a given time (for example, per second).
- **pitch** a tone's highness or lowness; depends on frequency.
- **middle ear** the chamber between the eardrum and cochlea containing three tiny bones (hammer, anvil, and stirrup) that concentrate the vibrations of the eardrum on the cochlea's oval window.
- **inner ear** the innermost part of the ear, containing the cochlea, semicircular canals, and vestibular sacs.
- **cochlea [KOHK-lee-uh]** a coiled, bony, fluid-filled tube in the inner ear through which sound waves trigger nerve impulses.

FIGURE **13.3**
How we transform sound waves into nerve impulses that our brain interprets

(a) The outer ear funnels sound waves to the eardrum. The bones of the middle ear amplify and relay the eardrum's vibrations through the oval window into the fluid-filled cochlea. (b) The resulting pressure changes in the cochlear fluid cause the basilar membrane to ripple, bending the hair cells on the surface. Hair cell movements trigger impulses at the bases of the nerve cells, whose fibers converge to form the auditory nerve. (For clarity, the cochlea is shown partially uncoiled.)

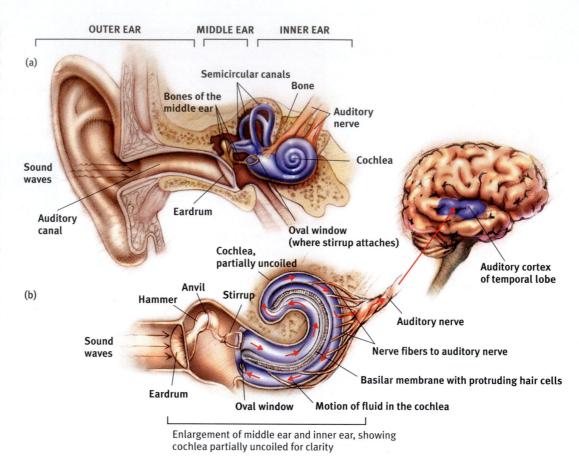

Enlargement of middle ear and inner ear, showing cochlea partially uncoiled for clarity

to the temporal lobe's auditory cortex. From vibrating air to moving piston to fluid waves to electrical impulses to the brain: Voila! We hear.

My vote for the most magical part of the hearing process is the hair cells, damage to which accounts for most hearing loss. A 1997 Howard Hughes Medical Institute report on these "quivering bundles that let us hear" marvels at their "extreme sensitivity and extreme speed." A cochlea only has 16,000 of them, which sounds like a lot until we compare that with an eye's 100 million or so photoreceptors. But consider their responsiveness. Deflect the tiny bundles of cilia on the tip of a hair cell by the width of an atom—the equivalent of displacing the top of the Eiffel Tower by only half an inch—and the alert hair cell triggers a neural response. Moreover, at the highest perceived frequency they can turn neural current on and off 20,000 times per second! As you might expect of something so sensitive, they are, however, delicate and fragile. Blast them with incessant jackhammer or headset sounds and the hair cell's cilia will begin to wither or fuse (see Close-Up: A Noisy Noise Annoys).

And how do we detect loudness? It is not as I would have guessed (from the intensity of a hair cell's response). Rather, a soft, pure tone activates only the few hair cells attuned to its frequency. Given louder sounds, its neighbor hair cells also respond. Thus, the brain can interpret loudness from the *number* of activated hair cells.

If a hair cell loses sensitivity to soft sounds, it may still respond to loud sounds. This helps explain another surprise: Really loud sounds may seem equally loud to people with and without hearing loss. This is why hard-of-hearing people do not want *all* sounds (loud and soft) amplified, as was the case with older hearing aids. They like sound *compressed*—which means soft sounds are amplified more than loud sounds.

CLOSE-UP:

A Noisy Noise Annoys

Modern life is noisy. Traffic roars. Factory machines clatter. Jackhammers tear up pavement. To escape into more pleasant sounds, runners stride to the beat of intense music on their headsets.

The intensity of all this noise causes a problem. Brief exposure to extremely intense sounds, such as gunfire near one's ear, and prolonged exposure to intense sounds, such as amplified music, can damage receptor cells and auditory nerves (Backus, 1977; West & Evans, 1990). Hair cells have been likened to shag carpet fibers. Walk around on them and they will pick up with a quick vacuuming. But leave a heavy piece of furniture on them for a long time and they may never rebound.

Small wonder that with industrialization, power tools, and loud recreations, the proportion of 45- to 64-year-old Americans who "cannot hear and understand normal speech" shot up by 87 percent in the two decades following 1971 (National Health Interview Survey, 1994). Ironically, even health clubs and fitness spas—which commonly blast 100+ decibel music—may be damaging their patrons' hearing health. They might take a cue from Pete Townshend of the Who, who sent Hearing Education and Awareness for Rockers a check for $10,000, acknowledging his own hearing loss. Although rock and roll may be here to stay, the sad truth for some rock musicians is that their hearing may not be.

As a general rule, if you cannot talk over a noise, it is potentially harmful, especially if prolonged (Roeser, 1998). (People who spend their day behind a power mower or above a jackhammer should be wearing earplugs.) And if we experience ringing of the ears after exposure to loud machinery or music we have been bad to our unhappy hair cells. As pain alerts us to possible bodily harm, ringing of the ears alerts us to possible hearing damage. It is hearing's equivalent of bleeding. "Condoms or, safer yet, abstinence," say sex educators. "Earplugs or walk away," say hearing educators.

Noise affects not only our hearing but also our behavior. On tasks requiring alert performance, people in noisy surroundings work less efficiently and make more errors (Broadbent, 1978). People who live with continual noise in factories, in homes near airports, and in apartments next to trains and highways suffer elevated rates of stress-related disorders: High blood pressure, anxiety, and feelings of helplessness are common (Evans & others, 1995).

But is it really the noise that causes the stress? Several laboratory experiments on the psychological effects of noise suggest an answer. In one such experiment, David Glass and Jerome Singer (1972) tape-recorded the chatter of office machines and of people speaking a mix of languages. While they did their various tasks, workers heard this noise, played either loudly or softly, either at predictable or unpredictable intervals. Regardless of the conditions, the people soon adapted to the predictable noise and performed well on most every task. However, having coped with the noise, those exposed to the *unpredictable* loud noise later made more errors on a proofreading task and reacted more quickly to frustration.

The conclusion: Noise is especially stressful when unanticipated or uncontrollable. That explains why the unpredictable and uncontrollable blaring of someone else's stereo can be so much more upsetting than the same decibels from your own. At such times we may wish that our ears had earlids.

Be kind to your inner ear's hair cells
When vibrating in response to sound, the 50 to 60 cilia shown here atop a hair cell produce an electrical signal.

How Do We Perceive Pitch?

How do we know whether a sound is the high-frequency, high-pitched chirp of a bird or the low-frequency, low-pitched roar of a truck? Current thinking on how we discriminate pitch, like current thinking on how we discriminate color, combines two theories.

■ **place theory** in hearing, the theory that links the pitch we hear with the place where the cochlea's membrane is stimulated.

■ **frequency theory** in hearing, the theory that the rate of nerve impulses traveling up the auditory nerve matches the frequency of a tone, thus enabling us to sense its pitch.

■ **conduction hearing loss** hearing loss caused by damage to the mechanical system that conducts sound waves to the cochlea.

■ **sensorineural hearing loss** hearing loss caused by damage to the cochlea's receptor cells or to the auditory nerves; also called *nerve deafness*.

Herman von Helmholtz's **place theory** presumes that we hear different pitches because different sound waves trigger activity at different places along the cochlea's basilar membrane. Thus, the brain can determine a sound's pitch by recognizing the place on the membrane from which it receives neural signals. When Nobel laureate-to-be Georg von Békésy (1957) cut holes in the cochleas of guinea pigs and human cadavers and looked inside with a microscope, he discovered a *travelling wave* that, for high frequencies, peaks near the beginning of the cochlea's membrane.

Although place theory explains how we hear high-pitched sounds, it doesn't explain how we hear low-pitched sounds, because the neural signals they generate are not so neatly localized on the basilar membrane. **Frequency theory** suggests an alternative explanation for how we detect pitch. The whole basilar membrane vibrates with the incoming sound wave, triggering neural impulses to the brain at the same rate as the sound wave. If the sound wave has a frequency of 100 waves per second, then 100 pulses per second travel up the auditory nerve. Thus, the brain can read pitch from the frequency of neural impulses.

Frequency theory can explain how we perceive low-pitched sounds. But it, too, is problematic: Individual neurons cannot fire faster than 1000 times per second. How then can frequency theory explain our sensing sounds with frequencies above 1000 waves per second (roughly the upper third of a piano keyboard and above)? Enter the *volley principle*: Like soldiers who alternate firing so that some can shoot while others reload, a group of neural cells can alternate firing. By firing in rapid succession they can achieve a combined frequency well above 1000 times per second.

Thus, place theory best explains how we sense high pitches, frequency theory best explains how we sense low pitches, and some combination of place and frequency seems to handle the pitches in the intermediate range.

How Do We Locate Sounds?

Why don't we have one big ear—perhaps above our one nose? The better to hear you, as the wolf said to Red Riding Hood. Just as the placement of our two eyes allows us to sense visual depth, the placement of our two ears allows us to enjoy stereophonic ("three-dimensional") hearing. The slightly different messages sensed by the two microphones used in creating a stereophonic recording mimic the slightly different sound messages received by our two ears.

Two ears are better than one for at least two reasons. If a car to the right honks, your right ear receives a more *intense* sound slightly *sooner* than your left ear (**FIGURE 13.4**). Because sound travels 750 miles per hour and our ears are but 6 inches apart, the intensity difference and the time lag are extremely small. However, our sensitive auditory system can actually detect such minute differences (Brown & Deffenbacher, 1979; Middlebrooks & Green, 1991). A just-noticeable difference in the direction from which two sounds come corresponds to a time difference of just 0.000027 second!

Some of today's digital hearing aids can, at the press of a button, use a similar strategy for selectively amplifying sound coming from the person one is looking at. They do it by using two microphones, one a half-inch in front of the other. Their microprocessor can then distinguish the voice sounds (which reach the front mike first) from the background

FIGURE 13.4
How we locate sounds
Sound waves strike one ear sooner and more intensely than the other. From this information, our nimble brains compute the sound's location. As you might therefore expect, people who lose all hearing in one ear often have difficulty locating sounds.

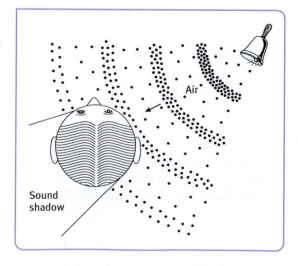

Air

Sound shadow

noise (which reaches both mikes simultaneously). The result, as my experience with two such aids verifies, is a nifty zoom microphone effect.

With auditory as with visual information, the brain uses parallel processing—by putting specialized neural teams to work simultaneously on different subtasks. Owls (and probably humans, too) process timing differences in one neural pathway and intensity differences in another before merging their information to pinpoint a sound's location (Konishi, 1993).

So how well do you suppose we do at locating a sound that is equidistant from our two ears, such as those that come from directly ahead, behind, overhead, or beneath us? Not very well. Why? Because such sounds strike the two ears simultaneously. Sit with closed eyes while a friend snaps fingers around your head. You will easily point to the sound when it comes from either side, but you will likely make some mistakes when it comes from directly ahead, behind, above, or below. That is why, when trying to pinpoint a sound, you cock your head, so that your two ears will receive slightly different messages.

Hearing Loss and Deaf Culture

Preview Questions: What breaks in our hearing system typically cause hearing loss? What is it like to live without hearing?

The ear's intricate and delicate structure makes it vulnerable to damage. Problems with the mechanical system that conducts sound waves to the cochlea cause **conduction hearing loss**. If the eardrum is punctured or if the tiny bones of the middle ear lose their ability to vibrate, the ear's ability to conduct vibrations diminishes. Digital hearing aids improve hearing by amplifying vibrations for frequencies (usually high frequencies) in which one's hearing is weakest.

Damage to the cochlea's hair cell receptors or their associated nerves can cause **sensorineural hearing loss** (or *nerve deafness*). Occasionally, disease causes sensorineural hearing loss, but more often biological changes linked with aging (**FIGURE 13.5**) and prolonged exposure to ear-splitting noise or music are the culprits. Once destroyed, these tissues remain dead, though a hearing aid may amplify enough sound to stimulate neighboring hair cells. In some animals, however, such as sharks and birds, hair cells can regenerate, and scientists have discovered ways to chemically stimulate hair cell regeneration in guinea pigs and rat pups (Forge & others, 1993; Warchol & others, 1993). These findings raise hopes that a way might someday be found to trick the human cochlea into regenerating hair cells—and thereby restore hearing among those with nerve deafness.

Good vibrations
Scotland's Evelyn Glennie, who has been profoundly deaf since she was 12 years old, is a full-time percussion soloist. In performance she relates to her instruments through her sense of touch (performing without shoes) and to the conductor through her keen visual sense.

FIGURE 13.5 Older people tend to hear low frequencies well but suffer hearing loss for high frequencies
This high-frequency loss results from nerve degeneration near the beginning of the basilar membrane. The finding supports place theory's assumption that different pitches activate different places on the basilar membrane. (From Wever, 1949.)

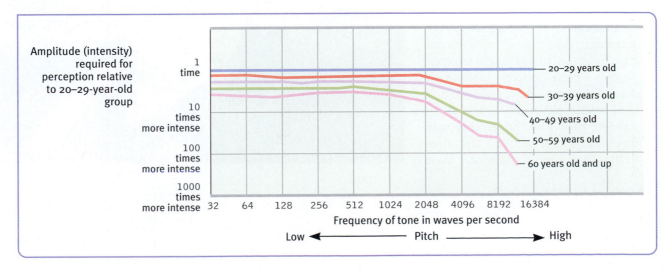

CLOSE-UP:

LIVING IN A SILENT WORLD

Those who live with hearing loss are a diverse group. Some are profoundly deaf; others have limited hearing. Some were deaf "prelingually" (before developing language); others have known the hearing world. Some sign and identify with the language-based Deaf Culture; others, especially those postlingually deaf, are "oral" and converse with the hearing world by reading lips or reading written notes. Still others move between the two cultures. Those who grow up around other deaf people more often identify with Deaf Culture and feel positive self-esteem. Deaf children raised in a signing household, whether by deaf or hearing parents, also express higher self-esteem and feel more accepted (Bat-Chava, 1993, 1994).

About one-fourth of deaf children attend residential schools. Half attend special education programs in public schools. The remaining fourth are partially or wholly mainstreamed into regular classrooms, sometimes aided by sign language interpreters (Kirk & Gallagher, 1989). Like their hearing counterparts, some of these students are slow learners, others are brilliant. Virtually all children, whether deaf or hearing, whether signers or speakers, display a remarkable ability to learn language (Meier, 1991).

Still, all deaf people face challenges (Braden, 1994). Because academic subjects are rooted in spoken languages, their school achievement may suffer. Social challenges are even greater. Unable to communicate in customary ways, deaf children and their hearing playmates struggle to coordinate their play. Adolescents may experience social exclusion and a resulting low self-confidence. Even adults whose hearing becomes impaired later in life may find that the challenges lead to a sort of shyness. "It's almost universal among the deaf to want to cause hearing people as little fuss as possible," reports Henry Kisor (1990, p. 244), a Chicago newspaper editor and columnist who lost his hearing at age 3. "We can be self-effacing and diffident to the point of invisibility. Sometimes this tendency can be crippling. I must fight it all the time."

I know. My mother, with whom we communicated by writing notes on an erasable "magic pad," spent her last dozen years in a silent world, withdrawn from the stress and strain of trying to interact with people outside a small circle of family and old friends. With my own hearing declining on a trajectory toward hers, I find myself sitting front and center at plays and meetings, seeking quiet corners in restaurants, using a special volume-controllable telephone, asking my wife to make necessary calls to friends whose accents differ from ours. But the greatest frustration comes when, with or without hearing aids, I can't hear the joke that everyone else is guffawing over; when, after repeated tries, I just can't catch that exasperated person's question and can't fake my way around it; when I can't hear the low frequencies of the bass that my son is playing in the school orchestra; when family members give up and say, "Oh, never mind" after trying three times to tell me something unimportant.

As she aged, my mother came to feel that seeking social interaction was simply not worth the effort. However, for newspaper columnist Kisor, communication is worth the effort. "So, for the most part, I will grit my teeth and plunge ahead" (p. 246). To reach out, to connect, to communicate with others, even across a chasm of silence, is to affirm our humanity and to affirm ourselves as social creatures.

Signs of success

The social challenges of hearing impairment are minimized for employees and patrons of the Ragin' Cajun restaurant in Seattle, where sign language is the primary mode of communication. Owner Danny Delcambre, shown here, is deaf and has made a special effort to hire other people with hearing impairments.

Until then, the only way to restore hearing among people with nerve deafness is a sort of bionic ear—a *cochlear implant*. This electronic device translates sounds into electrical signals that, wired into the cochlea's nerves, convey some information about sound to the brain. Learning to make sense of sound may take two or more years for a child who has never before heard sound (Fryauf-Bertschy & Gantz, 1994). The device enables some formerly deaf people to talk on the phone, but for others it gives only a rough approximation of hearing. For most, it can at least assist lipreading. The implant may also help children become less distractable and impulsive (Quittner & others, 1994).

The use of cochlear implants is hotly debated. More than 90 percent of deaf children have hearing parents, most of whom want their children to experience their world of sound and talk. The National Association of the Deaf, which takes pride in Deaf Culture, argues that deafness is *not* a disability, and it objects to using the implants on children deafened before learning to speak. Deaf-Culture advocates note that native signers are not linguistically disabled. Gallaudet University linguist William Stokoe confirmed this in his 1960 book, *Sign Language Structure*. He showed what even native signers had not fully understood: Sign is a complete language with its own grammar, syntax, and semantics.

Some Deaf-Culture advocates further contend that deafness could as well be considered "vision enhancement" as "hearing impairment." People who lose one channel of sensation seem to compensate with a slight enhancement of their other sensory abilities (Backman & Dixon, 1992; Levy & Langer, 1992). With one ear plugged, blind people are more accurate than sighted people at locating a sound source (Lessard & others, 1998). Starved for sensory input, deaf people's auditory cortex becomes responsive to touch (Levanen & others, 1998). As a result of her lifelong blindness and deafness, Helen Keller's brain had regions normally dedicated to visual and auditory inputs available for other uses, such as discriminating touch sensations. Although deaf people generally do not have superior reading ability, visual compensation may help explain why many are visually skilled engineers, architects, and mathematicians. Cosmologist Stephen Hawking has said that lacking a functional body forced him to use his brain for other activity, making his thinking more original (Uehling, 1998).

Those whose hearing has diminished with age or illness—who live outside the Deaf Culture and have known, then lost, hearing—are more likely to describe themselves as having an impairment or disability. Of the 9 percent of people who experience hearing loss, the National Center for Health Statistics estimates that only about 1 percent were born deaf. As noted earlier, losses that develop with age are greatest in the higher frequencies. Those who lose their hearing need not think of themselves as disabled *people* (which labels the person) to acknowledge that they are persons with a disability (describing the impairment). For individuals who have never learned to sign, the loss of hearing can indeed be socially disabling. Helen Keller said she "found deafness to be a much greater handicap than blindness. . . . Blindness cuts people off from things. Deafness cuts people off from people."

"By placing my hand on a person's lips and throat, I gain an idea of many specific vibrations, and interpret them: a boy's chuckle, a man's 'Whew!' of surprise, the 'Hem!' of annoyance or perplexity, the moan of pain, a scream, a whisper, a rasp, a sob, a choke, and a gasp."

Helen Keller, 1908

REVIEW AND REFLECT:

Hearing

What are the characteristics of the air pressure waves that we hear as meaningful sounds?

The pressure waves we experience as sound vary in frequency and amplitude, and correspondingly in perceived pitch and loudness.

How does the ear transform sound energy into neural messages that the brain interprets as a particular sound? How do we localize sounds as coming from a particular place?

Through a mechanical chain of events, sound waves traveling through the auditory canal cause minuscule vibrations in the eardrum. Transmitted via the bones of the middle ear to the fluid-filled cochlea, these vibrations create movement in tiny hair cells, triggering neural messages to the brain.

Research on how we hear pitch supports both the place theory, which best explains the sensation of high-pitched sounds, and frequency theory, which best explains the sensation of low-pitched sounds. We localize sound by detecting minute differences in the intensity and timing of the sounds received by each ear.

What breaks in our hearing system typically cause hearing loss? What is it like to live without hearing?

Hearing losses linked to conduction and nerve disorders can be caused by prolonged exposure to loud noise and by diseases and age-related disorders. Those who live with hearing loss face social challenges. Cochlear implants can enable some hearing by deaf children. But Deaf-Culture advocates, noting that sign is a complete language, question the enhancement.

Terms and Concepts to Remember

audition, p. 190
frequency, p. 190
pitch, p. 190
middle ear, p. 191
inner ear, p. 191

cochlea [KOHK-lee-uh], p. 191
place theory, p. 194
frequency theory, p. 194
conduction hearing loss, p. 194
sensorineural hearing loss, p. 194

Test Yourself

13.1. The amplitude of a light wave determines our perception of brightness. The amplitude of a sound wave determines our perception of
    a. loudness.   c. audition.
    b. pitch.   d. frequency.

13.2. The frequency of sound waves determines their pitch. The _____ the waves are, the lower their frequency is and the _____ the pitch.
    a. shorter; higher   c. lower; longer
    b. longer; lower   d. higher; shorter

13.3. Sound waves pass through the auditory canal to a tight membrane. Vibrations of this membrane are transmitted by three tiny bones to a snail-shaped tube in the inner ear, where the waves are converted into neural activity. This tube is called the
    a. anvil.   c. cochlea.
    b. basilar membrane.   d. eardrum.

13.4. Problems with the mechanical system that conducts sound waves to the cochlea cause
    a. sensorineural hearing loss.
    b. high-frequency hearing loss.
    c. nerve deafness.
    d. conduction hearing loss.

13.5. The difference in the sound waves received by our two ears enables us to
    a. translate sounds into electrical signals.
    b. locate sounds.
    c. hear low-pitched sounds.
    d. hear high-pitched sounds.

Review: In a nutshell, how do we transform sound waves into perceived sound?

Reflect: If you had been born deaf, do you think you would want to receive a cochlear implant? Does it surprise you that most natively deaf adults do not desire implants for themselves or any deaf children they may have? Why is it the Deaf community and its culture has no corresponding "blind community" or "blind culture"?

Answers to the Test Yourself and Review questions can be found in the green appendix at the end of the book.

The Other Senses

14

For humans, the major senses are seeing and hearing. We depend on them, particularly for communication. Our brains give these two senses priority in the allocation of cortical tissue. For other animals, the priorities differ. Sharks and dogs rely on their extraordinary sense of smell, aided by the large segment of their cortexes devoted to it. Nevertheless, without our sense of touch, our senses of taste and smell, and our senses of body motion and position, we humans would be seriously handicapped, and our capacities for enjoying the world would be devastatingly diminished.

Touch

Preview Question: How do we sense touch and feel pain?

If you had to lose one sense, which would you prefer it to be? If you could have only one, which would you want?

Although not the first sense to come to mind, touch could be our priority sense. Right from the start, touch is essential to our development. Premature babies gain weight faster and go home sooner if they are stimulated by hand massage. Infant rats deprived of their mothers' grooming touch produce less growth hormone and have a lower metabolic rate—a good way to keep alive until the mother returns, but a reaction that stunts growth if she's delayed. Infant monkeys allowed to see, hear, and smell—but not touch—their mothers become desperately unhappy; those separated by a screen with holes that allow touching are much less miserable. As lovers, we yearn to touch—to kiss, to stroke, to snuggle.

The precious sense of touch
As William James wrote in his *Principles of Psychology* (1890), "Touch is both the alpha and omega of affection."

Dave Barry may be right to say that the skin "keeps people from seeing the inside of your body, which is repulsive, and it prevents your organs from falling onto the ground." But skin does much more. Our "sense of touch" is actually a mix of at least four distinct skin senses—pressure, warmth, cold, and pain. Within the skin are different types of specialized nerve endings. Touching various spots on the skin with a soft hair, a warm or cool wire, and the point of a pin reveals that some spots are especially sensitive to pressure, others to warmth, others to cold, still others to pain. Does that mean that each nerve ending is a receptor for one of the basic skin senses, much as the eye's cone receptors correspond to light's basic colors?

Surprisingly, there is no simple relationship between what we feel at a given spot and the type of specialized nerve ending found there. Only pressure has identifiable receptors. The relationship between warmth, cold, and pain and the receptors that respond to them remains a mystery. Other skin sensations are variations of the basic four (pressure, warmth, cold, and pain):

+ Stroking adjacent pressure spots creates a tickle.
+ Repeated gentle stroking of a pain spot creates an itching sensation.
+ Touching adjacent cold and pressure spots triggers a sense of wetness, which you can experience by touching dry, cold metal.

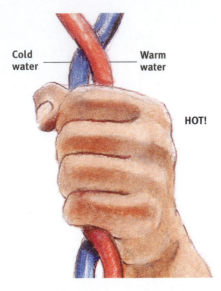

Cold water   Warm water

HOT!

FIGURE 14.1 Warm + cold = hot
When ice-cold water passes through one coil and comfortably warm water through another, we perceive the combined sensation as burning hot.

"When belly with bad pains doth swell, It matters naught what else goes well."

Sadi, *The Gulistan*, 1258

Putting pain out of mind
Vigorously rubbing sore feet helps reduce pain sensations, perhaps by stimulating the spinal cord's large fibers and closing the pain "gate" described in gate-control theory.

+ Stimulating nearby cold and warmth spots produces a feeling of "hot." Cold spots respond either to very low or very high temperatures. We sense hot when a stimulus activates both warm and cold spots (**FIGURE 14.1**).

Touch sensations involve more than tactile stimulation, however. A self-produced tickle produces less somatosensory cortex activation than the same tickle from something or someone else (Blakemore & others, 1998). The brain is wise enough to be most sensitive to stimulation it does not expect.

Pain

Be thankful for occasional pain. Pain is your body's way of telling you that something has gone wrong. Drawing your attention to a burn, a break, or a rupture, it tells you to change your behavior immediately. The rare people born without the ability to feel pain may experience severe injury without ever being alerted by pain's danger signals. Usually, they die by early adulthood. Without the discomfort that makes us occasionally shift position, their joints fail from excess strain, and without the warnings of pain, the effects of unchecked infections and injuries accumulate (Neese, 1991). More numerous are those who endure chronic pain. The suffering of people with persistent or recurring backaches, arthritis, headaches, and cancer-related pain prompts two questions: What is pain? How might it be controlled?

What Is Pain?

Pain is a property not only of the senses—of the region where we feel it—but of the brain as well. As the dreamer may see with eyes closed and the listener may hear a ringing during utter silence, so some 7 in 10 amputees may feel pain or movement in their nonexistent limbs (Melzack, 1992, 1993). (An amputee may also try to step off a bed onto a phantom limb or to lift a cup with a phantom hand.) Even those born without a limb sometimes perceive sensations from the absent limb. The brain, Melzack (1998) surmises, comes prepared to anticipate "that it will be getting information from a body that has limbs."

These *phantom limb sensations* indicate that with pain, as with sights and sounds, the brain can misinterpret the spontaneous central nervous system activity that occurs in the absence of normal sensory input. A similar phenomenon occurs with *tinnitus*, a ringing-in-the-ears sensation often experienced by people with hearing loss. Nerve damage in the taste system can similarly produce taste phantoms, such as ice water seeming sickeningly sweet (Goode, 1999). Others have ex-

perienced phantom smells, such as nonexistent rotten food. The moral: To see, hear, taste, smell, and feel, we require not only a body but also a brain. No brain, no pain.

Unlike vision, however, the pain system is not located in a simple neural cord running from a sensing device to a definable area in the brain. Moreover, there is no one type of stimulus that triggers pains (as light triggers vision), and there are no special receptors (like the retina's rods and cones) for pain. In fact, at low intensities, the stimuli that produce pain also cause other sensations, including warmth or coolness, smoothness or roughness.

MIND OVER MATTER: FIREWALKING

The popular media have at times made the phenomenon of firewalking a hot topic. For a fee we can take a "mind over matter" class that will supposedly enable us to alter our body's chemistry. The "proof": walking on red-hot coals without feeling pain or being burned. The psychological result: a newfound capacity to conquer one's fears. "If I can do something that's considered impossible," says the elated firewalker, "I can do almost anything."

Skeptical scientists have taken a cool look at firewalking (Leikind & McCarthy, 1985, 1988). The secret, they report, lies not in any mental power to alter the senses but in the poor heat conductivity of the wood coals. Think of a cake baking in a 350-degree oven. Touch the aluminum cake tin and you'll get burned; touch the cake—like wood, a poor conductor of heat—and you'll be okay. Cakes and coals do conduct some heat, so you better not stay in touch with them too long or you will get burned and learn the hard way that they who hesitate are lost. But the two seconds or less that it takes to quick-step across hot embers puts each foot in contact with the coals for only a fraction of a second and for less than a second in total time per foot. Wetting the feet on damp grass or in water before the firewalk provides further insulation (a phenomenon familiar to anyone who has used wet fingers to snuff a candle or test a hot iron). With these facts in mind, skeptical scientists have themselves performed the feat without "mind over matter" training.

World's longest firewalk At the University of Pittsburgh, Johnstown, physicist David Willey used 8 cords of wood to construct a 165-foot fire lane. That evening he explained heat-diffusion principles that permit firewalking, then joined several others in putting his feet where his mouth was.

Although no theory of pain explains all the available findings, psychologist Ronald Melzack and biologist Patrick Wall's (1965, 1983) **gate-control theory** provides a useful model. Melzack and Wall believe that the spinal cord contains a neurological "gate" that either blocks pain signals or allows them to pass on to the brain. The spinal cord contains small nerve fibers that conduct most pain signals, and larger fibers that conduct most other sensory signals. When tissue is injured, the small fibers activate and open the neural gate, and you feel pain. Large-fiber activity closes the pain gate, turning pain off.

Thus, one way to treat chronic pain is to stimulate (electrically, by massage, or by acupuncture) "gate-closing" activity in the large neural fibers. Rubbing the area around your stubbed toe will create competing stimulation that will block some of

■ **gate-control theory** theory that the spinal cord contains a neurological "gate" that blocks pain signals or allows them to pass on to the brain. The "gate" is opened by the activity of pain signals traveling up small nerve fibers and is closed by activity in larger fibers or by information coming from the brain.

The pain in sprain is mainly in the brain
Kerri Strug had just sprained her left ankle so severely that she would be unable to do gymnastics for months afterward. Yet with this near-perfect vault, she helped carry her team to a 1996 Olympic gold medal. Because pain is a phenomenon of the conscious brain, athletes sometimes endure serious injuries while focusing their attention outside their bodies.

"Pain is increased by attending to it."

Charles Darwin, *Expression of Emotions in Man and Animals*, 1872

"From there to here, from here to there, funny things are everywhere."

Dr. Seuss, *One Fish, Two Fish, Red Fish, Blue Fish*, 1960

the pain messages. If you place ice on a bruise, you not only will control the swelling but will also trigger cold messages that will close the gate on the pain signals. Some arthritic patients wear a small, portable electrical stimulation unit next to a painful area. When the unit stimulates nerves in the area, the patient feels a vibrating sensation rather than pain (T. Murphy, 1982).

Melzack and Wall believe the pain gate can also be closed by information from the brain. These brain-to-spinal-cord messages help explain some striking psychological influences on pain. When we are distracted from pain and soothed by the release of endorphins, our experience of pain may be greatly diminished. Sports injuries may go unnoticed, until the after-game shower. During a 1989 basketball game, Ohio State University player Jay Burson broke his neck—and kept playing. Clearly, there is more to pain than what stimulates the sense receptors.

That is also clear from people's perceiving more pain, and enduring it less, when others seem to be experiencing pain (Symbaluk & others, 1997). This phenomenon may help explain apparent social influences on pain, as when pockets of Australian keyboard operators during the mid 1980s suffered outbreaks of severe pain during typing or other repetitive work—without any discernible physical abnormalities (Gawande, 1998). René Descartes' idea, proposed centuries ago, is wrong. Pain is not merely a physical phenomenon of injured nerves sending impulses to the brain—like pulling on a rope to ring a bell. The brain creates pain. Pain-producing brain activity may be triggered with or without sensory input, says Melzack (1999) in qualifying his earlier gate-control theory. A brain in a jar could conceivably experience pain and other sensory experiences.

There is also more to our *memories* of pain than the pain we experienced. In experiments, and after medical procedures, people overlook a pain's duration. Their memory snapshots instead record its peak moment and how much pain they felt at the end. Daniel Kahneman and his co-researchers (1993) discovered this when they asked people to immerse one hand in painfully cold water for 60 seconds, and then the other hand in the same painfully cold water for 60 seconds followed by a slightly less painful 30 seconds more. Curiously, when asked which trial they would prefer to repeat, most preferred the longer trial, with more net pain—but less pain at the end. When patients recalled the pain of a colon examination a month later, their memories were similarly dominated by the final (and the worst) moments, not by how long the pain lasted.

For medical personnel, the implication is clear: It's better to taper down a painful procedure than to switch it off abruptly. In one experiment, a physician did this for some patients undergoing colon exams—lengthening the discomfort by a minute, lessening its intensity (Kahneman, 1999). Although this milder discomfort added to the net pain experience, patients given this "taper down" treatment later recalled the exam as less painful than those whose pain ended abruptly.

Pain Control

If pain is where body meets mind—if it is indeed a physical and a psychological phenomenon—then it should be treatable both physically and psychologically. Depending on the type of symptoms, pain control clinics select one or more therapies from a list that includes drugs, surgery, acupuncture, electrical stimulation, massage, exercise, hypnosis, relaxation training, and thought distraction.

The Lamaze method of childbirth combines several of these pain control techniques. Among them are relaxation (through deep breathing and muscle relaxation), counterstimulation (through gentle massage), and distraction (through focusing attention on, say, a pleasant photograph). After Everett Worthington and his colleagues (1983) trained women in the use of such pain control techniques, the women could more easily tolerate the pain of having their hand in ice water. Their pain tolerance was even greater when a trusted "coach" encouraged them, as husbands or an intimate friend encourage Lamaze-trained women during childbirth.

Distracting people with pleasant images ("Think of a warm, comfortable environment") or drawing their attention away from the painful stimulation ("Count backward by 3's") is an especially effective way to increase pain tolerance (Fernandez & Turk, 1989; McCaul & Malott, 1984). The principle works in health care situations. A well-trained nurse may distract needle-shy patients by chatting with them and asking them to look away when inserting the needle. For hospitalized patients, a pleasing window view of a natural landscape may have a similarly relaxing and distracting effect. In examining the records of one Pennsylvania hospital, Roger Ulrich (1984) discovered that surgery patients assigned to rooms looking out on trees required less pain medication and had shorter stays than did those assigned to identical rooms overlooking a brick wall. Because pain is in the brain, diverting the brain's attention may gain relief.

Although Lamaze training reduces labor pain, most Lamaze patients request a local anesthetic during labor. Some—having expected a "natural, painless birth"—feel needless guilt and failure (Melzack, 1984). Melzack therefore advocates—as does the Lamaze program itself—childbirth training that prepares a woman "to cope with an event which is often extremely painful and, at the same time, one of the most fulfilling peak experiences in her life."

Taste

Preview Question: How do we experience taste?

Like touch, our sense of taste involves four basic sensations—sweet, sour, salty, and bitter (McBurney & Gent, 1979). All other tastes are mixtures of these. Investigators have, however, been frustrated in their search for specialized nerve fibers for each of these four basic taste sensations.

Taste is a chemical sense. Inside each little bump on the top and sides of your tongue are 200 or more taste buds, each containing a pore that catches food chemicals. These molecules are sensed by 50 taste receptor cells that project antennalike hairs into the pore. Some of these receptors respond mostly to sweet-tasting molecules, others to salty-, sour-, or bitter-tasting ones. It doesn't take much to trigger a response. If a stream of water is pumped across your tongue, the addition of a concentrated salty or sweet taste for but one-tenth of a second will get your attention (Kelling & Halpern, 1983). When a friend asks for "just a taste" of your soft drink, you can squeeze off the straw after a mere fraction of a second.

Taste receptors reproduce themselves every week or two, so if you burn your tongue with hot food it hardly matters. However, as you grow older, the number of taste buds decreases, as does taste sensitivity (Cowart, 1981). (No wonder adults enjoy strong-tasting foods that children resist.) Also, smoking and alcohol use accelerate the decline in taste buds and sensitivities.

Taste buds are certainly essential for taste, but there's more to taste than meets the tongue. Hold your nose, close your eyes, and have someone feed you various foods. A slice of apple may be indistinguishable from a chunk of raw potato; a piece

■ **sensory interaction** the principle that one sense may influence another, as when the smell of food influences its taste.

of steak may taste like cardboard. To savor a taste, we normally breathe the aroma through our nose—which is why eating is not much fun when you have a bad cold, and why people who lose their sense of smell may think they have also lost their sense of taste. Smell not only adds to our perception of taste, it also changes it: A drink's strawberry odor enhances our perception of its sweetness. This is **sensory interaction** at work—the principle that one sense may influence another. Smell plus texture plus taste equals flavor. Similarly, we correctly perceive the location of the voice directly in front of us partly because we also *see* that the person is in front of us, not behind, above, or beneath us.

Taste researcher Linda Bartoshuk (1993) offers other fascinating facts about taste:

+ Our emotional responses to taste are hard-wired. Put a sweet or bitter substance on a newborn's tongue and the baby's tongue and face react like an adult's.
+ People without tongues can still taste—through receptors in the back and roof of the mouth.
+ If you lose taste sensation from one side of your tongue, you probably won't notice. That's because the other side will become correspondingly supersensitive. Also, the brain doesn't localize taste well: Although the middle of the tongue has few taste receptors, we perceive taste as coming from the whole tongue.
+ We can neither taste nor smell most nutrients—fat, protein, starch, and food vitamins. (Sugar is an exception.) But we do quickly associate the taste and smell of other food components with a food's nutritional or poisonous significance.

Smell

Preview Question: How do we smell, and how are we affected by this sense?

Inhale, exhale. Inhale, exhale. Breaths come in pairs—except at two moments: birth and death. Each day, you inhale and exhale nearly 20,000 breaths of life-sustaining air, bathing your nostrils in a stream of scent-laden molecules. The resulting experiences of smell (*olfaction*) are strikingly intimate ones: You inhale something of whatever or whoever it is you smell.

Like taste, smell is a chemical sense. We smell something when molecules of a substance carried in the air reach a tiny cluster of 5 million receptor cells at the top of each nasal cavity (**FIGURE 14.2**). These olfactory receptor cells, waving like sea anemones on a reef, respond selectively—to the aroma of a cake baking, to a wisp of smoke, to a friend's fragrance. Instantly they alert the brain through their axon fibers. Even nursing infants and their mothers have a literal chemistry to their relationship. They quickly learn to recognize each other's scents (McCarthy, 1986). Aided by smell, a mother fur seal returning to a beach crowded with pups will find her own. Our own sense of smell is less impressive than the acuteness of our seeing and hearing. Looking out across a garden we see its forms and colors in exquisite detail and hear a variety of birds singing, yet we smell little of it without settling our nose into the blooms.

Precisely how olfactory receptors work remains a mystery. Unlike light, which can be separated into its spectral colors, an odor cannot be separated into more elemental odors. The olfaction system has no parallel to the retina, which detects myriad colors with sensory cells dedicated to red, green, or blue. Olfactory receptors recognize odors individually.

Odor molecules come in many shapes and sizes, so many in fact that it takes many different receptors to detect them. A large family of some 1000 genes—some 1 percent of all our genes—design the 1000 or so receptor proteins that recognize particular odor molecules (Axel, 1995). As a key slips into a lock, so odor molecules slip into these receptors. Yet we seem not to have a distinct receptor for each detectable

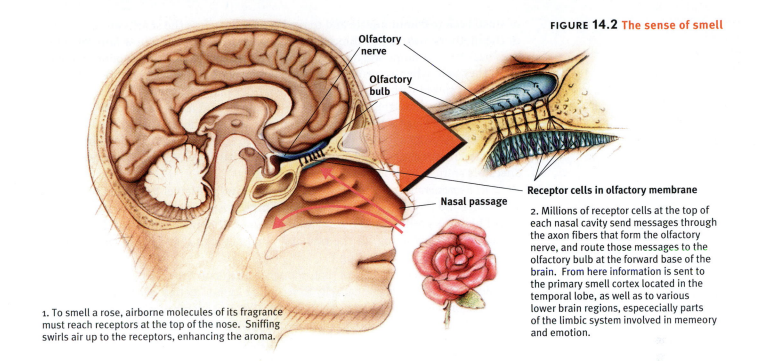

FIGURE 14.2 The sense of smell

Olfactory nerve

Olfactory bulb

Receptor cells in olfactory membrane

Nasal passage

1. To smell a rose, airborne molecules of its fragrance must reach receptors at the top of the nose. Sniffing swirls air up to the receptors, enhancing the aroma.

2. Millions of receptor cells at the top of each nasal cavity send messages through the axon fibers that form the olfactory nerve, and route those messages to the olfactory bulb at the forward base of the brain. From here information is sent to the primary smell cortex located in the temporal lobe, as well as to various lower brain regions, espececially parts of the limbic system involved in memeory and emotion.

odor. This suggests that some odors trigger a combination of receptors, whose activity the olfactory cortex interprets. As the alphabet's 26 letters can combine to form many words, so odor molecules bind to different receptor arrays, producing the 10,000 odors we can detect (Malnic & others, 1999).

The ability to identify scents peaks in early adulthood and gradually declines thereafter (**FIGURE 14.3**). Despite our skill at discriminating scents, we aren't nearly so good at describing them. Words more readily portray the sound of coffee brewing than its aroma. Compared with how we experience and remember sights and sounds, smells are almost primitive and certainly harder to describe (Richardson & Zucco, 1989).

As any dog or cat with a good nose could tell us, we each have our own identifiable chemical signature. (One noteworthy exception: A dog will follow the tracks of one identical twin as though they had been made by the other [Thomas, 1974].) Animals that have many times more olfactory receptors than we do also use their sense

Number of correct answers

Women and young adults have best sense of smell

Women

Men

Age group

FIGURE 14.3

Age, sex, and sense of smell

Among the 1.2 million people who responded to a *National Geographic* scratch and sniff survey, women and younger adults most successfully identified six sample odors. (From Wysocki & Gilbert, 1989.)

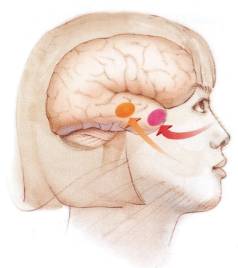

The olfactory brain
Information from the taste buds (orange arrow) travels to an area of the temporal lobe not far from that where olfactory information is received. The brain's circuitry for smell (red arrow) also connects with areas involved in memory storage, which helps explain why a smell can trigger a memory explosion.

of smell both to communicate and to navigate. Long before the shark can see its prey, or the moth its mate, odors direct their way. Migrating salmon follow faint olfactory cues back to their home stream. If exposed in a hatchery to one of two odorant chemicals, they will, when returning two years later, seek whatever stream near their release site is spiked with the familiar smell (Barinaga, 1999).

Odors also have the power to evoke memories and feelings. A hotline runs between the brain area that gets information from the nose and the brain's ancient limbic centers associated with memory and emotion. Smell is primitive. Eons before the elaborate analytical areas of our cerebral cortex had fully evolved, our mammalian ancestors sniffed for food—and for predators.

In *Remembrance of Things Past*, the French novelist Marcel Proust described how the aroma and flavor of a bit of cake soaked in tea resurrected long-forgotten memories of his aunt's bedroom in the old family house. "The smell and taste of things," he noted, "bears unfaltering, in the tiny and almost impalpable drop of their essence, the vast structure of recollection."

Laboratory studies confirm that, though it's difficult to recall odors by name, we do indeed have a remarkable capacity to recognize long-forgotten odors and their associated personal episodes (Engen, 1987; Schab, 1991). Students who do a word exercise while smelling the aroma of chocolate remember the words better the next day if the chocolate aroma is again present (Schab, 1990). And pleasant odors can evoke pleasant memories (Ehrlichman & Halpern, 1988). The smell of the sea, the scent of a perfume, or an aroma of a favorite relative's kitchen can bring to mind a happy time. Such is the power of an odor to switch on memories and to retrieve associated emotions.

Pleasant moods produced by pleasant scents may also boost workers' performance. That's what Robert Baron (1990) surmised after having students work in rooms with or without pleasant air scents. Pleasant scents boosted their moods and self-confidence, leading them to set slightly higher work goals on a clerical task and to negotiate more aggressively when bargaining.

Body Position and Movement

Preview Question: How do our senses monitor our body's position and movement?

With only the five familiar senses we have so far considered we could not put food in our mouths, stand up, or reach out and touch someone. We would be helpless. To know just how to move your arms to grasp someone's hand, you first need to know the current position of your arms and hands and then be aware of their changing positions as you move them. For you to take just one step requires feedback from and instructions to some 200 muscles.

We come equipped with millions of position and motion sensors. They are all over our bodies—in the muscles, tendons, and joints—and they are continually providing information to our brains. If we twist our wrists one degree, the sensors immediately report it. This sense of our body parts' position and movement is **kinesthesis** (kin-ehs-THEE-sehs).

One can momentarily imagine being blind or deaf. Close your eyes, plug your ears, and experience the dark stillness. But what would it be like to live without touch or kinesthesis—without, therefore, being able to sense the positions of your limbs when awakening during the night? Ian Waterman of Hampshire, England, knows. In 1972, at age 19, Waterman contracted a rare viral infection that destroyed the nerves that enabled his sense of light touch and of body position and movement. People with this condition report feeling disembodied, as though their body is dead, not real, not theirs (Sacks, 1985). With prolonged practice Waterman has learned to walk and eat—by visually focusing on his limbs and directing them accordingly. But if the lights go out, he crumples to the floor, unable to move until they come back on (Azar, 1998).

The intricate vestibular sense
Thank your inner ears for the information that enables your brain to monitor your body's position.

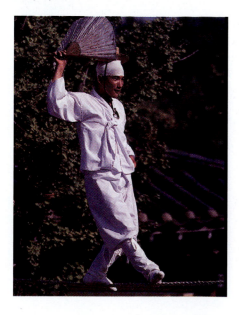

A companion **vestibular sense** monitors the head's (and thus the body's) position and movement. The biological gyroscopes for this sense of equilibrium are in the inner ear. In the *semicircular canals*, which look like a three-dimensional pretzel and the *vestibular sacs*, which connect the canals with the cochlea, are substances that move when the head rotates or tilts. This movement stimulates hairlike receptors in these organs of the inner ear. The receptors then send messages to the brain that enable us continually to sense our body position and to maintain our balance.

If you twirl around and then come to an abrupt halt, neither the fluid in your semicircular canals nor your kinesthetic receptors immediately return to their neutral state. The aftereffect fools your dizzy brain with the sensation that you're still spinning. This illustrates a principle that underlies *perceptual illusions*. Mechanisms that normally give us an accurate experience of the world can, under special conditions, fool us. Understanding how we get fooled provides clues to how our perceptual system works.

■ **kinesthesis [kin-ehs-THEE-sehs]** the system for sensing the position and movement of individual body parts.

■ **vestibular sense** the sense of body movement and position, including the sense of balance.

REVIEW AND REFLECT:

The Other Senses

How do we sense touch and feel pain?

Our sense of touch is actually four senses—pressure, warmth, cold, and pain—that combine to produce other sensations, such as "hot." One theory of pain is that a "gate" in the spinal cord either opens to permit pain signals traveling up small nerve fibers to reach the brain, or closes to prevent their passage. Because pain is both a physiological and a psychological phenomenon, it often can be controlled through a combination of physical and psychological treatments.

How do we experience taste?

Taste, a chemical sense, is likewise a composite of four basic sensations—sweet, sour, salty, and bitter—and of the aromas that interact with information from the taste buds. The influence of smell on our sense of taste is an example of sensory interaction.

How do we smell, and how are we affected by this sense?

Like taste, smell is a chemical sense, but there are no basic sensations for smell, as there are for touch and taste. Unlike the retina's receptor cells, the 5 million olfactory receptor cells with their 1000 different receptor proteins recognize individual odor molecules. Some odors trigger a combination of receptors. Like other stimuli, odors can spontaneously evoke memories and feelings.

How do our senses monitor our body's position and movement?

Our effective functioning requires a kinesthetic sense, which notifies the brain of the position and movement of body parts, and a sense of equilibrium, which monitors the position and movement of the whole body.

Terms and Concepts to Remember

gate-control theory, p. 201
sensory interaction, p. 204
kinesthesis [kin-ehs-THEE-sehs], p. 206
vestibular sense, p. 207

Test Yourself

14.1. At least four skin senses—pressure, warmth, cold, and pain—make up our sense of touch. Of all the skin senses, the only one that has its own identifiable receptor cells is
a. pressure.
b. warmth.
c. cold.
d. pain.

14.2. There is no one type of stimulus that triggers pain and no one definable spot in the brain that interprets pain. Although no theory fully explains our experience of pain, the gate-control theory is useful. According to this theory,
a. special pain receptors send signals directly to the brain.
b. pain is a property of the senses, not of the brain.
c. small nerve fibers in the spinal cord conduct most pain signals.
d. the stimuli that produce pain are unrelated to other sensations.

14.3. The taste of the food we eat is greatly enhanced by its smell or aroma. One sense influencing another is referred to as
a. sensory adaptation.
b. chemical sensation.
c. gate-control theory.
d. sensory interaction.

14.4. Kinesthesis is the body's way of sensing its position and movement, using millions of position and motion sensors found all over our bodies. The receptors for our companion vestibular sense are in the
a. skin.
b. brain.
c. inner ear.
d. skeletal muscles.

Review: How does our system for sensing smell differ from our sensory systems for vision, touch, and taste?

Reflect: Can you recall a time when, with your attention focused on some activity, you felt no pain from a wound or injury?

Answers to the Test Yourself and Review questions can be found in the green appendix at the end of the book.

Perceptual Organization

Perceptual Illusions

Preview Question: Why are psychologists so interested in perceptual illusions?

During the late 1800s, when psychology was emerging as a distinct discipline, perceptual illusions fascinated scientists. And they still do, because illusions reveal the ways we normally organize and interpret our sensations. Consider seven such perceptual puzzles:

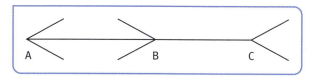

Puzzle 1 At left is an adaptation of a classic illusion created in 1889 by Franz Müller-Lyer. Does either line segment—AB or BC—appear longer? To most people the two segments appear to be the same length. Surprise! They are not. As your ruler can verify, line AB is a full one-third longer than line BC. Why did your eyes deceive you? (On page 220 you will discover one explanation.)

Puzzle 2 Below we have two unretouched photos of the same two girls, in the same room. The camera shows you these scenes much as you would see them if you were looking into the room through a single peephole. Why do the girls seem to change size when they switch places? (Page 221 will reveal why.)

Puzzle 3 Is the Gateway Arch in St. Louis taller than it is wide? Or wider than it is tall? To most it appears taller. In truth, its height and width are equal. Once again, seeing is deceiving. Why? (On page 216 we will meet this phenomenon again.)

Puzzle 4 Aircraft pilots, ship captains, and car drivers perceive their surroundings under varying visibility. When their perceptions or reactions err—as happens in most commercial airplane accidents (Adler, 1989)—the results can be devastating. To simulate distance judgments, psychologist Helen Ross (1975) asked passersby to estimate the distances of white disks she had placed on the lawn at Britain's Hull University. Those who judged the distance in the thick morning fog perceived the disks to be farther away than did those who made their estimates in the midday sunshine. What does this suggest about how we normally judge distances? (Pages 214–217 explain distance perception.)

Morning Fog

Midday Sunshine

Ross's distance judgment experiment

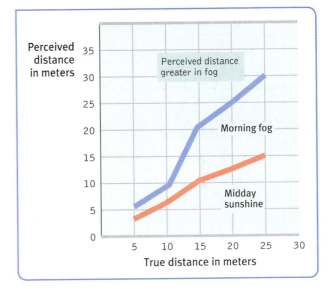

Puzzle 5 Here is another brain construction of virtual reality, described in 1935 by Hans Wallach. Do you see, on the right, below, a glowing blue worm? Measure the color between the lines and you will see there is no blue. The worm is merely the short blue lines of the left figure with black lines added. Anything else you perceive is a product of your "creative genius" (Hoffman, 1998). (See the discussion of grouping principles on pages 212–213.)

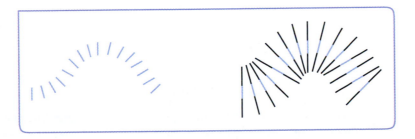

Puzzle 6 The real creators of virtual reality are not software developers, but the brains that developers trick into constructing virtual realities. The ripple at the top of the next page, from Donald Hoffman's *Visual Intelligence* (1998), is a flat two-dimensional drawing. But can you perceive it as flat? Not easily. Your brain will persist in creating a ripple that is not there. And it will construe it quite differently when you merely turn the book upside down. "Has your visual system gone off the deep end?" asks Hoffman. "It constructs from whole cloth a ripple in space and then proceeds to embellish it with mutable parts. Shall we

henceforth distrust the witness of vision, knowing now its penchant to perjure?" (p. 3). The ripple illusion is in part an assumption about light sources, as you will see on pages 216–217.

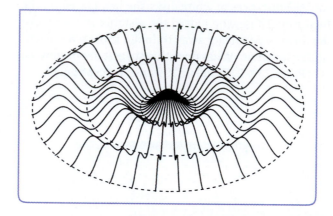

Puzzle 7 Illusions occur with the other senses, too, as the German psychologist Wilhelm Wundt pointed out more than a century ago. Wundt was puzzled by people's hearing the steady beat of a metronome or clock as if it were a repeating rhythm of two, three, or four beats. Rather than hearing an unaccented click-click-click-click, one might, for example, hear CLICK-click CLICK-click CLICK-click. Although a steady beat strikes the ear, each listener unconsciously shapes an auditory pattern. What perceptual principle is at work here? (See page 222.)

Psychology's emphasis on *visual* illusions reflects vision's preeminence among our senses. When vision conflicts with other sensations, vision usually dominates—a phenomenon called **visual capture**. People wearing prisms that displace the visual world to one side perceive their hand as where they *see* it, not where it really is. When the sound of a movie comes from a projector behind us, we nevertheless perceive it as coming from the screen, where we *see* the actors talking (much as we perceive a voice from the ventriloquist's dummy). While watching a roller coaster ride on a wrap-around movie screen, we may brace ourselves, though our other senses tell us we're not moving. In all three cases, vision *captures* the other senses.

Organizational Principles

Preview Question: What did the Gestalt psychologists contribute to our understanding of how the brain constructs perceptions from sensory information?

Early in the twentieth century, a group of German psychologists became intrigued with how the mind organizes sensations into perceptions. Given a cluster of sensations, the human perceiver organizes them into a **gestalt**, a German word meaning a "form" or a "whole." The Gestalt psychologists provided compelling demonstrations of gestalt perception and described principles by which we organize our sensations into perceptions. For example, look at **FIGURE 15.1**. Note that the individual elements of the figure are really nothing but eight blue circles, each containing three converging white lines. When we view them all together, however, we see a *whole*, a form, a Necker cube.

The Gestalt psychologists were fond of saying that in perception the whole may exceed the sum of its parts. Combine sodium, a corrosive metal, with chlorine, a poison gas, and something very different emerges—table salt. Likewise, a unique per-

- **visual capture** the tendency for vision to dominate the other senses.

- **gestalt** an organized whole. Gestalt psychologists emphasize our tendency to integrate pieces of information into meaningful wholes.

- **figure-ground** the organization of the visual field into objects (the *figures*) that stand out from their surroundings (the *ground*).

ceived form emerges from an object's components (Rock & Palmer, 1990). There is far more to perception than meets the senses.

Our yen for assembling visual features into complete forms involves *bottom-up* processing, starting with entry-level sensory analysis, as well as *top-down* processing that uses our experiences and expectations to interpret those sensations. However, the more we learn about this information-processing system, the fuzzier the distinction grows between *sensation* and *perception*. Sensation is not just bottom-up processing, and perception is not just top-down processing. Sensation and perception blend into one continuous process, progressing upward from specialized detector cells and downward from our assumptions. A monkey's cortex, for example, has specialized cells that respond to *illusory contours* similar to those shown in **FIGURE 15.2** (Wenderoth, 1992; Winckelgren, 1992). Surprisingly, these cells lie in a visual cortex area that receives signals from the eyes before much cognitive processing could have occurred (Grosof & others, 1993).

As you read further about the Gestalt psychologists' organizational principles, keep in mind the fundamental truth they illustrate: Our brains do more than merely register information about the world. Perception is not just opening a shutter and letting a picture print itself on the brain. We constantly filter sensory information and infer perceptions in ways that make sense to us. Mind matters.

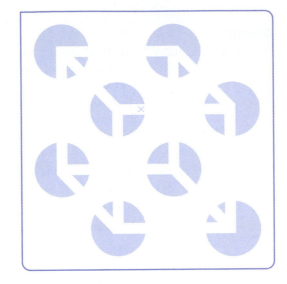

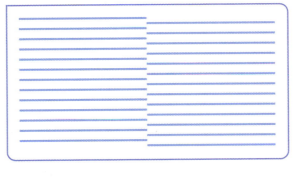

FIGURE 15.1 Necker cube
What do you see: circles with white lines, or a cube? If you stare at the cube, you may notice that it reverses location, moving the tiny X in the center from the front edge to the back. At times the cube may seem to float in front of the page, with circles behind it; other times the circles may become holes in the page through which the cube appears, as though it were floating behind the page. But note how our perceptual system always interprets this collection of lines and shading as a *gestalt* or whole form of some sort. (From Bradley & others, 1976.)

FIGURE 15.2 Illusory contours
You have to look closely to see there is no vertical line down the middle of this figure. The primary visual cortex of monkey brains contains cells that respond to such illusory contours.

Form Perception

Imagine designing a video/computer system that, like your eye/brain system, could read handwritten addresses or recognize faces at a glance. (Postal services are, in fact, hoping to develop such a scanner.) What abilities would it need?

Figure and Ground

To start with, the system would need to recognize the addresses and faces as distinct from their backgrounds. Likewise, our first perceptual task is to perceive any object, called the *figure*, as distinct from its surroundings, called the *ground*. Among the voices you hear at a party, the one you attend to becomes the figure; all others, part of the ground. As you read, the words are the figure; the white paper, the ground. In **FIGURE 15.3**, the **figure-ground** relationship continually reverses—but always we organize the stimulus into a figure seen against a ground. (Is it a vase, or profiles of a younger Prince Philip and Queen Elizabeth?) Such reversible figure-and-ground illustrations demonstrate again that the same stimulus can trigger more than one perception. Curiously, though, if you do not *know* the figure is reversible, it is not so likely to reverse (Rock & others, 1994).

FIGURE 15.3
Reversible figure and ground

Grouping

Having discriminated figure from ground, we (and our video/computer system) then have to organize the figure into a meaningful form. Some basic features of a scene—such as color, movement, and light/dark contrast—we process instantly and automatically (Treisman, 1987). To bring order and form to these basic sensations, our minds follow certain rules for **grouping** stimuli together (**FIGURE 15.4**). These rules, identified by the Gestalt psychologists, illustrate their idea that the perceived whole differs from the sum of its parts (Rock & Palmer, 1990):

Proximity We group nearby figures together. We see not six separate lines, but three sets of two lines.

Similarity Figures similar to each other we group together. We see the triangles and circles as vertical columns of similar shapes, not as horizontal rows of dissimilar shapes.

Continuity We perceive smooth, continuous patterns rather than discontinuous ones. This pattern could be a series of alternating semicircles, but we perceive it as two continuous lines—one wavy, one straight.

Connectedness When they are uniform and linked, we perceive spots, lines, or areas as a single unit.

FIGURE 15.4

Organizing stimuli into groups

We could perceive the stimuli shown here in many ways, yet people everywhere see them similarly. The Gestalt psychologists believed this shows that the brain uses "rules" to order sensory information into wholes.

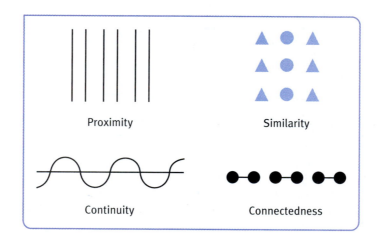

Proximity   Similarity

Continuity   Connectedness

Closure We fill in gaps to create a complete, whole object. Thus we assume that the circles (below, left) are complete but partially blocked by the (illusory) triangle. Add nothing more than little line segments that close off the circles (below, right) and now your brain stops constructing a triangle.

■ **grouping** the perceptual tendency to organize stimuli into coherent groups.

■ **depth perception** the ability to see objects in three dimensions although the images that strike the retina are two-dimensional; allows us to judge distance.

■ **visual cliff** a laboratory device for testing depth perception in infants and young animals.

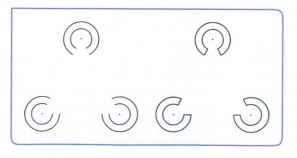

FIGURE **15.5** Grouping principles
You probably perceive this doghouse as a gestalt—a whole (though impossible) structure. Actually, your brain imposes this sense of wholeness on the picture. As the photo on page 222 shows, gestalt grouping principles such as closure and continuity are at work here. (Reprinted from GAMES Magazine [810 Seventh Avenue, New York, NY 10019]. Copyright © 1983 PSC Games Limited Partnership.)

Usually, these grouping principles help us construct reality. Sometimes, however, they can lead us astray, as with our perception of the neon worm in Puzzle 5, page 209, or when we look at the doghouse in FIGURE **15.5**.

Depth Perception

Two-dimensional images fall on our retinas, yet we somehow organize three-dimensional perceptions. Seeing objects in three dimensions, called **depth perception**, enables us to estimate their distance from us. At a glance, we estimate the distance of an oncoming car or the height of a house. This ability is partly innate. Eleanor Gibson and Richard Walk (1960) discovered this using a miniature cliff with a drop-off covered by sturdy glass. Gibson's inspiration for these experiments occurred while she was picnicking on the rim of the Grand Canyon. She wondered: Would a toddler peering over the rim perceive the dangerous drop-off and draw back?

Back in their Cornell University laboratory, Gibson and Walk placed 6- to 14-month-old infants on the edge of a safe canyon—a **visual cliff** (FIGURE **15.6**). Their mothers then coaxed them to crawl out onto the glass. Most refused to do so,

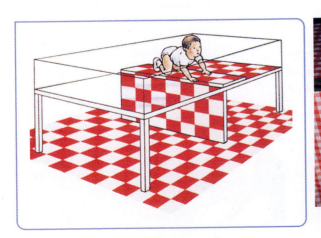

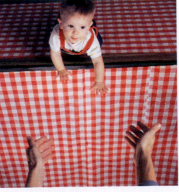

FIGURE **15.6** Visual cliff
Eleanor Gibson and Richard Walk devised this miniature cliff with a glass-covered drop-off to determine whether crawling infants and newborn animals can perceive depth. Even when coaxed, infants are reluctant to venture onto the glass over the cliff.

■ **binocular cues** depth cues, such as retinal disparity and convergence, that depend on the use of two eyes.

■ **monocular cues** distance cues, such as linear perspective and overlap, available to either eye alone.

■ **retinal disparity** a binocular cue for perceiving depth: The greater the disparity (difference) between the two images the retina receives of an object, the closer the object is to the viewer.

■ **convergence** a binocular cue for perceiving depth; the extent to which the eyes converge inward when looking at an object.

If you could switch your eyeballs (leaving their neural wiring intact), you would reverse the retinal disparity, making all objects reversed in depth. Close objects would appear distant, and distant objects would appear close (Wolf, 1996).

indicating that they could perceive depth. Perhaps by crawling age the infants had *learned* to perceive depth. Yet newborn animals with virtually no visual experience—including young kittens, a day-old goat, and newly hatched chicks—respond similarly. Each species, by the time it is mobile, has the perceptual abilities it needs. What is more, during the first month of life, human infants turn to avoid objects coming directly at them but remain unbothered by anything approaching at an angle that would not hit them (Ball & Tronick, 1971).

Biological maturation predisposes our wariness of heights. Experience amplifies it. Infants' wariness increases with their experiences of crawling, no matter when they begin to crawl. When infants' movement is enhanced by a walker, they become even more wary of heights (Campos & others, 1992).

How do we do it? How do we transform two-dimensional retinal images into three-dimensional perceptions? Some depth cues—**binocular cues**—require both eyes. Others—**monocular cues**—are available to each eye separately.

Binocular Cues

Because our eyes are about 2½ inches apart, our retinas receive slightly different images of the world. When the brain compares these two images, the difference between them—their **retinal disparity**—provides an important cue to the relative distance of different objects. When you hold your finger directly in front of your nose, your retinas receive quite different views. (You can see this if you close one eye and then the other, or create a finger sausage as in **FIGURE 15.7**.) At a greater distance—say, when you hold your finger at arm's length—the disparity is smaller.

The creators of three-dimensional (3-D) movies simulate or exaggerate retinal disparity by photographing a scene with two cameras placed a few inches apart (a feature we might want to build into our seeing computer). When we view through spectacles or a device that allows the left eye to see only the image from the left camera and the right eye only the image from the right camera, the 3-D effect mimics normal retinal disparity. Computer-generated 3-D "stereogram" images do the same by making two slightly differing images available for the brain to fuse.

Can you find the three-dimensional Greek letter psi (ψ) in the stereogram in **FIGURE 15.8**? Cross your eyes slightly (or look at a pencil tip 3 inches or so above the page), and see if you can perceive the psi image (at which point you will no longer feel that your eyes are crossed). The image looks so real you may be able to measure its distance from the page with a ruler.

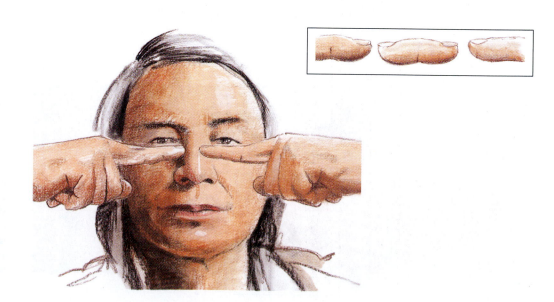

FIGURE 15.7
The floating finger sausage
Hold your two index fingers about 5 inches in front of your eyes, with their tips half an inch apart. Now look beyond them and note the weird result. Move your fingers out farther and the retinal disparity—and the finger sausage—will shrink.

But notice that you cannot trace the outline of the 3-D image on the page—because it isn't on the page. Notice also that if you close one eye, the image immediately disappears, illustrating that the image exists only in your brain. The perceived depth, from two slightly different images lying on top of one another, occurs as each eye focuses on one image and the brain integrates the two versions into a single 3-D image. This illustrates dramatically this module's fundamental lesson: Perception is not merely projecting the world onto our brains. Rather, sensations are disassembled into information bits that the brain then reassembles into its own functional model of the external world. *Our brains construct our perceptions.*

Another binocular cue to distance is **convergence**, a neuromuscular cue caused by the eyes' greater inward turn when they view a near object. The brain notes the angle of convergence, then computes whether you are focusing on this printed page or on something else across the room.

Monocular Cues

Try this: With both eyes open, hold two pens or pencils in front of you and touch their tips together. Now do so with one eye closed. The task should become noticeably more difficult, demonstrating the importance of binocular cues in judging the distance of nearby objects. Two eyes are better than one. How then do we judge whether a person is 10 or 100 meters away? In both cases, the retinal disparity while looking straight ahead is slight. At such distances we depend on monocular cues such as the following:

Interposition If one object partially blocks our view of another, we perceive it as closer. The painting at left purposely confuses figure and ground by interposition.

Relative size If we assume that two objects are similar in size, we perceive the one that casts the smaller retinal image as farther away.

Relative clarity Because light from distant objects passes through more atmosphere, we perceive hazy objects as farther away than sharp, clear objects. (Recall from Puzzle 4, page 209, the effects of fog on judging distance.)

FIGURE 15.8 **Two eyes + brain = depth**
If you are having trouble seeing the 3-D image, try holding the picture close to your face, so that the center of it touches your nose, then slowly move it backward without changing the focus of your eyes. About a foot from your face, the 3-D image should emerge. The image appears because the picture contains two views of the psi, from slightly different angles. When the brain fuses these two into one, you see the image in three dimensions. (Some people are able to reverse the depth by relaxing and looking through the image, as if to a point behind it.)

Interposition

Relative size

Texture gradient

Texture gradient   A gradual change from a coarse, distinct texture to a fine, indistinct texture signals increasing distance. Objects far away appear smaller and more densely packed.

Relative height   We perceive objects higher in our field of vision as farther away. (This reverses above the horizon, as when we perceive a higher bird as closer.) Relative height may contribute to the illusion that vertical dimensions are longer than identical horizontal dimensions (as we saw in Puzzle 3, page 208, the St. Louis Gateway Arch). Is the vertical line (below, left) longer, shorter, or equal in length to the horizontal line? Measure and see.

Relative motion (motion parallax)   As we move, objects that are actually stable may appear to move. If while riding in a train you fix your gaze on some object—say, a house—the objects closer than the house (the fixation point) appear to move backward. The nearer an object is, the faster it seems to move. Objects beyond the fixation point appear to move with you at a decreasing speed as the object gets farther away. Your brain uses these speed and direction clues to compute the objects' relative distances.

Linear perspective   Parallel lines, such as railroad tracks, appear to converge with distance. The more the lines converge, the greater their perceived distance. Linear perspective can contribute to rail-crossing accidents, by leading people to overestimate a train's distance (Leibowitz, 1985). (A train's massive size also makes it appear to be moving more slowly than it is.)

Light and shadow   Nearby objects reflect more light to our eyes. Thus, given two identical objects, the dimmer one seems farther away. This illusion can also contribute to accidents, as when a fog-shrouded vehicle, or one with only its parking lights on, seems farther away than it is. Shading, too, produces a sense of depth consistent with the assumed light source. (Recall the ripples of Puzzle 6.) Invert the top right illustration on the next page and the hollow becomes a hill, because our brains follow a simple rule: *Assume that light comes from above.*

Relative height

Relative motion

Fixation point

Direction of passenger's motion ➡

Linear perspective

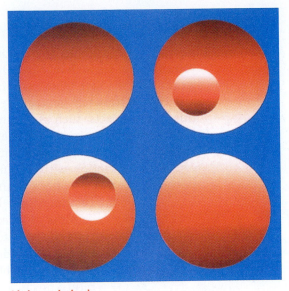

Light and shadow
(From "Perceiving Shape From Shading" by Vilayanur S. Ramachandran. Copyright © 1988 by Scientific American, Inc. All rights reserved.)

Artists use such monocular cues to convey depth on a flat canvas (**FIGURE 15.9**). So do people who must gauge depth with but one eye. In 1960, the University of Washington football team won the year's biggest game, thanks partly to the superb passing of Bob Schloredt. Schloredt, who was obviously skilled at judging his receiver's distance, used monocular cues for distance. He was blind in his left eye.

FIGURE 15.9
Perspective techniques
By the time that "Bristol, Broad Quay" was painted (c. 1730, Anonymous), techniques for depicting three dimensions on a flat surface were well established. Note the effective use of distance cues such as texture gradient, interposition, linear perspective, and relative size and height.

Illusory depth
What monocular depth cue did a photographer use to create this picture of illusory stairs? (See page 220.)

Motion Perception

Imagine that you could perceive the world as having color, form, and depth but that you could not see motion. Not only would you be unable to play cricket or drive a car, you might even have trouble writing, eating, and walking.

But fortunately you can perceive motion. You are by no means perfect at this. Large objects, such as a train, appear to move more slowly than smaller objects, such as a car moving at the same speed—an illusion that contributes to car-train crashes. Nevertheless, if you are a skilled baseball, softball, or cricket player you perceive motion with astounding speed and accuracy. As the ball leaves a pitcher's hand, the batter's brain detects the ball's speed, spin, and direction, computes in a literal eyeblink of time where it is going to be 4/10ths of a second later, and, before 0.15 seconds elapse, directs the arms to swing or not. As a fly ball arcs toward the outfield, the fielder's brain unconsciously computes the ball's trajectory, enabling the fielder to run through the point of its return precisely as it arrives (McBeath & others, 1995). A mathematical physicist working on a supercomputer could hardly compute more quickly or accurately.

Computing motion
This cricket fielder's brain computes the ball's trajectory with amazing speed and accuracy.

Our brain computes motion based partly on its assumption that shrinking objects are retreating (not getting smaller) and enlarging objects are approaching. But the changing size and position of a retinal image isn't our only clue to motion. Nod your head and the visual field's retinal position changes, but nothing appears to move. (Close one eye and gently move your other eyeball by pushing on the upper eyelid. Now the brain reads the changing retinal image as a moving world.)

As film animation artists know well, the brain will also interpret a rapid series of slightly varying images as movement (a phenomenon called *stroboscopic movement*). By flashing 24 still pictures each second, a motion picture creates perceived movement. The motion we see is not in the film. That just presents a superfast slide show. The motion is constructed in our heads.

Marquees and holiday lights sometimes create another illusion of movement using the **phi phenomenon**. When two adjacent stationary lights blink on and off in quick succession, we perceive a single light moving back and forth between them. Lighted signs exploit the phi phenomenon with a succession of lights that create the impression of, say, a moving arrow.

Perceptual Constancy

So far we have noted that our video/computer system must first perceive objects as we do—as having a distinct form, location, and perhaps motion. Its next task is even more challenging: to recognize the object without being deceived by changes in its size, shape, brightness, or color. **Perceptual constancy** enables us to perceive an object as unchanging even though the stimuli we receive from it change. Thus, we can identify things regardless of the angle, distance, and illumination by which we view them. You glance at someone ahead of you on the sidewalk and instantly recognize a classmate. In less time than it takes to draw a breath, information reaching your eyes has been sent to your brain, where work teams comprising millions of neurons have extracted the essential features, compared them with stored images, and identified the person. Replicating this human perceptual feat, which has intrigued perception researchers for decades, provides a monumental challenge for our seeing computer.

■ **phi phenomenon** an illusion of movement created when two or more adjacent lights blink on and off in succession.

■ **perceptual constancy** perceiving objects as unchanging (having consistent lightness, color, shape, and size) even as illumination and retinal images change.

Shape and Size Constancies

Sometimes an object whose actual shape cannot change *seems* to change shape with the angle of our view (**FIGURE 15.10**). More often, thanks to *shape constancy*, we perceive the form of familiar objects as constant even while our retinal images of them change. When a door opens, it casts a changing shape on our retinas, yet we still manage to perceive the door as having a constant doorlike shape (**FIGURE 15.11**).

Thanks to *size constancy* we perceive objects as having a constant size, even while our distance from them varies. Size constancy leads us to perceive a car as large enough to carry people, even when we see its tiny image from two blocks away. This illustrates the close connection between an object's perceived *distance* and perceived *size*. Perceiving an object's distance gives us cues to its size. Likewise, knowing its general size—that the object is, say, a car—provides us with cues to its distance.

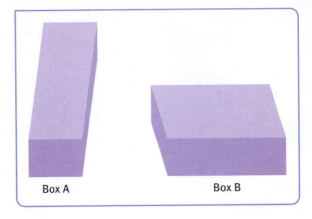

FIGURE 15.10

Perceiving shape

Do the tops of boxes A and B have different dimensions? They appear to. But—believe it or not—they are identical. (Measure and see.) With both boxes we adjust our perceptions relative to our viewing angle. (From Shepard, 1981.)

Box A   Box B

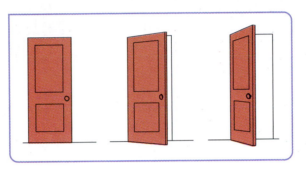

FIGURE 15.11

Shape constancy

A door casts an increasingly trapezoidal image on our retinas as it opens, yet we still perceive it as rectangular.

SIZE-DISTANCE RELATIONSHIP It is a marvel how effortlessly size perception occurs. Given the perceived distance of an object and the size of its image on our retinas, we instantly and unconsciously infer the object's size. Although the monsters in **FIGURE 15.12a** cast the same retinal images, the linear perspective tells our brain that the monster in pursuit is farther away. We therefore perceive it as larger.

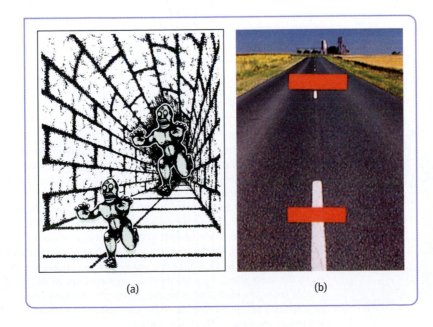

(a)   (b)

FIGURE 15.12

The interplay between perceived size and distance

(a) The monocular cues for distance make the pursuing monster look larger than the pursued. It isn't. (From Shepard, 1990.)
(b) This visual trick, called the Ponzo illusion, is based on the same principle as the fleeing monsters. The two red bars cast identical-sized images on our retinas. But experience tells us that a more distant object can create the same-sized image as a nearer one only if it is actually larger. As a result, we perceive the bar that seems farther away as larger.

Explanation of optical trick on page 217:
Photographer Walter Wick cut out pieces of
paper shaped to imitate stair patterns and
colored them to simulate *light* and *shadow*.

This interplay between perceived size and perceived distance helps explain several well-known illusions. For example, can you imagine why the moon looks up to 50 percent larger near the horizon than when high in the sky? For at least 22 centuries, scholars have wondered and have argued about reasons for the *moon illusion* (Hershenson, 1989). One reason is that cues to objects' distances at the horizon make the moon behind them seem farther away (Kaufman & Rock, 1962). Thus, the moon on the horizon seems larger, like the distant monster in Figure 15.12a and the distant bar in the *Ponzo illusion* in **FIGURE 15.12b**, page 219. Take away these distance cues—by looking at the horizon moon (or each monster or each bar) through a paper tube—and it immediately shrinks.

The size-distance relationship helps us understand two illusions demonstrated earlier. Puzzle 1 (page 208), the Müller-Lyer illusion concerning the lengths of straight lines between arrow tips, has been the subject of more than 1250 scientific publications, yet psychologists still debate its explanation. One is that our experience with the corners of rooms or buildings prompts us to interpret the vertical line on the ticket booth in **FIGURE 15.13a** as closer to us and therefore shorter, and the same-length vertical line by the door as farther away and therefore longer. Thus, what appears as an illusion when isolated in a line drawing actually enables correct depth perception in our three-dimensional world.

Experience supports this theory. People are more susceptible to the Müller-Lyer illusion if, unlike some rural Africans, they have lived in a carpentered world of rectangular shapes (Segall & others, 1990). The phenomenon reflects cultural experience, not race, for the same study showed that Africans who live in cities are more vulnerable to the illusion than are Africans in uncarpentered environments. Our experience in rectangular contexts provides a perspective that helps us construct our perceptions top-down.

Anthropologist Colin Turnbull (1961, p. 252) noted another effect of experience on perception when he took an African Pygmy guide, Kenge, on his first trip out of the dense forest. As they were crossing a wide plain, buffalo loomed several miles away.

(a)

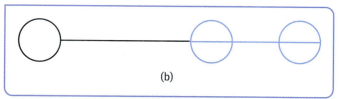

(b)

FIGURE 15.13 The Müller-Lyer illusion
(a) Richard L. Gregory (1968) suggested that the corners in our rectangularly carpentered world teach us to interpret "outward" or "inward" pointing arrowheads at the ends of a line as a cue to the line's distance from us and so to its length. The red line defined by the corner at the ticket booth looks shorter than the red line defined by the corner to the left. But if you measure them, you will see that both are the same length. (b) There is more to the Müller-Lyer illusion than size constancy, however, for if we replace the arrowheads with circles and judge whether the black or blue line segment seem longer, we still get much the same effect. Here the two line segments are equal. Most people judge the black line as longer, apparently because they perceptually adjust the lengths of the lines toward the distance separating the figures. (From Day, 1984.)

Kenge, unaccustomed to judging size over unbroken distances, wondered, "What insects are those?" "When I told Kenge that the insects were buffalo, he roared with laughter and told me not to tell such stupid lies," Turnbull reported. As they drove closer, the mystified Kenge became frightened when the buffalo grew bigger and bigger.

Anthropologists, missionaries, and cross-cultural psychologists also report that people who have never before seen photos or drawings may initially find them confusing (Deregowski, 1989). Shown a painting or a black-and-white picture of a familiar animal such as a tortoise, the inexperienced person may at first just not get it. More than we realize, our taken-for-granted perceptions of the world depend on our experience. We perceive the world not only as it is, but as we are.

Size-distance relationships also explain Puzzle 2, page 208, the shrinking and growing girls. As **FIGURE 15.14** reveals, the room is distorted. Viewed with one eye through a peephole, its trapezoidal walls produce the same images as those of a normal rectangular room viewed with both eyes. Presented with the camera's one-eyed view, the brain makes the reasonable assumption that the room *is* normal and that each of the girls is therefore the same distance from us. But given the different sizes of the images on the retina, our brain ends up calculating that the girls are very different in size.

FIGURE 15.14 The illusion of the shrinking and growing girls

This distorted room, designed by Adelbert Ames, appears to have a normal rectangular shape when viewed through a peephole with one eye. The girl in the near corner appears disproportionately large because we judge her size based on the false assumption that she is the same distance away as the girl in the far corner.

Our occasional misperceptions reveal the workings of our normally effective perceptual processes. The perceived relationship between distance and size is generally valid, but under special circumstances it can lead us astray—as when helping to create the moon illusion, the Müller-Lyer illusion, and the distorted-room illusion. Using distance cues to assess perceived size triggers illusions only if we aren't familiar with the object or if the distance cues are misleading. When we interpret the distance cues correctly—which we normally do—we also correctly perceive the object's size.

Lightness Constancy

White paper reflects 90 percent of the light falling on it; black paper, only 10 percent. In sunlight the black paper may reflect 100 times more light than does the white paper indoors, but it still looks black (McBurney & Collings, 1984). This illustrates *lightness constancy* (also called *brightness constancy*); we perceive an object as having a constant lightness even while its illumination varies. Perceived lightness depends on *relative luminance*—the amount of light an object reflects relative to its surroundings. If you view sunlit black paper through a narrow tube so nothing else is visible, it may look gray, because in bright sunshine it reflects a fair amount of light. View it without the tube and it is again black, because it reflects much less light than the objects around it. The phenomenon is similar to that of color constancy. As light changes, a red apple in a fruit bowl retains its redness, because our brain computes the light reflected by any object relative to its surrounding objects.

Perceived lightness stays roughly constant, given an unchanging context. But what happens when the surrounding context changes? As **FIGURE 15.15** shows, the visual system computes brightness and color relative to surrounding objects. Thus, perceived lightness changes with context.

Form perception, depth perception, motion perception, and perceptual constancy illuminate how we organize our visual experiences. Perceptual organization applies to other senses, too. It explains why we group the clock's steady clicks into patterns (Puzzle 7, page 210). Listening to an unfamiliar language, we have trouble hearing where one word stops and the next one begins. Listening to our own language, we automatically hear distinct words. This, too, is a form of perceptual organization. But it is more, for we even organize a string of letters—THEDOGATEMEAT—into words that make an intelligible phrase, more likely "The dog ate meat" than "The do gate me at" (McBurney & Collings, 1984). This process involves not only organization but interpretation—discerning meaning in what we perceive.

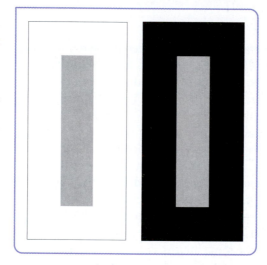

FIGURE 15.15
Brightness contrast
Although the interior rectangles are in fact identical, we perceive the right one as lighter because of the contrast with its dark surroundings. Like the effect of context on color perception, this phenomenon has great significance for artists and interior designers.

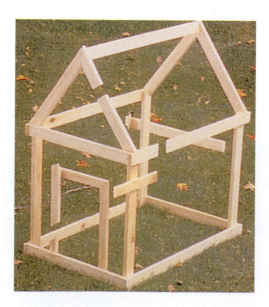

The solution
Another view of the impossible doghouse in Figure 15.5 (page 213.) reveals the secrets of this illusion. From the photo angle in Figure 15.5, the grouping principle of closure leads us to perceive the boards as continuous. (Reprinted from GAMES Magazine [810 Seventh Avenue, New York, NY 10019]. Copyright © 1983 PSC Games Limited Partnership.)

REVIEW AND REFLECT:

Perceptual Organization

Why are psychologists so interested in perceptual illusions?

Visual and auditory illusions were fascinating scientists even as psychology emerged. Explaining illusions required an understanding of how we transform sensations into meaningful perceptions, so the study of perception became one of psychology's first concerns. Conflict between visual and other sensory information is usually resolved with the mind's accepting the visual data, a tendency known as *visual capture*.

What did the Gestalt psychologists contribute to our understanding of how the brain constructs perceptions from sensory information?

The early Gestalt psychologists were impressed with the seemingly innate way we organize fragmentary sensory data into whole perceptions. Our minds structure the information that comes to us in several demonstrable ways:

- *Form Perception* To recognize an object, we must first perceive it (see it as a figure) as distinct from its surroundings (the ground). We must also organize the figure into a meaningful form. Several Gestalt principles—proximity, similarity, continuity, closure, and connectedness—describe this process.

- *Depth Perception* Research on the visual cliff revealed that many species perceive the world in three dimensions at, or very soon after, birth. We transform two-dimensional retinal images into three-dimensional perceptions by using binocular cues, such as retinal disparity, and monocular cues, such as the relative sizes of objects.

- *Motion Perception* Our brain computes motion as objects move across or toward the retina. A quick succession of images, as in a motion picture or on a lighted sign, can also create an illusion of movement.

- *Perceptual Constancy* Having perceived an object as a coherent figure and having located it in space, how then do we recognize it—despite the varying images that it may cast on our retinas? Size, shape, and lightness constancies describe how objects appear to have unchanging characteristics regardless of their distance, shape, or motion. These constancies explain several of the well-known visual illusions. For example, familiarity with the size-distance relationships in a carpentered world of rectangular shapes makes people more susceptible to the Müller-Lyer illusion.

Terms and Concepts to Remember

visual capture, p. 210
gestalt, p. 210
figure-ground, p. 211
grouping, p. 212
depth perception, p. 213
visual cliff, p. 213

binocular cues, p. 214
monocular cues, p. 214
retinal disparity, p. 214
convergence, p. 215
phi phenomenon, p. 218
perceptual constancy, p. 218

Test Yourself

15.1. When vision conflicts with other perceptions, vision usually dominates. This tendency is known as
  a. visual capture.
  b. the figure-ground relationship.
  c. virtual reality.
  d. shape constancy.

15.2. Gestalt psychologists identified the principles by which we organize our perceptions. Our tendencies to fill in the gaps and to perceive a pattern as continuous are two different examples of the organizing principle called
  a. figure-ground.
  b. depth perception.
  c. shape constancy.
  d. grouping.

15.3. In their experiments, Gibson and Walk used a visual cliff to test depth perception in infants and young animals. Their results suggest that
  a. infants have not yet developed depth perception.
  b. crawling infants perceive depth.
  c. depth perception depends on experience.
  d. humans differ significantly from animals in being able to perceive depth in infancy.

15.4. The images that fall on our retinas are two-dimensional, or flat. Yet we perceive the world as having three-dimensional depth. Depth perception underlies our ability to
  a. discriminate figure from ground.
  b. perceive objects as having a constant shape or form.
  c. judge distances.
  d. fill in the gaps in a figure.

15.5. In estimating distances we use both binocular cues, which depend on both eyes, and monocular cues, which are available to either eye alone. Examples of monocular cues are interposition and
  a. closure.
  b. retinal disparity.
  c. linear perspective.
  d. convergence.

15.6. In the Müller-Lyer illusion, we misperceive the length of the lines between arrowheads. We do so partly because
  a. distance cues do not help us assess size.
  b. the visual distance cues (implied by the arrowheads) mislead us.
  c. the perceived relationship between distance and size is generally illusory.
  d. of our linear perspective.

15.7. Form perception and perceptual constancy are organizing principles that apply to hearing as well as vision. For example, in listening to a concerto, you follow the solo instrument and perceive the orchestra as accompaniment; this illustrates the organizing principle of
  a. figure-ground.
  b. shape constancy.
  c. grouping.
  d. depth or distance perception.

Review: How does the study of illusions inform our understanding of normal perceptions?

Reflect: Try drawing a realistic depiction of the scene from your window using several of the monocular cues you have learned about.

Answers to the Test Yourself and Review questions can be found in the green appendix at the end of the book.

16 Perceptual Interpretation

Philosophers have debated the origins of our perceptual abilities: Is it nature or nurture? German philosopher Immanuel Kant (1724–1804) maintained that knowledge comes from our *inborn* ways of organizing sensory experiences. Indeed, we come equipped to process sensory information. But British philosopher John Locke (1632–1704) argued that through our experiences we also *learn* to perceive the world. Indeed, we learn to link an object's distance with its size. So, just how important is experience? How radically does it shape our perceptual interpretations?

> "Let us then suppose the mind to be, as we say, white paper void of all characters, without any ideas: How comes it to be furnished? . . . To this I answer, in one word, from EXPERIENCE."
>
> John Locke, *An Essay Concerning Human Understanding*, 1690

Sensory Deprivation and Restored Vision

Preview Question: What does research on sensory deprivation and restored vision reveal about the effects of experience on perception?

Writing to John Locke (1690), William Molyneux wondered whether "a man *born* blind, and now adult, taught by his *touch* to distinguish between a cube and a sphere" could, if made to see, visually distinguish the two. Locke's answer was no, because the man would *never* have *learned* to see the difference.

Molyneux's hypothetical case has since been put to the test with dozens of adults who, though blind from birth, have gained sight (Gregory, 1978; von Senden, 1932). Most had been born with cataracts—clouded lenses that allowed them to see only diffused light, rather as you or I might see a diffuse fog through a Ping-Pong ball sliced in half. When their cataracts were surgically removed, the patients could distinguish figure from ground and could sense colors—suggesting that these aspects of perception are innate. But much as Locke supposed, the formerly blind patients often could not recognize by sight objects that were familiar by touch.

Perhaps in these cases the surgery didn't completely restore the patients' visual equipment. Seeking to gain more control than is provided by clinical cases, researchers have conducted Molyneux's imaginary experiment with infant kittens and monkeys. In one experiment, they outfitted them with goggles through which the animals could see only diffuse, unpatterned light (Wiesel, 1982). After infancy, when their goggles were removed, these animals exhibited perceptual limitations much like those of humans born with cataracts. They could distinguish color and brightness, but not the form of a circle from that of a square. Their eyes had not degenerated; their retinas still relayed signals to their visual cortex. But lacking stimulation, the cortical cells had not developed normal connections. Thus, the animals remained functionally blind to shape.

In both humans and animals, a similar period of sensory restriction does no permanent harm if it occurs later in life. Cover the eye of an animal for several months during adulthood, and its vision will be unaffected after removing the eye patch. Remove cataracts that develop after early childhood, and a human, too, will enjoy normal vision. The effects of visual experiences during infancy in cats, monkeys, and humans suggest there is a *critical period* for normal sensory and perceptual development. Experience indeed does guide the organization of the brain's neural connections.

Human infants born with an opaque lens (cataract) will typically have corrective surgery within a few months. The brain network responsible for the corrected eye then rapidly develops, enabling improved visual acuity with as little as one hour's visual experience (Mauer & others, 1999). Congenitally deaf kittens and infants given cochlear implants exhibit a similar "awakening" of the pertinent brain area (Klinke & others, 1999; Siretenau, 1999). Nurture sculpts what nature has endowed.

We can also see the profound effects of early visual experience in experiments with young animals reared with restricted or altered visual input. Building on work by Richard Held and Alan Hein, Cambridge University researchers Colin Blakemore and Grahame Cooper (1970) reared kittens in darkness, except for 5 hours each day when they were placed in a horizontally or vertically striped environment (as in **FIGURE**

FIGURE 16.1

The experimental apparatus for the Blakemore and Cooper studies
From the time their eyes first opened, and until the age of 5 months, these kittens were removed from darkness each day to spend 5 hours alone in a black-and-white striped cylinder with a clear glass floor. A stiff collar prevented the kittens from seeing anything else, even their own bodies. Afterward, these kittens had difficulty perceiving horizontal forms, compared with other kittens exposed only to horizontal forms. (From Blakemore & Cooper, 1970.)

16.1). Remarkably, kittens raised without exposure to horizontal lines later had difficulty perceiving horizontal bars, and those raised without vertical lines had difficulty seeing vertical bars. While two of these kittens played, a researcher playfully shook a long black rod. The kitten reared in a world of vertical lines would play with the rod only when it was held upright. When the rod was held flat, that kitten ignored it while its companion—reared in a world of horizontal lines—ran to play with it. Eventually, their selective blindness diminished, but the kittens never regained normal sensitivity. By sampling the activity of the kittens' feature-detecting brain cells, Blakemore and Cooper found that whether such cells responded mostly to horizontal or to vertical lines depended on the kittens' early visual experience.

Newer experiments show that owls learn to adapt to a visual world that is shifted to the right or left by prisms fitted over their eyes during a sensitive early period. If again fitted with the prisms as adults, these owls—unlike other owls not given the early experience—can relearn to interact with this displaced world. Evidently, their brains retain the neural connections from their early experience (Knudsen, 1998).

Experiments on perceptual limitations and advantages produced by early sensory deprivation provide a partial answer to an important question: Does the effect of early experience last a lifetime? For some aspects of visual perception, the answer is clearly yes: "Use it *soon* or lose it." We retain the imprint of early visual experiences far into the future.

Sensory Restriction as Therapy

Preview Questions: What is it like to experience sensory restriction? How can this experience be beneficial?

The loss of a sense is one type of sensory restriction. Another is sensory monotony—the relatively unchanging sensory input experienced by prisoners in solitary confinement, by nighttime truck drivers and airline pilots, and by animals in barren zoos. To investigate the effects of sensory restriction, experimenters have put thousands of people through controlled, temporary simulations. Some spent several days in monotonous environments—small rooms where light and sound never changed. Others passed the time in the dark and silence, deprived of all normal sensory input. The first "sensory deprivation" experiments produced bizarre and widely publicized findings (Heron, 1957). The volunteers, lying on beds and wearing translucent goggles to

REST
Restricted environmental stimulation therapy can provide healing relaxation.

diffuse the light, typically began the experiment in good spirits. Here was a chance to make some easy money while relaxing and thinking creatively. But before long, they became disoriented, many even experiencing hallucinations, and some becoming susceptible to piped-in messages arguing for the reality of ghosts.

In science, manipulating one factor often simultaneously changes other factors. What really causes the effects of a monotonous environment? Sensory restriction? Social isolation? Or is it the stress of confinement? The dramatic reports from early experiments prompted many more investigations. Most of them produced less newsworthy results (Suedfeld & Kristeller, 1982).

It turns out that sensory restriction does not disturb most people. More often, it actually reduces stress and helps people become more open to positive influence. In University of British Columbia experiments with smokers and people who were overweight, Peter Suedfeld (1980) found that restricting sensory input helps people modify their behavior. Those wanting to alter their behavior often increased their self-control after 24 hours of what he aptly calls REST—restricted environmental stimulation therapy.

Allan Best and Suedfeld (1982) had smokers listen to antismoking messages for 24 hours while lying on beds in dark, quiet rooms (they got up only to sip a liquid diet through tubes or to use the toilets next to the beds). In the following week, none relapsed. A year later, two-thirds were still not smoking—double the number who had received the same instruction but without the day of REST.

Shorter REST periods can also pay dividends. In one experiment, heavy-drinking college students spent 2½ hours in REST. After 1½ hours, they were given 5 minutes of factual information about alcohol's negative effects. Unlike those in control conditions, the REST-plus-message group decreased their alcohol consumption by 55 percent during the ensuing 6 months (Cooper & others, 1988).

Periods of solitude and sensory restriction have traditionally fostered human fulfillment. Sensory restriction is a central component of the "quiet therapies" of Japan (Reynolds, 1982, 1986). Morita therapy for depression or anxiety sometimes begins with a week of bed rest and meditation, then moves to assigned light tasks. The religious visions of Moses, Mohammed, and Buddha reportedly occurred during times of solitude and contemplation. As living creatures we require sensory stimulation, but there are times when we benefit from the peace and relaxation of restricted stimulation.

Perceptual Adaptation

Preview Question: How adaptable is our ability to perceive the world around us?

Given a new pair of glasses, we may feel slightly disoriented, even dizzy. Within a day or two, we adjust. Our **perceptual adaptation** to changed visual input makes the world seem normal again. But imagine a far more dramatic new pair of glasses—one that shifts the apparent location of objects 40 degrees to the left. When you first put them on and toss a ball to a friend, it sails off to the left. Walking forward to shake hands with the person, you veer to the left.

Could you adapt to this distorted world? Chicks cannot. When fitted with such lenses, they continue to peck where food grains *seem* to be (Hess, 1956; Rossi, 1968).

■ **perceptual adaptation** in vision, the ability to adjust to an artificially displaced or even inverted visual field.

■ **perceptual set** a mental predisposition to perceive one thing and not another.

But we humans adapt to distorting lenses quickly. Within a few minutes your throws would again be accurate, your stride on target. Remove the lenses and you would experience an aftereffect: At first your throws would err in the *opposite* direction, sailing off to the right; but again, within minutes you would readapt.

Now imagine an even more radical pair of glasses—one that literally turns the world upside down. The ground is up, the sky is down. Could you adapt? Fish, frogs, and salamanders cannot. When Roger Sperry (1956) surgically turned their eyes upside down, they thereafter reacted to objects by moving in the wrong direction. But, believe it or not, kittens, monkeys, and humans can adapt to an inverted world. Psychologist George Stratton (1896) experienced this when he invented, and for 8 days wore, optical headgear that flipped left to right *and* up to down, making him the first person to experience a right-side-up retinal image while standing upright.

At first, Stratton felt disoriented. When he wanted to walk, he found himself searching for his feet, which were now "up." Eating was nearly impossible. He became nauseated and depressed. But Stratton persisted, and by the eighth day he could comfortably reach for something in the right direction and walk without bumping into things. When Stratton finally removed the headgear, he readapted quickly.

Later experiments replicated Stratton's experience (Dolezal, 1982; Kohler, 1962). After a period of adjustment, people wearing the optical gear have even been able to ride a motorcycle, ski the Alps, and fly an airplane. But how? Is it because through experience they perceptually reinvert their upside-down world to an upright position? Actually no. The street, ski slopes, and runway still seem above their heads. But by actively moving about in this topsy-turvy world, they adapt to the context and learn to coordinate their movements.

Perceptual adaptation
"Oops, missed," thinks Dr. Hubert Dolezal as he views the world through inverting goggles. Remarkably, people can learn to adapt to an upside-down visual world.

Perceptual Set

Preview Question: How do our assumptions and beliefs shape our interpretations, and thus our perceptions?

As everyone knows, to see is to believe. As many people also know, but do not fully appreciate, to believe is to see. Our experiences, assumptions, and expectations may give us a **perceptual set**, or mental predisposition, that greatly influences what we perceive. Is the image in the center picture of **FIGURE 16.2** a man playing the saxophone or a woman's face? What we see in such a drawing can be influenced by first looking at either of the two unambiguous versions (Boring, 1930).

Once we have formed a wrong idea about reality, we have more difficulty seeing the truth. Even scientists, striving for objectivity, perceive reality through the lenses of their theories. When first viewing the "canals" on Mars through telescopes, some people perceived them as the product of intelligent life. They were—but the intelligence was on the viewing end of the telescope.

"The temptation to form premature theories upon insufficient data is the bane of our profession."

Sherlock Holmes, in Arthur Conan Doyle's *The Valley of Fear*, 1914

FIGURE 16.2 Perceptual set
What do you see in the center picture: a male saxophonist or a woman's face? Glancing first at one of the two unambiguous versions of the picture is likely to influence your interpretation. (From Shepard, 1990.)

Everyday examples of perceptual set abound. In 1972, a British newspaper published genuine, unretouched photographs of a "monster" in Scotland's Loch Ness—"the most amazing pictures ever taken," stated the paper. If this information creates in you the same perceptual set it did in most of the paper's readers, you, too, will see the monster in the photo reproduced in **FIGURE 16.3a**. But when Steuart Campbell (1986) approached the photos with a different perceptual set, he saw a curved tree trunk—very likely the same tree trunk others had seen in the water the day the photo was shot. Moreover, with this different perceptual set, you may now notice that the object is floating motionless, without any rippling water or wake around it—hardly what we would expect of a lively monster. Aided by apparent perceptual set, thousands of others have marveled at a face on the moon, Mother Theresa on a cinnamon bun, Jesus on a pancake, and the word *Allah* on a sliced potato.

Our perceptual set can influence what we hear as well as what we see. Consider the kindly airline pilot who, on a takeoff run, looked over at his depressed co-pilot and said, "Cheer up." The co-pilot heard the usual "Gear up" and promptly raised the wheels—before they had left the ground (Reason & Mycielska, 1982). People listening to rock music or a Bill Clinton speech played backward often perceive an evil message *if* specifically told what to listen for (Vokey & Read, 1985). One Web site (www.kissthisguy.com) has offered some 2000 examples of misperceptions such as this one: Anna remembers her humiliation when her preschool classmates erupted in giggles as she recited, "Little Miss Muffet sat on a tuffet eating her curtains away." Clearly, much of what we perceive comes not just from the world "out there" but also from what's behind our eyes and between our ears.

Even when listening to Disney movies, sex-sensitive viewers have perceived supposedly subliminal messages, such as the letters S-E-X in a cloud of dust stirred up by Simba in *The Lion King,* or "All good teenagers take off your clothes," murmured by a voice in *Aladdin.* The latter message was first perceived by a testosterone-laden male university student, who told his sister, who told her mother, who wrote to *Movie Guide,* whose report (later retracted) was picked up by the American Life League newsletter, whose allegation was reported by Virginia's *Newport News*, from where it was picked up by the Associated Press. "If somebody is [perceiving] something, that's their perception," responded Rick Rhoades, a spokesperson for Disney, which had been inundated with letters of protest. "There's nothing there" (Bannon, 1995). Some things must be believed to be seen.

What determines our perceptual set? Through experience we form concepts, or *schemas*, that organize and interpret unfamiliar information. Our preexisting schemas for male saxophonists and women's faces, for monsters and tree trunks, for airplane lights and UFOs, all influence how we interpret ambiguous sensations with top-down processing. Confronted with an ambiguous moving object in the sky, different people may therefore apply different schemas: "It's a bird." "It's a plane." "It's Superman!"

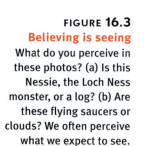

FIGURE 16.3
Believing is seeing
What do you perceive in these photos? (a) Is this Nessie, the Loch Ness monster, or a log? (b) Are these flying saucers or clouds? We often perceive what we expect to see.

(a)

(b)

Children's drawings give us a way to glimpse their developing perceptual schemas. A preschooler can draw circles and angled lines but cannot combine them to create an elaborate human figure. The child's difficulty is not clumsiness. A right-handed adult asked to draw with the left hand will create an awkward drawing, but it will be unlike the child's drawing in **FIGURE 16.4**. Part of the difference lies in the challenge for children to represent visually what they see. The main difference, however, lies in the child's simplified schema for essential human characteristics. To 3- and 4-year-olds, a face is a more important human feature than a body. From ages 3 to 8, children's schemas for bodies become more elaborate, and so do their drawings.

FIGURE 16.4 Schemas
Children's drawings reflect their schemas of reality, as well as their abilities to represent what they see. This drawing by 4-year-old Anna illustrates that the face has far greater importance than the body in young children's schemas of essential human characteristics.

Our schemas for faces prime us to see facial patterns in cartoonists' caricatures and even in random configurations, such as the lunar landscape. Peter Thompson (1980) at the University of York discovered that our face recognition is especially attuned to the expressive eyes and mouth. Portrait artists seem to understand this. Two-thirds of portraits sampled from the last five centuries have an eye at or within 5 percent of the painting's exact centerline (**FIGURE 16.5**). So attuned are we to eyes that we have trouble imagining what Madonna's inverted eyes and mouth will look like when we turn her face upright (**FIGURE 16.6**). But if we hold the eyes constant—by transferring

FIGURE 16.5 Aye for an eye
Christopher Tyler (1998) discovered that artists, when trying to capture a sense of the person, consciously or unconsciously place one eye on the painting's centerline.

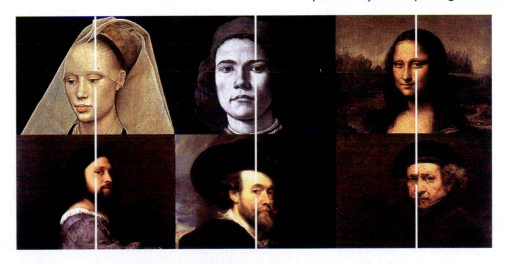

FIGURE 16.6 Face schemas
Which of these is the real Madonna? Slowly rotate the page to find out. As you do so, you will reach a point where you suddenly cannot assimilate her mouth and eyes into your schema for faces.

FIGURE 16.7
Bill Clinton and who?
Our brains are attuned to faces, and to eyes in particular. But head shape and hair style matter, too. After Pawan Sinha and Tomaso Poggio transferred Bill Clinton's eyes, nose, and mouth to Al Gore's face, we still quickly perceive the difference between them.

someone's eyes, nose, and mouth to another face—other head features obviously matter, too (**FIGURE 16.7**).

Context Effects

A given stimulus may trigger radically different perceptions, partly because of our differing schemas, but also because of the immediate context. Some examples:

✦ Imagine hearing a noise interrupted by the words "eel is on the wagon." Likely, you would actually perceive the first word as *wheel*. Given "eel is on the orange," you would hear *peel*. This curious phenomenon, discovered by Richard Warren, suggests that the brain can work backward in time to allow a later stimulus to determine how we perceive an earlier one. The context creates an expectation that, top-down, influences our perception as we match our bottom-up signal against it (Grossberg, 1995).

✦ Is the "magician's cabinet" in **FIGURE 16.8** sitting on the floor or hanging from the ceiling? How we perceive it depends on the context defined by the rabbits.

✦ Did the speaker say "cults and sects" or "cults and sex"? Did the critic advocate "attacks" or "a tax" on our politicians? In both instances, we must discern the meaning from the surrounding words.

Soviet film director Lew Kulechov believed that skilled directors evoke emotion in an audience by defining a context in which viewers interpret an actor's expressions. He once produced three short films, each depicting one of three contexts, followed by identical clips of an actor with a neutral expression (Wallbott, 1988). Shown a film of a dead woman, viewers of the clip were struck by the actor's sadness. Shown a dish of soup, viewers judged the actor thoughtful. Shown a playing child, viewers said the actor appeared happy. Even hearing sad rather than happy music can predispose people to perceive a sad meaning in spoken homophonic word meanings—*mourning* rather than *morning*, *die* rather than *dye*, *pain* rather than *pane* (Halberstadt & others, 1995).

In Seattle's county hospital where I was once an orderly, we occasionally faced the task of transporting a dead body through crowded hallways without alarming the patients or their visitors. Our solution was to exploit the "Kulechov effect" by creating a context that matched people's schemas for sleeping and sedated patients: With the body's face uncovered and the sheet turned down in normal fashion, we could wheel an apparently "sleeping" body past the unsuspecting.

In everyday life, perceptual sets—for example, stereotypes about gender or culture—can color the context. Without the obvious cues of pink or blue, people will struggle over whether to call the new baby "he" or "she." But told an infant is "David," people (especially children) may perceive "him" as bigger and stronger than

cathy®   **by Cathy Guisewite**

Given a perceptual set—"this is a girl"— people see a more feminine baby.

FIGURE 16.8 Context effects: The magician's cabinet
Is the box in the far left frame lying on the floor or hanging from the ceiling? What about the one on the far right? In each case, the context defined by the inquisitive rabbits guides our perceptions. (From Shepard, 1990.)

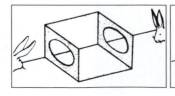

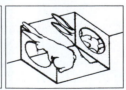

Culture and context effects
What is above the woman's head? In one study, nearly all those questioned from East Africa thought she was balancing a metal box or can on her head and that the family was sitting under a tree. Westerners, to whom corners and boxlike architecture are more common, were more likely to perceive the family as being indoors, with the woman sitting under a window. (Adapted from Gregory & Gombrich, 1973.)

if the same infant is called "Diana" (Stern & Karraker, 1989). Some gender differences, it seems, exist merely in the eyes of their beholders.

The effects of perceptual sets and context show how experience helps us construct perception. "We hear and apprehend only what we already half know," said Thoreau. The river of perception is fed by two streams, sensation and cognition. To return to the question—is perception innate or learned?—we can answer: It's both. "Simple" perceptions are the brain's creative products. The Close Up box on page 232 illustrates how product designs influence human perception and behavior.

Is There Extrasensory Perception?

Preview Questions: Can we perceive only what we sense? Or, without sensory input, are we capable of extrasensory perception?

Half or a little more of British and American adults and Japanese university students say they believe in **extrasensory perception (ESP)**, and another quarter aren't sure (Blackmore, 1997; Gallup & Newport, 1991; George, 1996; Nishizawa, 1996). The media overflow with reports of psychic wonders: crimes solved, dreams come true, futures foretold. Paranormal television (such as "Unsolved Mysteries" and "X-Files") and movies (such as *The Sixth Sense* and *The Blair Witch Project*) are big business. The dial-a-psychic industry tops $1 billion a year, much of it from low-income people (Nisbett, 1998). Are there indeed people—any people—who can read minds, see through walls, or foretell the future?

In laboratory experiments, **parapsychologists**—those who study paranormal (literally, beyond the normal) occurrences—have at times been astonished at psychics who seem capable of discerning the contents of sealed envelopes, influencing the roll of a die, or drawing a picture of what someone else is viewing at an unknown remote location. But other research psychologists and scientists—including 96 percent of the scientists in the National Academy of Sciences—have been skeptical (McConnell, 1991). If ESP is real, we would need to overturn the scientific understanding that we are creatures whose minds are tied to our physical brains and whose perceptual experiences of the world are built of sensations. However, sometimes new evidence does overturn our scientific preconceptions. So let's critically evaluate claims for ESP.

■ **extrasensory perception (ESP)** the controversial claim that perception can occur apart from sensory input. Said to include *telepathy*, *clairvoyance*, and *precognition*.

■ **parapsychology** the study of paranormal phenomena, including ESP and psychokinesis.

CLOSE-UP:

THE HUMAN FACTOR IN OPERATING MACHINES

I love our VCR, though I still haven't figured out how to make it "express record." Our stove is wonderful, except for the moments I spend puzzling over which control works which burner. The push-bar doors on our campus buildings are sturdy, though occasionally frustrating when I push the wrong end. The extra buttons on my computer-linked phone are handy, though when transferring a call I still must look up which button to press.

Human factors psychologists help to design appliances, machines, and work settings that harness rather than confound our natural perceptions. Psychologist Donald Norman (1988) suggests how simple design changes could reduce some of our frustrations. For example, by exploiting "natural mapping," we could design stove controls that require no labels.

Understanding human factors can do more than enable us to design for reduced frustration; it can help avoid disaster. After beginning commercial flights in the late 1960s, the Boeing 727 was involved in several landing accidents caused by pilot error. Psychologist Conrad Kraft (1978) noted a common setting for these accidents: All took place at night, and all involved landing short of the runway after crossing a dark stretch of water or unilluminated ground. Kraft reasoned that, beyond the runway, city lights would project a larger retinal image if on a rising terrain. This would make the ground seem farther away than it was. By re-creating these conditions in flight simulations, Kraft discovered that pilots were deceived into thinking they were flying safely, higher than their actual altitudes (**FIGURE 16.9**).

Aided by Kraft's finding, the airlines began corrective measures (such as requiring the co-pilot to monitor the altimeter and call out altitudes) and the accidents diminished.

Today's Boeing psychologists are at work on other human factors problems (Murray, 1998): How should airlines best train and manage mechanics to reduce the maintenance errors that underlie about 50 percent of flight delays and 15 percent of accidents? What illumination and typeface would make on-screen flight data easiest to read? How would warning messages be most effectively worded—as an action statement ("pull up") rather than a problem statement ("ground proximity")? In studying these and other human factors issues, psychologists strive to increase both safety and productivity.

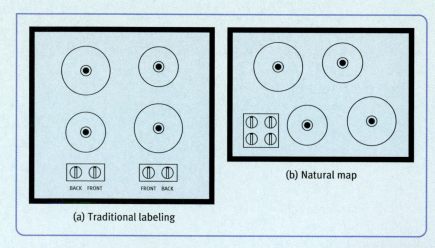

(a) Traditional labeling

(b) Natural map

Better labels

(a) With traditionally positioned stove controls, a person must read the labels to figure out which knob works which burner. (b) By positioning the controls in a natural map, which the brain understands at a glance, we can eliminate the need to ponder written instructions just to boil water.

FIGURE 16.9 Human factors problem
Lacking distance cues when approaching a runway from over a dark surface, pilots simulating a night landing tended to fly too low. (From Kraft, 1978.)

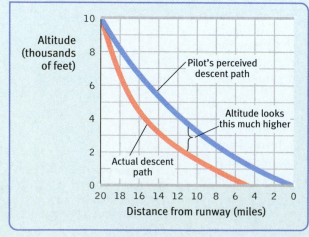

Claims of ESP

Claims of paranormal phenomena include astrological predictions, psychic healing, reincarnation, communication with the dead, and out-of-body experiences. Of these, the most respectable, testable, and—for a chapter on perception—relevant claims are for three varieties of ESP:

Telepathy, or mind-to-mind communication—one person sending thoughts to another or perceiving another's thoughts.

Clairvoyance, or perceiving remote events, such as sensing that a friend's house is on fire.

Precognition, or perceiving future events, such as a political leader's death or a sporting event's outcome.

Closely linked with these are claims of *psychokinesis*, or "mind over matter," such as levitating a table or influencing the roll of a die. (The claim is illustrated by the wry comment, "Will all those who believe in psychokinesis please raise my hand?")

Premonitions or Pretensions?

Can psychics see into the future? Although one might wish for a psychic stock forecaster, the tallied forecasts of "leading psychics" reveal meager accuracy. Between 1978 and 1985, the New Year's predictions of the *National Enquirer*'s favorite psychics yielded 2 accurate predictions out of 486 (Strentz, 1986). During the 1990s, tabloid psychics were all wrong in predicting surprising events (Madonna did not become a gospel singer, Bill Cosby did not become an ambassador to South Africa, Queen Elizabeth did not abdicate her throne to enter a convent). And they missed all the unexpected big-news events, such as specific terrorist bombings, Saddam Hussein's assault on Kuwait, and the O. J. Simpson case. If only the psychic whom Princess Diana consulted shortly before her death had foreseen the danger that lay ahead.

Analyses of psychic visions offered to police departments reveal that these, too, are no more accurate than guesses made by others (Reiser, 1982). Psychics working with the police do, however, generate dozens or even hundreds of predictions. This increases the odds of an occasional correct guess, which psychics can then report to the media. Moreover, vague predictions can later be interpreted ("retrofitted") to match events that provide a perceptual set for interpreting them. Nostradamus, a sixteenth-century French psychic, explained in an unguarded moment that his ambiguous prophecies "could not possibly be understood till they were interpreted after the event and by it." Police departments are wise to all this. When Jane Ayers Sweat and Mark Durm (1993) asked the police departments of America's 50 largest cities whether they ever used psychics, 65 percent said they never had. Of those that had, not one had found it helpful.

Are the spontaneous "visions" of everyday people any more accurate? Consider our dreams. Do they foretell the future, as about half of university students believe (Messer & Griggs, 1989)? Or do they only seem to do so because we are more likely to recall or reconstruct dreams that seem to have come true? Sixty years ago, two Harvard psychologists (Murray & Wheeler, 1937) tested the prophetic power of dreams. After aviator Charles Lindbergh's baby son was kidnapped and murdered but before the body was discovered, the researchers invited the public to report their dreams about the child. Of the 1300 dream reports submitted, how many accurately envisioned the child dead? Five percent. And how many also correctly anticipated the body's location—buried among trees? Only 4 of the 1300. Although this number was surely no better than chance, to those 4 dreamers the accuracy of their *apparent* precognitions must have seemed uncanny.

In 1996, Psychic Friends Network owner Michael Lasky spent $500,000 to purchase Eddie Murray's 500th home-run baseball (Dodd, 1996). One couldn't help but wonder not only about the poor souls whose money Lasky was spending, but why his psychics hadn't just told him when and where to sit to catch it himself.

"WOW"

"A person who talks a lot is sometimes right."

Spanish proverb

Which supposed psychic ability does Psychic Pizza claim?

Throughout the day, each of us imagines many events. Occasionally an unlikely imagining is bound to occur and to astonish us when it does. If you tell everyone in a group of 100 to think "heads" before each tosses six coins, someone is likely to get heads every time (whether thinking heads or not) and to feel eerie afterward. Random sequences will at times contain weird conjunctions or streaks. Given the billions of events in the world each day, and given enough days, some stunning coincidences are sure to occur. With enough time, the improbable becomes inevitable.

One skeptic, magician James Randi, long offered $10,000 to anyone who could demonstrate "*any* paranormal ability" before a group of competent experts. With pledges from others, his offer—"to anyone who proves a genuine psychic power under proper observing conditions"—several years ago was upped to $1 million, on deposit with Goldman-Sachs (Randi, 1999). Large as this sum is, the scientific seal of approval would be worth far more to anyone whose claims could be authenticated. To refute those who say there is no ESP, one need only produce a single person who can demonstrate a single, reproducible ESP phenomenon. So far, no such person has emerged. Randi's offer has been publicized for three decades and dozens of people have been tested, sometimes under the scrutiny of an independent panel of judges. Still, nothing.

> "Things that happen by chance are events in search of causes."
>
> K. C. Cole, *The Universe and the Teacup*, 1998

Putting ESP to Experimental Test

Finally, consider this, say the skeptics: If ESP existed, then surely someone out there could, when feeling the psychic spirit stirring, occasionally pick winning lottery numbers or blackjack outcomes (becoming fabulously wealthy or generous). If someone—anyone—out there has accurate spontaneous premonitions, why did they not (for the sake of charity if not out of greed) predict the outcome of the $195 million multistate Powerball lottery in May 1998? Enough people certainly tried. Some 130 million tickets were purchased, each an effort at precognition. With 80 million-to-1 odds against specifying the correct string of numbers, that number of tickets would lead us to expect one or two winners by chance alone. And sure enough, Frank Capaci of Chicago was the one lucky winner—without any reported psychic help.

Testing psychic powers in the British population
Hertfordshire University psychologist Richard Wiseman created a "mind machine" to see if people can influence or predict a coin toss. Using a touch-sensitive screen, visitors to festivals around the country were given four attempts to call heads or tails. Using a random-number generator, a computer then decided the outcome. When the experiment concluded in January 2000, nearly 28,000 people had predicted 110,972 tosses—with 49.8 percent correct.

After thousands of experiments, *a reproducible ESP phenomenon has never been discovered, nor has anyone produced any individual who can convincingly demonstrate psychic ability.* A National Research Council investigation of ESP similarly concluded that "the best available evidence does not support the contention that these phenomena exist" (Druckman & Swets, 1988). And in 1995, a CIA-commissioned report evaluated 10 years of military testing of psychic spies (a program previously abandoned by the CIA after having produced nothing). Twenty million dollars had been invested. The result? The program produced nothing. Given so many disappointing laboratory results and vague or erroneous psychic visions, the psychic spy program was finally scrapped (Hyman, 1996; Waller, 1995).

In the past, there have existed all kinds of strange ideas—that bumps on the head reveal character traits, that bloodletting is a cure-all, that each sperm cell contains a miniature person. When faced with such claims—or with claims of mind reading or out-of-body travel or communication with the dead—how can we separate

> "At the heart of science is an essential tension between two seemingly contradictory attitudes—an openness to new ideas, no matter how bizarre or counterintuitive they may be, and the most ruthless skeptical scrutiny of all ideas, old and new."
>
> Carl Sagan (1987)

bizarre ideas from those that sound bizarre but are true? At the heart of science is a simple answer: Test them to see if they work. If they do, so much the better for the ideas. If they don't, so much the better for our skepticism.

This scientific attitude has led both believers and skeptics to agree that what parapsychology needs to give it credibility is a reproducible phenomenon and a theory to explain it. Seeking a phenomenon, how might we test ESP claims in a controlled experiment? An experiment differs from a staged demonstration. On stage, the "psychic," like a magician, controls what the audience sees and hears. The "effects" are typically mind blowing. In the laboratory, the experimenter controls what the psychic sees and hears. Time and again, skeptics note, so-called psychics have exploited unquestioning audiences with amazing performances in which they *appeared* to communicate with the spirits of the dead, read minds, or levitate objects—only to have it revealed that their acts were a hoax, nothing more than the illusions of stage magicians. And why hasn't at least one psychic made billions in the stock market?

Knowing how easily we can be deceived, and lacking reproducible results, most research psychologists remain skeptical. Indeed, they are dismayed by all the shows, books, and magazines on paranormal topics. But some have become newly intrigued by findings published by social psychologist Daryl Bem and parapsychologist Charles Honorton (1994) using the *ganzfeld procedure*. The procedure would place you in a reclining chair, play hissing white noise through headphones, and shine diffuse red light through Ping-Pong ball halves strapped over your eyes. Ostensibly, this reduction of external distractions would put you in an ideal state to receive thoughts from someone else, which you may hear as small voices from within.

Building on earlier studies using this procedure, Bem and Honorton isolated a "sender" and "receiver" in separate, shielded chambers and had the sender concentrate for half an hour on one of four randomly selected visual images. The receivers were then asked which of four images best matched the images they experienced during the session. Over 11 studies, the receivers beat chance (25 percent accurately matched) by a bigger than usual margin (32 percent accurately matched).

Recall that psychology-based critical inquiry always asks two questions: What do you mean? And how do you know (what's your evidence)? Parapsychologists say the ganzfeld tests of ESP offer clear answers to both questions. Skeptic Ray Hyman (1994, 1996) granted that their methodology surpasses that of previous ESP experiments, but he questioned certain procedural details that may have introduced bias. Intrigued, other researchers set to work replicating these experiments. Would this be the first reliable ESP phenomenon? Or one more dashed hope?

Alas, Julie Milton and Richard Wiseman's (1999) statistical digest of 30 follow-up ganzfeld experiments found no effect. "We conclude that the ganzfeld technique does not at present offer a replicable method for producing ESP in the laboratory." But—hold the phone—one very recent study does find an effect (Milton, 1999).

Stay tuned, and remember: The scientific attitude blends curious skepticism with open-minded humility. It demands that extraordinary claims be supported by clear and reliable evidence. (If at 5'7" and age 57 I claim to be able to dunk a basketball, the burden of proof would be on me to show that I can do it, not on you to prove that I couldn't.) Given such evidence, science is open to nature's occasional surprises.

The scientific attitude involves skeptical but open-minded scrutiny of competing ideas. As critical thinkers, we can be open to new ideas without being gullible, discerning without being cynical. We can be critical thinkers, yet—knowing that our understanding of nature is incomplete—we can agree with Shakespeare's Hamlet that "there are more things in heaven and earth, Horatio, than are dreamt of in your philosophy."

Some things that we assume to be true—the reality of another's love, the existence or nonexistence of God, the finality of death or the reality of life after death—

The "effects" are typically too small for the naked eye to detect and unreliable (leading skeptics to mock that ESP stands for "error some place").

"A psychic is an actor playing the role of a psychic."

Psychologist-Magician Daryl Bem (1984)

The ganzfeld procedure
Hoping to detect faint telepathy signals, some parapsychologists use sensory deprivation to minimize distractions.

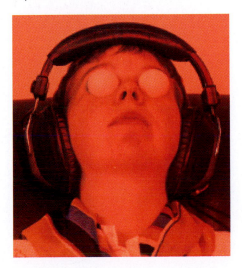

are beyond science. After clearing the decks of tested and rejected pseudomysteries, we can therefore retain a humble sense of wonder regarding life's untestable mysteries.

Why, then, are so many people predisposed to believe that ESP, which *should* be testable by science, exists? In part, such beliefs may stem from understandable misperceptions, misinterpretations, and selective recall. But some people also have an unsatisfied hunger for wonderment, an itch to experience the magical. In Britain and the United States, the founders of parapsychology were mostly people who, having lost their religious faith, began searching for a scientific basis for believing in the meaning of life and life after death (Alcock, 1985; Beloff, 1985). In the upheaval since the collapse of autocratic rule in Russia, there has come an "avalanche of the mystical, occult and pseudoscientific" (Kapitza, 1991). In Russia as elsewhere, "extrasensorial" healers and seers fascinate the awestruck public. "Many people," declared a statement by 32 leading Russian scientists (1999), "believe in clairvoyance, astrology, and other superstitions to compensate for the psychological discomforts of our time."

To feel awe and to gain a deep reverence for life, we do not need to look any further than our own perceptual system and its capacity for organizing formless nerve impulses into colorful sights, vivid sounds, and evocative smells. Within our ordinary perceptual experiences lies much that is truly extraordinary—surely much more than has so far been dreamt of in our psychology. A century of research has revealed many of the secrets of sensation and perception, yet for future generations of researchers there remain profound and genuine mysteries to solve. Between our sensing and acting lies an unimaginably complex information system that, more than ever, beckons explorers of our mind's inner space.

REVIEW AND REFLECT:

Perceptual Interpretation

What does research on sensory deprivation and restored vision reveal about the effects of experience on perception?

For many species, infancy is a critical period during which experience must activate the brain's innate visual mechanisms. If cataract removal restores eyesight to adults who were blind from birth, they remain unable to perceive the world normally. Generally, they can distinguish figure from ground and can perceive colors, but they are unable to recognize shapes and forms. In controlled experiments, animals have been reared with severely restricted visual input. When their visual exposure is returned to normal, they, too, suffer enduring visual handicaps.

What is it like to experience sensory restriction? How can this experience be beneficial?

Experiencing temporary sensory restriction often evokes a heightened awareness of all forms of sensation. Under supervision, sensory restriction may provide a therapeutic boost for seeking control over problems such as smoking.

How adaptable is our ability to perceive the world around us?

Human vision is remarkably adaptable. Given glasses that shift the world slightly to the left or right, or even turn it upside down, people manage to adapt their movements and, with practice, to move about with ease.

How do our assumptions and beliefs shape our interpretations, and thus our perceptions?

Clear evidence that perception is influenced by our experience—our learned assumptions and beliefs—as well as by sensory input comes from the many demonstrations of perceptual set and context effects. The schemas we have learned help us to interpret otherwise ambiguous stimuli, a fact that helps explain why some of us "see" monsters, faces, and UFOs that others do not.

Can we perceive only what we sense? Or, without sensory input, are we capable of extrasensory perception?

Many believe in or claim to experience extrasensory perception (ESP). Parapsychologists have tried to document several forms of ESP—telepathy, clairvoyance, and precognition—but for several reasons, especially the lack of a reproducible ESP effect, most research psychologists remain skeptical. New studies using the ganzfeld procedure raised hopes of a measurable telepathy phenomenon, but most follow-up studies have not supported the phenomenon's reliability.

Terms and Concepts to Remember

perceptual adaptation, p. 226
perceptual set, p. 227
extrasensory perception (ESP), p. 231
parapsychology, p. 231

Test Yourself

16.1. Locke believed that our perception of the world is learned through experience. Support for his view can be found in
   a. the writings of Immanuel Kant.
   b. research on depth perception.
   c. research on perceptual set and context.
   d. theories of color vision.

16.2. In some cases, surgeons have restored vision to patients who have been blind from birth. The newly sighted individuals were able to sense colors but had difficulty
   a. recognizing objects by touch.
   b. recognizing the shapes of objects.
   c. distinguishing figure from ground.
   d. distinguishing between bright and dim light.

16.3. Experiments in which research participants wear glasses that displace or invert their visual fields show that, after a period of disorientation, they learn to function quite well. This ability is called
   a. visual capture.
   b. perceptual set.
   c. sensory restriction.
   d. perceptual adaptation.

16.4. Our perceptual set influences what we perceive. This mental predisposition reflects our
   a. experiences, assumptions, and expectations.
   b. perceptual adaptation.
   c. objectivity, realism, and intelligence.
   d. perceptual constancy.

16.5. About half of British and American adults and Japanese university students believe in ESP (extrasensory perception). The response of psychologists to the claims of ESP has been to
   a. deny the possibility of perception apart from sensation.
   b. doubt the existence of mysteries and extraordinary phenomena.
   c. test and critique ESP claims.
   d. devise a theory that explains why ESP exists.

16.6. The most testable varieties of ESP involve perceiving future events, mind-to-mind communication, and perceiving remote events. In order, these refer to
   a. clairvoyance, telepathy, and precognition.
   b. telepathy, clairvoyance, and precognition.
   c. precognition, telepathy, and clairvoyance.
   d. precognition, clairvoyance, and telepathy.

Review

- What type of evidence shows that, indeed, "there is more to perception than meets the senses"?
- What psychic ability is being claimed by the sports channel in the cartoon on page 236?

Reflect

- Can you recall a time where your expectations have predisposed how you perceived a person (or group of people)?
- What do you think about claims of ESP—and what evidence might confirm or disconfirm your view?

Answers to the Test Yourself and Review questions can be found in the green appendix at the end of the book.

States of Consciousness

Now playing at an inner theater near you: the premiere showing of a sleeping person's vivid dream. This never-before-seen mental movie features captivating characters wrapped in a plot so original and unlikely, yet so intricate and so seemingly real, that the viewer later marvels at its creation.

Waking from a troubling dream, wrenched by its emotions, who among us has not wondered about this weird state of consciousness? How does our brain so creatively, colorfully, and completely construct this alternative, conscious world? In the shadowland between our dreaming and waking consciousness, we may even wonder for a moment which realm represents reality. And what shall we make of other altered states of consciousness—daydreaming, hypnosis, and drug-altered hallucinations?

Module 17 presents a historical view of consciousness, a discussion of various levels and functions of consciousness, and an in-depth look at sleep and dreams.

Module 18 discusses various beliefs about hypnosis, including research support for some of the claims related to hypnosis.

Module 19 details dependence, addiction, and the three main categories of psychoactive drugs.

17 Waking and Sleeping Rhythms

Waking Consciousness

Preview Question: How have psychologists viewed consciousness?

What is consciousness? In every science there are concepts so fundamental they are nearly impossible to define. Biologists agree on what is alive but not on precisely what life is. In physics, matter and energy elude simple definition. To psychologists, consciousness is similarly a fundamental yet slippery concept.

At its beginning, psychology was sometimes defined as "the description and explanation of states of consciousness" (Ladd, 1887). But the difficulty of scientifically studying consciousness led many psychologists during the first half of the twentieth century to turn to direct observations of behavior—an approach favored by an emerging school of psychology called *behaviorism*. By the 1950s, psychology no longer defined itself as the study of consciousness or "mental life" but rather as the science of behavior. Psychology had nearly lost consciousness. Consciousness was viewed as resembling a car's speedometer: "It doesn't make the car go, it just reflects what's happening" (Seligman, 1991, p. 24).

By 1960, mental concepts began to reenter psychology. Advances in neuroscience made it possible to relate brain activity to various mental states—waking, sleeping, dreaming. Researchers began studying consciousness altered by hypnosis and drugs. Psychologists of all persuasions were affirming the importance of mental processes (cognition). Psychology was regaining consciousness.

For most psychologists today, **consciousness** is our awareness of ourselves and our environment. When we learn a complex concept or behavior—say, driving a car—consciousness focuses our concentration on the car and the traffic. This awareness varies with our attentional spotlight. With practice, driving becomes automatic and no longer requires our undivided attention—freeing our consciousness to focus on other things. If I ask you to pay attention to the weight of your body pressing on your buttocks as you sit reading, you will momentarily stop reading.

> "Psychology must discard all reference to consciousness."
>
> **Behaviorist John B. Watson (1913)**

> "Neither [psychologist] Steve Pinker nor I can explain human subjective consciousness. . . . We don't understand it."
>
> **Evolutionary biologist Richard Dawkins (1999)**

Consciousness
Our awareness of ourselves and our environment is but the visible surface of our brain's information processing.

Levels of Information Processing

Preview Question: What are the levels and functions of consciousness?

■ **consciousness** our awareness of ourselves and our environments.

Conscious awareness enables us to exert voluntary control and to communicate our mental states to others, yet consciousness is but the tip of the information-processing iceberg. Research reported throughout this book reveals that we process a great deal of information outside our awareness. We register and react to stimuli we do not consciously perceive. We perform well-learned tasks automatically, as when keyboarding without attending to where the letters are. We change our attitudes and reconstruct our memories with no awareness of doing so.

Beneath the surface, subconscious information processing occurs simultaneously on many parallel tracks. When we look at a flying bird, we are consciously aware of the result of our cognitive processing but not of our subprocessing of the bird's color, form, movement, distance, and identity. When we meet someone, we instantly and unconsciously react to their gender, race, and appearance, and then become aware of our response.

Stephen Kosslyn and Olivier Koenig (1992) suggest that brain events are to consciousness what a guitar's individual notes are to a chord. As a chord emerges from the interaction of different notes, so consciousness emerges from the interaction of individual brain events. As we experience the chord an instant *after* all the notes are present, so consciousness is known to lag the brain events that evoke it (Libet, 1985). (When you lift a finger at will, your brain waves jump about 0.3 seconds ahead of your conscious perception of the decision!)

Unlike the parallel processing of subconscious information, conscious processing takes place in sequence (serially). Consciousness is relatively slow and has limited capacity, but is skilled at solving novel problems. It could be compared to a chief executive, whose many assistants automatically take care of routine business. Consider your hands. When not under conscious control, they have a life of their own, scanning your body for imperfections, grooming, gesturing. Traveling a familiar route, your hands and feet do the driving while your mind engages in conversation. Running on automatic pilot allows consciousness—the mind's CEO—to monitor the whole system and deal with new challenges.

Novel tasks do, however, require our conscious attention. At the wheel for the first time in a country where people drive on the other side of the road, driving will command your full attention. Or try this: If you are right-handed, you can move your right foot in a smooth counterclockwise circle, and you can write the number 3 repeatedly with your right hand—but probably not at the same time. (If you are musically inclined, try something equally difficult: Tap a steady three times with your left hand while tapping four times with your right hand.) Both tasks require conscious attention, which can be in only one place at a time. If time is nature's way of keeping everything from happening at once, then consciousness is nature's way of keeping us from thinking and doing everything at once.

Daydreams and Fantasies

Preview Question: Why do we daydream and fantasize?

In James Thurber's classic story "The Secret Life of Walter Mitty," the bland existence of mild-mannered Walter Mitty is spiced with gratifying fantasies. As he drives past a hospital, Mitty imagines himself as Dr. Mitty, rushing to an operating room where two renowned specialists plead for his help. Again and again, the bumbling Walter Mitty relieves the tedium of his life by imagining himself as the triumphant Walter Mitty—now the world's greatest target shooter, now a heroic pilot.

"This isn't a hasty decision. A lot of daydreaming went into it."

Thurber's story became a classic because most of us can identify with Walter Mitty. From interview and questionnaire studies with hundreds of adults, clinical psychologist Jerome L. Singer (1975) reported that nearly everyone has daydreams or waking fantasies every day—on the job, in the classroom, walking down the street—in fact, almost anywhere at any time. Compared with older adults, young adults spend more time daydreaming and admit to more sexual fantasies (Cameron & Biber, 1973; Giambra, 1974). About 95 percent of both men and women say they have had sexual fantasies. But men (whether gay or straight) fantasize about sex more often, more physically, and less romantically—and these tendencies influence their preferences for books and videos (Leitenberg & Henning, 1995). Sexual fantasies do *not* indicate sexual problems or dissatisfaction. (If anything, sexually active and satisfied people have more sexual fantasies.)

Not all daydreaming is as overtly escapist or dramatic as Walter Mitty's. Mostly it involves the familiar details of our lives—perhaps imagining an alternative approach to something we have to do, or picturing ourselves explaining to an instructor why a paper will be late, or replaying in our minds personal encounters that we relish or wish had gone differently.

Some individuals—perhaps 4 percent of the population—fantasize so vividly they are said to have **fantasy-prone personalities**. One study of 26 women in this category found that as children they had enjoyed unusually intense make-believe play with their dolls, stuffed animals, or imaginary companions (Wilson & Barber, 1983). As adults, they reported spending more than half their time fantasizing. They would relive experiences or imagine scenes so vividly that occasionally they would later have trouble sorting out their remembered fantasies from their memories of actual events. When watching or imagining violent or frightening scenes, they sometimes even felt ill. Three-fourths had experienced orgasms solely by sexual fantasy. Many reported profound mystical or religious experiences.

Although few daydream this intensively, we all daydream. Are the hours we spend in fantasy a way of escaping rather than facing reality? Sometimes. But daydreaming can also be adaptive. Some daydreams help us prepare for future events by keeping us aware of our unfinished business and giving us the chance to mentally rehearse. Playful fantasies enhance the creativity of scientists, writers, and artists. For children, daydreaming in the form of imaginative play nourishes social and cognitive development—a fact that makes the diversion of watching television a concern to some developmental psychologists (Singer, 1986). "When I examined myself, and my methods of thought, I came to the conclusion that the gift of fantasy has meant more to me than my talent for absorbing positive knowledge" (Albert Einstein, 1879–1955).

Daydreams may also substitute for impulsive behavior. People who are prone to delinquency and violence or who seek the artificial highs of dangerous drugs have fewer vivid fantasies (Singer, 1976). Perhaps Walter Mitty's imaginative reveries not only rescued him from boredom but also allowed him to indulge his impulses within the safety of his inner world.

Looking into the inner world
Daydreams and fantasies are a constructive part of everyone's repertoire of behaviors. For these Dutch commuters, daydreams may release tension, increase creativity, illuminate solutions to problems—and even lessen boredom.

"The art of living requires us to steer a course between the two extremes of external and internal stimulation."

Psychologist Jerome L. Singer (1976)

Sleep and Dreams

Sleep—the irresistible tempter to whom we must all succumb. Sleep—the mantle that covers human thought. Sleep—sweet, renewing, mysterious sleep. Sleep's age-old mysteries have intrigued us for centuries. Now, some of these mysteries are being solved. In laboratories throughout the world, thousands have slept attached to recording devices while others observe. By recording sleepers' brain waves and muscle movements, by observing and waking them from time to time, the sleep watchers glimpse things that a thousand years of common sense never told us. Perhaps you can anticipate some of their discoveries. Are the following statements true or false?

1. When people dream of performing some activity, their limbs often move in concert with the dream (page 249).
2. Older adults sleep more than young adults (Figure 17.8, page 257).
3. Sleepwalkers are acting out their dreams (page 247).
4. Sleep experts recommend treating insomnia with an occasional sleeping pill (page 253).
5. Some people dream every night; others seldom dream (page 249).

All these statements (adapted from Palladino & Carducci, 1983) are false. Let's see why.

> "I love to sleep. Do you? Isn't it great? It really is the best of both worlds. You get to be alive and unconscious."
>
> Comedian Rita Rudner, 1993

Biological Rhythms

Preview Question: How do our age-old biological rhythms influence our daily functioning and our sleep and dreams?

Like the ocean, life has its rhythmic tides. Over varying periods of time, our bodies fluctuate, and with them our minds. These **biological rhythms**, controlled by internal "biological clocks," include

- *annual cycles*: On an annual cycle, geese migrate, grizzly bears hibernate, and humans may experience seasonal variations in appetite, sleep length, and moods. For some people, especially in far northern regions, a depressed mood during winter's dark months may define a *seasonal affective disorder*.
- *twenty-eight-day cycles*: The female menstrual cycle averages 28 days. Does that cycle cause fluctuating moods? Many believe it indeed does, but some research psychologists are skeptical (see "Thinking Critically About PMS," page 244).
- *twenty-four-hour cycles*: Humans experience 24-hour cycles of varying and falling alertness, body temperature, and growth hormone secretion.
- *ninety-minute cycles*: We cycle through various stages of sleep.

The Rhythm of Sleep

Let's look more closely at two of those biological rhythms—our 24-hour biological clock and our 90-minute sleep cycle.

Circadian Rhythm

The rhythm of the day parallels the rhythm of life—from our waking to a new day's birth to our nightly return to what Shakespeare called "death's counterfeit." Our bodies roughly synchronize with the 24-hour cycle of day and night through a biological clock called the **circadian rhythm** (from the Latin *circa*, "about," and *dies*, "day"). Our body temperature, for example, rises as morning approaches, peaks during the day, dips for a time in early afternoon (when many people take siestas), and then begins to drop again before we go to sleep. Awake at 4:00 A.M., with a depressed body, we may fret over concerns: Does a lovers' spat signal a split? Does a child's

- **fantasy-prone personality** someone who imagines and recalls experiences with lifelike vividness and who spends considerable time fantasizing.

- **biological rhythms** periodic physiological fluctuations.

- **circadian rhythm** [ser-KAY-dee-an] the biological clock; regular bodily rhythms (for example, of temperature and wakefulness) that occur on a 24-hour cycle.

THINKING CRITICALLY ABOUT :

PMS

Are menstruating women more depressed, tense, and irritable during the two or three days before menstruation begins? People tend to notice and remember instances that confirm their beliefs and not to notice instances that contradict them. That, researchers Pamela Kato and Diane Ruble (1992) have maintained, helps explain why a woman who feels tense the day before the onset of her period may attribute the tension to her being premenstrual—the so-called premenstrual syndrome (PMS). But if the woman feels similarly tense a week later or does not feel tense the day her next period is about to start, she may be less likely to notice and remember these disconfirming instances.

Many researchers now believe that some women do indeed experience not only menstrual discomfort but also premenstrual tension (Hurt & others, 1992; Richardson, 1990). Thus, the American Psychiatric Association recognizes a severe form of PMS (called premenstrual dysphoric disorder). They do so despite objections from the American Psychological Association and from the Psychiatric Association's Committee on Women, which maintain that women's menstrual cycle problems should not be pathologized as a psychiatric disorder (DeAngelis, 1993).

Although many women *recall* feeling out of sorts just before their last period, their own day-to-day self-reports often reveal little emotional fluctuation across the menstrual cycle (FIGURE 17.1). In one study, those who reported severe premenstrual symptoms differed only slightly from other women in actual day-to-day reports throughout their menstrual cycles (Gallant & others, 1992). And contrary to the presumptions of some employers, women's physical and mental skills do not fluctuate noticeably with their menstrual cycles. Leta Hollingworth discovered this in her 1914 doctoral dissertation (using women's daily reports rather than their recollections), and many others since then have confirmed her finding (Choi, 1999; Sommer, 1992).

Moreover, PMS complaints vary with culture but not with any known biological differences among women. For most PMS patients, inactive placebos provide as much relief as actual drugs. All this is just what one would expect from a socially constructed disorder, say critics (Richardson, 1993; Rodin, 1992; Usher, 1992). With so many everyday symptoms on PMS checklists—lethargy, sadness, irritability, headaches, insomnia (or sleepiness), disinterest in sex (or heightened interest in sex)—"who wouldn't have 'PMS'?" asks Carol Tavris (1992). ■

FIGURE 17.1

Menstruation, actual mood, and perceived mood
Cathy McFarland and her colleagues (1989) found that Ontario women's daily mood reports did not vary across their menstrual cycle. Yet they *perceived* that their moods were generally worse just before and after menstruation and better at other times of the cycle.

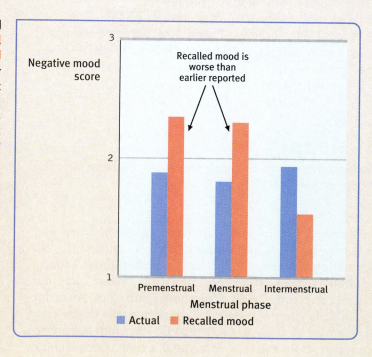

"When a man can't explain a woman's actions, the first thing he thinks about is the condition of her uterus."

Clare Boothe Luce, *Slam the Door Softly*, 1970

moodiness mean more trouble ahead? By midday, our body energized, we fret less. Pulling an all-nighter, we feel groggiest about 4:00 A.M., but we feel a second wind as our normal wake-up time arrives.

Recent evidence suggests that thinking is sharpest and memory most accurate when people are at their daily peak in circadian arousal. Some of us are morning-loving "larks," others evening-energized "owls." With age, we tend to shift from being owls to larks. Most university students are "evening persons," report Cynthia May and Lynne Hasher (1997). Their performance typically improves across the day. Most older adults are "morning persons," with their performance declining as the day wears on. In retirement homes, all is quiet by mid-evening; in university dorms, the day is far from over.

A transcontinental flight disrupts our circadian rhythm and we experience jet lag, mainly because we are awake when our circadian rhythm cries, "Sleep!" Studies in the laboratory and with shift workers reveal that bright light helps reset our biological clocks (Czeisler & others, 1986, 1989; Eastman & others, 1995). Thus, to speed the resetting of your biological clock after a long flight, spend the first day outdoors. Bright light in the morning facilitates awakening (and protects against depression). Bright light at night helps delay sleep (Oren & Terman, 1998).

Light tweaks the circadian clock as light-sensitive retinal proteins trigger signals to a brain region that controls the circadian clock (Miyamoto & Sancar, 1998). How then shall we explain the recent finding that our circadian clock can be manipulated by light administered to (I am not making this up) the back of the knee? In one experiment, researchers Scott Campbell and Patricia Murphy (1998), divided Cornell University volunteers into two groups. One group received light through a covered knee pad for varying 3-hour periods from midnight to noon. The other group wore the knee pads but received no light at all. (The volunteers were unaware which condition they were in.) Two nights later, those treated with light found that the dip in their body temperature had shifted by up to 3 hours. Those who received no light experienced no significant changes in their body rhythms.

Obviously, replication is needed before we start dreaming of administering light treatments to the skin of shift workers, jet setters, wintertime-depressed people, or insomniacs. But it could happen; the skin contains some of the same light-sensitive proteins that actuate the retina's messages to the brain's circadian clock.

There is a heartening lesson about science here, one that reminds us that science does not merely express our preconceived ideas. When our presumptions collide with observation, our presumptions need to change. Nature, even human nature, sometimes surprises us. As Agatha Christie's Miss Marple explained, "It wasn't what I expected. But facts are facts, and if one is proved to be wrong, one must just be humble about it and start again."

We can also reset our biological clocks by adjusting our sleep schedules. If we stay up late and sleep in on weekends, we may end up with "Sunday night insomnia" and "Monday morning blues." Those who sleep till noon on Sunday and then go to bed just 11 hours later in preparation for the new workweek often find sleep elusive. They are like New Yorkers whose biology is on California time, or like someone who has just flown east from Perth to Sydney.

Curiously—given that our ancestors' body clocks were attuned to the rising and setting sun of the 24-hour day—young adults isolated without clocks or daylight typically adopt a 25-hour day. For this, we can thank (or blame) Thomas Edison, inventor of the light bulb. Being bathed in light, even in a cave, is like traveling one time zone west—it nudges our 24-hour biological clock back (Czeisler & others, 1999; Dement, 1999). This helps explain why rotating shift workers adapt better to progressively later shifts than to earlier ones, and why until our later years we must discipline ourselves to get to bed on time and force ourselves to get up. Most animals, too, when placed under unnatural constant illumination, exceed a 24-hour day. Artificial light delays sleep.

If our natural circadian rhythm were attuned to a 23-hour cycle, would we instead need to discipline ourselves to stay up later at night and sleep in longer in the morning? Do older adults, who typically prefer an earlier waking and bedtime than university students, have a shorter circadian rhythm?

- **REM sleep** rapid eye movement sleep, a recurring sleep stage during which vivid dreams commonly occur. Also known as *paradoxical sleep* because the muscles are relaxed (except for minor twitches) but other body systems are active.

- **alpha waves** the relatively slow brain waves of a relaxed, awake state.

- **sleep** periodic, natural, reversible loss of consciousness—as distinct from unconsciousness resulting from a coma, general anesthesia, or hibernation (after Dement, 1999).

Sleep Stages

There is also a biological rhythm during our sleep. About every 90 or 100 minutes we pass through a cycle of five distinct sleep stages. This elementary fact was unknown until 8-year-old Armond Aserinsky went to bed one night in 1952. His father, Eugene, a University of Chicago graduate student, needed to test an electroencephalograph he had been repairing during the day (Aserinsky, 1988; Seligman & Yellen, 1987). He placed electrodes near Armond's eyes to record the rolling eye movements believed to occur during sleep. Before long, the machine went wild, tracing deep zigzags on the graph paper. Aserinsky thought the machine was still broken. But as the night proceeded, the activity periodically recurred, indicating, Aserinsky finally realized, fast, jerky eye movements accompanied by energetic brain activity. When he awakened Armond during one such episode, the boy reported he was having a dream. Aserinsky had discovered what we now know as **REM sleep** (rapid *eye movement* sleep).

To find out if similar cycles occur during adult sleep, Nathaniel Kleitman (1960) and Aserinsky pioneered procedures that have now been used with thousands of volunteers. To appreciate both their methods and findings, imagine yourself as a participant. As the hour grows late, you begin to fight sleepiness and yawn in response to reduced brain metabolism. Yawning stretches your neck muscles and increases your heart rate, thus increasing the bloodflow to your brain and your alertness (Moorcroft, 1993). When you are ready for bed, the researcher glues electrodes to your scalp (to detect your brain waves), just outside the corners of your eyes (to detect eye movements), and on your chin (to detect muscle tension) (**FIGURE 17.2**). Other devices allow the researcher to record your heart rate, your respiration rate, and the degree of your genital arousal.

When you are in bed with your eyes closed, the researcher in the next room sees on the EEG the relatively slow **alpha waves** of your awake but relaxed state (**FIGURE 17.3**). As you adapt to all this equipment and grow tired, you slip into **sleep**. Sleep is a state that we do not know we are in until we leave it. Our dive into sleep—marked by the slowed breathing and the irregular brain waves of Stage 1—happens in an unrecognized moment (**FIGURE 17.4**).

Sleep researcher William Dement (1999) observed the moment the perceptual door between the brain and outside world slammed shut in one of his 15,000 sub-

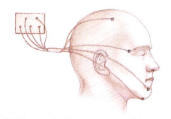
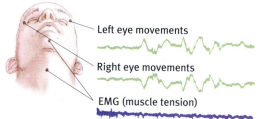
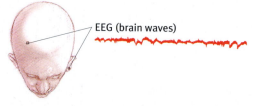

Left eye movements
Right eye movements
EMG (muscle tension)
EEG (brain waves)

FIGURE 17.2
Measuring sleep activity
Sleep researchers measure brain-wave activity, eye movements, and muscle tension by electrodes that pick up weak electrical signals from the brain, eye, and facial muscles.

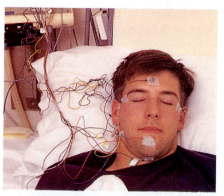

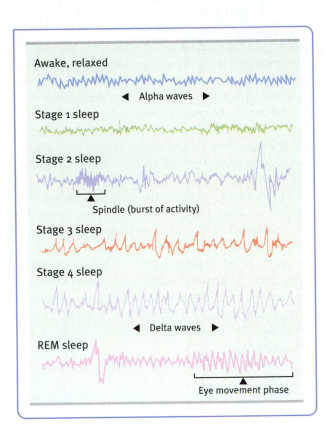

FIGURE 17.3

Brain waves and sleep stages

The regular alpha waves of an awake, relaxed stage are quite different from the slower, larger delta waves of deep Stage 4 sleep. Although the rapid REM sleep waves resemble the near-waking Stage 1 sleep waves, the body is more aroused during REM sleep than during Stage 1 sleep

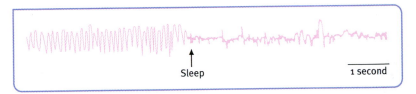

FIGURE 17.4

The moment of sleep

We seem unaware of the moment we fall into sleep, but someone eavesdropping on our brain waves could tell (from Dement, 1999).

jects. Dement asked this sleep-deprived young man, lying on his back with eyelids taped open, to press a button every time a strobe light flashed in his eyes (averaging about every 6 seconds). After a few minutes the subject missed one. Asked why, he said "because there was no flash." But there was a flash—which he missed because (his brain activity revealed) he had fallen asleep for two seconds. Unaware that he had done so, he had missed not only the flash 6 inches from his nose but also the abrupt moment of his entry into sleep.

During this light Stage 1 sleep, which lasts up to 5 minutes, you may experience fantastic images, resembling **hallucinations**—sensory experiences that occur without a sensory stimulus. You may have a sensation of falling (at which moment your body may suddenly jerk) or of floating weightlessly. Such "hypnogogic" sensations may later become incorporated into memories. People who claim to have been abducted by aliens—often shortly after getting in bed—commonly recall being floated off their beds.

Soon, you relax more deeply and begin about 20 minutes of Stage 2 sleep, characterized by the periodic appearance of *sleep spindles*—bursts of rapid, rhythmic brainwave activity. Although you can still be awakened without too much difficulty during this phase, you are now clearly asleep. Sleeptalking—usually garbled or nonsensical—can occur during this or any other sleep stage (Mahowald & Ettinger, 1990).

Then for the next few minutes you go through the transitional Stage 3 to the deep sleep of Stage 4. First in Stage 3, and increasingly in Stage 4, your brain emits large, slow **delta waves**. These stages together are called *slow-wave sleep*. They last for about 30 minutes, during which you are hard to awaken. Curiously, it is at the end of the deep sleep of Stage 4 that children may wet the bed or begin walking in their sleep. About 20 percent of 3- to 12-year-olds have at least one episode of sleepwalking, usually lasting 2 to 10 minutes; some 5 percent have repeated episodes (Giles & others, 1994).

Can you recall the moment you fell asleep last night? Or, at best, your last moments of waking?

■ **hallucinations** false sensory experiences, such as seeing something in the absence of an external visual stimulus.

■ **delta waves** the large, slow brain waves associated with deep sleep.

Even when you are deeply asleep, your brain somehow processes the meaning of certain stimuli. You move around on your bed, but you manage not to fall out of it. If you sleep with your babies, you will not roll over and suffocate them (assuming you are not intoxicated). The occasional roar of passing vehicles may leave deep sleep undisturbed, but the cry from a baby's nursery quickly interrupts it. So does the sound of your name—a stimulus our selective attention is ever alert for. EEG recordings confirm that the brain's auditory cortex responds to sound stimuli even during sleep (Kutas, 1990). All this reminds us of one of this book's basic lessons: *We process most information outside of conscious awareness.*

About an hour after you first fall asleep, a strange thing happens. Rather than continuing in deep slumber, you ascend from your initial sleep dive. Returning through Stage 3 and Stage 2 (where you spend about half your night), you enter the most intriguing sleep phase of all—REM sleep (**FIGURE 17.5**). For about 10 minutes, your brain waves become rapid and saw-toothed, more like those of the nearly awake Stage 1 sleep. But unlike Stage 1 sleep, REM sleep is a time when your heart rate rises, your breathing becomes rapid and irregular, and every half minute or so your eyes dart around in a momentary burst of activity behind closed lids. Because anyone watching a sleeper's eyes can notice these REM bursts, it is amazing that science was ignorant of REM sleep until 1952.

Curiously, small animals have shorter sleep cycles (rats, 10 minutes) than big animals (elephants, 100+ minutes) (Hobson, 1989).

FIGURE 17.5
The stages in a typical night's sleep
Most people pass through the five-stage sleep cycle several times, with the periods of Stage 4 sleep and then Stage 3 sleep diminishing and REM sleep periods increasing in duration. The second graph plots this increasing REM sleep and decreasing deep sleep based on data from 30 young adults.

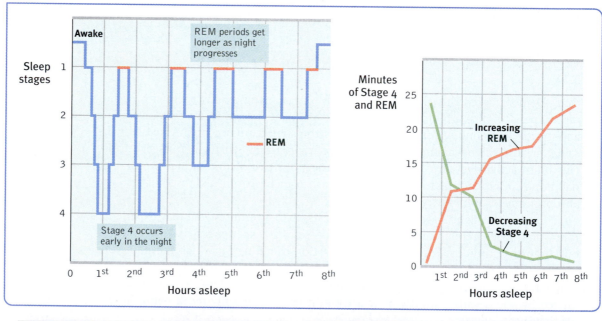

During REM sleep, your genitals become aroused and you have an erection or increased vaginal lubrication and clitoral engorgement. For example, the common "morning erection" stems from the night's last REM period, often just before waking. Except during very scary dreams, genital arousal always occurs, regardless of whether the dream's content is sexual (Karacan & others, 1966). The phenomenon has been studied mostly in men, from whom measurements are more easily recorded. In young men, sleep-related erections outlast REM periods, lasting 30 to 45 minutes on average (Karacan & others, 1983; Schiavi & Schreiner-Engel, 1988). A typical 25-year-old man therefore has an erection during nearly half his night's sleep, a 65-year-old man for one-quarter. Many men troubled by "erectile disorder" (impotence) have morning erections, suggesting that the problem is not between their legs.

Although your brain's motor cortex is active during REM sleep, your brainstem blocks its messages, leaving your muscles relaxed—so relaxed that, except for an occasional finger, toe, or facial twitch, you are essentially paralyzed. Moreover, you cannot easily be awakened. Thus, REM sleep is sometimes called *paradoxical* sleep; internally the body is aroused while externally it appears calm.

Even more intriguing than the paradoxical nature of REM sleep is what the rapid eye movements announce: the beginning of a dream. Even those who claim they never dream will, more than 80 percent of the time, recall a dream after being awakened during REM sleep. Unlike the fleeting images of Stage 1 sleep, REM sleep dreams are often emotional and usually storylike—but never acted out, thanks to REM's protective paralysis. (People occasionally recall dreams when awakened from stages other than REM sleep, but these dreams usually contain a single vague image, such as, "I was trying to borrow something from someone.")

Are the eye movements linked to a dream's visual aspects? Is the dreamer "watching" the dream as if it were a private movie projected in the mind's inner theater? Most researchers believe that is not the case: Darting eyes, like the occasional twitching of muscles, may merely reflect the overflow of the dreamer's active nervous system (Chase & Morales, 1983).

The sleep cycle repeats itself about every 90 minutes. As the night wears on, deep Stage 4 sleep gets progressively briefer and then disappears. The REM sleep period gets longer. By morning, 20 to 25 percent of our average night's sleep—some 100 minutes—has been REM sleep. This means that those who say, "I rarely dream" actually spend about 600 hours a year experiencing some 1500 dreams, or more than 100,000 dreams over a typical lifetime—dreams swallowed by the night.

© 1994 by Sidney Harris.

"Boy are my eyes tired! I had REM sleep all night long."

People rarely snore during dreams. When REM starts, snoring stops.

Some sleep deeply, some not
The fluctuating sleep cycle enables safe sleep for these soldiers on the battlefield. One benefit of communal sleeping is that someone will probably be awake or easily roused in the event of a threat during the night.

The Riddle of Sleep

Preview Question: Why must we sleep?

The idea that "everyone needs 8 hours of sleep" is not true. Newborns spend nearly two-thirds of their day asleep, most adults no more than one-third. Age-related differences in average time spent sleeping are rivaled by differences in the normal amount of sleep among individuals at any age. Some people thrive with fewer than 6 hours of sleep per night; others regularly sleep 9 hours or more. Sleep patterns may be genetically influenced. When Wilse Webb and Scott Campbell (1983) checked the pattern and duration of sleep among fraternal and identical twins, only the identical twins were strikingly similar.

Allowed to sleep unhindered, most humans will sleep 9 to 10 hours a night, reports Stanley Coren (1996). With that much sleep, we do not become groggy. We awake refreshed, sustain better moods, and perform more efficient and accurate work than do those who get less sleep. With a succession of 5-hour nights, however, we accumulate sleep debt that is not paid off by one 10-hour sleep—which explains why we can feel sleepy even after a long sleep. "The brain keeps an accurate count of sleep debt for at least two weeks," says William Dement (1999, p. 64). Deprived of sleep, we also begin to feel terrible, as our bodies yearn for sleep.

Obviously, then, we need sleep. Sleep commands roughly one-third of our lives—some 25 years, on average. But why? It seems an easy question to answer: Just keep people awake for several days and note how they deteriorate. If you were a volunteer in such an experiment, how do you think it would affect your body and mind?

Of course, you would become terribly drowsy at times—especially during the hours when your biological clock programs you to sleep. But could a lack of sleep physically damage you? Would it noticeably alter your biochemistry or body organs? Would you become emotionally disturbed? Intellectually disoriented?

Because of modern light bulbs, shift work, and social diversions, people in industrialized nations are able to sleep less than they did a century ago. People who a century ago would have gone to bed at 9:00 P.M. are now up until 11:00 P.M. Thomas Edison (1948, pp. 52, 178) was pleased to accept credit for this. For him, lost sleep meant more time and opportunity.

> When I went through Switzerland in a motor-car, so that I could visit little towns and villages, I noted the effect of artificial light on the inhabitants. Where water power and electric light had been developed, everyone seemed normally intelligent. When these appliances did not exist, and the natives went to bed with the chickens, staying there till daylight, they were far less intelligent.

Actually, a major effect of lessened sleep is not only sleepiness but a general malaise (Mikulincer & others, 1989). People today more than ever suffer from sleep patterns that thwart their having an energized feeling of well-being. Teenagers typically need 8 or 9 hours sleep, but they now average nearly 2 hours less sleep a night than their counterparts of 80 years ago (Holden, 1993; Maas, 1999). Many fill this need by using their first class for an early siesta and after-lunch study hall for a slumber party. Even when awake, they often function below their peak.

At Stanford University, William Dement (1997) reports, 80 percent of students are "dangerously sleep deprived." Those individuals "are at high risk for some sort of accident. . . . Sleep

---

1993 Time/CNN poll: "How many hours do you sleep each night?"

Under six	12%
Six	26
Seven	30
Eight	28
Over eight	3

In 1989, Michael Doucette was named America's Safest Driving Teen. In 1990, while driving home from college, he fell asleep at the wheel and collided with an oncoming car, killing both himself and the other driver. Michael's driving instructor later acknowledged never having mentioned sleep deprivation and drowsy driving (Dement, 1999).

A few of the unanswered questions about sleep: Why do we sleep more when we are young? Why do some animals sleep most of the day, others not at all? Why, when REM sleep paralyzes our muscles, do we twitch and jerk? Most important, what is sleep's function? (Adapted from UCLA Brain Research Institute, 1989.)

Sleepless and suffering
This fatigued, sleep-deprived person may also experience a depressed immune system, impaired concentration, and greater vulnerability to accidents.

deprivation [entails] difficulty studying, diminished productivity, tendency to make mistakes, irritability, fatigue." A large sleep debt "makes you stupid," says William Dement (1999, p. 231). But let's put this positively: To manage your life with enough sleep to awaken naturally and well rested is to be more alert, productive, healthy, and happy.

In experiments, the U.S. Navy and the National Institutes of Health have paid volunteers to spend 14 hours daily in bed for at least a week. For the first few days, the volunteers in both experiments averaged 12 hours sleep a day or more, apparently paying off a sleep debt that averaged 25 to 30 hours. That accomplished, they then settled back to 7.5 to 9 hours sleep a night and, with no sleep debt, felt energized and happier. "What this means to me," reflects Dement (1999, p. 72) "is that millions of us are living a less than optimal life and performing at a less than optimal level, impaired by an amount of sleep debt that we're not even aware we carry."

As a demonstration of the costs of widespread sleep deprivation among today's adolescents and adults, Stanley Coren capitalized on a naturally occurring experiment that manipulates sleep length—the "spring forward" to daylight time and "fall backward" to standard time. Searching millions of records, he found that in both Canada and the United States, accidents increase immediately after the shortened sleep associated with the spring time change. In Canada, for example, traffic accidents during 1991 and 1992 were 7 percent higher the Monday after the spring time change than on the Monday before, and they were 7 percent *lower* on the Monday following the extra sleep bestowed by the fall time change (**FIGURE 17.6**).

Similar effects were seen in accident patterns in the United States, but with less dramatic decreases in the fall. U.S. traffic deaths from 1986 through 1995 on the Monday after the spring shift were 17 percent higher than on the Monday before, but only 3 percent lower on the Monday following the fall shift. From 1986 to 1988 there was also a 7 percent increase in other forms of accidental deaths on the sleepy Monday after the spring shift, and only a 2 percent decrease in the fall. Coren (1998) speculates that we lose more sleep at the spring shift than we gain in the fall.

Sleep deprivation can also be devastating for driving and piloting. Some 30 percent of Australian highway deaths occur when drivers fall asleep on long, monotonous roads (Maas, 1999). "Rest. That's what I need is rest," said Eastern Airlines Captain James Reeves to the control tower on a September 1974 morning—30 minutes before crashing his airliner at low altitude, killing the crew and all 68 passengers (Moorcroft, 1993). Consider also the *Exxon Valdez* oil spill; Union Carbide's Bhopal,

"Tiger Woods said that one of the best things about his choice to leave Stanford for the professional golf circuit was that he could now get enough sleep."

Stanford sleep researcher William Dement, "What All Undergraduates Should Know About How Their Sleeping Lives Affect Their Waking Lives," 1997

To test whether you are one of the many sleep-deprived students, see Table 17.1, page 252.

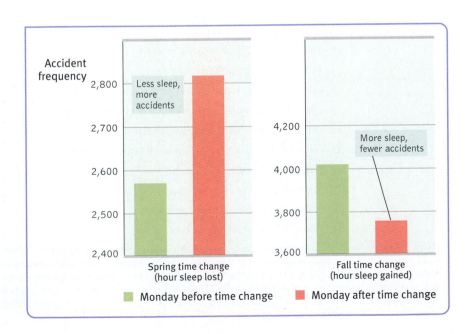

FIGURE 17.6
Canadian traffic accidents, 1991 and 1992
The Monday after the spring time change, when people lose sleep, accidents increased as compared with the Monday before. After the fall time change, they dropped.

"Drowsiness is red alert!"

William Dement, *The Promise of Sleep*, 1999

"The lion and the lamb shall lie down together, but the lamb will not be very sleepy."

Woody Allen, in the movie *Love and Death*, 1975

India, disaster; and the Three Mile Island and Chernobyl nuclear accidents—they all occurred after midnight, when operators in charge were likely to be drowsiest. Severely sleep-deprived, the *Exxon Valdez* mate at the helm was unresponsive to clear signals to turn his vessel back into the shipping lanes.

Other effects of sleep loss are subtle. One such effect is suppression of the disease-fighting immune system (Irwin & others, 1994; Beardsley, 1996). In rats, sleep deprivation increases the pathogens normally suppressed by the immune system. In humans, sleep deprivation suppresses immune cells that fight off viral infections and cancer, which helps explain why people who sleep 8 hours a night tend to outlive those chronically sleep-deprived (Dement, 1999). When infections do set in, we typically sleep more, boosting our immune cells. Chronic sleep debt also alters metabolic and hormonal functioning in ways that mimic aging and are conducive to obesity, hypertension, and memory impairment (Spiegel & others, 1999). Other effects include impaired creativity and concentration, slight hand tremors, irritability, slowed performance, and occasional misperceptions on monotonous tasks (Horne, 1989; Koslowsky & Babkoff, 1992).

Why, then, do we sleep? We have very few answers, but sleep may have evolved for at least two reasons: First, it suits our ecological niche. When darkness precluded our ancestors' hunting and food gathering and made travel treacherous, they were better off asleep in a cave, out of harm's way. Sleep *protects*. Animals with the most need to graze and the least ability to hide tend to sleep less. Elephants and horses sleep 3 to 4 hours a day, gorillas 12 hours, cats 15 hours, and bats 20 hours.

TABLE 17.1

ARE YOU SLEEP DEPRIVED?

Cornell University psychologist James Maas reports that most college students suffer the consequences of sleeping less than they should. To see if you are in that group, answer the following true-false questions:

True	False	
☐	☐	1. I need an alarm clock in order to wake up at the appropriate time.
☐	☐	2. It's a struggle for me to get out of bed in the morning.
☐	☐	3. Weekday mornings I hit the snooze bar several times to get more sleep.
☐	☐	4. I feel tired, irritable, and stressed out during the week.
☐	☐	5. I have trouble concentrating and remembering.
☐	☐	6. I feel slow with critical thinking, problem solving, and being creative.
☐	☐	7. I often fall asleep watching TV.
☐	☐	8. I often fall asleep in boring meetings or lectures or in warm rooms.
☐	☐	9. I often fall asleep after heavy meals or after a low dose of alcohol.
☐	☐	10. I often fall asleep while relaxing after dinner.
☐	☐	11. I often fall asleep within five minutes of getting into bed.
☐	☐	12. I often feel drowsy while driving.
☐	☐	13. I often sleep extra hours on weekend mornings.
☐	☐	14. I often need a nap to get through the day.
☐	☐	15. I have dark circles around my eyes.

If you answered "true" to three or more items, you probably are not getting enough sleep. To determine your sleep needs, Maas recommends that you "go to bed 15 minutes earlier than usual every night for the next week—and continue this practice by adding 15 more minutes each week—until you wake without an alarm clock and feel alert all day." (Quiz reprinted with permission from James B. Maas, *Power sleep: The revolutionary program that prepares your mind and body for peak performance* [New York: Harper Collins, 1999].)

Second, sleep helps us recuperate. It helps *restore* body tissues, especially those of the brain. During the time we are awake our active brain produces the chemical adenosine, which inhibits certain neurons, making us sleepy. (Caffeine blocks adenosine's activity.) During sleep, adenosine concentration declines (Porkka-Heiskanen & others, 1997). As we sleep, our brain is nevertheless active, repairing and reorganizing itself and consolidating memories.

Sleep may also play a role in the *growth* process. During deep sleep, the pituitary gland releases a growth hormone. As adults grow older, they release less of this hormone, and they spend less time in deep sleep (Pekkanen, 1982). These physiological discoveries are only beginning to solve the ongoing riddle of sleep.

Sleep Disorders

No matter what their normal need for sleep is, some 10 to 15 percent of adults complain of **insomnia**—persistent problems in falling or staying asleep. True insomnia is not the occasional inability to sleep that we experience when anxious or excited. For any stressed organism, being vigilant is natural and adaptive. Moreover, from middle age on, sleep is seldom uninterrupted. Being occasionally awakened becomes the norm, not something to fret over or treat with medication.

Some people fret unnecessarily about their sleep (Coren, 1996). In laboratory studies, insomnia complainers do get less sleep than others, but they typically overestimate—by about double—how long it took them to fall asleep. They also underestimate by nearly half how long they actually slept. Even if we have been awake only an hour or two, we may *think* we have had very little sleep, because it's the waking part we remember. When researchers awaken people repeatedly during the night, some recall having slept soundly.

The most common quick fixes for true insomnia, sleeping pills and alcohol, can aggravate the problem. Both reduce REM sleep and can leave a person with next-day blahs. Relying on such, one comes to need bigger doses to get an effect. Then when the drug is discontinued, the insomnia can worsen. Scientists are searching for natural chemicals that are abundant during sleep, hoping they might be synthesized as sleep aids without side effects. In the meantime, sleep experts offer other natural alternatives:

- Relax before bedtime, using dimmer light.
- Avoid caffeine (this includes chocolate) after late afternoon and avoid rich foods before bedtime. A glass of milk may help. (Milk provides raw materials for the manufacture of serotonin, a neurotransmitter that facilitates sleep.)
- Sleep on a regular schedule (rise at the same time even after a restless night) and avoid naps. A regular sleep schedule boosts daytime alertness, too, as shown in a recent experiment in which University of Arizona students slept 7.5 hours a night on either a varying or consistent schedule (Manber & others, 1996).
- Exercise regularly but not in the late evening (late afternoon is best).
- Reassure yourself that the temporary loss of sleep causes no great harm, certainly nothing worth losing sleep over. "Sleep is like love or happiness," notes Wilse Webb (1992, p. 170). "If you pursue it too ardently it will elude you."
- If nothing else works, aim for less sleep; go to bed later or get up earlier.

Rarer but also more severe than insomnia are the sleep disorders narcolepsy and sleep apnea. People who suffer **narcolepsy** (from *narco*, "numbness," and *lepsy*, "seizure") experience periodic, overwhelming sleepiness. This usually lasts less than 5 minutes, but sometimes occurs at the most inopportune times, perhaps just after taking a terrific swing at a softball or when laughing loudly, shouting angrily, or having sex (Dement, 1978, 1999). In severe cases, the person may collapse directly into a brief period of REM sleep, with its accompanying loss of muscular tension.

■ **insomnia** recurring problems in falling or staying asleep.

■ **narcolepsy** a sleep disorder characterized by uncontrollable sleep attacks. The sufferer may lapse directly into REM sleep, often at inopportune times.

"Sleep faster, we need the pillows."

Yiddish proverb

"In 1757 Benjamin Franklin gave us the axiom, 'Early to bed, early to rise, makes a man healthy, wealthy, and wise.' It would be more accurate to say 'consistently to bed and consistently to rise. . .'"

James B. Maas (1999)

Imagine observing a person with narcolepsy in medieval times. Might such symptoms and their associated hallucinations have seemed like demon possession?

■ **sleep apnea** a sleep disorder characterized by temporary cessations of breathing during sleep and consequent momentary reawakenings.

■ **night terrors** a sleep disorder characterized by high arousal and an appearance of being terrified; unlike nightmares, night terrors occur during Stage 4 sleep, within 2 or 3 hours of falling asleep, and are seldom remembered.

■ **dream** a sequence of images, emotions, and thoughts passing through a sleeping person's mind. Dreams are notable for their hallucinatory imagery, discontinuities, and incongruities, and for the dreamer's delusional acceptance of the content and later difficulties remembering it.

■ **manifest content** according to Freud, the remembered story line of a dream (as distinct from its latent content).

Those who suffer from narcolepsy—1 in 2000 people, estimates the Stanford University Center for Narcolepsy (1996)—must live with extra caution. As a traffic menace, "snoozing is second only to boozing," says the American Sleep Disorders Association, and those with narcolepsy are especially at risk (Aldrich, 1989). At the century's end, researchers discovered a gene causing narcolepsy in dogs (Lin & others, 1999). Physicians also began prescribing a new drug, Modafinil, to relieve narcolepsy's sleepiness in humans.

The National Heart, Lung, and Blood Institute reports that 1 in 25 people (mostly overweight men) suffer from **sleep apnea**—a disorder that was unknown before modern sleep research. They intermittently stop breathing during sleep. (*Apnea* means "stopping respiration.") After an airless minute or so, decreased blood oxygen arouses the sleeper to awaken and snort in air for a few seconds. The process can repeat more than 400 times a night, depriving the person of slow-wave sleep. Apart from complaints of sleepiness and irritability during the day—and their mates' complaints about their loud "snoring"—apnea sufferers are often unaware of their disorder. Sleep apnea leaves people tired and sometimes irritable during the day and therefore, like those who suffer narcolepsy, at increased risk of traffic accidents (Teran-Santos & others, 1999). Anyone who snores at night, who feels tired during the day, and who possibly has high blood pressure as well, should be checked for apnea (Dement, 1999).

Other sleepers, mostly children, experience **night terrors**. The person might sit up or walk around, talk incoherently, experience a doubling of heart and breathing rates, and appear terrified (Hartmann, 1981). The night-terror sufferer seldom wakes up fully during the episode and recalls little or nothing the next morning—at most, a fleeting, frightening image. Night terrors are not nightmares (which, like other dreams, typically occur during early morning REM sleep). As with sleepwalking, night terrors usually occur during the first few hours of Stage 4 (**FIGURE 17.7**). Family members often try to awaken and reassure the person with night terrors.

Sleepwalking and sleeptalking run in families. Finnish twin studies reveal that occasional childhood sleepwalking occurs for about one-third of those with a sleepwalking fraternal twin and half of those with a sleepwalking identical twin. The same is true for sleeptalking (Hublin & others, 1997, 1998). Sleepwalking is usually harmless and unrecalled the next morning. In rare cases of assault or homicide, courts have granted immunity to the perpetrators (Hobson & Silvestri, 1999). Sleepwalkers typically return to bed on their own or are guided there by a family member. Young children, who have the deepest and lengthiest Stage 4 sleep, are most likely to experience both night terrors and sleepwalking. As we grow older and deep Stage 4 sleep diminishes, so do night terrors and sleepwalking. After age 40, sleepwalking is rare.

FIGURE 17.7
Night terrors and nightmares
Night terrors occur within 2 or 3 hours of falling asleep, during Stage 4 sleep. Nightmares occur toward morning, during REM sleep. (From Hartmann, 1984.)

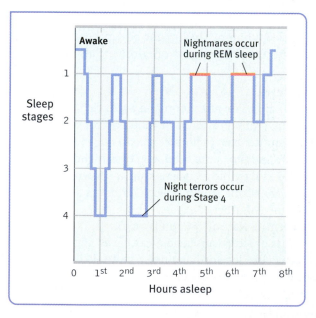

Dreams

Preview Question: What and why do we dream?

Discovering the link between REM sleep and dreaming opened a new era in dream research. Instead of relying on someone's hazy recall hours or days after having a dream, researchers could catch dreams as they happened. They could awaken people during a REM sleep period, or within 3 minutes afterward, and hear a vivid account.

What Do We Dream?

REM dreams—"hallucinations of the sleeping mind"—are vivid, emotional, and bizarre. Several times a night, you are the creator and producer of a surrealistic mental movie, in which events frequently occur in a jumbled sequence, scenes change suddenly, people appear and disappear, and physical laws, such as gravity, may be violated. Yet, **dreams** are so vivid we may confuse them with reality.

Occasionally, we may be sufficiently aware during a dream to wonder whether we are, in fact, dreaming. When experiencing such *lucid dreams*, some people are able to test their state of consciousness. If they can perform some absurd act, such as floating in the air, then they know they are dreaming.

We spend six years of our life in dreams, many of which are anything but sweet. For both women and men, 8 in 10 dreams are marked by negative emotions (Domhoff, 1999). People commonly dream of repeatedly failing in an attempt to do something; of being attacked, pursued, or rejected; or of experiencing misfortune (Hall & others, 1982). In the month after the San Francisco earthquake, 4 in 10 college students in the area (but only 1 in 20 students elsewhere) recalled one or more nightmares about an earthquake (Wood & others, 1992). And, when awakened during REM sleep, people report dreams with sexual imagery less often than you might think. In one study, only 1 in 10 dreams among young men and 1 in 30 among young women had sexual overtones (Domhoff, 1996.) More commonly, we dream of events in our daily lives, a meeting at work, taking an exam, relating to a family member or friend.

Across the world, people of all ages show a curious gender difference in dream content. Women dream of males and females equally often, whereas 65 percent of the characters in men's dreams are males. No one is sure why. Whatever its significance, dream researcher Calvin Hall (1984) believed we can add this fact to the short list of psychological gender differences.

The story line of our dreams—what Sigmund Freud called their **manifest content**—often incorporates experiences and preoccupations from the day's events, especially in our first dreams of the night. People in hunter-gatherer societies often dream of animals; urban Japanese rarely do (Mestel, 1997). The sensory stimuli of our sleeping environment may also intrude. A particular odor or the telephone's ringing may be instantly and ingeniously woven into the dream story. In one experiment, William Dement and Edward Wolpert (1958) lightly sprayed cold water on dreamers' faces. Compared with sleepers who did not get the cold-water treatment, these sleepers were more likely to dream about water—about a waterfall, a leaky roof, or even about being sprayed by someone. Even while in REM sleep, focused on internal stimuli, we maintain some awareness of changes in our external environment.

So, could we learn a foreign language by listening to tapes while we sleep? If only it were so easy. While sleeping we can learn to associate a sound with a mild electric shock (and to react to the sound accordingly). But we do not remember taped information played while we are soundly asleep (Eich, 1990; Wyatt & Bootzin, 1994). In fact, anything that happens during the 5 minutes just before we fall asleep is typically lost from memory (Roth & others, 1988). This explains why

Would you suppose that people dream if blind from birth? Studies of blind people in France, Hungary, Egypt, and the United States all found them dreaming of using their nonvisual senses—hearing, touching, smelling, tasting (Buquet, 1988; Taha, 1972; Vekassy, 1977).

A popular sleep myth: If you dream you are falling and hit the ground (or if you dream of dying), you die. (Unfortunately, those who could confirm these ideas are not around to do so. Some people, however, have had such dreams and are alive to report them.)

"For what one has dwelt on by day, these things are seen in visions of the night."

Menander of Athens (342–292 B.C.), *Fragments*

"I do not believe that I am now dreaming, but I cannot prove that I am not."

Philosopher Bertrand Russell (1872–1970)

■ **latent content** according to Freud, the underlying meaning of a dream (as distinct from its manifest content). Freud believed that a dream's latent content functions as a safety valve.

■ **REM rebound** the tendency for REM sleep to increase following REM sleep deprivation (created by repeated awakenings during REM sleep).

"When people interpret [a dream] as if it were meaningful and then sell those interpretations, it's quackery."

Sleep researcher J. Allan Hobson (1995)

Nocturnal mysteries
Marc Chagall's "I and the Village" captures the surrealism of many dreams. Psychologists study and debate why the brain creates such flights of fancy.

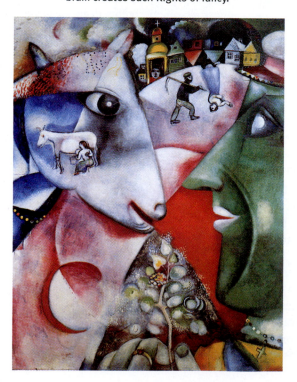

sleep apnea patients, who repeatedly awaken with a gasp and then immediately fall back to sleep, do not recall the episodes. It also explains why dreams that momentarily awaken us are mostly forgotten by morning. To remember a dream, get up and stay awake for a few minutes.

Why Do We Dream?

In his landmark book *The Interpretation of Dreams*, published in 1900, Freud offered "the most valuable of all the discoveries it has been my good fortune to make." He argued that by fulfilling wishes, a dream provides a psychic safety valve that discharges otherwise unacceptable feelings. According to Freud, a dream's manifest content is a censored, symbolic version of its **latent content**, which consists of unconscious drives and wishes that would be threatening if expressed directly. Although most dreams have no overt sexual imagery, Freud nevertheless believed that most adult dreams can be "traced back by analysis to *erotic wishes*." In Freud's view, a gun, for example, might be a disguised representation of a penis.

Freud considered dreams the key to understanding our inner conflicts. However, his critics say it is time to wake up from Freud's dream theory, which actually is one of his greatest failures. Dream interpretation, they say, is a nightmare. Some contend that even if dreams were symbolic, they could be interpreted any way one wished. Others maintain that dreams hide nothing. A dream about a gun is a dream about a gun. Legend has it that even Freud, who loved to smoke cigars, remarked that "sometimes, a cigar is just a cigar."

Freud's wish-fulfillment theory of dreams has in large part given way to other theories. Researchers who see dreams as *information processing* believe that dreams may help sift, sort, and fix the day's experiences in our memory. We have known for some time that REM sleep increases following stressful experiences or intense learning periods (Palumbo, 1978) and that REM sleep facilitates memory (McGrath & Cohen, 1978). In experiments, people have heard unusual phrases or learned to find hidden visual images before bedtime. If awakened every time they began REM sleep, they remembered less the next morning than if awakened during other sleep stages (Empson & Clarke, 1970; Karni & Sagi, 1994). A night of solid sleep (and dreaming) does, it seems, have an important place in our lives. As we sleep, our bodies consolidate the day's important memories.

Another explanation proposes that dreams may also serve a *physiological function*. Perhaps dreams—or the associated brain activity of REM sleep—provide the sleeping brain with periodic stimulation. Research on rats raised in enriched or impoverished environments indicates that stimulating experiences develop and preserve the brain's neural pathways. This theory of periodic brain stimulation during REM sleep makes sense from a developmental point of view. Infants, whose neural networks are fast developing, spend a great deal of time in REM sleep (**FIGURE 17.8**).

Other physiological theories propose that dreams erupt from neural activity that spreads upward from the brainstem (Antrobus, 1991; Hobson, 1988). According to one version—the *activation-synthesis* theory—this neural activity is random, and dreams are the brain's attempt to make sense of it. Much as a neurosurgeon can produce hallucinations by stimulating different parts of a patient's cortex, so can stimulation originating within the brain. Psychologists Martin Seligman and Amy Yellen (1987) note that the seconds-long bursts of rapid eye movements during REM sleep coincide with bursts of activity in the visual cortex. If awakened during one of these bursts of brain activity, people report vivid experiences, usually dramatic hallucinations. Given these visual scenes, what does our cognitive machinery do with it? It does what it usually does with meaningless stimuli—it

Average daily sleep (hours)

Marked drop in REM during infancy

Waking

REM sleep

Non-REM sleep

| 1–15 days | 3–5 mos. | 6–23 mos. | 2 yrs. | 3–4 yrs. | 5–13 yrs. | 14–18 yrs. | 19–30 yrs. | 31–45 yrs. | 90 yrs. |

Infancy | Childhood | Adolescence | Adulthood and old age

FIGURE 17.8 Sleep across the life span
As we age, our sleep patterns change. During our first few months, we spend progressively less time in REM sleep. During our first 20 years, we spend progressively less time asleep. (Adapted from Snyder & Scott, 1972.)

Rapid eye movements also stir the liquid behind the cornea; this delivers fresh oxygen to corneal cells, preventing their suffocation.

imposes meaning. Thus, say Seligman and Yellen, our ever-active brain weaves a story line from whatever is available—residues from the day's experiences, the alarm clock's ringing, or the brief visual hallucinations triggered by the brainstem. As Freud might have expected, the emotion-related limbic system also becomes active during REM sleep, while brain regions responsible for rational thought are idling. PET scans taken of sleeping people (if you can imagine sleeping while lying in a brain-scanning machine) reveal increased activity in several brain areas, especially the amygdala (Maquet & others, 1996). Add the limbic system's emotional tone to the brain's visual bursts and—voila!—we dream.

The activation-synthesis theory, then, is that dreams spring from the mind's relentless effort to make sense of unrelated visual bursts, which are given their emotional tone by the limbic system. Dreams are the brain's interpretation of its own activity.

The function of dreams provokes vigorous debate. Some dream researchers dispute both the Freudian and activation-synthesis theories, preferring instead to see dreams as part of cognitive development. For example, prior to age 7, children's dreams seem more like a slide show and less an active story in which the dreamer is an actor (Foulkes, 1999). But there is one thing the disputants all agree on: We *need* REM sleep. Deprived of it by repeatedly being awakened, people return more and more quickly to the REM stage after falling back to sleep. When finally allowed to sleep undisturbed, they literally sleep like babies—with increased REM sleep, a phenomenon called **REM rebound**. Withdrawing REM-suppressing sleeping medications also increases REM sleep, but with accompanying nightmares.

Most other mammals also experience REM sleep and REM rebound. Animals' need for REM sleep suggests that its causes and functions are deeply biological. That REM sleep occurs in mammals (and not in animals such as fish, whose behavior is less influenced by learning) also fits the information-processing theory of dreams. All of this reminds us once again of a basic lesson: *Biological and psychological explanations of behavior are partners, not competitors.*

But if dreams lack the disguised meanings that Freud supposed, and instead serve physiological functions, are they therefore psychologically meaningless? Not necessarily. Every psychologically meaningful experience involves an active brain. Moreover, say advocates of dream reflection, dreams may be akin to abstract art—amenable to more than one meaningful interpretation, and illuminating to ponder.

"Those dreams that on the silent night intrude, and with false flitting shapes our minds delude . . . are mere productions of the brain. And fools consult interpreters in vain."

Jonathan Swift, "On Dreams," 1727

REVIEW AND REFLECT:

Waking and Sleeping Rhythms

How have psychologists viewed consciousness?

Psychology began as the study of consciousness. Under the influence of behaviorism in the mid-twentieth century, the field turned to the study of observable behavior. Today scientific investigation of states of mind is again one of psychology's pursuits.

What are the levels and functions of consciousness?

Most psychologists today define *consciousness* as our awareness of ourselves and our environment. Speedy parallel processing handles subconscious information. Conscious processing of novel tasks is serial and much slower.

Why do we daydream and fantasize?

Virtually everyone daydreams, especially at times when our attention can be freed from the tasks at hand. Daydreaming can be adaptive; it can help us prepare for future events and may substitute for impulsive behavior. Those with fantasy-prone personalities have unusually vivid daydreams.

How do our age-old biological rhythms influence our daily functioning and our sleep and dreams?

Our bodies fluctuate in tune with a variety of annual, 28-day, 24-hour, and 90-minute cycles. Our daily schedule of waking and sleeping is timed by a body clock known as circadian rhythm. Each night's sleep also has a rhythm of its own, running from transitional Stage 1 sleep to deep Stage 4 sleep and back up to the more internally active REM sleep stage. This cycle repeats several times during a normal night's sleep, with periods of Stage 4 sleep progressively shortening and of dream-laden REM sleep lengthening.

Why must we sleep?

Depriving people of sleep has not conclusively revealed why, physiologically, we need sleep. Recent research reveals that sleep is linked with the release of pituitary growth hormone and that it may help to restore brain tissues and consolidate memories. Sleep may also have played a protective role in human evolution.

The disorders of sleep include insomnia (recurring wakefulness), narcolepsy (sudden uncontrollable sleepiness or lapsing into REM sleep), and sleep apnea (the stopping of breathing while sleeping).

What and why do we dream?

Although conscious thoughts can occur during any sleep stage, awakening people during REM sleep yields predictable "dreamlike" reports; awakening during other sleep stages yields only an occasional fleeting image. Our dreams are mostly of ordinary events and everyday experiences; they tend to involve some anxiety or misfortune more than an achievement.

Freud believed that a dream's manifest content, or story line, is a censored version of its latent content, some underlying meaning that gratifies our unconscious wishes. More recent explanations of why we dream suggest that dreams (1) help *process information* from the day and fix it in memory, (2) serve a *physiological function*, and/or (3) are the brain's efforts to *synthesize* periodic hallucinations (from activity bursts in the visual cortex) into a story line. Despite their differences, most theorists agree that REM sleep and its associated dreams serve an important function, as shown by the REM rebound that occurs following REM deprivation.

Terms and Concepts to Remember

consciousness, p. 240	delta waves, p. 247
fantasy-prone personality, p. 242	insomnia, p. 253
biological rhythms, p. 243	narcolepsy, p. 253
circadian rhythm [ser-KAY-dee-an], p. 243	sleep apnea, p. 254
	night terrors, p. 254
REM sleep, p. 246	dream, p. 255
alpha waves, p. 246	manifest content, p. 255
sleep, p. 246	latent content, p. 256
hallucinations, p. 247	REM rebound, p. 257

Test Yourself

17.1. Most people daydream every day. These daydreams serve several functions: They provide an escape from reality, they help us prepare for the future, they enhance creativity, and they may substitute for

a. a rich, complete life.   c. night dreams.

b. impulsive behavior.   d. meditative time.

17.2. Our body temperature tends to rise and fall in sync with a biological clock, which is referred to as

a. the circadian rhythm.   c. REM sleep.

b. narcolepsy.   d. hypnogogic sensations.

17.3. Stage 1 sleep is a twilight zone of light sleep. During Stage 1 sleep, a person is most likely to experience

a. sleep spindles.

b. hallucinations.

c. night terrors or nightmares.

d. rapid eye movements.

17.4. In the deepest stage of sleep—surprisingly, the stage when people sleepwalk—the brain emits large, slow delta waves. This deep stage of sleep is called

a. Stage 2.   c. REM sleep.

b. Stage 4.   d. paradoxical sleep.

17.5. An electroencephalograph shows that during sleep we pass through a cycle of five stages, each with characteristic brain waves. As the night progresses, the REM stage

a. gradually disappears.

b. becomes briefer and briefer.

c. remains about the same.

d. becomes progressively longer.

17.6. Various theories have been proposed to explain why we need sleep. They include all but which of the following?

a. Sleep has survival value.

b. Sleep helps us recuperate.

c. Sleep rests the eyes.

d. Sleep plays a role in the growth process.

17.7. Two relatively rare sleep disorders are narcolepsy and sleep apnea. With narcolepsy, the person _____; with sleep apnea, the person _____.

a. has persistent problems falling asleep; experiences a doubling of heart and breathing rates

b. experiences a doubling of heart and breathing rates; has persistent problems falling asleep

c. intermittently stops breathing; suffers periodic, overwhelming sleepiness

d. suffers periodic, overwhelming sleepiness; intermittently stops breathing

17.8. According to Sigmund Freud, dreams are the key to the understanding of our inner conflicts. In interpreting dreams, Freud was most interested in their

a. information-processing function.

b. physiological function.

c. manifest content, or story line.

d. latent content, or symbolic meaning.

17.9. Some theories of dreaming propose that dreams serve a physiological purpose. One such theory suggests that dreams

a. are the brain's attempt to make sense of random neural activity.

b. enable neurons to make new connections.

c. are manifestations of the sensory stimuli that intrude on our sleep.

d. prevent the brain from being disturbed by periodic stimulations.

17.10. The tendency for REM sleep to increase following REM sleep deprivation is referred to as

a. paradoxical sleep.

b. deep sleep.

c. REM rebound.

d. slow-wave sleep.

Review

- During psychology's history, what were the ups and downs of "consciousness"?

- Are you getting enough sleep? What might you ask yourself to answer this question?

Reflect

- Have you ever wondered how horses, dogs, and cats experience the world? Do you think they are consciously aware? If yes, are they also aware of being aware of the world?

- In some countries, such as Britain, the school day for teenagers runs from about 9:00 A.M. to 4:00 P.M. In other countries, such as the United States, the teen school day often runs from 8:00 A.M. to 3:00 P.M. or even 7:30 A.M. to 2:30 P.M. Early to rise isn't making kids wise, say critics—it's making them sleepy. For optimal alertness and well-being, teens need about 9 hours sleep a night. So, should early-start schools move to a later start time, even if it requires buying more buses or switching start times with elementary schools? Or is this impractical, and would it do little to remedy the tired-teen problem?

Answers to the Test Yourself and Review questions can be found in the green appendix at the end of the book.

18 Hypnosis

Preview Questions: What is hypnosis, and what powers does a hypnotist have over a hypnotized subject? Is hypnosis an altered state of consciousness or an extension of normal consciousness?

Imagine you are about to be hypnotized. The hypnotist invites you to sit back, fix your gaze on a spot high on the wall, and relax. In a quiet, low voice the hypnotist suggests, "Your eyes are growing tired. . . . Your eyelids are becoming heavy . . . now heavier and heavier. . . . They are beginning to close. . . . You are becoming more deeply relaxed. . . . Your breathing is now deep and regular. . . . Your muscles are becoming more and more relaxed. Your whole body is beginning to feel like lead."

After a few minutes of this hypnotic induction, your eyes are probably closed and you may undergo **hypnosis**—a social interaction in which one person (the hypnotist) suggests to another (the subject) that certain perceptions, feelings, thoughts, or behaviors will spontaneously occur. When the hypnotist suggests, "Your eyelids are shutting so tight that you cannot open them even if you try," your eyelids may stay closed and it may seem beyond your control to open them. Told to forget the number 6, you may be puzzled when you count 11 fingers on your hands. Invited to smell a sensuous perfume that is actually ammonia, you may linger delightedly over its pungent odor. Asked to describe a nonexistent picture the hypnotist claims to be holding, you may talk about it in detail. Told that you cannot see a certain object, such as a chair, you may indeed report that it is not there, although you manage to avoid the chair when walking around.

And if instructed to forget all these happenings once out of the hypnotic state, you may later report **posthypnotic amnesia**, a temporary memory loss rather like being unable to recall a familiar name. Although people *say* they don't remember "forgotten" material, subtle tests have led skeptics to doubt their reported amnesia (Coe, 1989a). The material must be "in there," for it can affect later behavior and be recalled at a prearranged signal (Kihlstrom, 1985; Spanos & others, 1985). A critical issue, then, is whether people are genuinely *unable* to recall the "forgotten" material, or whether people distract themselves or withhold information to meet the hypnotist's expectations.

Although hypnotic techniques have been used since antiquity, credit for their modern popularity goes to an Austrian physician, Anton Mesmer (1734–1815), who mistakenly thought he had discovered an "animal magnetism." With great flourish, Mesmer passed magnets over the bodies of ailing people, some of whom would lapse into a trancelike ("mesmerized") state, then awaken much improved. A French commission chaired by Benjamin Franklin found no evidence of animal magnetism and attributed Mesmer's "cures" to "mere imagination." Thus, hypnosis—or mesmerism, as it was then called—became linked with quackery.

Also working against the respectability of hypnosis were the grand claims made by its practitioners. Supposedly, mesmerized people could see with the backs of their heads, perceive others' internal organs, and communicate with the dead. Researchers now agree that hypnotized people can perform no such feats. Like unhypnotized people, those under hypnosis cannot leap tall buildings, run faster than a speeding bullet, or display superhuman

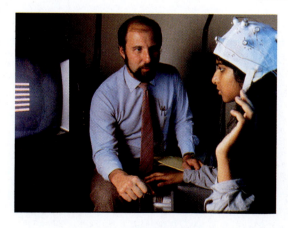

Subject to influence

As a deeply hypnotized woman sits before a TV screen, researcher David Spiegel asks her to imagine that a cardboard box is blocking the screen. When a stimulus appears on the screen, her brain waves do not display the normal response. Such findings, Spiegel argues, suggest that hypnosis can alter brain functioning.

strength. In experiments, their strength, stamina, learning, and perceptual abilities are like those of motivated unhypnotized people (Druckman & Bjork, 1994). Hypnotized people may surprise you by, say, extending their arms for 6 minutes straight—but unhypnotized people can also do this and other amazing feats (**FIGURE 18.1**).

Before considering whether the hypnotic state is actually an *altered* state of consciousness, let's first consider some areas of general agreement. Then, with the facts of hypnosis in mind, we can ponder two perplexing questions: What is hypnosis? And what does hypnosis tell us about human consciousness?

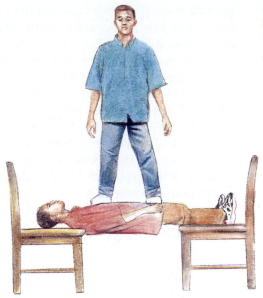

FIGURE 18.1
The "amazing" hypnotized "human plank"
Actually, unhypnotized people can also perform this feat.

Facts and Falsehoods

Those who study hypnosis agree that its power resides not in the hypnotist but in the subject's openness to suggestion (Bowers, 1984). Hypnotists have no magical mind-control power; they merely engage people's ability to focus on certain images or behaviors. But what powers does hypnosis have?

Can Anyone Experience Hypnosis?

To some extent, nearly everyone is suggestible. When people standing upright with their eyes closed are told repeatedly that they are swaying back and forth, most will indeed sway a little. In fact, postural sway is one of the items on the Stanford Hypnotic Susceptibility Scale that assesses a person's hypnotizability. The people who respond to such suggestions without hypnosis are the people who respond with hypnosis—only a little more so (Kirsch & Lynn, 1998a). During hypnosis, a hypnotist gives a brief hypnotic induction and then presents a series of suggested experiences that range from easy (one's outstretched arms will move together) to difficult (with eyes open one will see a nonexistent person).

Those who are highly hypnotizable—say, the 20 percent who can carry out a suggestion not to smell or react to a bottle of ammonia held under the nose—are still likely to be the most hypnotizable 25 years later (Piccione & others, 1989). These hypnotically susceptible people frequently become deeply absorbed in imaginative activities (Lynn & Rhue, 1986; Silva & Kirsch, 1992). Typically, they have rich fantasy lives and easily become absorbed in the imaginary events of a novel or movie. Many researchers therefore refer to hypnotic "susceptibility" as hypnotic *ability*, a label with more positive connotations. Few of us would care to be "susceptible" to hypnosis, but most of us would be glad to have the "ability" to focus our attention totally on a task, to become imaginatively absorbed in it, to entertain fanciful possibilities. That is exactly what fantasy-prone people with hypnotic ability can do.

Actually, anyone who can turn attention inward, relax, and imagine is able to experience some degree of hypnosis—because that's what hypnosis is. And virtually anyone will experience hypnotic responsiveness if led to *expect* it. To convince even skeptical University of Connecticut students that they were hypnotizable, Cynthia Wickless and Irving Kirsch (1989) played a clever stunt on them. After a standard

■ **hypnosis** a social interaction in which one person (the hypnotist) suggests to another (the subject) that certain perceptions, feelings, thoughts, or behaviors will spontaneously occur.

■ **posthypnotic amnesia** supposed inability to recall what one experienced during hypnosis; induced by the hypnotist's suggestion.

hypnotic induction, they suggested to the students that they would see red, then see green, then hear music, and so forth. After each suggestion, the merry prankster experimenters subtly projected appropriate stimuli—a very faint red or green light, or faint eerie music. Fooled by this weird experience of seeing and hearing what the hypnotist suggested, there were no doubters left. Thus, unlike those in control conditions not similarly persuaded, most scored as *highly* hypnotizable when later given the suggestions of the Stanford Hypnotic Susceptibility Scale.

Any real-life hypnotist does much the same in having people strain their eyes by staring at a high spot on the wall and then suggesting that "your eyes are growing tired . . . your eyelids are becoming heavy." With such strain, anyone's eyes would get tired. But if the hypnotist is successful, the subject will attribute the heavy eyelids to the hypnotist's powers.

Can Hypnosis Enhance Recall of Forgotten Events?

Can hypnotic procedures enable people to relive earlier experiences? To recall kindergarten classmates? To retrieve forgotten or suppressed details of a crime? Should testimony obtained under hypnosis be admissible in court?

Most people believe that our experiences are all "in there," that everything that happens to us gets recorded in our brains and can be recalled if only we are able to break through our own defenses (Loftus, 1980). (Although very popular, this belief is not supported by research on human memory.) Most university students, for example, agree that "under hypnosis a person [can] recall childhood events with very high accuracy" (Furnham, 1993). Testimonies to this come from *age regression* demonstrations, in which people supposedly relive experiences from their childhood. But 60 years of research dispute the claims of age regression: Hypnotized people are *not* more genuinely childlike than unhypnotized people who are asked to feign childlike behavior (Nash, 1987). Age-regressed people act as they *believe* children would, but they typically miss the mark by outperforming real children of the specified age (Silverman & Retzlaff, 1986). Age-regressed people may, for example, *feel* childlike and may print much as they know a 6-year-old would, but they sometimes do so with perfect spelling and typically without any change in their adult brain waves, reflexes, and perceptions.

On rare occasions, the relaxed, focused state of hypnosis has enabled witnesses to produce leads in criminal investigations. One instance occurred in 1977, when 26 children and their bus driver, Ed Ray, were kidnapped and forced into an abandoned trailer truck buried 6 feet underground. After their rescue, Ray, under hypnosis, recalled all but one digit of the kidnapper's license plate. With this crucial information, police tracked down the abductors. This anecdote is atypical, and it is unclear whether hypnosis enabled Ray to retrieve the memory. Nevertheless, many researchers believe that hypnotic procedures may have some value—or at least do little harm—when used as an investigative tool.

The problem comes in putting on the witness stand someone whose memories are "hypnotically refreshed." Researchers have found that hypnotically refreshed memories combine fact with fiction. Thus, American, Australian, and British courts increasingly ban testimony from witnesses who have been hypnotized (Druckman & Bjork, 1994; Gibson, 1995; McConkey, 1995).

Hypnosis has unpredictable effects. Sometimes the relaxed reflection boosts recall. But often hypnosis contaminates memory with false recollections or even increases one's confidence in false memories (Lynn & others, 1997; McConkey, 1992). When pressed under hypnosis to recall details, perhaps to "zoom in on your visual memory screen," people use their imaginations to construct their memories. Without either person being aware of what is going on, the hypnotist's hints—"Did you hear loud noises?"—can become the subject's pseudomemory. Previously hypnotized witnesses may end up testifying confidently to events they never experienced (Laurence & Perry, 1988). And whether hypnotized or not, highly hypnotizable (fantasy-prone) people are especially vulnerable to false memory suggestions (Barnier & McConkey, 1992).

So, hypnosis cannot change the rules by which we form, store, and retrieve memories. It distresses memory researchers that many therapists do not appreciate the unreliability of hypnotically induced memories. When hypnosis researcher Michael Yapko (1994) surveyed 869 therapists attending various therapy conventions, 47 percent agreed that "psychotherapists can have greater faith in details of a traumatic event when obtained hypnotically than otherwise." And 54 percent agreed that "hypnosis can be used to recover memories of actual events as far back as birth." Such ignorance "of the facts" left Yapko aghast: "I am deeply concerned that psychotherapy patients will be led to believe destructive ideas that are untrue . . . all in the name of 'psychotherapy.'"

Striking examples of memories created under hypnosis come from the tens of thousands of people who since 1980 have reported being abducted by UFOs, abused in satanic cults, or adulated during a past life. Under hypnosis, one woman

> remembered a light and a voice calling her out of bed. She obeyed against her will and went to a muddy field as a saucer-shaped craft neared the ground. Through the windows she saw beings and a piercing sound prevented her from moving. A warm beam of light then pulled her inside the craft. She found herself inside a white hospital room. Two small beings with tiny mouths and compelling eyes, dressed as if in motorcycle jackets, told her without speaking to undress and lie down on a table. She resisted but eventually gave in . . . at last the doctor entered and gave her an injection. He then inserted a needle into her navel. . . . One being . . . undressed himself and rubbed her with a jelly. It warmed her [and he] then raped her. (Bullard, 1987)

Studies reveal that most reports of UFOs have come from people who are predisposed to believe in aliens, are fantasy prone, and have undergone hypnosis (Newman & Baumeister, 1996; Nickell, 1996). Consider one hypnotic session with another supposed abductee:

Dr. Fiore: Now you're going to let yourself know if they put a needle in any part of your body, other than the rectum.

Sandi: No. They were carrying needles around, big ones, and I was scared for a while they were going to put one in me, but they didn't. [*Body tenses.*]

Dr. Fiore: Now just let yourself relax. At the count of three you're going to remember whether they put one of those big needles in you. If they did, know that you're safe. . . . And if they didn't you're going to remember that, too, at the count of three. One . . . two . . . three.

Sandi: They did. (Fiore, 1989, p. 26)

Can Hypnosis Force People to Act Against Their Will?

Researchers Martin Orne and Frederick Evans (1965) demonstrated that hypnotized people *could* be induced to perform an apparently dangerous act. The participants followed a request to dip one hand briefly into fuming acid, then throw the "acid" in a research assistant's face. When interviewed a day later, they exhibited no memory of their acts and emphatically denied they would ever follow orders to commit such an act.

"Hypnosis is not a psychological truth serum and to regard it as such has been a source of considerable mischief."

Researcher Kenneth Bowers (1987)

HYPNOTIC AGE REGRESSION: A TRUE STORY

Remembrances of Christmases Past?

What shall we make of a clever study by Robert True (1949)? He regressed hypnotized volunteers back to their Christmases and birthday parties at ages 10, 7, and 4. In each case, he asked them what day of the week it was. Without hypnosis, the odds that a person can name offhand the day of a long past date are but 1 in 7. Remarkably, the hypnotized subjects' answers were 82 percent correct.

But other investigators were unable to replicate True's results. When Martin Orne (1982) asked True why, he replied that *Science*, the journal that published his article, had shortened his key question to "What day is this?" Actually, he had asked his age-regressed subjects, "Is it Monday? Is it Tuesday?" and so forth until the subject stopped him with a yes. When Orne asked True if he knew the actual day of the week while posing the questions, True granted that he did but was puzzled why Orne would ask.

Can you see why? True's experiment appears to be a beautiful example of how hypnotists can subtly influence their subjects' memories. (It also illustrates how experimenters can subtly communicate their expectations and why they should be kept "blind" to the expected result.) "Given the eagerness of the hypnotized subject to fulfill the demands placed upon him," surmised Orne, it takes only the slightest change of inflection (in asking "Is it Wednesday?") for the subject to respond, "Yes."

The final blow to True's experiment came when Orne simply asked ten 4-year-olds what day of the week it was. To his surprise, none knew. If 4-year-olds typically do not know the day of the week, then True's adults were reporting information they probably didn't know when they were 4.

Remembrances of Lives Past?

If people's hypnotic regressions to childhood are partly imagined, then how believable are claims of hypnotic "regression to past lives"? Can the 25 percent of Americans who believe in reincarnation (Yankelovich, 1998) find support in such reports? Were the 36 percent of university students correct to agree, in a survey by Scott Brown and others (1996),

Will the real Joan of Arc please stand up? Under hypnosis, people who claim to remember a past life too often report being someone famous.

that "certain people can be age regressed to recall past lives"?

Nicholas Spanos (1987–1988; Spanos & others, 1991) reported that, when hypnotized, fantasy-prone people who believe in reincarnation will offer vivid details of "past lives." But they nearly always report being their same race—unless the researcher has informed them that different races are common. They often report being someone famous rather than one of the countless "nobodies." Some contradict one another by claiming to have been the same person, such as King Henry VIII (Reveen, 1987–1988). Moreover, they typically do not know things that any person of that time would have known. One subject who "regressed" to a "previous life" as a Japanese fighter pilot in 1940 could not name the emperor of Japan and did not know that Japan was already at war. Hypnotic regressions to past lives offer no credible evidence of reincarnation. ■

MY NAME IS EUNICE. I HAVE LIVED MANY PAST LIVES, MOST OF THEM IN TRENTON, NEW JERSEY....

CHANNELLING ON THE CHEAP

Had hypnosis given the hypnotist a special power to control these people against their will? To find out, Orne and Evans unleashed that enemy of so many illusory beliefs—the control group: Orne asked some other people to *pretend* they had been hypnotized. The laboratory experimenter, unaware that the control subjects had not been hypnotized, treated all the participants the same. The result? All the unhypnotized participants (perhaps believing that the laboratory context assured safety) performed the same acts as those who were hypnotized. Similarly, most hypnotized subjects can be induced to deface a sacred book, and a few will even steal an exam or sell illegal drugs. But most people asked to simulate hypnosis are equally likely to do the same (Levitt, 1986).

This illustrates a principle that is firmly established in social psychology's research findings: *An authoritative person in a legitimate context can induce people—hypnotized or not—to perform some unlikely acts.* Hypnosis researcher Spanos (1982) put it directly: "The overt behaviors of hypnotic subjects are well within normal limits."

Hypnosis may have one distinctive feature. Amanda Barnier and Kevin McConkey (1998) found that a person was equally likely to send them a daily postcard, whether requested to do so with a hypnotic suggestion or whether simply asked. But the University of New South Wales students who participated in the research reported that the act *felt* more compulsive and less effortful if done as a **posthypnotic suggestion** (a suggestion to be carried out after the hypnosis session has ended).

Can Hypnosis Be Therapeutic?

Hypnotherapists do nothing magical. They simply try to help patients harness their own healing powers (Baker, 1987). Posthypnotic suggestions have helped alleviate headaches, asthma, warts, and stress-related skin disorders. One woman, who for more than 20 years suffered from open sores all over her body, was asked to imagine herself swimming in shimmering, sunlit liquids that would cleanse her skin and to experience her skin as smooth and unblemished. Within three months her sores had disappeared (Bowers, 1984).

When hypnosis is applied to such problems with self-control as nail biting and smoking, the most hypnotizable people show no greater benefit than those least hypnotizable. This suggests that the benefits are not a result of the hypnosis per se (Bowers & LeBaron, 1986). Should we also then question whether hypnosis is the therapeutic agent when we hear of improvements in problems unrelated to willpower, such as skin disorders? Do the benefits of hypnosis surpass those of simply encouraging people to relax and to form positive images?

The answer remains in doubt. For example, hypnosis speeds the disappearance of warts, but in controlled studies, so do the same positive suggestions given without hypnosis (Spanos, 1991, 1996). Hypnosis and positive suggestions, like placebos, change people's expectations. But unlike placebos, notes Irving Kirsch (1999), "hypnosis does not require deception in order to be effective."

Can Hypnosis Alleviate Pain?

Yes, hypnosis *can* relieve pain (Druckman & Bjork, 1994; Kihlstrom, 1985). When unhypnotized subjects put their arms in an ice bath, they feel intense pain within 25 seconds. When hypnotizable subjects do the same after being given suggestions to feel no pain, they indeed report feeling little pain. As some dentists know, even light hypnosis can reduce fear, and thus hypersensitivity to pain. Nearly 10 percent of us can become so deeply hypnotized that even major surgery can be performed without anesthesia. And half of us can gain some pain relief from hypnosis.

How can this be? One theory of hypnotic pain relief finds the answer in **dissociation**, a split between different levels of consciousness. Hypnosis, it suggests, dissociates

■ **posthypnotic suggestion** a suggestion, made during a hypnosis session, to be carried out after the subject is no longer hypnotized; used by some clinicians to help control undesired symptoms and behaviors.

■ **dissociation** a split in consciousness, which allows some thoughts and behaviors to occur simultaneously with others.

The Lamaze method of childbirth
Like hypnosis, the Lamaze method uses breathing and concentration techniques that draw attention away from pain. Women for whom the method works tend to have high hypnotic ability (Venn, 1986).

the sensation of the pain stimulus (of which the subject is still aware) from the emotional suffering that defines our experience of pain. The ice water therefore feels cold—very cold—but not painful.

Another theory proposes that hypnotic pain relief results from selective attention, as when an injured athlete, caught up in the competition, feels little or no pain until the game ends. Support for this view comes from several studies showing that hypnosis relieves pain no better than does merely relaxing and distracting people (Chaves, 1989). With their attention distracted during hypnosis, some women can experience childbirth with minimal pain; but so can some women without hypnosis, especially if given childbirth training (D'Eon, 1989).

Both views of pain assume that at some level a hypnotized person does experience the pain stimulus. Indeed, people who report feeling no pain nevertheless may respond with a pounding heart to electric shock or a surgeon's knife. Similar disparities between self-reports and behavior involve seeing and hearing. Following a suggestion that they are deaf, hypnotized people will deny being able to hear their own voices. But when they hear their voice over a headset with a half-second delay, they respond as unhypnotized people do: The delayed feedback disrupts their ability to speak fluently. If told they are color-blind, hypnotized people do not respond to color-blindness tests as do people with actual color-deficient vision. In each of these cases, the hypnotized subjects *report* perceiving no pain, sound, or color. Yet the stimuli have quite obviously registered within their sensory systems. Thus, hypnosis does *not* block sensory input. What people *say* they experience just doesn't fit with their behavior.

The unanswered question of how hypnosis relieves pain—by *dissociating* the pain sensation from conscious awareness, or merely by focusing *attention* on other things—brings us to the basic issue: Is hypnosis a unique psychological state?

Is Hypnosis an Altered State of Consciousness?

We have seen that hypnosis involves heightened suggestibility. We have also seen that hypnotic procedures do not endow a person with special powers. But they can sometimes enhance a person's recall of real (and unreal) past events, aid in overcoming psychologically influenced ailments, and help alleviate pain. So, just what is hypnosis?

Hypnosis as a Social Phenomenon

Skeptics note that hypnosis is not a unique physiological state. Moreover, behaviors produced through hypnotic procedures can also be produced without them. This suggests that hypnotic phenomena may reflect the workings of normal consciousness (Lynn & others, 1990; Spanos & Coe, 1992).

We know that our interpretations of events exert a powerful influence on our ordinary perceptions. Especially in the case of pain, for which the effects of hypnosis seem most dramatic, our perceptions follow our attention. Moreover, imaginative people can manufacture vivid perceptions without hypnosis. Perhaps, then, "hypnotized" people are just acting the role of "good hypnotic subjects" and allowing the hypnotist to direct their fantasies.

It's not that people are consciously faking hypnosis. Rather, they're doing and reporting what's expected of them. Like actors who get caught up in their roles, they begin to feel and behave in ways appropriate to the hypnotic role. The more they like and trust the hypnotist and feel motivated to demonstrate hypnotic behavior, the more they do so (Gfeller & others, 1987). If told later to scratch their ear when they hear the word *psychology*, subjects will likely do so only if they think the experiment is still under way (and scratching is therefore expected). If an experimenter eliminates the motivation for their acting hypnotized—by stating that hypnosis reveals their "gullibility"—subjects become unresponsive.

Based on such findings, advocates of the *social influence theory* contend that hypnotic phenomena are *not* unique to hypnosis. They argue that hypnotic phenomena—like behavior associated with other supposed altered states, such as dissociative identity disorder and spirit or demon possession—are an extension of everyday social behavior (Spanos, 1994, 1996). Hypnotic subjects are imaginative actors caught up in playing the role of hypnotic subject.

Hypnosis as Divided Consciousness

Most hypnosis researchers grant that normal social and cognitive processes play a part in hypnosis, but they nevertheless believe hypnosis is more than imaginative acting. For one thing, hypnotized subjects will *sometimes* carry out suggested behaviors on cue, even when they believe no one is watching (Perugini & others, 1998). Their doing so shows that more may be at work than merely trying to be a "good subject." Moreover, many practitioners remain convinced that certain phenomena *are* unique to hypnosis. What else explains hypnotic experiences such as pain reduction and compelling hallucinations (Bowers, 1990)? Skeptics reply that hypnotists' livelihoods depend on maintaining an aura of mysterious power (Coe, 1989b).

To veteran researcher Ernest Hilgard (1986, 1992), hypnosis involves not only social influence but also a special state of dissociated (divided) consciousness. Hilgard views hypnotic dissociation as a vivid form of everyday mind splits. Putting a child to bed, we might read *Goodnight Moon* for the fourteenth time while mentally organizing a busy schedule for the next day. Under the influence of my dentist's nitrous oxide—a real gas—I hear her ask me to "open wide." As my conscious self contemplates her request, my mouth, much to my surprise, immediately obeys. As she says, "Turn toward me," my head instantly complies, as if controlled by some strange force.

One version of dissociation theory emphasizes such separations of behavior from conscious control (Woody & Bowers, 1994). With practice, you could even read and comprehend a short story while copying dictated words, much as you can doodle while listening to a lecture or finish typing a sentence while starting a conversation,

"The total possible consciousness may be split into parts which co-exist but mutually ignore each other."

William James, *Principles of Psychology*, 1890

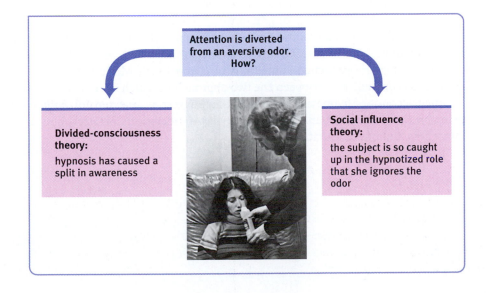

Explaining hypnosis
How can she do it? How can this hypnotized young woman show no reaction to the terrible smell of ammonia? Divided-consciousness theory and social influence theory offer possible explanations.

Demonstrating the "hidden observer"
A hypnotized subject being tested by Ernest Hilgard exhibits no pain when her arm is placed in an ice bath. But asked to press a key if some part of her feels the pain, she does so. To Hilgard, this suggests that hypnosis divides consciousness into one part that is unaware of pain and another part—a "hidden observer"—that is aware of it.

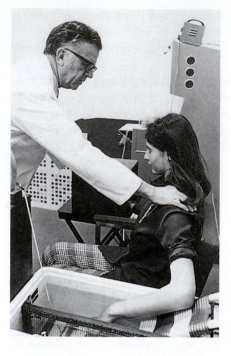

or as a skilled pianist can talk to an audience while playing a familiar piece (Hirst & others, 1978). In hypnosis as in life, *much of our behavior occurs on autopilot.* Thus, when hypnotized people write answers to questions about one topic while talking or reading about a different topic, they display an accentuated form of normal dissociation of cognition from behavior. So, when today's researchers refer to a "hypnotic state," note Irving Kirsch and Steven Jay Lynn (1995, 1998a,b), they merely refer to the subjective experience of hypnosis, not to a unique trance state.

Hilgard's discovery of hypnotic dissociation occurred dramatically. During a class demonstration of hypnosis, he induced deafness in someone and then set about showing the class that the person was now utterly unresponsive to questions, taunts, and even sudden loud sounds. When a student asked whether some part of the person might still be able to hear, Hilgard decided to show that the answer was no. He quietly asked the person to raise his right index finger if some part of him could still hear. To everyone's surprise—including Hilgard's and the subject's—the finger rose. When the person's hearing was restored, he explained that "it was a little boring just sitting here . . . when I suddenly felt my finger lift; that is what I want you to explain to me."

This phenomenon spurred further inquiry. Hypnotized subjects, as we noted earlier, report far less pain than others when they place their arms in ice water. But when asked to press a key if "some part" of them does feel the pain, they invariably press the key. To Hilgard, this suggests that a dissociated consciousness, a **hidden observer**, is passively aware of what is happening.

The divided-consciousness theory of hypnosis provoked controversy, because what the "hidden observer" reports varies with what the experimenter seems to want. But this much seems clear: You and I process much information without conscious awareness. Our information processing, which starts with selective attention, *is* divided into simultaneous conscious and subconscious realms. Without doubt, there is much more to thinking and acting than we are conscious of.

But still, there is also little doubt that social influences do play an important role in hypnosis. So, might the two views—social influence and divided consciousness—be bridged? Researchers John Kihlstrom and Kevin McConkey (1990) believe there is no contradiction between the two approaches, which are converging toward a "unified account of hypnosis." Hypnosis, they suggest, is an extension *both* of normal principles of social influence *and* of everyday dissociations between our conscious awareness and our automatic behaviors.

■ **hidden observer** Hilgard's term describing a hypnotized subject's awareness of experiences, such as pain, that go unreported during hypnosis.

REVIEW AND REFLECT:

Hypnosis

What is hypnosis, and what powers does a hypnotist have over a hypnotized subject?

Although hypnosis was historically linked with quackery, it has more recently become the subject of serious research. Psychologists now agree that hypnosis is a state of heightened suggestibility, and that people are subject to this state in varying degrees. Psychologists also believe that, although hypnotic procedures may help someone to recall past events, the hypnotist's beliefs frequently work their way into the subject's recollections. And they agree that hypnotized people can no more be made to act against their will than can nonhypnotized people. Hypnosis can be at least temporarily therapeutic, and hypnotizable people can enjoy significant pain relief.

Is hypnosis an altered state of consciousness or an extension of normal consciousness?

Hypnosis is at least partly a by-product of normal social and cognitive processes. Many researchers believe it also is an altered state of consciousness, perhaps involving a dissociation between levels of consciousness.

Terms and Concepts to Remember

hypnosis, p. 260
posthypnotic amnesia, p. 260
posthypnotic suggestion, p. 265

dissociation, p. 265
hidden observer, p. 268

Test Yourself

18.1. Hypnosis is a social interaction in which a hypnotist suggests to a subject that certain perceptions, feelings, thoughts, or behaviors will spontaneously occur. Subjects who are hypnotizable and will carry out a hypnotic suggestion usually

    a. are fantasy-prone.
    b. have low self-esteem.
    c. are subject to hallucinations.
    d. are hidden observers.

18.2. Although experts differ in their understandings of hypnosis, most agree that hypnosis can be effectively used to

    a. elicit testimony about a "forgotten" event.
    b. re-create childhood experiences.
    c. relieve pain.
    d. alter personality.

18.3. Ernest Hilgard believes hypnosis is not merely an extension of normal social influence but involves dissociation, which means

    a. nonconformity to social pressure.
    b. a state of paradoxical sleep.
    c. a state of divided consciousness.
    d. conscious enactment of a hypnotic role.

Review: When is the use of hypnosis potentially harmful, and when can hypnosis be used to help?

Reflect: Examples of dissociated consciousness may include talking while typing and thinking about something else while reading a favorite bedtime story. Can you think of a time when you have experienced dissociated consciousness?

Answers to the Test Yourself and Review questions can be found in the green appendix at the end of the book.

19 Drugs and Consciousness

There is controversy about whether hypnosis alters consciousness, but there is little dispute that drugs do. **Psychoactive drugs** are chemicals that change perceptions and moods. Let's imagine a day in the life of a legal drug user. It begins with a wake-up latté. By midday, several cigarettes have calmed frazzled nerves. Leaving work early makes time for a happy-hour drink, providing a relaxing and sociable prelude to a dental appointment, where nitrous oxide makes an otherwise painful experience mildly pleasurable. A diet pill before dinner helps stem the appetite, and its stimulating effects can later be partially offset with two Tylenol PMs. Before drifting off into REM-depressed sleep, our hypothetical drug user is dismayed by a news report of "rising drug abuse."

Dependence and Addiction

Preview Questions: What are dependence and addiction? Can substance abusers overcome their addictions?

Continued use of a psychoactive drug produces **tolerance**: The user requires larger and larger doses to experience the drug's effect. A person who rarely drinks alcohol might get tipsy on one can of beer, but an experienced drinker may not get tipsy until the second six-pack (**FIGURE 19.1**). Ironically, despite the connotations of "tolerance," alcoholics' brains, hearts, and livers suffer damage from the excessive alcohol they are "tolerating."

Users who stop taking psychoactive drugs may experience the undesirable side effects of **withdrawal**. As the body responds to the drug's absence, the user may feel physical pain and intense cravings, indicating a **physical dependence** on the drug. People can also develop **psychological dependence**, particularly for stress-relieving drugs. Although such drugs may not be physically addictive, they nevertheless become an important part of the user's life, often as a way of relieving negative emotions. With either physical addiction or psychological dependence, the user's primary focus becomes obtaining and using the drug.

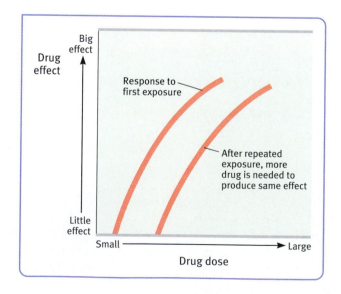

FIGURE 19.1 Drug tolerance
With repeated exposure to a psychoactive drug, the drug's effect lessens. Thus, it takes bigger doses to get the desired effect.

Misconceptions About Addiction

An "addiction" has traditionally meant a craving for a substance, with physical symptoms such as aches, nausea, and distress following sudden withdrawal. In recent pop psychology, the supposedly irresistible seduction of addiction has been extended to cover many behaviors formerly considered bad habits or even sins. Has the concept been stretched too far? Are addictions as irresistible as commonly believed? Many drug researchers believe the following three myths about addiction are *false*:

1. *Addictive drugs quickly corrupt; for example, morphine taken to control pain is powerfully addictive and often leads to heroin abuse.* After taking a psychoactive drug, some people—perhaps 10 percent—do indeed have a hard time using it in moderation or stopping altogether. However, there are many more controlled, occasional users than addicts of drugs such as alcohol, marijuana, and cocaine (Gazzaniga, 1988; Siegel, 1990). Moreover, people typically don't become addicted when using drugs medically. Those given morphine to control pain rarely develop the cravings of the addict who uses morphine as a mood-altering drug (Melzack, 1990).

2. *Addictions can't be overcome voluntarily; therapy is a must.* Some addicts do benefit from treatment programs. Alcoholics Anonymous, for example, has supported many people in overcoming their alcohol dependence. But, say critics, the recovery rates of treated and untreated groups differ less than one might suppose. Therapy or group support may be helpful, but people often recover on their own.

   Moreover, viewing addiction as a disease, as diabetes is a disease, can undermine self-confidence and the will to change cravings that, without treatment, "one can't fight." And that, critics say, would be unfortunate, for many people do voluntarily stop using addictive drugs, without treatment. Some 70 percent of smokers who seek treatment for their addiction later return to smoking, whereas most of America's 41 million ex-smokers kicked the habit on their own. Half of the U.S. soldiers in Vietnam tried heroin or opium, and 20 percent became regular users. And, of nearly 500 men whose urine revealed narcotic use upon their departure from Vietnam, one-third did try narcotics again (Robins & others, 1974). Yet, removed from the war's stressful setting and all the stimulus cues associated with their drug use (the place, the friends, the circumstances), only 7 percent of the 500 became readdicted.

3. *We can extend the concept of addiction to cover not just drug dependencies, but a whole spectrum of repetitive, pleasure-seeking behaviors.* We can, and we have, but should we? The addiction-as-disease-needing-treatment idea has been suggested for a host of driven behaviors, including overeating, shopping, exercise, sex, gambling, and work. Initially, we may use the term metaphorically ("I'm a science fiction addict"), but if we begin taking the metaphor as reality, addiction can become an all-purpose excuse. Those who embezzle to feed their "gambling addiction," who surf the Web half the night to satisfy their "Internet addiction," or who abuse or betray to indulge their "sex addiction" can then explain away their behavior as an illness. As Washington, D.C., Mayor Marion Barry replied when asked why he lied about being "chemically dependent," "That was the disease talking. I did not purposely do that to you. I was a victim" (Leo, 1991).

Bookstores now carry whole sections of books on addictive relationships, also known as "co-dependence." A supposedly co-dependent person—usually a woman—is said to be addicted to, or dependent on, a dysfunctional partner, at the cost of losing her own identity and self-fulfillment. Indeed, women whose parents abused alcohol may learn to meet exploitive people's expectations (Lyon & Greenberg, 1991). And women who live with a substance abuser do experience great stress and sometimes help to hide the abuser's addiction from public view. But, say critics, our individualistic

■ **psychoactive drug** a chemical substance that alters perceptions and mood.

■ **tolerance** the diminishing effect with regular use of the same dose of a drug, requiring the user to take larger and larger doses before experiencing the drug's effect.

■ **withdrawal** the discomfort and distress that follow discontinuing the use of an addictive drug.

■ **physical dependence** a physiological need for a drug, marked by unpleasant withdrawal symptoms when the drug is discontinued.

■ **psychological dependence** a psychological need to use a drug, such as to relieve negative emotions.

"About 70 percent of Americans have tried illicit drugs, but . . . only a few percent have done so in the last month. . . . Past age 35, the casual use of illegal drugs virtually ceases." Having sampled the pleasures and their aftereffects, "most people eventually walk away."

Neuropsychologist Michael Gazzaniga (1997)

© 1992 by Sidney Harris.

"Just tell me where you kids got the idea to take so many drugs."

■ **depressants** drugs (such as alcohol, barbiturates, and opiates) that reduce neural activity and slow body functions.

■ **stimulants** drugs (such as caffeine, nicotine, and the more powerful amphetamines and cocaine) that excite neural activity and speed up body functions.

■ **hallucinogens** psychedelic ("mind-manifesting") drugs, such as LSD, that distort perceptions and evoke sensory images in the absence of sensory input.

CALVIN AND HOBBES

NOTHING I DO IS MY FAULT.

MY FAMILY IS DYSFUNCTIONAL AND MY PARENTS WON'T EMPOWER ME! CONSEQUENTLY, I'M NOT SELF-ACTUALIZED!

MY BEHAVIOR IS ADDICTIVE FUNCTIONING IN A DISEASE PROCESS OF TOXIC CODEPENDENCY! I NEED HOLISTIC HEALING AND WELLNESS BEFORE I'LL ACCEPT ANY RESPONSIBILITY FOR MY ACTIONS!

ONE OF US NEEDS TO STICK HIS HEAD IN A BUCKET OF ICE WATER.

I LOVE THE CULTURE OF VICTIMHOOD.

culture often stretches "co-dependence" to include the lost freedoms of normal, mutually dependent wife-husband or parent-child relationships (Kaminer, 1992). Moreover, the co-dependent person often is *blamed*, and the dysfunctional partner's shame becomes hers as well. If people derive meaning from supporting and loving a troubled family member, are they really blameworthy or socially ill?

Sometimes, though, behaviors such as gambling do become compulsive and dysfunctional, much like abusive drug taking. Is there justification for stretching the addiction concept to cover social behaviors? Debates over the addiction-as-disease model continue.

Psychoactive Drugs

Preview Question: What types of drugs alter our perceptions and moods, and how do they work?

There are at least three categories of psychoactive drugs:

✛ **Depressants**, or "downers," calm neural activity and slow body functions.
✛ **Stimulants**, or "uppers," temporarily excite neural activity and arouse body functions.
✛ **Hallucinogens** distort perceptions and evoke sensory images in the absence of sensory input.

Drugs in all three categories do their work at the brain's synapses, by stimulating, inhibiting, or mimicking the activity of neurotransmitters, the brain's chemical messengers.

Depressants

Let's look first at drugs such as alcohol, barbiturates (tranquilizers), and opiates, those that slow our body's functions.

Alcohol

A University of Illinois campus survey showed that before sexual assaults, 80 percent of the male assailants and 70 percent of the female victims had been drinking (Camper, 1990). Another survey of 89,874 American collegians found alcohol or drugs involved in 79 percent of unwanted sexual intercourse experiences (Presley & others, 1997).

True or false? In large amounts, alcohol is a depressant; in small amounts, it is a stimulant.

False. Small doses of "spirits" may, indeed, enliven a drinker, but they do so by slowing brain activity that controls judgment and inhibitions. When provoked, people under alcohol's influence respond more aggressively than usual. If asked to help, people under alcohol's influence respond more willingly than usual. In everyday life, alcohol is an equal-opportunity drug: It *increases* harmful tendencies—as when sexually coercive college men lower their dates' sexual inhibitions by getting them to drink (Abbey, 1991; Mosher & Anderson, 1986)—and it increases helpful tendencies—as when tipsy restaurant patrons leave extravagant tips (M. Lynn, 1988). Thus, alcohol makes us more aggressive or helpful or self-disclosing or sexually daring—when such tendencies are already present. *The urges you feel when sober are the ones you are more likely to act upon when intoxicated.*

Low doses of alcohol relax the drinker by slowing sympathetic nervous system activity. With larger doses, alcohol can become a staggering problem: Reactions slow, speech slurs, and skilled performance deteriorates. Paired with sleep deprivation, alcohol becomes a potent sedative. (Although either sleep deprivation or booze can put a driver at risk, their combination is deadlier yet.) These physical effects, combined with lowered inhibitions, contribute to alcohol's worst consequences—the several hundred thousand lives claimed worldwide in alcohol-related accidents and violent crime each year. Accidents occur despite most drinkers' belief (when sober) that driving while under the influence of alcohol is wrong and despite their insisting that they wouldn't do so. Yet as their blood-alcohol level rises, people's moral judgments become less mature, their qualms about drinking and driving lessen—and virtually all will drive home from a bar, even if given a Breathalyzer test and told they are intoxicated (Denton & Krebs, 1990; MacDonald & others, 1995).

Alcohol not only affects judgment, it also affects memory. It impairs neither short-term recall for what just happened nor existing long-term memories. Rather, it disrupts the *processing* of recent experiences into long-term memories. Thus, the day after being intoxicated, heavy drinkers may not recall whom they met or what they said or did the night before. This memory blackout stems partly from an inability to transfer memories from the intoxicated to the sober state (Eich, 1980). Blackouts after drinking may also result from the way alcohol suppresses REM sleep, because people deprived of REM sleep have difficulty fixing their day's experiences into permanent memories.

Alcohol has another intriguing effect on consciousness: It reduces self-awareness (Hull & others, 1986). Compared with people who feel good about themselves, those who want to suppress their awareness of failures or shortcomings are more likely to drink. Losing a business deal, a game, or a romance will sometimes elicit a drinking binge.

Alcohol also focuses one's attention on the immediate situation and away from any future consequences. This facilitates urges that a person might otherwise resist (Steele & Josephs, 1990). In surveys, over half of rapists acknowledge drinking before committing their offense (Seto & Barbaree, 1995). The effect reaches onto college campuses. Sexually active university students are less likely to use condoms when intoxicated (MacDonald & others, 1996; in press). University women under alcohol's influence find an attractive but sexually promiscuous man a more appealing potential date than they do when sober. It seems, surmise Sheila Murphy and her colleagues (1998), "that when people have been drinking, the restraining forces of reason may weaken and yield under the pressure of their desires."

"That is not one of the seven habits of highly effective people."

Facts: College and university students drink more alcohol than their nonstudent peers, and they spend more on alcohol than on books and other beverages combined. Fraternity and sorority members drink three times as much as other students (Atwell, 1986; Malloy & others, 1994). Although few university students believe they have an alcohol problem, many meet the criteria for alcohol abuse (Marlatt, 1991). As students mature with age, they drink less.

Don't drink and drive
With an emphasis on the innocent victims of drunk driving, Mothers Against Drunk Driving (MADD) has vigorously promoted awareness of the dangers of alcohol abuse. They have also lobbied for stiffer penalties for drunk drivers.

As with other psychoactive drugs, alcohol's behavioral effects stem not only from its alteration of brain chemistry but also from the user's expectations. Many studies have found that when people *believe* that alcohol affects social behavior in certain ways, and *believe*, rightly or wrongly, that they have been drinking alcohol, they will behave accordingly (Leigh, 1989). In a driving simulator, "sensation-seeking" people drive more recklessly when they *believe* they have consumed alcohol (McMillen & others, 1989).

Another example: Although alcohol decreases sexual inhibitions, people become even more responsive to sexual stimuli if they *believe* alcohol promotes arousal and *believe* they have been drinking. From their review of research, Jay Hull and Charles Bond (1986) concluded that for some people alcohol serves "as an excuse to become sexually aroused."

Consider one such experiment by David Abrams and Terence Wilson (1983). They gave Rutgers University men who volunteered for a study on "alcohol and sexual stimulation" either an alcoholic or a nonalcoholic drink. (Both drinks had a strong taste that masked any alcohol.) In each group, half the participants thought they were drinking alcohol and half thought they were not. After being shown an erotic movie clip, the men who *thought* they had consumed alcohol were more likely to report having strong sexual fantasies and feeling guilt-free. Being able to *attribute* their sexual responses to alcohol released their inhibitions—whether they actually had drunk alcohol or not. If, as commonly believed, liquor is the quicker pick-her-upper, the effect lies partly in that powerful sex organ, the mind.

This research illustrates an important principle: A drug's psychological effects are powerfully influenced by the user's expectations. And that explains why drug experiences vary with cultures (Ward, 1994). If one culture assumes that a particular drug produces euphoria (or aggression or sexual arousal) and another does not, each culture may find its expectations fulfilled.

Barbiturates

The **barbiturate** drugs, or *tranquilizers*, mimic the effects of alcohol. Because they depress sympathetic nervous system activity, barbiturates such as Nembutal and Seconal are sometimes prescribed to induce sleep or reduce anxiety. In larger doses, they can lead to impaired memory and judgment. In combination with alcohol—as when people take a sleeping pill after an evening of heavy drinking—the total depressive effect on body functions can be lethal. With sufficient doses, barbiturates by themselves can also cause death, which makes them the drugs often chosen by those attempting suicide.

Opiates

The **opiates**—opium and its derivatives, morphine and heroin—also depress neural functioning. The pupils constrict, the breathing slows, and the user becomes lethargic. For a few hours, blissful pleasure replaces pain and anxiety. But for short-term pleasure one pays a long-term price, which for the heroin user is the gnawing craving for another fix, the need for progressively larger doses, the week-long physical anguish of withdrawal—and for some, the ultimate price: death by overdose.

The pathway to addiction is treacherous. When repeatedly flooded with artificial opiates, the brain eventually stops producing its own opiates, the endorphins. If the drug is then withdrawn, the brain lacks the normal level of these painkilling neurotransmitters. The result is the agony of withdrawal.

Stimulants

The most widely used stimulants are caffeine, nicotine, the powerful **amphetamines**, and the even more powerful cocaine. Stimulants speed up body functions, hence the nickname "speed" for amphetamines. Strong stimulants increase heart and

---

Fact: In a Harvard School of Public Health survey of 18,000 students at 140 colleges and universities, almost 9 in 10 students reported abuse by intoxicated peers, including sleep and study interruption, insults, sexual advances, and property damage (Wechsler & others, 1994).

Fact: Ten percent of U.S. drinkers account for half of the alcohol consumed (Centers for Disease Control, 1989).

Fact: Alcohol kills more people than all illegal drugs combined. So does tobacco (Siegel, 1990).

■ **barbiturates** drugs that depress the activity of the central nervous system, reducing anxiety but impairing memory and judgment.

■ **opiates** opium and its derivatives, such as morphine and heroin; they depress neural activity, temporarily lessening pain and anxiety.

■ **amphetamines** drugs that stimulate neural activity, causing speeded-up body functions and associated energy and mood changes.

Wake me up
Drive-through espresso stands are thriving in many places, including Anchorage, Alaska, where sleepy patrons seek out a caffeinated boost to get them through the dark winter days.

breathing rates. Pupils dilate, appetite diminishes (because blood sugar rises), and energy and self-confidence rise. For these reasons, people use stimulants to stay awake, lose weight, or boost mood or athletic performance. As with other drugs, the benefits come with a price. When drug stimulation ends, the user experiences a compensating slowdown and may "crash" into fatigue, headaches, irritability, and depression. Like the depressants, stimulants—including coffee and caffeinated sodas—can be addictive (Silverman & others, 1992).

In national surveys, 3 percent of U.S. adults and 3 percent of high school seniors reported having tried cocaine during the past year (Johnston & others, 1999; National Institute on Drug Abuse, 1999). Of the seniors, nearly half said they had smoked *crack*, a potent form of cocaine. During the 1990s the decade-long cocaine epidemic subsided, thanks partly to increased treatment and awareness and partly to the impoverishment, imprisonment, and deaths of many cocaine victims.

Cocaine addiction is a fast track from euphoria to crash. When animals and people chew coca leaves, only small amounts of cocaine enter the bloodstream, and they do so gradually, without seeming ill effects (Siegel, 1990). But when extracted cocaine is sniffed ("snorted"), and especially when injected or smoked ("free-based"), it enters the bloodstream quickly. The result: a "rush" of euphoria that lasts 15 to 30 minutes. Because the rush depletes the brain's supply of the neurotransmitters dopamine, serotonin, and norepinephrine, a crash of agitated depression occurs as the drug's effect wears off (**FIGURE 19.2**, page 276). Crack works even faster and produces a briefer but more intense high, a more intense crash, and a craving for more crack, which wanes after several hours but then returns several days later (Gawin, 1991).

To explore dopamine's role in cocaine addiction, researchers created a strain of mice in which they had "knocked out" the gene for a protein that mops up and recycles the excess dopamine released by a nerve cell (Giros & others, 1996). Like cocaine-hyped mice, these mice became hyperactive. They passed through a photocell beam five times as often as other mice. Moreover, cocaine did not affect the "knockout" mice. This suggests that cocaine raises dopamine concentrations by binding to the mop-up site, thus blocking its reuptake of dopamine. This effectively locks the brain's neural reward switches into the "on" position (Landry, 1997).

Regular cocaine users become addicted. Monkeys have become so strongly addicted that they will press a lever more than 12,000 times to gain each cocaine injection (Siegel, 1990). Human and animal cocaine users may experience emotional disturbance, suspiciousness, convulsions, cardiac arrest, or respiratory failure. In situations that trigger aggression, ingesting cocaine may increase aggressive reactions.

The recipe for Coca-Cola originally included an extract of the coca plant, creating a cocaine tonic for tired elderly people. Between 1896 and 1905, Coke was indeed "the real thing."

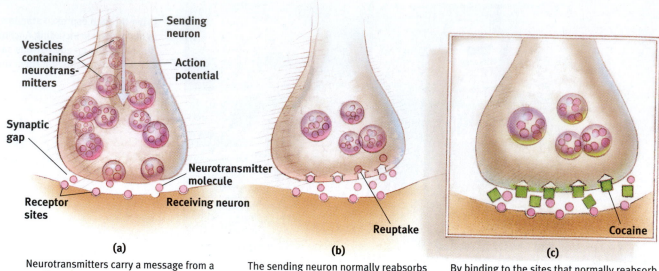

(a)

Neurotransmitters carry a message from a sending neuron across a synapse to receptor sites on a receiving neuron.

FIGURE **19.2**
Cocaine euphoria and crash

(b)

The sending neuron normally reabsorbs excess neurotransmitter molecules, a process called reuptake.

(c)

By binding to the sites that normally reabsorb neurotransmitter molecules, cocaine blocks reuptake of dopamine, norepinephrine, and serotonin (Ray & Ksir, 1990). The extra neurotransmitter molecules therefore remain in the synapse, intensifying their normal mood-altering effects and producing a euphoric rush. When the cocaine level drops, the absence of these neurotransmitters produces a crash.

Caged rats fight when given foot shocks, and they fight even more when given cocaine and foot shocks. Asked to determine how much electric shock one's opponent will receive in a laboratory competition, cocaine users who have ingested high-dose cocaine set higher levels than do those who have received a placebo (Licata & others, 1993).

As with all psychoactive drugs, cocaine's psychological effects depend not only on the dosage and form in which one takes the drug but also on one's expectations, one's personality, and the situation—a mix of factors. Given a placebo, cocaine users who *think* they are taking cocaine often have a cocainelike experience (Van Dyke & Byck, 1982).

Hallucinogens

Hallucinogens are psychoactive drugs that distort perceptions and evoke vivid images in the absence of sensory input (which is why these drugs are also called *psychedelics*, meaning "mind-manifesting"). Some are natural substances, such as the mild hallucinogen marijuana. Others are synthetic, the two best known of which are PCP ("angel dust"), a potent painkiller that has highly unpredictable and sometimes devastating psychological effects, and LSD.

LSD

In 1943, chemist Albert Hofmann, the creator of **LSD** (*lysergic acid diethylamide*) took the first "acid trip." After accidentally ingesting some of the chemical, Hofmann reported that he "perceived an uninterrupted stream of fantastic pictures, extraordinary shapes with intense, kaleidoscopic play of colors" (Siegel, 1984). LSD and other powerful hallucinogens are chemically similar to (and therefore block the actions of) a subtype of the neurotransmitter serotonin (Jacobs, 1987).

The emotions of an LSD trip vary from euphoria to detachment to panic. As with all drug use, a person's current mood and expectations color the LSD experience. Despite emotional variations, the resulting perceptual distortions and hallucinations do have commonalities. Psychologist Ronald Siegel (1982) reports that no matter whether you provoke your brain to hallucinate by loss of oxygen, extreme sensory deprivation, or drugs, "it will hallucinate in basically the same way." (See Close Up: Near-Death Experiences, page 278.) The experience typically begins with simple geometric forms, such as a lattice, a cobweb, or a spiral (**FIGURE 19.3**). The next phase consists of more meaningful images; some may be superimposed on a tunnel or funnel, others may be replays of past emotional experiences. When the hallucinogenic experience peaks, people frequently feel separated from their bodies and experience dreamlike scenes as though they were real—so real that users may become panic-stricken or even harm themselves.

FIGURE 19.3
Hallucinationlike patterns
Geometric forms, similar to those experienced by drug users during drug-induced hallucinations, can be seen in the embroidery of the Huichol. These Mexican Indians used peyote, from which the hallucinogen mescaline derives.

Marijuana

Marijuana consists of the leaves and flowers of the hemp plant, which for 5000 years has been cultivated for its fiber. Marijuana's major active ingredient is **THC**, the everyday name of the complex organic molecule delta-9-tetrahydrocannabinol. Whether smoked or eaten in such foods as chocolate brownies, THC produces a mix of effects that makes the drug difficult to classify. (Smoking gets the drug into the brain in about 7 seconds, producing a greater effect than does eating the drug, which causes its peak concentration to be reached at a slower, unpredictable rate.) Like alcohol, marijuana relaxes, disinhibits, and may produce a euphoric high. But marijuana also acts as a mild hallucinogen by amplifying sensitivity to colors, sounds, tastes, and smells.

As with other drugs, the marijuana user's experience varies, depending on the situation. If the person feels anxious or depressed, taking the drug may intensify these feelings. In other situations, using marijuana can be not only pleasurable but therapeutic. For those who suffer the pain, nausea, and severe weight loss associated with AIDS, or the nausea that sometimes accompanies cancer chemotherapy, marijuana may spell relief (Benson & Watson, 1999; Fackelmann, 1997). Such benefits have motivated legislation legalizing the drug for such patients. The medical uses are, however, compromised by the toxicity of marijuana smoke—which can cause cancer, lung damage, and pregnancy complications, reports the National Academy of Sciences (1999). If the drug becomes widely legalized for prescribed medical uses, capsules, patches, and inhalers may be developed to deliver the THC.

The National Academy of Sciences (1982, 1999) research reviews have identified other not-so-pleasant marijuana consequences. Like alcohol, marijuana impairs the motor coordination, perceptual skills, and reaction time necessary for safely operating an automobile or other machine. "THC causes animals to misjudge events," reports Ronald Siegel (1990, p. 163). "Pigeons wait too long to respond to buzzers or lights that tell them food is available for brief periods; and rats turn the wrong way in mazes." Marijuana also disrupts memory formation and interferes with immediate recall of information learned only a few minutes before. Such cognitive effects outlast the period of smoking (Pope & Yurgelun-Todd, 1996; Smith, 1995). Clearly, being stoned is not conducive to learning.

■ **LSD** a powerful hallucinogenic drug; also known as *acid* (*lysergic acid diethylamide*).

■ **THC** the major active ingredient in marijuana; triggers a variety of effects, including mild hallucinations.

CLOSE-UP:

NEAR-DEATH EXPERIENCES— MYSTICAL VISIONS OR HALLUCINATIONS?

A man . . . hears himself pronounced dead by his doctor. He begins to hear an uncomfortable noise, a loud ringing or buzzing, and at the same time feels himself moving very rapidly through a long dark tunnel. After this, he suddenly finds himself outside of his own physical body . . . and sees his own body from a distance, as though he is a spectator. . . . Soon other things begin to happen. Others come to meet and to help him. He glimpses the spirits of relatives and friends who have already died, and a loving, warm spirit of a kind he has never encountered before—a being of light—appears before him. . . . He is overwhelmed by intense feelings of joy, love, and peace. Despite his attitude, though, he somehow reunites with his physical body and lives. (Moody, 1976, pp. 23, 24)

This passage from Raymond Moody's bestselling book, *Life After Life*, is a composite description of a **near-death experience**. Near-death experiences are more common than you might suspect. Several inves-tigators each interviewed 100 or more people who had come close to death through such physical traumas as cardiac arrest. In each study, 30 to 40 percent of such patients recalled a near-death experience (Ring, 1980; Schnaper, 1980). When George Gallup, Jr. (1982; Gallup & O'Connell, 1986) interviewed a national sample of Americans, 15 percent reported having experienced a close brush with death. One-third of these people—representing some 8 million people by Gallup's estimate—reported an accompanying mystical experience. Some claimed to recall

things said while they lay unconscious and near death. (But then, anesthetized surgical patients in a "controlled coma" are sometimes not as out cold for the count as surgical teams might suppose. Occasionally, they can later recall operating room conversation or obscure facts or words presented over headphones [Bonke & others, 1986; Merikle & Daneman, 1996; Jelicic & others, 1992].)

Did Moody's description of the "complete" near-death experience sound familiar? The parallels with Ronald Siegel's (1977) descriptions of the typical hallucinogenic experience are striking: replay of old memories, out-of-body sensations, and visions of tunnels or funnels and bright lights or beings of light (**FIGURE 19.4**). Patients who have experienced temporal lobe seizures have also reported profound mystical experiences, as have solitary sailors and polar explorers while enduring monotony, isolation, and cold (Suedfeld & Mocellin, 1987). The twilight state between waking and

sleeping may similarly produce sensations of floating up off the bed. Oxygen deprivation can produce such hallucinations. As oxygen deprivation turns off the brain's inhibitory cells, neural activity increases in the visual cortex, notes Susan Blackmore (1991, 1993). The result is a growing patch of light, which looks much like what you would see moving through a tunnel.

Perhaps, then, the bored or stressed brain manufactures the near-death experience. The near-death experience, argued Siegel (1980), is best understood as "hallucinatory activity of the brain." It's like gazing out a window at dusk: We begin to see the reflected interior of the room as if it were outside, either because the light from outside is dimming (as in the near-death experience) or because the inside light is being amplified (as with LSD).

Some near-death investigators object. Those who have experienced both hallucinations and the near-death phenomenon typically deny their similarity. Moreover, a near-

FIGURE 19.4

Near-death vision or hallucination?

Psychologist Ronald Siegel (1977) reports that people under the influence of hallucinogenic drugs often see "a bright light in the center of the field of vision. . . . The location of this point of light create[s] a tunnel-like perspective." (From "Hallucinations" by R. K. Siegel. Copyright © 1977 Scientific American, Inc. All rights reserved.)

THE FAR SIDE

Before

After

And then suddenly I saw this bright light at the end of a tunnel!

death experience may change people in ways that a drug trip doesn't. Those who have been "embraced by the light" may become kinder, more spiritual, more believing in life after death. Skeptics reply that these effects stem from the death-related context of the experience. When near death, people worldwide sometimes report visions of another world, though the content of that vision often depends on the culture (Kellehear, 1996).

The controversy over interpreting near-death experiences raises a basic mind-body issue: Is the mind immaterial? Can it exist separate from the body? **Dualists** answer yes. They believe that the mind and body are interacting but distinct entities—the mind nonphysical, the body physical. As Socrates says in Plato's *Phaedo*, "Does not death mean that the body comes to exist by itself, separated from the soul, and that the soul exists by herself, separated from the body? What is death but that?"

For Socrates, as for those today who believe that near-death experiences are proof of immortality, death is not really the death of the person. Death is instead a person's liberation from the bodily prison, an occasion for rejoicing. (Carried to its extreme, this dualist view has given rise to glorifications of the afterlife trip under such titles as "The Thrill of Dying" and "The Wonderful World of Death.")

"The mind seems to act independently of the brain in the same sense that a programmer acts independently of his computer."

Neuroscientist Wilder Penfield, 1975

Monists answer no to the separation of mind and body. They contend that mind and body are different aspects of the same thing. The mind is what the brain does. In the Western world, monists include both scientists who assume the inseparability of mind and brain and theologians who affirm an afterlife that involves some form of bodily resurrection. Such monists generally believe that life is embodied, that death is real, and that without bodies we truly are nobodies.

"You, your joys and sorrows, your memories and your ambitions, your sense of personal identity and free will, are in fact no more than the behavior of a vast assembly of nerve cells and their associated molecules. As Lewis Carroll's Alice might have phrased it, 'You're nothing but a pack of neurons.'"

Geneticist Sir Francis Crick, *The Astonishing Hypothesis*, 1994

As debates over the significance of dreams, fantasy, hypnotic states, drug-induced hallucinations, and near-death experiences illustrate, science informs our wondering about human consciousness and human nature. Although there remain questions that it cannot answer, science nevertheless helps fashion our image of who we are—of our human potentials and our human limits.

■ **near-death experience** an altered state of consciousness reported after a close brush with death (such as through cardiac arrest); often similar to drug-induced hallucinations.

■ **dualism** the presumption that mind and body are two distinct entities that interact.

■ **monism** the presumption that mind and body are different aspects of the same thing.

TABLE 19.1

A GUIDE TO SELECTED PSYCHOACTIVE DRUGS

Drug	Type	Pleasurable Effects	Adverse Effects
Alcohol	Depressant	Initial high followed by relaxation and disinhibition	Depression, memory loss, organ damage, impaired reactions
Heroin	Depressant	Rush of euphoria, relief from pain	Depressed physiology, agonizing withdrawal
Caffeine	Stimulant	Increased alertness and wakefulness	Anxiety, restlessness, and insomnia in high doses; uncomfortable withdrawal
Methamphetamine ("speed," "crack," "ice")	Stimulant	Euphoria, alertness, energy	Irritability, insomnia, hypertension, seizures
Cocaine	Stimulant	Rush of euphoria, confidence, energy	Cardiovascular stress, suspiciousness, depressive crash
Nicotine	Stimulant	Arousal and relaxation, sense of well-being	Heart disease, cancer (from tars)
Marijuana	Mild hallucinogen	Enhanced sensation, relief of pain, distortion of time, relaxation	Lowered sex hormones, disrupted memory, lung damage from smoke

Unlike alcohol, which the body eliminates within hours, THC and its by-products linger in the body for a month or more. Thus, contrary to the usual tolerance phenomenon, regular users may achieve a high with smaller amounts of the drug than occasional users would take to get the same effect.

Uncertainty persists about marijuana's physical effects, but medical research suggests that long-term marijuana use may depress male sex hormone and sperm levels and damage the lungs more than does cigarette smoking (Wu & others, 1988). Large doses hasten the loss of brain cells (Landfield & others, 1988). Although marijuana is not as addictive as cocaine or nicotine, it changes brain chemistry, much as cocaine and heroin do, and it may make the brain more susceptible to cocaine and heroin addiction (Tanda & others, 1997). One study that followed 654 junior high students into their early twenties found that adolescents who heavily used marijuana developed more health and family problems than did nonusers (Newcomb & Bentler, 1988).

Despite their differences, the psychoactive drugs summarized in Table 19.1 share a common feature: They trigger negative aftereffects that offset their immediate positive effects. The aftereffects illustrate a more general principle: Emotions tend to produce opposing emotions, which linger after the original emotions disappear. With repetition, the opposing emotions grow stronger. This emotions-trigger-opposing-emotions principle parallels that of drug-induced pleasures; the pleasures wane as the drug exacts its compensatory price. That helps explain both tolerance and withdrawal. As the opposing, negative aftereffects get stronger, it takes larger and larger doses to produce the desired high (tolerance), causing the aftereffects to worsen in the drug's absence (withdrawal). This in turn creates a need to switch off the withdrawal symptoms by taking yet more of the drug.

"How strange would appear to be this thing that men call pleasure! And how curiously it is related to what is thought to be its opposite, pain! . . . Wherever the one is found, the other follows up behind."

Plato, *Phaedo,* **Fourth Century** B.C.

Influences on Drug Use

Preview Question: Why do some people become regular users of consciousness-altering drugs?

Drug use by North American youth increased during the 1970s. Then, with increased drug education and a more realistic and deglamorized media depiction of taking drugs, drug use declined sharply. But since the early 1990s the cultural antidrug voice has softened and drugs are once again being glamorized in some music and films. And drug use has rebounded, renewing public concern. Consider the trends:

+ In the University of Michigan's annual survey of 15,000 high school seniors, the proportion who believed there is "great risk" in regular marijuana use rose from 35 percent in 1978 to 79 percent in 1991, then retreated to 57 percent in 1999 (Johnston & others, 1999).

+ After peaking in 1978, marijuana use by this age group declined through 1992, but it has been rising since then (**FIGURE 19.5**).

+ In the UCLA/American Council on Education annual survey of new college and university students, support for the legalization of marijuana dropped from 53 percent in 1977 to 17 percent in 1989; support rebounded to 34 percent in 1999 (Astin & others, 1997; Sax & others, 1999).

Similar changes in attitude and usage since the late 1970s appear in surveys of Canadian teens (Smart & others, 1991). And in Britain, the number of 16- to 65-year-olds who acknowledged ever using marijuana similarly increased, from 2 percent in 1969 to 16 percent in 1993. By the mid-1990s, 57 percent of students surveyed at 10 British universities said they had tried marijuana (Conner & McMillan, 1999).

Other studies reveal a changing national attitude toward alcohol in the United States. More than at any time since Prohibition, health- and safety-conscious people see alcohol less as a beverage to be enjoyed than as a drug to be shunned. The number of new U.S. collegians who reported abstaining from drinking beer during the preceding year doubled, from 25 percent in 1981 to 49 percent in 1999. Four in 10 Americans declare themselves "a total abstainer" (Sourcebook, 1998). Hard liquor consumption per person dropped 40 percent from 1980 to 1994 in the United States and has similarly declined in Canada (Bureau of the Census, 1996; Statistics Canada, 1996). When the alcohol industry started substituting wine coolers for wine and nonalcoholic beer for alcoholic, it was clear that attitudes were changing.

Cigarette smoking, though addictive, has similarly plummeted among the general population. Recently, however, it has rebounded among teens. The drop is especially great among highly educated people, most of whom either never started or have stopped. The apparent lesson: Effectively inform people about the health hazards of using cocaine, marijuana, alcohol, or tobacco and—without therapy, support groups, or medicines—many will simply stop.

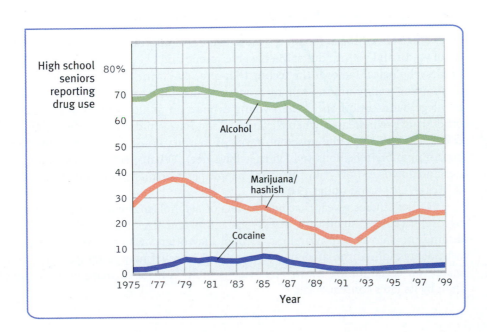

FIGURE 19.5 Trends in drug use
The percentage of high school seniors who report having used alcohol, marijuana, or cocaine during the past 30 days declined from the late 1970s to 1992. Since then drug use has been increasing and drug merchandise has become more openly available in stores and at concerts. (From Johnston & others, 1999.)

Why, then, do some people continue to use psychoactive drugs, and why is teen drug use increasing? Why, for example, do 42 percent of American high school seniors report having tried an illegal drug during the past year (Johnston & others, 1999)? For some adolescents, occasional drug use represents seeking a thrill. Why, though, do other adolescents become regular drug users?

Biological Influences

Some people may be biologically vulnerable to alcohol. For example, evidence accumulates that heredity influences alcohol use problems:

+ Adopted individuals are more susceptible to alcoholism if one or both of their biological parents has a history of alcoholism (Mirin & Weiss, 1989).
+ Having an identical twin with alcoholism puts a male at especially increased risk for alcohol problems (McGue, 1999; Prescott & others, 1994).
+ Boys who at age 6 are excitable, impulsive, and fearless (genetically influenced traits) are more likely as teens to smoke, drink, and use other drugs (Masse & Tremblay, 1997).
+ Compared with other children, children whose parents abuse alcohol have a higher tolerance for multiple alcoholic drinks taken over an hour or two (Schuckit & Smith, 1996). They also show a smaller evoked brain response to certain types of sensory stimulation (Polich & others, 1994).
+ Researchers have bred rats and mice that prefer alcoholic drinks to water (Azar, 1995; Holden, 1991; Goldman, 1996). One such strain has reduced levels of a brain chemical called NPY; mice engineered to overproduce NPY are very sensitive to alcohol's sedating effect and drink little (Thiele & others, 1998).
+ Molecular geneticists have identified a gene on chromosome 11 that is more common among people with alcoholism, especially in severe cases (Noble, 1993).

Such findings have fueled the search for a better understanding of genetic and biochemical influences on addiction. The most extensive study yet—a $25 million, 5-year analysis of 600 alcoholics and their relatives—is under way. If biological markers for being prone to addiction can be found, then perhaps young people at risk for specific addictions can be identified and counseled.

Psychological and Cultural Influences

Psychological and social factors may also exert an important influence. In their studies of youth and young adults, Michael Newcomb and L. L. Harlow (1986) found that one psychological factor is the feeling that one's life is meaningless and directionless, a common feeling among school dropouts who subsist without job skills, without privilege, with little hope. When young unmarried adults leave home, alcohol and other drug use increases; when they marry and have children, it decreases (Bachman & others, 1997). Yet the ups and downs of marijuana usage seem not due to youth becoming more rebellious (which they have not). What predicts usage is instead the ups and downs in how risky the young people perceive marijuana use to be (Bachman & others, 1998, and **FIGURE 19.6**)

Other studies reveal that heavy users of alcohol, marijuana, and cocaine often have experienced significant stress or failure and are depressed. By temporarily dulling the pain of self-awareness, alcohol may offer a way to avoid having to cope with depression, anger, anxiety, or insomnia. The relief may be temporary, but as research on conditioning shows, behavior is often controlled more by its immediate than by its later consequences.

Warning signs of alcoholism
- Drinking binges
- Regretting things done or said when drunk
- Feeling low or guilty after drinking
- Failing to honor a resolve to drink less
- Drinking to alleviate depression or anxiety
- Avoiding family or friends when drinking

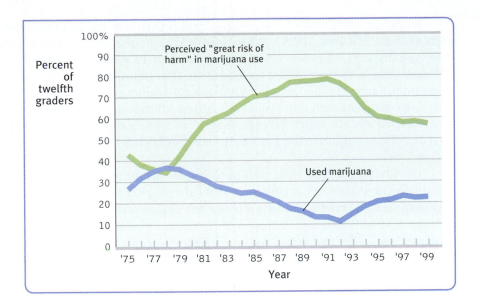

FIGURE 19.6
Perceived marijuana risk and actual use
As the percentage of twelfth graders perceiving a "great risk" in regular marijuana use increases, the percentage having used it in the previous 30 days decreases. (Data from Johnston & others, 1999.)

Especially for teenagers, drug use can also have social roots, evident in differing rates of drug use across cultural groups. In the United States, alcohol and other drug addiction rates are extremely low among the Amish, Mennonites, Mormons, and Orthodox Jews (Trimble, 1994). What do you suppose is the rate of drug usage among African American students—low or high? One of psychology's best-kept secrets is that, contrary to popular stereotypes, African American high school seniors "report the lowest rates of use for virtually all drugs" (Johnston & others, 1994, 1996). For example, nearly a third of white seniors, but only 13 percent of black seniors, report recently drinking heavily. Monthly smoking rates are 38 percent among white seniors, only 14 percent among black seniors. Although these data exclude high school dropouts, independent government studies of drug use in households nationwide and among 12,272 high schoolers in all 50 states confirms the finding: African American teens have sharply lower rates of drinking, smoking, and cocaine use (Bass & Kane-Williams, 1993; Kann & others, 1993). (Curiously, however, cocaine-related arrests and emergency room visits occur more often among African Americans [Bennett & DiIulio, 1996].)

Peer culture is a major social influence. By their words and examples, peers influence attitudes about drugs. They also throw the parties and provide the drugs. If an adolescent's friends use drugs, the odds are that he or she will, too. If the friends do not, the opportunity may not even arise. Indeed, the peer factor is so powerful that other predictors of adolescent drug use, such as family strength, religiousness, and school adjustment, seem to operate through their effects on peer associations.

Peer influence is not just a matter of what friends do and say but also of what adolescents *believe* their friends are doing and favoring. Young adolescents consume more alcohol when, as often happens, they overestimate their friends' use (Aas & Klepp, 1992; Graham & others, 1991). In one survey of sixth graders in 22 states, 14 percent believed their friends had smoked marijuana, though only 4 percent acknowledged doing so (Wren, 1999). At the university level, drinking dominates social occasions partly because students overestimate their fellow students' enthusiasm for alcohol (Prentice & Miller, 1993; Self, 1994). Thinking that few students share their concerns about the risks associated with alcohol, most students surrender to the perceived norm. Nearly half have engaged in binge drinking (Wechsler & others, 1994).

In the real world, alcohol accounts for one-sixth or less of beverage use. In television's world, drinking alcohol occurs more often than the combined drinking of coffee, tea, soft drinks, and water (Gerbner, 1990).

Annual Beer and Wine Consumption, Liters per Person

	Beer	Wine
France	41	67
Germany	143	25
Italy	23	57
New Zealand	110	15
Australia	102	19
United Kingdom	106	12
United States	87	7
Sweden	59	12

Source: *Australian Social Trends, 1995.*

Humorist Dave Barry (1995) recalling why he smoked his first cigarette the summer he turned 15: "Arguments against smoking: 'It's a repulsive addiction that slowly but surely turns you into a gasping, gray-skinned, tumor-ridden invalid, hacking up brownish gobs of toxic waste from your one remaining lung.' Arguments for smoking: 'Other teen-agers are doing it.' Case closed! Let's light up!"

People are more likely to stop using drugs if their use was influenced by their peers (Kandel & Raveis, 1989). When friends stop or the social network changes, they typically stop. As noted earlier, more than 9 in 10 soldiers who became drug-addicted while in Vietnam ceased their drug use after returning home. Teenagers who come from happy families and do well in school seldom use drugs, largely because they rarely associate with those who do (Oetting & Beauvais, 1987, 1990). As always with correlations, the traffic between friends' and one's own drug use may be two way: Our friends influence us, but we also select as friends those who share our likes and dislikes.

The findings suggest three possible channels of influence for drug prevention and treatment programs: (1) education about the long-term costs of a drug's temporary pleasures, (2) efforts to boost people's self-esteem and purpose in life, and (3) attempts to modify peer associations or to "inoculate" youth against peer pressures by training them in "refusal skills." Said more directly, people rarely abuse drugs if they understand the physical and psychological costs, feel good about themselves and the directions their lives are taking, and are in a peer group that disapproves of using drugs. These educational, psychological, and social factors help explain why 42 percent of American high school dropouts, but only 15 percent of college graduates, smoke (Ladd, 1998).

REVIEW AND REFLECT:

Drugs and Consciousness

What are dependence and addiction? Can substance abusers overcome their addictions?

Drugs often trigger withdrawal symptoms—negative aftereffects that oppose and offset their temporary pleasure. Such symptoms can lead to physical or psychological dependence. Medical use of drugs rarely creates addictions, however, and many who do suffer drug addictions overcome them when their social context changes.

What types of drugs alter our perceptions and moods, and how do they work?

The three main categories of psychoactive drugs are depressants, stimulants, and hallucinogens. All of them alter consciousness. Alcohol, barbiturates, and the opiates act by *depressing* neural functioning. Each offers pleasures, but at the cost of impaired memory and self-awareness or other physical consequences.

Caffeine, nicotine, the amphetamines, and cocaine act by *stimulating* neural functioning. As with nearly all psychoactive drugs, they act at the synapses by influencing the brain's neuro-transmitters, and their effects depend on dosage and the user's personality and expectations.

LSD and marijuana can distort the user's judgments of time and, depending on the setting, can alter sensations and perceptions.

Why do some people become regular users of consciousness-altering drugs?

Drug use among teenagers and young adults declined during the 1980s, as attitudes changed, and began a rebound during the mid-1990s. Psychological factors (such as stress, depression, and hopelessness) and social factors (such as peer pressure) combine to lead many people to experiment with—and become dependent on—drugs. Some people also appear to have a greater biological susceptibility to dependence on drugs such as alcohol.

Terms and Concepts to Remember

psychoactive drug, p. 270
tolerance, p. 270
withdrawal, p. 270
physical dependence, p. 270
psychological dependence, p. 270
depressants, p. 272
stimulants, p. 272
hallucinogens, p. 272
barbiturates, p. 274

opiates, p. 274
amphetamines, p. 274
LSD (lysergic acid diethylamide), p. 276
THC, p. 277
near-death experience, p. 278
dualism, p. 279
monism, p. 279

Test Yourself

19.1. Continued use of a psychoactive drug produces tolerance. This means that the user will
   a. feel physical pain and intense cravings.
   b. be irreversibly addicted to the substance.
   c. need to take bigger doses to get the desired effect.
   d. be able to take smaller doses to get the desired effect.

19.2. Depressants are drugs that reduce neural activity and slow down body functions. The depressants include alcohol, barbiturates,
   a. and opiates.
   b. cocaine, and morphine.
   c. caffeine, nicotine, and marijuana.
   d. and amphetamines.

19.3. Alcohol is a depressant that, in significant doses, powerfully affects behavior. For example, drinking alcohol may make a person more helpful or more self-disclosing; conversely, it may make a person more aggressive or more sexually daring. These alcohol effects result from

a. alcoholic blackouts or memory losses.

b. deprivation of REM sleep.

c. sensory arousal and hallucination.

d. the lowering of inhibitions.

19.4. Nicotine, caffeine, amphetamines, and cocaine stimulate neural activity, speed up body functions, and

a. induce sensory hallucinations.

b. interfere with memory.

c. induce a temporary sense of well-being.

d. lead to heroin use.

19.5. About one-third of those who have survived a brush with death have reported near-death experiences, which are strikingly similar to the hallucinations evoked by

a. amphetamines.   c. LSD.

b. barbiturates.   d. marijuana.

19.6. Smoking marijuana can relieve certain kinds of pain and nausea. It also

a. impairs motor coordination, perception, reaction time, and memory.

b. inhibits people's emotions.

c. increases male sex hormone levels.

d. stimulates brain cell development.

19.7. Drug use by young North Americans generally declined from the late 1970s until the early 1990s and then began to increase again. *Social* explanations for drug use today focus on the powerful effect of peer influence. An important *psychological* contributor to drug use is

a. inflated self-esteem.

b. the feeling that life is meaningless and directionless.

c. academic and job pressures.

d. overprotective parents.

Review: A U.S. government survey of 27,616 current or former alcohol drinkers found that 40 percent of those who began drinking before age 15 grow dependent on alcohol. The same was true of only 10 percent of those who first imbibed at ages 21 or 22 (Grant & Dawson, 1998). What possible explanations might there be for this correlation between early use and later abuse?

Reflect: Drinking dominates university parties when students overestimate other students' enthusiasm for alcohol. Do you think such misperceptions exist on your campus? How might you find out?

Answers to the Test Yourself and Review questions can be found in the green appendix at the end of the book.

Learning

When a chinook salmon first emerges from its egg in the gravel bed of a stream, its genes provide many of the behavioral instructions it needs for life. It knows instinctively how and where to swim, what to eat, and how to protect itself from predators. Following this built-in plan, the young salmon soon begins its trek to the sea. After some four years in the ocean, the mature salmon returns to its birthplace. It navigates hundreds of miles to the mouth of its home river and then, guided by the scent of its home stream, begins an upstream odyssey to its ancestral spawning ground. Once there, the salmon seeks out the exact conditions of temperature, gravel, and water flow that will facilitate its breeding. It then mates and dies.

Unlike the salmon, we are not born with a genetic blueprint for life. Much of what we do we must learn from experience. Although we struggle to find the life direction a salmon is born with, our learning gives us more flexibility. We can learn how to build grass huts or snow shelters, submarines or space stations, and thereby adapt to almost any environment. Indeed, nature's most important gift to us may be our *adaptability*—our capacity to learn new behaviors that enable us to cope with changing circumstances.

No topic is closer to the heart of psychology than *learning, a relatively permanent change in an organism's behavior due to experience.* Psychologists study the learning of moral ideas, of visual perceptions, of a drug's expected effect. Psychologists also consider how learning shapes our thought and language, our motivations and emotions, our personalities and attitudes.

Learning in all such realms breeds hope. What is learnable, we can potentially teach—a fact that encourages parents, educators, coaches, and animal trainers. What has been learned we can potentially change by new learning—an assumption that underlies counseling, psychotherapy, and rehabilitation programs. No matter how unhappy, unsuccessful, or unloving we are, that need not be the end of our story.

By definition, experience is key to learning. More than 200 years ago, philosophers such as John Locke and David Hume echoed Aristotle's conclusion from 2000 years earlier: We learn by association. Our minds naturally connect events that occur in sequence: We *associate* them. If, after seeing and smelling freshly baked bread, you eat some and find it satisfying, then the next time you see and smell fresh bread, your experience will lead you to expect that eating some will be satisfying again. And if you associate a sound with a frightening consequence, then your fear may be aroused by the sound itself. As one 4-year-old exclaimed after watching a TV character get mugged, "If I had heard that music, I wouldn't have gone around the corner!" (Wells, 1981).

"O! This learning, what a thing it is."

William Shakespeare,
The Taming of the Shrew, 1597

FIGURE **1**
Associative learning
By linking two events that occur close together, both the sea snail and the seals exhibit associative learning. The sea snail associates the squirt with impending shock; the seals associate slapping and barking with receiving a herring. In both cases, the animals learned something important to their survival: to associate the past with the immediate future.

EVENT 1   EVENT 2

Sea snail associates splash with a tail shock

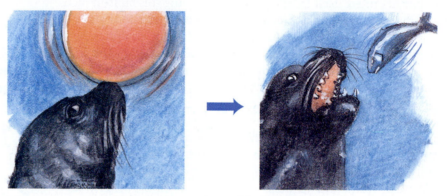

Seal learns to expect a snack for its showy antics

Simpler animals can learn simple associations (**FIGURE 1**). When disturbed by a squirt of water, the sea snail *Aplysia* will protectively withdraw its gill. If the squirts continue, as happens naturally in choppy water, the withdrawal response diminishes. (The snail's response "habituates.") But if the sea snail repeatedly receives an electric shock just after being squirted, its withdrawal response to the squirt alone becomes stronger. The animal associates the squirt with the impending shock. More complex animals can learn more complex associations, especially those that bring favorable consequences. Seals in an aquarium will repeat behaviors, such as slapping and barking, that prompt people to toss them a herring.

Learned associations influence people, too. During their first year, infants learn to associate different facial expressions with their accompanying behaviors and tones of voice—and thus to read a face (Walker-Andrews, 1997). Adults form similar associations. In one experiment, people rated neutral stimuli (Chinese characters) more positively when pressing their arms upward (as when lifting food or celebrating a triumphant moment) than they did when pressing them downward (as when pushing something or someone away). The positive associations of upward flexion infused the stimuli with more positive overtones (Cacioppo & others, 1993). (Can you feel a subtle emotional difference while lifting a table edge with upturned hands rather than pressing it down?)

Conditioning is the process of learning associations. In *classical conditioning*, the topic of Module 20, we learn to associate two stimuli and thus to anticipate events. We learn that a flash of lightning signals an impending crack of thunder, and so we start to brace ourselves when lightning flashes nearby (**FIGURE 2**).

In *operant conditioning*, the topic of Module 21, we learn to associate a response and its consequence and thus to repeat acts followed by rewards and avoid acts followed by punishment. We learn that pushing a vending machine button relates to the delivery of a candy bar (**FIGURE 3**).

"Learning is the eye of the mind."

Thomas Drake, *Bibliotheca Scholastica Instructissima*, 1633

Which type of conditioning does the sea snail illustrate? What about the seal?

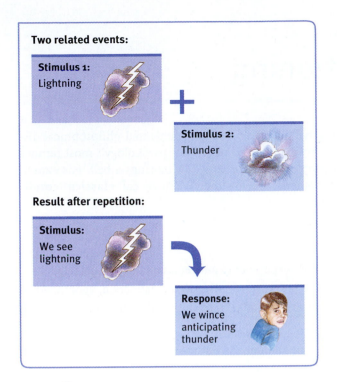

FIGURE 2
Classical conditioning

FIGURE 3
Operant conditioning

To simplify, we consider these two types of associative learning separately in Modules 20 and 21, but you should be aware that they often occur together in the same situation. A clever Japanese rancher reportedly herds cattle by outfitting them with electronic pagers, which he calls from his portable phone. After a week of training, the cows learned to associate two stimuli—the beep on their pager and the arrival of food (classical conditioning). But they also learned to associate their hustling to the food trough with the pleasure of eating (operant conditioning).

The concept of conditioning by association, however, leaves many questions: What principles influence the learning and the loss of associations? How can we apply these principles? And what really are the associations? Do associations form between neurons that are simultaneously active, such that firing one neuron cluster activates another? If so, does the first event also trigger a mental representation of the second? Does the beep on the cow's pager evoke a cognitive representation of food, to which the cow responds by coming to the trough? Or does it make little sense to explain conditioned associations in terms of cognitive processes?

Conditioning is not the only form of learning. As Module 22 explains, we learn from others' experiences and examples through *observational learning*. Complex animals, such as chimpanzees, sometimes learn behaviors merely by observing others perform them. If one animal watches another learn to solve a puzzle that gains a food reward, the observing animal may perform the trick more quickly.

In all these ways—by classical and operant conditioning and by observation—we humans learn and adapt to our environments. We learn to expect and prepare for significant events such as food or pain (classical conditioning). We also learn to repeat acts that bring good results and to avoid acts that bring bad results (operant conditioning). By watching others, we learn new behaviors (observational learning). And, through language, we also learn things we have neither experienced nor observed. Of all the world's creatures, we humans are the most capable of changing through learning.

Most of us would be unable to name the order of the songs on our favorite CD. Yet hearing the end of one piece cues (by association) an anticipation of the next. Likewise, when singing your national anthem, you associate the end of each line with the beginning of the next. (Pick a line out of the middle and notice how much harder it is to recall the *previous* line.)

Conditioned fear
Because of pain experienced during previous visits to the dentist chair, this young patient has learned to expect discomfort.

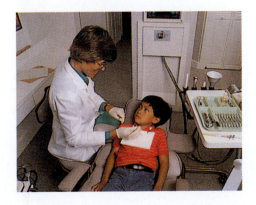

20 Classical Conditioning

Although the idea of **associative learning** had long generated philosophical discussion, it was only in the early twentieth century that psychology's most famous research verified it. For many people, the name Ivan Pavlov rings a bell. His experiments are classics, and the phenomenon he explored we justly call **classical conditioning** (or *Pavlovian conditioning*).

Pavlov's Experiments

Preview Questions: How did Pavlov's experiments on conditioning demonstrate learning by association? How do the processes of acquisition, extinction, spontaneous recovery, generalization, and discrimination affect a conditioned response?

Pavlov was driven by a lifelong passion for research. After setting aside his initial plan to follow his father into the Russian Orthodox priesthood, Pavlov received a medical degree at age 33 and spent the next two decades studying the digestive system. This work earned him Russia's first Nobel prize in 1904. But it was his novel experiments on learning, to which he devoted the last three decades of his life, that earned this feisty scientist his place in history.

Pavlov's new direction came when his creative mind seized on an incidental finding. After studying salivary secretion in dogs, he knew that when he put food in a dog's mouth the animal would invariably salivate. He also noticed that when he worked with the same dog repeatedly, the dog began salivating to stimuli associated with food—to the mere sight of the food, to the food dish, to the presence of the person who regularly brought the food, or even to the sound of that person's approaching footsteps. Because these "psychic secretions" interfered with his experiments on digestion, Pavlov considered them an annoyance—until he realized they pointed to a simple but important form of **learning**. From that time on, Pavlov studied learning, which he hoped might enable him to understand better the brain's workings.

At first, Pavlov and his assistants tried to imagine what the dog was thinking and feeling as it drooled in anticipation of the food. This only led them into fruitless debates. So to explore the phenomenon more objectively, they experimented. They paired various neutral stimuli with food in the mouth to see if the dog would begin salivating to the neutral stimuli alone. To eliminate the possible influence of extraneous stimuli, they isolated the dog in a small room, secured it in a harness, and attached a device that diverted its saliva to a measuring instrument (**FIGURE 20.1**).

■ **associative learning** learning that certain events (two stimuli in classical conditioning) occur together.

■ **classical conditioning** a type of learning in which an organism comes to associate stimuli. A neutral stimulus that signals an unconditioned stimulus (UCS) begins to produce a response that anticipates and prepares for the unconditioned stimulus. (Also called *Pavlovian conditioning*.)

■ **learning** a relatively permanent change in an organism's behavior due to experience.

Ivan Pavlov

"Experimental investigation . . . should lay a solid foundation for a future true science of psychology" (1927).

FIGURE 20.1
Pavlov's device for recording salivation
The dog's saliva was collected drop by drop in a tube. (Adapted from Goodwin, 1991.)

From an adjacent room they could present food—at first by sliding in a food bowl, later by blowing meat powder into the dog's mouth at a precise moment. If a neutral stimulus—something the dog could see or hear—now regularly signaled the arrival of food, would the dog associate the two stimuli? If so, would it begin salivating to the neutral stimulus in anticipation of the food?

The answers proved to be yes and yes. Just before placing food in the dog's mouth to produce salivation, Pavlov sounded a tone. After several pairings of tone and food, the dog began salivating to the tone alone, in anticipation of the meat powder. Using this procedure, Pavlov conditioned dogs to salivate to other stimuli—a buzzer, a light, a touch on the leg, even the sight of a circle.

Because salivation in response to food in the mouth was unlearned, Pavlov called it an **unconditioned response (UCR)**. Food in the mouth automatically, *unconditionally*, triggers a dog's salivary reflex (**FIGURE 20.2**). Thus, Pavlov called the food stimulus an **unconditioned stimulus (UCS)**.

Salivation in response to the tone was *conditional* upon the dog's learning the association between the tone and the food. One translation of Pavlov therefore calls the salivation the "conditional reflex" (Todes, 1997). More commonly, this learned response is known as the **conditioned response (CR)**. The previously irrelevant tone stimulus that now triggered the conditional salivation we call the **conditioned stimulus (CS)**. It's easy to distinguish these two kinds of stimuli and responses. Just remember: conditioned = learned; *un*conditioned = *un*learned.

If this demonstration of associative learning was so simple, what did Pavlov do for the next three decades? How did his research factory generate 532 papers on salivary conditioning (Windholz, 1997)? He and his associates explored the causes and effects of classical conditioning. Their experiments identified five major conditioning processes: acquisition, extinction, spontaneous recovery, generalization, and discrimination.

- **unconditioned response (UCR)** in classical conditioning, the unlearned, naturally occurring response to the unconditioned stimulus (UCS), such as salivation when food is in the mouth.

- **unconditioned stimulus (UCS)** in classical conditioning, a stimulus that unconditionally—naturally and automatically—triggers a response.

- **conditioned response (CR)** in classical conditioning, the learned response to a previously neutral conditioned stimulus (CS).

- **conditioned stimulus (CS)** in classical conditioning, an originally irrelevant stimulus that, after association with an unconditioned stimulus (UCS), comes to trigger a conditioned response.

FIGURE 20.2 Pavlov's classic experiment Pavlov presented a neutral stimulus (a tone) just before an unconditioned stimulus (food in mouth). The neutral stimulus then became a conditioned stimulus, producing a conditioned response.

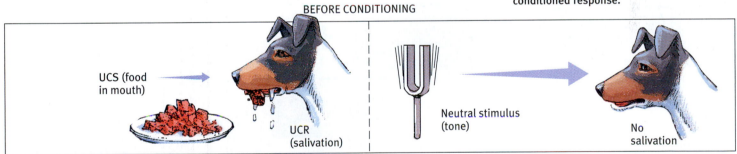

BEFORE CONDITIONING

UCS (food in mouth) → UCR (salivation)

An unconditioned stimulus (UCS) produces an unconditioned response (UCR).

Neutral stimulus (tone) → No salivation

A neutral stimulus produces no salivation response.

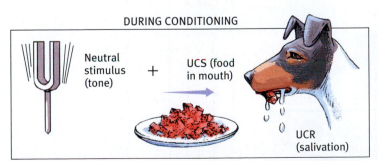

DURING CONDITIONING

Neutral stimulus (tone) + UCS (food in mouth) → UCR (salivation)

The unconditioned stimulus is repeatedly presented just after the neutral stimulus. The unconditioned stimulus continues to produce an unconditioned response.

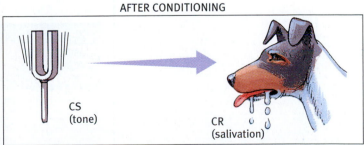

AFTER CONDITIONING

CS (tone) → CR (salivation)

The neutral stimulus alone now produces a conditioned response (CR), thereby becoming a conditioned stimulus (CS).

Acquisition

To understand the **acquisition**, or initial learning, of the stimulus-response relationship, Pavlov and his associates first had to confront the question of timing: How much time should elapse between presenting the neutral stimulus (the tone, the light, the touch, or whatever) and the unconditioned stimulus? They found that, in most cases, the answer was not much. With many species and procedures, half a second works well. What do you suppose would happen if the food (UCS) appeared *before* the tone (CS) rather than after? Would conditioning occur?

Not likely. Although there are exceptions, conditioning seldom occurs when the CS comes after the UCS. This finding fits the presumption that classical conditioning is biologically adaptive. It helps organisms *prepare* for good or bad events. Pavlov's tone (CS) signals an important biological event—the arrival of food (UCS). To a deer in the forest, the sound of a snapping twig (CS) may come to signal a predator (UCS). If the good or bad event had already occurred, the CS would not likely signal anything significant.

Michael Domjan (1992, 1994, 1997) showed how the CS signals an important biological event by conditioning the sexual arousal of male Japanese quail. Just before

Check yourself: If the aroma of cake baking sets your mouth to watering, what is the UCS? The CS? The CR? (See page 295.)

An unexpected CS
Onion breath does not usually produce sexual arousal. But when repeatedly paired with a passionate kiss it can become a CS and do just that.

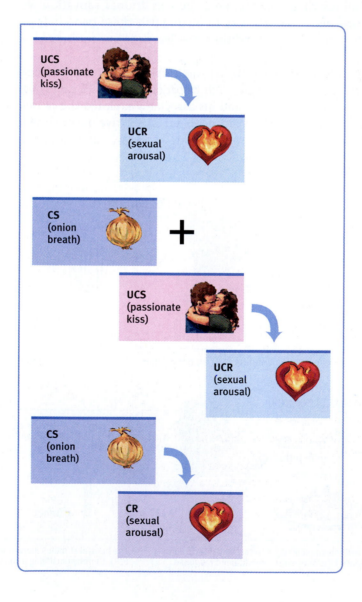

presenting an approachable female, the researchers turned on a red light. Over time, with the red light continuing to herald a female's impending arrival, it caused the male quail to become excited (and to copulate with her more quickly when she arrived). Moreover, the male quail developed a preference for their cage's red-light district. Exposure to sexually conditioned stimuli also caused them to release more semen and sperm (Domjan & others, 1998). All in all, the quail's capacity for classical conditioning gives them a reproductive edge. This illustrates the larger lesson that conditioning serves a function: It helps an animal survive and reproduce—by responding to cues that help it gain food, avoid dangers, defeat rivals, locate mates, and produce offspring (Hollis, 1997).

In humans, too, objects, smells, and sights associated with sexual pleasure become conditioned stimuli for sexual arousal. Psychologist Michael Tirrell (1990) recalls: "My first girlfriend loved onions, so I came to associate onion breath with kissing. Before long, onion breath sent tingles up and down my spine. Oh what a feeling!" (Questions: What is the unconditioned stimulus here? What is the conditioned response? See the diagram on page 292.) In laboratory experiments, even a geometric figure can become sexually arousing if repeatedly associated with an erotic stimulus (Byrne, 1982). (Note that in this case the figure is a CS, which gains its power to arouse by repeated pairing with a naturally erotic stimulus.)

Extinction and Spontaneous Recovery

After conditioning, what happens if the CS occurs repeatedly without the UCS? Will the CS continue to elicit the CR? Pavlov found that when he sounded the tone again and again without presenting food, the dogs salivated less and less. Their declining salivation illustrates **extinction**, the diminished responding that occurs when the CS (tone) no longer signals an impending UCS (food).

Pavlov found, however, that if he allowed several hours to elapse before sounding the tone again, the salivation to the tone would reappear spontaneously (**FIGURE 20.3**). This **spontaneous recovery**—the reappearance of a (weakened) CR after a rest pause—suggested to Pavlov that extinction was suppressing the CR rather than eliminating it.

After breaking up with his fire-breathing heartthrob, Tirrell also experienced extinction and spontaneous recovery. He recalls that "the smell of onion breath (CS), no longer paired with the kissing (UCS), lost its ability to shiver my timbers. Occasionally, though, after not sensing the aroma for a long while, smelling onion breath awakens a small version of the emotional response I once felt."

- **acquisition** in classical conditioning, the initial stage of learning; the phase associating a neutral stimulus with an unconditioned stimulus so that the neutral stimulus comes to elicit a conditioned response.

- **extinction** the diminishing of a conditioned response; in classical conditioning this occurs when an unconditioned stimulus (UCS) does not follow a conditioned stimulus (CS).

- **spontaneous recovery** the reappearance, after a rest period, of an extinguished conditioned response.

Remember:
UCS = UnConditioned Stimulus
UCR = UnConditioned Response
CS = Conditioned Stimulus
CR = Conditioned Response

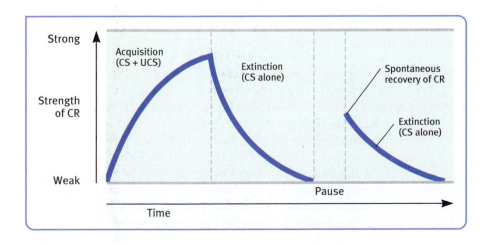

FIGURE 20.3
Idealized curve of acquisition, extinction, and spontaneous recovery
The rising curve shows that the CR rapidly grows stronger as the CS and UCS are repeatedly paired (acquisition), then weakens as the CS is presented alone (extinction). After a rest pause, the CR reappears (spontaneous recovery).

FIGURE 20.4 Generalization
Pavlov demonstrated generalization by attaching miniature vibrators to various parts of a dog's body. After conditioning salivation to stimulation of the thigh, he stimulated other areas. The closer a stimulated spot was to the thigh, the stronger the conditioned response. (From Pavlov, 1927.)

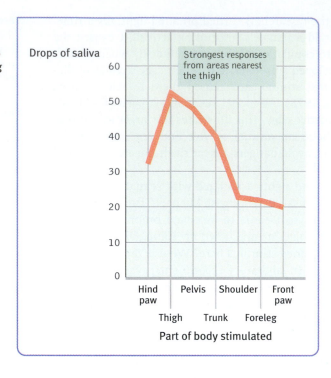

Drops of saliva

Strongest responses from areas nearest the thigh

Part of body stimulated

(Hind paw, Thigh, Pelvis, Trunk, Shoulder, Foreleg, Front paw)

Stimulus generalization

© The New Yorker Collection 1998 Sam Gross from cartoonbank.com. All Rights Reserved.

"I don't care if she's a tape dispenser. I love her."

■ **generalization** the tendency, once a response has been conditioned, for stimuli similar to the conditioned stimulus to elicit similar responses.

■ **discrimination** in classical conditioning, the learned ability to distinguish between a conditioned stimulus and other stimuli that do not signal an unconditioned stimulus.

Generalization

Pavlov and his students noticed that a dog conditioned to the sound of one tone also responded somewhat to the sound of a different tone never paired with food. Likewise, a dog conditioned to salivate when rubbed would also salivate some when scratched (Windholz, 1989) or when stimulated on a different body part (**FIGURE 20.4**). This tendency to respond to stimuli similar to the CS is called **generalization**.

Generalization can be adaptive, as when toddlers taught to fear moving cars in the street respond similarly to trucks and motorcycles, or when a child bitten by one dog may fear all dogs. So automatic is the generalization that one tortured Argentine writer still recoils with fear when he sees black shoes—his first glimpse of his torturers when they approached his cell. And a year after being shot in the shoulder and ribs during the 1995 massacre of 16 five-year-olds and their teacher in Dunblane, Scotland, Matthew Birnie similarly showed evidence of generalization. Matthew still responded with terror to the sight of toy guns and the sound of balloons popping, festive trappings that were excluded from his sixth birthday party (Craig & Shields, 1996). The phenomenon has been brought to the laboratory in studies comparing abused with nonabused children. Shown an angry face on a computer screen, abused children's brain-wave responses are dramatically stronger and longer lasting (Pollak & others, 1998).

Because of generalization, stimuli that are similar to naturally disgusting or appealing objects will, by association, evoke some disgust or liking. Normally desirable foods, such as fudge, are unappealing when presented in a disgusting form, as when shaped to resemble dog feces (Rozin & others, 1986). We perceive adults with childlike facial features (round face, large forehead, small chin, large eyes) as having childlike warmth, submissiveness, and naïveté (Berry & McArthur, 1986). In both cases, people's emotional reactions to one stimulus generalize to similar stimuli.

Discrimination

Pavlov's dogs also learned to respond to the sound of a particular tone and *not* to other tones. **Discrimination** is the learned ability to *distinguish* between a conditioned stimulus (which predicts the UCS) and other irrelevant stimuli. Like generalization, discrimination has survival value. Slightly different stimuli are at times followed by vastly different consequences. Being able to recognize these differences is adaptive. Confronted by a pit bull, your heart may race; confronted by a golden retriever, it likely will not. Facing an approaching group of skinheads, you may cross the street to avoid them; approaching some bald gentlemen, you don't.

Updating Pavlov's Understanding

Preview Question: What have we learned about the effects of cognitive processes and biological constraints on classical conditioning?

Pavlov's and Watson's disdain for "mentalistic" concepts such as consciousness has given way to a growing realization that they underestimated the importance of cognitive processes (thoughts, perceptions, expectations) and of biological constraints on an organism's learning capacity.

Cognitive Processes

The early behaviorists believed that the learned behaviors of various organisms could be reduced to mindless mechanisms. The idea that rats and dogs exhibit cognition therefore struck many psychologists as unnecessary. No longer. Robert Rescorla and Allan Wagner (1972) argued that when two significant events occur close together in time, an animal learns the *predictability* of the second event. If a shock always is preceded by a tone, and then sometimes also by a light that accompanies the tone, a rat will react with fear to the tone but not the light. Although the light is always followed by the shock, the tone better predicts impending shock. The more predictable the association, the stronger the conditioned response.

It's as if the animal learns an *expectancy*, an awareness of how likely it is that the UCS will occur. Rescorla (1988) surmised that classical conditioning "is not a stupid process by which the organism willy-nilly forms associations between any two stimuli that happen to occur." Conditioning occurs best when the CS and UCS have just the sort of relationship that would lead a scientist to conclude that the CS *causes* the UCS.

This principle helps explain why classical conditioning treatments that ignore cognition often have limited success. For example, people receiving therapy for alcoholism sometimes are given alcohol spiked with a nauseating drug. Will they then associate alcohol with sickness? If classical conditioning were merely a matter of "stamping in" stimulus associations, we might hope so, and—to some extent—this does occur. However, those receiving the drink are aware that they can blame their nausea on the drug, not on the alcohol. This cognition often weakens the association between alcohol and feeling sick. So, even in classical conditioning, it is not only the simple CS–UCS association but also the thought that counts.

> "All brains are, in essence, anticipation machines."
>
> Daniel C. Dennett, *Consciousness Explained*, 1991

Biological Predispositions

Ever since Darwin, scientists have assumed that all animals share a common evolutionary history and resulting commonalities in their makeup and functioning. Pavlov and Watson, for example, believed the basic laws of learning were essentially similar in all animals. So it should make little difference whether one studied pigeons or people. Moreover, it seemed that any natural response could be conditioned to any neutral stimulus. As learning researcher Gregory Kimble proclaimed in 1956, "Just about any activity of which the organism is capable can be conditioned and . . . these responses can be conditioned to any stimulus that the organism can perceive" (p. 195).

Twenty-five years later Kimble (1981) humbly acknowledged that "half a thousand" scientific reports had proven him wrong. More than the early behaviorists realized, an animal's capacity for conditioning is constrained by its biology. The biological predispositions of each species dispose it to learn the particular associations that enhance its survival. Environments are not the whole story.

Answer to questions on page 292: The cake (and its taste) are the UCS. The associated aroma is the CS. Salivation to the aroma is the CR.

John Garcia
As the laboring son of California farmworkers, Garcia attended school only in the off-season during his early childhood years. After entering junior college in his late twenties, and earning his Ph.D. in his late forties, he received the American Psychological Association's Distinguished Scientific Contribution Award "for his highly original, pioneering research in conditioning and learning." He was also elected to the National Academy of Sciences.

Taste aversion
If you became violently ill after eating mussels, you probably would have a hard time eating them again. Their smell and taste would have become a CS for nausea. This learning occurs readily because our biology prepares us to learn taste aversions to toxic foods.

Among those who challenged the prevailing behaviorist environmentalism was John Garcia. While researching the effects of radiation on laboratory animals, Garcia and Robert Koelling (1966) noticed that rats began to avoid drinking the water from the plastic bottles in radiation chambers. They wondered whether classical conditioning might be the culprit. Might the rats have linked the plastic-tasting water (a CS) to the sickness (UCR) triggered by the internal state (UCS)?

To test their hunch, Garcia and Koelling gave the rats a particular taste, sight, or sound (CS) and later also gave them radiation or drugs that led to nausea and vomiting (UCR). Two startling findings emerged: First, even if sickened as late as several hours after tasting a particular flavor, the rats thereafter avoided that flavor. This appeared to violate the notion that for conditioning to occur, the UCS must follow the CS immediately.

Second, the sickened rats developed aversions to the tastes but not to the sights or sounds. This contradicted the behaviorists' idea that any perceivable stimulus could serve as a CS. But it made adaptive sense, because for rats the easiest way to identify tainted food is to taste it. (If sickened after sampling a new food, they thereafter avoid the food—which makes it difficult to eradicate a population of "bait-shy" rats by poisoning.) Birds, which hunt by sight, appear biologically primed to develop aversions to the *sight* of tainted food (Nicolaus & others, 1983).

Humans, too, seem biologically prepared to learn some things rather than others. If you get violently ill four hours after eating contaminated mussels, you will probably develop an aversion to the taste of mussels but not to the sight of the associated restaurant, its plates, the people you were with, or the music you heard there. Similarly, we more easily learn an aversion to alcohol by associating its taste with nausea rather than with something unrelated to consumption, such as electric shock. We also more readily learn to fear snakes and spiders than to fear flowers (Cook & others, 1986). Again, it makes sense: Such animals harm us more frequently than do flowers.

All these cases support Darwin's principle that natural selection favors traits that aid survival. Nature prepares the members of each species to learn those things crucial to their survival. Someone who readily learns a taste aversion is unlikely to eat the same toxic food again and is more likely to survive and leave descendants. Indeed, all sorts of bad feelings, from nausea to anxiety to pain, serve good purposes. Like the low-oil light on a car dashboard, each alerts the body to a threat (Neese, 1991).

The philosopher Schopenhauer once said that important ideas are first ridiculed, then attacked, and finally taken for granted. So it was with Garcia's findings on taste aversion. At first, the leading journals refused to publish his work. The findings were impossible, said some critics. But as often happens in science, Garcia and Koelling's provocative findings stimulated new research, which confirmed their surprising findings and extended them to other species. In one well-known study, coyotes and wolves that were tempted into eating sheep carcasses laced with a sickening poison developed an aversion to sheep meat (Gustavson & others, 1974, 1976). Two wolves that were later penned with a live sheep seemed actually to fear it.

"Once bitten, twice shy."

G. F. Northall, *Folk-Phrases*, 1894

Such research suggests possible humane ways for controlling predators and agricultural pests. This is but one instance in which psychological research that began with the discomfort of some laboratory animals enhanced the welfare of many more animals. In this case, the research saved the sheep from the coyotes. The coyotes in turn were saved from angry ranchers and farmers who, with their livestock no longer endangered, were less adamant about destroying the coyotes. Later experiments revealed that conditioned taste aversion could successfully prevent baboons from raiding African gardens, racoons from attacking chickens, and ravens and crows from feeding on crane eggs—all while preserving predators who occupy an important ecological niche (Garcia & Gustavson, 1997).

Has research on biological constraints compelled researchers to abandon the search for universal principles of learning that generalize across species? No. Biological predispositions affirm a deeper principle: *Learning enables animals to adapt to their environments*. Adaptation shows us why animals would be responsive to stimuli that announce significant events, such as food or pain. Animals are generally predisposed to associate a CS with a UCS that follows predictably and immediately—for causes often immediately precede effects.

Adaptation also helps explain exceptions, such as the taste-aversion finding. In this case, effect need not follow cause immediately—poisoned food usually causes sickness quite a while after the food has been eaten. Similarly, cancer patients who suffer nausea and vomiting beginning more than an hour following chemotherapy often develop classically conditioned nausea to stimuli associated with taking the drug. After four or five clinic visits, they may react to its sight, sound, and smell with anxiety and anticipatory nausea (Hall, 1997). (Under normal circumstances, such revulsion to sickening stimuli is adaptive.) The conditioned stimuli elicit the associated nausea. Thus, merely returning to the clinic's waiting room or seeing the nurses can provoke sick feelings (Burish & Carey, 1986; Davey, 1992).

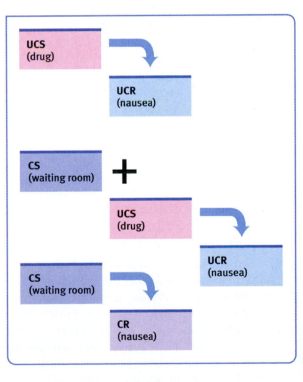

Nausea conditioning among cancer patients

Pavlov's Legacy

Preview Question: Why does Pavlov's work remain so important?

What, then, remains of Pavlov's ideas about conditioning? A great deal. All the researchers we have met so far in this module agree that classical conditioning is a basic form of learning. Judged by today's knowledge of cognitive processes and biological predispositions, Pavlov's ideas were incomplete. But if we see further than Pavlov did, it is because we stand on his shoulders.

If Pavlov had taught us only that old dogs can learn new tricks, his experiments would long ago have been forgotten. Why should anyone care that a dog can be conditioned to drool at the sound of a tone? The importance lies first in this fact: Many other responses to many other stimuli can be classically conditioned in many other organisms—in fact, in every species tested, from earthworms to fish to dogs to monkeys to people (Schwartz, 1984). Thus, classical conditioning is one way that virtually all organisms learn to adapt to their environment.

Second, Pavlov showed us how a process such as learning can be studied objectively. Pavlov was proud that his methods involved virtually no subjective judgments or guesses about what went on in the dogs' minds. The salivary response is an overt behavior measurable as so many drops or cubic centimeters of saliva. Pavlov's success therefore suggested a scientific model for how the young discipline of psychology might proceed—by isolating the elementary building blocks of complex behaviors and studying them with objective laboratory procedures.

Applications of Classical Conditioning

Psychologists have designed applications of Pavlov's principles of classical conditioning to improve human health and well-being in multiple contexts, including motivation, emotions, therapy for psychological disorders, and treatment of other health problems. Here are a few examples:

+ Former crack cocaine users often feel a craving when they again encounter cues (people, places) associated with previous highs. Thus, drug counselors advise addicts to steer clear of settings associated with the euphoria of previous drug use.

+ Counselors sometimes provide people who abuse alcohol with experiences that may reverse their positive associations with alcohol.

+ Classical conditioning even works on the body's disease-fighting immune system. When, say, a particular taste accompanies a drug that influences immune responses, the taste by itself may come to produce an immune response.

+ Animals deprived of the neurotransmitter acetylcholine have difficulty being conditioned to blink in response to a tone that has previously signaled an impending air puff. Alzheimer's patients' brains are similarly short of acetylcholine, and they, too, have difficulty with this conditioning. Diana Woodruff-Pak and Michelle Papka (1999) report that older adults who condition easily rarely have Alzheimer's disease and are unlikely soon to develop it. These findings motivate a new search for drugs that will enhance conditioning in animals—and perhaps help delay the onset of Alzheimer's (Azar, 1999).

Pavlov's work also provided a basis for John B. Watson's **behaviorism** (1913), the idea that human behavior, though biologically influenced, is mainly a bundle of conditioned responses. Watson urged his colleagues to discard reference to inner thoughts, feelings, and motives. The science of psychology should instead study how organisms respond to stimuli in their environments, said Watson. "Its theoretical goal is the prediction and control of behavior. Introspection forms no essential part of its methods." Simply said, psychology should be an objective science based on *observable behavior*. In one famous study, Watson and Rosalie Rayner (1920; Harris, 1979) showed how specific fears might be conditioned. Their subject was an 11-month-old infant named Albert. Like most infants, "Little Albert" feared loud noises but not white rats. Watson and Rayner presented him with a white rat and, as he reached to touch it, struck a hammer against a steel bar just behind his head. After seven repetitions of seeing the rat and then hearing the frightening noise, Albert burst into tears at the mere sight of the rat (an ethically troublesome study by today's standards). What is more, five days later Albert showed generalization of his conditioned response by reacting with fear to a rabbit, a dog, and a sealskin coat, but not to dissimilar objects such as toys.

"[Psychology's] factual and theoretical developments in this century—which have changed the study of mind and behavior as radically as genetics changed the study of heredity—have all been the product of objective analysis—that is to say, behavioristic analysis."

Psychologist Donald Hebb (1980)

John B. Watson

Watson (1924) admitted to "going beyond my facts" when offering his famous boast: "Give me a dozen healthy infants, well-formed, and my own specified world to bring them up in and I'll guarantee to take any one at random and train him to become any type of specialist I might select—doctor, lawyer, artist, merchant-chief, and, yes, even beggar-man and thief, regardless of his talents, penchants, tendencies, abilities, vocations, and race of his ancestors."

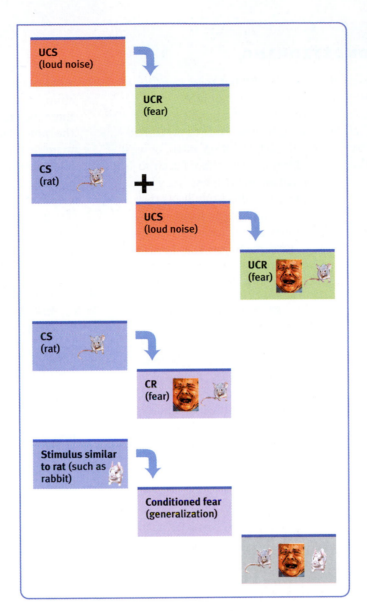

Little Albert's conditioning
The pairing of a laboratory rat with a terribly loud noise gave Little Albert a conditioned fear (the CR) of both rats (the CS) and similar furry things (generalization).

Although Little Albert's fate is unknown, Watson's is not. After losing his professorship at Johns Hopkins University over an affair with Rayner (whom he later married), he became the J. Walter Thompson advertising agency's resident psychologist. There he used his knowledge of associative learning to conceive many successful campaigns, including one for Maxwell House that helped make the "coffee break" an American custom (Hunt, 1993).

Although some psychologists had difficulty repeating Watson and Rayner's findings with other children, the work with Little Albert has had legendary significance for many psychologists. Some have wondered if each of us might not be a walking repository of conditioned emotions (see Close-Up on the aftermath of rape). Might our worst emotions be controlled by the application of extinction procedures or by conditioning new responses to emotion-arousing stimuli? Psychologists who use behavioral techniques to treat emotional disorders believe they could be. One therapist told a patient, who for 30 years had feared going into an elevator alone, to force himself to enter 20 elevators a day. Within 10 days, his fear nearly vanished (Ellis & Becker, 1982).

■ **behaviorism** the view that psychology (1) should be an objective science that (2) studies behavior without reference to mental processes. Most research psychologists today agree with (1) but not with (2).

CLOSE-UP:

RAPE AS CLASSICAL CONDITIONING

"A burnt child dreads the fire," says a medieval proverb. Experiments with dogs reveal that, indeed, if a painful stimulus is sufficiently powerful, a single event is sometimes enough to traumatize the animal when it again faces the situation. The human counterparts to these experiments can be tragic, as illustrated by one woman's experience of being attacked and raped, and thereby conditioned to a life of fear. Her fear (CR) is most powerfully associated with particular locations and people (CS), but it generalizes to other places and people. Note, too, how her traumatic experience has robbed her of the normally relaxing associations with such stimuli as home and bed.

Four months ago I was raped. In the middle of the night I awoke to the sound of someone outside my bedroom. Thinking my housemate was coming home, I called out her name. Someone began walking slowly toward me, and then I realized. I screamed and fought, but there were two of them. One held my legs, while the other put a hand over my mouth and a knife to my throat and said, "Shut up, bitch, or we'll kill you." Never have I been so terrified and helpless. They both raped me, one brutally. As they then searched my room for money and valuables, my housemate came home. They brought her into my room, raped her, and left us both tied up on my bed.

We never slept another night in that apartment. We were too terrified. Still, when I go to bed at night—always with the bedroom light left on—the memory of them entering my room repeats itself endlessly. I was an independent person who had lived alone or with other women for four years; now I can't even think about spending a night alone. When I drive by our old apartment, or when I have to go into an empty house, my heart pounds and I sweat. I am afraid of strangers, especially men, and the more they resemble my attackers the more I fear them. My housemate shares many of my fears, and is frightened when entering our new apartment. I'm afraid to stay in the same town, I'm afraid it will happen again, I'm afraid to go to bed. I dread falling asleep.

Eleven years later this woman could report—as do many trauma victims (Gluhoski & Wortman, 1996)—that her conditioned fears are gradually extinguishing:

The frequency and intensity of my fears have subsided. Still, I remain cautious about personal safety and occasionally have nightmares about my experience. But more important is my renewed ability to laugh, love, and trust—both old friends and new. Life is once again joyful. I have survived.

(From personal correspondence, with permission.)

REVIEW AND REFLECT:

Classical Conditioning

How did Pavlov's experiments demonstrate learning by association?

Although learning by association had been discussed for centuries, it remained for Ivan Pavlov to capture the phenomenon in his classic experiments on conditioning.

Pavlov repeatedly presented a neutral stimulus (such as a tone) just before an unconditioned stimulus (UCS, food) that triggered an unconditioned response (UCR, salivation). After several repetitions, the tone alone (now the conditioned stimulus, CS) began triggering a conditioned response (CR, salivation). Further experiments on acquisition revealed that classical conditioning was usually greatest when the CS was presented just before the UCS, thus preparing the organism for what was coming.

How do the processes of acquisition, extinction, spontaneous recovery, generalization, and discrimination affect a conditioned response?

The first stage in response learning involves the association of a CS with the UCS (acquisition). Responses are subsequently weakened if they are not reinforced (extinction), but they may reappear after a rest pause (spontaneous recovery). Responses may be triggered by stimuli similar to the conditioned stimulus (generalization) but not by dissimilar stimuli (discrimination).

Pavlov's work laid a foundation for John B. Watson's emerging belief that psychology, to be an objective science, should study only overt behavior, without considering unobservable mental activity. Watson called this position *behaviorism*.

What have we learned about the effects of cognitive processes and biological constraints on classical conditioning?

The behaviorists' optimism that learning principles would generalize from one response to another and from one species to another has been tempered. Conditioning principles, we now know, are cognitively influenced and biologically constrained. In classical conditioning, animals learn when to "expect" an unconditioned stimulus. Moreover, animals are biologically predisposed to learn associations between, say, a peculiar taste and a drink that will make them sick, which they will then avoid. They don't, however, learn to avoid a sickening drink announced by a noise.

Why does Pavlov's work remain so important?

Pavlov taught us that principles of learning apply across species, that significant psychological phenomena can be studied objectively, and that conditioning principles have important practical applications.

Terms and Concepts to Remember

associative learning, p. 290
classical conditioning (*Pavlovian conditioning*), p. 290
learning, p. 290
unconditioned response (UCR), p. 291
unconditioned stimulus (UCS), p. 291
conditioned response (CR), p. 291

conditioned stimulus (CS), p. 291
acquisition, p. 292
extinction, p. 293
spontaneous recovery, p. 293
generalization, p. 294
discrimination, p. 294
behaviorism, p. 298

Test Yourself

20.1. Learning is defined as "a relatively permanent change in behavior due to
   a. instinct."
   b. mental processes."
   c. experience with the environment."
   d. education or schooling."

20.2. Associative learning involves learning that certain events occur together. In classical conditioning, the organism associates
   a. a response and a consequence.
   b. an observed behavior with a stimulus.
   c. two stimuli.
   d. two responses.

20.3. Working with dogs, Pavlov paired a tone or other neutral stimulus with food in the mouth. The dogs then came to salivate when presented with the neutral stimulus alone. Salivation in response to food in the mouth occurs naturally in dogs, without conditioning; food is therefore the unconditioned stimulus (UCS). Salivation in response to a tone must be learned; the tone is therefore a/an

   a. conditioned stimulus.
   b. unconditioned stimulus.
   c. conditioned response.
   d. unconditioned response.

20.4. Dogs can learn to respond to one kind of stimulus and not to another—for example, to salivate at the sight of a circle (the CS) but not a square. Distinguishing between a CS and an irrelevant stimulus is
   a. generalization.
   b. discrimination.
   c. acquisition.
   d. spontaneous recovery.

20.5. Early behaviorists believed that for conditioning to occur, the unconditioned stimulus (UCS) must immediately follow the conditioned stimulus (CS). _____ demonstrated this was not always so.
   a. The Little Albert experiment
   b. Pavlov's experiments with dogs
   c. Watson's behaviorism theory
   d. Garcia and Koelling's taste-aversion studies

20.6. Research by Garcia and Koelling showed that rats developed aversions to certain tastes but not to sights or sounds, thus supporting
   a. Pavlov's demonstration of generalization.
   b. Darwin's principle that natural selection favors traits that aid survival.
   c. Watson's view that study should be limited to observable behavior.
   d. Kimble's original view that organisms can be conditioned to any stimulus.

20.7. Watson and Rayner classically conditioned a small child named Albert to fear a white rat. After Watson paired the rat with a frightening noise, Little Albert cried when the rat was presented (even without the noise). The child later showed fear in response to a rabbit, a dog, and a sealskin coat. Little Albert's fear of objects resembling the rat illustrates
   a. extinction.
   b. generalization of the conditioned response.
   c. spontaneous recovery.
   d. discrimination between two stimuli.

Review: In slasher movies, sexually arousing images of women are sometimes paired with violence against women. Based on classical conditioning principles, what might be an effect of this pairing?

Reflect: How have your emotions or behaviors been classically conditioned?

Answers to the Test Yourself and Review questions can be found in the green appendix at the end of the book.

21 Operant Conditioning

DENNIS THE MENACE

"I think Mom's using the can opener."

Classical conditioning associates neutral stimuli with important stimuli that produce responses which are often automatic. Another type of **associative learning** explains—and trains—more elaborate behaviors. It's one thing to teach an animal to salivate at the sound of a tone or a child to fear cars in the street; it's something else to teach an elephant to walk on its hind legs or a child to say *please*. Through **operant conditioning** people or animals associate behaviors with their consequences. Thus, they become more likely to repeat rewarded (reinforced) behaviors and less likely to repeat punished behaviors.

Both classical and operant conditioning involve acquisition, extinction, spontaneous recovery, generalization, and discrimination (Table 21.1). Yet their difference is straightforward: Classical conditioning forms associations between stimuli (a CS and the UCS it signals). It also involves **respondent behavior**—behavior that occurs as an *automatic* response to some stimulus (such as salivating in response to meat powder and later in response to a tone). Operant conditioning involves **operant behavior**, so-called because the act *operates* on the environment to produce rewarding or punishing stimuli. We can therefore distinguish classical from operant conditioning by asking: *Is the organism learning associations between events that it doesn't control (classical conditioning)? Or is it learning associations between its behavior and resulting events (operant conditioning)?*

TABLE 21.1

SOME DIFFERENCES BETWEEN CLASSICAL AND OPERANT CONDITIONING

	Classical Conditioning	Operant Conditioning
Basic idea	Organism learns associations between events it doesn't control.	Organism learns associations between its behavior and resulting events.
Acquisition	Initial stage in which a neutral stimulus is associated with an unconditioned stimulus (UCS) and comes to elicit a conditioned response (CR).	The strengthening of a reinforced response.
Extinction	The diminishing of a conditioned response; occurs when a UCS does not follow a CS.	The elimination of a response that is no longer reinforced.
Spontaneous recovery	The reappearance, after a rest period, of an extinguished CR.	The reappearance, after a rest period, of an extinguished response.
Generalization	The tendency, once a response has been conditioned, for stimuli similar to the CS to elicit similar responses.	Organism's response to stimuli that signal that a behavior will be reinforced.
Discrimination	The learned ability to distinguish between a CS and other stimuli that do not signal a UCS.	Organism's response to stimuli that do not signal that a behavior will be reinforced.

Skinner's Experiments

Preview Question: What did B. F. Skinner's research on operant conditioning teach us about how we learn to repeat or suppress many behaviors?

B. F. Skinner (1904–1990) was a college English major and an aspiring writer who, seeking a new direction, entered graduate school in psychology. He went on to become modern behaviorism's most influential and controversial figure. Skinner's work elaborated a simple fact of life that psychologist Edward L. Thorndike

The law of effect at Stingray City
For 35 years, Cayman Islands fishing crews have gathered conch and cleaned them over this barrier reef. Stingrays in the surrounding bay gradually became accustomed to these yummy treats. Noticing the rays congregating, scuba divers then began feeding the increasingly friendly rays by hand. Today, tourists can do the same and can even pet the rays as they graze past them.

(1874–1949) called the **law of effect**: Rewarded behavior is likely to recur. Using Thorndike's law of effect as a starting point, Skinner developed a "behavioral technology" that revealed principles of behavior control. These principles also enabled him to teach pigeons such unpigeonlike behaviors as walking in a figure 8, playing Ping-Pong, and keeping a missile on course by pecking at a target on a screen.

For his pioneering studies with rats (and later with pigeons), Skinner designed an **operant chamber**, popularly known as the *Skinner box*. The box is typically soundproof, with a bar or key that an animal presses or pecks to release a reward of food or water, and a device that records these responses.

Experiments by Skinner and other operant researchers did far more than teach us how to pull habits out of a rat. They explored the precise conditions that foster efficient and enduring **learning**.

Shaping

In his experiments, Skinner used **shaping**, a procedure in which reinforcers, such as food, gradually guide an animal's behavior toward a desired behavior. Imagine that you wanted to condition a rat to press a bar. After observing how the animal naturally behaves before training, you would build on its existing behaviors. You might give the rat a food reward each time it approaches the bar. Once the rat is approaching regularly, you would require it to move closer before rewarding it, then closer still; finally, you would require it to touch the bar before you gave it the food. With this method of *successive approximations*, you reward responses that are ever-closer to the final desired behavior, and you ignore all other responses. By making rewards contingent on desired behaviors, researchers and animal trainers gradually *shape* complex behaviors.

By shaping nonverbal organisms to discriminate between stimuli, a psychologist can also determine what they perceive. Can a dog distinguish colors? Can a baby discriminate sounds? If we can shape them to respond to one stimulus and not to another, then obviously they can perceive the difference. Experiments show that some animals are remarkably capable of forming concepts; they demonstrate this by discriminating between classes of events or objects. If an experimenter reinforces a pigeon for pecking after seeing a human face, but not after seeing other images, the pigeon will learn to recognize a face (Herrnstein & Loveland, 1964). After being trained to discriminate among flowers, people, cars, and chairs, pigeons can usually identify in which of these categories a new pictured object belongs (Bhatt & others, 1988; Wasserman, 1993). With training, pigeons have even been taught to discriminate between Bach's music and Stravinsky's (Porter & Neuringer, 1984).

associative learning learning that certain events (a response and its consequences in operant conditioning) occur together.

operant conditioning a type of learning in which behavior is strengthened if followed by reinforcement or diminished if followed by punishment.

respondent behavior behavior that occurs as an automatic response to some stimulus; Skinner's term for behavior learned through classical conditioning.

operant behavior behavior that operates on the environment, producing consequences.

law of effect Thorndike's principle that behaviors followed by favorable consequences become more likely, and that behaviors followed by unfavorable consequences become less likely.

operant chamber ("Skinner box") a chamber containing a bar or key that an animal can manipulate to obtain a food or water reinforcer, with attached devices to record the animal's rate of bar pressing or key pecking. Used in operant conditioning research.

learning a relatively permanent change in an organism's behavior due to experience.

shaping an operant conditioning procedure in which reinforcers guide behavior toward closer and closer approximations of a desired goal.

A discriminating creature
University of Windsor psychologist Dale Woodyard uses a food reward to train this manatee to discriminate between objects of different shapes, colors, and sizes. A manatee can remember such responses for as long as a year.

Parents can shape good table manners by using praise as a reward for eating behavior that is more and more adultlike. This sounds simple, but let's compare the essential features of shaping to what often happens at home and at school. In the shaping procedure, the trainer builds on the individual's existing behaviors by expecting and immediately rewarding successively closer approximations of a desired behavior. In everyday life, too, we continually reward and shape the behavior of others, said Skinner, but we often do so unintentionally. Sometimes we unthinkingly reward behaviors we find annoying. Billy's whining, for example, annoys his mystified parents, but look how they typically deal with Billy.

Billy: Could you tie my shoes?
Father: (Continues reading paper.)
Billy: Dad, I need my shoes tied.
Father: Uh, yeah, just a minute.
Billy: DAAAAD! TIE MY SHOES!
Father: How many times have I told you not to whine? Now, which shoe do we do first?

Or consider the way some teachers use rewards. On a wall chart, the teacher pastes gold stars after the names of children scoring 100 percent on spelling tests. All children take the same tests. As everyone can then see, some children, the academic all-stars, easily get 100 percent. The others, no matter how hard they try or how much they improve, get no reward. The teacher would be better advised to apply the principles of operant conditioning—to reward all spellers for gradual improvements (successive approximations toward perfect spelling of words they find challenging).

HI AND LOIS

Principles of Reinforcement

People often refer rather loosely to the power of "rewards." This idea gains a more precise meaning in Skinner's concept of **reinforcement**, any event that increases the frequency of a preceding response. A *positive* reinforcer may be a tangible reward. It may be praise or attention. Or it may be an activity—being able to use the car when the dishes are done, or to have a break after an hour of study.

Most people think of reinforcers as rewards. Actually, anything that serves to strengthen behavior is a reinforcer—even students being yelled at if yelling *increases* the offending behavior. There are two basic kinds of reinforcement (Table 21.2). One type (positive reinforcement) strengthens a response by *presenting* a stimulus after a response. Food is a positive reinforcer for animals; attention, approval, and money are positive reinforcers for most people. The other type (negative reinforcement) strengthens a response by reducing or *removing* an aversive stimulus. (Negative reinforcers, like negative numbers, subtract something.) Putting on a car seat belt may turn off the warning buzzer. Taking aspirin may relieve a headache. Dragging on a cigarette will reduce a nicotine addict's pangs. Pushing the snooze button silences the annoying alarm. All these involve negative reinforcement. When someone stops nagging or whining, that, too, is a reinforcer. (Note that contrary to popular usage, negative reinforcement is not aversive: It *removes* an aversive event.)

So imagine that whenever Billy throws a tantrum, his parents give in for the sake of peace and quiet. The child's tantrums will be reinforced when the parents give in. And the parents' behavior will be reinforced when Billy stops screaming. Or imagine a worried student who, after goofing off and getting a bad exam grade, studies harder for the next exam. The student's studying may be reinforced by reduced anxiety and by a better grade. Whether it works by giving something positive or by reducing something negative, *reinforcement is any consequence that strengthens behavior.*

Primary and Conditioned Reinforcers

Primary reinforcers—getting food or being relieved of electric shock—are innately satisfying. **Conditioned reinforcers**, also called *secondary reinforcers,* are learned. They get their power through association with primary reinforcers. If a rat in a Skinner box learns that a light reliably signals that food is coming, the rat will work to turn on the light. The light has become a secondary reinforcer associated with food. Our lives are filled with secondary reinforcers—money, good grades, a pleasant tone of voice, a word of praise—each of which has been linked with more basic rewards. Secondary reinforcers greatly enhance our ability to influence one another.

Immediate and Delayed Reinforcers

Let's return to the imaginary shaping experiment in which you were conditioning a rat to press a bar. Before performing this "wanted" behavior, the hungry rat will engage in a sequence of "unwanted" behaviors—scratching, sniffing, and moving around. Whichever of these behaviors immediately precedes the food reinforcer becomes more likely to recur. If you delay the reinforcement of bar pressing for longer than 30 seconds, allowing other behaviors to intervene and be reinforced, virtually no learning to press the bar will occur.

Unlike rats, humans do respond to reinforcers that are greatly delayed: the paycheck at the end of the week, the grade at the end of the semester, the trophy at the end of the season. Indeed, to function effectively we must learn to postpone immediate rewards for greater long-term rewards. Four-year-old children who in laboratory testing show an ability to delay gratification—who'd sooner have a big reward tomorrow than a small one right now—become more socially competent and more likely to be high achievers as adolescents (Mischel & others, 1989). A big step toward maturity—and toward gaining the most rewarding life—is learning to delay gratification, to control one's impulses in order to achieve more valued rewards (Logue, 1998a,b).

TABLE 21.2

WAYS TO INCREASE BEHAVIOR

Operant Conditioning Term	Description	Example
Positive reinforcement	*Add* a positive stimulus	a hug, TV on
Negative reinforcement	*Remove* an aversive stimulus	seat belt turns off buzzer

Positive reinforcement
An A grade positively reinforces this boy's effort, as do his classmates' smiles and his teacher's praise.

- **reinforcer** in operant conditioning, any event that *strengthens* the behavior it follows.

- **primary reinforcer** an innately reinforcing stimulus, such as one that satisfies a biological need.

- **conditioned reinforcer** (or *secondary reinforcer*) a stimulus that gains its reinforcing power through its association with a primary reinforcer.

"Oh, not bad. The light comes on, I press the bar, they write me a check. How about you?"

"The charm of fishing is that it is the pursuit of what is elusive but attainable, a perpetual series of occasions for hope."

Scottish author John Buchan (1875–1940)

■ **continuous reinforcement** reinforcing the desired response every time it occurs.

■ **partial (intermittent) reinforcement** reinforcing a response only part of the time; results in slower acquisition of a response but much greater resistance to extinction than does continuous reinforcement.

■ **fixed-ratio schedule** in operant conditioning, a schedule of reinforcement that reinforces a response only after a specified number of responses.

■ **variable-ratio schedule** in operant conditioning, a schedule of reinforcement that reinforces a response after an unpredictable number of responses.

But to our detriment, small but immediate reinforcements are sometimes more alluring than big but delayed reinforcements. Smokers, alcoholics, and other drug users may know that their immediate pleasure—the kick that often comes within seconds—is more than offset by future ill effects. Still, immediate reinforcement prevails. Thus, hangovers do not prevent further drinking, and drugs such as nicotine and cocaine that provide the most immediate reinforcement are the most strongly addictive (Marlatt, 1991). Likewise, for many teens the immediate gratification of risky, unprotected sex in passionate moments prevails over the delayed gratifications of safe sex or saved sex (Loewenstein & Furstenberg, 1991). And the hour-long enjoyment of staying up to watch another TV show may seem to outweigh the prospect of tomorrow's day-long sluggishness.

Reinforcement Schedules

So far, most of our examples assume **continuous reinforcement**: The desired response is reinforced every time it occurs. Under such conditions, learning occurs rapidly. But when the reinforcement stops—when we disconnect the food delivery chute—extinction also occurs rapidly. If the experimenter withholds food pellets, the rat soon stops pressing the bar. If a normally dependable candy machine fails to deliver a chocolate bar twice in a row, we stop putting money into it (although a week later we may exhibit spontaneous recovery by trying again).

Real life often does not provide continuous reinforcement. A salesperson does not make a sale with every pitch, nor does an angler get a bite with every cast. But they persist because their efforts have occasionally been rewarded. Researchers have explored several **partial (intermittent) reinforcement** schedules in which responses are sometimes reinforced, sometimes not (Nevin, 1988). Initial learning is typically slower with intermittent reinforcement, which makes continuous reinforcement preferable until a behavior is mastered. But intermittent reinforcement produces greater persistence—greater *resistance to extinction*—than is found with continuous reinforcement. Imagine a pigeon that has learned to peck a key to obtain food. When the experimenter gradually phases out the delivery of food until it occurs only rarely and unpredictably, pigeons may peck 150,000 times without a reward (Skinner, 1953). With intermittent reinforcement, hope springs eternal.

Corresponding human examples come readily to mind. Slot machines reward gamblers occasionally and unpredictably. This intermittent reinforcement affects them much as it affects pigeons: They keep trying, sometimes interminably. There is also a valuable lesson here for parents. *Occasionally* giving in to children's tantrums for the sake of peace and quiet puts the child on an intermittent reinforcement schedule. That is the very best procedure for making a behavior persist.

Skinner (1961) and his collaborators compared four schedules of partial reinforcement. Some are rigidly fixed, some unpredictably variable.

Fixed-ratio schedules reinforce behavior after a set number of responses. Like people paid on a piecework basis—say, for every 30 pieces—laboratory animals may be reinforced on a fixed ratio of, say, one reinforcer for every 30 responses. Once conditioned, the animal will pause only briefly after a reinforcer and will then return to a high rate of responding (**FIGURE 21.1**). Because resting while on a fixed-ratio schedule reduces rewards, employees often find such arrangements tiring. Unions have therefore pressured employers to replace piecework pay with hourly wage schedules.

Variable-ratio schedules provide reinforcers after an unpredictable number of responses. This is what gamblers and anglers experience—unpredictable reinforcement—and what makes gambling and fishing so hard to extinguish. Like the fixed-ratio schedule, the variable-ratio schedule produces high rates of responding, because reinforcers increase as the responding increases.

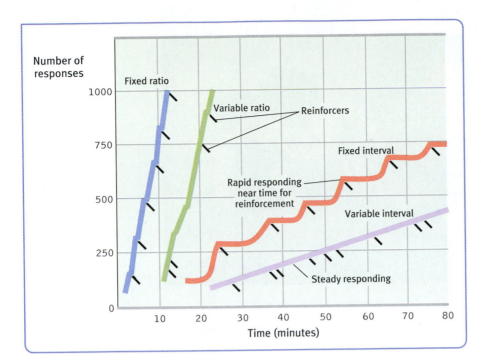

FIGURE 21.1
Intermittent reinforcement schedules
Skinner's laboratory pigeons produced these response patterns to each of four reinforcement schedules. (Reinforcers are indicated by diagonal marks.) For people, as for pigeons, reinforcement linked to number of responses (a ratio schedule) produces a higher response rate than reinforcement linked to amount of time elapsed (interval schedule). But the predictability of the reward also matters. A predictable (fixed) schedule produces a higher response rate than an unpredictable (variable) schedule. (Adapted from "Teaching Machines" by B. F. Skinner. Copyright © 1961, Scientific American, Inc. All rights reserved.)

Fixed-interval schedules reinforce the first response after a fixed time period. Like people checking more frequently for the mail as the delivery time approaches, or checking to see if the cookies are done or the Jell-O is set, pigeons on a fixed-interval schedule peck a key more frequently as the anticipated time for reward draws near, producing a choppy stop-start pattern (see Figure 21.1).

Variable-interval schedules reinforce the first response after *varying* time intervals. Like the unpredictable pop quiz that reinforces studying or the "Hello" that finally rewards persistence in redialing a busy phone number, variable-interval schedules tend to produce slow, steady responding. This makes sense, because there is no knowing when the waiting will be over. Should the pop quiz become predictable, students will begin the stop-start work pattern that characterizes fixed-interval schedules.

Animal behaviors differ, yet Skinner (1956) contended that these reinforcement principles of operant conditioning are universal. It matters little, he said, what response, what reinforcer, or what species you use. The effect of a given reinforcement schedule is pretty much the same: "Pigeon, rat, monkey, which is which? It doesn't matter. . . . Behavior shows astonishingly similar properties."

Punishment

The effect of **punishment** is opposite that of reinforcement. Reinforcement increases a behavior; punishment decreases it. Thus, a punisher is any consequence that *decreases* the frequency of a preceding behavior. Swift and sure punishers can powerfully restrain unwanted behavior. The dog that learns to come running at the sound of the electric can opener will learn to hide if its master starts running the can opener to attract and catch it for banishment to the basement. The rat that is shocked after touching the forbidden object and the child who loses a treat after running into the street will learn not to repeat the behavior.

Boys Town psychologist Robert Larzelere (1996, 1998, 1999) notes a problem with human punishment studies, which often find that spanked children are at increased risk for aggression, depression, and low self-esteem. Well, yes, says Larzelere, just as people who have received radiation treatments are more likely to die of cancer, and people who have undergone psychotherapy are more likely to suffer depression—

Door-to-door salespeople are reinforced by which schedule? People checking the oven to see if the cookies are done are on which schedule? Airline frequent-flyer programs that offer a free flight after every 25,000 miles of travel use which reinforcement schedule? (See page 309.)

■ **fixed-interval schedule** in operant conditioning, a schedule of reinforcement that reinforces a response only after a specified time has elapsed.

■ **variable-interval schedule** in operant conditioning, a schedule of reinforcement that reinforces a response at unpredictable time intervals.

■ **punishment** an event that *decreases* the behavior that it follows.

The problem with punishment
Swift and sure punishment can decrease unwanted behavior, but it can also evoke undesired responses, such as anger, fear, or resistance.

because they had preexisting problems that triggered the treatments. If one adjusts for preexisting cancer or depression—or antisocial behavior—then radiation, psychotherapy, or an occasional single swat or two of misbehaving 2- to 6-year-olds looks more effective. That is especially so if the swat is combined with a generous dose of reasoning and positive parenting, and if it is used only as a backup to enhance the effectiveness of milder disciplinary tactics such as reasoning and time-out.

Nevertheless, say advocates of nonviolent parenting, physical punishment has drawbacks. Punished behavior is not forgotten; it is suppressed. This temporary suppression may (negatively) reinforce the parents' punishing behavior. The child swears, the parent swats, the parent hears no more swearing from the child, and the parent feels the punishment was successful in stopping the behavior. But was it? If the punishment is avoidable, the punished behavior may reappear in safe settings. The child may simply learn not to swear around the house but to swear elsewhere. The driver who is hit with a couple of speeding tickets may buy a radar detector and speed freely when no radar patrol is around.

Punishment may also increase aggressiveness by demonstrating that aggression is a way to cope with problems. This helps explain why so many aggressive delinquents and abusive parents come from abusive families (Straus & Gelles, 1980; Straus & others, 1997). Moreover, punishment can create fear; the person receiving the punishment may associate the fear not only with the undesirable behavior but also with the person who administers it or with the situation in which it occurs. Thus, a child may come to fear the punitive teacher and want to avoid school. Worse, when punishments are unpredictable and inescapable, both animals and people may develop the sense that events are beyond their control. As a result, they may come to feel helpless and depressed. For these reasons, most European countries have banned hitting children in schools and child-care institutions (Leach, 1993, 1994). The Scandinavian countries and Austria have further outlawed physical punishment by parents, thereby extending to children the same legal protection given to spouses.

Even when punishment suppresses unwanted behavior, it often does not guide one toward more desirable behavior. Punishment tells you what *not* to do; reinforcement tells you what *to* do. Thus, punishment combined with reinforcement is usually more effective than punishment alone. This approach has been used with children who bite themselves or bang their heads. They may be mildly punished (say, with a squirt of water in the face) whenever they bite themselves, but also be rewarded with positive attention and food when they behave well. The approach also works in the classroom. The teacher whose feedback on a paper says "No, but try this . . ." and "Yes, that's it!" reduces unwanted behavior by reinforcing alternative behaviors.

Parents of delinquent youth often lack this awareness of how to reinforce desirable behavior without screaming or hitting (Patterson & others, 1982). Training programs for such parents help them reframe contingencies from dire threats to positive incentives—from "You clean up your room this minute or no dinner!" to "You're welcome at the dinner table after you get your room cleaned up." When you stop to think about it, many threats of punishment are just as forceful, and perhaps more effective, if rephrased positively. Thus, "If you don't get your homework done, there'll be no TV" would better be phrased as. . . .

To sum up, swift and sure punishment can be effective, and it may on occasion cause less pain than does the self-destructive behavior it suppresses. However, punished behavior may reappear if the threatened punishment can be avoided. (What punishment often teaches, said Skinner, is how to avoid it.) Punishment can also lead to undesirable side effects, such as creating fear and teaching aggression, and it often fails to teach how to act positively. Most psychologists therefore favor an emphasis on reinforcement rather than on punishment. Notice people doing something right and affirm them for it.

Updating Skinner's Understanding

Preview Question: What have we learned about the effect of cognitive processes and biological predispositions on operant conditioning?

Skinner granted the existence of private processes and the biological underpinnings of behavior. Nevertheless, many psychologists criticized him for discounting the importance of these processes and predispositions.

Cognition and Operant Conditioning

A mere eight days before dying of leukemia, Skinner (1990) stood before the American Psychological Association convention for one final critique of "cognitive science," which he viewed as a throwback to early twentieth-century introspectionism. Skinner died resisting the growing belief that cognitive processes—thoughts, perceptions, expectations—have a necessary place in the science of psychology and even in our understanding of conditioning. (He regarded thoughts and emotions as behaviors that follow the same laws as other behaviors.) Yet we have seen several hints that cognitive processes might be at work in operant learning. For example, animals on a fixed-interval reinforcement schedule respond more and more frequently as the time approaches when a response will produce a reinforcer. The animals behave as if they expect that repeating the response will soon produce the reward.

To a strict behaviorist, however, talk of "expectations" is unnecessary; it is enough to say that responses that are reinforced under certain conditions recur when those conditions recur. Moreover, talk of expectations and other cognitions begs the question of what causes them. It is not enough to say that evil thoughts predisposed Eric Harris and Dylan Klebold to murder 13 of their Littleton, Colorado, classmates. We want to know what would cause such thoughts and behavior.

Latent Learning

Evidence of cognitive processes has come from studying rats in mazes. Rats exploring a maze, with no obvious reward, are like people driving around a new town. The rats seem to develop a **cognitive map**, a mental representation of the maze. This occurs even if they are carried passively through the maze in a wire basket. When an experimenter then places a reward in the maze's goal box, the rats immediately perform as well as rats that have been reinforced with food for running the maze (**FIGURE 21.2**, page 310).

Answer to questions on page 307: Door-to-door salespeople are reinforced on a variable-ratio schedule (after varying numbers of rings). Cookie checkers are reinforced on a fixed-interval schedule. Frequent-flyer programs use a fixed-ratio schedule.

For more information on animal behavior, see books by (I am not making this up) Robin Fox and Lionel Tiger.

■ **cognitive map** a mental representation of the layout of one's environment. For example, after exploring a maze, rats act as if they have learned a cognitive map of it.

FIGURE 21.2 Latent learning
Animals, like people, can learn from experience, with or without reinforcement. After exploring a maze for 10 days, rats received a food reward at the end of the maze. They quickly demonstrated their prior learning of the maze—by immediately doing as well as (and even better than) rats that had been reinforced for running the maze. (From Tolman & Honzik, 1930.)

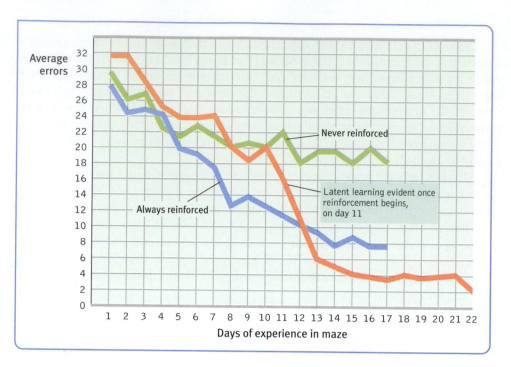

During their explorations, the rats seemingly experience **latent learning**—learning that becomes apparent only when there is some incentive to demonstrate it. The conclusion: Learning can occur without reinforcement. As the cognitive-mapping experiments suggest, there is more to learning than associating a response with a consequence. There is also cognition. Researchers have found striking evidence of animals' cognitive abilities in solving problems and in using aspects of language.

Overjustification

The cognitive perspective has also led to an important qualification concerning the power of rewards: Unnecessary rewards sometimes carry hidden costs. Most people think that offering tangible rewards will boost anyone's interest in an activity (Boggiano & others, 1987). Actually, promising children a reward for a task they already enjoy can backfire. People who begin to see the reward as their motive for an activity may lose their intrinsic interest in it. This phenomenon is called the **overjustification effect**, because an already justifiable activity becomes *over*justified by the promise of added reward.

In experiments, children promised a payoff for playing with an interesting puzzle or toy later play with the toy less than do children who are not paid to play (Tang & Hall, 1995; Deci & others, 1999). It is as if the children think, "If I have to be bribed into doing this, then it must not be worth doing for its own sake."

Wendy Grolnick and Richard Ryan (1987) showed how overjustification can affect teaching and learning. They invited fifth graders to read a passage from a social studies book. Some they instructed in a controlling way: "I'll be grading you on the test to see if you're learning enough." Others, treated in a less controlling manner ("You won't be graded on . . . I'm just interested in what children can remember"), learned as much *and found the passage more interesting.*

A person's interest also survives when a reward is used neither to bribe nor to control but to signal a job well done (Boggiano & others, 1985). If a reward boosts your feeling of competence after doing good work, your enjoyment of the task may increase. Children who are bribed into an activity will also sustain their interest if led to attribute their involvement to themselves and not the reward. One research team accomplished this by telling children, "You know, I thought you'd say you wanted to do this handwriting activity because you look like the kind of [girl/boy] who understands how important it is to write correctly, and who really wants to be good at it" (Cialdini & others, 1998). Rewards, rightly administered, have positive effects (Eisenberger & Cameron, 1996).

Biological Predispositions

As with classical conditioning, an animal's natural predispositions constrain its capacity for operant conditioning. When you reinforce a hamster's behavior with food, you can easily condition it to dig or to rear up, because these are among the animal's natural behaviors when searching for food. But it is difficult to use food as a reinforcer to shape hamster behaviors—such as face washing—that aren't normally associated with food or hunger (Shettleworth, 1973). Similarly, pigeons easily learn to flap their wings to avoid being shocked and to peck to obtain food, because it is natural for them to flee with their wings and eat with their beaks. However, they have a hard time learning to peck in order to avoid a shock or to flap their wings to obtain food (Foree & LoLordo, 1973). Biological constraints predispose organisms to learn associations that are naturally adaptive.

Skinner's former associates, Keller Breland and Marian Breland (1961), came to appreciate biological predispositions while using operant procedures to train animals for circuses, TV shows, and movies. The Brelands had originally assumed that operant principles would work on almost any response that any animal could make. But after training 6000 animals of 38 different species, from chickens to whales, they concluded that biological predispositions were more important than they had supposed. In one act, they trained pigs to pick up large wooden "dollars" and deposit them in a piggy bank. After learning this behavior, however, the animals began to drift back to their natural ways. They would drop the coin, push it with their snouts as pigs are prone to do, pick it up again, and then repeat the sequence—delaying their food reinforcer. As this "instinctive drift" illustrates, "misbehaviors" occurred when the animals reverted to their biologically predisposed patterns.

Natural athletes
Animals can most easily learn and retain behaviors that draw on their biological predispositions, such as cats' inborn tendency to leap high and land on their feet.

> "Never try to teach a pig to sing. It wastes your time and annoys the pig."
>
> Mark Twain (1835–1910)

Skinner's Legacy

Preview Question: In what ways are Skinner's operant principles used to influence people's behavior in schools, in the workplace, and at home?

B. F. Skinner was one of the most controversial intellectual figures of the late twentieth century. He stirred a hornet's nest by repeatedly insisting that external influences, not internal thoughts and feelings, shape behavior and by urging the use of operant principles to influence people's behavior at school, work, and home. To help or manage people effectively, Skinner said, we should worry less about their illusions of freedom and dignity. Recognizing that behavior is shaped by its consequences, we should administer rewards in ways that promote more desirable behavior.

Skinner's critics objected, saying that he dehumanized people by neglecting their personal freedom and by seeking to control their actions. Skinner's reply: People's behavior is already haphazardly controlled by external consequences, so why not administer those consequences for human betterment? In place of the punishments used in homes, schools, and prisons, wouldn't reinforcers be more humanitarian? And if it is humbling to think that we are shaped by our histories, this very idea also gives us hope that we can shape our future.

■ **latent learning** learning that occurs but is not apparent until there is an incentive to demonstrate it.

■ **overjustification effect** the effect of promising a reward for doing what one already likes to do. The person may now see the reward, rather than intrinsic interest, as the motivation for performing the task.

B. F. Skinner

"I am sometimes asked, 'Do you think of yourself as you think of the organisms you study?' The answer is yes. So far as I know, my behavior at any given moment has been nothing more than the product of my genetic endowment, my personal history, and the current setting" (1983).

Computer-assisted learning

Computers have helped realize Skinner's goal of individually paced instruction with immediate feedback.

Applications of Operant Conditioning

We have seen some applications of operant conditioning principles within this module. Psychologists also apply these principles to problems ranging from high blood pressure to social withdrawal. Behavioral economists are applying operant principles to their study of consumer behavior and drug use and abuse. Reinforcement technologies are also at work in schools, businesses, and homes.

At School

A generation ago, Skinner and others advocated teaching machines and textbooks that would shape learning in small steps and provide immediate reinforcement for correct responses. Such machines and texts, they said, would revolutionize education and free teachers to concentrate on their students' special needs.

To envision Skinner's idea, imagine two math teachers, each with a class of academically diverse students. Teacher A gives the whole class the same math lesson, knowing that some students will readily understand the concepts and that others will be frustrated. With so many different children, how can one teacher guide them individually? The whiz kids breeze through unchallenged; the slower learners experience failure. Faced with a similar class, Teacher B paces the material according to each student's rate of learning and provides prompt feedback with positive reinforcement to both slow and fast learners. Does the individualized instruction of Teacher B seem unrealistic?

Although the predicted revolution has not occurred, to the end of his life Skinner (1986, 1988, 1989) believed the ideal was achievable. "Good instruction demands two things," he said. "Students must be told immediately whether what they do is right or wrong and, when right, they must be directed to the step to be taken next." Computers were his final hope. For reading and math drills, the computer could be Teacher B—engaging the student actively, pacing material according to the student's rate of learning, quizzing the student to find gaps in understanding, providing immediate feedback, and keeping flawless records for the supervising teacher. With on-line testing systems improving and more and more interactive student software and Internet resources becoming available, we are closer than ever before to achieving Skinner's ideal.

Reinforcement principles can also enhance athletic abilities. Again, the key is to shape behavior, by first reinforcing small successes and then gradually increasing the challenge. Thomas Simek and Richard O'Brien (1981, 1988) applied these principles to teaching golf and baseball by starting with responses that are easily reinforced. Golf students begin with very short putts. As they build mastery, they eventually step back farther and farther until taking full swings off the tee. Likewise, novice batters begin with half swings at an oversized ball pitched from 10 feet away, giving them the immediate pleasure of smacking the ball. As the hitters' confidence builds with their success and they achieve mastery at each level, the pitcher gradually moves back—first to 15 feet, then 22 feet, 30 feet, and 40.5 feet—and eventually introduces a standard baseball. Compared with children taught by conventional methods, those trained by this behavioral method show, in both testing and game situations, faster improvement in their skill.

At Work

Believing reinforcers influence productivity, business managers have capitalized on psychological research. Many companies now enable their employees to share profits and to participate in company ownership. When workers' productivity boosts rewards for everyone, their motivation, morale, and cooperative spirit often increase (Deutsch, 1991). Reinforcement for jobs well done is especially effective in boosting productivity when the desired performance is *well-defined and achievable*. The message for managers? Reward is given for specific behaviors, not vaguely defined merit. Criticism, too, triggers the least resentment and the greatest performance boost when it is specific and considerate (Baron, 1988).

It is also wise to make the reinforcement *immediate*. When IBM legend Thomas Watson observed an achievement, he would write the employee a check on the spot (Peters & Waterman, 1982). But rewards need not be material, nor should

they be so substantial that they become political and a source of discouragement to those who don't receive them. An effective manager may simply walk the floor and praise people for good work, or write notes of appreciation for a completed project. As Skinner said, "How much richer would the whole world be if the reinforcers in daily life were more effectively contingent on productive work?"

Animals also can be trained to be useful. Imagine a self-propelled marine vehicle with a sonar system and on-board computer suitable for detecting, classifying, and manipulating targets. That pretty well describes how the U.S. Navy once viewed its dolphins and sea lions, which at various times have been trained to perform salvage duties, serve as watch dogs around a submarine base, or seek out mines in the Persian Gulf. The animals' trainers used food reinforcements to shape them toward the desired behavior (Holing, 1988; Morrison, 1988).

At Home

Many economists and psychologists believe people's spending behavior is controlled by its consequences (its costs and benefits). Compared with people who rent apartments in buildings where energy costs are paid by the landlord, those who live in comparable buildings but pay their own energy costs (therefore reaping the rewards of their own savings) use about 20 percent less energy. Similarly, those on an "energy diet" for their home electricity are helped by receiving frequent feedback that shows their current usage compared with their past consumption (Darley & others, 1979). In homes, as elsewhere, immediate consequences most effectively influence behavior. Al Gore (1992, p. 348) suggested how tax policies might harness the power of consequences:

> There is an economic rule of thumb: whatever we tax, we tend to get less of; whatever we subsidize, we tend to get more of. Currently, we tax work and we subsidize the depletion of natural resources—and both policies have contributed to high unemployment and the waste of natural resources. What if we lowered the tax on work and simultaneously raised it on the burning of fossil fuels?

Parents can also take helpful advantage of operant conditioning. Parent-training researchers Michelle Wierson and Rex Forehand (1994) remind us that when parents say "get ready for bed" and then cave in to protests or defiance, they reinforce such behaviors. Eventually, exasperated, they may yell at their child or gesture menacingly, at which point the child's fearful compliance in turn reinforces the parents' angry behavior. Over time, a destructive parent-child relationship develops. To disrupt this cycle, they have these recommendations for parents:

+ Give children attention and other reinforcers when they are behaving *well*. Target a specific behavior, reward it, and watch it increase.
+ Ignore whining. If whining has triggered attention in the past, it may temporarily increase when ignored. Over time, if not reinforced, it will diminish.

+ When children misbehave or are defiant, do not yell at or hit them. Simply explain the misbehavior and give them *time-out*—remove them from any reinforcing surroundings for a specified time.

Finally, we can use operant conditioning on ourselves, by reinforcing our most desired behaviors and extinguishing those undesired. To take charge of your own behavior, psychologists suggest these step-by-step procedures:

1. *State your goal*—say, to stop smoking, eat less, or study or exercise more—in measurable terms, and make your intention public. You might, for example, aim to boost your study time by an hour a day and announce that goal to some supportive friends.
2. *Monitor* how often you engage in the behavior you wish to promote. You might log your current study time, noting under what conditions you do and don't study. (When I began writing textbooks, I logged my time and was astonished to discover how much time I was wasting.)
3. *Reinforce* the desired behavior. To increase your study time, allow yourself a snack (or some other reinforcing activity) only after specified periods of study. Agree with your friends that you will join them for weekend activities only if you have met your weekly studying goal.
4. *Reduce the incentives* gradually while giving yourself a mental pat on the back as your new behaviors become more habitual.

Contrasting Conditioning Techniques

Preview Question: How does operant conditioning differ from classical conditioning?

The last four decades of research have changed psychologists' views of both classical and operant conditioning (summarized in Table 21.3). Learning, like so much else, depends on both nature and nurture. As we have seen, biological predispositions make learning some associations easier than learning others. Yet animals exhibit more sophisticated cognitive processes than once seemed likely. And rewarding people to do what they already enjoy may undermine their interest.

TABLE 21.3

COMPARISON OF CLASSICAL AND OPERANT CONDITIONING

	Classical Conditioning	**Operant Conditioning**
Response	Involuntary, automatic.	"Voluntary," operates on environment.
Acquisition	Associating events; CS announces UCS.	Associating response with a consequence (reinforcer or punisher).
Extinction	CR decreases when CS is repeatedly presented alone.	Responding decreases when reinforcement stops.
Cognitive processes	Subjects develop expectation that CS signals the arrival of UCS.	Subjects develop expectation that a response will be reinforced or punished; they also exhibit latent learning, without reinforcement.
Biological predispositions	Natural predispositions constrain what stimuli and responses can easily be associated.	Organisms best learn behaviors similar to their natural behaviors; unnatural behaviors instinctively drift back toward natural ones.

REVIEW AND REFLECT:

Operant Conditioning

What did B. F. Skinner's research on operant conditioning teach us about how we learn to repeat or suppress many behaviors?

Through operant conditioning, organisms learn to produce behaviors that are followed by reinforcing stimuli and to suppress behaviors that are followed by punishing stimuli. Skinner showed that when placed in an operant chamber, rats or pigeons can be shaped to display successively closer approximations of a desired behavior. Skinner and other researchers have also studied the effects of primary and secondary reinforcers, and of immediate and delayed reinforcers. Partial reinforcement schedules (fixed-ratio, variable-ratio, fixed-interval, and variable-interval) produce slower acquisition of the target behavior than does continuous reinforcement, but they also create more resistance to extinction. Punishment is most effective when it is strong, immediate, and consistent. However, it can have undesirable side effects.

What have we learned about the effect of cognitive processes and biological predispositions on operant conditioning?

Skinner's emphasis on external control of behavior made him both influential and controversial. Many psychologists criticized Skinner (as they did Pavlov) for underestimating the importance of cognitive and biological constraints. For example, research on latent learning and overjustification further indicates the importance of cognition in learning.

In what ways are Skinner's operant principles used to influence people's behavior in schools, in the workplace, and at home?

Skinner stimulated vigorous intellectual debate regarding the nature of human freedom and the strategies and ethics of managing people. Nevertheless, his operant principles are being applied in schools, the workplace, and homes. For example, computer-assisted instruction can embody the operant ideal of individualized shaping and immediate positive reinforcement.

How does operant conditioning differ from classical conditioning?

Both are forms of associative learning, and both involve acquisition, extinction, spontaneous recovery, generalizations, and discrimination. Through classical (Pavlovian) conditioning, an organism associates different stimuli that it does not control and responds automatically (respondent behaviors). Through operant conditioning, an organism associates its operant behaviors—those that act on its environment to produce rewarding or punishing stimuli—with their consequences. Cognitive processes and biological predispositions influence both classical and operant conditioning.

Terms and Concepts to Remember

associative learning, p. 302
operant conditioning, p. 302
respondent behavior, p. 302
operant behavior, p. 302
law of effect, p. 303
operant chamber (*Skinner box*), p. 303

learning, p. 303
shaping, p. 303
reinforcement, p. 305
primary reinforcer, p. 305
conditioned reinforcer (*secondary reinforcers*), p. 305
continuous reinforcement, p. 306

partial (intermittent) reinforcement, p. 306
fixed-ratio schedule, p. 306
variable-ratio schedule, p. 306
fixed-interval schedule, p. 307

variable-interval schedule, p. 307
punishment, p. 307
cognitive map, p. 309
latent learning, p. 310
overjustification effect, p. 310

Test Yourself

21.1. Salivating in response to a tone paired with food is a (an) _____; pressing a bar to obtain food is a(an) _____.
   a. primary reinforcer; secondary reinforcer
   b. secondary reinforcer; primary reinforcer
   c. operant behavior; respondent behavior
   d. respondent behavior; operant behavior

21.2. Thorndike's law of effect states that "rewarded behavior is likely to recur." This law became the basis for operant conditioning and the "behavioral technology" developed by
   a. Ivan Pavlov.   c. B. F. Skinner.
   b. John Garcia.   d. John B. Watson.

21.3. B. F. Skinner taught rats to press a bar to obtain a food pellet. To guide the rat's natural behavior toward the desired behavior, he used
   a. shaping.   c. taste aversion.
   b. punishment.   d. discrimination.

21.4. A reinforcer is a stimulus that is presented after a response and increases the frequency of that response. Imagine that your dog barks at every noise it hears. The barking disturbs you, so you put the dog outside when it starts to bark. The stopping of the barking is for you the termination of an aversive stimulus, or a
   a. positive reinforcer.   c. punishment.
   b. negative reinforcer.   d. primary reinforcer.

21.5. Continuous reinforcement—reinforcement of the desired response every time it occurs—makes for rapid learning and for rapid extinction when reinforcement stops. A partial reinforcement schedule that reinforces a response at unpredictable times—perhaps after 1 day or 2 days or even 15 days—is a
   a. fixed-interval schedule.   c. fixed-ratio schedule.
   b. variable-interval schedule. d. variable-ratio schedule.

21.6. A medieval proverb notes that "a burnt child dreads the fire." In behavioral terms, the burning is an example of a
   a. primary reinforcer.   c. punisher.
   b. negative reinforcer.   d. positive reinforcer.

21.7. Although Skinner disputed the idea, most researchers today believe that cognitive processes can play an important role in learning. Evidence for the effect of cognition (thoughts, perceptions, and expectations) comes from studies in which rats
   a. spontaneously recover previously learned behavior.
   b. develop cognitive maps.
   c. exhibit respondent behavior.
   d. generalize responses.

Continued

21.8. Animals, like people, can learn from experience, with or without reinforcement. After being carried passively through a maze and being given no reward, rats demonstrated their prior learning of the maze: In later trials involving food rewards, they immediately did as well as rats that had been reinforced for running the maze. The rats that had learned without reinforcement demonstrate

a. modeling.
b. biological predisposition.
c. shaping.
d. latent learning.

21.9. The overjustification effect occurs when people who enjoy an activity lose interest in it when offered a reward for performing the activity. Managers can best avoid this effect by

a. never rewarding employees.
b. rewarding all employees equally, regardless of their performance.
c. promising employees a reward if they do their job well.
d. telling employees that the reward represents the company's appreciation for their creativity and hard work.

Review: *Positive reinforcement, negative reinforcement,* and *punishment* are tricky concepts for many students. Can you fit the right term in the four boxes in this table? I'll do the first one (positive reinforcement) for you.

Type of Stimulus	Give It	Take It Away
Desired (for example, a compliment):	Positive reinforcement	
Undesired/aversive (for example, an insult):		

Reflect: Do you have any personal goals for this year? If so, can you see ways to apply reinforcement principles to help you attain them?

Answers to the Test Yourself and Review questions can be found in the green appendix at the end of the book.

Learning by Observation

Preview Question: What is observational learning?

From drooling dogs, running rats, and pecking pigeons psychologists have learned much about the basic processes of **learning**. But conditioning principles alone do not tell us the whole story. Among higher animals, especially humans, learning need not occur through direct experience. **Observational learning**, in which we observe and imitate others, also plays a big part. A child who sees his big sister burn her fingers on the stove has thereby learned not to touch it. The process of observing and imitating a specific behavior is often called **modeling**. We learn all kinds of social behaviors by observing and imitating models.

We can glimpse the roots of observational learning in other species. Shortly after a fight, stumptail macaque monkeys often reconcile with one another by approaching their opponent and making friendly contact. Rhesus macaque monkeys rarely make up quickly. If, however, rhesus monkeys grow up with forgiving older stumptails, then more often than not, their fights, too, are followed by reconciliation within three minutes (de Waal & Johanowicz, 1993). Monkey see, monkey do.

Imitation is all the more striking in humans. Indeed, so many of our ideas, fashions, and habits pass by imitation that researchers have given a name to these transmitted cultural elements: *memes*. We humans are the supreme meme machines, notes Susan Blackmore (1999). Our catch-phrases, hem lengths, ceremonies, foods, traditions, vices, and fads (think Pokemon) all spread by one person copying another.

The imitation of models shapes children's development. Shortly after birth, an infant may imitate an adult who sticks out his tongue. By 9 months, infants will imitate novel play behaviors. And by age 14 months they will imitate acts modeled on television (Meltzoff, 1988; Meltzoff & Moore, 1989, 1997). To persuade children to smoke, simply expose them to parents, older youth, and attractive media models who smoke. To encourage children to read, read to them and surround them with books and people who read them. To increase the odds of your children practicing your religion, worship and attend other religious activities with them.

Bandura's Experiments

Picture this scene from a famous experiment devised by Albert Bandura, the pioneering researcher of observational learning (Bandura & others, 1961). A preschool child is at work on a drawing. An adult in another part of the room is working with some Tinkertoys. The adult then gets up and for nearly 10 minutes pounds, kicks, and throws a large inflated Bobo doll around the room, while yelling such remarks as, "Sock him in the nose. . . . Hit him down. . . . Kick him."

After observing this outburst, the child is taken to another room where there are many appealing toys. Soon the experimenter interrupts the child's play and explains that she has decided to save these good toys "for the other children." She now takes the frustrated child to an adjacent room containing a few toys, including a Bobo doll. Left alone, what does the child do?

Compared with children not exposed to the adult model, those who observed the model's aggressive outburst were much more likely to lash out at the doll. Apparently, observing the adult model beating up the doll lowered their inhibitions. But something more than lowered inhibitions was at work, for the children also imitated the very acts they had observed and used the very words they had heard.

"We are, in truth, more than half what we are by imitation."

Lord Chesterfield (1694–1773)

Albert Bandura
"Learning would be exceedingly laborious, not to mention hazardous, if people had to rely solely on the effects of their own actions to inform them what to do" (1977).

■ **learning** a relatively permanent change in an organism's behavior due to experience.

■ **observational learning** learning by observing others.

■ **modeling** the process of observing and imitating a specific behavior.

■ **prosocial behavior** positive, constructive, helpful behavior. The opposite of antisocial behavior.

Applications of Observational Learning

The bad news from such studies is that antisocial models—in one's family or neighborhood, or on TV—may have antisocial effects. In the first eight days after the 1999 Columbine High School massacre, every U.S. state except Vermont had to deal with copycat threats or incidents. Pennsylvania alone had 60 threats of school violence (Cooper, 1999).

Observational learning helps us understand how abusive parents might have aggressive children and why men who beat their wives often had wife-battering fathers. The lessons we learn as children are not easily unlearned as adults, and they are sometimes visited on future generations. Critics note that the intergenerational transmission of abuse could be genetic. But with monkeys, at least, we know it can be environmental. In study after study, young monkeys that received high levels of aggression when reared apart from their mothers grew up to be perpetrators of aggression (Chamove, 1980).

The good news is that **prosocial** (positive, helpful) models can have prosocial effects. People who exemplify nonviolent, helpful behavior can prompt similar behavior in others. Mahatma Gandhi and Martin Luther King, Jr., both drew on the power of modeling, making nonviolent action a powerful force for social change. Parents are powerful models. Research indicates that European Christians who risked their lives to rescue Jews from the Nazis usually had a close relationship with at least one parent who modeled a strong moral or humanitarian concern, as did the 1960s U.S. civil rights activists (London, 1970; Oliner & Oliner, 1988).

Models are most effective when their actions and words are consistent. Sometimes, however, models say one thing and do another. Many parents seem to operate according to the principle "Do as I *say*, not as I do." Experiments suggest that children learn to do both (Rice & Grusec, 1975; Rushton, 1975). When exposed to a hypocrite, they tend to imitate the hypocrisy by doing what the model did and saying what the model said.

A model grandma

This boy is learning to cook by observing his grandmother. As the sixteenth-century proverb states, "Example is better than precept."

Learning from observation

This 14-month-old boy in Andrew Meltzoff's laboratory is imitating behavior he has seen on TV. In the top photo the infant leans forward and carefully watches the adult pull apart a toy. In the middle photo he has been given the toy. In the bottom photo he pulls the toy apart, imitating what he has seen the adult do.

What determines whether we will imitate a model? Bandura believes part of the answer is reinforcements and punishments—those received by the model as well as by the imitator. We look and we learn. By looking, we learn to anticipate a behavior's consequences in situations like those we are observing. By watching TV programs, children may "learn" that physical intimidation is an effective way to control others, that free and easy sex brings pleasure without later misery or disease, or that men are supposed to be tough and women gentle. We are especially likely to imitate those we perceive as similar to ourselves, as successful, or as admirable.

Bandura's work—like that of Pavlov, Watson, Skinner, and thousands of others who advanced our knowledge of learning principles—illustrates the impact that can result from single-minded devotion to a few well-defined problems and ideas. All of these researchers defined the issues and impressed on us the importance of learning. As their legacy demonstrates, intellectual history is often made by people who risk going to extremes in pushing ideas to their limits.

REVIEW AND REFLECT:

Learning by Observation

What is observational learning?

An important type of learning, especially among humans, is what Albert Bandura and others call *observational learning*. In experiments, children tend to imitate what a model both does and says, whether the behavior is social or antisocial. Such experiments have stimulated research on social modeling in the home, within the culture at large, and within peer groups. Children are especially likely to imitate those they perceive to be like them, successful, or admirable.

Terms and Concepts to Remember

learning, p. 317
observational learning, p. 317
modeling, p. 317
prosocial behavior, p. 318

Test Yourself

22.1. Children learn many social behaviors by imitating parents and other models. This type of learning is called
   a. observational learning.
   b. reinforced learning.
   c. operant conditioning.
   d. classical conditioning.

22.2. Parents are powerful models of behavior. They are *most* effective in getting their children to imitate them if
   a. their words and actions are consistent.
   b. they have outgoing personalities.
   c. the father works and the mother stays home to care for the children.
   d. they carefully explain why a behavior is acceptable in adults but not in children.

22.3. Bandura believes that modeling is not automatic. Whether a child will imitate a model depends in part on the
   a. child's closeness to the model.
   b. child's ability to distinguish right from wrong.
   c. rewards and punishments received by the model and by the imitator.
   d. child's age in relation to that of the model.

Review: Juan's parents and older friends all smoke, but they advise him not to. Jason's parents and friends don't smoke, but they say nothing to deter him from doing so. Will Juan or Jason be more likely to start smoking?

Reflect: Who have been significant role models for you? For whom are you a model?

Answers to the Test Yourself and Review questions can be found in the green appendix at the end of the book.

Memory

"I am memory alive."
Poet Joy Harjo, *"Skeleton of Winter"*

Be thankful for memory. We take it for granted, except when it malfunctions. But it's our memory, notes Rebecca Rupp (1998, p. xvii), that "allows us to recognize friends, neighbors, and acquaintances and call them by their names; to knit, type, drive, and play the piano; to speak English, Spanish, or Mandarin Chinese." It's our memory that enables us to sing our national anthem, find our way home, and locate the food and water we need for survival. It's our shared memories that bind us together as Muslims, Christians, or Jews; as Irish or Aussies; as Serbs or Albanians. And it is our memories that occasionally pit us against those whose offenses we cannot forget.

In large part, you are what you remember. Without memory, there would be no savoring joyful moments past, no guilt or anger over painful recollections. You would instead live in an enduring present. Each moment would be fresh. But each person would be a stranger, every language foreign, every task—dressing, cooking, biking—a novel challenge. You would even be a stranger to yourself, lacking that continuous sense of self that extends from your distant past to your momentary present.

Memories, unlike videotapes or photocopies, are personally constructed. And that is why two people can experience the same event and recall it differently. As a U.S. Supreme Court Justice nominee, Clarence Thomas was accused of sexual harassment by his former colleague Anita Hill. He vehemently denied it. People assumed one of them must be lying. But given the malleability and individuality of memory, notes Daniel Schacter (1999), Thomas and Hill may each have been recalling his or her own memory of the truth.

To think about memory, we first need a model of how it works. Module 23 introduces one classic and influential model—Richard Atkinson and Richard Shiffrin's three-stage model of memory. Modules 24 through 26 examine sensory memory, short-term memory (clarified by the newer concept of working memory), and long-term memory—thus reviewing how we move information into our memories, retain it, and later retrieve it. Module 27 looks at what happens when our memories fail us, as when we forget information, misremember it, or create false memories.

"Waiter, I'd like to order, unless I've eaten, in which case bring me the check."

23 Introduction to Memory

Preview Questions: What is memory? How do psychologists organize their own thinking about memory processes?

Your memory is your mind's storehouse, the reservoir of your accumulated learning. To the Roman statesman Cicero, memory was "the treasury and guardian of all things." To a psychologist, **memory** is any indication that learning has persisted over time. It is our ability to store and retrieve information.

Memory lost and found

Larry Treadgold, an engineer, invented a paging system that serves as a kind of artificial memory for his son Adrian. Brain-injured in an auto accident, the young man can retain information for as long as he pays attention. But as soon as he is distracted, the information fades. The paging system allows a central computer to take over memory functions, reminding him, for example, to "take your 8:00 A.M. medications; call 123–4567 to confirm." If Adrian fails to confirm, the computer continues to page him and eventually contacts an emergency number.

Studying memory's extremes has helped researchers understand this phenomenon. Talking with John, a former graduate student, you would be impressed by his wit, his intelligence (he might explain his master's thesis), and his skill at tasks such as typing. It might be some time before you noticed that John suffers a tragic defect, caused by a brain injury suffered in a motorcycle accident. He cannot form new memories. Although John remembers his life before the accident, he otherwise lives in an eternal present. Each morning when his rehabilitation therapist greets him she must reintroduce herself. She must listen patiently as over and over he retells anecdotes from his preaccident life. Each time the need arises, he inquires, "Where is the bathroom?" and is told anew.

MR. TOTAL RECALL

At the other extreme are some people who would be medal winners in a memory Olympics, such as Russian journalist Shereshevskii, or S, as psychologist Alexander Luria (1968) called him. S's memory not only allowed him merely to listen while other reporters were scribbling notes, it also earned him a place in virtually every modern book on memory. You and I can repeat back a string of about 7 digits—almost surely no more than 9. S could repeat up to 70 digits or words, provided they were read about 3 seconds apart in an otherwise silent room. Moreover, he could recall them backward as easily as forward. His accuracy was unerring, even when he was asked to recall a list as much as 15 years later, after having memorized hundreds of other lists. "Yes, yes," he might recall. "This was a series you gave me once when we were in your apartment. . . . You were sitting at the table and I in the rocking chair. . . . You were wearing a gray suit and you looked at me like this. . . ."

Which is more important—your experiences or your memories of them?

Do these memory feats make your own memory seem feeble? If so, just think: Your capacity for remembering countless voices, sounds, and songs; tastes, smells, and textures; faces, places, and happenings is pretty staggering in itself. Imagine viewing more than 2500 slides of faces and places, for only 10 seconds each. Later you see 280 of these slides one at a time, paired with a previously unseen slide. If you are like the subjects in this experiment by Ralph Haber (1970), you would recognize 90 percent of those you saw before.

Your memory ability is perhaps most apparent in your recall of unique and highly emotional moments in your past. One of my vivid memories is of my only hit in an entire season of Little League baseball. Perhaps yours is of a car accident, your first romantic kiss, your first day as an immigrant in a new country, or your surroundings when you heard some tragic news. Most Americans over 50 feel sure of exactly what they were doing when they heard the news of President Kennedy's assassination (Brown & Kulik, 1982). Seven months after Princess Diana's death, most Britishers could still recall what they had also reported the day after her death—their whereabouts on hearing the news (Wynn & Gilhooly, 1999). This clarity for our memories of surprising, significant events leads some psychologists to call them **flashbulb memories**, because it's as if the brain commands, "Capture this!"

How do we accomplish such memory feats? How can we remember things we have not thought about for years, yet forget the name of someone we met a minute ago? How can two people's memories of the same event be so different? How are memories stored in our brains? Why can even our flashbulb memories sometimes prove dead wrong? How can we improve our memories? To search for the answers to such questions, we first need a model of how memory works.

Information Processing

Building a memory is in some ways like my information processing in creating this book. For each edition I first glimpse countless items of information, including some 100,000 journal article titles. Most of it I ignore, but some things merit temporary storage in my briefcase for more detailed processing later. Most of these items I eventually discard. The rest—typically 2000 to 3000 articles and news items—gets organized and filed for long-term storage. Later, I retrieve this information and draw from it as I spin the story of today's psychology. In forming memories, you, too, must select, process, store, and retrieve information. You follow this process not only in the "cramming" you do to study in your college courses, but also in your processing of countless daily events.

Our memory is in some ways like a computer's information-processing system. To remember any event requires that we *get information into our brain* (**encoding**), *retain* that information (**storage**), and later *get it back out* (**retrieval**). Consider how a computer *encodes*, *stores*, and *retrieves* information. First, it

THE FAR SIDE

More facts of nature: All forest animals, to this very day, remember exactly where they were and what they were doing when they heard that Bambi's mother had been shot.

- **memory** the persistence of learning over time through the storage and retrieval of information.

- **flashbulb memory** a clear memory of an emotionally significant moment or event.

- **encoding** the processing of information into the memory system— for example, by extracting meaning.

- **storage** the retention of encoded information over time.

- **retrieval** the process of getting information out of memory storage.

Hours after the space shuttle *Challenger* explosion in 1986, people recalled where they had heard the news. Yet they were sometimes wildly inaccurate when again recalling their whereabouts 1 to 3 years later (McCloskey & others, 1988; Neisser, 1997). One woman recalled hearing it from someone running through her dorm screaming, "The space shuttle blew up." Actually, she had learned about it from friends over lunch.

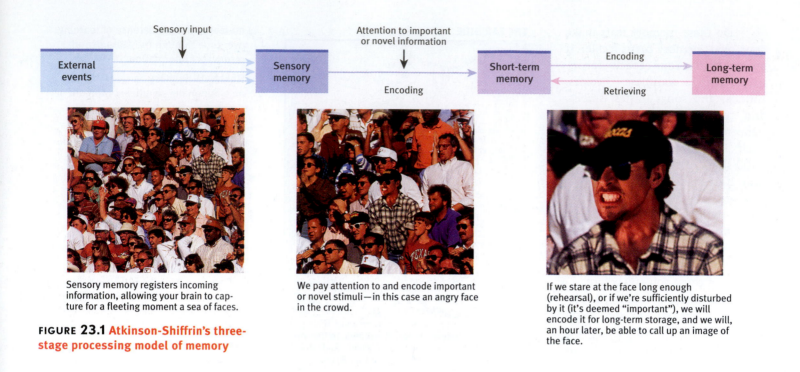

Sensory memory registers incoming information, allowing your brain to capture for a fleeting moment a sea of faces.

FIGURE 23.1 Atkinson-Shiffrin's three-stage processing model of memory

We pay attention to and encode important or novel stimuli—in this case an angry face in the crowd.

If we stare at the face long enough (rehearsal), or if we're sufficiently disturbed by it (it's deemed "important"), we will encode it for long-term storage, and we will, an hour later, be able to call up an image of the face.

- **sensory memory** the immediate, initial recording of sensory information in the memory system.

- **short-term memory** activated memory that holds a few items briefly, such as the seven digits of a phone number while dialing, before the information is stored or forgotten.

- **long-term memory** the relatively permanent and limitless storehouse of the memory system.

- **working memory** is a similar concept that focuses more on the processing of briefly stored information.

translates input (keystrokes) into an electronic language, much as the brain encodes sensory information into a neural language. The computer permanently stores vast amounts of information on a disk, from which it can later be retrieved. Like all analogies, the computer model has its limits, however. Our memories are less literal and more fragile than a computer's. Moreover, most computers process information sequentially but fast. The brain, as we have seen, is slower but does many things at once—in parallel.

In Modules 24 through 27, we will use Richard Atkinson and Richard Shiffrin's classic *three-stage processing model of memory* (1968), which suggests that we give birth to memories through three stages. We first record to-be-remembered information as a fleeting **sensory memory**, from which it is processed into a **short-term memory** bin, where we encode it for **long-term memory** and later retrieval (**FIGURE 23.1**).

This three-step process is limited and fallible. Bombarded with information, we cannot possibly focus on everything at once. Instead we shine the flashlight beam of our attention on certain incoming stimuli—often novel or important stimuli. These incoming stimuli, along with images we retrieve from our long-term memory, get displayed on our mental screen as conscious short-term memories. These rapidly decay unless used or rehearsed.

The newer concept of *working memory* clarifies the short-term memory concept by focusing more on our behind-the-scenes information processing. We do not just display information on-screen, we actively associate new and old information and solve problems. Working memory is roughly like a computer's random-access memory (RAM), which integrates information coming in from our keyboard with that retrieved from long-term storage on the hard drive. Part of this working memory is visible on our short-term screen.

Like short-term memory, **working memory** is quite limited. Alan Baddeley (1992) notes that working memory has a visual and a verbal component. These separate mental subsystems allow us to process images and words simultaneously en route to storage. Because each subsystem is limited, we cannot effectively engage in two conversations at once, though we can talk while playing chess.

REVIEW AND REFLECT:

Introduction to Memory

What is memory? How do psychologists organize their own thinking about memory processes?

Memory is the persistence of learning over time. Psychologists have proposed several information-processing models of memory. The influential three-stage processing model used in this text suggests that we (1) register fleeting *sensory memories*, some of which are (2) processed into on-screen *short-term* or *working memories*, a tiny fraction of which are (3) encoded for *long-term memory* and, possibly, later retrieval.

Terms and Concepts to Remember

memory, p. 322

flashbulb memory, p. 323

encoding, p. 323

storage, p. 323

retrieval, p. 323

sensory memory, p. 324

short-term memory, p. 324

long-term memory, p. 324

working memory, p. 324

Test Yourself

23.1. Many people have vivid memories of highly emotional moments—for example, what they were doing when they heard the news of an assassination or what kind of morning it was when they brought the new baby home from the hospital. These clear memories of emotional moments are called

a. short-term memories.

b. flashbulb memories.

c. inaccurate memories.

d. novel memories.

23.2. Short-term memory is an intermediate stage of memory where information is held before it is stored or forgotten. The newer concept of *working memory*

a. clarifies the idea of short-term memory by focusing on behind-the-scenes information processing.

b. splits short-term memory into two substages—sensory memory and working memory.

c. splits short-term memory into two areas—working (retrievable) memory and inaccessible memory.

d. clarifies the idea of short-term memory by introducing the element of rehearsal.

Review: Memory includes (in alphabetical order) long-term memory, sensory memory, and short-term memory. What's the correct order of these three memory stores?

Reflect: Do you have a flashbulb memory for an emotion-laden experience in your distant past?

Answers to the Test Yourself and Review questions can be found in the green appendix at the end of the book.

24 Encoding: Getting Information In

How We Encode

Preview Questions: What types of sensory information do we absorb incidentally? What types require intentional effort to be encoded and transferred into our memories?

Richard Atkinson and Richard Shiffrin's classic *three-stage processing model of memory* (1968) suggests that we give birth to memories through three stages. We first record to-be-remembered information as a fleeting *sensory memory*, from which it is processed into a *short-term memory bin*, where we encode it for *long-term memory* and later retrieval. Here we will focus on the *encoding* part of that process. Some encoding occurs automatically, freeing your attention to simultaneously process information that requires effort. Thus, your memory for the route you walked to your last class is handled by **automatic processing**. Your learning of psychology's concepts requires **effortful processing** (FIGURE 24.1). When we discuss effortful processing, I'll ask you to recall this sentence: *"The angry rioter threw the rock at the window."*

Automatic Processing

With little or no effort, you encode an enormous amount of information about *space*, *time*, and *frequency*: During an exam, you may recall the place on the textbook page where forgotten material appears. To guess where you left your coat, you can re-create a sequence of the day's events. You may realize that "this is the third time I've seen you this afternoon." Memories like these form almost automatically. In fact, not only does *automatic processing* occur effortlessly, it is difficult to shut off. When you hear or read a word in your native language, whether an insult or a compliment, it is virtually impossible not to register its meaning. Some types of automatic processing we learn. For example, learning to read reversed sentences at first requires effort:

.citamotua emoceb nac gnissecorp luftroffE

After practice, some *effortful processing* becomes more automatic, much as reading from right to left becomes easy for students of Hebrew (Kolers, 1975). Automatic processing occurs with little or no effort, without our awareness, and without interfering with our thinking about other things. (This is another example of our brain's capacity for parallel processing of multiple information streams.) If such processing requires no special attention, then asking people to attend to information they encode automatically, such as judging the frequency of words presented during an experiment, should be of little benefit. Lynn Hasher and Rose Zacks (1979, 1984) have shown that this is often the case. Although memory for such material may be modestly boosted by effort, our encoding is mostly automatic: We cannot switch it on and off at will.

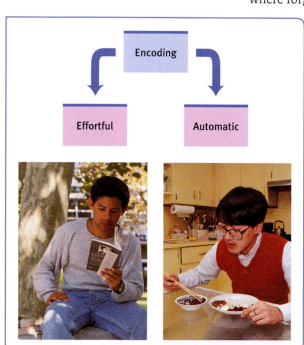

FIGURE 24.1
Automatic versus effortful processing
Some information, such as psychology's concepts, requires effort to encode and remember. Other information, like where you ate dinner yesterday, you process automatically.

Effortful Processing

We encode and retain vast amounts of information automatically, without any intentional effort. Other types of information, however, we remember only with effort and attention. When learning novel information such as names, we can boost our memory through **rehearsal**, or conscious repetition. This was shown long ago by the pioneering researcher of verbal memory, German philosopher Hermann Ebbinghaus (1850–1909). Ebbinghaus was to the study of memory what Ivan Pavlov was to the study of conditioning. Ebbinghaus became impatient with philosophical speculations about memory and decided to study it scientifically. To do so, he chose to study his own learning and forgetting of novel verbal materials.

Ebbinghaus needed to find verbal material that was not familiar. His solution was to form a list of all possible nonsense syllables created by sandwiching a vowel between two consonants. Then, for a particular experiment, he would randomly select a sample of the syllables. To get a feel for how Ebbinghaus tested himself, rapidly read aloud, eight times over, the following list (from Baddeley, 1982). Then try to recall the items:

> JIH, BAZ, FUB, YOX, SUJ, XIR, DAX, LEQ, VUM, PID, KEL, WAV, TUV, ZOF, GEK, HIW.

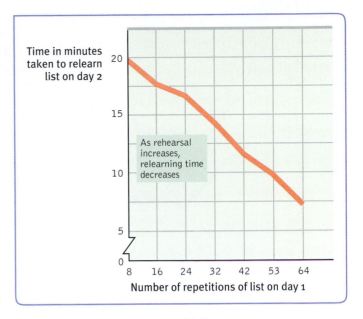

The day after learning such a list, Ebbinghaus could recall few of the syllables. But were they entirely forgotten? As **FIGURE 24.2** portrays, the more frequently he repeated the list aloud on day 1, the fewer repetitions he required to relearn the list on day 2. Here, then, was a simple beginning principle: *The amount remembered depends on the time spent learning.* Even after we learn material, additional rehearsal (*overlearning*) increases retention.

The point to remember is that for novel verbal information, practice—effortful processing—does indeed make perfect. And that helps us understand some other interesting phenomena:

+ The *next-in-line effect*: When people go around a circle reading words or saying their names, their poorest memories are for what was said by the person just before them (Bond & others, 1991; Brenner, 1973). When we are next in line, we focus on our own performance and often fail to process the last person's words.
+ Information presented in the seconds just before sleep seldom is remembered (Wyatt & Bootzin, 1994). When our consciousness fades before we've processed the information, all is lost. Information presented in the *hour* before sleep, as we will see, is well remembered.
+ Taped information played during sleep is registered by the ears but is not remembered (Wood & others, 1992). Without opportunity for rehearsal, "sleep learning" doesn't occur.

We also retain information better when our rehearsal is distributed over time (as when learning classmates' names), a phenomenon called the **spacing effect** (Dempster, 1988).

In a 9-year experiment, Harry Bahrick and three of his family members (1993) practiced foreign language word translations for a given number of times, at intervals ranging from 14 to 56 days. Their consistent finding: The longer the space between practice sessions, the better their retention, up to 5 years later. Reflecting on the spacing effect, Bahrick saw a practical implication: Restudying material for comprehensive final exams, capstone review courses, and senior examinations will enhance lifelong retention. Spreading out learning—say, over a semester or a year, rather than over shorter terms—should also help. Spaced study beats cramming.

That makes adaptive sense, note John Anderson and Lael Schooler (1991). In our environments, events that are spaced out *are* more likely to recur. Compared with a name we've heard or read five times in one month, the name we've read once a month for five months is a name we're more likely to read again. (They confirmed this by looking at such things as word frequencies in 730 consecutive *New York Times* headlines.) In such ways, our memory system, like so much else about us, is optimally designed to support our functioning and survival.

FIGURE 24.2
Ebbinghaus' retention curve
Ebbinghaus found that the more times he practiced a list of nonsense syllables on day 1, the fewer repetitions he required to relearn it on day 2. Said simply, the more time we spend learning novel information, the more we retain.

"The mind is slow in unlearning what it has been long in learning."

Roman philosopher Seneca (4 B.C.–A.D. 65)

■ **automatic processing** unconscious encoding of incidental information, such as space, time, and frequency, and of well-learned information, such as word meanings.

■ **effortful processing** encoding that requires attention and conscious effort.

■ **rehearsal** the conscious repetition of information, either to maintain it in consciousness or to encode it for storage.

■ **spacing effect** the tendency for distributed study or practice to yield better long-term retention than is achieved through massed study or practice.

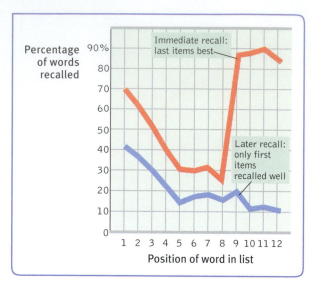

FIGURE 24.3

The serial position effect

After being presented with a list of words or names, people immediately recall the last items well (perhaps because they are still "on-screen"), and quite often the first few items nearly as well. But later they recall the first items best.

A phenomenon you have surely experienced further illustrates the benefits of rehearsal. Experimenters have shown people a list of items (words, names, dates) and then immediately asked them to recall the items in any order. As people struggle to recall the list, they often demonstrate the **serial position effect**: They remember the last and first items better than they do those in the middle (**FIGURE 24.3**). Perhaps because the last items are still in short-term memory, people briefly recall them especially quickly and well. But after a delay—after they shift their attention from the last items—their recall is best for the first items. As an everyday parallel, imagine being introduced to several people. As you meet each person, you repeat (rehearse) all their names starting from the beginning. By the time you meet the last person, you will have spent more time rehearsing the earlier names than the later ones; thus, the next day you will probably more easily recall the earlier names. Also, learning the first few names may interfere with your learning the later ones.

Rehearsal will not encode all information equally well. Sometimes merely repeating information, such as the new phone number we are about to dial, is not enough to store it for later recall (Craik & Watkins, 1973; Greene, 1987). How, then, do we encode information for processing into long-term memory? Processing our sensory input is like sorting through the day's mail. Some items we instantly discard. Others we process more thoughtfully: We open, read, and retain them. Our memory system processes information not just by repetitive rehearsal but also by encoding its significant features.

What We Encode

Preview Question: What strategies and devices help us remember information that requires effortful processing?

We process information in three key ways—by encoding its meaning, by visualizing it, and by mentally organizing it. To some extent we do these things automatically. But in each case there are effortful strategies for enhancing memory.

Encoding Meaning

Do you recall (from page 326) the sentence about the rioter? Can you now repeat that sentence: "The angry rioter threw . . ."? Your memory of the sentence may be affected by the way you stored it. When processing verbal information for storage, we usually encode its meaning. For example, we associate it with what we already know or imagine. Whether we hear "eye-scream" as "ice cream" or "I scream" depends on how the context and our experience guide us to interpret the sounds.

Perhaps, then, like the subjects in an experiment by William Brewer (1977), you recalled the rioter sentence as the meaning you encoded when you read it (for example, "The angry rioter threw the rock *through* the window") and not as it was written ("The angry rioter threw the rock *at* the window"). As such recall indicates, we tend not to remember things exactly as they were. Rather, *we remember what we encoded*. Studying for an exam, you may remember your lecture notes rather than the lecture itself. Likewise, as we hear or read about a situation, our minds construct a model of it. Gordon Bower and Daniel Morrow (1990) liken our minds to theater directors who, given a raw script, imagine a finished stage production. Asked later to recall what we heard or read, we recall not the literal text but the mental model we constructed from it.

What kind of encoding do you think yields the best memory of verbal information? **Semantic encoding** of meaning? **Acoustic encoding** of sound? **Visual en-**

- **serial position effect** our tendency to recall best the last and first items in a list.
- **semantic encoding** the encoding of meaning, including the meaning of words.
- **acoustic encoding** the encoding of sound, especially the sound of words.
- **visual encoding** the encoding of picture images.

coding of images? To find out, Fergus Craik and Endel Tulving (1975) flashed a word at people. Then they asked a question that required the people to process the words (1) visually (the appearance of the letters), (2) acoustically (the sound of the words), or (3) semantically (the meaning of the words). To experience the task yourself, rapidly answer the following questions:

Sample Questions to Elicit Processing	Word Flashed	Yes	No
1. Is the word in capital letters?	chair	___	___
2. Does the word rhyme with train?	BRAIN	___	___
3. Would the word fit in this sentence: The girl put the ___ on the table.	gun	___	___

Which type of processing would best prepare you to recognize the words at a later time? In Craik and Tulving's experiment, the deeper, semantic encoding—question 3—yielded much better memory than the "shallow processing" elicited by question 2 and especially by question 1 (**FIGURE 24.4**).

To experience the importance of meaning for verbal memory, put yourself in the place of the students whom John Bransford and Marcia Johnson (1972) asked to remember the following recorded passage:

> The procedure is actually quite simple. First you arrange things into different groups. Of course, one pile may be sufficient depending on how much there is to do. . . . After the procedure is completed one arranges the materials into different groups again. Then they can be put into their appropriate places. Eventually they will be used once more and the whole cycle will then have to be repeated. However, that is part of life.

When the students heard the paragraph you have just read, without a meaningful context, they remembered little of it. When told that the paragraph was about washing clothes (something additionally meaningful to them), they remembered much more of it—as you probably could now after rereading it.

Such research suggests the benefits of rephrasing what we read and hear into meaningful terms. From his experiments on himself, Ebbinghaus estimated that, compared with learning nonsense material, learning meaningful material required only one-tenth the effort. As memory researcher Wayne Wickelgren (1977, p. 346) noted, "The time you spend thinking about material you are reading and relating it to previously stored material is about the most useful thing you can do in learning any new subject matter."

We have excellent recall for information we can relate to ourselves. If asked how well certain adjectives describe someone else, we will often forget them; if asked to rate how well the adjectives describe ourselves, we remember the words well—a phenomenon called the *self-reference effect* (Symons & Johnson, 1997). So, you will profit from taking time to find personal meaning in what you are studying, for example, by taking the time to answer the Reflect questions found at the end of each module. Information deemed "relevant to me" is more likely to be processed deeply and to be accessible.

How many Fs are in the following sentence?
FINISHED FILES ARE THE RESULTS OF YEARS OF SCIENTIFIC STUDY COMBINED WITH THE EXPERIENCE OF YEARS. (See page 332.)

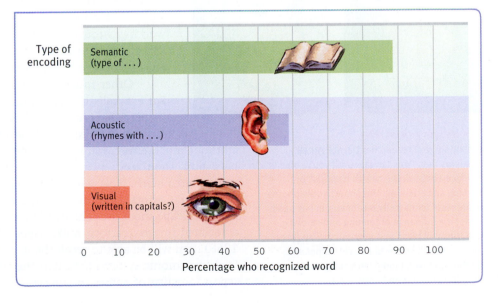

FIGURE 24.4 Levels of processing
Processing a word deeply—by its meaning (semantic encoding)—produces better recognition of it at a later time than does shallow processing by attending to its appearance or sound.

Type of encoding

Semantic (type of . . .)

Acoustic (rhymes with . . .)

Visual (written in capitals?)

0   10   20   30   40   50   60   70   80   90   100
Percentage who recognized word

Encoding Imagery

We struggle to memorize formulas, definitions, and dates, yet we can easily picture where we were yesterday, who was with us, where we sat, and what we wore. Our earliest memories—probably of something that happened at age 3 or 4—almost surely involve visual **imagery**, or mental pictures.

In a variety of experiments, researchers have documented the benefits of mental images. For example, we remember words that lend themselves to picture images better than we remember abstract, low-imagery words. (When I quiz you later, which three of these words—*typewriter, void, cigarette, inherent, fire, process*—will you most likely recall?) Similarly, you probably still recall the sentence about the rock-throwing rioter, not only because of the meaning you encoded but also because the sentence lent itself to a visual image. As the example suggests, and as certain memory experts believe, memory for concrete nouns is aided by encoding them *both* semantically and visually (Marschark & others, 1987; Paivio, 1986). Two codes are better than one.

Thanks to the durability of our most vivid images, we recall our experiences with mental snapshots of their best or worst moments. Thus, the best moment of a pleasure or joy, and the worst moment of a pain or frustration, often colors our memories more than does its duration (Fredrickson & Kahneman, 1993). Recalling the high points while forgetting the mundane moments may explain a phenomenon that Terrence Mitchell, Leigh Thompson, Erika Peterson, and Randy Cronk (1997) call *rosy retrospection*: People tend to recall events such as a camping holiday more positively than they evaluated them at the time. They remember their visit to Disney World less for the muggy heat and long lines than for the surroundings, food, and rides.

Imagery is at the heart of many memory aids. **Mnemonic** (nih-MON-ik) devices (so named after the Greek word for memory) were developed by ancient Greek scholars and orators as aids to remembering lengthy passages and speeches. Using the "method of loci," they imagined themselves moving through a familiar series of locations, associating each place with a visual representation of the to-be-remembered topic. Then, when speaking, the orator would mentally revisit each location and retrieve the associated image.

A variation on this method uses vivid stories to organize words to be memorized. Gordon Bower and Michael Clark (1969), using lists of unrelated nouns, asked one group to study the lists and another group to invent stories using the nouns. (A sample made-up story: "A LUMBERJACK DARTed out of a forest, SKATEd around a HEDGE past a COLONY of DUCKs. He tripped on some FURNITURE, tearing his STOCKING while hastening toward the PILLOW where his MISTRESS lay.") After working through 12 lists of 10 words each, the group that studied each list struggled to recall 13 percent of the words; the group that invented vivid stories recalled an astounding 93 percent.

Other mnemonic devices involve both acoustic and visual codes. For example, the "peg-word" system requires that you first memorize a jingle: *"One is a bun; two is a shoe; three is a tree; four is a door; five is a hive; six is sticks; seven is heaven; eight is a gate; nine is swine; ten is a hen."* Without much effort, you will soon be able to count by peg-words instead of numbers: bun, shoe, tree . . . and then to visually associate the peg-words with to-be-remembered items. Now you are ready to challenge anyone to give you a grocery list to remember. Carrots? Imagine them stuck into a bun. Milk? Fill the shoe with it. Paper towels? Drape them over the tree branch. Think "bun, shoe, tree" and you see their associated images: carrots, milk, paper towels. With few errors (Bugelski & others, 1968), you will be able to recall the items in any order and to name any given item. Such mnemonic systems are often the secret used by feats-of-memory experts who repeat long lists of names and objects.

> "A thing when heard, remember, strikes less keen on the spectator's mind than when 'tis seen."
>
> Horace, *Ars Poetica*, 8 B.C.

"You simply associate each number with a word, such as 'table' and 3,476,029."

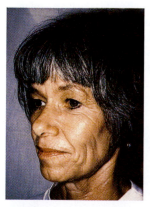

The imagery principle

Plastic surgery researcher Darrick Antell observes that "You can talk until you're blue in the face about all the health hazards" of tanning and smoking. But show people photos of identical twins, only one of whom has aged under the influence of tanning and smoking, and they will learn and remember. Sixty-year-old Gay Black, left, was an avid tanner and onetime smoker, unlike her younger-looking identical twin, Gwen Sirota, right.

Organizing Information for Encoding

Meaning and imagery enhance our memory partly by helping us organize information. When Bransford and Johnson's laundry paragraph (page 000) became meaningful, its sentences formed a sequence. Mnemonic devices help organize material for our later retrieval.

Chunking

To experience the importance of organization, glance for a few seconds at row 1 of **FIGURE 24.5**, then look away and try to reproduce what you saw. Impossible, yes? But you can easily reproduce the second row, which is no less complex. Similarly, I bet you found row 4 much easier to remember than row 3, although both contain the same letters. And you could remember the sixth cluster more easily than the fifth, although both contain the same words.

As this demonstrates, we organize easily remembered information into meaningful units, or chunks. **Chunking** information into meaningful units occurs so naturally that we take it for granted. If you are a native English speaker, you can reproduce perfectly the 150 or so line segments that make up the words in the three phrases of item 6 in Figure 24.5. It would astonish someone unfamiliar with the language.

I am similarly awed at the ability of someone literate in Chinese to glance at **FIGURE 24.6** and then to reproduce all the strokes; or of a chess master who, after a 5-second look at the board during a game, can recall the exact positions of most of the pieces (Chase & Simon, 1973); or of a varsity basketball player who, given a 4-second glance at a basketball play, can recall the positions of the players (Allard & Burnett, 1985). We all remember information best when we can organize it into personally meaningful arrangements.

Chunking also aids our recall of unfamiliar material. One mnemonic technique organizes it into a more familiar form by creating words (called *acronyms*) or sentences from the first letters of words to be remembered. Should you ever need to recall the names of North America's five Great Lakes, just remember HOMES (*H*uron, *O*ntario, *M*ichigan, *E*rie, *S*uperior). Want to remember the colors of the rainbow in order of wavelength? Think of ROY G. BIV (*r*ed, *o*range, *y*ellow, *g*reen, *b*lue, *i*ndigo, *v*iolet).

With chunking, you can increase your recall of digits, too. An impossible string of 16 numbers—1-4-9-2-1-7-7-6-1-8-1-2-1-9-4-1—becomes easy for an American when chunked into 1492, 1776, 1812, 1941 (as would 1066, 1688, 1815, and 1914 for those familiar with British history). After more than 200 hours of practice in the laboratory of Anders Ericsson and William Chase (1982), two Carnegie-Mellon University students even managed to increase their memory span from the typical 7 digits to more than 80. In another testing session, student Dario Donatelli heard the researcher read one digit per second in a monotonous voice: "1518593765502157841665850612094885686772731418186105462974801294 97965928." Motionless while learning the numbers, Donatelli then sprang alive. He

- **imagery** mental pictures; a powerful aid to effortful processing, especially when combined with semantic encoding.

- **mnemonics** [nih-MON-iks] memory aids, especially those techniques that use vivid imagery and organizational devices.

- **chunking** organizing items into familiar, manageable units; often occurs automatically.

1. ◁◀▷◖ᴎⵏᴎ◖
2. K L C I S N E

3. KLCISNE NVESE YNA NI CSTTIH TNDO
4. NICKELS SEVEN ANY IN STITCH DONT

5. NICKELS SEVEN ANY IN STITCH DONT SAVES AGO A SCORE TIME AND NINE WOODEN FOUR YEARS TAKE

6. DONT TAKE ANY WOODEN NICKELS FOUR SCORE AND SEVEN YEARS AGO A STITCH IN TIME SAVES NINE

FIGURE 24.5

Effects of chunking on memory
When we organize information into meaningful units, such as letters, words, and phrases, we recall it more easily.

FIGURE 24.6 An example of chunking—for those who read Chinese
After looking at these characters, can you reproduce them exactly? If so, you are literate in Chinese.

FIGURE 24.7
Organization benefits memory
When we organize words or concepts into hierarchical groups, as here, we remember them better than when we see them presented randomly.

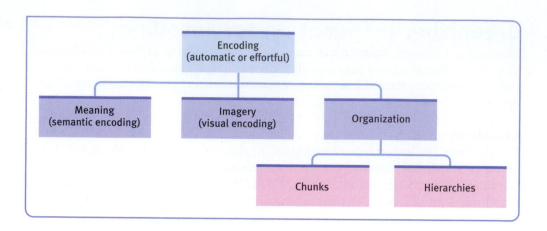

whispered numbers, rubbed his chin, tapped his feet, counted on his fingers, and ran his hands through his hair. "Okay," he announced almost 2 minutes later. "The first set is 1518. Then 5937. . . ." He repeated all 73 digits, in groups of 3 and 4.

How did he do it? By increasing the capacity of his short-term memory? No. When asked to remember letters, Donatelli fell back to about a seven-item capacity. Rather, he had developed a sophisticated strategy for number chunking. "First set was a 3-mile time," reported Donatelli, an All-American cross-country runner. "Second set was a 10-mile time. Then a mile. Half-mile. Two-mile time. An age. . . . Two mile. Age. Age. Age. Two-mile. . . ." (Wells, 1983).

Hierarchies

Answer to question on page 329: Partly because your initial processing of the letters was primarily acoustic rather than visual, you probably missed some of the six Fs, especially those that sound like a *V* rather than an *F*.

For Donatelli to reach his peak—106 digits—he retrieved the chunks of numbers by clustering them as a hierarchy (Waldrop, 1987). First came "three groups of four," he might think, and so forth. When people develop expertise in an area, they process information not only in chunks but also in hierarchies composed of a few broad concepts divided and subdivided into narrower concepts and facts. By organizing knowledge in hierarchies, we, too, can retrieve information efficiently. This module therefore aims not only to teach you some elementary facts of memory but also to help you organize these facts around broad principles, such as encoding; subprinciples, such as automatic and effortful processing; and still more specific concepts, such as meaning, imagery, and organization (**FIGURE 24.7**).

Gordon Bower and his colleagues (1969) demonstrated the benefits of hierarchical organization. They presented words either randomly or grouped into categories. When the words were organized into groups, recall was two to three times better. Such results show the benefits of organizing what you study—for instance giving special attention to this book's, Preview Questions, headings, review paragraphs, and "Review," "Reflect," and "Test Yourself" questions. If you can master a chapter's concepts with their overall organization, your recall should be effective at test time. Taking lecture and text notes in outline format—a type of hierarchical organization—may also prove helpful.

How many of the six quiz words on page 330 can you now recall? Of these, how many are high-imagery words? How many are low-imagery?

Encoding: Getting Information In

What types of sensory information do we absorb incidentally? What types require intentional effort to be encoded and transferred into our memory system?

Some types of information, notably information concerning space, time, and frequency, we encode mostly automatically. Other types of information, including much of our processing of meaning, imagery, and organization, require effort.

What strategies and devices help us remember information that requires effortful processing?

Mnemonic devices depend on the memorability of visual images and of information that is organized into chunks. Organizing information into chunks and hierarchies also aids memory.

Terms and Concepts to Remember

automatic processing, p. 326
effortful processing, p. 326
rehearsal, p. 326
spacing effect, p. 327
serial position effect, p. 328
semantic encoding, p. 328

acoustic encoding, p. 328
visual encoding, p. 328
imagery, p. 330
mnemonics [nih-MON-iks], p. 330
chunking, p. 331

Test Yourself

24.1. In his research on verbal memory, Hermann Ebbinghaus tested his ability to recall a list of nonsense syllables. He found that the more often he repeated the list aloud, the fewer repetitions he required to relearn the list. This increase in retention was due to additional rehearsal, or
   a. automatic processing.
   b. retrieval.
   c. overlearning.
   d. the flashbulb effect.

24.2. Rehearsal is the conscious repetition of information a person wants to remember, either in the short or long term. Rehearsal is part of
   a. automatic processing.
   b. effortful processing.
   c. forgetting.
   d. retrieval.

24.3. Psychologists have found that when people are shown a list of words and are immediately tested, they tend to recall the first and last items on the list more readily than those in the middle (called the serial position effect). When people are *re*tested after a delay, they are most likely to recall
   a. the first items on the list.
   b. the first and last items on the list.
   c. a few items at random.
   d. the last items on the list.

24.4. Many people use visual imagery to help them remember material that would otherwise be difficult to master. Memory aids that use visual imagery, peg-words, or other organizational devices are called
   a. acronyms.
   b. nonsense material.
   c. mental pictures.
   d. mnemonics.

24.5. Chunking is a way of organizing information into familiar and manageable units. A related technique involves organizing material into broad categories, which are then divided into subcategories. This technique, used in chapter outlines and organizational charts, is called
   a. serial position.
   b. peg-words.
   c. hierarchial organization.
   d. mental pictures.

Review: What would be the most effective strategy to learn and retain a list of historical names of key figures for a week? For a year?

Reflect: Can you think of three ways to employ the principles in this module to improve your own learning and retention of important things?

Answers to the Test Yourself and Review questions can be found in the green appendix at the end of the book.

25 Storage: Retaining Information

Preview Questions: What are the capacities and durations of storage for sensory memory, short-term memory, and long-term memory? How and where does the brain physically store memories?

If you later recall something you experienced, you must, somehow, have stored and retrieved it. Anything stored in long-term memory lies dormant, waiting to be reawakened by a cue. What is our temporary and our long-term memory storage capacity? Let's start with the first memory store noted in the three-stage processing model (**FIGURE 25.1**)—our fleeting sensory memory.

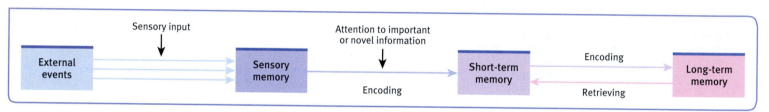

FIGURE 25.1
Atkinson-Shiffrin's three-stage processing model of memory

Sensory Memory

Consider what one intriguing memory experiment revealed about our sensory memory—the initial recording of sensory information in the memory system. As part of his doctoral research, George Sperling (1960) showed people three rows of three letters each for only 1/20th of a second (**FIGURE 25.2**). It was harder than reading by flashes of lightning. After the nine letters disappeared from the screen, the subjects could recall only about half of them.

Was it because they had insufficient time to glimpse them? No, Sperling cleverly demonstrated that even at faster than lightning-flash speed, people actually *can* see and recall all the letters, but only momentarily. Rather than ask them to recall all nine letters at once, Sperling would sound a high, medium, or low tone immediately *after* flashing the nine letters. This cue directed the subject to report only the letters of the top, middle, or bottom row, respectively. Now the subjects rarely missed a letter, showing that all nine letters were momentarily available for recall.

Sperling's experiment revealed that we have a fleeting photographic memory called **iconic memory**. For an instant, our eyes register an exact representation of a scene and we can recall any part of it in amazing detail—but only for a few tenths of a second. If Sperling delayed the tone signal by more than half a second, the iconic memory was gone and the subjects once again recalled only about half the let-

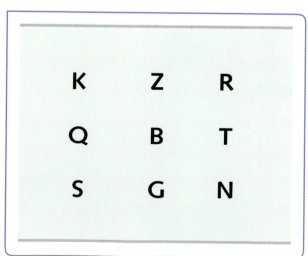

FIGURE 25.2
Momentary photographic memory
When George Sperling flashed a group of letters similar to this for 1/20th of a second, people could recall only about half of the letters. But when signaled to recall a particular row *immediately* after the letters had disappeared, they could do so with near-perfect accuracy.

ters. Our visual screen clears quickly, as it must, so that new images can be superimposed over old ones.

We also have an impeccable, though fleeting, memory for auditory sensory images, called **echoic memory** (Cowan, 1988; Lu & others, 1992). However, if partially interpreted, the auditory echo disappears more slowly. The last few words spoken seem to linger for 3 or 4 seconds. Sometimes, just as you ask, "What did you say?" you can hear in your mind the echo of what was said.

Short-Term Memory

Among the vast amounts of information registered by our sensory memory, we illuminate some with our attentional flashlight. We also retrieve information from long-term storage for "on-screen" display. But unless we meaningfully encode or rehearse that information, it quickly disappears. During your finger's trip from the phone book to the phone, your memory of a telephone number will disappear unless you work to maintain it in consciousness.

To find out how quickly a short-term memory will disappear, Lloyd Peterson and Margaret Peterson (1959) asked people to remember three-consonant groups, such as *CHJ*. To prevent subjects' rehearsal of the letters, the researchers asked them, for example, to start at 100 and count aloud backward by threes. After 3 seconds people recalled the letters only about half the time; after 12 seconds they seldom recalled them at all (**FIGURE 25.3**). Without active processing, short-term memories have a limited life.

Short-term memory is limited not only in duration but also in capacity, typically storing but seven or so chunks of information (give or take two). This recall capacity has been enshrined in psychology as the *Magical Number Seven, plus or minus two* (Miller, 1956).

Our short-term recall is slightly better for random digits (such as those of a phone number) than for random letters, which sometimes have similar sounds. It is slightly better for information we hear than for images we see. Both children and adults have short-term recall for roughly as many words as they can speak in 2 seconds (Cowan, 1994; Hulme & Tordoff, 1989). The basic principle: At any given moment, we can consciously process only a very limited amount of information.

- **iconic memory** a momentary sensory memory of visual stimuli; a photographic or picture-image memory lasting no more than a few tenths of a second.

- **echoic memory** momentary sensory memory of auditory stimuli; if attention is elsewhere, sounds and words can still be recalled within 3 or 4 seconds.

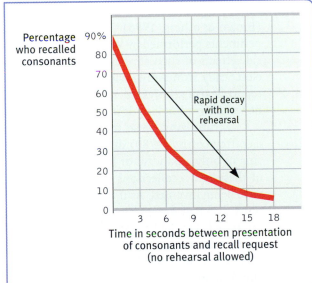

FIGURE 25.3
Short-term memory decay
Unless rehearsed, verbal information may be quickly forgotten.

Long-Term Memory

In Arthur Conan Doyle's *A Study in Scarlet*, Sherlock Holmes offers a popular theory of memory capacity:

> I consider that a man's brain originally is like a little empty attic, and you have to stock it with such furniture as you choose. . . . It is a mistake to think that that little room has elastic walls and can distend to any extent. Depend upon it, there comes a time when for every addition of knowledge you forget something that you knew before.

Clark's Nutcracker
Among animals, one contender for champion memorist would be a mere birdbrain—the Clark's Nutcracker—which during winter and early spring can locate up to 6000 caches of buried pine seeds (Shettleworth, 1993).

Contrary to Sherlock Holmes' belief, our capacity for storing long-term memories is essentially limitless. By one careful estimate, the average adult has about a billion bits of information in memory and a storage capacity that is probably a thousand to a million times greater (Landauer, 1986). So, our brains are *not* like attics, which once filled can store more items only if we discard old ones.

The point is vividly illustrated by those who have performed phenomenal memory feats. Consider Rajan Mahadevan, a University of Tennessee psychologist. Give him a block of 10 digits from the first 30,000 or so digits of pi and, after a few moments of mental searching for the string, he'll pick up the series from there, firing numbers like a machine gun (Delaney & others, 1999; Thompson & others, 1993). He also can repeat 50 random digits—backwards. It is not a genetic gift, he says; anyone could learn to do it. But given the genetic influence on so many human traits, and knowing that Rajan's father memorized Shakespeare's complete works, one wonders.

Storing Memories in the Brain

I marveled at my aging mother-in-law, a retired pianist and organist. At age 88 her blind eyes could no longer read music. But let her sit at a keyboard and she would flawlessly play any of hundreds of hymns, including ones she had not thought of for 20 years. Where did her brain store those thousands of sequenced notes? For a time, some memory researchers believed that brain stimulation during surgery provided evidence that our whole past, and not just well-practiced music, is "in there," in complete detail, just waiting to be relived. Even today, 6 in 10 university students agree that "everything we learn is permanently stored," although sometimes inaccessible (Brown & others, 1996). Perhaps some of them have heard of the brain surgery experiments performed by Wilder Penfield and other neurosurgeons. To predict possible side effects of such surgery, Penfield (1969) helped map the brain's motor cortex by electrically stimulating wide-awake patients. Occasionally, Penfield's patients would report hearing things, such as "a mother calling her little boy." Penfield assumed that he was activating long-lost experiences etched permanently on the brain.

Scrutinizing these famous reports, memory researchers Elizabeth Loftus and Geoffrey Loftus (1980) discovered that these flashbacks were extremely rare, occurring in only a handful of Penfield's 1100 stimulated patients. Moreover, the content of these few recollections suggested that the experiences were not being relived but were being invented. As if they had been dreaming, people would recall being in locations they had never visited. Although the brain's storage capacity may be essentially unlimited, Penfield's evidence did *not* suggest that we store most information with the exactness of a tape recorder. Rather, say memory researchers, forgetting occurs as new experiences interfere with our retrieval and as the physical memory trace gradually decays.

But what exactly is the "memory trace"? Since 1980, new clues to the physical basis of long-term memory have surfaced rapidly. While cognitive psychologists study our memory "software," neuroscientists are gaining new insights into our memory "hardware"—how and where we physically store information in our brains.

For several decades, neuroscientists have searched the brain for physical evidence of memory. The search has at times been exasperating. One psychologist, Karl Lashley (1950), trained rats to solve a maze, then cut out pieces of the rats' cortexes and retested their memory of the maze. He hoped eventually to locate where memory of the maze was stored. Alas, no matter what part of the cortex he removed, the rats retained at least a partial memory of how to solve the maze. Lashley's conclusion: Memories do not reside in single, specific spots.

Are memories instead rooted in the brain's ongoing electrical activity? If so, then temporarily shutting down that activity should eliminate them, much as a power failure eliminates the settings on a digital clock radio. To test this, Ralph Ger-

"Our memories are flexible and superimposable, a panoramic blackboard with an endless supply of chalk and erasers."

Elizabeth Loftus and Katherine Ketcham, *The Myth of Repressed Memory*, 1994

ard (1953) trained hamsters to turn right or left to get food. Then he lowered their body temperature until the brain's electrical activity ceased. When the hamsters were revived and their brains were active again, would they remember which way to turn? Yes. Their long-term memories survived the electrical blackout. In commenting on the elusiveness of the memory trace, one memory researcher, with tongue only partly in cheek, said "I must admit that memories are more of a spiritual than a physical reality. When you try to touch them, they turn to mist and disappear" (Loftus & Ketcham, 1994, p. 4). To know how our brain stores and effortlessly retrieves a flood of details "defies comprehension," says one awestruck neuroscientist (Doty, 1998).

Recently, the search for the physical basis of memory—information incarnated in matter—has focused on the firing potential of the synapses.

Synaptic Changes

Neuroscientists are expanding the search for the location of memories by exploring changes within and between single neurons. Memories begin as impulses whizzing through brain circuits, somehow leaving permanent neural traces. Where does the neural change occur? The available clues point to the synapses—the sites where nerve cells communicate with one another through their neurotransmitter messengers (Alkon & others, 1991). We know that experience modifies the brain's neural networks: Given increased activity in a particular pathway, neural interconnections form or strengthen.

Eric Kandel and James Schwartz (1982) observed actual changes in the sending neurons. Their subjects were among the simplest animals, the California sea snail, *Aplysia*. Its mere 20,000 or so nerve cells are unusually large and accessible, enabling the researchers to observe synaptic changes during learning. The sea snail can be classically conditioned (with electric shock) to reflexively withdraw its gills when squirted with water, much as a shell-shocked soldier jumps at the sound of a snapping twig. By observing the snails' neural connections before and after conditioning, the researchers were able to pinpoint changes. When learning occurs, the snail releases more of the neurotransmitter serotonin at certain synapses. These synapses then become more efficient at transmitting signals.

Increased synaptic efficiency makes for more efficient neural circuits. In experiments, rapidly stimulating certain memory-circuit connections has increased their sensitivity for hours or even weeks to come. The sending neuron now needs less prompting to release its neurotransmitter, and receptor sites may increase (**FIGURE 25.4**). This prolonged strengthening of potential neural firing, called **long-term potentiation (LTP)**, provides a neural basis for learning and remembering associations. We know now that drugs that block LTP interfere with learning (Lynch & Staubli, 1991). Mutant mice engineered to lack an enzyme needed for LTP can't learn their way out of a maze (Silva & others, 1992). And rats given a drug that enhances LTP will learn a maze with half the usual number of mistakes (Service, 1994). These findings raise hopes that researchers may someday discover a drug to enhance human memory, especially for those whose memory is fading.

After long-term potentiation has occurred, passing an electric current through the brain won't disrupt old memories. But the current will wipe out very recent experiences. Such is the experience both of laboratory animals and of depressed people given electroconvulsive therapy. A blow to the head can do the same. When football players who have been dazed or momentarily knocked unconscious are interviewed a few minutes later, they typically cannot recall the name of the play during which the incident occurred (Yarnell & Lynch, 1970). Likewise, a boxer knocked out in round 2 may have no memory of the round.

■ **long-term potentiation (LTP)** an increase in a synapse's firing potential after brief, rapid stimulation. Believed to be a neural basis for learning and memory.

What's next?
In the early stages of Alzheimer's disease, a loss of brain tissue that secretes important neurotransmitters results in considerable mental impairment. In recent years, social agencies have begun offering day-care services. At centers like the one shown here, patients are kept busy and their caretakers get a break.

FIGURE 25.4 Doubled receptor sites
Electron microscope images show just one receptor site (white) reaching toward a sending neuron before long-term potentiation (left) and two afterward (right).

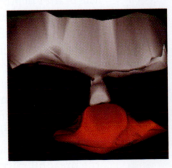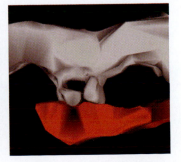

- **amnesia** the loss of memory.
- **implicit memory** retention without conscious recollection (of skills and dispositions). (Also called *procedural memory*.)
- **explicit memory** memory of facts and experiences that one can consciously know and "declare." (Also called *declarative memory*.)

(They are like sleepers who can't remember what they heard just before losing consciousness.) The information in short-term memory before the blow did not have time to consolidate into long-term memory.

Drugs that block neurotransmitters will also disrupt information storage (Squire, 1987). For example, alcohol impairs memory formation by disrupting serotonin's messenger activity (Weingartner & others, 1983). The morning after a night of heavy drinking, a person may have trouble remembering the previous evening.

Stress Hormones and Memory

The naturally stimulating hormones that humans and animals produce when excited or stressed also affect learning and retention—they boost it. When a rat receives an arousing hormone and then a mild foot shock, it forms an indelible memory—like the one it forms when an *intense* foot shock naturally triggers release of the same hormone (Gold, 1987, 1992; Martinez & others, 1991). By making more glucose energy available to fuel brain activity, the hormone surge signals the brain that something important has happened. The arousal sears the events onto the brain. Conversely, people given a drug that blocks the effects of stress hormones will later have more trouble remembering the details of an upsetting story (Cahill & others, 1994). No emotion means weaker memories.

Emotion-triggered hormonal changes help explain why we long remember exciting or shocking events, such as our first kiss, a political assassination, or an earthquake. People who have suffered traumatic experiences often relive the experience with vivid flashbacks. And people who experienced the 1989 San Francisco earthquake had perfect recall a year and a half later of where they were and what they were doing (as they had recorded within a day or two of the quake). Others' memories for the circumstances under which they *heard* about the quake were prone to errors (Neisser & others, 1991; Palmer & others, 1991). (A second important reason for the durability of dramatic experiences is our reliving and rehearsing them—as did most people who experienced the earthquake and told their stories to countless others.)

The point to remember, according to James McGaugh (1994), is that "stronger emotional experiences make for stronger, more reliable memories." After traumatic experiences—a wartime ambush, a house fire, a rape—vivid recollections of the horrific event intrude again and again. It is as if they were burned in.

There are, however, limits to stress-enhanced remembering. *Prolonged* stress—sometimes from sustained abuse or combat—acts like acid, corroding neural connections and shrinking a brain area that is vital for laying down memories. Moreover, when stress hormones are flowing, memories may get blocked. It is true for rats trying to find their way to a hidden target (de Quervain & others, 1998). And it is true for those of us whose minds have gone blank while speaking in public.

Stress hormones and memory
When we are greatly aroused, as are these Manila squatter colony residents fleeing typhoon Angela, our stress hormones help make memories indelible.

Storing Implicit and Explicit Memories

A memory-to-be enters the cortex through the senses, then winds its way into the brain's depths. Precisely where it goes depends on the type of information, as dramatically illustrated in **amnesic** patients. Neurologist Oliver Sacks (1985, pp. 26–27) describes one such patient, Jimmie, who had brain damage. Jimmie had no memories—thus, no sense of elapsed time—beyond his injury in 1945. Asked in 1975 to name the U.S. President, he replied, "FDR's dead. Truman's at the helm."

When Jimmie gave his age as 19, Sacks set a mirror before him: "Look in the mirror and tell me what you see. Is that a 19-year-old looking out from the mirror?"

Jimmie turned ashen, gripped the chair, cursed, then became frantic: "What's going on? What's happened to me? Is this a nightmare? Am I crazy? Is this a joke?" When his attention was diverted to some children playing baseball, his panic ended, the dreadful mirror forgotten.

Sacks showed Jimmie a photo from *National Geographic.* "What is this?" he asked.

"It's the moon," Jimmie replied.

"No, it's not," Sacks answered. "It's a picture of the earth taken from the moon."

"Doc, you're kidding? Someone would've had to get a camera up there!"

"Naturally."

"Hell! You're joking—how the hell would you do that?" Jimmie's wonder was that of a bright young man from 55 years ago reacting with amazement to his travel back to the future.

Careful testing of people with amnesia reveals something even stranger: Although incapable of recalling new facts or anything they have recently done, Jimmie and other similarly amnesic people can learn. They can be classically conditioned. Shown hard-to-find figures in pictures (where's Waldo?), they can quickly spot them again later. They can learn to read mirror-image writing or do a jigsaw puzzle, and they have even been taught complicated job skills (Schacter, 1992, 1996; Squire, 1987). However, *they do all these things with absolutely no awareness of having learned them.*

Consider what happens when such patients have learned to solve a Tower of Hanoi puzzle, which requires moving rings from one pole to another until they are stacked in order of size. Amnesia victims will deny having seen the puzzle before, insist it is silly for them to try, and then, like practiced experts, proceed to solve it. They are in some ways like people with brain damage who cannot consciously recognize faces but whose physiological responses to familiar faces reveal an implicit (unconscious) recognition.

These curious findings challenge the idea that memory is a single, unified system. Instead, we seem to have two memory systems operating in tandem (**FIGURE 25.5**). Whatever has destroyed conscious recall in these individuals with amnesia has not destroyed their unconscious capacity for learning. They can learn *how* to do something—called **implicit memory** (*procedural memory*). But they cannot know and declare *that* they know—called **explicit memory** (*declarative memory*). Having read a story once, they will read it faster a second time, showing implicit memory. But there will be no explicit memory, for they cannot recall having seen the story before. Having played golf on a new course, they will forget it completely, yet the more they play the course, the more their game will improve. If repeatedly shown the word *perfume*, they will not recall having seen it. But if asked the first word that comes to mind in response to the letters *per*, they surprise themselves by saying *perfume*, readily displaying their learning. They retain their past but do not explicitly recall it.

The two-track memory system reinforces an important principle of the way the brain handles information via parallel processing: Mental feats such as vision, thinking, and memory may seem to be single abilities, but they are not. Rather, we split information into different components for separate and simultaneous processing.

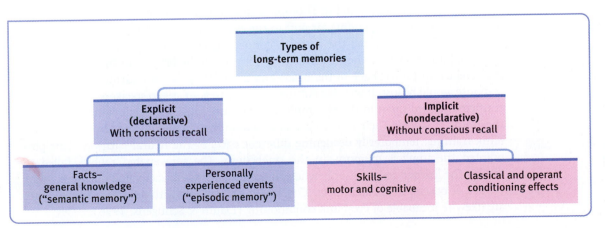

FIGURE 25.5
Memory subsystems
We process and store our explicit and implicit memories separately. Thus, one may lose explicit memory (becoming amnesic), yet display implicit memory for material one cannot consciously recall.

■ **hippocampus** a neural center located in the limbic system that helps process explicit memories for storage.

> "[Brain-scanning] technologies are revolutionizing the study of the brain and mind in the same way that the telescope revolutionized the study of the heavens."
>
> Endel Tulving (1996)

FIGURE 25.6 The hippocampus

Explicit memories for facts and episodes are processed in the hippocampus and fed to other brain regions for storage.

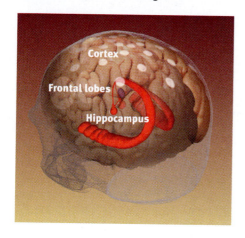

The Hippocampus

One way to discover how memory works is to study its malfunctions. For example, these remarkable patients provoke us to wonder: Do our explicit and implicit memory systems involve separate brain regions? Scans of the brain in action and autopsies of amnesic patients reveal that new explicit memories of names, images, and events are laid down via a limbic system structure called the **hippocampus** (FIGURE 25.6). When brain scans capture the brain giving birth to a memory they reveal activity in the hippocampus as well as in certain areas of the frontal lobes (Wagner & others, 1998). The hippocampus again lights up on a PET scan when people recall words (using explicit memory) (Squire, 1992).

Damage to the hippocampus disrupts some types of memory. Chickadees and other birds can store food in hundreds of places and return to these unmarked caches months later, but not if their hippocampus has been removed (Sherry & Vaccarino, 1989). Like the cortex, the hippocampus is lateralized. (You've got two of them, one just above each ear and about an inch and a half straight in.) Damage to the left or right hippocampus seems to produce different results. Patients with left hippocampus damage have trouble remembering verbal information, but they have no trouble recalling visual designs and locations. For those with right hippocampus damage, the problem is reversed (Schacter, 1996).

Monkeys who lose their hippocampus to surgery also lose most of their recall for things learned during the preceding month, though their older memories remain intact (Squire & Zola-Morgan, 1991). The hippocampus seems to act as a convergence zone where the brain registers and temporarily stores the elements of a remembered episode—the smells, feels, sounds, and place. It is also a play-back system that reactivates neurons that fired when we experienced the event, as if helping the brain strengthen connections among them.

Our brain's librarian assigns different information to different regions. Brain scans reveal that, once stored, our mental encores of past experience activate various parts of the frontal and temporal lobes (Fink & others, 1996; Gabrieli & others, 1996; Markowitsch, 1995). Calling up a telephone number and holding it in working memory activates a region of the left frontal cortex; recalling a party scene would more likely activate a region of the right hemisphere. There is no longer any doubt: Our memories are not in one place. Many brain regions are active as we encode, store, and retrieve different kinds of information. Savoring the memory of your first kiss requires a mental symphony conductor that retrieves snippets from various cortical storage sites and integrates them with the emotional associations provided by your amygdala.

The Cerebellum

Although your hippocampus is a temporary processing site for your explicit memories, you could lose it and still lay down memories for skills and conditioned associations. Hoping to locate such implicit memories, psychologist Richard Thompson and his fellow explorers David Krupa and Judith Thompson studied how a rabbit's brain learns to associate a tone with an impending air puff in the eye (and thus to blink in anticipation of the puff). First, they traced the pathway connecting the brain's reception of the tone with the blink response. They discovered that it runs to the brainstem through a part of the cerebellum (at the back of the head) and that if they cut this pathway, the learned response would be lost. It was like cutting the cords to your stereo speakers, which would confirm the cord's part in the electronic path but might still leave you wondering where the music is stored. Their next step was to administer a drug during the rabbits' eye-blink training, temporarily deadening different parts of the neural pathway. This pinpointed the implicit memory—in the cerebellum. The rejuvenated rabbits failed to display the learned response only when the cerebellum was deactivated during training (Krupa & others, 1993; Steinmetz, 1998). Human patients with a damaged cerebellum are likewise incapable of eye-blink conditioning (Daum & Schugens, 1996).

This dual explicit-implicit memory system helps explain infantile amnesia: The reactions and skills we learned during infancy reach far into our future, yet as adults we recall nothing (explicitly) of our first three years. Our conscious minds are blank, not only because we index so much of our explicit memory by words that nonspeaking children have not learned, but also because the hippocampus is one of the last brain structures to mature.

REVIEW AND REFLECT:

Storage: Retaining Information

What are the capacities and durations of storage for sensory memory, short-term memory, and long-term memory?

Information first enters the memory system through the senses. We register and briefly store visual images via iconic memory, and sounds via echoic memory. Our short-term memory span for information just presented is very limited—a seconds-long retention of up to about seven items, depending on the information and how it is presented. Our capacity for storing information permanently in long-term memory is essentially unlimited.

How and where does the brain physically store memories?

The search for the physical basis of memory has recently focused on the synapses and their neurotransmitters; on the long-term potentiation of brain circuits, such as those running through the hippocampus; and on the effects of stress hormones on memory. Studies of people with brain damage reveal that we have two types of memory—explicit (declarative) memories processed by the hippocampus, and implicit (nondeclarative) memories processed by more ancient brain regions. The differing types of memory loss reveal that the brain processes and stores information in differing ways.

Terms and Concepts to Remember

iconic memory, p. 334
echoic memory, p. 335
long-term potentiation (LTP), p. 337
amnesia, p. 338

implicit memory, p. 339
explicit memory, p. 339
hippocampus, p. 340

Test Yourself

25.1. Sensory information is initially recorded in our sensory memory. This memory may be visual (_____ memory) or auditory (_____ memory).
   a. implicit; explicit
   b. iconic; echoic
   c. declarative; nondeclarative
   d. long-term; short-term

25.2. Our capacity for storing long-term memories is essentially limitless. However, our short-term memory for new information is limited. When confronted with a list of novel items, most people can immediately recall
   a. only the first items on the list.
   b. a series of about 20 items.
   c. a series of about 7 items.
   d. only meaningful items.

25.3. The average adult probably has about a billion bits of information in long-term memory, which has a capacity perhaps a thousand to a million times greater than that. Evidence suggests that the best way to learn and remember new information is to
   a. undergo hypnosis.
   b. undergo electrical stimulation of the motor cortex.
   c. systematically forget or discard old memories.
   d. relate new information to old.

25.4. Researchers have found that long-term potentiation (LTP) provides a neural basis for learning and memory. LTP refers to
   a. emotion-triggered hormonal changes.
   b. the role of the hippocampus in processing explicit memories.
   c. an increase in a synapse's firing potential after brief, rapid stimulation.
   d. aging people's potential for learning.

25.5. A patient who has suffered damage to the hippocampus and is amnesic typically has difficulties in learning new facts and recalling recent events. However, the person may well be able to recall the more distant past and certain well-learned skills, such as how to ride a bicycle or hem a dress. Memories of skills are
   a. explicit memories.   c. iconic memories.
   b. implicit memories.   d. echoic memories.

25.6. The physical basis of memory—how and where memories are physically stored in the brain—is not yet well understood. However, research suggests that the hippocampus, a neural center in the limbic system of the brain, plays an important role. The hippocampus may function as
   a. a way station between short- and long-term explicit memories.
   b. a computer's hard disk.
   c. the cortex.
   d. a processing center for implicit memories.

Review: Your friend tells you that her father is suffering from the early signs of Alzheimer's. She wonders if psychology can explain why he can still play checkers very well but has a hard time holding a sensible conversation. What can you tell her?

Reflect: Can you name an instance where stress has *helped* you remember something, and another instance where stress has *interfered* with remembering something?

Answers to the Test Yourself and Review questions can be found in the green appendix at the end of the book.

26 Retrieval: Getting Information Out

Preview Question: What cues or associations help us access our stored memories?

To most people, memory is **recall**, the ability to retrieve information not in conscious awareness. To a psychologist, memory is any sign that something learned has been retained. So *recognizing* or more quickly *relearning* information also indicates memory.

Long after you cannot recall most of the people in your high school graduating class, you may still be able to recognize their yearbook pictures from a photographic lineup and pick their names from a list of names. Harry Bahrick and his colleagues (1975) reported that people who graduated 25 years earlier could not *recall* many of their old classmates, but they could *recognize* 90 percent of their pictures and names.

Our speed at relearning can reveal memory. If you once learned something and then forgot it, you probably will relearn it more quickly than you originally learned it.

When you study for a final exam or resurrect a language used in early childhood, the relearning is easier. Tests of **recognition** and of time spent **relearning** reveal that we remember more than we can recall.

Our recognition memory is impressively quick and vast. "Is your friend wearing a new or old outfit?" "Old." "Is this seconds-long movie clip from a film you've ever seen?" "Yes." "Have you ever before seen this person—this minor variation on the same old human features (two eyes, one nose, and so on)?" "No." Before the mouth can form our answer to any of millions of such questions, the mind knows, and knows that it knows.

Retrieval Cues

To retrieve a fact from a library, you need a way to access it. In recognition tests, retrieval cues (such as photographs) provide reminders of information (classmates' names) we could not otherwise recall. Retrieval cues also guide us to where to look. If you want to know what the pyramid on the back of an American dollar signifies, you might look in *Collier's Encyclopedia* under "dollar," "currency," or "money." But your efforts would be futile. To get the information you want, you would have to look under "Great Seal of the United States" (Hayes, 1981). Like information stored in encyclopedias, memories can't be accessed unless we have the right cues for retrieving them.

You can think of a memory as held in storage by a web of associations. To retrieve a specific memory, you first need to identify one of the strands that leads to it, a process called **priming**. Philosopher and psychologist William James referred to priming as the "wakening of associations." Often our associations are activated, or primed, without our awareness. As **FIGURE 26.1** indicates, seeing or hearing the word *rabbit* primes associations with *hare* even though we may not recall having seen or heard *rabbit*.

Priming has been called "memoryless memory"—memory without remembering, invisible memory. If, walking down a hallway, you see a poster of a missing child, you

---

Here is another sentence I will ask you about later: *The fish attacked the swimmer.*

Remembering things past
Even if Madonna and Paul Newman had not become famous, their high school classmates would most likely still recognize their yearbook photos.

"Memory is not like a container that gradually fills up; it is more like a tree growing hooks onto which memories are hung."

Psychologist Peter Russell,
The Brain Book, 1979

- **recall** a measure of memory in which the person must retrieve information learned earlier, as on a fill-in-the-blank test.

- **recognition** a measure of memory in which the person need only identify items previously learned, as on a multiple-choice test.

- **relearning** a memory measure that assesses the amount of time saved when learning material for a second time.

- **priming** the activation, often unconsciously, of particular associations in memory.

will then be "primed" to interpret an ambiguous adult-child interaction as a possible kidnapping (James, 1986). Although you don't consciously remember the poster, it predisposes your interpretation. (Researchers have shown that even subliminal stimuli can briefly prime responses to later stimuli.)

Retrieval cues often prime our memories of earlier experiences. Mnemonic devices (memory aids that use vivid images or organizational devices) provide us with handy retrieval cues. But the best retrieval cues come from the associations formed at the time we encode a memory, and those cues can be experiences as well as words. Tastes, smells, and sights often evoke our recall of associated episodes. To call up visual cues when trying to recall something, we may mentally place ourselves in the original context. For British theologian John Hull (1990, p. 174) this became difficult after losing his sight. On one occasion when his wife asked him what he had done that day he had difficulty recalling. "I knew I had been somewhere, and had done particular things with certain people, but where? I could not put the conversations I had had into a context. There was no background, no features against which to identify the place. Normally, the memories of people you have spoken to during the day are stored in frames which include the background."

Context Effects

It does help to put yourself back in the context where you experienced something. Duncan Godden and Alan Baddeley (1975) discovered this when they had scuba divers listen to a list of words in two different settings, either 10 feet underwater or sitting on the beach. As **FIGURE 26.2** illustrates, the divers recalled more words when they were retested in the same place.

FIGURE 26.1
Priming—awakening associations
After seeing or hearing *rabbit*, we are later more likely to spell the spoken word as *h-a-r-e*. The spreading of associations unconsciously activates related associations. This phenomenon is called priming.

Seeing or hearing the word *rabbit*

Activates concept

Primes spelling the spoken word *hair/hare* as *h-a-r-e*

Ask a friend two rapid-fire questions: (a) How do you pronounce the word spelled by the letters *s-h-o-p*? (b) What do you do when you come to a green light? If your friend answers "stop" to the second question, you have demonstrated priming.

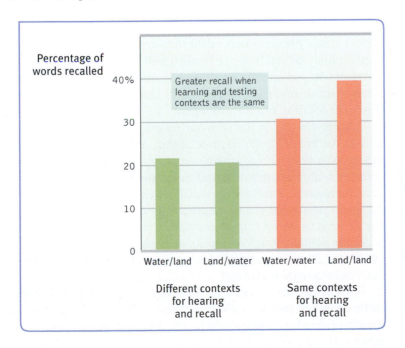

Percentage of words recalled

40%

Greater recall when learning and testing contexts are the same

30

20

10

0

Water/land Land/water Water/water Land/land

Different contexts for hearing and recall

Same contexts for hearing and recall

FIGURE 26.2
The effects of context on memory
Words heard underwater are best recalled underwater; words heard on land are best recalled on land.

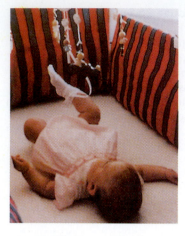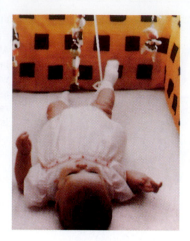

FIGURE 26.3
Familiar context activates memory
After learning to move a mobile by kicking, infants had their learning reactivated most strongly when retested in the same rather than a different context.

You have probably experienced similar context effects. You return to where you once lived or to the school you once attended and are flooded with retrieval cues and memories. Even taking an exam in the same room where you are taught may help a little. In several experiments, Carolyn Rovee-Collier (1993) found that a familiar context activates memories even in 3-month-olds. After infants learned that kicking a crib mobile would make it move (via a connecting ribbon from the ankle), the infants kicked more when tested again in the same crib with the same bumper (**FIGURE 26.3**).

Sometimes, being in a context similar to one we've been in before may trigger the experience of **déjà vu** (French for "already seen")—that eerie sense that "I've been in this exact situation before." The 60 percent of people who report having this experience (McAneny, 1996) often wonder, "How could I recognize a situation that I'm experiencing for the first time?" Those who suppose something paranormal is occurring may think of reincarnation ("I must have experienced this in a previous life") or precognition ("I viewed this scene in my mind before experiencing it"). If we pose the question differently ("Why do I feel as if I recognize this situation?"), we can see how our memory system might produce déjà vu (Alcock, 1981). If we have previously been in a similar situation, the current situation may be loaded with cues that unconsciously retrieve the earlier experience. Thus, if in such a context you see a stranger who looks and walks like one of your friends, the similarity may give rise to an eerie feeling of recognition. Because the feeling conflicts with your knowing that the person is a stranger, you may think, "I've seen that person in this situation before."

Moods and Memories

Associated words, events, and contexts are not the only retrieval cues. Events in the past may have aroused a specific emotion that later can prime us to recall its associated events. Cognitive psychologist Gordon Bower (1983) explained it this way: "A specific emotional state is like a specific room in a library into which the subject places memory records, and he can most easily retrieve those records by returning to that same room or emotional state." What we learn in one state—be it joyful or sad, drunk or sober—is sometimes more easily recalled when we are again in the same state, a subtle phenomenon called *state-dependent memory*. What is learned when depressed, high, or drunk is not recalled well in *any* state (depression and certain drugs interfere with encoding, and alcohol disrupts storage). But it is recalled slightly better when again drunk, high, or depressed. Someone who hides money when drunk may forget the location until drunk again.

More striking is the way our memories are *biased* by our moods (Eich, 1995; Ellis & Ashbrook, 1989; Matt & others, 1992). We seem to associate good or bad events with their accompanying emotions, which become retrieval cues. Thus, our memories are somewhat **mood-congruent**. Being depressed sours memories by priming negative associations, which we then use to explain our current mood. Conversely, if people are put in a buoyant mood—whether under hypnosis or just by the day's events (a World Cup soccer victory for the German subjects of one study)—they recall the world through rose-colored glasses (Forgas & others, 1984; Schwarz & others, 1987). They judge themselves competent and effective, other people benevolent, and life in general wonderful.

Knowing this connection, we should not be surprised that in some studies *currently* depressed people recall their parents as rejecting, punitive, and guilt-promoting, whereas *formerly* depressed people describe their parents much as do those who have never suffered depression (Lewinsohn & Rosenbaum, 1987; Lewis, 1992). No wonder

CALLAHAN

"I wonder if you'd mind giving me directions. I've never been sober in this part of town before."

Distributed by Levin Represents.

■ **déjà vu** that eerie sense that "I've experienced this before." Cues from the current situation may subconsciously trigger retrieval of an earlier experience.

■ **mood-congruent memory** the tendency to recall experiences that are consistent with one's current good or bad mood.

Robert Bornstein and others (1991) report that adolescents' ratings of parental warmth give little clue to how the same adolescents will rate their parents six weeks later. When teenagers are down, their world, including their parents, seems inhuman; as their mood brightens, their parents morph from devils into angels. You and I may nod our heads knowingly. Yet, in a good or bad mood, we persist in attributing to reality our own changing judgments and memories.

Moods also influence how we *interpret* other people's behavior. In a bad mood we read someone's look as a glare; in a good mood we encode the same look as interest. How we perceive the world depends on our mood. Passions exaggerate.

Your mood's effect on retrieval helps explain why moods persist. When happy, you recall happy events, which helps prolong the good mood. When depressed, you recall sad events, which in turn darkens your interpretations of current events. Unfortunately for those suffering from depression, this process maintains depression's vicious cycle.

Mood and memory
Elated, we remember other happy times. Mood serves as a retrieval cue, activating other memories tinged with the same emotion. These memories help sustain the current mood.

Do you recall the gist of the sentence I asked you to remember at the beginning of this module (on page 342)? If not, does the word *shark* help? Experiments show that *shark* more readily cues the image you stored than does the sentence's actual word, *fish* (Anderson & others, 1976).

REVIEW AND REFLECT:

Retrieval: Getting Information Out

What cues or associations help us to access our stored memories?

Psychologists interested in memory study not only our ability to retrieve information we have learned earlier (recall), but also our ability to identify items previously learned (recognition) and to relearn information quickly. To be remembered, information that is "in there" must be retrieved, with the aid of associations (cues) that prime the memory. Cues sometimes come from returning to the original context. Mood affects memory, too. While in a good or bad mood, we tend to retrieve memories congruent with that mood. This tendency helps explain why moods persist.

Terms and Concepts to Remember

recall, p. 342
recognition, p. 342
relearning, p. 342
priming, p. 342
déjà vu, p. 344
mood-congruent memory, p. 344

Test Yourself

26.1. To measure long-term memory, psychologists test a person's ability to *recall* information. They also test ability to *recognize* what has been learned, and they measure *relearning* time. A psychologist who asks you to write down as many objects as you can remember having seen a few minutes earlier is testing your
   a. recall.
   b. recognition.
   c. recall and recognition.
   d. relearning.

26.2. Multiple-choice questions test our _____; fill-in-the-blank questions test our _____.
   a. recall; relearning
   b. recognition; recall
   c. recall; recognition
   d. relearning; recognition

26.3. To gain access to a memory, a person activates an association that leads to that memory. The association may be activated by a specific odor, visual image, or mnemonic; all of these are examples of
   a. relearning.
   b. déjà vu.
   c. declarative memories.
   d. retrieval cues.

26.4. To retrieve a memory, it sometimes helps to return to the setting where the event occurred. In some cases, retrieval may be enhanced by a context similar to one you have already experienced. The resulting feeling that "you've been there before" is referred to as
   a. déjà vu.
   b. mood-congruent memory.
   c. relearning.
   d. the misinformation effect.

26.5. When happy, we tend to recall happy times. When depressed, we more often recall depressing events. This tendency to recall experiences that are consistent with our current emotions is called
   a. mnemonics.
   b. chunking.
   c. repression.
   d. mood-congruent memory.

Review: What is priming?

Reflect: What sort of mood have you been in lately? How has your mood colored your memories, perceptions, and expectations?

Answers to the Test Yourself and Review questions can be found in the green appendix at the end of the book.

27 Forgetting and Memory Construction

Amid all the applause for memory—all the efforts to understand it, all the books on how to improve it—have any voices been heard in praise of forgetting? William James (1890, p. 680) was such a voice: "If we remembered everything, we should on most occasions be as ill off as if we remembered nothing." To discard the clutter of useless or out-of-date information—where we parked the car yesterday, a friend's old phone number, restaurant orders already cooked and served—is surely a blessing (Bjork, 1978). The Russian memory whiz S accumulated a junk heap of memories and was haunted by them. They dominated his consciousness. He had difficulty thinking abstractly—generalizing, organizing, evaluating. A good memory is helpful, but so is the ability to forget.

More often, however, our memory dismays and frustrates us. Memories are quirky. My own memory can easily call up episodes like that wonderful first kiss with the woman I love or trivial facts like Sammy Sosa's current home run total. Then it abandons me when I'm trying to recall that new colleague's name or where I left my sunglasses.

Memory failures can occur in any of the stages of the memory system. They may be failures of encoding (the information never gets in), of storage (fading of the memory record), or of retrieval (from a lack of retrieval cues or from the interfering effects of other learning). Our memories may also become distorted or too persistent. Memory researcher Daniel Schacter (1999) enumerates seven ways our memories fail us—the seven sins of memory, he calls them. These include

Three sins of forgetting:

+ *Absent-mindedness*—inattention to details produces encoding failure (our mind is elsewhere as we lay down the car keys).
+ *Transience*—storage decay over time (unused information fades).
+ *Blocking*—inaccessibility of stored information (it may be on the tip of our tongue, but we experience retrieval failure—we cannot get it out).

Three sins of distortion:

+ *Misattribution*—confusing the source of information (putting words in someone else's mouth or remembering a movie scene as an actual happening).
+ *Suggestibility*—the lingering effects of misinformation (a leading question—"Did Mr. Jones touch your private parts?"—later becomes a young child's false memory).
+ *Bias*—belief-colored recollections (what were your initial feelings toward your fiancé?).

One sin of intrusion:

+ *Persistence*—unwanted memories (being haunted by images of a sexual assault).

Let's first consider the sins of forgetting, then those of distortion and persistence.

Forgetting

Preview Questions: What causes us to forget? At what points in the memory system can our memories fail us?

Encoding Failure

What causes us to forget? One answer is that we failed to encode the information (**FIGURE 27.1**). Thus, it never entered long-term memory. The same brain areas that jump into action when young adults are encoding new information are less respon-

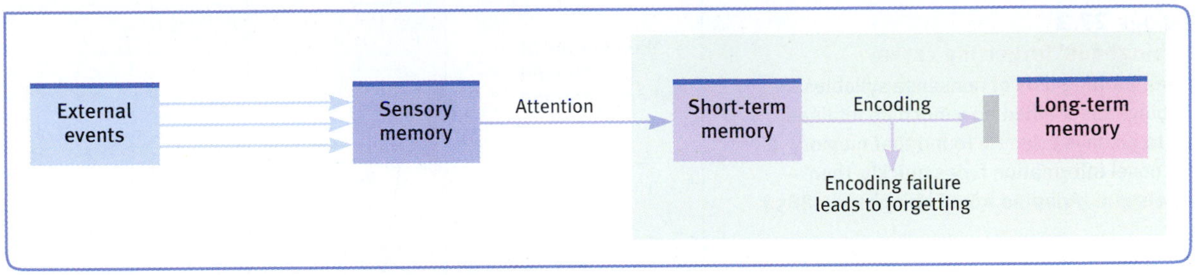

FIGURE **27.1**
Forgetting as encoding failure
We cannot remember what we have not encoded.

sive among older adults. This slower encoding helps explain age-related memory decline (Grady & others, 1995). (Although older people tend to recall less than younger adults do, they usually remember as well as younger people when given reminders or a recognition test.)

But no matter how young we are, we simply cannot attend to more than a few of the myriad sights and sounds continually bombarding us. In fact, much of what we sense we never even notice. Consider something you have looked at countless times: What letters accompany the number 5 on your telephone? Or where is the number 0 on your calculator? For most of us these are surprisingly difficult questions.

Here's another example of encoding failure. If you live in North America, Britain, or Australia, you have looked at thousands of pennies in your lifetime. You can surely recall the features (color and size) you use to distinguish coins. But can you recall what the side with the head looks like? If not, let's make the memory test easier: If you are familiar with U.S. coins, can you recognize the real thing in **FIGURE 27.2**? Raymond Nickerson and Marilyn Adams (1979) discovered that most people cannot. The U.S. Mint turns out about 40 million pennies a day. Yet of the eight critical features (Lincoln's head, date, "In God we trust," and so on) the average person spontaneously remembers only three. Likewise, few British people can draw from memory the one-pence coin (Richardson, 1993). The details of a penny are not very meaningful—nor are they essential for distinguishing pennies from other coins—and few of us have made the effort to encode them. We encode some information—where you ate dinner yesterday—automatically; other types of information—like the details of the penny—require effortful processing. Without effort, many memories never form.

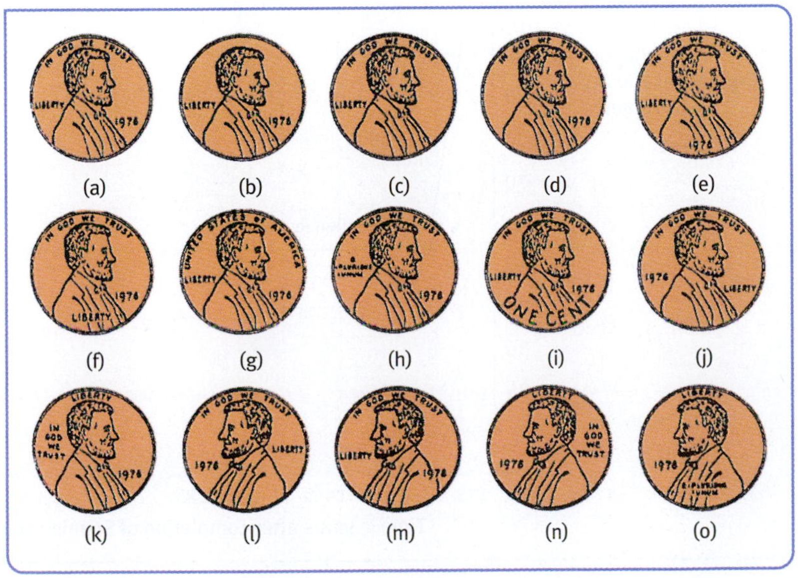

FIGURE **27.2 Test your memory**
Which one of these pennies is the real thing? (If you live outside the United States, try drawing one of your own country's coins.)

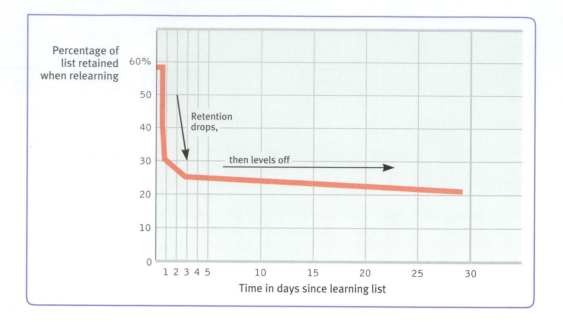

FIGURE 27.3

Ebbinghaus' forgetting curve
After learning lists of nonsense syllables, Ebbinghaus studied how much he retained up to 30 days later. He found that memory for novel information fades quickly, then levels out. (Adapted from Ebbinghaus, 1885.)

"Each of us finds that in [our] own life every moment of time is completely filled. [We are] bombarded every second by sensations, emotions, thoughts . . . nine-tenths of which [we] must simply ignore. The past [is] a roaring cataract of billions upon billions of such moments: any one of them too complex to grasp in its entirety, and the aggregate beyond all imagination. . . . At every tick of the clock, in every inhabited part of the world, an unimaginable richness and variety of 'history' falls off the world into total oblivion."

English novelist-critic C. S. Lewis (1967)

Storage Decay

Even after encoding something well, we sometimes later forget it. To study the durability of our stored memories, German philosopher Hermann Ebbinghaus (1885) learned lists of nonsense syllables and measured how much he retained when relearning each list, from 20 minutes to 30 days later. His famous "forgetting curve" (**FIGURE 27.3**) indicates that much of what we learn we may indeed quickly forget. Later experiments made the forgetting curve into one of psychology's laws: The course of forgetting is initially rapid, then levels off with time (Wixted & Ebbesen, 1991).

Harry Bahrick (1984) extended Ebbinghaus' finding. He examined the forgetting curve for Spanish vocabulary learned in school. By using the cross-sectional method (in which researchers test and compare people of different ages), Bahrick compared the knowledge of Spanish among people who had just taken Spanish with the knowledge of those who had studied it up to 50 years before. Compared with those just completing a high school or college Spanish course, those who had been out of school for 3 years had forgotten much of what they had learned (**FIGURE 27.4**).

FIGURE 27.4

The forgetting curve for Spanish learned in school
Compared with people just completing a Spanish course, those 3 years out of the course remembered much less. Compared with the 3-year group, however, those who studied Spanish even longer ago did not forget much more.

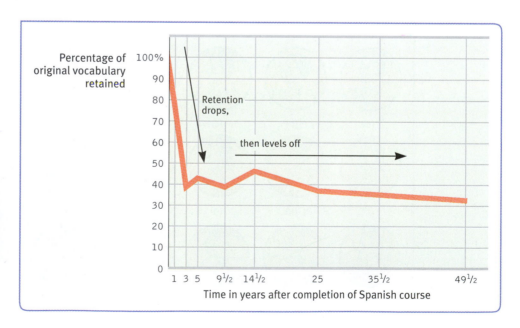

However, after roughly 3 years, their forgetting leveled off; what people remembered then, they still remembered 25 and more years later, even if they had not used their Spanish at all.

One explanation for these forgetting curves is a gradual fading of the physical memory trace. As we learn more about the physical storage of memory, we may come to understand better how memory storage can decay. But memories also fade because of the accumulation of other learning that disrupts our retrieval.

Retrieval Failure

We have seen that when we fail to encode information and when our stored memories decay, we forget. Forgotten events are like books you can't find in your campus library—some because they were never acquired, others because they were discarded.

But there is a third possibility: Even if the book is stored and available, it may be inaccessible. Perhaps you don't have the information needed to look it up and retrieve it. Information sometimes gets into our brain and, though we know it is there, we cannot get it out (**FIGURE 27.5**). A name may lie poised on the tip of the tongue, waiting to be retrieved. When people who cannot recall information get retrieval cues ("It begins with an *M*"), they often remember what they could not recall. Retrieval problems also lie behind the occasional memory failures of older adults. Forgetting is often not memories discarded but memories hard to find.

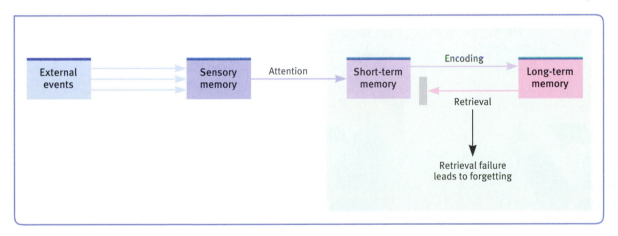

FIGURE 27.5
Retrieval failure
We store in long-term memory what's important to us, or what we've rehearsed. But sometimes even stored information cannot be accessed, which leads to forgetting.

Interference

Learning some items may interfere with retrieving others, especially when the items are similar. If someone gives you a phone number, you may be able to recall it later. But if two more people give you their numbers, each successive number will be more difficult to recall. Such **proactive** (*forward-acting*) **interference** occurs when something you learned earlier disrupts your recall of something you experience later. As you collect more and more information, your mental attic never fills, but it certainly gets cluttered.

For example, if you buy a new combination lock or get a new phone number, the old one may interfere. Benton Underwood (1957) found that those who learn different lists of words on successive days have more and more difficulty remembering each new list the next day. This proactive interference explains why Ebbinghaus, after memorizing countless lists of nonsense syllables during his career, could remember only about one-fourth of a new list of syllables on the day after he learned it—far fewer than you as a novice could remember after learning a single list.

- **proactive interference** the disruptive effect of prior learning on the recall of new information.

Retroactive (*backward-acting*) **interference** occurs when new information makes it harder to recall something you learned earlier (**FIGURE 27.6**). For example, learning new students' names typically interferes with a teacher's recall of the names of previous students.

You can minimize retroactive interference by reducing the number of interfering events—say, by going to sleep shortly after learning new information. This is what John Jenkins and Karl Dallenbach (1924) found in a classic experiment. Day after day, two people each learned some nonsense syllables, then tried to recall them after up to eight hours of being awake or asleep at night. As **FIGURE 27.7** shows, forgetting occurred more rapidly after being awake and involved with other activities. The investigators surmised that "forgetting is not so much a matter of the decay of old impressions and associations as it is a matter of interference, inhibition, or obliteration of the old by the new" (1924, p. 612). Later experiments have confirmed that the hour before a night's sleep (but not the minute before sleep) is a good time to commit information to memory (Fowler & others, 1973).

Interference is an important cause of forgetting, but we should not overstate the point. Sometimes old information can facilitate our learning of new information. Knowing Latin may help us to learn French—a phenomenon called *positive transfer*. It is when old and new information compete with each other that interference occurs.

Answer to question on page 347: The first penny (a) is the real penny.

FIGURE 27.6
Proactive and retroactive interference

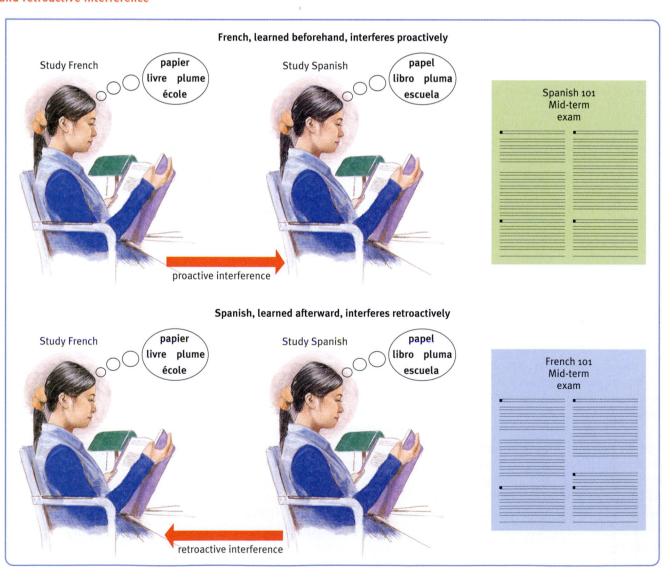

French, learned beforehand, interferes proactively

Study French

papier
livre   plume
école

Study Spanish

papel
libro   pluma
escuela

Spanish 101
Mid-term
exam

proactive interference

Spanish, learned afterward, interferes retroactively

Study French

papier
livre   plume
école

Study Spanish

papel
libro   pluma
escuela

French 101
Mid-term
exam

retroactive interference

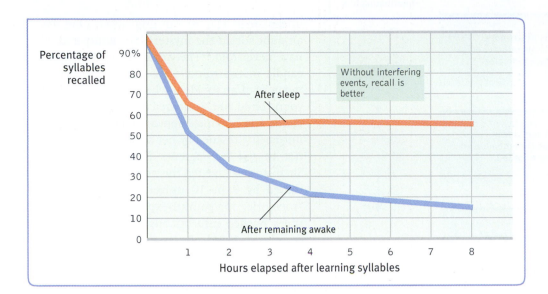

Motivated Forgetting

The huge cookie jar in our kitchen was jammed with freshly baked chocolate chip cookies. Still more were cooling across racks on the counter. Twenty-four hours later, not a crumb was left. Who had taken them? During that time, my wife, three children, and I were the only people in the house. So while memories were still fresh, I conducted a little memory test. Andy acknowledged wolfing down as many as 20. Peter admitted eating 15. Laura guessed she had stuffed her then-6-year-old body with 15 cookies. My wife, Carol, recalled eating 6, and I remembered consuming 15 and taking 18 more to the office. We sheepishly accepted responsibility for 89 cookies. Still, we had not come close; there had been 160.

In experiments that parallel the cookie-memory phenomenon, Michael Ross and his colleagues (1981) found that people unknowingly revise their own histories. After Ross persuaded a group of people that brushing their teeth frequently is desirable, they (more than other people) recalled having frequently brushed their teeth in the last two weeks. Having taken a highly touted study skills course, students later inflated their estimates of self-improvement. By *de*flating their evaluations of their previous study habits, they convinced themselves that they had really benefited (Conway & Ross, 1984). To remember our past is often to revise it. By recalling events as we wish, we protect and enhance our self-images.

Why do our memories fail us? Why did my family and I not encode, store, and retrieve the actual number of cookies each of us ate? As **FIGURE 27.8** (page 352) reminds us, we automatically encode sensory information in amazing detail. So was it a storage problem? Might our memories of cookies, like Ebbinghaus' memory of nonsense syllables, have vanished almost as fast as the cookies themselves? Or might the information still be intact but irretrievable because it would be embarrassing to remember?[1]

With his concept of **repression**, Sigmund Freud proposed that our memory systems do indeed self-censor painful information. To protect our self-concepts and to minimize anxiety, we supposedly repress painful memories. But the submerged memory lingers, said Freud, and with patience and effort may be retrieved by some later cue or during therapy. One reported case involved a woman with an intense,

"[It is] necessary to remember that events happened in the desired manner. And if it is necessary to rearrange one's memories . . . then it is necessary to forget that one has done so. The trick of doing this can be learned like any other mental technique. . . . It is called doublethink."

George Orwell, *Nineteen Eighty-Four*, 1948

■ **retroactive interference** the disruptive effect of new learning on the recall of old information.

■ **repression** in psychoanalytic theory, the basic defense mechanism that banishes anxiety-arousing thoughts, feelings, and memories from consciousness.

[1]One of my cookie-scarfing sons, on reading this in his father's textbook years later, confessed that he had fibbed "a little."

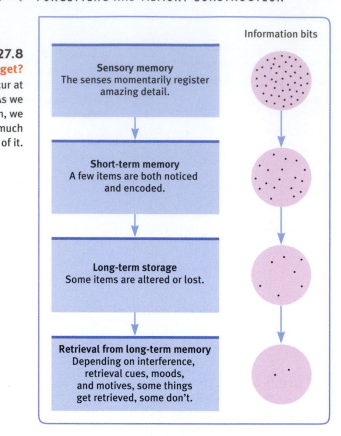

FIGURE 27.8
When do we forget?
Forgetting can occur at any memory stage. As we process information, we filter, alter, or lose much of it.

Information bits

Sensory memory
The senses momentarily register amazing detail.

Short-term memory
A few items are both noticed and encoded.

Long-term storage
Some items are altered or lost.

Retrieval from long-term memory
Depending on interference, retrieval cues, moods, and motives, some things get retrieved, some don't.

unexplained fear of running water. One day an aunt solved the mystery. She whispered, "I have never told." The words relit a blown-out candle in the mind; they cued the woman's memory of an incident when, as a disobedient young child, she wandered away from a family picnic and became trapped under a waterfall—until being rescued by her aunt, who promised not to tell her parents (Kihlstrom, 1990). Such stories have fed the now-common belief, shared by 9 in 10 university students, that "memories for painful experiences are sometimes pushed into unconsciousness" (Brown & others, 1996). Repression was central to Freud's psychology and became part of psychology's lore. Most everyone believes it. Therapists assume it often. Yet increasing numbers of memory researchers think repression rarely, if ever, occurs. People do forget negative (and positive) experiences. Do they repress them? Do people typically have difficulty remembering traumatic experiences, or forgetting them? Stay tuned.

Memory Construction

Preview Questions: What causes us to misremember, producing inaccurate or false memories? What does memory research tell us about the potential for inaccuracy in eyewitness memories and reports of repressed memories of abuse?

Picture yourself having this experience:

> You go to a fancy restaurant for dinner. You are seated at a table with a white tablecloth. You study the menu. You tell the server you want prime rib, medium rare, a baked potato with sour cream, and a salad with blue cheese dressing. You also order some red wine from the wine list. A few minutes later the server returns with your salad. Later the rest of the meal arrives. You enjoy it all, except the prime rib is a bit overdone.

Were I immediately to quiz you on this paragraph (adapted from Hyde, 1983), you could surely retrieve considerable detail. For example, without looking back, answer the following questions:

1. What kind of salad dressing did you order?
2. Was the tablecloth red checked?
3. What did you order to drink?
4. Did the server give you a menu?

You were probably able to recall exactly what you ordered, and maybe even the color of the tablecloth. Does retrieval therefore consist merely of "reading" the information stored in our brain's library? We do have an enormous capacity for storing and reproducing the incidental details of our daily experience. But we often construct our memories as we encode them, and we may also alter our memories as we withdraw them from the memory bank. Like a scientist who infers a dinosaur's appearance from its remains, we infer our past from stored information plus what we now assume. Did the server give you a menu? Not in the paragraph given. Nevertheless, many answer yes. By filtering information and filling in missing pieces, your schema for restaurants directed your memory construction.

■ **misinformation effect** *incorporating misleading information into one's memory of an event.*

Misinformation and Imagination Effects

In more than 200 experiments, involving more than 20,000 people, Elizabeth Loftus has shown how eyewitnesses similarly reconstruct their memories when questioned. In one experiment with John Palmer, Loftus showed a film of a traffic accident and then quizzed the viewers about what they saw (Loftus & Palmer, 1974). Those asked, "How fast were the cars going when they *smashed* into each other?" gave higher speed estimates than those asked, "How fast were the cars going when they *hit* each other?" A week later, the researchers asked the viewers if they recalled seeing any broken glass. Compared with those who had been asked the question with *hit*, those asked the question with *smashed* were more than twice as likely to say yes, they had seen broken glass (**FIGURE 27.9**). In fact, the film showed no broken glass.

In many follow-up experiments around the world, people have witnessed an event, received or not received misleading information about it, and then taken a memory test. The repeated result is a **misinformation effect**: After exposure to subtle misinformation, many people misremember. They have misrecalled a yield (give way) sign as a stop sign, hammers as screwdrivers, Coke cans as peanut cans, *Vogue* magazine as *Mademoiselle*, "Dr. Henderson" as "Dr. Davidson," breakfast cereal as eggs, and a clean-shaven man as a man with a mustache (Loftus & others, 1992). As a memory fades with time following an event, the injection of misinformation becomes easier (Loftus, 1992).

So unwitting are people of the misinformation effect that they later find it nearly impossible to discriminate between their memories of real and suggested events (Schooler & others, 1986). This difficulty was strikingly true among those who three years later misrecalled where they were when they heard of the space shuttle *Challenger's* explosion (Neisser & Harsch, 1992). When shown their own accounts, handwritten the day after the explosion, many were surprised. Some felt so sure of their false memories that they insisted their original version must have been flawed.

As we recount an experience, we fill in memory gaps with plausible guesses and assumptions. After more retellings, we often recall the guessed details, which have now been absorbed into our memories, as if we had actually observed them (Roediger & others, 1993). Others' vivid retelling of an event may also implant false memories.

Even repeatedly *imagining* nonexistent actions and events can create false memories. In one laboratory experiment, students who repeatedly imagined simple acts such as breaking a toothpick or picking up a stapler later experienced "imagination inflation"; they were more likely to think they had actually done such things during the experiment's first phase (Goff & Roediger, 1998). In another experiment, by Maryanne Garry and others (1996), university students noted whether they had experienced certain childhood events, such as breaking a window with their hand. Two weeks later, half were asked to imagine themselves experiencing four of these events—for example, running, tripping, falling, and cutting their hand as it crashed through a window. After vividly imagining the fictional event, one-fourth of them became more likely to believe that such events may actually have happened during their childhood.

Ira Hyman and his co-workers (1995, 1996) invited Western Washington University students to recall actual childhood events (reported to the researchers by their parents), along with a suggested false event, such as spilling a punch bowl at a wedding. By a third interview (after being encouraged to think about the events between interviews), one-fourth of the students had constructed false memories. For example, they were asked to recall something that happened "when you were six years old and you were attending a wedding." One student recalled, "It was an outdoor wedding and I think we were running around and knocked something over like the punch bowl or something and made a big mess and of course got yelled at for it." The take-home point: Given time, the mind's search for a fact may create a fiction.

Depiction of actual accident

Leading question:
"About how fast were the cars going when they *smashed* into each other?"

Memory construction

FIGURE 27.9 Memory construction
When people who saw the film of a car accident were asked a leading question, they recalled a more serious accident than they had witnessed.

"It isn't so astonishing, the number of things I can remember, as the number of things I can remember that aren't so."

Mark Twain (1835–1910)

"Memory is insubstantial. Things keep replacing it. Your batch of snapshots will both fix and ruin your memory. . . . You can't remember anything from your trip except the wretched collection of snapshots."

Annie Dillard, "To Fashion a Text," 1988

To see how far the mind will go in creating a fiction, Richard Wiseman and his University of Hertfordshire colleagues (1999) staged eight seances, each attended by 25 curious people. During the supposed seance, the medium—actually a professional actor and magician—asked everyone to concentrate on the moving table. Although it never moved, he suggested that it had: "That's good. Lift the table up. That's good. Keep concentrating. Keep the table in the air." When questioned two weeks later, 34 percent of the participants recalled having actually seen the table levitate.

We psychologists are not immune to memory construction:

+ Frederick Bartlett, a pioneer in studies of memory construction, recalled two decades later the "brilliant afternoon in May 1913" when the Cambridge University experimental psychology lab was opened. His colleague, Sir Godfrey Thompson, remembered that it poured rain (Ross, 1996).

+ Another memory researcher, Ulric Neisser (1982), vividly recalls hearing the announcement of the bombing of Pearl Harbor as an interruption to a baseball game broadcast. Years later he realized that American baseball games aren't played in December, when the bombing occurred. Although he knows the memory is false, he still "recalls" the incident.

+ The psychologist Jean Piaget was startled as an adult to learn that his vivid, detailed memory of his nursemaid's thwarting his kidnapping was utterly false. Piaget apparently constructed the memory from the many retellings of the story he had heard (later confessed by the nursemaid to have been false).

Source Amnesia

Piaget remembered, but attributed his memory to the wrong source (to his own experience rather than to his nursemaid's stories). When we encode memories, we distribute different aspects of them to different parts of the brain. Among the frailest parts of a memory is its source. Thus, we may recognize someone but have no idea where we have seen the person. Or we imagine or dream an event and later aren't sure if it really happened. In both cases, we retain the image, but not the context in which we acquired it.

Debra Poole and Stephen Lindsay (1995) replicated Piaget's **source amnesia** (also called *source misattribution*). They had preschoolers interact with "Mr. Science," who engaged them in demonstrations such as blowing up a balloon with baking soda

DOONESBURY

and vinegar. Three months later, their parents on three successive days read them a story about themselves and Mr. Science. The stories described some things they had experienced and some they had not. When asked by a new interviewer what Mr. Science had done with them, 4 in 10 children spontaneously recalled Mr. Science doing things that were only in the story.

Ronald Reagan's occasional source misattributions illustrated how fiction can be remembered as fact. During his three U.S. presidential campaigns, he told and retold a story of heroic sacrifice. A World War II gunner was terrified when his plane was hit by anti-aircraft fire and he could not eject from his seat. "Never mind, son," said his commander, "we'll ride it down together." With misty eyes, Reagan would conclude by telling how the brave commander received the Congressional Medal of Honor posthumously. A curious journalist later checked the 434 World War II Congressional Medal recipients. Finding no similar story, he kept digging. At last he found the episode—in the 1944 movie, *A Wing and a Prayer* (Loftus & Ketcham, 1994).

Discerning True and False Memories

Because memory is reconstruction as well as reproduction, we can't be sure whether a memory is real by how real it feels. Much as perceptual illusions may seem like real perceptions, unreal memories feel like real memories.

We also can't be sure whether a memory is real by how persistent it is. Memory researchers Charles Brainerd and Valerie Reyna (Brainerd & others, 1995, 1998) note that memories we derive from experience have more detail than memories we derive from imagination. Memories of imagined experiences are more restricted to the *gist* of the supposed event—the meanings and feelings we associate with it. Because gist memories are durable, children's false memories sometimes outlast their true memories (Brainerd & Poole, 1997). And when therapists or investigators ask for the gist rather than the details, they run a greater risk of eliciting false memories.

Although false memories created by suggested misinformation and misattributed sources may *feel* as real as true memories and may be very persistent, brain scans have revealed telltale signs of false memories. Imagine that I were to read aloud a list of words such as *candy, sugar, honey,* and *taste*. Later, I ask you to recognize the presented words from a larger list. If you are at all like the people tested by Henry Roediger and Kathleen McDermott (1995), you would err three out of four times—falsely remembering a nonpresented similar word such as *sweet*. In a follow-up study, PET scans revealed that the hippocampus is equally active whether the subject is truly or falsely recalling a word (Schacter & others, 1996). But other brain areas responded differently to true and false memories. Only when correctly remembering a spoken word such as *candy* did the brain light up in a left temporal lobe area that processes speech sounds. Because the falsely recognized word (*sweet*) was never heard, there was no sensory record to be activated from the temporal lobe. Although the people couldn't tell the difference between true and false memories, their brains could! (There currently is no way to use this technique as a truth detector for memories of one's more distant past.)

In experiments on eyewitness testimony, researchers have repeatedly found that the most confident and consistent eyewitnesses are the most persuasive; however, they often are not the most accurate. Eyewitnesses, whether right or wrong, express roughly similar self-assurance (Bothwell & others, 1987; Cutler & Penrod, 1989; Wells & Murray, 1984). Confidence also gives little clue to accuracy in studies of "earwitness" identifications of a previously heard voice among a lineup of voices (Yarmey, 1991).

Memory construction helps explain why "hypnotically refreshed" memories of crimes so easily incorporate errors, some of which originate with the hypnotist's leading questions. ("Did you hear loud noises?") It explains why dating partners who fall

■ **source amnesia** attributing to the wrong source an event that we have experienced, heard about, read about, or imagined. (Also called *source misattribution*.) Source amnesia, along with the misinformation effect, is at the heart of many false memories.

Authors and songwriters sometimes suffer source amnesia. They think an idea came from their own creative imagination, when in fact they are unintentionally plagiarizing something they earlier read or heard.

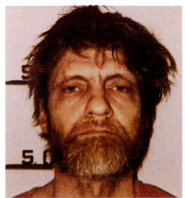

Eyewitness recollections
Our memories of witnessed events are fallible, especially when prompted by misleading questions. Even our relatively good memories of faces are not photographic, as this police sketch and photo of convicted Unabomber Theodore Kaczynski show.

in love *over*estimate their first impressions of one another ("It was love at first sight"), while those who break up *under*estimate their earlier liking ("We never really clicked") (McFarland & Ross, 1987). And it explains why people who are asked how they felt 10 years ago about marijuana or gender issues recall attitudes closer to their current views than to the views they actually reported a decade earlier (Markus, 1986).

Australian psychologist Donald Thompson found his own work on memory distortion ironically haunting him when authorities brought him in for questioning about a rape. Although he was a near-perfect match to the victim's memory of the rapist, he had an airtight alibi. Just before the rape occurred Thompson was being interviewed on live television. He could not possibly have made it to the crime scene. Then it came to light that the victim had been watching the interview—ironically about face recognition—and had experienced source amnesia, confusing her memories of Thompson with those of the rapist (Schacter, 1996).

Recognizing that the misinformation effect can occur as police and attorneys ask questions framed by their own understandings of an event, Ronald Fisher, Edward Geiselman, and their colleagues (1987, 1992) train police interviewers to ask less suggestive, more effective questions. To activate retrieval cues, the detective first asks witnesses to visualize the scene—the weather, time of day, lighting, sounds, smells, positions of objects, and their mood. Then the witness tells in detail, and without interruption, every point recalled, no matter how trivial. Only then does the detective ask evocative follow-up questions: "Was there anything unusual about the person's appearance or clothing?" When this "cognitive interview" technique is used, Fisher and Geiselman report, accurate recall increases by some 50 percent.

"Memory isn't like reading a book; it's more like writing a book from fragmentary notes."

Psychologist John F. Kihlstrom (1994)

Children's Eyewitness Recall

If memories can be sincere, yet so sincerely wrong, might children's recollections of sexual abuse be prone to error? Who is most often victimized—abused children whose recollections are disbelieved or falsely accused adults whose reputations are ruined?

At issue is the credibility of children's reports. As we have seen, interviewers who ask leading questions can plant false memories of a story they expect to hear. We also know that children sometimes are credible eyewitnesses in criminal cases, but that they tend to be suggestible. In 90 percent of studies making age comparisons, preschoolers were more suggestible than were older children or adults (Bruck & Ceci, 1999). In these studies, many young children have falsely reported that a nurse licked their knee, a man had put "something yucky" in their mouth, their doctor had put a stick in their genitals, and someone had touched their private parts. When suggestive interview techniques are combined, most preschoolers can be induced to report false events such as seeing a thief steal food in their day-care center (Bruck & others, 1998). Nevertheless, if questioned about their experiences in words they understand, children often accurately recall what happened and who did it (Goodman & others, 1990; Howe, 1997; Pipe, 1996). Children are especially credible when involved adults have not talked with them prior to the interview and when their disclosure is made in a first interview with a neutral person who asks nonleading questions.

So, depending on the questioning, children may or may not produce accurate eyewitness reports. To the children, both feel real. No wonder trained professionals, after viewing videotaped interviews, cannot discriminate between children's false and accurate reports (Bruck & Ceci, 1997).

Studies of children's recollections of physical examinations illustrate both reasonable accuracy and occasional lapses. Lynne Baker-Ward and her colleagues (1993) tested children's memories with general questions ("Tell me what the doctor did to check you") and specific questions ("Did the doctor shine a light in your eyes?"). Three to six weeks after the exam, 3-year-olds recalled about 60 percent and 7-year-olds about 90 percent of what the doctor did. Asked about things that didn't happen

("Did the doctor cut your hair?" "Did the nurse sit on top of you?"), 3-year-olds gave wrong answers nearly 30 percent of the time; 7-year-olds erred only about 15 percent of the time.

Stephen Ceci (1993) thinks "it would be truly awful to ever lose sight of the enormity of child abuse." Yet Ceci and Maggie Bruck's (1993a, 1995) studies of children's memories have sensitized them to children's suggestibility. In one study, they asked 3-year-olds to show on anatomically correct dolls where a pediatrician had touched them. Fifty-five percent of the children who had not received genital examinations pointed to either genital or anal areas.

In another study, Ceci and Bruck had a child choose a card from a deck of possible happenings and an adult then read from the card. For example, "Think real hard, and tell me if this ever happened to you. Can you remember going to the hospital with a mousetrap on your finger?" After 10 weekly interviews, with the same adult repeatedly asking children to think about several real and fictitious events, a new adult asked the same question. The stunning result: 58 percent of preschoolers produced false (often vivid) stories regarding one or more events they had never experienced. Here is one from a boy who initially had denied the mousetrap incident (Ceci & others, 1994):

> My brother Colin was trying to get Blowtorch [an action figure] from me, and I wouldn't let him take it from me, so he pushed me into the wood pile where the mousetrap was. And then my finger got caught in it. And then we went to the hospital, and my mommy, daddy, and Colin drove me there, to the hospital in our van, because it was far away. And the doctor put a bandage on this finger.

Given such detailed stories, professional psychologists who specialize in interviewing children were often fooled. They could not reliably separate real from false memories. Nor could the children themselves. The above child, reminded that his parents had told him several times that the mousetrap incident never happened—that he had imagined it—protested, "But it really did happen. I remember it!"

Repressed or Constructed Memories of Abuse?

During the 1990s, psychology's most intense controversy—the "memory wars"—concerned reports of repressed and recovered memories of childhood sexual abuse. Are clinicians who have guided people in "recovering" such memories triggering false memories that break apart families, or are they uncovering the truth? Without disputing the all-too-common reality and horror of such abuse, critics use principles of memory construction to question the reality of repressed and recovered memories.

Traumatic events *are* sometimes forgotten, perhaps aided by the toxic effects of sustained stress (Nadel & Jacobs, 1998). In 1974, four-year-old Rachel (not her real name) and two others were molested by her uncle. Rachel told her mother, who informed the mother of one of the others, who then stabbed and killed the uncle. Seventeen years later, psychologist Linda Meyer Williams (1995) tracked down Rachel and 128 other women who were recorded as having experienced childhood sexual abuse (sexual intercourse or fondling). When asked whether she had ever been sexually abused as a child or whether any family members had ever gotten into trouble for their sexual behavior, Rachel calmly said no, then added: "Oh wait a minute. . . . My uncle sexually assaulted someone. . . . I never met my uncle (my mother's brother), he died before I was born. You see, he molested a little boy. When the little boy's mother found out, she took a butcher knife and stabbed my uncle in the heart, killing him." Rachel was one of 49 victims—38 percent of those interviewed—who did not spontaneously recall the specific reported incident of their own abuse. (Most did recall experiencing other sexual traumas.)

"[The] research leads me to worry about the possibility of false allegations. It is not a tribute to one's scientific integrity to walk down the middle of the road if the data are more to one side."

Stephen Ceci (1993)

Cognitive psychologist Jennifer Freyd (1996, 1998, 1999) theorizes that memories may remain vivid for life-threatening traumas such as a hurricane or car accident, yet be dulled or blocked for traumas that involve repeated betrayal. Consider Eva Hart, who 84 years after surviving the sinking of the *Titanic* still remembers the event with chilling clarity: "I saw it, heard it, and nobody could possibly forget it" (Rupp, 1998, p. 70). But then there are Rachel and the others, who have not remembered. By repressing knowledge of a caregiver's sexual abuse, dependent children can maintain their relationship with the caregiver and ensure their survival.

Some who have forgotten claim later to have also *recovered* memories of abuse. In one recent five-year period in Washington state, 682 people who claimed repressed memories of sexual abuse and other crimes sought money for their therapy bills from the state's victim compensation fund (Hallinan, 1997).

Ellen Bass and Laura Davis (1988), authors of the popular incest-recovery manual *The Courage to Heal*, encouraged recovering and reporting such memories. They offered a long list of incest-survivor characteristics, including feelings of shame, powerlessness, unworthiness, vulnerability, perfectionism, and deficient goals and motivation. If you have some of these feelings, some therapists have said, don't be surprised if you have no memory of sexual abuse, because "denial" and "repression" are common. "If you are unable to remember any specific instances . . . but still have a feeling that something abusive happened to you, it probably did," said Bass and Davis (pp. 21–22). "If you think you were abused and your life shows the symptoms, then you were."

Accepting this, some therapists have reasoned with patients that "people who've been abused often have your symptoms, so you probably were abused. Let's see if, aided by hypnosis or drugs, or helped to dig back and visualize your trauma, you can recover it." In one American survey, the average therapist estimated that 11 percent of the population—some 34 million people—have repressed memories of childhood sexual abuse (Kamena, 1998). In another survey, of British and American doctoral-level therapists, 7 in 10 said they had used techniques such as hypnosis or drugs to help clients recover suspected repressed memories of childhood sexual abuse (Poole & others, 1995).

As we might expect from the research on source amnesia and the misinformation effect, many patients exposed to such techniques do form an image of a threatening person. With further visualization, the image grows more vivid, leaving the patient stunned, angry, and ready to confront or sue the equally stunned and devastated parent or other relative, who, as the therapist has predicted, vigorously denies the accusation. One woman in her thirty-second therapy session recalled that her father had abused her at age 15 months. After such aided recall, actress Roseanne Barr (1991) claimed to recall sexual abuse beginning in infancy.

Understandably, persuading adult women that their fathers or mothers were incestuous has torn apart many families. Thousands of such families have sought advice from the False Memory Syndrome Foundation. The foundation takes its name from the term John Kihlstrom (1996) defines as a disruptive condition in which a person's identity and relationships center around a false but strongly believed memory of traumatic experience. The person resists disconfirming information and may become so focused on the memory as to avoid coping with the real problems.

Without questioning the professionalism of most therapists, skeptics compare the uncorroborated accusations suggested by some therapists to a 1990s reenactment of the Salem witch trials. Clinicians who use "memory work" techniques such as "guided imagery," hypnosis, and dream analysis to recover such memories "are nothing more than merchants of mental chaos, and, in fact, constitute a blight on the entire field of psychotherapy," charge some scientific critics (Loftus & others, 1995). Irate clinicians counter that those who dispute recovered memories of abuse add to abused women's trauma and play into the hands of child molesters.

At the end of 1999, the False Memory Syndrome Foundation was tracking 800 lawsuits, 70 percent against accused parents (Freyd, 1999). Nine in ten accusers are women, most between ages 25 and 45. Eleven suits by former patients against therapists had gone to trial, with nine ending in a verdict against the therapist. Fifty-six more such suits were settled out of court.

The trouble with inferring child abuse from adult symptoms is that the symptom list is "general enough to include everybody at least sometimes," notes Carol Tavris (1993). People feel unworthy, ashamed, and perfectionistic for so many reasons that the symptoms hardly prove any one cause.

In an effort to find a sensible common ground that might resolve this ideological battle, study panels have been convened and public statements made by the American Medical, American Psychological, and American Psychiatric Associations; the Australian Psychological Society; the British Psychological Society; and the Canadian Psychiatric Association. Those committed to protecting abused children and those committed to protecting wrongly accused adults agree on the following:

+ *Injustice happens.* Some innocent people have been falsely convicted. Some guilty people have evaded responsibility by casting doubt on their truth-telling accusers.

+ *Incest happens.* And it happens more often than we once supposed. There is no characteristic "survivor syndrome" (Kendell-Tackett & others, 1993). However, sexual abuse can leave its victims predisposed to problems ranging from sexual dysfunction to depression.

+ *Forgetting happens.* Like Rachel, notes Elizabeth Loftus (1995), many of the women interviewed by Linda Meyer Williams either were very young when abused or may not have understood the meaning of their experience—circumstances under which forgetting is "utterly common." Forgetting isolated past events, both negative and positive, is an ordinary part of everyday life. With all sorts of memories, we tend over time to lose the peripheral details and retain the gist of the experience (Howe, 1998).

+ *Recovered memories are commonplace.* Cued by a remark or an experience, we recover memories of long-forgotten events, both pleasant and unpleasant. What is debated is whether the unconscious mind sometimes forcibly represses painful experiences and, if so, whether these can be retrieved by certain therapist-aided techniques.

+ *Memories "recovered" under hypnosis or the influence of drugs are especially unreliable.* "Age-regressed" hypnotized subjects, for example, easily incorporate suggestions into their memories, even memories of "past lives."

+ *Memories of things happening before age 3 are also unreliable.* People do not reliably recall happenings of any sort from their first 3 years—a phenomenon called *infantile amnesia.*

+ *Memories, whether real or false, can be emotionally upsetting.* If a false memory of abuse becomes a real part of one's history, the client as well as the family may suffer. Like real traumas, such experiences can then cause lasting suffering.

Without knowing a person's initial experience (as we do in memory experiments) it is difficult to assess the validity of a person's memory. As Mark Pendergrast (1996) notes, "It is ironic that no one can ethically conduct an experiment to replicate what is happening throughout the UK and the US in private therapy settings." Nevertheless, to many memory researchers, the idea that people literally record, then repress, then recover painful experiences is scientifically naive. All the ingredients for cooking false memories are potentially present in the therapy setting, notes Stephen Lindsay (1995): a credible authority, repeated suggestions, imagination-enhancing techniques, and affirmation for one's budding suspicions.

To more closely approximate therapist-aided recall, Elizabeth Loftus and her colleagues (1996) have experimentally implanted false memories of childhood traumas. In one study, she had a trusted family member recall for a teenager three real childhood experiences and a false one—a vivid account of the child's being lost for an extended time in a shopping mall at age 5 until being rescued by an elderly person.

"When memories are 'recovered' after long periods of amnesia, particularly when extraordinary means were used to secure the recovery of memory, there is a high probability that the memories are false."

Royal College of Psychiatrists Working Group on Reported Recovered Memories of Child Sexual Abuse (Brandon & others, 1998)

"Spend time imagining that you were sexually abused, without worrying about accuracy, proving anything, or having your ideas make sense. As you give rein to your imagination, let your intuitions guide your thoughts."

Wendy Maltz, *The Sexual Healing Journey*, 1991

TODAY'S SPECIAL GUEST

BRUNDAGE MORNALD, OF
BATTLE CREEK, MONTANA
UNDER HYPNOSIS, MR. MORNALD
RECOVERED LONG-BURIED
MEMORIES OF A PERFECTLY
NORMAL, HAPPY CHILDHOOD.

Elizabeth Loftus

"People in general and jurors in particular have a lot of misconceptions about the way memory works" (quoted by Monaghan, 1992).

Two days later, one subject, Chris, said, "That day I was so scared that I would never see my family again." Two days after that he began to visualize the flannel shirt, bald head, and glasses of the old man who supposedly had found him. Told the story was made up, Chris was incredulous: "I thought I remembered being lost . . . and looking around for the guys. I do remember that, and then crying, and Mom coming up and saying, 'Where were you? Don't you . . . ever do that again.'"

Such is the memory construction process by which people can recall being abducted by UFOs, victimized by a satanic cult, molested in a crib, or living a past life. Thousands of seemingly healthy people, notes Loftus, "speak in terror-stricken voices about their experience aboard flying saucers. They *remember*, clearly and vividly, being abducted by aliens. Or consider the fact that thousands of reasonable, normally functioning human beings relate in calm voices and with deeply felt conviction their past-life experiences. They *remember* having lived before" (Loftus & Ketcham, 1994, p. 66). There are likewise cases of medically certified virgins who *remember* being raped during satanic ritual abuse, and many thousands more who *remember* seeing babies murdered and eaten (but where, wonder skeptics, including the FBI, are the police reports of the missing babies?) (Pendergrast, 1996; Spanos & others, 1994).

Loftus knows firsthand the phenomenon she studies. At a recent family reunion, an uncle told her that at age 14, she found her mother's drowned body. Shocked, she denied it. But the uncle was adamant, and over the next three days she began to wonder if *she* had a repressed memory. "Maybe that's why I'm so obsessed with this topic." As the now-upset Loftus pondered her uncle's suggestion, she "recovered" an image of her mother lying in the pool, face down, and of herself finding the body. "I started putting everything into place. Maybe that's why I'm such a workaholic. Maybe that's why I'm so emotional when I think about her even though she died in 1959."

Then her brother called and said there was a mistake. Her uncle had later remembered what other relatives now confirmed. Aunt Pearl, not Loftus, had found the body (Loftus & Ketcham, 1994; Monaghan, 1992).

But then again, Loftus also knows firsthand the reality of sexual abuse. A male baby-sitter molested her when she was 6 years old. She has not forgotten. And that makes her wary of those whom she sees as trivializing real abuse by suggesting and seeking out uncorroborated traumatic experiences, then accepting them uncritically as fact. The enemies of the truly victimized are not only those who prey and those who deny, she says, but those whose writings and allegations "are bound to lead to an increased likelihood that society in general will disbelieve the genuine cases of childhood sexual abuse that truly deserve our sustained attention" (Loftus, 1993).

So, does repression ever occur? Psychologists continue to have heated debates on this topic, which is the cornerstone of Freudian theory and a recurring theme in so much popular psychology. But this much now appears certain: The most common response to a traumatic experience (witnessing the murder of a parent, experiencing the horrors of a Nazi death camp, being terrorized by a hijacker or a rapist) is not banishment of the experience into an active but inaccessible unconscious. Rather, such experiences are typically etched on the mind as vivid, persistent, haunting memories. "The things we remember best," noted Baltasar Gracian in 1647, "are those better forgotten."

Forgetting and Memory Construction

What causes us to forget? At what points in the memory system can our memories fail us?

One explanation of forgetting is that we fail to encode information for entry into our memory system. Without effortful processing, we never notice or process much of what we sense. Memories may also fade after storage—often rapidly at first, and then leveling off. Forgetting also results from retrieval failure. Retrieval-related forgetting may be caused by a lack of retrieval cues, by proactive or retroactive interference, or even, said Freud, by motivated forgetting.

What causes us to misremember, producing inaccurate or false memories?

Memories are not stored as exact copies, and they certainly are not retrieved as such. Rather, we construct our memories, using both stored and new information. Thus, when child or adult eyewitnesses are subtly exposed to misinformation after an event, they often believe they saw the misleading details as part of the event. People also exhibit source amnesia, by attributing something heard, read, or imagined to a wrong source. Because false memories feel like true memories and are equally durable, sincerity need not signify reality.

What does memory research tell us about the potential for inaccuracy in eyewitness memories and reports of repressed memories of abuse?

Memory researchers are especially suspicious of claims of long-repressed memories of sexual abuse, UFO abduction, or other traumas that are "recovered" with the aid of a therapist or suggestive book. More than we once supposed, incest and abuse happen. But unless the victim was a child too young to remember life experience, such traumas are usually remembered vividly, not banished into an active but inaccessible unconscious.

Terms and Concepts to Remember

proactive interference, p. 349
retroactive interference, p. 350
repression, p. 351

misinformation effect, p. 353
source amnesia, p. 354

Test Yourself

27.1. In some cases, forgetting may be due to encoding failure. That is meaningless information may not be transferred from
a. the environment into sensory memory.
b. sensory memory into long-term memory.
c. long-term memory into short-term memory.
d. short-term memory into long-term memory.

27.2. Forgetting may result from storage decay. Ebbinghaus found that about three days after a session of learning nonsense syllables, people have forgotten much of what they learned. Ebbinghaus' "forgetting curve" shows that as time goes on, retention of the nonsense syllables tends to
a. increase slightly.
b. decrease noticeably.
c. decrease greatly.
d. level out.

27.3. Experiments show that the hour before sleep is a good time to memorize information. For example, studying a vocabulary list before going to sleep minimizes the disrupting effects of all the other new words and terms that might, in the course of a school day, claim our attention. Going to sleep after learning new material minimizes
a. the misinformation effect.
b. amnesia.
c. retroactive interference.
d. proactive interference.

27.4. People unknowingly revise or rearrange their memories of events. According to Sigmund Freud, painful or unacceptable memories are self-censored, or blocked from consciousness, through a mechanism called
a. repression.
b. proactive interference.
c. anxiety.
d. memory decay.

27.5. Because we often alter information as we encode it and because we tend to fill in memory gaps with our assumptions about events, our memories are generally not exact reproductions of events. One reason for this memory reconstruction is
a. proactive interference.
b. the misinformation effect.
c. retroactive interference.
d. the eyewitness recall effect.

27.6. Aspects of our memories are distributed to different parts of the brain. Thus, while we may recognize a face in the crowd, we may not be able to recall where we know the person from. This is called
a. the misinformation effect.
b. amnesia.
c. source amnesia.
d. repression.

27.7. Memories we derive from experience have more details than memories we derive from imagination. Therapists run a great risk of eliciting false memories when they
a. use hypnotism to elicit memories.
b. ask for gist rather than details.
c. judge the accuracy of the memory by the confidence and consistency of the testimony.
d. All of the above are risky procedures.

Review

- Can you offer an example of proactive interference?

- What—given the commonality of source amnesia—might life be like if we remembered all our waking experiences and all our dreams?

Reflect

- Most people, especially as they grow older, wish for better memories. Is that true of you? Or do you more often wish you could discard old memories?

- Do you have an opinion on the controversy over reports of repressed and recovered memories? What evidence supports your view? Could you be an impartial jury member in a trial of a parent accused of sexual abuse based on such a memory, or of a therapist being sued for creating a false memory?

Answers to the Test Yourself and Review questions can be found in the green appendix at the end of the book.

Applying Memory Principles to Your Own Education

Now and then we are dismayed at our forgetfulness—at our embarrassing inability to recall someone's name, at forgetting to bring up a point in conversation, at forgetting to bring along something important, at finding ourselves standing in a room unable to recall why we are there (Herrmann, 1982). Is there anything we can do to minimize such misdeeds of our memory system? Much as biology benefits medicine and botany benefits agriculture, so can the psychology of memory benefit education. Here for easy reference is a summary of concrete suggestions for improving memory. The PRTR—*Preview, Read, Think critically, Review*—study technique used in this book incorporates several of these strategies.

Study repeatedly to boost long-term recall. Overlearn. To learn a name, say it to yourself after being introduced; wait a few seconds and say it again; wait longer and say it again. Provide yourself with many separate study sessions by taking advantage of life's little intervals—riding on the bus, walking across campus, waiting for class to start.

Spend more time rehearsing or actively thinking about the material. Speed-reading (skimming) complex material—with minimal rehearsal—yields little retention. Rehearsal and critical reflection help more. It pays to study actively!

> "I have discovered that it is of some use when you lie in bed at night and gaze into the darkness to repeat in your mind the things you have been studying. Not only does it help the understanding, but also the memory."
>
> **Leonardo da Vinci (1452–1519)**

Make the material personally meaningful. To build a network of retrieval cues, take thorough text and class notes in your own words. Mindlessly repeating information is relatively ineffective. It is better to form images, understand and organize information, relate the material to what you already know or have experienced, and put it in your own words. Without such cues, you may find yourself stuck when a question uses phrasing different from the rote forms you memorized. To increase retrieval cues, form as many associations as possible.

> "Knit each new thing on to some acquisition already there."
>
> **William James, *Principles of Psychology*, 1890**

To remember a list of unfamiliar items, use mnemonic devices. Associate items with peg-words. Make up a story that incorporates vivid images of the items. Chunk information into acronyms.

Refresh your memory by activating retrieval cues. Mentally re-create the situation and the mood in which the original learning occurred. Return to the same location. Jog your memory by allowing one thought to cue the next.

Recall events while they are fresh, before you encounter possible misinformation. If you are an eyewitness to an important event, record your memory before allowing others to suggest what may have occurred.

Minimize interference. Study before sleeping. Do not study in close proximity topics that are likely to interfere with each other, such as Spanish and French.

Test your own knowledge, both to rehearse it and to help determine what you do not yet know. If you must *recall* information later, do not be lulled into overconfidence by your ability to *recognize* it. Test your recall. Outline sections on a blank page. Define concepts listed at the end of a module or chapter *before* turning back to their definitions. Take practice tests; the study guides that accompany many texts, including this one, can help.

Without self-testing, one can easily become overconfident, as John Shaughnessy and Eugene Zechmeister (1992) found in an experiment with two groups of students. A "reread group" repeatedly read dozens of factual statements, then judged the likelihood that they would remember each fact, and then were tested on their recall. Students in this group felt fairly confident of their knowledge, even on the questions they later missed. Students in a "practice test group" also read the statements, but they then spent the rest of the time responding to tests requiring them to retrieve the facts. Compared with the "reread" group, the practice-test group did just as well on the final recall test. What is more, they could better discriminate what they did and did not know. It is clear that self-testing enhances recall and can help you to know what you know—and thus enable you to focus your study time on what you do not yet know. As former British Prime Minister Benjamin Disraeli once said, "To be conscious that you are ignorant is a great step to knowledge."

Thinking and memory
Most of what we know is not the result of efforts to memorize. We learn because we're curious and because we spend time thinking about our experiences. Actively thinking as we read, by rehearsing and relating ideas, yields the best retention.

Thinking, Language, and Intelligence

Throughout history, we humans have deplored our foolishness and celebrated our wisdom. The poet T. S. Eliot was struck by "the hollow men . . . Headpiece filled with straw." But Shakespeare's Hamlet extolled the human species as "noble in reason! . . . infinite in faculties! . . . in apprehension how like a god!" Psychologists, too, have sometimes marveled at our capabilities, sometimes at our propensity to err.

We have studied the human brain—a mere 3 pounds of tissue containing circuitry more complex than the planet's telephone networks. We have appreciated the competence of newborn infants. We have studied the human sensory system, which disassembles visual stimuli into millions of nerve impulses, distributes them for parallel processing, and then reassembles them into clear and colorful perceived images. We have acknowledged the seemingly limitless capacity of human memory and the ease with which we process information, consciously and unconsciously. Little wonder, then, that our species, by accumulating and refining ideas over time, has the collective genius to invent the camera, the car, and the computer; to unlock the atom and crack the genetic code; to travel into space and probe the oceans' depths.

At the same time, we have seen that our species is kin to the other animals, influenced by the same principles that produce learning in rats and pigeons. We have noted that we assimilate reality into our preconceptions and succumb to perceptual illusions. We have seen how easily we deceive ourselves about pseudopsychic claims, hypnotic regression, and false memories. It is also little wonder, then, that we sometimes imagine we can read minds and travel outside our bodies; that we form distorted images of other ethnic, age, and gender groups; that we are bound by the same biological principles as other creatures.

In Modules 28 and 29 we encounter further instances of these two images of the human condition—the rational and the irrational. We will see how we form concepts, solve problems, and make judgments. We will look at our flair for language and ask whether our species alone has this capability. And we will reflect on how deserving we are of our name, *Homo sapiens*—wise human.

In Modules 30 through 32, we focus on an ongoing debate about *intelligence*, in which psychologists and others pick sides on two major questions: (1) Does each of us have an inborn general mental capacity (intelligence), and (2) can we quantify this capacity as a meaningful number?

28 Thinking

Our brains receive, perceive, store, and retrieve information. How then does our cognitive system use this information as we organize our world, solve problems, make decisions, and form judgments? Thinking, or **cognition**, refers to all the mental activities associated with processing, understanding, and communicating. *Cognitive psychologists* study these mental activities.

By thinking about thinking, and alerting us to common errors in our thinking, cognitive psychologists aspire to help us think smart. Their research also suggests educational experiences that could help us to appreciate both the powers and the limits of our intuition and to reason more effectively when making practical decisions and everyday judgments. We begin with the building blocks of thinking: concepts.

Concepts

Preview Question: How do concepts help us to simplify the world around us and bring order to it?

To think about the countless events, objects, and people in our world, we simplify things. We form **concepts**—mental groupings of similar objects, events, and people. The concept *chair* sums up a variety of items—a baby's high chair, a reclining chair, the chairs around a dining room table, a dentist's chair.

Imagine life without concepts. We would need a different name for every object and idea. We could not ask a child to "throw the ball" because there would be no concept of *ball*. Instead of saying, "They were angry," we would have to describe facial expressions, vocal intensities, gestures, and words. Such concepts as *ball* and *angry* provide us with much information without much cognitive effort.

Animals, too, are capable of feats of concept formation. Pigeons demonstrate the surprising intelligence of bird brains by sorting objects according to their similarity. Shown pictures of cars, cats, chairs, and flowers, they readily learn to identify the categories. Shown a picture of a never-before-seen chair, the pigeon will reliably peck a key that represents "chairs" (Wasserman, 1995).

To simplify things further, humans organize concepts into hierarchies. Cab drivers organize their cities into geographical sectors, which subdivide into neighborhoods and again into blocks. The earliest naturalists simplified and ordered the overwhelming complexity of some 5 million living species by clustering them into two basic categories—the plant and animal kingdoms. Then they divided these basic categories into smaller and smaller subcategories—vertebrates, bony fish, and Atlantic salmon, for instance.

We form some concepts by definition. Told the rule that a triangle has three sides, we thereafter classify all three-sided geometric forms as triangles. More often, however, we form our concepts by developing **prototypes**—a mental image or best example that incorporates all the features we associate with a category (Rosch, 1978). The more closely something matches our prototype of a concept, the more readily we recognize it as an example of the concept. A robin and a goose both satisfy our definition of *bird*: an animal that has wings and feathers and hatches from an egg. Yet people agree more quickly that "A robin is a bird" than that "A goose is a bird." For most of us, the robin is the birdier bird; it more closely resembles our bird prototype. Likewise, "maternal love" and "self-love" both qualify as love. But people more instantly

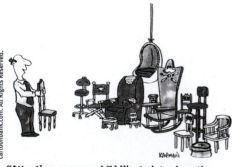

"Attention, everyone! I'd like to introduce the newest member of our family."

agree that "maternal love is a type of love," because it better matches their love prototype (Fehr & Russell, 1991).

If something fails to match our prototype, we may have trouble classifying it. Thus, we might be slow to recognize non-flying penguins and kiwis as birds. Similarly, we are slow to perceive an illness when our symptoms don't fit one of our disease prototypes (Bishop, 1991). People whose heart attack symptoms don't match their prototype of a heart attack may not seek help. And when discrimination doesn't fit our prejudice prototypes—of White against Black, male against female, young against old—we often fail to notice it. People more easily detect male prejudice against female than female against male or female against female (Inman & Baron, 1996).

A bird and a . . . ?
If asked to imagine a bird, most people quickly come up with a mental picture that is something like this American robin. It takes them a bit longer to conceptualize a penguin as a bird because it doesn't match their prototype of a small, feathered, flying creature.

Solving Problems

Preview Question: What strategies do we use to solve problems, and what obstacles hinder our problem solving?

One tribute to our rationality is our ability to form and use concepts. Another is our skill at solving problems as we cope with novel situations. What's the best route around this traffic jam? How shall we respond to a friend's criticism? How can we get into the house when we've lost our keys?

Some problems we solve through trial and error—Thomas Edison tried thousands of light bulb filaments before stumbling upon one that worked. For other problems, we may follow an **algorithm**, a step-by-step procedure that guarantees a solution. Told to find another word using all the letters in *SPLOYOCHYG*, we could try each letter in each position, but generating and examining the 907,208 resulting combinations would be exasperating. Because step-by-step algorithms can be laborious (well-suited to computers), we often solve problems with simple rule-of-thumb strategies, called **heuristics**. Thus, in rearranging the letters of *SPLOYOCHYG*, we might exclude letter combinations such as two *Y*'s together. By using rule-of-thumb heuristics and then applying trial and error, you may hit upon the answer (page 369).

Sometimes we are unaware of using any problem-solving strategy; the answer just comes to us. We can all recall occasions when we puzzled over a problem for some time. Then, suddenly, the pieces fell together and we perceived the solution. This facility for sudden flashes of inspiration we call **insight**. Ten-year-old Johnny Appleton displayed insight in solving a problem that had stumped construction workers: how to rescue a young robin that had fallen into a narrow 30-inch-deep hole in a cement block wall. Johnny's solution: to slowly pour in sand, giving the bird enough time to keep its feet on top of the constantly rising sand (Ruchlis, 1990). A tougher problem, "Fermat's Last Theorem," tantalized Princeton mathematician Andrew Wiles, as it had other brilliant minds for 350 years. Then "suddenly, totally unexpectedly, I had this incredible revelation" that combined two incomplete solutions:

It was so indescribably beautiful; it was so simple and so elegant. I couldn't understand how I'd missed it and I just stared at it in disbelief for twenty minutes. Then during the day I walked around the department, and I'd keep

■ **cognition** the mental activities associated with thinking, knowing, and remembering.

■ **concept** a mental grouping of similar objects, events, ideas, or people.

■ **prototype** a mental image or best example of a category. Matching new items to the prototype provides a quick and easy method for including items in a category (as when comparing feathered creatures to a prototypical bird, such as a robin).

■ **algorithm** a methodical, logical rule or procedure that guarantees solving a particular problem. Contrasts with the usually speedier—but also more error-prone—use of *heuristics*.

■ **heuristic** a rule-of-thumb strategy that often allows us to make judgments and solve problems efficiently; usually speedier but also more error-prone than *algorithms*.

■ **insight** a sudden and often novel realization of the solution to a problem; it contrasts with strategy-based solutions.

Heuristic searching

To search for horseradish in a supermarket you could search every aisle (an algorithm) or check the mustard, spice, and gourmet sections (heuristics). The heuristic approach is often speedier, but an algorithmic search guarantees you will find it eventually.

coming back to my desk looking to see if it was still there. It was still there. I couldn't contain myself, I was so excited. It was the most important moment of my working life (Wiles, quoted in Singh, 1998).

Insight provides a sense of satisfaction. After solving a difficult problem or discovering how to resolve a conflict, we feel happy. The joy of a joke may similarly lie in our capacity for insight—our sudden comprehension of an unexpected ending or a double meaning. We find double meaning in the story of the professor who complained to his colleagues that student interruptions had become a problem: "The minute I get up to speak, some fool begins to talk."

Obstacles to Problem Solving

Inventive as we can be in solving problems, the correct answer may elude us. Two cognitive tendencies—*confirmation bias* and *fixation*—often mislead our search for a solution.

Confirmation Bias

A major obstacle to problem solving is our eagerness to search for information that confirms our ideas, a phenomenon known as **confirmation bias**. In an experiment with British university students, Peter Wason (1960) demonstrated our reluctance to seek information that might disprove our beliefs. Wason gave students the three-number sequence 2-4-6 and asked them to guess the rule he had used to devise the series. (The rule was simple: any three ascending numbers.) Before submitting their answers, the students generated their own sets of three numbers, and each time Wason told them whether their sets conformed to his rule. Once they had done enough testing to feel *certain* they had the rule, they were to announce it.

> "The human understanding, when any proposition has been once laid down . . . forces everything else to add fresh support and confirmation."
>
> Francis Bacon, *Novum Organum*, 1620

The result? Seldom right but never in doubt. Most of Wason's students convinced themselves of a wrong rule. Typically, they formed a wrong idea ("Maybe it's counting by twos") and then searched only for confirming evidence (by testing 6-8-10, 100-102-104, and so forth). Such experiments reveal that we seek evidence that will verify our ideas more eagerly than we seek evidence that might refute them (Klayman & Ha, 1987; Skov & Sherman, 1986).

Business managers, for example, are more likely to follow the successful careers of those they once hired than to track the achievements of those they rejected, leading them to confirm their own perceived hiring ability. Individual jury members will early on construct a story that seems confirmed by the unfolding evidence—the defendant was angry or the defendant was afraid—and are often surprised to discover that other jurors have viewed the evidence with different stories (Kuhn & others, 1994; Pennington & Hastie, 1993). Reflecting on many experiments, Wason (1981) reported that once people have a wrong idea they often will not budge from their illogic: "Ordinary people evade facts, become inconsistent, or systematically defend themselves against the threat of new information relevant to the issue."

FIGURE 28.1 The matchstick problem

How would you arrange six matches to form four equilateral triangles? (From "Problem Solving" by M. Scheerer. Copyright © 1963 by Scientific American, Inc. All rights reserved.)

Fixation

Try your hand at these brainteasers drawn from classic experiments:

Arrange the six matches shown in **FIGURE 28.1** so they will form four equilateral triangles.

Suppose that you have a 21-cup jug, a 127-cup jug, and a 3-cup jug. Using these three jugs to draw and discard as much water as you like, how will you measure out exactly 100 cups of water? Solve the other problems presented in **FIGURE 28.2**, too.

Problem	Given jugs of these sizes			Measure out this much water:
	A	B	C	
1	21	127	3	100
2	14	46	5	22
3	18	43	10	5
4	7	42	6	23
5	20	57	4	29
6	23	49	3	20
7	15	39	3	18

FIGURE 28.2
The three-jugs problems
Using jugs A, B, and C with the capacities shown in the table, how would you measure out the volumes indicated in the right-hand column? (From Luchins, 1946.)

How can you use the box of matches, thumbtacks, and candle shown in **FIGURE 28.3** to mount the candle on a bulletin board? (Read on after trying these problems.)

A major obstacle to problem solving is **fixation**—the inability to see a problem from a fresh perspective. Once we incorrectly represent the problem, it's hard to restructure how we approach it. If your attempts to solve the matchstick problem were fixated on two-dimensional solutions, then the three-dimensional solution shown in **FIGURE 28.4**, page 370, will have eluded you.

FIGURE 28.3
The candle-mounting problem
Using these materials, how would you mount the candle on a bulletin board? (From Duncker, 1945.)

There is good reason why we become fixated on certain solutions. Those that worked in the past often work on new problems. Consider:

Given the sequence O-T-T-F-?-?-?, what are the final three letters?

Most people have difficulty recognizing that the three final letters are *F*(ive), *S*(ix), and *S*(even). But solving this problem may make the next one easier:

Given the sequence J-F-M-A-?-?-?, what are the final three letters? (If you don't get this one, ask yourself what month it is.)

Past success can indeed help solve present problems. But it may also interfere with our finding new solutions. This tendency to repeat solutions that have worked in the past is a type of fixation called **mental set**. As a *perceptual set* predisposes what we perceive, a *mental set* predisposes how we think. You probably ran into mental set in the water jug problems. For the first jug problem, you probably developed the following formula:

B – A – 2C = desired amount of water

This same formula works for all seven problems. Once you developed this mental set, you probably solved the later problems faster. But did this mental set cause you to miss the much simpler solutions for problems 6 and 7 (**FIGURE 28.5**, page 370)?

Flexible, rational thinking becomes even more difficult in times of stress and tension (Janis, 1989). During international crises, views of an enemy become fixed in simplified good-versus-bad terms. During personal crises, too, our thinking often becomes rigid. One Korean War paratrooper readying for a mission was given the last parachute—a left-handed one. "It's the same as the others," explained the ordnance sergeant, "but the rip cord hangs on the left side of the harness."

Answer to SPLOYOCHYG anagram on page 367: PSYCHOLOGY.

■ **confirmation bias** a tendency to search for information that confirms one's preconceptions.

■ **fixation** the inability to see a problem from a new perspective; an impediment to problem solving.

■ **mental set** a tendency to approach a problem in a particular way, especially a way that has been successful in the past but may or may not be helpful in solving a new problem.

FIGURE 28.4

Solution to the matchstick problem

To solve this problem, you must break the fixation of limiting your considerations to two-dimensional solutions. (From "Problem Solving" by M. Scheerer. Copyright © 1963 by Scientific American, Inc. All rights reserved.)

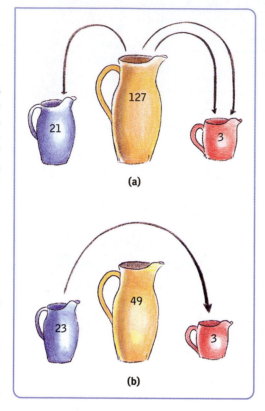

(a)

(b)

FIGURE 28.5

Solutions to the three-jugs problems

(a) All seven problems can be solved by the equation shown in (a): B − A − 2C = desired volume. (b) But simpler solutions exist for problems 6 and 7, such as A − C for problem 6. Did your mental set cause you to miss it? (From Luchins, 1946.)

FIGURE 28.6

Solution to the candle-mounting problem

Solving this problem requires recognizing that a box need not always serve as a container. (From Duncker, 1945.)

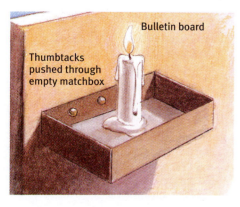

Bulletin board

Thumbtacks pushed through empty matchbox

At 8000 feet, the soldiers jumped one by one, and all went well—except for this one man who fell straight to his death. Investigators discovered that under the stress of the jump the man had become fixated on the familiar way to open a chute. The right side of his uniform, where he was accustomed to finding the rip cord, was completely torn off. Even the flesh on his chest had been gouged by his bloody right hand. Inches to the left was the rip cord, apparently untouched (Csikszentmihalyi, 1990).

Another type of fixation goes by the awkward but appropriate label **functional fixedness**. This is our tendency to perceive the functions of objects as fixed and unchanging. A person may ransack the house for a screwdriver when a dime would have turned the screw. Perhaps you experienced functional fixedness when you tried to solve the candle-mounting problem. If you thought of the matchbox as having only the function of holding matches, you may have overlooked its use shown in **FIGURE 28.6**. Perceiving and relating familiar things in new ways is part of creativity.

Making Decisions and Forming Judgments

Preview Question: How do we arrive at the hundreds of decisions and judgments we make each day?

When making each day's hundreds of judgments and decisions—Is it worth the bother to take an umbrella? Can I trust this person? Should I shoot the basketball or pass to the player who's hot?—we seldom take the time and effort to reason systematically. We just follow our intuition. After interviewing policymakers in government, business, and education, social psychologist Irving Janis (1986) concluded that they "often do not use a reflective problem-solving approach. How do they usually arrive at their decisions? If you ask, they are likely to tell you . . . they do it mostly by the *seat of their pants*."

Using and Misusing Heuristics

Those mental shortcuts we call heuristics often do help us make reasonable seat-of-the-pants decisions. Thanks to the mind's automatic information processing, intuitive judgments are instantaneous. But the price we sometimes pay for this efficiency can be costly bad judgments. To gain an idea of how heuristics determine our intuitive judgments—and how they occasionally lead even the smartest people into dumb decisions—consider two heuristics identified by cognitive psychologists Amos Tversky and Daniel Kahneman (1974): *representativeness* and *availability*.

The Representativeness Heuristic

To judge the likelihood of things in terms of how well they represent particular proto-types is to use the **representativeness heuristic**. To illustrate, consider:

> A stranger tells you about a person who is short, slim, and likes to read poetry, and then asks you to guess whether this person is more likely to be a professor of classics at an Ivy League university or a truck driver. Which would be the better guess? (Adapted from Nisbett & Ross, 1980)

If you are like most people, you answered "professor" because the description seems more *representative* of Ivy League scholars than of truck drivers. The representative-ness heuristic enabled you to make a snap judgment. But it also led you to ignore other relevant information, such as the total number of classics professors versus the number of truck drivers. When I help people think through this question, their own reasoning usually leads them to an answer that contradicts their immediate intu-ition. The typical conversation goes something like this:

Question: First, let's figure out how many professors fit the description. How many Ivy League universities do you suppose there are?

Answer: Oh, about 10, I suppose.

Question: How many classics professors would you guess there are at each?

Answer: Maybe 4.

Question: Okay, that's 40 Ivy League classics professors. What fraction of these are short and slim?

Answer: Let's say half.

Question: And, of these 20, how many like to read poetry?

Answer: I'd say half—10 professors.

Question: Okay, now let's figure how many truck drivers fit the description. How many truck drivers do you suppose there are?

Answer: Maybe 400,000.

Question: What fraction are short and slim?

Answer: Not many—perhaps 1 in 8.

Question: Of these 50,000, what percentage like to read poetry?

Answer: Truck drivers who like poetry? Maybe 1 in 100—oh, oh, I can see where this is going—that leaves me with 500 short, slim, poetry-reading truck drivers.

Question: Yup. So, although the person I've described may be much more repre-sentative of classics professors than of truck drivers, this person is still (even if we accept your stereotypes) 50 times more likely to be a truck driver than a classics professor.

This illustrates an illogical use of the representativeness heuristic. To judge the likelihood of something, we intuitively compare it with our mental representation of that category—of, say, what truck drivers are like. If the two match, then that fact usually overrides other considerations of statistics or logic.

The Availability Heuristic

The **availability heuristic** operates when we base our judgments on the availability of information in our memories. If instances of an event are easily available—if they come to mind readily—we presume such events are common. The faster people can remember an instance of some event ("a broken promise"), the more they expect it to recur (MacLeod & Campbell, 1992). Usually, cognitively available events *are* more likely to recur—but not always. To see this, make a guess: Does the letter *k* appear more often as the first or third letter in English usage?

■ **functional fixedness** the tendency to think of things only in terms of their usual functions; an impediment to problem solving.

■ **representativeness heuristic** a rule of thumb for judging the likelihood of things in terms of how well they seem to represent, or match, particular prototypes; may lead one to ignore other relevant information.

■ **availability heuristic** estimating the likelihood of events based on their availability in memory; if instances come readily to mind (perhaps because of their vividness), we presume such events are common.

THINKING CRITICALLY ABOUT :

RISKS—WHEN STATISTICS CLASH WITH HEURISTICS

"Most people reason dramatically, not quantitatively," said Oliver Wendell Holmes. With horrific television and magazine images of air crashes in mind, many people, petrified of air travel, prefer the safety of their own cars. One Gallup study (*Gallup Report*, 1989) found that, of those who do fly, 44 percent reported feeling fearful and 63 percent had "lost confidence" in airline safety.

Ironically, the statistical reality is that air travel is safer than ever. Mile for mile, U.S. travelers during the 1980s were 26 times more likely to die in a car crash than on a commercial flight (National Safety Council, 1991). In the 27 months following March 22, 1992, major U.S. airlines carried more than 1 billion passengers on *16 million* flights without a single death (Tolchin, 1994). For most air travelers, the most dangerous part of the journey is the drive to the airport. When a friend tells me of revising her will before flying, I cannot resist saying, "Much better to have done so before you drove to Kansas." For even if she were to board a random jet every day, she would (if her experience matched the average) have to live

Vivid events are more available to memory Photos of this July 1994 crash etched a sharper image in many minds than did the 16 million consecutive fatality-free flights on U.S. airlines during the preceding 27 months. Because such vivid happenings are more available to memory, they seem more common than they really are.

"The information-processing short-cuts—called heuristics—which are normally both highly efficient and immensely time-saving in day-to-day situations, work systematically against us in the market-place. . . . The tendency to underestimate or altogether ignore past probabilities in making a decision is undoubtedly the most significant problem of intuitive predictions."

David Dreman, *Contrarian Investment Strategy: The Psychology of Stock Market Success*, 1979

21,000 years before crashing to her death (Barnett, 1996).

Still, when overall statistics vie with vivid images of helpless crash victims, many find the memorable instances more persuasive. It is like judging the likelihood of shark attacks after watching the *Jaws* movies: Regardless of statistics, memorable images have a way of heightening swimmers' feelings of risk. People may *know* their fears are irrational, but no matter. Nightmarish images from horror movies may linger for months or years, causing anxiety over a creaking house. The available images of a plane death—which is 6900 times more likely to make the *New York Times* front page than a cancer death (Barnett, 1990)—protrude into consciousness. Even smokers (whose habit shortens their lives by about five years) may senselessly fret before flying (which shortens the average person's life by one day).

The 1988 terrorist bomb that exploded Pan Am Flight 103 and the 1996 fiery explosion of TWA Flight 800 caused many would-be international vacationers to stay home and risk the more dangerous highways. The same fearful public continues to smoke billions of cigarettes a year, guzzle alcohol, and devour foods that put people at risk for the greatest of killers—heart disease. All because *perceptions* of risk are virtually unrelated to actual risk (Slovic, 1987)—a phenomenon due partly to our greater fear of things we cannot control and partly to our overestimating the likelihood of dreaded, publicized, and cognitively available events. Thus, the public dreads a catastrophic nuclear accident (which after the 1986 Chernobyl disaster we can readily visualize). Yet it accepts the less dramatic risks of coal-generated power quietly fueling acid rain and global warming.

The point to remember: Whether making travel plans or choosing foods, defining safety standards or evaluating environmental hazards, smart thinkers will define risks based not on mentally available media images but on statistical reality.

Because words beginning with *k* come to mind more easily than words having *k* as their third letter, most people guess that *k* occurs more frequently as the first letter. Actually, *k* is two to three times more likely to appear as the third letter. So far in this module, words such as *know, kingdom,* and *kin* are outnumbered 47 to 17 by words such as *make, likely, asked,* and *acknowledged.*

The judgmental errors influenced by the availability heuristic are not always harmless. A lot of important decisions involve judgments of risk. Whether we favor using nuclear power or burning coal to produce energy depends partly on our judgments of their risks to our health and the environment. Our efforts to prevent various deadly diseases depend on our judgments of the likelihood of their occurrence. Our choice to buy or not to buy a lottery ticket depends on our hunch of the odds of striking it rich. Casinos entice us to gamble by signaling even small wins with bells and lights—making them vividly memorable—while keeping big losses soundlessly invisible. In such ways, hucksters can manipulate the hopes and risk perceptions of anyone naive about statistics.

Life and theft insurance salespeople sometimes exploit our tendency to believe that events are more likely if we can picture them readily (Cialdini & Carpenter, 1981). By having people imagine their families in mourning or their possessions stolen, they may cause the images of these disasters to linger. This makes such disasters seem more likely, motivating them to buy insurance.

The availability heuristic also affects our social judgments, as Ruth Hamill and her co-workers demonstrated (1980). They presented people with a single, vivid case of welfare abuse, in which a long-term welfare recipient had several unruly children. Statistically, this case was exceptional: Most people who receive welfare do so for four years or less (Duncan & others, 1988). Yet when the statistical reality was pitted against the single vivid case, the memorable case had greater influence on people's opinions about welfare recipients.

A memorable picture sometimes overwhelms a thousand statistics. When a little girl, Jessica McClure, fell into a Texas well, the attention of hundreds of millions of people worldwide was riveted on her three-day rescue. During those three days, more than 100,000 invisible children—"mere statistics" on some world health ledger—died of preventable starvation, diarrhea, and disease (Gore, 1992).

Based on the roughly 10-million-to-1 odds against a bet winning a state Lotto jackpot, one's chances are not much better than the odds of being struck by lightning. If you are an average British citizen and you place a bet in the National Lottery, the odds of your dying during the 20-minute National Lottery draw program on television are several times greater than the odds of your winning (*Chance News, 1999*).

"The human understanding is most excited by that which strikes and enters the mind at once and suddenly, and by which the imagination is immediately filled and inflated. It then begins almost imperceptibly to conceive and suppose that everything is similar to the few objects which have taken possession of the mind."

Francis Bacon, *Novum Organum,* 1620

Vivid events and mere statistics
When 12 teens were massacred in Littleton, Colorado, in April 1999, the Western world was aghast. "What has happened to America?" The less-noticed reality is that 12 teens, on average, die of gunshot wounds *every* day in the United States. In the last two decades, some 80,000 American children have been killed by firearms.

Overconfidence

Our use of intuitive heuristics when forming judgments, our eagerness to confirm the beliefs we already hold, and our knack for explaining away failures combine to create **overconfidence**, a tendency to overestimate the accuracy of our knowledge and judgments. Across various tasks, people overestimate what their performance was, is, or will be (Metcalfe, 1998).

In a classic study of overconfidence, Kahneman and Tversky (1979) asked people to answer obscure factual questions with a wide enough range to surely include the actual answer. The questions had this format: "I feel 98 percent certain that the population of New Zealand is more than _____ but less than _____." Nearly one-third of the time, people's estimates, made with 98 percent confidence, failed to include the correct answer (3.7 million as of 2000, in this instance). Although very sure of themselves, they were often wrong. Warning people against overconfidence

■ **overconfidence** the tendency to be more confident than correct—to overestimate the accuracy of one's beliefs and judgments.

Predict your own behavior
When will you finish reading this module?

"In creating these problems, we didn't set out to fool people. All our problems fooled us, too."

Amos Tversky (1985)

and urging them to broaden their estimates doesn't much reduce overconfidence. Exposing them to others' widely differing estimates does (Plous, 1996).

People are also more confident than correct when answering such questions as, "Is absinthe a liqueur or a precious stone?" (It's a licorice-flavored liqueur.) On questions where only 60 percent of people answer correctly, respondents typically feel 75 percent confident. Even when people feel 100 percent certain of their answers to such questions, they err about 15 percent of the time (Fischhoff & others, 1977).

Overconfidence plagues decisions outside the laboratory, too. It was an overconfident Hitler who invaded Russia, an overconfident Lyndon Johnson who waged war with North Vietnam, an overconfident Slobodan Milosovich who marched into Kosovo. Stockbrokers and investment managers market their services with confidence that they can outperform the market average in picking stocks, despite overwhelming evidence to the contrary (Malkiel, 1985, 1995). A purchase of stock X, recommended by a broker who judges this to be the time to buy, is usually balanced by a sale made by someone who judges this to be the time to sell. Despite their confidence, buyer and seller can't both be right.

To check people's confidence in making social judgments, David Dunning and his colleagues (1990) asked Stanford University students to guess a stranger's answers to 20 two-choice questions. Topics included whether the person studied for exams alone or with others, kept neat or messy lecture notes, and would pocket $5 found in a restaurant or turn it in. Knowing the type of questions (but not the actual questions), the students were first given a chance to interview the target person about academic interests, hobbies, family background, aspirations, strengths and weaknesses, astrological sign, anything they thought might prove helpful. Then the target person responded to the 20 questions, while the student interviewers predicted the answers.

The result? The interviewers were "markedly overconfident." Although they guessed right on 63 percent of their predictions, they felt, on average, 75 percent sure. When guessing their own roommates' responses to the 20 questions, students were somewhat more accurate—68 percent. But, again, their 78 percent confidence exceeded their accuracy. And the most confident people were also the most *over*confident. The same is true in studies where people have judged whether another is lying or telling the truth. On average, participants have been 5 percent accurate but 73 percent sure. Again, the most confident people are not more accurate (DePaulo & others, 1997).

Roger Buehler and his colleagues (1994) were struck by how routinely planners exhibit overconfidence in estimating how quickly and inexpensively they can do a project. In 1957, they predicted the Sydney Opera House would be completed in 1963 for $7 million. A reduced version actually opened in 1973 at a cost of $102 million. (Even as I wrote this we were moving into a new kitchen that our architect estimated would take one month, that our contractor estimated would take three months, and that actually took five months.) Buehler reports that students, too, are routinely overconfident about how quickly they can do assignments and write papers; they typically expect to finish projects ahead of schedule. But in fact, the projects generally get finished after about twice the number of days they predicted. Although people know they have often underestimated completion times, they remain overly confident of their next prediction.

Overconfidence does have adaptive value. Failing to appreciate one's potential for error when making military, economic, or political judgments can have devastating consequences, but so can a lack of self-confidence. People who err on the side of overconfidence live more happily and find it easier to make tough decisions (Baumeister, 1989; Taylor, 1989). Moreover, when given prompt and clear feedback on the accuracy of their judgments—as weather forecasters are after each day's predictions—people soon learn to assess their accuracy more realistically (Fischhoff, 1982). The wisdom to know when we know a thing and when we do not is born of experience.

Framing Decisions

A further test of rationality is whether the same issue, presented in two different but logically equivalent ways, will elicit the same answer. For example, one surgeon tells someone that 10 percent of people die while undergoing a particular surgery. Another tells someone that 90 percent survive. The information is the same. The effect is not. The risk seems greater to those who hear that 10 percent will die (Marteau, 1989; Rothman & Salovey, 1997).

The way we present an issue is called **framing**, and its effects are sometimes striking. Consumers respond more positively to ground beef described as "75 percent lean" rather than "25 percent fat" (Levin & Gaeth, 1988). Students are bothered more by hearing that 65 percent of their class had cheated than if told that 35 percent had not (Levin & others, 1988). People express more surprise when a "1 in 20" event happens than when an equivalent "10 in 200" event happens (Denes-Raj & others, 1995). And 9 in 10 college students rate a condom as effective if it has a supposed "95 percent success rate" in stopping the AIDS virus; only 4 in 10 think it successful when given a "5 percent failure rate" (Linville & others, 1992).

Consider how the framing effect influences economic and business decisions:

+ Merchants mark up their "regular prices" to appear to offer huge savings on "sale prices." A $100 coat marked down from $150 by Store X can seem like a better deal than the same coat priced regularly at $100 by Store Y (Urbany & others, 1988).

+ Many find taking a 7 percent pay cut in a period of zero inflation much more objectionable than receiving a 5 percent pay raise when inflation is 12 percent (Kahneman & others, 1986).

+ FedEx doesn't charge extra to pick up at your door; instead, they offer a "drop-off discount." Likewise, my dentist doesn't charge more if we pay later, though she does offer a 5 percent discount for immediate cash payment. FedEx and my dentist both understand that a fee framed as a forfeited discount irritates customers less than one framed as a surcharge, although they add up to the same thing.

That our judgments can flip-flop so dramatically is startling. It suggests that our judgments and decisions may not be well reasoned and that those who understand the power of framing can use it to influence important decisions—for example, by framing survey questions to support or reject a particular viewpoint.

"This CD player costs less than players selling for twice as much."

Belief Bias

Preview Question: What biases and tendencies put us at risk for error?

Intelligence is more than logical thinking. But logic matters. Philip Johnson-Laird (1999), an expert on logical reasoning, offers an example:

> If the test is to continue, then the turbines must be rotating fast enough.
> The turbine is not rotating fast enough.
> Therefore the test is *not* to continue.

■ **framing** the way an issue is posed; how an issue is framed can significantly affect decisions and judgments.

- **belief bias** the tendency for one's preexisting beliefs to distort logical reasoning, sometimes by making invalid conclusions seem valid, or valid conclusions seem invalid.

- **belief perseverance** clinging to one's initial conceptions after the basis on which they were formed has been discredited.

Deductions can be tricky, and the failure to draw this valid conclusion apparently contributed to the 1986 Chernobyl nuclear disaster. In Chernobyl as elsewhere, life requires us to venture deductions, and those who do it better, free of bias, more often succeed in the business of life.

We have seen that part of psychology's thinking about thinking emphasizes that we are prone to bias as we seek confirmation of our hunches, rely on efficient but fallible heuristics, display overconfidence, and fall prey to the effects of framing. But can we through logic escape the bias inflicted by our beliefs?

Logic helps, but we still find it easier to accept conclusions that agree with our opinions. Consider this logical argument:

Premise 1: Some communists are golfers.

Premise 2: All golfers are Marxists.

Conclusion: Some communists are Marxists.

In experiments, nearly everyone correctly recognized that the conclusion logically follows from the premises (Oakhill & others, 1989). But now consider this argument:

Premise 1: Some communists are golfers.

Premise 2: All golfers are capitalists.

Conclusion: Some communists are capitalists.

Many people had a harder time seeing that, given the premises, this conclusion is equally valid. Judge this next conclusion for yourself (adapted from Hunt, 1982):

Premise 1: Democrats support free speech.

Premise 2: Dictators are not democrats.

Conclusion: Dictators do not support free speech.

If that conclusion seems logical, you are experiencing **belief bias**—the tendency for our beliefs to distort our logic (Oakhill & others, 1990). (Premise 1 did not exclude the possibility that others, even dictators, can believe in free speech.) Consider another set of statements with *identical form and logic* and note how much easier it feels to refute the conclusion:

Premise 1: Robins have feathers.

Premise 2: Chickens are not robins.

Conclusion: Chickens do not have feathers.

Thus, belief bias: We more easily see the illogic of conclusions that run counter to our beliefs than of those that agree with our beliefs.

The Belief Perseverance Phenomenon

An additional source of irrationality is **belief perseverance**, our tendency to cling to our beliefs in the face of contrary evidence. Belief perseverance often fuels social conflict. Charles Lord and his colleagues (1979) revealed how this happens when they studied people with opposing views of capital punishment. Those on both sides studied two supposedly new research findings, one supporting and the other refuting the claim that the death penalty deters crime. Each side was more impressed by the study that supported its beliefs, and each readily disputed the other study. Thus, showing the pro- and anti–capital-punishment groups the *same* mixed evidence actually *increased* their disagreement.

If you want to rein in the belief perseverance phenomenon, a simple remedy exists: *Consider the opposite.* When Lord and his colleagues (1984) repeated the capital-punishment study, they asked some of their participants to be "as *objective* and

"God is love.
 Love is blind.
 Ray Charles is blind.
 Ray Charles is God."

Anonymous graffiti

"Once you have a belief, it influences how you perceive all other relevant information. Once you see a country as hostile, you are likely to interpret ambiguous actions on their part as signifying their hostility."

Political scientist Robert Jervis (1985)

unbiased as possible." The plea did nothing to reduce the biased evaluation of evidence. They asked another group to consider "whether you would have made the same high or low evaluations had exactly the same study produced results on the *other* side of the issue." Having imagined and pondered *opposite* findings, these people were much less biased in their evaluations of the evidence.

If people interpret ambiguous evidence as supporting their preexisting belief, would their belief be demolished by information that clearly discredits its basis? Not necessarily. Craig Anderson and Lee Ross discovered that it can be surprisingly difficult to change a false belief once a person has ideas that support it. In one study with Mark Lepper (1980), they asked people to consider whether risk-taking or cautious people make better fire fighters. Then they told half the people about a risk taker who was an excellent fire fighter and about a cautious person who was a poor fire fighter. From these cases, the participants surmised that risk takers tend to be better fire fighters. "Risk takers are braver," was the typical explanation. The researchers gave the other participants two cases suggesting the opposite conclusion, that cautious people are better fire fighters. These participants typically reasoned, "Cautious people think before they act. They're less likely to make foolish mistakes."

The researchers then discredited the basis for the beliefs by truthfully informing both groups that the cases were simply made up for the experiment. Did discrediting the evidence undermine the participants' newly formed beliefs? Not by much, because they held on to their explanations for why these new beliefs made sense. Although the evidence was gone, their theory survived.

The more we come to appreciate why our beliefs might be true, the more tightly we cling to them. Once people have explained to themselves why they believe that a child is "gifted" or "learning disabled," or that candidate X or Y will be more likely to preserve peace or start a war, or that women or men are naturally superior, they tend to ignore the evidence that undermines that belief. Prejudice persists.

Belief perseverance applies even to our beliefs about ourselves. Lepper and Ross, with Richard Lau (1986), encountered it after showing California high school students either an effective or a confusing instructional film. Each film demonstrated how to solve some reasoning problems. Those shown the effective film did well on a later test, felt successful, and surmised that they were good at solving such problems. Those shown the useless film did poorly, felt like failures, and surmised that they weren't very competent on that type of problem. Even when the researchers then explained that the *film* was responsible for their success or failure and showed them the other film as evidence, the students persisted in seeing themselves as either good or incompetent at that type of reasoning problem. (To prevent people from leaving the experiment feeling incompetent, the researchers more extensively debriefed and reassured them.)

And that, say the researchers, helps explain why early school failures can be so damaging. Even clearly demonstrating to children that their poor school performance "may well have been the consequence of an inept or biased teacher, a substandard school, or even prior social, cultural, or economic disadvantages" may fail to dent their feelings of incompetence. Once the belief that "I'm not very smart" forms, it tends to persist.

Belief perseverance

Do risk takers or cautious people make better fire fighters? Once we've formed opinions on a question like this and developed reasons for our views, we tend to cling to our beliefs—even if the basis for our opinion is undermined.

"I'm happy to say that my final judgment of a case is almost always consistent with my prejudgment of the case."

"To begin with, it was only tentatively that I put forward the views I have developed . . . but in the course of time they have gained such a hold upon me that I can no longer think in any other way."

Sigmund Freud, *Civilization and Its Discontents*, 1930

The belief perseverance phenomenon does not preclude our changing our beliefs. It's just that once beliefs form and get justified, it takes more compelling evidence to change them than it did to create them.

We have seen how our irrational thinking can plague our efforts to solve problems, make wise decisions, form valid judgments, and reason logically. From this we might conclude that our heads are indeed filled with straw. All in all, these and many other findings suggest "bleak implications for human rationality" (Nisbett & Borgida, 1975). Still, we should not forget that our cognition can be effective and wonderfully efficient: It enables our survival and our inventive genius.

In fact, one reason we function as well as we do is that in many real-life situations flawed reasoning *can* actually lead to correct conclusions (Funder, 1987). Physicians, for example, recognize the similarity between a patient's symptoms and those typical of a particular disease and then proceed to check out the hunch. In effect, their reasoning goes like this (Hunt, 1982):

+ Symptoms A, B, and C indicate disease X.
+ This patient has symptoms A, B, and C.
+ Therefore, I presume this patient has disease X.

The physician's conclusion is not necessarily logical. (Other diseases may also have symptoms A, B, and C.) Yet it is efficient and plausible, perhaps even probable. We reason, then, not so much by formal logic as by simplified, speedy heuristics, such as, "This situation reminds me of situations I have faced before, so what was true in those situations should be true here." Experts in other fields—even avid racetrack bettors who intuitively calculate the odds on horses (Ceci & Liker, 1986)—are similarly shrewd without necessarily knowing exactly how they reason.

Still, we should never underestimate the worth of sound reasoning. When we are deriving scientific hypotheses, playing chess, debating political issues, or evaluating a work of art, it helps to have the powers of reason at our disposal. This is why most college courses, including this one, aim to enhance your critical thinking. This is also why we psychologists study obstacles to problem solving and biases in reasoning. By expanding understanding of our irrational tendencies, we hope to steer people away from dumb decisions.

Simulating Thinking: Artificial Intelligence

Preview Questions: What is artificial intelligence? What are the relative advantages of artificial intelligence and human intelligence?

By 2040, speculates Carnegie Mellon robotics scientist Hans Moravec (1999), the soaring performance of computers and software will enable us finally to "achieve the original goal of robotics and a thematic mainstay of science fiction: a freely moving machine with the intellectual capabilities of a human being." And in the world beyond that, "it is likely that our descendants will cease to work in the sense that we do now. They will probably occupy their days with a variety of social, recreational and artistic pursuits, not unlike today's comfortable retirees and or the wealthy leisure classes." Time will judge this futurist vision, but this much seems sure: The better we understand our own brain, the more we realize what a grand model it provides of how future computers might work.

Indeed, it is a tribute to human cognition that there have been so many attempts to simulate human thinking on computers. **Artificial intelligence (AI)** is the science of designing computer systems to perform operations that mimic human thinking and do "intelligent" things. AI systems rely on massive stored information and rules for retrieving it. A hybrid of cognitive psychology and computer science, AI has two facets, one practical, the other theoretical.

■ **artificial intelligence (AI)** the science of designing and programming computer systems to do intelligent things and to simulate human thought processes such as intuitive reasoning, learning, and understanding language. Includes practical applications (chess playing, industrial robots, expert systems) and efforts to model human thinking inspired by our current understanding of how the brain works.

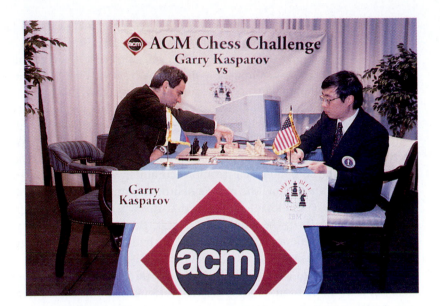

The practical side of AI includes the creation of industrial robots that can "sense" their environment; "expert systems" that can carry out chemical analyses, offer tax-planning advice, forecast weather, and help physicians diagnose their patients' diseases; and chess programs that now challenge or defeat the world's chess masters. Using voice-recognition software, my 91-year-old father, who does not type, can send e-mail. The words appear on a screen in response to his voice, correctly spelled as, say, *too*, *two*, or *to*, depending on the grammatical context.

The theoretical side of AI was pioneered by psychologist Herbert Simon. It studies how humans think by trying to design computer systems that mimic or rival human thought processes. The goal is a "unified theory of cognition" embodied in a computer system that can process information, solve problems, learn from experience, and remember.

Can computers mimic our thinking powers? In those areas where humans seem to have the most difficulty—manipulating huge amounts of numerical data, retrieving detailed information from memory, making decisions using specified rules—computers shine. Indeed, these areas of proficiency make computers indispensable to banks, libraries, and scientific laboratories. But even the most sophisticated computers are ironically dwarfed by the most ordinary of human mental abilities—recognizing a face; distinguishing a cat from a dog; knowing whether the word *line* refers to a rope or a fragment of poetry or a social come-on; exercising common sense; and experiencing emotions. "Human minds do more than process information," notes Donald Griffin (1984), "we experience beliefs, desires, fears, expectations, and many other subjective mental states."

Compare computer operations with the brain's. Electricity races through the computer's microcircuits millions of times faster than neural impulses travel through our systems. Yet most computers still process information serially—one step at a time (although their speed in jumping from task to task makes it *seem* they are doing multiple things at once). By contrast, the human brain actually does many things at once. One part of the brain analyzes speech while other parts recognize pictures, detect smells, or plan action. The visual system itself multitasks, splitting information about color, depth, movement, and form into separate channels, processing each channel simultaneously, and reassembling the information into a recognized image. The brain's capacity for parallel processing outclasses the traditional serial computer. Computer processing exceeds our thinking at tasks that use its unique strengths—vast memory and precise logic and retrieval. But computers have not duplicated the wide-ranging intelligence of a human

Discerning the difference between these two ads is much easier for a human than for a computer (from Schnitzer, 1984):

1. Car for sale. A classic! Lemon yellow coupe. Exterior is completely rustproof. Can be delivered upon request. No engine runs better. If the sun is out, you can remove the roof for the feel of the wind in your hair. Go ahead and kick the tires.

2. Car for sale. A classic lemon. Yellow coupe exterior is completely rust. Proof can be delivered upon request! No engine. Runs better if the sun is out. You can remove the roof. For the feel of the wind in your hair, go ahead and kick the tires.

■ **computer neural networks** computer circuits that mimic the brain's interconnected neural cells, performing tasks such as learning to recognize visual patterns and smells.

"Even though I am not religious, the amazement and wonder I have about the human mind is closer to religious awe than dispassionate analysis."

Bill Gates, 1997

"A $1000 personal computer will match the computing speed and capacity of the human brain by around the year 2020."

Ray Kuzweil, *The Age of Spiritual Machines: When Computers Exceed Human Intelligence*, 1999

mind, which can *all at once* converse naturally, recognize a caricatured face, use common sense, experience emotion, and consciously reflect on its own existence. Researchers who met in 1956 to chart AI never imagined that nearly a half-century later they would be struggling to simulate so many tasks that we find easy (Lenat, 1995). We still must learn computer languages, because they haven't learned ours.

Despite the "hype and bust" cycle of unfulfilled promises, excitement has grown over **computer neural networks**—computer systems designed to mimic the brain's interconnected neural units. As the brain has billions of neurons, each connected to thousands of others, so each computer processing unit can be connected to many others. The computer's electronic "neural network" can be programmed to execute rules that mimic how the brain's neurons communicate—with positive (excitatory) or negative (inhibitory) messages that fire when the signal strength reaches a certain threshold. As in the brain, the "neural" connections are programmed to gain strength with experience. The computer system's complex interaction is mind-boggling, but the basic idea is that simple.

The most exciting feature of artificial neural networks is their capacity to learn from experience, as some interconnections strengthen and others weaken. This feature, together with their capacity for parallel processing, enables neural network computers to learn to recognize particular shapes, sounds, and smells, tasks conventional computers find extremely difficult. The hoped-for payoffs are twofold. Neural network systems provide neuroscientists with new ways to test models of how living neural systems process sensations and memories. And they provide computer scientists with new insights into how to mimic the brain's thinking power.

A striking example: Thomas Landauer (1997, 1998) and his colleagues applied principles of computer neural networking to "read" another of my textbooks, the fifth edition of *Psychology* (1998). As their "Latent Semantic Analysis" program read the entire book, it associated all the individual words with one another. When then given many of the same multiple-choice questions that students using that text had encountered, the program got a passing grade. Moreover, the program reliably evaluated students' essay answers to factual questions. Because its evaluations are similar to those of actual professors, the program can give students helpful feedback on the content and coherence of their practice essays, as Landauer's University of Colorado students know well.

With computer software mimicking our amazing brains, we may someday benefit from robots that can learn or from telephone systems that can understand and translate speech, allowing, for example, an English speaker and a Spanish speaker to

Artificial reasoning
William McCune of Argonne National Laboratory has created a computer reasoning program. In 1996 it solved a problem that had stumped mathematicians for 60 years, offering a proof that would have been called creative if a human had thought of it (Kolata, 1996).

converse without an interpreter. If that sounds futuristic, think about the surprise our late–nineteenth-century ancestors would feel if they could return to see people flying through the air, watching sports live on a picture tube, or receiving their daily e-mail.

Let's pause to consider the question posed on page 365—how deserving are we of our name *Homo sapiens*? If we are getting graded on decision making and judgment, our error-prone species might rate a C+. On problem solving, where humans are inventive yet vulnerable to fixation, we would probably receive better marks, perhaps a B. On cognitive efficiency, our fallible but quick heuristics earn us an A.

What time is it now? On page 374, did you underestimate or overestimate how quickly you would finish the module?

REVIEW AND REFLECT:

Thinking

Our cognitive system receives, perceives, and retrieves information, which we then use to think and communicate, sometimes wisely, sometimes foolishly.

How do concepts help us to simplify the world around us and bring order to it?

Concepts simplify and order the world by organizing it into a hierarchy of categories. Concepts often form around prototypes, or best examples of a category. Matching objects and ideas with prototypes is an efficient way of making snap judgments about what belongs in a specific category.

What strategies do we use to solve problems, and what obstacles hinder our problem solving?

When faced with a novel situation for which no well-learned response will do, we may use such strategies as trial and error, algorithms, and rule-of-thumb heuristics. Sometimes the solution comes in a flash of insight. We do, however, face obstacles to successful problem solving. The confirmation bias predisposes us to verify rather than challenge our hypotheses. And fixations, such as mental set and functional fixedness, may prevent our taking a needed fresh perspective on a problem.

How do we arrive at the hundreds of decisions and judgments we make each day?

Our use of heuristics, such as representativeness and availability, provides highly efficient but occasionally misleading guides for making quick decisions and forming intuitive judgments. Our tendencies to seek confirmation of our hypotheses and to use quick and easy heuristics can blind us to our vulnerability to error, a phenomenon known as overconfidence. And the way someone poses, or frames, a question affects our responses.

What biases and tendencies put us at risk for error?

We tend to show a belief bias in our reasoning, accepting as more logical those conclusions that agree with our beliefs. We also exhibit belief perseverance, clinging to our ideas because the explanation we accepted as valid lingers in the mind even after the basis for the ideas has been discredited. Yet despite our capacity for error and our susceptibility to bias, human cognition is remarkably efficient and adaptive. As we gain expertise in a field, we grow adept at making quick, shrewd judgments.

What is artificial intelligence? What are the relative advantages of artificial intelligence and human intelligence?

AI is a hybrid science that combines cognitive psychology and computer science in an attempt to design and program computers that can simulate human thinking. Experimental computers and robots are performing operations that mimic intelligent thought. The most notable AI successes focus computer capacities for memory and precise logic on specific tasks, such as playing chess. For now, the brain's capacity for processing unrelated information simultaneously and the wide range of its abilities dwarf those of the most sophisticated computer. But hopes grow that a new generation of computer neural networks, mimicking the brain's neural networks, will produce more humanlike capabilities.

Terms and Concepts to Remember

cognition, p. 366
concept, p. 366
prototype, p. 366
algorithm, p. 367
heuristic, p. 367
insight, p. 367
confirmation bias, p. 368
fixation, p. 369
mental set, p. 369
functional fixedness, p. 370

representativeness heuristic, p. 371
availability heuristic, p. 371
overconfidence, p. 373
framing, p. 375
belief bias, p. 376
belief perseverance, p. 376
artificial intelligence (AI), p. 378
computer neural networks, p. 380

Test Yourself

28.1. We use the concept "bird" to think and talk about a variety of creatures, all of which have wings and feathers. A concept is
  a. a mental grouping of similar things.
  b. an example of insight.
  c. a fixation on certain characteristics.
  d. another word for "prototype."

28.2. Sometimes we solve problems through trial and error, trying hundreds or even thousands of solutions before finding one that works. At other times we are more methodical or systematic. The most systematic procedure for solving a problem is
  a. heuristics.   c. insight.
  b. an algorithm.   d. intuition.

28.3. A major obstacle to problem solving is confirmation bias, the tendency to search for information that confirms our preconceptions while ignoring information that might prove us wrong. Another obstacle to problem solving is fixation, which is
  a. an error we make when we base our judgments on certain vivid memories.
  b. the art of framing the same question in two different ways.
  c. the inability to view a problem from a new perspective.
  d. a rule of thumb for judging the likelihood of an event in terms of our mental image of it.

28.4. You move into a new neighborhood and notice that your next-door neighbor is very neatly dressed, wears glasses, and is reading a Greek play. Given a choice between her being a librarian and a store clerk, you incorrectly guess that she is a librarian. Your incorrect judgment is probably due to
  a. the availability heuristic.
  b. confirmation bias.
  c. overconfidence.
  d. the representativeness heuristic.

Continued

28.5. After a New York City bombing by foreign-born terrorists in 1993, many observers incorrectly assumed that the 1995 bombing of a federal building in Oklahoma City was probably the work of foreign-born terrorists. This assumption illustrates

a. belief perseverance.
b. the availability heuristic.
c. functional fixedness.
d. confirmation bias.

28.6. The way an issue is posed can affect our decisions and judgments. For example, one study found that people perceived student cheating to be worse if told that 65 percent of students had cheated than if told that 35 percent of students had not cheated. In this case people's reactions were influenced by

a. belief perseverance.   c. confirmation bias.
b. fixation.   d. framing.

28.7. Some biases and tendencies put us at risk for illogical thinking. Our tendency to cling to an idea in the face of overwhelming evidence that disproves it is known as

a. rule-of-thumb heuristics.   c. belief perseverance.
b. confirmation bias.   d. functional fixedness.

28.8. Computer neural networks are designed to mimic the brain's neural networks. Computer neural networks differ from earlier generations of artificial intelligence systems primarily in their abilities to

a. learn from experience and do parallel processing.
b. translate speech and do serial processing.
c. perform algorithms and do serial processing.
d. perform heuristics and do parallel processing.

Review: The availability heuristic is a quick-and-easy but sometimes misleading guide to judging reality. What is the availability heuristic?

Reflect: People's *perceptions* of risk, often biased by vivid images from movies or the news, are surprisingly unrelated to actual risks. (People may hide in the basement during thunderstorms but fail to buckle their seat belts in the car.) What are the things you fear? Are some of those fears out of proportion to statistical risk? Are you failing, in other areas of your life, to take reasonable precautions?

Answers to the Test Yourself and Review questions can be found in the green appendix at the end of the book.

Language and Thought

The most tangible indication of our thinking power is **language**—our spoken, written, or gestured words and the ways we combine them as we think and communicate. Humans have long and proudly proclaimed that language sets us above all other animals. "When we study human language," asserted linguist Noam Chomsky (1972), "we are approaching what some might call the 'human essence,' the qualities of mind that are, so far as we know, unique" to humans. To cognitive scientist Steven Pinker (1990), language is "the jewel in the crown of cognition." When the human vocal tract evolved the capacity to utter vowels, our capacity for language exploded, catapulting our species forward (Diamond, 1989). Whether spoken, written, or signed, language enables us to communicate complex ideas from person to person and to transmit civilization's accumulated knowledge across generations.

Language Structure

Preview Question: What are the three basic elements found in every language?

Consider how we might go about inventing a language. For a spoken language, we would need three building blocks. First, we would need a set of basic sounds, which linguists call **phonemes**. To say *bat* we utter the phoneme sounds *b, a,* and *t. Chat* also has three phonemes—*ch, a,* and *t.* Languages have varying numbers of phonemes. English has about 40; other languages have anywhere from half to twice that many.

Changes in phonemes produce changes in meaning. Variations in the vowel sound between *b* and *t* create 12 different meanings: *bait, bat, beat/beet, bet, bit, bite, boat, boot, bought, bout,* and *but* (Fromkin & Rodman, 1983). Generally, though, consonant phonemes carry more information than do vowel phonemes. The treth ef thes stetement shed be evedent frem thes bref demenstretien.

People who grow up learning one set of phonemes usually have difficulty pronouncing the phonemes of another language. The native English-speaker may smile at the native German-speaker's difficulties with the *th* sound, which often makes *this* sound like *dis.* But the German-speaker can smile at the problems English-speakers have rolling the German *r* or pronouncing the breathy *ch* in *Ich,* the German word for the personal pronoun *I.*

Sign language also has phonemelike building blocks defined by hand shapes and movements. Like speakers, native signers of one language may have difficulty with the phonemes of another. Chinese native signers who come to America and learn sign usually "sign with an accent," notes researcher Ursula Bellugi (1994).

The second building block is the **morpheme**, the smallest unit of language that carries meaning. In English, a few morphemes are also phonemes—the personal pronoun *I* and the article *a,* for instance. But most are combinations of two or more phonemes. Some morphemes, like *bat,* are words, but others are only parts of words. Morphemes include prefixes and suffixes, such as the *pre-* in *preview* or the *-ed* that shows past tense. *Undesirables* has four morphemes—*un-desir-able-s*—each of which adds to the word's total meaning.

Finally, our new language must have a **grammar**, a system of rules (called *semantics* and *syntax*) that enables us to communicate with and understand others. **Semantics** is the set of rules we use to derive meaning from morphemes, words, and even sentences. A semantic rule tells us that adding *-ed* to *laugh* means that it happened in the past. **Syntax** refers to the rules we use to order words into sentences. One rule of

■ **language** our spoken, written, or gestured words and the ways we combine them to communicate meaning.

■ **phoneme** in a spoken language, the smallest distinctive sound unit.

■ **morpheme** in a language, the smallest unit that carries meaning; may be a word or a part of a word (such as a prefix).

■ **grammar** a system of rules in a language that enables us to communicate with and understand others.

■ **semantics** the set of rules by which we derive meaning from morphemes, words, and sentences in a given language; also, the study of meaning.

■ **syntax** the rules for combining words into grammatically sensible sentences in a given language.

How many morphemes are in the word cats? (See page 387)

Language transmits culture
The actual words and grammar may differ from culture to culture, but every society has a history that it transmits in story form to its children. Here, a group of Ivory Coast boys listen as an elder retells a tribal legend.

From The Wall Street Journal—permission Cartoon Features Syndicate.

"Let me get this straight now. Is what you want to build a jean factory or a gene factory?"

A cultural universal: In every language, the commonest words are the shortest. As a word or phrase is used more and more, it often gets shortened. *Television* becomes *TV*, compact disc becomes *CD*, electronic mail becomes *e-mail* (Triandis, 1994).

Although you probably know about 80,000 words, you use only 150 words for about half of what you say.

English syntax says that adjectives usually come before nouns, so we say *white house*. Spanish adjectives usually come after nouns, so a Spanish speaker says *casa blanca*. The English rules of syntax allow the sentence *They are hunting dogs.* Given the context, semantics will tell us whether it refers to dogs that seek animals or people seeking dogs.

All 5000 human languages are intricately complex. "There are 'stone age' societies," says Steven Pinker (1995), "but they do not have 'stone age' languages." Contrary to the illusion that less-educated people speak ungrammatically, they simply speak a different dialect. To a linguist, "ain't got none" is grammatically equal to "doesn't have any."

Note, however, that language becomes more complex as you move from phoneme to morpheme to word to sentence. In English, the relatively small number of 40 or so phonemes can be combined to form more than 100,000 morphemes, which alone or in combination produce the 616,500 word forms in the *Oxford English Dictionary* (including 290,500 main entries such as *meat* and 326,000 subentries such as *meat eater*). We can then use these words to create an infinite number of sentences, most of which (like this one) are original. Like life itself constructed from the genetic code's simple alphabet, language is complexity built of simplicity.

Language Development

Preview Questions: When do children acquire language? Do humans have an inborn capacity for acquiring language, or is language development another instance of learning guided by association, imitation, and reinforcement?

Make a quick guess: How many words did you learn in one average day during the years between your first birthday and your high school graduation?

The average secondary school graduate knows some 80,000 words (Miller & Gildea, 1987). That averages (after age 1) to nearly 5000 words learned each year, or 13 each day! How you did it—how the 5000 words a year you learned could so far outnumber the roughly 200 words a year that your schoolteachers consciously taught you—is one of the great human wonders. Before children can add 2 + 2, they are creating their own original and grammatically appropriate sentences. Most parents would have trouble stating the rules of syntax. Yet their preschoolers comprehend and speak with a facility that puts to shame a college student struggling to learn a foreign language or a scientist struggling to simulate natural language on a computer. How does our astonishing facility for language unfold, and how can we explain it?

Acquiring Language

Children's language development mirrors language structure—it moves from simplicity to complexity. Infants start without language (*in fantis* means "not speaking"). Yet by 4 months of age, babies can read lips and discriminate speech sounds. They prefer to look at a face that matches a sound, so we know they can recognize that *ah* comes from wide open lips and *ee* from a mouth with corners pulled back (Kuhl & Meltzoff, 1982). At about this age, babies enter a **babbling stage** in which they spontaneously utter a variety of sounds such as *ah-goo*.

Babbling is not an imitation of adult speech, for it includes sounds from various languages, even sounds that do not occur in the household's language. From this early babbling, a listener could not identify an infant as being, say, French, Korean, or Ethiopian. Deaf infants babble (repeat syllablelike gestures), too (Petitto & Marentette, 1991). It seems, then, that before nurture molds our speech, nature enables a wide range of possible phonemes.

Eventually our babbling comes to resemble the characteristic sounds and intonations of our household language. By the time infants are about 10 months old, their babbling has changed so that a trained ear can identify the language of the household (de Boysson-Bardies & others, 1989). Phoneme sounds outside the infant's native tongue begin to disappear. And infants gradually lose their ability to discriminate sounds they never hear. Clever experiments by Janet Werker (1989) reveal that at 6 months infants can perceive subtle phoneme differences from other languages, but by 12 months they cannot (**FIGURE 29.1**). Without exposure to other languages, we became functionally deaf to speech sounds outside our native language. Thus, by adulthood those who speak only English cannot discriminate certain Japanese phonemes. Nor can Japanese adults with no training in English distinguish between the English *r* and *l*. Thus (believe it or not), *la-la-ra-ra* may sound like the same repeated syllable to a Japanese adult. This makes life challenging for the Japanese tourist who is told the train station is "just after the next light." The next what? After the street veering right or farther down, after the traffic light?

Around the first birthday (the exact age varies from child to child), most children enter the **one-word stage**. Having already learned that sounds carry meanings, they begin to use sounds to communicate meaning. Their first words usually contain only one syllable—*ma* or *da*, for instance—and may be barely recognizable. But family members quickly learn to understand the infant's language, and gradually it conforms more and more to the family's language. At this one-word stage, an inflected word may equal a sentence. "Doggy!" may mean "Look at the dog out there!"

- **babbling stage** beginning at 3 to 4 months, the stage of speech development in which the infant spontaneously utters various sounds at first unrelated to the household language.

- **one-word stage** the stage in speech development, from about age 1 to 2, during which a child speaks mostly in single words.

FIGURE 29.1

Testing for phoneme perception
We are all born with the ability to recognize speech sounds from all the world's languages. In Janet Werker's lab, an infant is reinforced with applause and by activating toy animals when he looks to the right after hearing a changed sound (as in *ba, ba, ba, ba, da, da*). Adult Hindi-speakers and young infants from English-speaking homes can easily discriminate two Hindi *t* sounds not spoken in English. By about age 1, however, English-speaking listeners rarely perceive the sound difference. (Adapted from Werker, 1989.)

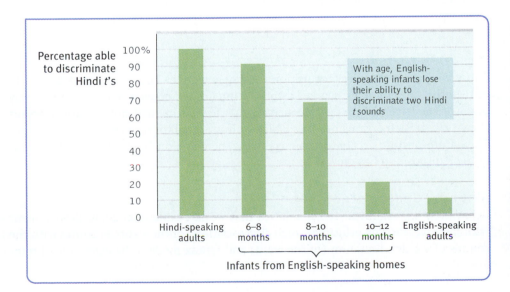

Percentage able to discriminate Hindi *t*'s

With age, English-speaking infants lose their ability to discriminate two Hindi *t* sounds

Hindi-speaking adults | 6–8 months | 8–10 months | 10–12 months | English-speaking adults

Infants from English-speaking homes

"Got idea. Talk better. Combine words. Make sentences."

Children typically use more and more single words during the second year. At about 18 months, their word learning begins to explode, from a word per week to a word per day. Before their second birthday, they usually enter the **two-word stage**, when they start uttering two-word sentences (Table 29.1). Language at this stage is characterized by **telegraphic speech**: Like telegrams (TERMS ACCEPTED. SEND MONEY), this early form of speech contains mostly nouns and verbs (*Want juice*). Also like telegrams, it follows rules of syntax; the words are in a sensible order. The English-speaking child typically says adjectives before nouns—*big doggy* rather than *doggy big*.

TABLE 29.1

SUMMARY OF LANGUAGE DEVELOPMENT

Month (approximate)	Stage
4	Babbles many speech sounds.
10	Babbling reveals household language.
12	One-word stage.
24	Two-word, telegraphic speech.
24+	Language develops rapidly into complete sentences.

Source: U.S. Department of Education

There seems to be no "three-word stage." Once children move out of the two-word stage, they quickly begin uttering longer phrases (Fromkin & Rodman, 1983). Although the sentences may still resemble a telegraphed message, they continue to follow the rules of syntax (*Mommy get ball*). By early elementary school, the child understands complex sentences and begins to enjoy the humor conveyed by double meanings: "You never starve in the desert because of all the sand-which-is there."

Explaining Language Development

Those who study language acquisition inevitably wonder how we do it. Attempts to answer this question have sparked a spirited intellectual controversy. The controversy parallels the larger debate over the behaviorist view of the malleable organism versus the view that each organism comes biologically prepared to learn certain associations. The nature-nurture debate surfaces again and, here as elsewhere, appreciation for innate predisposition has grown.

Skinner: Operant Learning

Behaviorist B. F. Skinner (1957) believed that we can explain language development with familiar learning principles, such as association (of the sights of things with the sounds of words), imitation (of the words and syntax modeled by others), and rein-

■ **two-word stage** beginning about age 2, the stage in speech development during which a child speaks mostly two-word statements.

■ **telegraphic speech** early speech stage in which the child speaks like a telegram—"go car"—using mostly nouns and verbs and omitting "auxiliary" words.

forcement (with success, smiles, and hugs when the child says something right). Thus, Skinner (1985) argued, babies learn to talk in many of the same ways that animals learn to peck keys and press bars: "Verbal behavior evidently came into existence when, through a critical step in the evolution of the human species, the vocal musculature became susceptible to operant conditioning."

Chomsky: Inborn Universal Grammar

The learning perspective in language goes well beyond Skinner's ideas, which linguist Noam Chomsky (1959, 1987) thinks were naive. Surely, Chomsky has said, a Martian scientist observing children in a single-language community would conclude that language is almost entirely inborn. But it isn't. Children do learn the language used in their environment. However, the rate at which they acquire words and grammar without being taught is too extraordinary to be explained solely by learning principles. Children generate all sorts of sentences they have never heard and, therefore, could not be imitating. (No parent teaches the sentence, "I hate you, Daddy.") They begin using morphemes in a predictable order. They begin adding -ing to words. Then they start using the prepositions in and on. Then come a and the, followed by is (Brown, 1973). There are 3,628,800 ways to arrange this sentence's 10 words. Only a handful of them make any sense. Yet any 4-year-old could pick them out from among the 3,628,700+ nonsensical orderings.

Answer to question on page 383: Two—*cat* and *-s*.

Moreover, many of the errors young children make result from overgeneralizing logical grammatical rules, such as adding -ed to make the past tense (from de Cuevas, 1990):

Child: My teacher holded the baby rabbits and we petted them.
Mother: Did you say your teacher held the baby rabbits?
Child: Yes.
Mother: Did you say she held them tightly?
Child: No, she holded them loosely.

Chomsky (1987) likens the behaviorist view of how language develops to filling a bottle with water. He instead views language development as "helping a flower to grow in its own way." It is, he believes, akin to sexual maturation: Given adequate nurture, it just "happens to the child." All human languages have the same grammatical building blocks, such as nouns and verbs, subjects and objects, negations and questions. Even sign language, whether produced by deaf Chinese or American children, has structural similarities (Goldin-Meadow & Mylander, 1998).

Our 5000 human languages are therefore dialects of the "universal grammar" for which our brains are prewired. Thanks to our inborn universal grammar, we readily learn the specific grammar of whatever language we hear. It happens so naturally—as naturally as birds learning to fly—that training hardly helps. Expose children to language and they will soak it up. If not exposed to a language, a group of children will make up their own. Without exposure to language, deaf children, too, will spontaneously create one with gestures, complete with sophisticated grammar (Horgan, 1995; Pinker, 1995).

Other worlds may have languages that, for us humans, are unlearnable, but our world does not. Chomsky maintains that our language acquisition capacity is like a box—a "language acquisition device"—in which grammar switches are thrown as children experience their language. Thus, English-speaking children learn to put the object of a sentence last ("She ate an apple"). Japanese-speaking children put the object before the verb ("She an apple ate"). We are born with the hardware and an operating system; experience writes the software (**FIGURE 29.2**, page 388).

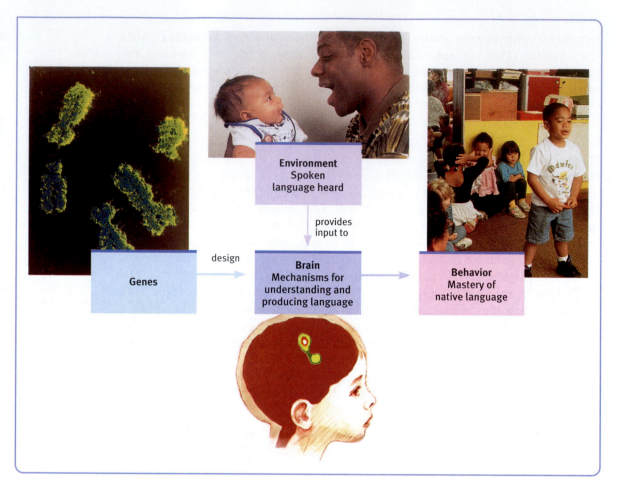

FIGURE 29.2
Nature and nurture
Genes design the mechanisms for a language, and experience activates them as it modifies the brain. Grow up in Paris and you will speak French (environment matters), but not if you are a cat (genes matter).

Creating a language
Brought together as if on a desert island (actually a school), Nicaragua's young deaf children created their own Nicaraguan Sign Language, complete with words and intricate grammar. Our biological predisposition to language does not create language in a vacuum. But activated by a social context, nature and nurture worked creatively together (Osborne, 1999).

Cognitive Neuroscientists: Statistical Learning

Cognitive neuroscientists still debate how much of our language capacity is inborn (Seidenberg, 1997). With experience (but with no "inborn" linguistic rules), computational models inspired by neural networks can learn to form past-tense verbs appropriately. They can learn, for example, to change words ending in *-ow* to *-ew*, as in *throw/threw*. To some scientists, this suggests the brain could be a blanker slate than Chomsky believes.

This network learning differs from the simple form of language learning envisioned by Skinner. It instead involves gradual changes in network connections based on experience. Given training through exposure to many language examples, a neuronlike network can learn a language's statistical structure. "Plane" and "left" have multiple possible meanings. But when put together—"The plane left for Melbourne"—we instantly know that the *plane* probably is an airplane and *left* is the past tense of *leave*.

It is not just computer models of neural networks but also human infants that display a remarkable ability to learn statistical aspects of human speech. When you or I listen to an unfamiliar language, the syllables all run together. Someone unfamiliar with English might, for example, hear the "United Nations" as the Uneye Tednay Shuns. Before our first birthday, our brains were discerning word breaks by statistically analyzing which syllables most often go together. Jenny Saffran and her colleagues (1996) showed this by exposing 8-month-old infants to a computer voice speaking an unbroken, monotone string of nonsense syllables (*bidakupadotigolabu-bidaku . . .*). After just two minutes of exposure, the infants were able to recognize (as indicated by their attention) three-syllable sequences that appeared repeatedly.

Follow-up research offers further testimony to infants' surprising knack for soaking up language:

+ Six-month-old infants seem to understand who "Mommy" and "Daddy" are. In one experiment, they watched two TV monitors, one showing their mother, the other their father. When a synthesized voice said *Mommy* or *Daddy*, the infants looked more at the named parent (Tincoff & Jusczyk, 1999).

+ Seven-month-old infants can learn simple sentence structures. After repeatedly hearing syllable sequences that follow one rule, such as *ga-ti-ga* and *li-na-li* (an ABA pattern), they listen longer to syllables in a different sequence, such as *wo-fe-fe* (an ABB pattern) rather than *wo-fe-wo*. Their detecting the difference between the two patterns suggests that babies come with a built-in readiness to learn grammatical rules (Marcus & others, 1999).

+ Infants who are 7.5 months old can detect familiar English words in the midst of fluent speech. They listen longer to passages with words they have repeatedly heard before than to sentences with unfamiliar words (Jusczyk, 1997).

The effect of language exposure during infancy illustrates the importance of learning. But Chomsky's view that our brain constrains how we learn language and that it may come prewired to look for grammatical rules seems to survive recent challenges. Moreover, a study of 2-year-old twins indicates that genes do play a role in determining how quickly children learn language (Plomin & Dale, 2000).

Nevertheless, our learning during life's first seven or so years is critical. Here's a dramatic example: Those who learn a second language as adults usually speak it with the accent of their first language. Do they master the foreign grammar better than the accent? To find out, Jacqueline Johnson and Elissa Newport (1991) gave Korean and Chinese immigrants to the United States a grammar test, requiring them to identify each of 276 sentences ("Yesterday the hunter shoots a deer") as grammatically correct or incorrect. Some of the test-takers had immigrated in early childhood, others as adults. Regardless of their age at immigration, each had been in the United States for approximately 10 years. Nevertheless, as **FIGURE 29.3** reveals, those who learned their second language early learned it best. Chomsky would say that once the grammar switches are thrown during a child's developing years, mastering another grammar becomes more difficult.

*Brain scans reveal a difference in how the brain records a second language learned early versus later in life. Adults who learned a second language early in life use the *same* patch of frontal lobe tissue when recounting an event in one language, then another. Those who learned their second tongue after childhood display activity in an *adjacent* brain area while using their second language (Kim & others, 1997).*

Just as a flower's growth will be stunted without nourishment, so, too, will children become linguistically stunted if isolated from language during the critical period for its acquisition. Consider Genie, who spent most of her early years tied to a chair without being spoken to. When discovered by Los Angeles authorities in 1970 at age 13, she was mute and uncomprehending (Curtiss, 1977, 1981). In the years that followed, Genie learned some individual words but not how to construct grammatically correct sentences. Today, she lives in a home for mentally impaired adults (Rymer, 1993).

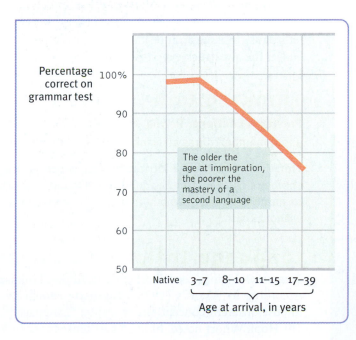

Percentage correct on grammar test

The older the age at immigration, the poorer the mastery of a second language

Native 3–7 8–10 11–15 17–39

Age at arrival, in years

FIGURE 29.3 New language learning gets harder with age
Young children have a readiness to learn language. Ten years after coming to the United States, Asian immigrants took a grammar test. Those who arrived before age 8 understood grammar as well as native speakers. Those who arrived later did not. (From Johnson & Newport, 1991.)

Little statistician
Human infants come with a remarkable capacity to analyze language statistically and to discern words and grammatical rules. This is a tribute to both nature and nurture—to our biological machinery for learning language.

The impact of early experience is also evident in comparisons of deaf and hearing children. Hearing children of hearing-speaking parents and deaf children of deaf-signing parents have much in common. Both groups babble as infants—hearing children by repeating sounds, deaf children by repeating elementary sign gestures (Petitto & Marentette, 1991). Both groups develop vocabularies at comparable rates (Meier, 1991). For both groups, later-than-usual exposure to language (at age 2 or 3) unleashes their brain's idle language capacity, producing a rush of language. But consider the 90+ percent of deaf children born to hearing-nonsigning parents. These children typically do not experience language during their early years. Compared with deaf children exposed to sign language from birth, those who learn to sign as teens or adults are like immigrants who learn English after childhood. They can master the basic words and learn to order them, but they never become as fluent as native signers in producing and comprehending subtle grammatical differences (Newport, 1990).

To summarize, children's genes design complex brain wiring that prepares them to learn language as they interact with their caregivers. Skinner's emphasis on learning helps explain why infants acquire the language they hear and how they add new words. (So does infants' ability to learn statistical probabilities in speech.) Chomsky's emphasis on our built-in readiness to learn grammar rules helps explain why preschoolers acquire language so readily and use grammar so well. Once again, we see biology and experience working together.

Returning to our debate about how deserving we are of our name *Homo sapiens*, let's pause to issue an interim report card. When it comes to learning and using language, the awestruck experts would surely award the human species an A+.

"Childhood is the time for language, no doubt about it. Young children, the younger the better, are good at it; it is child's play. It is a onetime gift to the species."

Lewis Thomas, *The Fragile Species*, 1992

No means no! No matter how you say it
Deaf children of deaf-signing parents and hearing children of hearing parents have much in common. They develop language skills at about the same rate, and they are equally effective at opposing parental wishes and demanding their way.

Thinking and Language

Preview Questions: To what extent does language control what we think, perceive, and remember? Does all thinking depend on language?

Thinking and language intricately intertwine. Asking which comes first is one of psychology's chicken-and-egg questions. Do our ideas come first and we wait for words to name them? Or are our thoughts conceived in words and therefore unthinkable without them?

Language Influences Thinking

Linguist Benjamin Lee Whorf contended that language determines the way we think. According to Whorf's (1956) **linguistic relativity** hypothesis, different languages impose different conceptions of reality: "Language itself shapes a man's basic ideas." The Hopi, Whorf noted, have no past tense for their verbs. Therefore, he contended, a Hopi could not so readily *think* about the past.

Whorf's relativity hypothesis would probably not occur to people who speak only one language and view that language as simply a vehicle for thought. But to those who speak two dissimilar languages, such as English and Japanese, it seems obvious that a person thinks differently in different languages (Brown, 1986). Unlike English, which has a rich vocabulary for self-focused emotions such as anger, Japanese has many words for interpersonal emotions such as sympathy (Markus & Kitayama, 1991). Many bilinguals report that they even have a different sense of self, depending on which language they are using (Matsumoto, 1994). After emigrating from Asia to North America, bilinguals may even reveal different personalities when taking the same personality test in their two languages (Dinges & Hull, 1992). Learn a language and you learn about a culture. When a language becomes extinct—the likely fate of most of the world's 5000 remaining languages—the world loses the culture and thinking that hang on that language. "To destroy a people, destroy their language," observed poet Joy Hajo.

To say that language *determines* the way we think is much too strong. People who speak the same language often think very differently. A conservative and a liberal may know the same words, use the same grammar, yet have conflicting attitudes. Moreover, a Papua New Guinean without our words for shapes and colors nevertheless perceives them much as we do (Rosch, 1974).

Our words, however, have some *influence* on what we think (Hardin & Banaji, 1993). Whether living in Britain or New Guinea, people use their language when classifying and remembering colors (Davidoff & others, 1999). Imagine that while viewing three colors you called (using your color words) two of them yellow and one of them blue. Later you would likely see and recall the yellows as being more similar. People in the Berinmo tribe, which has words for two different shades of yellow, would better recall the distinctions between the two yellows.

Given the subtle influence of words on thinking, we do well to choose our words carefully. Referring to women as *girls*—as in "the girls at the office"—perpetuates a view of women's having lower status, does it not? Or consider the generic use of the pronoun *he*. Does it make any difference whether I write "A child learns language as *he* interacts with *his* caregivers" or "Children learn language as *they* interact with *their* caregivers"? Some argue it makes no difference because every reader knows "the masculine gender shall be deemed and taken to include females" (as the British Parliament declared in 1850).

But is the generic *he* always taken to include females? Twenty studies consistently found that it is not (Henley, 1989). For example, Janet Hyde (1984) asked children to finish stories for which she gave them a first line, such as "When a kid goes to school, _____ often feels excited on the first day." When Hyde used *he* in the blank, the children's stories were nearly always about males. *He or she* in the blank resulted in female characters about one-third of the time. Studies with adolescents and adults in North America and New Zealand have found similar effects of the generic *he* (Hamilton, 1988; Martyna, 1978; Ng, 1990). Sentences about "the artist and his work" tend to conjure up images of a man. Similarly, ambiguous actions taken by a "chairman of the board" seem to reveal an assertive and independent personality. The same actions taken by a "chairperson of the board" seem to reveal a warmer, more caring personality (McConnell & Fazio, 1996).

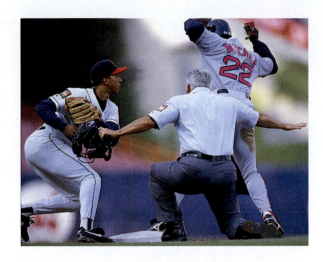

A safe sign
We have outfielder William Hoy to thank for baseball sign language. The first deaf player to join the major leagues in 1892, he invented hand signals for "Strike!" "Safe!" (shown here) and "Yerr Out!" (Pollard, 1992). Such gestures worked so well that referees in all sports now use invented signs, and fans are fluent in sports sign language.

"All words are pegs to hang ideas on."

Henry Ward Beecher, *Proverbs from Plymouth Pulpit*, 1887

"To call forth a concept, a word is needed."

Antoine Lavoisier, *Elements of Chemistry*, 1789

■ **linguistic relativity** Whorf's hypothesis that language determines the way we think.

Consider, too, that people use generic pronouns selectively, as in "the doctor . . . he" and "the secretary . . . she" (MacKay, 1983). If *he* and *his* were truly gender-free, we shouldn't skip a beat when hearing that "a nurse must answer his calls" or that "man, like other mammals, nurses his young." That we are startled indicates that *his* carries a gender connotation that clashes with our idea of *nurse*.

Language's power to influence thought makes vocabulary building a crucial part of education. To expand language is to expand the ability to think. In young children, thinking develops hand in hand with language (Gopnik & Meltzoff, 1986). And what is true for preschoolers is true for everyone: *It pays to increase your word power.* That's why most textbooks, including this one, introduce new words—to teach new ideas and new ways of thinking.

Increased word power helps explain what McGill University researcher Wallace Lambert (1992; Lambert & others, 1993) calls the "bilingual advantage." Bilingual children in Canada, Switzerland, Israel, South Africa, and Singapore outperform monolinguals on intelligence tests. Knowing this, Lambert helped devise a Canadian program that enables English-speaking children to be immersed in French. (From 1981 to 1999, the number of non-Quebec Canadian children immersed in French rose from 65,000 to 280,000 [Commissioner, 1999].) For most of their first three years in school, the English-speaking children are taught entirely in French, and thereafter gradually shift by the end of their schooling to classes mostly in English. Not surprisingly, the children attain a natural French fluency unrivaled by other methods of language teaching. Moreover, compared with similarly capable children in control conditions, they do so without detriment to their English fluency, and with increased aptitude scores, math scores, and appreciation for French-Canadian culture.

So, for English-speaking Canadians, immersion followed by bilingual education pays dividends. Does bilingual education for children in a linguistic minority also pay dividends? Advocates of "English-only" education doubt it. They argue that bilingual programs are expensive, ineffective, and detrimental to non–English-speaking children's assimilation into their English-based cultures (Porter, 1998). But some studies find that such children benefit from bilingual education, if in "two-way" schools where they, together with English-speaking children, experience half their classes in English and half in their native language. Compared with non–English-speaking children dropped into English-only schools, those in the two-way schools tend to develop higher self-esteem. They drop out less frequently. And they eventually attain higher levels of academic achievement and English proficiency (August & Hakuta, 1998; Padilla & Benavides, 1992; Thomas & Collier, 1998).

Increasing word power through sign language has also had great benefits for deaf people, who for thousands of years were viewed as incompetent to inherit property, marry, be educated, or have challenging work (Sacks, 1990). Since the spread of signed instruction, deaf people have shown that, when exposed to signing as preschoolers and then schooled in their language, they become fully literate. Deaf children with native sign fluency—learned, for example, as children of signing deaf parents—outperform other signing deaf children on measures of intelligence and academic achievement (Isham & Kamin, 1993). Whether we are deaf or hearing, language transforms experience. Language connects us to the past and the future. Language fuels our imagination. Language links us to one another.

Thinking Without Language

When you are alone, do you talk to yourself? Is "thinking" simply conversing with yourself? Without a doubt, words convey ideas. But aren't there times when ideas precede words? To turn on the cold water in your bathroom, in which direction do you turn the handle? To answer this question, you probably thought not in words but with a mental picture. Indeed, we often think in images. Artists think in images. So do composers, poets, mathematicians, athletes, and scientists. Albert Einstein reported that he achieved some of his greatest insights through visual images and later put them into words.

Pianist Liu Chi Kung showed the value of thinking in images. One year after placing second in the 1958 Tchaikovsky piano competition, Liu was imprisoned during China's Cultural Revolution. Soon after his release, after seven years without touching a piano, he was back on tour, the critics judging his musicianship better than ever. How did he continue to develop without practice? "I did practice," said Liu, "every day. I rehearsed every piece I had ever played, note by note, in my mind" (Garfield, 1986).

Athletes in many fields now supplement physical with mental practice. For Olympic athletes, "mental practice has become a standard part of training," reports Richard Suinn (1997). Golf great Jack Nicklaus has said that he would "watch a movie" in his head before each shot. In a laboratory test, Georgia Nigro (1984) demonstrated the wisdom of mental practice. She had people actually throw darts 24 times at a target, then had half the people throw 24 darts mentally, and, finally, had everyone throw another 24 darts. Only those who had mentally practiced showed any improvement.

Young members of the U.S. Figure Skating Association have exhibited similar improvement in their performance ratings for jumps and spins following mental practice while listening to their skating music (Garza & Feltz, 1998). And several experiments on mental practice and basketball foul shooting have found comparable benefits. In one such experiment (Savoy & Beitel, 1996), conducted with the University of Tennessee women's team over 35 games, the team's free-throw shooting increased from approximately 52 percent in games following standard physical practice to some 65 percent after mental practice. During the mental practice, players repeatedly imagined making foul shots under various conditions, including being "trash-talked" by their opposition. The experiment's dramatic conclusion occurred when Tennessee won the national championship game in overtime, thanks in part to their foul shooting.

Mental rehearsal can also help you achieve an academic goal. In one study, Shelley Taylor and her UCLA colleagues (1998) engaged introductory psychology students who were a week away from facing a midterm exam. Some were told to visualize themselves scanning the posted grade list, seeing their A, beaming with joy, and feeling proud. Repeating this "outcome simulation" 5 minutes each day until the exam had little effect, adding only 2 points to their exam scores, compared with scores of student counterparts not engaging in any mental simulation. But the researchers had another group visualize themselves effectively studying—reading the chapters, going over notes, eliminating distractions, declining an offer to go out. Repeating this "process simulation" for 5 minutes each day had a beneficial effect. Compared with the control students, this second group of students began studying sooner, spent more time at it, and beat the control group average by 8 points. From such experiments, the researchers conclude that it is better to spend your fantasy time planning how to get somewhere than to dwell on the imagined destination.

More evidence of thinking without language comes from research on information processing outside of consciousness, beyond language. Inside the ever-active brain, many streams of activity flow in parallel, function automatically, are remembered implicitly, and only occasionally surface as conscious words. "Thinking lite," this unconscious processing has been called—one-fourth the effort of regular thinking. So, yes, there certainly is cognition without language.

What, then, should we say about the relationship between thinking and language? As we have seen, language does influence our thinking. But if thinking did not also affect language, there would never be any new words. And new words and new

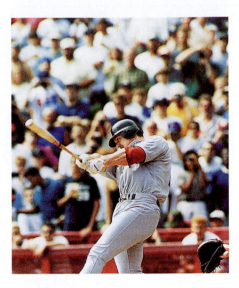

Mental practice
Before each turn at bat during his 1998, record-breaking 70–home-run season, Mark McGwire would imagine the pitcher throwing the baseball, imagine how the ball would move, and "imagine smashing the ball with his Paul Bunyan swing" (Olney, 1998).

A thoughtful art
Playing the piano engages thinking without language. In the absence of a piano, practice on an imaginary piano can sustain one's skill.

The interplay of thought and language
The traffic runs both ways between thinking and language. Thinking affects our language, which affects our thought.

Chimpanzee inventiveness
A wild chimp shows ingenuity by using a stick to fish for ants living in the tree.

conbinations of old words express new ideas. The basketball term *slam dunk* was coined after the act itself had become fairly common. So, let us say that *thinking affects our language, which then affects our thought.*

Psychological research on thinking and language mirrors the mixed reviews given our species in literature and religion. The human mind is simultaneously capable of striking intellectual failures and of vast intellectual power. Some misjudgments have disastrous consequences, so we do well to appreciate our capacity for error. Yet our efficient thinking skills often serve us well. Moreover, our ingenuity at problem solving and our extraordinary power of language surely, among the animals, rank humankind as almost "infinite in faculties."

Animal Thinking and Language

Preview Questions: Do animals—in some sense that we can identify with—think? Do other species exhibit language, or is language unique to humans?

If in our use of language we humans are, as the psalmist long ago rhapsodized, "little lower than God," where do other animals fit in the scheme of things? Are they "little lower than human"? In part, the answer lies in the extent to which animals share our capacity for thinking and language.

Do Animals Think?

Animals, especially the great apes, display remarkable capacities for thinking. Some experimenters have monkeyed with numbers. In one experiment, monkeys were shown four screens containing one to four objects each (perhaps two bananas, one triangle, four apples, and three hearts). Across variations in sizes and shapes, the monkeys quickly learned to touch pictures in ascending numerical order and then to receive a food reward. When then shown a display containing five to nine objects, they could order these, too (Brannon & Terrace, 1998). One female chimp named Ai could even order five random numbers between 0 and 9 after they were hidden (Kawai & Matsuzawa, 2000). After the first number was touched, the four others were covered by white squares on a screen. More than 90 percent of the time, Ai could remember and order the numbers by touching squares in the right sequence. Monkey see, monkey count.

We aren't the only creatures that display insight. German psychologist Wolfgang Köhler (1925) observed apparent insight while studying chimpanzees placed on an island off the coast of Africa. In one experiment with a caged chimp named Sultan, Köhler placed a piece of fruit and a long stick well beyond reach, and a short stick inside the cage. Spying the short stick, the chimp grabbed it and tried to reach the fruit. But the stick, by design, was too short. After several unsuccessful attempts, Sultan dropped the stick and paused to survey the situation. Then suddenly, as if thinking "Aha!" he jumped up, seized the short stick again, and used it to pull in the longer stick—which he then used to reach the fruit. Sultan's actions displayed animal cognition, claimed Köhler, and showed that there is more to learning than conditioning.

Thanks to problem solving shaped by reinforcement, forest-dwelling chimpanzees have become natural tool users (Boesch-Achermann & Boesch, 1993). They can select appropriate branches or stones to use as hammers in cracking nuts. They can also break off a reed or a stick, strip the twigs and leaves, carry it to a termite mound, fish for termites by twisting it just so, and then carefully remove it without scraping off many termites. One anthropologist, trying to mimic the chimpanzee's deft termite fishing, failed miserably.

Researchers have found at least 39 local customs related to chimp tool use, grooming, and courtship (Gibbons, 1992; Whiten & others, 1999). One group of chimps may slurp ants directly from the stick, while another plucks them off individually. One group may break nuts with a stone hammer, another with a wooden hammer. Such group differences, along with differing dialects and hunting styles, occur within subspecies and thus seem not to be genetic. Rather, they are the chimpanzee equivalent of cultural diversity. Like humans, chimps—often younger chimps—invent customs and pass them on to their peers.

If primates can count, exhibit insight, use tools, and transmit cultural innovations, do they have a "theory of mind"? Can they infer mental states in themselves and their peers? Chimps and orangutans have been observed using mirrors to inspect themselves and touching a colored spot that a researcher has dabbed on their face (Gallup, 1998). Chimps and baboons have also been observed using deception, as when a young baboon feigns having been attacked as a seeming tactic for getting its mother to drive a competing baboon away from its food. Do such observations indicate that primates are capable of self-recognition and of comprehending others' perceptions? Many researchers think yes, but some behaviorists are unconvinced (Heyes, 1998). For example, unlike young children, chimpanzees do not know to beg food from someone who could see them—with a blindfold over the mouth rather than the eyes (Povinelli, 1999).

Do Animals Exhibit Language?

Without doubt, animals communicate. Vervet monkeys have different alarm cries for different predators: a barking call for a leopard, a cough for an eagle, and a chuttering for a snake. Hearing the leopard alarm, other vervets climb the nearest tree. Hearing the eagle alarm, they rush into the bushes. Hearing the snake chutter, they stand up and scan the ground (Byrne, 1991). Whales also communicate, with clicks and wails. The question is, however, do animals' communications make up a language?

The Case of the Honeybee

More than 2000 years ago, the Greek philosopher Aristotle observed that once a lone honeybee discovers a source of nectar, other bees soon leave the hive and go straight to the newfound food source. Aristotle surmised that the original explorer must return to the hive and lead other bees back to the food. He was wrong. In 1901, a clever German researcher followed the explorer bee back to the hive and trapped it as it left to return to the food source. Although deprived of their guide, the new recruits still flew straight to the nectar.

How did the bees know where to go? Intrigued, Austrian biologist Karl von Frisch (1950) undertook experiments for which he later shared the Nobel prize. The experiments revealed that the explorer bee communicates with the other worker bees by means of an intricate dance. The direction and duration of the dance, Frisch discovered, informs other bees of the direction and distance of the food source (**FIGURE 29.4**). Using robotic honeybees that perform a credible song and dance act, experimenters have since discovered that it takes a combination of dance and sound to tell nestmate bees where to fly to find food (Kirchner & Towne, 1994).

Impressive? Yes. But the honeybees' song and dance hardly challenges the complexity, flexibility, and power of human language. The honeybee communicates, but not with the elements of language.

The Case of the Apes

The greatest challenge to humanity's claim to be the only language-using species has come from reports of apes that "talk" with people. Genetically speaking, our closest relatives are the chimpanzees, and the chimpanzees' closest relatives are not other apes, but us (Sagan & Druyan, 1992). Knowing

Smart bird brain
Alex, an African gray parrot trained and tested by University of Arizona professor Irene Pepperberg (1994, 2000), displays numerical competence when shown novel assortments of objects. Asked, for example, "How many red blocks?" or "How many green balls?" Alex, with a brain the size of a walnut, answers correctly more than 80 percent of the time.

FIGURE 29.4
The dance of the honeybee
The straight-line part of the dance points in the direction of a nectar source relative to the sun, and the duration of the dance indicates the distance. The other bees, who cannot see the dance in the dark hive, huddle close to feel what is going on. (From von Frisch, 1974.)

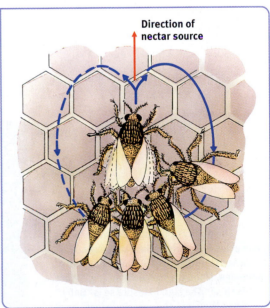

Direction of nectar source

Gestured communication
For hearing people, today's gestures may be less central to communication than for those who first used hand signals. Yet gestures remain naturally associated with spontaneous speech, especially speech that has spatial content.

Seeing a doll floating in her water, Washoe signed, "Baby in my drink."

Gesture researcher Robert Krauss (1998) recalls his grandfather telling of two men walking on a bitter winter day. One chattered away while the second nodded, saying nothing. "Schmuel, why aren't you saying anything?" the first friend finally wondered. "Because," replied Schmuel, "I forgot my gloves."

that chimpanzees could not vocalize more than a few words, University of Nevada researchers Allen Gardner and Beatrice Gardner (1969) tried to teach sign language words to a chimp named Washoe, as though she were a deaf human child. After four years, Washoe could use 132 signs. At age 32, Washoe had a vocabulary of 181 signs (Sanz & others, 1998). The Gardners' announcement of the success of their efforts aroused enormous scientific and public interest. One *New York Times* reporter, having learned sign language from his deaf parents, visited Washoe and exclaimed, "Suddenly I realized I was conversing with a member of another species in my native tongue."

Human language appears to have evolved from gestured communications (Corballis, 1999). So it is no wonder that our ape relatives have produced many gestured words but few spoken words. It is no wonder that gestures survive as part of hearing people's speech (even when talking on the phone!). It is no wonder that signing so readily developed among deaf people as an alternative to speech. It is no wonder that congenitally blind people produce gestures similar to those of sighted people, even if they believe the listener is also blind (Iverson & Goldin-Meadow, 1998). And it is no wonder that prohibiting gestures disrupts speech that has spatial content (for example, when describing an apartment layout). For both humans and apes, communication entails gestures.

Further evidence of gestured "ape language" surfaced during the 1970s. Usually apes signed just single words, but sometimes they strung signs together to form intelligible sentences. Washoe signed, "You me go out, please." Apes even appeared to combine words creatively. Washoe designated a swan as a "water bird." Koko, a gorilla trained by Francine Patterson (1978), reportedly described a long-nosed Pinocchio doll as an "elephant baby." Lana is a chimpanzee that "talks" by punching buttons wired to a computer that then translates her punches into English. One day, she wanted her trainer's orange, but she had no word for *orange*. She did, however, know

But is this language?
The ability of chimpanzees to express themselves in American Sign Language (ASL) raises questions about the very nature of language. Here, the trainer is asking, "What is this?" The sign in response is "Baby." Does the response constitute language?

her colors and the word for *apple*, so she improvised: "?Tim give apple which-is orange" (Rumbaugh, 1977).

As reports of ape language accumulated, it seemed that they might indeed be "little lower than human." Granted, their vocabularies and sentences are simple, rather like those of a 2-year-old child, yet the apes do seem to share what we humans have considered our unique ability.

But Can Apes Really Talk?

By the late 1970s, fascination with "talking apes" turned toward cynicism: Were the chimps language champs or were the researchers chumps? The ape language researchers were making monkeys out of themselves, said the skeptics, who raised the following arguments:

+ Apes gain their limited vocabularies only with great difficulty. They are hardly like speaking or signing children, who effortlessly soak up dozens of new words a week. Saying that apes can learn language because they can sign words is like saying humans can fly because they can jump.

+ Chimps can make signs or push buttons in sequence to get a reward, just as Moscow circus bears can learn to ride unicycles. But pigeons, too, can peck a sequence of keys to get grain (Straub & others, 1979). No one says the pigeon is "talking."

+ Apes can certainly use symbols meaningfully. But "Give orange me give eat orange me eat orange. . ." is a far cry from the exquisite syntax of a 3-year-old (Pinker, 1995). To the child, "you tickle" and "tickle you" communicate different ideas. A chimp might sign the phrases interchangeably.

+ After training a chimp whom he named Nim Chimsky, Herbert Terrace (1979) concluded that much of chimpanzees' signing is nothing more than apes aping their trainers' signs.

+ Research on perceptual set tells us that when people are presented with ambiguous information, they tend to see what they want or expect to see. Interpreting chimpanzee signs as language may be little more than wishful thinking on the part of their trainers, claimed Terrace. (When Washoe signed *water bird*, she perhaps was separately naming *water* and *bird*.)

"Chimps do not develop language," concludes Steven Pinker (1995). "But that is no shame on them; humans would surely do no better if trained to hoot and shriek like chimps, to perform the waggle-dance of the bee, or any of the other wonderful feats in nature's talent show."

In science as in politics, controversy can stimulate progress. The provocative claim that "apes share our capacity for language" and the skeptical rejoinder that "apes no use language" (as Washoe might have put it) have moved psychologists toward a greater appreciation of both apes' remarkable capabilities and our own. Everyone agrees: Humans alone possess language, if by the term we mean verbal or signed expression of complex grammar. If we mean, more simply, the ability to communicate through a meaningful sequence of symbols, then apes are indeed capable of language.

Although chimpanzees do not have our facility for language, their abilities to think and communicate continue to impress their trainers. After her second infant died, a depressed Washoe repeatedly asked "Baby?" and became withdrawn when told "Baby dead, baby gone, baby finished." Two weeks later, caretaker-researcher Roger Fouts (1992, 1997) had better news for Washoe: "I have baby for you." Washoe reacted to the signed news with instant excitement, her hair on end, swaggering and panting while signing over and again, "Baby, my baby." When Fouts then introduced the foster infant, Loulis, it took several hours for them to warm to each other, whereupon Washoe broke the ice by signing, "Come baby" and cuddling Loulis. In the months that followed, Loulis picked up 68 signs simply by observing Washoe and three other language-trained chimps.

Moreover, Washoe, Loulis, and the others now sign spontaneously. They ask one another to *chase, tickle, hug, come,* or *groom.* People who sign can actually eavesdrop on these chimp-to-chimp conversations with near-perfect agreement about what the chimps are saying, 90 percent of which pertains to social interaction, reassurance, or

Another "talking" chimpanzee
Lana has learned to speak by punching word symbols on a computer keyboard. When she presses a key, the symbol lights up.

"Although humans make sounds with their mouths and occasionally look at each other, there is no solid evidence that they actually communicate with each other."

"[Our] egocentric view that [we are] unique from all other forms of animal life is being jarred to the core."

Duane Rumbaugh and Sue Savage-Rumbaugh (1978)

"He says he wants a lawyer."

play (Fouts & Bodamer, 1987). The chimps are even modestly bilingual; they can translate spoken English words into signs (Shaw, 1989–1990).

Most stunning still is the discovery by Sue Savage-Rumbaugh and her colleagues (1993) that pygmy chimpanzees can learn to comprehend the semantic nuances of spoken English. Kanzi, one such chimp with the grammatical abilities of a 2½-year-old, happened onto language while observing his adoptive mother being language trained. Kanzi behaves intelligently whether asked, "Can you show me the light?" or "Can you bring me the [flash]light?" or "Can you turn the light on?" Kanzi also knows the spoken words *snake, bite,* and *dog.* Given stuffed animals and asked—for the first time—to "make the dog bite the snake," he put the snake to the dog's mouth. For chimps as for humans, early life is the critical time for learning language. If raised without early exposure to speech or word symbols, the chimps are unable as adults to gain language competence (Rumbaugh & Savage-Rumbaugh, 1994).

Yes, trained apes' language capabilities are modest by human standards. Yet their cognitive powers remain impressive. If Kanzi "had a vocal tract, he would be talking," exclaims Duane Rumbaugh (1994). Realizing this, we see once again how animal research can increase our respect for the creatures studied. Believing that animals could not think, Descartes and other philosophers argued that they were living robots without any moral rights. Animals, it has been said at one time or another, cannot plan, conceptualize, count, use tools, show compassion, or use language (Thorpe, 1974). Today, we know better. We have seen primates exhibit insight, show family loyalty, communicate with one another, display altruism, transmit cultural patterns across generations, and comprehend the syntax of human speech. Accepting and working out the moral implications of all this is an unfinished task for our own thinking species.

REVIEW AND REFLECT:

Language and Thought

What are the three basic elements found in every language?

Language is built of basic speech sounds, called *phonemes*; elementary units of meaning, called *morphemes*; and the semantics (meaning) and syntax (rules for word order) that make up *grammar.*

When do children acquire language? Do humans have an inborn capacity for acquiring language, or is language development another instance of learning guided by association, imitation, and reinforcement?

Among the marvels of nature is a child's ability to acquire language. The ease with which children progress from the babbling stage (at 4 months) through the one-word stage (at 1 year) to the telegraphic speech of the two-word stage (at 2 years) and beyond has sparked a lively debate concerning how they do it. Behaviorist B. F. Skinner explained that we learn language by the familiar principles of association, imitation, and reinforcement. Challenging this claim, linguist Noam Chomsky argued that children are biologically prepared to learn words and use grammar. Cognitive neuroscientists emphasize that, for mastery of grammar, the learning that occurs during life's first few years is critical.

To what extent does language control what we think, perceive, and remember?

Thinking and language are very hard to separate. Words convey ideas, and different languages embody different ways of thinking. Although the linguistic relativity hypothesis suggested that language *determines* thought, it is more accurate to say that language *influences* thought. Studies of the effects of the generic pronoun *he* and the ability of vocabulary enrichment to enhance thinking reveal the influence of words.

Does all thinking depend on language?

Some ideas, such as the ability to perceive and remember different colors, do not depend on language. We sometimes think in images rather than in words, and we invent new words or new combinations of old words to describe new ideas. So we might say that our thinking affects our language, which then affects our thought.

Do animals—in some sense that we can identify with—think?

Evidence accumulates that primates at some level count, display insight, create tools, and transmit cultural innovations.

Do other species exhibit language, or is language unique to humans?

Whether language is uniquely human is a vigorously debated issue. Animals obviously communicate. Bees, for example, communicate the location of food through an intricate combination of dance and sound. And several teams of psychologists have taught various species of apes, including a number of chimpanzees, to communicate with humans by signing or by pushing buttons wired to a computer. Apes have developed considerable vocabularies. They string words together to express meaning and to make and follow requests. Skeptics point out important differences between apes' and humans' facilities with language, especially in their respective abilities to order words using proper syntax. Nevertheless, these studies reveal that apes have considerable cognitive ability.

Terms and Concepts to Remember

language, p. 383
phoneme, p. 383
morpheme, p. 383
grammar, p. 383
semantics, p. 383
syntax, p. 383

babbling stage, p. 385
one-word stage, p. 385
two-word stage, p. 386
telegraphic speech, p. 386
linguistic relativity, p. 390

Test Yourself

29.1. All languages have phonemes, morphemes, and grammar, which itself is made up of syntax and semantics. _____ are the smallest distinctive sound units in a language; _____ are the smallest meaningful units.

a. Semantics; syntaxes
b. Morphemes; phonemes
c. Phonemes; morphemes
d. Syntaxes; semantics

29.2. children progress from babbling to the one-word stage and then to two-word sentences. The one-word stage of speech development is usually reached at about

a. 4 months.   c. 1 year.
b. 6 months.   d. 2 years.

29.3. B. F. Skinner believed that we learn language the same way we learn other behaviors—through association, imitation, and reinforcement. Skinner's behaviorist view is most helpful in explaining

a. the onset of babbling.
b. the speech behavior of deaf infants.
c. the seemingly effortless mastery of grammatical rules by very young children.
d. why children learn their household's language.

29.4. According to Noam Chomsky, we are biologically prepared to acquire language and are born with a readiness to learn the grammatical rules of the language we hear. He believes that all we need to acquire language is

a. instruction in grammar.
b. exposure to language in early childhood.
c. reinforcement for babbling and other early verbal behaviors.
d. imitation and drill.

29.5. According to Benjamin Lee Whorf, our language determines the way we perceive and think about the world. His linguistic relativity hypothesis suggests an explanation for why

a. a person who learns a second language thinks differently in that language.
b. children have a built-in readiness to learn grammatical rules.
c. apes are able to communicate through sign language.
d. artists, athletes, and others are able to think in visual images.

29.6. There is much controversy over whether apes can be taught to use language in the way that humans do. However, most researchers of ape sign language agree that apes can

a. communicate through symbols.
b. reproduce most human speech sounds.
c. create new sentences and meanings.
d. surpass a human 3-year-old in language skills.

Review

• If children are not yet speaking, is there any reason to think they would benefit from parents and other caregivers reading to them? Why or why not?

• To say that "words are the mother of ideas" assumes the truth of what concept?

• If your dog barks at a stranger at the front door, does this qualify as *language*? What if the dog yips in a telltale way to let you know she needs to go out?

Reflect

• There has been controversy at some universities about allowing fluency in sign language to fulfill a second-language requirement for an undergraduate degree. What is your opinion?

• Can you think of examples of how our language is alive and constantly evolving? For example, do you use certain words or gestures that only your family or closest circle of friends would understand? What are they?

• Can you think of a time when you felt an animal was communicating with you? How might you put such intuition to a test?

Answers to the Test Yourself and Review questions can be found in the green appendix at the end of the book.

30 Introduction to Intelligence

Intelligence is a slippery concept. Psychologists debate whether we should define *intelligence* as an inherent cognitive capacity, an achieved level of intellectual performance, or an ascribed quality that, like beauty, is in the eye of the beholder. Reading all the conflicting ideas about intelligence can leave you feeling as Alice in Wonderland felt after reading "Jabberwocky": "Somehow it seems to fill my head with ideas—only I don't exactly know what they are."

We have had more than a century to educate ourselves since psychologists constructed the first **intelligence test**—an instrument for assessing a person's mental abilities and comparing them with the abilities of other people, by means of numerical scores. Intelligence experts do agree on this: Intelligence is not a "thing." When we refer to someone's "IQ" as if it were a fixed and objectively real trait like height, we commit a reasoning error called *reification*—viewing an abstract, immaterial concept as if it were a concrete thing. To reify is to invent a concept, give it a name, and then convince ourselves that such a thing objectively exists in the world. When someone says, "She has an IQ of 120," they are reifying IQ; they are imagining IQ to be a thing one *has*, rather than a score once obtained on a particular test. The abbreviation *IQ* is a clue that we are reifying intelligence. *IQ* is a short-hand form of *intelligence quotient*, a numerical score reached by means of a formula used in one of the early intelligence tests. Thus, to be accurate—and to avoid reification—one should say, "Her score on the intelligence test was 120."

Intelligence is a socially constructed concept. Cultures deem "intelligent" whatever attributes enable success in those cultures (Sternberg & Kaufman, 1998). In rural Kenya it may be a gift for discerning which native herbs are effective medicines for which diseases. In Asian cultures, social skill is a valued part of intelligence. In Western countries, a superior performance on cognitive tasks is considered an important aspect of intelligence. In each context, **intelligence** is the ability to learn from experience, solve problems, and use knowledge to adapt to new situations. Practically, intelligence (in research studies) is whatever intelligence tests measure, which historically has tended to be school smarts.

Despite this general agreement about the concept, two controversies remain:

1. Is intelligence a single overall ability or several specific abilities?
2. With the tools of modern neuroscience, can we now measure intelligence as the brain's information-processing speed?

Is Intelligence One General Ability or Several Specific Abilities?

Preview Question: Do we have one general aptitude that forms the foundation of all our abilities, or do our individual talents represent independent types of intelligence?

We all know some people talented in science, others in the humanities, and still others in athletics, art, music, or dance. Perhaps you have known a talented artist who is dumbfounded by the simplest mathematical problems, or a brilliant math student who has little aptitude for literary discussion. We may therefore wonder whether people's mental abilities are too diverse to justify labeling them with the single word *intelligence* or quantifying them with a number from some single scale.

The Factor-Analysis Approach

To find out whether there might be a general ability factor that runs throughout our specific mental abilities, psychologists study how various abilities relate to one another. A statistical method called **factor analysis** enables researchers to identify clusters of test items that measure a common ability. For example, people who do well on vocabulary items often do well on paragraph comprehension, a cluster that helps define a verbal intelligence factor. Other clusters include a spatial ability factor and a reasoning ability factor.

Charles Spearman (1863–1945), who helped develop factor analysis, believed there is also a **general intelligence**, or **g**, factor that underlies the specific factors. Spearman granted that people often have special abilities that stand out. But he also noted that those who score high on one factor, such as verbal intelligence, typically score higher than average on other factors, such as spatial or reasoning ability. So there is at least a tendency for different abilities to come in the same package. Spearman believed that this commonality, the *g* factor, underlies all of our intelligent behavior, from navigating the sea to excelling in school.

This idea of a general mental capacity expressed by a single intelligence score was controversial in Spearman's day, and it remains so in our own. One of Spearman's early opponents was L. L. Thurstone (1887–1955). He gave 56 different tests to people and mathematically identified eight clusters of "primary mental abilities," such as word fluency, memory, and reasoning. Thurstone did not rank his subjects on a single scale of general aptitude. But when other investigators studied the profiles of his subjects, they detected a small tendency for those who excelled in one of the eight clusters to score well on the others. So, they concluded, there was still some evidence of a *g* factor.

We might, then, liken mental abilities to physical abilities. Athleticism is not one thing but many. The ability to run fast is distinct from the strength needed for power lifting, which is distinct from the eye-hand coordination required to throw a ball on target. A champion weightlifter rarely has the potential to be a skilled ice skater. Yet there remains some tendency for good things to come packaged together—for running speed and throwing accuracy to correlate, thanks to general athletic ability. Similarly, intelligence involves several distinct abilities, which cluster together in the same individual often enough to define a small general intelligence factor.

Broadened Theories of Intelligence

Since the mid-1980s some psychologists have sought to extend the definition of intelligence beyond academic smarts.

Multiple Intelligences

Howard Gardner (1983, 1993, 1995) supports Thurstone's idea that intelligence comes in different packages. He notes that brain damage may diminish one type of ability but not others. He observes that different abilities enabled our ancestors to cope with different environmental challenges (finding their way home, reading others' emotions, solving problems). And he studies people with exceptional abilities, including those who excel in only one. People with **savant syndrome**, for example, often score low on intelligence tests but have an island of brilliance—some incredible ability, as in computation, drawing, or musical memory (**FIGURE 30.1**, page 402). These people may have virtually no language ability, yet may be able to compute numbers as quickly and accurately as an electronic calculator, or identify almost instantly the day of the week that corresponds to any given date in history (Miller, 1999).

Athleticism, like intelligence, is many things
Some football and basketball coaches have therefore encouraged players to develop their finesse by taking dance classes.

"*g* is one of the most reliable and valid measures in the behavioural domain . . . and it predicts important social outcomes such as educational and occupational levels far better than any other trait."

Robert Plomin (1999)

■ **intelligence test** a method for assessing an individual's mental aptitudes and comparing them with those of others, using numerical scores.

■ **intelligence** mental quality consisting of the ability to learn from experience, solve problems, and use knowledge to adapt to new situations.

■ **factor analysis** a statistical procedure that identifies clusters of related items (called *factors*) on a test; used to identify different dimensions of performance that underlie one's total score.

■ **general intelligence (g)** a general intelligence factor that Spearman and others believed underlies specific mental abilities and is therefore measured by every task on an intelligence test.

■ **savant syndrome** a condition in which a person otherwise limited in mental ability has an exceptional specific skill, such as in computation or drawing.

FIGURE 30.1 Savant syndrome
Although hardly able to speak coherently, Britain's Stephen Wiltshire can draw intricate scenes after just one good look. This drawing is of St. Mark's Cathedral in Venice, Italy. By age 13, Stephen was famous for his ability to "draw, with greatest ease, any street he had seen; but he could not, unaided, cross one by himself" (Sacks, 1995).

Gardner (1998) also speculates about a ninth possible intelligence—"existential intelligence"—the ability "to ponder large questions about life, death, existence."

Using such evidence, Gardner argues that we do not have *an* intelligence but instead have *multiple* intelligences, each relatively independent of the others. In addition to the verbal and mathematical aptitudes assessed by the standard tests, he identifies distinct aptitudes for musical accomplishment, for spatially analyzing the visual world, for mastering movement skills (as in dance), and for insightfully understanding ourselves, others, and our natural environment. In simple words, you can think of these eight intelligences as word smarts, number smarts, music smarts, space smarts, body smarts, self smarts, people smarts, and nature smarts. If you are not a candidate for the high-IQ group, MENSA, you might still have a genius for leadership.

As exemplars of these alternative intellects Gardner offers poet T. S. Eliot, scientist Albert Einstein, composer Igor Stravinsky, artist Pablo Picasso, dancer Martha Graham, psychiatrist Sigmund Freud, leader Mahatma Gandhi, and naturalist Charles Darwin. According to Gardner, the computer programmer, the poet, the street-smart adolescent who becomes a crafty executive, and the point guard on the basketball team exhibit different kinds of intelligence. He notes (1998),

> If a person is strong (or weak) in telling stories, solving mathematical proofs, navigating around unfamiliar terrain, learning an unfamiliar song, mastering a new game that entails dexterity, understanding others, or understanding himself, one simply does not know whether comparable strengths (or weaknesses) will be found in other areas.

Spatial intelligence genius
In 1998, World Checkers Champion Ron "Suki" King of Barbados set a new record by simultaneously playing 385 players in 3 hours and 44 minutes. Thus, while his opponents often had hours to plot their game moves, King could devote only about 35 seconds to each game. Yet he still managed to win all 385 games!

A general intelligence score is therefore like the overall rating of a city—which doesn't give you much specific information about its schools, streets, or nightlife.

Wouldn't it be wonderful if the world were so just, responds intelligence researcher Sandra Scarr (1989), that being weak in any area would often be compensated by genius in some other area? Alas, the world is not just, for there remains some tendency for different skills to correlate. For example, people with mental disadvantages often have lesser physical abilities as well; thus, we hold Special Olympics to give them a chance to enjoy fair competition.

Moreover, Gardner's critics question, does it really make sense to lump all sorts of abilities under the concept of intelligence? Are not some, such as verbal and reasoning skills, really more crucial than others? Intelligence is *mental* ability, they say. The abilities that we can manage without, as in music and athletics, are better considered *talents* than intelligences. If people lack physical talent, do we consider them as lacking an *intelligence*? Gardner counters that all forms of intelligence have intrinsic value—it is one's culture and context that place greater value on some capacities than on others. Indeed, definitions of intelligence—whether the traditional predictor of school achievement or a broader definition—tend to express what people value in a human being.

"You're wise, but you lack tree smarts."

Aspects of Successful Intelligence

While Robert Sternberg (1985, 1997) agrees with Gardner's idea of multiple intelligences, he distinguishes more simply among three aspects of intelligence:

+ **Analytical (academic problem-solving) intelligence**—assessed by intelligence tests, which present well-defined problems having a single right answer.
+ **Creative intelligence**—demonstrated in reacting adaptively to novel situations and generating novel ideas.
+ **Practical intelligence**—often required for everyday tasks, which are frequently ill-defined, with multiple solutions.

Traditional intelligence tests assess academic intelligence. They predict school grades reasonably well but do less well in predicting vocational success. People who demonstrate keen practical intelligence may or may not have distinguished themselves in school. Managerial success, for example, depends less on the academic abilities assessed by an intelligence test score (assuming the score is average or above) than on a shrewd ability to manage oneself, one's tasks, and other people. Sternberg and Richard Wagner's (1993, 1995) test of practical managerial intelligence measures whether the test-taker knows how to write effective memos, how to motivate people, when to delegate tasks and responsibilities, how to read people, and how to promote one's own career. Business executives who score high on this test tend to earn higher salaries and receive better performance ratings than do those who score low. In a similar finding, Stephen Ceci and Jeffrey Liker (1986) report that racetrack fans' expertise in handicapping horses—a practical but complex cognitive task—is unrelated to their intelligence test scores.

Although Sternberg (1998, 1999) and Gardner (1998) differ on specific points, they agree that multiple abilities can contribute to life success. They also agree that the differing varieties of giftedness add spice to life and challenges for education. Under Gardner's or Sternberg's influence, many teachers have been trained to appreciate the varieties of ability and to apply multiple intelligence theory in their classrooms. Evaluations of these programs are under way.

Emotional Intelligence

Also distinct from academic intelligence is what Nancy Cantor and John Kihlstrom (1987) first called *social intelligence*—the know-how involved in comprehending social situations and managing oneself successfully. Seymour Epstein and Petra Meier

"You have to be careful, if you're good at something, to make sure you don't think you're good at other things that you aren't necessarily so good at. . . . Because I've been very successful at [software development] people come in and expect that I have wisdom about topics that I don't."

Bill Gates (1998)

■ **emotional intelligence** the ability to perceive, express, understand, and regulate emotions.

(1989) agreed. If academic aptitude signifies social competence, they asked, why then are high-aptitude people "not, by a wide margin, more effective . . . in achieving better marriages, in successfully raising their children, and in achieving better mental and physical well-being?" Consistent with this distinction between academic and social intelligence is the repeated finding that college grades only modestly predict later work achievement (Bretz, 1989; Dye & Reck, 1989).

A critical part of social intelligence is what Peter Salovey and John Mayer (1990; Mayer & Salovey, 1993, 1995, 1997) call **emotional intelligence**—the ability to perceive, express, understand, and regulate emotions. Emotionally intelligent people are especially self-aware. They manage their emotions without being hijacked by overwhelming depression, anxiety, or anger. They can delay gratification in pursuit of long-range rewards, rather than being overtaken by immediate impulses. Their empathy enables them to read others' emotions. They handle others' emotions skillfully, knowing what to say to a grieving friend, how to encourage colleagues, and how to manage conflicts well. Simply said, they are emotionally smart, and thus they often succeed in careers, marriages, and parenting where other academically smarter (but emotionally less intelligent) people fail.

Given the significance of practical, creative, and emotional intelligence, researchers are now wondering: Can we assess these alternative intelligences? Can we teach practical and emotional intelligence to schoolchildren? Can we stimulate their creative problem-solving abilities and their abilities to read and manage emotions (Goleman, 1995)? Such questions define a new frontier in the study of intelligence. Although popular emotional intelligence measures seem unreliable, researchers are searching for insights. Michaela Davies and her co-workers (1998), for example, offer hope for measures of the emotional perceptiveness component of emotional intelligence.

Other scholars, however—including even multiple intelligence man Howard Gardner (1999)—think that concepts such as *emotional intelligence* and *moral intelligence* stretch *intelligence* too far. It is wise to stretch the concept to include not only our processing of words, numbers, and logic, but also space, music, and information about ourselves and others, says Gardner. But let us also, he says, respect emotional sensitivity, creativity, motivation, and morality as important but different. Stretch a word to mean everything we prize and it will lose its meaning.

In defense of academic smarts—the *g* factor—researchers point to studies in which traditional intelligence scores *do* to some extent predict both occupational status and job performance (Brody, 1997; Schmidt & Hunter, 1998). For example, intelligence matters most in mentally demanding jobs. Meteorology more than meter reading requires intelligence to excel. However, once admitted to a vocation, those who become highly successful have other traits as well—they are conscientious, well-connected, and doggedly energetic. Thus, high intelligence does more to get you into a profession (via the schools and training programs that take you there) than it does to make you successful, once there.

So it seems that the academic aptitude tapped by intelligence tests is indeed important. Yet our competence in everyday living requires much that traditional intelligence tests do not measure.

Emotional intelligence
Some people, even if they don't score high on standard intelligence tests, are gifted at perceiving, understanding, and expressing emotions.

Is Intelligence Neurologically Measurable?

Preview Question: Could brain size, structure, or functioning explain differences in intelligence?

Might there soon, as some have predicted, be neurological tests of intelligence? Using today's neuroscience tools, might we link differences in people's intelligence test performance to dissimilarities in the heart of smarts—the brain?

Brain Size and Intelligence

In the early 1800s, phrenologist Franz Gall realized that human intelligence surpasses animal intelligence because the human cortex is more developed. He therefore wondered whether intelligence differences among humans might similarly be due to differing brain structures, detectable in skull protrusions. Although his efforts to gauge mental abilities failed, 25 modern studies do reveal a slight +.15 correlation between head size (relative to body size) and intelligence score (Jensen & Johnson, 1994).

Maybe the correlation from modern studies of brain size and intelligence is so near zero (and was therefore undetectable in the nineteenth-century analyses) because head size is a weak proxy for brain size. There is, after all, more inside the skull than cortical tissue. Newer studies that directly measure brain volume using MRI scans reveal a more significant correlation of +.44 between brain size (adjusted for body size) and intelligence score (Rushton & Ankney, 1996). Moreover, as adults age, brain size and nonverbal intelligence test scores fall in concert (Bigler & others, 1995).

If intelligence does correlate with brain size, the cause could be differing genes, nutrition, environmental stimulation, some combination of these, or perhaps something else. We know that experience does alter the brain. Rats raised in a stimulating rather than deprived environment develop thicker, heavier cortexes. And learning leaves detectable traces in the brain's neural connections.

Efforts to link brain structure with cognition continue. One ongoing project gives tests of abilities and personality to cancer patients with poor prognoses and then after their deaths receives their brains for study (Witelson & McCulloch, 1991). With the brains of 91 Canadians as a comparison base, Sandra Witelson and her colleagues (1999) seized an opportunity to study Einstein's brain. Although not notably heavier or larger than the typical Canadian's brain, Einstein's brain was 15 percent larger in the parietal lobe's lower region—which just happens to be a center for processing mathematical and spatial information. Certain other areas were a tad smaller than average. With different mental functions competing for the brain's real estate, these observations may offer a clue to why Einstein, like some other great physicists such as Richard Feynman and Edward Teller, was slow in learning to talk (Pinker, 1999). They also are consistent with the idea that the brain is a modular system with multiple intelligences.

> Correlations do not indicate cause and effect, but they do tell us whether two things are associated in some way. The lowest correlation, –1.0, represents perfect disagreement between two sets of scores—as one score goes up, the other goes down. A correlation of zero represents no consistency. The highest correlation, +1.0, represents perfect consistency—as the first score goes up, so does the second.

Brain Function and Intelligence

Even if the modest correlations between brain anatomy and intelligence prove reliable, they hardly explain intelligence differences. Searching for other explanations, neuroscientists are studying the brain's functioning.

Brain Glucose Consumption

R. J. Haier (1993) and Randolph Parks and his colleagues (1988) have done PET scans while people with high or low abilities perform cognitive tasks. High performers' brains are *less* active (they guzzle less glucose energy). This link between ability on a task and neurological efficiency holds true whether one compares more intelligent people with less intelligent people, or compares those who have had more opportunity to master the task with those who have had less opportunity.

Are more intelligent people literally more quick-witted, much as today's speedy computer chips enable more powerful computing than did their predecessors? On some tasks they seem to be. Earl Hunt (1983) found that verbal intelligence scores are predictable from the speed with which people retrieve information from memory. Those who recognize quickly that *sink* and *wink* are different words, or that *A* and *a* share the same name, tend to score high in verbal ability. Extremely precocious 12- to 14-year-old college students are especially quick in responding to such tasks (Jensen, 1989). To try to define "quick-wittedness," researchers are taking a close look at speed of perception and speed of neural processing of information.

Perceptual Speed

Across many studies, the correlation between intelligence score and the speed of taking in perceptual information tends to be about +.4 (Deary & Stough, 1996, 1997). A typical experiment flashes an incomplete stimulus, as in **FIGURE 30.2**. Its lingering afterimage is immediately masked by a stimulus that overrides it. The subject is then asked whether the long side appeared on the right or left. How much stimulus inspection time does one need to answer correctly 80 percent of the time? Perhaps .01 second? Or .02 second? Those who perceive quickly tend to score somewhat higher on intelligence tests, particularly tests based on perceptual rather than verbal problem solving.

Neurological Speed

Do the quicker perceptions of highly intelligent people reflect greater neurological speed? Repeated studies have found that their brain waves register a simple stimulus (such as a flash of light or a tone beep) more quickly and with greater complexity (Caryl, 1994; Deary & Caryl, 1993; Reed & Jensen, 1992). The evoked brain response also tends to be slightly faster when people with high rather than low intelligence scores perform a simple task, such as pushing a button when an *X* appears on a screen (McGarry-Roberts & others, 1992).

Neural processing speed on a simple task seems far removed from the untimed responses to complex intelligence test items, such as "In what way are *wool* and *cotton* alike?" As yet, notes intelligence expert Nathan Brody (1992), we have no firm understanding of *why* fast reactions on simple tasks should predict intelligence test performance. Philip Vernon (1983) has speculated that "faster cognitive processing may allow more information to be acquired." Perhaps people who more quickly process information accumulate more information—about wool, cotton, and millions of other things.

The neurological approach to understanding intelligence (and so many other things in psychology) is currently in its heyday. Will this new research reduce what we now call the *g* factor to simple measures of underlying brain activity? Or are these efforts totally wrongheaded because what we call intelligence is not a single general trait but several culturally adaptive skills? The controversies surrounding the nature of intelligence are a long way from resolution.

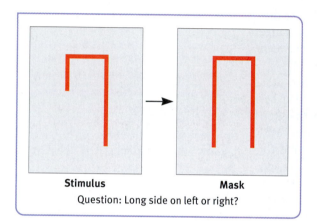

Stimulus   **Mask**

Question: Long side on left or right?

FIGURE 30.2 An inspection time task
How long would you need to glimpse the stimulus at the left to answer the question? People who can perceive the stimulus very quickly tend to score somewhat higher on intelligence tests. (Adapted from Deary & Stough, 1996.)

REVIEW AND REFLECT:

Introduction to Intelligence

It is misleading to reify concepts such as "intelligence" and "gift-edness"—to regard these abstract concepts as if they were real, concrete things. To most psychologists, *intelligence* is defined as the ability to learn from experience, solve problems, and adapt to new situations.

Do we have one general aptitude that forms the foundation of all our abilities, or do our individual talents represent independent types of intelligence?

Psychologists agree that people have specific abilities, such as verbal and mathematical aptitudes. However, they debate whether a general intelligence (*g*) factor runs through them all. Factor analysis and studies of special conditions, such as the savant syndrome, have identified clusters of mental aptitudes.

Could brain size, structure, or functioning explain differences in intelligence?

Several studies report a very slight correlation between head size (adjusted for body size) and intelligence test score, and a slightly greater (though still modest) correlation between brain size and intelligence test score. Other studies suggest that the brains of highly skilled people require less glucose energy while performing certain cognitive tasks. Highly intelligent people also tend to take in information more quickly and to show faster brain-wave responses to simple stimuli such as a flash of light. Time will tell whether these new neurological approaches to intelligence will bear important fruit. If they do, researchers will surely debate the extent to which nature and nurture affect the brain's structure and functioning.

Terms and Concepts to Remember

intelligence test, p. 400
intelligence, p. 400
factor analysis, p. 401
general intelligence (*g*), p. 401
savant syndrome, p. 401
emotional intelligence, p. 404

Test Yourself

30.1. Intelligence is a socially constructed concept. This means that different cultures
   a. necessarily have different definitions of intelligence.
   b. have the same definition of intelligence because we all belong to the same species.
   c. tend to view as intelligent those traits that enable success in their own way of life.
   d. tend to view as intelligent those traits that put society's interests above the interests of the individual.

30.2. Factor analysis is a statistical procedure that identifies clusters of related items on a test. Using this procedure, _____ identified _____.
   a. Thurstone; eight clusters of "primary mental abilities"
   b. Spearman; independent clusters of social and emotional intelligence

   c. Gardner; three aspects of intelligence—analytical, creative, and practical
   d. Sternberg; one general intelligence factor

30.3. People with savant syndrome have limited mental abilities except for an incredible ability in one specific area. The existence of savant syndrome seems to support
   a. Sternberg's distinction among three aspects of intelligence.
   b. Spearman's notion of general intelligence, or *g* factor.
   c. Gardner's theory of multiple intelligences.
   d. Thurstone's clusters of primary mental abilities.

30.4. Traditional intelligence tests predict school grades reasonably well but are less successful at predicting achievement in other areas. Robert Sternberg has therefore identified three aspects of intelligence, which are
   a. spatial, academic, and artistic intelligence.
   b. musical, athletic, and academic intelligence.
   c. academic, practical, and creative intelligence.
   d. emotional, practical, and spatial intelligence.

30.5. Emotionally intelligent people are characterized by
   a. the tendency to seek immediate gratification.
   b. the ability to understand their own emotions but not those of others.
   c. high practical intelligence.
   d. self-awareness.

30.6. Neuroscientists have shown that people who quickly perceive and process stimuli during simple tasks also tend to receive high scores on intelligence tests. Knowing this, we can say that
   a. intelligent people accumulate more information than their less intelligent counterparts.
   b. there is no *g* factor.
   c. multiple intelligences are not possible.
   d. this correlation exists; any other conclusion is speculation since we don't know *why* fast reactions are associated with high intelligence test scores.

Review: For the second time in a week, José and Miguel encountered a barking dog on their walk to class. Miguel picked up a stick and was about to yell at the dog when José began talking gently to the dog, and the dog began wagging its tail. Why was José's response more "intelligent" according to the definition in this section?

Reflect: The modern concept of multiple intelligences (à la Howard Gardner or Robert Sternberg) assumes that the analytical word smarts and number smarts measured by traditional intelligence tests are important abilities but that other abilities are also important. Different people have different gifts. What are yours?

Answers to the Test Yourself and Review questions can be found in the green appendix at the end of the book.

Assessing Intelligence

How do we assess intelligence? Movie hero Forrest Gump's answer, "Stupid is as stupid does," catches the spirit of psychology's simplest answer: Intelligent is as intelligent does on an intelligence test. In other words, intelligence is whatever intelligence tests measure. So, what are these tests, and what makes a test credible? The answer to that question begins with a look at why psychologists created tests of mental abilities and how they have used them.

The Origins of Intelligence Testing

Preview Question: When psychologists invented the first tests of mental ability, what were they trying to measure?

> "People are trapped in history, and history is trapped in them."
>
> James Baldwin, *Notes of a Native Son*

Some societies concern themselves with promoting the collective welfare of the family, community, and society. Other societies emphasize individual opportunity. A pioneer of this individualist tradition, Plato wrote more than 2000 years ago in *The Republic* that "no two persons are born exactly alike; but each differs from the other in natural endowments, one being suited for one occupation and the other for another." As heirs to Plato's individualism, people in Western societies have pondered how and why individuals differ. Western attempts to assess individual differences in mental ability began in earnest about a century ago. Our present concept of intelligence is in large part a product of the history of those attempts. The history of intelligence testing also illustrates an important lesson: Although science itself strives for objectivity, individual scientists are affected by their own attitudes.

Alfred Binet: Predicting School Achievement

The modern intelligence-testing movement began when the pioneering French psychologist Alfred Binet (1857–1911) began assessing intellectual abilities. When the French government passed a law requiring that all children attend school, teachers soon faced an overwhelming range of individual differences. Some children, including many newcomers to Paris, seemed incapable of benefiting from the regular school curriculum and in need of special classes. But how could the schools objectively identify children with special needs?

The government was reluctant to trust teachers' subjective judgments of children's learning potential. Academic slowness might merely reflect inadequate prior education. Also, teachers might prejudge children on the basis of their social backgrounds. To minimize bias, France's minister of public education in 1904 commissioned Binet and others to study the problem. In response, Binet and his collaborator, Théodore Simon, decided to develop an objective test to identify children likely to have difficulty in the regular classes.

Binet and Simon began by assuming that all children follow the same course of intellectual development but that some develop more rapidly. "Dull" children, they presumed, were merely "retarded" in their development. On tests, therefore, a "dull" child should perform as does a typical younger child, and a "bright" child as does a typical older child.

- **mental age** a measure of intelligence test performance devised by Binet; the chronological age that most typically corresponds to a given level of performance. Thus, a child who does as well as the average 8-year-old is said to have a mental age of 8.

- **Stanford-Binet** the widely used American revision (by Terman at Stanford University) of Binet's original intelligence test.

- **intelligence quotient (IQ)** defined originally as the ratio of mental age (ma) to chronological age (ca) multiplied by 100 [thus, IQ = (ma/ca) × 100]. On contemporary intelligence tests, the average performance for a given age is assigned a score of 100.

Binet and Simon set out to measure what came to be called a child's **mental age**, the chronological age typical of a given level of performance. The average 9-year-old has a mental age of 9. But many 9-year-olds have mental ages below or above 9. Children below average, such as 9-year-olds who perform at the level of a typical 7-year-old, would struggle with schoolwork considered normal for their age.

To measure mental age, Binet and Simon theorized that mental aptitude, like athletic aptitude, is a general capacity that shows up in various ways. They then developed varied reasoning and problem-solving questions that might predict school achievement. By testing "bright" and "backward" Parisian schoolchildren on these questions, Binet and Simon succeeded: They found items that did predict how well the children handled schoolwork.

Note that Binet and Simon made no assumptions concerning *why* a particular child was slow, average, or precocious. Binet personally leaned toward an environmental explanation. To raise the capacities of low-scoring children, he recommended "mental orthopedics" that would train them to develop their attention span and self-discipline. He refused to speculate about what the test was actually measuring, but he insisted that it did not measure inborn intelligence as a meterstick measures height. Rather, the test had a single practical purpose: to identify French schoolchildren needing special attention. Binet hoped his test would be used to improve children's education, but he also feared it would be used to label children and limit their opportunities (Gould, 1981).

Lewis Terman: The Innate IQ

Binet might have been dismayed to discover that the test he designed as a practical guide for identifying slow learners in need of special help would soon be used as a numerical measure of inherited intelligence. After Binet's death in 1911, Stanford University professor Lewis Terman (1877–1956) attempted to use Binet's test but found that the Paris-developed age norms worked poorly with California schoolchildren. So Terman revised the test. He adapted some of Binet's original items, added others, established new age norms, and extended the upper end of the test's range from teenagers to "superior adults." Terman gave his revision the name it retains today—the **Stanford-Binet**.

For such tests, German psychologist William Stern derived the famous **intelligence quotient**, or **IQ**. The IQ was simply a person's mental age divided by chronological age and multiplied by 100 to get rid of the decimal point:

$$IQ = \frac{\text{mental age}}{\text{chronological age}} \times 100$$

Thus, an average child, whose mental and chronological ages are the same, has an IQ of 100. But an 8-year-old who answers questions as would a typical 10-year-old has an IQ of 125.

Most current intelligence tests, including the Stanford-Binet, no longer compute an IQ. The original IQ formula works fairly well for children but not for adults. Consider: Should a 40-year-old who does as well on the test as an average 20-year-old be assigned an IQ of only 50? Obviously, something is

Alfred Binet
"The scale, properly speaking, does not permit the measure of intelligence, because intellectual qualities . . . cannot be measured as linear surfaces are measured" (Binet & Simon, 1905).

"The IQ test was invented to predict academic performance, nothing else. If we wanted something that would predict life success, we'd have to invent another test completely."

Social psychologist Robert Zajonc (1984b)

Lewis Terman
"The children of successful and cultured parents test higher than children from wretched and ignorant homes for the simple reason that their heredity is better" (1916, p. 115).

"You did very well on your IQ test. You're a man of 49 with the intelligence of a man of 53."

out of whack. Today's intelligence tests therefore produce a mental ability score based on the test-taker's performance relative to the average performance of others the same age. As on the original Stanford-Binet, current tests define this score so that 100 is average, with about two-thirds of all people scoring between 85 and 115. Although there is no longer any intelligence *quotient*, the term "IQ" still lingers in everyday vocabulary as a shorthand expression for "intelligence test score."

Terman promoted the widespread use of intelligence testing. His motive was to "take account of the inequalities of children in original endowment" by assessing their "vocational fitness." In sympathy with the eugenics movement—a nineteenth-century movement that proposed measuring human traits and using the results to encourage or discourage people from reproducing—Terman (1916, pp. 91–92) lamented what he believed was the "dullness" and "unusually prolific breeding" of certain ethnic groups. He envisioned that the use of intelligence tests would "ultimately result in curtailing the reproduction of feeble-mindedness and in the elimination of an enormous amount of crime, pauperism, and industrial inefficiency" (p. 7).

With Terman's help, the U.S. government developed new tests to evaluate newly arriving immigrants and 1.7 million World War I army recruits—the world's first mass administration of an intelligence test. To some psychologists, the results indicated the inferiority of people not sharing their Anglo-Saxon heritage. Such findings were part of the cultural climate that led to the 1924 immigration law, which reduced immigration quotas for Southern and Eastern Europe to less than a fifth of those for Northern and Western Europe.

Binet would have been horrified at his test being adapted and used to draw such conclusions. Indeed, such sweeping judgments did become an embarrassment to most of those who championed testing. Terman, for instance, came to appreciate that test scores reflect not only people's innate mental abilities but also their education and their familiarity with the culture assumed by the test. Nevertheless, abuses of the early intelligence tests serve to remind us that science can be value-laden. Influenced by his ideology, Terman (1916, pp. 91–92) had expected "enormously significant racial differences in intelligence." Behind a screen of scientific objectivity, ideology sometimes lurks.

> "Science must be understood as a social phenomenon, a gutsy, human enterprise, not the work of robots programmed to collect pure information."
>
> Stephen Jay Gould (1981)

Modern Tests of Mental Abilities

Preview Question: What is the difference between an aptitude test and an achievement test?

Matching patterns
Block design puzzles test the ability to analyze patterns. Wechsler's individually administered intelligence test comes in forms suited for adults (WAIS) and children (WISC).

Today's most widely used intelligence test, the **Wechsler Adult Intelligence Scale (WAIS)**, was created by psychologist David Wechsler, who, as a 6-year-old Romanian, was among the supposedly feeble-minded Eastern European immigrants of the early 1900s. Later he developed a similar test for school-age children, called the *Wechsler Intelligence Scale for Children (WISC)*, and still later a test for preschool children. The WAIS consists of 11 subtests, as illustrated in **FIGURE 31.1**. It yields not only an overall intelligence score, as does the Stanford-Binet, but also separate "verbal" and "performance" (nonverbal) scores. Striking differences between the two scores alert the examiner to possible learning problems. For example, a verbal score much lower than the same person's performance score might indicate a reading or language disability. The tests also provide clues to cognitive strengths that a teacher or an employer might build upon.

By this point in your life, you've faced dozens of ability tests: elementary school tests of basic reading and math skills, course examinations, intelligence tests, driver's license examinations, and college entrance examinations, to name just a few. Psychologists classify such tests as either **aptitude tests**, intended to

VERBAL

General Information
What day of the year is Independence Day?

Similarities
In what way are *wool* and *cotton* alike?

Arithmetic Reasoning
If eggs cost 60 cents a dozen, what does 1 egg cost?

Vocabulary
Tell me the meaning of corrupt.

Comprehension
Why do people buy fire insurance?

Digit Span
Listen carefully, and when I am through, say the numbers right after me.

7 3 4 1 8 6

Now I am going to say some more numbers, but I want you to say them backward.

3 8 4 1 6

PERFORMANCE

Picture Completion
I am going to show you a picture with an important part missing. Tell me what is missing.

'85

SUN	MON	TUE	WED	THU	FRI	SAT
1	2	3	4	5	6	7
8	9	10	11	12	13	14
15	16	17	18	19	20	21
22	23	24	25	26	27	28
29	30					

Picture Arrangement
The pictures below tell a story. Put them in the right order to tell the story.

Block Design
Using the four blocks, make one just like this.

Object Assembly
If these pieces are put together correctly, they will make something. Go ahead and put them together as quickly as you can.

Digit-Symbol Substitution

Code

△	○	⃟	✕	8
1	2	3	4	5

Test

△	8	✕	○	△	⃟	8	✕	△	8

FIGURE 31.1

Sample items from the Wechsler Adult Intelligence Scale (WAIS) subtests (From Thorndike & Hagen, 1977.)

predict your ability to learn a new skill, or **achievement tests**, intended to *reflect* what you have learned. Thus, a college entrance exam, which seeks to predict your ability to do college work, is an aptitude test—a "thinly disguised intelligence test," says Howard Gardner (1999). Exams covering what you have learned in this course are achievement tests.

Actually, the differences between aptitude tests and achievement tests are not so clear-cut. Your achieved vocabulary influences your score on most aptitude tests. Similarly, your aptitudes for learning and test-taking influence your grades on tests for achievement. Most tests, whether labeled aptitude or achievement, assess both ability and its development. Practically speaking, however, aptitude tests (such as the WAIS and WISC) predict future performance, and achievement tests (such as your final exams this term) assess current performance. And whether a test is an aptitude or an achievement test, its design is governed by the same set of stringent requirements.

Principles of Test Construction

Preview Question: What do we mean when we say a test is standardized, reliable, and valid?

To be widely accepted, psychological tests must meet three criteria: They must be *standardized*, *reliable*, and *valid*. The Stanford-Binet and Wechsler tests meet these requirements.

■ **Wechsler Adult Intelligence Scale (WAIS)** the WAIS is the most widely used intelligence test; it contains verbal and performance (nonverbal) subtests.

■ **aptitude test** a test designed to predict a person's future performance; *aptitude* is the capacity to learn.

■ **achievement test** a test designed to assess what a person has learned.

standardization defining meaningful scores by comparison with the performance of a pretested "standardization group."

normal curve the symmetrical bell-shaped curve that describes the distribution of many physical and psychological attributes. Most scores fall near the average, and fewer and fewer scores lie near the extremes.

reliability the extent to which a test yields consistent results, as assessed by the consistency of scores on two halves of the test, on alternate forms of the test, or on retesting.

Standardization

The number of questions you answered correctly on an intelligence test would tell us almost nothing. To evaluate your performance, we need a basis for comparing it with others' performance. To enable meaningful comparisons, test-makers first give the test to a representative sample of people. When others take the test following the same procedures, their scores can be compared with the standards defined by the sample. This process of defining meaningful scores relative to a pretested group is called **standardization**.

Recall that Terman and his colleagues recognized that items developed for Parisians did not provide a satisfactory standard for evaluating Americans. So they revised the test and standardized the new version by testing 2300 native-born, white Americans of differing socioeconomic levels. Ironically, they then used this standard to evaluate nonwhite American and immigrant groups (Van Leeuwen, 1982).

Standardized test results typically form a *normal distribution*, a bell-shaped pattern of scores that forms the **normal curve** (FIGURE 31.2). No matter what we measure—people's heights, weights, or mental aptitudes—scores often form a roughly symmetrical, bell-shaped distribution clustered around the average. On an intelligence test, we call this average score 100. As we move out from the average (toward either extreme) we find fewer and fewer people. Within each age group, the Stanford-Binet and the Wechsler tests assign any person a score according to how much that person's performance deviates above or below the average. As Figure 31.2 shows, a performance higher than all but 2 percent of all scores earns an intelligence score of 130. A raw score that is comparably *below* 98 percent of all the scores earns an intelligence score of 70.

To keep the average score near 100, the Stanford-Binet and the Wechsler scales are periodically restandardized. If you took the revised WAIS recently, your performance was compared with a standardization sample who took the test between 1976 and 1980, not to David Wechsler's initial 1930s sample. If you compared the performance of the most recent standardization sample with that of the 1930s sample, do you suppose you would find rising or declining test performance? Amazingly—given that college entrance aptitude scores were dropping during the 1960s and 1970s—intelligence test performance has been *improving*. This worldwide phenomenon is called the *Flynn effect* in honor of New Zealand researcher James Flynn (1987, 1999), who first calculated its magnitude. As FIGURE 31.3 indicates, the average person's IQ score 80 years ago was—by today's standard—only a 76! Such rising performance has been observed in 20 countries. The increase seems real and is now widely accepted as an

FIGURE 31.2 The normal curve Scores on aptitude tests tend to form a normal, or bell-shaped, curve. For example, the Wechsler scale calls the average score 100.

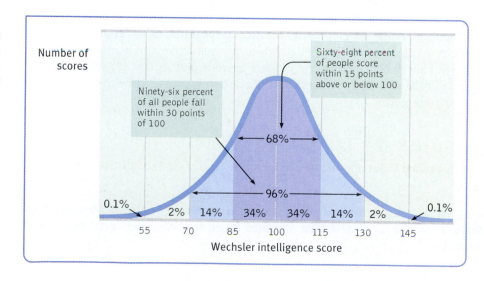

Number of scores

Sixty-eight percent of people score within 15 points above or below 100

Ninety-six percent of all people fall within 30 points of 100

68%

96%

0.1%   2%   14%   34%   34%   14%   2%   0.1%

55   70   85   100   115   130   145

Wechsler intelligence score

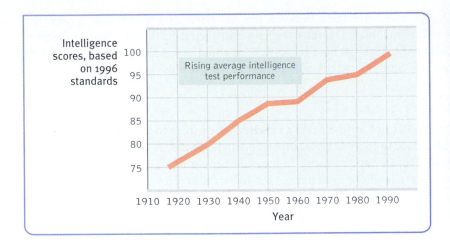

FIGURE **31.3**
Getting smarter?
In every country studied, intelligence test performance has been rising, as shown here with American Wechsler and Stanford-Binet test performance between 1918 and 1989. In Britain, test scores have risen 27 points since 1942. (From Hogan, 1995.)

important phenomenon, because it suggests either that a problem exists with the tests or that intelligence is changeable.

The Flynn effect's cause is a mystery (Neisser, 1997a, 1998). Does it result from greater test sophistication? (But the gains began before testing was widespread.) From better nutrition? (People have gotten taller as well as smarter.) From more education? More stimulating environments? Less childhood disease? Regardless of what combination of factors explains the rise in intelligence test scores, the phenomenon counters one concern of some hereditarians—that the higher twentieth-century birthrates among those with lower scores would shove human intelligence scores downward. Such may still happen as the twentieth-century nutritional and educational gains max out, say pessimists (Lynn, 1997). In human history, the long-term future has always belonged to the fertile, they argue—to those who propagate and populate. Nevertheless, for most of the century, the social-class gap in intelligence scores *shrank* (Williams & Ceci, 1997).

What an intriguing puzzle: Are aptitudes decreasing, as some have inferred from the decline in college aptitude test scores, or are they rising, as intelligence test data suggest? The college aptitude decline is due partly to the greater academic diversity of the students who began taking the test during the 1960s. The WAIS, however, has always been standardized on a more diverse and broadly representative group. Such people—people in general—have become more literate and better educated since the 1930s. These facts help explain why performance on the more complex college aptitude tests dropped while performance rose on the basic skills tested by the WAIS. The IQ score gain has probably occurred at the lower end—fewer 70s and 80s, speculates David Lykken (1998)—given that genius scores have not increased. Mysteriously, the gains are greatest on nonverbal tests, tests that improved schooling should least affect. (Perhaps playing with Legos, mazes, and video games has helped, though the increase began before all these became popular.) Flynn finds it hard to imagine that his generation is so much smarter than his grandparents', yet he finds the data hard to dismiss. "I'm baffled," he says.

Reliability

Comparing your test scores to those of the standardizing group still won't tell us much about you unless the test has **reliability**. A good test must yield dependably consistent scores. To check a test's reliability, researchers retest people using either the same test or another form of it. If the two scores generally agree, or *correlate*, the test is reliable. As an alternative, the researcher may split a test in half and see whether scores derived from odd and even questions agree.

Correlations indicate whether two sets of measurements are associated in some way. The lowest correlation, –1.0, represents perfect disagreement between the two sets—as one measurement goes up, the other goes down. A correlation of zero represents no consistency. The highest correlation, +1.0, represents perfect consistency—as the first measurement goes up, so does the second.

The higher the correlation between the *test-retest* or the *split-half* scores, the higher the test's reliability. The tests we have considered so far—the Stanford-Binet, the WAIS, and the WISC—all have reliabilities of about +.9, which is very high. When retested, people's scores generally match their first score closely.

Validity

High reliability does not ensure a test's **validity**—the extent to which the test actually measures what it is supposed to measure or predicts what it is supposed to predict. If you use an inaccurate tape measure to measure people's heights, your height report would have high reliability (consistency) but low validity. How, then, is a test's validity determined? It is enough for some tests that they have **content validity**, meaning the test taps the pertinent behavior. The road test for a driver's license has content validity because it samples the tasks a driver routinely faces. Course exams have content validity if they assess one's mastery of a representative sample of course material.

Other tests are evaluated in terms of how well they agree with some **criterion**, an independent measure of what the test aims to assess. For some tests, the criterion is future performance. For example, aptitude tests must have **predictive validity** (also called *criterion-related validity*), which means they predict future achievement.

Are general aptitude tests as predictive as they are reliable? As critics are fond of noting, the answer is plainly no. The predictive power of aptitude tests is fairly strong in the early grades, but later it weakens. Academic aptitude test scores are reasonably good predictors of achievement in elementary school, where the correlation between intelligence score and grades is about +.60 (Jensen, 1980). The Scholastic Assessment Test (SAT), used in the United States as a college entrance exam, is less successful in predicting first-year college grades; here, the correlation is less than +.50 (Willingham & others, 1990). By the time we get to the Graduate Record Examination (GRE; an aptitude test similar to the SAT but for those applying to graduate school), the correlation with graduate school grades is an even more modest +.30 (GRE, 1990).

Why does the predictive power of aptitude scores diminish as students move up the educational ladder? Consider a parallel situation: Among all football linemen, body weight correlates with success. A 270-pound player tends to overwhelm a 190-pound opponent. But within the narrow 250- to 290-pound range typically found at the professional level, the correlation between weight and success becomes negligible (**FIGURE 31.4**). The narrower the *range* of weights, the lower the predictive power of body weight becomes.

FIGURE 31.4

Diminishing predictive power

Let's imagine a correlation between football linemen's body weight and their success on the field. Note how insignificant the relationship becomes when we narrow the range of weights to 250 to 290 pounds. As the range of data under consideration narrows, its predictive power diminishes.

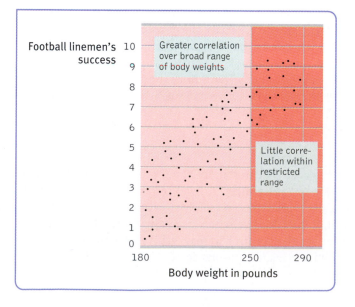

Likewise, if an elite university takes only students with very high aptitude scores, their scores, hardly varying, cannot possibly predict much. A similar narrowing of range explains why the GRE is only a modest predictor of graduate school grades. If a graduate school admits only those students whose aptitude scores fall within a narrow range, it should not surprise us that their aptitude scores will not closely predict their grades. This will be true even if the test has excellent predictive validity with a more diverse sample of students. So, when we validate a test using a wide range of people but then use it with a restricted range of people, it loses much of its predictive validity. A narrowed range of grades—as in graduate school departments that award mostly As and Bs—similarly reduces predictive validity.

The Dynamics of Intelligence

Preview Question: How stable is human intelligence over the life span?

Stability or Change

If we retested people periodically throughout their lives, would their intelligence scores be stable? This question has led to a search for indicators of infants' later intelligence that has left few stones unturned. Unable to talk with infants, developmental researchers have assessed what they can observe—everything from birth weight, to whether the third toe was longer than the second, to age of sitting up alone. None of these measures provides any useful prediction of intelligence scores at much later ages (Bell & Waldrop, 1989; Broman, 1989). Perhaps, as developmental psychologist Nancy Bayley reflected in 1949, "we have not yet found the right tests." Someday, she speculated, we might find "infant behaviors which are characteristic of underlying intellectual functions" and which will predict later intelligence.

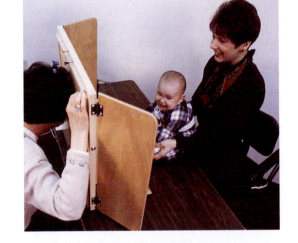

Such a test may have been found. Two dozen studies by Joseph Fagan, Marc Bornstein, John Columbo, and others reveal that 2- to 7-month-old babies who quickly grow bored with a picture—who, given a choice, prefer to look at a new one—score higher on tests of brain speed and intelligence up to 11 years later (McCall & Carriger, 1993; Neisser & others, 1996; Rose & Feldman, 1997). Although the prediction is crude, the tests can help identify children likely to be extremely below or above average.

So, can everyday observations or intelligence test scores now predict preschoolers' future performance and educational needs? The question is especially interesting to new parents wondering about their baby's intelligence and to educators wanting an early identification of children with special needs. Those anxious about comparing their baby with others can relax. Except for extremely impaired or very precocious children, casual observation and intelligence tests before age 3 predict children's future aptitudes only minimally (Humphreys & Davey, 1988). For example, children who are early talkers—speaking in sentences typical of 3-year-olds by age 20 months—are *not* especially likely to be reading by age 4½ (Crain-Thoreson & Dale, 1992). (A better predictor of early reading is having parents who have read lots of stories to their child.) Even Albert Einstein was slow in learning to talk (Quasha, 1980).

validity the extent to which a test measures or predicts what it is supposed to. (See also *content validity* and *predictive validity*.)

content validity the extent to which a test samples the behavior that is of interest (such as a driving test that samples driving tasks).

criterion the behavior (such as college grades) that a test (such as the SAT) is designed to predict; thus, the measure used in defining whether the test has predictive validity.

predictive validity the success with which a test predicts the behavior it is designed to predict; it is assessed by computing the correlation between test scores and the criterion behavior. (Also called *criterion-related validity*.)

How smart is this baby?
Infants' preference for novel stimuli is a moderate predictor of future intelligence. This researcher in Joseph Fagan's laboratory briefly shows an infant a previously seen picture alongside a new picture, recording the number of seconds the child looks at each.

By age 3, however, children's performances on intelligence tests begin to predict their adolescent and adult scores. Moreover, high-scoring adolescents tend to have been early readers. One study surveyed the parents of 187 seventh- and eighth-graders who had taken a college aptitude test as part of a seven-state talent search and had scored considerably higher than most high school seniors. If their parents' memories can be trusted, more than half of this precocious group of adolescents began reading by age 4 and more than 80 percent were reading by age 5 (Van Tassel-Baska, 1983). Not surprisingly, then, intelligence tests given in kindergarten begin to predict school achievement (Tramontana & others, 1988).

After about age 7, intelligence test scores, though certainly not fixed, stabilize (Bloom, 1964). Thus, the consistency of scores over time increases with the age of the child. The remarkable stability of aptitude scores by late adolescence is seen in an Educational Testing Service study of 23,000 students who took the SAT and then later took its more advanced counterpart, the GRE, a test taken by many college seniors (Angoff, 1988). On either test, verbal scores correlate only modestly with math scores—revealing that these two aptitudes are distinct. Yet scores on the SAT verbal test correlated +.86 with the scores on GRE verbal tests taken four to five years later. An equally astonishing +.86 correlation occurred between the two math tests. Given the time lapse and differing educational experiences of these 23,000 students, the stability of their aptitude scores is remarkable—surely beyond what anyone would have predicted.

The stability of intelligence test scores tends to continue throughout later life and into old age. Current research indicates, however, that the relationship between intelligence test scores and age may depend in part on what we assess. Test scores of *crystallized intelligence*—one's accumulated knowledge as reflected in vocabularies and analogies tests—seem to remain stable or even increase slightly as we age. Crystallized intelligence is reflected in the verbal scores of traditional intelligence tests, such as the Wechsler Adult Intelligence Scale. Scores on tests that measure *fluid intelligence*—one's ability to reason speedily or abstractly, as when solving novel logic problems—tend to decrease slightly up to about age 75, when they fall off more rapidly (Cattell, 1963; Horn, 1982). Such tests, because they assess speed of thinking, may place older adults at a disadvantage because of their slower neural mechanisms for processing information.

Extremes of Intelligence

Preview Question: What can comparisons of people who score at the extremes on an intelligence test tell us about that test?

One way to glimpse the validity and significance of any test is to compare people who score at the two extremes of the normal curve. The two groups should differ noticeably, and they do.

The Low Extreme

At one extreme are those whose intelligence test scores fall below 70. To have a developmental disability that the *Diagnostic and Statistical Manual* labels **mental retardation**, a child must have both a low test score *and* difficulty adapting to the normal demands of independent living. Only about 1 percent of the population meets both criteria, with males outnumbering females by 50 percent (American Psychiatric Association, 1994). As Table 31.1 indicates, most individuals with mental retardation can, with support, live in mainstream society.

Mental retardation sometimes has a known physical cause. One such case is **Down syndrome**, a disorder of varying severity caused by an extra chromosome in the person's genetic makeup.

> "My dear Adele, I am 4 years old and I can read any English book. I can say all the Latin Substantives and Adjectives and active verbs besides 52 lines of Latin poetry."
>
> Francis Galton, letter to his sister, 1827

Ironically, SAT and GRE scores correlate better with each other than either does with its intended criterion, school achievement. Thus, their reliability far exceeds their predictive validity. If either test was much affected by coaching, luck, or how one feels on the test day (as so many people believe), such reliability would be impossible.

A young man with Down syndrome
In the past, people with this condition were often institutionalized. Today, with a supportive family environment and special education, many people with Down syndrome learn to care for themselves and hold a job.

TABLE **31.1**

DEGREES OF MENTAL RETARDATION

Level	Typical Intelligence Scores	Percentage of Persons with Retardation	Adaptation to Demands of Life
Mild	50–70	85%	May learn academic skills up to sixth-grade level. Adults may, with assistance, achieve self-supporting social and vocational skills.
Moderate	35–49	10%	May progress to second-grade level academically. Adults may contribute to their own support by laboring in sheltered workshops.
Severe	20–34	3–4%	May learn to talk and to perform simple work tasks under close supervision but are generally unable to profit from vocational training.
Profound	Below 20	1–2%	Require constant aid and supervision.

Source: Reprinted with permission from the *Diagnostic and Statistical Manual of Mental Disorders*, Fourth Edition. Copyright 1994 American Psychiatric Association.

■ **mental retardation** a condition of limited mental ability, indicated by an intelligence score below 70 and difficulty in adapting to the demands of life; varies from mild to profound.

■ **Down syndrome** a condition of retardation and associated physical disorders caused by an extra chromosome in one's genetic makeup.

During the last two centuries, the pendulum of opinion about how best to care for people with mental retardation has made a complete swing. Until the mid-nineteenth century, they were cared for at home. Many of those with the most severe disabilities died, but people with milder forms of retardation often found a place in a farm-based society. Then, residential schools for slow learners were established. By the twentieth century, many of these institutions had become warehouses, providing residents no privacy, little attention, and no hope. Parents often were told to separate themselves permanently from their impaired child before they became attached.

In the last half of the twentieth century, the pendulum swung back to normalization—encouraging people to live in their own communities as normally as their functioning permits. Children with mild retardation are now educated in less restrictive environments, and many are integrated, or *mainstreamed*, into regular classrooms. Most grow up with their own families, then move into a protected living arrangement, such as a group home. The hope, and often the reality, is a happier and more dignified life.

The High Extreme

In one famous project begun in 1921, Lewis Terman studied more than 1500 California schoolchildren with IQ scores over 135. Contrary to the popular notion that intellectually gifted children are frequently maladjusted because they are "in a different world" from their nongifted peers, Terman's high-scoring children were healthy, well adjusted, and unusually successful academically. When restudied over the next seven decades, most had attained high levels of education (Holahan & Sears, 1995). The group included many doctors, lawyers, professors, scientists, and writers. Johns Hopkins University studies have similarly tracked mathematically precocious youngsters into early scientific achievement (Lubinski & Benbow, 2000; Stanley, 1997). These whiz kids remind one of Jean Piaget, who by age 7 was devoting his free time to studying birds, fossils, and machines; who by 15 began publishing scientific articles on mollusks; and who later went on to become the twentieth century's most famous developmental psychologist (Hunt, 1993).

A gifted child
At age 10, Lenny Ng became the youngest child to score a perfect 800 on the SAT math test. At age 16, his math project won a $20,000 scholarship in the 1993 Westinghouse Science Talent Search. By age 20, he was a second-year graduate student in mathematics at MIT, after graduating with highest honors from Harvard and winning a national math competition. Contrary to the notion that such precocious children suffer socially, high-aptitude children are typically well adjusted.

■ **creativity** the ability to produce novel and valuable ideas.

Nevertheless, there are critics who question many of the assumptions of currently popular "gifted child" programs, such as the belief that only 3 to 5 percent of children are gifted and that it pays to identify and label these special few—segregating them and giving them academic enrichment not available to the "ungifted" other 95 percent. This is an example of "tracking"—placing students in separate classes with others who share their level of aptitude score. Defenders say that this is preferable to teaching all students at the same level, as if holding top students back will bring less achieving students up. Other researchers, however, have concluded that the academic achievement scores of students tracked by aptitude are hardly higher than those of similar untracked students. Moreover, tracking by aptitude tends to lower students' self-esteem and sometimes creates a self-fulfilling prophecy: Those labeled "ungifted" can be influenced to become so (Lipsey & Wilson, 1993; Slavin & Braddock, 1993).

A report of the Carnegie Council on Adolescent Development (1989) condemned academic tracking as "one of the most divisive and damaging school practices in existence." Denying "low-ability" students opportunities for enriched education widens the achievement gap between the two groups and increases their social isolation from one another, one reason why there is no tracking in the elementary schools of Japan and China (Stevenson & Lee, 1990). Because minority and low-income youth are more often placed in lower academic groups, tracking can also promote segregation and prejudice—hardly a healthy preparation for working and living in a multicultural society.

Sorting children into gifted and nongifted groups often presumes that giftedness is a single trait—measured by an intelligence test—rather than just one of many potentials. Newspaper and magazine articles advise parents on how to spot "the signs of giftedness" in their children, as if it were an objective quality, like blue eyes, that a child either has or lacks. This reifies giftedness—by creating the concept and then presuming that it has a concrete reality. It ignores the fact that we, not nature, are deciding the criteria for giftedness.

Critics and proponents of gifted education do, however, agree on this much: Children have differing gifts. Some are especially good at math, others at verbal reasoning, others at art, still others at social leadership. It is a maxim of biology that nature prefers diversity. By packaging different gifts in different bodies, nature enhances a group's welfare and the odds that some will survive environmental challenges. Educating children as if all were alike is as naive as assuming that giftedness is something you either have or don't have. One need not hang value-laden labels on children to affirm their special talents and to challenge them all at the frontiers of their own abilities and understandings. By providing "appropriate developmental placement" suited to their talents, we can promote both equity and excellence for all (Benbow & Stanley, 1998; Lubinski & Benbow, 2000).

> "Joining Mensa means that you are a genius. . . . I worried about the arbitrary 132 cutoff point, until I met someone with an I.Q. of 131 and, honestly, he was a bit slow on the uptake."
>
> **Steve Martin, 1997**

> "Alpha children wear grey. They work much harder than we do, because they're so frightfully clever. I'm really awfully glad I'm a Beta, because I don't work so hard. And then we are much better than the Gammas and Deltas. Gammas are stupid."
>
> **Aldous Huxley, *Brave New World*, 1932**

Creativity and Intelligence

Preview Question: Is creativity linked to intelligence?

Creativity is the ability to produce ideas that are both novel and valuable. The forms for creativity vary by culture. Samoan culture encourages creativity in dance, Balinese culture in music, the African Ashanti culture in wood carvings (Lubart, 1990). In each, creativity means expressing familiar themes in novel and valuable ways.

Results from tests of intelligence and creativity suggest that a certain level of aptitude is necessary but not sufficient for creativity. In general, people with high intelligence scores also do well on creativity tests. ("How many uses can you think of for a brick?") But beyond a certain level—a score of about 120—the correlation between intelligence scores and creativity shrivels. Exceptionally creative architects, mathematicians, scientists, and engineers usually score no higher on intelligence tests than do their less creative peers (MacKinnon & Hall, 1972). So clearly there is more to creativity than that which intelligence tests reveal. Studies of creative people suggest five other components of creativity (Sternberg, 1988; Sternberg & Lubart, 1991, 1992):

+ The first is *expertise*—a well-developed base of knowledge. "Chance favors only the prepared mind," observed Louis Pasteur. The more ideas, images, and phrases we have to work with, through our accumulated learning, the more chances we have to combine these mental building blocks in novel ways.

+ *Imaginative thinking skills* provide the ability to see things in new ways, to recognize patterns, to make connections. To be creative you must first master the basic elements of a problem, then redefine or explore the problem in a new way. Copernicus first developed expertise regarding the solar system and its planets and then defined the system as revolving around the Sun, not the Earth.

+ A *venturesome personality* tolerates ambiguity and risk, perseveres in overcoming obstacles, and seeks new experiences rather than following the pack. Inventors, for example, have a willingness to persist after failures. Thomas Edison tried countless substances for his light bulb filament.

+ *Intrinsic motivation* is creativity's fourth component. As psychologist Teresa Amabile points out, "People will be most creative when they feel motivated primarily by the interest, enjoyment, satisfaction, and challenge of the work itself—rather than by external pressures" (Amabile & Hennessey, 1992). Creative people focus not so much on extrinsic motivators—meeting deadlines, impressing people, or making money—as on the intrinsic pleasure and challenge of their work.

+ A *creative environment* sparks, supports, and refines creative ideas. After studying the careers of 2026 prominent scientists and inventors, Dean Keith Simonton (1992) noted that the most eminent among them were in fact not lone geniuses. Rather they were mentored, challenged, and supported by their relationships with colleagues. Such people often have the emotional intelligence needed to network effectively with peers.

Amabile's (1983, 1987) experiments demonstrated that creative environments also free people from concern about social approval. In one experiment, she asked college students to make paper collages, telling half beforehand that experts would evaluate their work. Those unaware that their work would be evaluated produced collages that judges later rated as more creative. Unworried about being evaluated, they felt freer to be creative.

Managers wanting to foster innovation at work should keep the intrinsic motivation principle in mind, observed Amabile (1988). They should set employees to work on what naturally interests them. And they can emulate managers who have successfully nurtured creativity—by providing their subordinates with time, freedom, and support to attain set goals. At the 3M company, where the Eleventh Commandment has been "Thou shalt not kill a new product idea," researchers are encouraged to spend 15 percent of their time pursuing creative projects that have no immediate payoff. From this creativity-nurturing environment have come such products as the removable Post-it notes (Kreitner,1992).

On his way home from picking up a Nobel prize in Stockholm, physicist Richard Feynman stopped in Queens, New York, to look at his high school record. "My grades were not as good as I remembered," he reported, "and my IQ was [a good, though unexceptional] 124" (Faber, 1987).

Reprinted with permission of Paul Soderblom.

Everyone held up their crackers as David threw the cheese log into the ceiling fan.

REVIEW AND REFLECT:

Assessing Intelligence

Among the most controversial issues in psychology is the debate over intelligence testing: whether tests can measure and quantify a person's abilities and how widely the results can be used fairly.

When psychologists invented the first tests of mental ability, what were they trying to measure?

More than a century ago in France, Alfred Binet started the modern intelligence-testing movement by developing questions that helped predict children's future progress in the Paris school system. Lewis Terman of Stanford University revised Binet's work for use in the United States. Terman believed his Stanford-Binet could help guide people toward appropriate opportunities, but—unlike Binet—he was biased by his belief that intelligence was inherited. During the early part of the twentieth century, intelligence tests were sometimes used in ways that, in hindsight, even their designers regretted—to "document" a presumed innate inferiority of certain ethnic and immigrant groups.

What is the difference between an aptitude test and an achievement test?

Aptitude tests are designed to predict learning ability, as is the Wechsler. Achievement tests are designed to assess current competence.

What do we mean when we say a test is standardized, reliable, and valid?

A good test must be *standardized*, so that any person's performance can be meaningfully compared to others'; *reliable*, so it yields dependably consistent scores; and *valid*, so it measures what it is supposed to measure. Test scores usually fall into a bell-shaped distribution, the normal curve. The average score is assigned an arbitrary number (such as 100 on an intelligence test). Aptitude tests tend to be highly reliable, but they are weak predictors of success in life. However, their predictive validity for academic success in the early grades is fairly strong. Test validity weakens for predicting grades in college and even more so in graduate school, as the range of student abilities becomes more restricted.

How stable is human intelligence over the life span?

The stability of intelligence test scores increases with age, with practical predictive value beginning by age 3 and scores becoming fairly stable by age 7. Among infants, those who quickly become bored with a picture, preferring to look at a new one, tend to score well on later intelligence tests.

What can comparisons of people who score at the extremes of an intelligence test tell us about that test?

Comparing those who score extremely low with those who score extremely high magnifies a test's apparent validity. The groups should differ markedly.

Is creativity linked to intelligence?

Intelligence correlates weakly with creativity. Increases in intelligence beyond a necessary threshold level are not linked with increased creativity.

Terms and Concepts to Remember

mental age, p. 409
Stanford-Binet, p. 409
intelligence quotient (IQ), p. 409
Wechsler Adult Intelligence Scale (WAIS), p. 410
aptitude test, p. 410
achievement test, p. 411
standardization, p. 412

normal curve, p. 412
reliability, p. 413
validity, p. 414
content validity, p. 414
criterion, p. 414
predictive validity, p. 414
mental retardation, p. 416
Down syndrome, p. 416
creativity, p. 418

Test Yourself

31.1. Intelligence quotient, or IQ, was originally defined as the ratio of mental age to chronological age multiplied by 100. By this definition, a 6-year-old child with a measured mental age of 6 would have an IQ of 100. Likewise, a 6-year-old with a measured mental age of 9 would have an IQ of
   a. 67.
   b. 133.
   c. 86.
   d. 150.

31.2. The Wechsler Adult Intelligence Scale (WAIS) yields an overall intelligence score as well as separate verbal and performance (nonverbal) scores. The WAIS is best able to tell us
   a. what part of an individual's intelligence is determined by genetic inheritance.
   b. whether the test-taker will succeed in a job.
   c. how the test-taker compares with other adults in vocabulary and arithmetic reasoning.
   d. whether the test-taker has specific skills for music and the performing arts.

31.3. Aptitude and achievement tests are tests of mental abilities. Aptitude tests are designed to _____, whereas achievement tests are designed to _____.
   a. predict ability to learn; reflect what has been learned
   b. assess adaptive behavior; identify level of intelligence
   c. uncover undeveloped skills; objectively evaluate adaptability
   d. measure performance; differentiate slow learners from all others

31.4. Standardization is the process of defining meaningful scores relative to a pretested group. Standardized test results typically form a
   a. Flynn effect.
   b. restricted range.
   c. bell-shaped curve.
   d. test-retest correlation.

31.5. The Stanford-Binet, the Wechsler Adult Intelligence Scale, and the Wechsler Intelligence Scale for Children are known to have very high reliability (about +.9). This means that
a. a pretest has been given to a representative sample.
b. the test yields consistent results, for example on retesting.
c. the test measures what it is supposed to measure.
d. the results of the test will be distributed on a bell-shaped curve.

31.6. After about age 7, an individual's intelligence test scores tend to _____ over the person's life span.
a. increase
b. decrease
c. fluctuate
d. remain stable

31.7. Creativity is the ability to produce novel and valuable ideas. Which of the following is not a characteristic of a creative person?
a. expertise
b. extrinsic motivation
c. a venturesome personality
d. imaginative thinking skills

Review

- How did Terman's motives for creating tests of mental abilities differ from Binet's?

- Does leg strength predict running speed? To find out, Fiona correlates the muscular strength of the 10 fastest youth in her school with their 100-meter times—and finds only a weak correlation. But even if strong muscles do enable speed, we could have expected this result. Why?

- The Smiths have enrolled their 2-year-old son, whom they believe is gifted, in a special program that claims to "give your child a superior mind." Why is this endeavor of questionable value?

Reflect

- Scientists' personal beliefs sometimes bias their interpretations. Consider your personal beliefs. How might they bias your interpretations of what you read and hear?

- Are you working to the potential reflected in your college entrance exam scores? What, other than your aptitude, is affecting your college performance?

- How do you feel about mainstreaming children of all ability levels in the same classroom? What evidence are you using to support your view?

Answers to the Test Yourself and Review questions can be found in the green appendix at the end of the book.

32 Genetic and Environmental Influences on Intelligence

What exactly determines intelligence? Our genes? Our environment? Psychologists have long recognized that intelligence seems to run in families. Moreover, we know that intelligence seems modestly predictable from infants' boredom with familiar pictures or from the complexity and speed of a person's brain-wave responses to a flash of light. But why? Are our intellectual abilities mostly inherited? Or primarily molded by our environment?

Few issues arouse such passion or have such serious political implications. Consider: If we mainly inherit our differing mental abilities, and if success reflects those abilities, then people's socioeconomic standing will correspond to their inborn differences. This could lead to those on top believing that their intellectual birthright justifies their social positions.

If, on the other hand, mental abilities are primarily nurtured by the environments that raise and inform us, then children from disadvantaged environments can expect to lead disadvantaged lives. In this case, people's standing will result from their unequal opportunities, a situation often regarded as basically unjust. For now, as best we can, let us set aside such political implications and examine the evidence.

Genetic Influences

Preview Question: How much credit do our genes get for our scores on intelligence tests?

Do people who share the same genes also share comparable mental abilities? As you can see from **FIGURE 32.1**, which summarizes many studies, the answer is clearly yes. In support of the genetic contribution to intelligence, researchers cite four sets of findings:

+ Across five studies, the intelligence test scores of 163 identical twins reared apart are virtually as similar as those of the same person taking the same test twice (Lykken, 1999). Fraternal twins, who share only half their genes, are much less similar in their scores.
+ Even identical twins whose parents do not dress or treat them identically are virtual carbon copies of each other in intelligence test scores (Loehlin & Nichols, 1976). Likewise, identical twins reared separately have similar scores—similar enough to lead twin researcher Thomas Bouchard (1996) to estimate that "about 70 percent" of intelligence score variation "can be attributed to genetic variation." Other researchers have offered estimates nearer 50 percent (Devlin & others, 1997; Plomin, 1999).
+ Among the many genes that combine to influence intelligence, one, located on chromosome 6, has recently been identified. In two studies, the gene was carried by about one-third of children with very high intelligence scores but only one-sixth of those with average scores (Chorney & others, 1998).
+ By inserting an extra gene into fertilized mouse eggs, researchers have produced smarter mice—mice that excel at learning and remembering the location of a hidden underwater platform or recognizing cues that signal impending shock (Tsien, 2000). The gene engineers a neural receptor involved in memory.

But there is also some evidence pointing to an effect of environment. Fraternal twins, who are genetically no more alike than any other siblings but who are

Smart scientist, smart mouse
Working with Ya-Ping Tang and others, Princeton University biologist Joe Z. Tsien genetically engineered a strain of smart mice. Such work may shed new light on the biology of human intelligence.

Similarity of intelligence scores (correlation)

Lower correlation than identical twins reared together shows some environmental effect

Lower correlation than identical twins shows genetic effects

| | Identical twins reared together | Identical twins reared apart | Fraternal twins reared together | Siblings reared together | Unrelated individuals reared together |

(Bar graph: y-axis "Similarity of intelligence scores (correlation)" from 0 to 1.00; bars approximately 0.86, 0.72, 0.60, 0.46, 0.33)

FIGURE 32.1

Intelligence: Nature and nurture

The most genetically similar people have the most similar intelligence scores. Remember: 1.0 indicates a perfect correlation; zero indicates no correlation at all. (Data from McGue & others, 1993.)

treated more alike because they are the same age, tend to score more alike than other siblings.

Seeking to disentangle genes and environment, researchers have also asked whether adopted children and their siblings, thanks to their shared environment, share similar aptitudes. During childhood, the intelligence test scores of adoptive siblings correlate modestly. Researchers have also compared the intelligence test scores of adopted children with those of their biological parents, the people from whom they received their genes, and with those of their adoptive parents, the providers of their home environment. Over time, adopted children accumulate experience in their differing adoptive families. So would you expect the family environment effect to grow with age and the genetic legacy effect to shrink?

If, like many people, you would, behavior geneticists have a surprise for you. With age, mental similarities between adopted children and their adoptive families disappear as the effect of common rearing wanes; by adulthood, the correlation is roughly zero (McGue & others, 1993). Such findings contradict the widely held belief that, as we accumulate life experience, the environmental influence on traits such as intelligence increases. In fact, the *opposite* seems true: With age, genetic influences become more apparent (Bouchard, 1995, 1996a). Adopted children's intelligence scores become more like their biological parents', and identical twins' similarities continue or increase into their eighties (McClearn & others, 1997; Plomin & others, 1997; see **FIGURE 32.2**, page 424).

Given such findings, one might be tempted to make statements about the heritability of intelligence. But be very careful how you use the word *heritability*. To say that the heritability of intelligence—

"I told my parents that if grades were so important they should have paid for a smarter egg donor."

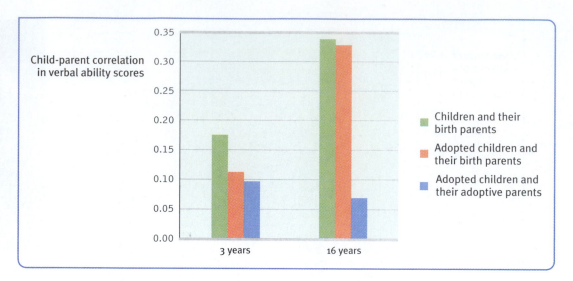

FIGURE **32.2**
Who do adopted children resemble?
As the years went by in their adoptive families, Colorado Adoption Project children's verbal ability scores became modestly more like their *biological* parents' scores. (Adapted from Plomin & Defries, 1998.)

the variation in intelligence test scores attributable to genetic factors—is roughly 50 percent does *not* mean that your genes are responsible for 50 percent of your intelligence and your environment for the rest. It means that we can attribute to heredity 50 percent *of the variation in intelligence within a group of people*. This point is so often misunderstood that I repeat: We can never say what percentage of an *individual's* intelligence is inherited. Heritability refers instead to the extent to which *differences among people* are attributable to genes. Heritability *never* pertains to an individual, only to why people differ.

Even this conclusion must be qualified, because heritability can vary from study to study. For example, environmental differences are more predictive of intelligence scores among children of less-educated parents—among whom family environments may vary widely (Rowe & others, 1999). Mark Twain once proposed that boys should be raised in barrels and fed through a hole. Given the boys' equal environments, differences in their individual intelligence test scores at age 12 could be explained only by their heredity. Thus, heritability for their differences would be nearly 100 percent. But if we raise people with similar heredities in drastically different environments (barrels versus advantaged homes), heritability—differences due to genes—will be low.

Remember, too, that genes and environment interact. For example, students with a natural aptitude for mathematics are more likely to select math courses in high school and later to score well on math aptitude tests—thanks *both* to their natural math aptitude *and* to their math experience. Our genes shape the experiences that shape us.

Environmental Influences

Preview Question: To what extent are our scores on intelligence tests attributable to our life experiences?

We have seen that our genes make a difference. Even if we were all raised in the same intellectually stimulating environment, we still would not have the same aptitudes. But we have also seen that heredity doesn't tell the whole story. Within the limits dictated by our genes, our life experiences do matter. The environment that siblings share doesn't much influence their aptitudes, but it significantly influences their scholastic achievement (Thompson & others, 1991).

Human environments are rarely as impoverished as the dark and barren cages inhabited by deprived rats that develop thinner-than-normal brain cortexes (Rosenzweig and others, 1972). Yet severe life experiences do leave marks on us.

Early Intervention Effects

Psychologist J. McVicker Hunt (1982) both observed the dramatic effects of early experiences and demonstrated the impact of early intervention effects in a destitute Iranian orphanage in Tehran. The typical child Hunt observed there could not sit up unassisted at age 2 or walk at age 4. The little care the infants received was not in response to their crying, cooing, or other behaviors. The children were therefore not developing any sense of personal control over their environment. As a result, they were becoming passive "glum lumps." Extreme deprivation was bludgeoning native intelligence.

Aware of the benefits of responsive caregiving, Hunt began a program of "tutored human enrichment." For instance, he trained caregivers to play vocal games with the infants. They first imitated the babies' babbling. Then they led the babies in vocal follow-the-leader by shifting from one familiar sound to another. Then they began to teach sounds from the Persian language.

The results were dramatic. All 11 infants who received these language-fostering experiences could name more than 50 objects and body parts by 22 months. So charming had the infants become that most were adopted—an unprecedented success for the orphanage.

Hunt's findings testify to the importance of environment. There is no doubt that severe disadvantage takes a toll on children (Ramey & Ramey, 1992). And when the infant malnutrition associated with severe poverty is relieved with nutritional supplements, poverty's effect on physical and cognitive development lessens (Brown & Pollitt, 1996).

Do such findings indicate a way to "give your child a superior intellect"? Some popular books claim that with intensive preschool training such is possible, but most experts are doubtful (Bruer, 1999). Although malnutrition, sensory deprivation, and social isolation can retard normal brain development, the difference between normal and "enriched" environments matters less. There is no environmental recipe for superbabies, beyond normal exposure to sights, sounds, and speech. Sandra Scarr's (1984) verdict still is widely shared: "Parents who are very concerned about providing special educational lessons for their babies are wasting their time." Parents of children with high intelligence test scores may have been more likely to hang crib mobiles, take the children to the theater, or whatever. Did such experiences boost the children's scores a notch or two? We don't know, stated Scarr (1986). Parents supply their children with both genes and environments. So even if the environments of children with high scores on intelligence tests are noticeably different from those with low scores, we cannot be sure how much difference their environments make.

Hunt would probably agree with Scarr that extra instruction has little effect on the intellectual development of children from stimulating environments. But he was optimistic when it came to children from disadvantaged environments. Indeed, his 1961 book, *Intelligence and Experience*, helped launch Project Head Start in 1965. Head Start, a $4 billion U.S. government–funded preschool program, serves some 800,000 children, most of whom come from families below the poverty level (Ripple & others, 1999). It aims to enhance children's chances for success in school and beyond by boosting their cognitive and social skills.

Does it succeed? Researchers study Head Start and other preschool programs by comparing children who do experience the program with their counterparts who don't. Research findings indicate that high-quality programs for disadvantaged children produce at least short-term cognitive gains, even on intelligence tests (Haskins, 1989). Quality programs also increase school readiness, decreasing the likelihood of a

Getting a head start
To increase readiness for schoolwork and expand children's notions of where school might lead them, Project Head Start offers educational activities. Here children in a classroom learn about colors and those on a field trip learn what fire fighters do.

"There is a large body of evidence indicating that there is little if anything to be gained by exposing middle-class children to early education."

Developmental psychologist
Edward F. Zigler (1987)

child's repeating a grade or being placed in special education. Although the aptitude benefits dissipate over time (reminding us that life experience *after* Head Start matters, too), psychologist Edward Zigler, the program's first director, believes there are long-term benefits (Zigler & Muenchow, 1992). High-quality preschool programs improve emotional intelligence—creating better attitudes toward learning and reducing school dropouts and criminality.

One intervention program provided year-round quality day care for the children of poor and uneducated North Carolina families from infancy to age 5. Craig Ramey and Sharon Ramey (1998) report that at age 15, the intervention group maintained an intelligence test score advantage of five points over their peers in a control group, were still performing better on math and reading achievement tests, and were less likely to have repeated a school grade. Compared to less effective intervention programs, they conclude, the most effective intervention programs

+ begin earlier and continue longer.
+ are more intensive (more hours a day and days per year).
+ provide children with direct educational experiences (rather than relying on parent training).
+ offer a support program for maintaining the positive attitudes and behaviors gained during the program.

Schooling Effects

Schooling itself is an intervention that pays dividends reflected in intelligence scores. Stephen Ceci and Wendy Williams (1997) have amassed evidence that schooling and intelligence contribute to each other (and that both enhance later income). High intelligence is conducive to prolonged schooling. But it is also true that intelligence scores tend to rise during the school year and drop over the summer months. They decline when students' schooling is discontinued. Completing high school elevates intelligence scores over those obtained by comparable children who leave school early. And consider this: Children whose birthdays just make the cutoff point for school entrance temporarily have higher intelligence scores than those born just slightly later, who are a year behind them in school (**FIGURE 32.3**). The worldwide increase in intelligence test performance since the 1920s (known as the Flynn effect [Flynn, 1987, 1999]) is probably partly due to increasing years of schooling during that period—and to the more stimulating home environments provided by today's better-educated parents.

FIGURE 32.3
The schooling effect
On a test of nonverbal intelligence administered by Sorel Cahan and Nora Cohen of Hebrew University, older children within a grade tend to score slightly higher than their younger classmates. The large gap between the end of one line and the beginning of the next reflects the extra year of schooling among children who are virtually the same age. (From Neisser, 1997.)

Group Differences in Intelligence Test Scores

Preview Question: How should we interpret ethnic and gender group differences in average scores on intelligence tests?

If there were no group differences in aptitude scores, psychologists could politely debate hereditary and environmental influences in their ivory towers. But there are group differences. What are they? And what shall we make of them?

Ethnic Similarities and Differences

Fueling this discussion are two disturbing but agreed-upon facts:

+ Racial groups differ in their average scores on intelligence tests.
+ High-scoring people (and groups) are more likely to attain high levels of education and income.

A statement by 52 intelligence researchers explains: "The bell curve for Whites is centered roughly around IQ 100; the bell curve for American Blacks roughly around 85; and those for different subgroups of Hispanics roughly midway between those for Whites and Blacks" (Avery & others, 1994). Comparable results come from other academic aptitude tests, such as the SAT. In recent years, the Black-White difference has diminished somewhat, and among children has dropped to 10 points in some recent studies (Neisser & others, 1996). Yet the test score gap persists.

There are differences among other groups as well. European New Zealanders outscore native Maori New Zealanders. Israeli Jews outscore Israeli Arabs. Most Japanese outscore the stigmatized Japanese minority, the Burakumin. And those who can hear outscore those born deaf (Braden, 1994; Steele, 1990a; Zeidner, 1990).

Everyone further agrees that such *group* differences provide little basis for judging individuals. Women outlive men by six years, but knowing someone's sex doesn't tell us with any precision how long that person will live. Even Charles Murray and Richard Herrnstein (1994), whose writings have drawn attention to Black-White differences, reminded us that "millions of Blacks have higher IQs than the average White."

If heredity contributes to individual differences in intelligence, does it also contribute to group differences? Some psychologists believe it does (Herrnstein & Murray, 1994; Rowe, 1997). Some have speculated that different climates and survival challenges could have led to racial differences in aptitudes (Lynn, 1991; Rushton, 1990, 1995). But it's also clear that, as in our earlier barrel-versus-home-reared boys example, group differences in a heritable trait may be entirely environmental. Consider one of nature's experiments: Allow some children to grow up hearing their culture's dominant language, while others, born deaf, do not. Then give them an intelligence test rooted in that language, and (no surprise) those with expertise in the test's language will score highest. Although individual performance differences may be substantially genetic, the group difference is not (**FIGURE 32.4**, page 428).

Consider: If each identical twin were exactly as tall as his or her co-twin, heritability would be 100 percent. Imagine that we then separated some young twins and gave only half of them a nutritious diet, and that the well-nourished twins all grew to be exactly 3 inches taller than their counterparts—an environmental effect comparable to that actually observed in both Britain and America, where adolescents are several inches taller than their counterparts were half a century ago (Angoff, 1987; Lynn, 1987). What would the heritability of height be now for our well-nourished twins? Still 100 percent, because the variation in height within the group would remain entirely predictable from the heights of their malnourished identical siblings. So even perfect heritability within groups would not eliminate the possibility of a strong environmental impact on the group differences.

The culture of scholarship
The children of Indochinese refugee families studied by Nathan Caplan, Marcella Choy, and James Whitmore (1992) typically excel in school. On weekday nights after dinner, the family clears the table and begins homework. Family cooperation is valued, and older siblings help younger ones.

Since 1850, the average Dutch man has grown from 5 feet 4 inches to today's 5 feet 10 inches (Bogin, 1997).

In prosperous country X everyone eats all they want. In country Y the rich are well fed, but the semistarved poor are often thin. In which country will the heritability of body weight be the greatest? (See page 431.)

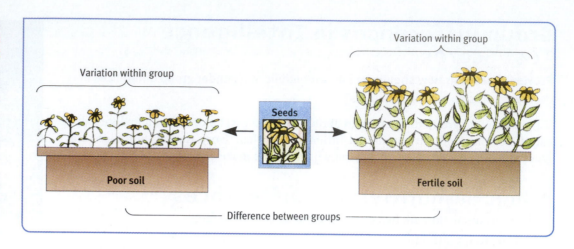

FIGURE 32.4
Group differences and environmental impact
Even if the variation between members within a group reflects genetic differences, the average difference between groups may be wholly due to the environment. Imagine that seeds from the same mixture are sown in poor and fertile soil. Although height differences within each pot will be genetic, the height difference between the two groups will be environmental. (From Lewontin, 1976.)

> "Do not obtain your slaves from Britain, because they are so stupid and so utterly incapable of being taught."
>
> Cicero 106–43 B.C.

So, is there evidence that the racial gap may be similarly environmental? Consider these findings:

+ Genetics research reveals that under the skin, the races are remarkably alike (Cavalli-Sforza & others, 1994; Lewontin, 1982). Individual differences within a race are much greater than differences between races. The average genetic difference between two Icelandic villagers or between two Kenyans greatly exceeds the difference between Icelanders and Kenyans. Moreover, looks can deceive. Europeans and Africans are genetically closer than are Africans and Aboriginal Australians.

+ Asian students outperform North American students on math achievement and aptitude tests. But this difference appears to be a recent phenomenon and may reflect conscientiousness rather than competence. Asian students also attend school 30 percent more days per year and spend much more time in and out of school studying math (Geary & others, 1996; Larson & Verma, 1999; Stevenson, 1992).

+ The intelligence test performance of today's better-fed and better-educated population exceeds that of the 1930s population (the Flynn effect) by the same margin that the intelligence test score of the average white today exceeds that of the average black. No one attributes the generational group difference to genetics.

+ White and black infants have scored equally well on an infant intelligence measure (preference for looking at novel stimuli—a predictor of future intelligence scores; Fagan, 1992).

+ In different eras, different ethnic groups have experienced golden ages—periods of remarkable achievement. Twenty-five hundred years ago it was the Greeks and the Egyptians, then the Romans; in the eighth and ninth centuries, genius seemed to reside in the Arab world; 500 years ago it was the Aztec Indians and the peoples of Northern Europe. Today, people marvel at Asians' technological genius. Cultures rise and fall over centuries; genes do not. That fact makes it difficult to attribute a natural superiority to any race.

Moreover, consider the striking results of a national study that looked back over the mental test performances of white and black young adults after graduation from college. From eighth grade through the early high school years, the average aptitude score of the white students increased, while those of the black students decreased—creating a gap that reached its widest point at about the time that high school students take college admissions tests. But during college, the black students' scores increased "more than four times as much" as those of their white counterparts, thus greatly *decreasing* the aptitude gap. "It is not surprising," concluded researcher Joel Myerson and his colleagues (1998), "that as black and white students complete more grades in high school environments that differ in quality, the gap in cognitive test scores widens. At the college level, however, where black and white students are exposed to educational environments of comparable quality . . . many Blacks are able to make remarkable gains, closing the gap in test scores."

Gender Similarities and Differences

In science, as in everyday life, differences, not similarities, excite interest. Compared with the anatomical and physiological similarities between men and women, our sex differences are relatively minor. Yet it is the differences we find exciting. Similarly, in the psychological domain, gender similarities vastly outnumber gender differences, but the differences often capture our attention. To some, it is news that there is no gender gap in overall intelligence scores. But most people find differences more newsworthy. Girls are better spellers: At the end of high school, only 30 percent of males spell better than the average female (Lubinski & Benbow, 1992). Girls are more verbally fluent and more sensitive to touch, taste, and odor (Halpern, 1997). Boys outnumber girls at the low extremes and therefore in special education classes (Kleinfeld, 1998). Boys tend to talk later and to stutter more often. In remedial reading classes, boys outnumber girls three to one (Finucci & Childs, 1981). In high school, underachieving boys outnumber girls by two to one (McCall & others, 1992).

Math and Spatial Aptitudes

In math grades, the average girl typically equals or surpasses the average boy (ETS, 1992; Kimball, 1989). And on math tests given to more than 3 million representatively sampled people in 100 independent studies, males and females obtained nearly identical average scores (Hyde & others, 1990). But again—despite greater diversity within the genders than between them—group differences make the news. Although females have an edge in math computation, males in 20 of 21 countries scored higher in math problem solving (Bronner, 1998; Hedges & Nowell, 1995). For example, male high school seniors average 45 points higher on the 200- to 800-point SAT math test (literally meaning that they average 4 more correct answers on the 60-question test). Because U.S. National Merit Scholarships are based on SAT scores, only about 35 percent of these awards have gone to girls (despite their generally higher grades).

The score differences are sharpest at the extremes. Among precocious 12-year-olds scoring extremely high on SAT math, boys have outnumbered girls 13 to 1 (Lubinski & Benbow, 1992). In other Western countries, virtually all math prodigies participating in the International Mathematics Olympiad have been males. Female math prodigies have, however, reached the top levels in non-Western countries such

"African-Americans, from a condition of mass illiteracy 50 years ago, are now among the most educated groups of people in the world, with median years of schooling and college completion rates higher than those of most European nations."

Sociologist Orlando Patterson, *The Ordeal of Integration*, 1997

Despite the gender equivalence in intelligence test scores, males are more likely than females to overestimate their own test scores. Both males and females tend to rate their fathers' scores higher than their mothers', and their sons' scores higher than their daughters' (Furnham & Gasson, 1998; Furnham & Rawles, 1995).

World Math Olympics Champs
After outscoring 350,000 of their U.S. peers, these boys all had perfect scores in competition with math whizzes from 68 other countries.

FIGURE 32.5
The mental rotation test
This is a test of spatial abilities. Which two responses show a different view of the standard? (From Vandenberg & Kuse, 1978.) (See page 432 for answers.)

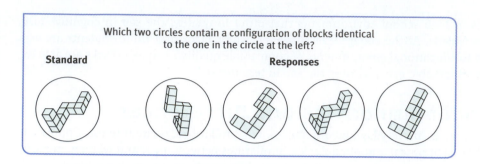

Which two circles contain a configuration of blocks identical to the one in the circle at the left?

Standard   Responses

In the first 56 years of the Putnam Mathematical Competition—the Olympics of college math—all of the nearly 300 awardees were men (Arenson, 1997). In 1997, a woman broke the male grip by joining 5 men in the winner's circle.

as China (Halpern, 1991). The average male edge seems most reliable in tests like the one shown in **FIGURE 32.5**, which involve speedily rotating three-dimensional objects in one's mind (Collins & Kimura, 1997; Masters & Sanders, 1993; Voyer & others, 1995). Such spatial ability helps when fitting suitcases into a car trunk, playing chess, or doing certain types of geometry problems.

Working from an evolutionary perspective, David Geary (1995, 1996) and Irwin Silverman and his colleagues (1992, 1998) speculate that skills in navigating within three-dimensional space also helped our ancestral fathers in tracking their prey and making their way home. In contrast, the survival of our ancestral mothers was enhanced by keen memory for the location of edible plants—a legacy that lives today in women's superior memory for objects and their location.

In studies of more than 100,000 American adolescents, girls also modestly surpassed boys in memory for picture associations (Hedges & Nowell, 1995). And among nearly 200,000 students taking Germany's Test for Medical Studies, young women year after year have surpassed men in remembering facts from short medical cases (Stumpf & Jackson, 1994). (My wife, who remembers many of my experiences for me, tells me that if she died I'd be a man without a past.)

Do natural sex differences therefore explain why most mathematicians and more than 9 in 10 rated chess players and American architects, engineers, and mapmakers are men? Or why the world chess body has therefore found it necessary to hold separate competitions for men and women? Exposure to high levels of male sex hormones during the prenatal period does enhance spatial abilities (Berenbaum & others, 1995). But social expectations also shape boys' and girls' interests and abilities (Crawford & others, 1995; Eccles & others, 1990). Traditionally, math and science have been considered masculine subjects. For example, many parents send their sons to computer camps and give their daughters more encouragement in English. Thus, the male edge in math problem solving grows with age, becoming detectable only after elementary school. In the United States it also persists in the male edge on the annual physics and computer science Advanced Placement exams (Stumpf & Stanley, 1998). But as more and more girls are encouraged to develop their abilities in math and science, the gender gap is narrowing (Nowell & Hedges, 1998).

Who wants to be a millionaire?
In the first half year of this wildly popular quiz show, only one in 10 American contestants who made it to the hot seat were women. The qualifying questions—requiring a competitive, speed-based, sequential ordering of information—seemed to favor men. A different format, such as challenging contestants to detect facial emotions, might have favored women.

Emotion-Detecting Ability
Recall that part of emotional intelligence is empathic accuracy in reading others' emotions. Some of us are more sensitive to emotional cues. Robert Rosenthal, Judith Hall, and their colleagues (1979) demonstrated this by showing hundreds of

people brief film clips of portions of a person's emotionally expressive face or body, sometimes with a garbled voice added. For example, after a two-second scene revealing only the face of an upset woman, the researchers asked whether the woman was criticizing someone for being late or was talking about her divorce. Rosenthal and Hall reported that some people are much better emotion detectors than others are, and that women are better at it than men.

Some psychologists speculate that women's ability to detect emotions helped our ancestral mothers read emotions in their infants and would-be lovers, which may in turn have fueled cultural tendencies to encourage women's empathic skills. Such skills may explain women's somewhat greater responsiveness in both positive and negative emotional situations.

The Question of Bias

Preview Questions: Are intelligence tests biased? Are they a vehicle for discrimination against certain groups?

Knowing there are group differences in intelligence test scores leads us to wonder whether intelligence tests are biased. The answer depends on two very different definitions of *bias*. One meaning is that the tests detect not only innate differences in intelligence but also differences caused by cultural experiences. In this sense, everyone agrees that intelligence tests are biased. No one claims that heritability is 100 percent responsible for any test score. An intelligence test measures a person's developed abilities at a particular time. These abilities necessarily reflect that person's experiences *and* environment.

You may have read examples of intelligence test items that make middle-class assumptions (for example, that a cup goes with a saucer, or that people buy fire insurance to protect the value of their homes and possessions). Do such items bias the test against those who do not use saucers or do not have enough possessions to make the cost of fire insurance relevant? Could such questions explain racial differences in test performance? If so, are tests a vehicle for discrimination, consigning potentially capable children to dead-end classes and jobs?

Defenders of aptitude testing have in turn observed that racial group differences occur on nonverbal items, such as counting digits backward, as well as on verbal items, such as vocabulary knowledge (Jensen, 1983). Moreover, they add, blaming the test for a group's lower scores is like blaming a messenger for bad news. Why blame the tests for exposing unequal experiences and opportunities? If, because of malnutrition, people were to suffer stunted growth, would you blame the measuring stick that reveals it? If unequal past experiences predict unequal future achievements, a valid aptitude test will detect such inequalities.

Another meaning of *bias* hinges on whether a test is less valid for some groups than for others. If the SAT accurately predicts the college achievement of one race but not that of another, then the test would be biased. The near-consensus among psychologists, as summarized by the National Research Council's Committee on Ability Testing and the American Psychological Association's Task Force on Intelligence, is that the major aptitude tests are *not* biased in this statistical meaning of the term (Neisser & others, 1998; Wigdor & Garner, 1982). The predictive validity of the SAT or of a standard intelligence test is roughly the same for blacks and whites and for rich and poor. If an intelligence test score of 95 predicts C grades, the rough prediction usually applies equally to all ethnic and economic groups. If anything, the SAT overpredicts the college achievements of non-Asian minority students (Steele, 1997).

To predict school performance accurately, an aptitude test must mirror any gender or racial bias in school teaching and testing. Among students given a difficult math test by Steven Spencer and his colleagues (1997), men outperformed equally

Answer to question on page 427:
Heritability—differences due to genes—will be greater in country X, where environmental differences in nutrition are minimal.

Untested compassion
Intelligence test scores are only one part of the picture of a whole person. They don't measure the abilities, talent, and commitment of, for example, people who devote their lives to helping others.

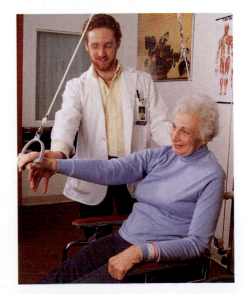

capable women—except when the women had been led to expect that women usually do as well as men on the test. Otherwise, the women apparently felt apprehensive and despairing, affecting their test. Claude Steele and Joshua Aronson (1996) observed the same self-fulfilling effect of negative beliefs. They found black students' verbal aptitude scores were lower when they took tests under conditions designed to make black students feel threatened. Steele (1995, 1997) concluded that if you tell students they probably won't succeed (as remedial "minority support" programs often do), this stereotype will eventually erode their performance both on aptitude tests and in school. Over time, such students may "disidentify" with school achievement. They may detach their self-esteem from academics and look for self-esteem elsewhere—which would explain why they tend to underachieve relative to their abilities. (Indeed, as African-American boys progress from eighth to twelfth grade, the disconnect between their grades and their self-esteem becomes pronounced [Osborne, 1997].) Minority students in university programs that instead challenge them to believe in their potential produce markedly higher grades and have lower dropout rates.

What then can we realistically conclude about aptitude tests and bias? The tests do seem biased in one sense—sensitivity to performance differences caused by cultural experience. But they are not biased in another—statistical prediction for different groups.

Does this mean the tests are discriminatory? Again, the answer can be yes or no. In one sense, yes, their purpose is to discriminate—to distinguish among individuals. In another sense, their purpose is to reduce discrimination by reducing reliance on subjective criteria for school and job placement—criteria such as whom you know, what you look like, or how much the interviewer happens to like "your kind of person." Many pioneers of mental testing saw themselves as social progressives who were sometimes uncovering abilities—diamonds in the rough—when few expected to find them. (The educational system is very good at finding those who score in the top 1 or 2 percent on intelligence-related tests and then offering a first-class education that may lead to a first-class job.) Banning aptitude tests would lead those who decide on admissions and jobs to rely more on other considerations, such as their personal opinions. Civil service tests, for example, were devised to discriminate more fairly and objectively, by reducing the political, racial, and ethnic discrimination that preceded their use.

Perhaps, then, our aim should be threefold. First, we should realize the benefits that French psychologist Alfred Binet, founder of the intelligence-testing movement, foresaw for tests of mental abilities—to enable schools to recognize who might best benefit from early intervention. At the same time, we must remain alert to Binet's fear that test scores may be misinterpreted as literal measures of a person's worth and fixed potential. And finally, we must remember that *intelligence test scores reflect only one aspect of personal competence.* Our practical and emotional intelligence matter, too, as do other forms of talent and character. The competence that intelligence tests sample is important but far from all-inclusive. The spatial ability of the carpenter differs from the logical ability of the computer programmer, which differs from the verbal ability of the poet. Differences are not deficits. Because there are many ways of being successful, our personal and cultural differences—regardless of their origins—are variations on the human theme of adaptability.

"Math class is tough!"

"Teen talk" Barbie doll (introduced February 1992, recalled October 1992)

Answers to the mental rotation test on page 430: the first and fourth alternatives.

"Almost all the joyful things of life are outside the measure of IQ tests."

Madeleine L'Engle, *A Circle of Quiet,* 1972

REVIEW AND REFLECT:

Genetic and Environmental Influences on Intelligence

Because of its political and racial overtones, the debate over the nature and nurture of intelligence is an ongoing controversy.

How much credit do our genes get for our scores on intelligence tests?

Studies of twins, family members, and adopted children together point to a significant hereditary contribution to intelligence scores. Heritability, the proportion of person-to-person variation attributable to genes, can vary, depending on the range of populations and environments studied.

To what extent are our scores on intelligence tests attributable to our life experiences?

These same studies, plus others that compare children reared in extremely impoverished or enriched environments or in different cultures, indicate that life experiences also significantly influence intelligence test performance.

How should we interpret ethnic and gender differences in average scores on intelligence tests?

Like individuals, groups vary in intelligence test scores. Hereditary variation *within* a group need not signify a hereditary explanation of *between*-group differences. In the case of the racial gaps in test scores, the evidence suggests that environmental differences are largely, perhaps entirely, responsible. Psychologists debate evolutionary and cultural explanations of gender differences in specific aptitudes.

Are intelligence tests biased? Are they a vehicle for discrimination against certain groups?

Aptitude tests aim to predict how well a test-taker will perform in a given situation. So they are necessarily "biased" in the sense that they are sensitive to performance differences caused by cultural experience. But *bias* can also mean what psychologists commonly mean by the term—that a biased test predicts less accurately for one group than for another. In this sense of the term, most experts do not consider the major aptitude tests to be significantly biased.

Test Yourself

32.1. A current view is that between 50 and 70 percent of intelligence score variation among individuals can be attributed to heredity. The strongest support for the hereditary influence on intelligence is the finding that
   a. identical twins, but not other siblings, have nearly identical IQ scores.
   b. the correlation between IQ scores of fraternal twins is higher than that for other siblings.
   c. unrelated people living in the same environment tend not to have similar IQ scores.
   d. the IQ scores of adopted children do not closely correlate with those of their biological or adoptive parents.

32.2. The heritability of a trait may vary, depending on the range of populations and environments studied. To say that the heritability of intelligence is 50 percent means that 50 percent of
   a. intelligence is due to genetic factors.
   b. the similarities among groups of people are attributable to genes.
   c. the variation in intelligence within a group of people is attributable to genetic factors.
   d. intelligence is due to the mother's genes and the rest is due to the father's genes.

32.3. Within the limits set by heredity, experiences help shape intelligence. The experience that has the clearest, most profound effect on intellectual development is
   a. being enrolled in a Head Start program.
   b. growing up in an economically disadvantaged home or neighborhood.
   c. being raised in a very neglectful home or institution.
   d. being exposed to very stimulating toys and lessons in infancy.

32.4. Racial group differences exist in average scores on tests of aptitude and intelligence. Some people have assumed that these differences are attributable to heredity. Those who believe the differences are due to environmental influences note that
   a. genetic differences within races are far greater than those between races.
   b. white and black infants score equally well on infant intelligence measures.
   c. black and white students exposed to educational environments of comparable quality at the college level tend to have similar scores.
   d. All of the above are true.

32.5. Psychologists tend to agree that aptitude tests
   a. are *not* in any way biased.
   b. *are* biased because they distinguish among individuals.
   c. *are* biased because they are less valid for some groups than for others because they predict achievement for only some groups.
   d. are *not* biased because they are not sensitive to performance differences caused by cultural experience.

Review: As society succeeds in creating equality of opportunity, it will also increase the heritability of ability. The heritability of intelligence scores will be greater in a society marked by equal opportunity than in a society of peasants and aristocrats. Why?

Reflect: How have genetic and environmental influences shaped *your* intelligence?

Answers to Test Yourself and Review questions can be found in the green appendix at the end of the book.

Motivation

"What's my motivation?" the actor asks the director. In our everyday conversation, the question "What motivated you to do that?" is a way of asking "What *caused* your behavior? *Why* did you act that way?" To psychologists, a *motivation* is a need or desire that serves to *energize* behavior and to *direct* it toward a goal. Motivation is a hypothetical concept: We infer it from behaviors we observe. Consider motivation in these situations:

+ David Mandel (1983), a former Nazi concentration camp inmate, re-called how a starving "father and son would fight over a piece of bread. Like dogs." One father, whose 20-year-old son stole his bread from under his pillow while he slept, went into a deep depression, asking over and over again how his son could do such a thing. The next day the fa-ther died. "Hunger does something to you that's hard to describe," Mandel explained. "I can't believe it myself today, so how can I expect anyone else to understand it?"

+ In the Old Testament's *Song of Solomon* love poems, a man and a woman express their intense sexual passion for one another. "I am sick with love," she declares. "O that his left hand were under my head, and that his right hand embraced me!" He, in turn, pronounces her "delec-table." "You are stately as a palm tree, and your breasts are like its clus-ters. I say I will climb the palm tree and lay hold of its branches."

+ In Texas, a school truant officer discovers Alfredo Gonzales, age 14, picking fruit and sends him off to the first day of school in his life. Al-though placed at the lowest skill level and paddled for asking questions in Spanish—he knows no English—Alfredo decides "I could do better." Today he is a highly educated college administrator who works to moti-vate youth to wake up, as he did, to "their own potential and to gain a desire to achieve it."

In Modules 34 through 36, we explore motivation by focusing on these three motives—hunger, sex, and achievement. Although other identifiable motives exist (including thirst and curiosity), a close look at these three re-veals the interplay between nature (the physiological "push") and nurture (the cognitive and cultural "pulls"). Before considering hunger, sex, and achievement, we take time in Module 33 to see how psychologists have ap-proached the study of motivation.

33 Introduction to Motivation

A **motivation** is a need or desire that serves to *energize* behavior and to *direct* it toward a goal. Three perspectives have particularly influenced psychologists' study of motivation: instinct theory (now replaced by an evolutionary perspective), drive-reduction theory (emphasizing the interaction between inner pushes and external pulls), and arousal theory (emphasizing the urge for an optimum level of stimulation). A fourth perspective, Abraham Maslow's hierarchy of needs, addresses the question of why some motives are more compelling than others at certain points in our lives.

Instincts and Evolutionary Psychology

Preview Question: What is the underlying assumption shared by instinct theory and evolutionary psychology?

Early in the twentieth century, as the influence of Charles Darwin's evolutionary theory grew, it became fashionable to classify all sorts of behaviors as instincts. If people criticized themselves, it was because of their "self-abasement instinct." If they boasted, it reflected their "self-assertion instinct." After scanning 500 books, one sociologist compiled a list of 5759 supposed human instincts! Before long, this fad for naming instincts collapsed under its own weight. Rather than *explaining* human behaviors, the early instinct theorists were simply *naming* them. It was like "explaining" a bright child's low grades by labeling the child an "underachiever." To name a behavior is *not* to explain it.

To qualify as an **instinct**, a complex behavior must have a fixed pattern throughout a species and be unlearned (Tinbergen, 1951). Such behaviors are common in other species (such as imprinting in birds and the return of salmon to their birthplace). Human behavior, too, exhibits certain innate tendencies, including simple fixed patterns such as an infant's rooting and sucking. Most psychologists, though, view human behavior as directed by physiological needs *and* psychological wants.

Although instinct theory failed to explain human motives, the underlying assumption that genes predispose species-typical behavior remains as strong as ever. Evolutionary psychology is now in its heyday, and psychologists working from this perspective search for explanations of some human behaviors in the genetic blueprint shared by our species. They are interested, for example, in how evolution might influence our phobias, our helping behaviors, and our romantic attractions.

"What do you think . . . should we get started on that motivation research or not?"

Same motive, different wiring
The more complex the nervous system, the more adaptable the organism. Both the woman and the weaverbird satisfy their need for shelter in ways that reflect their inherited capacities. The woman's behavior is flexible; she can learn whatever skills she needs to build a house. The bird's behavior pattern is fixed; it can build only this kind of nest.

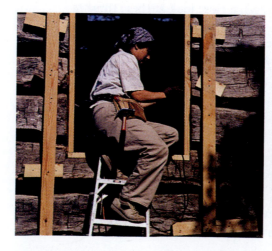

Drives and Incentives

Preview Question: How does drive-reduction theory help us understand the forces that energize and direct some of our behaviors?

When the original instinct theory of motivation collapsed, it was replaced by **drive-reduction theory**—the idea that a physiological need creates an aroused state that *drives* the organism to reduce the need by, say, eating or drinking. With few exceptions, when a physiological need increases, so does a psychological drive—an aroused, motivated state.

The physiological aim of drive reduction is **homeostasis**—the maintenance of a steady internal state. An example of homeostasis (literally "staying the same") is the body's temperature-regulation system, which works like a thermostat. Both systems operate through feedback loops: Sensors feed room temperature to a control device. If room temperature cools, the control device switches on the furnace. Likewise, if our body temperature cools, blood vessels constrict to conserve warmth, and we feel driven to put on more clothes or seek a warmer environment. Similarly, if the water level in our cells drops, sensors detect our need for water and we feel thirsty (**FIGURE 33.1**).

Not only are we *pushed* by our "need" to reduce drives, we also are *pulled* by **incentives**—positive or negative stimuli that lure or repel us. This is one way our individual learning histories influence our motives. Depending on our learning, the aroma of fresh roasted peanuts (or toasted ants), the sight of someone we find attractive, and the threat of disapproval can all motivate our behavior. Our internal needs energize and direct our behavior, but these external incentives do as well. The lure of money may energize us quite apart from any need-based drive.

When there is both a need and an incentive, we feel strongly driven. The food-deprived person who smells baking bread feels a strong hunger drive. In the presence of that drive, the baking bread becomes a compelling incentive. For each motive, we can therefore ask, "How is it pushed by our inborn physiological needs and pulled by incentives in the environment?"

- **motivation** a need or desire that energizes and directs behavior.

- **instinct** a complex behavior that is rigidly patterned throughout a species and is unlearned.

- **drive-reduction theory** the idea that a physiological need creates an aroused tension state (a drive) that motivates an organism to satisfy the need.

- **homeostasis** a tendency to maintain a balanced or constant internal state; the regulation of any aspect of body chemistry, such as blood glucose, around a particular level.

- **incentive** a positive or negative environmental stimulus that motivates behavior.

| Need (e.g., for food, water) | → | Drive (hunger, thirst) | → | Drive-reducing behaviors (eating, drinking) |

FIGURE 33.1 Drive theory

Optimum Arousal

Preview Question: What types of motivated behavior does arousal theory attempt to explain?

We are much more than homeostatic systems, however. Our biological rhythms cycle through times of arousal. Also, far from reducing a physiological need or minimizing tension, some motivated behaviors *increase* arousal. Well-fed animals will leave their shelter to explore, seemingly in the absence of any need-based drive. From taking such risks, animals may, however, gain information and resources (Renner, 1992).

Driven by curiosity

Baby monkeys and small people are fascinated by things they've never handled before. Their drive to explore the relatively unfamiliar is one of several motives that do not fill any immediate physiological need.

■ **hierarchy of needs** Maslow's pyramid of human needs, beginning at the base with physiological needs that must first be satisfied before higher-level safety needs and then psychological needs become active.

Curiosity drives monkeys to monkey around trying to figure out how to unlock a latch that opens nothing, or how to open a window that allows them to see outside their room (Butler, 1954). It drives the 9-month-old infant who investigates every accessible corner of the house. It drives the scientists whose work this text discusses. And it drives the explorers and adventurers. Asked why he wanted to climb Mount Everest, George Mallory answered, "Because it is there." Those who, like Mallory, enjoy high arousal are most likely to enjoy intense music, novel foods, and risky behaviors (Zuckerman, 1979).

In experiments on sensory restriction, volunteers have spent hour after hour isolated in a monotonous chamber. Their experience—though peaceful and quiet—sensitized them to any available stimulation. Despite having all our biological needs satisfied, we feel driven to experience stimulation. Without it, we feel bored and look for a way to increase arousal to some optimum level. However, with too much stimulation comes stress, and we then look for a way to decrease arousal.

A Hierarchy of Motives

Preview Question: What is the organizing principle for Maslow's hierarchy of needs?

Some needs take priority over others. At this moment, with your needs for air and water satisfied, other motives—such as your desire to achieve—energize and direct your behavior. Let your need for water go unsatisfied and your thirst will preoccupy you. But if you were deprived of air, your thirst would disappear.

Abraham Maslow (1970) described these priorities as a **hierarchy of needs** (FIG-URE 33.2). At its base are our physiological needs, such as those for food and water. Only if these needs are met are we prompted to meet our need for safety, and then to meet the uniquely human needs to give and receive love and to enjoy self-esteem. Beyond this, said Maslow (1971), lies the highest of human needs: to actualize one's full potential.

Maslow's hierarchy is somewhat arbitrary. Moreover, the order of such needs is not universally fixed. People have starved themselves to make a political statement. Nevertheless, the simple idea that some motives are more compelling than others does provide a framework for thinking about motivation. Moreover, surveys of life satisfaction in 39 nations have confirmed what Maslow would have predicted: Financial satisfaction is more strongly predictive of subjective well-being in poorer nations, whereas home-life satisfaction matters more in wealthy nations and self-esteem in individualist nations (Oishi & others, 1999). Where there is little money, money—which buys shelter and food—matters.

FIGURE 33.2
Maslow's hierarchy of needs
Once our lower-level needs are met, we are prompted to satisfy our higher-level needs. (From Maslow, 1970.)

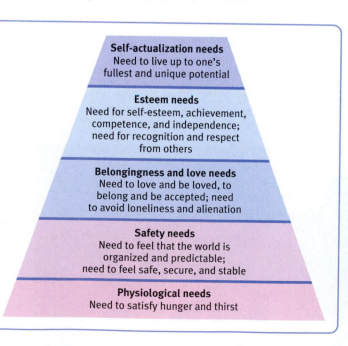

Self-actualization needs
Need to live up to one's fullest and unique potential

Esteem needs
Need for self-esteem, achievement, competence, and independence; need for recognition and respect from others

Belongingness and love needs
Need to love and be loved, to belong and be accepted; need to avoid loneliness and alienation

Safety needs
Need to feel that the world is organized and predictable; need to feel safe, secure, and stable

Physiological needs
Need to satisfy hunger and thirst

REVIEW AND REFLECT:

Introduction to Motivation

Motivation is the energizing and directing of behavior, the force behind our yearning for food, our longing for sexual intimacy, our need to belong, and our desire to achieve.

What is the underlying assumption shared by instinct theory and evolutionary psychology?

Under Darwin's influence, early theorists viewed behavior as controlled by biological forces, such as specific instincts. When it became clear that people were naming, not explaining, various behaviors by calling them instincts, this approach fell into disfavor. The underlying assumption—that genes predispose species-typical behavior—is, however, still influential in evolutionary psychology.

How does drive-reduction theory help us understand the forces that energize and direct some of our behaviors?

Most physiological needs create aroused psychological states that drive us to reduce or satisfy those needs. The aim of drive reduction is internal stability, or homeostasis. Thus, drive reduction motivates survival behaviors, such as eating and drinking. Not only are we pushed by our internal drives, we are also pulled by external incentives. Depending on our personal and cultural experiences, some stimuli (for example, certain foods or erotic images) will arouse our desires.

What types of motivated behaviors does arousal theory attempt to explain?

Rather than reducing a physiological need or tension state, some motivated behaviors increase arousal. Curiosity-driven behaviors, for example, suggest that too little as well as too much stimulation can motivate people to seek an optimum level of arousal.

What is the organizing principle for Maslows hierarchy of needs?

Maslow's hierarchy of needs expresses the idea that, until satisfied, some motives are more compelling than others.

Terms and Concepts to Remember
motivation, p. 436
instinct, p. 436
drive-reduction theory, p. 437
homeostasis, p. 437
incentive, p. 437
hierarchy of needs, p. 438

Test Yourself

33.1. Although instinct theory fails to explain most human behavior, the existence of simple fixed patterns such as an infant's rooting and sucking suggest some innate tendencies in humans. Indeed, the underlying assumption of instinct theory—that _____—is as strong as ever.
 a. physiological needs arouse psychological states
 b. genes predispose species-typical behavior
 c. physiological needs increase arousal
 d. external needs energize and direct behavior

33.2. Drive reduction motivates many behaviors necessary for survival. A need, or deprivation (for example, a lack of water), leads to an aroused state or drive; this in turn motivates the organism to act to reduce this drive (drink a glass of water) and restore internal stability. Drive reduction also motivates behaviors such as
 a. eating and breathing.
 b. satisfaction of curiosity.
 c. nest building and other instincts.
 d. pursuit of stimulation.

33.3. The aim of drive reduction is internal stability. For example, if we are too hot, we perspire; if we are dehydrated, we feel thirsty—and drink. The maintenance of a balanced internal state is called
 a. instinct.   c. a hierarchy of needs.
 b. sensory restriction.   d. homeostasis.

33.4. Motivated behaviors satisfy a variety of needs. Experiments on sensory restriction indicate that one such need can be to
 a. reduce physiological needs.
 b. search out respect from others.
 c. increase arousal.
 d. ensure stability.

33.5. Behavior is also influenced by incentives in the environment. For example, a pile of leaves in the driveway may motivate you to get out the rake; your neighbor's disapproval may motivate you to turn down your radio. To explain the effects of external incentives, we must refer to
 a. biological needs.   c. individual learning histories.
 b. instinct.   d. homeostasis.

33.6. According to Abraham Maslow, we are not prompted to satisfy psychological needs, such as the need to be accepted or loved, until we have satisfied more basic needs. The most basic needs are physiological needs, including the need for food, water, and oxygen; just above these are
 a. safety needs.   c. belongingness needs.
 b. self-esteem needs.   d. psychological needs.

Review: While on a long road trip, your stomach is growling with hunger. So, you pull off to eat at the nearest restaurant. What motivational perspective would most easily explain this behavior and why?

Reflect: Consider your own experiences with Maslow's hierarchy of needs. Have you ever experienced true hunger or thirst, which displaced your concern for other, higher-level needs? Do you usually feel safe? Loved? Confident? How often do you feel you are able to address what Maslow called your "self-actualization" needs?

Answers to the Test Yourself and Review questions can be found in the green appendix at the end of the book.

34 Hunger

A vivid demonstration of the supremacy of physiological needs came about following reports of starvation in World War II prison camps and occupied areas. To learn more about the results of semistarvation, scientist Ancel Keys and his colleagues (1950) solicited volunteers for an experiment. More than 100 conscientious objectors to the war volunteered and from them the researchers selected 36 men. First, they fed them just enough to maintain their initial weight. Then, for six months, they cut this food level in half.

The effects soon became visible. Without thinking about it, the men began conserving energy; they appeared listless and apathetic. Their body weights dropped rapidly, eventually stabilizing at about 25 percent below their starting weights. But the psychological effects were especially dramatic. Consistent with Abraham Maslow's idea (1970) that we are not prompted to satisfy psychological needs until we have satisfied more basic needs, the men became obsessed with food. They talked food. They daydreamed food. They collected recipes, read cookbooks, and feasted their eyes on delectable forbidden foods. At the same time, they lost interest in sex and social activities. They became preoccupied with their unfulfilled basic needs. As one participant reported, "If we see a show, the most interesting part of it is contained in scenes where people are eating. I couldn't laugh at the funniest picture in the world, and love scenes are completely dull."

> "Nobody wants to kiss when they are hungry."
>
> Dorothea Dix, 1801–1887

The Physiology of Hunger

Preview Question: What physiological factors cause us to feel hungry?

Keys' semistarved subjects felt their hunger in response to a homeostatic system. *Homeostasis* is our body's attempt to maintain some constant or balanced internal state—in this case, to maintain normal body weight and an adequate nutrient supply. But what precisely triggers hunger? Is it the pangs of an empty stomach? That is how it feels. And so it seemed after A. L. Washburn, working with Walter Cannon (Cannon & Washburn, 1912), intentionally swallowed a balloon. When inflated in his stomach, the balloon transmitted his stomach contractions to a recording device (**FIGURE 34.1**). While his stomach was being monitored, Washburn pressed a key each time he felt hungry. The discovery: Washburn was indeed having stomach contractions whenever he felt hungry. Some diet aids reduce this feeling of an empty stomach by filling the stomach with indigestible fibers that swell as they absorb water.

GARFIELD

THE TV ADVERTISERS DIDN'T WASTE ANY TIME

I'VE BEEN ON A DIET ONE DAY AND THEY'RE ALREADY RUNNING MORE FOOD COMMERCIALS

JIM DAVIS   © 1986 PAWS, INC./Distributed by Universal Press Syndicate   3-19

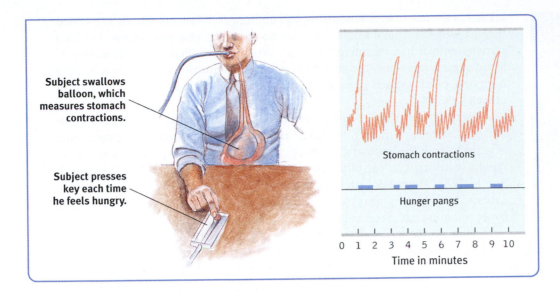

FIGURE 34.1
Monitoring stomach contractions
Using this procedure, Washburn showed that stomach contractions (transmitted by the stomach balloon) accompany our feelings of hunger (indicated by a key press). (From Cannon, 1929.)

Alas, there is more to hunger than the pangs of an empty stomach. Researchers discovered this a quarter-century later when they removed some rats' stomachs and attached their esophagi to their small intestines (Tsang, 1938). Without stomach pangs, did hunger persist? Did the rats continue to eat regularly? Indeed they did. Hunger persists similarly in humans whose ulcerated or cancerous stomachs have been removed. In fact, one can feel hungry even on a full stomach. Animals that fill their stomachs by eating low-calorie food will eat more than animals that consume a less filling, high-calorie diet (McHugh & Moran, 1978). If the pangs of an empty stomach are not the only source of our hunger, what else matters?

"The full person does not understand the needs of the hungry."

Irish proverb

Body Chemistry

Changes in body chemistry also affect hunger. People and other animals automatically regulate their caloric intake to prevent energy deficits and maintain a stable body weight. This suggests that the body is somehow, somewhere, keeping tabs on its available resources. One such resource is the blood sugar **glucose**. Increases in the insulin hormone diminish blood glucose, partly by converting it to stored fat. The body is normally adept at maintaining blood glucose levels. But if the blood glucose level drops, hunger increases. As we will soon see, however, insulin and glucose are not the only hunger-regulating chemicals.

The Brain

Low blood glucose triggers hunger. But you do not consciously feel this change in your blood chemistry. Rather, the brain automatically monitors information on your body's internal state. Signals from the stomach, the intestines, and the liver (indicating whether glucose is being deposited or withdrawn) all signal the brain to motivate eating or not. But where in the brain are these messages integrated? During the 1940s and 1950s, researchers located hunger controls within the hypothalamus, a small but complex neural traffic intersection buried deep in the brain (**FIGURE 34.2**).

Actually, there are two distinct hypothalamic centers that help control eating. Experiments during the 1960s suggested that activity along the sides of the hypothalamus,

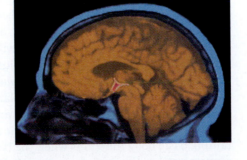

FIGURE 34.2
The hypothalamus
The hypothalamus (colored red) performs various body maintenance functions, including control of hunger. Blood vessels supply the hypothalamus, enabling it to respond to our current blood chemistry as well as to incoming neural information about the body's state.

■ **glucose** the form of sugar that circulates in the blood and provides the major source of energy for body tissues. When its level is low, we feel hunger.

Evidence for the brain's control of eating
A lesion near the ventromedial (middle) area of the hypothalamus caused this rat's weight to triple. At 92.05 grams, it weighs about three times more than normal.

known as the *lateral hypothalamus*, brings on hunger. When electrically stimulated there, a well-fed animal would begin to eat; when the area was destroyed, even a starving animal had no interest in food. When a rat is deprived of food and its blood sugar levels wane, the lateral hypothalamus churns out a hunger-triggering hormone, orexin. When given orexin, rats become ravenously hungry (Sakurai & others, 1998).

Activity in the lower middle of the hypothalamus, the *ventromedial hypothalamus*, depresses hunger. Stimulate this area and an animal will stop eating; destroy it and the animal's stomach and intestines will process food more rapidly, causing it to eat more often and to become extremely fat (Duggan & Booth, 1986; Hoebel & Teitelbaum, 1966). This discovery explained why some patients with tumors near the base of the brain (in what we now realize is the hypothalamus) eat excessively and become very overweight (Miller, 1995).

How do these complementary areas of the hypothalamus work? One theory is that they influence how much glucose is converted to fat and how much is left available to fuel immediate activity (and minimize hunger). After ventromedial lesions, rats produce more fat and use less fat for energy, rather like a miser who runs every bit of extra money to the bank and resists taking any out (Pinel, 1993). Recent experiments also suggest that a distributed brain system monitors the body's state and reports to the hypothalamus, which processes the information and sends it along to the frontal lobes, which decide behavior (Winn, 1995).

To estimate body fat, the hypothalamus monitors levels of leptin, a protein produced by bloated fat cells. When leptin levels rise in mice, the brain curbs eating and increases activity. When researchers inject leptin into obese mice (who are short on leptin), the mice eat less, become more active, and lose weight (Halaas & others, 1995). Research is under way with obese human volunteers who inject themselves with leptin. In one study, participants lost significant amounts of weight only when taking large doses that produced unpleasant side effects (Heymsfield & others, 1999). Further tests of new leptin formulations are under way.

An older theory is that manipulating the lateral and ventromedial hypothalamus alters the body's "weight thermostat," which predisposes us to keep our body at a particular weight level, called its **set point** (Keesey & Corbett, 1983). When semistarved rats fall below their normal weight, biological pressures act to restore the lost weight: Hunger increases and energy expenditure decreases. If body weight rises—as happens when rats are force-fed—hunger decreases and energy expenditure increases. This stable weight toward which semistarved and overstuffed rats return is their set point. In rats and in humans, heredity influences body type and set point.

Human bodies regulate weight much as rats' bodies do—through the control of food intake and energy output. Despite day-to-day variations in your eating, your body regulates your weight much better than you could through conscious efforts to control food intake precisely. If your body weight rises above its set point, you will tend to feel less hungry; if your weight drops below, you will tend to eat more. Consider that over the next 40 years you will eat about 20 tons of food. If during those years you increase your daily intake by just .01 ounce more than required for your energy needs, you will gain 24 pounds (Martin & others, 1991). With astonishing precision, your body will automatically balance your energy intake and expenditure.

To maintain its set-point weight, your body adjusts not only food intake and energy output but also its **basal metabolic rate**—its rate of energy expenditure in maintaining basic body functions when the body is at rest. By the end of their 24 weeks of semistarvation, the subjects in the World War II experiment had stabilized at three-quarters of their normal weight—while eating half of what they previously did. The stabilization resulted from reduced energy expenditure, achieved partly by physical lethargy and partly by a 29 percent drop in their basal metabolic rate. In a reverse ex-

■ **set point** the point at which an individual's "weight thermostat" is supposedly set. When the body falls below this weight, an increase in hunger and a lowered metabolic rate may act to restore the lost weight.

■ **basal metabolic rate** the body's resting rate of energy expenditure.

periment—in which volunteers were overfed 1000 calories a day for eight weeks—those who gained the least weight tended to spend the caloric energy by fidgeting more (Levine & others, 1999).

Some researchers, however, doubt that the body has a precise set point that drives hunger. They believe that slow, sustained changes in body weight can, for example, alter one's set point. Given unlimited access to tasty foods, people and other animals tend to overeat and gain weight. This casts doubt on the idea that our bodies have a preset tendency to maintain optimum weight (Assanand & others, 1998). Hunger is determined by many factors, including learned incentives.

The Psychology of Hunger

Preview Question: What psychological influences affect our eating behavior and feelings of hunger?

Our eagerness to eat is indeed pushed by our physiological state—our body chemistry and hypothalamic activity. Yet there is more to hunger than meets the stomach. This was strikingly apparent when Paul Rozin and his trickster colleagues (1998) tested two patients with amnesia who had no memory for events occurring more than a minute ago. If, 20 minutes after eating a normal lunch, the patients were offered another, both readily consumed it . . . and usually a third meal offered 20 minutes after the second was finished. This suggests that part of knowing when to eat is our memory of our last meal. As time accumulates since we last ate, we anticipate eating again and start feeling hungry.

External Incentives and Hunger

Like Pavlov's dogs, people learn to salivate in anticipation of appealing foods. As the hours pile up since last eating, food becomes a strong incentive. Anticipating pleasure from eating, we eat. Some people are especially responsive to appealing foods, and tend to gain the most weight, when food is abundant.

Consider the 9- to 15-year-old girls studied by Judith Rodin and Joyce Slochower (1976) at an eight-week summer camp. During the first week of camp, some could not resist munching readily visible M&M's, even after a full meal. These girls were typical of a category the researchers called *externals*—people whose eating is triggered more by the presence of food than by internal factors. In the seven weeks that followed, the "external" girls gained the most weight.

In a delicious demonstration of how internal and external factors interact, Rodin (1984) invited other research subjects to her laboratory for lunch. They had gone 18 hours without food. While blood samples were being taken, a large, juicy steak was wheeled in, crackling as it finished grilling. As the hungry subjects sat watching, hearing, and smelling the soon-to-be-eaten steak, Rodin monitored their rising blood insulin levels and their accompanying feelings of hunger. When stimulated by the sight, sound, and aroma of the steak, "externals" had the greatest insulin increase and accompanying hunger response. This illustrates how certain individuals' psychological experience of an external incentive (the steak) can affect their internal physiological state.

PEANUTS

Drawing by Charles Schulz; © 1989 United Feature Syndicate, Inc. Reprinted by permission of UFS, Inc.

An acquired taste
For Alaskan Eskimos, but not for most other North Americans, whale blubber is a tasty treat. People everywhere learn to enjoy the fatty, bitter, or irritating foods that are prescribed by their culture.

Taste Preference: Biology or Culture?

Psychologists have studied how we eat and how our eating is influenced by hunger and taste. As our hunger diminishes, our eating behavior changes. Eliot Stellar (1985) discovered this after outfitting people with a special dental retainer engineered to record each chew and swallow. The device answers questions about our eating that you may never have thought to ask. During a meal of sandwich snacks, how often does the average person swallow? Every 14 seconds. How many chews per swallow? On average, 19. How fast do people chew? Some 1.8 chews per second. As the meal progresses and both hunger and food tastiness decrease, people chew more. Ironically, the better a food tastes, the *less* time we leave it in our mouth.

Body chemistry and environmental factors together influence not only when we feel hunger, but what we feel hungry for—our taste preference. When feeling tense or depressed, do you crave sweet or starchy carbohydrate-laden foods? Carbohydrates help boost levels of the neurotransmitter serotonin, which has calming effects.

Our preferences for sweet and salty tastes are genetic and universal. Other taste preferences are conditioned, as when people given highly salted foods develop a liking for excess salt (Beauchamp, 1987) or when people develop an aversion to a food eaten before becoming violently ill. (The frequency of children's illnesses provides many chances for them to learn food aversions.)

Culture affects taste, too. Bedouins enjoy eating the eye of a camel, which most North Americans would find repulsive. Similarly, most North Americans and Europeans shun dog, rat, and horse meat, all of which are prized elsewhere, but welcome beef, which Hindus would not think of eating. Such preferences vary with exposure (Pliner & Pelchat, 1991; Rozin, 1976). We humans have a natural dislike of many things that are unfamiliar, including novel foods (especially novel animal-based rather than vegetarian foods). Rats, too, prefer long-familiar foods (Sclafani, 1995). This "neophobia" surely was adaptive for our ancestors, protecting them from potentially toxic substances. In experiments, people have tried novel fruit drinks or ethnic foods. With repeated exposure, their appreciation for the new taste typically increases; moreover, exposure to one set of novel foods increases our willingness to try another (Pliner, 1982; Pliner & others, 1993).

Eating Disorders

Psychological influences on eating behavior are strikingly evident in those for whom normal homeostatic pressures are overwhelmed by a motive for abnormal thinness. Consider two eating disorder cases.

Mary is a 5 foot 3 inch 15-year-old who, having reached 100 pounds, decided she needed to lose weight to enhance her attractiveness. After gradually reducing her food intake to a few vegetables a day and then adding a vigorous exercise program, she now weighs a mere 80 pounds. Yet she still feels "fat" and plans to continue dieting. Mary has been having difficulty sleeping, has at times been depressed, and no longer has regular menstrual periods. She is socially inactive, but she is very successful academically. Mary does not regard herself as ill or needing treatment.

Alice is a 5 foot 9 inch 17-year-old who weighs 160 pounds and says she has always been a little chubby. For the last five years, she has often eaten in binges, followed by vomiting. She will eat a quart of ice cream or an entire pie and then, to control her weight, make herself vomit in secret. Alice wants to date, but she doesn't, partly because she is so self-conscious about her looks. She has at times taken diet pills to try to lose weight.

Mary is diagnosed as having **anorexia nervosa**—a disorder in which a person becomes significantly underweight (typically, 15 percent or more) yet feels fat and is obsessed with losing weight. Even when emaciated, the person continues to limit food intake. The disorder usually develops in adolescence, 9 times out of 10 in females.

Alice's condition is a more common one. **Bulimia nervosa** is a disorder marked by repeated episodes of overeating followed by compensatory vomiting, laxative use, fasting, or excessive exercise. Bulimia patients eat the way some alcoholics drink—in spurts, sometimes under the influence of friends who are bingeing (Crandall, 1988). Most binge-purge eaters are women in their late teens or early twenties. Like those with anorexia, they are preoccupied with food (craving sweet and high-fat foods), are fearful of becoming overweight, and are depressed or anxious (Hinz & Williamson, 1987). Their depression and shame are felt most keenly during and following binges. About half of those with anorexia also display the binge-purge-depression symptoms of bulimia. But unlike anorexia, bulimia is marked by weight fluctuations within or above normal ranges, making the condition easy to hide.

Dying to be thin
Champion U.S. gymnast Christy Henrich, shown here at the 1989 World Games, was plagued by anorexia and bulimia. She was at times training nine hours a day and eating one apple. "My life is a horrifying nightmare. It feels like there's a beast inside of me," she exclaimed before dying in 1994, a 60-pound tragedy who barely dented her hospital mattress (Deardorff, 1994).

Researchers report that the families of bulimia patients have a higher-than-usual incidence of alcoholism, obesity, and depression. In contrast, anorexia patients often come from families that are competitive, high-achieving, and protective (Pate & others, 1992; Yates, 1989, 1990). They set high standards, fret about falling short of expectations, and are intensely concerned with how others perceive them (Heatherton & Baumeister, 1991; Striegel-Moore & others, 1993). Eating disorders do *not*, however, provide (as some have speculated) a telltale sign of childhood sexual abuse (Kinzi & others, 1994; Pope & others, 1992, 1994; Rorty & others, 1994).

Genetics, too, may influence susceptibility to eating disorders. If twins are identical rather than fraternal, the chances of the other twin's sharing the disorder are much greater (Fichter & Noegel, 1990). People with eating disorders may also have abnormal supplies of certain neurotransmitters that put them at risk for anxiety or depression (Fava & others, 1989).

"Diana remained throughout a very insecure person at heart, almost childlike in her desire to do good for others, so she could release herself from deep feelings of unworthiness, of which her eating disorders were merely a symptom."

Charles, Ninth Earl of Spencer, eulogizing his sister Princess Diana, 1997

There is, however, a cultural explanation for the fact that anorexia and bulimia occur mostly in women and mostly in weight-conscious cultures. Mothers of girls with eating disorders are themselves often focused on their own weight and on their daughters' weight and appearance (Pike & Rodin, 1991). Anorexia nervosa always begins as a weight-loss diet, and the self-induced vomiting of bulimia nearly always begins after a dieter has broken diet restrictions and gorged. Facing a diet, the person's body seems to revolt and overcomes the dieter's willpower by demanding food to restore lost fat. Those whose natural weight is well above their thin-ideal weight are especially vulnerable (Seligman, 1994).

Ideals of beauty have varied over the centuries, but women in every era have struggled to make their bodies conform to the particular ideal of their day. The sickness of today's eating disorders lies not just within the victims but also within our weight-obsessed culture—a culture that says, in countless ways, "Fat is bad," that motivates millions of women to be "always dieting," and that encourages eating binges by pressuring women to live in a constant state of semistarvation. "You can't be too rich or too thin," declared the Duchess of Windsor. Eating disorder specialists disagree. As obesity researchers Susan Wooley and Orland Wooley (1983) noted, "An increasingly stringent cultural standard of thinness for women has been accompanied by a steadily increasing incidence of serious eating disorders in women."

■ **anorexia nervosa** an eating disorder in which a normal-weight person (usually an adolescent female) diets and becomes significantly (15 percent or more) underweight, yet, still feeling fat, continues to starve.

■ **bulimia nervosa** an eating disorder characterized by episodes of overeating, usually of highly caloric foods, followed by vomiting, laxative use, fasting, or excessive exercise.

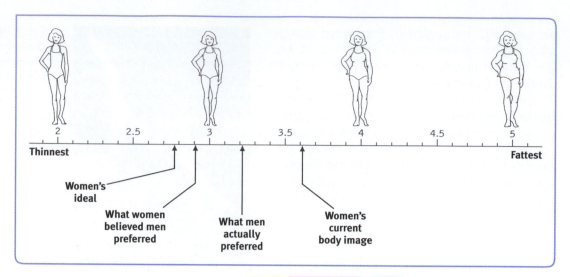

FIGURE 34.3
Women's body images
Many U.S. women students tend to idealize—and misperceive men as idealizing—a body shape considerably thinner than their actual shape (Fallon, 1990; Fallon & Rozin, 1985).

A recent analysis of 222 studies of 141,000 people over 50 years revealed "dramatic increases in the numbers of women . . . who have poor body image" (Feingold & Mazzella, 1998). In one 1993 national survey, nearly one-half of U.S. women reported feeling negative about their appearance and preoccupied with being or becoming overweight (Cash & Henry, 1995). In one lighthearted experiment, a research team led by Barbara Fredrickson (1998) had University of Michigan men and women put on a sweater or a swimsuit and complete a math test while alone in a changing room. For the women but not the men, wearing the swimsuit triggered self-consciousness and shame that disrupted their math performance. Other research confirms that those vulnerable to eating disorders are indeed those with greater body dissatisfaction (Cash & Deagle, 1997).

Women's perceptions are distorted in part by their impression of the body shapes that men find attractive. In one study of nearly 500 University of Pennsylvania students, April Fallon and Paul Rozin (1985) found not only that women's ideal body weight was less than their current weight, but also that the weight they thought men preferred was less than the weight men actually preferred (**FIGURE 34.3**). The researchers found no such discrepancies in the men's self-ratings. Men more often judged their current weight, their ideal weight, and the weight they thought women preferred as all quite similar. Women's greater self-dissatisfaction stems from their perceiving their cheeks, waist, and hips as looking larger than they do (Thompson, 1986).

Part of the cultural pressure is surely transmitted by the view of women exemplified in fashion magazines, advertisements, and even in some toys. What do you suppose happens when young women repeatedly encounter magazine images of fashion models, who tend to be unnaturally thin (Tovee & others, 1997)? Eric Stice and Heather Shaw (1994) and Heidi Posavac and colleagues (1998) report that women tend to feel more ashamed, depressed, and dissatisfied with their own bodies—the very attitudes that predispose eating disorders. Further evidence of the effect of cultural pressure on ideal body image came in 1995, when satellites began beaming television signals to a remote region of Fiji in the South Pacific. Within three years, the percentage of teen girls who induced vomiting to control their weight had quintupled. Those who watched TV three or more nights a week were 50 percent more likely to describe themselves as "too big or fat" and 30 percent more likely to be dieting, which was uncommon before 1995 (Goode, 1999). But even ultra-thin actresses and models do not define the impossible standard of the Barbie fashion doll. Adjusted to a height of 5 feet 7 inches, her 32-16-29 figure (in centimeters, 82 bust, 41

"Gee, I had no idea you were married to a supermodel."

waist, and 73 hips) defines a body shape approximated by fewer than 1 in 100,000 women (Norton & others, 1996).

Women with low self-esteem are particularly likely to have a negative body image and are especially vulnerable to eating disorders (Mintz & Betz, 1986; Strauman & others, 1991; Striegel-Moore & others, 1986). By controlling their eating and weight, some clinicians speculate, these women may feel greater control over their lives.

Body ideals vary across culture and time. In India, women students rate their ideals as close to their actual shape. In Western cultures, however, the rise in eating disorders has coincided with a dramatic increase over the past 50 years in women having a poor body image (Feingold & Mazzella, 1996). Moreover, eating disorders have plagued mainly *white* women (Dolan, 1991).

"Why do women have such low self-esteem? There are many complex psychological and societal reasons, by which I mean Barbie."

Dave Barry, 1999

REVIEW AND REFLECT:

Hunger

What physiological factors cause us to feel hungry?

Hunger's inner push primarily originates not from the stomach's contractions but from variations in body chemistry. For example, we are likely to feel hungry when our glucose levels are low. This information is integrated by the hypothalamus, which regulates the body's weight as it influences our feelings of hunger and satiety. To maintain weight, the body also adjusts its metabolic rate of energy expenditure.

What psychological influences affect our eating behavior and feelings of hunger?

Our preferences for certain tastes are partly genetic and universal, but also partly learned in a cultural context. Especially in "external" people, the sight and smell of food can trigger hunger and eating, in part by stimulating a rise in insulin level. The impact of psychological factors, such as challenging family settings and weight-obsessed societal pressures, on eating behavior is dramatic in people with anorexia nervosa, who keep themselves on near-starvation rations, and in those with bulimia nervosa, who binge and purge in secret. In the past half-century a dramatic increase in poor body image has coincided with a rise in eating disorders among women in Western cultures.

Terms and Concepts to Remember

glucose, p. 441
set point, p. 442
basal metabolic rate, p. 442

anorexia nervosa, p. 444
bulimia nervosa, p. 445

Test Yourself

34.1. The hypothalamus, a structure deep within the brain, controls feelings of hunger and fullness, in part by evaluating changes in blood chemistry. Hunger occurs in response to high blood insulin and
a. high blood glucose.
b. low blood glucose.
c. decreased energy expenditure.
d. stimulation of any part of the hypothalamus.

34.2. One theory maintains that our bodies tend to stay at a particular weight level, or set point. Changes in the basal metabolic rate help keep us at this weight. For example, when our weight falls below the set point, we feel hungrier (and eat more) and lethargic (and reduce our energy expenditure). The operation of this "weight thermostat" is an example of
a. homeostasis.   c. individual learning.
b. an eating disorder.   d. binge-purge episodes.

34.3. Some of our responses to food and to eating are learned; others are genetic and universal. Which of the following are genetic responses to food?
a. An aversion to eating dogs and cats
b. An interest in novel foods
c. A preference for sweet and salty foods
d. An aversion to carbohydrates

34.4. Both anorexia nervosa and bulimia nervosa are eating disorders characterized by excessive weight loss. Which of the following is true regarding bulimia nervosa?
a. People with bulimia continue to want to lose weight even when they are underweight.
b. Bulimia is marked by weight fluctuations within or above normal ranges.
c. Bulimia patients often come from middle-class families that are competitive, high-achieving, and protective.
d. If one twin is diagnosed with bulimia, the chances of the other twin's sharing the disorder are greater if they are fraternal rather than identical twins.

Review: You are traveling and have not eaten anything in eight hours. As your long-awaited favorite dish is placed in front of you, your mouth waters. Even imagining this may set your mouth to watering. What triggers this anticipatory drooling?

Reflect: Do you feel in touch with your body's hunger signals? Do you eat when your body needs food? Or do you tend to be more externally influenced by enticing foods even when you're full?

Answers to Test Yourself and Review questions can be found in the green appendix at the end of the book.

Sexual Motivation

Sex is part of life. Had this not been so for all your ancestors, you would not be reading this book. Sexual motivation is nature's clever way of making people procreate, thus enabling our species' survival. When two people feel attracted, they hardly stop to think of themselves as guided by their genes. As the pleasure we take in eating is nature's inventive method of getting our body nourishment, so the pleasure of sex is our genes' way of preserving and spreading themselves.

Describing Sexual Behavior

Preview Question: What behavior patterns must a theory of sexual motivation explain?

Unable to answer his students' questions about people's sexual practices, Indiana University biologist Alfred Kinsey and his colleagues (1948, 1953) set out to find some answers. Kinsey's confidential interviews with 18,000 people—85 percent conducted by himself or his associate Wardell Pomeroy—asked more than 350 rapid-fire questions. Social scientists were quick to point out what Kinsey readily acknowledged—that his nonrandom sample contained an overrepresentation of well-educated white urbanites. Nevertheless, his statistics-laden volumes became bestsellers. Here readers learned the surprising news that most of the men and nearly half the women reported having had premarital sexual intercourse; that most women and virtually all men reported masturbating; and that women who reported masturbating to orgasm before marriage seldom had difficulties experiencing orgasm after marriage. The books also revealed that sexual behavior is enormously varied. Kinsey found some men and women who said they had never had an orgasm and others who said they had four or more a day. For those who evaluate themselves by comparisons with others, Kinsey's findings—and others showing wide variations in "normal" sexual behavior around the world—are reassuring. Given the range of sex drives and the variety of sexual behaviors, our own sexual interests probably fall well within the range of "normal."

Because we do not know whether Kinsey's sample accurately represented the nation's sexual practices in the 1940s, let alone those of today, his precise findings can be misleading. Moreover, Kinsey and Pomeroy's questioning encouraged (some say, demanded) admission of sexual activity. They never asked subjects *whether* they had engaged in a particular activity; they asked them *when* they had first engaged in it (thus making it easier for people to divulge their behavior). Pomeroy (1972, pp. 113, 124, 127) reported that he and Kinsey "went on the broad assumption that everybody had done everything." If Kinsey or Pomeroy doubted a subject's denial, they might respond, "Yes, I know you have never done that, but how old were you the *first* time you did it?" or even "Look, I don't give a damn what you've done, but if you don't tell me the straight of it, it's better that we stop this history right here. Now, how old were you the first time this or that happened?" Even his motives are suspect. Kinsey, his biographers report, was driven by a desire to overthrow the "Victorian repression" of his father's strict Methodist morality and to justify his own sexual compulsions (Ericksen, 1998; Jones, 1997a,b).

By today's standards of random sampling and nonleading questioning, Kinsey's tactics, and thus his results, are suspect. Yet his surveys were less misleading than some of the haphazard sexual surveys reported more recently in the popular press. Some of these popular "sex reports" have relied on biased samples of people (such as

"I love the idea of there being two sexes, don't you?"

■ **sexual response cycle** the four stages of sexual responding described by Masters and Johnson—excitement, plateau, orgasm, and resolution.

subscribers to selected magazines) and have received replies from 3 percent of their nonrandom sample—good reason to doubt the generality of their findings.

Better information is becoming available. Despite the media image of rampant marital infidelity—an image reinforced by media psychologist Joyce Brothers' (1990) pronouncement that two-thirds of married men and half of married women have affairs—eight recent surveys of randomly sampled U.S. adults provide a different view (Smith, 1998). Some 84 percent of married adults claim (even when responding anonymously) to have had sex only with their spouse during their present marriage. And 96 percent say they have been faithful during the past year. Faithful attractions overwhelmingly outnumber fatal attractions. Moreover, at 91 percent, disapproval of extramarital sex runs as high as ever among adult Americans (Smith, 1994).

Alfred Kinsey
The controversial biologist, shown here conducting one of his interviews, did not begin with sexually explicit questions. Rather, he first helped people feel at ease by asking nonthreatening questions about family background, health, and education.

The Physiology of Sex

Preview Questions: What are the stages of the human sexual response cycle? How do sex hormones influence human sexual development and arousal?

Like hunger, sexual arousal depends on the interplay of internal and external stimuli. To understand sexual motivation, we must consider both.

The Sexual Response Cycle

The headlines created by Kinsey's 1940s surveys reappeared after some 1960s studies in which scientists recorded the physiological responses of volunteers who masturbated or had intercourse. With the help of 382 female and 312 male volunteers—a somewhat atypical sample, consisting only of people able and willing to display arousal and orgasm while being observed in a laboratory—gynecologist-obstetrician William Masters and his collaborator Virginia Johnson (1966) monitored or filmed more than 10,000 sexual "cycles."

Their description of the **sexual response cycle** identified four stages, similar in men and women. During the initial *excitement phase*, the genital areas become engorged with blood, causing the man's penis to become partially erect and the woman's clitoris to swell and the inner lips covering her vagina to open up. Her vagina also expands and secretes lubricant, and her breasts and nipples may enlarge.

In the *plateau phase*, excitement peaks as breathing, pulse, and blood pressure rates continue to increase. The penis becomes fully engorged and some fluid—frequently containing enough live sperm to enable conception—may appear at the tip of the penis. Vaginal secretion continues to increase, the clitoris retracts, and orgasm feels imminent.

Masters and Johnson observed muscle contractions all over the body during *orgasm*; these were accompanied by further increases in breathing, pulse, and blood pressure rates. A woman's arousal and orgasm facilitate conception by helping propel semen from the penis, positioning the uterus to receive sperm, and drawing the sperm farther inward. A woman's orgasm therefore not only reinforces intercourse, which is essential to natural reproduction, it also increases retention of deposited sperm (Furlow & Thornhill, 1996). In the excitement of the moment, men and women are hardly aware of all this but are more aware of their rhythmic genital contractions that create a pleasurable feeling of sexual release. The feeling apparently is much the same for both sexes. In one study, a panel of experts could not reliably distinguish between descriptions of orgasm written by men and those written by women (Vance & Wagner, 1976).

After orgasm, the body gradually returns to its unaroused state as the engorged genital blood vessels release their accumulated blood—relatively quickly if orgasm has

A nonsmoking 50-year-old male has about a 1 in a million chance of a heart attack during any hour. This increases to merely 2 in a million during the hour following sex (with no increase for those who exercise regularly). Compared with risks associated with heavy exertion or anger, this risk seems not worth losing sleep (or sex) over (Muller & others, 1996).

- **refractory period** a resting period after orgasm, during which a man cannot achieve another orgasm.

- **estrogen** a sex hormone, secreted in greater amounts by females than by males. In nonhuman female mammals, estrogen levels peak during ovulation, promoting sexual receptivity.

- **testosterone** the most important of the male sex hormones. Both males and females have it, but the additional testosterone in males stimulates the growth of the male sex organs in the fetus and the development of the male sex characteristics during puberty.

occurred, relatively slowly otherwise. (It's like the nasal tickle that goes away rapidly if you have sneezed, slowly otherwise.) During this *resolution phase*, the male enters a **refractory period**, lasting from a few minutes to a day or more, during which he is incapable of another orgasm. The female's refractory period is not very long, which may make it possible for her to have another orgasm if restimulated during or soon after resolution.

Hormones and Sexual Behavior

Sex hormones have two effects: They direct the development of male and female sex characteristics, and (especially in nonhuman animals) they activate sexual behavior. In most mammals, nature neatly synchronizes sex with fertility. The female becomes sexually receptive ("in heat") when production of the female hormone **estrogen** peaks at ovulation. (In experiments, researchers stimulate receptivity by injecting female animals with estrogen.) Male hormone levels are more constant, and researchers cannot so easily manipulate the sexual behavior of male animals by hormone treatments (Feder, 1984). Nevertheless, castrated male rats—having lost their testes, which manufacture the male sex hormone **testosterone**—gradually lose much of their interest in receptive females. They gradually regain it if injected with testosterone.

Hormones do not, however, so neatly control human sexual behavior. At ovulation, women's sexual desire is only slightly higher than at other times (Harvey, 1987; Meuwissen & Over, 1992). Women's sexuality also differs from that of other mammalian females in being more responsive to testosterone level than to estrogen level (Andersen & Cyranowski, 1995; Reichman, 1998). If a woman's testosterone level is low, her sexual interest may wane, but it can be restored by a testosterone replacement drug.

In men, normal fluctuations in testosterone levels, from man to man and hour to hour, have little effect on sexual drive (Byrne, 1982). Indeed, fluctuations in male hormones are partly a response to sexual stimulation. When James Dabbs and his colleagues (1987) had male collegians converse separately with a male and with a female student, the men's testosterone levels rose with the social arousal, but especially after talking with the female. Thus, sexual arousal can be a cause as well as a consequence of increased testosterone levels.

Although normal short-term hormonal changes have little effect on men's and women's desire, large hormone shifts over the life span have a greater effect. A person's interest in dating and sexual stimulation usually increases with the pubertal surge in sex hormones. If the hormonal surge is precluded—as happened during the 1600s and 1700s with prepubertal boys who were castrated to preserve their soprano voices for Italian opera—the normal development of sex characteristics and sexual desire does not occur (Peschel & Peschel, 1987). Among adult men who suffer castration, sex drive typically falls along with declining testosterone levels (Hucker & Bain, 1990). Likewise, male sex offenders lose much of their sexual urge when voluntarily taking Depo-Provera, a drug that reduces testosterone level to that of a prepubertal boy (Money & others, 1983). In later life, as sex hormone levels decline, the frequency of sexual fantasies and intercourse declines as well (Leitenberg & Henning, 1995).

Hormones influence sexual arousal via the hypothalamus, which both monitors variations in blood hormone levels and activates the appropriate neural circuits. In rats, destroying a key area of the hypothalamus may extinguish sexual activity; stimulating this area, either electrically or by directly inserting minute quantities of hormones, may activate sexual behavior.

"Fill'er up with testosterone."

To summarize: We might compare human sex hormones, especially testosterone, to the fuel in a car. Without fuel, a car will not run. But if the fuel level is minimally adequate, adding more fuel to the gas tank won't change how the car runs. The analogy is imperfect, because the interaction between hormones and sexual motivation is two-way. However, the analogy correctly suggests that biology is a necessary but not sufficient explanation of human sexual behavior. The hormonal fuel is essential, but so are the psychological stimuli that turn on the engine, keep it running, and shift it into high gear.

The Psychology of Sex

Preview Question: How do internal and external stimuli contribute to sexual arousal?

Hunger and sex are different sorts of motives. Hunger responds to a *need*. If we do not eat, we die. Sex is not in this sense a need. If we do not have sex, we may feel like dying, but we do not. Nevertheless, there are similarities between hunger and sexual motivation. Both depend on internal physiological factors. And both are influenced by external stimuli.

External Stimuli

Many studies confirm that men become aroused when they see, hear, or read erotic material. Surprising to many (because sexually explicit materials are sold mostly to men) is that most women—at least the less-inhibited women who volunteer to participate in such studies—report nearly as much arousal to the same stimuli (Stockton & Murnen, 1992).

In one study, psychologist Julia Heiman (1975) had sexually experienced university volunteers attach instruments that detected arousal (changes in penis circumference or in vaginal color). The students then listened to one of four tapes: a sexually explicit erotic tape, a romantic tape (of a couple expressing love without physical contact), a combined erotic-romantic tape, or a neutral control tape. Which do you suppose the men were most aroused by? And the women? Both found the tape of explicit sex most arousing, especially when a woman initiated the sex and the depiction centered on her responses. In other studies both sexes have shown arousal to sexual stimuli, though men's arousal has tended to exceed women's somewhat (Murnen & Stockton, 1997).

People may find such arousal either pleasing or disturbing. (Those who find it disturbing often limit their exposure to such materials, just as those wishing to control hunger limit their exposure to tempting cues.) With repeated exposure, the emotional response to any erotic stimulus often "habituates" (lessens). During the 1920s, when Western women's hemlines first reached the knee, an exposed leg was a mildly erotic stimulus, as were modest (by today's standards) two-piece swimsuits and movie scenes of a mere kiss.

Can sexually explicit materials have adverse effects? Research indicates that it can. Depictions of women being sexually coerced—and enjoying it—tend to increase the viewers' acceptance of the false idea that women enjoy rape and tend to increase male viewers' willingness to hurt women (Malamuth & Check, 1981; Zillmann, 1989). Images of sexually attractive women and men may also lead people to devalue their own partners and relationships. After male collegians watch TV or magazine depictions of sexually attractive women, they often find an average woman, or their own girlfriends or wives, less attractive (Kenrick & Gutierres, 1980; Kenrick & others, 1989; Weaver & others, 1984). Viewing X-rated sex films similarly tends to diminish people's satisfaction with their own sexual partners (Zillmann, 1989). Some sex researchers fear that reading or watching erotica may create expectations that few men and women can hope to live up to.

"Ours is a society which stimulates interest in sex by constant titillation. . . . Cinema, television, and all the formidable array of our marketing technology project our very effective forms of titillation and our prejudices about man as a sexy animal into every corner of every hovel in the world."

Germaine Greer, 1984

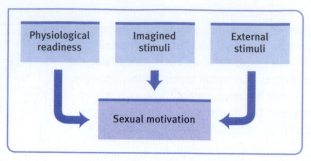

FIGURE 35.1
Forces affecting sexual motivation
Physiology, imagination, and the environment all affect sexual motivation.

"There is no difference between being raped and being run over by a truck except that afterward men ask if you enjoyed it."

Marge Piercy, "Rape Poem," 1976

Imagined Stimuli

Sexual motivation arises from the interplay of our physiology and our environment. But the stimuli inside our heads—our imaginations—also influence sexual arousal and desire (**FIGURE 35.1**). The brain, it has been said, is our most significant sex organ. People who, because of a spinal cord injury, have no genital sensation, can still feel sexual desire (Willmuth, 1987). Consider, too, the erotic potential of dreams. Sleep researchers have discovered that genital arousal accompanies all types of dreams, even though most dreams have no sexual content. But in nearly all men and some 40 percent of women (Wells, 1986), dreams sometimes do contain sexual imagery that leads to orgasm. In men, these nocturnal emissions ("wet dreams") are more likely when orgasm has not occurred recently.

Wide-awake people become sexually aroused not only by memories of prior sexual activities but also by fantasies. Fantasies need not correspond to actual behavior. In one survey of masturbation-related fantasies (Hunt, 1974), 19 percent of women and 10 percent of men reported imagining being taken by someone overwhelmed with desire for them. Fantasy is not reality, however. To paraphrase Susan Brownmiller (1975), for women there's a big difference between fantasizing that Leonardo DiCaprio just won't take no for an answer and having a hostile stranger actually force himself on you.

About 95 percent of both men and women say they have had sexual fantasies. But men (whether gay or straight) fantasize about sex more often, more physically, and less romantically—and prefer less personal and faster-paced sex content in books and videos (Leitenberg & Henning, 1995). Fantasizing about sex does *not* indicate a sexual problem or dissatisfaction. (If anything, sexually active people have more sexual fantasies.)

CLOSE-UP:

SEXUAL DISORDERS AND THERAPY

Masters and Johnson sought not only to describe the human sexual response cycle but also to understand and treat the inability to complete it. **Sexual disorders** are problems that consistently impair sexual functioning. Some involve sexual motivation, especially lack of sexual energy and arousability. In a national survey of 18- to 59-year-old Americans, 3 in 10 men reported *premature ejaculation* (before they or their partners wish) and 1 in 10 acknowledged *impotence* (the in-ability to have or maintain an erection) (Laumann & others, 1999). Among women respondents, 3 in 10 reported low sexual desire and 1 in 4 acknowledged *orgasmic disorder* (infrequently or never experiencing orgasm).

What causes such problems? The idea that personality disorders are to blame has been largely discounted. Men who experience premature ejaculation are similar, even in their sexual arousal patterns, to men who do not; they simply ejaculate at lower levels of arousal—something that often occurs with young men who have had long periods of sexual abstinence (Grenier & Byers, 1995; Spiess & others, 1984).

When Barbara Andersen (1983) reviewed research on the diagnosis and treatment of orgasmic disorder in women, she, too, could find no associated personality traits. Furthermore, she reported that treating orgasmic disorder through traditional psychotherapy (as though it were a disorder of personality) has been unsuccessful.

She did, however, report a nearly 100 percent success rate with a behavioral treatment that trains women to enjoy their bodies and to give themselves orgasms, with a vibrator if necessary. Women who undergo such training are then sometimes able to generalize their new sexual responsiveness to interactions with their mates (Rosen & Leiblum, 1995; Wakefield, 1987). Some success has also been reported in training men to control their premature ejaculations by repeatedly stimulating the penis and then stopping stimulation (or even firmly squeezing the head of the penis) when the urge to ejaculate arises. Alternatively, men can reduce their excitability by simply having more orgasms (LoPicolo & Stock, 1986).

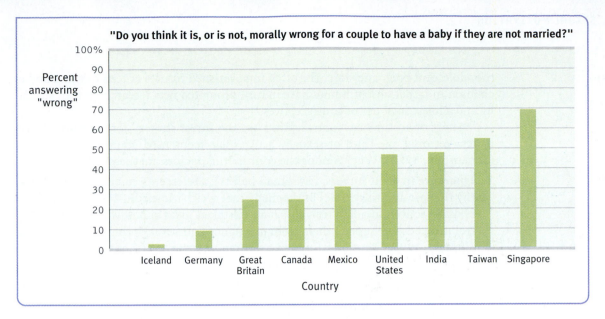

FIGURE 35.2
Same drives, different attitudes
People around the world have widely varying attitudes about nonmarital childbearing (Gallup poll, 1997).

Adolescent Sexuality

Preview Question: What factors influence teenagers' sexual attitudes and behaviors?

Adolescents' physical maturation fosters a sexual dimension to their emerging identity. Yet sexual expression also varies dramatically with time and culture.

Culture

We humans are one species, driven by similar motives that enhance our survival and spread our genes. Yet our attitudes toward behaviors such as premarital sex and nonmarital childbearing vary widely across the planet (**FIGURE 35.2**). These cultural differences in sexual attitudes are manifest in sexual behavior. In the United States, about half of ninth- to twelfth-graders report having had sexual intercourse, as do 42 percent of Canadian 16-year-olds (Boroditsky & others, 1995; Smith, 1998). Teen intercourse rates are higher in Western Europe but much lower in Arab and Asian countries and among North Americans of Asian descent (McLaughlin & others, 1997). In one survey only 2.5 percent of 4688 unmarried Chinese students entering Hong Kong's six universities reported having had sexual intercourse (Meston & others, 1996). The variations in sexual standards from country to country help to explain the cultural differences in rates of nonmarital childbearing (**FIGURE 35.3**).

Sexual attitudes and behaviors also vary with time within the same culture. Among American women born before 1900, a mere 3 percent had experienced premarital sex by age 18; among today's 18-year-old women, slightly more than half have done so (Smith, 1998). This increase in sexual activity has led to an increase in

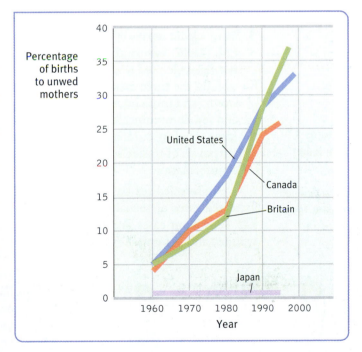

FIGURE 35.3
Births to unwed parents
Since 1960, the percentage of babies born to unmarried Canadian, British, and American women—one-third of whom were teens—has more than quintupled. This increase stems from two trends: a decreasing birthrate among married women and a doubling of the birthrate among unmarried women. (Data from National Center for Health Statistics; Bureau of the Census [1998], Table 1347; and British Annual Abstract of Statistics, 1999.)

■ **sexual disorder** a problem that consistently impairs sexual arousal or functioning.

the adolescent pregnancy rate. The often impoverished futures of teen mothers and of children in father-absent homes have in turn prompted new research on teen sexuality and adolescents' use of contraceptives.

Short of abstinence, contraceptives are the surest strategy for preventing pregnancy. Yet only one-third of sexually active male teens used condoms consistently (Sonenstein, 1992). Why? Among the contributing factors are these:

1. *Ignorance* In eight surveys, fewer than half the adolescents could correctly identify the safe and risky times of the menstrual cycle (Morrison, 1985). Half of sexually active Canadian teen girls have mistaken ideas about which birth control methods will protect them from pregnancy and sexually transmitted diseases (Immen, 1995). Thus, most unwed teens report surprise at finding themselves pregnant (Brooks-Gunn & Furstenberg, 1989).

2. *Guilt related to sexual activity* Although sexual inhibitions reduce sexual activity, they also result in lack of planned birth control for those who do engage in sex (Gerrard & Luus, 1995). Not wanting to appear deliberately sexual or promiscuous, teens may hesitate to carry and produce a condom. When, as sometimes happens, passion overwhelms intentions, the result may be conception.

3. *Minimal communication about birth control* Many teenagers are uncomfortable discussing contraception with their parents, partners, and peers (Kotva & Schneider, 1990; Milan & Kilmann, 1987). Teens who talk freely with friends or parents and are in an exclusive relationship with a partner with whom they communicate openly are more likely to use contraceptives.

4. *Alcohol use* Sexually active teens are typically alcohol-using teens (National Research Council, 1987). By depressing the brain centers that control judgment, inhibition, and self-awareness, alcohol tends to break down normal restraints, a phenomenon well known to sexually coercive males.

5. *Mass media norms of unprotected promiscuity* The Planned Parenthood Federation (1986) has complained that television and movies help define sexual norms, which today are "Go for it *now*." An average hour of prime-time television on the three major U.S. networks contains approximately 15 sexual acts, words, and innuendos. Nearly all of these instances involve unmarried partners, and few communicate any concern for birth control or sexually transmitted disease (Sapolsky & Tabarlet, 1991). Planned Parenthood contends that repeated portrayals of unsafe sex, without consequence, amounts to a campaign of sex disinformation.

Unprotected sex has led not only to an increase in teen pregnancies but also to increased rates of sexually transmitted disease (STD). The United States alone has had 12 million cases annually, not including bacterial diseases such as chlamydia, syphilis, and gonorrhea (Guttmacher Institute, 1993). More than 60 percent of new infections occur in persons under 25. Teenage girls, because of their less mature biological development and lower levels of protective antibodies, seem especially vulnerable to STD and associated risks of becoming infertile and developing certain cancers (Guttmacher Institute, 1994; Morell, 1995). One response to these facts of life has been a shift to include teen abstinence within comprehensive sex education.

To comprehend the mathematics of sexually transmitted disease, imagine an island on which all people were virgins until they first began having sex a

"Will your child learn to multiply before she learns to subtract?"

Anti–teen-pregnancy poster, Children's Defense Fund

"All of us who make motion pictures are teachers, teachers with very loud voices."

Film producer George Lucas, Academy Award ceremonies, 1992

FEIFFER

year ago. Pat has sex with 9 people, each of whom over the same time period has sex with 9 other people, who in turn have sex with 9 others. How many "phantom" sex partners (past partners of partners) will Pat have? Ohio State researchers Laura Brannon and Timothy Brock (1994) report that the actual number—511—is more than five times what the average student guess is.

Given these odds, the rapid spread of STDs is not surprising. Although condoms sometimes fail, they reduce tenfold the risk of contracting HIV from an infected partner (Pinkerton & Abramson, 1997). With certain other skin-to-skin STDs—notably the human papilloma virus, which is responsible for most genital cancers—condoms are virtually useless (Medical Institute, 1994).

Throughout history, the pendulum of sexual values has swung—from the European eroticism of the early 1800s to the conservative Victorian era of the late 1800s, from the libertine flapper era of the 1920s to the family values period of the 1950s. With new voices decrying family disintegration and calling for a balance between sexual expression and restraint, the pendulum may have begun a new swing toward commitment in the twenty-first century. In West Germany, the percentage of teens who link sex with committed love is up significantly since 1970 (Schmidt & others, 1994). And would you agree or disagree that "if two people like each other, it's all right for them to have sex even if they've known each other for a very short time"? The percentage of first-year American college and university students who agree dropped from 52 percent in 1987 to 41 percent in 1999 (Sax & others, 1999).

Sexual Orientation

Preview Question: What does current research tell us about why some people are attracted to members of their own sex and others are attracted to members of the other sex?

To motivate is to energize and direct behavior. So far, we have considered the energizing of sexual motivation but not its direction. We express the direction of our sexual interest in our **sexual orientation**—our enduring sexual attraction toward members of a particular gender. Cultures vary in their attitudes toward homosexuality. As far as we know, all cultures in all times have been predominantly heterosexual (Bullough, 1990). Whether a culture condemns or accepts homosexuality, heterosexuality prevails and homosexuality survives.

Gay men and lesbians often recall childhood play preferences like those of the other sex (Bailey & Zucker, 1995). But most homosexual people report not becoming aware of same-gender sexual feelings until during or shortly after puberty, and not thinking of themselves as gay or lesbian until around age 20 (Garnets & Kimmel, 1990).

How many people are exclusively homosexual? Until recently, the popular press assumed a homosexuality rate of 10 percent. But in both Europe and the United States, more than a dozen national surveys in the early 1990s explored sexual orientation, using methods that protected the respondent's anonymity. Their results agree in suggesting that a more accurate figure is about 3 or 4 percent of men and 1 or 2 percent of women (Laumann & others, 1994; National Center for Health Statistics, 1991; Smith, 1998). Fewer than 1 percent of the respondents reported being actively bisexual, but a larger number of adults reported having had an isolated homosexual experience. And most people said they had had an occasional homosexual fantasy.

Health experts find it helpful to know sexual statistics, but numbers do not decide issues of human rights. Similarly, it's helpful in manufacturing school desks to know that about 10 percent of people are left-handed. But whether left-handers are 3 percent or 10 percent of the population doesn't answer the moral question of whether lefties should enjoy equal rights.

■ **sexual orientation** an enduring sexual attraction toward members of either one's own gender (homosexual orientation) or the other gender (heterosexual orientation).

"It has been maintained for years that we each use only about 10 percent of our brain capacity; that the condom failure rate is 10 percent; and until just last year, that 10 percent of Americans are homosexual. Such statistics are partly artifacts, I suspect, of our decimal system; in a base 12 system, we'd no doubt show a similar affinity for statistics that were multiples of 8.333 percent."

John Allen Paulos,
"Counting on Dyscalculia," 1993

What does it feel like to be homosexual in a heterosexual culture? If you are heterosexual, one way to understand is to imagine how you would feel if you were ostracized or fired for openly admitting or displaying your feelings toward someone of the other sex; if you overheard people making crude jokes about heterosexual people; if most movies, TV shows, and advertisements portrayed (or implied) homosexuality; and if your family members were pleading with you to change your heterosexual lifestyle and to enter into a homosexual marriage.

Facing such reactions, homosexual people often struggle with their sexual orientation. They may at first try to ignore or deny their desires, hoping they will go away. But they don't. Then they may try to change, through psychotherapy, willpower, or prayer. But the feelings typically persist, as do those of heterosexual people—who are similarly incapable of becoming homosexual (Haldeman, 1994). Eventually, homosexuals may accept their orientation—by electing celibacy (as do some heterosexuals); by engaging in promiscuous sex (a choice more commonly made by men than by women); by attempting suicide (which homosexual people are at increased risk for); or by entering into a committed, long-term love relationship (a choice more often made by women than by men) (Peplau, 1982; Remafedi, 1999; Weinberg & Williams, 1974).

Most psychologists today view sexual orientation as neither willfully chosen nor willfully changed. Sexual orientation in some ways is like handedness: Most people are one way, some (mostly men) the other. A very few are truly ambidextrous. Regardless, the way one is endures. Nor is sexual orientation linked with psychological disorder or sexual crime. "Child molester" is not a sexual orientation. Some child molesters are homosexual, but most are heterosexual males (Gonsiorek, 1982). Partly for these reasons, the American Psychiatric Association in 1973 dropped homosexuality from its list of "mental illnesses."

Understanding Sexual Orientation

If our sexual orientation is indeed something we do not choose and cannot change, then where do these preferences come from? How do we move toward either a heterosexual or a homosexual orientation? See if you can anticipate the consensus that has emerged from hundreds of research studies by responding yes or no to the following questions:

1. Is homosexuality linked with problems in a child's relationships with parents, such as with a domineering mother and an ineffectual father, or a possessive mother and a hostile father?
2. Does homosexuality involve a fear or hatred of people of the other gender, leading individuals to direct their sexual desires toward members of their own sex?
3. Is sexual orientation linked with levels of sex hormones currently in the blood?
4. As children, were many homosexuals molested, seduced, or otherwise sexually victimized by an adult homosexual?

Contrary to widely held ideas about homosexuality, the answer to all these questions is no (Storms, 1983). Consider the findings of lengthy Kinsey Institute interviews with nearly 1000 homosexuals and 500 heterosexuals (Bell & others, 1981; Hammersmith, 1982). The investigators assessed nearly every imaginable psychological cause of homosexuality—parental relationships, childhood sexual experiences, peer relationships, dating experiences. Their findings: Apart from homosexuals' somewhat greater nonconformity, the reported backgrounds of homosexuals and heterosexuals were similar. Homosexuals were no more likely to have been smothered by maternal love, neglected by their father, or sexually abused. And consider this: If "distant fathers" were more likely to produce homosexual sons, then shouldn't boys growing up in father-absent homes more often be gay? (They are not.) And shouldn't

Personal values affect sexual orientation less than they affect other forms of sexual behavior. Compared with people who rarely attend church, for example, those who attend regularly are one-third as likely to have cohabited before marriage, and they report having had many fewer sex partners. But (if male) they are just as likely to be homosexual (Smith, 1998).

Note that the scientific question is not "What causes homosexuality?" (or "What causes heterosexuality?") but "What causes differing sexual orientation?" In pursuit of answers, psychological science compares the backgrounds and physiology of people whose sexual orientations differ.

the rising number of such homes have led to a noticeable increase in the gay population? (It has not.)

More recent studies have also found that sons of homosexual men were *not* more likely to become gay if they lived with their gay dad, and that 9 in 10 children of lesbian mothers developed into heterosexuals (Bailey & others, 1995; Golombok & Tasker, 1996). If even being reared by a homosexual parent has no appreciable influence on sexual orientation, then having a gay or lesbian teacher or bus driver also seems unlikely to have an appreciable influence.

Homosexual people do, however, appear more often in certain populations:

+ In America's dozen largest cities, the percentage of men identifying themselves as gay jumps to 9 percent, compared with only 1 percent in rural areas (Binson & others, 1995; Laumann & others, 1994).
+ One study (Ludwig, 1995) of the biographies of 1004 eminent people found homosexual and bisexual people overrepresented (11 percent of the sample), especially among poets (24 percent), fiction writers (21 percent), and artists and musicians (15 percent).
+ Men who have older brothers are somewhat more likely to be gay, reports Ray Blanchard (1997). Assuming the odds of homosexuality are roughly 3 percent among first sons, they rise to 4 percent among second sons and 5 percent for third sons. The reason for this curious phenomenon is unclear, though Blanchard suspects a maternal immune response that becomes stronger after each pregnancy with a male fetus.

So, what then does determine sexual orientation? One theory proposes that people develop same-sex erotic attachments if segregated by gender at the time their sex drive matures (Storms, 1981). But even in a tribal culture in which homosexual behavior is expected of all boys before marriage, heterosexuality prevails (Money, 1987). (As this illustrates, homosexual *behavior* does not always indicate a homosexual *orientation*.) Another theory proposes the opposite: that people develop romantic attachments to those who *differ* from, and thus are more fascinating than, the peers they associated with while growing up (Bell, 1982). The bottom line from a half-century's theory and research: If there are environmental factors that influence sexual orientation, we do not yet know what they are. If someone were to ask me, "What can I do to influence my child's sexual orientation?" my answer would have to be "I haven't a clue."

The Brain and Sexual Orientation

New research indicates that sexual orientation is at least partly physiological. Researcher Simon LeVay (1991) discovered this while studying sections of the hypothalamus taken from deceased heterosexual and homosexual people. As a gay scientist, LeVay wanted to do "something connected with my gay identity." He knew he had to avoid biasing the results, so he did the study "blind," without knowing which donors were gay. For nine months he peered through his microscope at a cell cluster he thought might be important. Then one morning, LeVay sat down and broke the codes. His discovery: The cell cluster was reliably larger in heterosexual men than in women and homosexual men. As the brain difference became apparent, "I was almost in a state of shock. . . . I took a walk by myself on the cliffs over the ocean. I sat for half an hour just thinking what this might mean" (LeVay, 1994).

It should not surprise us that brains differ with sexual orientation. Although we find it convenient to talk separately of psychological and biological explanations, *everything psychological is simultaneously biological.* The critical question is, when did the brain difference begin? At conception? In the womb? During childhood or adolescence? Did experience produce the difference? Or did genes or prenatal hormones (or genes via prenatal hormones)?

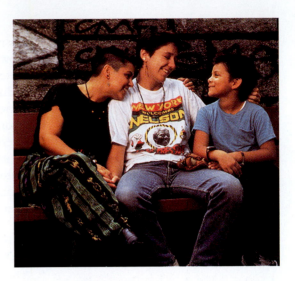

Erick has two moms
Maria Christina Vlassidis (left) and Marie Tatro (center), who are lesbians, tell playmates of their son Erick, 8, that they are both his moms. Both women attend school conferences and support other aspects of his life. Studies suggest that being reared by lesbian or gay parents does not appreciably affect a child's sexual orientation.

LeVay does not view this neural center as a sexual orientation center; rather, he sees it as an important part of the neural pathway engaged in sexual behavior. He acknowledges that it's possible that sexual behavior patterns influence the brain's anatomy. In fish, birds, rats, and humans, brain structures vary with experience—including sexual experience, reports Marc Breedlove (1997—and yes, that is his real name). But LeVay believes it more likely that brain anatomy influences sexual orientation. Laura Allen and Roger Gorski (1992) offered a similar conclusion after discovering that a section of the fibers connecting right and left hemispheres is one-third larger in homosexual men than in heterosexual men. "The emerging neuroanatomical picture," notes Brian Gladue (1994), "is that, in some brain areas, homosexual men are more likely to have female-typical neuroanatomy than are heterosexual men."

Genes and Sexual Orientation

The evidence suggests that genetic influence plays a role in sexual orientation (Hershberger, 1997; Whitam & others, 1993). One research team studied the twin brothers of homosexual men. Among their identical twin brothers, 52 percent were homosexual, as were 22 percent of fraternal twin brothers (Bailey & Pillard, 1991, 1995). In a follow-up study of homosexual women, a similar 48 percent of their identical twins were homosexual, as were 16 percent of their fraternal twins (Bailey & others, 1993). With half the identical twin pairs differing, we know that genes are not the whole story. Moreover, a new study using a diverse sample of Australian twins found somewhat lower rates of sexual similarity—although, again, identical twins were more likely than fraternal twins to share homosexual feelings (Bailey & others, 1997). This is the sort of pattern we expect to see when genes are having an *influence*. Moreover, with a single transplanted gene, scientists can now cause male fruit flies to display homosexual behavior (Zhang & Odenwald, 1995).

Prenatal Hormones and Sexual Orientation

The elevated rate of homosexual orientation even in fraternal twins might also result from their sharing the same prenatal environment. In animals and some exceptional human cases, sexual orientation has been altered by abnormal prenatal hormone conditions. German researcher Gunter Dorner (1976, 1988) pioneered this research by manipulating a fetal rat's exposure to male hormones, thereby "inverting" its sexual behavior toward rats of the other sex. Female sheep will likewise show homosexual behavior if their pregnant mothers are injected with testosterone during a critical gestation period (Money, 1987).

With humans, a critical period for the brain's neural-hormonal control system may exist between the middle of the second and fifth months after conception (Ellis & Ames, 1987; Gladue, 1990; Meyer-Bahlburg, 1995). Exposure to the hormone levels typically experienced by female fetuses during this time appears to predispose the person (whether female or male) to be attracted to males in later life. Some tests reveal that homosexual men have spatial abilities like those typical of heterosexual women—a pattern consistent with the hypothesis that homosexuals were exposed to atypical prenatal hormones (Gladue, 1994; McCormick & Witelson, 1991; Sanders & Wright, 1997).

Curiously, gay men also have fingerprint patterns rather like those of heterosexual women. Most people have more fingerprint ridges on their right hand than on their left. Jeff Hall and Doreen Kimura (1994) observed that this difference is less true of females and gay males than of heterosexual males—a difference these researchers believe is due to prenatal hormones.

Lesbians may likewise have more male-typical anatomy. For example, the cochlea and hearing system of lesbians develop in a way that is "intermediate to those of heterosexual females and heterosexual males" (McFadden & Pasanen, 1998, 1999).

Because the physiological evidence is preliminary and controversial, some scientists remain skeptical. Rather than specifying sexual orientation, perhaps biological factors predispose a temperament that influences sexuality "in the context of individual learning and experience" (Byne & Parsons, 1993). Perhaps, theorizes Daryl Bem (1996, 1998), genes code for prenatal hormones and brain anatomy, which predispose *temperaments* that lead children to prefer sex-typical or sex-atypical activities and friends. These preferences may later lead children to feel attracted to whichever sex feels different from their own. The dissimilar-seeming sex (whether or not it conforms to one's own anatomy) becomes associated with anxiety and other forms of arousal, which eventually gets transformed into romantic arousal. The exotic becomes erotic.

Regardless of the process, the consistency of the genetic, prenatal, and brain findings has swung the pendulum toward a physiological explanation. Nature more than nurture, most psychiatrists now believe, predisposes sexual orientation (Vreeland & others, 1995). If biological influences prove critical (perhaps especially so in certain environmental contexts), such would explain why sexual orientation is so difficult to change.

Still, some people wonder: Should the cause of sexual orientation matter? Perhaps it shouldn't, but people's assumptions matter. Those who believe, as do most homosexual people, that sexual orientation is a biological given—an enduring identity, not a choice—express more accepting attitudes toward homosexual persons (Allen & others, 1996; Furnham & Taylor, 1990; Whitley, 1990). In American surveys, agreement that homosexuality is "something a person is born with" rose from 13 to 31 percent between 1977 and 1998 (Newport, 1998). Over roughly the same period, support for equal job rights for gays and lesbians increased from 59 to 80 percent (Moore, 1993). And agreement "that homosexuality should be an acceptable alternative life-style" increased between 1982 and 1996 from 34 to 44 percent (Gallup, 1996; see also **FIGURE 35.4**). Acceptance is most common among women and those with a gay or lesbian friend or relative (Herek & Capitanio, 1996; Kite & Whitley, 1996).

To gay and lesbian activists, the new biological research is a double-edged sword (Diamond, 1993). If sexual orientation, like skin color and sex, is genetically influenced, that offers a further rationale for civil rights protection. Moreover, it may alleviate parents' concerns about their children having gay teachers and role models. It does, however, raise the haunting possibility that genetic markers of sexual orientation could someday be identified through fetal testing, and the fetus be aborted simply for being homosexual.

Sex and Human Values

Preview Question: Is scientific research on sexual motivation value-free?

Recognizing that values are both personal and cultural, most sex researchers and educators strive to keep their writings on sexuality value-free.

But can the study of sexual behavior and what motivates it ever be free of values? Those who think not say that the very words we use to describe behavior often reflect our personal values. When sex researchers label sexually restrained individuals as "erotophobic" and as having "high sex guilt," they express their own values. Whether we label sexual acts we do not practice as "perversions," "deviations," or part of an "alternative sexual life-style" depends on our attitudes toward the behaviors. Labels describe, but they also evaluate.

When education about sex is separated from the context of human values, some students may get the idea that sexual intercourse is simply a recreational activity. Diana Baumrind (1982), a University of California child-rearing expert, has

> "Biological theories of sexual orientation are far more promising than any current alternatives."
>
> J. Michael Bailey and Richard C. Pillard (1994)

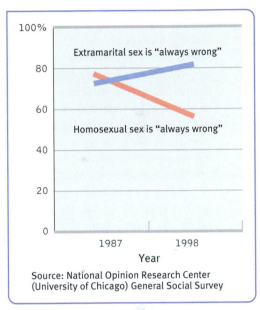

FIGURE 35.4 Changing attitudes
National Opinion Research Center surveys indicate that attitudes remain conservative regarding extramarital sex but are becoming more tolerant of homosexual sex under at least some circumstances.

CLOSE-UP:

THE NEED TO BELONG

We are what Aristotle called "the social animal." We have a need to affiliate with others, even to become strongly attached to certain others in enduring, close relationships. Human beings, contended the personality theorist Alfred Adler, have an "urge to community" (Ferguson, 1989). Roy Baumeister and Mark Leary (1995) have assembled evidence for this deep *need to belong*.

Aiding Survival

Social bonds boosted our ancestors' survival rate. By keeping children close to their caregivers, attachments served as a powerful survival impulse. As adults, those who formed attachments were more likely to come together to reproduce and to stay together to nurture their offspring to maturity.

Cooperation in groups also enhanced survival. In solo combat, our ancestors were not the toughest predators. But as hunters they learned that six hands were better than two. Those who foraged in groups also gained protection from predators and enemies. If those who felt a need to belong were also those who survived and reproduced most successfully, their genes would in time predominate. The inevitable result: an innately social creature. People in every society on earth belong to groups and tend to prefer and favor "us" over "them."

Wanting to Belong

The need to belong colors our thoughts and emotions. We spend a great deal of time thinking about our actual and hoped-for relationships. When relationships form, we often feel joy. Falling in mutual love, people have been known to feel their cheeks ache from their irrepressible grins. Asked, "What is necessary for your happiness?" or "What is it that makes your life meaningful?" most people mention—before anything else—close, satisfying relationships with family, friends, or romantic partners (Berscheid, 1985). Happiness hits close to home.

Acting to Increase Social Acceptance

When we feel included, accepted, and loved by those important to us, our self-esteem rides high. Indeed, say Mark Leary and his colleagues (1998), our self-esteem is a gauge of how valued and accepted we feel. Much of our social behavior therefore aims to increase our belonging—our social acceptance and inclusion.

To avoid rejection, we generally conform to group standards and seek to make favorable impressions. To win friendship and esteem, we monitor our behavior, hoping to create the right impressions. Seeking love and belonging, we spend billions on clothes, cosmetics, and diet and fitness aids—all motivated by our quest for acceptance.

Like sexual motivation, which feeds both love and exploitation, the need to belong feeds both deep attachments and menacing threats. Out of our need to define a "we" come loving families, faithful friendships, and team spirit, but also teen gangs, ethnic rivalries, and fanatic nationalism.

Maintaining Relationships

For most of us, familiarity breeds liking, not contempt. We resist breaking social bonds. Thrown together at school, at summer camp, on a vacation cruise, people resist the group's dissolution. Hoping to maintain our relationships, we promise to call, to write, to come back for reunions. Parting, we feel distress. The dark side of this is that attachments can keep people in abusive relationships; the fear of being alone may seem worse than the pain of

A sharing of love

For most adults, a sexual relationship fulfills not only a biological motive, but a social need for intimacy.

observed that adolescents interpret sex education that pretends to be "value-free" as meaning that adults are neutral about adolescent sexual activity. Such an implication is unfortunate, she added, because "promiscuous recreational sex poses certain psychological, social, health, and moral problems that must be faced realistically."

Other researchers have found that teenagers who have had formal sex education are no more likely to engage in premarital sex than those who have not (Furstenberg & others, 1985; Zelnik & Kim, 1982). Moreover, we enrich our lives by knowing ourselves, by realizing that others share our feelings, by understanding what is likely to please or displease our loved one. Witness the crumbling of falsehoods about homosexuality. Witness the growing realization that certain sexually explicit material can lead people to devalue and hurt others.

Perhaps we can agree that the knowledge provided by sex research is preferable to ignorance and yet also agree that researchers' values should be stated openly, en-

emotional or physical abuse. The fear has some basis in reality. Children who move through a series of foster homes, with repeated disruption of budding attachments, may come to have difficulty forming deep attachments.

When something threatens or dissolves our social ties, negative emotions overwhelm us. For children, even a brief time-out in isolation can be an effective punishment. For adults as well as children, social ostracism can be even more painful. To be shunned—given the cold shoulder or the silent treatment, with others' eyes avoiding yours—is to have one's need to belong threatened, observe Kipling Williams and Lisa Zadro (in press). People often respond to social ostracism with depressed moods, initial efforts to restore their acceptance, and then withdrawal. "It's the meanest thing you can do to someone, especially if you know they can't fight back. I never should have been born," said Lea, a lifelong victim of the silent treatment by her mother and grandmother. "I came home every night and cried. I lost 25 pounds, had no self-esteem and felt that I wasn't worthy," reported Richard, after two years of silent treatment by his employer.

Exile, imprisonment, and solitary confinement are progressively more severe forms of punishment. The bereaved often feel life is empty, pointless. Children reared in institutions without a sense of belonging to anyone, or locked away at home under extreme neglect, become pathetic crea-

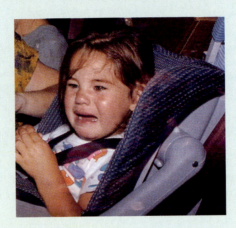

The need to belong

Separated from friends or family—isolated in prison, alone at a new school, living in a foreign land—most people feel keenly their lost connections with important others. Wrenched from the only family she has ever known by a 1993 court decision in an adoption dispute, 2½-year-old Jessica DeBoer sobs enroute to her biological parents' home hundreds of miles away.

tures—withdrawn, frightened, speechless. Adults denied acceptance and inclusion may feel depressed. Anxiety, jealousy, loneliness, and guilt all involve threatened disruptions of our need to belong. Even when bad relationships break, people suffer. In one 16-nation survey, separated and divorced people were only half as likely as married people to say they were "very happy" (Inglehart, 1990). After such separations, feelings of loneliness and anger—and sometimes even a strange desire to be near the former partner—are commonplace.

Fortifying Health

Do you have close friends—people with whom you freely disclose your ups and downs? People who feel supported by close relationships live with better health and at lower risk for psychological disorders and premature death than do those who lack social support. Married people, for example, are less at risk for depression, suicide, and early death than are unattached people. All this evidence affirms Baumeister and Leary's (1995) contention that "human beings are fundamentally and pervasively motivated by a need to belong."

abling us to debate them and to reflect on our own values. We should remember that scientific research on sexual motivation does not aim to define the personal meaning of sex in our own lives. You could know every available fact about sex—that the initial spasms of male and female orgasm come at 0.8-second intervals, that the female nipples expand 10 millimeters at the peak of sexual arousal, that systolic blood pressure rises some 60 points and the respiration rate to 40 breaths per minute—but fail to understand the human significance of sexual intimacy.

Surely one significance of sexual intimacy is its expression of our profoundly social nature. Sex is a socially significant act. Men and women can achieve orgasm alone, yet most people find greater satisfaction while embracing their loved one. There is a yearning for closeness in sexual motivation, and that yearning blurs the boundary between sexual motivation and our need to belong (see the Close-Up feature, "The Need to Belong"). Sex at its human best is life-uniting and love-renewing.

"The relationship between women and men should be characterized not by patronizing behavior or exploitation, but by love, partnership, and trustworthiness. . . . Sexuality should express and reinforce a loving relationship lived by equal partners."

Towards a Global Ethic, 1993 **Parliament of the World's Religions**

REVIEW AND REFLECT:

Sexual Motivation

What behavior patterns must a theory of sexual motivation explain?

Although early data-collection efforts by Alfred Kinsey and others have been criticized for their methodology, information about human sexual practices continues to accumulate. We do know that sexual behaviors vary across both place and time and that the range of "normal" sexual interests and behaviors is very broad.

What are the stages of the human sexual response cycle?

Physiologically, the human sexual response cycle normally follows a pattern of excitement, plateau, orgasm, and resolution. A refractory period occurs during the resolution stage. During this resting period, renewed arousal and orgasm are impossible for males.

How do sex hormones influence human sexual development and arousal?

Sex hormones (testosterone and estrogen), in combination with the hypothalamus, help our bodies develop and function as either male or female. In nonhuman animals, hormones also help stimulate sexual activity. In humans, they influence sexual behavior more loosely, especially once sufficient hormone levels are present.

How do internal and external stimuli contribute to sexual arousal?

External stimuli can trigger sexual arousal in both men and women. Sexually explicit materials may also lead people to perceive their partners as comparatively less appealing and to devalue their relationships. In combination with the internal hormonal push and the external pull of sexual stimuli, fantasies (imagined stimuli) influence sexual arousal. Sexual disorders, such as premature ejaculation and female orgasmic disorder, are being successfully treated by new methods, which assume that people learn and can modify their sexual responses.

What factors influence teenagers' sexual attitudes and behaviors?

Adolescents' physical maturation fosters a sexual dimension to their emerging identity. But culture is a big influence, too, as is apparent from varying rates of teen intercourse and pregnancy. Epidemic rates of sexually transmitted diseases have triggered new research and educational programs pertinent to adolescent sexuality.

What does current research tell us about why some people are attracted to members of their own sex and others are attracted to members of the other sex?

One's heterosexual or homosexual orientation seems neither willfully chosen nor willfully changed. Preliminary new evidence links sexual orientation with genetic influences, prenatal hormones, and certain brain structures.

Is scientific research on sexual motivation value-free?

Sex research and education are not value-free. Some say that sex-related values should therefore be openly acknowledged, recognizing the emotional significance of sexual expression. Human sexuality at its life-uniting and love-renewing best affirms our deep need to belong.

Terms and Concepts to Remember

sexual response cycle, p. 449
refractory period, p. 450
estrogen, p. 450

testosterone, p. 450
sexual disorder, p. 452
sexual orientation, p. 455

Test Yourself

35.1. In the 1940s, Alfred Kinsey and his colleagues used questionnaires to investigate human sexual behavior. Their results have been criticized because
a. their sample was not large enough.
b. their sample was not representative of the population as a whole.
c. they asked leading questions.
d. both *b.* and *c.* are true.

35.2. In describing the sexual response cycle, Masters and Johnson noted that
a. a plateau phase follows orgasm.
b. men experience a refractory period during which they cannot experience orgasm.
c. the feeling that accompanies orgasm is stronger in men than in women.
d. testosterone is released in the female as well as in the male.

35.3. Daily and monthly fluctuations in hormone levels do not greatly affect sexual desire in humans. Over the life span, however, hormonal changes have significant effects. A striking effect of hormonal changes on human sexual behavior is the
a. arousing influence of erotic materials.
b. sharp rise in sexual interest at puberty.
c. increase in women's sexual desire at the time of ovulation.
d. increase in testosterone levels in castrated males.

35.4. Sexual behavior is motivated by internal biological factors, by external stimuli, and by imagined stimuli. An example of an external stimulus that might influence sexual behavior is
a. blood level of testosterone.
b. the onset of puberty.
c. a sexually explicit film.
d. an erotic fantasy or dream.

35.5. Sexual disorders are problems that consistently impair sexual functioning. In some cases, they involve sexual motivation, especially lack of arousability. The cause of such problems is

a. personality traits, because psychotherapy has been used successfully to treat such problems.
b. genetic factors, because no treatment has successfully eliminated the problem.
c. physiological factors, because exercise has been found to help people with such problems.
d. unknown, although behavioral therapy has been used successfully to treat such problems.

35.6. Aside from abstinence, contraception is the surest way of preventing pregnancy. More than half of all sexually active teens, however, either do not use contraceptives or do not use them regularly. Factors contributing to the epidemic of teen pregnancies include ignorance about reproduction and contraception, guilt about sexual behavior, mass media norms of promiscuity, insufficient communication about contraception, and

a. the "just say no" attitude.
b. the unavailability of abortion.
c. the decreased rates of sexually transmitted disease.
d. alcohol use.

35.7. Sexual orientation refers to our enduring sexual attraction to members of a particular gender. Current research suggests several possible contributors to sexual orientation. Which of the following is NOT one of those contributors?

a. Certain cell clusters in the hypothalamus
b. Gender segregation during the time the sex drive matures
c. A section of fibers connecting the right and left hemispheres of the brain
d. Exposure to hormone levels typically experienced by female fetuses

Review: Research on sexual attitudes and behaviors has relied extensively on volunteers. How might this factor bias the results of such studies?

Reflect: What do you think would be an effective strategy for reducing teen pregnancy?

Answers to the Test Yourself and Review questions can be found in the green appendix at the end of the book.

36 Achievement Motivation

The biological perspective on motivation—the idea that physiological needs drive us to satisfy those needs—only partially explains what energizes and directs our behavior. Hunger and sex have both social and physiological components. Moreover, there are motives that, unlike hunger and sex, do not appear to satisfy any physical need. Billionaire entrepreneurs may be motivated to make ever more money, celebrities to become even more famous, dictators to achieve more power, daredevils to seek greater thrills. When fed, such motives, like our need to belong, seem not to diminish. The more we achieve, the more we may need to achieve.

Identifying Achievement Motivation

Preview Question: What characteristics are shared by people with a high need to achieve?

Think of someone you know who strives to succeed by excelling at any task where evaluation is possible. Now think of someone who is less driven. Psychologist Henry Murray (1938) defined the first person's high need for achievement, or **achievement motivation**, as a desire for significant accomplishment, for mastering skills or ideas, for control, and for rapidly attaining a high standard.

To study this motive, we first need a way to measure it. If driven by hunger, we begin to fantasize about food. Our sexual orientation directs our prevalent sexual fantasies. If socially isolated, we think about those we love. Do these examples suggest a way to assess a person's need to achieve?

Murray and investigators David McClelland and John Atkinson presumed that people's fantasies would reflect their concern for achievement. So they asked research participants to invent stories about ambiguous pictures. If a person who was shown the daydreaming boy in **FIGURE 36.1** said the boy was preoccupied with pursuit of a goal, that he imagined himself performing a heroic act, or that he was feeling pride about some success, the researchers scored the response as indicating achievement concerns. If people's stories consistently included such themes, McClelland and Atkinson regarded them as having a high need for achievement.

Would you expect people whose stories express high achievement to prefer tasks that are easy, moderately challenging, or very difficult? People whose stories suggest low achievement motivation tend to choose either very easy or very difficult tasks, where failure is either unlikely or not embarrassing (Geen, 1984). Those whose stories express high achievement motivation tend to prefer moderately difficult tasks, where success is attainable yet attributable to their skill and effort. In a ring-toss game they often stand at an intermediate distance from the stake, enabling some successes while providing a suitable challenge. When things get difficult, people with a strong need to achieve

What is your greatest achievement to date? What is your greatest future ambition—to attain fame? Fortune? Creative accomplishment? Security? Love? Power? Wisdom? Spiritual wholeness?

FIGURE 36.1
What is this boy daydreaming about?
By analyzing responses to ambiguous photos like this, motivation researchers have sought clues to people's level of achievement motivation.

do persist more (Cooper, 1983). By contrast, high school underachievers persist less in completing college degrees, holding on to jobs, and maintaining their marriages (McCall, 1994).

As you might expect from their persistence and eagerness for realistic challenges, people with high achievement motivation do achieve more. One study followed the lives of 1528 California children whose intelligence test scores were in the top 1 percent. Forty years later, when researchers compared those who were most and least successful professionally, they found a motivational difference. Those most successful were more ambitious, energetic, and persistent. As children, they had more active hobbies. As adults, they participated in more groups and favored participating in sports over being a spectator (Goleman, 1980).

Another study of outstanding scholars, athletes, and artists found that all were highly motivated and self-disciplined, willing to dedicate hours every day to the pursuit of their goals (Bloom, 1985). These superstar achievers were distinguished not so much by their extraordinary natural talent as by their extraordinary daily discipline. When their preparation met an opportunity, the result was success.

By their early twenties, top violinists have accumulated some 10,000 lifetime practice hours—double the practice time of other violin students aiming to be teachers (Ericsson & others, 1993). From his studies, Herbert Simon (1998), a psychologist who won the Nobel prize for economics, estimates that world-class experts in a field typically have invested "at least 10 years of hard work—say, 40 hours a week for 50 weeks a year." Great achievement, it seems, mixes a teaspoon of inspiration with a gallon of perspiration.

Analyses of the life histories of great scientists, philosophers, political leaders, writers, and musicians confirm the importance of disciplined motivation. Great achievers, consumed by a passion to perfect their gift, are often continuously productive from an early age, notes Dean Keith Simonton (1994). So much so that a small proportion of contributors to any field produce most of its achievements. Intelligence is distributed like a *bell curve*—most scores fall near the average, with fewer and fewer scores lying near the extreme high or low ends of the scale. Achievements do not follow the same pattern—and that tells us that achievement involves much more than raw ability.

Sources of Achievement Motivation

Preview Question: Why are some of us driven to excel but others are not?

Why, despite having similar potentials, does one person become more motivated to achieve than another? Highly motivated children (and those least likely to drop out of school) often have parents and teachers who encourage their independence from an early age and praise and reward them for their successes (Teevan & McGhee, 1972; Vallerand & others, 1997). Such parents encourage their children to dress and feed themselves and to do well in school. When their children achieve, they express delight. The independence of achievement-driven people can be seen in the higher

The image of achievement
What motivates a person to study to the level of a Ph.D., learn five languages, and become a leading expert in international issues—as did Madeleine Albright, before becoming the U.S. representative to the United Nations and then the U.S. secretary of state?

"The more I practice the luckier I get."

Gary Player, golf professional

■ **achievement motivation** a desire for significant accomplishment: for mastery of things, people, or ideas; for attaining a high standard.

"They can because they think they can."

Virgil, *Aeneid*, 19 B.C.

achievement motivation scores of those Albanian, Czech, and Slovakian university students who are seeking to leave their country and of American students wanting to migrate to a new region (Boneva & others, 1998).

Theorists speculate that the high achievement motivation displayed by such children has *emotional* roots. They learn to associate achievement with positive emotions. There may also be *cognitive* roots, as children learn to attribute their achievements to their own competence and effort, raising their expectations (Dweck & Elliott, 1983). Even children who are bribed into an activity such as writing will sustain their interest if led to attribute their involvement internally. In one experiment this was effectively accomplished by telling children, "You know, I thought you'd say you wanted to do this handwriting activity because you look like the kind of [girl/boy] who understands how important it is to write correctly, and who really wants to be good at it" (Cialdini & others, 1998).

Intrinsic Motivation and Achievement

Preview Question: How does intrinsic motivation differ from extrinsic motivation?

In the classroom, at work, and on the athletic field, two types of achievement motivation operate. **Intrinsic motivation** is the desire to perform a behavior for its own sake and to be effective. Intrinsically motivated people approach work or play seeking enjoyment, interest, self-expression, or challenge. **Extrinsic motivation** is seeking external rewards and avoiding punishments.

To sense the difference between extrinsic and intrinsic motivation, you might reflect on your own current experience. Are you feeling pressured to get this reading finished before a deadline? Worried about your course grade? Eager for rewards that depend on your doing well? If yes, then you are extrinsically motivated (as, to some extent, almost all students are). Are you also finding the course material interesting? Does learning it lead you to feel more competent? If there were no grade at stake, might you be curious enough to want to learn the material for its own sake? If yes, intrinsic motivation also fuels your efforts.

In sports, as in other activities, excessive external pressures and incentives can undermine our intrinsic enjoyment. When researcher Dean Ryan (1980) studied university football players, he found that those on athletic scholarships (who were, in a sense, playing for pay) enjoyed playing less than did the nonscholarship players. Had pay and pressure turned play into labor? Perhaps. But rewards can increase intrinsic motivation if their effect is to inform the players of their athletic competence (as with a "most improved player" award).

So, should coaches emphasize extrinsic pressures, rewards, and competition? Studies by motivation researchers Edward Deci and Richard Ryan indicate that it also depends on the goal (1985, 1992). For some, as for legendary football coach Vince Lombardi, "Winning isn't everything; it's the only thing." If so, it may pay to control the players with pressures and rewards for winning. But what if the goal is—as it should be for most programs of physical education, fitness, and amateur sports—the promotion of an enduring interest and participation in physical activity? In that case, as Deci and Ryan observed, "External pressures, competitive emphasis, and evaluative feedback are in contradiction to this goal." If children's soccer coaches want the kids to continue playing in the future, they should focus not on winning but on the joy of playing one's best.

Researchers in the psychology of religion have also explored intrinsic versus extrinsic motivation (Bergin, 1991; Gorsuch, 1988). Some religiously active people score high on tests of *extrinsic* religious motivation, by reporting their religion is a means to other ends. (They might agree, for example, that "a primary reason for my

Tiger Woods

"I remember a daily ritual that we had: I would call Pop at work to ask if I could practice with him. He would always pause a second or two, keeping me in suspense, but he'd always say yes. . . . In his own way, he was teaching me initiative. You see, he never pushed me to play" (quoted in *USA Weekend*, 1997).

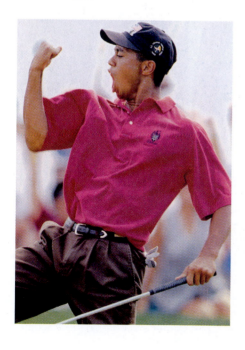

interest in religion is that my church is a congenial social activity.") Others score high on *intrinsic* religious motivation, by reporting their religion is an end in itself. ("My religious beliefs are what really lie behind my whole approach to life.") Compared with the extrinsically religious, intrinsically religious people tend to score lower on tests of prejudice and anxiety. They also tend to live with a greater sense of control over their lives and a clearer sense of purpose (Wulff, 1991).

Motivating People

Preview Question: How can effective leaders motivate others to seek higher levels of achievement?

Industrial/organizational psychology includes studies of how managers might best

+ promote teamwork and group achievement.
+ match people with jobs, by identifying motivated, well-suited personnel.
+ make jobs suit people, by creating work environments that boost morale and output.
+ evaluate performance and create incentives for excellence.

What every leader wants to know is "How can I manage in ways that enhance people's motivation, productivity, satisfaction?" (Satisfied workers aren't always more productive, but they are less likely to be absent or to quit.) Effective leaders cultivate intrinsic motivation, attend to people's motives, set goals, and choose an appropriate leadership style.

Cultivate Intrinsic Motivation

Given that intrinsic motivation stimulates achievement, especially in situations where people work independently (as students, teachers, executives, artists, and scientists often do), how can we encourage it? Here, from hundreds of studies, are the consistent answers: First, provide tasks that challenge and trigger curiosity (Malone & Lepper, 1986). Second, avoid snuffing out people's sense of self-determination with an overuse of controlling extrinsic rewards (Deci & Ryan, 1987).

Note that we can use extrinsic rewards in two ways: to *control* ("If you clean up your room, you can have some ice cream") or to *inform* someone of successes ("That was outstanding—congratulations!"). Attempts to *control* people's behaviors through rewards and surveillance may be successful as long as these controls are present. But, if taken away, people's interest in the activity often drops. Teachers who try hardest to boost their students' achievement on competency tests tend to be most controlling, thus ironically undermining their students' intrinsic interest.

On the other hand, rewards that *inform* people that their efforts are paying off can boost their feelings of competence and intrinsic motivation. Rewarding employees for high performance can boost intrinsic motivation (Eisenberger & others, 1999). In one experiment, Thane Pittman and his colleagues (1980) asked college students to work on puzzles. Those given informative compliments ("Compared with most of my subjects, you're doing really well") usually continued playing with the puzzles when they were left alone. Those given either no praise or a controlling form of praise ("If you keep it up, I'll be able to use your data") were less likely to continue. So, depending on whether we use rewards to inform or control, they can either raise or lower intrinsic motivation (**FIGURE 36.2**).

■ **intrinsic motivation** a desire to perform a behavior for its own sake and to be effective.

■ **extrinsic motivation** a desire to perform a behavior due to promised rewards or threats of punishment.

■ **industrial/organizational psychology** a subfield of psychology that studies and advises on workplace behavior. Industrial/organizational (I/O) psychologists help organizations select and train employees, boost morale and productivity, and design products and assess responses to them.

FIGURE 36.2 Rewards
The type of reward affects motivation.

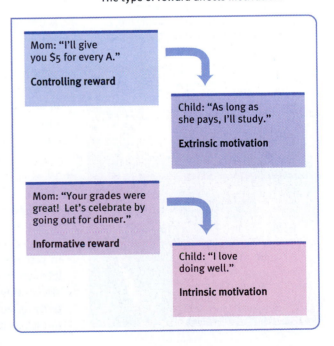

Toys "R" everywhere
Hiring Japanese top executives who know their own culture and listening to what they have to say has enabled Toys "R" Us and some other Western firms to succeed in Japanese markets.

It also pays to praise effort more than ability. That is the conclusion of Claudia Mueller and Carol Dweck (1998) after giving a large and diverse group of elementary school students a test with some fairly easy problems. Some they told, "You must be smart at these problems," while others they told, "You must have worked hard at these problems." After then struggling with some more difficult problems, those who had been praised for their intelligence enjoyed the task less and gave up sooner. By comparison, those praised for their effort stayed more focused, tried new strategies, and were less defeated by knowing that they had not done well.

There is an important practical principle here. Because the use of rewards to control undermines intrinsic motivation, parents, teachers, and managers should take care not to be overcontrolling. It is important to expect, support, challenge, and inform, but if you want to encourage internally motivated, self-directed achievements, do not overly control.

Attend to People's Motives

Effective managerial styles vary with the people managed. To motivate people, Martin Maehr and Larry Braskamp (1986; Braskamp, 1987) advised managers to assess their people's motives and then adjust their managerial style accordingly. Challenge employees who value *accomplishment* to try new things and to strive for excellence. Give those who value *recognition* the attention they desire. Place those who value *affiliation* in a unit that has a family feeling and shares decision making. Motivate those who value *power* with competition and opportunities for triumphant success. Different strokes for different folks, but for each a way to motivate.

Set Specific, Challenging Goals

In study after study, specific, challenging goals have motivated higher achievement, especially when combined with progress reports (Locke & Latham, 1990; Mento & others, 1987; Tubbs, 1986). Clear objectives, such as those you might set in planning your course work, serve to direct attention, promote effort, and stimulate creative strategies. When people find a goal reasonable, their reaching it or not affects their self-evaluation (White & others, 1995). So, to motivate high productivity, effective leaders work with people to define explicit goals and elicit commitments, and they provide feedback on progress.

"I knew exactly where I wanted to go and I focused on getting there. . . . Whether it's golf, basketball, business, family life, or even baseball, I set goals—realistic goals—and I focus on them."
Michael Jordan,
I Can't Accept Not Trying, 1994

Choose an Appropriate Leadership Style

Whether a directive or a democratic leadership style works best depends on the situation and the leader. The best leadership style for leading a discussion is not the best style for leading troops on a charge (Fiedler, 1981). Moreover, different leaders are suited to different styles. Some excel at **task leadership**—setting standards, organizing work, and focusing attention on goals. Being goal-oriented, task leaders are good at keeping a group centered on its mission. Typically, they have a directive style, which can work well if the leader is bright enough to give good orders (Fiedler, 1987).

Other managers excel at **social leadership**—mediating conflicts and building the sort of team spirit that leads to high performance (Evans & Dion, 1991). Social leaders often have a democratic style: They delegate authority and welcome the participation of team members. Many experiments show that social leadership is good for morale. Subordinates usually feel more satisfied and motivated when they can participate in decision making (Burger, 1987; Spector, 1986).

John Williams and Deborah Best (1990, p. 15) have suggested an imaginary scenario in which we hear about two people: One is "adventurous, autocratic, coarse, dominant, forceful, independent, and strong." The other is "affectionate, dependent, dreamy, emotional, submissive, and weak." Did you picture the first person as a woman and the second as a man? If so, you are likely nearly alone. The world around, people perceive the first set of traits as more descriptive of men, the second set more of women. As leaders, men indeed tend to be directive, even autocratic, and women tend to be more democratic (Eagly & Johnson, 1990). When people interact, men are more likely to utter opinions, women to express support (Aries, 1987; Wood, 1987). In everyday behavior, men are more likely than women to act the ways powerful people do—to talk assertively, to interrupt, to initiate touching, to smile less, to stare (J. Hall, 1987; Major & others, 1990). Thus, despite great variations within each gender, women do more often excel at social leadership, men at task leadership (Eagly & Karau, 1991).

Because effective leadership styles vary with the situation and the person, the once-popular "great person" theory of leadership—that all great leaders share certain traits—fell out of favor. However, Peter Smith and Monir Tayeb (1989) have compiled data from studies in India, Taiwan, and Iran indicating that effective managers—whether in coal mines, banks, or government offices—often exhibit a high degree of *both* task and social leadership. As achievement-minded people, effective managers certainly care about how well work is done, yet at the same time they are sensitive to their subordinates' needs.

Effective leaders of laboratory groups, work teams, and large corporations also tend to exude a self-confident "charisma" (House & Singh, 1987; Shamir & others, 1993). Their charisma is a mix of a *vision* of some goal, an ability to *communicate* it clearly and simply, and enough optimism and faith in their group to *inspire* others to follow. Leadership of this kind motivates others to identify with and commit themselves to the group's mission.

Whether managers favor a participative/democratic approach depends not only on their personality but also on their assumptions about human motivation. Douglas McGregor (1960)

> "Good leaders don't ask more than their constituents can give, but they often ask—and get—more than their constituents intended to give or thought it was possible to give."
>
> John W. Gardner, *Excellence*, 1984

Participative management

The employees of Herman Miller, Inc., share in decision making, share in the profits, and have made the firm very profitable.

identified two contrasting views. **Theory X** managers assume that workers are basically lazy, error-prone, and extrinsically motivated by money. Thus, they need simple tasks, close monitoring, and incentives to work harder. **Theory Y** managers make very different assumptions—that people are intrinsically motivated to work for reasons beyond money—for example, to promote self-esteem, enjoy satisfying relations with others, and fulfill their potential. Thus, given enough freedom and challenge, employees will strive to demonstrate their competence and creativity. Theory Y managers are more likely to give employees control over work procedures, to welcome employee participation in decision making, and to have creative and satisfied subordinates (Deci & others, 1989).

Theory Y is one guiding force behind the contemporary move by many businesses to increase employee participation in making decisions, a management style common in Sweden and Japan (Naylor, 1990; Sundstrom & others, 1990). Partly because managers tend to think better of work they directly supervised, many have been slow to empower workers (Pfeffer, 1998).

Ironically, a major influence on the "Japanese-style participative management" that has grown increasingly popular in North America was MIT social psychologist Kurt Lewin. In laboratory and factory experiments, Lewin and his students demonstrated the effects of worker participation on productivity. Shortly before World War II, Lewin visited Japan and explained his findings to industrial and academic leaders (Nisbett & Ross, 1991). Back in the United States, some companies did, however, quietly begin implementing Lewin's participative management. One of these pioneer companies was Michigan's Herman Miller, Inc., now the world's second-largest manufacturer of office furniture. That success may be attributable in part to the belief of Herman Miller's now-retired chairman, Max DePree (1987), who invested in the idea that workers want to be effective and productive, to feel they are making a meaningful contribution, to have control over their own destinies, and to be appreciated. When workers share in corporate profits and become part owners, they become invested in their company's success. When workers participate in decision making and know that they and their managers are mutually accountable, labor-versus-management hostility is replaced by a shared commitment to corporate and personal goals. Workers who feel respected, cared about, and involved find their work more satisfying. And, thanks to their productivity, their company benefits. Between 1974 and 1999 Herman Miller's annual sales grew from $40 million to $1.7 billion.

Although identifiable physiological mechanisms drive some motives, such as hunger (though external incentives and learned tastes matter, too), it is clear that other motives, such as achievement, are driven by psychological factors, such as an intrinsic quest for mastery and the external rewards of recognition. What unifies all motives, however, is their common effect: the energizing and directing of behavior.

■ **Theory X** assumes that workers are basically lazy, error-prone, and extrinsically motivated by money and, thus, should be directed from above.

■ **Theory Y** assumes that, given challenge and freedom, workers are motivated to achieve self-esteem and to demonstrate their competence and creativity.

REVIEW AND REFLECT:

Achievement Motivation

What traits characterize people with a high need to achieve?

Some human behaviors are energized and directed without satisfying any obvious physiological need. Achieving personal goals, for example, may be motivated by a person's need for competence and self-determination. People with a high need to achieve tend to prefer moderately challenging tasks and to persist in accomplishing them. They are highly motivated and self-disciplined.

Why are some of us driven to excel but others are not?

To understand why people with similar abilities often differ widely in their achievements, psychologists have studied highly motivated children. Many achievement-oriented children have parents and teachers who encourage and affirm independent achievement rather than overly controlling them with rewards and threats.

How does intrinsic motivation differ from extrinsic motivation?

Intrinsic motivation is the desire to be effective and to perform a behavior for its own sake. Extrinsic motivation is the desire to receive external rewards and avoid punishments.

How can effective leaders motivate others to seek higher levels of achievement?

Industrial/organizational psychologists explore how best to create a motivated, productive, and satisfied workforce. Rewards may increase intrinsic motivation if used not to control people but to boost their sense of competence or to inform them of improvement. Effective managers adjust their managerial style in response to workers' motives; set specific, challenging goals; and combine goal-oriented task leadership with group-oriented social leadership, according to the needs of the situation.

Terms and Concepts to Remember

achievement motivation, p. 464
intrinsic motivation, p. 466
extrinsic motivation, p. 466
industrial/organizational
  psychology, p. 467
task leadership, p. 469

social leadership, p. 469
Theory X, p. 470
Theory Y, p. 470

Test Yourself

36.1. Achievement motivation is defined as a desire for significant accomplishment, for mastering skills or ideas, for control, and for rapidly attaining a high standard. Given a choice of tasks, high achievers would select one that is

a. very difficult, so they have an excuse for failure.

b. very easy, so that they can avoid failure.

c. moderately challenging, so that their success will be attributed to their skill and effort.

d. extremely difficult, so that when they do complete the task, they can feel superior to others performing the same task.

36.2. Psychologists know that achievements are not distributed in a bell curve, as intelligence scores are. Achievement therefore must be more than just raw ability. Studies of highly motivated children have found that

a. their parents tend to encourage their independence and praise and reward their successes.

b. their teachers and caretakers use primarily extrinsic rewards.

c. these children are aggressive, antisocial, and self-absorbed.

d. these children are distinguished by extraordinary natural talent.

36.3. Psychologists identify two types of achievement motivation: extrinsic and intrinsic. Intrinsic motivation is a desire to perform a behavior because it is enjoyable and leads to feelings of mastery. For a violinist, an example of an intrinsic motive is the desire to

a. earn enough to maintain an extravagant life-style.

b. be promoted to concertmaster.

c. perfect a difficult piece of music.

d. obtain a positive grade or evaluation.

36.4. Task leadership is goal-oriented, while social leadership is group-oriented. Research indicates that effective managers exhibit

a. only task leadership.

b. only social leadership.

c. task leadership for building teams and social leadership for setting standards.

d. both task and social leadership, depending on the situation and the person.

Review: If a couple asked you, "What is the best way to motivate achievement in my child?" what two tips could you give them after reading this section?

Reflect: Are you highly motivated, or not highly motivated, to achieve in school? How has this affected your academic success? How might you improve upon your own achievement levels?

Answers to Test Yourself and Review questions can be found in the green appendix at the end of the book.

Emotion

No one needs to tell you that feelings add color to your life, or that in times of stress they can disrupt your life or save it. Of all the species, we seem the most emotional (Hebb, 1980). More often than any other creature, we express fear, anger, sadness, joy, and love.

Fictional characters help us imagine life without emotion. Data, the human-appearing android in *Star Trek: The Next Generation*, embodied cool, rational, emotionless intelligence. Data's brilliance and cool logic gave him superhuman analytical intelligence. And yet he realized something was missing. He tried to write poetry, but without the passions of the heart it fell flat. Data's intellectual curiosity led him to wonder about fear, anger, and joy. But try as he might, he could not create such feelings. Data was all cognition, no emotion.

Back in the real world, consider the case of Elliot. Elliot has normal intelligence and memory. But since the removal of a brain tumor he has lived without emotion. "I never saw a tinge of emotion in my many hours of conversation with him," reported neuroscientist Antonio Damasio (1994, p. 45), "no sadness, no impatience, no frustration." Shown disturbing pictures of injured people, destroyed communities, and natural disasters, Elliot shows—and realizes he feels—no emotion. He knows but he cannot feel. And lacking emotional signals, his social intelligence plummeted. He lost his job. He went bankrupt. His marriage collapsed. He remarried and divorced again. And he is now dependent on custodial care from a sibling and a disability check.

So, how do psychologists think about and study these emotions so important to our well-being? In Module 37, we examine three classic theories of emotion that explore the interplay of physiological activation, expressive behavior, and conscious experience. Module 38 then turns to the topic of how we experience and express our emotions, with an in-depth look at fear, anger, and happiness.

37 Theories of Emotion

Where do emotions come from? What are they made of? Imagine that, while walking home along a deserted street late at night, you hear the rumble of an engine and think someone in a car is stalking you. Emotions are your body's adaptive response. They focus your attention and prepare you for action. Your heart begins to race, you quicken your pace, you wonder about the driver's intent, and you feel scared. As this illustrates, **emotions** are a mix of (1) physiological activation (heart pounding), (2) expressive behaviors (quickened pace), and (3) conscious experience (interpreting the person's intent and feeling fearful). The puzzle is how these three pieces fit together: Did you first notice your heart racing and your faster step, and then feel afraid? Or did your sense of fear come first, stirring your heart and legs to respond?

> Not only emotion, but most psychological phenomena (vision, sleep, memory, sex, and so forth) can be approached these three ways—physiologically, behaviorally, and cognitively.

The James-Lange and Cannon-Bard Theories

Preview Questions: Does physiological arousal precede or follow an emotional experience? (Does your heart pound because you are afraid, or are you afraid because you feel your heart pounding?)

Common sense tells most of us that we cry because we are sad, lash out because we are angry, tremble because we are afraid. First comes conscious awareness, then the physiological trimmings. But to pioneering psychologist William James this commonsense view of emotion was 180 degrees out of line. According to James, "We feel sorry because we cry, angry because we strike, afraid because we tremble" (1890, p. 1066). After you evade an oncoming car in your lane, you may notice your racing heart and then feel shaken with fright. Your feeling of fear follows your body's response. James' idea, which was also proposed by Danish physiologist Carl Lange, is called the **James-Lange theory**.

The James-Lange theory struck U.S. physiologist Walter Cannon (1871–1943) as implausible. Cannon thought the body's responses were not distinct enough to evoke the different emotions. Does a racing heart signal fear, anger, or love? Also, changes in heart rate, perspiration, and body temperature seemed too slow to trigger sudden emotion. Cannon, and later another physiologist, Philip Bard, concluded that physiological arousal and our emotional experience occur simultaneously: The emotion-triggering stimulus is routed simultaneously to the brain's cortex, causing the subjective awareness of emotion, and to the sympathetic nervous system, causing the body's arousal. Thus, this **Cannon-Bard theory** implies that your heart begins pounding *as* you experience fear; one does not cause the other (**FIGURE 37.1**).

As long as the evidence suggested that our physiological reactions to different emotions were much the same, the James-Lange assumption that we experience our emotions through differing body states seemed improbable. But then new evidence showed subtle physiological distinctions among the emotions, and the James-Lange theory again became plausible. James struggled with his own feelings of depression and grief, and in doing so he came to believe that we can control emotions by going "through the outward motions" of whatever emotion we want to experience. "To feel cheerful," he advised, "sit up cheerfully, look around cheerfully, and act as if cheerfulness were already there." The last few decades' findings concerning emotional effects of facial expressions, as we will see, are precisely what James might have predicted.

> "Whenever I feel afraid
> I hold my head erect
> And whistle a happy tune."
>
> **Richard Rodgers and Oscar Hammerstein,**
> *The King and I*, 1958

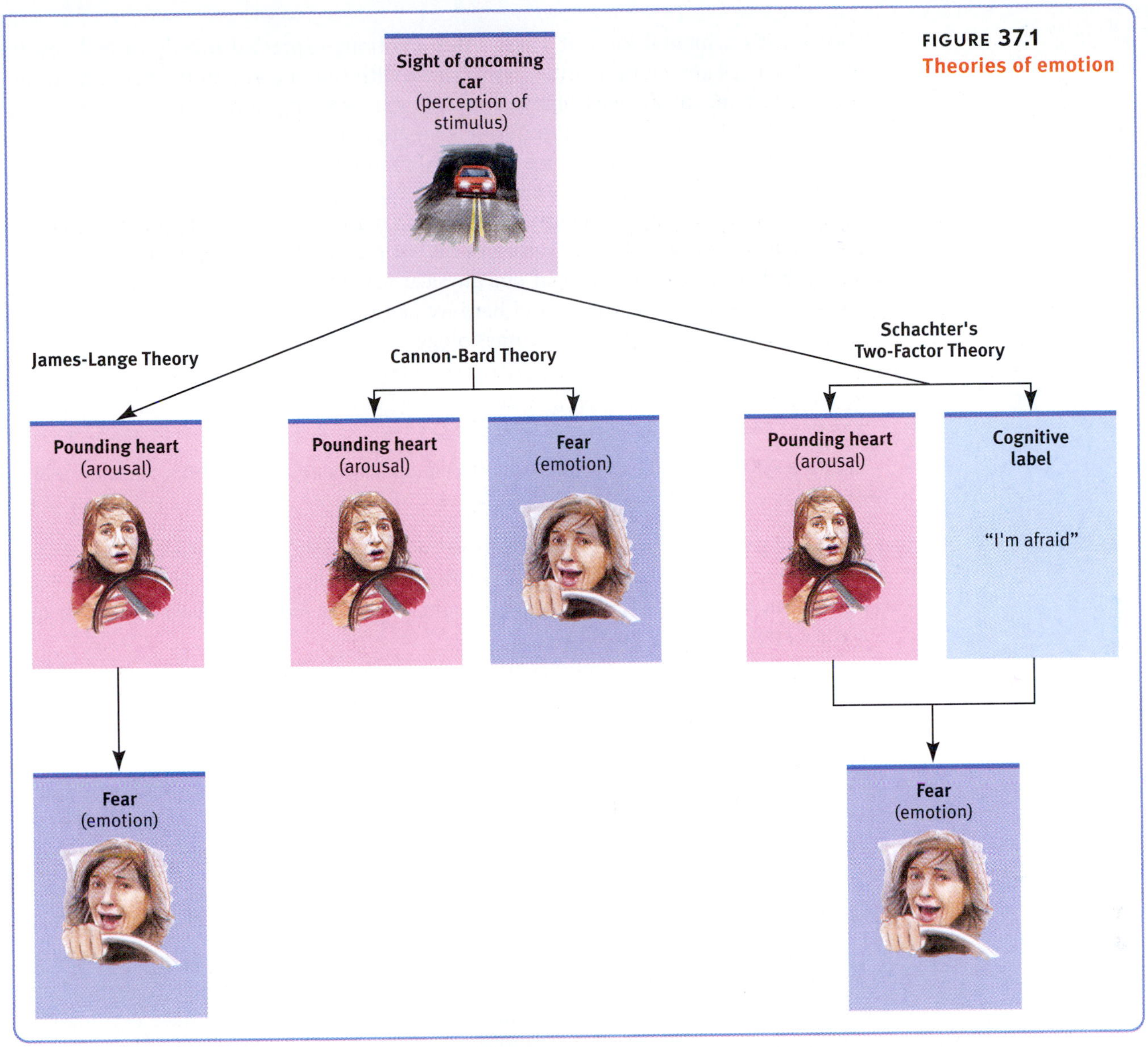

FIGURE **37.1**
Theories of emotion

Let's check your understanding of the James-Lange and Cannon-Bard theories. Imagine that your brain could not sense your heart pounding or your stomach churning. According to each theory, how would this affect your experienced emotions?

Cannon and Bard would have expected you to experience emotions normally, because they believed emotions occur separately from (though simultaneously with) the body's arousal. James and Lange would have expected greatly diminished emotions because they believed that to experience emotion you must first perceive your body's arousal.

The condition you imagined actually exists in people with severed spinal cords. Psychologist George Hohmann (1966) interviewed 25 soldiers who suffered such injuries in World War II. He asked them to recall emotion-arousing incidents that occurred before and after their spinal injuries. Those with injuries in the lower part of the spine, who had lost sensation only in their legs, reported little change in their emotions. Those who could feel nothing below the neck reported a considerable decrease in emotional intensity (as James and Lange would have expected). These soldiers said that although they might act much the same as before in emotional situations, the anger, as one man confessed, "just doesn't have the heat to it that it

■ **emotion** a response of the whole organism, involving (1) physiological arousal, (2) expressive behaviors, and (3) conscious experience.

■ **James-Lange theory** the theory that our experience of emotion is our awareness of our physiological responses to emotion-arousing stimuli.

■ **Cannon-Bard theory** the theory that an emotion-arousing stimulus simultaneously triggers (1) physiological responses and (2) the subjective experience of emotion.

used to. It's a mental kind of anger." But emotions expressed mostly in body areas above the neck are felt more intensely by those with spinal cord injury. Virtually all the men Hohmann interviewed reported increases in weeping, lumps in the throat, and getting choked up when saying good-bye, worshipping, or watching a touching movie.

Although such evidence breathed new life into the James-Lange theory, most researchers agree with Cannon and Bard that our experienced emotions also involve cognition (Averill, 1993). Whether we fear the man behind us on the dark street depends entirely on whether we interpret his actions as threatening or friendly. With James and Lange we can say that our physical reactions are an important ingredient of emotion. And with Cannon and Bard we can say that there is more to the experience of emotion than reading our physiology.

> "Every moment is more intense."
>
> Paralyzed actor Christopher Reeve (1995)

Cognition and Emotion

Preview Question: To experience emotions, must we consciously interpret and label them?

Now, the second and most recent controversy: Put simply, what is the connection between what we *think* and how we *feel*? Which is the chicken and which the egg? Do our emotions always grow from our thoughts? Are our feelings always subject to our mind's appraisal of a situation?

We know that our emotions affect our thinking. When we *feel* like singing "Oh, what a beautiful morning!" we *see* the world and the people around us as wonderful. If the following day we find ourselves singing the blues, we perceive the same world and the same people as less than wonderful.

Can we experience emotion apart from thinking? The issue has practical implications for self-improvement. Can we change our emotions by changing our thinking? Is it true that we become what we think?

Schachter's Two-Factor Theory of Emotion

Most psychologists today believe that our cognitions—our perceptions, memories, and interpretations—are an essential ingredient of emotion. One such theorist, Stanley Schachter, proposed a **two-factor theory**, in which emotions have two ingredients: physical arousal and a cognitive label (Figure 37.1). Like James and Lange, Schachter presumed that our experience of emotion grows from our awareness of our body's arousal. Yet like Cannon and Bard, Schachter also believed that emotions are physiologically similar. Thus, in his view, an emotional experience requires a conscious interpretation of the arousal.

Sometimes our arousal response to one event spills over into our response to the next event. Imagine that after an invigorating run you arrive home to find a message that you got a longed-for job. With arousal lingering from the run, would you feel more elated than if you received this news after awakening from a nap?

To find out whether this spillover effect exists, Schachter and Jerome Singer (1962) aroused college men with injections of the hormone epinephrine. Picture yourself as one of their subjects: After receiving the injection, you go to a waiting room, where you find yourself with another person (actually an accomplice of the experimenters) who is acting either euphoric or irritated. As you observe this person, you begin to feel your heart race, your body flush, and your breathing become more rapid. If told to expect these effects from the injection, what would you feel? Schachter and Singer's subjects felt little emotion—because they attributed their arousal to the drug. But if told the injection

The spillover effect
Arousal from a soccer match can fuel anger, as in the 1989 match at Hillsborough, England, where 96 people were crushed to death in the ensuing riot.

would produce no effects, what would you feel? Perhaps you would react, as another group of subjects did, by "catching" the apparent emotion of the person you are with—becoming happy if the accomplice is acting euphoric, and testy if the accomplice is acting irritated.

This discovery—that a stirred-up state can be experienced as one emotion or another very different one, depending on how we interpret and label it—has been replicated in dozens of experiments. Although emotional arousal is not as undifferentiated as Schachter believed, arousal can intensify just about any emotion (Reisenzein, 1983; Sinclair & others, 1994). Insult people who have just been aroused by pedaling an exercise bike or watching rock videos and they will find it easy to misattribute their arousal to the provocation. Their feelings of anger will be greater than those of people who were similarly provoked but were not previously aroused. Arousal from emotions as diverse as anger, fear, and sexual excitement can spill from one emotion to another (Zillmann, 1986). In anger-provoking situations, sexually aroused people react with more hostility; and the arousal that lingers after an intense argument or a frightening experience may intensify sexual passion (Palace, 1995). Arousal fuels emotion; cognition channels it.

Must Cognition Precede Emotion?

So, to experience an emotion, must we first label our arousal? If Robert Zajonc (pronounced ZI-yence; 1980, 1984a) is right, the answer is no. He argues that our emotional reactions can be quicker than our interpretations of a situation; we therefore feel some emotions *before* we think. For example, when people repeatedly view stimuli flashed too briefly for them to perceive and recall, they nevertheless come to prefer these stimuli. Without being consciously aware of having seen the stimuli, they rather like them. A subliminally flashed smiling or angry face can also prime us to feel better or worse about a follow-up stimulus (Murphy & others, 1995).

Research on neurological processes shows how we can experience emotion before cognition. Some neural pathways involved in emotion bypass the cortical areas involved in thinking. One such pathway runs from the eye or ear via the thalamus to the amygdala, an emotional control center. This shortcut enables a quick, precognitive emotional response before the intellect intervenes. Indeed, the amygdala sends more neural projections up to the cortex than it receives back; this makes it easier for our feelings to hijack our thinking than for our thinking to rule our feelings, note Joseph LeDoux and Jorge Armony (1999). After the cortex has further interpreted a threat, the thinking brain can take over (**FIGURE 37.2**). In the forest, we jump at the sound of rustling leaves nearby, leaving the cortex to decide later whether the sound was made by a predator or just the wind. Such an experience supports Zajonc's belief that *some* of our emotional reactions involve no deliberate thinking and that cognition is not always necessary for emotion. The heart is not always subject to the mind.

Emotion researcher Richard Lazarus (1991, 1998) disagrees. He does concede that our brains process and react to vast amounts of information without our conscious awareness, and he willingly grants that some emotional responses do not require *conscious* thinking. Nevertheless, he points out, even instantaneously felt emotions require some sort of cognitive appraisal of the situation;

■ **two-factor theory** Schachter's theory that to experience emotion one must (1) be physically aroused and (2) cognitively label the arousal.

Can you recall liking something or someone immediately, without knowing why?

FIGURE 37.2

The brain's shortcut for emotions

Sensory input may be routed both to the cortex and directly to the amygdala for a more instant emotional reaction.

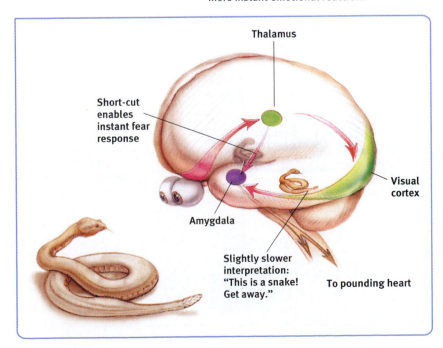

Thalamus

Short-cut enables instant fear response

Visual cortex

Amygdala

Slightly slower interpretation: "This is a snake! Get away."

To pounding heart

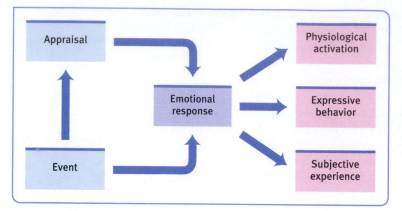

FIGURE 37.3 Two routes to emotion
As Zajonc emphasizes, some emotional responses are immediate, before any conscious appraisal. As Lazarus and Schachter emphasize, our appraisal and labeling of events also determine our emotional responses.

otherwise, how do we *know* what we are reacting to? The appraisal may be effortless and we may not be conscious of it, but it is still a mental function (**FIGURE 37.3**). Emotions arise when we *appraise* an event as beneficial or harmful to our well-being, whether we truly know it is or not. We appraise the sound of the rustling leaves as the presence of a predator. We learn after the appraisal that it was "just the wind."

Complex emotions such as guilt, happiness, and love most clearly arise from our interpretations and expectations. Highly emotional people are intense partly because of their interpretations. They *personalize* events as being somehow directed at them, and they *generalize* their experiences by blowing single incidents out of proportion (Larsen & others, 1987). Whether we feel irritated, depressed, or accepting depends on whether we attribute a low grade to an unfair exam, bad luck, our own inability, or lack of preparation (Weiner, 1985). Attributing failure to our inability erodes our motivation: "If I just don't have it, why try?" If we attribute our failure to unfairness, we instead feel angry.

For us, the important conclusion concerns what Lazarus and Zajonc agree on: Some emotional responses—especially simple likes, dislikes, and fears—involve no conscious thinking. We may fear the spider, even if we "know" it is harmless. Such responses are difficult to alter by changing our thinking.

Other emotions—including moods such as depression and complex feelings such as hatred and love—are greatly affected by our interpretations, memories, and expectations. For these emotions, learning to *think* more positively about ourselves and the world around us helps us *feel* better.

Two Dimensions of Emotion

Preview Question: What are the two basic dimensions by which we can describe an emotion?

FIGURE 37.4
Two dimensions of emotion
James Russell, David Watson, Auke Tellegen, and others describe emotions as variations on two dimensions—low versus high arousal and unpleasant versus pleasant valence.

Our feelings are "obscure and confused," noted Benjamin Constant de Rebecque in 1816. To cut through the obscurity, psychologists have asked people to report their experiences of different emotions. Estonians, Poles, Greeks, Chinese, and Canadians all seem to place emotions along the two dimensions illustrated in **FIGURE 37.4**—pleasant versus unpleasant (the emotion's *valence*) and high versus low arousal (Russell & others, 1989, 1999a,b; Watson & others, 1999).

The valence dimension can be seen in successful Olympic gymnasts and in exam takers who—more than their less successful counterparts—label arousal as energizing, as giving them an edge, rather than as threatening (Raglin, 1992). For them arousal has *positive valence*, while for those suffering stage fright it has *negative valence*. Experienced professors and public speakers similarly welcome prelecture arousal as meaning they are "up" or "on" rather than flat. On the arousal dimension, *terrified* is more frightened than *afraid*, *enraged* is angrier than *angry*, *delighted* is happier than *happy*.

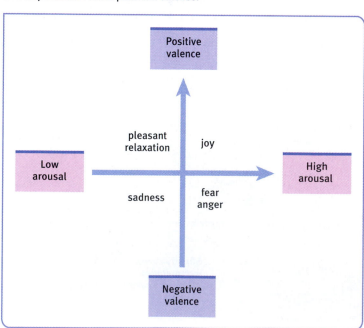

REVIEW AND REFLECT:

Theories of Emotion

Does physiological arousal precede or follow an emotional experience? (Does your heart pound because you are afraid, or are you afraid because you feel your heart pounding?)

This is one of the oldest theoretical controversies regarding emotion. William James and Carl Lange proposed that we feel emotion *after* we notice our physiological responses. Walter Cannon and Philip Bard believed that we feel emotion *at the same time* that our bodies respond. Most researchers today agree with Cannon and Bard but also note that, as James and Lange pointed out, physical reactions are an important ingredient of emotion.

To experience emotions, must we consciously interpret and label them?

A more recent controversy among emotion researchers concerns whether we can experience human emotions apart from cognition. Can we feel before we think? Stanley Schachter's two-factor theory of emotion contends that the cognitive labels we put on our states of arousal are an essential ingredient of emotion. Richard Lazarus agrees that cognition is essential: Many important emotions arise from our interpretations or inferences. Robert Zajonc, however, believes that some simple emotional responses occur instantly, not only outside of conscious awareness but before any cognitive processing occurs. The issue has practical implications: To the degree that emotions are rooted in thinking, we can hope to change them by changing our thinking. Richard Solomon's opponent-process theory tries to explain why our emotions tend to balance in the long run. He proposes that every emotion triggers an opposing emotion.

What are the two basic dimensions by which we can describe an emotion?

Many emotions can be placed along two basic dimensions: arousal (high versus low) and valence (pleasant versus unpleasant).

Terms and Concepts to Remember

emotion, p. 474
James-Lange theory, p. 474
Cannon-Bard theory, p. 474
two-factor theory, p. 476

Test Yourself

37.1. Two important theories of emotion are the James-Lange theory and the Cannon-Bard theory. The James-Lange theory states that our experience of an emotion is a consequence of our physiological response to a stimulus; we are afraid because our heart pounds. The Cannon-Bard theory proposes that the physiological response (like heart pounding) and the subjective experience of, say, anger
   a. are unrelated.
   b. occur simultaneously.
   c. occur in the opposite order (with feelings of fear first).
   d. are regulated by the thalamus.

37.2. Assume that after spending an hour on a treadmill, you receive a letter saying that your scholarship to college has been approved. The two-factor theory of emotion would predict that your physical arousal will
   a. weaken your happiness.
   b. intensify your happiness.
   c. transform your happiness into relief.
   d. have no particular effect on your happiness.

37.3. Research suggests that we can experience an aroused state as one of several different emotions, depending on how we interpret and label the arousal. If physically aroused by swimming, then heckled by an onlooker, we may interpret our arousal as anger and
   a. become less physically aroused.
   b. feel angrier than usual.
   c. feel less angry than usual.
   d. feel sexually aroused.

37.4. Robert Zajonc maintains that some of our emotional reactions occur before we have had the chance to label or interpret them. Richard Lazarus disagrees. The two psychologists differ about whether emotional responses occur in the absence of
   a. physical arousal.   c. cognitive processing.
   b. the hormone epinephrine.   d. learning.

37.5. Psychologists have asked people in many parts of the world to describe their emotions. The two dimensions used in these studies are
   a. low versus high arousal and unpleasant verses pleasant valence.
   b. low versus high valence and unpleasant versus pleasant arousal.
   c. objective appraisal versus subjective appraisal.
   d. cognitive appraisal versus physiological experience.

Review: Christine is holding her 8-month-old baby when a fierce dog appears out of nowhere and, with teeth bared, leaps for the baby's face. Christine immediately ducks for cover to protect the baby, screams at the dog, then notices that her heart is banging in her chest and she's broken out in a cold sweat. How would the James-Lange, Cannon-Bard, and two-factor theories explain Christine's emotional reaction?

Reflect: Schachter's and Lazarus's theories of emotion would support the idea that we can change some of our emotional reactions by changing our cognitive responses to various situations. Would you like to change any of your emotional responses? Do you feel you are too easily provoked to anger or fear, for instance? How might you go about changing your thinking so that you can change your emotional reactions?

Answers to the Test Yourself and Review questions can be found in the green appendix at the end of the book.

38 Experiencing and Expressing Emotion

Physiological Arousal

Preview Question: What physiological changes accompany emotions?

Emotion physically arouses you. Some physical responses you easily notice. As you hear a motorcycle rumbling up alongside you on a dark street, your muscles tense, your stomach develops butterflies, your mouth becomes dry.

Your body also mobilizes for action in less noticeable ways. To provide energy, your liver pours extra sugar into your bloodstream. To help burn the sugar, your respiration increases to supply needed oxygen. Your digestion slows, diverting blood from your internal organs to your muscles. With blood sugar driven into the large muscles, running becomes easier. Your pupils dilate, letting in more light. To cool your stirred-up body, you perspire. If you were wounded, your blood would clot more quickly. After your next crisis, think of this: Without any conscious effort, your body's response to danger was wonderfully coordinated and adaptive—preparing you to fight or flee.

Our *autonomic nervous system* controls our arousal (**FIGURE 38.1**). Its sympathetic division activates arousal by directing the adrenal glands atop the kidneys to release the stress hormones epinephrine (adrenaline) and norepinephrine (noradrenaline). The surge in epinephrine and norepinephrine increases heart rate, blood pressure, and blood sugar levels. When the crisis passes, the parasympathetic neural centers become active, calming the body. Even after the parasympathetic division inhibits further release of stress hormones, those already in the bloodstream linger awhile, so arousal diminishes gradually.

Prolonged arousal, produced by sustained stress, taxes the body, but in many situations arousal is adaptive. Too little arousal (say, sleepiness) can be as disruptive as extremely high levels of arousal. When you're taking an exam, it pays to be moderately aroused—alert but not trembling with nervousness.

> "Fear lends wings to his feet."
>
> Virgil, *Aeneid*, 19 B.C.

One explanation of sudden death caused by a voodoo "curse" is that the terrified person's parasympathetic nervous system, which calms the body, overreacts to the extreme arousal by slowing the heart to a stop (Seligman, 1974).

FIGURE 38.1 Emotional arousal
Emotional arousal involves autonomic nervous system activation.

Autonomic nervous system controls physiological arousal		
Sympathetic division (arousing)		Parasympathetic division (calming)
Pupils dilate	EYES	Pupils contract
Decreases	SALIVATION	Increases
Perspires	SKIN	Dries
Increases	RESPIRATION	Decreases
Accelerates	HEART	Slows
Inhibits	DIGESTION	Activates
Secrete stress hormones	ADRENAL GLANDS	Decrease secretion of stress hormones

Although we usually perform best when our arousal is moderate, the level of arousal for optimal performance varies for different tasks. With easy or well-learned tasks, peak performance comes with relatively high arousal, which enhances the dominant, usually correct, response. With more difficult or unrehearsed tasks, the optimal arousal is somewhat lower (**FIGURE 38.2**). Runners, who are performing a well-learned task, usually achieve their peak performances when highly aroused by competition. Basketball players shooting free throws—a less automatic skill—may not perform quite as well if a packed fieldhouse makes them hyperaroused (Sokoll & Mynatt, 1984). Likewise, students who feel great anxiety during exams perform more poorly than those equally able but more confident. Teaching anxious students how to relax before an exam often enables them to perform better (Hembree, 1988).

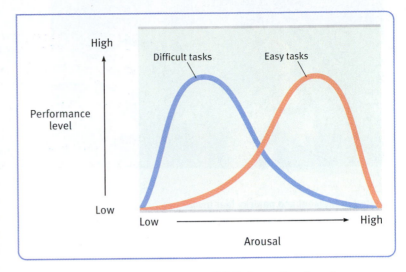

FIGURE 38.2 Arousal and performance
Performance peaks at lower levels of arousal for difficult tasks and at higher levels for easy or well-learned tasks.

Physiological States Accompanying Specific Emotions

Preview Question: Do different emotions activate different physiological responses?

Imagine conducting an experiment exploring physiological signs of arousal. In each of four rooms, you have someone watching a movie: In the first the person is viewing a horror show; in the second, a film sure to provoke anger; in the third, a sexually arousing film; in the fourth, an utterly boring movie. From the control center you monitor each person's physiological responses, examining their perspiration, breathing, and heart rates. Do you think you could tell who was frightened? Who was angry? Who was sexually aroused? Who was bored?

With training, you could probably pick out the bored viewer. But discerning physiological differences among fear, anger, and sexual arousal, with their similar arousal but differing valences, is much more difficult (Cacioppo & others, 1997; Zillmann, 1986).

Fear, anger, and sexual arousal certainly *feel* different (and, as we shall see, cognitively *are* different). If you are terrified, you may feel a clutching, sinking sensation in your chest and a knot in your stomach. If angry, you may feel "hot under the collar" and will likely experience a pressing inner tension. If sexually stimulated, you will experience a genital response. Yet despite similar arousal, frightened and angry people also *look* different—"paralyzed with fear" and "ready to explode." Knowing this, is it possible to pinpoint some distinct physiological indicators of each emotion?

The finger temperatures and hormone secretions that accompany fear and rage sometimes differ (Ax, 1953; Levenson, 1992). The arousal that accompanies negative fear and positive excitement may lead to similar increases in heart rate but different versions of muscle tension, recorded above the eyes in a subtle frown or below them in a smile (Witvliet & Vrana, 1995). Different emotions also arise through different brain circuits (Kalin, 1993; Panksepp, 1982). Stimulate one area of a cat's limbic system and it will pull back in terror at the sight of a mouse. Stimulate another limbic area and the cat will look enraged—pupils dilated, fur and tail erect, claws out, hissing furiously.

As people experience negative emotions such as disgust, their right hemisphere becomes more electrically active. One man, having lost part of his right frontal lobe in brain surgery, became, his not-unhappy wife reported, less irritable and more affectionate (Goleman, 1995). The left hemisphere activates when processing positive emotions (Davidson, 1999). For some infants and adults, the left frontal lobe shows more activity than the right. These individuals are typically more cheerful and less readily threatened or depressed than those with more active right frontal lobes. The left frontal lobe's

"No one ever told me that grief felt so much like fear. I am not afraid, but the sensation is like being afraid. The same fluttering in the stomach, the same restlessness, the yawning. I keep on swallowing."

C. S. Lewis, *A Grief Observed*, 1961

In 1966, a young man named Charles Whitman killed his wife and mother and then climbed to the top of a tower at the University of Texas and shot 38 people. An autopsy later revealed a tumor in his limbic system.

Emotional arousal
Elated excitement and panicky fear involve similar physiological arousal. That allows us to flip rapidly between the two emotions.

rich supply of dopamine receptors may help explain why a peppy left hemisphere correlates with a perky disposition.

So, although emotions as varied as fear and anger involve a similar general autonomic arousal (thanks to the sympathetic nervous system), there are real, if subtle, physiological differences that help explain why we experience them so differently. Moreover, the physical accompaniments of emotion appear innate and universal—the same in a village on Sumatra as in one in North America (Levenson & others, 1991).

Expressing Emotion

Preview Questions: How do we communicate nonverbally? Are nonverbal expressions of emotion universally understood? Do our facial expressions influence our experienced emotions?

There is another, simpler method of deciphering people's emotions: We read their bodies, listen to their tone of voice, and study their faces.

Nonverbal Communication

All of us communicate nonverbally as well as verbally. If irritated, we may tense our bodies, press our lips together, and turn away. With a gaze, an averted glance, or a stare we can communicate intimacy, submission, or dominance (Kleinke, 1986). Among those passionately in love, gazing into one another's eyes is typically prolonged and mutual (Rubin, 1970). Joan Kellerman, James Lewis, and James Laird (1989) wondered if such intimate gazes would stir such feelings between strangers. To find out, they asked unacquainted male-female pairs to gaze intently for two minutes either at one another's hands or into one another's eyes. After separating, the couples reported feeling a greater tingle of attraction and affection.

Most of us are good enough at reading nonverbal cues to decipher the emotions in an old silent film. We are especially good at detecting nonverbal threats. In a crowd of faces, a single angry face will "pop out" faster than a single happy one (Hansen & Hansen, 1988). By exposing different parts of emotion-laden faces, Robert Kestenbaum (1992) discovered that we read fear and anger mostly from the eyes, happiness from the mouth.

Some of us are more sensitive than others to these cues. Robert Rosenthal, Judith Hall, and their colleagues (1979) discovered this by showing hundreds of people brief film clips of portions of a person's emotionally expressive face or body, sometimes adding a garbled voice. For example, after a 2-second scene revealing only the face of an upset woman, the researchers would ask whether the woman was criticizing someone for being late or was talking about her divorce. Rosenthal and Hall reported that some people are much better than others at detecting emotion. Introverts tend to do better at reading others' emotions, although extraverts are themselves easier to read (Ambady & others, 1995).

"Your face, my thane, is a book where men may read strange matters."

Lady Macbeth to her husband, in William Shakespeare's *Macbeth*.

Gender and Nonverbal Behavior

Studies also consistently find females better at reading people's emotional cues (Hall, 1987). Women's nonverbal sensitivity, perhaps a by-product of traditional gender roles, helps explain their greater emotional responsiveness in positive and negative situations (Grossman & Wood, 1993; Sprecher & Sedikides, 1993; Stoppard & Gruchy, 1993).

When surveyed, women are far more likely than men to describe themselves as empathic. If you have empathy, you identify with others. You rejoice with those who rejoice and weep with those who weep. You imagine what it must feel like to live with that problem, what it must be like to try so hard to impress people, what a thrill it must be to win that award. Physiological measures of empathy, such as one's heart rate while seeing another's distress, reveal a much smaller gender gap than reported in surveys (Eisenberg & Lennon, 1983). Nevertheless, females are more likely to *express* empathy—to cry and to report distress when observing someone in distress. Ann Kring and Albert Gordon (1998) observed this gender difference from videotapes of men and women students as they watched film clips that were sad (children with a dying parent), happy (slapstick comedy), or frightening (a man nearly falling off the ledge of a tall building). As **FIGURE 38.3** shows, the women reacted more visibly to each of the films.

Women and men also differ in the emotions they express best. Erik Coats and Robert Feldman (1996) demonstrated this when they asked students to recall and talk about times when they were happy, sad, and angry. They then showed silent 5-second videos of their reports of the three emotional states to participants who acted as judges. The judges correctly discerned women's recall of being happy nearly two-thirds of the time, but they were able to spot it less than half the time when observing men. Men, however, slightly surpassed women in conveying their anger.

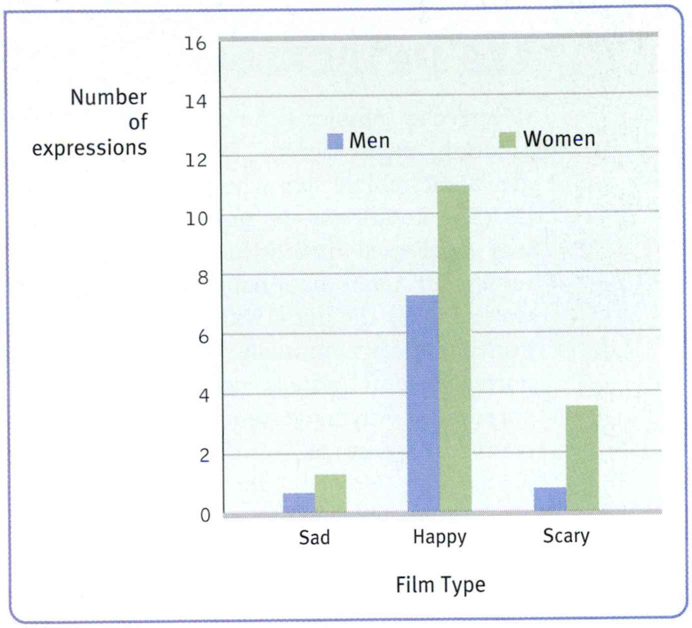

Detecting and Computing Emotion

Working with high-tech equipment, psychologists are now linking various emotions with specific facial muscles (**FIGURE 38.4**). Hard-to-control facial muscles reveal signs of emotions you may be trying to conceal. Lifting just the inner part of your eyebrows, which few people do consciously, reveals distress or worry. Eyebrows raised and pulled together signal fear. Activated muscles under the eyes and raised cheeks suggest a natural smile. A feigned smile, such as one we make for a photographer, often continues for more than four or five seconds. Most authentic expressions have faded by that time. Feigned smiles also get switched on and off more abruptly than a genuine smile (Bugental, 1986).

Unless trained in recognizing such subtle signals, most people find it difficult to detect deceiving expressions. For example, Paul Ekman and Maureen O'Sullivan (1991) videotaped university students for a minute each as they watched either a nature film or an upsetting gruesome film. Regardless of which film they watched, the students were asked to talk and act as if they were watching and enjoying the nature film. Telltale signs of lying, such as raising the pitch of one's voice, enabled the researchers to guess correctly 86 percent of the time whether a participant was lying or telling the truth. Using our intuition, could the rest of us do as well? Not likely. Ekman and O'Sullivan challenged 39 college students, 67 psychiatrists, 110 court judges, 126 police officers, and 90 federal polygraphers to spot the liars. All five groups' guesses were near chance (50 percent). Only a sixth group of experienced crowd-scanners—U.S. Secret Service agents—beat chance. But even they were only 64 percent correct.

FIGURE 38.3
Gender and expressiveness
Although male and female students did not differ dramatically in self-reported emotions or physiological responses while viewing emotional films, the women's faces *showed* much more emotion. (From Kring & Gordon, 1998)

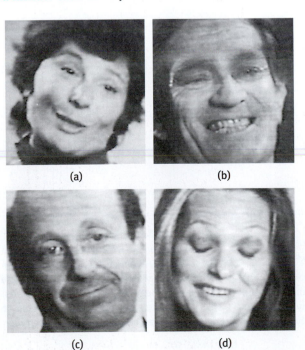

FIGURE 38.4
Smiles as indicators of emotions
Paul Ekman's system for classifying a particular smile consists of a specific code for each facial muscle used to create it. Notice how different these smiles are. (a) A smile that masks anger (the woman has just been told she is being dismissed). (b) An overly polite smile (the man is telling a patient to enjoy her hospital stay). (c) A smile softening verbal criticism ("I'd appreciate it if you wouldn't come to rehearsal drunk"). And (d) a reluctant, compliant smile ("I guess I don't have any choice, so OK").

(a)　(b)

(c)　(d)

THINKING CRITICALLY ABOUT:

LIE DETECTION

Given the physical indicators of emotion, might we, like Pinocchio, give some telltale sign whenever we lie? The *lie detector*, or **polygraph**, was once used mainly in law enforcement and national security work. But by the mid-1980s, 2 million Americans annually were reportedly being tested, usually by corporations trying to screen applicants for honesty or to uncover employee theft (Holden, 1986a).

Just what does a polygraph do? First of all, it does not literally detect lies. Rather, it measures several of the arousal responses that accompany emotion, such as changes in breathing, pulse rate, blood pressure, and perspiration. While you try to relax, the examiner measures your physiological responses as you answer questions. Some of these, called control questions, are designed to make anyone a little nervous. If asked, "In the last

20 years, have you ever taken something that didn't belong to you?" many people will tell a white lie and say no, causing arousal that the polygraph would detect. If your physiological reactions to the critical questions ("Did you ever steal anything from your previous employer?") are weaker than to the control questions, the examiner infers you are telling the truth. The assumption is that only a thief becomes agitated when denying a theft (**FIGURE 38.5**).

But there is a problem: An innocent person might also respond with heightened tension to the accusations implied by the relevant questions. When a Yakima, Washington, mother of a 4-year-old boy was accused by her ex-husband's new wife of sexually abusing her son, she gladly accepted a police offer of a polygraph test "to prove her innocence." Asked, "Did you

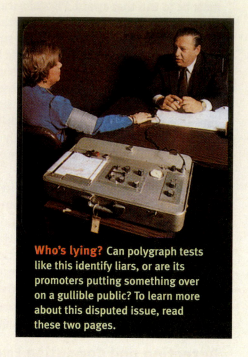

Who's lying? Can polygraph tests like this identify liars, or are its promoters putting something over on a gullible public? To learn more about this disputed issue, read these two pages.

take Tommy's penis in your mouth?" the accused mother understandably reacted with greater perspiration and blood pressure than when asked "Have you ever told a lie

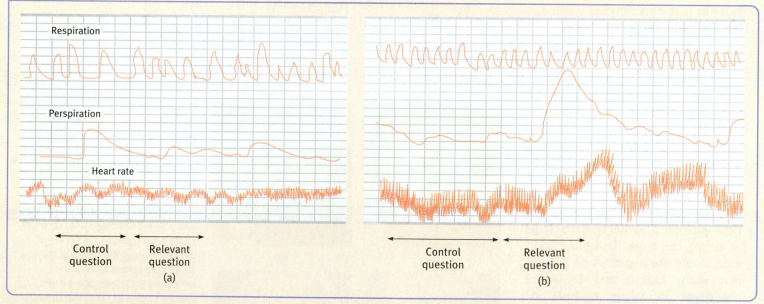

(a)

(b)

FIGURE 38.5

Physiological responses to a lie detector test

(a) This is the record of a witness who supported an accused murderer's alibi. She reacted more strongly when answering no to a control question, "Up to age 18, did you ever deceive anyone?" than when answering yes to the relevant question, "Was [the accused] at another location at the time of the murder?" As a result, the examiner concluded she was telling the truth. (b) This is the record of an accused murderer judged to be lying when he pleaded self-defense. He reacted less strongly in answering no to the control question, "Up to age 18, did you ever physically harm anyone?" than when answering yes to the relevant question, "Did [the deceased] threaten to harm you in any way?" (From Raskin, 1982.)

to get out of trouble?" (Physiologically, the fear of being disbelieved looks a lot like the fear of being caught lying.) This revealed her guilt, explained the police-sergeant-turned-polygrapher to the jury. (Fortunately for the mother, her attorney managed to locate a scientific expert who persuaded the jury that, by itself, this was not credible evidence of guilt.) Many rape victims similarly "fail" lie detector tests when reacting emotionally while telling the truth about their assailant (Lykken, 1992).

The major adversaries of lie detector tests have been psychologists David Lykken (1983, 1992) and Leonard Saxe (1994). They note that our physiological arousal is much the same from one emotion to another. The polygraph cannot distinguish among anxiety, irritation, and guilt—they all appear as arousal. Thus, these tests err about one-third of the time. The "lie detector" could more accurately be called a fear detector. The test more often labels the innocent guilty—when the relevant question upsets the honest person—than the guilty innocent (**FIGURE 38.6**). Good advice, then, would be never to take a lie detector test if you are innocent.

Skeptics therefore applauded when the American and British Psychological Associations in 1986 expressed great reservations about polygraph tests. They applauded when in 1988 the U.S. Congress prohibited most nongovernment polygraph testing. And they applauded again when the U.S. Supreme Court in 1998 upheld a ban on polygraph tests in military trials. But then they groaned when the U.S. Secretary of Energy in 1999 ordered polygraph screening of all its nuclear weapons scientists at Los Alamos National Laboratory. Because the polygraph cannot discriminate the arousal of guilty lying from fearful honesty, "tens of thousands

of polygraph screening exams administered by the CIA, the FBI, and the National Security Agency have yet to uncover a single spy," noted Robert Park (1999). Meanwhile Aldrich Ames, who enjoyed an unexplained lavish life-style while a Russian spy within the CIA, went undetected. Ames "took scores of polygraph tests and passed them all," notes Park. "Nobody thought to investigate the source of his sudden wealth—after all, he was passing the lie detector tests." The truth is, lie detectors can lie.

Although too error-prone for use in testing applicants and employees, the polygraph can serve as a tool in criminal investigation. Police sometimes use it to induce confessions from criminals by scaring them into thinking that any lies will be transparent.

In a recent survey, however, more than 9 in 10 psychophysiologists and research psychologists agreed that savvy criminals and spies could beat the test by augmenting their arousal to control questions, such as biting their tongue (Iacono & Lykken, 1997). A more effective approach uses the *guilty knowledge test*, which assesses

a suspect's physiological responses to the details of a crime known only to the police and the guilty person. If a camera and money had been stolen, the polygraph examiner could notice whether the suspect reacts strongly to the specific brand name of the camera and the dollar amounts. Presumably, only one guilty of the crime would have such responses. Given enough such specific probes, an innocent person will seldom be wrongly accused. Thus, while more than 9 in 10 informed research psychologists believe lie detection tests can be beaten by criminals and spies, nearly as many judge the guilty knowledge test as "scientifically sound" (Iacono & Lykken, 1997). ■

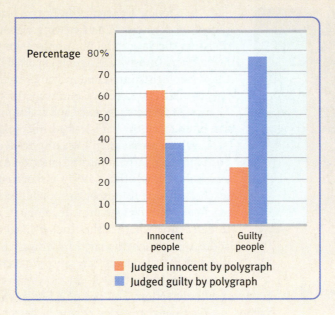

FIGURE 38.6 How often do lie detectors lie? Benjamin Kleinmuntz and Julian Szucko (1984) had polygraph experts study the polygraph data of 50 theft suspects who later confessed to being guilty and 50 suspects whose innocence was later established by someone's confession. Had the polygraph experts been the judges, more than one-third of the innocent would have been declared guilty, and almost one-fourth of the guilty would have been declared innocent.

polygraph a machine, commonly used in attempts to detect lies, that measures several of the physiological responses accompanying emotion (such as perspiration, heart rate, blood pressure, and breathing changes).

A silent language of emotion
The art of nonverbal communication reached a pinnacle early in the twentieth century as silent films became widely available. For a nickel, enraptured audiences could watch performers mime a wide range of unmistakable emotions. Here Chester Conklin woos a woman on horseback while Louise Fazenda fumes.

In a follow-up study, the Ekman team (1999) found three more groups of skilled lie-catchers. When viewing videotapes of people stating their opinions on issues such as capital punishment—or the opposite of their opinions—federal law officers (mostly CIA agents) spotted the liars 73 percent of the time. Clinical psychologists interested in lying research did so 68 percent of the time, and street-smart Los Angeles County sheriff's interrogators scored an almost equal 67 percent. With experience and training, it seems, people as well as computers can often catch the liar's leaking microexpressions of guilt, despair, and fear.

When people aren't seeking to deceive us, we do much better. In fact, our brains are rather amazing emotion detectors. Elisha Babad, Frank Bernieri, and Robert Rosenthal (1991) discovered just *how* amazing after videotaping teachers talking to unseen schoolchildren. A mere 10-second clip of either the teacher's voice or face provided enough clues for both young and old viewers to determine whether the teacher liked and admired the child he or she was addressing. Teachers may think they can conceal their feelings and stay objective, but their students can sense what their expressions and gestures reveal.

Subtle facial indicators of emotion may someday enable a new behavioral approach to lie detection. For example, given mild emotional stimuli, electrodes attached to your facial muscles can now detect your hidden reactions (Tassinary & Cacioppo, 1992). Your face may not look any different, but voltage changes on the skin reveal underlying micromuscular smiles or frowns. They can also reveal whether a frown reflects a bad mood or focused concentration.

A camera may do the same. Research teams are now at work developing high-speed computer software that analyzes videotaped microexpressions by comparing them with a person's face devoid of expression. Any change from neutral—even the eyebrow's momentary lowering in anger preceding a counterfeit smile—gets detected (Bartlett & others, 1999). In initial tests, the computer outperformed human nonexperts, with 91 percent accuracy in recognizing six facial expressions. When further developed to register all facial muscle movements, might computer image analysis, combined with measures of arousal, better identify emotional valences—and unmask lies? Stay tuned.

The growing awareness that we communicate through the body's silent language has led to studies of how job applicants and interviewers communicate (or miscommunicate) nonverbally. Popular guidebooks and articles offer advice on how to interpret nonverbal signals when negotiating a business deal, selling a product, or flirting. It pays to be able to read feelings that leak through via subtle facial expressions, body movements, and postures. Fidgeting, for example, may reveal anxiety or boredom. It's important to remember that more specific interpretations of postures and gestures are risky because different expressions may convey the same emotion: Either a cold stare or the avoidance of eye contact may signify hostility. And a single given expression can convey very different emotions: Folded arms, for example, can signify either irritation or relaxation.

Such gestures, facial expressions, and tones of voice are all absent in computer-based communication. E-mail communications sometimes include sideways "emoticons," such as ;-) for a knowing wink and :-(for a frown. But e-mail letters and Internet discussions otherwise lack nonverbal cues to status, personality, and age. Nobody knows what you look or sound like, or anything about your background—you are judged solely on your words. It's no wonder then that when first meeting an e-mail pen pal face to face, people are often surprised at the person they encounter.

It's also easy to misread e-mailed communications. The absence of expressive e-motion can make for ambiguous emotion. So can the absence of those vocal nuances by which we signal that a statement is serious, kidding, or sarcastic. Research by Justin Kruger and his colleagues (1999) shows that communicators often think their "just kidding" intent is equally clear, whether e-mailed or spoken. But they commonly exhibit egocentrism by not foreseeing misinterpretations in the absence of nonverbal cues. The result can be flaming hostilities.

Open Palm Greece: an insult dating to ancient times; West Africa: You have five fathers, an insult akin to calling someone a bastard

Thumbs-up Australia: up yours; Germany: the number one; Japan: the number five; Saudi Arabia: I'm winning; Ghana: an insult; Malaysia: the thumb is used to point rather than the finger

Thumb and forefinger Most countries: money; France: something is perfect; Mediterranean: a vulgar gesture

OK Sign France: you're a zero; Japan: please give me coins; Brazil: an obscene gesture; Mediterranean countries: an obscene gesture

Understanding gestures
Volunteers working with international visitors during the 1996 Olympics were briefed on the cultural meanings of gestures.

Culture and Emotional Expression

The meaning of gestures varies with the culture. Some years ago, psychologist Otto Klineberg (1938) observed that in Chinese literature people clapped their hands to express worry or disappointment, laughed a great "Ho-Ho" to express anger, and stuck out their tongues to show surprise. Similarly, the North American "thumbs up" and "A-OK" signs would be insults in certain other cultures. (When former U.S. President Nixon made the latter sign in Brazil, he didn't realize he was saying "Let's have sex.") Just how important cultural definitions of gestures can be was demonstrated in 1968, when North Korea photographed supposedly happy officers from a captured U.S. Navy spy ship. In the photo, three of the men raised their middle-fingers; they had told captors it was a "Hawaiian good luck sign" (Fleming & Scott, 1991).

Do facial expressions also have different meanings in different cultures? To find out, two investigative teams—one led by Paul Ekman and Wallace Friesen (1975, 1987, 1994), the other by Carroll Izard (1977, 1994)—showed photographs of different facial expressions to people in different parts of the world and asked them to guess the emotion. You can try this yourself. Match the six emotions with the six faces of **FIGURE 38.7**.

You probably did pretty well regardless of your cultural background. A smile's a smile the world around. Ditto for anger, and to a lesser extent the other basic expressions (Elfenbein & Ambady, 1999). (There is no culture where people frown when they are happy.) Despite some differences, cultures and languages share many similarities in the ways they categorize emotions—as anger, fear, and so on. The physiological indicators of emotion also cross cultural boundaries (Levenson & others, 1992; Mesquita & Frijda, 1992).

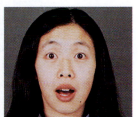
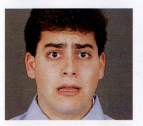
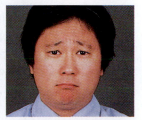

FIGURE 38.7 Culture-specific or culturally universal expressions?
As people of differing cultures and races, do our faces speak differing languages? Which face expresses disgust? Anger? Fear? Happiness? Sadness? Surprise? The answers are on page 489.

While weightless, astronauts' fluids move toward their upper body and their faces become puffy. This makes nonverbal communication more difficult, increasing the risks of misunderstanding, especially among multinational crews (Gelman, 1989).

Do people from different cultures make and interpret facial expressions similarly because they experience similar influences, such as American movies, the BBC, and CNN? Apparently not. Ekman and his team asked isolated people in New Guinea to display various emotions in response to such statements as, "Pretend your child has died." When the researchers showed videotapes of the New Guineans' facial reactions to North American collegians, the students read them easily. Children's facial expressions—even those of blind children who have never seen a face—are also universal (Eibl-Eibesfeldt, 1971). People blind from birth spontaneously exhibit the common facial expressions associated with such emotions as joy, sadness, fear, and anger (Galati & others, 1997). The world over, children cry when distressed, shake their heads when defiant, and smile when they are happy.

The discovery that the facial muscles speak a fairly universal language would have come as no surprise to pioneering emotion researcher Charles Darwin (1809–1882). He speculated that in prehistoric times, before our ancestors communicated in words, their ability to convey threats, greetings, and submission with facial expressions helped them survive. That shared heritage, he believed, is why all humans express the basic emotions with similar facial expressions. A sneer, for example, retains elements of an animal's baring its teeth in a snarl.

Smiles, too, are social phenomena as well as emotional reflexes. Bowlers don't smile when they score a strike—they smile when they turn to face their companions (Jones & others, 1991; Kraut & Johnston, 1979). Even euphoric winners of Olympic gold medals typically don't smile when they are awaiting their ceremony but do when interacting with officials and facing the crowd and cameras (Fernádez-Dols & Ruiz-Belda, 1995).

It has also been adaptive for us to *interpret* faces in particular contexts. People judge an angry face set in a frightening situation as afraid. They judge a fearful face set in a painful situation as pained (Carroll & Russell, 1996). Movie directors harness this phenomenon by creating contexts and soundtracks that amplify our perceptions of particular emotions.

Emotional expressions may enhance our survival in other ways, too. Surprise raises the eyebrows and widens the eyes, enabling us to take in more information. Disgust wrinkles the nose, closing it from foul odors.

Although cultures share a universal facial language for basic emotions, they do differ in how much emotion they express. In cultures that encourage individuality, as in Western Europe, Australia, New Zealand, and North America, emotional displays often are intense and prolonged. People focus on their own goals and attitudes and express themselves accordingly. Watching a film of someone's hand being cut, Americans grimace (whether alone or with other viewers). In contrast, Japanese viewers hide their emotions when in the presence of others (Triandis, 1994). Asians rarely and briefly display negative or self-aggrandizing emotions that might disrupt communal feeling within close-knit groups (Markus & Kitayama, 1991; Matsumoto & others, 1988). Moreover, in Asian and other cultures that emphasize social connections and interdependence, displays of emotions such as sympathy, respect, and shame are more common than in the West.

The Effects of Facial Expressions

Expressions not only communicate emotion, they also amplify and regulate it. In his 1872 book, *The Expression of the Emotions in Man and Animals*, Darwin contended that "the free expression by outward signs of an emotion intensifies it. . . . He who gives way to violent gestures will increase his rage."

Was Darwin right? I was driving in my car one day when the song "Put On a Happy Face" came on the radio. How phony, I thought. But I tested Darwin's hypothesis anyway, as you can, too. Fake a big grin. Now scowl. Can you feel the "smile therapy" difference?

The subjects in dozens of experiments have felt a difference. For example, James Laird and his colleagues (1974, 1984, 1989) subtly induced students to make a frowning expression by asking them to "contract these muscles" and "pull your brows together" (supposedly to help the researchers attach facial electrodes). The results? The students reported feeling a little angry. Students similarly induced to smile felt happier, found cartoons more humorous, and recalled happier memories than did the frowners. People instructed to mold their faces in ways that mimicked expressions of other basic emotions also experienced those emotions. For example, they reported feeling more fear than anger, disgust, or sadness when made to construct an expression of fear: "Raise your eyebrows. And open your eyes wide. Move your whole head back, so that your chin is tucked in a little bit, and let your mouth relax and hang open a little" (Duclos & others, 1989). Going through the motions awakens the emotions.

In the absence of competing emotions, this "facial feedback" effect is subtle, yet detectable. Consider these findings:

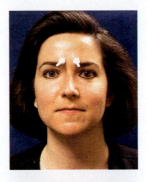
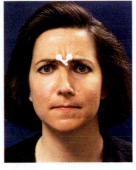

FIGURE **38.8** **How to make people frown without telling them to frown** Randy Larsen, Margaret Kasimatis, and Kurt Frey's (1992) solution: Attach two golf tees above the eyebrows and ask the subjects to make the tee tips touch. Subjects felt sad while viewing scenes of war, sickness, and starvation, and even sadder with their "sad face" muscles activated.

+ If subtly manipulated into furrowing their brows (**FIGURE 38.8**), people feel sadder while looking at sad photos.

+ Saying the phonemes *e* and *ah*, which activate smiling muscles, puts people—believe it or not—in a better mood than saying the German *ü* (rather like saying the English *e* and *u* together), which activates muscles associated with negative emotions (Zajonc & others, 1989).

+ Just activating one of the smiling muscles by holding a pen in the teeth (rather than with the lips, which activates a frowning muscle) is enough to make cartoons seem more amusing (Strack & others, 1988). A heartier smile, made not just with the mouth but with raised cheeks as well, works even better (Ekman & others, 1990). Looking at oneself in a mirror further amplifies the effect (Kleinke & others, 1998). Smile warmly on the outside and you feel better on the inside. Scowl and the whole world seems to scowl back.

Sara Snodgrass and her associates (1986) observed the behavior feedback phenomenon with walking. You can duplicate her subjects' experience: Walk for a few minutes while taking short, shuffling steps, keeping your eyes downcast. Now walk around taking long strides, with your arms swinging and your eyes looking straight ahead. Can you feel your mood shift?

If assuming an emotional expression triggers a feeling, then would imitating others' expressions help us feel what they are feeling? Again, the laboratory evidence is supportive. Kathleen Burns Vaughn and John Lanzetta (1981) asked some students but not others to make a pained expression whenever an electric shock was apparently delivered to someone they were watching. With each apparent shock, the grimacing observers perspired more and had a faster heart rate than the other observers. So one small way to become more empathic—to feel what others feel—is to let your own face mimic the other person's expression. Acting as another acts helps us feel what another feels.

"Refuse to express a passion and it dies. . . . If we wish to conquer undesirable emotional tendencies in ourselves, we must . . . go through the outward movements of those contrary dispositions which we prefer to cultivate."

William James, *Principles of Psychology*, 1890

A request from your author: Smile often as you read this book.

Which smile makes Paul Ekman feel happy? The smile on the right, which engages the face muscles of a natural smile.

Answers to the questions in Figure 38.7 (page 487): From left to right, top to bottom: happiness, surprise, fear, sadness, anger, disgust.

Experiencing Emotion

Preview Questions: What are the functions, causes, and consequences of fear? Of anger? Of happiness?

How many distinct emotions are there? Carroll Izard (1977) isolated 10 such basic emotions (joy, interest-excitement, surprise, sadness, anger, disgust, contempt, fear, shame, and guilt), most of which are present in infancy (**FIGURE 38.9**). Izard reported that other emotions are combinations of these 10. Although Phillip Shaver and his colleagues (1996) believe that love, too, may be a basic emotion, Izard viewed it as a mixture of joy and interest-excitement.

We focus on three important emotions: fear, anger, and happiness. What functions do they serve? What influences our experience of them?

Fear

Fear can be poisonous. It can torment us, rob us of sleep, and preoccupy our thinking. People can be literally scared to death. Fear can also be contagious. In 1903, someone yelled "Fire!" as a fire broke out in Chicago's Iroquois Theater. Eddie Foy, the comedian on stage at the time, tried to reassure the crowd by calling out, "Don't get excited. There's no danger. Take it easy!" Alas, the crowd panicked. During the 10 minutes it took the fire department to arrive and quickly extinguish the flames, more than 500 people perished, most of them trampled or smothered in a stampede. Bodies were piled 7 or 8 feet deep in the stairways, and many of the faces bore heel marks (Brown, 1965).

More often, fear is adaptive. It's an alarm system that prepares our bodies to flee danger. Fear of real or imagined enemies binds people together as families, tribes, and nations. Fear of injury can protect us from harm. Fear of punishment or retaliation can constrain us from harming one another. Fear triggers worry, which helps us focus on a problem and rehearse coping strategies.

> "He who fears all snares falls into none."
>
> Publius Syrus, *Sententiae*, 43 B.C.

FIGURE 38.9

Infants' naturally occurring emotions
To identify the emotions present from birth, Carroll Izard analyzed the facial expressions of very young infants.

(a) Joy (mouth forming smile, cheeks lifted, twinkle in eye)

(b) Anger (brows drawn together and downward, eyes fixed, mouth squarish)

(c) Interest (brows raised or knitted, mouth softly rounded, lips may be pursed)

(d) Disgust (nose wrinkled, upper lip raised, tongue pushed outward)

(e) Surprise (brows raised, eyes widened, mouth rounded in oval shape)

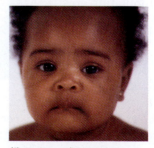

(f) Sadness (brow's inner corners raised, mouth corners drawn down)

(g) Fear (brows level, drawn in and up, eyelids lifted, mouth corners retracted)

Learning Fear

People can be afraid of almost anything—"afraid of truth, afraid of fortune, afraid of death, and afraid of each other," observed Ralph Waldo Emerson. Why so many fears? Psychologists note that we can actually learn to fear almost anything—infants can learn to fear furry objects associated with frightening noises, and adults can become terrified of incidental stimuli linked with traumatic experiences such as rape. As infants become mobile they experience falls and near-falls—and become increasingly afraid of heights (Campos & others, 1992). Through such conditioning, the short list of naturally painful and frightening events can multiply into a long list of human fears—fear of driving or flying, fear of mice or cockroaches, fear of closed or open spaces, fear of failure, fear of success, fear of another race or nation.

Learning by observation extends the list. Susan Mineka (1985) sought to explain why nearly all monkeys reared in the wild fear snakes, yet lab-reared monkeys do not. Surely, most wild monkeys do not actually suffer snake bites. Do they learn their fear through observation? To find out, Mineka experimented with six monkeys reared in the wild (all strongly fearful of snakes) and their lab-reared offspring (virtually none of which feared snakes). After repeatedly observing their parents or peers refusing to reach for food in the presence of a snake, the younger monkeys developed a similar strong fear of snakes. When retested three months later, their learned fear persisted, suggesting that our fears may reflect not only our own past traumas but also the fears we learn from our parents and friends.

The Biology of Fear

Moreover, we may be biologically prepared to learn some fears more quickly than others. Monkeys learn to fear snakes even by watching videotapes of monkeys reacting fearfully to a snake; but they *don't* learn to fear flowers when video splicing transposes the seemingly feared stimulus into a flower (Cook & Mineka, 1991). We humans quickly learn to fear snakes, spiders, and cliffs—fears that probably helped our ancestors survive. We are less predisposed to fear cars, electricity, bombs, and global warming, all of which are now far more dangerous (Lumsden & Wilson, 1983; McNally, 1987). Stone Age fears leave us unprepared for high-tech dangers.

A key to fear learning lies in the amygdala, a limbic system neural center deep in the brain (**FIGURE 38.10**). The amygdala plays a key role in associating various emotions, including fear, with certain situations (Barinaga, 1992). Rabbits learn to react with fear to a tone that predicts an impending small shock—unless their amygdala is damaged. If rats have their amygdala deactivated by a drug that blocks the strengthening of neural connections, they, too, show no fear learning. Not only does the amygdala link situations with fear responses, its output is wired to all the parts of the brain that produce the bodily symptoms of extreme fear, such as diarrhea and shortness of breath.

The amygdala is similarly involved in human fears. If an experimenter repeatedly blasts people with a blaring horn after showing a blue slide, they will begin to react emotionally to the slide (as measured by their perspiring skin conducting electricity). If they have suffered damage to the hippocampus, they still show the emotional reaction but won't be able to remember why. If they have suffered amygdala damage, they will remember the conditioning but will show no emotional effect of it (Schacter, 1996).

Researchers are now mapping these circuits, showing which activate as animals and humans learn fears. If people are subjected to an aversive sound while viewing faces (either perceptibly or subliminally), amygdala fear pathways will

Hard-wired fears
Entertainment businesses exploit our survival circuits. Although we can *know* that amusement park deaths are extremely rare, our fear alarm system nevertheless gives us an adrenaline rush and sweaty palms during a free-flying fair ride.

FIGURE 38.10 The amygdala— a neural key to fear learning
Nerves running out from these knots of neural tissue, one on either side of the brain's center, carry messages that control heart rate, sweating, stress hormones, attention and other engines that rev up in threatening situations.

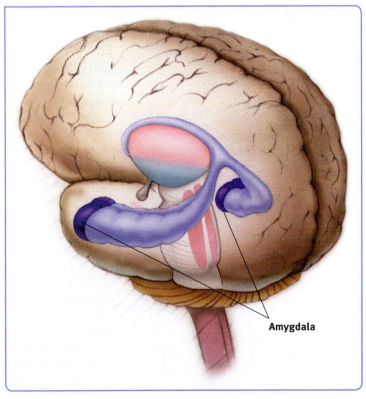

Amygdala

become active on future viewings of the face (Buchel & others, 1998; Morris & others, 1998). Patients who have lost use of the amygdala are unusually trusting of scary-looking people (Adolphs & others, 1998).

Of course, there are people whose fears (*phobias*) seem to fall outside the average range. Their intense fears of specific objects (such as bugs) or situations (such as public speaking) disrupt their ability to cope. They may be very fearful of threatening or embarrassing situations. To be ever-attentive to potential threats is to be chronically anxious (Mineka & Sutton, 1992). But others—courageous heroes and remorseless criminals—are less fearful than most of us. Astronauts and adventurers who have "the right stuff"—who can keep their wits and can function coolly and effectively in times of severe stress—seem to thrive on risk. So, too, do con artists and killers who charm their intended victims without a hint of nervousness. In laboratory tests, they exhibit little fear of a tone that predictably precedes a painful electric shock.

Experience helps shape such fearfulness or fearlessness, but so do our genes. We now know that genes influence our temperament—our emotional reactivity. Even among identical twins reared separately, one twin's level of fearfulness is similar to the other's (Lykken, 1982).

Anger

Anger, the sages have said, is "a short madness" (Horace, 65–8 B.C.) that "carries the mind away" (Virgil, 70–19 B.C.) and that can be "many times more hurtful than the injury that caused it" (Thomas Fuller, 1654–1734). But they have also said, "noble anger" (William Shakespeare, 1564–1616) "makes any coward brave" (Cato, 234–149 B.C.) and "brings back . . . strength" (Virgil).

What makes us angry? To find out, James Averill (1983) asked people to recall or keep careful records of their experiences with anger. Most reported becoming at least mildly angry several times a week, some several times a day. The anger was often a response to friends' or loved ones' perceived misdeeds and was especially common when another person's act seemed willful, unjustified, and avoidable. But blameless annoyances—foul odors, high temperatures, a traffic jam, aches and pains—also have the power to make us angry (Berkowitz, 1990).

What do we do with our anger? And what *should* we do with it? When anger fuels physically or verbally aggressive acts we later regret, it becomes maladaptive. And chronic hostility is linked with heart disease. But Averill's subjects recalled that when they were angry they often reacted assertively rather than hurtfully. Their anger frequently led them to talk things over with the offender, thereby lessening the aggravation. Controlled expressions of anger are more adaptive than either hostile outbursts or pent-up angry feelings.

Popular books and articles on aggression at times advise that even releasing angry feelings as hostile outbursts can be better than internalizing them. When irritated, should we go ahead and curse, tell a person off, or retaliate? Was Ann Landers (1969) right that "youngsters should be taught to vent their anger"? Are "recovery movement" leaders right in encouraging us to rage at our dead parents, imaginatively curse the boss, or confront our childhood abuser?

Such encouragement to vent our rage is typical in individualized cultures, but it would seldom be heard in cultures where people's identity is centered more on the group. People who keenly sense their *inter*dependence see anger as a threat to group harmony (Markus & Kitayama, 1991). In Tahiti, for instance, people learn to be considerate and gentle. From infancy on in Japan, expressions of anger are less common than in Western cultures.

But even in Western cultures "vent your anger" advice presumes that emotional expression provides emotional release, or **catharsis**. The catharsis hypothesis maintains that we reduce anger by releasing it through aggressive action or fantasy. Experimenters report that this sometimes occurs. When people retaliate against someone

"I thought it would be nice if we had a forum where we could get together and have screaming tantrums."

"Anger will never disappear so long as thoughts of resentment are cherished in the mind."

The Buddha, 500 B.C.

■ **catharsis** emotional release. In psychology, the catharsis hypothesis maintains that "releasing" aggressive energy (through action or fantasy) relieves aggressive urges.

who has provoked them, they may indeed calm down—*if* their counterattack is directed against the provoker, *if* their retaliation seems justifiable, and *if* their target is not intimidating (Geen & Quanty, 1977; Hokanson & Edelman, 1966). In short, expressing anger can be *temporarily* calming *if* it does not leave us feeling guilty or anxious.

However, despite the afterglow—people sometimes feel better for hours afterward—catharsis usually fails to cleanse one's rage. More often, expressing anger breeds more anger. For one thing, it may provoke retaliation, thus escalating a minor conflict into a major confrontation. For another, expressing anger can magnify anger. (Recall Darwin's suggestion that violent gestures increase anger.) Ebbe Ebbesen and his colleagues (1975) saw this when they interviewed 100 frustrated engineers and technicians just laid off by an aerospace company. They asked some of the workers questions that released hostility, questions such as, "What instances can you think of where the company has not been fair with you?" When these people later filled out a questionnaire that assessed their attitudes toward the company, did this opportunity to "drain off" their hostility reduce it? Quite the contrary. Compared with those who had not vented their anger, those who had let it all out exhibited *more* hostility. Even when provoked people hit a punching bag *believing* it will be cathartic, the effect is the opposite—leading them to exhibit *more* cruelty (Bushman & others, 1999).

Thus, although "blowing off steam" may temporarily calm us, it may also amplify the underlying hostility. And—ironically—when angry outbursts actually do calm us, they may actually be reinforcing and therefore habit forming. If stressed managers find they can drain off some of their tension by berating their employees, then the next time they feel irritated and tense they may be more likely to explode again. Think about it: The next time you are angry you are likely to do whatever has relieved your anger in the past.

What then is the best way to handle our anger? Experts offer two suggestions. First, wait. You can bring down the level of physiological arousal of anger by waiting. "It is true of the body as of arrows," noted Carol Tavris (1982), "what goes up must come down. Any emotional arousal will simmer down if you just wait long enough." Second, deal with anger in a way that involves neither being chronically angry over every little annoyance nor passively sulking, merely rehearsing your reasons for your anger. Ruminating inwardly about the causes of your anger serves only to increase it (Rusting & Nolen-Hoeksema, 1998). Don't join those who stifle their feelings over a series of provocations and then suddenly overreact to a single incident (Baumeister & others, 1990). Calm yourself in other ways, such as by exercising, playing an instrument, or confiding your feelings to a friend.

Anger can actually benefit a relationship when it expresses a grievance in ways that promote reconciliation rather than retaliation. Civility means not only keeping silent about trivial irritations but also communicating important ones clearly and assertively. A nonaccusing statement of feeling—perhaps letting one's housemate know that "I get irritated when you leave your dirty dishes for me to clean up"—can help resolve the conflicts that cause anger.

Happiness

"How to gain, how to keep, how to recover happiness is in fact for most men at all times the secret motive for all they do," observed William James (1902, p. 76). Understandably so, for one's state of happiness or unhappiness colors everything. People who are happy perceive the world as safer (Johnson & Tversky, 1983), make decisions more easily (Isen & Means, 1983), rate job applicants more favorably (Baron, 1987), are more cooperative (Forgas, 1998), and report greater satisfaction with their whole lives (Schwarz & Clore, 1983). When your mood is gloomy and your thinking preoccupied,

A cool culture
Caregivers who turn abusive against other family members are rare in Micronesia. This photo of community life on Pulap Island suggests one possible reason: Family life takes place in the open in the South Pacific. Relatives and neighbors who witness angry outbursts can step in before the emotion escalates into child, spouse, or elder abuse.

Faced with adversity
In 1995, an accident transformed *Superman* actor Christopher Reeve into an immobile person needing others to feed, dress, and care for him. "Maybe I should just check out," he told his wife, Dana, shortly after the accident. But within four months he reported in a Barbara Walters interview "genuine joy in being alive."

■ **feel-good, do-good phenomenon**
people's tendency to be helpful when
already in a good mood.

■ **subjective well-being** self-perceived
happiness or satisfaction with life. Used
along with measures of objective well-
being (for example, physical and
economic indicators) to evaluate
people's quality of life.

"Everything important has been said
before."

**Philosopher Alfred North Whitehead
(1861–1947)**

"Weeping may tarry for the night, but
joy comes with the morning."

Psalms 30:5

"If I couldn't know the joy of dancing,
I could know the ecstasy of creating."

Christy Brown, *My Left Foot*, 1954

life as a whole seems depressing. Let your mood brighten and your thinking broadens
and becomes more playful and creative (Fredrickson, 1998, 2000). Your relationships,
your self-image, and your hopes for the future also seem more promising.

Moreover—and this is one of psychology's most consistent findings—when we feel
happy we are more willing to help others. In study after study, a mood-boosting experience (finding money, succeeding on a challenging task, recalling a happy event) made
people more likely to give money, pick up someone's dropped papers, volunteer time, and
so forth. Psychologists call it the **feel-good, do-good phenomenon** (Salovey, 1990).

Despite the significance of happiness, psychology throughout its history has
more often focused on negative emotions. Since 1887, *Psychological Abstracts* (a guide
to psychology's literature) has included 8072 articles mentioning anger, 57,800 mentioning anxiety, and 70,856 mentioning depression. For every 14 articles on these
topics, only one dealt with the positive emotions of joy (851), life satisfaction
(5701), or happiness (2958). There is, of course, good reason to focus on negative
emotions; they can make our lives miserable and drive us to seek help. But researchers are becoming increasingly interested in **subjective well-being**, assessed either as feelings of happiness (sometimes defined as a high ratio of positive to negative
feelings) or as a sense of satisfaction with life. "Positive psychology" is on the rise.

On this subject, as on so many others, whatever psychological research reveals
will have been anticipated by someone. We have inherited any number of contradictory maxims concerning happiness: that it comes from knowing the truth, or
from preserving illusions; from living for the present, or from living for the future;
from being with others, or from living in peaceful solitude (Tatarkiewicz, 1976).
The list goes on, and the scientific task is clear: to ask which of these competing
ideas fit reality. Sifting the actual predictors of happiness from the plausible
hunches requires research.

In their research on happiness, psychologists have studied influences on both
our temporary moods and our long-term life satisfaction. Studying people's reports of
daily moods confirms that stressful events—an argument, a sick child, a car problem—trigger bad moods. No surprise there. But by the next day, the gloom nearly always lifts (Affleck & others, 1994; Bolger & others, 1989; Stone & Neale, 1984). If
anything, people tend to rebound from bad days to a *better*-than-usual good mood
the following day. When in a bad mood, can you usually depend on rebounding
within a day or two? Are your times of elation similarly hard to sustain? Over the
long ride, our emotional ups and downs tend to balance.

Apart from prolonged grief over the loss of a loved one or lingering anxiety
after a trauma (such as child abuse, rape, or the terrors of war), even tragedy is
not permanently depressing. The finding is surprising but reliable. Those who become blind or paralyzed usually recover near-normal levels of day-to-day happiness. Consider these findings:

+ Able-bodied University of Illinois students described themselves as happy 50 percent of the time, unhappy 22 percent of the time, and neutral 29 percent of the
  time. To within 1 percentage point, students with disabilities rated their emotions identically (Chwalisz & others, 1988).
+ Students perceive their friends with disabilities as just as happy as their other
  friends (Allman, 1989).
+ In one survey of 128 people with all four limbs paralyzed, most acknowledged
  having considered suicide after their injury. However, more than a year later,
  only 10 percent rated their quality of life as poor; most described it as good or excellent (Whiteneck & others, 1985). When 233 emergency room caregivers
  imagined how they would feel about themselves years after such an injury, only
  39 percent guessed they would feel "satisfied with myself, on the whole." But
  that is exactly how 95 percent of the actual patients felt (Gerhart & others,
  1994). And 98 percent of them agreed that "I feel I am a person of worth."

In less time than most people suppose, the emotional impact of significant events dissipates. Learning that one is HIV-positive is devastating. Yet after five weeks of adapting to the grim news, those who tested positive felt less emotionally distraught than they had expected (Sieff & others, 1999). Likewise, faculty members up for tenure expected their lives would be deflated by a negative decision. Actually, 5 to 10 years later, those denied are not noticeably unhappier than those who were awarded tenure, report Daniel Gilbert and colleagues (1998). The same is true of romantic breakups, which at the time may seem to have ruined one's life. The surprising reality: We overestimate the long-term emotional impact of very bad news and underestimate our capacity to adapt.

It may come as a disappointment, but the effect of dramatically positive events is similarly temporary. Once their rush of euphoria wears off, state lottery winners typically find their overall happiness unchanged (Brickman & others, 1978). Other research confirms that there is much more to well-being than being well-off. Many people (including most new collegians, as **FIGURE 38.11** suggests) believe they would be happier if they had more money. They probably would be—temporarily. But in the long run, increased affluence hardly affects happiness. Within most affluent countries, people with lots of money are not much happier than those with just enough to afford life's necessities. Wealth is like health: Its utter absence breeds misery, yet having it is no guarantee of happiness.

Most people agree that money can't buy happiness, but they do believe that a *little* more money would make them a *little* more happy, secure, and comfortable. So, over time, does our happiness grow, little by little, with our paychecks? No, it doesn't. During the last four decades, the average U.S. citizen's buying power doubled. The 1957 per-person after tax income, inflated to 1995 dollars, was $8500; by 1998, thanks partly to the rich getting richer and to women's increasing employment, it was $20,000. Did this doubled wealth—enabling twice as many cars per capita, and color TVs, VCRs, personal computers, air conditioning, and answering machines galore—also buy more happiness? As **FIGURE 38.12** shows, the average American is now twice as rich but not a bit happier. In 1957, some 35 percent said they were "very happy," as did slightly fewer—32 percent—in 1998.

Indeed, if we can judge from statistics—a doubled divorce rate, tripled teen suicide and teen violent crime rates, and mushrooming depression—contemporary Americans seem to be more often miserable. The same is true of the European countries and of Japan: In these countries, people enjoy better nutrition, health care, education, and science, and are somewhat happier

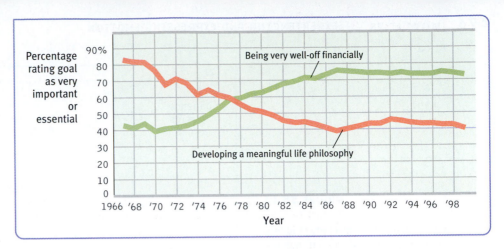

FIGURE 38.11 The changing materialism of entering college students
From 1970 through most of the 1980s, annual surveys of more than 200,000 entering U.S. college students revealed an increasing desire for wealth. (From *The American Freshman* surveys, UCLA, 1966 to 1999.)

FIGURE 38.12
Does money buy happiness?
It surely helps us to avoid certain types of pain. Yet, though buying power has doubled since the 1950s, the average American's reported happiness has remained almost unchanged. (Happiness data from Niemi & others, 1989, and T. Smith, personal correspondence; income data from *Historical Statistics of the United States* and *Economic Indicators*.)

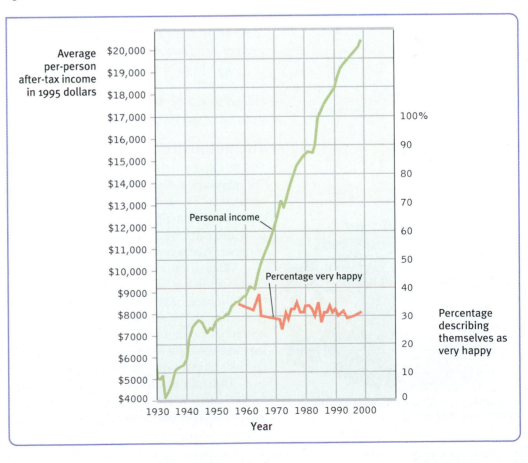

FIGURE 38.13

Values and life satisfaction
Among college and university students worldwide, those who report high life satisfaction give priority to love over money. (From Diener & Oishi, 2000.)

"This lovely car has not brought us happiness. You agree, Morris? That is why I am now thinking in terms of having the entire house recarpeted."

"No happiness lasts for long."

Seneca, *Agamemnon*, A.D. 60

"Shortly after I realized I had plenty, I realized there was plenty more."

than those in very poor countries, and yet the increasing real incomes have *not* produced increasing happiness. The findings lob a bombshell at modern materialism: *Economic growth in affluent countries has provided no apparent boost to morale or social well-being.*

A further bombshell comes from studies showing that individuals who strive most for wealth tend to live with a lower sense of well-being, a finding that "comes through very strongly in every culture I've looked at," reports Richard Ryan (1999). His collaborator, Tim Kasser (in press), concludes from their studies that those who instead strive for "intimacy, personal growth, and contribution to the community" experience a higher quality of life. Ryan and Kasser's research echoes an earlier finding by H. W. Perkins (1991): Among 800 college alumni surveyed, those with "Yuppie values"—preferring a high income and occupational success and prestige to having very close friends and a close marriage—were twice as likely as their former classmates to describe themselves as "fairly" or "very" *un*happy. A similar correlation appears among 7167 college students surveyed in 41 countries. Those who value love more than money report much higher satisfaction with life than do their money-hungry peers (**FIGURE 38.13**).

Two psychological principles explain why, for all but the very poor, more money buys no more than a temporary surge of happiness and why our emotions seem attached to elastic bands that pull us back from highs or lows. In its own way, each principle suggests that happiness is relative.

The Adaptation-Level Principle: Happiness Is Relative to Our Prior Experience

The **adaptation-level phenomenon** describes our tendency to judge various stimuli relative to those we have previously experienced. As psychologist Harry Helson explained, we adjust our "neutral" levels—the points at which sounds seem neither loud nor soft, temperatures neither hot nor cold, events neither pleasant nor unpleasant—based on our experience. We then notice and react to variations up or down from these levels.

Adaptation researcher Allen Parducci (1995) recalls a striking example: "On the Micronesian island of Ponope, which is almost on the equator, I was told of a bitter night back in 1915 when the temperature dropped to a record-breaking 69 degrees [Fahrenheit; 21 degrees Celsius]!" In the United States, Midwesterners, perhaps after watching too many "Baywatch" episodes, see sunny California as a happy place to live. But contrary to Midwesterners' intuitions, Californians—much as they may prefer their climate—are no happier (Schkade & Kahneman, 1998).

Thus, if our current condition—income, grade-point average, or social prestige, for example—increases, we feel an initial surge of pleasure. We then adapt to this new level of achievement, come to consider it as normal, and require something even better to give us another surge of happiness. From my childhood, I can recall the thrill of watching my family's first 12-inch, black-and-white television set. Now, if the color goes out on our 25-inch TV, I feel deprived. Having adapted upward, I perceive as negative what I once experienced as positive. The point to remember: Satisfaction and dissatisfaction, success and failure—all are relative to our recent experience. Satisfaction, as Richard Ryan (1999) says, "has a short half-life."

So, could we ever create a permanent social paradise? Donald Campbell (1975) answered no: If you woke up tomorrow to your utopia—perhaps a world with no bills, no ills, all A's, someone who loves you unreservedly—you would feel euphoric, for a time. But before long, you would soon recalibrate your adaptation level. Before long you would again sometimes feel gratified (when achievements surpass expectations), sometimes feel deprived (when they fall below), and sometimes feel neutral. That helps explain why, despite the realities of triumph and tragedy, million-dollar lottery winners and people who are paralyzed report roughly similar levels of happiness. It also explains why material wants can be insatiable—why many a child "needs" just one more Nintendo game. Or why Imelda Marcos, surrounded by poverty while living in splendor as wife of the Philippines' president, bought 1060 pairs of shoes. When the victor belongs to the spoils and the possessor is possessed by possessions, adaptation level has run amuck.

Seeking happiness through material achievement requires an ever-increasing abundance of things. At the end of his *Chronicles of Narnia*, C. S. Lewis depicts heaven as a place where good things do continually increase, where life is a never-ending story "in which every chapter is better than the one before." Here on Earth the unavoidable ups and downs of real life preclude a perpetual high.

The Relative Deprivation Principle: Happiness Is Relative to Others' Attainments

Happiness is relative not only to our past experience but also to our comparisons with others. We are always comparing ourselves with others. And whether we feel good or bad depends on who those others are. We are slow-witted or clumsy only when others are smart or agile.

An example: To explain the frustration expressed by U.S. Air Corps soldiers during World War II, researchers formulated the concept of **relative deprivation**—the sense that we are worse off than others with whom we compare ourselves. Despite a relatively rapid promotion rate for the group, many soldiers were frustrated about their own promotion rates (Merton & Kitt, 1950). Apparently, seeing so many others being promoted inflated the soldiers' expectations. And when expectations soar above attainments, the result is disappointment. When the Oakland Athletics signed baseball outfielder Jose Canseco to a $4.7 million annual salary, his fellow outfielder Rickey Henderson became openly dissatisfied with his $3 million salary and refused to show up on time for spring training (King, 1991).

Such comparisons help us understand why the middle- and upper-income people in a given country, who can compare themselves with the relatively poor, tend to be slightly more satisfied with life than their less fortunate compatriots. Nevertheless, once people reach a moderate income level, further increases do little to increase their happiness. Why? Because as people climb the ladder of success they mostly compare themselves with peers who are at or above their current level (Gruder, 1977; Suls & Tesch, 1978). For Rickey Henderson, Jose Canseco was the standard of comparison. For average people, athletes' salaries are emotionally irrelevant. "Beggars do not envy millionaires, though of course they will envy other beggars who are more successful," noted Bertrand Russell (1930, p. 90). Thus, "Napoleon envied Caesar, Caesar envied Alexander, and Alexander, I daresay, envied Hercules, who never existed. You cannot, therefore, get away from envy by

> "Continued pleasures wear off. . . . Pleasure is always contingent upon change and disappears with continuous satisfaction."
>
> **Dutch psychologist Nico Frijda (1988)**

> "I have also learned why people work so hard to succeed: It is because they envy the things their neighbors have. But it is useless. It is like chasing the wind. . . . It is better to have only a little, with peace of mind, than be busy all the time with both hands, trying to catch the wind."
>
> **Ecclesiastes 4:4,6**

> "Our poverty became a reality. Not because of our having less, but by our neighbors having more."
>
> **Will Campbell, *Brother to a Dragonfly*, 1977**

■ **adaptation-level phenomenon** our tendency to form judgments (of sounds, of lights, of income) relative to a "neutral" level defined by our prior experience.

■ **relative deprivation** the perception that one is worse off relative to those with whom one compares oneself.

CLOSE-UP:

OPPONENT-PROCESS THEORY OF EMOTION

The adaptation-level phenomenon helps explain why, in the long run, our emotional ups and downs tend to balance. University of Pennsylvania psychologist Richard Solomon (1980) showed that emotions balance in the short run as well, and he developed a theory to explain why. Solomon was intrigued by the emotional price tag that so often follows pleasure and by the emotional dividends that can compensate for past suffering. For the pleasure of a drug high, one pays the price of discomfort when the drug wears off. For the pain of hard exercise or a hot sauna bath, one afterward receives the dividend of a pleasurable feeling of well-being.

Solomon proposed, with support from laboratory studies of human and animal emotions, that *every emotion triggers an opposing emotion*. He called this the *opponent-process theory* of emotion. Imagine that you are about to take your first parachute jump. Solomon said that the primary emotion you experience before the jump—fear—triggers an opposing emotion—elation—as you land. Once the opposing emotion activates, perhaps to keep the initial emotion under control, you experience a diminishing of the initial emotion's intensity. This happens because you experience the primary emotion minus the opposing emotion. As the primary emotion subsides, the opposing emotion lingers a while. After parachutists survive their first free-fall, which for many is a terrifying experience, the fear switches off and they feel elated. For some women, the pain and fear of labor and childbirth may enhance a sense of euphoric relief afterward.

Repetitions of the emotion-arousing event strengthen the opposing emotion. Thus, the primary emotional experience, such as the pleasure derived from drug use or the fear aroused by parachuting, diminishes. This helps explain drug tolerance: With repetition, the initial high lessens.

With repetition, the afterreaction, such as the pain of drug withdrawal, remains strong or becomes stronger. This helps explain both drug hangovers (the opponent feelings that knock down the initial pleasure and linger afterward) and drug addiction (the craving for more of the drug to switch off the pain of withdrawal).

As Solomon noted, opponent-process theory and the research that supports it are good news for puritans and bad news for hedonists: Those who seek pleasure pay for it later. With every kick comes a kickback, and with repetition even pleasure will lose much of its intensity. "Take what you want," says an old Spanish saying. "Take it, and pay for it." But those who suffer will receive some reward. With most pain comes a gain.

Looking over the whole of psychology, we can see a deep principle emerging: Human nature is a battlefield of opposing tendencies. Our sympathetic and parasympathetic nervous systems, our neural balance between excitation and inhibition, our endorphin responses to pain, our opponent neural processes that create color and negative afterimages, our regulation of hunger and satiety, and our experiences of pleasure and misery—all involve carefully negotiated truces between opposing forces.

"I wish I came in first more often."

Michael Jordan, *Newsweek*, February 17, 1992

The effect of comparison with others helps explain why students of a given level of academic ability tend to have a higher academic self-concept if they attend a school where most other students are not exceptionally able (Marsh & Parker, 1984). If you were near the top of your class in high school, you might feel inferior upon entering a college where everyone was near the top of their class.

means of success alone, for there will always be in history or legend some person even more successful than you are" (pp. 68–69).

By "counting our blessings" when we compare ourselves with those less fortunate, we can, however, increase our satisfaction. Just as comparing ourselves with those who are better off creates envy, so comparing ourselves with those less well off boosts our contentment. Marshall Dermer and his colleagues (1979) demonstrated this by asking University of Wisconsin-Milwaukee women to study others' deprivation and suffering. After viewing vivid depictions of how grim life was in Milwaukee in 1900, or after imagining and then writing about various personal tragedies, such as being burned and disfigured, the women expressed greater satisfaction with their own lives. Similarly, when mildly depressed people read about someone who is even more depressed, they feel somewhat better (Gibbons, 1986). "I cried because I had no shoes," states a Persian saying, "until I met a man who had no feet."

Predictors of Happiness

If, as the adaptation-level phenomenon implies, our emotions tend to balance around normal, why do some people seem so filled with joy and others so gloomy day after day? What makes one person normally happy and another less so? Research re-

TABLE 38.1

HAPPINESS IS...

Researchers Have Found That Happy People Tend to	However, Happiness Seems Not Much Related to Other Factors, Such as
Have high self-esteem (in individualistic countries)	Age
Be optimistic, outgoing, and agreeable	Gender (women are more often depressed, but also more often joyful)
Have close friendships or a satisfying marriage	Education levels
Have work and leisure that engage their skills	Parenthood (having children or not)
Have a meaningful religious faith	Physical attractiveness
Sleep well and exercise	

Source: Summarized from DeNeve and Cooper (1998), Myers (1993, 2000), and Myers and Diener (1995, 1996).

veals several predictors of happiness (Table 38.1). Again, keep in mind that knowing that two variables correlate does not tell us whether one causes the other. For example, many studies indicate that religiously active people tend to report greater happiness and life satisfaction. Is happiness then conducive to faith? Or does faith enhance happiness?

Whether at work or leisure, most of us derive our greatest enjoyment from engaging, challenging activities. Mihaly Csikszentmihalyi (1990) and his colleagues discovered this after giving research volunteers a pager. When beeped, the people would note what they were doing and how they were feeling. Usually, they felt happier if mentally engaged by work or active leisure than if passively vegetating. Ironically, the less expensive a leisure activity is, the more absorbed and happy people often are while doing it. People are happier gardening than sitting on a power boat. They're happier when talking to friends than when watching TV. Happy, says Csikszentmihalyi, are those whose work and leisure absorb them, enabling them to "flow" unselfconsciously in focused activity.

Satisfying tasks and relationships affect our happiness, but always within the limits imposed by our genetic leash. From their study of 254 identical and fraternal twins, David Lykken and Auke Tellegen (1996) estimated that 50 percent of the difference among people's happiness ratings is heritable. Even identical twins raised apart are often similarly happy. Depending on our outlooks and recent experiences, our happiness fluctuates around our "happiness set point," which disposes some people to be ever upbeat, and others down. Our happiness, it seems, is like our cholesterol level—genetically influenced yet also influenced by factors under our control.

"I could cry when I think of the years I wasted accumulating money, only to learn that my cheerful disposition is genetic."

"The optimist is as often wrong as the pessimist, but far happier."

Anonymous

A recent study of 137 chimpanzees in zoos revealed that happiness in chimps, as in humans, is genetically influenced (Weiss & others, 1999).

REVIEW AND REFLECT:

Experiencing and Expressing Emotion

What physiological changes accompany emotions?

Emotions are psychological responses that involve physiological reactivity controlled by the autonomic nervous system and a positive or negative valence. Our performance on a task is usually best when arousal is moderate, though this varies with the difficulty of the task.

Do different emotions activate different physiological responses?

The physiological arousal that occurs with one emotion is, in most ways, indistinguishable from the arousal that occurs with another. However, scientists have discovered subtle differences in the brain pathways and hormones associated with different emotions.

Polygraphs measure several physiological indicators of emotion. They detect lies at a rate better than chance but not nearly well enough to justify their widespread use in business and government.

How do we communicate nonverbally?

Much of our communication is through the body's silent language. Psychologists have studied people's abilities to detect emotion, even from thin slices of behavior. High-tech equipment may enable researchers to make more precise linkages between emotions and facial muscles.

Are nonverbal expressions of emotions universally understood?

Although some gestures are culturally determined, facial expressions, such as those of happiness and fear, are common the world over. In communal cultures that value interdependence, intense displays of potentially disruptive emotions are infrequent.

Do our facial expressions influence our experienced emotions?

Expressions do more than communicate emotion. They also amplify the felt emotion and signal the body to respond accordingly.

What are the functions, causes, and consequences of fear?

Fear is an adaptive emotion, but it can be traumatic. Although we seem biologically predisposed to acquire some fears, what we learn through experience and observation best explains the variety of human fears.

What are the functions, causes, and consequences of anger?

Anger is most often evoked by events that not only are frustrating or insulting but also are interpreted as willful, unjustified, and avoidable. Blowing off steam may be temporarily calming, but in the long run it does not reduce anger. Expressing anger can actually cause more anger.

What are the functions, causes, and consequences of happiness?

A good mood boosts people's perceptions of the world and their willingness to help others. The moods triggered by the day's good or bad events seldom last beyond that day. Even significant good events, such as a substantial rise in income, seldom increase happiness for long. We can explain the relativity of happiness with the adaptation-level phenomenon and the relative deprivation principle. Nevertheless, some people are usually happier than others, and researchers have identified factors that predict such happiness.

Terms and Concepts to Remember

polygraph, p. 484
catharsis, p. 492
feel-good, do-good
  phenomenon, p. 494

subjective well-being, p. 494
adaptation-level phenomenon, p. 496
relative deprivation, p. 497

Test Yourself

38.1. Emotions such as fear and anger involve a general autonomic arousal that is orchestrated by the sympathetic nervous system. In many situations, arousal is adaptive. For example, with a challenging task, such as taking an exam, performance is likely to be best when arousal is
a. very high. c. low.
b. moderate. d. diminishing.

38.2. Although feelings of fear and anger involve a similar general autonomic arousal, they involve different brain areas. For example, stimulate one area of a cat's _____ and the cat draws back in terror; stimulate another area and the cat hisses with rage.
a. cortex c. reticular formation
b. hypothalamus d. limbic system

38.3. We can successfully interpret nonverbal threats and certain other silent messages regardless of the national origin of the sender. However, some nonverbal behaviors are *not* universal. People in different cultures are most likely to differ in their interpretations of
a. adults' facial expressions. c. smiles.
b. children's facial expressions. d. postures and gestures

38.4. When people are induced to assume fearful expressions, they will feel their heart rates increase. This suggests that the autonomic nervous system responds to
a. signals from the facial muscles.
b. conscious feelings of emotion.
c. physiological responses involved in deception.
d. electrical stimulation.

38.5 In some situations, venting anger–"blowing up"–seems to calm a person temporarily. In other cases, acting angry increases hostility. Experts suggest that to bring down anger, a good first step is to
a. retaliate verbally or physically.
b. wait or "simmer down."
c. express anger in action or fantasy.
d. review the grievance silently.

38.6 After graduating from college, you get a job and move into a large metropolitan city. At first, you find the street noise irritatingly loud, but after a while, it no longer bothers you, thus illustrating the
a. relative deprivation principle.
b. adaptation-level principle.
c. feel-good, do-good phenomenon.
d. catharsis principle.

38.7 A philosopher notes that one cannot escape envy by means of success alone: There will always be someone more successful, more accomplished, or richer with whom to compare oneself. In psychology this observation is embodied in the
a. relative deprivation principle.
b. adaptation-level principle.
c. list of predictors of happiness.
d. feel-good, do-good phenomenon.

38.8. When happy and unhappy people are compared, researchers find that happy people are optimistic, outgoing, and likely to have satisfying close relationships. One of the most consistent findings of psychological research is that happy people are also
a. more likely to express anger.
b. generally luckier than others.
c. concentrated in the wealthier nations.
d. more likely to help others.

38.9. Age, race, and gender seem not to be predictably related to subjective feelings of happiness or well-being. However, researchers have found that happy people tend to

a. have children.
b. score high on intelligence tests.
c. have a meaningful religious faith.
d. complete high school and some college education.

Review

- How would an evolutionary psychologist explain our autonomic nervous system's reaction (increased heart rate and respiration, tense muscles, slowed digestion, and so on) to an alarming situation?

- Who tends to express more emotion—men or women? How do we know the answer to that question?

- What things do (and don't) predict self-reported happiness?

Reflect

- Can you think of a recent time when you noticed your body's reactions to an emotionally charged situation, such as a difficult social setting or perhaps even a test or game you were worrying about in advance? Did you perceive the situation as a challenge or a threat? How well did you do as a result?

- Think of one situation in which you would like to change the way you feel, and create a simple plan for doing so. For instance, if you would like to feel more cheerful on your way to class tomorrow morning rather than dragging yourself there, you might try walking briskly—with head held high and a pleasant expression on your face.

- Does the new happiness research suggest any new priorities or behaviors that might enhance your own well-being?

Answers to the Test Yourself and Review questions can be found in the green appendix at the end of the book.

Personality

Novelist William Faulkner was a master at creating characters with vivid personalities.[1] One of his creations, Ike McCaslin, who appears at various ages in more than a dozen novels and short stories, is highly principled, and consistently so. At age 10 he feels a deep reverence for the wilderness and its creatures. At 21 he forfeits a "tainted" inheritance. In his late seventies he counsels his nephew to use his land responsibly. Ike the adult is clearly an extension of Ike the child.

Another Faulkner character, Jason Compson, is a selfish, whining 4-year-old at the beginning of *The Sound and the Fury*, and a selfish, screaming 34-year-old as the novel closes. As head of the Compson household, he verbally abuses family members and household servants. Lying, threatening, conniving, he was a self-centered child who became a self-centered adult.

Faulkner's characters, as they appear and reappear throughout his fiction, exhibit the distinctiveness and consistency that define personality. Psychology often emphasizes our similarity—how we all develop, perceive, learn, remember, think, and feel. To study personality is to study our individuality. Your individual *personality* is your characteristic pattern of thinking, feeling, and acting. If your behavior pattern is strikingly distinctive and consistent—if you are always outgoing, whether at a party or in a classroom—people are likely to say that you have a "strong" personality.

Personality is important to psychologists in many different realms: biological influences on personality; personality development across the life span; personality-related aspects of learning, motivation, and emotion; disorders of personality; personality's influence on health; social influences on personality.

These modules explore and evaluate four major perspectives on personality:

+ Sigmund Freud's *psychoanalytic* theory, which proposes that childhood sexuality and unconscious motivations influence personality (Module 39).
+ The *trait* perspective, in which researchers identify personality dimensions that account for our consistent behavior patterns (Module 40).
+ The *humanistic* approach, which focuses on our inner capacities for growth and self-fulfillment (Module 41).
+ The *social-cognitive* approach, which emphasizes how we shape and are shaped by our environment (Module 42).

"There is no man who is not, at each moment, what he has been and what he will be."

Oscar Wilde, 1854–1900

[1] Faulkner scholar Nancy Nicodemus assisted with these examples.

39 The Psychoanalytic Perspective

Sigmund Freud, 1856–1939
"I was the only worker in a new field."

Ask 100 people on the street to name a notable deceased psychologist, suggests Keith Stanovich (1996, p. 1), and "Sigmund Freud would be the winner hands down." Freud's current influence in psychological science has diminished (Robins & others, 1999). But his influence lingers in literary and film interpretation, psychiatry, and pop psychology . . . and Woody Allen movies. So, who was Freud, and what did he teach?

Well before entering the University of Vienna in 1873, a youthful Sigmund Freud showed signs of independence and brilliance. He had a prodigious memory and so loved reading plays, poetry, and philosophy that he once ran up a bookstore debt beyond his means. As a teen he often took his evening meal in his tiny bedroom in order to lose no time from his studies.

Freud went to medical school and after graduation set up a private practice, specializing in nervous disorders. Before long, however, he faced patients whose disorders made no neurological sense. For example, a patient might have lost all feeling in a hand—yet there is no sensory nerve that, if damaged, would numb the entire hand and nothing else. Freud's search for a cause for such disorders set his mind running in a direction destined to change human self-understanding. His views, which evolved as he treated patients and analyzed himself, eventually filled 24 volumes published between 1888 and 1939. Following his first solo book, *The Interpretation of Dreams* (1900), his ideas gradually began to attract both dedicated followers and intense criticism. Love his ideas or not, "Freud has left an important—and I believe indelible—mark on human self-understanding," observes Drew Westen (1998). For now, let's reserve judgment on Freud's theory and instead try to see things as he did. It is impossible to summarize 24 volumes in these few pages, but we can highlight Freud's psychoanalytic theory—the first comprehensive theory of **personality**.

- **personality** an individual's characteristic pattern of thinking, feeling, and acting.

- **free association** in psychoanalysis, a method of exploring the unconscious in which the person relaxes and says whatever comes to mind, no matter how trivial or embarrassing.

- **psychoanalysis** Freud's theory of personality that attributes our thoughts and actions to unconscious motives and conflicts; the techniques used in treating psychological disorders by seeking to expose and interpret unconscious tensions.

- **unconscious** according to Freud, a reservoir of mostly unacceptable thoughts, wishes, feelings, and memories. According to contemporary psychologists, information processing of which we are unaware.

- **preconscious** information that is not conscious but is retrievable into conscious awareness.

Exploring the Unconscious

Preview Question: What was Freud's view of human personality and its development and dynamics?

Freud wondered whether some neurological disorders might have psychological rather than physiological causes. To explore this possibility, he spent several months in Paris studying with a neurologist who was using hypnosis to treat patients. On returning to Vienna, Freud began to hypnotize his patients, encouraging them while hypnotized to talk freely about themselves and the circumstances surrounding the onset of their symptoms. The patients often responded openly, at times becoming quite agitated during the hypnotic experience. Sometimes their symptoms diminished or even disappeared.

While experimenting with hypnosis, Freud "discovered" the unconscious. Piecing together his patients' accounts of their lives, he decided that the loss of feeling in one's hand might be caused by a fear of touching one's genitals; that blindness or deafness might be caused by not wanting to see or hear something that aroused intense anxiety. Given his patients' uneven capacity for hypnosis, he turned to **free association**—in which he merely told the patient to relax and say whatever came to mind, no matter how embarrassing or trivial. Freud seemed to assume that a line of mental dominoes had fallen from his patients' distant past to their troubled present. Free association, he believed, allowed him to trace that line back, producing a chain of thought leading into the patient's unconscious, thereby retrieving and releasing

Freud's office was rich with antiquities from around the world, including artwork related to his ideas about unconscious motives. His famous couch, piled high with pillows, placed patients in a comfortable reclining position facing away from him to help them focus inward.

painful unconscious memories, often from childhood. Freud called his theory and associated techniques **psychoanalysis**.

Underlying Freud's psychoanalytic conception of personality was his belief that the mind is like an iceberg—mostly hidden. Our conscious awareness is the part of the iceberg that floats above the surface. Below the surface is the much larger, **unconscious** region containing thoughts, wishes, feelings, and memories, of which we are largely unaware. Some of these thoughts we store temporarily in a **preconscious** area, from which we can retrieve them into conscious awareness. Of greater interest to Freud was the mass of unacceptable passions and thoughts that he believed we *repress*, or forcibly block from our consciousness because they would be too unsettling to acknowledge. Freud believed that, although we are not consciously aware of them, these troublesome feelings and ideas powerfully influence us. In his view, our unacknowledged impulses express themselves in disguised forms—the work we choose, the beliefs we hold, our daily habits, our troubling symptoms. In such ways, the unconscious seeps into our thoughts and actions.

For Freud the determinist, nothing was ever accidental. He believed he could glimpse the seepage of the unconscious not only in people's free associations, beliefs, habits, and symptoms but also in their dreams and slips of the tongue and pen. He illustrated with a financially stressed patient who, not wanting any large pills, said, "Please do not give me any bills, because I cannot swallow them." Similarly, Freud viewed jokes as expressions of repressed sexual and aggressive tendencies, and dreams as the "royal road to the unconscious." The remembered content of dreams (their *manifest content*) he believed to be a censored expression of the dreamer's unconscious wishes (the dream's *latent content*). By analyzing people's dreams, Freud believed, he could reveal the nature of their inner conflicts and release their inner tensions.

"Good morning, beheaded—uh, I mean beloved."

Personality Structure

In Freud's view, human personality—including its emotions and strivings—arises from a conflict between our aggressive, pleasure-seeking biological impulses and the internalized social restraints against them. Personality is the result of our efforts to resolve this basic conflict—to express these impulses in ways that bring satisfaction without also bringing guilt or punishment.

"I remember your name perfectly but I just can't think of your face."

Oxford professor W. A. Spooner, 1844–1930, famous for his linguistic flip-flops ("spoonerisms"). Spooner rebuked one student for "fighting a liar in the quadrangle" and another who "hissed my mystery lecture," adding "You have tasted two worms."

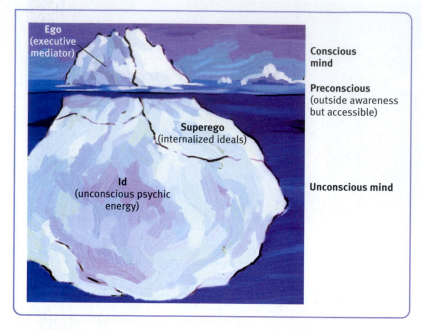

FIGURE 39.1

Freud's idea of the mind's structure
Consciousness is like an iceberg's visible tip. Note that the id is totally unconscious, but ego and superego operate both consciously and unconsciously. (Adapted from Freud, 1933, page 111.)

Freud theorized that the conflict centers on three interacting systems: id, ego, and superego (**FIGURE 39.1**). These abstract psychological concepts are, said Freud, "useful aids to understanding" the mind's dynamics.

The **id** has a reservoir of unconscious psychic energy constantly striving to satisfy basic drives to survive, reproduce, and aggress. The id operates on the *pleasure principle*: If not constrained by reality, it seeks immediate gratification. Think of newborn infants. Governed by the id, they cry out for satisfaction the moment they feel a need, caring nothing for the outside world's conditions and demands.

As the **ego** develops, the young child learns to cope with the real world. The ego, operating on the *reality principle*, seeks to gratify the id's impulses in realistic ways that will bring long-term pleasure rather than pain or destruction. (Imagine what would happen if, lacking an ego, we expressed our unrestrained sexual or aggressive impulses whenever we felt them.) The ego contains our partly conscious perceptions, thoughts, judgments, and memories, making it the personality "executive," mediating the impulsive demands of the id, the restraining demands of the superego, and the real-life demands of the external world.

Beginning around age 4 or 5, Freud theorized, a child's ego recognizes the demands of the newly emerging **superego**, the voice of conscience that forces the ego to consider not only the real but the ideal, and that focuses solely on how one *ought* to behave. The superego strives for perfection, judging actions and producing positive feelings of pride or negative feelings of guilt. Someone with an exceptionally strong superego may be virtuous yet, ironically, guilt-ridden; another with a weak superego may be wantonly self-indulgent and remorseless. Because the superego's demands often oppose the id's, the ego struggles to reconcile the two. The chaste student who is sexually attracted to someone may satisfy both id and superego by joining a volunteer organization to which the desired person belongs.

Personality Development

Analysis of his patients' histories convinced Freud that personality forms during life's first few years. Again and again his patients' symptoms seemed rooted in unresolved conflicts from early childhood. He concluded that children pass through a series of **psychosexual stages** during which the id's pleasure-seeking energies focus on distinct pleasure-sensitive areas of the body called *erogenous zones* (Table 39.1).

"Fifty is plenty."   "Hundred and fifty."

TABLE 39.1

FREUD'S PSYCHOSEXUAL STAGES

Stage	Focus
Oral (0–18 months)	Pleasure centers on the mouth—sucking, biting, chewing
Anal (18–36 months)	Pleasure focuses on bowel and bladder elimination; coping with demands for control
Phallic (3–6 years)	Pleasure zone is the genitals; coping with incestuous sexual feelings
Latency (6 to puberty)	Dormant sexual feelings
Genital (puberty on)	Maturation of sexual interests

During the *oral stage*, which lasts throughout the first 18 months, the infant's sensual pleasures focus on sucking, biting, and chewing.

During the *anal stage*, from about 18 months to 3 years, the sphincter muscles become sensitive and controllable, and bowel and bladder retention and elimination become a source of gratification.

During the *phallic stage*, from roughly 3 to 6 years, the pleasure zone shifts to the genitals. Freud believed that during this stage boys seek genital stimulation and develop both unconscious sexual desires for their mother and jealousy and hatred for their father, whom they consider a rival. Given these feelings, boys would also feel guilt and a lurking fear of punishment, perhaps by castration, from their father. Freud called this collection of feelings the **Oedipus complex** after the Greek legend of Oedipus, who unknowingly killed his father and married his mother. Although some psychoanalysts believed that girls experience a parallel *Electra complex*, Freud (1931, p. 229) said no: "It is only in the male child that we find the fateful combination of love for the one parent and simultaneous hatred for the other as a rival."

Children eventually cope with threatening feelings, said Freud, by repressing them and by identifying with (trying to become like) the rival parent. It's as though something inside the child decides, "If you can't beat 'em (the parent of the same sex), join 'em." Through this **identification** process, children's superegos gain strength as they incorporate many of their parents' values. Freud believed that identification with the same-sex parent provides what we now call our *gender identity*—our sense of being male or female.

With their sexual feelings repressed and redirected, children enter a *latency stage*. Freud maintained that during latency, extending from around age 6 to puberty, sexuality is dormant and children play mostly with peers of the same sex.

At puberty, latency gives way to the final stage, the *genital stage*, as the person begins to experience sexual feelings toward others.

In Freud's view, maladaptive behavior in the adult results from conflicts unresolved during earlier psychosexual stages. At any point in the oral, anal, or phallic stage, strong conflict can lock, or **fixate**, the person's pleasure-seeking energies in that stage. For example, people who were either orally overindulged or deprived (perhaps by abrupt, early weaning) might fixate at the oral stage. Orally fixated adults are said to exhibit either passive dependence (like that of a nursing infant) or an exaggerated denial of this dependence—perhaps by acting tough and uttering biting sarcasm. Or they might continue to seek oral gratification by excessively smoking and eating. Similarly, those who never quite resolve the anal conflict between the desire to eliminate at will and the demands of toilet training may be messy and disorganized (*anal expulsive*) or highly controlled and compulsively neat (*anal retentive*). In such ways, believed Freud, the twig of personality is bent at an early age.

"Oh, for goodness' sake! Smoke!"

Identification

Freud believed that children cope with threatening feelings of competition with their same-sex parent by identifying with that parent.

- **id** contains a reservoir of unconscious psychic energy that, according to Freud, strives to satisfy basic sexual and aggressive drives. The id operates on the pleasure principle, demanding immediate gratification.

- **ego** the largely conscious, "executive" part of personality that, according to Freud, mediates among the demands of the id, superego, and reality. The ego operates on the *reality principle*, satisfying the id's desires in ways that will realistically bring pleasure rather than pain.

- **superego** the part of personality that, according to Freud, represents internalized ideals and provides standards for judgment (the conscience) and for future aspirations.

- **psychosexual stages** the childhood stages of development (oral, anal, phallic, latency, genital) during which, according to Freud, the id's pleasure-seeking energies focus on distinct erogenous zones.

- **Oedipus [ED-uh-puss] complex** according to Freud, a boy's sexual desires toward his mother and feelings of jealousy and hatred for the rival father.

- **identification** the process by which, according to Freud, children incorporate their parents' values into their developing superegos.

- **fixation** according to Freud, a lingering focus of pleasure-seeking energies at an earlier psychosexual stage, where conflicts were unresolved.

- **defense mechanisms** in psychoanalytic theory, the ego's protective methods of reducing anxiety by unconsciously distorting reality.

- **repression** in psychoanalytic theory, the basic defense mechanism that banishes anxiety-arousing thoughts, feelings, and memories from consciousness.

- **regression** defense mechanism in which an individual faced with anxiety retreats to a more infantile psychosexual stage, where some psychic energy remains fixated.

- **reaction formation** defense mechanism by which the ego unconsciously switches unacceptable impulses into their opposites. Thus, people may express feelings that are the opposite of their anxiety-arousing unconscious feelings.

- **projection** defense mechanism by which people disguise their own threatening impulses by attributing them to others.

"The lady doth protest too much, methinks."

William Shakespeare, *Hamlet*, 1600

Defense Mechanisms

To live in social groups, we cannot spontaneously act out our sexual and aggressive impulses willy-nilly. We must control them. When the ego fears losing control of the inner war between the demands of the id and the superego, the result is a dark cloud of unfocused anxiety. Anxiety, said Freud, is the price we pay for civilization. Anxiety is hard to cope with, as when we feel unsettled but are unsure why. Freud proposed that the ego protects itself against anxiety with **defense mechanisms**. These reduce or redirect anxiety in various ways, all of them distorting reality. Some examples:

Repression banishes anxiety-arousing thoughts and feelings from consciousness. According to Freud, *repression underlies all the other defense mechanisms*, each of which disguises threatening impulses and keeps them from reaching consciousness. Freud believed that repression explains why we do not remember our childhood lust for our parent of the other sex. However, he also believed that repression is often incomplete, that repressed urges seep out in dream symbols and slips of the tongue.

We also cope with anxiety through **regression**—retreating to an earlier, more infantile stage of development. Thus, when facing the anxious first days of school, a child may regress to the oral comfort of thumb-sucking. Juvenile monkeys, when anxious, retreat to infantile clinging to their mothers or to one another (Suomi, 1987). Even homesick new college students may long for the security and comfort of home.

In **reaction formation**, the ego unconsciously makes unacceptable impulses look like their opposites. En route to consciousness, the unacceptable proposition "I hate him" becomes "I love him." Timidity becomes daring. Feelings of inadequacy become bravado.

Projection disguises threatening impulses by attributing them to others. Thus, "He doesn't trust me" may be a projection of the actual feeling "I don't trust him" or "I don't trust myself." An El Salvadoran saying captures the idea: "The thief thinks everyone else is a thief."

The familiar mechanism of **rationalization** occurs when we unconsciously generate self-justifying explanations in order to hide from ourselves the real reasons for our actions. Thus, habitual drinkers may say they drink with their friends "just to be sociable." Students who fail to study may rationalize, "All work and no play makes Jack [or Jill] a dull person."

Displacement diverts one's sexual or aggressive impulses toward an object or person that is psychologically more acceptable than the one that aroused the feelings. Children who fear expressing anger against their parents may displace it by kicking the family pet. Students upset over an exam may snap at a roommate.

Sublimation is the transformation of unacceptable impulses into socially valued motivations. Freud suggested that Leonardo da Vinci's paintings of Madonnas were a sublimation of his longing for intimacy with his mother, who was separated from him at an early age.

Note that all these defense mechanisms function indirectly and unconsciously, reducing anxiety by disguising our threatening impulses. We would never say, "I'm feeling anxious; I'd better project my sexual or hostile feelings onto someone else." Defense mechanisms would not work if we recognized them. Just as the body unconsciously defends itself against disease, so also, believed Freud, does the ego unconsciously defend itself against anxiety.

Regression

Faced with a mild stress, children and young monkeys will regress, retreating to the comfort of earlier behaviors.

Assessing the Unconscious

Preview Question: What are projective tests, and what do clinicians in the Freudian tradition hope to learn from them?

Those who study personality or provide therapy need ways to evaluate personality characteristics. As a result, different personality theories have developed different methods of assessment.

Freud's theory maintains that the significant influences on our personalities arise from the unconscious, which contains residues from early childhood experiences. The interpretation of dreams, he said, provides the road into the unconscious mind. Psychoanalysts therefore dismiss objective assessment tools, such as agree-disagree or true-false questionnaires, as merely tapping the conscious surface. Their tool of choice would be a sort of psychological x-ray—a test that sees through our surface pretensions and reveals our hidden conflicts and impulses.

Projective tests aim to provide such a view by presenting an ambiguous stimulus and then asking test-takers to describe it or tell a story about it. The stimulus has no inherent significance, so any meaning people read into it presumably is a projection of their interests and conflicts. Henry Murray (1933) demonstrated a possible basis for such a test at a party hosted by his 11-year-old daughter. Murray engaged the children in a frightening game called "Murder." When shown some photographs after the game, the children perceived the photos as more malicious than they had before the game. These children, it seemed to Murray, had *projected* their inner feelings into the pictures.

A few years later, Murray introduced the **Thematic Apperception Test (TAT)**—a test in which people view ambiguous pictures and then make up stories about them. One use of storytelling has been to assess achievement motivation. Shown a daydreaming boy, those who imagine he is fantasizing about an achievement are presumed to be projecting their own goals. "As a rule," said Murray, "the subject leaves the test happily unaware that he has presented the psychologist with what amounts to an x-ray of his inner self" (quoted by Talbot, 1999).

Various projective tests ask test-takers to draw a person, to complete sentences ("My mother. . . ."), or to provide the first word that comes to mind after the examiner says a test word. Most widely used is the famous **Rorschach inkblot test**, introduced in 1921 by Swiss psychiatrist Hermann Rorschach [ROAR-shock]. The test assumes that what we see in its 10 inkblots reflects our inner feelings and conflicts. If we see predatory animals or weapons, the examiner may infer we have aggressive tendencies.

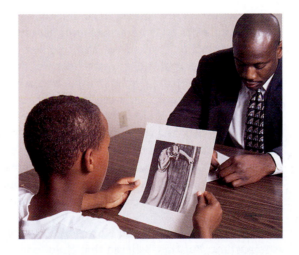

Is this reasonable? If so, can a psychologist use the Rorschach to understand one's personality and diagnose an emotional disorder? The two primary criteria of a good test are *reliability* (consistency of results) and *validity* (predicting what it's supposed to). On those criteria, how good is the Rorschach?

The "almost universal agreement among the scientific community" is that it is not very good (Sechrest & others, 1998). No one accepted system for scoring and interpreting the test has been developed. If two raters were not trained in the same scoring system, their agreement on the results of any given test would be minimal. Nor

■ **rationalization** defense mechanism that offers self-justifying explanations in place of the real, more threatening, unconscious reasons for one's actions.

■ **displacement** defense mechanism that shifts sexual or aggressive impulses toward a more acceptable or less threatening object or person, as when redirecting anger toward a safer outlet.

■ **sublimation** in psychoanalytic theory, the defense mechanism by which people rechannel their unacceptable impulses into socially approved activities.

■ **projective test** a personality test, such as the Rorschach or TAT, that provides ambiguous stimuli designed to trigger projection of one's inner dynamics.

■ **Thematic Apperception Test (TAT)** a projective test in which people express their inner feelings and interests through the stories they make up about ambiguous scenes.

■ **Rorschach inkblot test** the most widely used projective test, a set of 10 inkblots, designed by Hermann Rorschach; seeks to identify people's inner feelings by analyzing their interpretations of the blots.

The TAT

This psychologist presumes that the hopes, fears, and interests expressed in this boy's descriptions of a series of ambiguous pictures in the Thematic Apperception Test (TAT) are projections of his inner feelings.

"If a professional psychologist is 'evaluating' you in a situation in which you are at risk and asks you for responses to ink blots . . . walk out of that psychologist's office."

Robyn Dawes, *House of Cards: Psychology and Psychotherapy Based on Myth*, 1994

has the test been very successful at predicting behavior or at discriminating between groups (for example, identifying who is suicidal and who is not). The Rorschach is not an emotional MRI.

With all the criticisms, the Rorschach remains "simultaneously, the most cherished and the most reviled of all psychological assessment tools" (Hunsley & Bailey, 1999). Some clinicians remain confident of the test's validity—not as a device that by itself can provide a diagnosis, but as a source of suggestive leads that supplement other information. Other clinicians use the test as an icebreaker and a revealing interview technique. There is even a research-based, computer-aided scoring and interpretation tool that aims to improve agreement among raters and enhance the test's validity (Erdberg, 1990; Exner, 1993). But the evidence is insufficient to satisfy critics, who still find "no scientific basis for justifying the use of Rorschach scales in psychological assessments" (Hunsley & Bailey, 1999). Freud himself probably would have been uncomfortable with trying to assign each patient a test score and more interested in the therapist–patient interactions that take place during the test.

The Rorschach test
In this projective test, people tell what they see in a series of symmetrical inkblots. Some who use this test are confident that the interpretation of ambiguous stimuli will reveal unconscious aspects of the test-taker's personality. Others use it as an icebreaker or to supplement other information.

Evaluating the Psychoanalytic Perspective

Preview Questions: Which of Freud's ideas did his followers accept or reject? How do Freud's ideas hold up today?

Freud's Early Descendants and Dissenters

Freud's writings were controversial, but they soon attracted followers, mostly young, ambitious physicians who formed an inner circle around their strong-minded leader. From time to time sparks flew, and one member or another would leave or be cast out. Even the ideas of the outcasts, however, reflected Freud's influence.

These pioneering psychoanalysts and others, whom we now call *neo-Freudians*, accepted Freud's basic ideas: the personality structures of id, ego, and superego; the importance of the unconscious; the shaping of personality in childhood; and the dynamics of anxiety and the defense mechanisms. But they did veer away from Freud in two important ways: They placed more emphasis on the role of the conscious mind both in interpreting experience and in coping with the environment. And they doubted that sex and aggression were all-consuming motivations. Instead, they placed more emphasis on loftier motives and on social interaction. The following examples illustrate.

Alfred Adler and Karen Horney [HORN-eye] agreed with Freud that childhood is important. But they believed that childhood *social*, not sexual, tensions are crucial for personality formation. Adler, who himself struggled to overcome childhood illnesses and accidents, said that much of our behavior is driven by efforts to conquer childhood feelings of inferiority, feelings that trigger our strivings for superiority and power. (Adler proposed the still-popular idea of the "inferiority complex.") Horney said childhood anxiety, caused by the dependent child's sense of helplessness, triggers our desire for love and security. Horney countered Freud's assumptions that women have weak superegos and suffer "penis envy," and she attempted to balance the bias she detected in this masculine view of psychology.

Alfred Adler
"The individual feels at home in life and feels his existence to be worthwhile just so far as he is useful to others and is overcoming feelings of inferiority" (*Problems of Neurosis*, 1964).

"The female . . . acknowledges the fact of her castration, and with it, too, the superiority of the male and her own inferiority; but she rebels against this unwelcome state of affairs."

Sigmund Freud, *Female Sexuality*, 1931

Karen Horney

"The view that women are infantile and emotional creatures, and as such, incapable of responsibility and independence is the work of the masculine tendency to lower women's self-respect" (*Feminine Psychology*, 1932).

Carl Jung

"We can keep from a child all knowledge of earlier myths, but we cannot take from him the need for mythology" (*Symbols of Transformation*, 1912).

Unlike other neo-Freudians, Carl Jung—Freud's disciple-turned-dissenter—placed less emphasis on social factors and agreed with Freud that the unconscious exerts a powerful influence. But to Jung (pronounced Yoong), the unconscious contains more than our repressed thoughts and feelings. He believed we also have a **collective unconscious**, a common reservoir of images derived from our species' universal experiences. Jung said that the collective unconscious explains why, for many people, spiritual concerns are deeply rooted and why people in different cultures share certain myths and images, such as mother as a symbol of nurturance. (Today's psychologists discount the idea of inherited experiences. But many do believe that our shared evolutionary history shaped some universal dispositions.)

Freud died in 1939. Since then some of his ideas have been incorporated into *psychodynamic theory*. "Most contemporary dynamic theorists and therapists are not wedded to the idea that sex is the basis of personality," notes Drew Westen (1996). They "do not talk about ids and egos, and do not go around classifying their patients as oral, anal, or phallic characters." What they do assume, with Freud, is that much of our mental life is unconscious, that childhood shapes our personalities and ways of becoming attached to others, and that we often struggle with inner conflicts among our wishes, fears, and values.

© 1983 by Sidney Harris; American Scientist Magazine.

"The forward thrust of the antlers shows a determined personality, yet the small sun indicates a lack of self-confidence. . . ."

Freud's Ideas in the Light of Modern Research

We can also critique Freud from the perspective of the beginning of the twenty-first century, a perspective that is itself subject to revision. Freud did not have access to all that we have since learned about human development, thinking, and emotion. Thus, say Freud's admirers, to criticize his theories by comparing them with current concepts is like comparing Henry Ford's Model T with today's Taurus. To Freud's critics, however, his ideas are psychology's historical equivalent of astronomy's flat-earth theory.

Both admirers and critics could agree that recent research contradicts many of Freud's specific ideas. Today's developmental psychologists see our development as lifelong, not fixed in childhood. They doubt that infants' neural networks are mature enough to sustain as much emotional trauma as Freud assumed. Some think Freud overestimated parental influence and underestimated peer influence (and abuse). They also question Freud's idea that conscience and gender identity form as the child resolves the Oedipus complex at age 5 or 6. We gain our gender identity earlier and become strongly masculine or feminine even without a same-sex parent present (Frieze & others, 1978). Freud's ideas about childhood sexuality arose from his rejection of stories of childhood sexual abuse told by his female patients—stories that some scholars believe he suggested or coerced and then attributed to their own

"Many aspects of Freudian theory are indeed out of date, and they should be: Freud died in 1939, and he has been slow to undertake further revisions."

Psychologist Drew Westen (1998)

■ **collective unconscious** Carl Jung's concept of a shared, inherited reservoir of memory traces from our species' history.

"Studies have begun to converge toward a verdict . . . : there is literally nothing to be said [for] the entire Freudian system."

Frederick Crews (1996)

childhood sexual wishes and conflicts (Powell & Boer, 1994). Today, we understand how Freud's questioning might have created false memories, and we also know that childhood sexual abuse does happen. Freud's ideas about the natural superiority of men have been thoroughly discounted.

New ideas about why we dream—to consolidate memories, or to make sense of random neural activity, for example—dispute Freud's belief that dreams disguise and fulfill wishes. And slips of the tongue can be explained as competition between similar verbal choices in our memory network. Someone who says "I don't want to do that—it's a lot of brothel" may simply be blending *bother* and *trouble* (Foss & Hakes, 1978). Researchers find little support for Freud's idea that defense mechanisms disguise sexual and aggressive impulses (though our cognitive gymnastics do work to protect our self-esteem). And Jerome Kagan (1989b) notes that history does not support another of Freud's ideas—that sexual repression causes psychological disorder. From Freud's time to ours, sexual repression has diminished; psychological disorders have not.

Is Repression a Myth?

Sigmund Freud's entire psychoanalytic theory rests on his assumption that the human mind often *represses* painful experiences, banishing them into the unconscious. Freud and his followers thought if we could somehow uncover our past experiences, we would find them intact, like long-lost books in a dusty attic. Recover and resolve the painful repressed memories of our childhood and emotional healing would follow. Under Freud's influence, repression has been used to explain hypnotic phenomena, psychological disorders, and apparent lost and recovered memories of childhood traumas (Chert, 1998). It became one of popular psychology's most widely accepted concepts. In one survey, 88 percent of university students believed that painful experiences commonly get pushed out of awareness and into the unconscious (Garry & others, 1994).

Actually, contend many of today's researchers, repression, if it ever occurs, is a rare mental response to terrible trauma. "Repression folklore is . . . partly refuted, partly untested, and partly untestable," says Elizabeth Loftus (1995). Consider: If the human mind indeed commonly banishes painful experiences, how do we explain these odd findings?

+ Shouldn't we expect children who have witnessed a parent's murder to repress the experience? A study of sixteen 5- to 10-year-old children who had this horrific experience found that not one repressed the memory (Malmquist, 1986).

+ Shouldn't survivors of Nazi death camps have banished the atrocities from consciousness? With rare exceptions they remember all too well—although many do benefit from disclosing and talking through their experiences (Helmreich, 1992, 1994; Pennebaker, 1990).

+ Shouldn't we expect children who have been terrorized while their school bus was hijacked or pinned down by sniper fire to repress the experience? In separate incidents every child remembered it (Pope & Hudson, 1995).

+ Shouldn't we expect victims and observers to black out the image of the horrific collapse of two hotel skywalks in which 114 died and more than 200 were injured? Not only do they recall it, nearly 90 percent later said they remembered it repeatedly (Wilkinson, 1983).

+ Shouldn't battle-scarred veterans suffer amnesia for their worst experiences? In one neurological unit in a British hospital, 35 percent of military patients arrived with amnesia after severe combat during World War II (Arrigo & Pezdek, 1997; Karon & Widener, 1997, 1998). But such cases often appear to be either concussion-related or a "false amnesia" tactic for escaping intolerable situations (Holmes, 1990, 1994). Folklore regarding recovered battlefield memories is either unconfirmed or related to therapists' use of suggestive techniques.

"Warning. Despite seventy years of research, there is no objective evidence to support the concept of repression."

Psychologist David S. Holmes (1994)

+ Shouldn't people who have kept a diary of everyday life events later recall negative events significantly less well than positive events? "The memory for the two types of events [is] almost the same," report Charles Thompson and his colleagues (1996).

There are exceptions—one death camp survivor reportedly forgot for over 30 years the snatching and shooting of her infant son (Kraft, 1996). Some researchers believe that extreme, prolonged stress, such as the stress some severely abused children experience, might disrupt memory by damaging the hippocampus (Schacter, 1996). But the far more common reality? High stress enhances memory, and negative emotional events are therefore remembered well (Christianson, 1992; Shobe & Kihlstrom, 1997). In fact, too well: Traumatic events, such as rape and torture, haunt survivors, who experience unwanted flashbacks. They are seared onto the soul.

After studying 400 hours of recollections by 120 witnesses to the Holocaust, psychologist Robert Kraft (1996) reported that "the nearly universal response is persistent, intrusive, extended, vivid memory for personally-experienced events." "You see the babies," said survivor Sally H. (1979). "You see the screaming mothers. You see hanging people. You sit and you see that face there. It's something you don't forget."

The Unconscious Mind

History has been kinder to Freud's "iceberg" view of the mind, at least in part. We now know that we indeed have limited access to all that goes on in our minds (Erdelyi, 1985, 1988; Kihlstrom, 1990; Lewicki & others, 1992). As Freud supposed, mental processes can operate in parallel and sometimes opposing ways. Our thoughts and emotions are sometimes out of sync.

However, the "iceberg" notion held by today's research psychologists differs from Freud's—so much so, argues Anthony Greenwald (1992), that it is time to abandon Freud's view of the unconscious. Many researchers think of the unconscious not as seething passions and repressive censoring but as cooler information processing that occurs without our awareness. To them, the unconscious involves

+ the schemas that automatically control our perceptions and interpretations.
+ the priming by stimuli to which we have not consciously attended.
+ the right-hemisphere activity that enables the split-brain patient's left hand to carry out an instruction the patient cannot verbalize.
+ the parallel processing of different aspects of vision and thinking.
+ the implicit memories that operate without conscious recall, even among those with amnesia.
+ the emotions that activate instantly, before conscious analysis.
+ the self-concept and stereotypes that automatically and unconsciously influence how we process information about ourselves and others (Bargh, 1997).

More than we realize, we fly on autopilot. This understanding of unconscious information processing is more like the pre-Freudian view of an underground stream of thought from which spontaneous creative ideas surface.

Recent history has supported Freud's idea that we defend ourselves against anxiety. Again, however, the contemporary idea differs from Freud's. Jeff Greenberg, Sheldon Solomon, and Tom Pyszczynski (1997) believe that one source of anxiety is "the terror resulting from our awareness of vulnerability and death." Experiments testing their *terror-management theory* show that thinking about one's mortality—by writing a short essay on dying and its associated emotions—provokes enough anxiety to intensify prejudices. Anxiety motivates contempt for others and esteem for oneself. To feel self-esteem is to feel more secure in a threatening world.

Recent research has also provided some support for Freud's idea of defense mechanisms (even if they don't work exactly as Freud supposed). Roy Baumeister and his colleagues (1999) illustrate:

"During the Holocaust, many children . . . were forced to endure the unendurable. For those who continue to suffer [the] pain is still present, many years later, as real as it was on the day it occurred."

Eric Zillmer, Molly Harrower, Barry Ritzler, and Robert Archer, *The Quest for the Nazi Personality*, 1995

"Two passengers leaned against the ship's rail and stared at the sea. 'There sure is a lot of water in the ocean,' said one. 'Yes,' answered his friend, 'we've only seen the top of it.'"

Psychologist George A. Miller (1962)

+ If confronted with their sexism, racism, or incompetence, people often react with views and actions that seek to prove the opposite. For example, white research participants previously accused of racism give more money to a black panhandler than do their nonaccused counterparts. This curious generosity is akin to Freud's *reaction formation*, which states that we sometimes behave in ways opposite to our true feelings.

+ People tend to see their foibles and attitudes in others, a phenomenon called the *false consensus effect*. People who cheat on their taxes or break speed limits tend to think many others do likewise. Moreover, when trying to suppress thinking about our own faults we become more likely to see them in others (Newman & others, 1997). The evidence has not, however, confirmed Freud's idea that this *projection* has a defensive purpose—to conceal our own bad traits (Holmes, 1978, 1981). Having a target for projection doesn't help us suppress or repress the self-awareness.

Supportive evidence is, however, meager for defenses (such as displacement and sublimation) that are tied to instinctual energy. More evidence exists for defenses (such as reaction formation) that defend self-esteem. Defense mechanisms, Baumeister concludes, are motivated less by the seething impulses that Freud presumed than by our need to protect our self-image.

Freud's Ideas as Scientific Theory

Psychologists also criticize Freud's theory for its scientific shortcomings, noting that good scientific theories explain observations and offer testable hypotheses. Freud's theory rests on few objective observations and offers few hypotheses to verify or reject. (For Freud, his own recollections and interpretations of patients' free associations, dreams, and slips were evidence enough.)

What is the most serious problem with Freud's theory? It offers after-the-fact explanations of any characteristic (of one person's smoking, another's fear of horses, another's sexual orientation) yet fails to *predict* such behavior and traits. If you feel angry at your mother's death, you illustrate his theory because "your unresolved childhood dependency needs are threatened." If you do not feel angry, you again illustrate his theory because "you are repressing your anger." That, said Calvin Hall and Gardner Lindzey (1978, p. 68), "is like betting on a horse after the race has been run." Using after-the-fact interpretation, some Freud-influenced theorists have counted the *absence* of conscious memory of child abuse as evidence that abuse occurred. After-the-fact interpretation is appropriate for some historical and literary scholars, which helps explain Freud's lingering influence on certain forms of literary criticism. But psychological research is governed by the rules of science: A good theory makes testable predictions.

For such reasons, some of Freud's critics offer harsh words. They see a decaying Freudian edifice built on the swamplands of childhood sexuality, repression, dream analysis, and after-the-fact speculation. "When we stand on

> "Sigmund Freud is an empirical void."
>
> **Anonymous**

> "We are arguing like a man who should say, 'If there were an invisible cat in that chair, the chair would look empty; but the chair does look empty; therefore there is an invisible cat in it.'"
>
> **C. S. Lewis,** *Four Loves***, 1958**

[Freud's] shoulders, we only discover that we're looking further in the wrong direction," says John Kihlstrom (1997). Freud's most searing critic, Frederick Crews (1998), likens Freud to Peter Sellers' bumbling Inspector Clouseau, albeit with a unique talent for bamboozling an entire century. What is original about Freud's ideas is not good, and what is good is not original (the unconscious mind is an idea that dates back to Plato).

Freud's supporters object. "To reject psychodynamic thinking because Freud's instinct theory or his view of women is dated," says Drew Westen (1998), "is like rejecting modern physics because Newton did not understand relativity." Moreover, to criticize Freudian theory for not making testable predictions is like criticizing baseball for not being an aerobic exercise. Is it fair to fault something for not being what it was never intended to be? Unlike many later psychoanalysts, Freud never claimed that psychoanalysis was predictive science. He merely claimed that, looking back, psychoanalysts could find meaning in our state of mind (Rieff, 1979).

Freud's supporters also note that some of his ideas *are* enduring. It was Freud who drew our attention to the unconscious and the irrational, to our defenses against anxiety, to the importance of human sexuality, and to the tension between our biological impulses and our social well-being. It was Freud who challenged our self-righteousness, punctured our pretensions, and reminded us of our potential for evil.

Freud's legacy lives on. Some ideas that many people assume to be true—that childhood experiences mold personality, that many behaviors have disguised motives—are part of that legacy. His early-twentieth-century concepts penetrate our twenty-first-century language. Without realizing their source, we may speak of *ego*, *repression*, *projection*, *sublimation*, *complex* (as in "inferiority complex"), *sibling rivalry*, *Freudian slips*, and *fixation*. "Freud's premises may have undergone a steady decline in currency within academia for many years," notes Martin Seligman (1994), "but Hollywood, the talk shows, many therapists, and the general public still love them."

REVIEW AND REFLECT:

The Psychoanalytic Perspective

What was Freud's view of human personality and its development and dynamics?

Sigmund Freud's treatment of emotional disorders led him to believe that they spring from unconscious dynamics, which he sought to analyze through his own free associations and dreams and those of his patients. Freud saw personality as composed of pleasure-seeking psychic impulses (the id), a reality-oriented executive (the ego), and an internalized set of ideals (the superego).

Freud believed that children develop through psychosexual stages—the oral, anal, phallic, latency, and genital stages. He suggested that our personalities are influenced by how we have resolved conflicts associated with these stages and whether we have remained fixated at any stage.

Tensions between demands of the id and superego cause anxiety. The ego copes by using defense mechanisms, of which repression is the most basic.

What are projective tests, and what do clinicians in the Freudian tradition hope to learn from them?

Projective tests are tests that attempt to assess personality by presenting ambiguous stimuli that are designed to reveal the unconscious. Although projective tests, such as the Rorschach inkblots, have questionable reliability or validity, many clinicians continue to use them.

Which of Freud's ideas did his followers accept or reject? How do Freud's ideas hold up today?

Neo-Freudians Alfred Adler and Karen Horney accepted many of Freud's ideas, as did Carl Jung. But they also argued that we have motives other than sex and aggression, and that the ego's conscious control is greater than Freud supposed.

Today's research psychologists find some of Freud's specific ideas implausible, unvalidated, or contradicted by new research, and they note that his theory offers only after-the-fact explanations. Many researchers now believe that repression rarely, if ever, occurs. Nevertheless, Freud drew psychology's attention to the unconscious, to the struggle to cope with anxiety and sexuality, and to the conflict between biological impulses and social restraints. His cultural impact has been enormous.

Continued

Terms and Concepts to Remember

personality, p. 504
free association, p. 504
psychoanalysis, p. 505
unconscious, p. 505
preconscious, p. 505
id, p. 506
ego, p. 506
superego, p. 506
psychosexual stages, p. 506
Oedipus [ED-uh-puss]
  complex, p. 507
identification, p. 507
fixation, p. 507

defense mechanisms, p. 508
repression, p. 508
regression, p. 508
reaction formation, p. 508
projection, p. 508
rationalization, p. 508
displacement, p. 508
sublimation, p. 508
projective test, p. 509
Thematic Apperception Test
  (TAT), p. 509
Rorschach inkblot test, p. 509
collective unconscious, p. 511

Test Yourself

39.1. According to Freud, we block from consciousness the thoughts, wishes, feelings, and memories that are unacceptable or unbearably painful. The blocked material surfaces in disguised forms, for example, in physical symptoms, dreams, or slips of the tongue. This unconscious blocking of unacceptable thoughts is

a. free association.
b. repression.
c. anxiety.
d. reaction formation.

39.2. According to Freud's view of personality structure, the "executive" system, the _____, seeks to gratify impulses of the _____ in more realistic ways.

a. id; ego
b. ego; superego
c. ego; id
d. id; superego

39.3. Freud proposed an Oedipus complex, which is resolved through a process called identification, during which the child incorporates parental values. This process is closely associated with the development of the "voice of conscience," the part of the personality that internalizes ideals and that Freud called the

a. ego.
b. superego.
c. reality principle.
d. sublimation.

39.4. According to the psychoanalytic view of development, the oral, anal, and phallic stages are followed by a latency stage during which sexuality is largely dormant or submerged. The latency stage extends roughly through

a. the preschool years.
b. the early school years.
c. adolescence.
d. infancy.

39.5. Defense mechanisms identified by Freud include regression (in which a person copes with anxiety by retreating to an earlier stage of development) and projection (in which a person disguises threatening impulses by attributing them to others). There are many other defense mechanisms. All of them have in common some distortion or disguising of reality, and all of them are

a. conscious.
b. unconscious.
c. preconscious.
d. rationalizations.

39.6. In general, neo-Freudians such as Adler and Horney accepted many of Freud's views but they placed more emphasis on

a. development throughout the life span.
b. the collective unconscious.
c. the role of the id.
d. social interactions.

39.7. Projective tests are personality tests that present test-takers with an ambiguous stimulus and ask them to respond to it, for example, by describing it or telling a story about it. One well-known projective test, which uses inkblots as stimuli, was created by

a. the neo-Freudians.
b. Henry Murray.
c. Carl Jung.
d. Hermann Rorschach.

39.8. Many of Freud's specific ideas—for example, his ideas on the formation of gender identity and the function of dreams—have been modified by the neo-Freudians or challenged by recent research. However, psychodynamic psychologists would agree with Freud about

a. the existence of unconscious mental processes.
b. the Oedipus and Electra complexes.
c. the predictive value of Freudian theory.
d. adult psychological problems being the result of inadequate psychosexual development.

Review: What, according to Freud, were some of the important defense mechanisms, and what do they defend against?

Reflect: What understanding and impressions of Freud did you bring to this module? Have they changed in any way after reading it?

Answers to the Test Yourself and Review questions can be found in the green appendix at the end of the book.

The Trait Perspective

40

Sigmund Freud's *psychoanalytic theory* attempts to explain personality in terms of the dynamics that underlie behavior. It peers beneath the surface searching for hidden motives. In 1919, Gordon Allport, a curious 22-year-old psychology student, interviewed Freud in Vienna and discovered just how preoccupied the founder of psychoanalysis was with finding hidden motives.

> Soon after I had entered the famous red burlap room with pictures of dreams on the wall, he summoned me to his inner office. He did not speak to me but sat in expectant silence, for me to state my mission. I was not prepared for silence and had to think fast to find a suitable conversational gambit. I told him of an episode on the tram car on my way to his office. A small boy about 4 years of age had displayed a conspicuous dirt phobia. He kept saying to his mother, "I don't want to sit there . . . don't let that dirty man sit beside me." To him everything was *schmutzig* (filthy). His mother was a well-starched *Hausfrau*, so dominant and purposive looking that I thought the cause and effect apparent.
>
> When I finished my story Freud fixed his kindly therapeutic eyes upon me and said, "And was that little boy you?" Flabbergasted and feeling a bit guilty, I contrived to change the subject. While Freud's misunderstanding of my motivation was amusing, it also started a deep train of thought. (1967, pp. 7–8)

That train of thought ultimately led Allport to do what Freud did not do: to describe personality in terms of fundamental **traits**—people's characteristic behaviors and conscious motives (such as the professional curiosity that actually motivated Allport to see Freud). Meeting Freud, said Allport, "taught me that [psychoanalysis], for all its merits, may plunge too deep, and that psychologists would do well to give full recognition to manifest motives before probing the unconscious." Allport came to define personality in terms of identifiable behavior patterns. He was concerned less with *explaining* individual traits than with *describing* them.

How then do psychologists describe and classify personalities? An analogy may help. Imagine you want to describe and classify apples. Someone might correctly say that every apple is unique. Still, you might find it useful to begin by classifying apples as distinct *types*—Granny Smith, McIntosh, Red or Golden Delicious, and so forth. That is precisely how the ancient Greeks described personality—by classifying people according to four types. Depending on which of one's bodily "humors," or fluids, they believed to predominate, they declared people either melancholic (depressed), sanguine (cheerful), phlegmatic (unemotional), or choleric (irritable).

We now have other ideas of basic personality types. Based on children's physiological and psychological reactivity, Jerome Kagan (1989b) has classified children's temperaments as either shy-inhibited or fearless-uninhibited types. Some health psychologists classify people as intense, *Type A*, or as laid back, *Type B*, personalities.

Psychologist William Sheldon (1954) classified people by body type. Santa Claus typifies the plump *endomorph*: relaxed and jolly. Superman typifies the muscular *mesomorph*: bold and physically active. Sherlock Holmes typifies the thin *ectomorph*: high strung and solitary. But are different body types actually associated with different personalities? When researchers assess people's body types and personalities separately, there is a linkage, but it is modest. The stereotypes of the chubby happy-go-lucky person and of the muscular confident person turn out to be just that—stereotypes that exaggerate a mere kernel of truth (Tucker, 1983).

■ **trait** a characteristic pattern of behavior or a disposition to feel and act, as assessed by self-report inventories and peer reports.

Whoopi the extravert
Whoopi Goldberg seems as outgoing as her stage name implies. Trait labels such as extraversion can describe our temperaments and typical behaviors.

More popular today, especially in business and career counseling, is an effort to classify people according to Carl Jung's personality types, based on their responses to 126 questions written by Isabel Briggs Myers (1987) and her mother, Kathleen Briggs. The *Myers-Briggs Type Indicator* is quite simple. It offers choices, such as "Do you usually value sentiment more than logic, or value logic more than sentiment?" Then it counts the test-taker's preferences, labels them as indicating, say, a "feeling" or "thinking" type, and feeds them back to the person in complimentary terms. Feeling types, for example, are told they are sensitive to values and "sympathetic, appreciative, and tactful"; thinking types are told they "prefer an objective standard of truth" and are "good at analyzing."

Most people agree with their announced type profile. It, after all, mirrors their declared preferences. They may also accept their label as a basis for being matched with work partners and tasks that supposedly suit their temperaments (although critics wonder if labeling people creates self-fulfilling prophecies). A National Research Council report, however, noted that the test's initial use outran research on its value as a predictor of job performance and that "the popularity of this instrument in the absence of proven scientific worth is troublesome" (Druckman & Bjork, 1991, p. 101; see also Pittenger, 1993). With more than 300 articles on the Myers-Briggs now published in the *Journal of Psychological Type* (Carskadon & McCarley, 1997), advocates hope that verdict may change.

Exploring Traits

Preview Question: How do psychologists use traits to describe personality, and which aspects of human traits seem to provide the most useful information about personality variation?

Classifying people as one or another distinct personality type fails to capture their full individuality. So how else could we describe their personalities? To return to our apple analogy, we might describe an apple along several trait dimensions—relatively large or small, red or yellow, sweet or sour. We know that variations on just three color dimensions—hue, saturation, and brightness—create many thousands of colors. Similarly, by placing people on several trait dimensions simultaneously, psychologists can describe countless individual personality variations.

What trait dimensions describe personality? Allport and his associate H. S. Odbert (1936) literally counted all the words in an unabridged dictionary with which one could describe people. How many were there? Almost 18,000! How, then, could psychologists condense the list to a manageable number of basic traits?

Factor Analysis

One way has been to propose traits, such as anxiety, that some theory regards as basic. A newer technique is *factor analysis*, a statistical procedure that has been used to identify clusters of test items that tap basic components of intelligence (such as spatial ability, reasoning ability, or verbal skill). Imagine that people who describe themselves as outgoing also tend to say that they like excitement and practical jokes and dislike quiet reading. Such a statistically correlated cluster of behaviors reflects a basic trait, or factor—in this case, a trait called *extraversion*.

British psychologists Hans Eysenck and Sybil Eysenck [EYE-zink] believe that we can reduce many of our normal individual variations to two or three genetically influenced dimensions, including *extraversion-introversion* and *emotional stability-instability* (**FIGURE 40.1**). Their *Eysenck Personality Questionnaire* has been given to people in 35 countries around the world, from China to Uganda to Russia. When people's answers are analyzed, the extraversion and emotionality factors inevitably emerge as basic personality dimensions (Eysenck, 1990, 1992).

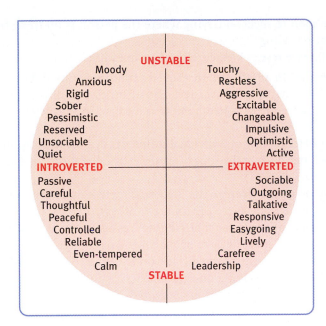

UNSTABLE

Moody   Touchy
Anxious   Restless
Rigid   Aggressive
Sober   Excitable
Pessimistic   Changeable
Reserved   Impulsive
Unsociable   Optimistic
Quiet   Active

INTROVERTED — **EXTRAVERTED**

Passive   Sociable
Careful   Outgoing
Thoughtful   Talkative
Peaceful   Responsive
Controlled   Easygoing
Reliable   Lively
Even-tempered   Carefree
Calm   Leadership

STABLE

FIGURE 40.1
Two personality factors
Mapmakers can tell us a lot by using two axes (north-south and east-west). Hans Eysenck and Sybil Eysenck use two primary personality factors—extraversion-introversion and stability-instability—as axes for describing personality variation. Varying combinations define other, more specific traits. (From Eysenck & Eysenck, 1963.)

The Big Five

Most researchers believe that while the Eysencks' dimensions are important, they do not tell the whole story. A slightly expanded set of factors—dubbed the *Big Five*—does a better job (Goldberg, 1993; John, 1990; Wiggins, 1996). If a test specifies where you are on the five dimensions of Table 40.1, it has said much of what there is to say about your personality. Around the world, people describe others in terms roughly consistent with the Big Five—how agreeable they are, how extraverted they are, and so forth. The Big Five is not the last word: Other theorists wonder whether we should add dimensions such as self-consciousness, masculinity-femininity, or positive-negative emotion. But for now the winning number in the personality lottery is five. The Big Five was the most active personality research topic during the 1990s and is currently our best approximation of the basic trait dimensions (Endler & Speer, 1998). If you could ask five questions about the personality of a stranger—

TABLE 40.1

THE "BIG FIVE" PERSONALITY FACTORS

Trait Dimension	Endpoints of the Dimension
Emotional stability	Calm ⇄ anxious Secure ⇄ insecure Self-satisfied ⇄ self-pitying
Extraversion	Sociable ⇄ retiring Fun-loving ⇄ sober Affectionate ⇄ reserved
Openness	Imaginative ⇄ practical Preference for variety ⇄ preference for routine Independent ⇄ conforming
Agreeableness	Soft-hearted ⇄ ruthless Trusting ⇄ suspicious Helpful ⇄ uncooperative
Conscientiousness	Organized ⇄ disorganized Careful ⇄ careless Disciplined ⇄ impulsive

Source: Adapted from McCrae & Costa (1986, p. 1002).

say, a blind date you were soon to meet—querying where the person is on these five dimensions would be most revealing.

The recent wave of Big Five research explores various questions:

+ ***How stable are these traits?*** In adulthood, the Big Five traits are quite stable, with some tendencies (neuroticism, extraversion, and openness) waning a bit in the decades after college, and others (agreeableness and conscientiousness) rising (McCrae & others, 1999).

+ ***How heritable are they?*** Heritability of individual differences varies with the diversity of people studied, but it generally runs 50 percent or a tad more for each dimension (Loehlin & others, 1998).

+ ***How well do they apply to other cultures?*** The Big Five dimensions describe personality in various cultures reasonably well (McCrae & others, 1998).

+ ***Do the Big Five traits predict other personal attributes?*** Yes again. An example: Highly conscientious people are more likely to be morning types ("larks"); evening types ("owls") are marginally more extraverted (Jackson & Gerard, 1996). Another example: When one's partner scores lower on agreeableness, stability, and openness, marital and sexual satisfaction may suffer (Botwin & others, 1997).

By exploring such questions, Big Five research has rejuvenated trait psychology and renewed appreciation for the importance of personality.

Biology and Personality

Genetic predispositions influence most personality traits. Extraverts, the researchers contend, seek stimulation because their normal levels of brain arousal are relatively low. PET scans confirm that a frontal lobe area that inhibits behavior is less active in extraverts than in introverts (Johnson & others, 1999). Emotionally stable people react calmly because their autonomic nervous systems are less active than those of unstable people.

Many other trait theorists also view personality traits as biologically rooted. Jerome Kagan attributes differences in children's shyness and inhibition to their autonomic nervous system reactivity. Our genes have much to say about the temperament and the behavioral style that help define our personality—more, it seems, than the way our parents handled us (although parents also have an influence and are very important for other internal realities such as beliefs and values). New molecular genetic studies are beginning to isolate genes that predispose babies to welcome novelty and to grow into adults who seek sensation and take risks (Ebstein & others, 1998). The fearless, curious child may become the rock-climbing or fast-driving adult. And studies comparing identical and fraternal twins, comparing identical twins reared apart, and comparing adoptees with their adoptive and biological parents all remind us: Personality forms under the influence of genes.

Assessing Traits

Preview Question: What are personality inventories, and what are their strengths and weaknesses as trait-assessment tools?

Assessment techniques derived from trait concepts do not reveal hidden personality dynamics. Rather, they profile a person's behavior patterns. Many trait scales provide quick assessments of a single trait, such as extraversion, anxiety, or self-esteem. Alternatively, psychologists can assess several traits at once by administering **personality inventories**—longer questionnaires on which people respond to items covering a wide range of feelings and behaviors.

The most extensively researched and widely used personality inventory is the **Minnesota Multiphasic Personality Inventory (MMPI)**. Although it assesses "abnormal" personality tendencies rather than normal personality traits, the MMPI il-

■ **personality inventory** a questionnaire (often with true-false or agree-disagree items) on which people respond to items designed to gauge a wide range of feelings and behaviors; used to assess selected personality traits.

■ **Minnesota Multiphasic Personality Inventory (MMPI)** the most widely researched and clinically used of all personality tests. Originally developed to identify emotional disorders (still considered its most appropriate use), this test is now used for many other screening purposes.

■ **empirically derived test** a test (such as the MMPI) developed by testing a pool of items and then selecting those that discriminate between groups.

lustrates a good way of developing a personality inventory. One of its creators, Starke Hathaway (1960), compared his effort to that of Alfred Binet. Binet developed the first intelligence test by selecting items that discriminated children who would have trouble progressing normally in French schools. The MMPI items, too, were **empirically derived**. That is, from a large pool of items Hathaway and his colleagues selected those that discriminated particular diagnostic groups. They then grouped the questions into 10 clinical scales.

They initially gave hundreds of true-false statements ("No one seems to understand me"; "I get all the sympathy I should"; "I like poetry") to groups of psychologically disordered patients and to "normal" people. They retained any statement—no matter how silly it sounded—on which the patient group's answer differed from that of the normal group. "Nothing in the newspaper interests me except the comics" may seem senseless, but it just so happened that depressed people were more likely to answer "true." (Nevertheless, people have had fun spoofing the MMPI with their own mock items, such as: "Weeping brings tears to my eyes," "Frantic screams make me nervous," and "I stay in the bathtub until I look like a raisin" [Frankel & others, 1983].)

Today's new "MMPI-2," renormed on a full cross-section of Americans and containing revised items, still contains 10 clinical scales (**FIGURE 40.2**). Like its predecessor, it has several validity scales, including the so-called lie scale that assesses the extent to which a person is faking in order to make a good impression (by responding "false" to statements such as "I get angry sometimes"). And it has 15 content scales assessing, for instance, work attitudes, family problems, and anger.

In contrast to the subjectivity of projective tests, personality inventories are scored objectively—so objectively that a computer can administer and score them. (The computer can also provide descriptions of people who previously responded similarly.) Objectivity does not, however, guarantee validity. For example, sophisticated test-takers taking the MMPI for employment purposes can give fake answers to create a good impression. (They consistently answer in socially desirable ways, except on those items like "I get angry sometimes," for which nearly any honest person would say yes.) Moreover, the ease of computerized testing tempts untrained administrators—including many personnel officers, educational admissions officers, and physicians—to use the test in ways for which it has not been validated (Matarazzo, 1983). Nevertheless, for better or worse, the objectivity of the MMPI contributes to its popularity and to its translation into more than 100 languages.

Self-report personality tests are the most widely used method of assessing traits. But psychologist David Funder (1991, 1995) believes that peer reports provide more trustworthy information. Friends who have observed you repeatedly in everyday situations provide the acid test for judging, say, how extraverted you are. More often than not, self-reports and peer reports tend to agree (Borkenau & Liebler, 1993). But when they disagree, Funder would put his money on peer reports. If everyone who knows you agrees you are outgoing, then, regardless of what you think, you *are* outgoing.

FIGURE 40.2

Minnesota Multiphasic Personality Inventory (MMPI) test profile
This graph plots the scores of Ed, a depressed and anxious young man, before and after psychotherapy. Scores are converted to a "T-scale," such that an average score is called 50 and about two-thirds of people fall between 40 and 60. T-scores above 60 suggest a psychological disorder. (Adapted from Butcher, 1990.)

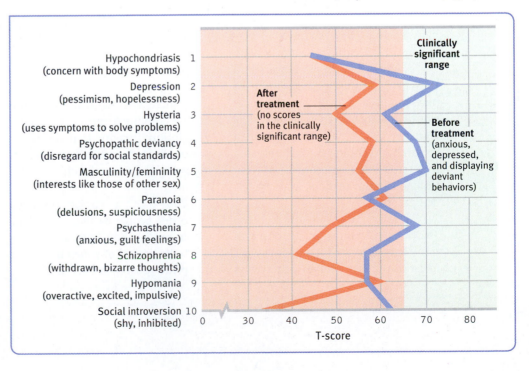

How to Be a "Successful" Astrologer or Palm Reader

How should we evaluate alternative ways of assessing traits? Does the alignment of the stars and planets at the time of one's birth affect who we are? Is one's handwriting revealing? Do our palms expose deep secrets?

While astronomers scoff at the naiveté of astrology—the constellations have shifted in the millennia since astrologers formulated their predictions (Kelly, 1997, 1998)—psychologists ask questions. Does it work? Are birth dates correlated with character traits? Given someone's birth date, can astrologers surpass chance when asked to identify the person from a short lineup of different personality descriptions? Can people pick out their own horoscopes from a lineup of horoscopes? The consistent answers have been: no, no, no, and no (British Psychological Society, 1993; Carlson, 1985; Kelly, 1997). Graphologists, who make predictions from handwriting samples, have similarly been found to do no better than chance when trying to discern people's occupations from examining several pages of their handwriting (Beyerstein & Beyerstein, 1992; Dean & others, 1992).

How, then, do astrologers and the like persuade thousands of newspapers and millions of people worldwide to buy their advice? Ray Hyman (1981), palm reader turned research psychologist, has revealed the suckering methods of astrologers, palm readers, and crystal-ball gazers.

Their first technique, the "stock spiel," builds on the observation that each of us is in some ways like no one else and in other ways

just like everyone. That some things are true of us all enables the "seer" to offer statements that seem impressively accurate: "I sense that you're nursing a grudge against someone; you really ought to let that go." "You worry about things more than you let on, even to your best friends." "You are adaptable to social situations and your interests are wide-ranging."

pendent thinker and do not accept other opinions without satisfactory proof. You have found it unwise to be too frank in revealing yourself to others. At times you are extraverted, affable, sociable; at other times you are introverted, wary, and reserved. Some of your aspirations tend to be pretty unrealistic (Davies, 1997; Forer, 1949).

Such generally true statements can be combined into a personality description. Imagine that you take a personality test and then receive the following character sketch:

You have a strong need for other people to like and to admire you. You have a tendency to be critical of yourself. . . . You pride yourself on being an inde-

In experiments, college students have received stock assessments like this one, drawn from statements in a newsstand astrology book. When they think the bogus feedback was prepared just for them and when it is favorable and pretty general, they nearly always rate the description as either "good" or "excellent" (Davies, 1997). Peter Glick and his co-workers (1989) found that even skeptics of astrology, when given a flattering description attributed to an astrologer, begin to think that "maybe there's something to this astrology stuff after all."

French psychologist Michael Gauguelin placed an ad in a Paris newspaper offering a free personal horoscope. Ninety-four percent of those receiving the horoscope praised the description as accurate. Whose horoscope had they all actually received? That of France's Dr. Petiot, a notorious mass murderer (Kurtz, 1983).

This acceptance is called *the Barnum effect*, named in honor of master showman P. T. Barnum's dictum, "There's a sucker born every minute." So powerful is the Barnum effect that, given a choice between this stock spiel and an individualized personality description actually based on a real test, most people choose the phony description as being more accurate.

Even some popular psychological labels are made plausible by Barnum statements. Mary Beth Logue and her colleagues (1992) report that adult children of alcoholics rate descriptions of their supposed traits ("You are sensitive to the difficulties of others" or "You sometimes project a front, hiding your true feelings") as accurate. But people who are *not* children of alcoholics rate the same statements as descriptive of *themselves*.

A second technique used by seers is to "read" our clothing, physical features, nonverbal gestures, and reactions to what they are saying. Imagine yourself as the character reader who was visited by a young woman in her late twenties or early thirties. Hyman described the woman as "wearing expensive jewelry, a wedding band, and a black dress of cheap material. The obser-

vant reader noted that she was wearing shoes which were advertised for people with foot trouble." Do these clues suggest anything?

Drawing on these observations, the character reader proceeded to amaze his client with his insights. He assumed that the woman had come to see him, as did most of his female customers, because of a love or financial problem. The black dress and the wedding band led him to reason that her husband had died recently. The expensive jewelry suggested that she had been financially comfortable during the marriage, but the cheap dress suggested that her husband's death had left her impoverished. The therapeutic shoes signified that she was now on her feet more than she had been used to, implying that she had been working to support herself since her husband's death.

If you are not as shrewd as this character reader (who correctly guessed that the woman was wondering if she should remarry in hope of ending her economic hardship), Hyman says it hardly matters. If

people seek you out for a reading, start with some safe sympathy: "I sense you're having some problems lately. You seem unsure what to do. I get the feeling another person is involved." Then tell them what they want to hear. Memorize some Barnum statements from astrology and fortune-telling manuals and use them liberally. Tell people it is their responsibility to cooperate by relating your message to their specific experiences. Later they will recall that you predicted the specifics. Phrase statements as questions, and when you detect a positive response assert the statement strongly. Be a good listener, and later, in different words, reveal to people what they earlier revealed to you. If you dupe them, they will come.

Better yet, beware of those who, by exploiting people with these techniques, are fortune takers rather than fortune tellers. ■

"Madame Zelinski can provide an even more accurate reading with your date of birth and social security number."

Evaluating the Trait Perspective

Preview Question: Does research support the consistency of personality traits over time and across situations?

Are our personality traits stable and enduring? Or does our behavior depend on where we are and whom we are with? William Faulkner created characters, like the self-centered Jason Compson, whose personality traits were consistent across various times and places. The Italian playwright Luigi Pirandello had a different view. For him, personality was ever-changing, tailored to the particular role or situation. In one of Pirandello's plays, Lamberto Laudisi describes himself to Signora Sirelli: "I am really what you take me to be; though, my dear madam, that does not prevent me from also being really what your husband, my sister, my niece, and Signora Cini take me to be—because they also are absolutely right!" To which she responds, "In other words you are a different person for each of us."

The Person-Situation Controversy

Who, then, most represents human personality, Faulkner's consistent Jason Compson or Pirandello's inconsistent Laudisi? Both. Our behavior is influenced by the interaction of our inner disposition with our environment. Still, the question lingers: Which is *more* important? Are we *more* as Faulkner or as Pirandello imagined us to be? Forced to choose, most people would probably side with Faulkner. Until the late 1960s, most psychologists would have, too. Isn't it obvious that some people are dependably conscientious and others unreliable, some cheerful and others dour, some outgoing and others shy?

When we explore this *person-situation controversy*, we look for genuine personality traits that persist over time *and* across situations. If we are to consider friendliness a trait, friendly people must act friendly at different times and places. Do they? In considering research that has followed lives through time, some scholars (especially those who study infants) are impressed with personality change; others are struck by personality stability during adulthood. Data from 152 long-term studies reveal that personality trait scores correlate with scores obtained seven years later as follows: children = 0.31, collegians = 0.54, 30-year-olds = 0.54, and 50- to 70-year-olds = 0.74 (Roberts & DelVecchio, 2000). Interests may change—the avid collector of tropical fish may become the avid gardener. Careers may change—the determined salesperson may become a determined social worker. Relationships may change—the hostile spouse may start over with a new partner. But most people recognize their traits as their own, note Robert McCrae and Paul Costa (1994), "and it is well that they do. A person's recognition of the inevitability of his or her one and only personality is . . . the culminating wisdom of a lifetime." Faulkner would not have been surprised.

The consistency of specific *behaviors* from one situation to the next is another matter. As Walter Mischel (1968, 1984) has pointed out, people do not act with predictable consistency. In one of the first studies to reveal this, Hugh Hartshorne and Mark May (1928b) gave thousands of children opportunities to lie, cheat, and steal while at home, at play, and in the classroom. Were some children consistently honest, others dishonest? Generally not. "Most children will deceive in certain situations and not in others," the researchers reported. A child's "lying, cheating, and stealing as measured by the test situations used in these studies are only very loosely related" (p. 411). More than a half-century later, Mischel's studies of college students' conscientiousness revealed a similar finding. There was virtually no relation between a student's being conscientious on one occasion (say, showing up for class on time) and being similarly conscientious on another occasion (say, turning in assignments on time). Pirandello would not have been surprised.

Mischel has also pointed out that people's scores on personality tests only mildly predict their behaviors. For example, people's scores on an extraversion test do

"There is as much difference between us and ourselves, as between us and others."

Michel de Montaigne, *Essays*, 1588

Roughly speaking, the temporary, external influences on behavior are the focus of social psychology, and the enduring, inner influences are the focus of personality psychology. In actuality, behavior always depends on the interaction of persons with situations.

not neatly predict how sociable they actually will be on any given occasion. If we remember such results, says Mischel, we will be more cautious about labeling and pigeonholing individuals. We will be more restrained when asked to predict whether someone is likely to violate parole, commit suicide, or be an effective employee. Years in advance, science can tell us the phase of the moon for any given date. A day in advance, meteorologists can often predict the weather. But we are much further from being able to predict how *you* will feel and act tomorrow.

"Mr. Coughlin over there was the founder of one of the first motorcycle gangs."

In defense of traits, Seymour Epstein (1983a,b) maintained that trying to predict a specific act on the basis of a personality test result is like trying to predict your answer to a specific aptitude question on the basis of an intelligence test result. Your answer to any given question is unpredictable because it depends on so many variables (your reading of the question, your understanding of the topic, your concentration level at the moment, luck). Your *average* accuracy over many questions on several tests is more predictable. Similarly, people's *average* outgoingness, happiness, or carelessness over *many* situations is predictable, Epstein observed. When rating someone's shyness or agreeableness, this consistency enables people who know someone well to agree (Kenrick & Funder, 1988). As our best friends can verify, we *do* have personality traits—genetically influenced traits, we now know. Moreover, our traits are socially significant. They influence our health, our thinking, and our job performance (Deary & Matthews, 1993; Hogan, 1998).

Consistency of Expressive Style

In unfamiliar, formal situations—perhaps when a guest in the home of a person from another culture—our traits may remain hidden as we attend carefully to social cues. In familiar, informal situations—just hanging out with friends—we feel less constrained, allowing our traits to emerge (Buss, 1989). In such situations, our expressive styles are impressively consistent. Thus, we often form lasting impressions within a few moments of meeting someone and noting the person's animation, manner of speaking, and gestures. Nalini Ambady and Robert Rosenthal (1992, 1993) videotaped 13 Harvard University graduate students teaching undergraduate courses. Observers then viewed three thin slices of each teacher's behavior—mere 10-second clips from the beginning, middle, and end of a class—and rated each teacher's level of confidence, activeness, warmth, and so forth. These behavior ratings, based on 30 *seconds* of teaching from an entire semester, predicted amazingly well the teacher's average student ratings at the semester's end. Observing even thinner slices—three 2-second clips—yielded ratings that still correlated as high as +.72 with the student evaluations. Some people's first impressions, derived from expressive behavior, predicted other people's lasting impressions!

Mere glimpses of someone's behavior can be revealing because of the potency of traits such as expressiveness. Some people are naturally expressive (and therefore talented at pantomime and charades); others are less expressive (and therefore better poker players). To evaluate people's voluntary control over their expressiveness, Bella DePaulo and her colleagues (1992) asked people to *act* as expressive or inhibited as possible while stating opinions. Their remarkable findings: Inexpressive people, even when feigning expressiveness, were less expressive than expressive people acting naturally. Similarly, expressive people, even when trying to seem inhibited, were less inhibited than inexpressive people acting naturally. It's hard to be someone you're not, or not to be what you are.

The irrepressibility of expressiveness explains why we can size up how outgoing someone is within seconds. Picture this experiment by Maurice Levesque and David Kenny (1993). They seated groups of four university women around a table and asked each woman merely to state her name, year in school, hometown, and college residence. Judging from just these few seconds of verbal and nonverbal behavior, the women were then to guess one another's talkativeness. (How do you think you would do in guessing someone's talkativeness based on such a small glimpse of their behavior?) When later correlated with how talkative each woman actually was during a series of one-on-one videotaped conversations, the snap judgments proved reasonably accurate. When we judge an expressive trait such as outgoingness, thin slices of behavior can be revealing.

To sum up, we can say that at any moment the immediate situation powerfully influences a person's behavior, especially when the situation makes clear demands. We can better predict drivers' behavior at traffic lights from knowing the color of the lights than from knowing the drivers' personalities. Thus, professors may perceive certain students as subdued (based on their classroom behavior), but friends may perceive them as pretty wild (based on their party behavior). Averaging our behavior across many occasions does, however, reveal that we do have distinct personality traits. Moreover, we can quickly perceive individual differences in some traits, such as expressiveness.

REVIEW AND REFLECT:

The Trait Perspective

How do psychologists use traits to describe personality, and which aspects of human traits seem to provide the most information about personality variation?

Rather than explain the hidden aspects of personality, trait researchers describe the predispositions that underlie our actions. For example, through factor analysis, researchers have isolated five important dimensions of personality. Genetic predispositions influence most such traits.

What are personality inventories, and what are their strengths and weaknesses as trait-assessment tools?

Personality inventories (like the MMPI-2) are questionnaires on which people respond to items designed to gauge a wide range of feelings and behaviors. Items on the tests are empirically derived, and the tests are objectively scored. But people can fake their answers, and peer reports may provide more trustworthy clues to a person's behavioral traits.

Does research support the consistency of personality traits over time and across situations?

Critics of the trait perspective question the consistency with which traits are expressed. Although people's traits persist over time, human behavior varies widely from situation to situation. Despite these variations, a person's *average* behavior across different situations tends to be fairly consistent.

Terms and Concepts to Remember
trait, p. 517
personality inventory, p. 520
Minnesota Multiphasic Personality Inventory (MMPI), p. 520
empirically derived test, p. 521

Test Yourself

40.1. Trait theory describes personality in terms of characteristic behaviors, or traits, such as agreeableness or extraversion. A pioneering trait theorist was
   a. Sigmund Freud.   c. Gordon Allport.
   b. Alfred Adler.   d. Henry Murray.

40.2. Hans Eysenck and Sybil Eysenck define personality in terms of two primary factors—extraversion-introversion and stability-instability. Most researchers today believe that the Eysenck dimensions are too limiting and prefer the so-called Big Five personality factors. Which of the following is *not* one of the Big Five?
   a. conscientiousness   c. extraversion
   b. anxiety   d. agreeableness

40.3. Trait theorists assess personality by developing a profile of a person's traits. For example, they administer personality inventories, long questionnaires that ask people to report their characteristic feelings and behaviors. The most widely used of all personality inventories is the
   a. extraversion-introversion scale.   c. MMPI.
   b. TAT.   d. Rorschach.

40.4. The items of the MMPI were empirically derived. This means, for example, that the designers of the test figured out which responses indicated schizophrenia by
   a. taking case histories before and after the test.
   b. analyzing the content of the items in the light of their understanding of the disorder.
   c. comparing the responses of people known to have schizophrenia with the responses of "normal" people.
   d. assessing the degree of deception, using validity scales.

40.5. People's scores on personality tests are only mildly predictive of their behavior. Such tests best predict
   a. a person's behavior on a specific occasion.
   b. a person's average behavior across many situations.
   c. behavior involving a single trait, such as conscientiousness.
   d. behavior that depends on situation or context.

Review: How many trait dimensions are typically used to describe personality, and what are those dimensions?

Reflect: Where would you place yourself on these dimensions?

Answers to the Test Yourself and Review questions can be found in the green appendix at the end of the book.

41

The Humanistic Perspective

Exploring the Self

Preview Question: What do humanistic psychologists view as the central feature of personality, and what is their goal in studying personality?

By 1960, some personality psychologists had become discontented both with Sigmund Freud's negativity and with trait psychology's objectivity. In contrast to Freud's study of the base motives of "sick" people, these *humanistic psychologists* focused on the ways "healthy" people strive for self-determination and self-realization. Two pioneering theorists—Abraham Maslow (1908–1970) and Carl Rogers (1902–1987)—illustrate these emphases on human potential and seeing the world through the person's (not the researcher's) eyes.

Abraham Maslow's Self-Actualizing Person

Maslow proposed that we are motivated by a hierarchy of needs. If our physiological needs are met, we become concerned with personal safety; if we achieve a sense of security, we then seek to love, to be loved, and to love ourselves; with our love needs satisfied, we seek self-esteem. Having achieved self-esteem, we ultimately seek **self-actualization**, the process of fulfilling our potential.

Maslow (1970) developed his ideas by studying healthy, creative people rather than troubled clinical cases. He based his description of self-actualization on a study of those who seemed notable for their rich and productive lives—among them, Abraham Lincoln, Thomas Jefferson, and Eleanor Roosevelt. Maslow reported that these people shared certain characteristics: They were self-aware and self-accepting, open and spontaneous, loving and caring, and not paralyzed by others' opinions. Secure in their sense of who they were, their interests were problem-centered rather than self-centered. They focused their energies on a particular task, one they often regarded as their mission in life. Most enjoyed a few deep relationships rather than many superficial ones. Many had been moved by spiritual or personal *peak experiences* that surpassed ordinary consciousness.

These, said Maslow, are mature adult qualities, ones found in those who have learned enough about life to be compassionate, to have outgrown their mixed feelings toward their parents, to have found their calling, to have "acquired enough courage to be unpopular, to be unashamed about being openly virtuous, etc." Maslow's work with college students led him to speculate that those likely to become self-actualizing adults were likable, caring, "privately affectionate to those of their elders who deserve it," and "secretly uneasy about the cruelty, meanness, and mob spirit so often found in young people."

Abraham Maslow
"Any theory of motivation that is worthy of attention must deal with the highest capacities of the healthy and strong person as well as with the defensive maneuvers of crippled spirits" (*Motivation and Personality*, 1970).

Carl Rogers' Person-Centered Perspective

Fellow humanistic psychologist Carl Rogers agreed with much of Maslow's thinking. Rogers believed that people are basically good and are endowed with self-actualizing tendencies. Unless thwarted by an environment that inhibits growth, each of us is like an acorn, primed for growth and fulfillment. Rogers (1980) believed that a growth-promoting climate required three conditions—genuineness, acceptance, and empathy.

■ **self-actualization** according to Maslow, the ultimate psychological need that arises after basic physical and psychological needs are met and self-esteem is achieved; the motivation to fulfill one's potential.

The picture of empathy
Being open and sharing confidences is easier when the listener shows real understanding. Within such relationships people can relax and fully express their true selves.

According to Rogers, people nurture our growth by being *genuine*—by being open with their own feelings, dropping their facades, and being transparent and self-disclosing.

People also nurture growth by being *accepting*—by offering us what Rogers called **unconditional positive regard**. This is an attitude of grace, an attitude that values us even knowing our failings. It is a profound relief to drop our pretenses, confess our worst feelings, and discover that we are still accepted. We hope to enjoy this gratifying experience in a good marriage, a close family, or an intimate friendship in which we no longer feel a need to explain ourselves. In the best of relationships, we are free to be spontaneous without fearing the loss of others' esteem.

Finally, people nurture growth by being *empathic*—by sharing and mirroring our feelings and reflecting our meanings. "Rarely do we listen with real understanding, true empathy," said Rogers. "Yet listening, of this very special kind, is one of the most potent forces for change that I know."

Genuineness, acceptance, and empathy are the water, sun, and nutrients that enable people to grow like vigorous oak trees, according to Rogers. For "as persons are accepted and prized, they tend to develop a more caring attitude toward themselves" (Rogers 1980, p. 116). As persons are empathically heard, "it becomes possible for them to listen more accurately to the flow of inner experiencings."

Rogers believed that genuineness, acceptance, and empathy nurture growth not only in the relationship between therapist and client but also between parent and child, leader and group, teacher and student, administrator and staff member—in fact, between any two human beings. He would have been pleased by a finding published shortly after his death: Preschool children whose parents exhibit such attitudes usually become creative adolescents (Harrington & others, 1987).

For Maslow, and even more for Rogers, a central feature of personality is one's **self-concept**—all the thoughts and feelings we have in response to the question, "Who am I?" If our self-concept is positive, we tend to act and perceive the world positively. If it is negative—if in our own eyes we fall far short of our "ideal self"—said Rogers, we feel dissatisfied and unhappy. A worthwhile goal for therapists, parents, teachers, and friends is therefore, he said, to help others know, accept, and be true to themselves.

College of Positive Self-Image 7. University of Low Self-Esteem o.

Assessing the Self

Preview Questions: How do humanistic psychologists assess a person's sense of self? What have we learned from more than three decades of research on the self?

If a humanistic psychologist were to assess your personality, you might be asked to fill out a questionnaire that would evaluate your self-concept. One questionnaire, inspired by Carl Rogers, asks people to describe themselves both as they would ideally like to be and as they actually are. When the ideal and the actual self are nearly alike, said Rogers, the self-concept is positive. When assessing his clients' personal growth during therapy, he looked for successively closer ratings of actual and ideal self.

Some humanistic psychologists believe that any standardized assessment of personality is depersonalizing, that even a questionnaire detaches the psychologist from the living human. Rather than forcing the person to respond to narrow categories, these humanistic psychologists believe that interviews and intimate conversation enable a better understanding of each person's unique experiences.

■ **unconditional positive regard** according to Rogers, an attitude of total acceptance toward another person.

■ **self-concept** all our thoughts and feelings about ourselves, in answer to the question, "Who am I?"

■ **self-esteem** one's feelings of high or low self-worth.

Research on the Self

Psychology's concern with people's sense of self dates back at least to William James, who, in his 1890 *Principles of Psychology*, devoted more than 100 pages to the topic. By 1943, Gordon Allport lamented that the self had become "lost to view." Even humanistic psychology's emphasis on the self did not instigate much scientific research, but it did help renew the concept of self and keep it alive. Now, more than a century after

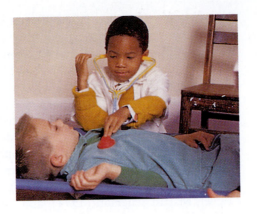

Possible selves
By giving them a chance to try out many possible selves, pretend games offer children important opportunities to grow emotionally, socially, and cognitively. Although this young boy may not grow up to be a physician, playing adult roles will certainly bear fruit in terms of an expanded vision of what he might become.

James and outside humanistic psychology, the self is one of Western psychology's most vigorously researched topics. Every year, new studies galore appear on self-esteem, self-disclosure, self-awareness, self-schemas, self-monitoring, and so forth—more than 110,000 articles in all since 1967.

An example of more recent thinking about self is the concept of *possible selves* put forth by Hazel Markus and her colleagues (Inglehart & others, 1989; Markus & Nurius, 1986). Your possible selves include your visions of the self you dream of becoming—the rich self, the successful self, the loved and admired self. They also include the self you fear becoming—the unemployed self, the lonely self, the academically failed self. Such possible selves motivate us by laying out specific goals and calling forth the energy to work toward them. University of Michigan students in a combined undergraduate/medical school program earn higher grades if they undergo the program with a clear vision of themselves as successful doctors. Dreams do often give birth to achievements.

Underlying this research is an assumption (shared by humanistic psychologists) that the self, as organizer of our thoughts, feelings, and actions, is a pivotal center of personality. From our self-focused perspective we too readily presume that others are noticing and evaluating us. Thomas Gilovich (1996) demonstrated this "spotlight effect" by having individual Cornell University students don Barry Manilow T-shirts before entering a room with other students. Feeling self-conscious, the T-shirt wearers guessed that nearly half of their peers would take note of the shirt as they walked in. In reality, only 23 percent did. This absence of attention applies not only to our dorky clothes and bad hair but also to our nervousness, irritation, or attraction—fewer people notice than we presume (Gilovich & Savitsky, 1999).

Self-focus affects our recall too, but in a more constructive way: We remember information better if we encode it in terms of ourselves. Tory Higgins and John Bargh (1987) asked people to consider whether some specific words such as *friendly* described them, and whether the words described someone else. The participants better recalled words they had considered in relation to themselves.

How we *feel* about ourselves is also important. Research studies confirm the benefits of positive self-esteem and also hint at the hazards of pride.

"The first step to better times is to imagine them."

Chinese fortune cookie

The Benefits of Self-Esteem

High **self-esteem**—a feeling of self-worth—pays dividends. People who feel good about themselves (who strongly agree with self-affirming questionnaire statements) have fewer sleepless nights, succumb less easily to pressures to conform, are less likely to use drugs, are more persistent at difficult tasks, are less shy and lonely, and are just plain happier (Crocker & Wolfe, 1999; Leary, 1999; Tafarodi & Vu, 1997).

Psychotherapy researcher Hans Strupp (1982) noted that "As soon as one listens to a patient's story, one encounters unhappiness, frustration, and despair. . . . Basic to all these difficulties are impairments in self-acceptance and self-esteem."

Those whose self-esteem is low do not necessarily see themselves as worthless or wicked, but they seldom say good things about themselves. Such low self-esteem exacts costs. Unhappiness and despair often coexist with low self-esteem.

Low self-esteem comes in different forms. Those vulnerable to depression often feel they are falling short of their *hopes*. Those vulnerable to anxiety often feel they are falling short of what they *ought* to be (Higgins, 1987). For such people, the pain of anticipated social rejection, experienced as low self-esteem, is sometimes adaptive. As with other forms of pain, it may aid survival by motivating them to behave in ways that sustain their inclusion within a supportive group (Leary & others, 1995).

The correlational links between low self-esteem and personal problems have other possible interpretations. Psychologists William Damon (1995), Robyn Dawes (1994), Martin Seligman (1994), and Mark Leary (1999) doubt that self-esteem is really "the armor that protects kids" from life's problems. Could it not be the other way around? Couldn't problems and failures cause low self-esteem? Maybe self-esteem simply reflects reality. Maybe feeling good *follows* doing well. Maybe it's a side effect of meeting challenges and surmounting difficulties. Maybe self-esteem is a gauge that reads out the state of our relationships with others. If so, isn't pushing the gauge artificially higher akin to forcing a car's low fuel gauge to display "full"? And will the best boost to self-esteem therefore come not so much from our repeatedly telling children how wonderful they are as from their own effective coping and hard-won achievements?

However, an *effect* of low self-esteem does appear in experiments. Temporarily deflate people's self-image (say, by telling them they did poorly on an aptitude test or by disparaging their personality) and they will be more likely to disparage others or to express heightened racial prejudice (Ybarra, 1999). Those who are negative about themselves also tend to be thin-skinned and judgmental (Baumeister, 1993; Baumgardner & others, 1989; Pelham, 1993). Some "love their neighbors as themselves"; others loathe their neighbors as themselves. In experiments, those made to feel insecure often become excessively critical, as if to impress others with their own brilliance (Amabile, 1983). Such findings are consistent with Maslow's and Rogers' presumptions that a healthy self-image pays dividends. Accept yourself and you'll find it easier to accept others.

Culture and Self-Esteem

Is it true, as so many assume, that ethnic minorities, people with disabilities, and women live lives handicapped by impoverished self-esteem? The accumulated evidence says no. For example, 261 comparisons of more than half a million people have revealed slightly *higher* self-esteem scores for black than for white children, adolescents, and young adults (Gray-Little & Hafdahl, 2000). The National Institute of Mental Health's 1980s study of *Psychiatric Disorders in America* similarly reveals that the rates of depression and alcoholism among African- and Hispanic-Americans are roughly comparable of those among other Americans (if anything, America's ethnic minorities suffer slightly less depression).

Some people wonder: How can this be? Some members of "stigmatized" groups (people of color, those with disabilities, women) have faced discrimination and lower status, yet maintain their self-esteem in three ways, according to Jennifer Crocker and Brenda Major (1989):

+ They value the things at which they excel.
+ They attribute problems to prejudice.
+ They do as everyone does—they compare themselves to those in their own group.

These findings help us understand why, despite the realities of prejudice, such groups report roughly comparable levels of happiness.

> "There's a lot of talk about self-esteem these days. It seems pretty basic to me. If you want to feel proud of yourself, you've got to do things you can be proud of."
>
> Oseola McCarty, Mississippi washerwoman, after donating $150,000 to the University of Southern Mississippi

The Pervasiveness of Self-Serving Bias

Carl Rogers (1958) once objected to the religious doctrine that humanity's problems arise from excessive self-love, or pride. He noted that most people he had known "despise themselves, regard themselves as worthless and unlovable." Mark Twain had the idea: "No man, deep down in the privacy of his heart, has any considerable respect for himself."

Actually, most of us have a good reputation with ourselves. In studies of self-esteem, even those who score low respond in the midrange of possible scores. (A "low" self-esteem person responds to statements such as "I have good ideas" with qualifying adjectives such as *somewhat* or *sometimes*.) Moreover, one of psychology's most provocative and firmly established recent conclusions concerns our potent **self-serving bias**—our readiness to perceive ourselves favorably (Brown, 1991; Myers, 1999). Consider these findings:

People accept more responsibility for good deeds than for bad, and for successes than for failures. Athletes often privately credit their victories to their own prowess and their losses to bad breaks, lousy officiating, or the other team's exceptional performance. After receiving poor grades on an exam, most students in a half-dozen studies criticized the exam, not themselves. On insurance forms, drivers have explained accidents in such words as: "An invisible car came out of nowhere, struck my car, and vanished." "As I reached an intersection, a hedge sprang up, obscuring my vision, and I did not see the other car." "A pedestrian hit me and went under my car." The question "What have I done to deserve this?" is one we usually ask of our troubles, not our successes—those, we assume we deserve.

Most people see themselves as better than average. This is true for nearly any subjective and socially desirable dimension. In national surveys, most business executives say they are more ethical than their average counterpart. In several studies, 90 percent of business managers and more than 90 percent of college professors rated their performance as superior to that of their average peer. In Australia, 86 percent of people rate their job performance as above average, and only 1 percent as below average. Although the phenomenon is notably less striking in Asia, where people value modesty, self-serving biases have been observed worldwide: among Dutch, Australian, and Chinese students; Japanese drivers; Indian Hindus; and French people of most all walks of life. The world, it seems, is Garrison Keillor's Lake Wobegon writ large—a place where "all the women are strong, all the men are good-looking, and all the children are above average."

And who is at least "somewhat likely" to go to heaven? Of Americans surveyed by *U.S. News* (1997), 19 percent thought O. J. Simpson would make it. They were more optimistic about Bill Clinton (52 percent), Princess Diana (60 percent), and Michael Jordan (65 percent). The public figure closest to a perceived heavenly shoo-in was Mother Teresa (79 percent). But she was topped by the survey's respondents, 87 percent of whom believed *they* themselves were destined to enter the Pearly Gates.

Self-serving bias flies in the face of today's pop psychology. "All of us have inferiority complexes," wrote John Powell (1989, p. 15). "Those who seem not to have such a complex are only pretending." But additional findings remove any doubts (Myers, 1999):

+ We remember and justify our past actions in self-enhancing ways.
+ We exhibit an inflated confidence in the accuracy of our beliefs and judgments.

■ **self-serving bias** a readiness to perceive oneself favorably.

"To love oneself is the beginning of a life-long romance."

Oscar Wilde, *An Ideal Husband*, 1895

PEANUTS reprinted by permission of UFS, Inc.

PEANUTS

"The [self-]portraits that we actually believe, when we are given freedom to voice them, are dramatically more positive than reality can sustain."

Shelley Taylor, *Positive Illusions*, 1989

+ We overestimate how desirably *we* would act in situations where most people behave less than admirably.
+ We often seek out favorable, self-enhancing information.
+ We are quicker to believe flattering descriptions of ourselves than unflattering ones, and we are impressed with psychological tests that make us look good.
+ We shore up our self-image by overestimating how much others support our opinions and share our foibles, and by *under*estimating the commonality of our strengths.
+ We exhibit group pride—a tendency to see our group (our school, our country, our race) as superior.

Moreover, pride does often go before a fall. Self-serving perceptions underlie conflicts ranging from blaming one's spouse for marital discord to arrogantly promoting one's own ethnic superiority. "Aryan pride" fueled Nazi atrocities. It was national self-righteousness that led both the Americans and Soviets during the arms race to say, "Your weapons threaten us, ours are for our defense." No wonder religion and literature so often warn against the perils of excessive pride.

Finding their self-esteem threatened, people with large egos may do more than put others down; they may react violently. Someone with a swelled head that gets deflated by insult or rejection is potentially dangerous. Brad Bushman and Roy Baumeister (1998) experimented with this dark side of high self-esteem. They had 540 undergraduate volunteers write a paragraph, in response to which another supposed student gave them either praise ("Great essay!") or stinging criticism ("One of the worst essays I have read!"). Then the essay writers played a reaction-time game against the other student. After wins, they could assault their opponent with noise of any intensity for any duration.

Can you anticipate the result? After criticism, those with unrealistically high self-esteem were "exceptionally aggressive." They delivered three times the auditory torture of those with normal self-esteem. It is "threatened egotism," not low self-esteem, that predisposes aggression, the researchers concluded. Moreover, people with excessive self-regard are prone to excessive risks (Baumeister & others, 1993). Would you rather ride with people who overestimate or underestimate their ability to maintain control while driving fast?

Despite the demonstrated perils of pride, many people reject the idea of self-serving bias, insisting it overlooks those who feel worthless and unlovable and seem to despise themselves. If self-serving bias prevails, why do so many people disparage themselves? For at least two reasons. Sometimes self-directed put-downs are subtly strategic: They elicit reassuring strokes. Saying "No one likes me" may at least elicit "But not everyone has met you!" At other times, such as before a game or an exam, self-disparaging comments prepare us for possible failure. The coach who extols the superior strength of the upcoming opponent makes a loss understandable, a victory noteworthy.

Even so, it's true: All of us some of the time, and some of us much of the time, *do* feel inferior—especially when we compare ourselves with those who are a step or two higher on the ladder of status, looks, income, or ability. The deeper and more frequently we have such feelings, the more unhappy, even depressed, we are. But for most people—the 98 percent who at anytime are *not* suffering depression (Diener, 1993; Gotlib, 1992)—thinking has a naturally positive bias.

We can therefore affirm what humanistic psychologists rightly emphasize: For the individual, self-affirming thinking is generally adaptive. To a point, our positive illusions are beneficial. They maintain our self-confidence, protect against anxiety and depression, and sustain our sense of well-being. "Life is the art of being well-deceived," observed the English essayist William Hazlitt.

"The enthusiastic claims of the self-esteem movement mostly range from fantasy to hogwash. The effects of self-esteem are small, limited, and not all good."

Roy Baumeister (1996)

"If you compare yourself with others, you may become vain and bitter; for always there will be greater and lesser persons than yourself."

Max Ehrmann, "Desiderata," 1927

Recognizing both the perils of self-righteousness and the dividends of positive self-esteem, psychologists Roy Baumeister (1989), Jonathan Brown (1991), and Shelley Taylor (1989) have all suggested that humans function best with modest self-enhancing illusions. Like the Japanese and European magnetic levitation trains, Brown noted, we function optimally when riding just off the rails—not so high that we gyrate and crash, yet not so in touch that we grind to a halt.

Culture and the Individual Self

If someone were to rip away your social connections, making you a solitary refugee in a foreign land, how much of your identity would remain intact? The answer might depend in large part on whether your culture gives greater priority to the independent self that marks **individualism** or the interdependent self that marks **collectivism**.

If the solitary travelers were individualists, a great deal of their identity would remain intact—the very core of their being, their sense of "me," their awareness of their personal convictions and values. Individualists give relatively greater priority to personal goals and define their identity mostly in terms of personal attributes. They strive for personal control and individual achievement. Although individualism varies from person to person within any culture, cross-cultural psychologists have mostly studied how it varies across cultures, ranging from the extreme individualism of the United States outside the Deep South to the extreme collectivism of rural Asia (Hofstede, 1980; Triandis, 1994; Vandello & Cohen, 1999).

Those collectivists, if set adrift in a foreign land, might experience a much greater loss of identity. Cut off from family, groups, and loyal friends, they would lose connections that have defined who they are. In a collectivist culture, a social network provides one's bearings. What is most important is not "me" but "we." Collectivists give priority to the goals of their groups—often their family, clan, or company—and define their identity accordingly. By their group identifications, collectivists gain a sense of belonging, a set of values, a network of caring individuals, an assurance of security.

The individual identity that is usually primary for Westerners gives way to a collective identity that is more often primary for Asians. Compared with American students, for example, students in Japan, China, and India are much less likely to complete the sentence "I am. . ." with personal traits ("I am sincere," "I am confident") and are much more likely to declare their social identities ("I am a Keio University student," "I am the third son in my family") (Cousins, 1989; Dhawan & others, 1995; Triandis, 1989a,b). And the individualized latté—"decaf, single shot,

individualism giving priority to one's own goals over group goals, and defining one's identity in terms of personal attributes rather than group identifications.

collectivism giving priority to the goals of one's group (often one's extended family or work group) and defining one's identity accordingly.

Like athletes who take more pleasure in their team's victory than in their own performance, collectivists find satisfaction in advancing their groups' interests, even at the expense of personal needs.

Collectivism
By identifying with family and other groups, these yak herders in India gain a sense of "we," a set of values, a network of care.

skinny, extra hot"—that feels so good to a North American in an espresso shop might sound more like a selfish demand in Seoul, note Heejung Kim and Hazel Markus (1999). In Korea, their studies confirm, people place less value on uniqueness and more on tradition and shared practices.

The contrast between individualist and collectivist cultures also appears in people's names. Individualist cultures give priority to personal identity by putting the personal name first ("Christine Brune"). Collectivist cultures often give priority to one's family identity ("Hui Harry"). Family loyalty also appears in popular Chinese songs, which much more often than in Western pop music express positive feelings for one's parents. To those from an individualist culture, a typical Chinese song may sound quaint (Rothbaum & Xu, 1995):

> I am mamma's short poem
> Composed of mother's painstaking effort,
> Mamma has suffered so much pain for me . . .
> How much I wish there would be good news tomorrow
> To repay mother's deep feeling for me.

To a rural Chinese, songs like "I Gotta Be Me" would seem equally odd, even embarrassing.

Being more self-contained, individualists more easily move in and out of social groups. They feel relatively free to switch churches, leave one job for another, or even to leave their extended families and migrate to a new place. Marriage is often for as long as they both shall love. In contrast, collectivists may act shy in new groups and are more easily embarrassed (Singelis & others, 1995, 1999). They have deeper, more stable attachments to their familiar groups and friends. Relationships are long-term. Loyalties run strong between employer and employees.

Valuing communal solidarity, people in collectivist cultures place a premium on maintaining harmony and making sure others never lose face. Direct confrontation and blunt honesty are rare, as are expressions of personal egotism. What people say reflects not only what they feel (their inner attitudes) but also what they presume others feel (Kashima & others, 1992). Elders and superiors are given respect. To preserve group spirit, people avoid uncomfortable topics, defer to others' wishes, and display a polite, self-effacing humility (Kitayama & Markus, in press; Markus & Kitayama, 1991). People remember those who have done them favors, and reciprocation becomes a social art. The collectivist self is not independent but *inter*dependent (Table 41.1). Among collectivists—especially those influenced by the Confucian idea of self as embedded in "a web of interrelatedness"—no one is an island (Kim & Lee, 1994). Happiness is being attuned to others (Kitayama & Markus, 2000).

Both individualism and collectivism offer benefits and come at a cost. People in competitive, individualistic cultures have more personal freedom, take more pride in personal achievements, are less geographically bound to their families, and enjoy more privacy. Their less-unified cultures offer a smorgasbord of life-styles and invite individuals to construct their own identities. These cultures also celebrate innovation and creativity, and they tend to respect individual human rights. Such may help explain Ed Diener, Marissa Diener, and Carol Diener's (1995) finding that people in individualistic cultures report experiencing greater happiness than do those in collectivist cultures. When individualists pursue their own ends and all goes well, life can seem rewarding.

Curiously, though, within individualist cultures, people with the strongest social ties express greatest satisfaction with their lives (Bettencourt & Door, 1997). Moreover, the seeming benefits of individualism can come at the cost of more loneliness, more divorce, more homicide, and more stress-related disease (Popenoe, 1993; Triandis & others, 1988). Individualists demand more romance and personal fulfillment in marriage, which subjects the marriage relationship to more pressure (Dion

No wonder, says Harry Triandis (1989b), that modern world colonization was led not by Asians, who were reluctant to cut social and family ties, but by the more individualist Europeans. And no wonder that countries colonized by Europeans willing to leave friends and family are today highly individualistic.

TABLE 41.1

VALUE CONTRASTS BETWEEN INDIVIDUALISM AND COLLECTIVISM

Concept	Individualism	Collectivism
Self	Independent (identity from individual traits)	Interdependent (identity from belonging)
Life task	Discover and express one's uniqueness	Maintain connections, fit in
What matters	Me—personal achievement and fulfillment; rights and liberties; self-esteem	We—group goals and solidarity; social responsibilities and relationships
Coping method	Change reality	Accommodate to reality
Morality	Defined by individuals (self-based)	Defined by social networks (duty-based)
Relationships	Many, often temporary or casual; confrontation acceptable	Few, close and enduring; harmony valued
Attributing behavior	Behavior reflects one's personality and attitudes	Behavior reflects social norms and roles

Sources: Adapted from Thomas Schoeneman (1994) and Harry Triandis (1994).

& Dion, 1993). In one survey, "keeping romance alive" was rated as important to a good marriage by 78 percent of American women but only 29 percent of Japanese women (*American Enterprise*, 1992). In China, love songs often express enduring commitment and friendship (Rothbaum & Tsang, 1998). As one song put it, "we will be together from now on . . . I will never change from now to forever."

In recent decades, Western individualism has increased, while the priority placed on social obligations and family ties has decreased (Yankelovich, 1993). Martin Seligman (1988) has argued that "rampant individualism carries with it two seeds of its own destruction. First, a society that exalts the individual to the extent ours now does will be ridden with depression. . . . Second, and perhaps most important, is meaninglessness [which occurs when there is no] attachment to something larger than you are."

> "One needs to cultivate the spirits of sacrificing the *little me* to achieve the benefits of the *big me*."
>
> **Chinese saying**

Evaluating the Humanistic Perspective

Preview Questions: How has the humanistic perspective on personality influenced psychology? What criticisms have been leveled against humanistic psychology?

One thing said of Freud can also be said of the humanistic psychologists: Their impact, though waning, has been pervasive. Their ideas have influenced counseling, education, child-rearing, and management. They have also influenced—sometimes in ways they did not intend—much of today's popular psychology.

Through popular psychology many people have absorbed some of what Maslow and Rogers taught—that a positive self-concept is the key to happiness and success, that acceptance and empathy help nurture positive feelings about oneself, and that people are basically good and capable of self-improvement. One study found that, by a four-to-one margin, Americans believe "human nature is basically good" rather than "fundamentally perverse and corrupt" (NORC, 1985). Humanistic psychologists can also take satisfaction in the changed response to one of the MMPI items: Among those in the 1930s normal standardization sample, only 9 percent agreed that "I am an important person"; in the mid-1980s, more than half agreed (Holden, 1986b). Responding to a 1989 Gallup poll, 85 percent of Americans rated "having a good self-image or self-respect" as *very* important; 0 percent rated it unimportant. And 89 percent of people responding to a 1992 *Newsweek* Gallup poll rated self-esteem as very important for "motivating a person to work hard and succeed." Humanistic psychology's message has been heard.

"We do pretty well when you stop to think that people are basically good."

Perhaps one reason that message has been so well received is that its emphasis on the individual self reflects and reinforces Western cultural values. As self-reliant individualism has grown, with increased priority given to personal identity and aspirations, the popular media have celebrated the rugged individual. Movie plots feature heroes who, true to themselves, buck social convention or take the law into their own hands. Popular songs proclaim "I Did It My Way" and remind us that to love yourself is "The Greatest Love of All" (Schoeneman, 1994).

The prominence of the humanistic perspective set off a backlash of criticism. First, said the critics, its concepts are vague and subjective. Consider the description of self-actualizing people as open, spontaneous, loving, self-accepting, and productive. Is this a scientific description? Isn't it merely a description of Maslow's personal values and ideals? Maslow, noted M. Brewster Smith (1978), offered impressions of his own personal heroes. Imagine another theorist who began with a different set of heroes—perhaps Napoleon, Alexander the Great, and John D. Rockefeller, Sr. This theorist would likely describe self-actualizing people as "undeterred by the needs of others," "motivated to achieve," and "obsessed with power."

Critics raised a second objection to the idea that, as Carl Rogers put it, "The only question which matters is, 'Am I living in a way which is deeply satisfying to me, and which truly expresses me?'" (quoted by Wallach & Wallach, 1985). The individualism encouraged by humanistic psychology—trusting and acting on one's feelings, being true to oneself, fulfilling oneself—can lead to self-indulgence, selfishness, and an erosion of moral restraints (Campbell & Specht, 1985; Wallach & Wallach, 1983). Indeed it is those who focus beyond themselves who are most likely to experience social support, to enjoy life, and to cope effectively with stress (Crandall, 1984).

How have humanistic psychologists answered such objections? They counter that belligerence, hostility, and insensitivity are often traceable to a poor self-concept. Moreover, they argue, a secure, nondefensive self-acceptance is actually the first step toward loving others.

A final accusation leveled against humanistic psychology is that it fails to appreciate the reality of our human capacity for evil. Faced with assaults on the environment, overpopulation, and the spread of nuclear weapons, we may become apathetic from either of two rationalizations. One is a naive optimism that denies the threat ("People are basically good; everything will work out"). The other is a dark despair ("It's hopeless; why try?"). Action requires enough realism to fuel concern and enough optimism to provide hope. Humanistic psychology, say the critics, encourages the needed hope but not the equally necessary realism about evil.

Even within humanistic psychology there has been debate over whether people are basically good. Carl Rogers clearly thought so. Although aware of the "incredible amount" of cruel, destructive behavior in the world, he did "not find that this evil is inherent in human nature." He stated that he had never known an individual who—given growth-promoting conditions—had chosen "the cruel or destructive path" (Rogers, 1981). Evil, in his view, springs not from human nature but from toxic cultural influences, including "the constricting, destructive influence of our educational system, the injustice of our distribution of wealth, [and] our cultivated prejudices against individuals who are different."

Fellow humanistic psychologist Rollo May dissented. Of course the cultural context matters, he said. But "Who makes up the culture except persons like you and me? The culture is evil as well as good because we, the human beings who constitute it, are evil as well as good." May agreed with the critics who saw people joining the humanistic movement seeking "a community of like-minded persons who also are playing possum to the evils about us." Accepting the reality of human evil requires "the age-old religious truths of mercy and forgiveness," he said, "and it leaves no place for self-righteousness" (May, 1982).

REVIEW AND REFLECT:

The Humanistic Perspective

What do humanistic psychologists view as the central feature of personality, and what is their goal in studying personality?

Humanistic psychologists have sought to turn psychology's attention from baser motives and environmental conditioning to the growth potential of healthy people, as seen through the individual's own experiences. Abraham Maslow believed that if basic human needs are fulfilled, people will strive to actualize their highest potential. To describe self-actualization, he studied some exemplary personalities and summarized his impressions of their qualities. To nurture growth in others, Carl Rogers advised being genuine, accepting, and empathic. In such a climate, people can develop a deeper self-awareness and a more realistic and positive self-concept.

How do humanistic psychologists assess a person's sense of self? What have we learned from more than three decades of research on the self?

Humanistic psychologists assess personality through questionnaires on which people report their self-concept and in therapy by seeking to understand others' subjective personal experiences. Research on the self documents the importance of high self-esteem and the potency of self-serving bias. Individuals and cultures vary in giving priority to "me" or "we"—to personal control and individual achievement or to social connections and solidarity. Self-reliant *individualism* defines identity in terms of personal goals and attributes; socially connected *collectivism* gives priority to group goals and to one's social identity and commitments.

How has the humanistic perspective on personality influenced psychology? What criticisms have been leveled against humanistic psychology?

Humanistic psychology helped to renew psychology's interest in the self. Nevertheless, humanistic psychology's critics complain that its concepts are vague and subjective, its values individualist and self-centered, and its assumptions naively optimistic.

Terms and Concepts to Remember

self-actualization, p. 527
unconditional positive regard, p. 528
self-concept, p. 528
self-esteem, p. 529

self-serving bias, p. 531
individualism, p. 533
collectivism, p. 533

Test Yourself

41.1. Abraham Maslow theorized that human beings are motivated by a hierarchy of needs. When basic physiological and psychological needs are satisfied, he wrote, people become motivated to fulfill their potential through self-actualization. Maslow based his ideas on
a. people from many cultures.
b. his experiences with patients.
c. a series of laboratory experiments.
d. his study of healthy, creative people.

41.2. According to Carl Rogers, a growth-promoting environment is one that offers genuineness, acceptance, and empathy. The total acceptance Rogers advocated is called
a. self-concept.
b. unconditional positive regard.
c. self-actualization.
d. the "ideal self."

41.3. Researchers have found that high self-esteem is beneficial, noting that people who feel good about themselves have fewer sleepless nights, are less likely to use drugs, and are happier, for example. On the other hand, low self-esteem is linked with life problems. How should this link between low self-esteem and life problems be interpreted?
a. Life problems cause low self-esteem.
b. The answer isn't clear because the link is correlational and does not indicate cause and effect.
c. Low self-esteem leads to life problems.
d. Because of the self-serving bias, we must assume that external factors cause low self-esteem.

41.4. Researchers have found that people tend to accept responsibility for their successes or good qualities and blame circumstances or luck for their failures. This is an example of
a. low self-esteem.
b. self-actualization.
c. self-serving bias.
d. empathy.

41.5. Individualists and collectivists have differing identities. Compared with collectivists, individualists more often define themselves in terms of their
a. family connections.
b. nationality.
c. social roles.
d. personal achievements.

41.6. The humanistic perspective is most concerned with the potential for human growth and self-fulfillment; ideas of the humanistic psychologists have found their way into counseling, education, child-rearing, and popular psychology. The humanistic perspective has been so well received because
a. its emphasis on the individual fits well with the erosion of moral restraints in modern society.
b. it feeds people's optimism about the good in human nature.
c. it negates the idea that humans have a basic capacity for evil.
d. its emphasis on the individual self reflects and reinforces Western cultural values.

Review: In a 1997 Gallup poll, white Americans estimated 44 percent of their fellow white Americans to be high in prejudice (scoring them 5 or higher on a 10-point scale). How many rated themselves similarly high in prejudice? Just 14 percent. What phenomenon does this illustrate?

Reflect: What possible future selves do you envision? To what extent do these imagined selves motivate you now?

Answers to the Test Yourself and Review questions can be found in the green appendix at the end of the book.

42 The Social-Cognitive Perspective

A major perspective on personality that applies psychological principles of learning, cognition, and social behavior was called the *social-cognitive perspective* by psychologist Albert Bandura (1986), and the *cognitive social learning perspective* by others. Its proponents emphasize the importance of external events and how we interpret them.

Exploring Behavior in Situations

Preview Question: In the view of social-cognitive psychologists, what three influences shape an individual's personality?

Like learning theorists, social-cognitive theorists believe we learn many of our behaviors either through conditioning or by observing others and modeling our behavior after theirs. They also emphasize the importance of mental processes: What we think about our situations affects our behavior. Instead of focusing solely on how our environment controls us (behaviorism), social-cognitive theorists focus on how we and our environment interact: How do we interpret and respond to external events? How do our schemas, our memories, and our expectations influence our behavior patterns?

Reciprocal Influences

Bandura (1986) called the process of interacting with our environment **reciprocal determinism**. "Behavior, internal personal factors, and environmental influences," he said, "all operate as interlocking determinants of each other" (**FIGURE 42.1**). For example, children's TV-viewing habits (past behavior) influence their viewing preferences (personal factor), which influence how television (environmental factor) affects their current behavior. The influences are mutual.

FIGURE 42.1
Reciprocal determinism
The social-cognitive perspective proposes that our personalities are shaped by the interaction of personal/cognitive factors (our thoughts and feelings), our environment, and our behaviors.

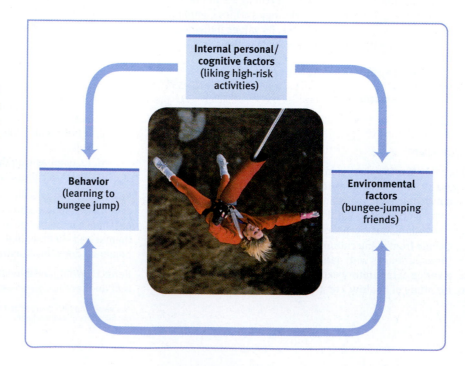

Internal personal/cognitive factors (liking high-risk activities)

Behavior (learning to bungee jump)

Environmental factors (bungee-jumping friends)

Consider three specific ways in which individuals and environments interact:

1. **Different people choose different environments.** The school you attend, the reading you do, the television programs you watch, the music you listen to, the friends you associate with—all are part of an environment you have chosen, based partly on your dispositions (Ickes & others, 1997). *You choose your environment and it then shapes you.*

2. **Our personalities shape how we interpret and react to events.** Anxious people, for example, are more likely to be attuned to potentially threatening events than are nonanxious people (Eysenck & others, 1987). Thus, anxious people perceive the world as more threatening than do those who are nonanxious, and they react accordingly.

3. **Our personalities help create situations to which we react.** Many experiments reveal that how we view and treat people influences how they in turn treat us. If we expect someone to be angry with us, we may give the person a cold shoulder, touching off the very behavior we expect. If we have an easygoing temperament we will likely enjoy close, supportive friendships (Kendler, 1997).

In such ways, we are both the products and the architects of our environments.

If all this has a familiar ring, it may be because it parallels and reinforces a pervasive theme in psychology and in this book: Behavior emerges from the interplay of external and internal influences. Boiling water turns an egg hard and a potato soft. A threatening environment turns one person into a hero, another into a scoundrel. *At every moment*, our behavior is determined by our genes, our experiences, and our personalities.

Personality is seen in individual differences, as it shapes how people interpret and react to events.

Personal Control

In studying how we interact with our environment, social-cognitive psychologists emphasize our sense of **personal control**—whether we learn to see ourselves as controlling, or as controlled by, our environment. Psychologists have two basic ways to study the effect of personal control (or any personality factor). One: *Correlate* people's feelings of control with their behaviors and achievements. Two: *Experiment*, by raising or lowering people's sense of control and noting the effects. Let's take these one at a time.

Locus of Control

Consider your own feelings of control. Do you feel that your life is beyond your control? That the world is run by a few powerful people? That getting a good job depends mainly on being in the right place at the right time? Or do you more strongly believe that what happens to you is your own doing? That the average person can influence government decisions? That being a success is a matter of hard work, not luck?

Hundreds of studies have compared people who differ in their perceptions of control. On the one side are those who have what psychologist Julian Rotter called an **external locus of control**—the perception that chance or outside forces determine their fate. On the other are those who perceive an **internal locus of control** and believe that to a great extent they control their own destiny. In study after study, "internals" achieve more in school, act more independently, enjoy better health, and feel less depressed than do "externals" (Lachman & Weaver, 1998; Lefcourt, 1982; Presson & Benassi, 1996). Moreover, they are better able to delay gratification and cope with various stresses, including marital problems (Miller & others, 1986).

Learned Helplessness Versus Personal Control

People who feel helpless and oppressed often perceive control as external. This perception may then deepen their feelings of resignation. In fact, this is precisely what researcher Martin Seligman (1975, 1991) and others found in experiments with both

■ **reciprocal determinism** the interacting influences between personality and environmental factors.

■ **personal control** our sense of controlling our environment rather than feeling helpless.

■ **external locus of control** the perception that chance or outside forces beyond one's personal control determine one's fate.

■ **internal locus of control** the perception that one controls one's own fate.

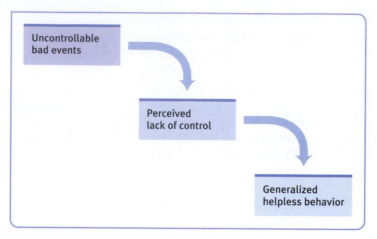

FIGURE 42.2
Learned helplessness When animals and people experience no control over repeated bad events, they often learn helplessness.

Uncontrollable bad events

Perceived lack of control

Generalized helpless behavior

animals and people. Dogs strapped in a harness and given repeated shocks, with no opportunity to avoid them, learned a sense of helplessness. Later placed in another situation where they *could* escape the punishment by simply leaping a hurdle, the dogs cowered without hope. Repeatedly faced with traumatic events over which they have no control, people, too, come to feel helpless, hopeless, and depressed. Psychologists call this passive resignation **learned helplessness** (**FIGURE 42.2**). In contrast, animals able to escape the shocks in the first situation learned personal control and easily escaped the shocks in the new situation.

In concentration camps, in prisons, even in factories, colleges, and well-meaning nursing homes, people given little control experience a similar lowering of their morale and an increase in stress. Part of the shock we feel in an unfamiliar culture comes from a diminished sense of control when unsure how people in the new environment will respond (Triandis, 1994). Measures that increase control—allowing prisoners to move chairs and control room lights and the TV, having workers participate in decision making, offering nursing home patients choices about their environment—noticeably improve health and morale (Miller & Monge, 1986; Ruback & others, 1986; Wener & others, 1987). In one famous study of nursing home patients, 93 percent of those encouraged to exert more control became more alert, active, and happy (Rodin, 1986). As researcher Ellen Langer (1983, p. 291) concluded, "Perceived control is basic to human functioning." She recommended that "for the young and old alike," it is important that we create environments that enhance our sense of control and personal efficacy.

The verdict of these studies is reassuring: Under conditions of democracy, personal freedom, and empowerment, people thrive. Small wonder that the citizens of stable democracies report higher levels of happiness (Inglehart, 1990). Shortly before the democratic revolution in the former East Germany, psychologists Gabriele Oettingen and Martin Seligman (1990) compared the telltale body language of working-class men in East and West Berlin bars. Compared with their counterparts on the other side of the Wall, the empowered West Berliners much more often laughed, sat upright rather than slumped, and had upward- rather than downward-turned mouths. To paraphrase the Roman philosopher Seneca, happy are those who choose their own path.

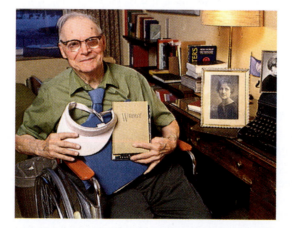

Control affects well-being
Nursing home residents who can arrange their own possessions, control other aspects of their daily lives, and pursue their own interests are more vigorous and happy than those who do not have these opportunities.

Optimism

One measure of how helpless or effective you feel is where you stand on the optimism-pessimism continuum. How do you characteristically explain negative and positive events? Perhaps you have known students whose *attributional style* is negative—who attribute poor performance to their lack of ability ("I can't do this") or to situations

CLOSE-UP:

TOWARD A MORE POSITIVE PSYCHOLOGY

During its first century, psychology understandably focused much of its attention on understanding and alleviating negative states. We have studied abuse and anxiety, depression and disease, prejudice and poverty. Articles on selected negative emotions since 1887 have outnumbered those on positive emotions by 14 to 1. Similarly, the 14,964 articles on "crime" dwarf the 1155 articles on "virtue." "Anger" (8166 articles) has outstripped "forgiveness" (416). And "fear" (18,602 articles) has triumphed over "courage" (671).

In ages past, noted 1998 American Psychological Association president Martin Seligman (1998a,b), times of relative peace and prosperity have enabled cultures to turn their attention from repairing weakness and damage to promoting "the highest qualities of life." Prosperous fifth-century Athens nurtured philosophy and democracy. Flourishing fifteenth-century Florence nurtured great art. Victorian England, flush with the bounty of the British empire, nurtured honor, discipline, and duty. In the new millennium, Seligman believes that thriving Western cultures have a parallel opportunity to create, as a "humane, scientific monument," a more

positive psychology—a psychology concerned not only with weakness and damage but also with strength and virtue.

Positive psychology shares with humanistic psychology an interest in advancing human fulfillment, but its origins and methodology are scientific. From these roots have grown not only the new studies of happiness and health but also the shift in emphasis from learned helplessness and depression to optimism and thriving. Taken together, satisfaction with the past, happiness with the

Martin E. P. Seligman
"The main purpose of a positive psychology is to measure, understand and then build the human strengths and the civic virtues."

present, and optimism about the future define the movement's first pillar: *positive subjective well-being.*

The second pillar, *positive character*, focuses on exploring and enhancing virtues such as creativity, courage, compassion, integrity, self-control, leadership, wisdom, and spirituality. Current research examines the roots and fruits of such virtues, sometimes by studying individuals who exemplify them in extraordinary ways.

The third pillar, *positive groups, communities, and cultures*, seeks to foster a positive social ecology, including healthy families, communal neighborhoods, effective schools, socially responsible media, and civil dialogue.

Will psychology have a more positive mission in this new century? Without slighting the need to repair damage and cure disease, the supporters of positive psychology hope so. With *American Psychologist* millennial issues (January 2000 and January 2001) devoted to this topic, and with a forthcoming *Handbook of Positive Psychology* (Snyder & Lopez, in press), an upcoming book series, and new prizes for outstanding positive psychology scholarship, these psychologists have reason to be positive.

---

beyond their control ("bad" teachers, textbooks, or exam questions). Such students are more likely to persist in getting low grades than are students who adopt the more hopeful attitude that effort, good study habits, and self-discipline can make a difference (Noel & others, 1987; Peterson & Barrett, 1987).

In their study of professional achievement, Seligman and Peter Schulman (1986) compared sales made by new life insurance representatives who were more or less optimistic in their outlooks. Those who put an optimistic spin on their setbacks—seeing them as flukes or as a means to learning a new approach, rather than viewing them as signs of incompetence—sold more policies during their first year and were half as likely to quit. Seligman's finding came to life for him when Bob Dell, one of the optimistic recruits who began selling for Metropolitan Life after taking Seligman's optimism test, later dialed him up and sold him a policy.

Health, too, benefits from a basic optimism. A depressed hopelessness dampens the body's disease-fighting immune system. In repeated studies, optimists have been found to outlive pessimists or to live with fewer illnesses.

If positive thinking in the face of adversity pays dividends, so, too, can a dash of realism. Anxiety over possible failure can actually fuel energetic efforts to avoid the

- **learned helplessness** the hopelessness and passive resignation an animal or human learns when unable to avoid repeated aversive events.

- **positive psychology** the scientific study of optimal human functioning; aims to discover and promote conditions that enable individuals and communities to thrive.

"We just haven't been flapping them hard enough."

"O God, give us grace to accept with serenity the things that cannot be changed, courage to change the things which should be changed, and the wisdom to distinguish the one from the other."

Reinhold Niebuhr, "The Serenity Prayer," 1943

"I didn't think it could happen to me."

Earvin "Magic" Johnson, *My Life*, 1993 (after contracting the HIV virus)

"Ignorance more freely begets confidence than does knowledge."

Charles Darwin, *The Descent of Man*, 1871

dreaded fate (Cantor & Norem, 1989; Goodhart, 1986; Showers, 1992). Overconfident students often perform less well than their equally able peers who, concerned about bombing the upcoming exam, study thoroughly and get a top grade. Edward Chang (1996) reports that, compared with European-American students, Asian-American students express somewhat greater pessimism—which he suspects helps explain their more impressive academic achievements. Success requires enough optimism to provide hope and enough pessimism to prevent complacency.

Excessive optimism can also blind us to real risks. Neil Weinstein (1980, 1982, 1996) has shown how our natural positive-thinking bias can promote "an unrealistic optimism about future life events." Most college students perceive themselves as less likely than their average classmate to develop drinking problems, drop out of school, or have a heart attack by age 40. Most late adolescents see themselves as much less vulnerable than their peers to the AIDS virus (Abrams, 1991). Our natural positive-thinking bias does seem to vanish, however, when we are bracing ourselves for feedback, as when we are about to receive exam results (Taylor & Shepperd, 1998). (Have you ever noticed that, as a game nears its end the outcome seems more in doubt when your team is ahead than when it is behind?) Positive illusions also vanish after a traumatic personal experience—as they did for California victims of a catastrophic earthquake, who had to give up their illusions of being less vulnerable than others to earthquakes (Helweg-Larsen, 1999).

Given illusory optimism, documented in some 200 research reports, people may fail to take sensible precautions. Most young Americans know that half of U.S. marriages end in divorce, but they are confident that *theirs* will not (Lehman & Nisbett, 1985). Most cigarette smokers smoke high-tar brands, but only 17 percent believe their brand has a more hazardous tar level than most others (Segerstrom & others, 1993). Compared with other women at their university, sexually active undergraduate women—especially those who do *not* consistently use effective contraception—perceive themselves as *less* vulnerable to unwanted pregnancy (Burger & Burns, 1988). Individuals who optimistically venture into ill-fated relationships, deny the effects of smoking, or engage in unprotected sex remind us that, like pride, blind optimism may go before a fall.

Ironically, people often are most overconfident when most incompetent. That's because it often takes competence to recognize competence, note Justin Kruger and David Dunning (1999). They found that most students scoring at the low end of tests of grammar and logic believed they had scored in the top half. If you do not know what good grammar is, you may be unaware that your grammar is poor. The difficulty in recognizing one's own incompetence helps explain why so many low-scoring students are dumbfounded after doing badly on an exam.

DOONESBURY   **BY GARRY TRUDEAU**

Assessing Behavior in Situations

Preview Question: What underlying principle guides social-cognitive psychologists in their assessment of people's behavior and beliefs?

Social-cognitive researchers explore the effect of differing situations on people's behavior patterns and attitudes. They study, for example, how viewing aggressive or nonaggressive models affects behavior. They assess the impact of dehumanizing situations on people's attitudes. And they examine the consistency of people's personalities in varying circumstances.

An ambitious example of such research, and one that predates social-cognitive theory, is the U.S. Army's World War II strategy for assessing candidates for spy missions. Rather than using paper-and-pencil tests, army psychologists subjected the candidates to simulated undercover conditions. They tested their ability to handle stress, solve problems, maintain leadership, and withstand intense interrogation without blowing their covers. Although it was time-consuming and expensive, this assessment of behavior in a realistic situation helped predict later success on actual spy missions (OSS Assessment Staff, 1948).

Military and educational organizations and 4 in 5 Fortune 500 companies are continuing this strategy in their evaluations of hundreds of thousands of people each year in assessment centers (Bray & others, 1991, 1997). AT&T observes prospective managers doing simulated managerial work. Many colleges assess potential faculty members' teaching abilities by observing them teach. Armies assess their soldiers by observing them during military exercises. Most American cities with populations of 50,000 or more use assessment centers in evaluating police and fire officers (Lowry, 1997).

These procedures exploit the principle that the best means of predicting future behavior is neither a personality test nor an interviewer's intuition. Rather, it is the person's past behavior patterns in similar situations (Mischel, 1981; Oullette & Wood, 1998; Schmidt & Hunter, 1998). As long as the situation and the person remain much the same, the best predictor of future job performance is past job performance; the best predictor of future grades is past grades; the best predictor of future aggressiveness is past aggressiveness; the best predictor of drug use in young adulthood is drug use in high school. If you can't check the person's past behavior, the next-best thing is to create an assessment situation that simulates the demands of the task so you can see how the person handles them.

Evaluating the Social-Cognitive Perspective

Preview Question: What has the social-cognitive perspective contributed to the study of psychology, and what criticisms have been leveled against it?

The social-cognitive perspective on personality sensitizes researchers to how situations affect, and are affected by, individuals. More than do the other perspectives, it builds from psychological research on learning and cognition.

One criticism is that the theory focuses so much on the situation that it fails to appreciate the person's inner traits. Where is the person in this view of personality, ask the dissenters (Carlson, 1984); and where are human emotions? True, the situation does guide our behavior. But, say the critics, in many instances our unconscious motives, our emotions, and our pervasive traits shine through. Consider Percy Ray Pridgen and Charles Gill. They each faced the same situation: They jointly won a $90 million lottery jackpot (Harriston, 1993). When he learned of the winning numbers, Pridgen began trembling uncontrollably, huddled with a friend behind a bathroom door while confirming the win, then sobbed. Gill told his wife and then went to sleep.

REVIEW AND REFLECT:

The Social-Cognitive Perspective

In the view of social-cognitive psychologists, what three influences shape an individual's personality?

The social-cognitive perspective applies principles of learning, cognition, and social behavior to personality, with particular emphasis on the ways in which our personality influences and is influenced by our interaction with the environment. It assumes reciprocal determinism—that personal-cognitive factors combine with the environment to influence people's behavior. By studying how people vary in their perceived locus of control and in their experiences of learned helplessness, researchers have found that a sense of personal control helps people to cope with life. Research on learned helplessness has evolved into research on optimism and now into a broader positive psychology movement.

What underlying principle guides social-cognitive psychologists in their assessment of people's behavior and beliefs?

Social-cognitive researchers observe how people's behaviors and beliefs both affect and are affected by their situations. They have found that the best way to predict someone's behavior in a given situation is to observe that person's behavior pattern in similar situations.

What has the social-cognitive perspective contributed to the study of psychology, and what criticisms have been leveled against it?

Although faulted for slighting the importance of unconscious dynamics, emotions, and inner traits, the social-cognitive perspective builds on psychology's well-established concepts of learning and cognition and reminds us of the power of social situations.

Terms and Concepts to Remember

reciprocal determinism, p. 538　　internal locus of control, p. 539
personal control, p. 539　　learned helplessness, p. 540
external locus of control, p. 539　　positive psychology, p. 541

Test Yourself

42.1. Albert Bandura, a social-cognitive theorist, believes that interacting with our environment involves reciprocal determinism, or mutual influences among personal factors, environmental factors, and behavior. An example of an environmental factor is

　a. the presence of books in a home.
　b. a preference for outdoor play.
　c. the ability to read at a fourth-grade level.
　d. the fear of violent action on television.

42.2. Researchers have found that when elderly patients are given an active part in the management of their care and surroundings, their morale and health tend to improve. The assumption is that the patients do better when they perceive

　a. learned helplessness.
　b. an external locus of control.
　c. an internal locus of control.
　d. reciprocal determinism.

42.3. Martin Seligman described an attitude of passive resignation, which he called learned helplessness. Working with animals and people, Seligman identified the circumstances under which learned helplessness develops. For example, a dog will respond with learned helplessness if it has received repeated shocks and has had

　a. the opportunity to escape.
　b. no control over the shocks.
　c. pain or discomfort.
　d. no food or water prior to the shocks.

42.4. The social-cognitive perspective holds that the best means of predicting future behavior is a person's past behavior in similar situations. An assessment procedure based on this principle is

　a. the road test in a driving exam.
　b. the written test in a driving exam.
　c. an essay in which you predict what kind of a driver you will be.
　d. the driving instructor's intuition about your future road behavior.

42.5. Social-cognitive theory applies principles of learning, cognition, and social behavior to personality. This perspective has been criticized for ignoring the influence of

　a. the environment.
　b. social situations.
　c. people's beliefs.
　d. emotions and unconscious motives.

Review: How do learned helplessness and optimism influence behavior?

Reflect: Are you a pessimist? Do you readily catastrophize, have low expectations, and attribute bad events to your inability or to circumstances beyond your control? Or are you an optimist, perhaps even someone who frequently exhibits "illusory optimism"? How did either tendency influence your choice of school or major?

Answers to the Test Yourself and Review questions can be found in the green appendix at the end of the book.

Reflections on the Four Perspectives on Personality

Each perspective summarized in the Table can teach us something. The psychoanalytic perspective draws our attention to the unconscious and irrational aspects of human existence. The trait perspective systematically describes and classifies important components of personality. The humanistic perspective reminds us of the importance of our sense of self and of our potential for self-actualization. The social-cognitive perspective teaches us that we always act in the context of situations that we help to create.

Seldom in life does a single perspective on any issue give us a complete picture of another human being. Human personality reveals its different aspects when we view it from different perspectives, and each perspective can enlarge our vision of the whole person.

"Nature is always more subtle, more intricate, more elegant than what we are able to imagine."

Carl Sagan, "Science—Who Cares?" 1991

THE FOUR PERSPECTIVES ON PERSONALITY

Perspective	Explanation of Behavior	Assessment Techniques	Evaluation
Psychoanalytic	Unconscious conflicts between pleasure-seeking impulses and social restraints	Projective tests aimed at revealing unconscious motivations	A speculative, hard-to-test theory with enormous cultural impact
Trait	Expressing biologically influenced dispositions, such as extraversion or introversion	Personality inventories that assess the strengths of different traits	A descriptive approach criticized as sometimes underestimating the variability of behavior from situation to situation
Humanistic	Processing conscious feelings about oneself in the light of one's experiences and needs	Questionnaire assessments of self-concept	A theory that reinvigorated contemporary interest in the self; criticized as subjective and sometimes naively self-centered and optimistic
Social-cognitive	Reciprocal influences between people and their situations, colored by perceptions of control	Correlational and experimental studies of people's feelings of control	An interactive theory that integrates research on learning, cognition, and social behavior; criticized as underestimating the importance of emotions and enduring traits

Psychological Disorders

I felt the need to clean my room at home in Indianapolis every Sunday and would spend four to five hours at it. I would take every book out of the bookcase, dust and put it back. At the time I loved doing it. Then I didn't want to do it anymore, but I couldn't stop. The clothes in my closet hung exactly two fingers apart. . . . I made a ritual of touching the wall in my bedroom before I went out because something bad would happen if I didn't do it the right way. I had a constant anxiety about it as a kid, and it made me think for the first time that I might be nuts.

Marc, diagnosed with obsessive-compulsive disorder (From Summers, 1996)

Whenever I get depressed it's because I've lost a sense of self. I can't find reasons to like myself. I think I'm ugly. I think no one likes me. . . . I become grumpy and short-tempered. Nobody wants to be around me. I'm left alone. Being alone confirms that I am ugly and not worth being with. I think I'm responsible for everything that goes wrong.

Greta, diagnosed with depression (From Thorne, 1993, p. 21)

Voices, like the roar of a crowd came. I felt like Jesus; I was being crucified. It was dark. I just continued to huddle under the blanket, feeling weak, laid bare and defenseless in a cruel world I could no longer understand.

Stuart, diagnosed with schizophrenia (From Emmons & others, 1997)

People are fascinated by the exceptional, the unusual, the abnormal. But why such fascination with disturbed people? Do we see in them something of ourselves? At various moments, all of us feel, think, or act the way disturbed people do much of the time. We, too, get anxious, depressed, withdrawn, suspicious, deluded, or antisocial, just less intensely and more briefly. It's no wonder then that studying psychological disorders may at times evoke an eerie sense of self-recognition, one that illuminates the dynamics of our own personality. "To study the abnormal is the best way of understanding the normal," proposed William James (1842–1910).

Another reason for our curiosity is that so many of us have felt, either personally or through friends or family members, the bewilderment and pain of a psychological disorder—which can bring unexplained physical symptoms, irrational fears, or even the feeling that life is not worth living.

Module 43 introduces psychological disorders, explaining the major perspectives and categories and the risks of labeling, and the prevalance of the various disorders. Module 44 describes *anxiety disorders*, which are characterized by persistent distressing anxiety or maladaptive behaviors that reduce anxiety. Module 45 focuses on the rare and controversial *dissociative disorders*, and the problematic *personality disorders*, which impair social functioning. Module 46 examines the emotional extremes of *mood disorders* in depth. And Module 47 outlines the symptoms and characteristics of those suffering from *schizophrenia*, a frightening split from reality.

> "The sun shines and warms and lights us and we have no curiosity to know why this is so, but we ask the reason of all evil, of pain, and hunger, and [unusual] people."
>
> **Ralph Waldo Emerson, 1803–1882**

Introduction to Psychological Disorders

Most people would agree that someone who is too depressed to get out of bed for weeks at a time has a psychological disorder. But what about those who, having experienced a loss, are unable to resume their usual social activities? Where should we draw the line between sadness and depression? Between zany creativity and bizarre irrationality? Between normality and abnormality? How should we *define* psychological disorders? Equally important, how should we *understand* disorders—as sicknesses that need to be diagnosed and cured, or as natural responses to a troubling environment? Finally, how might we *classify* psychological disorders? Can we do so in a way that allows us to help disturbed people without stigmatizing them with labels?

Defining Psychological Disorders

Preview Question: Where should we draw the line between normality and disorder?

Many mental health workers view **psychological disorders** as *harmful dysfunctions* (Spitzer, 1997; Wakefield, 1997). *Dysfunction* refers to not functioning as natural selection predisposes our species to behave, and *harmful* is a judgment of undesirability. Thus, they label behavior as disordered when they judge it to be *atypical, disturbing, maladaptive,* and *unjustifiable.*

Being different from most other people in one's culture is *part* of what it takes to define a psychological disorder. As the reclusive poet Emily Dickinson observed in 1862,

A benign obsession
British street cleaner Snowy Farr's eccentric behavior may indeed be atypical, but clinicians would not label it disordered because it is neither particularly disturbing nor maladaptive.

Assent—and you are sane—
Demur—you're straightaway dangerous—
and handled with a Chain.

But there is more to a disorder than being atypical. Olympic gold medalists are abnormal in their physical abilities, and they are heroes. To be considered disordered, an atypical behavior must also be one that other people find *disturbing.*

Standards of acceptability for behaviors vary. In some cultures, people routinely behave in ways (such as going about naked) that in other cultures would be grounds for arrest. In at least one cultural context—wartime—even mass killing may be viewed as heroic. One person's homicidal "terrorist" is another person's "freedom fighter." Standards of acceptability also vary over time. Sex experts William Acton, writing in the late 1800s, and William Masters and Virginia Johnson, writing in the late 1900s, all knew that some women have orgasms during intercourse but that others don't (Wakefield, 1992). For Acton, orgasm was a disorder (resulting from overstimulation); for Masters and Johnson, lack of orgasm was a disorder (resulting from inadequate stimulation).

On December 9, 1973, homosexuality was an illness. By day's end on December 10 it was not. The American Psychiatric Association had dropped homosexuality as a disorder (because it no longer equated being gay with having psychological problems). Later it *added* nicotine dependence (because it deemed smoking both addictive and self-destructive).

Atypical and disturbing behaviors are more likely to be considered disordered when judged harmful. Indeed, many clinicians define disorders as behaviors that are *maladaptive*—as when a smoker's nicotine dependence causes physical damage. By this yardstick, even typical behaviors, such as the occasional despondency that many college students feel, may signal a psychological disorder—if they become disabling. Maladaptiveness, then, is a key element in defining a disorder: The behaviors must be distressing or disabling or put one at greatly increased risk of suffering or death. An intense fear of spiders may be irrational, but if it doesn't impair your life it's not a disorder.

Finally, abnormal behavior is most likely to be considered disordered when others find it rationally *unjustifiable*. Actress Shirley MacLaine could wear a crystal on her neck and say, "See the outer bubble of white light watching you. It is part of you," and not be seen as disordered because enough people found her rational (Friedrich, 1987).

> "If a man is in a minority of one, we lock him up."
>
> Oliver Wendell Holmes, 1841–1935

Understanding Psychological Disorders

Preview Question: What theoretical models or perspectives can help us to understand psychological disorders?

To explain puzzling behavior, people in earlier times often presumed that strange forces—the movements of the stars, godlike powers, or evil spirits—were at work. "The devil made him do it," you might have said, if you had lived during the Middle Ages. The cure might have been to get rid of the evil force—by placating the great powers or exorcising the demon. Until the last two centuries, "mad" people were sometimes caged in zoolike conditions or given "therapies" appropriate to a demon: They were sometimes beaten, burned, or castrated. In other times, the therapy included pulling teeth, removing lengths of intestines, and cauterizing the clitoris. Some people considered "mad" even had their own blood removed and replaced with transfusions of animal blood (Farina, 1982).

The Medical Perspective

In opposition to such brutal treatment, reformers such as Philippe Pinel (1745–1826) in France insisted madness was not demon possession but a sickness caused by severe stresses and inhumane conditions. For Pinel and other reformers, treatment included boosting patients' morale by unchaining them, talking with them, and replacing brutality with gentleness, isolation with activity, and filth with clean air and sun.

When physicians later discovered that syphilis infects the brain and distorts the mind, health reformers and medical workers began to focus on physical causes for disorders and treatments that would cure them. Today, the medical perspective is familiar and recognizable to us in the terminology of the mental *health* movement: A mental *illness* (also called a *psychopathology*) needs to be *diagnosed* on the basis of its *symptoms* and *cured* through *therapy*, which may include *treatment* in a psychiatric *hospital*. In the 1800s, the assumption of this **medical model**—that psychological disorders are sicknesses—provided the impetus for much-needed reform. Comfort replaced chains, therapy replaced torture, and hospitals replaced asylums.

■ **psychological disorder** a "harmful dysfunction" in which behavior is judged to be atypical, disturbing, maladaptive, and unjustifiable.

■ **medical model** the concept that diseases have physical causes that can be diagnosed, treated, and, in most cases, cured. When applied to psychological disorders, the medical model assumes that these "mental" illnesses can be diagnosed on the basis of their symptoms and cured through therapy, which may include treatment in a psychiatric hospital.

The medical perspective has gained credibility from recent discoveries. As we will see, genetically influenced abnormalities in brain structure and biochemistry contribute to a number of disorders. "Mental illnesses are diagnosable disorders of the brain," declares a White House fact sheet on mental illness (1999). Two of the most troubling, depression and schizophrenia, are often treated medically. But psychological factors, such as traumatic stress, also play an important role.

The Bio-Psycho-Social Perspective

Today's psychologists contend that *all* behavior, whether called normal or disordered, arises from the interaction of nature (genetic and physiological factors) and nurture (past and present experiences). To presume that a person is "mentally ill" attributes the condition solely to an internal problem—to a "sickness" that must be found and cured. Maybe there *is* no deep, internal problem. Maybe instead there is a growth-blocking difficulty in the person's environment, in the person's current interpretations of events, or in the person's bad habits and poor social skills.

Evidence of environmental effects comes from links between disorder and culture. Some major disorders such as depression and schizophrenia occur worldwide. From Asia to Africa and across the Americas, the core symptoms of schizophrenia include irrationality and incoherent speech (Brislin, 1993; Draguns, 1990b). Other disorders are culture-bound (Beardsley, 1994; Castillo, 1997). Different cultures have different sources of stress and produce different ways of coping. The eating disorders anorexia nervosa and bulimia, for example, occur mostly in Western cultures. *Susto*, marked by severe anxiety, restlessness, and a fear of black magic, is a disorder found in Latin America. *Taijin-kyofusho*, which combines social anxiety about one's appearance with a readiness to blush and a fear of eye contact, appears in Japan. Such disorders may share an underlying dynamic (such as anxiety) while differing in the symptoms (an eating problem or a type of fear) manifested in a particular culture.

Today, most mental health workers assume that disorders are influenced by genetic predispositions and physiological states. And by inner psychological dynamics. And by social and cultural circumstances. To get the whole picture, we need an interdisciplinary **bio-psycho-social perspective** (**FIGURE 43.1**).

"Who in the rainbow can draw the line where the violet tint ends and the orange tint begins? Distinctly we see the difference of the colors, but where exactly does the one first blendingly enter into the other? So with sanity and insanity?"

Herman Melville, *Billy Budd, Sailor,* **1924**

"It's no measure of health to be well adjusted to a profoundly sick society."

Krishnamurti, 1895–1986

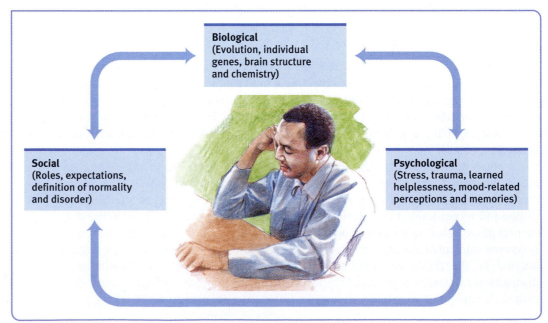

FIGURE 43.1
The bio-psycho-social perspective
Today's psychology studies how biological, psychological, and social factors interact to produce specific psychological disorders.

Biological
(Evolution, individual genes, brain structure and chemistry)

Social
(Roles, expectations, definition of normality and disorder)

Psychological
(Stress, trauma, learned helplessness, mood-related perceptions and memories)

Classifying Psychological Disorders

Preview Question: How and why do clinicians classify psychological disorders?

In biology and the other sciences, classification creates order. To classify an animal as a mammal says a great deal—that it is warm-blooded, has hair or fur, and nourishes its young with milk. In psychiatry and psychology, too, classification both orders and describes clusters of symptoms. To classify a person's disorder as "schizophrenia" suggests that the person talks incoherently, hallucinates or has delusions (bizarre beliefs), shows either little emotion or inappropriate emotion, or is socially withdrawn. Thus, the diagnostic term simply provides a handy shorthand for describing a complex disorder.

In psychiatry and psychology, diagnostic classification ideally aims to describe a disorder, predict its future course, imply appropriate treatment, and stimulate research into its causes. Indeed, to study a disorder we must first name and describe it. The current authoritative scheme for classifying psychological disorders is the American Psychiatric Association's *Diagnostic and Statistical Manual of Mental Disorders (Fourth Edition)*, nicknamed **DSM-IV**. This 1994 volume and an accompanying book of case illustrations provide the basis for much of the material in this chapter. DSM-IV was developed in coordination with the tenth edition of the World Health Organization's *International Classification of Diseases* (ICD-10).

The very idea of "diagnosing" people's problems in terms of their "symptoms" presumes a mental "illness." As a result, some practitioners are not enthralled with this medical terminology, but most find DSM-IV a helpful and practical tool. It is also a financially necessary one: Most North American health insurance companies require a DSM-IV diagnosis before they will pay for therapy.

DSM-IV defines 17 major categories of "mental disorder," describing the disorders and listing their prevalence without presuming to explain their causes. The once-popular term *neurosis*, for example, is no longer a diagnostic category—because neurosis was Freud's idea of the process by which unconscious conflicts cause anxiety. DSM-IV does mention **neurotic disorders**—psychological disorders that, although distressing, still allow one to think rationally and function socially. But even this term is so vague that psychologists use it minimally, usually as a contrast to the more bizarre and debilitating **psychotic disorders**, marked by irrationality.

For a DSM-IV category to be valid, it must first be reliable. If one psychiatrist or psychologist diagnoses someone as having, say, "catatonic schizophrenia," what are the chances that another mental health worker will independently give the same diagnosis? With the DSM-IV's diagnostic guidelines, the chances are good. The guidelines work by asking clinicians a series of objective questions about observable behaviors, such as, "Is the person afraid to leave home?" In one study, 16 psychologists used this structured-interview procedure to diagnose 75 psychiatric patients as suffering from (1) depression, (2) generalized anxiety, or (3) some other disorder (Riskind & others, 1987). Without knowing the first psychologist's diagnosis, another psychologist viewed a videotape of each interview and offered a second opinion. For 83 percent of the patients, the two opinions agreed.

Some critics fault the manual for casting too wide a net and bringing "almost any kind of behavior within the compass of psychiatry" (Eysenck & others, 1983). These critics point to behaviors ranging from irrational fear of humiliation and embarrassment (social phobia) to persistently breaking rules at home or school (conduct disorder). As the number of disorder categories has swelled, from 60 in the 1950s' DSM to 400 in today's, so has the number of adults who meet the criteria for at least one psychiatric ailment—nearly 30 percent in one recent year according to one national survey (Regier & others, 1998).

Other DSM critics register a more fundamental complaint—that these labels are at best arbitrary and at worst value judgments masquerading as science.

"I'm always like this, and my family was wondering if you could prescribe a mild depressant."

© 1992 by Sidney Harris.

■ **bio-psycho-social perspective** a contemporary perspective which assumes that biological, psychological, and sociocultural factors combine and interact to produce psychological disorders.

■ **DSM-IV** the American Psychiatric Association's *Diagnostic and Statistical Manual of Mental Disorders (Fourth Edition)*, a widely used system for classifying psychological disorders.

■ **neurotic disorder** a psychological disorder that is usually distressing but that allows one to think rationally and function socially. Freud saw the neurotic disorders as ways of dealing with anxiety.

■ **psychotic disorder** a psychological disorder in which a person loses contact with reality, experiencing irrational ideas and distorted perceptions.

Labeling Psychological Disorders

Preview Question: Why do some psychologists criticize the use of diagnostic labels?

Once we label a person, we view that person differently (Farina, 1982). Labels create preconceptions that can bias our perceptions and our interpretations. It is better, some clinicians say, to study the roots of specific symptoms, such as delusions or hallucinations, than to study catchall categories, such as schizophrenia (Persons, 1986).

In the most controversial demonstration of the biasing power of diagnostic labels, David Rosenhan (1973) and seven of his friends and Stanford University colleagues went to mental hospital admissions offices, complaining of "hearing voices" that were saying "empty," "hollow," and "thud." Apart from this complaint and giving false names and occupations, they answered all the questions truthfully. All eight were diagnosed as mentally ill.

That these normal people were misdiagnosed is not really surprising. As one psychiatrist noted, if someone swallowed blood, went to an emergency room, and spat it up, would we fault the doctor for diagnosing a bleeding ulcer? What followed the diagnosis, however, *was* startling. Until being released (an average of 19 days later), the "patients" exhibited no further symptoms. Yet the clinicians were able to "discover" the causes of their disorders after analyzing their (quite normal) life histories. They said one person was reacting to mixed emotions about his parents. Even the normal behaviors of the "patients," such as taking notes, were often misinterpreted as symptoms.

Other studies also confirm that labels affect how we perceive one another. Ellen Langer and her colleagues (1974, 1980) had people rate an interviewee they thought was either normal (a job applicant) or out of the ordinary (a psychiatric or cancer patient). All the raters saw the identical videotape. Those who watched unlabeled interviewees perceived them as normal; those who watched supposed patients perceived them as "different from most people." Therapists (who thought they were evaluating a psychiatric patient) perceived the interviewee as "frightened of his own aggressive impulses," a "passive, dependent type," and so forth. A label can serve a useful purpose. But as Rosenhan discovered, it can also have "a life and an influence of its own."

The power of labels to stigmatize people in others' eyes was illustrated when a female associate of psychologist Stewart Page (1977) called 180 people in Toronto who were advertising furnished rooms for rent. When she merely asked if the room was still available, the answer was nearly always yes. When she said she was about to be released from a mental hospital, the answer three times out of four was no (as it was when she said she was calling for her brother who was about to be released from jail). When some who answered no were later called by a second person who simply asked if the room was still available, the advertiser nearly always said it was. Surveys in Western Europe have uncovered similar attitudes toward those labeled mentally ill. But as we have come to understand psychological disorders as diseases of the brain, not failures of character, the stigma seems to be lifting (Solomon, 1996). More and more public figures are feeling free to "come out" and speak with candor about their struggles with disorders such as depression. And, the more often people have contact with mental health patients, the more accepting their attitudes are (Kolodziej & Johnson, 1996).

If people also form their impressions of psychological disorder from the popular media, then it is hardly surprising that stereotypes linger. Television researcher George Gerbner (1985) reported that 1 in 5 prime-time and daytime programs depicts a psychologically disordered person, and 7 in 10 of such programs portray this character as violent or criminal. Movies, too, stereotype mental health patients, sometimes as homicidal (Anthony Hopkins' role in *Silence of the Lambs*) or as freaks (Woody Allen

"One of the unpardonable sins, in the eyes of most people, is for a man to go about unlabelled. The world regards such a person as the police do an unmuzzled dog, not under proper control."

T. H. Huxley, *Evolution and Ethics*, 1893

Tipper Gore

"I had clinical depression, recognized it, and went to a social worker. I got diagnosed and then successfully treated. I hope that will encourage people to seek treatment if they think they are suffering from depression."

Tipper Gore (1999)

as *Zelig*) (Hyler & others, 1991; Wahl, 1992). As Unabomber Theodore Kaczynski vividly illustrated, people with schizophrenia are indeed more likely than others to commit violent crime, especially if they also abuse alcohol (Citrome & Volavka, 1999; Tiihonen & others, 1997). However, at least 9 in 10 people with disorders are *not* dangerous; instead, they are anxious, depressed, or withdrawn. And *if* they steer clear of alcohol and drugs, those released from mental hospitals are no more prone to violence than are their neighbors (Steadman & others, 1998). Indeed, reports the U.S. Surgeon General's Office (1999, p. 7), "There is very little risk of violence or harm to a stranger from casual contact with an individual who has a mental disorder."

Labels not only can bias perceptions, they can also change reality. When teachers are told certain students are "gifted," when students expect someone to be "hostile," or when interviewers check to see whether someone is "extraverted," they may act in ways that elicit the very behavior expected (Snyder, 1984). Someone who was led to think you are nasty may treat you coldly, leading you to respond as a mean-spirited person would. Labels can serve as self-fulfilling prophecies.

But let us remind ourselves of the benefits of diagnostic labels. As Robert Spitzer (1975), a chief author of the current diagnostic system explained, "There is a purpose to psychiatric diagnosis. It is to enable mental health professionals to (a) communicate with each other about the subject matter of their concern, (b) comprehend the pathological processes involved in psychiatric illness, and (c) control psychiatric outcomes."

Rates of Psychological Disorders

Preview Questions: How many people suffer, or have suffered, a psychological disorder? Does the risk vary with ethnicity or gender?

Each year there are nearly 2.1 million inpatient admissions to U.S. mental hospitals and psychiatric units (Bureau of the Census, 1999). Some 2.4 million others, troubled but not disabled, seek help as outpatients from mental health organizations and clinics. Many more—1 in 5 in both America and Australia, according to government reports—are judged to need such help in any given year, as have twice that many at some time in their lives (Australian Bureau of Statistics, 1999; Surgeon General, 1999). Such problems are not peculiar to the United States. No known culture is free of depression and schizophrenia (Castillo, 1997; Draguns, 1990a,b, 1997). Some 400 million people worldwide suffer psychological disorders, according to the World Health Organization's mental health director (Sartorius, 1994). The WHO also reports that, worldwide, mental disorders account for 15.4 percent of the years of life lost due to death or disability—scoring slightly below cardiovascular conditions and slightly above cancer (Murray & Lopez, 1996). As members of the human family, few of us go through life unacquainted with the reality of psychological disturbance. Table 43.1 shows the relative prevalence of some selected disorders among three ethnic groups, among men and women, and in the whole population.

"We are all mad at some time or another."

Battista Mantuanus, *Eclogues*, 1500

TABLE **43.1**

PERCENTAGE OF AMERICANS WHO HAVE EVER EXPERIENCED PSYCHOLOGICAL DISORDERS

Disorder	Ethnicity			Gender		
	White	Black	Hispanic	Men	Women	Total
Alcohol abuse or dependence	13.6%	13.8%	16.7%	23.8%	4.6%	13.8%
Generalized anxiety	3.4	6.1	3.7	2.4	5.0	3.8
Phobias	9.7	23.4	12.2	10.4	17.7	14.3
Obsessive-compulsive disorder	2.6	2.3	1.8	2.0	3.0	2.6
Mood disorder	8.0	6.3	7.8	5.2	10.2	7.8
Schizophrenia	1.4	2.1	0.8	1.2	1.7	1.5
Antisocial personality	2.6	2.3	3.4	4.5	0.8	2.6

Source: Data from Robins & Regier, 1991. Similar gender differences, though with somewhat higher rates of disorder, come from the U.S. National Comorbidity Survey (Kessler & others, 1994).

INSANITY AND RESPONSIBILITY

My brain . . . my genes . . . my bad upbringing made me do it. Such defenses were anticipated by Shakespeare's *Hamlet*. If I wrong someone when not myself, he explained, "then Hamlet does it not, Hamlet denies it. Who does it then? His madness." And such is the essence of the legal insanity defense, created in 1843 after a deluded Scotsman tried to shoot the prime minister (who he thought was persecuting him) but killed an assistant by mistake. The Scotsman, Daniel M'Naughten, was—like John Hinckley, who almost a century and a half later shot U.S. President Ronald Reagan and his assistant—sent to a mental hospital rather than to prison.

In both cases, the public was outraged. "Hinckley Insane, Public Mad," declared one headline. And they were mad again when a deranged Jeffrey Dahmer in 1991 admitted murdering 15 young men and eating parts of their bodies. They were mad when withdrawn and paranoid Unabomber Theodore Kaczynski murdered 3 and injured 23. They were mad in 1998 when 15-year-old Kip Kinkel, driven by "those voices in my head," killed his parents and 2 fellow Springfield, Oregon, students and wounded 25 others. And they were mad when angry white supremacist and former mental patient Buford Furrow, Jr., in 1999 opened fire on schoolchildren in a Los Angeles Jewish community center. The public was mad enough that all of these people were sent to jails, not hospitals, following their arrests.

These cases are not uncommon. A 1999 U.S. Justice Department study found 283,000 jail and prison inmates with severe mental disorders—about 16 percent of the American inmate population and considerably more than the 190,000 psychiatric inpatients in all types of hospitals (Bureau of the Census, 1998; Butterfield, 1999). Many people who have been executed or are on death row have been limited by mental retardation or motivated by delusional voices. Larry Robison (1999) was twice hospitalized for paranoid schizophrenia, as were his brother, sister, uncle, and grandfather. When denied further treatment after insurance coverage ran out, Robison was discharged and killed five people. On January 21, 2000, he was executed by the state of Texas.

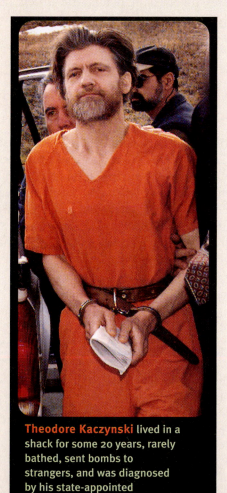

Theodore Kaczynski lived in a shack for some 20 years, rarely bathed, sent bombs to strangers, and was diagnosed by his state-appointed psychiatrist with paranoid schizophrenia. Should Kaczynski be jailed as a criminal or hospitalized as mentally ill?

Questions to consider: Who should be held responsible for such crimes? The people who commit them, or the "madness" that clouds their vision? Where do normalcy and personal responsibility shade into a disorder that precludes people's appreciating the wrongfulness of their acts, thus making them *insane* by legal judgment? Should we treat or punish executives who sexually harass their employees and then plead guilty to alcoholism or "sex addiction" (not to being jerks)? Should we fire the nasty co-worker who behaves with "disregard for, and violation of, the rights of others" (the definition of antisocial personality disorder) or protect him because he suffers from a disability?

Many sick crimes are the products of sick minds—and the malfunctioning brains and abusive nurturing that often produced them. Where do we draw the line? How can society show compassion for people with mental disorders who commit violent crimes? If the heinousness of a crime becomes synonymous with mental incompetence, does this create a social basis for evading responsibility (like the person who, having just killed his parents, then demands mercy because he is an orphan)?

We all, thanks to our self-serving bias, tend to attribute our good deeds to ourselves while shucking responsibility for our misdeeds. "It is only our bad temper that we put down to being tired or worried or hungry," reflected C. S. Lewis. "We put our good temper down to ourselves." Yet we *are* the sum of all our traits and behaviors, good and bad. If some superpsychologist were to understand the biological and environmental basis for everything—for generosity and for vandalism—society would probably still wish to hold people responsible for both. ■

The incidence of serious psychological disorders is doubly high among those below the poverty line (Centers for Disease Control, 1992). Like so many other correlations, the poverty–disorder association raises a chicken-and-egg question: Does poverty cause disorders? Or do disorders cause poverty? It's both, though the answer varies with the disorder. Schizophrenia—a psychotic disorder in which a person loses contact with reality—understandably leads to poverty. Yet the stresses and demoralization of poverty can also precipitate disorders, especially depression in women and substance abuse in men (Dohrenwend & others, 1992).

Those who experience a psychological disorder usually do so by early adulthood. "Over 75 percent of our sample with any disorder had experienced its first symptoms by age 24," reported Robins and Regier (1991, p. 331). The symptoms of antisocial personality disorder and of phobias appear earliest, by a median age of 8 and 10, respectively. Symptoms of alcohol abuse, obsessive-compulsive disorder, bipolar disorder (formerly known as manic-depressive disorder), and schizophrenia appear at a median age near 20. Major depression often hits somewhat later, at a median age of 25. Such findings make clear the need for research and treatment to help the growing number of people, especially teenagers and young adults, who suffer the bewilderment and pain of a psychological disorder.

Although mindful of the pain, we can also be encouraged by the many successful people—including Leonardo da Vinci, Isaac Newton, and Leo Tolstoy—who pursued brilliant careers while enduring psychological difficulties. The bewilderment, fear, and sorrow caused by psychological disorders are real. But hope, too, is real as our understanding of these disorders continues to grow.

REVIEW AND REFLECT:

Introduction to Psychological Disorders

Psychological disorders fascinate us, partly because most of us will at some time experience or witness them close at hand.

Where should we draw the line between normality and disorder?

Between normality and abnormality there is not a gulf but a somewhat arbitrary line. Where we draw this line depends on how atypical, disturbing, maladaptive, and unjustifiable a person's behavior is.

What theoretical models or perspectives can help us to understand psychological disorders?

The medical model's assumption that psychological disorders are mental illnesses displaced earlier views that demons and evil spirits were to blame. Recent interest in the link between disorders and genetically influenced abnormalities in brain structure and biochemistry has renewed interest in the medical model. However, critics question the medical model's labeling of psychological disorders as sicknesses. Most mental health workers today adapt a bio-psycho-social perspective. They assume that disorders are influenced by genetic predisposition, physiological states, psychological dynamics, and social circumstances.

How and why do clinicians classify psychological disorders?

Many psychiatrists and psychologists use the *Diagnostic and Statistical Manual of Mental Disorders* (DSM-IV) for naming and describing psychological disorders to facilitate treatment and research. Diagnostic labels facilitate mental health professionals' communications and research, and most health insurance policies in North America require DSM-IV diagnoses before they will pay for therapy.

Why do some psychologists criticize the use of diagnostic labels?

Critics point out the price we pay for the benefits of classifying disorders: Labels can create preconceptions that unfairly stigmatize people and bias our perceptions of their past and present behavior.

How many people suffer, or have suffered, a psychological disorder? Does the risk vary with ethnicity or gender?

A 1980s NIMH survey of nearly 20,000 institutionalized and community residents revealed that one in three U.S. adults had experienced a psychological disorder, and that one in five was currently experiencing a disorder. The three most common were phobic disorder, alcohol abuse or dependence (with men outnumbering women five to one), and mood disorder (with women outnumbering men two to one).

Continued

Terms and Concepts to Remember

psychological disorder, p. 548   DSM-IV, p. 551
medical model, p. 549   neurotic disorder, p. 551
bio-psycho-social   psychotic disorder, p. 551
  perspective, p. 550

Test Yourself

43.1. To be labeled "disordered," a behavior must usually be atypical, disturbing, unjustifiable, and maladaptive. For example, we all wash our hands; physicians may well wash their hands 100 times a day. But if a person washes his hands 100 times a day for no apparent reason and is unable to do much else, the behavior will be labeled disordered because it is, among other things,
   a. unjustifiable and maladaptive.
   b. not explained by the medical model.
   c. harmful to others.
   d. untreatable.

43.2. In the past, people considered to be mad or insane were beaten, punished, or caged. A more modern approach is to equate psychological disorders with sickness and to refer the "mentally ill" to hospitals, where they can be treated as patients. This more modern approach is called the
   a. social-cultural perspective.   c. medical model.
   b. psychological model.   d. diagnostic model.

43.3. Many psychologists adhere to the idea that psychological disorders are sicknesses arising from an internal problem. Others contend that other factors may be involved—for example, a growth-blocking difficulty in the person's environment or the person's bad habits and poor social skills. Psychologists who take this approach to psychological disorders are said to be advocates of the _____ perspective.
   a. medical   c. bio-psycho-social
   b. biomedical   d. social-cultural

43.4. Although some psychological disorders are culture-bound, others are universal. For example, in every known culture there are people who suffer
   a. bulimia nervosa.   c. schizophrenia.
   b. anorexia nervosa.   d. susto.

43.5. The American Psychiatric Association's system of classifying psychological disorders is found in the DSM-IV. The DSM-IV system is more reliable than its predecessors; one study found that psychologists using the manual's structured-interview procedure agreed on a diagnosis for more than 80 percent of patients. The DSM-IV has improved reliability because it helps mental health workers base their diagnoses on
   a. a few well-defined categories.
   b. in-depth histories of the patients.
   c. the patients' observable behaviors.
   d. the theories of Pinel, Freud, and others.

43.6. Labels such as "schizophrenia" and "generalized anxiety" may be useful in clinical situations. In other contexts, however, labels create preconceptions and biases. From watching television dramas you would never guess that most people with psychological disorders, when encountered in the real world, seem
   a. antisocial and amoral.
   b. violent or homicidal.
   c. accomplished in the arts and literature.
   d. anxious, depressed, or withdrawn.

43.7. On the basis of an NIMH report, researchers note that 32 percent of American adults have experienced a psychiatric disorder at some time in their lives. Despite differences in the prevalence of disorders among ethnic groups and between men and women, all groups are vulnerable. One factor that crosses ethnic and gender lines and is closely correlated with serious psychological disorder is
   a. age.   c. poverty.
   b. education.   d. religious faith.

Review

- What is the bio-psycho-social perspective, and why is it important?

- Does poverty cause psychological disorders? Explain.

Reflect

- How would you draw the line between sending disturbed criminals to prisons or to mental hospitals? Would the person's history (for example, having suffered child abuse) influence your decisions?

Answers to the Test Yourself and Review questions can be found in the green appendix at the end of the book.

Anxiety Disorders

Preview Questions: What are anxiety disorders, and what are their symptoms? What causes the anxious feelings and cognitions that characterize these disorders?

Anxiety is part of life. When speaking in front of a class, or peering down from a ledge, or waiting to play in a big game, any one of us might feel anxious. At one time or another, most of us feel enough anxiety that we fail to make eye contact or we avoid talking to someone—"shyness" we call it. Fortunately for most of us, our uneasiness is not intense and persistent. If it becomes so, we may have one of the **anxiety disorders**, marked by distressing, persistent anxiety or maladaptive behaviors that reduce anxiety. In this module we focus on four of these disorders:

+ **Generalized anxiety disorder**, in which a person is unexplainably and continually tense and uneasy
+ **Panic disorder**, in which a person experiences sudden episodes of intense dread
+ **Phobias**, in which a person feels irrationally afraid of a specific object or situation
+ **Obsessive-compulsive disorder**, in which a person is troubled by repetitive thoughts or actions

Taken together, these are the most common mental disorders.

Generalized Anxiety Disorder and Panic Disorder

Tom, a 27-year-old electrician, complains of dizziness, sweating palms, heart palpitations, and ringing in his ears. He feels edgy and sometimes finds himself shaking. With reasonable success he hides his symptoms from his family and co-workers. Nevertheless, he has had few social contacts since the symptoms began two years ago. He occasionally has to leave work. His family doctor and a neurologist can find no physical problem.

Tom's unfocused, out-of-control, negative feelings suggest generalized anxiety disorder. The symptoms of this disorder are commonplace; their persistence is not. Sufferers, two-thirds of whom are women, are continually tense and jittery, worried about bad things that might happen, and experience symptoms of autonomic nervous system arousal (racing heart, clammy hands, stomach butterflies, sleeplessness). The tension and apprehension may leak out through furrowed brows, twitching eyelids, trembling, perspiration, or fidgeting. One of the worst characteristics of generalized anxiety disorder is that the person cannot identify, and therefore cannot deal with or avoid, its cause. To use Freud's term, the anxiety is "free-floating."

Panic disorder takes anxiety to the extreme. For the 1 person in 75 who suffers from this disorder, anxiety suddenly escalates into a terrifying *panic attack*—a minutes-long episode of intense fear that something horrible is about to happen to them. Heart palpitations, shortness of breath, choking sensations, trembling, or dizziness typically accompany the panic. The experience is unpredictable and so frightening that the sufferer often comes to fear the fear itself and to avoid situations where the panic has struck before. Smokers have a fourfold risk of a first-time panic attack (Breslau & Klein, 1999).

■ **anxiety disorders** psychological disorders characterized by distressing, persistent anxiety or maladaptive behaviors that reduce anxiety.

■ **generalized anxiety disorder** an anxiety disorder in which a person is continually tense, apprehensive, and in a state of autonomic nervous system arousal.

■ **panic disorder** an anxiety disorder marked by a minutes-long episode of intense dread in which a person experiences terror and accompanying chest pain, choking, or other frightening sensations.

■ **phobia** an anxiety disorder marked by a persistent, irrational fear and avoidance of a specific object or situation.

■ **obsessive-compulsive disorder** an anxiety disorder characterized by unwanted repetitive thoughts (obsessions) and/or actions (compulsions).

Lighting up doesn't lighten up
Perhaps due to the fact that nicotine is a stimulant, daily smokers are at increased risk of a first panic attack.

One woman recalled suddenly feeling "hot and as though I couldn't breathe. My heart was racing and I started to sweat and tremble and I was sure I was going to faint. Then my fingers started to feel numb and tingly and things seemed unreal. It was so bad I wondered if I was dying and asked my husband to take me to the emergency room. By the time we got there (about 10 minutes) the worst of the attack was over and I just felt washed out." (Greist & others, 1986)

Agoraphobia is fear or avoidance of situations in which escape might be difficult or help unavailable when panic strikes. Given such fear, people may avoid being outside the home, being in a crowd, being on a bus or even on an elevator. After spending five years sailing the world, Charles Darwin began suffering panic disorder at age 28. Because of the attacks, he moved to the country, avoided social gatherings, and traveled only in his wife's company. But the relative seclusion did free him to focus on developing his evolutionary theory. "Even ill health," he reflected, "has saved me from the distraction of society and its amusements" (quoted in Ma, 1997).

Phobias

Phobias *focus* anxiety on a specific object, activity, or situation. (See **FIGURE 44.1** for one ranking of some common and less common fears.) Phobias are irrational fears that disrupt behavior. They are a common psychological disorder that many people accept and live with. Some *specific phobias*, however, are incapacitating. Marilyn, a 28-year-old homemaker, so fears thunderstorms that she feels anxious as soon as a weather forecaster mentions possible storms later in the week. If her husband is away and a storm is forecast, she sometimes stays with a close relative. During a storm, she hides from windows and buries her head to avoid seeing the lightning. She is otherwise healthy and happy.

Some people suffer from irrational fears of specific animals or insects, or of heights, or blood, or tunnels. Sometimes it is possible to avoid the stimulus that arouses the fear: One can hide during thunderstorms or avoid high places. With a *social phobia*, an intense fear of being scrutinized by others, the anxious person will avoid potentially embarrassing social situations. The person may avoid speaking up, eating out, or going to parties—or will sweat, tremble, or have diarrhea when doing so. Social phobia is shyness taken to an extreme.

FIGURE 44.1
Some common and uncommon fears
This national survey ranked the relative fear levels of Americans to some sources of anxiety. A fear becomes a phobia if it provokes a compelling but irrational desire to avoid the dreaded object or situation. (From *Public Opinion*, 1984.)

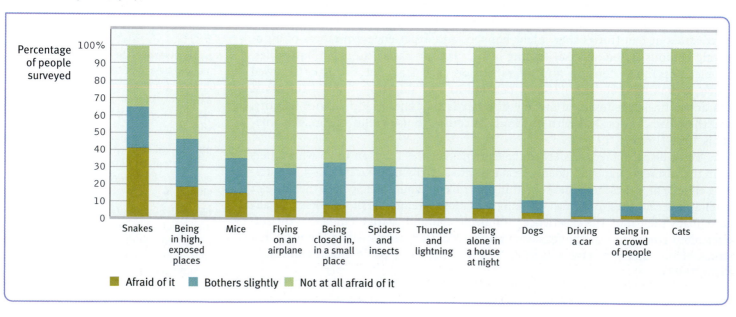

TABLE 44.1

COMMON OBSESSIONS AND COMPULSIONS AMONG CHILDREN AND ADOLESCENTS WITH OBSESSIVE-COMPULSIVE DISORDER

Thought or Behavior	Percentage* Reporting Symptom
Obsessions (repetitive thoughts)	
Concern with dirt, germs, or toxins	40
Something terrible happening (fire, death, illness)	24
Symmetry, order, or exactness	17
Compulsions (repetitive behaviors)	
Excessive hand washing, bathing, tooth brushing, or grooming	85
Repeating rituals (in/out of a door, up/down from a chair)	51
Checking doors, locks, appliances, car brake, homework	46

*Seventy children and adolescents reported their symptoms.
Source: Adapted from Rapoport, 1989.

Obsessive-Compulsive Disorder

As with generalized anxiety and phobias, we can see aspects of our own behavior in obsessive-compulsive disorder. We may at times be obsessed with senseless or offensive thoughts that will not go away. Or we may engage in compulsive, rigid behavior—checking, ordering, cleaning, hoarding. We recheck a locked door, step over cracks in the sidewalk, or line up our books and pencils "just so" before studying.

Obsessive thoughts and compulsive behaviors cross the fine line between normality and disorder when they become so persistent that they interfere with the way we live or when they cause distress. Checking to see that the door is locked is normal; checking 10 times is not. Washing your hands is normal; washing so often that your skin becomes raw is not. (Table 44.1 offers more examples.) At some time during their lives, often during their late teens or twenties, 2 to 3 percent of people cross that line from normal preoccupations and fussiness to debilitating disorder (Karno & others, 1988). The obsessive thoughts become so haunting, the compulsive rituals so senselessly time-consuming, that effective functioning becomes impossible.

One such person was billionaire Howard Hughes. Hughes compulsively dictated the same phrases over and over again. Under stress, he developed an obsessive fear of germs. Hughes became reclusive and insisted his assistants carry out elaborate hand-washing rituals and wear white gloves when handling any document he would later touch. He ordered tape around doors and windows and forbade his staff to touch or even look at him. "Everybody carries germs around with them," he explained. "I want to live longer than my parents, so I avoid germs" (Fowler, 1986).

Although Hughes' symptoms worsened with age, older people are less often plagued by obsessive-compulsive disorder than are teens and young adults (Samuels & Nestadt, 1997). A 40-year follow-up study of 144 Swedish people diagnosed around 1950 found that for most, the obsessions and compulsions had gradually lessened, though only 1 in 5 completely recovered (Skoog & Skoog, 1999). Anxiety disorders all engage our anticipation of future events, about which older adults, it seems, are less apprehensive.

Explaining Anxiety Disorders

Anxiety is both a feeling and a cognition—a doubt-laden appraisal of one's safety or social skill. How do these anxious feelings and cognitions arise? Freud's psychoanalytic perspective assumed that, beginning in childhood, people repress intolerable impulses, ideas, and feelings and that this submerged mental energy sometimes produces mystifying symptoms such as anxiety. However, many of today's psychologists have turned away from Freud to two contemporary perspectives—learning and biological.

The Learning Perspective

Fear Conditioning

When bad events happen unpredictably and uncontrollably, anxiety often develops (Chorpita & Barlow, 1998). Researchers have linked general anxiety with classical conditioning of fear. In the laboratory, they have created chronically anxious, ulcer-prone rats by giving them unpredictable electric shocks (Schwartz, 1984). Like assault victims who report feeling anxious when entering the neighborhood in which they were attacked, the rats become apprehensive in their lab environment. For many victims of post-traumatic stress disorder, anxiety swells with any reminder of their trauma (see the Close-Up at the right). Such experiences might help explain why anxious people are hyperattentive to possible threats (Mineka & Zinbarg, 1996). In one survey, 58 percent of those with social phobia experienced their disorder after a traumatic event (Ost & Hugdahl, 1981).

When experimental shocks become predictable—when preceded by a particular conditioned stimulus—the animals' fear focuses on *that* stimulus and when it is absent, they relax. Decades of research on conditioning have demonstrated that dogs learn to fear neutral stimuli associated with shock, that infants come to fear furry objects associated with frightening noises, and that adults can become terrified of incidental stimuli linked with traumatic experiences. As infants become mobile they experience falls and near-falls—and become increasingly afraid of heights (Campos & others, 1992).

Through such conditioning, the short list of naturally painful and frightening events can multiply into a long list of human fears. Recently, my car was struck by another whose driver missed a stop sign. For months afterward, I felt a twinge of unease when any car approached from a side street. Marilyn's phobia may have been similarly conditioned during a terrifying or painful experience associated with a thunderstorm.

Stimulus Generalization

Conditioned fears may remain long after we have forgotten the experiences that produced them (Jacobs & Nadel, 1985). Moreover, some fears arise from *stimulus generalization*. A person who fears heights after a fall may be afraid of airplanes without ever having flown.

Reinforcement

Once phobias and compulsions arise, reinforcement helps maintain them. Avoiding or escaping the feared situation reduces anxiety, thus reinforcing the phobic behavior. Feeling anxious or fearing a panic attack, a person may go or stay inside (Antony & others, 1992). Compulsive behaviors similarly reduce anxiety. If washing your hands relieves your feelings of unease, you will likely wash your hands again when the feelings return.

Observational Learning

We might also learn fear through observational learning—by observing others' fears. As Susan Mineka (1985) demonstrated, wild monkeys transmit their fear of snakes to their lab-reared offspring. Human parents similarly transmit their fears to their children.

The Biological Perspective

There is more to anxiety than simple conditioning, as evident from how few people develop lasting phobias after suffering traumas. The biological perspective helps explain why we learn some fears more readily and why some individuals are more vulnerable.

CLOSE-UP:

THE WOUNDS OF WAR: POST-TRAUMATIC STRESS DISORDER

During the fighting in Vietnam, Jack's platoon was repeatedly under fire. In one ambush, his closest friend was killed while Jack was standing a few feet away. Jack himself killed one of his enemies in a brutal assault. Years later, images of these events intrude on him as flashbacks and nightmares. He still jumps at the sound of a cap gun or the backfire of a car. When annoyed by his family or friends, he lashes out in ways he seldom did before Vietnam. To calm his continuing anxiety, he drinks more than he should.

Such has been the experience of many combat veterans, accident and disaster survivors, and sexual assault victims, including an estimated two-thirds of prostitutes (Brewin & others, 1999; Farley & others, 1998; Taylor & others, 1998). Traumatic stress—experiencing or witnessing severely threatening, uncontrollable events with a sense of fear, helplessness, or horror—can produce *post-traumatic stress disorder*, symptoms of which include haunting memories and nightmares, a numbed social withdrawal, jumpy anxiety, or depression (Goodman & others, 1993; Kaylor & others, 1987; Wilson & others, 1988).

After witnessing atrocities or living in life-threatening circumstances, children of the world's war zones and violent neighborhoods show similar symptoms (Garbarino, 1991, 1992). Their sense of basic trust erodes; many experience fearful wariness, troubled sleep, nightmares, and a sense of hopelessness about their future. This "learned helplessness" on the part of children who have repeatedly suffered abuse appears to make them more vulnerable to post-traumatic stress if assaulted as adults (Mineka & Zinbarg, 1996).

To pin down the frequency of post-traumatic stress disorder, the U.S. Centers for Disease Control (1988) compared 7000 Vietnam combat veterans with 7000 noncombat veterans who served during the same years. Combat stress more than doubled a veteran's risk of alcohol abuse, depression, or anxiety. More than a decade after the war, another study located 2095 identical twins among Vietnam-era veterans (Goldberg & others, 1990). Compared with their twins who served noncombat roles in Vietnam, individuals who experienced heavy combat were 5.4 times more likely to suffer post-traumatic stress disorder.

Studies of U.S. and Israeli soldiers reveal that the more terrifying and prolonged the battle experience, the greater the psychological casualties (King & King, 1991; Solomon, 1990). Roughly 15 percent of all Vietnam veterans, for example, showed post-traumatic stress symptoms. This rate was halved among those who never saw combat and tripled among those who experienced heavy combat. And among soldiers held captive in Vietnam, the more torture they suffered, the greater its psychological toll (Mollica & others, 1998).

Researchers have also found that psychological disorders and suicide attempts were most common among vets who felt responsible for a trauma, because they had either killed someone or failed to prevent a death (Fontana & others, 1992). Many still experience nightmares, have trouble sleeping and concentrating, and find themselves easily startled. This is especially so for those exposed to savage mutilation, torture, or the sight of a friend's death.

Much as they might wish to avoid or suppress the memory, it continues to intrude.

Despite such symptoms, some psychologists believe post-traumatic stress disorder is a fad diagnosis. The disorder, the skeptics say, actually is infrequent (Young, 1996). Most combat-stressed veterans live productive lives. Most rescuers cope well afterwards, as did all the Sioux City firefighters who rescued people and charred bodies from a flaming DC-10 crash in 1989 (Gist & others, 1998, 1999; Redburn & others, 1993). Most political dissidents who survive dozens of episodes of torture do *not* later exhibit post-traumatic stress disorder (Mineka & Zinbarg, 1996). And, although suffering some lingering stress symptoms, most American Jews who survived the Holocaust trauma—experiencing starvation, beatings, lost freedom, the murders of loved ones—went on to live productive lives. In fact, compared with other American Jews of the same age, these survivors have been *less* likely to have seen a psychotherapist (18 percent versus 31 percent) and *more* likely to have had stable marriages (83 percent versus 62 percent). Moreover, virtually none has committed a criminal act. Researcher William Helmreich (1992, p. 276) reflects on their successes:

The story of the survivors is one of courage and strength, of people who are living proof of the indomitable will of human beings to survive and of their tremendous capacity for hope. It is not a story of remarkable people. It is a story of just how remarkable people can be.

An emotional high
Although we humans seem biologically predisposed to fear heights—certainly an adaptive response—this construction worker seems fearless. The biological perspective helps us understand why most people would be terrified in this situation.

Evolution

Human behavior was road tested in the Stone Age. We humans therefore seem biologically prepared to fear dangers faced by our ancestors, and most of our phobias focus on such objects: spiders, snakes, closed spaces, heights, storms. (Those fearless about these occasional threats were less likely to survive and leave ancestors.) It is easy to condition but hard to extinguish fears of such stimuli (Davey, 1995; Ohman, 1986). Many of our modern fears may also have an evolutionary explanation. For example, a fear of flying may also come from our biological past, which predisposes us to fear confinement and heights.

Moreover, consider what people tend *not* to learn to fear. World War II air raids produced remarkably few lasting phobias. As the air blitz continued, the British, Japanese, and German populations did not become more panicked, but rather indifferent to planes not in their immediate neighborhood (Mineka & Zinbarg, 1996). Evolution has not prepared us to learn to fear bombs dropping from the sky.

Just as our phobias focus on dangers faced by our ancestors, our compulsive acts typically exaggerate behaviors that contributed to our species' survival. Grooming gone wild becomes hair pulling. Washing up becomes ritual hand washing. Checking territorial boundaries becomes checking and rechecking an already locked door (Rapoport, 1989).

Genes

Some people more than others seem genetically predisposed to particular fears and high anxiety. Identical twins often develop similar phobias, in some cases even when raised separately (Carey, 1990; Eckert & others, 1981). One pair of 35-year-old identical female twins independently developed claustrophobia. They also became so afraid of water that each would gingerly wade backward into the ocean, and then only up to the knees. Among monkeys, fearfulness runs in families. Individual monkeys react more strongly to stress if their close biological relatives are anxiously reactive (Suomi, 1986). Among humans, vulnerability to anxiety disorder rises when the afflicted relative is an identical twin (Barlow, 1988; Kendler & others, 1992, 1999; Roy & others, 1995).

Physiology

General anxiety, panic attacks, and even obsessions and compulsions are biologically measurable as an overarousal of brain areas involved in impulse control and habitual behaviors. PET scans of persons with obsessive-compulsive disorder reveal unusually high activity in an area of the frontal lobes just above the eyes (**FIGURE 44.2**) (Rauch & Jenike, 1993; Resnick, 1992). Fear-learning experiences also serve to solder fear circuits within the amygdala, deep in the brain (Armony & others, 1998). Some antidepressant drugs dampen this fear-circuit activity, and the associated obsessive-compulsive behavior, by increasing the neurotransmitter serotonin.

FIGURE 44.2
A PET scan of the brain of a person with obsessive-compulsive disorder
The scan reveals abnormally high metabolic activity (red areas) in the frontal lobes, seen at the top of the photo. This is visible in a region of the left hemisphere's frontal lobe involved in directing attention.

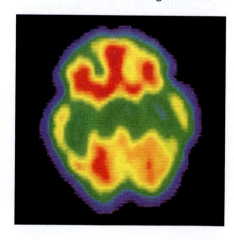

REVIEW AND REFLECT:

Anxiety Disorders

What are anxiety disorders, and what are their symptoms?

Anxiety is part of our everyday experience. It is classified as a psychological disorder only when it becomes distressing or persistent or is characterized by maladaptive behaviors intended to reduce it.

Those who suffer a *generalized anxiety disorder* may for no clear reason feel persistently and uncontrollably tense and uneasy. Anxiety escalates into periodic episodes of intense dread for those suffering *panic disorder*. Those with a *phobic disorder* may be irrationally afraid of a specific object or situation. Persistent and repetitive thoughts and actions characterize *obsessive-compulsive disorder*.

What causes the anxious feelings and cognitions that characterize these disorders?

The psychoanalytic perspective viewed anxiety disorders as the discharging of repressed impulses. Psychologists now tend to consider these disorders from the learning and biological perspectives. The learning perspective sees anxiety disorders as a product of fear conditioning, stimulus generalization, reinforcement, and observational learning. The biological perspective considers possible evolutionary, genetic, and physiological influences.

Terms and Concepts to Remember

anxiety disorders, p. 557
generalized anxiety disorder, p. 557
panic disorder, p. 557

phobia, p. 557
obsessive-compulsive disorder, p. 557

Test Yourself

44.1. When anxiety is so distressing, uncontrollable, or persistent that it results in maladaptive behavior, the person is said to have an anxiety disorder. If a person's anxiety takes the form of an irrational fear of a specific object or situation—for example, an irrational fear of dogs, thunderstorms, or closed spaces—the disorder is called
   a. a phobia.
   b. a panic attack.
   c. generalized anxiety.
   d. obsessive-compulsive disorder.

44.2. The experience of anxiety often involves physical symptoms, such as trembling, dizziness, chest pains, or choking sensations. An episode of intense dread, which is typically accompanied by such symptoms and by feelings of terror, is called
   a. generalized or chronic anxiety.
   b. a social phobia.
   c. a panic attack.
   d. an obsessive fear.

44.3. Marina has always been concerned with cleanliness and neatness. Her mother never had to remind her to clean up her room. When Marina became consumed with the need to clean the entire house and refused to participate in any other activities, her family consulted a therapist, who diagnosed her as having
   a. obsessive-compulsive disorder.
   b. generalized anxiety disorder.
   c. a phobia.
   d. dissociative fugue.

44.4. Rats subjected to unpredictable shocks in the laboratory become chronically anxious. To the learning researcher this suggests that anxiety is a response to
   a. a phobia.
   b. biological factors.
   c. the pressures of the superego.
   d. helplessness.

44.5. Psychologists have different ideas about the causes of phobias. For example, some psychologists stress the importance of biological predispositions, noting that we seem predisposed to fear certain stimuli. Psychologists of the learning perspective, on the other hand, maintain that phobias are
   a. the result of individual genetic makeup.
   b. a way of repressing unacceptable impulses.
   c. conditioned fears.
   d. a symptom of having been abused as a child.

Review: Can you distinguish between generalized anxiety disorder, phobias, and obsessive-compulsive disorder?

Reflect: Can you recall a fear that you have learned? What role, if any, was played by fear conditioning and by observational learning?

Answers to the Test Yourself and Review questions can be found in the green appendix at the end of the book.

45 Dissociative and Personality Disorders

Dissociative Disorders

Preview Question: What are dissociative disorders, and why are they controversial?

Among the most intriguing disorders are the rare **dissociative disorders**, in which a person appears to experience a sudden loss of memory or change in identity. When a situation becomes overwhelmingly stressful, people are said to dissociate themselves from it. Their conscious awareness becomes separated from painful memories, thoughts, and feelings. (Note that this explanation presumes the existence of repressed memories, which have recently been questioned.)

Certain symptoms of dissociation are not so rare. Now and then, many people may have a sense of being unreal, of being separated from their body, of watching themselves as if in a movie. Perhaps you can recall getting in your car and driving to some unintended location while your mind was preoccupied elsewhere. Facing trauma, such detachment may actually protect a person from being overwhelmed by emotion. Only when such experiences are severe and prolonged do they suggest a dissociative disorder.

The king of dissociative disorders is the massive dissociation of self from ordinary consciousness in those with **dissociative identity disorder**. These people are said to have two or more distinct identities that alternately control the person's behavior. The person with this disorder may be prim and proper one moment and loud and flirtatious the next. Each personality has its own voice and mannerisms, and the original one typically denies any awareness of the other(s).

Although people diagnosed as having multiple personalities are usually not violent, there have been cases in which the person reportedly became dissociated into a "good" and a "bad" or aggressive personality—a modest version of the Dr. Jekyll/Mr. Hyde split immortalized in Robert Louis Stevenson's story. Freud would have said that, rid of the original "good" personality's awareness, the wanton second personality is free to discharge forbidden impulses. One unusual case that for a time seemed to support this interpretation involved Kenneth Bianchi, who was on trial for the "Hillside Strangler" rapes and murders of 10 California women. During a hypnosis session with Bianchi, psychologist John Watkins (1984) "called forth" a hidden personality: "I've talked a bit to Ken, but I think that perhaps there might be another part of Ken that I haven't talked to, another part that maybe feels somewhat differently from the part that I've talked to. . . . Would you talk with me, Part, by saying, 'I'm here'?" Bianchi answered "Yes" and then claimed to be "Steve."

When speaking as Steve, Bianchi stated that he hated Ken because Ken was nice and that he (Steve), aided by a cousin, had murdered women. He also claimed that Ken knew nothing about his existence and that Ken was innocent of the murders. Was Bianchi's second personality a ruse, simply a way of disavowing responsibility for his actions? Yes. Bianchi—a practiced liar who had read about multiple personality in psychology books—was later convicted.

Exploring our capacity for personality shifts, Nicholas Spanos (1986, 1994, 1996) asked college students to pretend they were accused murderers being examined by a psychiatrist. When given the same hypnotic treatment Bianchi received, most spontaneously expressed a second personality. This discovery made Spanos wonder: Are dissociative identities simply a more extreme version of our normal human capacity to vary the "selves" we present—as when we might display a goofy, loud self while hanging out with friends, and a subdued, respectful self around grandparents. Are clinicians who discover multiple personalities merely triggering fantasy-prone people's enactment of a role? If so, can such people then convince themselves of the authenticity of their own role enactments? Are they like actors, who commonly report "losing themselves" in their roles?

Spanos was no stranger to this line of thinking. In a related area of research, he had also raised these questions about the hypnotic state. Given that most multiple personality patients are highly hypnotizable, whatever explains one condition—dissociation or role playing—may help explain the other.

Those who accept dissociative identity as a genuine disorder find support in the distinct brain and body states associated with differing personalities (Putnam, 1991). Handedness, too, sometimes switches with personality (Henninger, 1992). Subtle memories of one personality's experience sometimes fail to transfer to another personality (Eich & others, 1997). In one study, ophthalmologists detected shifting visual acuity and eye-muscle balance as patients switched personalities. These changes did not occur among control subjects trying to simulate multiple personality (Miller & others, 1991).

Skeptics nevertheless find it suspicious that the disorder became so popular in the late 1900s. In North America, the number of diagnoses exploded from only 2 reported cases per decade from 1930 to 1960 to more than 20,000 in the 1980s (McHugh, 1995a). The average number of displayed personalities also mushroomed—from 3 to 12 per patient (Goff & Sims, 1993). How could such a dramatic disorder have gone unnoticed for so long? Isn't the sudden increase just what one would expect after the role of multiple personality was well publicized in books and films of that time, including *The Three Faces of Eve* and *Sybil*? Many clinicians have never encountered a case of dissociative identity, and the disorder is almost nonexistent outside North America, although in other cultures some people are said to be "possessed" by an alien spirit (Aldridge-Morris, 1989; Kluft, 1991). In Britain, the diagnosis—which some consider "a wacky American fad" (Cohen, 1995)—is rare. In India and Japan it is essentially nonexistent.

To skeptics, these findings point to a cultural phenomenon—a disorder created by therapists in a particular social context (Merskey, 1992). Skeptics note how some therapists go fishing for it: "Have you ever felt like another part of you does things you can't control? Does this part of you have a name? Can I talk to the angry part of you?" Once patients permit a therapist to talk, by name, "to the part of you that says those angry things" they have begun acting out the fantasy. Moreover, say skeptics, "It is no coincidence" that multiple personality studies began among practitioners of hypnosis and that symptoms are most dramatic after beginning therapy (Goff, 1993; Piper, 1998).

With the dissociative disorders, as with the anxiety disorders, both psychoanalytic and learning perspectives see the symptoms as ways of dealing with anxiety. Psychoanalysts see them as defenses against the anxiety caused by the eruption of unacceptable impulses. Learning theorists see them as behaviors reinforced by anxiety reduction.

Others view dissociative disorders as what psychiatrist Frank Putnam (1995) calls "post-traumatic disorders"—a natural, protective response to "histories of childhood trauma." Researchers debate whether most dissociative identity disorder patients suffered physical, sexual, or emotional abuse as children (Gleaves, 1996; Lilienfeld & others, 1999). One study of 12 murderers diagnosed with dissociative identity disorder did find that 11 of them had suffered severe, torturous child abuse (Lewis & others, 1997). One was set afire by his parents. Another was used in child pornography and was scarred from being made to sit on a stove burner. Perhaps, then, multiple personalities are the desperate efforts of the traumatized to flee inward.

But then why, wonder the skeptics, did the children of the Holocaust, after enduring boxcars, concentration camps, and their parents' murders, not develop dissociative

■ **dissociative disorders** disorders in which conscious awareness becomes separated (dissociated) from previous memories, thoughts, and feelings.

■ **dissociative identity disorder** a rare dissociative disorder in which a person exhibits two or more distinct and alternating personalities. Also called *multiple personality disorder*.

"Pretense may become reality."

Chinese Proverb

The "Hillside Strangler"
Kenneth Bianchi is shown here at his trial.

identity disorders? Is it because the condition is either contrived by fantasy-prone, emotionally variable people, or constructed out of the therapist-patient interaction? If so, history's verdict will not be sympathetic. "This epidemic will end in the way that the witch craze ended in Salem," predicts psychiatrist Paul McHugh (1995b). "The [multiple personality phenomenon] will be seen as manufactured, the 'repressed memory' explanation will be recognized as misguided, and psychiatrists will become immunized against the practices that generated these artifacts."

Personality Disorders

Preview Question: What characteristics are typical of personality disorders?

Personality disorders are inflexible and enduring patterns of behavior that impair one's social functioning. One cluster of disorders expresses anxiety, such as a fearful sensitivity to rejection that predisposes the withdrawn *avoidant personality disorder*. A second cluster expresses eccentric behaviors, such as the social disengagement of the *schizoid personality disorder*.

A third cluster exhibits dramatic or impulsive behaviors. A person with a *histrionic personality disorder* displays shallow, attention-getting emotions and goes to great lengths to gain others' praise and reassurance. Those with *narcissistic personality disorder* exaggerate their own importance, aided by success fantasies. They find criticism hard to accept, often reacting with rage or shame. Those with *borderline personality disorder* have an unstable identity, unstable relationships, and unstable emotions. If personality is one's enduring pattern of thinking, feeling, and acting, then a markedly unstable sense of self defines a "borderline personality."

The most troubling of these impulsive personality disorders is the **antisocial personality disorder**. The person (formerly called a *sociopath* or a *psychopath*) is typically a male whose lack of conscience becomes plain before age 15, as he begins to lie, steal, fight, or display unrestrained sexual behavior. About half of such children become antisocial adults—unable to keep a job, irresponsible as a spouse and parent, and assaultive or otherwise criminal (Farrington, 1991). When the antisocial personality combines a keen intelligence with amorality, the result may be a charming and clever con artist—or worse.

Interestingly enough, despite their antisocial behavior, most criminals do not fit the description of antisocial personality disorder. Why? Because most criminals actually show responsible concern for their friends and family members. Antisocial personalities feel little and fear little, and in extreme cases, the results can be horrifyingly tragic. Henry Lee Lucas reported that at age 13 he strangled a woman who refused to have sex with him. He at one time confessed to having bludgeoned, suffocated, stabbed, shot, or mutilated some 360 women, men, and children during his 32 years of crime. During the last 6 years of his reign of terror, Lucas teamed with Elwood Toole, who reportedly slaughtered about 50 people whom he "didn't think was worth living anyhow." It ended when Lucas confessed to stabbing and dismembering his 15-year-old common-law wife, who was Toole's niece.

The antisocial personality expresses little regret over violating others' rights. "Once I've done a crime, I just forget it," said Lucas. Toole was equally matter-of-fact: "I think of killing like smoking a cigarette, like another habit" (Darrach & Norris, 1984).

The antisocial personality disorder is woven of both biological and psychological strands. No single gene codes for a complex behavior such as crime, but twin and adoption studies reveal that biological relatives of certain individuals are at increased risk for criminality (Brennan & Mednick, 1991; DiLalla & Gottesman, 1991; Lyons & others, 1995). Their genetic vulnerability appears as a fearless approach to life. When they await

FIGURE 45.1 Cold-blooded arousability and risk of crime
Levels of the stress hormone adrenaline were measured in two groups of 13-year-old Swedish boys. In both stressful and nonstressful situations, those who were later convicted of a crime (as 18- to 26-year-olds) showed relatively low arousal.

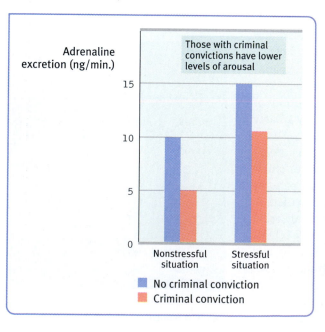

Those with criminal convictions have lower levels of arousal

Adrenaline excretion (ng/min.)

- No criminal conviction
- Criminal conviction

aversive events, such as electric shocks or loud noises, they show little autonomic nervous system arousal (Hare, 1975). Even as youngsters, before committing any crime, they react with lower levels of stress hormones than do others their age (**FIGURE 45.1**).

Some studies have detected the early signs of antisocial behavior in children as young as ages 3 to 6 (Caspi & others, 1996; Tremblay & others, 1994). Boys who later became aggressive or antisocial as adolescents tended, as young children, to have been impulsive, uninhibited, unconcerned with social rewards, and low in anxiety. If channeled in more productive directions, such fearlessness may lead to courageous heroism or adventurism. Lacking a sense of social responsibility, the same disposition produces a cool con artist or killer (Lykken, 1995).

Genetic influences help wire the brain. Adrian Raine (1999) compared PET scans of 41 murderers' brains with those from people of similar age and sex. Raine found reduced activity in the murderers' frontal lobe, which helps control impulses (**FIGURE 45.2**). This was especially true for those who murdered impulsively. Frontal lobe damage can impair people's discerning right from wrong (Anderson & others, 1999).

Perhaps a biologically based fearlessness, as well as early environment, helps explain the reunion of long-separated sisters Joyce Lott, 27, and Mary Jones, 29—in a South Carolina prison where both were sent on drug charges. After a newspaper story about their reunion, their long-lost half-brother Frank Strickland called. He explained it would be a while before he could come see them—because he, too, was in jail, on drug, burglary, and larceny charges (Shepherd & others, 1990).

Genetics alone is hardly the whole story of antisocial crime, however. Relative to 1960, the average American in 1995 (before the late 1990s crime decline) was twice as likely to be murdered, four times as likely to report being raped, four times as likely to report being robbed, and five times as likely to report being assaulted (FBI, *Uniform Crime Reports*). Violent crime was also surging in other Western nations. Yet the human gene pool had hardly changed. Or consider the British social experiment begun in 1787, exiling 160,000 criminals to Australia. The descendants of these exiles, carrying their ancestors' supposed "criminal genes," have helped create a civilized democracy whose crime rate is similar to Britain's. Genetic predispositions do put some individuals more at risk for antisocial conduct than others; biological as well as environmental influences explain why 5 to 6 percent of offenders commit 50 to 60 percent of crimes (Lyman, 1996). But we must look to sociocultural factors to explain the modern epidemic of violence.

A study of criminal tendencies among young Danish men illustrates the usefulness of a complete bio-psycho-social perspective. A research team led by Adrian Raine (1996) checked criminal records on nearly 400 men at ages 20 to 22, knowing that all had experienced either biological risk factors at birth, such as premature birth, or had come from family backgrounds marked by poverty and family instability. The researchers compared each of these groups with a "biosocial" group whose lives were marked by *both* the biological and social risk factors. The biosocial group had double the risk of committing crime (**FIGURE 45.3**). Other studies confirm that with antisocial behavior, as with so much else, nature and nurture interact (Rutter, 1997).

- **personality disorders** psychological disorders characterized by inflexible and enduring behavior patterns that impair social functioning.

- **antisocial personality disorder** a personality disorder in which the person (usually a man) exhibits a lack of conscience for wrongdoing, even toward friends and family members. May be aggressive and ruthless or a clever con artist.

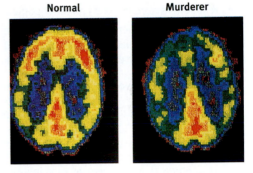

FIGURE 45.2 Murderous minds
PET scans illustrate reduced activation in a murderer's frontal cortex—a brain area that helps brake impulsive, aggressive behavior.

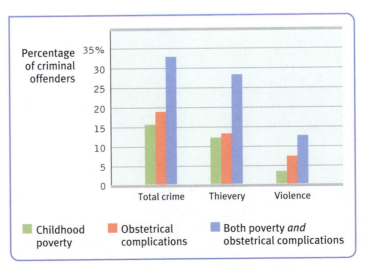

FIGURE 45.3 Bio-psycho-social roots of crime
Danish male babies whose backgrounds were marked *both* by obstetrical complications and social stresses associated with poverty were twice as likely to be criminal offenders by ages 20 to 22 as those in either the biological or social risk groups.

REVIEW AND REFLECT:

Dissociative and Personality Disorders

What are dissociative disorders, and why are they controversial?

Dissociative disorders occur when, under stress, a person's conscious awareness becomes dissociated (separated) from previous memories, thoughts, and feelings. Most mysterious of all dissociative disorders are cases of dissociative identity (*multiple personality*). The afflicted person is said to have two or more distinct personalities, with the original typically unaware of the other(s). Skeptics question whether this disorder may be a cultural phenomenon, finding it suspicious that the disorder has just recently become popular and is virtually nonexistent outside North America.

What characteristics are typical of personality disorders?

Personality disorders are enduring, maladaptive patterns of behavior that impair social functioning. For society, the most troubling of these is the remorseless and fearless antisocial personality.

Terms and Concepts to Remember

dissociative disorders, p. 564

dissociative identity disorder, p. 564

personality disorders, p. 566

antisocial personality disorder, p. 566

Test Yourself

45.1. Some disorders involve gaps in awareness—for example, sudden loss of memory. These psychological disorders are called

a. anxiety disorders.

b. dissociative disorders.

c. mood disorders.

d. memory disorders.

45.2. Dissociative identity disorder is relatively rare. This disorder is controversial because

a. criminals have used it as a defense.

b. it was reported frequently in the 1920s but rarely today.

c. it is almost never reported outside North America.

d. its symptoms are nearly identical to those of obsessive-compulsive disorder.

45.3. Unlike other psychological disorders, personality disorders need not involve any apparent anxiety, depression, or loss of contact with reality. A personality disorder, such as antisocial personality, is characterized by

a. the presence of multiple personalities.

b. disorganized thinking.

c. enduring and maladaptive personality traits.

d. mood disturbances.

Review: Does a full moon trigger "madness" in some people? How could you test that question?

Reflect: How would you evaluate the relative contributions of nature and nurture to antisocial personality disorder?

Answers to the Test Yourself and Review questions can be found in the green appendix at the end of the book.

Mood Disorders

Preview Questions: What are mood disorders, and what forms do they take? What might explain depression and its rising incidence among young people in the Western world?

The emotional extremes of **mood disorders** come in two principal forms: (1) *major depressive disorder*, in which the person experiences prolonged hopelessness and lethargy until usually rebounding to normality; and (2) *bipolar disorder* (formerly called *manic depressive disorder*), in which the person alternates between depression and *mania*, an overexcited, hyperactive state.

Major Depressive Disorder

Perhaps you know what depression feels like. If you are like most college students, at some time during this year—more likely the dark months of winter than the bright days of summer—you will probably experience a few of the symptoms of depression (Beck & Young, 1978). You may feel deeply discouraged about the future, dissatisfied with your life, or isolated from others. You may lack the energy to get things done or even to force yourself out of bed; be unable to concentrate, eat, or sleep normally; or even wonder if you would be better off dead. Perhaps academic success came easily to you in high school, and now you find that disappointing grades jeopardize your goals. You may feel lonely and isolated as a "nontraditional" student—returning after attending to other work or family commitments. Maybe social stresses, such as feeling you don't belong or the breakup of a romance, have plunged you into despair. And maybe brooding has at times only worsened your self-torment.

You are not alone. Depression is the "common cold" of psychological disorders—an expression that effectively describes its pervasiveness but certainly not its seriousness. Although phobias are more common, depression is the number one reason people seek mental health services.

As anxiety is a response to threat of future loss, depression is often a response to past and current loss. To feel bad in reaction to profoundly sad events (such as a significant loss) is to be in touch with reality. In such times, depression is like a car's low-oil-pressure light—a signal that warns us to stop and take protective measures. Recall that, biologically speaking, life's purpose is not happiness but survival and reproduction. To this end, coughing, vomiting, and various forms of pain are unpleasant, but they protect the body from dangerous toxins. Similarly, depression is a sort of psychic hibernation: It slows us down, avoids attracting predators, and evokes support. To grind temporarily to a halt and ruminate, as depressed people do, is to reassess one's life when feeling threatened. From this perspective, there is sense to suffering.

But when does this response become seriously maladaptive? The line separating life's normal "downs" from major depression is difficult to draw. Joy, contentment, sadness, and despair are different points on a continuum, points at which any of us may be found at any given moment. On that continuum, between the temporary blue moods we all experience and the crushing impact of major depression, is a condition called *dysthymic disorder*—a down-in-the-dumps mood that fills most of the day, nearly every day, for two years or more. Although less disabled than people with major depression, those with dysthymic disorder tend to experience chronic low energy and self-esteem, have difficulty concentrating or making decisions, and sleep and eat too much or too little.

For some people, recurring depression during winter's dark months constitutes a seasonal affective disorder. For others, winter darkness means more blue moods. When asked, "Have you cried today?" Americans answered "yes" more often in the winter:

	Men (answered "yes")	Women (answered "yes")
August	4%	7%
December	8%	21%

Source: Time/CNN survey, 1994

■ **mood disorders** psychological disorders characterized by emotional extremes. See *major depressive disorder, manic episode*, and *bipolar disorder.*

"My life had come to a sudden stop. I was able to breathe, to eat, to drink, to sleep. I could not, indeed, help doing so; but there was no real life in me."

Leo Tolstoy, *My Confession*, 1887

"All the people in history, literature, art, whom I most admire: Mozart, Shakespeare, Homer, El Greco, St. John, Chekhov, Gregory of Nyssa, Dostoevsky, Emily Brontë: not one of them would qualify for a mental-health certificate."

Madeleine L'Engle, *A Circle of Quiet*, 1972

Major depressive disorder occurs when signs of depression (including lethargy, feelings of worthlessness, or loss of interest in family, friends, and activities) last two weeks or more without any notable cause. The difference between a blue mood after bad news and a mood disorder is like the difference between gasping for breath for a few minutes after a hard run and being chronically short of breath. To sense what depression feels like, suggest some clinicians, imagine combining the anguish of grief with the sluggishness of jet lag.

Bipolar Disorder

With or without therapy, episodes of major depression usually end, and people temporarily or permanently return to their previous behavior patterns. However, some people rebound to or from the opposite emotional extreme—a euphoric, hyperactive, wildly optimistic **manic episode**. If depression is living in slow motion, mania is fast forward. Alternation between depression and mania signals **bipolar disorder**. During the manic phase of bipolar disorder, the person is typically overtalkative, overactive, elated (though easily irritated if crossed); has little need for sleep; and shows fewer sexual inhibitions. Speech is loud, flighty, and hard to interrupt.

One of mania's maladaptive symptoms is grandiose optimism and self-esteem, which may lead to reckless investments and spending sprees. Although people in a manic state find advice irritating, they need protection from their own poor judgment. In milder forms, however, the energy and free-flowing thinking of mania can fuel creativity. History offers many examples of creative bipolar people, from Walt Whitman and Ernest Hemingway to actress Margot Kidder. Bipolar disorder is especially common among creative artists (Jamison, 1993, 1995). George Frederic Handel (1685–1759), who many believe suffered a mild form of bipolar disorder, composed his nearly four-hour-long *Messiah* during three weeks of intense, creative energy (Keynes, 1980). Creative professionals who rely on precision and logic (architects, designers, journalists) are less vulnerable to bipolar disorder than are those who rely on emotional expression and vivid imagery (poets, novelists, entertainers), reports Arnold Ludwig (1995).

It is as true of emotions as of everything else: What goes up comes down. Before long, the elated mood either returns to normal or plunges into a depression. Though as maladaptive as major depression, bipolar disorder is much less common, occurring in about 1 percent of the population. Unlike major depression, it afflicts as many men as women.

Creativity and bipolar disorders
History has given us many creative artists, composers, and writers with bipolar disorder, including Walt Whitman, Virginia Woolf, Edgar Allan Poe, Samuel Clemens (Mark Twain), Ernest Hemingway, and Margot Kidder.

Explaining Mood Disorders

Because depression profoundly affects so many people, it understandably has been the subject of thousands of studies. Psychologists are working to develop a theory of mood disorders that will suggest ways to treat and prevent them. Researcher Peter Lewinsohn and his colleagues (1985, 1998) summarized the facts that any theory of depression must explain. Among them are the following:

+ **Many behavioral and cognitive changes accompany depression.** Depressed people are inactive and feel unmotivated. They are especially sensitive to negative happenings, expect negative outcomes, and are more likely to recall negative information. When the depression lifts, these behavioral and cognitive accompaniments disappear. Nearly half the time they exhibit symptoms of another disorder, such as anxiety or drug or alcohol abuse.

+ **Depression is widespread.** Its commonality suggests that its causes, too, must be common.

+ **Compared with men, women are twice as vulnerable to major depression, even more so if they have been depressed before** (FIGURE **46.1**). In general, women are most vulnerable to passive disorders—internalized states, such as depression, anxiety, and inhibited sexual desire. Men's disorders are more active—alcohol abuse, antisocial conduct, lack of impulse control (Robins & Regier, 1991; Kessler & others, 1994). When women get sad they often get sadder than men do. When men get mad, they often get madder than women do. Curiously, the gender difference in depression is quite small among college students (Regeth & Lewis, 1995).

+ **Most major depressive episodes last less than six months.** Therapy can speed recovery, yet most people suffering major depression return to normal without professional help. The plague of depression comes and, a few weeks or months later, it usually goes.

+ **Stressful events related to work, marriage, and close relationships often precede depression.** A family member's death, a job loss, a marital crisis, or a physical assault increase one's risk of depression. One study followed 2000 people over time. It found that the risk of the onset of depression in the ensuing month ranged from less than 1 percent among those who had experienced no stressful life event to 24 percent among those with three such stresses (Kendler & others, 1998). National samples of Israelis, whose tiny nation has been a living stress laboratory, revealed greater feelings of depression after the outbreak of the 1982 Israel-Lebanon war (Hobfoll & others, 1989). The early loss of a parent due to death or separation also increases later vulnerability to depression (Agid & others, 1999).

To these facts we can add one more: With each new generation, the rate of depression is increasing and the disorder is striking earlier (now often in the late teens). This is true not only in Canada and the United States but also in Germany, Italy, France,

- **major depressive disorder** a mood disorder in which a person, for no apparent reason, experiences two or more weeks of depressed moods, feelings of worthlessness, and diminished interest or pleasure in most activities.

- **manic episode** a mood disorder marked by a hyperactive, wildly optimistic state.

- **bipolar disorder** a mood disorder in which the person alternates between the hopelessness and lethargy of depression and the overexcited state of mania.

About 50 percent of those who recover from depression will suffer another episode within two years. Recovery is more likely to be enduring the longer patients stay well, the fewer their previous episodes, the less stress they experience, and the more social support they have (Belsher & Costello, 1988).

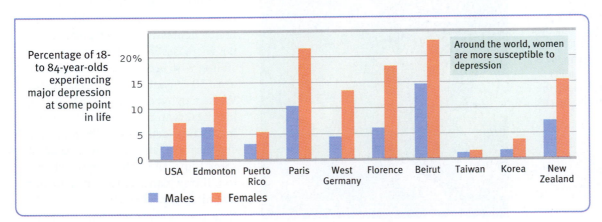

FIGURE **46.1**
Gender and depression
Interviews with 38,000 adults in 10 countries confirm what many smaller studies have found: Women's risk of major depression is double that of men's. Note, too, that lifetime risk of depression varies by culture—from 1.5 percent in Taiwan to 19 percent in Beirut. (Data from Weissman & others, 1996.)

Percentage of 18- to 84-year-olds experiencing major depression at some point in life

Around the world, women are more susceptible to depression

USA Edmonton Puerto Rico Paris West Germany Florence Beirut Taiwan Korea New Zealand

■ Males ■ Females

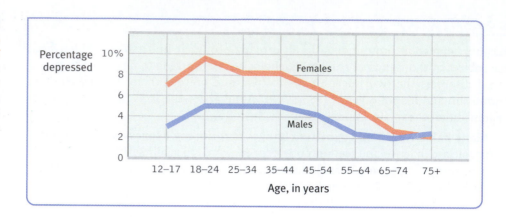

FIGURE 46.2
Canadian depression rates, by age and gender

Among the 1 to 3 million Canadians who acknowledge having suffered depression for at least two weeks in the previous year, young adults and women were most at risk (*Statistics Canada*, 1999).

Lebanon, New Zealand, Taiwan, and Puerto Rico (Cross-National Collaborative Group, 1992). In North America, today's young adults are three times as likely as their grandparents to report recently—or ever—suffering depression (despite the grandparents' having had many more years at risk). In one National Institute of Mental Health study of 18,244 Americans, only 1 percent of those born before 1905 had suffered major depression by age 75. Of those born since 1955, 6 percent had experienced depression by age 25. The increase appears authentic, *not* simply the result of younger adults being more willing to disclose depression. Young adult Canadians are similarly most vulnerable to depression (**FIGURE 46.2**).

As you might expect, researchers understand and interpret these facts in ways that reflect their different perspectives. Psychoanalytic theory applies Freud's ideas about the importance of early childhood experiences and unconscious impulses. It suggests that depression occurs when significant losses evoke feelings associated with losses experienced in childhood. Loss of a romantic relationship or a job might evoke feelings associated with the loss of the intimate relationship with one's mother. Alternatively, unresolved anger toward one's parents might be turned inward against the self. Today's bio-psycho-social perspective is replacing these Freudian explanations with biological and cognitive explanations.

The Biological Perspective

Most recent mental health research dollars have funded explorations of biological influences on mood disorders. Depression is a whole-body disorder. It involves genetic predispositions, biochemical imbalances, melancholy mood, and negative thoughts.

Gene-hunters' pursuit of bipolar-DNA links

Linkage studies seek to identify aberrant genes in family members suffering the disorder. These Pennsylvania Amish family members—an isolated population sharing a common life-style and some vulnerability to the disorder—have been among the volunteer subjects.

Genetic influences

We have long known that mood disorders run in families. The risk of major depression and bipolar disorder increases if you have a parent or sibling who became depressed before age 30 (Pauls & others, 1992; Weissman & others, 1986). If one identical twin is diagnosed as suffering major depressive disorder, the chances are about 1 in 2 that at some time the other twin will be, too. If one identical twin has bipolar disorder, the chances are 7 in 10 that the other twin will at some point be diagnosed similarly. Among fraternal twins, the corresponding odds are just under 1 in 5 (Tsuang & Faraone, 1990). The greater similarity of identical twins' depressive tendencies even occurs among twins reared apart (DiLalla & others, 1996). Moreover, adopted people who suffer a mood disorder often have close biological relatives who suffer mood disorders, become dependent on alcohol, or commit suicide (Wender & others, 1986).

A search for the genes that put people at risk for depression is now under way. At least 15 groups worldwide are sleuthing the genes that make one vulnerable to bipolar disorder (Veggeberg, 1996). To tease out which genes are implicated, researchers use *linkage analysis*. First, they find families that have had the disorder across several generations. Then they draw blood from both affected and unaffected family members and examine their DNA, looking for differences.

The Depressed Brain

Genes act by directing biochemical events that, down the line, influence behavior. The biochemical key is the neurotransmitters, those messenger molecules that shuttle signals between nerve cells. Norepinephrine, a neurotransmitter that increases arousal and boosts mood, is overabundant during mania and scarce during depression. A second neurotransmitter, serotonin, also appears to be scarce during depression. Drugs that alleviate mania reduce norepinephrine; drugs that relieve depression tend to increase norepinephrine or serotonin supplies by blocking either their reuptake (as Prozac, Zoloft, and Paxil do with serotonin) or their chemical breakdown. Repetitive physical exercise, such as jogging, also increases serotonin and helps reduce depression (Jacobs, 1994).

Using modern scanning machines, researchers are also spotting neurological signs of depression. Many recent studies have found the brains of depressed people to be less active, indicating a slowed-down state (**FIGURE 46.3**). The left frontal lobe, which is active during positive emotions, is likely to be inactive in depressed states (Davidson, 1999). MRI scans have even shown the frontal lobes to be 7 percent smaller in severely depressed patients (Coffey & others, 1993).

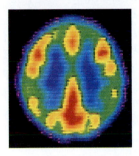

FIGURE 46.3

The ups and downs of bipolar disorder
PET scans show that brain energy consumption rises and falls with the patient's emotional switches. Red areas are where the brain rapidly consumes glucose.

Depressed state
(27-May-83)

Manic state
(18-May-83)

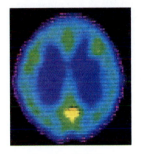

Depressed state
(17-May-83)

The Social-Cognitive Perspective

Some people slide into depression for no obvious reason, even when life has been going well. Often, however, biological factors accompany psychological reactions to experience (**FIGURE 46.4**). The mind's negative thoughts somehow influence biochemical events that in a vicious cycle amplify depressing thoughts.

Recent research reveals how *self-defeating beliefs* feed the vicious cycle. Depressed people view life through dark glasses. Their intensely negative assumptions about themselves, their situations, and their futures lead them to magnify bad experiences and minimize good ones. Listen to Norman, a Canadian college professor, recalling his depression:

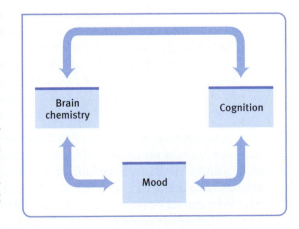

FIGURE 46.4 Depression—an ailing mind in an ailing body
Altering any one component of the chemistry-cognition-mood circuit can alter the others.

CLOSE-UP:

SUICIDE

"But life, being weary of these worldly bars, Never lacks power to dismiss itself."
William Shakespeare, *Julius Caesar*, 1599

Each year some three-quarters of a million despairing people worldwide will say no to life by electing a permanent solution to what may be a temporary problem (Retterstøl, 1993). To find out who commits suicide, researchers have compared the suicide rates of different groups.

+ ***National differences*** The suicide rates of England, Italy, and Spain are little more than half those of Canada, Australia, and the United States; Austrian, Danish, and Finnish suicide rates are about double (U.S. Bureau of the Census, 1998). Within Europe, the most suicide-prone people (Hungarians) are 20 times more likely to kill themselves than the least (Albanians) (Schmidtke, 1997).

+ ***Racial differences*** White Americans are nearly twice as likely as black Americans to kill themselves (U.S. Bureau of the Census, 1998).

+ ***Gender differences*** Women are much more likely than men to attempt suicide. But men are two to four times more likely (de-

pending on the country) to succeed (**FIGURE 46.5**). (There is one exception—China—whose 500 daily female suicides account for at least half the world total [Rosenthal, 1999].) Men are more likely to use lethal methods, such as firing a bullet into the head, the method of choice in 6 of 10 U.S. suicides. (A study of 238,000 California handgun purchasers found them 57 times

FIGURE 46.5

Suicide rates by gender and age

In the United States, suicide rates are higher among males than among females. The highest rates of all are found among older men. (From Centers for Disease Control, 1999.)

more likely than other Californians to kill themselves in the week following their purchase [Wintemute & others, 1999].)

+ ***Age differences*** Due partly to improved reporting (Gist & Welch, 1989), the known suicide rate among 15- to 19-year-olds has more than doubled in the United States since 1950. It now nearly equals the traditionally higher suicide rate among adults (**FIGURE 46.6**). In Canada, the suicide rate among 15- to 18-year-olds has increased sixfold since 1955 (NFFRE, 1996).

+ ***Other group differences*** Suicide rates are much higher among the rich, the nonreligious, and those

I [despaired] of ever being human again. I honestly felt subhuman, lower than the lowest vermin. Furthermore, I was self-deprecatory and could not understand why anyone would want to associate with me, let alone love me. . . . I was positive that I was a fraud and a phony and that I didn't deserve my Ph.D. I didn't deserve to have tenure; I didn't deserve to be a Full Professor. . . . I didn't deserve the research grants I had been awarded; I couldn't understand how I had written books and journal articles. . . I must have conned a lot of people. (Endler, 1982, pp. 45–49)

Self-defeating beliefs may arise from *learned helplessness.* Studies show that both dogs and humans act depressed, passive, and withdrawn after experiencing uncontrollable painful events. Gender differences in uncontrollable stress help explain why women have been twice as vulnerable to depression. Women more often than men have been abused or made to feel helpless (Hamida & others, 1998; Nolen-Hoeksema, 1990). Thirty-nine percent of women and 20 percent of men entering American col-

"I have learned to accept my mistakes by referring them to a personal history which was not of my making."

B. F. Skinner (1983)

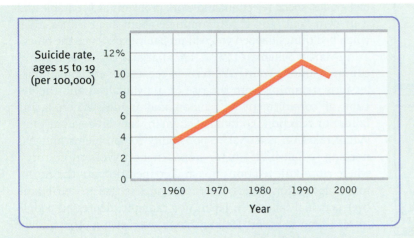

FIGURE 46.6

Increasing rates of teen suicide

Teen suicide soared from 1960 to 1990, and then tapered off. (From National Center for Health Statistics.)

who are single, widowed, or divorced (Hoyer & Lund, 1993; Stack, 1992; Stengel, 1981). In both the United States and Australia, the teen suicide surge was almost entirely among males (Hassan & Carr, 1989).

People seldom commit suicide while in the depths of depression, when energy and initiative are lacking. It is when they begin to rebound and become capable of following through that the risk increases. Teenage suicides may follow a trau-matic event, such as a romantic breakup or a guilt-provoking antisocial act; they are often linked with drug and alcohol abuse (Fowler & others, 1986; Kolata, 1986). Compared with people who suffer no disorder, those addicted to alcohol are roughly 100 times more likely to commit suicide; some 3 percent of them do (Murphy & Wetzel, 1990). Even among those who have attempted suicide, those who abuse alcohol are five times more likely than others to kill themselves eventually (Beck & Steer, 1989).

Social suggestion may trigger the final act. Following highly publicized suicides and TV programs featuring suicide, known suicides increase. So do fatal auto "accidents" and private airplane crashes.

Among the elderly, suicide is sometimes chosen as an alternative to current or future suffering. In people of all ages, suicide is not necessarily an act of hostility or revenge, but may instead be a way of switching off unendurable pain (Shneidman, 1987).

In retrospect, families and friends may recall signs that they believe should have forewarned them—verbal hints, giving possessions away, or withdrawal and preoccupation with death. Most people who commit suicide have been depressed. One-third have tried before to kill themselves.

Few who talk of suicide or think suicidal thoughts (a number that includes one-third of all adolescents and college students) actually attempt suicide, and few of those who attempt it complete the act (Yip, 1998). The United States, for example, records about 30,000 suicides annually and half a million emergency room visits for attempted suicide (Surgeon General, 1999). Still, most who do commit suicide had talked of it. And anyone who does threaten suicide is at least sending a signal of being desperate or feeling despondent. So, if a friend talks suicide, it's important to listen and to direct them to professional help.

leges feel "frequently overwhelmed by all I have to do" (Sax & others, 1999). (Men report spending more of their time in "light anxiety" activities such as sports, TV watching, and partying, possibly avoiding activities that might make them feel overwhelmed.)

Negative Thoughts Feed Negative Moods

Why do life's unavoidable failures lead some people, but not others, to become depressed? The difference lies partly with people's *attributions* of blame. We have some choice of whom or what to blame for our failures. If you fail a test and blame yourself, you may feel stupid and depressed. If you externalize the blame—perhaps attributing your failure to an unfair test—you are more likely to feel angry.

Depressed people tend to explain bad events in terms that are *stable* ("It's going to last forever"), *global* ("It's going to affect everything I do"), and *internal* ("It's all my fault"). Lyn Abramson, Gerald Metalsky, and Lauren Alloy (1989) theorize that

Drawing by Charles Schulz; © 1956 United Feature Syndicate, Inc.

the result of these pessimistic, overgeneralized, self-blaming attributions is a depressing sense of hopelessness. If you tend to see bad grades, social rejection, and work problems as inevitable and your own fault, and if you ruminate about such things, then when bad things happen you will probably experience the blues.

Martin Seligman (1991, 1995) argues that depression is common among young Westerners because of epidemic hopelessness stemming from the rise of individualism and the decline of commitment to religion and family. When facing failure or rejection, contends Seligman, the self-focused individual takes on personal responsibility for problems and has nothing to fall back on for hope. In non-Western cultures, where close-knit relationships and cooperation are the norm, major depression is less common and less tied to self-blame over personal failure. In Japan, for example, depressed people instead tend to report feeling shame over letting others down (Draguns, 1990a).

Negative Moods Feed Negative Thoughts

There is, however, a chicken-and-egg problem with the social-cognitive explanation of depression. Self-defeating beliefs, self-blame, and negative attributions surely do support depression. But do they *cause* depression, any more than a speedometer's reading 70 mph causes a car's speed? Peter Barnett and Ian Gotlib (1988) note that such cognitions are *indicators* of depression. Depressing thoughts *coincide* with a depressed mood. But before or after being depressed, people's thoughts are less negative. Perhaps this is because a depressed mood triggers negative thoughts, a phenomenon known as state-dependent memory. If you temporarily put people in a bad or sad mood, their memories, judgments, and expectations suddenly become more pessimistic.

Joseph Forgas and his associates (1984) provided a striking demonstration of the mood effect. Subjects who had been put in a good or bad mood via hypnosis watched a videotape of themselves talking with someone the day before. The happy subjects detected in themselves more positive than negative behaviors; the unhappy subjects more often saw themselves behaving negatively (**FIGURE 46.7**). Thus, even when watching themselves on videotape, people judge themselves more negatively when they feel depressed.

FIGURE 46.7 The mood effect
A happy or depressed mood strongly influences people's rating of their own behavior. In this experiment, those in a hypnotically induced good mood detected many more positive than negative behaviors. The reverse was true for those in a bad mood.

Percentage of observations

Good moods breed positive self-perceptions

35%

Bad mood

30

25

20

Good mood

15

Negative behaviors — Positive behaviors

Self-ratings

Depression's Vicious Cycle

"A recipe for severe depression is preexisting pessimism encountering failure," notes Martin Seligman (1991, p. 78). Depression, as we have seen, is often brought on by stressful experiences—losing a job, getting divorced or rejected, suffering physical trauma—anything that disrupts your sense of who you are and why you are a worthy human being. Such brooding after failure can be adaptive; one may gain insights during times of depressed inactivity that can later lead to more effective strategies for interacting with the world. But depression-prone people respond to bad events in an especially self-focused, self-blaming way (Pyszczynski & others, 1991; Wood & others, 1990a,b). Their self-esteem fluctuates up more rapidly with boosts and down with threats (Butler & others, 1994). When down, their brooding amplifies their negative feelings, which in turn trigger depression's other cognitive and behavioral symptoms.

This phenomenon also helps explain women's doubled risk of depression. When trouble strikes, women tend to think, men tend to act. Women often have vivid recall for both wonderful and horrid ex-

CLOSE-UP:

LONELINESS

Loneliness—the painful awareness that one's social relationships are deficient—is both a contributor to depression and its own problem. The deficiency stems from a mismatch between one's actual and desired social contacts. One person may feel lonely when isolated, another when in a crowd.

Aloneness often breeds loneliness. People who are alone—unmarried, unattached, and often young—are more likely to feel lonely. Dutch psychologist Jenny de Jong-Gierveld (1987) has speculated that the emphasis on individual fulfillment and the downgrading of stable relationships and commitment to others are "loneliness-provoking factors." Work-related moves also make for fewer long-term family and social ties and increased loneliness (Dill & Anderson, 1999).

People commonly experience one or more of four types of loneliness (Beck & Young, 1978). To be lonely is to feel *excluded* from a group you would like to belong to; to feel *unloved* and uncared about by those around you; to feel *constricted* and unable to share your private concerns with anyone; or to feel *alienated*, or different, from those in your community.

Like people suffering from depression, lonely people tend to blame themselves, attributing their deficient social relationships to their own inadequacies (Snodgrass, 1987). There may be a basis for this self-blame: Chronically lonely people tend to be shy, self-conscious, and lacking in self-esteem, and to be perceived as less socially competent and attractive (Cheek & Melchior, 1990; Lau & Gruen, 1992; Vaux, 1988). They often find it hard to introduce themselves, make phone calls, and participate in groups (Rook, 1984; Spitzberg & Hurt, 1987). In addition, believing in their own social unworthiness restricts them from noticing and remembering positive feedback and from taking steps that would reduce their loneliness (Frankel & Prentice-Dunn, 1990). Thus, the very factors that work to create and maintain the cycle of depression can also produce a cycle of loneliness.

periences; men more vaguely recall such experiences (Seidlitz & Diener, 1998). This gender difference in emotional recall may feed women's greater rumination over negative events. A woman may fret and act anxious or depressed, while a man may distract himself by drinking, acting out, delving into work, or watching sports (Nolen-Hoeksema, 2000; Seligman, 1994).

None of us is immune to the dejection, diminished self-esteem, and negative thinking brought on by rejection or defeat. As Edward Hirt and his colleagues (1992) demonstrated, even small losses can temporarily sour our thinking. They studied some avid Indiana University basketball fans who seemed to regard the team as an extension of themselves. After the fans watched their team lose or win, the researchers asked them to predict the team's future performance, and their own. After a loss, the morose fans offered bleaker assessments not only of the team's future, but also of their own likely performance at throwing darts, solving anagrams, and getting a date. When things aren't going our way, it may seem as though they never will.

When bad events happen, those who ruminate and catastrophize with pessimistic, self-blaming thoughts are more at risk for depression. In research demonstrating this effect, Susan Nolen-Hoeksema and Jannay Morrow (1991) happened to assess Stanford University students' moods and ruminations 2 weeks before the 1989 earthquake devastated much of their area. Those identified as prone to brood over negative events showed more symptoms of depression both 10 days and 7 weeks after the earthquake. If you have an optimistic way of interpreting events, a failure or stress is unlikely to provoke depression (Seligman, 1991). And even if you do fall prey to depression, you are more likely to recover quickly (Metalsky & others, 1993; Needles & Abramson, 1990).

And what might you expect of new college students who are not depressed but do exhibit a pessimistic cognitive style (some of whom are about to satisfy Martin Seligman's depression recipe: pessimism encountering failure)? Lauren Alloy and her collaborators (1999) monitored Temple University and University of Wisconsin students every 6 weeks for 2.5 years. Among those identified as having optimistic thinking

"Man never reasons so much and becomes so introspective as when he suffers, since he is anxious to get at the cause of his sufferings."

Luigi Pirandello, *Six Characters in Search of an Author*, 1922

Surviving depression
CBS correspondent Mike Wallace became debilitated by severe depression during a tough libel trial. "Depression is palpable," he says. "You begin to feel like a fake and a fraud. You second-guess everything about everything."

FIGURE 46.8
The vicious cycle of depression
This cycle can be broken at any point. A variety of therapeutic techniques attempt to intervene at one or more of the four points in the cycle. (Adapted from Lewinsohn & others, 1985.)

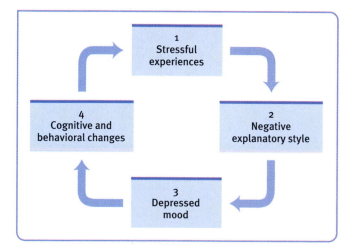

styles only 1 percent had a first episode of major depression, as did 17 percent of those who began college with pessimistic thinking styles. Their simple conclusion: Negative thinkers are vulnerable to depression.

So there is two-way traffic between depressed mood and negative thinking. Depression causes self-focused negative thinking. And a self-focused, self-blaming style of explaining events puts one at risk for depression when bad events strike.

Knowing this, might we train depression-prone people to think more positively? That is one aim of cognitive therapy. It's also the aim of the Penn Optimism Program for 9- to 13-year-old children targeted as at risk for depression. The program puts children through 12 small-group sessions, each lasting two hours, in which they learn to tune into their thoughts when facing tough situations and to imagine alternatives to negative thoughts. The leader might, for example, present a cartoon depicting a child being called a name and invite the children to brainstorm positive ways to cope. In early experiments, the training has halved the proportion of children suffering depression for up to two ensuing years (Gillham & Reivich, 1999).

When successful, such therapy helps disrupt depression's vicious cycle. Being withdrawn, self-focused, and complaining elicits rejection (Furr & Funder, 1998; Gotlib & Hammen, 1992). In one study, researchers Stephen Strack and James Coyne (1983) noted that "depressed persons induced hostility, depression, and anxiety in others and got rejected. Their guesses that they were not accepted were not a matter of cognitive distortion." Weary of the person's fatigue, hopeless attitude, and lethargy, a spouse may threaten to leave or a boss may begin to question the person's competence. Indeed, people in the throes of depression are at high risk for divorce, job loss, and other stressful life events. (This provides another example of genetic–environmental interaction: People genetically disposed to depression more often experience depressing events.) The losses and stress only serve to compound the original depression. Misery may love another's company, but company does not love another's misery.

We can now assemble the pieces of the depression puzzle (**FIGURE 46.8**): (1) Negative, stressful events interpreted through (2) a ruminating, pessimistic explanatory style create (3) a hopeless, depressed state that (4) hampers the way the person thinks and acts. This, in turn, fuels (1) more negative experiences. It's a cycle we can all recognize. Bad moods feed on themselves: When we *feel* down, we *think* negatively and remember bad experiences. On the brighter side, we can break the cycle of depression at any of these points—by moving to a different environment, by reversing our self-blame and negative attributions, by turning our attention outward, or by engaging in more pleasant activities and more competent behavior.

Winston Churchill called depression a "black dog" that periodically hounded him. Poet Emily Dickinson was so afraid of bursting into tears in public that she spent much of her adult life in seclusion (Patterson, 1951). Abraham Lincoln was so withdrawn and brooding as a young man that his friends feared he might take his own life (Kline, 1974). As each of these lives reminds us, people can and do struggle through depression. Most regain their capacity to love, to work, and even to succeed at the highest levels

REVIEW AND REFLECT:

Mood Disorders

What are mood disorders, and what forms do they take?

Mood disorders are characterized by emotional extremes. The two principal forms are *major depressive disorder* and *bipolar disorder*. In major depressive disorder, the person—without apparent reason—descends for weeks or months into deep unhappiness, lethargy, and feelings of worthlessness before rebounding to normality. Although less disabling, *dysthymic disorder* is marked by chronic low energy and poor self-esteem.

In the less common bipolar disorder, the person alternates between the hopelessness and lethargy of depression and the hyperactive, wildly optimistic, impulsive phase of mania.

What might explain depression and its rising incidence among young people in the Western world?

Current research on depression is vigorously exploring two sets of influences. The first focuses on genetic predispositions and neurotransmitter abnormalities. The second views the cycle of depression from a social-cognitive perspective, in light of cyclic self-defeating beliefs, learned helplessness, negative attributions, and aversive experiences.

Terms and Concepts to Remember

mood disorders, p. 569
major depressive disorder, p. 570
manic episode, p. 570
bipolar disorder, p. 570

Test Yourself

46.1. With bipolar disorder, the person alternates between the lethargy of depression and the overexcited state of mania. Although bipolar disorder is as maladaptive as depression, it is much less common and it affects
   a. all ethnic groups equally.
   b. primarily scientists and doctors.
   c. as many men as women.
   d. younger people more than older people.

46.2. Depression affects many people, often following a stressful event, such as divorce or job change. In a depressive episode, a person tends to be inactive and unmotivated and overly sensitive to negative happenings. In most cases the depressive episode lasts
   a. less than three months.
   b. six months.
   c. six months to one year.
   d. two years.

46.3. Depression tends to run in families. It can often be alleviated by drugs that block the reuptake of the neurotransmitters norepinephrine and serotonin. These statements suggest that an explanation for depression may well be found in
   a. psychoanalytic theory.
   b. learned helplessness.
   c. stressful events.
   d. biological factors.

46.4. In linkage analysis, researchers study families that have had a disorder across several generations. Researchers focus on
   a. brain-structure differences between affected and unaffected family members.
   b. DNA differences between affected and unaffected family members.
   c. life-style differences between affected and unaffected members.
   d. DNA similarities between the families and the general population.

46.5. Depressed people are more likely than others to blame themselves, rather than external factors, for their failures. Such self-defeating beliefs often arise from feelings of helplessness or futility. Psychologists who emphasize the importance of negative perceptions, beliefs, and thoughts in depression are working within the _____ perspective.
   a. psychoanalytic
   b. biological
   c. behavioral
   d. social-cognitive

Review: When you show your depressed friend Figure 46.8 on page 578, he responds, "You see? Depression is a vicious cycle and there's no way out!" What hope could you offer?

Reflect: Has your entry into college life been a challenging time for you? What advice would you have for future collegians?

Answers to the Test Yourself and Review questions can be found in the green appendix at the end of the book.

47 Schizophrenia

Preview Questions: What are the symptoms of schizophrenia, and what forms does it take? What are the possible causes of schizophrenia?

If depression is the common cold of psychological disorders, chronic schizophrenia is the cancer. Nearly 1 in 100 people will develop schizophrenia, joining the millions across the world who have suffered one of humanity's most dreaded disorders. It typically strikes as young people are maturing into adulthood, it knows no national boundaries, and it affects males and females about equally often (though men tend to be struck earlier and more severely).

Symptoms of Schizophrenia

Literally translated, **schizophrenia** means "split mind." It refers not to a multiple-personality split but rather to a split from reality that shows itself in disorganized thinking, disturbed perceptions, and inappropriate emotions and actions.

Disorganized Thinking

Imagine trying to communicate with Maxine, a young woman whose thoughts spill out in no logical order. Her biographer, Susan Sheehan (1982, p. 25), observed her saying aloud to no one in particular,

> This morning, when I was at Hillside [Hospital], I was making a movie. I was surrounded by movie stars. The X-ray technician was Peter Lawford. The security guard was Don Knotts. That Indian doctor in Building 40 was Lou Costello. I'm Mary Poppins. Is this room painted blue to get me upset? My grandmother died four weeks after my eighteenth birthday.

As this strange monologue illustrates, the thinking of a person with schizophrenia is fragmented, bizarre, and distorted by false beliefs, called **delusions** ("I'm Mary Poppins"). Jumping from one idea to another may occur even within sentences, creating a sort of "word salad." One young man begged for "a little more allegro in the treatment," and suggested that "liberationary movement with a view to the widening of the horizon" will "ergo extort some wit in lectures." Those with *paranoid* tendencies are particularly prone to delusions of persecution.

Many psychologists believe disorganized thoughts result from a breakdown in selective attention. We normally have a remarkable capacity for selective attention—for, say, giving our undivided attention to one voice at a party while filtering out competing sensory stimuli. Schizophrenia sufferers cannot do this (Gjerde, 1983). They also have difficulty clearing their working memory of distracting information (Schooler & others, 1997). Thus, an irrelevant stimulus or an extraneous part of the preceding thought easily distracts them. Minute stimuli, such as the grooves on a brick or the inflections of a voice, may distract their attention from the whole scene or from the speaker's meaning. As one former patient recalled, "What had happened to me . . . was a breakdown in the filter, and a hodge-podge of unrelated stimuli were distracting me from things which should have had my undivided attention" (MacDonald, 1960, p. 218).

- **schizophrenia** a group of severe disorders characterized by disorganized and delusional thinking, disturbed perceptions, and inappropriate emotions and actions.

- **delusions** false beliefs, often of persecution or grandeur, that may accompany psychotic disorders.

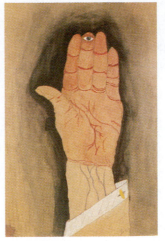

Art by people diagnosed with schizophrenia
Commenting on the kind of art work shown here, poet and art critic John Ashbery wrote: "The lure of the work is strong, but so is the terror of the unanswerable riddles it proposes."

Disturbed Perceptions

A person with schizophrenia may perceive things that are not there. Such *hallucinations* (sensory experiences without sensory stimulation) are usually auditory. The person may hear voices that make insulting statements or give orders. The voices may tell the patient that she is bad or that he must burn himself with a cigarette lighter. Less commonly, people see, feel, taste, or smell things that are not there. Such hallucinations have been compared to dreams breaking into waking consciousness. When the unreal seems real, the resulting perceptions are at best bizarre, at worst terrifying.

Inappropriate Emotions and Actions

The emotions of schizophrenia are often utterly inappropriate. Maxine's emotions seemed split off from reality. She laughed after recalling her grandmother's death. On occasion, she became angry for no apparent reason or cried when others laughed. Other victims of schizophrenia sometimes lapse into *flat affect*, a zombielike state of apparent apathy.

Motor behavior may also be inappropriate. The person may perform senseless, compulsive acts, such as continually rocking or rubbing an arm. Those who exhibit *catatonia* may remain motionless for hours on end and then become agitated.

As you can imagine, such disorganized thinking, disturbed perceptions, and inappropriate emotions and actions profoundly disrupt social relationships. During their most severe periods, people with schizophrenia live in a private inner world, preoccupied with illogical ideas and unreal images. Given a supportive environment, some recover to enjoy a normal life or experience bouts of schizophrenia only intermittently. Others remain socially withdrawn and isolated throughout much of their lives. Rarely is schizophrenia a one-time episode that is "cured," never to return.

Types of Schizophrenia

We have thus far described schizophrenia as if it were a single disorder. Actually, it is a cluster of disorders. The subtypes share some common features, but they also have some distinguishing symptoms (Table 47.1). Schizophrenia patients with *positive symptoms* may experience hallucinations, are often disorganized and deluded in their talk, and may exhibit inappropriate laughter, tears, or rage. Those with *negative symptoms* have toneless voices, expressionless faces, or mute and rigid bodies. Thus positive symptoms are the *presence* of inappropriate behaviors and negative symptoms are the *absence* of appropriate behaviors. Because schizophrenia is more than one disorder, these varied symptoms could have more than one cause.

TABLE 47.1

SUBTYPES OF SCHIZOPHRENIA

Paranoid:	Preoccupation with delusions or hallucinations
Disorganized:	Disorganized speech or behavior, or flat or inappropriate emotion
Catatonic:	Immobility (or excessive, purposeless movement), extreme negativism, and/or parrotlike repeating of another's speech or movements
Undifferentiated:	Many and varied symptoms
Residual:	Withdrawal, after hallucinations and delusions have disappeared

CLOSE-UP:

EXPERIENCING SCHIZOPHRENIA

These recollections of a schizophrenia patient illustrate some of the thoughts and feelings of those who suffer the positive symptoms of schizophrenia. Note the hallucinations and the delusions of persecution and grandeur.

One night I was invited to listen to a talk by a worker in the foreign service. I was suspicious of him and thought he thought I was a Communist spy. I didn't say anything. I just leaned over and stared at him.

I thought the Government was spying on my room with a telescope in a building across the street. I thought people were loading down my food in the cafeteria with salt. In criminology class I thought the professor and the other students were laughing about me. I thought they were directing the poisoning of my food in the cafeteria.

When I went to the cafeteria my hand shook as the waitress poured what I thought was poisonous coffee into my cup. I thought everyone in the cafeteria knew I was going to die. They all thought it was too bad but I was so evil it was necessary.

On a Saturday I drank lemonade to try to neutralize the poison. Then I would take showers to try to sweat the poison out. I was so nervous I could hardly think. I thought I might only have hours left to live. I thought of taking a bus home to my parents. But no, I thought, it was too late for that.

One day when my strange behavior landed me in a jail cell, the walls began to buzz like bees. I felt there were thousands of bees in the walls buzzing. The buzzing went on and on. There was no relief. It was maddening. Finally, I felt my father's hand rest on my head and I felt peace.

When someone asks me to explain schizophrenia, I tell them, you know how sometimes in your dreams you are in them yourself and some of them feel like real nightmares? My schizophrenia was like I was walking through a dream. But everything around me was real. At times, today's world seems so boring and I wonder if I would like to step back into the schizophrenic dream, but then I remember all the scary and horrifying experiences. (*Excerpted and paraphrased with permission from Stuart Emmons, Craig Geisler, Kalman J. Kaplan, and Martin Harrow,* Living With Schizophrenia. *Muncie, IN: Taylor & Francis, 1997.*)

Sometimes, as in the case of Maxine, schizophrenia develops gradually, emerging from a long history of social inadequacy (which partially explains why those predisposed to schizophrenia often end up in the lower socioeconomic levels, or even homeless). Other times it appears suddenly, seemingly as a reaction to stress. One rule holds true around the world (World Health Organization, 1979): When the schizophrenia is a slow-developing process (called *chronic*, or *process*, schizophrenia), recovery is doubtful. When, in reaction to particular life stresses, a previously well-adjusted person develops schizophrenia rapidly (*acute*, or *reactive*, schizophrenia), recovery is much more likely. Those with chronic schizophrenia often exhibit the negative symptom of withdrawal. The outlook is better for those exhibiting positive symptoms—they more often have a reactive condition that responds to drug therapy (Fenton & McGlashan, 1991, 1994; Fowles, 1992). (For one person's experiences with positive symptoms, see the Close-Up: Experiencing Schizophrenia, above.)

Understanding Schizophrenia

Schizophrenia is not only the most dreaded psychological disorder but also one of the most heavily researched. Most of the new research studies link it with brain abnormalities and genetic predispositions. Schizophrenia is a disease of the brain exhibited in symptoms of the mind.

Brain Abnormalities

The idea that imbalances in brain chemistry might underlie schizophrenia has long intrigued scientists. Strange behaviors, they knew, could have strange chemical causes. The saying "mad as a hatter" refers to the psychological deterioration of

British hatmakers whose brains, it was later discovered, were slowly poisoned as they moistened the brims of mercury-laden felt hats with their lips (Smith, 1983). Scientists are beginning to understand the mechanism by which chemicals such as LSD produce hallucinations. These discoveries hint that schizophrenia symptoms might have a biochemical key.

Dopamine Overactivity

One such key to schizophrenia involves the neurotransmitter dopamine. When researchers examined patients' brains after death, they found an excess of receptors for dopamine—in fact, a sixfold excess for the so-called D4 dopamine receptor (Seeman & others, 1993; Wong & others, 1986). The researchers speculate that such a high level may intensify brain signals in schizophrenia, creating positive symptoms such as hallucinations and paranoia. As we might therefore expect, drugs that block dopamine receptors often lessen the symptoms; drugs that increase dopamine levels, such as amphetamines and cocaine, sometimes intensify them (Swerdlow & Koob, 1987). Dopamine overactivity may underlie patients' overreacting to irrelevant external and internal stimuli.

Brain Anatomy

Modern brain-scanning techniques reveal that many people with chronic schizophrenia have abnormal brain activity. Some have abnormally low brain activity in the frontal lobes (Pettegrew & others, 1993; Resnick, 1992). One recent study took PET scans of brain activity while people were hallucinating (Silbersweig & others, 1995). When participants heard a voice or saw something, their brains became vigorously active in several core regions, including the thalamus, a structure deep in the brain that filters incoming sensory signals and transmits them to the cortex.

Enlarged, fluid-filled areas and a corresponding shrinkage of cerebral tissue seem characteristic of schizophrenia, especially in men (Cannon & Marco, 1994; Elkis & others, 1995). The greater the shrinkage, often involving the hippocampus and amygdala in the limbic system, the worse the thought disorder tends to be (Nelson & others, 1998; Shenton & others, 1992). The thalamus, too, is smaller than normal, which may explain why people with schizophrenia have difficulty filtering sensory input and focusing attention (Andreasen & others, 1994). The bottom line of various brain studies, reports Nancy Andreasen (1997), is that schizophrenia involves not a single brain abnormality but problems with several brain regions and their interconnections.

Naturally, scientists wonder what causes these brain abnormalities. One possibility is a prenatal problem. Low birth weight and birth complications are known risk factors for schizophrenia (Buka & others, 1999). People conceived during the peak of the Dutch wartime famine also later displayed a doubled rate of schizophrenia (Susser & others, 1996). A midpregnancy viral infection that might impair fetal brain development is another possible culprit (Waddington, 1993).

Can you imagine some ways to test this fetal-virus idea? Scientists exploring this possibility have asked the following questions:

+ **Are people at increased risk of schizophrenia if, during the middle of their fetal development, their country experienced a flu epidemic?** The repeated answer is yes (Mednick & others, 1994; Murray & others, 1992; Wright & others, 1995).

+ **Are people born in densely populated areas, where viral diseases spread more readily, at greater risk for schizophrenia?** The repeated answer, confirmed in a new study of 1.75 million Danes, is yes (Jablensky, 1999; Mortensen & others, 1999).

+ **Are those born during the winter and spring months—after the fall-winter flu season—also at increased risk?** The answer is again yes, at 5 to 8 percent increased risk (Torrey & others, 1997).

Studying the neurophysiology of schizophrenia
Psychiatrist E. Fuller Torrey is collecting the brains of hundreds of those who died as young adults and suffered disorders such as schizophrenia and bipolar disorder. Torrey is making tissue samples available to researchers worldwide.

+ **In the Southern Hemisphere, where the seasons are the reverse of the Northern Hemisphere, are the months of above-average schizophrenia births similarly reversed?** Again, the answer is yes, though somewhat less so. In Australia, for example, people born between August and October are at greater risk—unless they migrated from the Northern Hemisphere, in which case their risk is greater if they were born between January and March (McGrath & others, 1995, 1999).

+ **As infectious disease rates have declined, has there been a correlated decline in the later incidence of schizophrenia?** Once again, the answer is yes (Eagles, 1991).

Although schizophrenia has other causes (as genetics research makes plain), these converging lines of evidence suggest that prenatal viral infections do play a contributing role. If more evidence supports this association, future schizophrenia prevention programs might include immunizing women of childbearing age against influenza.

Genetic Factors

Might people also inherit a predisposition to certain brain abnormalities? The evidence strongly suggests that, yes, some do. The nearly 1 in 100 odds of any person's being diagnosed with schizophrenia become 1 in 10 among those who have an afflicted sibling or parent, and close to 1 in 2 among those who have an afflicted identical twin (**FIGURE 47.1**). Although there are barely more than a dozen such known cases, it appears that an identical twin of a person with schizophrenia retains that 1-in-2 chance, whether the twins are reared together or apart (Plomin & others, 1997).

Curiously, though, even with identical twins there may be a prenatal environmental component. About two-thirds of identical twins share the same placenta and blood. (They usually also have opposite handedness to their co-twin.) If one has an identical twin with schizophrenia, the odds are 6 in 10 that the co-twin will be similarly afflicted if they shared a single placenta, but only 1 in 10 if the twins had separate placentas (Davis & others, 1995a,b; Phelps & others, 1997). Twins who share a placenta are more likely to experience the same prenatal viruses. So it's possible that shared germs as well as shared genes produce identical twin similarities.

FIGURE 47.1

Risk of developing schizophrenia
The lifetime risks of developing schizophrenia vary with one's genetic relatedness to someone having this disorder. (From family and twin studies conducted between 1920 and 1987 in Europe, Irving Gottesman, 1991.)

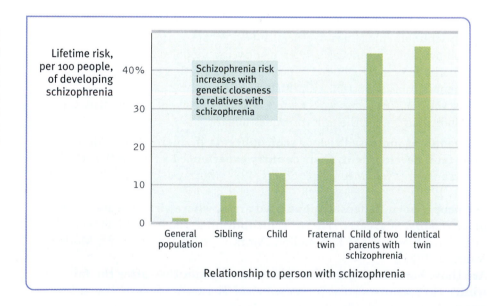

Adoption studies, however, confirm that the genetic link is real (Gottesman, 1991). Children adopted by someone who develops schizophrenia seldom "catch" the disorder. Rather, adopted children have an elevated risk if a biological parent is diagnosed with schizophrenia.

With the genetic factor established, researchers are now sleuthing specific genes that, in some combination, might predispose schizophrenia-inducing brain abnormalities. So far, the evidence has produced a confusing mix of findings. But several linkage studies have implicated chromosomes 6, 8, and 22 as sites of genes that make some people susceptible (DeLisi, 1999).

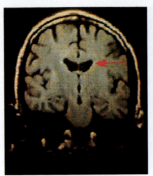
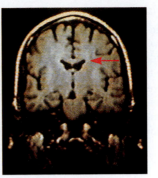

Schizophrenia   No schizophrenia

Schizophrenia in identical twins
When twins differ, only the one afflicted with schizophrenia typically has enlarged, fluid-filled cranial cavities (Suddath & others, 1990). The difference between the twins implies some nongenetic factor, such as a virus, is also at work.

The genetic contribution to schizophrenia is beyond question. But the genetic role is not straightforward like the inheritance of eye color. After all, about half the twins who share identical genes with a schizophrenia victim do *not* develop the disorder. Thus, behavior geneticists Susan Nicol and Irving Gottesman (1983) concluded that some people "have a genetic predisposition to the disorder but that this predisposition by itself is not sufficient for the development of schizophrenia." Other factors—including prenatal viral infections, nutritional deprivation, and oxygen deprivation at birth—also may be ingredients for the disease.

Our knowledge of the human genome and of genetic influences upon maladies such as schizophrenia and bipolar disorder is exploding. So, can scientists develop genetic tests that reveal who is at risk? If so, will people in the future subject their embryos to genetic testing (and gene repair or abortion if they are at risk for a psychological or physical malady)? Or might they take their egg and sperm to the genetics lab for screening before combining them to produce an embryo? Or will children be tested for genetic risks and given appropriate preventive treatments? Although there is a growing possibility of such a test, the patterns of inheritance seem too complex to expect that a single gene abnormality will prove predictive (Gottesman, 1993). Yet given the explosion in gene and brain research technologies, scientists are optimistic that schizophrenia will soon be better understood.

Psychological Factors

If genetically predisposed physiological abnormalities do not, by themselves, cause schizophrenia, neither do prenatal and psychological factors alone. It remains true, as Nicol and Gottesman (1983) noted nearly two decades ago, that "no environmental causes have been discovered that will invariably, or even with moderate probability, produce schizophrenia in persons who are not related to a schizophrenic." Psychologists long ago ceased blaming cold and capricious "refrigerator mothers."

Nevertheless, if genes predispose some people to *react* to particular experiences by developing schizophrenia, then there must be identifiable triggering experiences. Researchers have asked: Can stress trigger schizophrenia? Can difficulties in family communications be a contributing factor?

The answer to each question is a strong maybe. The psychological triggers of schizophrenia have proved elusive, partly because they may vary with the type of schizophrenia and its speed of onset—whether it is a slow-developing, chronic schizophrenia, or a sudden, acute reaction to stress. True, young people with schizophrenia tend to have unusually disturbed communications with their parents.

The Genain quadruplets
The odds of any four people picked at random all being diagnosed with schizophrenia are 1 in 100 million. But Nora, Iris, Myra, and Hester Genain all have the disease. Two of the sisters have more severe forms of the disorder than the others, suggesting the influence of environmental as well as biological factors.

But is this a cause or a result of their disorder? True, stressful experiences, biochemical abnormalities, and schizophrenia's symptoms often occur together. But as the bio-psycho-social perspective emphasizes, the traffic between brain biochemistry and psychological experiences runs both ways. True, schizophrenic withdrawal often occurs in adolescence or early adulthood, coinciding with the stresses of having to become independent, assert oneself, and achieve social success and intimacy. So, is schizophrenia the maladaptive coping reaction of biologically vulnerable people? For example, abnormalities in the dopamine system and in brain anatomy may render a patient hypersensitive to stress, which worsens symptoms by augmenting dopamine activity (Walker & Diforio, 1997).

Hoping to identify the psychological causes of schizophrenia, several investigators are now following the development of "high-risk" children, such as those born to a parent with schizophrenia or exposed to prenatal risks (Freedman & others, 1998; Olin & Mednick, 1996; Susser, 1999). By comparing the experiences of high-risk and low-risk children who do and do not develop schizophrenia, these researchers are seeking early warning signs. So far, these seem to include the following:

+ A mother whose schizophrenia was severe and long-lasting
+ Birth complications, often involving oxygen deprivation, and low birth weight
+ Separation from parents
+ Short attention span and poor muscle coordination
+ Disruptive or withdrawn behavior
+ Emotional unpredictability
+ Poor peer relations

Most of us can relate more easily to the ups and downs of mood disorders than to the strange thoughts, perceptions, and behaviors of schizophrenia. Sometimes our thoughts do jump around, but we do not talk nonsensically. Occasionally we feel unjustly suspicious of someone, but we do not fear that the world is plotting against us. Often our perceptions err, but rarely do we see or hear things that are not there. We have felt regret after laughing at someone's misfortune, but we rarely giggle in response to bad news. At times we just want to be alone, but we do not live in social isolation. However, millions of people around the world do talk strangely, suffer delusions, hear nonexistent voices, see things that are not there, laugh or cry at inappropriate times, or withdraw into private imaginary worlds. The quest to solve the cruel puzzle of schizophrenia therefore continues.

REVIEW AND REFLECT:

Schizophrenia

Schizophrenia typically strikes during late adolescence. It affects men and women about equally, and it seems to occur in all cultures.

What are the symptoms of schizophrenia?

Schizophrenia shows itself in disorganized thinking (nonsensical talk and delusions, which may stem from a breakdown of selective attention); disturbed perceptions (including hallucinations); and inappropriate emotions and actions. It is rarely a one-time episode.

What forms does schizophrenia take?

Schizophrenia is a set of disorders that emerge either gradually from a chronic history of social inadequacy (in which case the outlook is dim) or suddenly in reaction to stress (in which case the prospects for recovery are brighter).

What are the possible causes of schizophrenia?

Multiple factors converge to create schizophrenia. Researchers have linked certain forms of schizophrenia with brain abnormalities, such as enlarged, fluid-filled cerebral cavities or increased receptors for the neurotransmitter dopamine, known to be a major player in schizophrenia. Twin and adoption studies also point to a genetic predisposition that, in conjunction with environmental factors, may bring about a schizophrenia disorder.

Terms and Concepts to Remember

schizophrenia, p. 580   delusions, p. 580

Test Yourself

47.1. Schizophrenia patients often show disorganized thinking and disturbed perceptions. They may speak illogically and may hear voices urging self-destruction. Hearing voices in the absence of any auditory stimulation is an example of a(n)
   a. delusion or false belief.   c. word salad.
   b. inappropriate emotion.   d. hallucination.

47.2. Many psychologists believe that the disorganized thoughts that characterize schizophrenia may be the result of a breakdown in selective attention. People with schizophrenia cannot

   a. filter out competing stimuli or clear their working memory of distracting information.
   b. mimic another person's speech or movements.
   c. react to stressful events.
   d. see, feel, taste, or smell sensory stimuli.

47.3. Schizophrenia is actually a cluster of disorders characterized by positive or negative symptoms. A person with positive symptoms is most likely to experience
   a. catatonia.   c. withdrawal.
   b. delusions.   d. flat emotion.

47.4. Stressful events, faulty family communications, and, especially, inherited abnormalities in brain chemistry and structure are all possible factors in the development of schizophrenia. Chances for recovery are best when
   a. onset is sudden, in response to stress.
   b. deterioration occurs gradually, during childhood.
   c. no environmental causes can be identified.
   d. there is a detectable brain abnormality.

47.5. Most recent research studies link schizophrenia with brain abnormalities and genetic predispositions. Drugs that block dopamine receptors tend to
   a. intensify positive symptoms.
   b. lessen positive symptoms.
   c. intensify negative symptoms.
   d. lessen negative symptoms.

Review: What are the five subtypes of schizophrenia?

Reflect: Civil libertarians defend the right of schizophrenia patients not to be hospitalized against their will. E. Fuller Torrey (1998), a psychiatrist who views schizophrenia as a brain disorder, objects: "If a person with Alzheimer's wanted to go outside with no shoes in the winter, we wouldn't say, 'That's fine, he should have free choice.'" Do you think patients with schizophrenia should be hospitalized and treated against their will? Or do they always have the right to live free, even if under bridges or in shelters?

Answers to the Test Yourself and Review questions can be found in the green appendix at the end of the book.

Therapy

Today we comprehend deep outer space and can state with certainty the chemical composition of Jupiter's atmosphere. But in understanding and treating the disturbances of deep inner space—the psychological disorders that continue to plague humankind—we are only beginning to make real progress. Consider: In the 2200 years since Eratosthenes correctly estimated the Earth's circumference, we have charted the heavens, explored the solar system, reconstructed the basic history of life on Earth, cracked the genetic code, and eliminated or found cures for all sorts of diseases. Meanwhile, we have treated psychological disorders with a bewildering variety of methods, harsh and gentle: by cutting holes in the head and by giving warm baths and massages; by restraining, bleeding, or "beating the devil" out of people; by placing them in sunny, serene environments; by administering drugs and electric shocks; and by talking—talking about childhood experiences, about current feelings, about maladaptive thoughts and behaviors.

The transition from brutal to gentler treatments occurred thanks to the efforts of reformers such as Philippe Pinel in France and Dorothea Dix in the United States, Canada, and Scotland. Both advocated constructing mental hospitals to offer more humane methods of treatment. As we shall see, however, the introduction of therapeutic drugs and community-based treatment programs has largely emptied mental health hospitals since the mid-1950s.

Today's favored treatment depends on the therapist's viewpoint. Those who believe that psychological disorders are learned will tend to favor psychological therapies. Those who view disorders as biologically rooted are likely to advocate medication as well. Those who believe that disorders are responses to social conditions will, in addition, want to reform the "sick" environment. Many therapists seek to integrate insights from each of these views.

We can classify therapies into two main categories: The *psychological therapies* (Modules 48 and 49) employ structured interactions (usually verbal) between a trained professional and a client with a problem. The *biomedical therapies* (Module 50) act directly on the patient's nervous system.

48 The Psychological Therapies

Psychological therapy, or **psychotherapy**, is "a planned, emotionally charged, confiding interaction between a trained, socially sanctioned healer and a sufferer" (Frank, 1982). There are 250 or more types of psychotherapy (Parloff, 1987). We will look at only the most influential. Each is built on one or more of psychology's major personality theories: psychoanalytic, humanistic, behavioral, and cognitive. We will also consider the use of these techniques in group therapies.

While each technique is distinctive, there are common threads. Therapists who view disorders as an interplay of bio-psycho-social influences may welcome a combination of treatments. Indeed, half of psychotherapists describe themselves as taking an **eclectic approach**, by using a blend of therapies (Beitman & others, 1989; Castonguay & Goldfried, 1994). Depending on the client and the problem, an eclectic therapist will draw from a variety of techniques. Closely related to eclecticism is *psychotherapy integration*. Rather than picking and choosing methods, integration advocates aim to combine them into a single, coherent system.

The history of treatment
William Hogarth's (1697–1764) engraving (near right) of St. Mary of Bethlehem hospital in London (commonly called Bedlam) depicts the treatment of mental disorders in the eighteenth century. Visitors paid to gawk at the patients as if they were viewing zoo animals. The chair on the far right was designed by Benjamin Rush (1746–1813) "for the benefit of maniacal patients." Rush, a founder of the movement for more humane treatment of the mentally ill, believed that they required restraint to regain their sensibilities.

Psychoanalysis

Preview Question: What are the aims and methods of psychoanalysis and psychodynamic therapy?

Although few of today's therapists practice therapy as Sigmund Freud did, many of his psychoanalytic techniques survive. **Psychoanalysis** is part of our modern vocabulary, and its assumptions influence many other therapies. To understand the Freud-influenced "psychodynamic" therapies, let's first look at classical psychoanalysis as practiced by Freud himself.

Aims

Sigmund Freud believed that the mind was like an iceberg, with the *unconscious* region below the surface and the *preconscious* close enough to the surface for its contents to be retrievable. He saw personality as composed of a reservoir of pleasure-seeking psychic impulses (the *id*), a reality-oriented executive (the *ego*), and an internalized set of ideals (the *superego*).

Freud believed that children develop through several formative *psychosexual stages*, which he labeled the oral, anal, phallic, latency, and genital stages. He suggested that people's later personalities were influenced by how they resolved conflicts associated with these stages and whether they remained *fixated* at any stage.

Classical psychoanalysis
The placement of the analyst's chair out of view is thought to minimize distraction and make it easier for the patient—relaxed on a couch—to verbalize whatever comes to mind.

Psychoanalysis assumes that many psychological problems are fueled by childhood's residue of supposedly repressed impulses and conflicts. Psychoanalysts try to bring these repressed feelings into conscious awareness where the patient can deal with them. By gaining insight into the origins of the disorder—by fulfilling the ancient imperative to "know thyself" in a deep way—the patient "works through" the buried feelings. The theory presumes that healthier, less anxious living becomes possible when patients release the energy they had previously devoted to id-ego-superego conflicts.

Methods

Psychoanalysis is historical reconstruction, its goal being to unearth the past in hope of unmasking the present. But how?

Freud came to believe that one path to the past was *free association*. Imagine yourself as a patient using the free association technique. The analyst invites you to relax, perhaps by lying on a couch. He or she will probably sit out of your line of vision, helping you focus attention on your thoughts and feelings. Beginning with a childhood memory, a dream, or a recent experience, you say aloud whatever comes to your mind from moment to moment. It sounds easy, but soon you notice how often you edit your thoughts as you speak, omitting what seems trivial, irrelevant, or shameful. Even in the safe presence of the analyst, you may pause momentarily before uttering an embarrassing thought. You may make a joking remark or change the subject to something less threatening. Sometimes your mind may go blank or you may find yourself unable to remember important details.

To the psychoanalyst, these blocks in the flow of your free associations indicate **resistance**. They hint that anxiety lurks and that you are repressing sensitive material. The analyst will want to explore these sensitive areas, first making you aware of your resistances and then interpreting their underlying meaning. The analyst's **interpretations**—suggestions of underlying wishes, feelings, and conflicts—aim to provide you with *insight*. If offered at the right moment, the analyst's interpretation—of, say, your not wanting to talk about your mother—may illuminate what you are avoiding. You may then discover what your resistances mean and how they fit with other pieces of your psychological puzzle.

Freud believed that another clue to repressed impulses is your dreams' *latent content*—its underlying but censored meaning.

- **psychotherapy** an emotionally charged, confiding interaction between a trained therapist and someone who suffers from psychological difficulties.

- **eclectic approach** an approach to psychotherapy that, depending on the client's problems, uses techniques from various forms of therapy.

- **psychoanalysis** Sigmund Freud's therapeutic technique. Freud believed the patient's free associations, resistances, dreams, and transferences—and the therapist's interpretations of them—released previously repressed feelings, allowing the patient to gain self-insight.

- **resistance** in psychoanalysis, the blocking from consciousness of anxiety-laden material.

- **interpretation** in psychoanalysis, the analyst's noting supposed dream meanings, resistances, and other significant behaviors in order to promote insight.

Thus, after inviting you to report a dream, the analyst may offer a dream analysis, suggesting its meaning.

During many such sessions you will probably disclose to your analyst more of yourself than you have ever revealed to anyone. Because psychoanalytic theory emphasizes the formative power of childhood experiences, much of what you reveal will pertain to your earliest memories. You will also probably find yourself experiencing strong positive or negative feelings for your analyst. Such feelings may express the dependency or mingled love and anger that you earlier experienced toward family members or other important people in your life. When this happens, Freud would say you are actually *transferring* your strongest feelings from those other relationships to the analyst. Analysts and other therapists believe that this **transference** exposes long-repressed feelings, giving you a belated chance to work through them with your analyst's help. But psychoanalysis is not just about excavating your childhood past. By examining your feelings toward the analyst you may also gain insight into your current relationships.

Note how much of psychoanalysis is built on the assumption that repressed memories exist, an assumption that is now questioned. This challenge—to an assumption so basic to much of professional and popular psychology—is provoking intense debate.

Critics also say psychoanalysts' interpretations are hard to refute. If, in response to the analyst's suggested interpretation, you say, "Yes! I see now," your acceptance confirms the analyst's interpretation. If you emphatically say, "No! That just doesn't ring true," your denial may be taken as more resistance, also confirming the interpretation. Psychoanalysts acknowledge it's hard to prove or disprove their interpretations. But they insist that interpretations often are a great help to patients.

Traditional psychoanalysis takes time, up to several years of several sessions a week, and it is expensive. (Three times a week for just two years at $100 or more per hour comes to $30,000 or more.)

Psychodynamic Therapy

Although there are relatively few traditional psychoanalysts, psychoanalytic assumptions influence many therapists, especially those who make *psychodynamic* assumptions. Psychodynamic therapists try to understand a patient's current symptoms by exploring childhood experiences. They probe for supposed repressed, emotion-laden information, seeking to help the person gain insight into the unconscious roots of problems and work through newly resurrected feelings. Although influenced by Freud's psychoanalysis, these therapists may talk to the patient face to face (rather than out of the line of vision), once a week (rather than several times weekly), and for only a few weeks or months (rather than several years).

No brief excerpt can exemplify psychodynamic therapy's probing of the past, but we can illustrate these therapists' goal of enabling insight via their interpretations. In the following interaction, therapist David Malan responds to all that he has heard from a depressed patient by suggesting insights into her problems. Note how Malan interprets the woman's earlier remarks and suggests that her relationship with him reveals a characteristic pattern of behavior (1978, pp. 133–134).

Malan: I get the feeling that you're the sort of person who needs to keep active. If you don't keep active, then something goes wrong. Is that true?

Patient: Yes.

Malan: I get a second feeling about you and that is that you must, underneath all this, have an awful lot of very strong and upsetting feelings. Somehow they're there but you aren't really quite in touch with them. Isn't this right? I feel you've been like that as long as you can remember.

Patient: For quite a few years, whenever I really sat down and thought about it I got depressed, so I tried not to think about it.

Woody Allen, after awakening from suspended animation in the movie *Sleeper*: "I haven't seen my analyst in 200 years. He was a strict Freudian. If I'd been going all this time, I'd probably almost be cured by now."

Malan: You see, you've established a pattern, haven't you? You're even like that here with me, because in spite of the fact that you're in some trouble and you feel that the bottom is falling out of your world, the way you're telling me this is just as if there wasn't anything wrong.

Interpersonal psychotherapy, a brief (12- to 16-session) alternative to psychodynamic therapy has been shown to be effective with depressed patients (Weissman, 1999). Like psychodynamic therapies, interpersonal psychotherapy aims to help people gain insight into the roots of their difficulties. But rather than focusing on undoing past hurts and offering interpretations, this approach focuses on current relationships, and assists people in improving their relationship skills. Its goal is not personality change but symptom relief in the here and now.

Interpersonal psychotherapy goals can be illustrated with the case of Anna (not her real name), a 34-year-old married businesswoman. Five months after receiving a promotion, with accompanying increased responsibilities and longer hours, Anna experienced increased tensions with her husband over his wanting a second child. She began feeling depressed, had trouble sleeping, became irritable, and was gaining weight. A psychodynamic therapist would likely help Anna gain insight into her angry impulses and her defenses against anger. An interpersonal therapist would similarly want the patient to gain insight but would also engage Anna's thinking on immediate issues—how to balance work and home, how to resolve the dispute with her husband, and how to express emotion more effectively (Markowitz & others, 1998).

Face-to-face therapy
In this type of therapy session the couch has disappeared. But the influence of psychoanalytic theory may not have, especially if the therapist probes for the origin of the patient's symptoms by seeking information from the patient's childhood.

Humanistic Therapies

Preview Question: What are the basic themes of humanistic therapy, such as Rogers' person-centered approach?

The humanistic perspective emphasizes people's inherent potential for self-fulfillment. Not surprisingly, then, humanistic therapists aim to boost self-fulfillment by helping people grow in self-awareness and self-acceptance. Unlike psychoanalytic therapists, humanistic therapists tend to focus on

+ the *present* and *future* instead of the past. They explore feelings as they occur, rather than achieving insights into the childhood origins of the feelings.
+ *conscious* rather than unconscious thoughts.
+ taking immediate *responsibility* for one's feelings and actions rather than uncovering hidden determinants.
+ promoting *growth* instead of curing illness. Thus, those in therapy are "clients" rather than "patients."

The most widely used humanistic technique is Carl Rogers' (1961, 1980) **client-centered therapy**. A client-centered therapist focuses on the person's conscious self-perceptions rather than on the therapist's own interpretations. The therapist listens, without judging or interpreting, and refrains from directing the client toward certain insights, a strategy labeled *nondirective* therapy.

Believing that most people already possess the resources for growth, Rogers encouraged therapists to exhibit *genuineness, acceptance,* and *empathy.* When therapists drop their facades and genuinely express their true feelings, when they enable their clients to feel unconditionally accepted, and when they empathically sense and reflect their clients' feelings, the clients may increase in self-understanding and self-acceptance. As Rogers (1980, p. 10) explained,

Hearing has consequences. When I truly hear a person and the meanings that are important to him at that moment, hearing not simply his words, but him, and

■ **transference** in psychoanalysis, the patient's transfer to the analyst of emotions linked with other relationships (such as love or hatred for a parent).

■ **client-centered therapy** a humanistic therapy, developed by Carl Rogers, in which the therapist uses techniques such as active listening within a genuine, accepting, empathic environment to facilitate clients' growth. (Also called *person-centered therapy.*)

Active listening
The late Carl Rogers (right) empathizes with a client during a group therapy session.

when I let him know that I have heard his own private personal meanings, many things happen. There is first of all a grateful look. He feels released. He wants to tell me more about his world. He surges forth in a new sense of freedom. He becomes more open to the process of change.

I have often noticed that the more deeply I hear the meanings of the person, the more there is that happens. Almost always, when a person realizes he has been deeply heard, his eyes moisten. I think in some real sense he is weeping for joy. It is as though he were saying, "Thank God, somebody heard me. Someone knows what it's like to be me."

"Hearing" refers to Rogers' technique of **active listening**—echoing, restating, and seeking clarification of what the person expresses (verbally or nonverbally) and acknowledging the expressed feelings. Active listening is now an accepted part of therapeutic counseling practices in many schools, colleges, and clinics. The counselor listens attentively and interrupts only to restate and confirm the client's feelings, to accept what the client is expressing, or to seek clarification. In counseling a male client, Rogers illustrates active listening:

> **Client:** I just ain't no good to nobody, never was, and never will be.
>
> **Rogers:** Feeling that now, hm? That you're just no good to yourself, no good to anybody. Never will be any good to anybody. Just that you're completely worthless, huh?—Those really are lousy feelings. Just feel that you're no good at all, hm?
>
> **Client:** Yeah. (Muttering in low, discouraged voice) That's what this guy I went to town with just the other day told me.
>
> **Rogers:** This guy that you went to town with really told you that you were no good? Is that what you're saying? Did I get that right?
>
> **Client:** M-hm.
>
> **Rogers:** I guess the meaning of that if I get it right is that here's somebody that—meant something to you and what does he think of you? Why, he's told you that he thinks you're no good at all. And that just really knocks the props out from under you. (Client weeps quietly.) It just brings the tears. (Silence of 20 seconds)
>
> **Client:** (Rather defiantly) I don't care though.
>
> **Rogers:** You tell yourself you don't care at all, but somehow I guess some part of you cares because some part of you weeps over it. (Meador & Rogers, 1984, p. 167)

This brief excerpt illustrates how the client-centered counselor seeks to provide a psychological mirror that helps clients see themselves more clearly. But can a thera-

"We have two ears and one mouth that we may listen the more and talk the less."

Zeno, 335–263 B.C., *Diogenes Laertius*

"You say, 'Off with her head,' but what I'm hearing is, 'I feel neglected.'"

pist be a perfect mirror, without selecting and interpreting what is reflected? Rogers conceded that one cannot be *totally* nondirective. Nevertheless, he believed that the therapist's most important contribution is to accept and understand the client. Given a nonjudgmental, grace-filled environment that provides *unconditional positive regard*, people internalize unconditional positive self-regard; they may accept even their worst traits and feel valued and whole.

If you want to listen more actively in your own relationships, three hints may help (keep in mind that practicing these is not easy):

1. *Paraphrase.* Check your understandings by summarizing the speaker's words in your own words.
2. *Invite clarification.* "What might be an example of that?" may encourage the speaker to say more.
3. *Reflect feelings.* "That must be frustrating" might mirror what you're sensing from the speaker's body language and intensity.

Behavior Therapies

Preview Question: What are the assumptions and techniques of the behavior therapies?

All the therapies we have considered so far assume that, for rational people at least, psychological problems diminish as self-awareness grows. The psychoanalyst expects problems to subside as people gain insight into their unresolved and unconscious tensions. The humanistic therapist expects problems to abate as people "get in touch with their feelings." Behavior therapists, however, do not believe that self-awareness is a magic bullet. They assume that the problem behaviors *are* the problems. You can, for example, become aware of why you are highly anxious during exams and still be anxious. So, instead of trying to alleviate distressing behaviors by resolving a presumed underlying problem, **behavior therapy** applies well-established learning principles to eliminate the unwanted behavior. To treat phobias or sexual disorders, behavior therapists do not delve deep below the surface looking for inner causes. Rather, they try to replace problem thoughts and maladaptive behaviors with constructive ways of thinking and acting.

Classical Conditioning Techniques

One cluster of behavior therapies derives from principles developed in Ivan Pavlov's early twentieth-century conditioning experiments. As Pavlov and others showed, we learn various behaviors and emotions through classical conditioning—a type of learning in which we come to associate certain stimuli with each other. So, are maladaptive symptoms also conditioned responses? If, say, a claustrophobic fear of elevators is a learned response to the stimulus of being in an enclosed space, then might one unlearn the fear by counterconditioning the fear response? **Counterconditioning** pairs the trigger stimulus with a new response that is incompatible with fear. For example, if we repeatedly pair the enclosed space of the elevator with a relaxed response, the fear response may be displaced.

Another classical conditioning therapy was developed by learning theorist O. H. Mowrer for chronic bed-wetters. The child sleeps on a liquid-sensitive pad connected to an alarm. Moisture on the pad triggers the alarm, waking the child. With sufficient repetition, this association of urinary relaxation with waking up stops the bed-wetting. In three out of four cases the treatment is effective, and the success provides a boost to the child's self-image (Christophersen & Edwards, 1992; Houts & others, 1994).

Two specific counterconditioning techniques are *systematic desensitization* and *aversive conditioning.*

- **active listening** empathic listening in which the listener echoes, restates, and clarifies. A feature of Rogers' client-centered therapy.

- **behavior therapy** therapy that applies learning principles to the elimination of unwanted behaviors.

- **counterconditioning** a behavior therapy procedure that conditions new responses to stimuli that trigger unwanted behaviors; based on classical conditioning. Includes *systematic desensitization* and *aversive conditioning.*

What might a psychoanalyst say about this therapy for bed-wetting? How might a behavior therapist reply?

Systematic Desensitization

Picture this scene reported in 1924 by Mary Cover Jones, an associate of the behaviorist John B. Watson: Three-year-old Peter is petrified of rabbits and other furry objects. Jones aims to replace Peter's fear of rabbits with a conditioned response that is incompatible with fear. Her strategy is to associate the fear-evoking rabbit with the pleasurable, relaxed response associated with eating. As Peter begins his midafternoon snack, Jones introduces a caged rabbit on the other side of the huge room. Peter, eagerly munching away on his crackers and drinking his milk, hardly notices. On succeeding days, she gradually moves the rabbit closer and closer. Within two months, Peter is tolerating the rabbit in his lap, even stroking it while he eats. Moreover, his fear of other furry objects subsides as well, having been "countered," or replaced, by a relaxed state that cannot coexist with fear (Fisher, 1984; Jones, 1924).

Unfortunately for those who might have been helped by her counterconditioning procedures, Jones' story of Peter and the rabbit did not immediately become part of psychology's lore. It was not until more than 30 years later that psychiatrist Joseph Wolpe (1958; Wolpe & Plaud, 1997) refined Jones' technique into what has become the most widely used method of behavior therapy: **systematic desensitization**. Wolpe assumed, as did Jones, that you cannot simultaneously be anxious and relaxed. Therefore, if you can repeatedly relax when facing anxiety-provoking stimuli, you can gradually eliminate your anxiety. The trick is to proceed gradually.

Let's see how this might work with a common phobia. Imagine yourself afraid of public speaking. A behavior therapist might first ask for your help in constructing a hierarchy of anxiety-triggering speaking situations. Your anxiety hierarchy could range from mildly anxiety-provoking situations, such as speaking up in a small group of friends, to panic-provoking situations, such as having to address a large audience.

Using *progressive relaxation*, the therapist trains you to relax one muscle group after another, until you achieve a drowsy state of complete relaxation and comfort. Then the therapist asks you to imagine, with your eyes closed, a mildly anxiety-arousing situation: You are having coffee with a group of friends and are trying to decide whether to speak up. If imagining the scene causes you to feel any anxiety, you signal your tension by raising your finger, and the therapist instructs you to switch off the mental image and go back to deep relaxation. This imagined scene is repeatedly paired with relaxation until you can feel no trace of anxiety.

The therapist progresses up the client's anxiety hierarchy, using the relaxed state to desensitize the person to each imagined situation. After several therapy sessions,

Virtual reality exposure therapy
Within the confines of a room, virtual reality technology exposes patients to vivid simulations of feared stimuli, such as a plane's takeoff.

you practice what you had imagined in actual situations, beginning with relatively easy tasks and gradually moving to more anxiety-filled ones. Conquering your anxiety in an actual situation, not just in your imagination, raises your self-confidence (Foa & Kozak, 1986; Williams, 1987). Eventually, you may even become a confident public speaker.

Desensitization is a prime example of *exposure therapy*—a therapy that exposes someone, in imagination or actuality, to a feared situation. More aggressive than systematic desensitization is another exposure therapy called *flooding*, an extinction procedure that forces a person to confront feared stimuli. When dogs are forced to face situations in which they have previously received shocks, it floods them with fear. When no shocks occur, their fear begins to extinguish. People, too, when guided to experience or vividly imagine a feared situation often come to realize that no real danger exists.

Virtual reality technology can now expose clients to situations more vividly than their own imaginations could. The individual wears a head-mounted display unit that projects a three-dimensional virtual world, immersing its wearer into a lifelike series of scenes. For those unable to vividly imagine the anxiety-arousing situation and too terrified or embarrassed to experience the situation in reality, virtual reality offers an efficient middle ground. Experiments led by several research teams in Atlanta and elsewhere have treated people with fears of flying, fears of heights, fears of particular animals, and fears of public speaking (North & others, 1998; Rothbaum & others, 1995, 1997; Vincelli & Molinari, 1998). For example, patients with a fear of flying can experience peering out a virtual window of a simulated plane, feeling vibrations, and hearing the engine roar as the plane taxis down the runway and takes off. In initial experiments, those experiencing this *virtual reality exposure therapy* have experienced greater relief from their fears—in real life—than those in control groups.

Therapists sometimes combine systematic desensitization with other techniques. For clients with phobias, they may have someone model appropriate behavior in a fear-arousing situation. If you were afraid of snakes, you would first observe someone handling a snake. Then you would be coaxed in gradual steps to approach, touch, and handle it yourself (Bandura & others, 1969). By applying this principle of observational learning, therapists have helped people overcome disruptive fears of snakes, spiders, and dogs (**FIGURE 48.1**, page 598).

Notice that the systematic desensitization and modeling procedures make no attempt to help you achieve insight into your fear's underlying cause. If you are afraid of

■ **systematic desensitization** a type of counterconditioning that associates a pleasant relaxed state with gradually increasing anxiety-triggering stimuli. Commonly used to treat phobias.

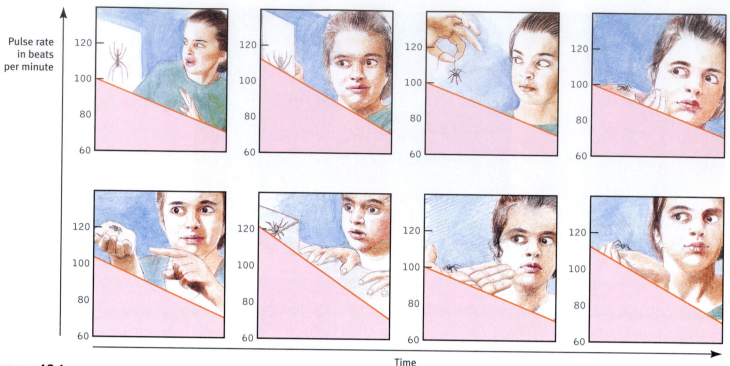

Pulse rate in beats per minute

Time

FIGURE 48.1

Systematic desensitization of a phobia

Beverly, who is terribly afraid of spiders, is exposed to stimuli that are progressively more threatening, but she adapts to each one in turn, as shown by her fairly consistent pulse rate. She tolerates first a picture of a spider, then a toy spider, then a dead spider, and finally a live one.

heights, the therapist will not spend much time probing when you first experienced the fear or what may have caused it. Nor do behavior therapists worry (as psychoanalysts might) that eliminating your fear of heights will leave an underlying problem that may now be expressed as, say, a fear of elevators. On the contrary, they find that overcoming maladaptive behaviors helps people feel better about themselves.

Aversive Conditioning

In systematic desensitization, the therapist helps the client substitute a positive (relaxed) response for a negative (fearful) response to a harmless stimulus. In **aversive conditioning**, the therapist tries to replace a positive response to a harmful stimulus (such as alcohol) with a negative (aversive) response. Thus, aversive conditioning is the reverse of systematic desensitization.

The procedure is simple: It associates unpleasant feelings with the unwanted behavior. To treat nail biting, one can paint the fingernails with a yucky-tasting nail polish (Baskind, 1997). Similarly, by giving child molesters electric shocks as they view photos of nude children, aversion therapists try to eliminate the molesters' sexual response to children. And, by giving withdrawn and self-abusing autistic children harmless "aversives," such as a spray of cold water in the face, therapists hope to suppress the child's self-injury while reinforcing more appropriate behavior. Because this therapy involves an unpleasant experience, it is practiced sparingly, with the appropriate consent.

Aversion therapy has also been used to treat alcoholism. To that end, the therapist offers the client appealing drinks laced with a drug that produces severe nausea. By linking the drinking of alcohol with violent nausea, the therapist seeks to transform the person's reaction to alcohol from positive to negative (**FIGURE 48.2**). Arthur Wiens and Carol Menustik (1983) studied 685 alcoholic patients who completed an aversion therapy program at a Portland, Oregon, hospital. One year later, after returning for several booster treatments of alcohol-sickness pairings, 63 percent were still successfully abstaining. But after three years, only 33 percent had remained abstinent.

Does aversive conditioning work? In the short run it may. But, in therapy (as in research experiments), cognition influences conditioning. People know that outside the therapist's office they can drink without fear of nausea or engage in sexually deviant behavior without fear of shock. A person's ability to discriminate between the aversive conditioning situation and all other situations can limit the treatment's effectiveness. Thus, it is often used in combination with another treatment.

Operant Conditioning

The work of B. F. Skinner and others teaches us a basic principle of operant conditioning—voluntary behaviors are strongly influenced by their consequences. This simple fact enables behavior therapists to reinforce desired behaviors and to withhold reinforcement for, or to punish, undesired behaviors. Using operant conditioning to solve specific behavior problems has raised hopes for some cases thought to be hopeless. Children with mental retardation have been taught to care for themselves. Socially withdrawn children with autism have learned to interact. People with schizophrenia have been helped to behave more rationally in their hospital ward. In such cases, therapists use positive reinforcers to shape behavior by rewarding closer and closer approximations of the desired behavior.

In extreme cases, treatment must be intensive. In one study (Lovaas, 1987), 9 withdrawn, uncommunicative 3-year-olds with autism participated in a 2-year, 40-hour-a-week program in which their parents attempted to shape their behavior. The combination of positive reinforcing of desired behaviors and ignoring or punishing aggressive and self-abusive behaviors worked wonders. By first grade, 9 of the 19 children were functioning successfully in school and exhibiting normal intelligence. Only 1 of 40 comparable children who did not undergo this treatment showed similar improvement.

The rewards used to modify behavior vary. For some people, the reinforcing power of attention or praise is sufficient. Others require concrete rewards, such as food. In institutional settings, therapists may create a **token economy**. When patients display appropriate behavior, such as getting out of bed, washing, dressing, eating, talking coherently, cleaning up their rooms, or playing cooperatively, they receive a token or plastic coin as a positive reinforcer. Later, they can exchange their accumulated tokens for various rewards, such as candy, watching television, trips to town, or better living quarters. Token economies have been successfully applied in various settings (homes, classrooms, hospitals, institutions for the delinquent) and among members of various populations (including disturbed children and people with schizophrenia and other mental disabilities).

Critics of such *behavior modification* express two concerns. One concern is practical: What happens when the reinforcers stop, as when the person leaves the institution? Could the person become so dependent on extrinsic rewards that the appropriate behaviors quickly disappear? If so, how can behavior therapists make the appropriate behaviors durable? Proponents of behavior modification respond that they may wean patients from the tokens by shifting them toward rewards, such as social approval, that are more typical of life outside the institution. They may also train patients to behave in ways that are intrinsically rewarding. For example, as a withdrawn person becomes more socially competent, the intrinsic satisfactions of social interaction may help the person maintain the behavior.

The second concern is ethical: Is it right for one human to control another's behavior? Those who set up token economies typically deprive people of something they desire and then decide which behaviors they will reinforce. To critics, the whole

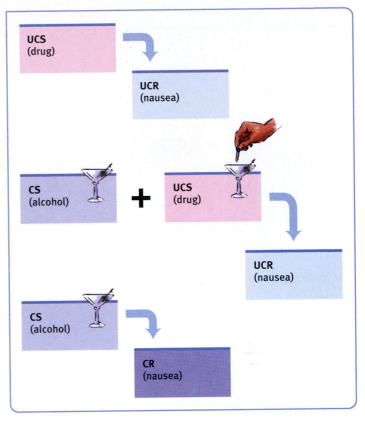

FIGURE 48.2
Aversion therapy for alcoholism
After repeatedly imbibing an alcoholic drink mixed with a drug that produces severe nausea, some people with a history of alcohol abuse develop at least a temporary conditioned aversion to alcohol.

■ **aversive conditioning** a type of counterconditioning that associates an unpleasant state (such as nausea) with an unwanted behavior (such as drinking alcohol).

■ **token economy** an operant conditioning procedure that rewards desired behavior. A patient exchanges a token of some sort, earned for exhibiting the desired behavior, for various privileges or treats.

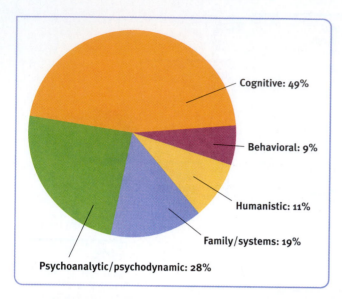

FIGURE 48.3 The cognitive revolution
Half of all faculty in accredited clinical psychology doctoral programs now align themselves with a cognitive or cognitive-behavior therapy orientation. (Data from Mayne & others, 1994. Note: Some faculty identify with more than one perspective.)

"Life does not consist mainly, or even largely, of facts and happenings. It consists mainly of the storm of thoughts that are forever blowing through one's mind."

Mark Twain, 1835–1910

behavior modification process has an authoritarian taint. Advocates reply that control already exists; rewards and punishers are already maintaining destructive behavior patterns. So why not reinforce adaptive behavior instead? They argue that treatment with positive rewards is more humane than being institutionalized or punished, and that the right to effective treatment and to an improved life justifies temporary deprivation.

Cognitive Therapies

Preview Question: What are the goals and techniques of the cognitive therapies?

We have seen how behavior therapists treat specific fears and problem behaviors. But how do they deal with major depression or general anxiety? One can reinforce healthier behaviors and train people to avoid "high-risk" situations. Still, when anxiety has no focus, developing a hierarchy of anxiety-triggering situations is difficult. The cognitive revolution that has profoundly changed psychology during the last four decades has also influenced how therapists treat these less clearly defined psychological problems (**FIGURE 48.3**).

The **cognitive therapies** assume that our thinking colors our feelings (**FIGURE 48.4**), that between the event and our response is the mind. Self-blaming and over-generalized explanations of bad events are an integral part of the vicious cycle of depression. The person with depression interprets a suggestion as criticism, disagreement as dislike, praise as flattery, friendliness as pity. Ruminating on such thoughts sustains the bad mood. (That explains why distracting oneself, perhaps by getting absorbed in a task, can alleviate a bad mood [Erber & Tesser, 1992; Lyubomirsky & Nolen-Hoeksema, 1994].) If depressing thinking patterns are learned, then surely they can be replaced. Cognitive therapists try in various ways to teach people new, more constructive ways of thinking.

FIGURE 48.4

A cognitive perspective on psychological disorders

The person's emotional reactions are produced not directly by the event but by the person's thoughts in response to the event.

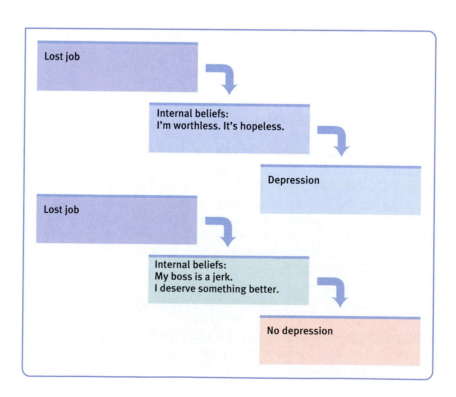

Cognitive Therapy for Depression

Cognitive therapist Aaron Beck was originally trained in Freudian techniques. As Beck analyzed the dreams of patients with depression, he found recurring negative themes of loss, rejection, and abandonment that extended into their waking thoughts. So in his form of cognitive therapy, Beck and his colleagues (1979) seek to reverse clients' catastrophizing beliefs about themselves, their situations, and their futures. They attempt to convince depressed people to take off the dark glasses through which they view life, and their technique is a gentle questioning that aims to help people discover their irrationalities (Beck & others, 1979, pp. 145–146):

Patient: I agree with the descriptions of me but I guess I don't agree that the way I think makes me depressed.

Beck: How do you understand it?

Patient: I get depressed when things go wrong. Like when I fail a test.

Beck: How can failing a test make you depressed?

Patient: Well, if I fail I'll never get into law school.

Beck: So failing the test means a lot to you. But if failing a test could drive people into clinical depression, wouldn't you expect everyone who failed the test to have a depression? . . . Did everyone who failed get depressed enough to require treatment?

Patient: No, but it depends on how important the test was to the person.

Beck: Right, and who decides the importance?

Patient: I do.

Beck: And so, what we have to examine is your way of viewing the test (or the way that you think about the test) and how it affects your chances of getting into law school. Do you agree?

Patient: Right.

Beck: Do you agree that the way you interpret the results of the test will affect you? You might feel depressed, you might have trouble sleeping, not feel like eating, and you might even wonder if you should drop out of the course.

Patient: I have been thinking that I wasn't going to make it. Yes, I agree.

Beck: Now what did failing mean?

Patient: (tearful) That I couldn't get into law school.

Beck: And what does that mean to you?

Patient: That I'm just not smart enough.

Beck: Anything else?

Patient: That I can never be happy.

Beck: And how do these *thoughts* make you feel?

Patient: Very unhappy.

Beck: So it is the meaning of failing a test that makes you very unhappy. In fact, believing that you can never be happy is a powerful factor in producing unhappiness. So, you get yourself into a trap—by definition, failure to get into law school equals "I can never be happy."

Another variety of cognitive therapy builds on the finding that depressed people do not exhibit the self-serving bias common in nondepressed people—the tendency to judge ourselves favorably, to take more responsibility for good deeds than for bad, and to credit ourselves for our successes and

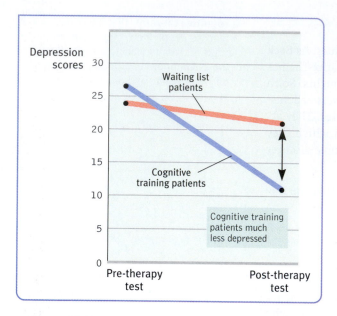

FIGURE 48.5
Cognitive therapy for depression
After undergoing a program that trained them to think more like nondepressed people—by noticing and taking personal credit for good events and by not taking blame for or overgeneralizing from bad events—patients' depression dropped dramatically. (From Rabin & others, 1986.)

others for our failures. Instead, depressed people often attribute their failures to themselves and attribute their successes to external circumstances. Thus, Adele Rabin and her colleagues (1986) explained to 235 depressed adults the advantages of interpreting events as nondepressed people do. She then trained the participants to reform their habitually negative patterns of thinking and labeling. For example, she gave them homework assignments that required them to record each day's positive events and to write down how they contributed to each. Compared with people who remained on a waiting list to receive therapy for depression, those who went through the positive-thinking exercises found their depression dropped dramatically (**FIGURE 48.5**). The more people change their negative thinking styles, the more their depression lifts (Seligman, 1989).

Cognitive therapists often combine the reversal of self-defeating thinking with efforts to modify behavior. This integrated therapy, called **cognitive-behavior therapy**, aims to alter the way people act (behavior therapy) and to alter the way they think (cognitive therapy). It seeks to make people aware of their irrational negative thinking, to replace it with new ways of thinking, *and* to practice the more positive approach in everyday settings.

An example: In one study, patients with obsessive-compulsive behavior learned to relabel their compulsions (Schwartz & others, 1996). Feeling the urge to wash their hands again, they would tell themselves, "I'm having a compulsive urge," and attribute it to their brain's abnormal activity, as shown in PET scans. Instead of giving in to the urge, they then engaged for 15 minutes in an enjoyable, alternative behavior, such as practicing an instrument, taking a walk, or gardening. This helped "unstick" the brain by shifting attention and engaging other parts of the brain. For two or three months the weekly therapy sessions continued, with relabeling and refocusing practice at home. By the study's end, most patients' symptoms had diminished and their PET scans revealed normalized brain activity.

Another example: We often think in words. Therefore, getting people to change what they say to themselves is an effective way to change their thinking. Perhaps you can identify with the anxious students who before an exam make matters worse with self-defeating thoughts: "This exam's probably going to be impossible. All these other students seem so relaxed and confident. I wish I were better prepared. Anyhow, I'm so nervous I'll forget everything." To change such negative patterns, Donald Meichenbaum (1977, 1985) offers *stress inoculation training*. He trains people to restructure their thinking in stressful situations. Sometimes it may be enough simply to say more positive things to oneself: "Relax. The exam may be hard, but it will be hard for everyone else, too. I studied harder than most people. Besides, I don't need a perfect score to get a good grade."

Group and Family Therapies

Preview Question: In what group contexts do people receive therapy?

Except for traditional psychoanalysis, the therapies we have considered may also occur in therapist-led small groups. Group therapy does not provide the same degree of therapist involvement with each client; however, it saves therapists' time and clients' money—and it often is no less effective than individual therapy (Fuhriman & Burlingame, 1994). Therapists often suggest group therapy for people experiencing family conflicts or those whose behavior is distressing to others. For up to 90 minutes a week, the therapist guides the interactions of 6 to 10 people as they engage issues and react to one another.

Family therapy
This type of therapy often acts as a preventive mental health strategy. The therapist helps family members understand how their ways of relating to one another create problems. The treatment's emphasis is not on changing the individuals but on changing their relationships and interactions.

Group sessions are often valuable because the social context allows people both to discover that others have problems similar to their own and to try out new ways of behaving. As you have perhaps experienced, receiving honest feedback—being reassured that you look poised even though you feel anxious and self-conscious, for example—can be very helpful. And it can be a great relief to find that you are not alone—to learn that others, despite their apparent composure, share your problems and your troublesome feelings.

This has been the experience of a wide range of participants in self-help and support groups (Yalom, 1985). In an individualistic age, with more and more people living alone or feeling isolated, the popularity of support groups—for the bereaved, the divorced, the addicted, and those simply seeking fellowship and growth—reflects a longing for community and connectedness. More than 100 million Americans belong to small religious, interest, or self-help groups that meet regularly—and 9 in 10 report that group members "support each other emotionally" (Gallup, 1994). The grandparent of self-help groups, Alcoholics Anonymous (AA), reportedly has 60,000 chapters in 112 countries. Its famous 12-step strategy, emulated by many other self-help groups, asks members to admit their powerlessness, to seek help from a higher power and from one another, and (the twelfth step) to take the message to others in need of it. In one eight-year, $27 million investigation, people seeking treatment for alcoholism reduced their drinking sharply and to roughly the same degree whether randomly assigned to a therapy based on AA principles and AA participation or to cognitive-behavior therapy or a "motivational therapy" (Project Match, 1997).

One special type of group interaction, **family therapy**, assumes that no person is an island, that we live and grow in relation to others, especially our families. We do struggle to differentiate ourselves from our families but we also need to connect with them emotionally. Some of our problem behaviors arise from the tension between these two tendencies, which often creates family stress. Patients often come to therapists seeking help in their relationships with family members.

Unlike most psychotherapy, which focuses on what happens inside the person's own skin, family therapists work with family groups to heal relationships and to mobilize family resources. Their aim is to help family members discover the role they play within their family's social system. A child's rebellion, for example, affects and is affected by other family tensions. Family therapists also attempt—usually with some success, research suggests (Hazelrigg & others, 1987; Shadish & others, 1993)—to open up communication within the family or to help family members discover new ways of preventing or resolving conflicts.

■ **cognitive-behavior therapy** a popular integrated therapy that combines cognitive therapy (changing self-defeating thinking) with behavior therapy (changing behavior).

■ **family therapy** therapy that treats the family as a system. Views an individual's unwanted behaviors as influenced by or directed at other family members; attempts to guide family members toward positive relationships and improved communication.

REVIEW AND REFLECT:

The Psychological Therapies

The major psychotherapies derive from the familiar psychoanalytic, humanistic, behavioral, and cognitive perspectives on psychology.

What are the aims and methods of psychoanalysis and psychodynamic therapy?

Those influenced by the psychoanalytic perspective try to help people gain insight into the unconscious origins of their disorders and to work through the accompanying feelings. To do so, a therapist may draw on techniques such as free association and dream analysis, and interpret resistance and the transference to the therapist of long-repressed feelings. Traditional psychoanalysis, which is no longer practiced widely, is criticized for assuming repression, for after-the-fact interpretations, and for being time consuming and costly. The more common psychodynamic therapy is influenced by the psychoanalytic perspective's concern for providing insight into childhood experiences and defense mechanisms. But it offers a briefer treatment form and often incorporates other techniques into the therapy sessions.

What are the basic themes of humanistic therapy, such as Rogers' person-centered approach?

Unlike psychoanalysts, humanistic therapists focus on clients' current conscious feelings and on their taking responsibility for their own growth. Carl Rogers, in his client-centered therapy, used active listening to express genuineness, acceptance, and empathy.

What are the assumptions and techniques of the behavior therapies?

Behavior therapists worry less about promoting self-awareness and more about directly modifying problem behaviors. Thus, they may countercondition behaviors through systematic desensitization or aversive conditioning. Or they may apply operant conditioning principles with behavior modification techniques, such as token economies.

What are the goals and techniques of the cognitive therapies?

The cognitive therapies, such as Aaron Beck's cognitive therapy for depression, aim to change self-defeating thinking by training people to look at themselves in new, more positive ways.

In what group contexts do people receive therapy?

Many therapeutic techniques can also be applied in a group context. Self-help and support groups, such as AA, engage many millions of people. Family therapy treats the family as an interactive system from which problems may arise.

Terms and Concepts to Remember

psychotherapy, p. 590
eclectic approach, p. 590
psychoanalysis, p. 590
resistance, p. 591
interpretation, p. 591
transference, p. 592
client-centered therapy, p. 593
active listening, p. 594

behavior therapy, p. 595
counterconditioning, p. 595
systematic desensitization, p. 596
aversive conditioning, p. 598
token economy, p. 599
cognitive therapy, p. 600
cognitive-behavior therapy, p. 602
family therapy, p. 603

Test Yourself

48.1. Many therapists view disorders as an interplay of biopsychosocial influences, and they therefore tend to use a combination of treatments. Their approach is best described as
   a. eclectic or integrated.
   b. psychoanalytic or psychodynamic.
   c. humanistic or Rogerian.
   d. cognitive or cognitive behavioral.

48.2. All of the psychological therapies involve verbal interactions between a trained professional and a client with a problem. A therapist who encourages clients to relate their dreams and searches for the unconscious roots of their problems is drawing from
   a. psychoanalysis.   c. person-centered therapy.
   b. humanistic therapies.   d. nondirective therapy.

48.3. According to psychoanalytic theory, a patient's emotional relationship with the therapist mirrors other important relationships in the patient's life—for example, an early relationship with a parent. In psychoanalysis, the development of strong feelings for the therapist is an important part of the therapeutic process and is called
   a. transference.   c. interpretation.
   b. resistance.   d. empathy.

48.4. Interpersonal therapy, like psychodynamic therapy, aims to help clients gain insight into the roots of their feelings and behaviors. The goal of interpersonal therapy stresses _____ more than _____.
   a. empathy; active listening
   b. active listening; empathy
   c. symptom relief; personality change
   d. personality change; symptom relief

48.5. Humanistic therapists focus on present experience—on becoming aware of feelings as they arise and taking responsibility for them. Compared with psychoanalytic therapists, humanistic therapists are more likely to emphasize
   a. hidden or repressed feelings.
   b. childhood experiences.
   c. psychological disorders.
   d. self-fulfillment and growth.

48.6. Especially important to Carl Rogers' person-centered therapy is the technique of active listening. The therapist who practices active listening
   a. engages in free association.
   b. exposes the patient's resistances.
   c. restates and clarifies the client's statements.
   d. directly challenges the client's self-perceptions.

48.7. Behavior therapies apply learning principles to the treatment of problems such as sexual disorders, phobias, and alcoholism. In treating people with these problems, the goal of the behavior therapist is to
   a. identify and treat the underlying causes of the problem.
   b. improve learning and insight.
   c. eliminate the unwanted behavior.
   d. improve communication and social sensitivity.

48.8. Behavior therapists assume that phobias and other maladaptive behaviors are conditioned responses. Behaviorists attempt either to extinguish these responses or to countercondition a client by conditioning a new response to stimuli that trigger maladaptive or unwanted responses. Two counterconditioning techniques are systematic desensitization and
a. positive reinforcement.
b. aversive conditioning.
c. rational-emotive therapy.
d. token economy.

48.9. The technique of systematic desensitization, developed by Joseph Wolpe, teaches people to relax in the presence of progressively more anxiety-provoking stimuli. Systematic desensitization has been found to be especially effective in the treatment of
a. phobias.
b. depression.
c. alcoholism.
d. bed-wetting.

48.10. Some institutions, such as homes for people who are mentally retarded or delinquent, use a token economy to shape behavior. They hand out tokens, which may later be exchanged for other rewards, to a person who displays a desired behavior or takes a step in the right direction. The token economy is an application of
a. classical conditioning.
b. counter conditioning.
c. cognitive therapy.
d. operant conditioning.

48.11. Aaron Beck's form of cognitive therapy teaches people to stop attributing failures to personal inadequacy, and success to external circumstances. This form of cognitive therapy has been shown to be especially effective in treating
a. mental retardation.
b. phobias.
c. alcoholism.
d. depression.

48.12. Psychotherapy is in large part an individual process, although most therapies may occur in therapist-led small groups. The social context of this group therapy tells people that others have problems similar to theirs and allows them to act out alternative behaviors. One type of group therapy, family therapy, serves as a
a. source of psychoanalysis.
b. preventive mental health strategy.
c. self-help group.
d. type of behavior therapy.

Review: What is the major distinction between psychoanalytic therapies and behavior therapies?

Reflect: Without trying to play therapist, how might you use the helping principles discussed in this chapter with a friend who is anxious?

Answers to the Test Yourself and Review questions can be found in the green appendix at the end of the book.

Evaluating Psychotherapies

Advice columnist Ann Landers frequently advises her troubled letter writers to get professional help. One response urged the writer "not to give up. Hang in there until you find [a psychotherapist] who fills the bill. It's worth the effort." On the same day, she advised a second letter writer, "There are many excellent mental health facilities in your city. I urge you to make an appointment at once" (Farina & Fisher, 1982). Therapy advocate Tipper Gore (1994) would concur: "The data show high levels of success in treating large numbers of people suffering [mental illnesses]." Many share Ann Landers' and Tipper Gore's confidence in psychotherapy's effectiveness. The National Institute of Mental Health estimates that 15 percent of Americans seek help for psychological and addictive disorders each year (**FIGURE 49.1**).

Before 1950, the primary mental health providers were psychiatrists. Since then, demand has outgrown the psychiatric profession, and now most psychotherapy is done by clinical and counseling psychologists; clinical social workers; pastoral, marital, abuse, and school counselors; and psychiatric nurses. Much of it is done through *community mental health* programs, which provide outpatient therapy, crisis phone lines, and halfway houses for those making the transition from hospitalization to independent living. With such an enormous outlay of time, money, effort, and hope, it is important to ask: Is the faith that Ann Landers and millions of others worldwide place in these therapists justified? And is the *Wall Street Journal* (1999) therefore wrong to suppose that including psychotherapy in health insurance plans would lead to "endless payments for dubious benefits of apparently marginal problems"?

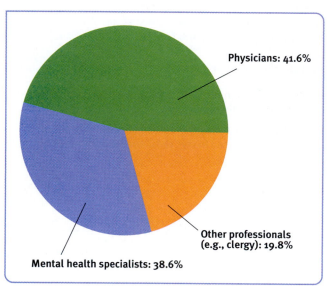

FIGURE 49.1

Where do people turn for help?

The National Institute of Mental Health reports that 19 million Americans a year seek help for psychological difficulties. About two in five seek out a mental health worker, such as a psychologist or psychiatrist. (Data from Regier & others, 1993.)

Is Psychotherapy Effective?

Preview Question: Does psychotherapy work?

The question, though simply put, is not simply answered. For one thing, measuring therapy's effectiveness is not like taking your body's temperature to see if your fever has gone away. If you and I were to undergo psychotherapy, how would we gauge its effectiveness? By how we feel about our progress? How our therapist feels about it? How our friends and family feel about it? How our behavior has changed? Some other way?

Clients' Perceptions

If clients' testimonials were the only yardstick, we could strongly affirm the effectiveness of psychotherapy. Three out of four clients have reported themselves satisfied, and one in two have said they are "very satisfied" (Lebow, 1982). When 2900 readers of *Consumer Reports* (1995; Kotkin & others, 1996; Seligman, 1995) reported on their experiences with mental health professionals, 89 percent were at least "fairly well satisfied." Among those who recalled feeling *fair* or *very poor* when beginning therapy, 9 in 10 now were feeling *very good, good,* or at least *so-so*. We have their word for it—and who should know better?

We should not dismiss these testimonials lightly. People enter therapy because they are suffering, and most leave feeling better about themselves. But there are several reasons why client testimonials do not persuade psychotherapy's skeptics:

+ ***People often enter therapy in crisis.*** When, with the normal ebb and flow of events, the crisis passes, people may attribute their improvement to the therapy.

+ ***Clients may need to believe the therapy was worth the effort.*** To admit investing time and money in something ineffective is like admitting to having one's car serviced repeatedly by a mechanic who never fixes it. Self-justification is a powerful human motive.

+ ***Clients generally like their therapists and speak kindly of them.*** Even if the clients' problems remain, say the critics, "they work hard to find something positive to say. The therapist had been very understanding, the client had gained a new perspective, he learned to communicate better, his mind was eased, anything at all so as not to have to say treatment was a failure" (Zilbergeld, 1983, p. 117).

Testimonials can be misleading. As research findings continue to document, we are prone to selective and biased recall and to making judgments that confirm our beliefs. Consider a massive experiment with over 500 Massachusetts boys, aged 5 to 13 years, many of whom seemed bound for delinquency. By the toss of a coin, half the boys were assigned to a five-year treatment program. Counselors visited them twice a month, they were involved in community programs such as the Boy Scouts, and, as the need arose, they received academic tutoring, medical attention, and family assistance. Some 30 years after the end of the program, Joan McCord (1978, 1979) located 97 percent of the participants. To assess the treatment's impact, she sent them questionnaires and checked public records from courts, mental hospitals, and other sources.

Assessing the treatment program with client testimonials yielded encouraging results. Many of the men offered glowing reports. Some noted that had it not been for their counselors, "I would probably be in jail"; "My life would have gone the other way"; or "I think I would have ended up in a life of crime." The court records offered apparent support for these testimonials. Even among the "difficult" boys in the program, 66 percent had no official juvenile crime record.

But recall psychology's most powerful tool for sorting reality from wishful thinking: the *control group.* For every boy who was counseled, there was a similar boy in a control group who was not. McCord tracked down these untreated people and found that among the predelinquent boys in the control group, *70 percent* had no juvenile record. Moreover, on some measures, such as a record of having committed a second crime, alcoholic tendencies, death rate, and job satisfaction, the untreated men exhibited slightly *fewer* problems. The glowing testimonials of those treated had been unintentionally deceiving.

Clinicians' Perceptions

If clinicians' perceptions accurately reflected therapeutic effectiveness, we would have even more reason to celebrate. Case studies of successful treatment abound. Furthermore, every therapist treasures compliments from clients as they say good-bye or later express their gratitude. The problem is that clients justify entering psychotherapy by emphasizing their woes, justify leaving therapy by emphasizing their well-being, and stay in touch only if satisfied. Therapists are aware of failures, but they are mostly the failures of *other* therapists—those whose clients, having experienced only temporary relief, are now seeking a new therapist for their recurring problems. Thus, the same person with the same recurring difficulty—the same old weight problem, depression, or marital difficulty—may represent "success" stories in several therapists' files.

Because people enter therapy when they are extremely unhappy, and usually leave when they are less extremely unhappy, most therapists, like most clients, testify to therapy's success—regardless of the treatment. Although "treatments" have varied widely, from chains to counseling, every generation views its own approach as more enlightened.

"REGRESSING" FROM UNUSUAL TO USUAL

Clients' and therapists' perceptions of therapy's effectiveness are vulnerable to inflation from two phenomena. One is the power of *belief* in a treatment, called the *placebo effect*. An inert placebo is often used as a control treatment in drug experiments. If you *think* a treatment is going to be effective, it just may be (thanks to the healing power of your positive expectation).

The second phenomenon is **regression toward the mean**—the tendency for unusual events (or emotions) to "regress" (return) toward their average state. Thus, extraordinary happenings (feeling low) tend to be followed by more ordinary ones (a return to our more usual state). Because we returned to that more usual state, anything we tried in the interim may seem effective. Indeed, when things hit bottom, we may try anything, and whatever we try—going to a psychotherapist, starting yoga, doing aerobic exercise—is more likely to be followed by improvement than by further descent.

"The real purpose of [the] scientific method is to make sure Nature hasn't misled you into thinking you know something that you actually don't."

Robert Pirsig, *Zen and the Art of Motorcycle Maintenance*, 1974

The point may seem obvious, yet we regularly miss it: We sometimes attribute what may be a normal regression (the expected falling back to normal) to something we have done. Consider:

+ Students who score much lower or higher on an exam than they usually do are likely, when retested, to return to their average.
+ Unusual ESP subjects who defy chance when first tested nearly always lose their "psychic powers" when retested (a phenomenon parapsychologists have called the "decline effect").
+ After a sudden crime wave, the town council initiates a "stop crime" drive and the crime rate then returns to previous levels. The drive may therefore appear more successful than it was.
+ Coaches who yell at their players after an unusually bad first half may feel rewarded for having done so when the team's performance improves (returns to normal) during the second half.
+ Scientists who win a Nobel prize—an extraordinary accomplishment—almost always experience diminished accomplishments thereafter, leading some to believe that winning a Nobel hinders creativity.
+ Some people also believe there is a "*Sports Illustrated* jinx"—that athletes whose peak performances get them on the cover of the magazine will then suffer a decline in their performance.

"Once you become sensitized to it, you see regression everywhere."

Psychologist Daniel Kahneman (1985)

In each case, the effect may be genuine. More likely, however, each represents the natural tendency for behavior to regress from the unusual to the more usual. And this defines a task for therapy effectiveness research: to discern whether improvement following a particular therapy exceeds what we could expect from the placebo and regression effects. ■

■ **regression toward the mean** the tendency for extremes of unusual scores to fall back (regress) toward the average.

Outcome Research

How, then, can we objectively measure the effectiveness of psychotherapy? What types of people and problems are best helped, and by what type of psychotherapy? The questions have both academic and personal relevance. If you or someone you care about feels anxious or depressed, or suffers some psychological disorder, it is crucial for you to understand the likelihood of psychotherapy's being of help.

In hopes of better assessing psychotherapy's effectiveness, psychologists have turned to controlled research studies. Similar research in the 1800s transformed medicine from concocted treatments (bleeding, purging, infusions of plant and metal substances) into a science. The transformation occurred when skeptical physicians began to realize that many patients got better on their own, that most of the fashionable treatments were doing no good, and that sorting fact from superstition required following illnesses closely—with and without a particular treatment. Typhoid fever patients, for example, often improved after being bled, convincing most physicians that the treatment worked. Not until a control group was given mere bed rest—and 70 percent were observed to improve after five weeks of fever—did physicians learn, to their shock, that their treatments were, at best, worthless (Thomas, 1992).

In psychology, the opening challenge in what became a spirited debate over such research was issued by British psychologist Hans Eysenck (1952). He summarized studies showing that after undergoing psychotherapy, two-thirds of those suffering nonpsychotic disorders improve markedly. To this day, no one disputes that optimistic estimate.

So why then are we still debating psychotherapy's effectiveness? Because Eysenck also reported similar improvement among *untreated* persons, such as those who were on waiting lists. With or without psychotherapy, he said, roughly two-thirds improved noticeably. Time was a great healer.

The avalanche of criticism prompted by Eysenck's conclusions did reveal shortcomings in his analyses. Also, in 1952 Eysenck could find only 24 studies of psychotherapy outcomes to analyze. Today, there are hundreds. The best of these studies randomly assign people on a waiting list to therapy or to no therapy. Afterward, researchers evaluate everyone, using tests and the reports of friends and family or of psychologists who don't know whether therapy was given. The results of such studies are then digested by a technique called **meta-analysis**, a procedure for statistically combining the results of many different studies as if they had come from one huge study with thousands of participants.

In the first of more than five dozen meta-analyses of psychotherapy outcome studies, Mary Lee Smith and her colleagues (1980) combined the results of 475 investigations. For psychotherapists, the welcome result was that "the evidence overwhelmingly supports the efficacy of psychotherapy" (p. 183). **FIGURE 49.2** depicts their finding—that the average therapy client ends up better off than 80 percent of the untreated individuals on waiting lists. The claim is more modest than it first appears—by definition, about 50 percent of untreated people also are better off than the average untreated person. Nevertheless, Smith and her collaborators exulted that "psychotherapy benefits people of all ages as reliably as schooling educates them, medicine cures them, or business turns a profit" (p. 183).

Newer research summaries confirm this optimism. As one put it, "Hundreds of studies have shown that psychotherapy works better than nothing" (Kopta & others, 1999). In one ambitious study, the National Institute of Mental Health compared three depression treatments: cognitive therapy, interpersonal therapy, and a standard drug therapy. Twenty-eight experienced therapists at research sites in Norman, Oklahoma; Washington, DC; and Pittsburgh, Pennsylvania, were trained in one of the three methods and randomly assigned their share of the 239 people with depression who participated. Patients in all three groups improved more than did those in a control group who received merely an inert medication and supportive attention, encouragement, and advice.

■ **meta-analysis** a procedure for statistically combining the results of many different research studies.

"Fortunately, [psycho]analysis is not the only way to resolve inner conflicts. Life itself still remains a very effective therapist."

Karen Horney, *Our Inner Conflicts*, 1945

FIGURE 49.2

Treatment versus no treatment
These two normal distribution curves based on data from 475 studies show the improvement of untreated people and psychotherapy clients. The outcome for the average therapy client surpassed that for 80 percent of the untreated people.

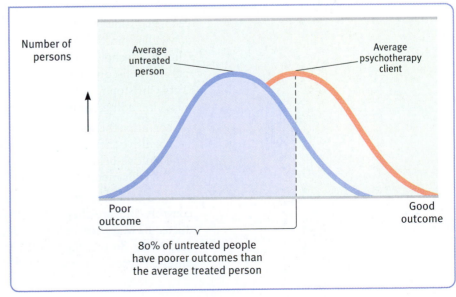

Among patients who completed a full 16-week treatment program, the depression had lifted for slightly more than half of those in each treatment group—but for only 29 percent of those in the control group (Elkin & others, 1989). This verdict echoes the results of the earlier outcome studies: *Those not undergoing therapy often improve, but those undergoing therapy are more likely to improve.*

Often, however, the improvement was not permanent. Only one in four patients undergoing psychotherapy and one in six undergoing drug therapy both recovered and experienced no relapse within 18 months (Shea & others, 1992). So, extravagant expectations that psychotherapy will transform your life and personality seem unwarranted. Still, Eysenck's pessimism also seems unwarranted. *On average,* psychotherapy is somewhat effective—and is also cost-effective when compared with the greater costs of medical care for psychologically related ailments. When people seek psychological treatment, their search for medical treatment drops—by 16 percent in one digest of 91 studies (Chiles & others, 1999). The annual cost of psychological disorders and substance abuse—including crime, accidents, lost work, and treatment—is staggering. Thus, just as an investment in prenatal and well-baby care *reduces* long-term costs, so will an investment in almost any effective treatment for psychological problems. Anything that boosts employees' psychological well-being will reduce medical costs, improve work efficiency, and diminish absenteeism. Studies by health insurers show that mental health treatment can more than pay for itself with reduced medical costs (American Psychological Association, 1991).

But note that *on average* refers to no one therapy in particular. It is like saying, "Surgery is somewhat effective," or like reassuring lung-cancer patients that "on the average" medical treatment of health problems is effective. What people want to know is not the effectiveness of therapy in general but the effectiveness of particular treatments for their particular problems.

In general, therapy is most effective when the problem is clear-cut (Singer, 1981). Those who experience phobias, who are unassertive, or who are frustrated by sexual performance problems can hope for improvement. Those who have chronic schizophrenia or who wish to change their whole personality are unlikely to benefit from psychotherapy alone (Zilbergeld, 1983). The more specific the problem, the more hope there is.

The Relative Effectiveness of Different Therapies

Preview Question: Are some therapies more effective than others?

People considering therapy, and those paying for it, want to know *which* psychotherapy will be most effective for their problem. To help answer that question, a Society of Clinical Psychology task force has worked to identify treatments shown to be beneficial in "well-controlled treatment studies" (Chambless & others, 1998; DeRubeis & Crits-Christoph, 1998). The task force offers lists of "empirically supported therapies," including, for example,

+ cognitive therapy, interpersonal therapy, and behavior therapy for depression.
+ cognitive therapy, exposure therapy, and stress inoculation training for anxiety.
+ cognitive-behavior therapy for bulimia.
+ behavior modification for bed-wetting.

So some therapies are known to be effective when tested against no-treatment controls. But are they more effective than other therapies? The meta-analysis conducted by Mary Lee Smith and her colleagues (1977, 1980) compared different therapies. What do you suppose it revealed? Despite claims of superiority by advocates of different types of therapy, Smith's comparison of therapies revealed no one type of therapy that was actually superior. (*Consumer Reports* [1995] readers, too, were equally satisfied, no matter what type of therapy they received and whether treated by a psychiatrist, psychologist, or social worker.) Moreover—and more astonishing—the group or individual context of the therapy made no discernible difference, nor did the level of training and experience of the therapist. Now, two decades after Smith's analysis, the evidence still indicates little if any connection between clinicians' experience, training, supervision, and licensing and their clients' outcomes (Bickman, 1999). It seems as though the dodo bird in *Alice in Wonderland* was right: "Everyone has won and all must have prizes."

Some therapies are, however, well suited to particular disorders. For example, behavioral conditioning therapies achieve especially favorable results with specific behavior problems such as phobias, compulsions, or sexual disorders (Bowers & Clum, 1988; Giles, 1983). Just as physicians offer particular treatments for specific medical problems, so psychotherapists are aiming toward particular treatments for specific psychological problems.

Evaluating Alternative Therapies

Preview Question: How do alternative therapies stand up to psychology's critical thinking methods?

The tendency of abnormal states of mind to "regress" to normal, combined with the *placebo effect*, creates fertile soil for pseudotherapies. Bolstered by anecdotes, heralded by the media, praised on the Internet, alternative therapies can spread like wildfire. Princess Diana typified the modern fascination with alternative healers by seeking out spiritualists, a hypnotherapist, an "anger-release" therapist, reflexologists, aromatherapists, colonic irrigationists, and a "mind-body" therapist (Smith, 1999).

What can we say of such alternative therapies? Testimonials aside—every therapy, whether effective or not, will *seem* effective to some—what does the evidence say? Which are empirically validated?

About most, there is no evidence, because their proponents and devotees feel no need for controlled research. For them, personal experience is evidence enough. So which therapies do get systematically evaluated? To gauge scientific versus popular interest in various treatments and assessment techniques, clinical researcher Scott Lilienfeld (1998) suggests comparing the number of times each is mentioned in electronic searches of psychology's literature and on the World Wide Web. As Table 49.1 shows, some topics exist mostly in one realm or the other.

> "Whatever differences in treatment efficacy exist, they appear to be extremely small, at best."
>
> **Bruce Wampold and colleagues (1997)**

> "Different sores have different salves."
>
> **English proverb**

TABLE **49.1**

COMPARISON OF PSYCHOLOGY CITATIONS AND WEB SITES

Topic	Psychology Journal Citations*	Web Sites**	Ratio
Systematic desensitization	2,205	715	3 to 1
Cognitive-behavior therapy	4,727	1,714	3 to 1
Interpersonal psychotherapy	3,529	411	9 to 1
St. John's wort (herbal remedy)	27	17,722	1 to 656
Enneagram (personality typing)	13	29,010	1 to 2,232
Therapeutic touch	227	5,409	1 to 24

*Using PsychInfo
**Using AltaVista

Testing the energy field

Could therapeutic touch practitioners detect a nearby hand? To find out, Emily Rosa tossed a coin and held a hand over the subject's obscured right or left hand.

Let's evaluate three alternative therapies—therapeutic touch, eye movement desensitization and reprocessing (EMDR), and light-exposure therapy. As we do, remember that sifting sense from nonsense requires the scientific attitude: being skeptical but not cynical, open to surprises but not gullible.

Therapeutic Touch

Among the most popular recent alternative therapies is *therapeutic touch*. Its tens of thousands of practitioners worldwide (many of whom are nurses) move their hands a few inches from a patient's body, purportedly "pushing energy fields into balance." Advocates say these manipulations help heal everything from headaches to burns to cancer (Krieger, 1993). Skeptics say the evidence shows no healing power beyond the placebo effect (Scheiber & Selby, 1997).

To put therapeutic touch to the test, fourth-grader Emily Rosa and her mother, a nurse, schemed a simple experiment (Rosa & others, 1998). Why not test healers' ability to detect the supposed energy field by inviting them to rest their hands, palms up, on a flat surface? (Thanks to a screen, the healers wouldn't see their or Emily's hands.) After the toss of a coin, Emily would hover a hand over one of the practitioner's hands (the experimental hand) to see if the practitioner could detect that this hand rather than the other (the control hand) was receiving the energy field. Shortly before, skeptic James Randi had offered $742,000 to anyone who could detect a human energy field under similar conditions. Only one person agreed to be tested by Randi, and that volunteer had left the experiment in a huff after achieving only chance results in guessing which hand was close to another's.

Apparently less threatened by a 9-year-old girl doing a science fair project, and not fully realizing that this was a serious research project, 21 practitioners agreed to be tested by Emily for 10 trials each. Could they beat chance—50 percent? They could not, averaging but 47 percent correct. A year later when the trials were repeated—this time allowing each practitioner to "feel" Emily's energy field in each hand and then choose which hand Emily would use—the practitioners got 41 percent correct. The results, published in the prestigious *Journal of the American Medical Association*, caused its editor to conclude that the supposed human energy field "does not exist" and that, barring new evidence, patients should "save their money." Perhaps, say critics of this experiment, Emily's hands were held too far from the practitioner's hands. But other research suggests that, when body heat is shielded by a thin sheet of glass, people cannot detect the presence of unseen hands (Long & others, 1999). Thus, the tentative scientific verdict is that therapeutic touch (actually not-touch) does not work, nor is there any credible theory that predicts why it might.

Eye Movement Desensitization and Reprocessing (EMDR)

Walking in a park one day, Francine Shapiro (1989) observed that anxious thoughts vanished as her eyes spontaneously darted about. From this experience she developed a novel anxiety treatment. While patients imagine traumatic scenes, the therapist triggers eye movements by waving a finger in front of their eyes. When Shapiro tried this on 22 people who were haunted by old traumatic memories, all experienced marked reductions in their distress after just one therapeutic session. This extraordinary result triggered an enormous response from mental health professionals, 22,000 of whom have reportedly paid $350 or more to attend Shapiro's training workshops (McNally, 1999; Rosen & Lohr, 1997). Not since the similarly charismatic Franz

Anton Mesmer introduced "animal magnetism" (hypnosis) more than two centuries ago (also after feeling inspired by an outdoor experience) has a new therapy attracted so many devotees so quickly.

Does it work? For 84 to 100 percent of single-trauma victims participating in four recent studies, the answer is yes, reports Shapiro (1999). (When EMDR did not fare well in other trials, Shapiro argued that the therapists were not properly trained.) Moreover, the treatment need take no more than three 90-minute sessions. The Society of Clinical Psychology task force on empirically validated treatments acknowledges that the treatment is "probably efficacious" for the treatment of civilian post-traumatic stress disorder (Chambless & others, 1998). Encouraged by their seeming successes, EMDR therapists are now applying the technique to other anxiety disorders, such as panic disorder, and, with Shapiro's (1995) encouragement, to a wide range of complaints including pain, grief, paranoid schizophrenia, rage, and guilt.

EMDR is a therapy that thousands adore, and thousands more dismiss as a sham. Why should rapidly moving one's eyes while recalling traumas be therapeutic, wondered skeptics. Indeed, when they tested the therapy without the eye movements—with finger tapping, for example, or with eyes fixed straight ahead while the therapist's finger wagged—the therapeutic results were the same (Cahill & others, 1999; Lohr & others, 1999). Eye movements, it seems, are not the therapeutic ingredient. What is therapeutic, the skeptics suspect, is the combination of exposure therapy—repeatedly reliving traumatic memories in a safe and reassuring context—and a robust placebo effect. Had Mesmer's pseudotherapy been compared with no treatment at all, notes Richard McNally (1999), it, too (thanks to the healing power of positive belief), could have been found "probably efficacious."

Light-Exposure Therapy

Have you ever found yourself oversleeping, gaining weight, and feeling lethargic during the dark mornings and overcast days of winter? For some people, especially women and those living far from the equator, the wintertime blahs constitute a form of depression known as *seasonal affective disorder*, for which the appropriate acronym is SAD. To counteract these dark spirits, National Institute of Mental Health researchers in the early 1980s had a bright idea: Give SAD people a timed daily dose of intense light. Light exposure can tweak the circadian clock. When clinical experience indicated that light exposure could also relieve symptoms associated with wintertime depression, manufacturers produced "light boxes" that can now be rented or purchased from health supply and lighting stores.

Is this another placebo effect, attributable to people's expectations? Three new studies shed light on this therapy. In one, Charmane Eastman and her colleagues (1998) exposed some SAD patients to 90 minutes of bright light and others to a sham placebo treatment—a hissing "negative ion generator" about which the staff expressed similar enthusiasm (but which unknown to the patients was not turned on). After four weeks of exposure, 61 percent of those exposed to morning light had greatly improved, as had 50 percent of those exposed to evening light and 32 percent of those exposed to the placebo treatment. Another study, led by Michael Terman (1998), found that 30 minutes of light exposure produced relief for 54 percent of people receiving morning light therapy and 33 percent receiving evening light therapy. The third study, led by Alfred Lewy (1998), replicated the morning light effect and identified a possible biological mechanism. With SAD patients, morning light exposure shifted secretion of the hormone melatonin, which helps regulate circadian rhythm, to an earlier time. The verdict: For many people, morning bright light does indeed dim SAD symptoms.

Light therapy

To counteract winter depression, some people spend time each morning in front of a box that emits intense light that mimics natural outdoor light.

"I utilize the best from Freud, the best from Jung, and the best from my Uncle Marty, a very smart fellow."

Commonalities Among Psychotherapies

Preview Question: What three elements are shared by all forms of psychotherapy?

Despite their differences, each therapy's effectiveness may derive from certain underlying commonalities. Jerome Frank (1982), Marvin Goldfried (Goldfried & Padawer, 1982), and Hans Strupp (1986) studied the common ingredients of various therapies and suggested that they all offer at least three benefits: hope for demoralized people; a new perspective on oneself and the world; and an empathic, trusting, caring relationship. These "nonspecific" factors aren't all that therapy offers, but they are important (Barker & others, 1988; Jones & others, 1988; Roberts & others, 1993). They are part of what the growing numbers of self-help and support groups offer their members. And they have been part of what traditional healers offer (Jackson, 1992). Healers—special people to whom others disclose their suffering—have for centuries listened in order to understand and to empathize, reassure, advise, console, interpret, or explain.

Hope for Demoralized People

People who seek therapy typically feel anxious, depressed, devoid of self-esteem, and incapable of turning things around. What any therapy offers is the expectation that, with commitment from the patient, things can and will get better. Apart from the particular therapeutic technique, this belief may itself promote improved morale, new feelings of self-efficacy, and diminished symptoms (Prioleau & others, 1983). This benefit derived from a person's belief in a treatment is, of course, the placebo effect. In psychotherapy experiments, the placebo treatment may be listening to inspirational tapes, attending group discussions, or taking a fake pill.

The finding that improvement is greater for placebo-treated people than for untreated people (although not as great as for those receiving actual psychotherapy) suggests that one reason therapies help is that they offer hope. Said another way, therapy outcomes vary with the client's attitude—the client's motivation, confidence, and commitment. Each therapy, in its individual way, may harness the client's own healing powers. And that, says psychiatrist Jerome Frank, helps us understand why all sorts of treatments—including some folk healing rites known to be powerless apart from the patient's belief—may in their own time and place produce cures. Until the 1800s, most medicines and the healers who prescribed them owed their good reputations to natural recoveries—and to placebo effects.

A New Perspective

Every therapy offers people a plausible explanation of their symptoms and an alternative way of looking at themselves or responding to their worlds. Therapy can offer new experiences as well, ones that help people change their behaviors and their views of themselves. Armed with a believable fresh perspective, they may approach life with a new attitude.

An Empathic, Trusting, Caring Relationship

To say that all therapies are about equally effective is not to say all *therapists* are equally effective. Regardless of their therapeutic technique, effective therapists are empathic people who seek to understand another's experience; whose care and concern the client feels; and whose respectful listening, reassurance, and advice earn the client's trust and respect. In a National Institute of Mental Health depression-treatment study, the most effective therapists were those who were perceived as most empathic and caring and who established the closest therapeutic bonds with their clients (Blatt & others, 1996). In another study, Marvin Goldfried and his associates (1998) ana-

"All successful therapy has two things in common: It is forward-looking and it requires assuming responsibility. Therapy that reviews childhood endlessly has a century-long history of being ineffective. All therapy that works for depression, anxiety, and sexual problems focuses on exactly what is going wrong now and on how to correct it."

Martin E. P. Seligman, *What You Can Change and What You Can't*, 1994

CLOSE-UP:

A CONSUMER'S GUIDE TO PSYCHOTHERAPISTS

When should a person seek the help of a mental health professional? Life for everyone is marked by a mix of serenity and stress, blessing and bereavement, good moods and bad. When troubling thoughts and emotions interfere with your normal living, you might consider talking to a professional. The American Psychological Association offers these common trouble signals:

+ Feelings of hopelessness
+ Deep and lasting depression
+ Self-destructive behavior such as alcohol and drug abuse
+ Disruptive fears
+ Sudden mood shifts
+ Thoughts of suicide
+ Compulsive rituals such as hand washing
+ Sexual difficulties

If you are looking for a therapist, it may be wise to first have a preliminary consultation with two or three. You can describe your problem and learn each therapist's treatment approach. You can ask questions about the therapist's values, credentials (Table 49.2), and fees. And you can assess your own feelings about each one.

TABLE **49.2**

THERAPISTS AND THEIR TRAINING

Type	Description
Clinical psychologists	Most are psychologists with a Ph.D. and expertise in research, assessment, and therapy, supplemented by a supervised internship. About half work in agencies and institutions, half in private practice.
Clinical or psychiatric social workers	A two-year Master of Social Work graduate program plus postgraduate supervision prepares some social workers to offer psychotherapy, mostly to people with everyday personal and family problems. About half have earned the National Association of Social Workers' designation of clinical social worker.
Counselors	Marriage and family counselors specialize in problems arising from family relations. Pastoral counselors provide counseling to countless people. Abuse counselors work with substance abusers and with spouse and child abusers and their victims.
Psychiatrists	Physicians who specialize in the treatment of psychological disorders. Not all psychiatrists have had extensive training in psychotherapy, but as M.D.s they can prescribe medications. Thus, they tend to see those with the most serious problems. Many have a private practice.

lyzed taped therapy sessions from 36 recognized master therapists. Some were cognitive-behavior therapists, others were psychodynamic-interpersonal therapists. Regardless, the striking finding was how *similar* the therapists were during the parts of their sessions they considered most significant. At key moments, the empathic therapists of both persuasions would help clients evaluate themselves, link one aspect of their lives with another, and gain insight into their interactions with others. Indeed, some believe that warmth and empathy are hallmarks of healers everywhere, whether psychiatrists, witch doctors, or shamans (Torrey, 1986).

That all therapies offer *hope* through a *fresh perspective* offered by a *caring person* is supported by a meta-analysis of 39 studies. Each study compared treatment offered by professional therapists with treatment offered by laypeople: friendly professors, people who had had a few hours' training in empathic listening skills, and college students supervised by a professional clinician. The result? The "paraprofessionals," as these briefly trained people are called, typically proved as effective as the professionals (Christensen & Jacobson, 1994). Although most of the problems they treated were mild, the trained paraprofessionals were—believe it or not—as effective as professionals even when dealing with more disturbed adults, such as those diagnosed with serious depression.

To recap, people who seek help usually improve. And yet so do many of those who do not undergo psychotherapy, a tribute to our human resourcefulness and to our capacity to care for one another. Nevertheless, though the therapist's orientation and experience appear not to matter much, people who receive some psychotherapy usually improve more than those who do not. Mature, articulate people with specific emotional or behavioral problems often improve the most.

A caring relationship
Effective therapists form a bond of trust with their patients.

CLOSE-UP:

PREVENTING PSYCHOLOGICAL DISORDERS BY TREATING THE SOCIAL CONTEXTS THAT BREED THEM

"It is better to prevent than to cure."

Peruvian folk wisdom

We infer that people who act cruelly must be cruel and that people who act "crazy" must be "sick." We attach labels to such people, thereby distinguishing them from "normal" folks. It follows, then, that we try to treat "abnormal" people by giving them insight into their problems, by changing their thinking, and/or by controlling them with drugs.

There is an alternative viewpoint: We could interpret many psychological disorders as understandable responses to a disturbing and stressful society. According to this view, it is not just the person who needs treatment, but also the person's social context. Better to prevent a problem by reforming a sick situation and by developing people's coping competencies than to wait for a problem to arise and then treat it.

A story about the rescue of a drowning person from a rushing river illustrates this viewpoint: Having successfully administered first aid to the first victim, the rescuer spots another struggling person and pulls her out, too. After a half-dozen repetitions, the rescuer suddenly turns and starts running away while the river sweeps yet another floundering person into view. "Aren't you going to rescue that fellow?" asks a bystander. "Heck no," the rescuer replies. "I'm going upstream to find out what's pushing all these people in."

Preventive mental health is upstream work. It seeks to prevent psychological casualties by identifying and alleviating the conditions that cause them. George Albee (1986) believes there is abundant evidence that poverty, meaningless work, constant criticism, unemployment, racism, and sexism undermine people's sense of competence, personal control, and self-esteem. Such stresses increase their risk of depression, alcoholism, and suicide.

Albee contends that we who care about preventing psychological casualties should therefore support programs that alleviate poverty, discrimination, and other demoralizing situations. We eliminated smallpox not by treating the afflicted but by inoculating the unafflicted. We conquered yellow fever by controlling mosquitos. Prevention of psychological problems means empowering those who have learned an attitude of helplessness, changing environments that breed loneliness, renewing the disintegrating family, and bolstering parents' and teachers' skills at nurturing children's achievements and resulting self-esteem. Indeed, "Everything aimed at im-proving the human condition, at making life more fulfilling and meaningful, may be considered part of primary prevention of mental or emotional disturbance" (Kessler & Albee, 1975, p. 557). That includes such programs as cognitive training to promote positive thinking in children at risk for depression.

There is, however, more to the story of psychological disorders than toxic environments and pessimism. Anxiety disorders, major depression, bipolar disorder, and schizophrenia are known biological events. Yet Albee reminds us again of one of this book's themes: *A human being is an integrated bio-psycho-social system.* For years we have trusted our bodies to physicians and our minds to psychiatrists and psychologists. That neat separation no longer seems valid. Stress affects body chemistry. And chemical imbalances, whatever their cause, can produce schizophrenia and depression. And anger, depression, and stress can threaten our physical health. *"Mens sana in corpore sano,"* says an ancient Latin adage: A healthy mind in a healthy body.

"Mental disorders arise from physical ones, and likewise physical disorders arise from mental ones."

The Mahabharata, c. A.D. 200

Part of what all therapies offer is hope, a fresh way of looking at life, and an empathic, caring relationship. That may explain why the empathy and friendly counsel of paraprofessionals are often as helpful as professional psychotherapy. And that may also explain why people who feel supported by close relationships—who enjoy the fellowship and friendship of caring people—are less likely to need or seek therapy (Frank, 1982; O'Connor & Brown, 1984).

Culture and Values in Psychotherapy

Preview Question: How do differences in culture and values influence the relationship between a therapist and a client?

All therapies offer hope, and nearly all therapists attempt to enhance their clients' sensitivity, openness, personal responsibility, and sense of purpose (Jensen & Bergin, 1988). But on certain matters of moral and cultural diversity, therapists may differ from one another and from their clients (Kelly, 1990). In Canada and the United States, for example, about 1 person in 25 is a self-proclaimed atheist or agnostic, as are (depending on the survey) one-fifth to one-half of psychiatrists and clinical psychologists (Gallup, 1993; Lukoff & others, 1992). In Britain, two-thirds of psychiatrists say they are atheists (Neeleman & Persaud, 1995). That raises an issue: What values prevail in psychotherapy? What values *should* prevail? Should it matter that highly religious people prefer religiously similar therapists (Worthington & others, 1996)?

Albert Ellis, a well-known therapist, and Allen Bergin, co-editor of the *Handbook of Psychotherapy and Behavior Change*, illustrate how sharply values can differ. Ellis (1980) assumes that "no one and nothing is supreme," that "self-gratification" should be encouraged, and that "unequivocal love, commitment, service, and . . . fidelity to any interpersonal commitment, especially marriage, leads to harmful consequences." Bergin (1980) assumes the opposite—that "because God is supreme, humility and the acceptance of divine authority are virtues," that "self-control and committed love and self-sacrifice are to be encouraged," and that "infidelity to any interpersonal commitment, especially marriage, leads to harmful consequences." Granted, Bergin and Ellis disagree more radically than most therapists regarding what values are healthiest. In so doing, however, they illustrate what they agree on: that psychotherapists' personal beliefs and values influence their practice. Knowing that clients tend to adopt their therapists' values (Worthington & others, 1994), Bergin and Ellis also agree that therapists should divulge their values more openly.

Value differences also can become significant when a therapist from one culture meets a client from another. In North America, Europe, and Australia, for example, most therapists reflect their culture's individualism (often giving priority to personal desires and identity). Clients who are immigrants from Asian countries, which expect people to be mindful of others' expectations, may therefore have problems with therapies that require them to think only of their own well-being. Such differences help explain the reluctance of some minority populations to use mental health services (Sue, 1990). Recognizing that therapists and clients may differ in values, communication styles, and language, many therapy training programs now provide training in cultural sensitivity and recruit members of underrepresented culture groups.

REVIEW AND REFLECT:

Evaluating Psychotherapies

Does psychotherapy work?

Because the positive testimonials of clients and therapists cannot prove that therapy is actually effective, psychologists have conducted hundreds of studies of psychotherapy's outcomes. Meta-analyses of these studies reveal that (1) people who remain untreated often improve; (2) those who receive psychotherapy are more likely to improve, regardless of what kind of therapy they receive and for how long; (3) mature, articulate people with specific behavior problems often receive the greatest benefits from therapy; but (4) placebo treatments or the sympathy and friendly counsel of paraprofessionals also tend to produce more improvement than occurs when people receive no treatment.

Are some therapies more effective than others?

All types of psychotherapy seem to offer three benefits: new hope, a fresh perspective, and an empathic, trusting, caring relationship. Therapists do, however, differ in the values that influence their aims.

Terms and Concepts to Remember

regression toward the mean, p. 608   meta-analysis, p. 609

Test Yourself

49.1. The question "Is psychotherapy effective?" has been the subject of hundreds of scientific studies and innumerable personal accounts. The most enthusiastic or optimistic view of psychotherapy comes from
   a. outcome research.
   b. psychologist Hans Eysenck.
   c. reports of clinicians and clients.
   d. a government study of treatment for depression.

49.2. On average, troubled people who undergo therapy are more likely to improve than those who do not, and therapy tends to be most effective when the problem is clear-cut and specific. Studies show that _____ therapy is most effective overall.
   a. behavior   c. individual as opposed to group
   b. humanistic   d. no one type of

49.3. Psychologists have observed that people's belief that a treatment will help them is often sufficient to cause some improvement. A neutral treatment, such as an inert pill, that results in improved morale and diminished symptoms is called
   a. a placebo effect.   c. an empathic perspective.
   b. preventive mental health.   d. clinical treatment.

49.4. Regression toward the mean, in the context of therapy, means that our unusual behaviors or emotions tend to be followed by more ordinary ones. Given this tendency, researchers evaluating the effectiveness of therapy must ensure that improvement following therapy
   a. is equal to that of people who receive no treatment.
   b. is greater than it would be for people who receive no treatment.
   c. is significant, observable, and permanent.
   d. is attested to by both the client and the therapist.

49.5. Those who offer or receive alternative therapies usually feel that testimonials are enough evidence of the success of the therapy. One alternative therapy that has passed the test of critical evaluation is
   a. hypnotherapy.
   b. light-exposure therapy.
   c. eye movement desensitization and reprocessing.
   d. therapeutic touch.

49.6. Being poor or unemployed undermines a person's self-esteem and sense of competence. An approach that seeks to alleviate poverty and other demoralizing situations that put people at high risk for developing psychological disorders is
   a. biomedical therapy.
   b. the humanistic approach.
   c. empathy and active listening.
   d. preventive mental health.

Review: How do psychologists evaluate the effectiveness of the multitude of treatment options available?

Reflect: Do you feel differently about therapy than when you entered this course? How have your own views changed?

Answers to the Test Yourself and Review questions can be found in the green appendix at the end of the book.

The Biomedical Therapies

Drug Therapies

Preview Questions: What are the most common forms of drug therapy? What criticisms have been leveled against drug therapies?

By far the most widely used biomedical treatments today are the drug therapies. When introduced in the 1950s, drug therapy greatly reduced the need for psychosurgery or hospitalization. The discoveries in **psychopharmacology** (the study of drug effects on mind and behavior) revolutionized the treatment of people with severe disorders, liberating hundreds of thousands from confinement in mental hospitals. Thanks to drug therapy—and to political and legal efforts to minimize involuntary hospitalization and to return hospitalized people to their communities, aided by community mental health programs—the resident population of state and county mental hospitals in the United States today is but 20 percent of what it was half a century ago (**FIGURE 50.1**).

For those unable to care for themselves, however, release from hospitals has meant homelessness, not liberation. If home is the place where, as Robert Frost said, when you go there, they have to take you in, then some 200,000 Americans and many thousands of Europeans with mental disorders have no place to call home (Fichter & others, 1996; Leshner, 1992). Studies suggest that about one-third of the homeless have a disabling psychological disorder (Fischer & Breakey, 1991; Levine & Rog, 1990; McCarty & others, 1991). And that doesn't include alcohol or drug abuse, which also plague at least one in three homeless people.

Almost any new treatment, including drug therapy, is greeted by an initial wave of enthusiasm as many people apparently improve. But that enthusiasm often diminishes after researchers subtract the rate of (1) normal recovery among untreated persons and (2) recovery due to the placebo effect, which arises from the positive expectations of patients and mental health workers alike. So, to evaluate the effectiveness of any new drug, researchers use the *double-blind technique*. Half the patients receive the drug, the other half a similar-appearing placebo. Neither the staff nor the patients know who gets which. The good news is that in double-blind studies, several types of drugs have proved useful in treating psychological disorders.

■ **psychopharmacology** the study of the effects of drugs on mind and behavior.

"The mentally ill were out of the hospital, but in many cases they were simply out on the streets, less agitated but lost, still disabled but now uncared for."

Lewis Thomas, *Late Night Thoughts on Listening to Mahler's Ninth Symphony*, 1983

FIGURE 50.1 The emptying of U.S. mental hospitals

After the widespread introduction of antipsychotic drugs, starting in about 1955, the number of residents in state and county mental hospitals declined sharply. But in the rush to deinstitutionalize the mentally ill, many people who were ill-equipped to care for themselves were left homeless on city streets. (Data from the National Institute of Mental Health and Bureau of the Census, 1999.)

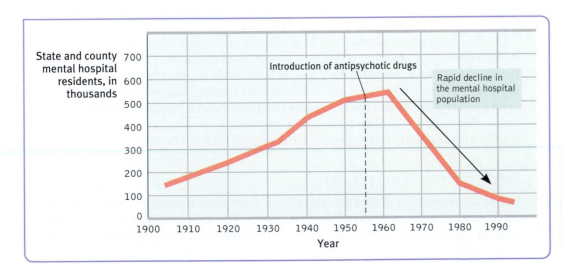

Herself renewed

Thanks to clozapine, Daphne Moss went "from hating the sunshine in the morning to loving it." No longer suffering from the paranoid delusion that her parents were witches, Moss began teaching school and living independently.

Antipsychotic Drugs

The revolution in drug therapy for psychological disorders began with the accidental discovery that certain drugs, used for other medical purposes, calmed psychotic patients. These antipsychotic drugs, such as chlorpromazine (sold as Thorazine), dampen responsiveness to irrelevant stimuli. Thus they provide the most help to schizophrenia patients experiencing positive symptoms such as auditory hallucinations and paranoia (Lehman & others, 1998; Lenzenweger & others, 1989). Patients exhibiting negative symptoms such as apathy and withdrawal often do not respond well to these antipsychotic drugs. A newer drug, clozapine (marketed as Clozaril), does sometimes enable "awakenings" in such people. It also sometimes helps those who have positive symptoms but have not responded to other drugs. In 1 or 2 percent of cases, clozapine has a toxic effect on white blood cells, necessitating regular blood tests. While researchers continue testing possible cousin drugs that would offer the same benefits without the blood problem, clozapine remains the most effective schizophrenia treatment available (Wahlbeck & others, 1999).

The molecules of antipsychotic drugs are similar enough to molecules of the neurotransmitter dopamine to occupy its receptor sites and block its activity (Pickar & others, 1984; Taubes, 1994). (Clozapine also blocks serotonin activity.) This finding—that most antipsychotic drugs block dopamine receptors—reinforces the idea that an overactive dopamine system contributes to schizophrenia.

Antipsychotics such as Thorazine are powerful drugs. They can produce sluggishness, tremors, and twitches similar to those of Parkinson's disease, which is marked by too little dopamine (Kaplan & Saddock, 1989). (Clozapine, thankfully, has few such side effects.) Another complication is that what is an effective dose for some people may be an overdose for others. Asians, for example, seem to require lower doses than do Caucasians (Holden, 1991). Only by carefully monitoring the dosage and its effects can therapist and patient tread the fine line between relieving symptoms and causing extremely unpleasant side effects. But with the appropriate dosage, combined with life-skills programs and family support, hundreds of thousands of people with schizophrenia who had been consigned to the back wards of mental hospitals have returned to work and to near-normal lives.

Antianxiety Drugs

Among the most heavily prescribed and also abused drugs are the antianxiety agents, such as Valium and Librium. Like alcohol, these drugs depress central nervous system activity. Because they reduce tension and anxiety without causing excessive sleepiness, they have been prescribed for even minor emotional stresses. Used in combination with other therapy, an antianxiety drug can help a person learn to cope with frightening situations and fear-triggering stimuli.

The criticism sometimes made of the behavior therapies—that they reduce symptoms without resolving underlying problems—is also made of antianxiety drugs. Unlike the behavior therapies, they may be used as an ongoing treatment. However, routinely "popping a Valium" at the first sign of tension can produce psychological dependence on the drug. (The immediate relief reinforces a person's tendency to take drugs when anxious.) When heavy users stop taking the drug, they may experience both increased anxiety and insomnia, driving them back to the drug for relief.

Antidepressant Drugs

Just as the antianxiety drugs can calm people down from a state of anxiety, the antidepressants sometimes lift people up from a state of depression. Most antidepressants work by increasing the availability of the neurotransmitters norepinephrine or serotonin, which elevate arousal and mood and appear scarce during depression. Consider fluoxetine, which users worldwide know as Prozac. Prozac and other serotonin-enhancing drugs have been prescribed not only to patients with depression but also to those with obsessive-compulsive disorder, two-thirds of whom respond with "partial symptom reduction" (Pigott & Seay, 1997). Prozac blocks the reabsorption and removal of serotonin from synapses (**FIGURE 50.2**). Prozac, and its cousins Zoloft and Paxil, are therefore called serotonin-reuptake-inhibitor drugs. The 77 million prescriptions written for these drugs in 1998 (at a cost of $5.6 billion) made them the world's most widely prescribed psychiatric drugs (Kaufman, 1999). Other antidepressants work by blocking the reabsorption of both norepinephrine and serotonin or by inhibiting an enzyme that breaks down neurotransmitters such as serotonin. These drugs, though no less effective, have more potential side effects, such as dry mouth, weight gain, or dizzy spells (Muldrow & others, 1999).

But be advised: Patients who begin taking antidepressants do not wake up the next day singing "Oh, what a beautiful morning!" Although the influence of antidepressants on neurotransmission does occur within hours, their full psychological effect often requires four weeks, sometimes aided by cognitive therapy to help the patient reverse a now-habitual negative thinking style. Antidepressant drugs are not the only way to give the body a lift. Aerobic exercise, which helps calm people who feel anxious and energize those who feel depressed, does about as much good, and with positive side effects that include increased arousal, increased serotonin levels, and decreases in blood pressure.

Everyone agrees that people with depression often improve after a month on antidepressants. But after allowing for natural recovery (the regression to normal called "spontaneous recovery") and the placebo effect, how big is the drug effect? Not big, report Irving Kirsch and Guy Sapirstein (1998) from their meta-analysis of 19 double-blind clinical trials: "Inactive placebos produced improvement that was 75 percent of the effect of the active drug." Moreover, they report, some of the 25 percent difference seems due to an additional placebo effect derived from drug side effects. Side effects tell patients they're getting an active drug, thus raising their expectations. Placebos that mimic the side effects of antidepressants are nearly as effective as the drugs themselves (Fisher & Greenberg, 1997).

Many who have witnessed or experienced the healing power of antidepressants question these findings. "It would be very miraculous if all the people I've seen getting better were getting better only by virtue of placebo," says the National Institute

"If this doesn't help you don't worry, it's a placebo."

FIGURE 50.2
Biology of antidepressants

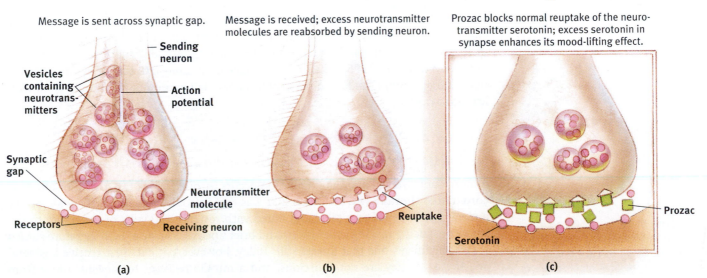

Message is sent across synaptic gap.

- **Sending neuron**
- **Vesicles containing neurotransmitters**
- **Action potential**
- **Synaptic gap**
- **Receptors**
- **Neurotransmitter molecule**
- **Receiving neuron**

(a)

Message is received; excess neurotransmitter molecules are reabsorbed by sending neuron.

- **Reuptake**

(b)

Prozac blocks normal reuptake of the neurotransmitter serotonin; excess serotonin in synapse enhances its mood-lifting effect.

- **Prozac**
- **Serotonin**

(c)

"First of all I think you should know that last quarter's sales figures are interfering with my mood-stabilizing drugs."

"No twisted thought without a twisted molecule."

Attributed to psychologist Ralph Gerard

of Mental Health's director, Steven Hyman (1999). But this much seems assured: Our expectations have surprisingly powerful effects not only on our perceptions and our responses to such external stimuli as alcohol, hypnosis, and sexual situations, but also on our health and well-being (Kirsch & Lynn, 1999). The mind matters.

Skeptics of the biomedical therapies are unsurprised. Yesterday, says neuroscientist Elliot Valenstein (1998), we blamed mothers and sought to heal their children's inner wounds. Today, hardly wiser, we blame brain chemistry and circuitry and pump in "molecules of the mind." But our knowledge of the biochemical roots of disorder and recovery is elementary, he contends. Psychotherapeutic drugs are not "'smart missiles' that can correct the precise biochemical error responsible for each mental illness" without side effects (p. 5). The chemistry and circuitry—and life experiences—that underlie behavior are too complex for that.

Although the effects of drug therapy are less exciting than many news stories would have us believe, they also are less frightening than other stories have suggested. Some people taking Prozac, for example, have committed suicide, but their numbers seem fewer than we would expect from millions of people with depression who are not taking the medication. Prozac users who commit suicide are like cellular phone users who get brain cancer. Given the millions of people taking Prozac and using cellular phones, alarming anecdotes tell us nothing. The question critical thinkers want answered is this: Do these groups suffer an elevated *rate* of suicide and brain cancer? The answer in each case appears to be no (Paulos, 1995; Tollefson & others, 1993, 1994).

Current drug therapies reduce or increase activity at all the receptors for a given neurotransmitter. This has been likened to watering one's garden by closing and opening floodgates. Drug researchers hope that the next generation of therapeutic drugs will target specific receptors that control specific symptoms, rather like watering individual plants. If so, such drugs may offer greater potency with fewer side effects (Goleman, 1996). One type of drug currently under development aims to block receptors for a brain chemical called substance P, which helps transmit pain messages (Kramer & others, 1998). Two dozen studies also indicate unexplained antidepressant effects of an herb, St. John's wort, which ancient Greeks used to drive off evil spirits and which modern Europeans have used as a natural antidote for mild depression (Josey & Tackett, 1999; Kim & others, 1999).

For those suffering the manic-depressive mood swings of a bipolar disorder, the simple salt **lithium** can be an effective mood stabilizer. Australian physician John Cade discovered this in the 1940s when he administered lithium to a severely manic patient. Although his reason for doing so was misguided—he thought lithium had calmed excitable guinea pigs when actually it had made them sick—Cade found that in less than a week the patient became perfectly well (Snyder, 1986). With continued lithium use, emotional highs and lows typically level. After suffering mood swings for years, about 7 in 10 people with bipolar disorder benefit from a long-term daily dose of this cheap salt (Solomon & others, 1995). Their risk of suicide is but one-sixth that of bipolar patients not taking lithium (Tondo & others, 1997). Although we do not fully understand why, lithium works.

Electroconvulsive Therapy

Preview Questions: What is electroconvulsive therapy? When is it used?

The medical use of electricity is an ancient practice. Physicians treated the Roman Emperor Claudius (10 B.C.–A.D. 54) for headaches by pressing electric eels to his temples.

A more controversial brain manipulation occurs through shock treatment, or **electroconvulsive therapy (ECT)**. When ECT was first introduced in 1938, the wide-awake patient was strapped to a table and jolted with roughly 100 volts of electricity to the brain, producing racking convulsions and brief unconsciousness. ECT therefore gained a barbaric image, one that lingers still. Today, however, patients first receive a general anesthetic so they are not conscious, and a muscle relaxant to prevent injury from convulsions. Then a psychiatrist momentarily electrically shocks the unconscious patient's brain. Within 30 minutes the patient awakens and remembers nothing of the treatment or of the hours preceding it.

Psychiatrists usually limit ECT to treatment of severe depression. (It is usually ineffective in treating other psychological disorders.) After three such sessions each week for two to four weeks, 80 percent or more of people receiving ECT improve markedly, showing some memory loss for the treatment period but no discernible brain damage (Bergsholm & others, 1989; Coffey, 1993). "A miracle had happened in two weeks," reported noted research psychologist Norman Endler (1982) after ECT alleviated his deep depression. A 1999 report of the U.S. Surgeon General, as well as earlier research reviews, confirm that ECT is an effective treatment for severe depression in patients who have not responded to

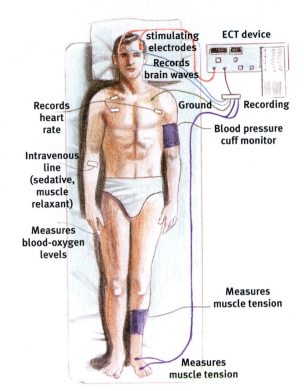

stimulating electrodes
ECT device
Records brain waves
Records heart rate
Ground
Recording
Intravenous line (sedative, muscle relaxant)
Blood pressure cuff monitor
Measures blood-oxygen levels
Measures muscle tension
Measures muscle tension

FIGURE 50.3
Electroconvulsive therapy
Although ECT is controversial, it is the preferred treatment for depression that does not respond to drug therapy.

drug therapy (Consensus Conference, 1985; Parker & others, 1992). Thus, reports the American Psychiatric Association (1990), ECT has regained respectability as a "major treatment" for depression (**FIGURE 50.3**).

How does ECT work? After more than 50 years, no one knows for sure (Kapur & Mann, 1993). One recipient likened ECT to smallpox vaccine, which was saving lives before we knew how it worked. Perhaps electrical shock increases the release of norepinephrine, a neurotransmitter that elevates arousal and mood and seems in short supply during depression. Or perhaps the shock-induced seizures cause the brain to react by calming neural centers where overactivity produces depression.

ECT is credited with saving many from suicide and is now administered with briefer pulses that disrupt memory less (Fink, 1998, 2000). Yet, despite its use with 100,000 people annually in the United States alone, ECT's Frankensteinlike image continues. No matter how impressive the results, the idea of electrically shocking people into convulsions still strikes many as barbaric, especially given our ignorance about why ECT works. Moreover, ECT-treated patients, like other patients with a history of depression, are vulnerable to relapse. Nevertheless, electroconvulsive therapy is, in the minds of many psychiatrists and patients, a lesser evil than depression's misery, anguish, and risk of suicide.

At the century's turn, hopes are rising for a gentler alternative for jump-starting the depressed brain. Depressed moods seem to improve when repeated pulses surge through a magnetic coil held close to a person's skull above the right eyebrow. The painless procedure—called repetitive transcranial magnetic stimulation (rTMS)—is performed on wide-awake patients. Unlike ECT, the rTMS procedure produces no seizures, memory loss, or other side effects. In one double-blind experiment, 67 Israelis with major depression were randomly assigned to two groups (Klein & others, 1999). One group received 10 daily stimulations over a two-week period while the other received sham treatments (without magnetic stimulation). At the end of the two weeks, half of the stimulated patients showed at least a 50 percent improvement in their scores on a depression scale, as did only a quarter of the placebo group. Other studies with animals are identifying the electrochemical changes induced by rTMS.

■ **lithium** a chemical that provides an effective drug therapy for the mood swings of bipolar (manic-depressive) disorders.

■ **electroconvulsive therapy (ECT)** a biomedical therapy for severely depressed patients in which a brief electric current is sent through the brain of an anesthetized patient.

■ **psychosurgery** surgery that removes or destroys brain tissue in an effort to change behavior.

■ **lobotomy** a now-rare psychosurgical procedure once used to calm uncontrollably emotional or violent patients. The procedure cut the nerves that connect the frontal lobes to the emotion-controlling centers of the inner brain.

Psychosurgery

Preview Question: Under what conditions might psychosurgery be considered for changing behavior or moods?

Because its effects are irreversible, **psychosurgery**—surgery that removes or destroys brain tissue—is the most drastic and the least-used biomedical intervention for changing behavior. In the 1930s, Portuguese physician Egas Moniz developed what became the best-known psychosurgical operation: the **lobotomy**. Moniz found that cutting the nerves connecting the frontal lobes with the emotion-controlling centers of the inner brain calmed uncontrollably emotional and violent patients. After shocking the patient into a coma, a neurosurgeon would hammer an icepicklike instrument through each eye socket into the brain, then wiggle it to sever connections running up to the frontal lobes. The whole procedure was crude but easy and inexpensive, and it took only about 10 minutes. During the 1940s and 1950s, tens of thousands of severely disturbed people were "lobotomized," and Moniz was honored with a Nobel prize (Valenstein, 1986).

Although the intention was simply to disconnect emotion from thought, the effect was often more drastic: The lobotomy produced a permanently lethargic, immature, impulsive personality. During the 1950s, after some 35,000 people had been lobotomized in the United States alone, calming drugs became available and psychosurgery was largely abandoned. Today, lobotomies are almost never performed, and other psychosurgery is used only in extreme cases. For example, if a patient suffers uncontrollable seizures, surgeons can deactivate the specific nerve clusters that cause or transmit the convulsions. MRI-guided precision surgery is also occasionally done to cut the circuits involved in severe obsessive-compulsive disorder (Sachdev & Sachdev, 1997). Because such beneficial operations are irreversible, however, neurosurgeons perform them only as a last resort.

The effectiveness of the biomedical therapies reminds us of a fundamental lesson: We find it convenient to talk of separate psychological and biological influences, but everything psychological is also biological. Every thought and feeling depends on the functioning brain. Every creative idea, every moment of joy or anger, every period of depression emerges from the electrochemical activity of the living brain. The influence is two-way: When therapy relieves obsessive-compulsive behavior, PET scans reveal a calmer brain (Schwartz & others, 1996).

Mind-body interaction

The biomedical therapies assume that mind and body are a unit: Affect one and you will affect the other.

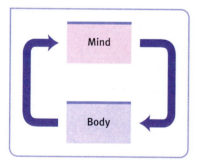

REVIEW AND REFLECT:

The Biomedical Therapies

What are the most common forms of drug therapy? What criticisms have been leveled against drug therapies?

The most widely used biomedical therapies are the antipsychotic, antianxiety, and antidepressant drugs. Although a few drugs, such as lithium for bipolar disorder, have proven very effective in double-blind studies, many drugs are hardly more effective than placebo treatments, and some have serious side effects.

What is electroconvulsive therapy? When is it used?

ECT is a biomedical therapy in which a brief electric current is sent through the brain of an anesthetized patient. Although controversial, ECT remains an effective, last-resort treatment for many people with severe depression who have not responded to drug therapy.

Under what conditions might psychosurgery be considered for changing behavior or moods?

Although radical psychosurgical procedures such as lobotomy were once popular, neurosurgeons now rarely perform brain surgery to alleviate specific problems. Even when MRI-guided precision surgery is considered, it is a treatment of last resort because its effects are irreversible.

Terms and Concepts to Remember

psychopharmacology, p. 619

lithium, p. 622

electroconvulsive therapy (ECT), p. 622

psychosurgery, p. 624

lobotomy, p. 624

Test Yourself

50.1. Antipsychotic drugs are used to calm schizophrenia patients so that they can live outside the hospital. The drugs often bring relief from auditory hallucinations and other troubling symptoms. However, some of them can have unpleasant side effects, most notably

a. hyperactivity.

b. convulsions and momentary memory loss.

c. sluggishness, tremors, and twitches.

d. paranoia.

50.2. Valium and Librium, which depress central nervous system activity, are among the most heavily prescribed and abused drugs. These drugs are referred to as _____ drugs.

a. antipsychotic

b. antianxiety

c. antidepressant

d. antineurotic

50.3. The antidepressant drugs seem to increase the availability of the neurotransmitters norepinephrine or serotonin, which appear to be scarce during depression. One antidepressant drug that often brings relief to patients suffering the manic-depressive mood swings of bipolar disorder is

a. dopamine.

b. Librium.

c. lithium.

d. Valium.

50.4. Two controversial biomedical therapies are electroconvulsive therapy (shock treatment) and lobotomy (a type of psychosurgery). Lobotomy, once used to treat uncontrollably violent patients, is no longer an accepted treatment. Electroconvulsive therapy, however, remains in use as a treatment for

a. depression.

b. severe depression.

c. schizophrenia.

d. anxiety disorders.

Review: What is the placebo effect? Include an example in your answer.

Reflect: Can you think of a time when you may have been affected by your expectations for relief?

Answers to the Test Yourself and Review questions can be found in the green appendix at the end of the book.

Stress and Health

No one needs to be told that psychological states cause physical reactions. Nervous about an important encounter, we feel stomach butterflies. Anxious over speaking in public, we frequent the bathroom. Smoldering over a conflict with a family member, we develop a splitting headache.

If such stress endures, it may also bring on (in those physiologically predisposed) skin rashes, asthma attacks, or high blood pressure. This mind-body connection was strikingly apparent in an inadvertent experiment conducted by British Airways on an April 23, 1999, flight from San Francisco to London. Three hours after takeoff, a mistakenly played message told passengers the plane was about to crash into the sea. Although the flight crew immediately recognized the error and tried to calm the terrified passengers, several required medical assistance (Associated Press, 1999).

If prolonged, stress—together with unhealthy behaviors—can put us at serious risk. The National Academy of Sciences' Institute of Medicine has traced half the mortality from the 10 leading causes of death in the United States to people's behavior—to cigarette smoking, alcohol abuse, unprotected sex, ignoring doctors' orders, insufficient exercise, use of illicit drugs, and poor nutrition. If we could understand and modify these behavioral sources of illness, we might lessen people's suffering, increase their life expectancy, and enrich their quality of life. To pursue these goals, psychologists and physicians created the interdisciplinary field of *behavioral medicine*, integrating behavioral and medical knowledge.

Health psychology provides psychology's contribution to behavioral medicine. Its numbers include many of the 3900 psychologists now on the faculties of Canadian and U.S. medical schools (Williams & Kohut, 1999). In the early 1950s, the average medical school had two faculty psychologists; today it has about 30 (Sheridan, 1999). For psychologists, health is more than "merely the slowest possible rate at which one can die" (Prairie Home Companion, 1999). As we will see in Module 51, health psychologists ask: How do our emotions and personality influence our risk of disease? How do our perceptions of a situation determine the stress we feel? How can we reduce or control stress? And as we will see in Module 52, health psychologists also ask: What attitudes and behaviors help prevent illness and promote health and well-being?

51 Stress and Illness

Walking along the path toward his Rocky Mountain campsite, Karl hears a rustle at his feet. As he glimpses a rattlesnake, his body mobilizes for fight or flight: His muscles tense, his adrenaline flows, his heart pounds, and he flees, racing to the security of camp. Once there, Karl's muscles gradually relax and his heart rate and breathing ease.

Karen leaves her suburban apartment one morning and, delayed by road construction, arrives at the parking lot of the commuter train station just in time to see the 8:05 pull away. Catching the next train, she arrives in the city late and elbows her way through crowds of rush-hour pedestrians. Once at her bank office, she apologizes to her first client, who wonders where Karen has been and why his quarterly investment report is not ready. Karen does her best to mollify the client. Afterward, she notices her tense muscles, clenched teeth, and churning stomach.

Karl's response to stress saved his life; Karen's, if chronic, could increase her risk of heart disease, high blood pressure, and other stress-linked health problems. Moreover, feeling under pressure, she might sleep and exercise less and smoke and drink more, further endangering her long-term health.

Worldwide, reports the World Health Organization, nearly a quarter of health care contacts are prompted by psychological problems (Sartorius, 1994).

Stress and Stressors

Preview Questions: What is stress? What events tend to provoke stress responses?

Stress is a slippery concept. It is sometimes used to describe threats or challenges ("Karen was under a lot of stress"), other times to describe our responses ("When Karl saw the rattler, he experienced acute stress"). Most psychologists would define Karen's missed train as a "stressor," Karl's physical and emotional responses as a "stress reaction," and the process by which Karen and Karl related to their environments as stress.

Thus, **stress** is not just a stimulus or a response. It is the process by which we appraise and cope with environmental threats and challenges (**FIGURE 51.1**). The events of our lives flow through a psychological filter. Stress arises less from events per se than from how we appraise them (Lazarus, 1998). One person, alone in a house, dismisses its creaking sounds and experiences no stress; someone else suspects an intruder and becomes alarmed. One person regards a new job as a welcome challenge; someone else appraises it as risking failure.

FIGURE 51.1 Stress appraisal
How we appraise an event influences how much stress we experience and how effectively we respond.

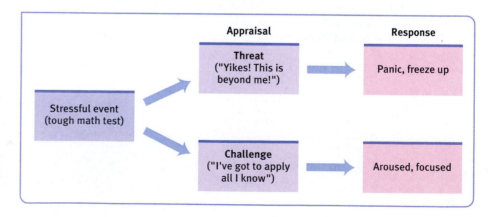

When perceived as challenges, stressors can have positive effects, arousing and motivating us to conquer problems. Championship athletes, successful entertainers, and great teachers and leaders all thrive and excel when aroused by a challenge. Having conquered cancer or rebounded from a lost job, some people emerge with stronger self-esteem and a deepened spirituality and sense of purpose. Indeed, among humans and other animals, some stress and physical stimulation early in life is conducive to later emotional resilience and physical growth (Landauer & Whiting, 1979). As many of us have experienced, bad things sometimes work for good. Adversity sometimes begets growth. The Chinese character for *crisis*, note Virginia O'Leary and Jeannette Ickovics (1995), combines the symbols for *danger* and for *opportunity*.

But stressors can also threaten our resources—our status and security on the job, our loved ones' health or well-being, our deeply held beliefs, our self-image (Hobfoll, 1989). And experiencing severe or prolonged stress may harm us. Those who had post-traumatic stress reactions to heavy combat in the Vietnam war went on to suffer greatly elevated rates of circulatory, digestive, respiratory, and infectious diseases (Boscarino, 1997).

The Stress Response System

Although medical interest in stress dates back to Hippocrates (460–377 B.C.), it was not until the 1920s that physiologist Walter Cannon (1929) confirmed that the stress response is part of a unified mind-body system. He observed that extreme cold, lack of oxygen, and emotion-arousing incidents all trigger an outpouring of epinephrine (adrenaline) and norepinephrine (noradrenaline). These stress hormones enter the bloodstream from sympathetic nerve endings in the inner part of the adrenal glands. This outpouring is but one part of the sympathetic nervous system's response. When alerted by any of a number of brain pathways, the sympathetic nervous system increases heart rate and respiration, diverts blood from digestion to the skeletal muscles, dulls pain, and releases sugar and fat from the body's stores—all to prepare the body for what Cannon called *fight or flight*. All in all, this stress response struck Cannon as wonderfully adaptive. Physiologists have also identified a second stress response system (**FIGURE 51.2**). On orders from the cerebral cortex (via the hypothalamus and pituitary gland), the outer (cortical) part of the adrenal gland secretes the stress hormone cortisol.

Canadian scientist Hans Selye's (1936, 1976) 40 years of research on stress extended Cannon's findings and helped make stress a major concept in both psychology and medicine. The story of how Selye arrived at his concept of the stress response is one worth remembering in times of intellectual discouragement. Hoping to discover a new sex hormone, Selye injected rats with ovarian hormone extract. He detected three effects: enlargement of the adrenal cortex, shrinkage of the

stress the process by which we perceive and respond to certain events, called *stressors*, that we appraise as threatening or challenging.

FIGURE 51.2 Dual-response system
The adrenal glands (atop the kidneys) release stress hormones on orders received through a dual-track system.

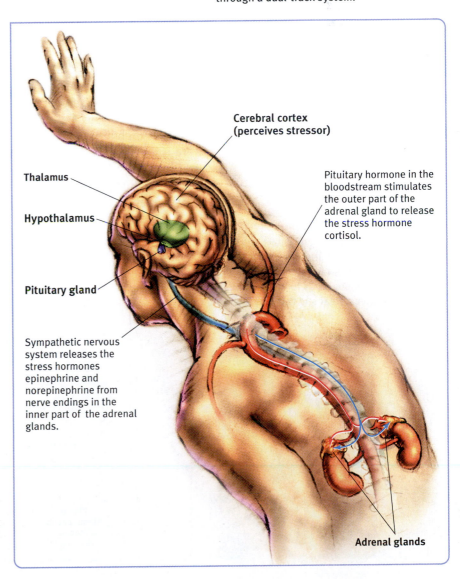

Cerebral cortex (perceives stressor)

Thalamus

Hypothalamus

Pituitary gland

Pituitary hormone in the bloodstream stimulates the outer part of the adrenal gland to release the stress hormone cortisol.

Sympathetic nervous system releases the stress hormones epinephrine and norepinephrine from nerve endings in the inner part of the adrenal glands.

Adrenal glands

thymus gland (which contains disease-fighting white blood cells), and bleeding ulcers. Because no known hormone had ever produced such symptoms, Selye was elated. "At the age of 28, I seemed to be already on the track of a new hormone."

Before long, Selye's elation turned to disappointment. When he injected the rats with other fluids, he observed the same effects: adrenal enlargement, thymus shrinkage, and bleeding ulcers. Alas, he concluded, the effects were *not* due to a new hormone:

> All my dreams of discovering a new hormone were shattered. All the time and all the materials that went into this long study were wasted. . . . I became so depressed that for a few days I could not do any work at all. I just sat in my laboratory, brooding. . . . The ensuing period of introverted contemplation turned out to be the decisive factor in my whole career; it pointed the way for all my subsequent work. . . . As I repetitiously continued to go over my ill-fated experiments and their possible interpretation, it suddenly struck me that one could look at them from an entirely different angle. If there was such a thing as a single non-specific reaction of the body to damage of any kind, . . . the general medical implications of the syndrome would be enormous! (1976, pp. 24–26)

To verify his hunch, Selye studied animals' reactions to various other stressors, such as electric shock, surgical trauma, and immobilizing restraint. He discovered that the body's adaptive response to stress was so general—like a single burglar alarm that sounds no matter what intrudes—that he called it the **general adaptation syndrome (GAS)**.

Selye saw the GAS as having three phases (**FIGURE 51.3**). Let's say you suffer a physical or emotional trauma. In Phase 1, you experience an *alarm reaction* due to the sudden activation of your sympathetic nervous system. Your heart rate zooms. Blood is diverted to your skeletal muscles. You feel the faintness of shock. With your resources mobilized, you are now ready to fight the challenge during Phase 2, *resistance*. Your temperature, blood pressure, and respiration remain high, and there is a sudden outpouring of hormones. If persistent, the stress may eventually deplete your body's reserves during Phase 3, *exhaustion*. With exhaustion, you are more vulnerable to illness or even, in extreme cases, collapse and death.

FIGURE 51.3

Selye's general adaptation syndrome

After a trauma, the body enters an alarm phase of temporary shock. From this it rebounds, as stress resistance rises. If the stress is prolonged, as for these Kurdish refugees, wear and tear may lead to exhaustion.

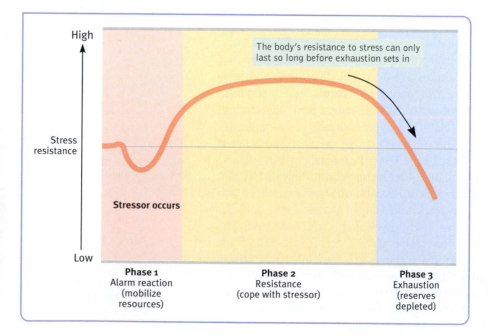

High

The body's resistance to stress can only last so long before exhaustion sets in

Stress resistance

Low

Stressor occurs

Phase 1
Alarm reaction
(mobilize
resources)

Phase 2
Resistance
(cope with stressor)

Phase 3
Exhaustion
(reserves
depleted)

Newer research reveals subtle differences in the body's reactions to different stressors. Nevertheless, few medical experts today quarrel with Selye's basic point: Although the human body comes designed to cope with temporary stress, prolonged stress can produce physical deterioration. Several recent studies have taken MRI brain scans of people who have experienced a prolonged flood of stress hormones, due to sustained child abuse, combat, or an endocrine disease (Sapolsky, 1999). Most have a shrunken hippocampus, the inner brain structure vital to laying down explicit (declarative) memories. In animals, too, various stresses—being subordinate in a group, being physically restrained, being isolated—can cause hippocampal tissue to shrink (McEwen, 1998). Such findings serve as further incentives to today's **health psychologists**, who have joined with physicians to create the interdisciplinary field of **behavioral medicine**. Health psychologists are actively exploring such questions as, What causes stress? What are the effects of stress? And how can we alleviate those effects?

Stressful Life Events

Research has focused on our responses to three types of stressors: catastrophes, significant life changes, and daily hassles.

Catastrophes

Catastrophes are unpredictable, large-scale events such as war and natural disasters that nearly everyone appraises as threatening. Although people often provide one another with aid as well as comfort after such events, the health consequences can be significant. Two examples:

+ On the day of its 1994 earthquake, Los Angeles experienced a fivefold increase in sudden-death heart attacks—especially in the first two hours after the quake and near its epicenter. Physical exertion (running, lifting debris) was a factor in only 13 percent of the deaths, leaving stress as the likely trigger for the others (Muller & Verrier, 1996).

+ In the year following the crash of a 747 jumbo jet at Lockerbie, Scotland, police officers—after being pressed into recovering human remains and patrolling the disaster zone—suffered a 38 percent increase in short-term illnesses (Paton, 1992).

Do other community disasters usually produce effects this great? After digesting data from 52 studies of catastrophic floods, hurricanes, and fires, Anthony Rubonis and Leonard Bickman (1991) found the typical effect more modest but nonetheless genuine. In disaster's wake, rates of psychological disorders such as depression and anxiety rose an average 17 percent. The nuclear accident at Three Mile Island produced similar stress symptoms in area residents (Baum & Fleming, 1993). Refugees fleeing their homeland also suffer increased rates of psychological disorder. Their stress stems from the trauma of uprooting and family separation, and from the challenges of adjusting to a foreign culture's new language, ethnicity, climate, and social norms (Williams & Berry, 1991). In all these cases, the health consequences often come only after prolonged stress.

Significant Life Changes

The second type of life event stressor is a significant personal life change—leaving home, the death of a loved one, the loss of a job, a marriage or divorce. Life transitions and insecurities are often keenly felt during young adulthood. That helps explain why, when 15,000 Canadian adults were

■ **general adaptation syndrome (GAS)** Selye's concept of the body's adaptive response to stress in three stages—alarm, resistance, exhaustion.

■ **health psychology** a subfield of psychology that provides psychology's contribution to behavioral medicine.

■ **behavioral medicine** an interdisciplinary field that integrates behavioral and medical knowledge and applies that knowledge to health and disease.

Toxic stress
Researchers have found that catastrophes such as flooding increase rates of psychological disorders.

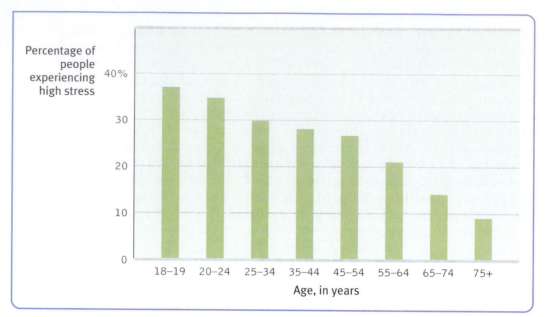

FIGURE 51.4
Chronic stress, by age
As Canadians age, feelings of chronic stress tend to subside. (Data from Statistics Canada, 1999.)

asked whether "You are trying to take on too many things at once," responses indicated highest stress levels among the youngest adults (**FIGURE 51.4**).

Some psychologists study the health effects of life changes by following people over time to see if such events precede illnesses. Others compare the life changes recalled by those who have or have not suffered a specific health problem, such as a heart attack. A review of these studies commissioned by the U.S. National Academy of Sciences revealed that people recently widowed, fired, or divorced are more vulnerable to disease (Dohrenwend & others, 1982). A Finnish study of 96,000 widowed people confirmed the phenomenon: Their risk of death doubled in the week following their partner's death (Kaprio & others, 1987). Experiencing a cluster of crises puts one even more at risk.

Daily Hassles

Our happiness tends to stem less from enduring good fortune than from our response to daily events—an A on an exam, a gratifying letter, your team's winning the big game. This principle works for negative events, too. Everyday annoyances may be the most significant sources of stress (Kohn & Macdonald, 1992; Lazarus, 1990; Ruffin, 1993). These daily hassles include rush-hour traffic, aggravating housemates, long lines at the bank or store, too many things to do, and misplacing things. Although some people can simply shrug them off, others are "driven up the wall" by such inconveniences. In fact, 6 in 10 people say they feel "great stress" at least once a week (Harris, 1987).

Over time, these little stressors can add up and take a toll on our health and well-being. Hypertension (high blood pressure) rates are high among residents of urban ghettos, where the stresses that accompany poverty, unemployment, solo parenting, and overcrowding are part of daily life for some people. And these daily pressures may be compounded by racism, which—like other stressors—can have both psychological and physical consequences. Imagine thinking that some people distrust you, do not like you, or doubt your abilities. Might you not find daily life stressful? Might such stress eventually take a toll on your health, perhaps driving up your blood pressure? Well, that describes the experiences

No end in sight
"It's not the large things that send a man to the madhouse . . . no, it's the continuing series of small tragedies . . . not the death of his love but the shoelace that snaps with no time left" (Charles Bukowski, cited by Lazarus in Wallis, 1983).

of many African Americans as they perceive racism in their daily lives, note Rodney Clark and his colleagues (1999).

The dramatic effects of high levels of stress became apparent in Russia from 1990 to 1993, following the collapse of socialism in the former Soviet Union. During that period, Russia experienced mushrooming divorce, murder, suicide, and stress-related disease rates. Life expectancy for Russian men also plummeted by nearly 5 years, to 58.9 years (Holden, 1996).

Persistent on-the-job hassles can lead to a condition of mental, physical, and emotional exhaustion called **burnout** (Maslach, 1982). Teachers, nurses, social workers, parents, and police officers—indeed, anyone facing persistent work hassles—may become worn down from the never-ending stress of their job. The result may be a sharp drop in performance caused by the fatigue of physical exhaustion, the depression of emotional exhaustion, and the cynicism of mental exhaustion.

■ **burnout** physical, emotional, and mental exhaustion brought on by persistent job-related stress.

Perceived Control

Catastrophes, important life changes, and daily hassles and conflicts are especially stressful when we appraise them as both negative *and* uncontrolled. If two rats receive simultaneous shocks, but one can turn a wheel to stop the shocks, the helpless rat becomes more susceptible to ulcers and lowered immunity to disease (Laudenslager & Reite, 1984) (**FIGURE 51.5**). In humans, a bacterial infection often combines with uncontrollable stress to produce the most severe ulcers (Overmier & Murison, 1997). To cure the ulcer, kill the bug with antibiotics and control the acid secretions with reduced stress.

Perceiving a loss of control, we become vulnerable to ill health. Judith Rodin (1986), for example, has shown that elderly nursing home patients who have little perceived control over their activities tend to decline faster and die sooner than do those given more control over their activities. And workers given control over their work environments—by being able to adjust office furnishings and control interruptions and distractions—experience less stress (O'Neill, 1993). This helps explain why British civil service workers at the executive grades outlive those at clerical or laboring grades. The more control workers have, the longer they live (Bosma & others, 1997, 1998; Marmot & others, 1997).

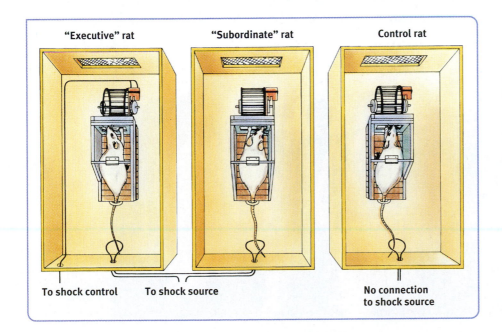

FIGURE 51.5 Health consequences of a loss of control
The "executive" rat at the left can switch off the tail shock by turning the wheel. Because it has control over the shock, it is no more likely to develop ulcers than is the unshocked control rat on the right. The "subordinate" rat in the center receives the same shocks as the executive rat. But because the subordinate rat has no control over the shocks, it is more likely to develop ulcers. (Adapted from Weiss, 1977.)

Poverty and Inequality

Control may help explain a well-established link between economic status and longevity. In one study of 843 grave markers in an old graveyard in Glasgow, Scotland, those with the costliest, highest pillars (indicating the most affluence) tended to live the longest (Carroll & others, 1994). Likewise, Scottish regions with the least overcrowding and unemployment have the greatest longevity. In the United States and Canada, too, poorer people are more at risk for premature death. Even among primates, those at the bottom of the social pecking order are more likely than their higher-status companions to become sick when exposed to a coldlike virus (Cohen & others, 1997).

People also tend to die younger in areas where there is greater income *inequality* (Kawachi & others, 1999; Lynch & others, 1998; Marmot & Wilkinson, 1999). Among developed countries, Britain and the United States, which have large income disparities between rich and poor, have life expectancies two to four years lower than those in Japan and Sweden, where the differences in income are less extreme. And as income inequality has grown over the last decade in Eastern Europe and Russia, life expectancy has decreased. The effect is not confined to nations. Cities and U.S. states with relatively disparate incomes also tend to have lower life expectancy than those where incomes are more equal.

Does the inequality–mortality correlation occur merely because extreme differences in income are flags of substantial poverty? No, the correlation remains after adjusting for average income and for the proportion of the population with low incomes. In fact, report John Lynch and his colleagues (1998, 2000), people at every income level are at greater risk of death if they live in a community with great income inequality.

Researchers are now pondering *why* inequality predicts mortality. Is it because the risk of violent death is greater? Because receiving relatively low income evokes feelings of frustration and worthlessness? Because investment in public health, education, and housing is lower in such regions? Stay tuned for some answers.

Optimism-Pessimism

A control-related factor that also influences our vulnerability to stress is optimism. Psychologists Michael Scheier and Charles Carver (1992) report that optimists—people who agree with statements such as, "In uncertain times, I usually expect the best"—not only perceive more control, they cope better with stressful events and

Equal incomes lead to longer lives
In Kerala state, India, incomes are low, yet life expectancy is greater than in other Indian states. "Indeed," report John Lynch and his co-researchers, thanks to relative equality and to "investment in human resources, . . . [life expectancy approximates] levels seen in rich industrialized countries."

enjoy better health. During the last month of a semester, students previously identified as optimistic report less fatigue and fewer coughs, aches, and pains. During the stressful first few weeks of law school, those who are optimistic ("It's unlikely that I will fail") enjoy better moods and stronger infection-thwarting immune systems (Segerstrom & others, 1998). Optimists also respond to stress with smaller increases in blood pressure, and they recover more quickly from heart bypass surgery. One study that followed 2428 middle-aged Finnish men for up to 10 years discovered that the number of deaths among men with a bleak, hopeless outlook was more than double that found among their optimistic counterparts (**FIGURE 51.6**).

Why do perceived loss of control and pessimism predict health problems? Animal studies show—and human studies confirm—that losing control provokes an outpouring of stress hormones. When rats cannot control shock or when humans feel unable to control their environment, stress hormone levels rise and immune responses drop (Rodin, 1986). Captive animals therefore experience more stress and are more vulnerable to disease than are wild animals (Roberts, 1988). The crowding that occurs in high-density neighborhoods, prisons, and college dorms is another source of diminished feelings of control—and of elevated levels of stress hormones and blood pressure (Fleming & others, 1987; Ostfeld & others, 1987).

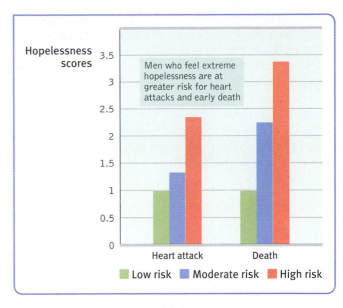

FIGURE 51.6 Toxic hopelessness
Compared with Finnish middle-aged men scoring low in hopelessness, those scoring high were two to four times more vulnerable to a heart attack over the ensuing six years and three to four times more likely to die. (Data from Everson & others, 1996.)

Stress and Heart Disease

Preview Questions: To what extent does stress contribute to heart disease? Why are some of us more prone to coronary heart disease than others are?

In the past century, behavior-related illnesses have emerged as the major causes of death. Stress, it seems, can put us at risk for one of today's four leading causes of serious illness and death: heart disease, cancer, stroke, and chronic lung disease (**FIGURE 51.7**).

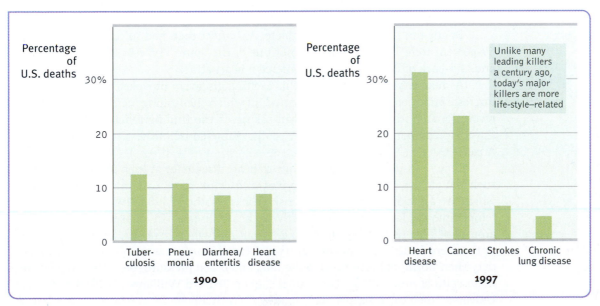

FIGURE 51.7
The four leading causes of death in the United States in 1900 and 1997
With the conquering of the major infectious diseases, diseases influenced by behavior have now emerged as the major causes of death. The story is much the same in Canada, Australia, New Zealand, and most European countries. (From National Center for Health Statistics, *World Health Statistics Annual*, and Statistics Canada, 1999.)

■ **coronary heart disease** the clogging of the vessels that nourish the heart muscle; the leading cause of death in the United States.

■ **Type A** Friedman and Rosenman's term for competitive, hard-driving, impatient, verbally aggressive, and anger-prone people.

■ **Type B** Friedman and Rosenman's term for easygoing, relaxed people.

In both India and America, Type A bus drivers are literally hard-driving: They brake, pass, and honk their horns more often than their more easygoing Type B colleagues (Evans & others, 1987).

Although infrequent before 1900, **coronary heart disease**—the closing of the vessels that nourish the heart muscle—became by the 1950s North America's leading cause of death and remains so today. In addition to family history of the disease, many behavioral and physiological factors increase the risk of heart disease—smoking, obesity, a high-fat diet, physical inactivity, elevated blood pressure, and an elevated cholesterol level. The psychological factors of stress and personality also play a big role.

In 1956, cardiologists Meyer Friedman, Ray Rosenman, and their colleagues stumbled upon an indication of how big that role is (Friedman & Ulmer, 1984). While studying the eating behavior of white San Francisco Junior League women and their husbands, Friedman and Rosenman discovered that the women consumed as much cholesterol and fat as their husbands did, yet they were far less susceptible to heart disease. Was it because of their female sex hormones? No, the researchers surmised, because African American women with the same sex hormones but facing more stress than the Junior Leaguers are as prone to heart disease as their husbands are.

The Junior League president thought she knew the answer. "If you really want to know what is going to give our husbands heart attacks, I'll tell you. It's stress," she said sadly, "the stress they have to face in their businesses, day in, day out. Why, when my husband comes home at night, it takes at least one martini just to unclench his jaws."

To test the idea that stress increases vulnerability to heart disease, Friedman and Rosenman measured the blood cholesterol level and clotting speed of 40 tax accountants. From January through March, both of these coronary warning indicators were completely normal. Then, as the accountants began scrambling to finish their clients' tax returns before the April 15 filing deadline, their cholesterol and clotting measures rose to dangerous levels. In May and June, with the deadline past, the measures returned to normal. The researchers' hunch had paid off: Stress predicted heart attack risk.

The stage was set for Friedman and Rosenman's classic nine-year study of more than 3000 healthy men aged 35 to 59. At the start of the study, they interviewed each man for 15 minutes about his work and eating habits. During the interview, they noted the man's manner of talking and other behavioral patterns. Those who seemed the most reactive, competitive, hard-driving, impatient, time-conscious, supermotivated, verbally aggressive, and easily angered they called **Type A**. A roughly equal number who were more easygoing they called **Type B**. Which group do you suppose turned out to be the most coronary-prone?

By the time the study was complete, 257 of the men had suffered heart attacks; 69 percent were Type A. Moreover, not one of the "pure" Type Bs—the most mellow and laid-back of their group—had suffered a heart attack.

As happens often in science, this exciting discovery provoked enormous public interest. But after the honeymoon period, in which the finding seemed definitive and revolutionary, other researchers began asking, Is the finding reliable? If so, what is the toxic component of the Type A profile: Time-consciousness? Competitiveness? Anger?

Type A people may be more prone to heart disease for at least two reasons. First, such individuals smoke more, sleep less, and drink more caffeinated drinks, all of which are associated with coronary risk (Hicks & others, 1982, 1983). Second, their temperament may contribute directly to heart disease. In relaxed situations, the arousal of Type As and Type Bs is no different. But when harassed, given a challenge, or threatened with a loss of control, Type A individuals are more physiologically reactive. Their hormonal secretions, pulse rate, and blood pressure soar, while Type Bs remain calm (Lyness, 1993). For example, when Redford Williams (1989) asked Duke University men to do simple math problems (with a prize for the fastest), the Type A students' stress-hormone levels rose to more than double those of their Type B classmates. These hormones accelerate the buildup of plaques (scarlike masses formed by cholesterol deposits) on the artery walls, producing atherosclerosis, or "hardening" of the arteries. Atherosclerosis also makes reactive people vulnerable to high blood pressure, a risk factor for strokes and heart attacks (Schneiderman & others, 1989).

These findings suggest that reactive Type A individuals are more often "combat ready." When harassed or challenged, their active sympathetic nervous system redistributes bloodflow to the muscles and away from internal organs such as the liver, which removes cholesterol and fat from the blood. Thus, their blood may contain excess cholesterol and fat that later get deposited around the heart. Further stress—sometimes conflicts brought on by their own abrasiveness—may trigger the altered heart rhythms that, in those with weakened hearts, can cause sudden death (Kamarck & Jennings, 1991). In such ways, the hearts and minds of people interact.

More recent research has revealed that rather than a fast-paced life-style, Type A's toxic core is negative emotions—especially the anger associated with an aggressively reactive temperament (Miller & others, 1996; Williams, 1993). The effect of an anger-prone personality appears most noticeably in studies in which interviewers assess verbal assertiveness and emotional intensity. (If you pause in the middle of a sentence, an intense, anger-prone person may jump in and finish it for you.) Among young and middle-aged adults, those who react with anger over little things are the most coronary-prone. One study followed Duke University law students over 25 years. Those inclined to be hostile and cynical were five times more likely than their gentler, trusting classmates to die by middle age (Williams, 1989). As Charles Spielberger and Perry London (1982) put it, rage "seems to lash back and strike us in the heart muscle."

> "The fire you kindle for your enemy often burns you more than him."
>
> Chinese proverb

Anger is not the only toxic emotion. Depression, too, can be lethal. Centers for Disease Control researchers studied adults who were feeling a sense of hopelessness or at least mild depression. Compared with those without such feelings, these downhearted people were more vulnerable to heart disease in the ensuing 12 years. This was true even after controlling for differences in age, sex, smoking, and other factors linked to heart ailments (Anda & others, 1993). Another study (Whooley & Browner, 1998), of 7406 women age 67 or older with varying levels of depression, found significant differences in mortality, due partly to increased heart disease. Of those with no depressive symptoms, 7 percent died within six years, as did 17 percent of those with three to five depressive symptoms and 24 percent of those with six or more depressive symptoms. In the years following a heart attack, depressed people have a quadrupled risk of further heart problems (Pratt & others, 1996; Frasure-Smith & others, 1995, 1999). The depression that follows a spouse's death similarly increases one's risk of having a heart attack or stroke (National Academy of Sciences, 1984). All in all, the evidence from 57 studies suggests that "depression substantially increases the risk of death, especially death by unnatural causes and cardiovascular disease" (Wulsin & others, 1999).

The toxic effects of negative emotions help explain why about a quarter of medical inpatients suffer a mood or anxiety disorder, and why 4 in 10 chronically ill patients suffer or have suffered a psychiatric disorder (Cohen & Rodriguez, 1995; Katon & Sullivan, 1990). Negative emotions have physical consequences. The fats released during stress linger in the bloodstream and help form the plaques that clog arteries. While making blood available to the extremities, stress also constricts blood vessels in the heart, decreasing blood flow to parts of the heart. Negative emotions may also influence a person's poor health practices and health-related decisions. (The correlation between physical and psychological disorder may additionally reflect the effect of illness. Chronic or terminal illness can be demoralizing.)

Stress and Susceptibility to Disease

Preview Question: How does stress make us more vulnerable to disease?

Not so long ago, the term *psychosomatic* described psychologically caused physical symptoms. To laypeople, the term implied that the symptoms were unreal—they were "merely" psychosomatic. To avoid such connotations and to describe better the genuine physiological effects of psychological states, most experts today refer instead to **psychophysiological illnesses**. These illnesses, such as hypertension and some headaches, are stress-related. A person under stress may retain excess sodium and fluids, which, together with constriction of the arteries' muscle walls, contribute to increased blood pressure (Light & others, 1983).

Stress and the Immune System

Evidence for the reality of psychophysiological ailments comes from hundreds of new experiments that reveal the nervous and endocrine systems' influence on the immune system. Your immune system is a complex surveillance system that defends your body by isolating and destroying bacteria, viruses, and other foreign substances. This system includes two types of white blood cells, called **lymphocytes**. *B lymphocytes* form in the bone marrow and release antibodies that fight bacterial infections. *T lymphocytes* form in the thymus and other lymphatic tissue and attack cancer cells, viruses, and foreign substances—even "good" ones, such as transplanted organs. Another agent of the immune system is the *macrophage* ("big eater"), which identifies, pursues, and ingests harmful invaders. Age, nutrition, genetics, body temperature, and stress all influence the immune system's activity.

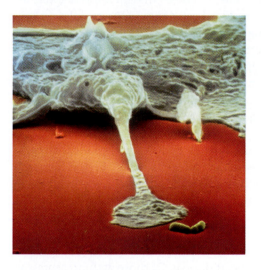

The immune system in action
A large macrophage (at top) is about to trap and ingest a tiny bacterium (lower right). Macrophages constantly patrol our bodies in search of invaders—such as this *Escherichia coli* bacterium—and debris, such as worn-out red blood cells.

Your immune system can err in two directions. Responding too strongly, it may attack the body's own tissues, causing arthritis or an allergic reaction. Or it may underreact, allowing, say, a dormant herpes virus to erupt or cancer cells to multiply. Women are immunologically stronger than men (Morell, 1995), making them less susceptible to infections. But this very strength also makes them more susceptible to self-attacking diseases, such as lupus and multiple sclerosis.

Your immune system is not a headless horseman. Rather, it exchanges information with your brain and your hormone-secreting endocrine system. The brain regulates the secretion of stress hormones, which in turn suppress the disease-fighting lymphocytes. Thus, when animals are physically restrained, given unavoidable electric shocks, or subjected to noise, crowding, cold water, social defeat, or maternal separation, their immune systems become less active (Maier & others, 1994). One study monitored immune responses in 43 monkeys over six months (Cohen & others, 1992). Twenty-one were stressed by being housed with new roommates—three or four new monkeys—each month. (To empathize with the monkeys, recall the stress of leaving home to attend school or summer camp, and imagine having to repeat this experience monthly.) Compared with monkeys left in stable groups, the socially disrupted monkeys experienced weakened immune systems.

"In the eyes of God or biology or what have you, it is just very important to have women."

Immunologist Normal Talal (1995)

Does stress similarly depress the immune system of humans? Consider:

+ In three separate *Skylab* missions, the immune systems of the astronauts showed reduced effectiveness immediately after the stress of reentry and splashdown (Kimzey, 1975; Kimzey & others, 1976).

+ Marital spats are not good for health. As 90 healthy newlywed couples spent a half-hour discussing problem areas in their marriage, some became angrier than others—and suffered more immune system suppression during the next day (Kiecolt-Glaser & others, 1993).

+ Surgical wounds heal more slowly in stressed animals and humans. In one experiment, dental students received "punch wounds" (punching a precise small hole in the skin). Compared with wounds placed during summer vacation, those placed three days before a major exam healed 40 percent more slowly. In fact, report Janice Kiecolt-Glaser and her co-researchers (1998), "no student healed as rapidly during this stressful period as during vacation."

+ Students' disease-fighting mechanisms are weaker during high-stress times, such as exam weeks, and on days when they are upset (Jemmott & Magloire, 1988; Stone & others, 1987). In one experiment, 47 percent of subjects living stress-filled lives developed colds after a virus was dropped in their noses, but only 27 percent of those living relatively free of stress caught colds (Cohen & others, 1991). Follow-up experiments confirm the link between stress and severity of cold symptoms (Cohen & others, 1993, 1995, 1998, 1999).

+ Managing stress may be life-sustaining. The one personality trait shared by 169 centenarians (people over 100) was their ability to manage stress well (Silver & Perls, 1999).

The stress effect on immunity makes physiological sense (Maier & others, 1994). As we have seen, stress involves an aroused, fight-or-flight response. Stress diverts energy to the muscles and brain, mobilizing the body for action. The immune response to disease is a competing energy system. It takes energy to fight infections, produce inflammations, and maintain fevers. Thus, when diseased, our bodies reduce muscular energy output by inactivity and increased sleep. Stress diverts energy from the disease-fighting system, rendering us more vulnerable to illness. The bottom line: Stress does not make us sick, but it does restrain our immune functioning, making us more vulnerable to foreign invaders.

Stress and AIDS

AIDS has become the world's fourth leading cause of death and the number one killer in Africa, where in 1998 it took 1.83 million lives (Balter, 1999). AIDS, as its name tells us, is an immune disorder—an *acquired immune deficiency syndrome* caused by the human immunodeficiency virus (HIV), which is spread by the exchange of bodily fluids, primarily semen and blood. If a disease that is spread by human contact kills very quickly it likely will not kill many. If, as with HIV, it kills slowly, it ironically can be lethal to more people: Those who carry the disease have time to spread it, often without realizing they are infected. When the HIV infection becomes manifest as AIDS, some years after the initial infection, the person has difficulty fighting off other diseases, such as pneumonia. Worldwide, reports the United Nations, 33 million people were infected with HIV in 1999, 2.6 million of whom died of AIDS that year (*New York Times*, 1999).

So if chronic stress serves to suppress immune functioning, could it also exacerbate the course of AIDS? Researchers have found that stress and negative emotions do correlate with a progression from HIV infection to AIDS and with the speed of decline in those infected (Bower & others, 1998; Kiecolt-Glaser & Glaser, 1995; Leserman & others, 1999). HIV-infected men faced with stressful life circumstances, such

■ **psychophysiological illness** literally, "mind-body" illness; any stress-related physical illness, such as hypertension and some headaches. *Note:* This is distinct from *hypochondriasis*—misinterpreting normal physical sensations as symptoms of a disease.

■ **lymphocytes** the two types of white blood cells that are part of the body's immune system: *B lymphocytes* form in the *bone* marrow and release antibodies that fight bacterial infections; *T lymphocytes* form in the *thymus* and, among other duties, attack cancer cells, viruses, and foreign substances.

"When the heart is at ease, the body is healthy."

Chinese proverb

as the loss of a partner, exhibit somewhat greater immune suppression and a faster disease progression.

Would efforts to reduce stress help control the disease? Although the benefits are small compared with available drug treatments, the answer appears again to be yes. Educational initiatives, bereavement support groups, cognitive therapy, and exercise programs that reduce distress have all had positive consequences for HIV-positive individuals (Baum & Posluszny, 1999; Schneiderman, 1999).

Stress and Cancer

Stress and negative emotions such as anger and depression have also been linked to cancer's rate of progression. To explore a possible connection between stress and cancer, experimenters have implanted tumor cells into rodents or given them cancer-producing substances. Those rodents also exposed to uncontrollable stress, such as inescapable shocks, were more prone to cancer (Sklar & Anisman, 1981). With their immune systems weakened by stress, their tumors developed sooner and grew larger.

In people, some researchers have found no link between stress and cancer (Edelman & Kidman, 1997; Fox, 1998; Petticrew & others, 1999). Concentration camp and prisoner of war survivors, for example, have not exhibited elevated cancer rates. However, other investigators report that people are at increased risk for cancer within a year after experiencing depression, helplessness, or bereavement. For example, cancer occurs slightly more often than usual among those widowed, divorced, or separated. A study of the husbands of women with terminal breast cancer pinpointed a possible reason: During the first two months after their wives' deaths, the bereaved men's lymphocyte responses dropped (Schleifer & others, 1979).

Supporting survival
Can support groups delay the course of cancer? One experiment has suggested that they can. Other research, currently under way, will reveal whether this finding is replicable.

Another study gave a personality test to 2018 middle-aged men employed by the Western Electric Company in 1958. During the next 20 years, 7 percent of those with no symptoms of depression died of cancer, as did 12 percent of those who were somewhat depressed (Persky & others, 1987). A large Swedish study revealed that people with a history of workplace stress had 5.5 times greater risk of colon cancer than those who reported no such problems (Courtney & others, 1993). In both studies, the cancer difference was not attributable to differences in age, smoking, drinking, or physical characteristics.

In the first weeks after receiving their diagnosis, cancer patients understandably feel anxious and depressed (Andersen, 1989). Might promoting their fighting spirit aid their survival? Can hope boost the body by alleviating negative emotions that suppress the cancer-fighting immune system?

Although the jury is still out, some studies suggest that mastectomy patients who display a determination to conquer their breast cancer survive longer than do those who are stoic or feel hopeless (Hall & Goldstein, 1986; Pettingale & others,

"A cheerful heart is a good medicine, but a downcast spirit dries up the bones."

Proverbs 17:22

1985). What is more, in some studies, cancer patients who bottle up their negative emotions have had a somewhat lower chance of survival than those who verbalized their feelings (McKenna & others, 1999; O'Leary, 1990; Temoshok, 1992).

One danger in publicizing reports on attitudes and cancer is that they may lead some patients to blame themselves for their illness—"If only I had been more expressive, relaxed, and hopeful." A corollary danger is a "wellness macho" among the healthy, who credit their health to their healthy character and lay a guilt trip on the ill: "She has cancer? That's what you get for holding your feelings in and being so nice." Dying thus becomes the ultimate failure.

In noting the modest link between emotions and cancer prognosis, we must remember that stress does not create cancer cells. Rather, it affects their growth by weakening the body's natural defenses against a few proliferating, malignant cells. Although a relaxed, hopeful state may enhance these defenses, we should be aware of the thin line that divides science from wishful thinking. The physiological processes at work in advanced cancer or AIDS are not likely to be derailed by avoiding stress or by a relaxed but determined spirit (Kessler & others, 1991).

When organic causes of illness are unknown, it is tempting to invent psychological explanations. Before the germ that causes tuberculosis was discovered, personality explanations of TB were popular (Sontag, 1978).

Conditioning the Immune System

A hay fever sufferer sees the flower on the restaurant table and, not realizing it is plastic, begins to sneeze. Such experiences hint that stress is not the only psychological influence on the body's ailments. Simple classical conditioning may be an added influence. This raises an intriguing question: If conditioning affects the body's overt physiological responses, might it affect the immune system as well?

Psychologist Robert Ader and immunologist Nicholas Cohen (1985) discovered that the answer is yes. Ader came upon this discovery while researching taste aversion in rats. He paired the rats' drinking of saccharin-sweetened water with injections of a drug that happened to suppress immune functioning. After repeated pairings, sweetened water alone triggered immune suppression, as if the drug had been given (**FIGURE 51.8**). Such conditioned immune suppression can triple an animal's likelihood of growing a tumor when fed a carcinogen (Blom & others, 1995).

Many questions about the role of the immune system and ways to harness its healing potential remain unanswered. If it is possible to condition the immune system's suppression, should it not also be possible to condition its enhancement? Might this be one way in which placebos—treatments that have no biochemical effect—promote healing? Can a placebo sometimes elicit the same healthful state produced by an actual drug? Research now under way is hoping to answer such questions.

For now, we can view the toll that stress sometimes takes on our resistance to disease as a price we pay for the adaptive benefits of stress (**FIGURE 51.9**, page 642). Stress invigorates our lives by arousing and motivating us. An unstressed life would hardly be challenging or productive. Moreover, spending our resources in fighting or fleeing an external threat aids our immediate survival. But it does so at the cost of diminished resources for fighting internal threats to our body's health. When the stress is momentary, the cost is negligible. When uncontrollable aggravations persist, however, the cost may become considerable.

FIGURE 51.8 The conditioning of immune suppression
After Ader and Cohen (1985) associated sweetened water with a drug that causes immune suppression in rats, the inert substance alone triggered the conditioned immune response.

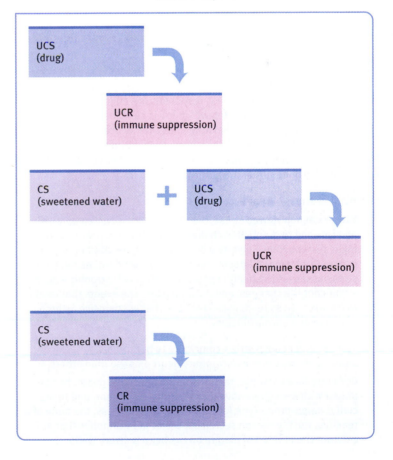

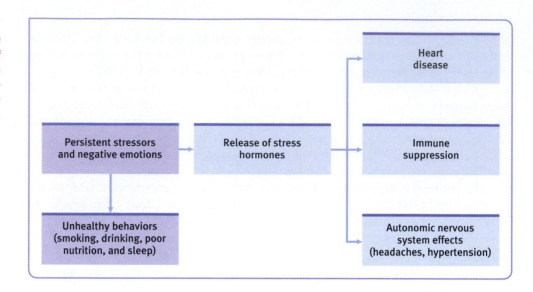

FIGURE 51.9

Negative emotions can have a variety of health-related consequences
This is especially so when experienced by "disease-prone" angry, depressed, or anxious persons.

This new behavioral medicine research provides yet another reminder of one of contemporary psychology's overriding themes. *Mind and body continuously interact. Everything psychological is simultaneously physiological.* Psychological states are physiological events that can influence other parts of our physiological system. Just pausing to *think* about biting into an orange section—the sweet, tangy juice from the pulpy fruit flooding across your tongue—can trigger salivation. As the Indian sage Santi Parva recognized more that 4000 years ago, "Mental disorders arise from physical causes, and likewise physical disorders arise from mental causes."

REVIEW AND REFLECT:

Stress and Illness

People's behaviors and stress responses are major influences on health and disease. Health psychology is contributing to the interdisciplinary field of behavioral medicine, which provides new avenues for the prevention and treatment of illness. Among health psychology's concerns are the effects of stress and the promotion of healthier living.

What is stress? What events tend to provoke stress responses?

Walter Cannon viewed stress, the process by which we appraise and respond to events that challenge or threaten us, as a fight-or-flight system. Hans Selye saw it as a three-stage (alarm-resistance-exhaustion) general adaptation syndrome. Modern research on stress assesses the health consequences of catastrophic events, significant life changes, and daily hassles. The events that tend to provoke stress responses are those that we perceive as both negative and uncontrollable.

To what extent does stress contribute to heart disease? Why are some of us more prone to coronary heart disease than others are?

Coronary heart disease, the number one cause of death, has been linked with the competitive, hard-driving, impatient, and (especially) anger-prone Type A personality. Under stress, the body of a reactive, hostile person secretes more of the hormones that accelerate the buildup of plaque on the heart's artery walls.

How does stress make us more vulnerable to disease?

Stress diverts energy from the immune system, making a person more vulnerable to infections and malignancy. Although stress does not cause diseases such as cancer, it may influence the disease's progression. Research indicates that conditioning also influences the immune system's responses.

Terms and Concepts to Remember

stress, p. 628
general adaptation syndrome (GAS), p. 630
health psychology, p. 631
behavioral medicine, p. 631
burnout, p. 633

coronary heart disease, p. 636
Type A, p. 636
Type B, p. 636
psychophysiological illness, p. 638
lymphocytes, p. 638

Test Yourself

51.1. The physiologist Walter Cannon described the role of the sympathetic nervous system in preparing the body for fight or flight. Hans Selye extended Cannon's findings by describing the body's adaptive response to stress in general. Selye's general adaptation syndrome (GAS) consists of an alarm reaction followed by

a. fight or flight.
b. resistance and exhaustion.
c. challenge and recovery.
d. stressful life events.

51.2. In the months following a catastrophe, such as an earthquake or a nuclear accident, there is a higher than usual number of short-term illnesses and stress-related psychological disorders. Following widowhood, there is an increased risk of illness and death. These findings suggest that

a. daily hassles have adverse health consequences.

b. experiencing a very stressful event increases one's vulnerability to illness and death.

c. the amount of stress felt is directly related to the number of stressors involved.

d. having a negative outlook has an adverse effect on recovery from illness.

51.3. Stressors are events that we appraise as threatening or challenging. Research suggests that the most significant sources of stress are

a. catastrophes.

b. traumatic events, such as the loss of a loved one.

c. daily hassles.

d. threatening events that we witness.

51.4. The stress we experience depends on how we perceive the events of our lives. A person (or animal) is most likely to find an event stressful and to suffer reduced immunity and other adverse health effects if the event seems

a. painful or harmful.

b. predictable and negative.

c. uncontrollable and negative.

d. both repellent and attractive.

51.5. Cardiologists Meyer Friedman, Ray Rosenman, and their colleagues observed that heart attacks were more frequent in Type A men—in those who appeared to be hard-driving, verbally aggressive, and anger-prone. The component of Type A behavior linked most closely to coronary heart disease is

a. living a fast-paced life-style.

b. working in a competitive area.

c. meeting deadlines and challenges.

d. feeling angry and negative much of the time.

51.6. Evidence suggests that disease-fighting mechanisms are weakened during times of high stress—for example, following the death of a loved one. Stress hormones suppress the lymphocytes, which ordinarily attack bacteria, viruses, cancer cells, and other foreign substances. The stress hormones are released mainly in response to a signal from the

a. lymphocytes and macrophages.

b. brain.

c. upper respiratory tract.

d. adrenal glands.

51.7. Research has shown people are at increased risk for cancer a year or so after experiencing depression, helplessness, or bereavement. In describing this link between emotions and cancer, researchers are quick to point out that

a. accumulated stress that is not relieved by positive emotions poses the greatest threat to people who are genetically vulnerable to cancer.

b. anger is the negative emotion most closely linked to cancer.

c. stress does not create cancer cells, but it weakens the body's natural defenses against them.

d. feeling optimistic about chances of survival ensures that a cancer patient will get well.

51.8. In testing taste aversion in rats, researchers paired the rats' drinking of saccharin-sweetened water with injections of a drug that suppressed immune functioning. After repeated pairings, sweetened water *alone* triggered immune suppression. These results suggest that

a. the immune system is under the direct control of the hypothalamus.

b. classical conditioning may influence the body's ailments.

c. placebos are as effective as actual drugs in treating the body's ailments.

d. external threats diminish our body's ability to fight internal threats.

Review: Describe our stress response system.

Reflect: What are the stresses of your own life? How intensely do you respond to them? Are there changes you could make to avoid the persistent stressors in your life?

Answers to the Test Yourself and Review questions can be found in the green appendix at the end of the book.

Promoting Health

Traditionally, people have sought out physicians for the diagnosis and treatment of disease. That, say health psychologists, is like ignoring a car's maintenance and going to a mechanic only when the car breaks down. Now that we realize that our attitudes and behaviors affect our health, attention is turning to health maintenance—on ways of coping with stress, preventing illness, and promoting well-being.

"Is there anyone here who specializes in stress management?"

Coping With Stress

Preview Question: What tactics can we use to reduce stress-related ailments?

Stressors are unavoidable. This fact, coupled with the growing awareness that recurring stress correlates with heart disease, lowered immunity, and other bodily ailments, gives us a clear message. If we cannot eliminate stress by changing or ignoring a situation, we had best learn to manage it—by confronting or escaping the problem and taking steps to prevent its recurrence. Stress management may include aerobic exercise, biofeedback, relaxation, and social support.

Aerobic Exercise

Aerobic exercise is sustained exercise that increases heart and lung fitness. Clearly, such exercise strengthens the body. Does it also boost the spirit?

Exercise and Mood

Many studies suggest that aerobic exercise can reduce stress, depression, and anxiety. One in 3 Americans and about 4 in 10 Canadians exercise regularly, and studies indicate that they also cope better with stressful events, exhibit more self-confidence, feel more vigor, and feel depressed and fatigued less often than those who exercise less (Brown, 1991; *Prevention*, 1995; Statistics Canada, 1999). But if we state this observation the other way around—that stressed and depressed people exercise less—cause and effect become unclear.

Experiments have resolved this ambiguity by randomly assigning stressed, depressed, or anxious people either to aerobic exercise or to other treatments. In one such experiment, Lisa McCann and David Holmes (1984) assigned one-third of a group of mildly depressed female college students to a program of aerobic exercise and another third to a treatment of relaxation exercises; the remaining third, a control group, received no treatment. As **FIGURE 52.1** shows, 10 weeks later the women in the aerobic exercise program reported the greatest decrease in depression. Many of them had, quite literally, run away from their troubles.

More than 100 other studies confirm that exercise reduces depression and anxiety (Craft & Landers, 1998; Long & van Stavel, 1995). Repeated surveys, some by government health agencies, reveal that Canadians and Americans are more self-confident, self-disciplined, and psychologically resilient if physically fit (Stephens, 1988). Just a 10-minute walk stimulates two hours of increased well-being by raising energy levels and lowering tension (Thayer, 1987, 1993).

The mood boost
Aerobic exercise, such as running, appears to counteract depression partly by increasing arousal (replacing depression's low-arousal state) and by doing naturally what Prozac does—increasing the brain's serotonin activity.

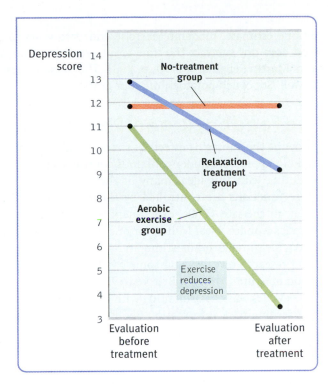

FIGURE 52.1
Aerobic exercise and depression
Mildly depressed college women who participated in an aerobic exercise program showed markedly reduced depression, compared with those who did relaxation exercises or received no treatment. (From McCann & Holmes, 1984.)

Researchers are now wondering *why* aerobic exercise alleviates the effects of stress and negative emotions. They know that exercise

+ strengthens the heart, increases blood flow, and lowers both blood pressure and the blood pressure reaction to stress (Perkins & others, 1986; Roviario & others, 1984).
+ orders up chemicals from our body's internal pharmacy by increasing production of mood-boosting neurotransmitters such as norepinephrine, serotonin, and the endorphins (Jacobs, 1994).
+ modestly enhances cognitive abilities, such as memory (Etnier & others, 1997).
+ promotes the growth of new brain cells in mice exercising daily on a running wheel regimen (Kempermann & Gage, 1999).

Perhaps the emotional benefits of exercise are also a side effect of increased body arousal and warmth or of the muscle relaxation and sounder sleep that occur afterward. Or perhaps a sense of accomplishment and an improved physique enhance one's emotional state.

Exercise and Health
Other research reveals that exercise not only boosts our mood, but also benefits our physical health.

+ One 16-year study of 17,000 middle-aged Harvard alumni found that those who exercised regularly were likely to live longer (Paffenbarger & others, 1986).
+ A study of 15,000 Control Data Corporation employees found that those who exercised had 25 percent fewer hospital days than those who didn't (Anderson & Jose, 1987).
+ A digest of data from 43 studies revealed that, compared with inactive adults, people who exercise suffer half as many heart attacks (Powell & others, 1987). Exercise makes the muscles hungry for the "bad fats" that contribute to clogged arteries (Barinaga, 1997).
+ A study following adult Finnish twins for nearly 20 years revealed that, other things being equal, occasional exercise reduced the risk of death by 29 percent, compared with no exercise. Daily conditioning exercise reduced death risk by 43 percent (Kujala & others, 1998).

■ **aerobic exercise** sustained exercise that increases heart and lung fitness; may also alleviate depression and anxiety.

■ **biofeedback** a system for electronically recording, amplifying, and feeding back information regarding a subtle physiological state, such as blood pressure or muscle tension.

By one estimate, moderate exercise adds two years to one's expected life. "Perhaps God does not subtract the time spent exercising from your allotted time on earth," jests Martin Seligman (1994, p. 193). The "mood boost" is reaping health dividends as well. So, couch potatoes, off your duffs!

Biofeedback and Relaxation

Knowing the damaging effects of stress, could we train people to bring their heart rate and blood pressure under conscious control? When a few psychologists started experimenting with this idea, many of their colleagues thought them foolish. After all, these functions are controlled by the autonomic ("involuntary") nervous system. Then, in the late 1960s, experiments by respected psychologists began to make the skeptics wonder. Neal Miller, for one, found that rats could modify their heartbeat if given pleasurable brain stimulation when their heartbeat increased or decreased. Later research revealed that some paralyzed humans could also learn to control their blood pressure (Miller & Brucker, 1979).

Miller was experimenting with **biofeedback**, a system of recording, amplifying, and feeding back information about subtle physiological responses. Biofeedback instruments have been likened to a mirror (Norris, 1986). The instruments no more control one's body than a mirror combs one's hair. Rather, by reflecting the results of a person's own efforts, they allow the person to assess which techniques are most effective in controlling a particular physiological response.

In the example in **FIGURE 52.2**, a sensor records tension in the forehead muscle of a person with chronic headaches. A computer processes this physiological information and instantly feeds it back to the person in some easily understood signal. As the person relaxes the forehead muscle, the pointer on the display screen (or a tone) may go lower. The patient's task is to learn to control the pointer or tone and thereby learn to control the tension in the forehead muscle and the accompanying headaches.

Initially, biofeedback researchers and practitioners reported that people could learn to increase their production of alpha brain waves, warm their hands, and lower their blood pressure—all signs of a more relaxed state. These reports triggered both excitement and some 4000 follow-up studies, including more than 400 in Russia (Sokhadze & Shtark, 1991). After a decade of study, researchers stepped back to assess the results and decided the initial claims for biofeedback were overblown and over-

FIGURE 52.2 Self monitoring Biofeedback systems—such as this one, which records tension in the forehead muscle of a headache sufferer—allow people to monitor their subtle physiological responses.

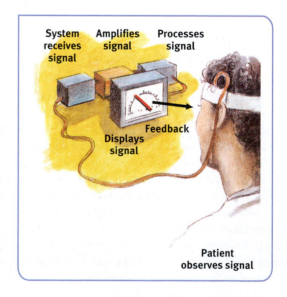

Learning the "relaxation response"
Relaxation training is a component of many stress-reduction programs. At Boston's Deaconess Hospital, hypertension patients learn meditation techniques that counteract stress.

sold (Miller, 1985). Biofeedback does enable some people to influence their finger temperature and forehead-muscle tension, and it can help somewhat in reducing the intensity of migraine headaches and chronic pain (King & Montgomery, 1980; Qualls & Sheehan, 1981; Turk & others, 1979). A 1995 National Institutes of Health panel declared that biofeedback works best on tension headaches. But other, simpler methods of relaxation, which require no expensive equipment, produce many of the same benefits.

If relaxation is an important part of biofeedback, then wouldn't relaxation exercises alone be a natural antidote for stress? Cardiologist Herbert Benson (1996) became intrigued with this possibility when he found that experienced meditators could decrease their blood pressure, heart rate, and oxygen consumption and raise their fingertip temperature. You can experience the essence of this *relaxation response*, as Benson calls it, right now: Assume a comfortable position, breathe deeply, and relax your muscles from foot to face. Now, concentrate on a single word or a phrase. (About 80 percent of Benson's patients choose to focus on a favorite prayer.) Close your eyes and let other thoughts drift away when they intrude as you repeat your phrase continually for 10 to 20 minutes.

Many of those who simply set aside a quiet time or two each day report enjoying the tranquility. Stress worsens pain, infertility, and insomnia, and it suppresses the immune system. Meditative relaxation counteracts all these effects, Benson reports. One astonishing study assigned 73 residents of homes for the elderly either to daily meditation or to none. After three years, one-fourth of the nonmeditators had died, while all the meditators were still alive (Alexander & others, 1989).

Another interesting study focused on Type A heart attack victims. If these competitive, hard-driving, impatient, and (especially) anger-prone people could be taught to relax, might their risk of another attack be reduced? To find out, Meyer Friedman and his colleagues randomly assigned hundreds of middle-aged heart attack survivors in San Francisco to one of two groups. The first group received standard advice from cardiologists concerning medications, diet, and exercise habits. The second group received similar advice plus continuing counseling on modifying their life-styles—how to slow down and relax by walking, talking, and eating more slowly; by smiling at others and laughing at themselves; by admitting mistakes; by taking time to enjoy life; and by renewing their religious faith. As **FIGURE 52.3** (page 648) indicates, during the ensuing three years, the second group experienced half as many repeat heart attacks as the first group. This, wrote the exuberant Friedman, is an unprecedented, spectacular reduction in heart attack recurrence. A smaller-scale British study similarly divided

Meditation is a modern phenomenon with a long history: "Sit down alone and in silence. Lower your head, shut your eyes, breathe out gently, and imagine yourself looking into your own heart. . . . As you breathe out, say 'Lord Jesus Christ, have mercy on me.'. . . Try to put all other thoughts aside. Be calm, be patient and repeat the process very frequently" (Gregory of Sinai, died 1346).

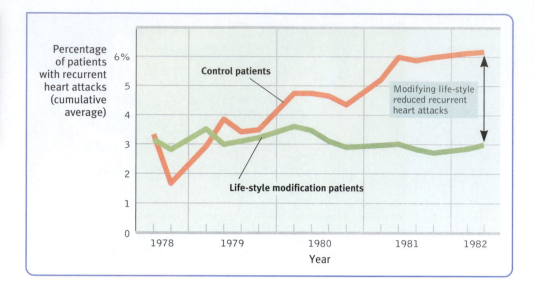

FIGURE 52.3 Recurrent heart attacks and life-style modification
The San Francisco Recurrent Coronary Prevention Project offered survivors of heart attacks counseling from a cardiologist. Those who were also guided in modifying their Type A life-style suffered fewer repeat heart attacks. (From Friedman & Ulme, 1984.)

heart-attack–prone people into control and life-style modification groups (Eysenck & Grossarth-Maticek, 1991). During the next 13 years, it also found a 50 percent reduction in death rate among those trained to alter their thinking and life-style.

Researchers are now seeking to identify which of Friedman's dozens of stress-reduction drills are beneficial. Even while Friedman was collecting his data, other investigators were studying specific stress buffers. For example, laughter seems to work in ways similar to exercise—it arouses us, massages muscles, and then leaves us feeling relaxed (Robinson, 1983). The "inner jogging" of hearty laughter exercises the muscles of the abdomen, diaphragm, shoulders, and face. This may help explain findings that stressful life events and even physical ailments, such as arthritis, are less disturbing to good-humored people (Lefcourt & Davidson-Katz, 1991; Nezu & others, 1988; Skevington & White, 1998). Although it would probably be an overstatement to suggest that "laughter is the best medicine," there is reason to suspect that those who laugh, last.

> "There ain't much fun in medicine, but there's a heck of a lot of medicine in fun."
>
> Humorist Josh Billings, 1818–1885

Social Support

Linda and Emily had much in common. When interviewed for a study conducted by UCLA social psychologist Shelley Taylor (1989), both Los Angeles women had married, raised three children, suffered comparable breast tumors, and recovered from surgery and six months of chemotherapy. But there was a difference. Linda, a widow in her early fifties, was living alone, her children scattered in Atlanta, Boston, and Europe. "She had become odd in ways that people sometimes do when they are isolated," reported Taylor. "Having no one with whom to share her thoughts on a daily basis, she unloaded them somewhat inappropriately with strangers, including our interviewer."

Interviewing Emily was difficult in a different way. Phone calls interrupted. Her children, all living nearby, were in and out of the house, dropping things off with a quick kiss. Her husband called from his office for a brief chat. Two dogs roamed the house, greeting visitors enthusiastically. All in all, Emily "seemed a serene and contented person, basking in the warmth of her family."

Three years later, the researchers tried to reinterview the women. Linda, they learned, had died two years before. Emily was still lovingly supported by her family and friends and was as happy and healthy as ever.

Because no two cancers are identical, we can't be certain that different social situations led to Linda's and Emily's fates. But they do illustrate a conclusion drawn

> Humans aren't the only source of stress-buffering comfort. After stressful events, Medicare patients who have a dog or other companionable pet are less likely to visit their doctor (Siegel, 1990).

from several large studies: Social support—feeling liked, affirmed, and encouraged by intimate friends and family—promotes not only happiness, but also health.

However, relationships can sometimes be stressful, especially in living conditions that are crowded and lack privacy (Evans & others, 1989). "Hell is others," wrote Jean-Paul Sartre. Peter Warr and Roy Payne (1982) at the University of Sheffield asked a representative sample of British adults what, if anything, had emotionally strained them the day before. Their most frequent answer? "Family." Even when well-meaning, family intrusions can be stressful. And stress, as we have seen, contributes to heart disease, hypertension, and a suppressed immune system.

On balance, however, close relationships more often contribute to health and happiness. Asked what prompted yesterday's times of pleasure, the same British sample, by an even larger margin, again answered, "Family." For most of us, family relationships provide not only our greatest heartaches but also our greatest comfort and joy. Moreover, seven massive investigations, each following thousands of people for several years, revealed that close relationships affect health. Compared with those having few social ties, people are less likely to die prematurely if supported by close relationships with friends, family, fellow workers, members of a religious group, or other support groups (Cohen, 1988; House & others, 1988; Nelson, 1988). Some additional examples:

+ In a study that followed leukemia patients preparing to undergo bone marrow transplants, only 20 percent of those who said they had little social support from their family or friends were still alive 2 years later. Among those who felt strong emotional support, the 2-year survival rate was 54 percent (Colon & others, 1991).
+ A study of 1234 heart attack patients found nearly a doubled rate of a recurring attack within 6 months among those living alone (Case & others, 1992).
+ A study of 1965 heart disease patients revealed a 5-year survival rate of 82 percent among those married or having a confidant, but only 50 percent among those having no one (Williams & others, 1992).
+ A 70-year study that followed 1528 California children with high IQ scores found that those whose parents did not divorce during their childhood outlived children of divorce by about 4 years (Schwartz & others, 1995). Controlling for the family's economic status and the child's personality did little to diminish the family-stability factor.

There are several possible reasons for the link between social support and health (Helgeson & others, 1998). Perhaps after symptoms appear family members who offer social support also help patients to receive medical treatment more quickly. Perhaps people eat better and exercise more because their partners guide and goad them into adhering to treatment regimens. Perhaps they smoke and drink less. One study following 50,000 young adults through time found that such unhealthy behaviors drop precipitously after marriage (Marano, 1998). Perhaps such relationships help us evaluate and overcome stressful events, such as social rejection. Perhaps they help bolster our self-esteem. When we are wounded by someone's dislike or by the loss of a job, a friend's advice, assistance, and reassurance may be good medicine (Cutrona, 1986; Rook, 1987).

Environments that support our need to belong also foster stronger immune functioning. Given ample social support, spouses of cancer patients exhibit stronger immune functioning (Baron & others, 1990). Social ties even confer resistance to cold viruses. Sheldon Cohen and his colleagues (1997) demonstrated this after putting 276 healthy volunteers in quarantine for five days after administering nasal drops laden with a cold virus. (The volunteers were paid $800 each to endure this experience.) The cold fact is that the effect of social ties is nothing to sneeze at. Age, race, sex, smoking, and other health habits being equal, those with the most social ties were least likely to catch a cold and they produced less mucus. More than 50

"Woe to one who is alone and falls and does not have another to help."

Ecclesiastes 4:10

"I get by with a little help from my friends."

John Lennon and Paul McCartney, *Sgt. Pepper's Lonely Hearts Club Band*, 1967

studies further reveal that social support calms the cardiovascular system, lowering blood pressure and stress hormones (Uchino & others, 1996, 1999).

Close relationships also provide the opportunity to *confide* painful feelings, a social support component that has now been extensively studied. In one study, health psychologists James Pennebaker and Robin O'Heeron (1984) contacted the surviving spouses of people who had committed suicide or died in car accidents. Those who bore their grief alone had more health problems than those who could express it openly. Talking about our troubles can be "open heart therapy." Older people, many of whom have lost a spouse and close friends, are somewhat less likely to enjoy such confiding (**FIGURE 52.4**).

Actively suppressing thoughts can cause them to bubble up intrusively, preoccupying the person (Wegner, 1990). Disclosing suppressed thoughts may stop the cycle. In a simulated confessional, Pennebaker asked volunteers to share with a hidden experimenter some upsetting events that had been preying on their minds. He asked some of the volunteers to describe a trivial event before they divulged the troubling one. Physiological measures revealed that their bodies remained tense the whole time they talked

about the trivial event; they relaxed only when they later confided the cause of their turmoil. Even writing about personal traumas in a diary can help. When volunteers in other experiments did this, they had fewer health problems during the ensuing four to six months (Pennebaker, 1990). As one subject explained, "Although I have not talked with anyone about what I wrote, I was finally able to deal with it, work through the pain instead of trying to block it out. Now it doesn't hurt to think about it." Even arthritis and asthma symptoms lessened after three periods of writing, but only when the writer recorded personal traumas rather than plans for the next day (Smyth & others, 1999).

Friendships are good medicine
Several long-term studies of thousands of people have found that individuals with close supportive relationships are less likely than socially isolated people to die prematurely.

Suppressed traumas sometimes eat away at us and affect our physical health. Consider:

+ When Pennebaker surveyed more than 700 undergraduate women, he found that about 1 in 12 reported a traumatic sexual experience in childhood. Compared with women who had experienced nonsexual traumas, such as parental death or divorce, the sexually abused women—especially those who had kept their secret to themselves—reported more headaches and stomach ailments.

FIGURE 52.4
Social support across the life span
Do you have someone you can confide in? Someone to count on in a crisis? Someone to count on for advice? Someone who makes you feel loved and cared for? In a national health survey, 9 in 10 young adult Canadians, but only 7 in 10 over the age of 75, indicated high social support by answering yes to all four questions (data from Statistics Canada, 1999, page 133).

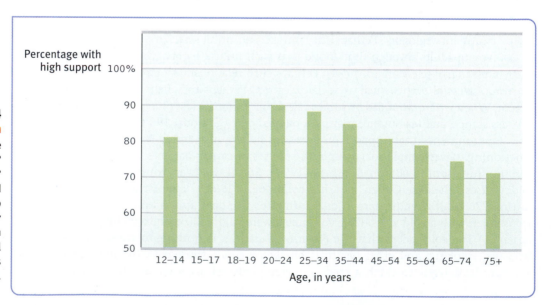

+ After the 1989 San Francisco Bay Area earthquake, residents talked nonstop about the upheaval for about two weeks. Then the talking died down as people tired of hearing others' opinions and feelings. ("Thank you for not sharing your earthquake experience," read one popular T-shirt.) But for another month people kept thinking about the quake. During this inhibition phase—when people kept ruminating but disclosed less of their anxieties and feelings—hostility, nightmares, and health problems peaked (Pennebaker & Harber, 1993).

+ Pennebaker and his colleagues (1989) also invited 33 Holocaust survivors to spend two hours recalling their experiences. Many did so in intimate detail never before disclosed. Most watched and showed family and friends a videotape of their recollections in the weeks following. Again, those who were most self-disclosing had the most improved health 14 months later. Talking about a stressful event can temporarily arouse people, but in the long run it calms them (Mendolia & Kleck, 1993). Confiding is good for the soul.

Sustained emotional reactions to stressful events can be debilitating. However, the level of stress experienced depends on the person and the environment. Nothing is stressful until we appraise it as such. Thus, when stressful things happen, our personalities and interpretations influence how we react emotionally. Moreover, the toxic impact of stressful events can be buffered by a relaxed, healthy life-style and by the comfort and aid provided by supportive friends and family (**FIGURE 52.5**).

Spirituality and Faith Communities

Throughout history, humans have suffered ills and sought healing. In response, the two healing traditions—religion and medicine—historically have joined hands in care of the sick. Religious and healing efforts were often conducted by the same person; the priest was also the healer. Maimonides was a twelfth-century rabbi and a renowned physician. Hospitals were first established in monasteries, then spread by missionaries.

As medical science matured, however, healing and religion diverged. Rather than simply asking God to spare their children from smallpox, people began vaccinating them. Rather than seeking a spiritual healer when burning with bacterial fever, they turned to antibiotics.

This wall between religion and medicine is now breaking down again. "Spirituality" has made a comeback. Pollster George Gallup (1994) detected "the search for spiritual moorings" as a "dominant trend" in the mid-1990s. Since 1995, Harvard Medical School has annually attracted nearly 2000 health professionals from across North America to its Spirituality and Healing in Medicine conferences. Duke University has established a Center for the Study of Religion/Spirituality and Health. And 61 of America's 126 medical schools were offering spirituality and health courses in 1999, up from 3 in 1994 (Levin & others, 1997; McVeigh, 1999). A Yankelovich survey found 94 percent of HMO professionals and 99 percent of family physicians agreeing that "personal prayer, meditation, or other spiritual and religious practices" can enhance medical treatment. This renewed convergence of religion and medicine was also evident in such books as *The Faith Factor* (Viking, 1998), *The Healing Power of Faith* (Simon & Schuster, 1999), and *Religion and Health* (Oxford University Press, 2000). *Time* magazine, not to be left out, devoted a 1996 cover story to "Faith and Healing."

FIGURE 52.5
Coping with stress
Life events can be debilitating or not. It all depends on how we appraise them and whether the stresses are buffered by a stress-resistant disposition, healthy habits, and enduring social support.

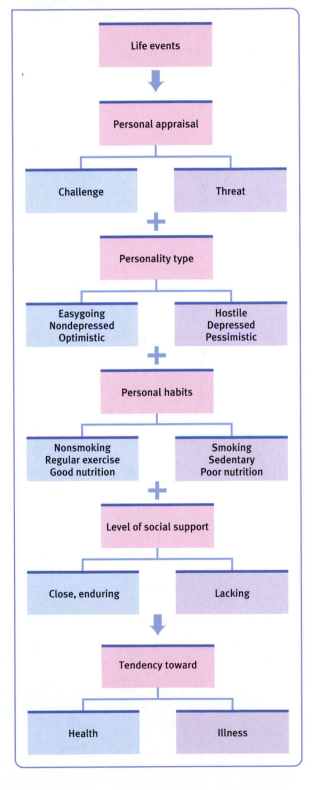

Alternative Medicine: New Ways to Health or Old Snake Oil?

One health care growth market is **complementary and alternative medicine**, which encompasses acupuncture, massage therapy, homeopathy, spiritual healing, herbal remedies, chiropractic, aromatherapy, and the like. In Germany, herbal remedies and homeopathy are enormously popular. In China, herbal therapies have long flourished, as have acupuncture and acupressure therapies that claim to correct "imbalances of energy flow" (called *Qi* or *Chi*) at identifiable points close to the skin. In the United Kingdom, sales of alternative medical remedies were predicted to double in the five years surrounding 2000 (Ernst, 1998). In the United States, Andrew Weil's eight books on alternative medicine have sold millions of copies, putting him on the cover of *Time* magazine and gaining his Web site a reported 2.5 million monthly hits (Relman, 1998). Facing political pressure to explore such things, the National Institutes of Health established the National Center for Complementary and Alternative Medicine, which the center defines as health care treatments not taught widely in medical schools, not used in hospitals, and not usually reimbursed by insurance companies (Table 52.1). Furthering the alternative medicine boom, Congress increased the center's funding from $20 million in 1998 to $50 million in 1999.

So what shall we make of alternative medicine? Some aspects, such as life-style and stress management, have acknowledged validity. Do the other aspects offer, as some believe, a new medical paradigm for a new millennium? Or do they represent, as others maintain, "voodoo medicine"—a retreat from rationality and science?

Supporters of alternative medicine offer inspirational cases, such as these from Andrew Weil's books (Relman, 1998):

+ A young woman diagnosed with bone cancer starts a vigorous exercise program (biking 500 miles and running 60 miles weekly), becomes vegetarian (consuming fresh fruit, juices, and whole grains), and shucks the alleged cancer.

+ A woman uses "respiratory biofeedback" to end her Parkinson's-induced seizures.

+ A man with scleroderma, a progressive and fatal disease of the skin and internal organs, cures himself with vinegar, lemons, aloe vera juice, and vitamin E.

But critics point out that people consult physicians for diagnosable, curable diseases and employ

> "Sickness is the manifestation of evil in the body."
>
> Andrew Weil, *Health and Healing*, 1998

TABLE 52.1

SUBFIELDS OF ALTERNATIVE MEDICINE

Alternative systems of medical practice	Health care ranging from self-care according to folk principles, to care rendered in an organized health care system based on alternative traditions or practices
Bioelectromagnetic applications	The study of how living organisms interact with electromagnetic (EM) fields
Diet, nutrition, life-style changes	The knowledge of how to prevent illness, maintain health, and reverse the effects of chronic disease through dietary or nutritional intervention
Herbal medicine	Employing plant and plant products from folk medicine traditions for pharmacological use
Manual healing	Using touch and manipulation with the hands as a diagnostic and therapeutic tool
Mind-body control	Exploring the mind's capacity to affect the body, based on traditional medical systems that make use of the interconnectedness of mind and body
Pharmacological and biological treatments	Drugs and vaccines not yet accepted by mainstream medicine

Source: Offered without endorsement by the National Center for Complementary and Alternative Medicine (nccam.nih.gov)

alternative medicine when they either are incurably ill or are basically well but feeling subpar. So an otherwise healthy person with a cold, for example, may try an herbal remedy and then credit the subsequent return to good health to alternative medicine, rather than to the body's natural regression to normal. Alternative medicine will seem especially effective with cyclical diseases, such as arthritis and allergies, as people seek therapy during the downturn and presume its effectiveness during the ensuing upturn. Add to this the healing power of belief—the placebo effect—plus the natural disappearance ("spontaneous remission") of many diseases, and voila: Alternative medicine practices are bound to seem effective, whether they are or not. In the 1700s, even bloodletting *seemed* effective. Sometimes people improved despite the treatment; when they did not, the practitioner inferred the disease was too far advanced to be reversed.

The National Council Against Health Fraud and the editors of leading medical journals and of the *Scientific Review of Alternative Medicine* doubt the efficacy of alternative medicine therapies. They note that for most alternative medicine claims the scientific jury is not out; it hasn't yet convened. Although the U.S. government's National Center for Complementary and Alternative Medicine is funding research, the 30 research grants it awarded in 1993 had, almost six years later, produced only four studies found among the 3500 medical journals—

and none of these controlled for placebo effects (Angell & Kassirer, 1998).

In November 1998, the *Journal of the American Medical Association* published seven new research studies. Three showed alternative medicine treatments to be useless (chiropractic manipulation for tension headaches, a popular herb for weight loss, and acupuncture to control nerve pain caused by HIV). Four other treatments—an herb mixture for inflammatory bowel syndrome, an herbal remedy for bladder problems, yoga for carpal tunnel syndrome pain, and a Chinese method for inducing fetuses in the breech position to turn—showed some benefits. Each now awaits replication, with new controls. As always, the way to discern what works and what does not is to experiment: Randomly assign patients to receive the therapy or a placebo control. Then ask the critical question: When neither the therapist nor the patient knows who is getting the real therapy, is the real therapy effective?

Much of today's mainstream medicine began as yesterday's alternative medicine, not all of which, like bloodletting, was refuted by controlled experiments. Natural botanical life has given us

"In God we trust. All others must have data."

George Lundberg, Editor, *Journal of the American Medical Association*, 1998

■ **complementary and alternative medicine** unproven health care treatments not taught widely in medical schools, not used in hospitals, and not usually reimbursed by insurance companies.

digitalis (from purple foxglove), morphine (from the opium poppy), and penicillin (from penicillium mold). In each case, the active ingredient was isolated, synthesized, and carefully verified in controlled trials. We have medical science, not alternative medicine, to thank for the antibiotics, vaccines, surgical procedures, and emergency medicine that helped lengthen our life expectancy by three decades during the last century. If you have acute chest pain, find a lump in your chest, cough up blood, or develop a high fever, you would do well to seek out someone trained in medical science—someone undergirded by research on what treatments really work best for what ailments at what doses for what lengths of time.

Indeed, said *New England Journal of Medicine* editors Marcia Angell and Jerome Kassirer (1998), "There cannot be two kinds of medicine—conventional and alternative. There is only medicine that has been adequately tested and medicine that has not, medicine that works and medicine that may or may not work. Once a treatment has been tested rigorously, it no longer matters whether it was considered alternative at the outset."

Is there fire underneath all this smoke? Do religion and spirituality actually relate to health, as polls show 4 in 5 Americans believe (Matthews, 1997)? More than a thousand studies have sought to correlate "the faith factor" with health and healing. Consider two:

+ Jeremy Kark and his colleagues (1996) compared the death rates for 3900 Israelis either in one of 11 religiously orthodox or in one of 11 matched, nonreligious collective settlements (kibbutz communities). The researchers reported that over a 16-year period, "belonging to a religious collective was associated with a strong protective effect" not explained by age or economic differences. In every age group, those belonging to the religious communities were about half as likely as their nonreligious counterparts to have died. This is roughly comparable to the gender difference in mortality. (In every age group, 64 British and 60 American women die for every 100 men [*Chance News*, 1997].)

+ An earlier study of 91,909 persons in one Maryland county found that those who attended religious services weekly were less likely to die during the study period than those who did not—53 percent less from coronary disease, 53 percent less due to suicide, and 74 percent less from cirrhosis of the liver (Comstock & Partridge, 1972).

In response to such findings, Richard Sloan and his skeptical colleagues (1999) remind us that mere correlations can leave many factors uncontrolled. Consider one obvious possibility: Women are more religiously active than men, and women outlive men. So perhaps religious involvement is merely an expression of the gender effect on longevity.

However, several new studies find the religiosity-longevity correlation among men alone, and even more strongly among women (McCullough & others, 2000). One study that followed 5286 Californians over 28 years found that, after controlling for age, gender, ethnicity, and education, frequent religious attendees were 36 percent less likely to have died in any year (**FIGURE 52.6**). Another followed 3968 elderly North Carolinians for 6 years. It found that 23 percent of those attending religious services at least weekly had died, as had 37 percent of infrequent attendees (Koenig & others, 1999). A National Health Interview Survey (Hummer & others, 1999) followed 21,204 people over 8 years. After controlling for age, sex, race, and region, researchers found that nonattenders were 1.87 times more likely to have died than were those attending more than weekly. This translated into a life expectancy at age 20 of 83 years for frequent attenders and 75 years for infrequent attenders (**FIGURE 52.7**)

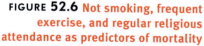

FIGURE 52.6 Not smoking, frequent exercise, and regular religious attendance as predictors of mortality
Epidemiologist William Strawbridge and his co-workers (1997, 1999) followed 5286 Alameda, California, adults over 28 years. After adjusting for age and education, the researchers found that not smoking, regular exercise, and religious attendance all predicted a lowered risk of death in any given year. Women attending weekly religious services, for example, were only 54 percent as likely to die in a typical study year as were nonattenders.

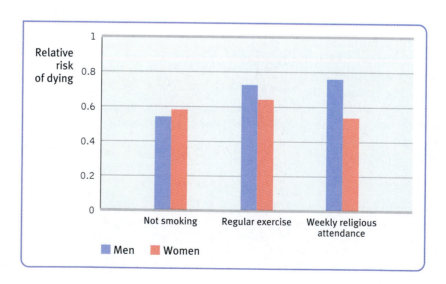

These correlational findings do not indicate that if nonattenders start attending, and change nothing else, they will live 8 years longer. But they do indicate that as a *predictor* of health and longevity, religious involvement rivals nonsmoking and exercise effects. Such findings demand explanation. Can you imagine what "intervening variables" might account for the correlation?

First, in all the available studies, the beliefs of religiously active people motivate healthier life-styles; for example, they smoke and drink less. Health-oriented, vegetarian Seventh Day Adventists have a longer-than-usual life expectancy (Berkel & de Waard, 1983). Religiously orthodox Israelis eat less fat than do their nonreligious compatriots. But such differences are not great enough to explain the dramatically reduced mortality in the religious kibbutzim, argued the Israeli researchers. In the recent American studies, too, about a 75 percent longevity difference remains after controlling for unhealthy behaviors such as inactivity and smoking (Musick & others, 1999).

Social support is another variable that helps explain the "faith factor." For Judaism, Christianity, and Islam, faith is not solo spirituality but a communal experience that helps satisfy the need to belong. The more than 350,000 faith communities in North America and the millions more elsewhere provide support networks for their active participants—people who are there for one another when stress strikes. Moreover, religion encourages another predictor of health and longevity—marriage. In the religious kibbutzim, for example, divorce is almost nonexistent.

But even after controlling for gender, unhealthy behaviors, social ties, and pre-existing health problems, the mortality studies find much of the mortality reduction remaining. Researchers therefore speculate that a third set of intervening variables is the stress protection and enhanced well-being associated with a coherent worldview, a sense of hope for the long-term future, feelings of ultimate acceptance, and the relaxed meditation of prayer or Sabbath observance (**FIGURE 52.8**). These variables might also help to explain other recent findings, such as healthier immune functioning and fewer hospital admissions among religiously active people (Koenig & Larson, 1998; Koenig & others, 1997).

Although the religion-health correlation is yet to be fully explained, Harold Pincus (1997), deputy medical director of the American Psychiatric Association, believes these findings "have made clear that anyone involved in providing health care services . . . cannot ignore . . . the important connections between spirituality, religion, and health."

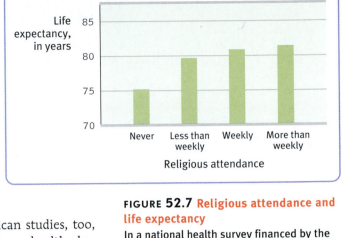

FIGURE 52.7 Religious attendance and life expectancy
In a national health survey financed by the Centers for Disease Control and Prevention, religiously active people had longer life expectancies. (Data from Hummer & others, 1999.)

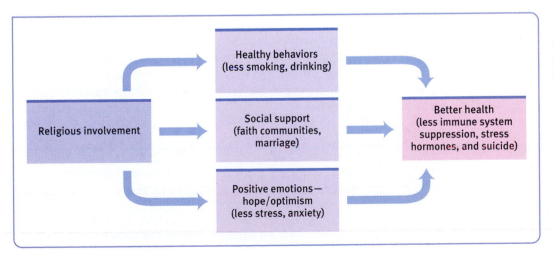

FIGURE 52.8
Possible explanations for the correlation between religious involvement and health/longevity
The religion factor is multidimensional.

Modifying Illness-Related Behaviors

Preview Questions: How can we modify health-destructive behaviors such as smoking? How effective are programs that aim to help people stop smoking or lose weight?

Researchers are persuaded that health-promotion programs cost far less than many countries now spend to treat diseases. With combined annual expenditures of more than $1 trillion (not counting lost workdays), Britain now spends 7 percent, Australia 8 percent, Canada 10 percent, and the United States 14 percent of gross domestic product on health care (Bureau of the Census, 1998). Moreover, among patients visiting their primary care physicians with such typical complaints as fatigue, headache, chest or abdominal pain, dizziness, constipation, and insomnia, fewer than 20 percent have a clear organic problem. Medical researchers presume many of these problems involve *psychosocial factors* (Kroenke & Mangelsdorff, 1989). It is clear that even modestly successful health-promotion programs could save more money than they cost.

In corporate organizations, such programs commonly provide health assessments and support fitness training, quitting smoking, and stress management. Because most employees are there five days per week, the workplace is an ideal location for the promotion of health and vitality. Employers can actively participate by encouraging healthy behaviors through social support, arranging for competition among work groups, and awarding bonuses or days off for sticking to an exercise or smoking-cessation regimen.

Are such programs effective? Several careful evaluations revealed that they can be. At Prudential Insurance Company, for example, a fitness program reduced sick days by 20 percent and major medical costs by 46 percent. The company actually saved $1.93 for every dollar it spent operating the program (Bowne & others, 1984). Control Data Corporation also found that its StayWell health program improved employee health and the company's balance sheet. Compared with other Control Data sites, sites that implemented the program reported decreases in smoking by 20 percent, in the number of overweight employees by 25 percent, and in the number of nonexercising employees by 32 percent—with corresponding reductions in health care claims and sick leave (Jose & Anderson, 1991). Other studies reveal decreases in seeking expensive medical care for minor illnesses, acute asthma, and arthritis (Sobel, 1993).

What makes health-promoting programs successful? Let's take a closer look at smoking, nutrition, and weight control.

Smoking

Imagine that cigarettes were harmless—except for an occasional innocent-looking one in every 50,000 packs that is filled with dynamite. Not such a bad risk of having your head blown off, you might say. But with 250 million packs a day consumed worldwide, we could expect more than 5000 gruesome deaths daily—surely enough to have cigarettes banned everywhere.[1]

Ironically, the lost lives from these dynamite-loaded cigarettes would be far less than from today's actual cigarettes. Each year throughout the world, tobacco kills some 3 million of its best customers. That is equivalent to 20 loaded jumbo jets daily (Peto & others, 1992, 1994). And the worst is yet to come. Given present trends, according to a 1994 report by the World Health Organization and a 1999 update, the

The United States spends nearly three times more per person on health care than does Great Britain (partly because the average income of a U.S. doctor is nearly four times that of a British doctor). In the United States, average life expectancy at birth is 76.1; in Britain it is 77.2 (Bureau of the Census, 1998).

Smokers repay society for the health, disability, and fire risk costs of their habit by dying earlier, which saves Social Security and retirement pension payments (Manning & others, 1989).

"There is an overwhelming medical and scientific consensus that cigarette smoking causes lung cancer, heart disease, emphysema, and other serious diseases in smokers. Smokers are far more likely to develop serious diseases, like lung cancer, than nonsmokers."

Philip Morris Companies Inc., 1999

---

[1]This analogy, adapted here with world-based numbers, was suggested by mathematician Sam Saunders, as reported by K. C. Cole (1998).

3 million annual deaths will soon grow to 10 million, meaning that *half a billion* people alive today will be killed by tobacco (Lopez, 1999). A teen-to-the-grave smoker has a 50 percent chance of dying from the habit, and the death is often agonizing and premature. Smoke a cigarette and nature will charge you 12 minutes—or 4 hours every pack—off your life expectancy (*Discover*, 1996). The elimination of smoking would do more to increase life expectancy than would any other preventive measure (**FIGURE 52.9**).

These facts are hardly secrets. A national survey of Canadian teens and adults found almost everyone agreeing that smoking is associated with lung cancer (97 percent), respiratory ailments (95 percent), and heart disease (94 percent) (Statistics Canada, 1999). In the United States, 96 percent of people (though only 58 percent of tobacco farmers) believe that "smoking is harmful to people" (Altman & others, 1997).

Nonsmokers not only live healthier, they live happier. Smoking correlates with higher rates of depression, chronic disabilities, and divorce (Doherty & Doherty, 1998; Vita & others, 1998). Healthy living seems to add both years to life and life to years.

When and Why Do People Start Smoking?

Smoking is a "pediatric disease." It usually begins during early adolescence and is especially common among those who get low grades, who drop out of school, who feel less competent and in control of their future, and whose friends, parents, and siblings smoke (Chassin & others, 1987; Schulenberg & others, 1994). If by now the cigarette manufacturers haven't attracted your business, the odds are overwhelming that they never will.

Social-cognitive theory, which explains how we learn behaviors through the models we imitate and the social rewards we receive, can help us understand an adolescent's vulnerability to the allure of smoking. Teenage smokers have traditionally been perceived as tough, precocious, and sociable (Barton & others, 1982). Indeed, teen smokers are a somewhat rebellious, risk-taking group. The National Center for Health Statistics (1995) reports they are twice as likely as nonsmokers to have had sex, three times as likely to drink alcohol, and 17 times more likely to use marijuana.

Adolescents are self-conscious and often think the world is watching their every move. So, they may begin smoking to imitate cool models, to get the social reward of being accepted by them, and to project a mature image (Covington & Omelich, 1988). Cigarette ads have effectively modeled smoking with youth-oriented themes: independence, adventure-seeking, social approval, sophistication—and no wonder, given that so many people decide on smoking and establish their brand loyalty during their teens. Typically, teens who start smoking also have friends who smoke, who suggest its pleasures, and who offer them cigarettes (Eiser, 1985; Evans & others, 1988; Rose & others, 1999). Among teens whose parents and best friends are nonsmokers, the smoking rate is close to zero (Moss & others, 1992).

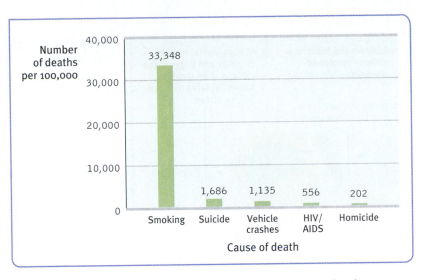

FIGURE 52.9 Premature deaths per 100,000 Canadians who were smoking by age 15

Smoking-related early deaths will eventually claim nine times more Canadian teen smokers than will suicide, car accidents, AIDS, and homicide combined (Statistics Canada, 1999).

Nic-a-teen

Aware that virtually all smokers start as teenagers—and that sales would plummet if no teens were enticed to smoke—cigarette companies target teens. By portraying tough, appealing, socially adept smokers, they entice teens to imitate. They are supported by the resurgence of Hollywood's modeling of smoking. With such stars as Vanessa Williams, Winona Rider, Sharon Stone, Bruce Willis, and Arnold Schwarzennegger all looking cool or rebellious while dragging on a cigarette or cigar, teens in the mid-1990s were getting the message and becoming addicted in increasing numbers.

A correlation–causation question: Does the close link between teen smoking and friends' smoking reflect peer influence? Teens seeking similar friends? Or both?

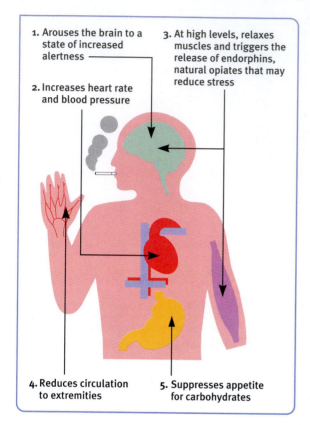

1. Arouses the brain to a state of increased alertness

2. Increases heart rate and blood pressure

3. At high levels, relaxes muscles and triggers the release of endorphins, natural opiates that may reduce stress

4. Reduces circulation to extremities

5. Suppresses appetite for carbohydrates

FIGURE 52.10 **Where there's smoke . . . : the physiological effects of nicotine**
Nicotine reaches the brain within 7 seconds, twice as fast as intravenous heroin. Within minutes, the amount in the blood soars.

Why Do People Not Stop Smoking?

Three in four have tried (Niemi & others, 1989). However, once addicted to nicotine we find it very hard to quit. Tobacco products are as addictive as heroin and cocaine. Indeed, some who have kicked the heroin habit have been unable to also stop smoking. Surveys in Britain and the United States show that at least 1 in 3 of those who try cigarettes become hooked—a higher addiction rate than for heroin and cocaine (Heishman & others, 1997).

As with other addictions, the smoker becomes *dependent*; each year fewer than 1 of every 7 smokers who want to quit will do so. A smoker also develops *tolerance*, eventually needing larger and larger doses to get the same effect. A sad irony is that those who are initially most sensitive to nicotine—and most likely to feel sick or dizzy on first smoking—tend to develop a tolerance quickly and to become most strongly addicted (Pomerleau & others, 1993). Quitting causes *withdrawal* symptoms. Craving, insomnia, anxiety, and irritability all accompany nicotine withdrawal. And all it takes to relieve these aversive states is a cigarette (**FIGURE 52.10**). For those who endure, the acute craving and withdrawal symptoms of the first week or two gradually dissipate over the ensuing six months (Ward & others, 1997).

As with all addictive drugs, nicotine use is not only compulsive and mood-altering, it is also reinforcing. After an hour or a day without smoking, the habitual smoker finds a cigarette—a portable nicotine dispenser—powerfully reinforcing. Even if given low-nicotine cigarettes, the smoker will end up smoking more of them to maintain a roughly constant level of nicotine in the blood.

Smoking reinforces smoking by both terminating the aversive craving and offering a pleasurable lift. Nicotine triggers the release of epinephrine and norepinephrine, which in turn diminish appetite and boost alertness and mental efficiency. More importantly, nicotine also stimulates the central nervous system to release neurotransmitters that calm anxiety and reduce sensitivity to pain. For example, nicotine, like cocaine, increases dopamine—cocaine by blocking its reuptake, nicotine by stimulating its release (Nowak, 1994). Therefore, people who are anxious or depressed often find it especially hard to forgo smoking's rewards (Mansnerus, 1992). Over time, smokers who are abstaining feel increasing tension and stress, which a cigarette temporarily relieves (Parrott, 1999). These rewards keep people smoking even when they wish they could stop—indeed, even when they know they are committing slow-motion suicide.

Consistent with the bio-psycho-social perspective, genes also influence one's propensity to cigarette addiction. A meta-analysis of twin studies indicates a 60 percent heritability (Heath & Madden, 1995). Two recent studies have further discovered that smokers and nonsmokers tend to differ in a gene that influences responses to the neurotransmitter dopamine (Lerman & others, 1999; Sabol & others, 1999).

How Effective Are Programs to Stop Smoking?

The efforts to help people stop smoking include public health warnings, counseling, drug treatments, hypnosis, aversive conditioning (for example, having people sicken themselves by rapidly smoking cigarette after cigarette), operant conditioning, cognitive therapy, and support groups. In the short run, these treatments are often effective. But the bad news is that all but one-fifth of the participants eventually succumb to the habit again (Schelling, 1992). For those quitting solo, the odds are even less. With a pack of cigarettes seldom more than minutes away, a single moment of weakness can be enough to break the resolve.

Better news comes from a Centers for Disease Control report that half of Americans who have ever smoked have quit. More than 90 percent did so on their own, often after repeated attempts. Because so many people have stopped or not started

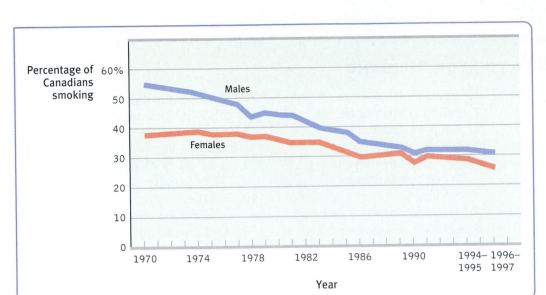

FIGURE 52.11

Fewer Canadian smokers
From 1970 to 1990, Canadian smoking rates among people 15 years of age or older fell sharply, especially for males (Statistics Canada, 1999).

smoking, the percentage of Americans who smoke is down to 25 percent, well below the 42 percent rate in 1965. In Canada, too, smoking has declined sharply (**FIGURE 52.11**). Most public places are no longer aswirl with tobacco smoke.

Still, among high school dropouts and those of lower socioeconomic levels, smoking rates remain higher. But among college students and graduates, smoking has become gauche rather than cool; in the United States, nearly 9 in 10 are non-smokers. In Canada, 30 percent of those not completing high school but only 15 percent of university-educated people light up within 5 minutes of waking (Statistics Canada, 1999). The drop has been most pronounced in the male smoking rate, which now barely exceeds that of women. Thanks in part to such trends, the death rate due to coronary heart disease has declined by about 30 percent since the mid-1960s. Smoking-related cancer deaths have also been declining, especially among men (Wingo & others, 1999).

For the tobacco industry, the news is not all bad. Smoking rebounded among U.S. teens during the mid-1990s (**FIGURE 52.12**), and a similar comeback occurred among Canadian teens (Brooke, 2000). And despite the declining cigarette sales among educated adults in Western countries and the new restrictions on cigarette advertising, sales, and smoking, per-person cigarette consumption worldwide is near an all-time high.

Smoking has skyrocketed in Asia. In China, where 7 in 10 men but no more than 1 in 10 women smoke, cigarette consumption has soared from 100 billion cigarettes a year in the early 1950s to 1.8 trillion today (McDonald, 1997; Schwartz & Pomfret, 1998). In Japan, 35 percent (50 percent of men) are smokers (Coleman, 1997). And countries like Kenya and Zimbabwe, with their relatively low per-person consumption rates, are developing markets. In other developing countries where smoking is also on the increase, British and U.S. tobacco companies are more than making up for declining domestic consumption (Shenon, 1994). In so doing, they are putting hundreds of millions of unsuspecting people at risk for ill health and premature death. The World Health Organization predicts that in the next three decades, 70 percent of tobacco-related deaths will occur in developing countries where many people are unaware of the dangers of smoking (Lopez, 1999; Schwartz & Pomfret, 1998).

In 1998, 5.61 trillion cigarettes were sold worldwide.

FIGURE 52.12

U.S. teen smoking comeback
Adult smoking has dropped sharply over the last quarter-century, especially among educated people, but smoking has made a partial comeback among U.S. teens. (Data from Johnston & others, 1999.) A similar 1990s smoking comeback occurred among Canadian teens (Brooke, 2000).

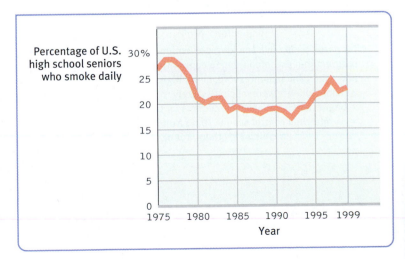

CLOSE-UP:

FOR THOSE WHO WANT TO STOP SMOKING

Would you, or someone you love, like to stop smoking? Most smokers want to quit, and nearly half try each year, but fewer than 1 in 7 permanently succeed, reports an expert panel appointed by the U.S. Agency for Health Care Policy and Research. The panel's smoking-cessation guidelines do, however, offer some helpful pointers (Wetter & others, 1998).

1. Set a quit date.
2. Inform family and friends.
3. Remove all cigarettes.
4. Review things you learned from previous attempts to quit and anticipate challenges.
5. Use a nicotine patch or gum.
6. Be totally abstinent—not even a single puff.
7. Abstain from or greatly limit alcohol (which facilitates relapse).
8. If other smokers live or work with you, quit together.
9. Avoid places where others are likely to smoke.
10. Exercise. In recent experiments, quitters assigned to regular exercise have had higher success rates (Bock & others, 1999).

How Can We Prevent Smoking?

It is vastly easier never to begin smoking than to stop once addicted. Drawing on social psychological analyses of why youngsters start smoking, several research teams have devised strategies for averting the behavior patterns that lead to smoking (Evans & others, 1984; Murray & others, 1984). In one such study, a research team led by Alfred McAlister (1980) had high school students "inoculate" seventh-graders (13-year-olds) against peer pressure to smoke. The older peers taught the youngsters to respond to ads implying that liberated women smoke by saying, "She's not really liberated if she is hooked on tobacco." They also role-played calling someone a "chicken" for not trying a cigarette and responding with statements like, "I'd be a real chicken if I smoked just to impress you." After several sessions during the seventh and eighth grades, the "inoculated" students were only half as likely to begin smoking as were their noninoculated counterparts at a neighboring school, even though the parents of both sets of students had the same smoking rate (**FIGURE 52.13**).

This experiment as well as others like it have generated curricular programs that teachers can implement easily and inexpensively. According to a National Cancer Institute panel, the key ingredients of such programs are information about the effects of smoking; information about peer, parent, and media influences; and training in refusal skills, through modeling and role playing. The informational ingredients can

FIGURE 52.13
Results of a smoking "inoculation" program
After participating in a smoking-prevention program that prepared them to cope with smoking ads and peer pressure, junior high school students were much less likely to begin smoking than were students at a matched control school. (Data from McAlister & others, 1980).

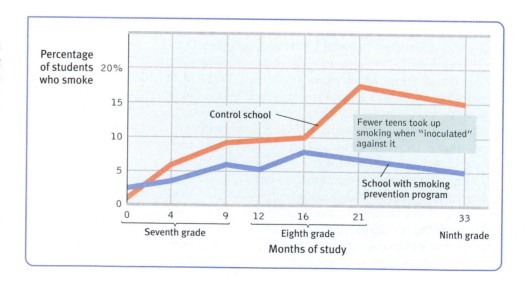

also be offered through the mass media, which Australia has effectively used to discourage smoking across educational levels (Macaskill & others, 1992). In 1998, Florida initiated a massive youth-oriented media campaign to reduce the allure of smoking—and by early 1999 the number of 12- to 14-year-olds who reported smoking had dropped 19 percent from those of the previous year (*MMWR*, 1999).

To be permanently effective, smoking-prevention programs may require follow-up booster sessions in later years (Murray & others, 1989). Nevertheless, the plummeting overall rate of smoking suggests that such programs are succeeding.

There is one other way to discourage smoking: Make it more immediately costly. Operant conditioning principles tell us that the most effective rewards and punishments are immediate. When the delayed rewards of exercise compete with the immediate discomfort of doing so, the immediate consequences often win out. Likewise, even *knowing* that in the long run smoking is often suicidal, many continue to smoke. If we could only raise the immediate costs, consumption would surely decline. For example, raising cigarette taxes (and therefore prices) cuts consumption—by about 4 percent for each 10 percent rise, according to the Centers for Disease Control (Brown & others, 1993). The effect is even greater among teenagers—the age when 90 percent of smokers start their habit.

Effective prevention

The state of Florida directed a huge, youth-oriented 1998 anti-smoking campaign, which produced reduced rates of smoking in teens by 1999.

Nutrition

Does the saying "You are what you eat" hold some truth? The discovery that specific neurotransmitters affect emotion and behavior has definitely fueled speculation: Might eating foods that provide the biochemical building blocks for those neurotransmitters affect our mood and behavior?

For example: The body synthesizes the neurotransmitter serotonin from the amino acid tryptophan. Several studies have found that high-carbohydrate foods (such as bread, potatoes, and pasta) increase the relative amount of tryptophan reaching the brain via the bloodstream. That, in turn, raises the level of serotonin, which makes us feel relaxed, sleepy, and less sensitive to pain. And that helps explain why people feeling tense or in a bad mood, including those on nicotine withdrawal, often snack on carbohydrate-rich foods for a mood lift (Christensen, 1993, 1996). And when we instead desire food for thought, a high-protein meal improves our concentration and alertness. Deprived of adequate protein, malnourished young children may suffer enduring cognitive deficits (Lozoff, 1989).

Other nutritional issues are also generating vigorous research and debate:

+ **Are children hyped by a diet high in sugar and calmed by one that is low in sugar?** Researchers doubt this folk wisdom (Spring & others, 1987). They have, however, found that well-nourished children are more active and happy at play (Espinoza & others, 1992). Moreover, nutritionally empty sugar calories added to cereal, fruit drinks, soft drinks, yogurt, and the like—accounting for a huge increase in sugar consumption over the last quarter-century—displace more nutritious foods. The result is not only tooth decay but also increased risk of osteoporosis, cancer, diabetes, high blood pressure, and heart disease (Brody, 1999). A sweet tooth contributes to sour health.
+ **What are the links between diet and high blood pressure?** Hypertensive people tend to have a higher than normal salt intake and a lower than normal calcium intake (Feinleib & others, 1984; McCarron & others, 1984).
+ **Does skipping breakfast matter?** Three studies by Bonnie Spring and her colleagues (1992) suggest it does. Those who eat a balanced breakfast are, by late morning, more alert and less fatigued.

Percentage of Canadians regarding nutrition as "very" or "extremely" important in choosing foods (Statistics Canada, 1999):

Males	41%
Females	73%

✛ ***Do some nutrients reduce depression?*** Depressed patients have recently been observed to have lower levels in their diet and blood of a "good" fat, omega-3 fatty acid, believed to enhance brain function (Edwards & others, 1998; Maes & others, 1999). Countries such as Japan where people eat omega-3–rich fish tend to have low depression rates (Hibbeln, 1998). Future research may determine whether eating more fish, walnuts, and other foods rich in omega-3 supports mental health.

As debate continues on these issues, other researchers are working on a problem that now affects millions.

Obesity and Weight Control

People wonder: Why do some people gain weight while others eat the same amount and seldom add a pound? And why do so few overweight people win the battle of the bulge? What hope is there for the one American in three who is, according to the National Center for Health Statistics, overweight?

First, the good news about fat. It is an ideal form of stored energy that provides the body with a high-caloric fuel reserve to carry it through periods when food is scarce—a common occurrence in the feast-or-famine existence of our prehistoric ancestors. Eating three or more meals every day is actually a relatively recent phenomenon and a luxury hundreds of millions of people still do not enjoy. In circumstances of alternating feast and famine, overeating and storing the excess as fat is adaptive; it prepares the body to withstand famine. Think of that spare tire around the middle as an energy storehouse—biology's counterpart to a hiker's waist-borne snack pack. This may explain why in most developing societies today, as in Europe in earlier centuries—in fact, wherever people face famine—obesity is a sign of affluence and social status (Furnham & Baguma, 1994).

Cultures without a thin-ideal for women are also cultures without eating disorders. For example, Ghanians idealize a larger body size than do Americans—and experience fewer eating disorders (Cogan & others, 1996). The same is true of African-American women compared with European-American women (Parker & others, 1995).

The bad news is that in those parts of the world where food and sweets are now abundantly available, the adaptive tendency to store fat has become maladaptive. Being slightly overweight poses no health risks (Ernsberger & Koletsky, 1999; Miller, 1999). Fitness matters more than being a little overweight. But the National Institutes of Health reports that significant obesity increases the risk of diabetes, high blood pressure and heart disease, gallstones, arthritis, sleep disorders, and certain types of cancer. This is more true for apple-shaped people who carry their weight in pot bellies than for pear-shaped people with ample hips and thighs (Greenwood, 1989).

Not surprisingly, then, a massive recent study—following more than 1 million Americans over 14 years—revealed that being signficantly overweight can cut life short (Calle & others, 1999). This was especially true for white men: White men with the highest body mass index (BMI) were 2 to 6 times more likely to have died than were those with a BMI of 24. The heaviest white women were twice as likely to have died as those with a BMI of 23, while the heaviest black men and women had lower relative risks of death (1.4 and 1.2) than their counterparts who were not significantly overweight. For all men and women, being moderately over or under normal weight was less of a risk factor (**FIGURE 52.14**).

Obesity is not just a threat to physical health. Being perceived as obese can affect both how you are treated and how you feel about yourself. People often stereo-

Rubens' *The Garden of Love*
In other times and places, fatter bodies have been idealized.

Government guidelines encourage a body mass index (BMI) under 25.

$$BMI = \frac{\text{weight in kg (pounds x .45)}}{\text{squared height in meters (inches divided by 39.4)}}$$

The World Health Organization and many countries define obesity as a BMI of 30 or more.

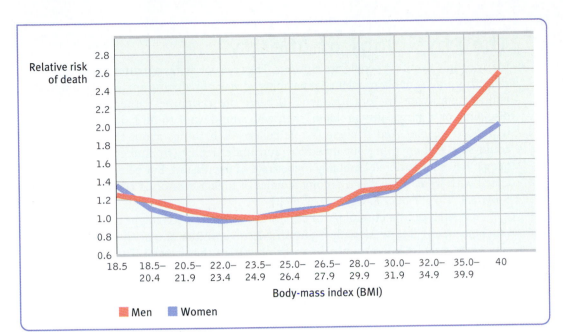

FIGURE **52.14**
Obesity and mortality
Relative risk of death among healthy nonsmokers rises with extremely high or low body mass index. (Data from 14-year study of 1.05 million Americans; Calle & others, 1999.)

type anyone who is obese as slow, lazy, and sloppy (Crandall, 1994, 1995; Ryckman & others, 1989). Widen people's images on a video monitor (making them look fatter) and they suddenly seem less sincere, less friendly, meaner, and more obnoxious (Gardner & Tockerman, 1994). Curiously, black women are less denigrating of large black women than white women are of large white women (Hebl & Heatherton, 1998).

Obese people—sometimes victims of ridicule and job discrimination—know the stereotype. In studies of patients who were especially unhappy with their weight—those who had lost an average of 100 pounds after short-cutting digestion with intestinal bypass surgery—4 in 5 said their children had asked them not to attend school functions. Nine in 10 said they would rather have a leg amputated than be obese again (Rand & Macgregor, 1990, 1991). As the parents of Samuel Graham—5 feet 4 inches and weighing 174 pounds—can testify, overweight children suffer, too. No longer able to bear classmates' taunts about his weight, Samuel, age 12, hanged himself (Cogan & Ernsberger, 1999).

The social effects of obesity were clear in a study that followed 370 obese 16- to 24-year-old women (Gortmaker & others, 1993). When restudied seven years later, two-thirds of the women were still obese. They also were less likely to be married, and they were making less money than a comparison group of some 5000 other women. Even after correcting for aptitude test scores, race, and parental income, the obese women's incomes were $7000 a year below average.

In one clever experiment, Regina Pingitore and her colleagues (1994) videotaped job interviews in which professional actors appeared as either normal-weight or overweight applicants. In one condition, they wore makeup and prostheses that made them look 30 pounds heavier. When appearing overweight, the same person, using the same lines, intonation, and gestures, was rated as less worthy of hiring. The weight bias was especially strong against women applicants (**FIGURE 52.15**). Other studies reveal that weight discrimination is greater than race and gender discrimination, and that it occurs at every stage of the employment cycle—hiring, placement, promotion, compensation, discipline, and discharge (Roehling, 2000).

FIGURE **52.15**
Gender and weight discrimination
When women applicants were made to look overweight, university students were less willing to think they would hire them. Among men applicants, weight mattered less. (Data from Pingitore & others, 1994.)

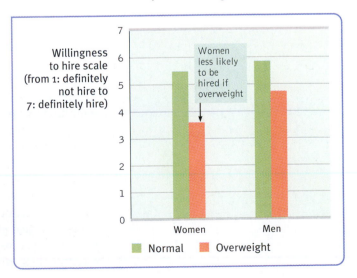

The Physiology of Obesity

Many people think fat people are gluttons. They see obesity as a matter of choice or as reflecting a personality problem—a maladjusted way of reducing anxiety, dealing with guilt, or gratifying an "oral fixation." If being obese signifies either a lack of self-discipline or a personality problem, then who would want to hire, date, or associate with such people? And if obese people believe such things about themselves, how could they feel anything but unworthy and undesirable? (In studies to date, obese people have not suffered a notably higher rate of depression, but being heavy is associated with lower self-esteem among females of higher economic class [Friedman & Brownell, 1995; Miller & Downey, 1999].)

Research on the physiology of obesity challenges the stereotype of severely overweight people being weak-willed gluttons. First, consider the arithmetic of weight gain: People get fat by consuming more calories than they expend. The energy equivalent of a pound of fat is 3500 calories; therefore, dieters have been told they will lose a pound for every 3500-calorie reduction in their diet. Surprise: This conclusion is false. Why? The answer lies in the physiology of fat.

Fat Cells

The immediate determinants of body fat are the size and number of fat cells. A typical adult has about 30 billion of these miniature fuel tanks, half of which lie near the skin's surface. A fat cell can vary from relatively empty, like a deflated balloon, to overly full. In an obese person, fat cells may swell to two or three times their normal size and then divide. Once the number of fat cells increases—due to genetic predisposition, early childhood eating patterns, or adult overeating—it never decreases. Fat cells may shrink on a diet, but they never disappear (Sjöstrom, 1980).

This unyielding nature of our fat cells is but one way, once we become fat, our bodies maintain fat. Another way is that fat tissue has a low metabolic (energy expenditure) rate. Compared with other tissue, fat takes less food energy to maintain. Thus, once we become fat, we require less food to maintain our weight than we did to attain it.

Set Points and Metabolism

There is another reason why most obese people find it so difficult to lose weight permanently. Their bodies' "weight thermostats" are set to maintain body weight within a higher-than-average range. When their weight drops below the set-point range, their hunger increases and metabolism decreases.

As many a dieter can testify, the drop in resting metabolic rate can be particularly frustrating. After the rapid weight losses that occur during the initial three weeks or so of a rigorous diet, any further weight loss comes slowly. In a classic experiment (Bray, 1969), obese patients whose daily food intake was reduced from 3500 to 450 calories lost only 6 percent of their weight—partly because their metabolic rates dropped about 15 percent (**FIGURE 52.16**). Thus, the body adapts to starvation by burning off fewer calories, and to extra calories by burning off more. That is why reducing your food intake by 3500 calories may not reduce your weight by 1 pound. And that is why when a diet ends and the body is still conserving energy, amounts of food that worked to maintain weight before the diet may now increase it.

Individual differences in resting metabolism explain why—contrary to the stereotype of the overweight glutton—it is possible for two people of the same height, age, and activity level to maintain the same weight, even if one of them eats much more than the other does. Or why it is possible for a person to eat less than another similarly active person, yet weigh more. This appears true despite findings that people—obese people, especially—tend to overestimate their physical activity and underestimate their caloric intake (Brownell & Wadden, 1992; Lichtman & others, 1992).

Caloric intake in calories per day

3000

2000

1000

0

Calorie intake plunges

8   16   24   32
Days

Body weight in kilograms

165

160

155

150

145

140

Weight drops a little but then levels off

8   16   24   32
Days

Metabolism: Oxygen consumption in liters per hour

26

25

24

23

22

21

A sharp drop in metabolism is responsible for the limited weight loss

8   16   24   32
Days

The Genetic Factor

Studies of adoptees and twins reveal a genetic influence on body weight. Consider:

+ Despite shared family meals, the body weights of adoptive siblings are uncorrelated with one another and with those of their adoptive parents. Rather, people's weights resemble those of their biological parents (Grilo & Pogue-Geile, 1991).

+ Identical twins have closely similar weights, even when reared apart (Plomin & others, 1997; Stunkard & others, 1990). Across studies, their weight correlates .74. The much lower .32 correlation among fraternal twins suggests that genes explain two-thirds of our varying BMI (Maes & others, 1997). Being overweight is therefore *not* simply a matter of scarfing too many hot fudge sundaes. And losing weight is not merely a matter of mind over platter.

The genetic influence is surely complex, with some genes influencing when our intestines signal "full," others dictating how efficiently we burn calories or convert extra calories to fat, or how much we fidget. But recent experiments do reveal one genetic mechanism for weight control. As a normal mouse's fat cells become bloated, its genes produce leptin, a protein that is monitored by the brain. When researchers injected obese mice with daily doses of leptin, the mice then ate less, became more active, and lost weight. So, might injections of leptin similarly serve as virtual fat for humans, fooling the brain into making a fat body trimmer? Or, as newer research suggests, are the leptin receptors of obese humans insensitive to leptin (Considine & others, 1996)? If so, might a slightly different drug be designed that activates insensitive leptin receptors? Or might we look forward to a drug that blocks hypothalamic receptors that activate eating (Gerald & others, 1996)? Given the huge potential market for such drugs, the race to define them is on.

Genes aren't the whole story behind obesity, however. Genes cannot explain why obesity is six times more common among lower-class than among upper-class women, more common among Americans than among Europeans, and more common among Americans today than in 1900. Exercise and diet—Big

FIGURE 52.16

The effects of a severe diet on obese patients' body weight and metabolism

After seven days on a 3500-calorie diet, six obese patients were given only 450 calories a day for the next 24 days. Body weight declined only 6 percent and then leveled off, because metabolism dropped about 15 percent. (From Bray, 1969.)

Fat-signaling hormone

The obese mouse at left has a defective gene for producing the fat-signaling hormone, leptin. When the genetically similar mouse at right was treated with leptin, it shed 40 percent of its body weight.

In Britain, as elsewhere, not all pounds are sterling
We humans were not designed for a world filled with energy-saving cars and tools, and high-calorie foods. In hunting and gathering societies, obesity is almost unknown (Brown, 1993).

Gulps, Double Whoppers, and Frosted Flakes—can. Compared with their counterparts in the early 1900s, people are eating a higher-fat, higher-sugar diet, expending fewer calories, and suffering more diabetes at younger ages (Thompson, 1998).

Across the developed world, the increase in population pudginess has accelerated. In Britain, the average woman's dress size has increased from size 12 in 1951 to size 16 today (Merriman, 1999). And so it goes, pretty much everywhere this book is being read. As recently as 1960, 43 percent of Americans were classified as overweight, with a BMI of 25 or over; today 55 percent are, and nearly twice as many—23 percent—are obese, at a BMI of 30 or more (Flegal & others, 1998; NIH, 1998). Australia, too, classifies 55 percent of its population as overweight (Australian Bureau of Statistics, 1999). In Canada, the proportion of people classified as overweight has increased by 60 percent since 1985 (Statistics Canada, 1999). Public seating is now expanding to accommodate this population growth. As the century turned, airlines and theaters were offering wider seats for today's wider bodies. The Washington State Ferries abandoned its 50-year-old standard of 18 inches per person. "Eighteen-inch butts are a thing of the past," explained a spokesperson (Shepherd, 1999).

Note how these findings reinforce a familiar lesson: There can be high levels of heritability (genetic influence on individual differences) without heredity explaining group differences. Genes mostly determine why one person today is heavier than another. Environment mostly determines why people are heavier today than 50 years ago.

Ironically, the expanding waistlines of the American population coincide with an increasing idealization of the thin-and-fit look. Consider:

+ Most models and actresses have hardly more than half the 22 to 26 percent body fat of an average woman (Brownell, 1991). When young women look at magazine pictures of ultra-thin models, they report an increase in their feelings of shame, guilt, and body dissatisfaction (Stice & Shaw, 1994).
+ In 1950, department-store mannequins looked nearly like real women. Since then, they have lost about 3 inches around their hips, which now average only 31 inches—quite unlike today's average young adult woman's 37 inches. In fact, women with as little body fat as these mannequins likely would not menstruate (University of California, 1993).
+ While the average North American woman weighs more than her counterpart of 40 years ago and obesity rates are increasing, today's average Miss America contestant weighs about 15 pounds less.

The lean look
Contemporary clothing ads and films present an ideal of thinness that most women cannot attain. The message is so pervasive in Western cultures that even those of flawless appearance are often worried about their bodily "imperfections."

Losing Weight

Perhaps you shake your head in sympathy with obese people: "Slim chance they (or we) have of becoming and staying thin. If they lose weight on a diet, their metabolism slows and their hungry fat cells cry out, 'Feed me!'" Indeed, the condition of an obese person's body reduced to average weight is much like that of a semistarved body. Held under normal set point, each body "thinks" it is starving. Having lost weight, formerly obese people look normal, but their fat cells may be abnormally small, their metabolism slowed, and their minds obsessed with food.

All this explains why most people who succeed on a weight-loss program eventually gain nearly all of the weight back (Garner & Wooley, 1991; Wing & Jeffery, 1979). One study followed 207 obese patients who had lost large amounts of weight during a 2-month hospital fast (Johnson & Drenick, 1977). Within 3 years, half had gained back all the weight they had lost, and virtually all were again obese within 9 years. Programs that modify one's life-style and ongoing eating behavior have better carryover to postdiet weight management. Yet the participants in these programs, too, typically regain much of their lost weight (**FIGURE 52.17**). When cultural ideals of slimness collide with hunger, hunger usually wins. Commercial weight-loss programs can justifiably proclaim that they help people lose weight, *temporarily*. For most people, however, the only long-term result is a thinner wallet.

And yet, the battle of the bulge rages on as intensely as ever, especially in North America, where weight concern and dieting have been a greater preoccupation than in, say, Australia or developing countries (Rothblum, 1990; Tiggemann & Rothblum, 1988). Americans spend $30 billion a year trying to lose weight (Gura, 1997). In 1999, 52 percent of Americans—up from 31 percent in 1951—said they would like to lose weight (Gallup, 1999).

The battle of the bulge is most intense among people with two X chromosomes. In one survey of 108,000 adults, 29 percent of men and 44 percent of women were actively trying to lose weight (Serdula & others, 1999). Asked if they would rather "be five years younger or weigh 15 pounds less," 29 percent of men and 48 percent of women said they would prefer losing the weight (*Responsive Community*, 1996). The gender difference for teenagers is even larger: 15 percent of boys and 44 percent of girls report trying to lose weight (Centers for Disease Control, 1991).

Bottom Liners

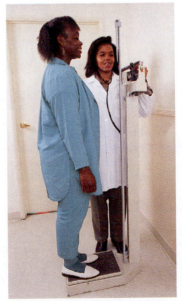

"It works as well as most other diet plans. . . . I've lost over $200 in less than three weeks."

"After years of research, after tens of millions of dieters, after tens of billions of dollars, no one has found a diet that keeps the weight off in any but a small fraction of dieters."

Martin E. P. Seligman, *What You Can Change and What You Can't*, 1994

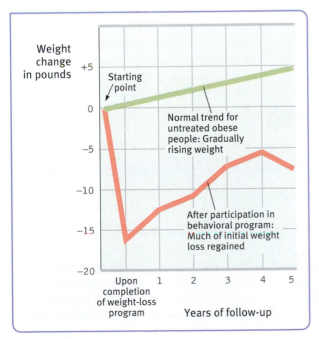

FIGURE **52.17 Weight-loss programs and weight change**
Behavior management weight-loss programs promote weight loss, but most lost weight is regained. (From Brownell & Jeffrey, 1987.)

CLOSE-UP:

HELPFUL HINTS FOR LOSING WEIGHT

Minimize exposure to tempting food cues.

Keep tempting foods out of the house or out of sight. Stay out of the sweets and chips shops. Go to the supermarket only on a full stomach.

Take steps to boost your metabolism.

Inactive people are often overweight (**FIGURE 52.18**). Exercise, such as brisk walking, running, and swimming, not only empties fat cells, builds muscle, and makes you feel better, it also temporarily speeds up metabolism and can help lower your set point (Bennett, 1995; Kolata, 1987; Thompson & others, 1982). Even brief bouts of exercise—four 10-minute walks a day—provide benefits

(Jakicic & others, 1999). Lack of exercise helps explain why so few succeed in losing weight permanently. In a Centers for Disease Control study of 107,000 adults, only one in five of those trying to lose weight were following the government recommendation to both count calories and exercise 150 minutes weekly (Serdula & others, 1999).

Be realistic and moderate.

Being moderately heavy is less risky than being extremely thin (Ernsberger & Koletzky, 1999). Permanent weight loss is not easy. Take it gradually. "A reasonable *time line* for a 10 percent reduction in body weight is six months," advises the National Institutes of Health (1998).

"I looked at you and thought, I bet this man runs marathons."

Modify both your metabolic rate and your hunger by changing the food you eat.

Findings suggest that complex carbohydrates (pasta, grains, potatoes) increase metabolism and are less readily converted to body fat than are the same calories eaten as fats (Rodin, 1979, 1985). Complex carbohydrates and fructose (the sugar in fruits) stimulate less of the hunger-producing insulin jump than does refined sugar (sucrose).

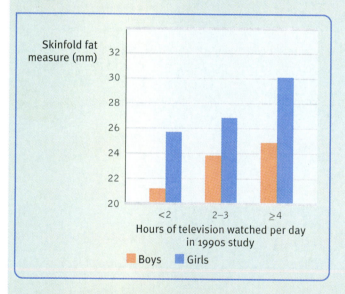

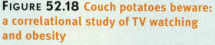

Don't starve all day and eat one big meal at night.

This eating pattern, common among overweight people, slows metabolism.

Beware of the binge.

Among people who consciously restrain their eating, drinking alcohol or feeling anxious or depressed can unleash the urge to eat (Herman & Polivy, 1980). Once the diet is broken, the person often thinks "what the heck" and then binges (Polivy & Herman, 1985, 1987). A lapse need not become a full collapse: Remember, most people occasionally lapse. Remind yourself that you've succeeded before, and continue with your plan.

Set realistic goals.

Targeting an ambitiously low weight usually dooms a person to eventual defeat. Setting a realistic objective—such as walking several times a week—can promote effort and persistence.

FIGURE 52.18 Couch potatoes beware: a correlational study of TV watching and obesity
In a 1980s study of 6671 young people 12 to 17 years old, and in a 1990s follow-up study of 4063 individuals 8 to 16 years old, obesity was more common among those who watched the most television (From Andersen & others, 1998; Deitz & Gortmaker, 1985). Of course, overweight people may avoid activity, preferring to sit and watch TV. But the association between TV watching and obesity remained when many other factors were controlled, suggesting that inactivity and snacking while watching TV do contribute to obesity. Also, as life-styles have become more sedentary and TV watching has increased, so has the percentage of overweight people in Britain, North America, and elsewhere (Vines, 1995). When California children were placed in a TV-reduction educational program, they watched less—and lost weight (Robinson, 1999).

An unusual success story
Tammy and Jeffrey Munson—two volunteers in the National Weight Control Registry—shown before and after she lost 147 pounds and he lost 100 pounds.

With fat cells, set points, metabolism, and genetic factors all tirelessly conspiring to make losing weight a big problem, what advice can psychology offer if you wish to shed any excess pounds? First, begin only if you feel motivated and self-disciplined enough to restrict your eating or continue your exercise program permanently. For most people, permanent weight loss requires making a career of staying thin—a lifelong change in eating habits combined with gradually increased exercise. In fact, sustained exercise can be a weapon against the body's normal metabolic slowdown when eating less. One of the few predictors of successful long-term weight loss is exercise both during and after changing your eating patterns (Foreyt & others, 1996; McGuire & others, 1999; Wadden & others, 1998).

Although preserving weight loss is a constant challenge, Stanley Schachter (1982) was less pessimistic than most obesity researchers about the likelihood of doing it successfully. While he recognized the overwhelming rate of failure among those in structured weight-loss programs, he also noted that these are a special group of people, probably people who have been unable to help themselves. Moreover, the failure rates recorded for these programs are based on single attempts at weight loss. Perhaps when people try repeatedly to lose weight, more of them do eventually succeed. When Schachter interviewed a haphazard sample of people, he found that one-fourth had at one time been significantly overweight and had tried to slim down. Of these, 6 out of 10 had *succeeded*: They weighed at least 10 percent less than their maximum prediet weight (an average loss of 35 pounds) and were no longer obese. A 1993 survey of 90,000 *Consumer Reports* readers found 25 percent of dieters claiming an enduring weight loss. Aided by media publicity, the National Weight Control Registry has identified 2500 Americans who have maintained a weight loss for at least one year and are being studied over time (Fritsch, 1999; McGuire & others, 1999).

Two other studies, however, reveal less encouraging results: Fewer than one-third of formerly overweight people had maintained their weight loss (Jeffery & Wing, 1983; Rzewnicki & Forgays, 1987). But the findings do hint that prospects for losing weight may be somewhat brighter than the dismal conclusions drawn from following patients who undergo a single weight-loss program. If all this has a familiar ring, recall that stop-smoking programs tend to be (1) effective in the short run and (2) ineffective in the long run, but that (3) many people are former smokers.

There is another option for overweight people, and one chosen by 13 percent of the people Schachter interviewed—simply to accept one's weight. We all do well to note that researchers have *not* identified guilt, hostility, oral fixation, or any similar personality maladjustment as causes of obesity. Nor is obesity simply a matter of a lack of willpower. If dieters are more likely to binge when under stress or after breaking their diets, this may be largely a consequence of their constant dieting. Indeed, the relentless pursuit of thinness puts people at risk not only for binge eating and food obsession, but also for taxing weight fluctuations, malnutrition, smoking, depression, and harmful side effects of weight-loss drugs (Cogan & Ernsberger, 1999).

"Fat is not a four-letter word," proclaims the National Association to Advance Fat Acceptance, so "a waist is a terrible thing to mind." Such statements discount the health risks linked with significant obesity, but they do convey a valid point: It is surely better to accept oneself as a bit chubby than to diet and binge and feel continually out of control and guilty. Fans loved Oprah Winfrey before she lost 67 pounds. They loved her after she put them back on. They loved her when she shed them again. And they will love her still, chubby or not.

While working to clarify the precise relationships among diet, behavior, and health, health psychologists continue their efforts to persuade us to adopt healthier life-styles. Doing so is quite a challenge, however. Happy people tend to see themselves as relatively invulnerable to health problems, especially those that might arise from their own actions (Salovey & Birnbaum, 1989; Weinstein, 1987). They also typically believe their own life-style is healthier than other people's—that they drink less alcohol, consume less fat and cholesterol, and get more exercise. Often they are fooling themselves. Furthermore, many individuals who admit to behaviors known to increase health risks will deny that the behaviors actually make them personally more vulnerable to illness or injury. Unlike people who are told they have normal blood pressure, those told they have high blood pressure tend to dismiss its seriousness (Croyle & Ditto, 1990). And smokers may delude themselves by saying that their exercising counteracts smoking's effects.

Because of people's optimistic denials of health risks, the first hurdle health-promotion programs must surmount is to get us to realize our vulnerability to stress- and behavior-related health problems. Only then will we make an effort to control stress, stop smoking, moderate our drinking, eat wisely, exercise regularly, and even buckle our seat belts.

"Fat! So?"

Popular T-shirt at the 1999 convention of the National Association to Advance Fat Acceptance

REVIEW AND REFLECT:

Promoting Health

Preventing illness and promoting health through stress management and behavior change is far easier and more cost-effective than attempting to treat problems after they occur.

What tactics can we use to reduce stress-related ailments?

Among the components of stress-management programs are training in aerobic exercise, biofeedback, and relaxation. Although the degree of mind control over the body that can be gained through biofeedback has fallen short of early expectations, it sometimes helps control tension headaches and high blood pressure. Simple relaxation exercises offer some of the same benefits. Counseling Type A heart-attack survivors to slow down and relax has helped lower rates of recurring attacks. Social support also helps people cope, partly by buffering the impact of stress. Researchers are now trying to understand the active components of the religion-health correlation.

How can we modify health-destructive behaviors such as smoking? How effective are programs that aim to help people stop smoking or lose weight?

The largest preventable cause of death in North America is cigarette smoking, a fact that motivates health psychologists to study the social influences that cause adolescents to start smoking, the negative and positive reinforcers that maintain the habit, and possible ways to stop and prevent smoking.

Researchers are now exploring how certain foods, by providing the building blocks for specific neurotransmitters, affect mood and behavior.

Fat is a concentrated fuel reserve stored in fat cells. It is the number and size of these cells, influenced by genetics, that determines one's body fat. Obese people find it difficult to lose weight permanently because the number of fat cells is not reduced by dieting, because the energy expenditure necessary for tissue maintenance is lower in fat than in other tissues, and because overall metabolic rate decreases when body weight drops below the set point. To improve success rates, those who need to lose weight should minimize exposure to food cues, boost energy expenditure through exercise, and make a lifelong change in eating patterns.

Terms and Concepts to Remember

aerobic exercise, p. 644
biofeedback, p. 646

complementary and alternative
medicine, p. 652

Test Yourself

52.1. A number of studies reveal that aerobic exercise raises energy levels and helps alleviate depression and anxiety. The reasons for these emotional effects of exercise are unclear. Once explanation is that exercise triggers the release of mood-boosting neurotransmitters such as norepinephrine, serotonin, and
   a. the placebos.
   b. the endorphins.
   c. epinephrine.
   d. acetylcholine.

52.2. Neal Miller found that rats could learn to control their heartbeat when they were rewarded with pleasurable brain stimulation for doing so. Later research showed that some paralyzed humans could also learn to control blood pressure through biofeedback. Biofeedback was thought to help people exercise control over functions that are usually controlled by
   a. the autonomic nervous system.
   b. conscious thought.
   c. the immune system.
   d. external stimuli.

52.3. Long-term studies of thousands of people have shown that people who have close relationships—a strong social support system—are less likely to die prematurely than those who do not. These studies provide evidence that
   a. social ties can be a source of stress.
   b. people who lose a close relationship are at risk for illness.
   c. Type A behavior is responsible for many premature deaths.
   d. social support has a beneficial effect on health.

52.4. Smokers tend to begin smoking as teenagers. Over the past 25 years, smoking among _____ has risen, but smoking among _____ has dropped.
   a. men; women
   b. college-educated people; high school dropouts
   c. teenagers; adults
   d. American women; Chinese men

52.5. One theory of weight control maintains that an obese person's body is set to maintain body weight within a higher-than-normal range. This view is known as the _____ theory.
   a. leptin
   b. set point
   c. physiology of fat cells
   d. metabolic

Review: Nonsmokers, the text reports, are less likely to become depressed and get divorced. What type of research finding is this, and what explanations might it have?

Reflect: To promote health by discouraging smoking, many governments now heavily tax cigarettes. Would you concur with the suggestion of Kelly Brownell (1997), director of Yale's Center for Eating and Weight Disorders, to slap a similar tax on fatty foods to decrease their consumption? Explain your perspective on this issue.

Answers to the Test Yourself and Review questions can be found in the green appendix at the end of the book.

Social Psychology

"We cannot live for ourselves alone," remarked the novelist Herman Melville. "Our lives are connected by a thousand invisible threads." Social psychologists explore these connections by scientifically studying how we think about, influence, and relate to one another.

+ *Social thinking:* How do we explain people's behavior? How do we form our beliefs and attitudes? What is the relationship between what we think and what we do? (Module 53)
+ *Social influence:* What invisible social threads pull us? How strong are they? How do they operate? (Module 54)
+ *Social relations:* What makes us harm or help or fall in love? What can we do to transform the closed fists of aggression into the open arms of compassion? (Module 55)

53 Social Thinking

Especially when the unexpected occurs, we analyze why people act as they do. Does her warmth reflect romantic interest, or is that how she relates to everyone? Does his absenteeism signify illness, laziness, or a stressful work atmosphere? These are just a few of the questions that intrigue social psychologists. Just as personality psychologists study the enduring, inner determinants of behavior that help to explain why different people act differently in a given situation, so **social psychologists** study the social influences that help explain why the same person will act differently in different situations.

Attributing Behavior to Persons or to Situations

Preview Questions: How do we tend to explain others' behavior? How do we explain our own behavior?

After studying how people explain others' behavior, Fritz Heider (1958) proposed an **attribution theory.** Heider noted that people usually attribute others' behavior either to their internal dispositions or to their external situations. A teacher, for example, may wonder whether a child's hostility reflects an aggressive personality (*a dispositional attribution*) or a reaction to stress or abuse (*a situational attribution*).

In class, we notice that Julie seldom talks; over coffee, Jack talks nonstop. Attributing their behaviors to their personal dispositions, we decide Julie is shy and Jack is outgoing. Because people do have enduring personality traits, such attributions are sometimes valid. However, we often overestimate the influence of personality and underestimate the influence of situations. In class, Jack may be as quiet as Julie. Catch Julie at a party and you may hardly recognize your quiet classmate. Underestimating such situational influences is known as the **fundamental attribution error**.

An experiment by David Napolitan and George Goethals (1979) illustrates the phenomenon. They had Williams College students talk, one at a time, with a young woman who acted either aloof and critical or warm and friendly. Beforehand, they told half the students the woman's behavior would be spontaneous. They told the other half the truth—that she had been instructed to *act* friendly (or unfriendly). What effect do you suppose this information had?

None. The students disregarded the information. If the woman acted friendly, they inferred she really was a warm person. If she acted unfriendly, they inferred she really was a cold person. In other words, they attributed her behavior to her personal disposition *even when told that her behavior was situational*—that she was merely acting that way for purposes of the experiment.

The fundamental attribution error is almost irresistible. In a high school play I once attended, a talented 16-year-old girl convincingly played the part of a bitter old woman—so convincingly that, although I reminded myself of the fundamental attribution error, I still assumed that the young actress was typecast because she was well-suited for the part. Meeting her later at a cast party, I discovered she actually has a very pleasant disposition. I then remembered that several months earlier I had seen her play the part of a charming 10-year-old in *The Sound of Music*. Leonard Nimoy of "Star Trek" fame would not have been surprised by my error. He titled one of his books *I Am Not Spock*.

- **social psychology** the scientific study of how we think about, influence, and relate to one another.

- **attribution theory** the theory that we tend to give a causal explanation for someone's behavior, often by crediting either the situation or the person's disposition.

- **fundamental attribution error** the tendency for observers, when analyzing another's behavior, to underestimate the impact of the situation and to overestimate the impact of personal disposition.

You, too, have surely committed the fundamental attribution error. In judging, say, whether your psychology instructor is shy or outgoing, you have perhaps by now inferred that he or she has an outgoing personality. But you know your instructor only from the classroom, a situation that demands outgoing behavior. Catch the instructor in a different situation and you might be surprised (as some of my students are when confronting me in a pick-up basketball game). Outside their assigned roles, professors seem less professorial, presidents less presidential, servants less servile.

The instructor, on the other hand, observes his or her own behavior in many different situations—in the classroom, in meetings, at home—and so might say, "Me, outgoing? It all depends on the situation. In class or with good friends, yes, I'm outgoing. But at conventions I'm really rather shy."

So, when explaining *our own* behavior, we are sensitive to how our behavior changes with the situations we encounter. When explaining *others'* behavior, particularly after observing them in only one type of situation, we often commit the fundamental attribution error: We disregard the situation and leap to unwarranted conclusions about their personality traits. We do so partly because we have learned to focus our attention more on the person than on the situational context. Meanwhile, the person's own attention focuses more on the situation to which he or she is reacting. Reverse the perspectives of actor and observer—by having each view a videotape replay of the situation from the other's perspective—and this reverses the attributions (Lassiter & Irvine, 1986; Storms, 1973). By seeing the world from the actor's perspective, the observers better appreciate the situation. Given an observer's point of view, the actors better appreciate their own personal style.

The Effects of Attribution

In everyday life we often struggle to explain others' actions. To what should we attribute them? A jury must decide whether a shooting was malicious or in self-defense. An unhappy wife and husband each ponder why the other behaves so selfishly. An interviewer must judge whether the applicant's geniality is genuine. When we make such judgments, our attributions—either to the person or to the situation—have important consequences (Fincham & Bradbury, 1993; Fletcher & others, 1990). Happily married couples attribute their spouse's tart-tongued remark to a temporary situation ("She must have had a bad day at work"). Unhappily married persons attribute the same remark to a mean disposition ("Why did I marry such a hostile person?").

Or consider the political effects of attribution: How do you explain poverty or unemployment? Researchers in Britain, India, Australia, and the United States (Furnham, 1982; Pandey & others, 1982; Wagstaff, 1982; Zucker & Weiner, 1993) report that political conservatives tend to attribute such social problems to the personal dispositions of the poor and unemployed themselves: "People generally get what they deserve. Those who don't work are often freeloaders. Anybody who takes the initiative can still get ahead." "Society is not to blame for crime, criminals are," said one U.S. presidential candidate (Dole, 1996). Political liberals (and social scientists) are more likely to blame past and present situations: "If you or I had to live with the same poor education, lack of opportunity, and discrimination, would we be any better off?"

Managers also have to make attributions. In evaluating employees, they are likely to attribute poor performance to personal factors, such as low ability or lack of motivation. On the other hand, workers doing poorly on a job recognize situational influences: inadequate supplies, poor working conditions, difficult co-workers, impossible demands (Rice, 1985).

Cultures also vary in how they make attributions. An example comes from the 1990s' "rogue trader" scandals, causing huge losses for several banks and investment firms when employees made unauthorized trades.

"Otis, shout at that man to pull himself together."

FIGURE **53.1**
Attributions and attitudes
How we explain someone's behavior affects how we react to it.

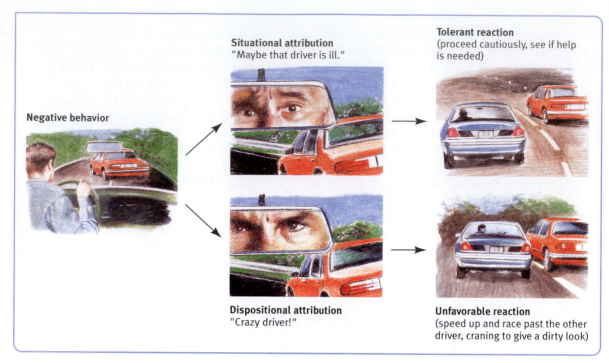

Negative behavior

Situational attribution
"Maybe that driver is ill."

Tolerant reaction
(proceed cautiously, see if help is needed)

Dispositional attribution
"Crazy driver!"

Unfavorable reaction
(speed up and race past the other driver, craning to give a dirty look)

Who was to blame? American newspapers attributed the mess-ups to the individuals ("Salomon's errant cowboy," was the *New York Times'* description of one trader). Japanese papers attributed the problems to lack of organizational controls (Menon & others, 1999).

The point to remember: Our attributions—to individuals' dispositions or to their situations—have real consequences. (**FIGURE 53.1**).

Attitudes and Actions

Preview Question: Does what we think predict what we will do, or does what we do shape what we will think?

Attitudes are beliefs and feelings that predispose our reactions to objects, people, and events. If we *believe* that someone is mean, we may *feel* dislike for the person and *act* unfriendly. "Change the way people think," said South African civil rights martyr Steve Biko, "and things will never be the same." Such is the power of persuasion.

Do Our Attitudes Guide Our Actions?

Although most people assume that changing someone's attitudes can indeed change behavior, dozens of studies during the 1960s challenged this idea (Wicker, 1971). Moreover, studies of attitudes and behaviors regarding cheating, religion, and racial minorities revealed that people often talk and act a different game.

But this seeming hypocrisy did startle social psychologists, most of whom shared Biko's belief that there is a close connection between thought and action, character and conduct, private words and public deeds. So during the 1970s and 1980s they conducted many follow-up studies (Kraus, 1991; Wallace & others, 1996). Each revealed that our attitudes *will* guide our actions, if—

+ **Outside influences on what we say and do are minimal.** Facing pressures from motorists and truckers, politicians may voice opposition to a gas tax increase that, privately, they believe would help conserve resources and reduce greenhouse emissions (**FIGURE 53.2**).

"Thinking is easy, acting difficult, and to put one's thoughts into action, the most difficult thing in the world."

German poet Goethe, 1749–1832

■ **attitude**   a belief and feeling that predisposes one to respond in a particular way to objects, people, and events.

■ **foot-in-the-door phenomenon**   the tendency for people who have first agreed to a small request to comply later with a larger request.

+ **The attitude is specifically relevant to the behavior.** People readily profess *general* attitudes that contradict their behavior. They proclaim love while yelling at their mate, cherish honesty while cheating on their income tax returns, and value good health while smoking and not exercising. Attitudes about the specific act do, however, guide action. Your attitudes toward running help predict whether you will run if you do exercise.
+ **We are keenly aware of our attitudes.** When we mindlessly follow habit or social expectations, our attitudes lie dormant. If, however, something makes us self-conscious or reminds us of how we feel, we are truer to our convic-tions. For example, Martha Powell and Russell Fazio (1984) report that repeatedly expressing an attitude makes it come to mind more quickly. Moreover, the attitudes that do come quickly to mind are the ones more likely to guide our behavior (Fazio, 1990). When we know and are conscious of what we believe, we are true to ourselves.

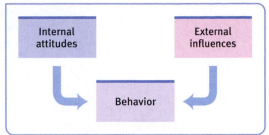

FIGURE 53.2 Attitudes, external influences, and behavior
Our behavior is affected by our inner attitudes as well as by external social influences.

Do Our Actions Affect Our Attitudes?

So attitudes will affect behavior under certain circumstances: when other influences are minimal, when the attitude is specific to the behavior, and when we are mindful of our attitudes. Now consider a more surprising principle: People also come to believe in what they have stood up for. Many streams of evidence confirm that *attitudes follow behavior*. Here are two.

The Foot-in-the-Door Phenomenon

During the Korean War, many captured U.S. soldiers were imprisoned in war camps run by Chinese communists. Without using brutality, the captors secured the collaboration of hundreds of their prisoners in various activities. Some merely ran errands or accepted favors. Others made radio appeals and false confessions. Still others informed on fellow prisoners and divulged military information. When the war ended, 21 prisoners chose to stay with the communists. More returned home "brainwashed"—convinced that communism was a good thing for Asia.

A key ingredient of the Chinese "thought-control" program was its effective use of the **foot-in-the-door phenomenon**—a tendency for people who agree to a small request to comply later with a larger one. The Chinese harnessed this phenomenon by gradually escalating their demands on the prisoners, beginning with harmless requests (Schein, 1956). Having "trained" the prisoners to speak or write trivial statements, the communists then asked them to copy or create something more important, noting, perhaps, the flaws of capitalism. The prisoners then participated in group discussions, wrote self-criticisms, or uttered public confessions. Once they had done so, perhaps to gain privileges, the prisoners then often adjusted their beliefs toward consistency with their public acts.

The point is simple, says Robert Cialdini (1993): To get people to agree to something big, "Start small and build." And be wary of those who would exploit you with the tactic. This chicken-and-egg spiral of actions feeding attitudes feeding actions enables behavior to escalate. A trivial act makes the next act easier. Succumb to a temptation and you will find the next temptation harder to resist.

In dozens of experiments simulating part of the war prisoners' experience, people have been coaxed into acting against their attitudes or violating their moral standards. The nearly inevitable result: Most subjects begin to rationalize their behavior, persuading themselves that they were justified in saying or doing what they did. If induced to speak or

Attitudes follow behavior
Cooperative actions, such as those performed by people on sports teams, feed mutual liking. Such attitudes, in turn, promote positive behavior.

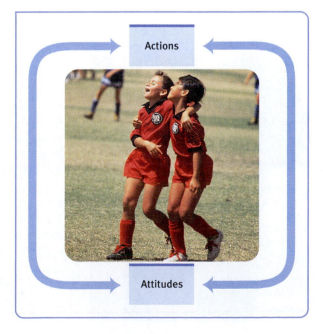

"If the King destroys a man, that's proof to the King it must have been a bad man."

Thomas Cromwell, in Robert Bolt's *A Man for All Seasons*, 1960

write on behalf of a point of view they have doubts about, they begin to believe their own words. Saying becomes believing. Similarly, subjects induced to harm an innocent victim—by making cutting comments or by delivering electric shocks—typically begin to disparage their victim.

Fortunately, the attitudes-follow-behavior principle works as well for good deeds as for bad. The foot-in-the-door tactic helps boost charitable contributions, blood donations, and product sales. In one experiment, researchers posing as safe-driving volunteers asked Californians to permit the installation of a large, poorly lettered "Drive Carefully" sign in their front yards. Only 17 percent consented. They approached other home owners with a small request first: Would they display a 3-inch high "Be a Safe Driver" sign? Nearly all readily agreed. When reapproached two weeks later to allow the large, ugly sign in their front yards, 76 percent consented (Freedman & Fraser, 1966).

In the years immediately following the introduction of school desegregation and the passage of the Civil Rights Act of 1964, white Americans expressed diminishing racial prejudice. And as Americans in different regions came to act more alike— thanks to more uniform national standards against discrimination—they began to think more alike. Experiments confirm that moral action has positive effects on the actor, and that doing favors for another person often leads to greater liking of the person. We love people for the good we do them as well as for the good they do us. Evil acts certainly shape the self. But so do acts of good will. Act as if you like someone, and you soon will.

Role Playing Affects Attitudes

When you adopt a new role—when you become a college student, marry, or begin a new job—you strive to follow the social prescriptions. At first, your behaviors may feel phony, because you are *acting* the role. The first weeks in the military feel artificial—as if one is pretending to be a soldier. The first weeks of a marriage may feel like "playing house." Before long, however, your behavior no longer feels forced. What began as play-acting in the theater of life becomes *you*. This helps explain why women who do administrative or professional work develop, over time, more confident and assertive personalities (Roberts, 1997).

Researchers have confirmed this effect. They have assessed people's attitudes before and after they adopt a new role, sometimes in laboratory situations, sometimes in everyday situations, such as before and after taking a job. In one laboratory study, college students volunteered to spend time in a simulated prison devised by psychologist Philip Zimbardo (1972). Some he randomly designated as guards; he gave them uniforms, billy clubs, and whistles and instructed them to enforce certain rules. The remainder became prisoners; they were locked in barren cells and forced to wear humiliating outfits. After a day or two in which the volunteers self-consciously "played" their roles, the simulation became real—too real. Most of the guards developed disparaging attitudes, and some devised cruel and degrading routines. One by one, the prisoners broke down, rebelled, or became passively resigned, causing Zimbardo to call off the study after only six days.

In real life, the military junta then in power in Greece was training another group of men to become torturers (Staub, 1989). The men's indoctrination into their roles occurred in small steps. First, the trainee stood guard outside the interrogation cells—the "foot in the door." Next, he stood guard inside. Only then was he ready to become actively involved in the questioning and torture. As the nineteenth-century writer Nathaniel Hawthorne noted, "No man, for any considerable period, can wear one face to himself and another to the multitude without finally getting bewildered as to which may be true." Behavior affects attitudes. What we do, we gradually become.

Social roles are powerful
Initially both the obedient recruit and the abusive sergeant may have consciously adopted the behavior expected of them. In time, they may become the characters they are playing.

Why Do Our Actions Affect Our Attitudes?

Without doubt, then, actions can affect attitudes, sometimes turning prisoners into collaborators, doubters into believers, or mere acquaintances into friends. But why? One explanation is that we feel motivated to justify our actions. When we are aware that our attitudes and actions don't coincide, we experience tension, called *cognitive dissonance*. To relieve this tension, according to the **cognitive dissonance theory** proposed by Leon Festinger, we often bring our attitudes into line with our actions. It is as if we rationalize, "If I chose to do it (or say it), I must believe in it." The less coerced and more responsible we feel for a troubling act, the more dissonance we feel. The more dissonance we feel, the more motivated we are to find consistency, such as changing our attitudes to help justify the act.

Dozens of experiments have confirmed cognitive dissonance by making people feel responsible for behavior that is inconsistent with their attitudes and that has foreseeable consequences. As a participant in one of these experiments, you might agree for a measly $2 to help a researcher by writing an essay that supports something you don't believe in (perhaps a tuition increase). Feeling responsible for the statements (which are not consistent with your attitudes), you would probably feel dissonance, especially if you thought an administrator would be reading your essay. How would you reduce the uncomfortable dissonance? One way would be to start believing your phony words. Let your pretense become your reality (**FIGURE 53.3**).

■ **cognitive dissonance theory** the theory that we act to reduce the discomfort (dissonance) we feel when two of our thoughts (cognitions) are inconsistent. For example, when our awareness of our attitudes and of our actions clash, we can reduce the resulting dissonance by changing our attitudes.

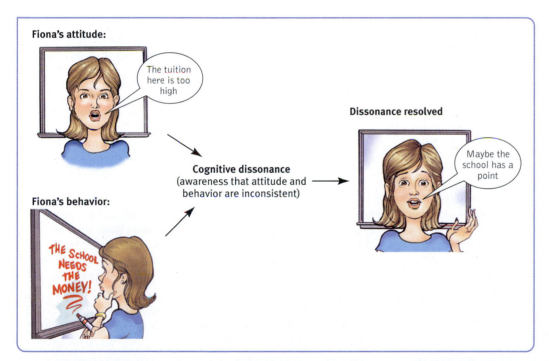

FIGURE 53.3
When attitudes follow behavior, cognitive dissonance lessens

The attitudes-follow-behavior principle has some heartening implications. Although we cannot directly control all our feelings, we can influence them by altering our behavior. If we are unloving, we can become more loving by behaving as if we were so—by doing thoughtful things, expressing affection, giving affirmation. If we are down in the dumps, we can do as cognitive therapists advise and talk in more positive, self-accepting ways with fewer self–put-downs. *The point to remember:* Changing our behavior can change how we think and how we feel. Just do it.

"Sit all day in a moping posture, sigh, and reply to everything with a dismal voice, and your melancholy lingers. . . . If we wish to conquer undesirable emotional tendencies in ourselves, we must . . . go through the outward movements of those contrary dispositions which we prefer to cultivate."

William James, *Principles of Psychology*, 1890

Social Thinking

Social psychology is the study of how people think about, influence, and relate to one another.

How do we tend to explain others' behavior? How do we explain our own behavior?

We generally explain people's behavior by attributing it either to internal dispositions or to external situations. In accounting for others' actions, we often underestimate the influence of the situation, thus committing the fundamental attribution error. When we explain our own behavior, however, we more often point to the situation and not to ourselves.

Does what we think predict what we will do, or does what we do shape what we will think?

Attitudes predict behavior only under certain conditions, as when other influences are minimized, when the attitude is specific to the behavior, and when people are aware of their attitudes. Studies of the foot-in-the-door phenomenon and of role playing reveal that our actions can also modify our attitudes, especially when we feel responsible for those actions. Cognitive dissonance theorists explain that behavior shapes attitudes because people feel discomfort when their actions go against their feelings and beliefs; they reduce the discomfort by bringing their attitudes more into line with what they have done.

Terms and Concepts to Remember

social psychology, p. 674
attribution theory, p. 674
fundamental attribution
   error, p. 674

attitude, p. 676
foot-in-the-door phenomenon, p. 677
cognitive dissonance theory, p. 679

Test Yourself

53.1. In explaining a person's behavior we tend to make the fundamental attribution error—we overestimate the impact of internal factors (such as disposition or personality) and underestimate the impact of the situation in which the behavior occurs. Thus, if we encounter a person seemingly high on drugs, we might attribute the person's behavior to
   a. moral weakness or an addictive personality.
   b. peer pressure.
   c. the easy availability of the drug on city streets.
   d. society's acceptance of drug use.

53.2. Whether our actions are really guided by our attitudes depends on several factors. For example, attitudes that are

specifically relevant to a behavior are most likely to predict that behavior. Thus, we could best predict whether someone will vote in a mayoral election if we knew the person's attitude on
   a. the value of democracy.
   b. the benefits of efficient city government.
   c. corruption in municipal affairs.
   d. the importance of this particular election.

53.3. During the Korean War, the Chinese "brainwashed" soldiers to think that communism was a good thing for Asia. A key ingredient in their "thought-control" program was their ability to make use of the tendency of people who have first agreed to a small request to comply later with a larger request. This tendency is called
   a. the fundamental attribution error.
   b. the foot-in-the-door phenomenon.
   c. the behavior-follows-attitudes principle.
   d. role playing.

53.4. When we are aware that there is a discrepancy between our attitudes and our behavior, cognitive dissonance theory predicts that we will act to reduce the discomfort or dissonance we feel. The theory explains why
   a. people who act against their attitudes tend to change their attitudes.
   b. attitudes predict actions when social pressures are minimized.
   c. changing an attitude—through persuasion—often fails to result in behavioral changes.
   d. people are hypocritical, talking one way and acting another.

Review: Driving to school one wintry day, Marco narrowly misses a car that slides through a red light. "Slow down! What a terrible driver," he thinks to himself. Moments later, Marco himself slips through an intersection and yelps, "Wow! These roads are awful. The city snow plows need to get out here." What social psychology principle has Marco just demonstrated? Explain.

Reflect: Do you have an attitude or tendency you would like to change? Using the attitudes-follow-behavior principle, how might you go about changing that attitude?

Answers to the Test Yourself and Review questions can be found in the green appendix at the end of the book.

Social Influence

54

Social psychology's great lesson is the enormous power of social influence on our attitudes, beliefs, decisions, and actions. This influence can be seen in our conformity, compliance, and group behavior. Suicides, bomb threats, airplane hijackings, and UFO sightings all have a curious tendency to come in clusters. Armed with principles of social influence, advertisers, salespeople, and campaign workers aim to sway our decisions to buy, to donate, to vote. Isolated with others who share their grievances, dissenters may gradually become rebels and rebels may become terrorists. During a lengthy stay in another part of the world, we may struggle with the new cultural norms. On campus, we wear blue jeans; on New York's Wall Street or London's Bond Street, we wear suits and ties. Let's examine the pull of these social strings. How strong are they? How do they operate?

Conformity and Obedience

Preview Question: What do experiments on conformity and compliance reveal about the power of social influence?

Behavior is contagious. One person giggles, coughs, or yawns, and others in the group are soon doing the same. A cluster of people stand gazing upward, and passersby pause to do likewise. Laughter, even canned laughter, can be infectious. Bartenders and street musicians know to "seed" their tip containers with money to suggest that others have given.

Unconsciously mimicking others' expressions, postures, and voice tones helps us feel what they are feeling. This helps explain why we feel happier around happy people than around depressed ones, and why studies of groups of British nurses and accountants reveal "mood linkage"—sharing up and down moods (Totterdell & others, 1998). Tanya Chartrand and John Bargh (1999) call our natural mimicry "the chameleon effect." They had students work in a room alongside someone—a confederate working for the experimenter—who rubbed his or her face and, on another occasion, alongside a confederate who shook his or her foot. Participants tended to rub their own faces when with the face-rubbing person and shake their own feet with the foot-shaking person. Such mimicry is part of empathy, and the most empathic people mimic—and are liked—the most.

Sometimes the effects of suggestibility are more serious. In the eight days following the 1999 shooting rampage at Colorado's Columbine High School, every U.S. state except Vermont experienced threats of copycat violence. Pennsylvania alone recorded 60 such threats (Cooper, 1999). Sociologist David Phillips and his colleagues (1985, 1989) found that suicides, too, sometimes increase following a highly publicized suicide. In the wake of Marilyn Monroe's suicide on August 6, 1962, the number of August suicides in the United States exceeded the usual count by 200. Although not all studies have confirmed the copycat suicide phenomenon, suicides have sometimes occurred in local clusters. Within an 18-day span, one 1500-student high school recorded 2 completed suicides, 7 attempted suicides, and 23 students with suicidal thoughts. Within a one-year period, one London psychiatric unit experienced 14 patient suicides (Joiner, 1999).

Niche conformity
Are these students asserting their individuality or identifying themselves with others of the same microculture?

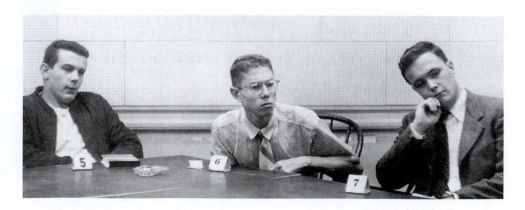

What caused these suicide clusters? Do people act similarly because of their influence on one another? Or because they are simultaneously exposed to the same events and conditions? Seeking answers, social psychologists have conducted experiments on group pressure and conformity.

Group Pressure and Conformity

Suggestibility is a subtle type of **conformity**—adjusting our behavior or thinking to bring it into line with some group standard. To study conformity, Solomon Asch (1955) devised a simple test. As a participant in the study, you arrive at the experiment location in time to take a seat at a table where five people are already seated. The experimenter asks which of three comparison lines is identical to a standard line (**FIGURE 54.1**). You see clearly that the answer is Line 2 and await your turn to say so after the others. Your boredom with this experiment begins to show when the next set of lines proves equally easy.

Now comes the third trial, and the correct answer seems just as clear-cut, but the first person gives what strikes you as a wrong answer: "Line 3." When the second person and then the third and fourth give the same wrong answer, you sit up straight and squint. When the fifth person agrees with the first three, you feel your heart begin to pound. The experimenter then looks to you for your answer. Torn between the unanimity of your five fellow students and the evidence of your own eyes, you feel tense and much less sure of yourself than you were moments ago. You hesitate before answering, wondering whether you should suffer the discomfort of being viewed as an oddball. What answer do you give?

In the experiments conducted by Asch and others after him, thousands of college students have experienced this conflict. Answering such questions alone, they erred less than 1 percent of the time. But it was a different story when several others—confederates working for the experimenter—answered incorrectly. Asch reports that more than one-third of the time, the "intelligent and well-meaning" college students were then "willing to call white black," by going along with the group.

FIGURE 54.1

Asch's conformity experiments
Which of the three comparison lines is equal to the standard line? What do you suppose most people would say after hearing five others say, "Line 3"? In this photo from one of Asch's experiments, the research participant (center) shows the severe discomfort that comes from disagreeing with the responses of other group members.

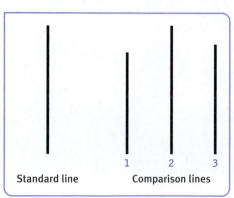

Standard line   Comparison lines

Conditions That Strengthen Conformity

Asch's procedure became the model for later investigations. Although experiments have not always found such a high degree of blind conformity, they do reveal that conformity increases when

+ one is made to feel incompetent or insecure.
+ the group has at least three people. (Further increases in group size yield not much more conformity.)
+ the group is unanimous. (The support of a single fellow dissident greatly increases social courage.)
+ one admires the group's status and attractiveness.
+ one has made no prior commitment to any response.
+ others in the group observe one's behavior.
+ the particular culture strongly encourages respect for social standards.

Thus, we might predict the behavior of Joe, an enthusiastic but insecure new fraternity member: Noting that the 40 other members appear unanimous in their plans for a fund-raiser, Joe is unlikely to voice his dissent.

Reasons for Conforming

Why do we clap when others clap, eat as others eat, believe what others believe, even see what others see? Frequently, it is to avoid rejection or to gain social approval. In such cases, we are responding to what social psychologists call **normative social influence**. We are sensitive to social norms—understood rules for accepted and expected behavior—because the price we pay for being different may be severe. Marco Lokar knows. During the 1991 Persian Gulf War, Lokar, an Italian, was the only Seton Hall University basketball player who chose not to display an American flag on his uniform. As the team traveled, the fans' abusive responses to his nonconforming behavior became unbearable, so he left the team and returned to Italy.

Respecting norms is not the only reason we conform: The group may provide valuable information. Only an uncommonly stubborn person will *never* listen to others. When we accept others' opinions about reality, we are responding to **informational social influence**. "Those who never retract their opinions love themselves more than they love truth," observed the eighteenth-century French essayist, Joseph Joubert.

Robert Baron and his colleagues (1996) cleverly demonstrated how we become open to informational influence on tough, important judgments. They modernized the Asch experiment by showing University of Iowa students a slide of a stimulus person, followed by a slide of a four-person lineup (**FIGURE 54.2**). Their experiment made the task either easy (viewing the lineup for five seconds) or difficult (viewing the lineup for but half a second). It also construed their judgments as either unimportant (just a preliminary test of some eyewitness identification procedures) or as important (establishing norms for an actual police procedure, with a $20 award to the most accurate participants). When the task was unimportant, people conformed about a third of the time to the judgments of two confederates who gave a wrong answer. When the accuracy of their judgments seemed important, people rarely conformed when the task was easy, but conformed half the time when the task was difficult. When we are unsure of what is right, and when being right matters, we become receptive to others' opinions.

conformity adjusting one's behavior or thinking to coincide with a group standard.

normative social influence influence resulting from a person's desire to gain approval or avoid disapproval.

informational social influence influence resulting from one's willingness to accept others' opinions about reality.

"Have you ever noticed how one example—good or bad—can prompt others to follow? How one illegally parked car can give permission for others to do likewise? How one racial joke can fuel another?"

Marian Wright Edelman, *The Measure of Our Success*, 1992

FIGURE 54.2
Informational influence
Sample task: After seeing Slides 1 and 2, participants judged which person in Slide 2 was the same as the person in Slide 1. (From Baron, Vandello, & Brunsman, 1996.)

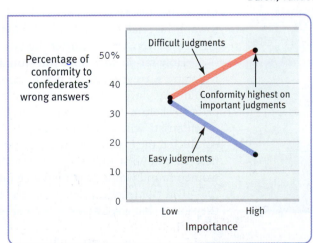

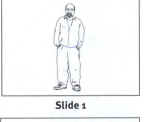

Our perception of social influence as negative or positive depends on our values. When influence supports what we approve, we applaud those who are "open-minded" and "sensitive" enough to be "responsive." When influence supports what we disapprove, we scorn the "submissive conformity" of those who comply with others' wishes. Cultures also vary in the value they place on conformity, depending on the extent to which they stress individualism or collectivism. Western Europeans and people in most English-speaking countries tend to prize individualism more than conformity and obedience. These values are reflected in social influence experiments that have been conducted in 17 countries: Conformity rates ran lower in individualistic cultures (Bond & Smith, 1996).

Obedience

Social psychologist Stanley Milgram (1965, 1974) knew that people often comply with social pressures. But how would they respond to outright commands? To find out, he undertook what have become social psychology's most famous and controversial experiments. Imagine yourself as one of the nearly 1000 participants in Milgram's 20 experiments.

Responding to an advertisement, you come to Yale University's psychology department to participate in an experiment. Professor Milgram's assistant explains that the study concerns the effect of punishment on learning. You and another person draw slips from a hat to see who will be the "teacher" (which your slip says) and who will be the "learner." The learner is then led to an adjoining room and strapped into a chair that is wired through the wall to an electric shock machine. You sit in front of the machine, which has switches labeled with voltages. Your task: to teach and then test the learner on a list of word pairs. You are to punish the learner for wrong answers by delivering brief electric shocks, beginning with a switch labeled "15 Volts—Slight Shock." After each of the learner's errors, you are to move up to the next higher voltage. With each flick of a switch, lights flash, relay switches click on, and an electric buzzing fills the air.

If you comply with the experimenter's instructions, you hear the learner grunt when you flick the third, fourth, and fifth switches. After you activate the eighth switch (labeled "120 Volts—Moderate Shock"), the learner shouts that the shocks are painful. After the tenth switch ("150 Volts—Strong Shock"), he cries, "Get me out of here! I won't be in the experiment anymore! I refuse to go on!" When you hear these pleas, you draw back. But the experimenter prods you: "Please continue—the experiment requires that you continue." If you still resist, he insists, "It is absolutely essential that you continue," or "You have no other choice, you *must* go on."

If you obey, you hear the learner's protests escalate to shrieks of agony as you continue to raise the shock level with each succeeding error. After the 330-volt level, the learner refuses to answer and soon falls silent. Still, the experimenter pushes you toward the final, 450-volt switch, ordering you to ask the questions and, if no correct answer is given, to administer the next shock level.

How far do you think you would follow the experimenter's commands? When Milgram surveyed people before conducting the experiment, most declared they would stop playing such a sadistic role soon after the learner first indicated pain and certainly before he shrieked in agony. This also was the prediction made by each of 40 psychiatrists whom Milgram asked to guess the outcome. When Milgram actually conducted the experiment with men aged 20 to 50, he was astonished to find that 63 percent complied fully—right up to the last switch. Ten later studies that included women found women's compliance rates were similar to men's (Blass, 1999).

Did the teachers figure out the hoax—that no shock was being delivered? Did they guess that the learner was a confederate who only pretended to feel the shocks?

Stanley Milgram (1933–1984)
The late social psychologist's obedience experiments now "belong to the self-understanding of literate people in our age" (Sabini, 1986).

Did they realize that the experiment was really testing their willingness to comply with commands to inflict punishment? No, the teachers typically displayed genuine agony: They sweated, trembled, laughed nervously, and bit their lips.

Milgram's use of deception and stress triggered a debate over his research ethics. In his own defense, Milgram pointed out that, after the participants learned of the deception and actual research purposes, virtually none regretted taking part. When 40 of the teachers who had agonized most were later interviewed by a psychiatrist, none appeared to be suffering emotional aftereffects. All in all, said Milgram, the experiments provoked less stress than university students experience when facing and sometimes failing big exams (Blass, 1996).

Wondering whether the participants obeyed because the learners' protests were not convincing, Milgram repeated the experiment, with 40 new teachers. This time his confederate mentioned a "slight heart condition" while being strapped into the chair, and then he complained and screamed more intensely as the shocks became more punishing. Still, 65 percent of the new teachers complied fully (**FIGURE 54.3**).

In later experiments, Milgram discovered that subtle details of a situation powerfully influence people. When he varied the social conditions, the proportion of fully compliant subjects varied from 0 to 93 percent. Obedience was highest when

+ the person giving the orders was close at hand and was perceived to be a legitimate authority figure.
+ the authority figure was supported by a prestigious institution. (Milgram got somewhat less compliance when he dissociated his experiments from Yale University.)
+ the victim was depersonalized or at a distance, even in another room. (Similarly, in combat with an enemy they can see, many soldiers either do not fire their rifles or do not aim them properly. Such refusals to kill are rare among those who operate the more distant weapons of artillery or aircraft [Padgett, 1989].)
+ there were no role models for defiance; that is, no other subjects were seen disobeying the experimenter.

The power of legitimate, close-at-hand authorities is dramatically apparent in stories of those who complied with orders to carry out the atrocities of the Holocaust, and those who didn't. In the summer of 1942 nearly 500 middle-aged German

FIGURE 54.3 Milgram's follow-up obedience experiment
In a repeat of the earlier experiment, 65 percent of the adult male "teachers" fully obeyed the experimenter's commands to continue. They did so despite the "learner's" earlier mention of a heart condition and despite hearing cries of protest after 150 volts and agonized protests after 330 volts. (Data from Milgram, 1974.)

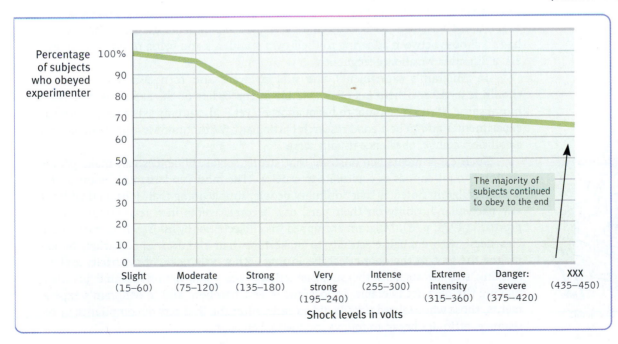

Percentage of subjects who obeyed experimenter

The majority of subjects continued to obey to the end

Shock levels in volts
Slight (15–60), Moderate (75–120), Strong (135–180), Very strong (195–240), Intense (255–300), Extreme intensity (315–360), Danger: severe (375–420), XXX (435–450)

Standing up for democracy
Some individuals—roughly one in three in Milgram's experiments—resist social coercion, as did this unarmed man in Beijing, by single-handedly challenging an advancing line of tanks the day after the 1989 Tiananmen Square student uprising was crushed.

reserve police officers were dispatched to Jozefow, Poland, in German-occupied territory. On July 13, the group's visibly upset commander informed his recruits, mostly family men, that they had been ordered to round up the village's Jews, who were said to be aiding the enemy. Able-bodied men were to be sent to work camps, and all the rest were to be shot on the spot. Given a chance to refuse participation in the executions, only about a dozen immediately did so. Within 17 hours, the remaining 485 officers killed 1500 helpless women, children, and elderly by shooting them in the back of the head as they lay face down. Hearing the pleadings of the victims, and seeing the gruesome results, some 20 percent of the officers did eventually dissent, managing either to miss their victims or to wander away and hide until the slaughter was over (Browning, 1992). But in real life, as in Milgram's experiments, the disobedient were the minority.

Another story was being played out in the French village of Le Chambon, where French Jews destined for deportation to Germany were being sheltered by villagers who openly defied orders to cooperate with the "New Order." The villagers' ancestors had themselves been persecuted and their pastors had been teaching them to "resist whenever our adversaries will demand of us obedience contrary to the orders of the Gospel" (Rochat, 1993). Ordered by police to give a list of sheltered Jews, the head pastor modeled defiance: "I don't know of Jews, I only know of human beings." Without realizing how long and terrible the war would be, or how much punishment and poverty they would suffer, the resisters made an initial commitment to resist. Supported by their beliefs, their role models, their interaction with one another, and their own initial acts, they remained defiant to the war's end.

Lessons From the Conformity and Obedience Studies

What do the Asch and Milgram experiments teach us about ourselves? How does judging the length of a line or flicking a shock switch relate to everyday social behavior? This research, like all psychological experiments, aimed not to re-create the literal behaviors of everyday life but to capture and explore the underlying processes that shape those behaviors. Asch and Milgram devised experiments in which the subjects had to choose between adhering to their own standards and being responsive to others, a dilemma we all face frequently.

In Milgram's experiments, the subjects were also torn between what they should respond to—the pleas of the victim or the orders of the experimenter. Their moral sense warned them not to harm another, yet it also prompted them to obey the experimenter and to be a good research participant. With kindness and obedience on a collision course, obedience usually won.

Such experiments demonstrate that strong social influences can make people conform to falsehoods or capitulate to cruelty. "The most fundamental lesson of our study," Milgram noted, is that "ordinary people, simply doing their jobs, and without any particular hostility on their part, can become agents in a terrible destructive process" (1974, p. 6). Milgram entrapped his subjects not by asking them first to zap "learners" with enough electricity to make their hair stand on end. Rather, he exploited the foot-in-the-door effect, beginning with a little tickle of electricity and escalating step by step. In the subjects' minds, the small action became justified, making the next act tolerable. In Jozefow, in Le Chambon, and in Milgram's experiments, those who resisted usually did so early. After the first acts of compliance or resistance, attitudes began to follow and justify behavior.

Drawing by Mel Yauk.

"Drive off the cliff, James, I want to commit suicide."

So it happens when people succumb, gradually, to evil. In any society, great evils sometimes grow out of people's compliance with lesser evils. The Nazi leaders suspected that most German civil servants would resist shooting or gassing Jews directly, but they found them surprisingly willing to handle the paperwork of the Holocaust (Silver & Geller, 1978). Likewise, when Milgram asked 40 men to administer the learning test while someone else did the shocking, 93 percent complied. Contrary to images of devilish villains, evil does not require monstrous characters; all it takes is ordinary people corrupted by an evil situation—ordinary soldiers who follow orders to shoot, ordinary students who follow orders to haze initiates into their group, ordinary employees who follow orders to produce and market harmful products.

Group Influence

Preview Questions: How does the presence of others influence our actions? How does our behavior change when we act as part of a group?

How do groups affect our behavior? To find out, social psychologists study the various influences that operate in the simplest of groups—one person in the presence of another—and those that operate in more complex groups, such as families, teams, and committees.

Individual Behavior in the Presence of Others

Appropriately, social psychology's first experiments focused on the simplest of all questions about social behavior: How are we influenced by the mere presence of others—by people watching us or joining us in various activities?

Social Facilitation

Having noticed that cyclists' racing times were faster when they competed against each other than when they competed with a clock, Norman Triplett (1898) hypothesized that the presence of others boosts performance. To test his hypothesis, Triplett had adolescents wind a fishing reel as rapidly as possible. He discovered that they wound the reel faster in the presence of someone who was doing the same thing. This phenomenon of stronger performance in the presence of others is called **social facilitation**. For example, after a light turns green, drivers take about 15 percent less time to travel the first 100 yards when another car is beside them at the intersection than when they are alone (Towler, 1986). But on tougher tasks (learning nonsense syllables or solving complex multiplication problems), people perform less well when observers or others working on the same task are present.

Further studies revealed why the presence of others sometimes helps and sometimes hinders performance (Guerin, 1986; Zajonc, 1965). When others observe us, we become aroused. This arousal strengthens the most likely response—the correct one on an easy task, an incorrect one on a difficult task. Thus, when we are being observed, we perform well-learned tasks more quickly and accurately and unmastered tasks less quickly and less accurately. James Michaels and his associates (1982) found that expert pool players who made 71 percent of their shots when alone made 80 percent when four people came to watch them. Poor shooters, who made 36 percent of their shots when alone, made only 25 percent when watched. The energizing effect of an enthusiastic audience probably contributes to the home advantage enjoyed by various sports teams. Studies of more than 80,000 college and professional athletic events in Canada, the United States, and England reveal that home teams win about 6 in 10 games (somewhat fewer for baseball and football, somewhat more for basketball and soccer—see Table 54.1).

■ **social facilitation** improved performance of tasks in the presence of others; occurs with simple or well-learned tasks but not with tasks that are difficult or not yet mastered.

> "I was only following orders."
>
> **Adolf Eichmann, Director of Nazi deportation of Jews to concentration camps**

TABLE 54.1

HOME ADVANTAGE IN MAJOR TEAM SPORTS

Sport	Games Studied	Home Team Winning Percentage
Baseball	23,034	53.5%
Football	2,592	57.3
Ice hockey	4,322	61.1
Basketball	13,596	64.4
Soccer	37,202	69.0

From Courneya & Carron, 1992

SOCIAL INFLUENCE

Many social influences are so subtle that we don't notice them. Or if we do, we think ourselves immune. "Yes, TV affects others," most people say, "but not me." Peer examples don't intimidate us. Role models don't sway us. Ads don't persuade us. We are not slaves to fads, fashions, and opinions; we are true to ourselves.

Or so we may think. The reality, as social influence research has more than a thousand times demonstrated, is that the influence others have on us, and we on them, is real, though often unnoticed. The extent to which influences go unnoticed, even by those looking for them, appears in studies of "facilitated communication" with children with autism. *Autism*, which appears during the preschool years, is marked by minimal intelligible speech, restricted interests and activities, and apparent indifference to others. Hoping to break down the walls that isolate such children, a facilitator holds or steadies the arm of a child, who then uses one finger to type words on a keyboard.

The technique is said to have produced breathtaking results with thousands of children, who suddenly begin typing intelligible words

FIGURE 54.4

Testing facilitated communication
The child responds after the facilitator and child see the same or different pictures. (Adapted from Wheeler & others, 1993.)

(sometimes elaborate sentences) which supposedly report their experiences and feelings. In several dozen cases where a person other than the parent was a facilitator, children have typed accusations of sexual abuse by their parents.

These spectacular findings and serious accusations led some to question who was doing the communicating and the accusing—the child or the facilitator? To find out, Douglas Wheeler and his colleagues (1993) had 12 children with autism

view pictures of everyday objects (a shoe, a book, a comb) and then type what they saw. When their facilitators saw the same picture, the children often typed the correct answer. When the facilitators saw a different picture, or no picture, the children were *never* correct (**FIGURE 54.4**).

More than two dozen other experiments have produced similar results (Burgess & others, 1998; Jacobson & others, 1995). Whatever the facilitator believed (right or wrong) is what was typed. Facilitated communication proponents replied (as have ESP proponents) that the pressure of the testing situation obliterated the delicate phenomenon. But to the researchers, the more logical conclusion is the one reluctantly drawn by some of the shocked facilitators: The communication comes not from the child but from the facilitator (who misattributes the action to the child). The results stunned the well-meaning facilitators. Until the controlled experiment, they were completely unaware of their influence on the child's movements. In this situation, as in so many others, human influence is subtle, unnoticed, even disbelieved, yet it is very real. ■

Social facilitation
Skilled athletes often find they are "on" before an audience. What they do well, they do even better when people are watching.

The point to remember: What you do well, you are likely to do even better in front of an audience, especially a friendly audience; what you normally find difficult may seem all but impossible when you are being watched.

Social facilitation also helps explain a funny effect of crowding: Comedy records that are mildly amusing to people in an uncrowded room seem funnier in a densely packed room (Aiello & others, 1983; Freedman & Perlick, 1979). As comedians and actors know, a "good house" is a full one. The arousal triggered by crowding amplifies other reactions, too. If sitting close to one another, participants in experiments like a friendly person even more, an unfriendly person even less (Schiffenbauer & Schiavo, 1976; Storms & Thomas, 1977).

Social Loafing

Social facilitation experiments test the effect of others' presence on performance on an individual task, such as shooting pool. But what happens to performance when people perform the task as a group? In a team tug-of-war, for example, do you suppose the effort that a person puts forth would be more than, less than, or the same as the effort he or she would exert in a one-on-one tug-of-war? To find out, Alan Ingham and his fellow researchers (1974) asked blindfolded University of Massachusetts students to "pull as hard as you can" on a rope. When Ingham fooled the students into believing three others were also pulling behind them, they exerted only 82 percent as much effort as when they knew they were pulling alone.

To describe the diminished effort by those in a group, Bibb Latané and his colleagues (1981; Jackson & Williams, 1988) coined the term **social loafing**. In 78 experiments conducted in the United States, India, Thailand, Japan, China, and Taiwan, social loafing occurred on various tasks, though it was especially common among men in individualistic cultures (Karau & Williams, 1993). In one of Latané's experiments, blindfolded subjects seated in a group clapped or shouted as loud as they could while listening through headphones to the sound of loud clapping or shouting. When told they were doing it with the others, the subjects produced about one-third less noise than when they thought their individual efforts were identifiable.

Why? First, people acting as part of a group feel less accountable and therefore worry less about what others think. Second, they may view their contribution as dispensable (Harkins & Szymanski, 1989; Kerr & Bruun, 1983). As many leaders of organizations know, if group members share equally in the group's benefits regardless of how much they contribute, some may slack off. Unless highly motivated and identified with their group, they may "free-ride" on the other group members' efforts.

Deindividuation

So the presence of others can arouse people (as in the social facilitation experiments) or can diminish their feelings of responsibility (as in the social loafing experiments). But sometimes the presence of others both arouses people *and* diminishes their sense of responsibility. The result can be uninhibited behavior ranging from a food fight in the dining hall or screaming at a basketball referee to vandalism or rioting. Abandoning normal restraints to the power of the group is termed **deindividuation**. To be deindividuated is to be less self-conscious and less restrained when in a group situation.

Deindividuation often occurs when group participation makes people feel aroused and anonymous. In one experiment, New York University women dressed in depersonalizing Ku Klux Klan-style hoods delivered twice as much electric shock to a victim as did identifiable women (Zimbardo, 1970). (As in all such experiments, the "victim" did not actually receive the shocks.) Similarly, tribal warriors who depersonalize themselves with face paints or masks are more likely than those with exposed faces to kill, torture, or mutilate captured enemies (Watson, 1973). Whether in a mob, at a rock concert, at a ballgame, or at worship, to lose self-consciousness (to become deindividuated) is to become more responsive to the group experience.

Effects of Group Interaction

We have examined the conditions under which the presence of others can

+ make easy tasks easier and difficult tasks harder.
+ tempt people to free-ride on the efforts of others or motivate them to exert themselves.
+ enhance humor or fuel mob violence.

Research shows how group interaction, too, can have both bad and good effects.

Group Polarization

Educational researchers have noted that, over time, initial differences between groups of college students tend to grow. If the first-year students at College X tend to be more intellectually oriented than those at College Y, that difference will probably be amplified by the time they are seniors. Similarly, if the political conservatism of students who join fraternities and sororities is greater than that of students who do not, the gap in the political attitudes of the two groups will probably widen as they progress through college (Wilson & others, 1975).

social loafing the tendency for people in a group to exert less effort when pooling their efforts toward attaining a common goal than when individually accountable.

deindividuation the loss of self-awareness and self-restraint occurring in group situations that foster arousal and anonymity.

FIGURE **54.5**
Group polarization
If a group is like-minded, discussion strengthens its prevailing opinions. Talking over racial issues increased prejudice in a high-prejudice group of high school students and decreased it in a low-prejudice group. (Data from Myers & Bishop, 1970.)

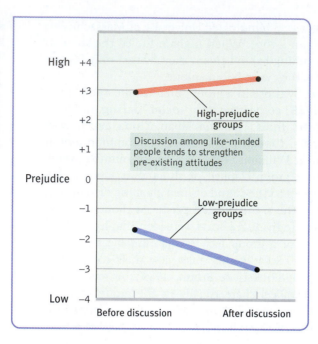

High-prejudice groups

Discussion among like-minded people tends to strengthen pre-existing attitudes

Low-prejudice groups

Before discussion   After discussion

This enhancement of a group's prevailing tendencies—called **group polarization**—occurs when people within a group discuss attitudes that most of them either favor or oppose. Group polarization can have beneficial results, as when it amplifies a sought-after spiritual awareness or strengthens the resolve of those in a self-help group. But it can also have dire consequences. For example, George Bishop and I discovered that when a low-prejudice group of high school students discussed racial issues, their attitudes became more accepting. When high-prejudice students discussed the same issues, they became more prejudiced (**FIGURE 54.5**).

Similarly, well-meaning programs that bring together adolescents at risk for delinquency have sometimes *increased* their negative behaviors (Dishion & others, 1999). And psychologists Clark McCauley and Mary Segal (1987), who have analyzed terrorist organizations around the world, note that the terrorist mentality does not erupt suddenly. Rather, it arises among people who get together because of a grievance and then become more and more extreme as they interact in isolation from any moderating influences.

The Internet provides a new medium for group polarization. Its tens of thousands of virtual groups enable bereaved parents, peacemakers, and teachers to find solace and support from kindred spirits. But the Internet also enables people who share interests in government cover-ups, extraterrestrial visitors, white supremacy, Y2K collapse, or citizen militias to find one another and to find support for their shared suspicions (McKenna & Bargh, 1998). Future experiments will reveal whether electronic discussions mirror the polarizing effects of face-to-face discussions. With their views echoing one another's, do nerds become nerdier, goths gothier, conspiracy wackos wackier?

Groupthink

Does group interaction ever distort important decisions? Social psychologist Irving Janis began to think so as he read historian Arthur M. Schlesinger, Jr.'s account of how President John F. Kennedy and his advisers blundered into an ill-fated plan to invade Cuba with 1400 CIA-trained Cuban exiles. When the invaders were easily captured and soon linked to the U.S. government, Kennedy wondered in hindsight, "How could we have been so stupid?"

To find out, Janis (1982) studied the decision-making procedures that led to the fiasco. He discovered that the soaring morale of the recently elected president and his advisers fostered undue confidence in the plan. To preserve the good group feeling, any dissenting views were suppressed or self-censored, especially after the president voiced his enthusiasm for the scheme. Since no one spoke strongly against the idea, everyone assumed consensus support. To describe this harmonious but unrealistic group thinking, Janis coined the term **groupthink**.

Janis and others then examined other historical fiascos—the failure to anticipate the 1941 Japanese attack on Pearl Harbor, the escalation of the Vietnam

"One's impulse to blow the whistle on this nonsense was simply undone by the circumstances of the discussion."

Arthur M. Schlesinger, Jr. (1965, p. 255)

War, the U.S. Watergate cover-up, the Chernobyl nuclear reactor accident (Reason, 1987), and the U.S. space shuttle *Challenger* explosion (Esser & Lindoerfer, 1989). They discovered that in these cases, too, groupthink was fed by overconfidence, conformity, self-justification, and group polarization. Buoyed by a string of successful space shuttle launches, the NASA (National Aeronautics and Space Administration) management team approached the 1985 *Challenger* mission brimming with confidence but frustrated by launch delays. When the rocket booster's engineers opposed the launch because of dangers posed by freezing temperatures, group pressures to go ahead effectively overrode their warnings. Unless the engineers could *prove* that the rocket seals would not hold, the management group would not agree to another delay. Moreover, managers shielded the NASA executive who made the final "Go" decision from information about the warnings. Assuming—wrongly—that support was unanimous, he launched the *Challenger* on its one-way flight to annihilation.

Despite such fiascos and tragedies, Janis also knew that, with some types of problems, two heads are better than one. So he also studied instances in which U.S. presidents and their advisers collectively made good decisions, such as when the Truman administration formulated the Marshall Plan, which offered assistance to Europe after World War II, and when the Kennedy administration worked to keep the Soviets from installing missiles in Cuba. In such instances—and in the business world, too, Janis believed—groupthink is prevented when a leader welcomes various opinions, invites experts' critiques of developing plans, and assigns people to identify possible problems. Just as the suppression of dissent bends a group toward bad decisions, so open debate often shapes good ones. None of us is as smart as all of us.

The Power of Individuals

In affirming the power of social influence, we must not overlook our power as individuals. *Social control* (the power of the situation) and *personal control* (the power of the individual) interact. People aren't billiard balls. When feeling pressured, we may react by doing the opposite of what is expected, thereby reasserting our sense of freedom (Brehm & Brehm, 1981).

Self-Fulfilling Prophecies

Many situations that influence us are ones we actually helped create. If we expect people to be uncooperative and hostile, we may treat them in ways that elicit such behavior. Thus, our expectations may become **self-fulfilling prophecies**. In one experiment, men talked more charmingly by phone to women they believed to be beautiful. This led the women to respond more warmly—confirming the men's idea that attractive people are likeable (Snyder & others, 1977). In a follow-up experiment, Robert Ridge and Jeffrey Reber (1998) led some university men to believe that a female fellow student was attracted to them, and others to believe she was not attracted to them. Later analysis of conversations between them revealed a self-fulfilling prophecy: When the man *believed* the woman found him attractive, she was more likely to act as if she did. Seek and ye shall find.

In long-term relationships, does idealizing our partner set us up for later disappointment? Actually, report Sandra Murray and her colleagues (1996, 2000), positive illusions about partners tend to be prophetic. Those who idealize their dating partners as having many virtues and few faults tend to have more satisfying and longer-lasting relationships. Moreover, idealized perceptions tend to be self-fulfilling; people come to accept their partner's perceptions. Love is not blind, Murray concludes. Rather, it helps create the reality it presumes.

- **group polarization** the enhancement of a group's prevailing attitudes through discussion within the group.

- **groupthink** the mode of thinking that occurs when the desire for harmony in a decision-making group overrides a realistic appraisal of alternatives.

- **self-fulfilling prophecy** occurs when one person's belief about others leads one to act in ways that induce the others to appear to confirm the belief.

"Truth springs from argument among friends."

Philosopher David Hume, 1711–1776

"Love to faults is always blind."

William Blake, *Poems*, 1791–1792

Gandhi

As the life of Mahatma Gandhi powerfully testifies, a consistent and persistent minority voice can sometimes sway the majority. The nonviolent appeals and fasts of the Hindu nationalist and spiritual leader were instrumental in winning India's independence from Britain in 1947.

Minority Influence

The power of committed individuals also appears in their influence on their groups. Social history is often made by a minority that sways the majority. Were this not so, communism would have remained an obscure theory, Christianity would be a small Middle Eastern sect, and Rosa Parks' refusal to sit at the back of the bus would not have ignited the civil rights movement. Technological history, too, is often made by innovative minorities who overcome the majority's resistance to change. To many, the railroad was a nonsensical idea; some farmers even feared that train noise would prevent hens from laying eggs. People derided Robert Fulton's steamboat as "Fulton's Folly." As Fulton later said, "Never did a single encouraging remark, a bright hope, a warm wish, cross my path." Much the same reaction greeted the printing press, the telegraph, the incandescent lamp, and the typewriter (Cantril & Bumstead, 1960).

To better understand how minorities can sway majorities, European social psychologists led by Serge Moscovici (1985) investigated groups in which one or two individuals consistently express a controversial attitude or an unusual perceptual judgment. They repeatedly found that a minority that unswervingly holds to its position is far more successful in swaying the majority than is a minority that waffles. Holding consistently to a minority opinion will not make you popular, but it may make you influential. This is especially so if your self-confidence stimulates others to consider why you react as you do. Although people often follow the majority view publicly, they may privately develop sympathy for the minority view. Even when a minority's influence is not yet visible, it may be persuading some members of the majority to rethink their views (Wood & others, 1994). The powers of social influence are enormous; but so are the powers of the committed individual.

REVIEW AND REFLECT:

Social Influence

What do experiments on conformity and compliance reveal about the power of social influence?

As suggestibility studies demonstrate, when we are unsure about our judgments, we are likely to adjust them toward the group standard. Solomon Asch found that under certain conditions people will conform to a group's judgment even when it is clearly incorrect. We may conform either to gain social approval (normative social influence) or because we welcome the information that others provide (informational social influence). In Stanley Milgram's famous experiments, people torn between obeying an experimenter and responding to another's pleas to stop the shocks usually chose to obey orders, even though obedience supposedly meant harming the other person. Social influence is potent.

How does the presence of others influence our actions?

Experiments on social facilitation reveal that the presence of either observers or co-actors can arouse individuals, boosting their performance on easy tasks but hindering it on difficult ones.

How does our behavior change when we act as part of a group?

When people pool their efforts toward a group goal, social loafing may occur as some individuals take a free ride on others' efforts. When a group experience arouses people and makes them anonymous, they may become less self-aware and self-restrained, a psychological state known as deindividuation. Within groups, discussions among like-minded members often produce group polarization, an enhancement of the group's prevailing attitudes. This is one cause of groupthink, the tendency for harmony-seeking groups to make unrealistic decisions after suppressing dissenting information.

The power of the group is great, but so is the power of the person. Even a small minority sometimes sways a group, especially when the minority expresses its views consistently.

Terms and Concepts to Remember

conformity, p. 682
normative social influence, p. 683
informational social influence, p. 683
social facilitation, p. 687
social loafing, p. 689
deindividuation, p. 689
group polarization, p. 690
groupthink, p. 690
self-fulfilling prophecy, p. 691

Test Yourself

54.1 Conformity involves adjusting our thinking and behavior toward others in the group. Conformity studies have found that a person is most likely to conform to a group if
a. the group members have diverse opinions.
b. the person feels competent and secure.
c. the group consists of a least three people.
d. other group members will not observe the person's behavior.

54.2. In a classic experiment on obedience, Stanley Milgram tested his subjects' willingness to comply with a command to deliver painful high-voltage shocks to another person. Al-though no shocks were given, the subjects believed they were—and more than 60 percent complied with the experimenter's instruction to deliver stronger and stronger shocks. In subsequent experiments, Milgram's obedience studies showed that the rate of compliance was highest when
a. the victim was at a distance.
b. the experimenter was in another room.
c. other subjects refused to go along with the experimenter.
d. the subjects believed the victim had a heart condition.

54.3. In the presence of others we become aroused: Before an audience, a swimmer swims faster. Social facilitation—improved performance in the presence of others—occurs with
a. any physical task.   c. a well-learned task.
b. new learning.   d. competitive sports only.

54.4. When people are part of a group working toward a common goal, their individual efforts are diminished. Latané and his colleagues called this
a. minority influence.   c. social loafing.
b. social facilitation.   d. group polarization.

54.5. In a group situation that fosters arousal and anonymity, a person sometimes loses self-consciousness and self-control. This phenomenon, called deindividuation, is best illustrated by
a. improved performance in front of an audience.
b. unrestrained behavior at a mass rally.
c. evasion of responsibility in a group clean-up effort.
d. denial of one's own perceptions in the face of an opposing consensus.

54.6. If a group is like-minded, discussion strengthens its prevailing opinion. This effect is called
a. groupthink.   c. group polarization.
b. minority influence.   d. social facilitation.

54.7. Group interaction has the potential of distorting important group decisions. For example, when a group's desire for harmony overrides its realistic appraisal of alternatives, _____ has occurred.
a. group polarization   c. social facilitation
b. groupthink   d. deindividuation

Review: You are organizing a Town Hall–style meeting of fiercely competitive political candidates. To add to the fun, friends have suggested handing out masks of the candidates' faces for supporters to wear. What phenomenon might these masks engage?

Reflect: Name two examples of social influence you have experienced this week (remembering that influence may be informational).

Answers to the Test Yourself and Review questions can be found in the green appendix at the end of the book.

55

Social Relations

W hat can social psychology teach us about how we *relate* to one another? We will ponder the bad and the good: from prejudice, aggression, and conflict, to attraction, altruism, and peacemaking.

Prejudice

Preview Question: What are the social, emotional, and cognitive roots of prejudice?

Prejudice means "prejudgment." It is an unjustifiable and usually negative attitude toward a group—typically a different cultural, ethnic, or gender group. Like all attitudes, **prejudice** is a mixture of beliefs (often overgeneralized and called **stereotypes**), emotions (hostility, envy, or fear), and predispositions to action (to discriminate). To *believe* that overweight people are gluttonous, to *feel* antipathy for an overweight person, and to be hesitant to hire or date an overweight person is to be prejudiced.

Like other forms of prejudgment, prejudices are schemas that influence how we notice and interpret events. In one study, most white participants perceived a white man shoving a black man as "horsing around." When they saw a black man shove a white man, they interpreted the act as "violent" (Duncan, 1976). Our preconceived ideas about people bias our impressions of their behavior. Prejudgments color perceptions.

How prejudiced are people? To find out, we can assess what they say and what they do. To judge by what Americans say, racial and gender attitudes have changed dramatically in the last half-century (**FIGURE 55.1**). Nearly everyone agrees that children of all races should attend the same schools and that women and men should receive the same pay for the same job. In Western Europe, where many "guest workers" and refugees have settled in recent years, "modern prejudice" (exaggerating ethnic differences, rejecting minorities for supposedly nonracial reasons) is replacing blatant prejudice (Pettigrew, 1998).

As blatant prejudice wanes, subtle prejudice lingers. In socially intimate settings (dating, dancing, marrying), many people admit they would feel uncomfortable with someone of another race. This fact helps explain why, in a survey of students at 390 colleges and universities, 53 percent of African-American students felt excluded from school activities (Hurtado & others, 1994). (Similar feelings were reported by 24 percent of Asian-Americans, 16 percent of Mexican-Americans, and 6 percent of European-Americans.) On NBA basketball teams, where most of the players and all the top scorers have been African-American in recent years, a similar majority–minority dynamic can lead some white minority players to feel lonely or disrespected (Schoenfeld, 1995).

Two recent studies illustrate that prejudice can be not only subtle but apparently unconscious. In one, Anthony Greenwald and his colleagues (1998) showed that even people who deny harboring racial or gender prejudice may carry negative associations. For example, 9 in 10 white respondents took longer to identify pleasant words (such as *peace, paradise*) as "good" when good was associated with black rather than white faces. In the other, Kent Harbert (1998) asked white university women to evaluate a flawed essay said to be written by a black or a white fellow student. When the writer was said to be black, the ratings were markedly *higher*. Harsh criticisms—

Does perception change with race?
The Italian clothing manufacturer Benetton asked this question with altered photographs in their company magazine. Skin color and facial features are, however, mere frosting on the physiological cake. On average, any two randomly chosen humans are 99.8 percent alike in the alphabetic sequence in their genetic code. Only 6 percent of their 0.2 percent difference is racial; 9 percent represents ethnic differences within races (for example, between French and Italians); 85 percent is individual differences within one's group (Hoffman, 1994; Vines, 1995).

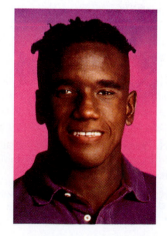

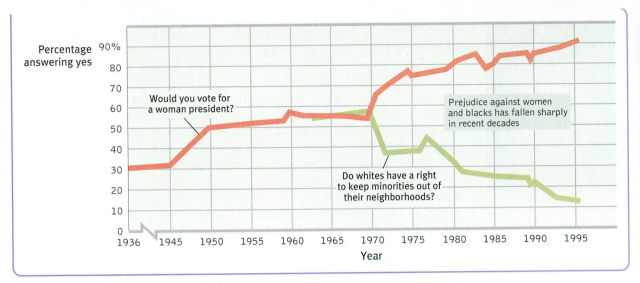

FIGURE 55.1
Prejudice over time
Americans today express much less racial and gender prejudice than they did two and three decades ago. (Niemi & others, 1989; T. Smith, 1994, personal communication.)

"When I read college work this bad I just want to lay my head down on the table and cry"—were never given the supposedly black-authored essays. Did the evaluators calibrate their evaluations to their racial stereotypes, Harbert wondered, leading them to patronize the black writers with less exacting standards? If so, such low expectations and the resulting "inflated praise and insufficient criticism" may hinder minority student achievement.

But lest we think blatant prejudice is behind us, we should be aware that prejudice has at times resurfaced since the late 1980s, in public settings as well as in private. In several American states where black motorists are a minority of the drivers and speeders on interstate highways, they have been the majority of those stopped and searched by state police (Lamberth, 1998; Staples, 1999a,b). In one New Jersey turnpike study, African-Americans were 13.5 percent of the car occupants, 15 percent of the speeders, and 35 percent of the drivers stopped. Elmo Randolph, a New Jersey dentist, knew it all along. After being stopped more than 100 times over four years while driving his gold BMW from his home to his office, Dr. Randolph, guilty of nothing more than "driving while black," sold the car.

Elsewhere, hate has raged openly—between Israel's Palestinians and Jews, Kosovo's Serbs and Albanians, Rwanda's Tutsis and Hutus. In 1997, the world was plagued by one major armed conflict between countries (India–Pakistan) and 24 armed conflicts between warring groups within countries (Mutiso, 1998).

Around the world, gender prejudice and discrimination persist, too. Worldwide, women are more likely to live in poverty (Lipps, 1999). And, worldwide, two-thirds of children without basic schooling are girls. Thus, there are some 350 million illiterate men and 600 million illiterate women (United Nations, 1991, 1993). In Saudi Arabia, women are not allowed to drive. In Western countries, we pay more to those (usually men) who take care of our garbage than to those (usually women) who take care of our children. And despite gender equality in intelligence scores, people tend to perceive their fathers as more intelligent than their mothers (Furnham & Rawles, 1995).

Nowhere are female infants left out on a hillside to die of exposure, as was the practice in ancient Greece. Yet even today boys are often valued more than their sisters. During the 1970s Bangladesh famine, preschool girls were more malnourished than boys were, and in many developing countries death rates are higher for girls than for boys (Bairagi, 1987). And with testing that enables sex-selective abortions, South Korean male births now exceed female births by 14 percent (instead of the normal 5 percent). China now has 120 boys for every 100 girls (Fathalla, 1999;

"Unhappily the world has yet to learn how to live with diversity."

Pope John Paul II, Address to the United Nations, 1995

■ **prejudice** an unjustifiable (and usually negative) attitude toward a group and its members. Prejudice generally involves stereotyped beliefs, negative feelings, and a predisposition to discriminatory action.

■ **stereotype** a generalized (sometimes accurate but often overgeneralized) belief about a group of people.

(a)   (b)

FIGURE 55.2 Who do you like best? Which one placed an ad seeking a long-term relationship?
Research suggests that subtly feminized features convey a likeable image, which people tend to associate more with committed dads than with promiscuous cads. Thus, most people picked computer-generated face (b) in response to both questions.

Nando Times, 1999). Sex-selective neglect and abortions have resulted in China and India together having 76 million fewer females than they should have (Klasen, 1994). Globally, up to 100 million women are missing (Fathalla, 1999). (You read that right: 100 *million* "missing women.")

But the news isn't all bad for girls and women. Most people *feel* more positively about "women" in general than they do about "men" (Eagly, 1994; Haddock & Zanna, 1994). People see women as having some traits, such as nurturance, sensitivity, and less aggressiveness, that most people prefer (Swim, 1994). Perhaps that's why people prefer slightly feminized computer-generated men's and women's faces to slightly masculinized faces. Researcher David Perrett and his colleagues (1998) speculate that a slightly feminized male face connotes kindness, cooperativeness, and other traits of a good father. When the British Broadcasting Company invited 18,000 women to guess which of the men in **FIGURE 55.2** was most likely to place a personal ad seeking a "special lady to love and cherish forever," 66 percent guessed the slightly feminized face B. No wonder Leonardo DiCaprio has seemed so appealing to young girls.

Why does prejudice arise? Inequalities, social divisions, and emotional scapegoating are partly responsible. But so are the natural cognitive mechanisms by which we simplify our worlds.

Social Inequalities

When some people have money, power, and prestige and others do not, the "haves" usually develop attitudes that justify things as they are. In the extreme case, slave owners perceived slaves as innately lazy, ignorant, and irresponsible—as having the very traits that "justified" enslaving them. More commonly, women are perceived as unassertive but sensitive and therefore suited for the caretaking tasks they have traditionally performed (Hoffman & Hurst, 1990). In short, prejudice rationalizes inequalities.

Discrimination also increases prejudice through the reactions it provokes in its victims, another example of a self-fulfilling prophecy. In his classic 1954 book, *The Nature of Prejudice*, Gordon Allport noted that being a victim of discrimination can produce either self-blame or anger. Both reactions may create new grounds for prejudice through the classic *blame-the-victim* dynamic. If the circumstances of ghetto life breed a higher crime rate, someone can then use the higher crime rate to justify continuing the discrimination that helped to create the ghetto.

"You cannot oppress people for over three centuries and then say it is all over and expect them to put on suits and ties and [be] attaché-carrying citizens and go to work on Wall Street."

Shelby Steele, "The New Segregation," 1992

Us and Them: Ingroup and Outgroup

Thanks to our ancestral need to belong, we are a group-bound species. We cheer on our groups, kill for them, die for them. Indeed, we define who we are—our identities—partly in terms of our groups. Australian psychologists John Turner (1987) and Michael Hogg (1996) note that through our *social identities* we associate ourselves with certain groups and contrast ourselves with others. When Ian identifies himself as a man, an Aussie, a Labourite, a University of Sydney student, a Catholic, and a MacGregor, he knows who he is.

The social definition of who you are also implies who you are not. Mentally drawing a circle that defines "us" (the **ingroup**) excludes "them" (the **outgroup**). Such group identifications typically promote an **ingroup bias**—a favoring of one's own group. Even arbitrarily creating an us–them distinction—by grouping people with the toss of a coin—leads people to show favoritism to their own group when dividing any rewards (Tajfel, 1982; Wilder, 1981).

The urge to distinguish enemies from friends and to have one's group be dominant predisposes prejudice against strangers (Whitely, 1999). To Greeks of the classi-

"All good people agree,
 And all good people say
 All nice people, like us, are We
 And everyone else is They.
 But if you cross over the sea
 Instead of over the way
 You may end by (think of it)
 looking on We
 As only a sort of They."

Rudyard Kipling, "We and They," 1926

cal era, all non-Greeks were "barbarians." Most citizens in the coalition of countries fighting in the 1991 Persian Gulf War felt more pain over the few hundred dead Allied soldiers than over the reported 100,000 Iraqi dead. In Africa, where some 700 traditional societies cluster into fewer than 50 nations, people typically like and admire their own group and direct their hostility toward other groups (Segall & others, 1990). Most children believe their school is better than the other schools in town. In high schools, students often form cliques—jocks, preppies, stoners, skaters, gangsters, freaks, geeks—and disparage those outside their group. Even chimpanzees have been seen to wipe clean the spot where they were touched by a chimp from another group (Goodall, 1986).

- **ingroup** "us"—people with whom one shares a common identity.
- **outgroup** "them"—those perceived as different or apart from one's ingroup.
- **ingroup bias** the tendency to favor one's own group.
- **scapegoat theory** the theory that prejudice provides an outlet for anger by providing someone to blame.

Scapegoating

Prejudice springs not only from the divisions of society but also from the passions of the heart. Prejudice may express anger: When things go wrong, finding someone to blame can provide a target, a scapegoat, for one's anger. Evidence for this **scapegoat theory** of prejudice comes from high prejudice levels among economically frustrated people and from experiments in which a temporary frustration intensifies prejudice. Nazi leader Hermann Rausching once explained the Nazis' need to scapegoat: "If the Jew did not exist, we should have to invent him" (quoted by Koltz, 1983). Pernicious passions produce poisonous prejudice.

In addition to providing a convenient emotional outlet for anger, despised outgroups can also boost ingroup members' self-esteem. In experiments, students who experience failure or are made to feel insecure will often restore their self-esteem by disparaging a rival school or another person (Cialdini & Richardson, 1980; Crocker & others, 1987). To boost our own sense of status, it helps to have others to denigrate. That is why a rival's misfortune sometimes provides a twinge of pleasure.

"If the Tiber reaches the walls, if the Nile does not rise to the fields, if the sky doesn't move or the Earth does, if there is famine, if there is plague, the cry is at once: 'The Christians to the lion!'"

Tertullian, *Apologeticus*, A.D. 197

Cognitive Roots of Prejudice

Prejudice springs from the divisions of society, the passions of the heart, and also from the mind's natural workings. Stereotyped beliefs are a by-product of how we cognitively simplify the world.

Categorization

One way we simplify our world is to categorize. A chemist categorizes molecules as organic and inorganic. A mental health professional categorizes psychological disorders by types. In categorizing people into groups, however, we often stereotype them. Stereotypes may contain a germ of truth, but they bias our perceptions. Jeff Stone and his colleagues (1997) demonstrated this by having Princeton University students listen to a radio broadcast of a university basketball game while evaluating the performance of one player. Influenced by their expectations, those introduced to him with a photo of a black player gave him a better performance evaluation than did those who had been shown a photo of a white player.

Categorization also biases our perceptions of diversity. We view ourselves as individuals, but we overestimate the similarity of people within groups other than our own. "They"—the members of some other group—seem to look and act alike, but "we" are diverse (Bothwell & others, 1989). If we could see ourselves from a penguin's perspective, we would all look alike—much as penguins all look alike to us (though not to their fellow penguins). We are keenly sensitive to differences within our group, less so to

Do racial stereotypes influence perceptions?
At Illinois' Augustana College black students' and white students' reactions to the O.J. Simpson "not guilty" criminal trial verdict mirrored the nation's racial difference in perceptions of his guilt or innocence. In part, people's reactions reflected their stereotypes of white police officers as either honest or oppressive.

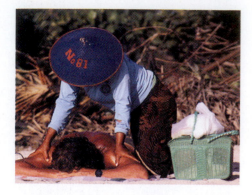

Do people of another race look alike?
Foreign sunbathers on Bali's beaches may think they do. Balinese masseuses wear identifying numbers on their hats, enabling visitors to recognize them easily.

differences within other groups. To those in one ethnic group, members of another often seem more alike in appearance, personality, and attitudes than they are. With experience, however, people get better at recognizing individual faces from another group. For example, people of European descent more accurately identify individual African faces if they have watched a great deal of basketball on television, exposing them to many African-heritage faces (Li & others, 1996).

Vivid Cases

The *availability heuristic*—one of the mental shortcuts we use to make decisions—refers to our tendency to judge the frequency of events by instances that readily come to mind. In a classic experiment, Myron Rothbart and his colleagues (1978) showed how we can overgeneralize from vivid, memorable cases. They divided University of Oregon student volunteers into two groups, then showed them information about 50 men. The first group's list included 10 men arrested for nonviolent crimes, such as forgery. The second group's list included 10 men arrested for violent crimes, such as assault. Later when both groups recalled how many men on their list had committed any sort of crime, the second group overestimated the number. Vivid (violent) cases are readily available to our memory and therefore influence our judgments of a group.

The Just-World Phenomenon

As we noted earlier, people often justify their prejudice by blaming its victims. Bystanders, too, may blame victims by assuming the world is just and therefore "people get what they deserve." In experiments, merely observing someone receive painful shocks has led many people to think less of the victim (Lerner, 1980). This **just-world phenomenon** reflects an idea we commonly teach our children—that good is rewarded and evil is punished. From this it is but a short leap to assume that those who succeed must be good and those who suffer must be bad. Such reasoning enables the rich to see both their own wealth and the poor's misfortune as justly deserved. As one German civilian is said to have remarked when visiting the Bergen-Belsen concentration camp shortly after World War II, "What terrible criminals these prisoners must have been to receive such treatment."

Hindsight bias is also at work here (Carli & Leonard, 1989). Have you ever heard people say that rape victims, abused spouses, or people with AIDS got what they deserved? An experiment by Ronnie Janoff-Bulman and her collaborators (1985) illustrates this phenomenon of blaming the victim. When given a detailed account of a date that ended with the woman's being raped, people perceived the woman's behavior as at least partly to blame. In hindsight, they thought, "She should have known better." (Blaming the victim also serves to reassure people that it couldn't happen to them.) Others who were given the same account, with the rape ending deleted, did not perceive the woman's behavior as inviting rape. Only when victimized was she faulted for her behavior.

Aggression

Preview Question: What biological and psychological factors make us more prone to harm one another?

The most destructive force in our social relations is aggression. In psychology, *aggression* has a more precise meaning than it does in everyday usage. The assertive, persistent salesperson is not aggressive. Nor is the dentist who makes you wince with pain. But the person who passes along a vicious rumor about you, the person who verbally assaults you, and the attacker who mugs you are aggressive. In psychology, **aggression** is any physical or verbal behavior intended to hurt or destroy, whether done reactively out of hostility or proactively as a calculated means to an end. Thus, murders and assaults that occurred as hostile outbursts are aggression. So were the 110 million war-related deaths that took place during the last century, many of which were cool and calculated.

Why is it that some countries, and some individuals, are so violence-prone? If you are living outside the United States, your risk of being murdered is *much* lower than if you are within the U.S. borders—one-fifth if you are a Canadian or an Australian, one-sixth if you are a New Zealander, and, on average, one-tenth if you are British (United Nations, 1997).

To answer this question, we turn once again down a familiar path. Research on aggression affirms that behavior emerges from the interaction of biology and experience. For a gun to fire, the trigger must be pulled; with some people, as with hair-trigger guns, it doesn't take much to trip an explosion. Let us look first at biological factors that influence our thresholds for aggressive behavior, then at the psychological factors that pull the trigger.

The Biology of Aggression

According to one view, argued by Sigmund Freud and others, our species has a volcanic potential to erupt in aggression. Freud thought that we harbor not only positive survival instincts but also a self-destructive "death instinct," which we usually displace toward others as aggression or release in socially approved activities such as the arts or sports.

Aggression varies too widely from culture to culture and person to person to be considered an unlearned instinct, as Freud supposed. But biology does influence aggression. Stimuli that trigger aggressive behavior operate through our biological system. We can look for biological influences at three levels—genetic, neural, and biochemical. Our genes engineer our individual nervous systems, which operate electrochemically.

Genetic Influences

Animals have been bred for aggressiveness—sometimes for sport, sometimes for research. Twin studies suggest that genes influence human aggression as well (Miles & Carey, 1997; Rowe & others, 1999). If one identical twin admits to "having a violent temper," the other twin will often independently admit the same. Fraternal twins are much less likely to respond similarly.

Neural Influences

Animal and human brains have neural systems that, when stimulated, inhibit or produce aggressive behavior (Moyer, 1983). Consider:

+ The domineering leader of a caged monkey colony had a radio-controlled electrode implanted in a brain area that, when stimulated, inhibits aggression. When researchers placed the button that activated the electrode in the colony's cage, one small monkey learned to push it every time the boss became threatening.
+ A mild-mannered woman had an electrode implanted in her brain's limbic system (in the amygdala) by neurosurgeons seeking to diagnose a disorder. Because the brain has no sensory receptors, she was unable to feel the stimulation. But at the flick of a switch she snarled, "Take my blood pressure. Take it now," then stood up and began to strike the doctor.
+ Intensive evaluation of 15 death-row inmates revealed that all 15 had suffered a severe head injury. Although most neurologically impaired people are not violent, researcher Dorothy Lewis and her colleagues (1986) inferred that unrecognized neurological disorders may be part of the violence recipe.

In the last 25 years in the United States, guns have caused 800,000 suicidal, homicidal, and accidental deaths. Compared with people of the same sex, race, age, and neighborhood, those who keep a gun in the home (ironically, often for protection) are nearly three times more likely to be murdered in the home—nearly always by a family member or close acquaintance. For every self-defense use of a gun in the home, there are four unintentional shootings, seven criminal assaults or homicides, and eleven attempted or completed suicides (Kellermann & others, 1993, 1997, 1998).

■ **just-world phenomenon** the tendency of people to believe the world is just and that people therefore get what they deserve and deserve what they get.

■ **aggression** any physical or verbal behavior intended to hurt or destroy.

A lean, mean fighting machine—the testosterone-laden female hyena
The hyena's unusual embryology pumps testosterone into female fetuses. The result is revved-up young female hyenas who seem born to fight.

"It's a guy thing."

"We could avoid two-thirds of all crime simply by putting all able-bodied young men in cryogenic sleep from the age of 12 through 28."

David T. Lykken, *The Antisocial Personalities*, 1995

Group anonymity + competition + alcohol = aggression
A 1985 riot at a soccer game in Brussels left 38 dead and 437 injured. Aroused by the competition and loaded with alcohol, English fans lost all restraint when provoked by Italian fans. They attacked the Italians, who retreated and were then crushed against a wall.

So, does the brain have a "violence center" that produces aggression when stimulated? Actually, no one spot in the brain controls aggression, because aggression is a complex behavior that occurs in particular contexts. Rather, the brain has neural systems that facilitate aggression, making it more likely given the presence of provocation and the absence of deterrents.

Biochemical Influences

Hormones, alcohol, and other substances in the blood influence the neural systems that control aggression. A raging bull will become a gentle Ferdinand when its testosterone level is reduced by castration. The same is true of castrated mice. When injected with testosterone, the castrated mice once again become aggressive.

Although humans are less sensitive to hormonal changes, violent criminals tend to be muscular young males with lower-than-average intelligence scores, low levels of the neurotransmitter serotonin, and higher-than-average testosterone levels (Dabbs, 1992; Pendick, 1994). Drugs that sharply reduce their testosterone levels also subdue their aggressive tendencies. High testosterone correlates with irritability, low tolerance for frustration, and impulsiveness, qualities that predispose somewhat more aggressive responses to provocation (Harris, 1999). Among both teenage boys and adult men, high testosterone levels correlate with delinquency, hard drug use, and aggressive-bullying responses to frustration (Berman & others, 1993; Dabbs & Morris, 1990; Olweus & others, 1988). With age, testosterone levels—and aggressiveness—diminish.

The traffic between hormones and behavior is two-way. Testosterone heightens dominance and aggressiveness, but dominating or defeating behavior also boosts testosterone levels (Mazur & Booth, 1998). One study measured testosterone levels in the saliva of male college basketball fans before and after a big game. Testosterone levels swelled among the victorious fans and sank among the dejected ones (Bernhardt & others, 1998).

Alcohol, for biological and psychological reasons, unleashes aggressive responses to frustration (Bushman, 1993; Ito & others, 1996; Taylor & Chermack, 1993). (Just *thinking* you've imbibed alcohol has some effect; but so, too, does unknowingly ingesting alcohol slipped into a drink.) Police data and prison surveys reinforce conclusions drawn from experiments on alcohol and aggression. Aggression-prone people are more likely to drink and to become violent when intoxicated (White & others, 1993). People who have been drinking commit 4 in 10 violent crimes and 3 in 4 acts of spousal abuse (Greenfeld, 1998).

■ **frustration-aggression principle** the principle that frustration—the blocking of an attempt to achieve some goal—creates anger, which can generate aggression.

The Psychology of Aggression

Biological factors influence the ease with which aggression is triggered. But what psychological factors pull the trigger?

Aversive Events

Although suffering sometimes builds character, it may also bring out the worst in us. Studies in which animals or humans experience unpleasant events reveal that those made miserable often make others miserable (Berkowitz, 1983, 1989).

Being blocked short of a goal also increases people's readiness to aggress. This phenomenon is called the **frustration-aggression principle**: Frustration creates anger, which may in some people generate aggression, especially in the presence of an aggressive cue, such as a gun. Like frustration, other aversive stimuli—physical pain, personal insults, foul odors, hot temperatures, cigarette smoke, and a host of others—can also evoke hostility. For example, violent crime and spousal abuse rates are higher during hotter years, seasons, months, and days (**FIGURE 55.3**). When people are hot, they think, feel, and act more aggressively. From the available data, Craig Anderson and his colleagues (1999) project that, other things being equal, global warming of 4 degrees Fahrenheit (about 2 degrees centigrade) would induce more than 50,000 additional assaults and murders in the United States alone.

So near, but . . .
Being blocked from achieving a goal can trigger aggression. This is especially likely when the frustration can be blamed on the "other." In Canada and the United States, more than 40 deaths since 1978 have reportedly been caused by shaken vending machines toppling over and crushing frustrated patrons (Mckelvie, 1999).

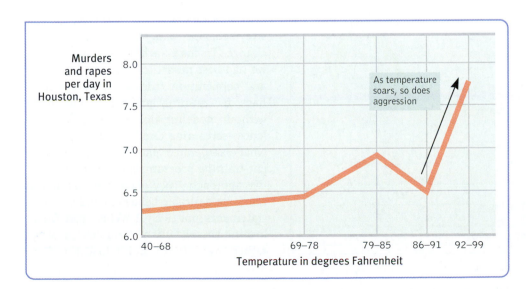

FIGURE 55.3 Uncomfortably hot weather and aggressive reactions
Between 1980 and 1982 in Houston, murders and rapes were more common on days over 91 degrees Fahrenheit (33 degrees centigrade), as shown in the graph. This finding is consistent with those from laboratory experiments in which people working in a hot room react to provocations with greater hostility. (From Anderson & Anderson, 1984.)

Learning to Express and Inhibit Aggression

Aggression may be a natural response to aversive events, but learning can alter natural reactions. Animals naturally eat when they are hungry. But if appropriately rewarded or punished, they can be taught either to overeat or to starve.

Our reactions are more likely to be aggressive in situations where experience has taught us that aggression pays. Children whose aggression successfully intimidates other children may become more aggressive. Animals that have successfully fought to get food or mates become increasingly ferocious. Aggressive behavior can be learned not only through direct rewards but also by observation. Children who grow up observing aggressive models often imitate what they see. Parents of delinquent youngsters typically discipline with beatings, thus modeling aggression as a method of dealing with problems (Patterson & others, 1982, 1992). They also frequently cave into (reward) their children's tears and temper tantrums.

Different cultures model, reinforce, and evoke different tendencies toward violence. For example, crime rates are higher in countries marked by a great disparity between rich and poor (Triandis, 1994). Richard Nisbett and Dov Cohen (1996) show how violence can vary by culture within a country. They analyzed violence among white Americans in southern U.S. towns settled by Scottish-Irish herders whose tradition emphasized "manly honor," the use of arms to protect one's flock, and a history of coercive slavery. To this day, their cultural descendants have triple the homicide rates and are more supportive of physically punishing children, of warfare initiatives, and of uncontrolled gun ownership than are their white counterparts in New England towns settled by Puritan, Quaker, and Dutch farmer-artisans.

Social influence also appears in high violence rates among cultures and families that experience minimal father care (Triandis, 1994). For example, the U.S. Bureau of Justice Statistics reports that 70 percent of imprisoned juveniles did not grow up with two parents (Beck & others, 1988). (Because an absent parent is usually a father, most grew up with minimal father care.) The correlation between father absence and violence in the United States holds for all races, income levels, and locations (Myers, 2000). The correlation also appears over time. From 1960, when just over 1 in 10 American children did not live with two parents, to 1997, when more than 3 in 10 did not, the U.S. juvenile violent crime rate more than tripled (**FIGURE 55.4**).

It is important, however, to note how many individuals are leading gentle, even heroic lives amid social stresses, reminding us again that individuals differ. The person matters. That people differ over time and place reminds us that environments differ. Situations matter. Aggressive behavior, like all behavior, arises from the interaction of persons and situations.

Once established, however, aggressive behavior patterns are difficult to change. To foster a kinder, gentler world we had best model and reward sensitivity and cooperation from an early age, perhaps by training parents to discipline without modeling violence. Modeling violence—screaming and hitting—is precisely what exasperated parents often do. Parent-training programs advise a more positive approach. They encourage parents to reinforce desirable behaviors and to frame statements positively ("When you finish loading the dishwasher you can go play," rather than "If you don't load the dish-

> "Why do we kill people who kill people to show that killing people is wrong?"
>
> National Coalition to Abolish the Death Penalty, 1992

FIGURE 55.4

Juvenile arrest rates for violent crime
In 1997 American 15- to 17-year-olds were 3.3 times more likely than their 1960 counterparts to have been arrested for violent crime. (Bureau of Justice Statistics data assembled in Myers, 2000.)

washer, there'll be no playing.") One "aggression-replacement program" that brought down re-arrest rates of juvenile offenders and gang members taught the youth and their parents communication skills, trained them in how to control anger, and encouraged more thoughtful moral reasoning (Goldstein & Glick, in press).

Television Watching and Aggression

Parents are hardly the only models of aggression. During their first 18 years, most children spend more time watching television than they spend in school. In the United States, the average household has a TV on 51 hours a week (Elliot, 1996). Two-thirds of homes have three or more sets, which helps explain why parents' reports of what their children watch hardly correlate with children's reports of what they watch (Donnerstein, 1998). In urban homes across the world, including those of South America and Asia, television is now commonplace. In Beijing, for example, the percentage of homes with television skyrocketed from 32 percent in 1980 to 95 percent by the end of the decade (Lull, 1988). With more than 1 billion TV sets now in homes around the world, CNN reaching 150 countries, and MTV videos seen from Alaska to Bangladesh, television has created a global pop culture (Lippman, 1992). One can watch American programs in Perth or Prague and watch the latest rock videos from New Delhi to Newfoundland. But television does not reflect the world we live in. On evening dramas broadcast in the United States during the 1980s and early 1990s and often exported to the rest of the world, only one-third of the characters were women. Fewer than 3 percent were visibly old. One percent were Hispanic. Only 1 in 10 was married (Gerbner, 1993).

In 1993, U.S. network programs offered about 3 violent acts per hour during prime time, and 18 per hour during children's Saturday morning programs (Gerbner & others, 1994). During the late twentieth century the average child viewed some 8000 TV murders and 100,000 other acts of violence before finishing elementary school (Huston & others, 1992). If one includes cable programming and video rentals, the violence numbers escalate. (Popular rental films like *Die Hard 1*, with its 264 deaths, are much more violent than major network programs.) Half of television's violent interactions don't show the harm done to victims and 6 in 10 don't show the victims' pain (Mediascope, 1995). This is life as rendered by a rather peculiar storyteller, one who reflects the culture's mythology but not its reality.

Does viewing televised aggression influence some people to commit aggression? Was the judge who in 1993 tried two British 10-year-olds for their murder of a 2-year-old right to suspect that one possible influence was the aggressors' exposure to "violent video films"? Were the American media right to think that the teen assassins who killed 13 of their Columbine High School classmates had been influenced by repeated viewings of *Natural Born Killers* and by frequently playing splatter games such as *Doom*? To answer similar questions, researchers have conducted both correlational and experimental studies (Hearold, 1986; Wood & others, 1991).

Correlational studies do link young children's viewing of violence and their combativeness as teenagers and young adults (Eron, 1987; Turner & others, 1986). In the United States and Canada, homicide rates doubled between 1957 and 1974, coinciding with the introduction and spread of television. Moreover, census regions that were late in acquiring television had their homicide rate jump correspondingly later. White South Africans were first introduced to television in 1975. A similar near-doubling of the homicide rate began after 1975 (Centerwall, 1989). "There is absolutely no doubt," concluded the 1993 American Psychological Association Commission on Violence and Youth, "that higher levels of viewing violence on television are correlated with increased acceptance of aggressive attitudes and increased aggressive behavior."

"The problem with television is that the people must sit and keep their eyes glued to a screen: The average American family hasn't time for it. Therefore the showmen are convinced that . . . television will never be a serious competitor of [radio] broadcasting."

New York Times, 1939

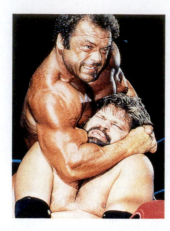
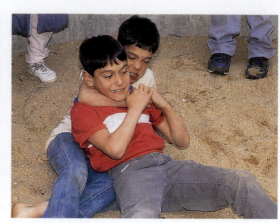

Violence viewing leads to violent play
Research has shown that viewing media violence does lead to increased expression of aggression in the viewers, as with these boys imitating pro wrestlers.

TV's greatest effect may stem from what it displaces. Children and adults who spend four hours a day watching television spend four fewer hours in active pursuits—talking, studying, playing, reading, or socializing with friends. What would you have done with your extra time if you had never watched television, and how might you therefore be different?

"Thirty seconds worth of glorification of a soap bar sells soap. Twenty-five minutes worth of glorification of violence sells violence."

U.S. Senator Paul Simon, Remarks to the Communitarian Network, 1993

But we know that correlation does not imply causation. So these correlational studies do not prove that viewing violence *causes* aggression (Freedman, 1988; McGuire, 1986). Maybe aggressive children prefer violent programs. Maybe children of neglectful or abusive parents are both more aggressive and more often left in front of the TV. Maybe television simply reflects, rather than affects, violent trends.

To pin down causation, experimenters have randomly assigned some viewers to view violence and others to view entertaining nonviolence. Does viewing cruelty prepare people to react more cruelly when irritated? To some extent, it does. "The consensus among most of the research community," reported the National Institute of Mental Health (1982), "is that violence on television does lead to aggressive behavior by children and teenagers who watch the programs." This is especially so when an attractive person commits justified, realistic violence that goes unpunished and causes no visible pain or harm (Donnerstein, 1998).

The violence effect stems from a combination of factors—from *arousal* by the violent excitement, from the strengthening of violence-related *ideas*, from the erosion of one's *inhibitions*, and from *imitation* (Geen & Thomas, 1986). One research team observed a sevenfold increase in violent play immediately after children viewed the "Power Rangers" (Boyatzis & others, 1995). Boys often precisely imitated the characters' flying karate kicks and other violent acts.

Television's unreal world, a world in which acts of aggression greatly outnumber acts of affection, can also affect our *thinking* about the real world. Those who avidly watch prime-time crime regard the world as much more dangerous than it actually is (Gerbner & others, 1993; Heath & Petraitis, 1987; Singer & Singer, 1986).

Also, prolonged exposure to violence desensitizes viewers; they become more indifferent to it when later viewing a brawl, whether on TV or in real life (Rule & Ferguson, 1986). While spending three evenings watching sexually violent movies, male viewers in one experiment became progressively less bothered by the rapes and slashings. Three days later, they also expressed less sympathy for domestic violence victims than did research participants who had not been exposed to the films, and they rated the victims' injuries as less severe (Mullin & Linz, 1995). Indeed, as Edward Donnerstein and his co-researchers (1987) suggested, an evil psychologist could hardly imagine a better way to make people indifferent to brutality than to expose them to a graded series of scenes, from fights to killings to the mutilations in slasher movies. Watching cruelty fosters indifference.

Sexual Aggression and the Media

A woman's risk of rape has varied across cultures and times but is generally greater today than half a century ago (Koss & others, 1994). Recent surveys of both women and men reveal that unreported rapes—four in five committed by

"**Don't you understand? This is *life*, this is what is happening. We *can't* switch to another channel.**"

THINKING CRITICALLY ABOUT :

DO VIDEO GAMES TEACH OR RELEASE VIOLENCE?

The recent explosion in violent video game sales became an issue for public debate in 1999 after teen assassins in Paducah, Kentucky, and Littleton, Colorado, seemed to mimic the carnage in the splatter games they had so often played. When youths play games like Mortal Kombat, Doom, Quake, Resident Evil, and Twisted Metal—attacking or dismembering people—do they learn social scripts? When someone assumes the video game identity of Clare Redfield in Resident Evil 2 and sprays bullets into Zombie cops, whose bodies slump, twitch, and hemorrhage, is anything being learned?

Most pack-a-day smokers don't die of lung cancer. Most abused children don't become abusive adults. And most young people who spend hundreds of hours in these mass murder simulators won't become teen assassins. Still, mindful that smoking and child abuse are risk factors, we wonder: If passively viewing violence elevates aggressive responses to provocation and lowers sensitivity to cruelty, what will be the effect of actively role-playing aggression?

Researchers are beginning to address such questions. Mary Ballard and Rose Wiest (1998) observed a rising level of arousal and feelings of hostility in college men as they played Mortal Kombat. Other studies have

found that video games can prime aggressive thoughts and increase aggression. Consider this report from Craig Anderson and Karen Dill (2000): University men who have spent the most hours playing violent video games tend to be the most physically aggressive (for example, to have acknowledged hitting or attacking someone else). And, in an experiment, those randomly assigned to play a game involving bloody murders with groaning victims (rather than to play nonviolent Myst) became more

hostile. On a follow-up task, they also were more likely to blast intense noise at a fellow student.

Although much remains to be learned, these studies again disconfirm the *catharsis hypothesis*—the idea that we reduce anger by releasing it through action or fantasy. They challenge the rationalization of one video game company's CEO—that we are "violent by nature [and] need release valves." Expressing anger breeds more anger, and practicing violence breeds more violence. ■

dates or acquaintances—greatly outnumber those reported (Schafran, 1995). In other surveys, about one-fifth of women report that a man has forced them to do something sexually, about one-half report some form of unwanted sexual coercion, and most report experiencing verbal sexual harassment (Craig & others, 1989; Laumann & others, 1994; Sandberg & others, 1985). Similar levels of sexual coercion have been reported in Canadian, Australian, and New Zealand surveys (Koss & others, 1994; Patton & Mannison, 1995).

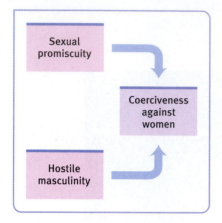

FIGURE 55.5

Men who sexually coerce women

The recipe for coercion against women combines an impersonal approach to sex with a hostile masculinity. (Adapted from Malamuth, 1996.)

Pornography means different things to different people. Following Webster's dictionary, some define pornography as erotic depictions intended to excite sexual arousal. Others define it as sexual materials that exploit, degrade, or subordinate women.

In follow-up studies, Zillmann (1989) found that after massive exposure to X-rated sexual films, men and women became more accepting of extramarital sex, of women's sexual submission to men, and of a man's seducing a 12-year-old girl. As people heavily exposed to televised crime perceive the world as more dangerous, so people heavily exposed to pornography see the world as more sexual.

What factors might explain this epidemic of sexual aggression? Alcohol consumption—often linked with aggression—has not increased. We do know that sexually coercive men typically are sexually unrestrained and hostile in their relationships with women (**FIGURE 55.5**). Might changes in the media have contributed to such tendencies?

Coinciding with the increase in sexual aggression has been the rise of the home video business, giving easier access to R-rated "slasher films" and X-rated films. Content analyses reveal that most X-rated films depict quick, casual sex between strangers, but that scenes of rape and sexual exploitation of women by men are also common (Cowan & others, 1988; NCTV, 1987; Yang & Linz, 1990).

Rape scenes often portray the victim at first fleeing and resisting her attacker, but then becoming aroused and finally driven to ecstasy. In less graphic form, the same unrealistic script—she resists, he persists, she melts—is commonplace on TV and in romance novels. The woman who first thwarts the insistent man ends up passionately kissing him. In *Gone with the Wind*, Scarlett O'Hara is carried to bed screaming and wakes up singing. Most rapists accept this "rape myth"—the idea that some women invite or enjoy rape and get "swept away" while being "taken" (Brinson, 1992). In actuality, rape is very traumatic, and it frequently harms women's reproductive and sexual health (Golding, 1996).

Do images of sexual exploitation influence sexual aggression? When interviewed, Canadian and U.S. sex offenders (rapists, child molesters, and serial killers) do report a greater-than-usual appetite for sexually explicit and sexually violent materials—materials typically labeled as "pornography" (Marshall, 1989; Ressler & others, 1988). For example, the Los Angeles Police Department reports that pornography was "conspicuously present" or used in 62 percent of its extrafamilial child sexual abuse cases during the 1980s (Bennett, 1991). But are the sexual offenders merely, as sex researcher John Money (1988) suspects, using pornography "as an alibi to explain to themselves and their captors what otherwise is inexplicable"?

Laboratory experiments reveal that repeatedly watching X-rated films (even if nonviolent) makes one's own partner seem less attractive (Zillmann, 1989), makes a woman's friendliness seem more sexual, and makes sexual aggression seem less serious (Harris, 1994). In one such experiment, Dolf Zillmann and Jennings Bryant (1984) showed undergraduates six brief, sexually explicit films each week for six weeks. A control group viewed nonerotic films during the same six-week period. Three weeks later, both groups read a newspaper report about a man convicted but not yet sentenced for raping a hitchhiker. When asked to suggest an appropriate prison term, those who had viewed sexually explicit films recommended sentences half as long as those recommended by the control group.

In another study, Neil Malamuth and James Check (1981) found that men who viewed films with some sexual violence were more accepting of the rape myth. The experimenters had one group of University of Manitoba men watch two nonsexual movies, and another watch two movies depicting a man sexually overpowering a woman. When surveyed a week later, the men who had seen the films in which the woman was overpowered reported themselves a little more likely to commit rape if they were sure they could get away with it. Further studies have shown that viewing slasher movies, such as *The Texas Chainsaw Massacre*, can also lead viewers to trivialize rape.

Experiments cannot study actual sexual violence, but they can assess a man's willingness to hurt a woman. Often the research gauges the effect of violent versus nonviolent films on men's willingness to deliver supposed electric shocks to women who had earlier provoked them. These experiments suggest that it's not the eroticism but rather the depictions of sexual *violence* (whether in R-rated slasher films or X-rated films) that most directly affect men's acceptance and performance of aggression against women. A 1986 conference of 21 social scientists, including many of the researchers who conducted these experiments, produced a consensus (Surgeon General, 1986): "Pornography that portrays sexual aggression as pleasurable for the victim increases the acceptance of the use of coercion in sexual relations." Contrary to much popular opinion, viewing such depictions does not provide an outlet for bottled-up impulses. Rather, "in laboratory studies measuring short-term effects, exposure to violent pornography increases punitive behavior toward women."

TV Violence, Pornography, and Society

Significant behaviors such as violence usually have many determinants, making any single explanation an oversimplification. Asking what causes violence is therefore like asking what causes cancer. Those who study, say, the effects of asbestos exposure on cancer rates may remind us that asbestos is indeed a cancer cause, but only one among many. Likewise, report Neil Malamuth and his colleagues (1991, 1995), several factors can create a predisposition to sexual violence; they include not only the media but also dominance motives, disinhibition by alcohol, and a history of child abuse. Still, if media depictions of violence can disinhibit and desensitize; if viewing sexual violence fosters hostile, domineering attitudes and behaviors; and if viewing pornography leads viewers to trivialize rape, devalue their partners, and engage in uncommitted sex, then media influence is not a minor issue.

Social psychologists attribute the media's influence partly to the *social scripts* they provide. When we find ourselves in new situations, uncertain how to act, we rely on social scripts provided by our culture. After so many episodes of "Power Rangers," followed by Bruce Willis and Arnold Schwarzenegger action films, youngsters may acquire a script—a mental tape for how to act—that gets played when they face real-life conflicts. Challenged, they may "act like a man" by intimidating or eliminating the threat. Likewise, after viewing 15 sexual innuendoes and acts per prime-time TV hour—nearly all involving impulsive, short-term relationships—youths may acquire sexual scripts they later enact in real-life relationships (Sapolsky & Tabarlet, 1991).

Might public consciousness be raised by making people aware of the information you have just been reading? In the 1940s, movies often depicted African-Americans as childlike, superstitious buffoons. Today, we would not tolerate such images. In the 1960s and 1970s, some rock music and movies glamorized drug use. Responding to a tidal change in cultural attitudes, the entertainment industry now more often portrays the dark side of drug use. Even cigarette smoking in movies largely disappeared until the 1990s, when its reappearance was accompanied by a new surge in teen smoking rates. In response to growing public concern about violence in the media, television violence levels declined in the early 1990s (Gallup, 1993; Gerbner & others, 1993). The growing sensitivity to violence has raised hopes that entertainers, producers, and audiences might someday look back with embarrassment on the days when movies "entertained" people with scenes of torture, mutilation, and sexual coercion.

Conflict

Preview Question: What social processes fuel conflict?

We live in surprising times. With astonishing speed, democratic movements have swept away totalitarian rule in Eastern European countries, and hopes for a new world order have displaced the Cold War chill. And yet, the world spends $2 billion every day for arms and armies, money that could be used for housing, nutrition, education, and health. Knowing that, as the UNESCO motto declares, wars begin in human minds, psychologists have wondered, What in the human mind causes destructive conflict? How might the perceived threats of social diversity be replaced by a spirit of cooperation?

As U.S. First Lady, Hillary Rodham Clinton voiced concerns shared by many when she worried about media models of an "impulsive sexuality" that encourage uncommitted sex (a predictor of sexual violence) and father-absent families (a predictor of juvenile violence).

"What we're trying to do is raise the level of awareness of violence against women and pornography to at least the level of awareness of racist and Ku Klux Klan literature."

Gloria Steinem (1988)

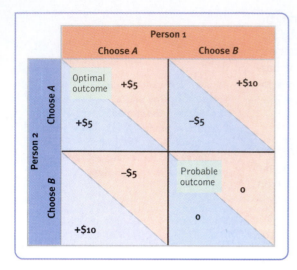

FIGURE 55.6

Social trap game matrix

By pursuing our self-interest and not trusting others, we can end up losers. To illustrate this, imagine playing the game at left. The orange triangles show the outcomes for Person 1, which depend on the choices made by both persons. If you were Person 1, would you choose *A* or *B*? (This game is called a "non–zero-sum game" because the outcomes need not add up to zero; both sides can win or both can lose.)

To a social psychologist, a **conflict** is a seeming incompatibility of actions, goals, or ideas. The elements of conflict are much the same at all levels, from nations at war to cultural disputes within a society to individuals in a marital dispute. In each situation, people become enmeshed in a potentially destructive social process that can produce results no one wants. Among the destructive processes are social traps and distorted perceptions.

Social Traps

In some situations, we can enhance our collective well-being by pursuing our personal interests. As capitalist Adam Smith wrote in *The Wealth of Nations* (1776), "It is not from the benevolence of the butcher, the brewer, or the baker that we expect our dinner, but from their regard to their own interest." In other situations, the parties involved may become caught up in mutually harmful behavior as they pursue their own ends. Such situations are **social traps**.

Consider the simple game matrix in **FIGURE 55.6**, which is similar to those that have been used in experiments with thousands of people. In this game, both sides can win or both can lose, depending on the players' individual choices. Pretend you are Person 1, and that you and Person 2 will each receive the amount shown after you separately choose either *A* or *B*. (You might invite someone to look at the matrix with you and take the role of Person 2.) Which do you choose—*A* or *B*?

As you ponder the game, you will discover that you and Person 2 are caught in a dilemma. If you both choose *A*, you both benefit, making $5 each. Neither of you benefits if you both choose *B*, for neither of you makes anything. Nevertheless, on any single trial you serve your own interests if you choose *B*: You can't lose, and you might make $10. But the same is true for the other person. Hence, the social trap: As long as you both pursue your own immediate best interest and choose *B*, you will both end up with nothing—the typical result—when you could have made $5.

Many real-life situations similarly pit our individual interests against our communal well-being. Individual whalers reason that the few whales they take will not threaten the species and that if they didn't take them other whalers would anyway. The result: A species of whales becomes endangered. The individual car owner and home owner reasons, "It would cost me comfort or money to buy a more fuel-efficient car and furnace. Besides, the fossil fuels I burn don't noticeably add to the greenhouse gases." When enough others reason similarly, the collective result threatens disaster—global warming.

Social traps challenge us to find ways of reconciling our right to pursue our personal well-being with our responsibility for the well-being of all. Psychologists are therefore exploring ways to convince people to cooperate for their

A social trap

In the Atlantic waters off Newfoundland, those who fished knew that their individual catch was their livelihood and, by itself, hardly depleted the whole fish population. Such reasoning by everyone, including outsiders, depleted fish stocks. The result: Newfoundland's fishing fleet sits idle and an economy is in ruins during a 1990s fishing moratorium. This unemployed fisherman has been forced to use his boat for firewood.

mutual betterment—through agreed-upon *regulations*, through better *communication*, and through promoting *awareness* of our responsibilities toward community, nation, and the whole of humanity (Dawes, 1980; Linder, 1982; Sato, 1987). Under such conditions, people more often cooperate, whether it be in playing a laboratory game or the real game of life.

Enemy Perceptions

Psychologists have noted that those in conflict have a curious tendency to form diabolical images of one another. These distorted images are ironically similar, so similar in fact that we call them *mirror-image perceptions*: As we see "them"—as untrustworthy and evil intentioned—so "they" see us. Thus, during the early 1980s, the U.S. government viewed the communist support of guerrillas trying to overthrow the government of El Salvador as evidence of an "evil empire" at work. Meanwhile, the Soviets saw the U.S. support of guerrillas trying to overthrow the government of Nicaragua as the work of "imperialist warmongers." As enemies change, so do perceptions. In American minds and media, the "bloodthirsty, cruel, treacherous" Japanese of World War II later became our "intelligent, hardworking, self-disciplined, resourceful allies" (Gallup, 1972).

Biased perceptions—whether of individuals or of groups or nations—have deep psychological roots. The *self-serving bias* leads each party to accept credit for good deeds and to shuck the blame for bad deeds. Although two nations admit to a buildup of military forces, the *fundamental attribution error* leads each to see the other's actions as arising from an aggressive disposition, and to view its own buildup as necessary self-defense. Information about each other's actions is then filtered, interpreted, and remembered through preconceived *stereotypes*. Group interaction among like-minded policymakers may *polarize* these tendencies, leading to *groupthink*, whereby each sees its own group as more moral, thereby justifying retaliation. In Soviet-U.S. relations, such biases resulted in the social perceptions that fueled the arms race: Each side (1) wished for mutual arms reduction, but (2) wanted above all to avoid disarming while the other armed, and (3) perceived the other side as wanting above all to gain an arms advantage (Plous, 1993).

Another result of such perceptions is a vicious cycle of hostility. If Victor believes Samantha is annoyed with him, he may snub her, causing her to act in ways that justify his perception. As with individuals, so with countries. Perceptions confirm themselves by influencing the other country to react in ways that seem to justify them. The self-fulfilling prophecy rides again.

We have pondered the bad side of our social relations—prejudice, aggression, and conflict. Is there a good side? There is—attraction, altruism, and peacemaking.

Attraction

Preview Questions: Why do we become friends with some people but not with others? Does our love for a partner remain the same as time passes?

Pause a moment and think about your relationships with two people—a close friend, and someone who stirred in you feelings of romantic love. What leads to friendship and to romance? What helps us sustain these relationships?

We endlessly wonder how we can win others' affection and what makes our own affections flourish or fade. Do birds of a feather flock together? Or do opposites attract? Does familiarity breed contempt, or does it intensify our affection? Does absence make the heart grow fonder, or is out of sight out of mind? Social psychology suggests some answers.

- **conflict** a perceived incompatibility of actions, goals, or ideas.
- **social trap** a situation in which the conflicting parties, by each rationally pursuing their self-interest, become caught in mutually destructive behavior.

"Why do you see the speck that is in your brother's eye, but do not notice the log that is in your own eye?"

Jesus, Luke 6:41–42

The Psychology of Attraction

What is the psychological chemistry that binds two people together in that special sort of friendship that helps us cope with all other relationships? Consider three ingredients of our liking for one another.

Proximity

Before friendships become close, they must begin. *Proximity*—geographic nearness—is perhaps the most powerful predictor of friendship. Proximity provides opportunities for aggression, but much more often it breeds liking. Study after study reveals that people are most likely to like, and even to marry, those who live in the same neighborhood, who sit nearby in class, who work in the same office, who share the same parking lot. Look around.

Why is proximity so conducive to liking? Obviously, part of the answer is the greater availability of those we often meet. But there is more to it than that. For one thing, repeated exposure to novel stimuli—be they nonsense syllables, musical selections, geometric figures, Chinese characters, human faces, or the letters of our own name—increases our liking for them (Moreland & Zajonc, 1982; Nuttin, 1987). This phenomenon, exploited by advertisers, we call the **mere exposure effect**. Within certain limits (Bornstein, 1989, 1999), familiarity breeds fondness. Richard Moreland and Scott Beach (1992) demonstrated this by having four equally attractive women silently attend a 200-student class for zero, 5, 10, or 15 class sessions. At the end of the course, students were shown slides of each woman and asked to rate each one's attractiveness. The most attractive? The ones they'd seen most often. The phenomenon will come as no surprise to the young Taiwanese man who wrote more than 700 letters to his girlfriend, urging her to marry him. She did marry—the mail carrier (Steinberg, 1993).

For our ancestors, the mere exposure phenomenon was adaptive. What was familiar was generally safe and approachable. What was unfamiliar was more often dangerous and threatening. Robert Zajonc (1998) concludes that evolution has hard-wired into us the tendency to bond with those who are familiar and to be wary of those who are unfamiliar. Gut-level prejudice against those culturally different may thus be a primitive, automatic emotional response (Devine, 1995).

Physical Attractiveness

Once proximity affords you contact, what most affects your first impressions: The person's sincerity? Intelligence? Personality? Hundreds of experiments reveal that it is something far more superficial: Appearance.

For people taught that "beauty is only skin deep" and that "appearances can be deceiving," the power of physical attractiveness is unnerving. In one early study, Elaine Hatfield and her co-workers (Walster & others, 1966) randomly matched new

Familiarity breeds acceptance
When this rare white penguin was born in the Sydney, Australia, zoo, his tuxedoed peers ostracized him. Zookeepers thought they would need to dye him black to gain acceptance. But after three weeks of contact, the other penguins came to accept him.

The mere exposure effect
The mere exposure effect applies even to ourselves. Because the human face is not perfectly symmetrical, the face we see in the mirror is not the same as the one our friends see. Most of us prefer the familiar mirror image, while our friends like the reverse (Mita & others, 1977). The Prime Minister Tony Blair known to the British is shown at the top. The person Blair sees in the mirror each morning is shown at the bottom, and that's the photo he would probably prefer.

"Personal beauty is a greater recommendation than any letter of introduction."

Aristotle, *Apothegems*, 330 B.C.

University of Minnesota students for a Welcome Week dance. Before the dance, each took a battery of personality and aptitude tests. On the night of the blind date, the couples danced and talked for more than two hours and then took a brief intermission to rate their dates. What determined whether they liked each other? So far as the researchers could determine, only one thing mattered: Physical attractiveness (which had been rated by the researchers beforehand). Both the men and the women liked good-looking dates best. Although women are more likely than men to *say* that another's looks don't affect them, a man's looks do affect women's behavior (Feingold, 1990; Sprecher, 1989; Woll, 1986).

People's physical attractiveness has wide-ranging effects. It predicts their frequency of dating, their feelings of popularity, and others' initial impressions of their personalities. We perceive attractive people to be healthier, happier, more sensitive, more successful, and more socially skilled, though not more honest or compassionate (Eagly & others, 1991; Feingold, 1992; Hatfield & Sprecher, 1986). Attractive, well-dressed people are more likely to make a favorable impression on potential employers (Cash & Janda, 1984; Solomon, 1987).

An analysis of 100 top-grossing films since 1940 found that attractive characters were portrayed as morally superior to unattractive characters (Smith & others, 1999). But Hollywood modeling doesn't explain why, to judge from their gazing times, even babies prefer attractive over unattractive faces (Langlois & others, 1987). So do some blind people, discovered University of Birmingham professor John Hull (1990, p. 23) after going blind. A colleague's remarking on a woman's beauty would strangely affect his feelings. He finds this "deplorable . . . but I still feel it. . . . What can it matter to me what sighted men think of women . . . yet I do care what sighted men think, and I do not seem able to throw off this prejudice."

That looks are important may seem unfair and unenlightened. Two thousand years ago the Roman statesman Cicero felt the same way: "The final good and the supreme duty of the wise person is to resist appearance." Cicero might be reassured by two other findings about attractiveness.

First, people's attractiveness is surprisingly unrelated to their self-esteem and happiness (Diener & others, 1995; Major & others, 1984). One reason may be that, except after comparing themselves with superattractive people, few people view themselves as unattractive (Thornton & Moore, 1993). (Thanks, perhaps, to the mere exposure effect, most of us become accustomed to our faces.) Another reason is that strikingly attractive people are sometimes suspicious that praise for their work may simply be a reaction to their looks. When less attractive people are praised, they are more likely to accept it as sincere (Berscheid, 1981).

Cicero might also find comfort in knowing that attractiveness judgments are relative. The standards by which judges crown Miss Universe hardly apply to the whole planet. Rather, beauty is in the eye of the culture—most accepted standards of beauty are influenced by one's place and time. Hoping to look attractive, people in different cultures have pierced their noses, lengthened their necks, bound their feet, dyed or painted their skin and hair, gorged themselves to achieve a full figure or liposuctioned fat to achieve a slim one, strapped on leather garments to make their breasts seem smaller or surgically filled their breasts with silicone and put on Wonder Bras to make them look bigger. In North America, the ultra-thin ideal of the Roaring Twenties gave way to the soft, voluptuous Marilyn Monroe ideal of the 1950s, only to be replaced by the lean yet busty ideal of the 1990s. Americans now spend more on beauty supplies than on education and social services combined, and when still not satisfied undergo nearly 1 million facial plastic surgeries a year (Etcoff, 1999; Sharlet, 1999). Yet since 1970 the number of women unhappy with their appearance has substantially increased (Feingold & Mazella, 1998).

■ **mere exposure effect** the phenomenon that repeated exposure to novel stimuli increases liking of them.

"Love comes in at the eye."

William Butler Yeats, "A Drinking Song," 1909

Percentage of Men and Women Who "Constantly Think About Their Looks"

	Men	Women
Canada	18%	20%
United States	17	27
Mexico	40	45
Venezuela	47	65

per Starch survey, reported by McCool (1999).

When Neanderthals fall in love.

New York Times columnist Maureen Dowd on liposuction (January 19, 2000):

"Women in the 50's vacuumed. Women in the 00's are vacuumed. Our Hoovers have turned on us!"

Pleasing with plastic surgery

In affluent, beauty-conscious cultures, increasing numbers of people—including President Clinton's sexual harassment accuser, Paula Jones—have turned to cosmetic surgery to improve their looks. If money were no concern, might you ever do the same?

Some aspects of attractiveness, however, do cross place and time. Men in 37 cultures, from Australia to Zambia, judge women as more attractive if they have a youthful appearance. Women feel attracted to healthy-looking men, but especially to those who seem mature, dominant, and affluent.

People also seem to prefer physical features—noses, legs, physiques—that are neither unusually large or small. In one clever demonstration of this, Judith Langlois and Lori Roggman (1990) digitized the faces of up to 32 college students and used a computer to average them. Students judged the averaged, composite faces as more attractive than 96 percent of the individual faces. One reason (but not the only one) is that averaged faces are symmetrical, and people with symmetrical faces and bodies are more sexually attractive (Rhodes & others, 1999; Singh, 1995b; Thornhill & Gangestad, 1995).

Eggs for sale

"Choosing eggs from beautiful women will profoundly increase the success of your children and your children's children, for centuries to come," said one entrepreneur in offering the eggs of beautiful models in an on-line auction.

PERM AND DYE JOB   DENTAL WORK   RHINOPLASTY

MAKEUP AND GIRDLE   BREAST IMPLANTS   WE'LL PAY YOU $50,000 FOR YOUR EGGS!

"Love is a dirty trick played on us to achieve the continuation of the species."

Novelist W. Somerset Maugham, 1874–1965

An averaged face is attractive. But more attractive yet, observed David Perrett and his colleagues (1994) from studies with British and Japanese students, is a face that is averaged from a set of attractive individuals. And still more attractive are faces that exaggerate the subtle differences between average and attractive faces. So sensitive is our radar for facial attractiveness that we can judge someone's looks after but a 0.15-second glimpse (Zajonc, 1998).

In the eye of the beholder

Conceptions of attractiveness vary by culture and across time. What may be deemed attractive in one culture may seem strange or unattractive in another. And the current concept of attractiveness in Kenya, Morocco, and the United States may well change in the future.

Cultural standards aside, attractiveness also depends on our feelings about the person. In a Rodgers and Hammerstein musical, Prince Charming asks Cinderella, "Do I love you because you're beautiful, or are you beautiful because I love you?" Chances are it's both. As we see someone again and again, and come to like them, their physical imperfections grow less noticeable and their attractiveness grows more apparent (Beaman & Klentz, 1983; Gross & Crofton, 1977). As Shakespeare put it in *A Midsummer Night's Dream*, "Love looks not with the eyes, but with the mind." Until you got to know him, E.T. was uglier than Darth Vader.

Similarity

Let's say that proximity has brought you into contact with someone and that your appearance has made a favorable first impression. What now influences whether acquaintances develop into friends? For example, as you get to know someone better, is the chemistry better if you are opposites or if you are alike?

It makes a good story—extremely different types living in harmonious union: Rat, Mole, and Badger in *The Wind in the Willows*, Frog and Toad in Arnold Lobel's books. The stories delight us by expressing what we seldom experience, for we tend *not* to like dissimilar people (Rosenbaum, 1986). In real life, opposites retract. Birds that flock together usually *are* of a feather. Friends and couples are far more likely to share common attitudes, beliefs, and interests (and, for that matter, age, religion, race, education, intelligence, smoking behavior, and economic status) than are randomly paired people. Much as you and I may dismiss such differences, seeing ourselves as one human family in a global village, we can't hang out with 6 billion people. Moreover, the more alike people are, the more their liking endures (Byrne, 1971). Journalist Walter Lippmann was right to suppose that love is best sustained "when the lovers love many things together, and not merely each other." Similarity breeds content.

Proximity, attractiveness, and similarity are not the only determinants of attraction. We also like those who like us, especially when our self-image is low. When we believe someone likes us, we respond to them more warmly, which leads them to like us even more (Curtis & Miller, 1986). To be liked is powerfully rewarding.

Indeed, a simple reward theory of attraction—that we will like those whose behavior is rewarding to us and that we will continue relationships that offer more rewards than costs—can explain all the findings we have considered so far. When a person lives or works in close proximity with someone else, it costs less time and effort to develop the friendship and enjoy its benefits. Attractive people are aesthetically pleasing, and associating with them can be socially rewarding. Those with similar views reward us by validating our own.

Romantic Love

Occasionally, people move quickly from initial impressions to friendship to the more intense, complex, and mysterious state of romantic love. Elaine Hatfield (1988) distinguishes two types of love: temporary passionate love and a more enduring companionate love.

Beautiful symmetry
Beautiful people are blessed with almost perfectly symmetrical faces and bodies, as illustrated in this "beauty mask" created by a plastic surgeon.

"Love has ever in view the absolute loveliness of that which it beholds."

George MacDonald, *Unspoken Sermons*, 1867

"I don't think, David, that agreeing to disagree is a good foundation for marriage."

Passionate Love

Noting that arousal is a key ingredient of **passionate love**, Hatfield suggests that the *two-factor theory of emotion* can help us understand this intense positive absorption in another. The theory assumes that (1) emotions have two ingredients—physical arousal plus cognitive appraisal—and that (2) arousal from any source can enhance one emotion or another, depending on how we interpret and label the arousal.

In tests of this theory, college men have been aroused by fright, by running in place, by viewing erotic materials, or by listening to humorous or repulsive monologues. They are then introduced to an attractive woman and asked to rate her (or their girlfriend). Unlike unaroused men, those who are stirred up attribute some of their arousal to the woman or girlfriend and feel more attracted to her (Carducci & others, 1978; Dermer & Pyszczynski, 1978; White & Kight, 1984).

Outside the laboratory, Donald Dutton and Arthur Aron (1974, 1989) went to two bridges across British Columbia's rocky Capilano River. One, a swaying footbridge, was 230 feet above the rocks; the other was low and solid. An attractive young female accomplice intercepted men coming off each bridge, sought their help in filling out a short questionnaire, and then offered her phone number in case they wanted to hear more about her project. Far more of those who had just crossed the high bridge—which left their hearts pounding—accepted the number and later called the woman. To be revved up and to associate some of that arousal with a desirable person is to feel the pull of passion. As lovers who take a thrilling roller coaster ride together know, adrenaline makes the heart grow fonder.

HI & LOIS

Reprinted with special permission of King Features Syndicate.

Companionate Love

Inevitably, the passion of romantic love subsides. The intense absorption in the other, the thrill of the romance, the giddy "floating on a cloud" feeling fades. JUST MARRIED becomes just married. Recognizing the short duration of passionate love, some societies have deemed such feelings an irrational reason for marrying. Better, such cultures say, to choose (or have someone choose for you) a partner with a compatible background and interests. And in fact, non-Western cultures, where people rate love less important for marriage, indeed have lower divorce rates (Levine & others, 1995).

So, are the French correct in saying that "love makes the time pass and time makes love pass"? Or can friendship and commitment keep a relationship going after the passion cools? Hatfield notes that as love matures it becomes a steadier **companionate love**—a deep, affectionate attachment. There may be adaptive wisdom to this change from passion to affection. Passionate love often produces children, whose survival is aided by the parents' waning obsession with one another. Social psychologist Ellen Berscheid and her colleagues (1984) note that the failure to appreciate passionate love's limited half-life can doom a relationship: "If the inevitable odds against eternal passionate love in a relationship were better understood, more people might choose to be satisfied with the quieter feelings of satisfaction and contentment."

One key to a gratifying and enduring relationship is **equity**: Both partners receive in proportion to what they give. When equity exists—when both partners freely give and receive, when they share decision making—their chances for sustained and satisfying companionate love are good (Gray-Little & Burks, 1983; Van Yperen & Buunk, 1990). Mutually sharing self and possessions, giving and getting emotional support, promoting and caring about one another's welfare are at the core of every type of loving relationship (Sternberg & Grajek, 1984). It's true for lovers, for parent and child, and for intimate friends.

"When two people are under the influence of the most violent, most insane, most delusive, and most transient of passions, they are required to swear that they will remain in that excited, abnormal, and exhausting condition continuously until death do them part."

George Bernard Shaw, *Man and Superman*, 1903

"When a match has equal partners then I fear not."

Aeschylus, *Prometheus Bound*, 478 B.C.

Passionate love to companionate love
The quality of love changes as a relationship matures from passionate absorption to affectionate attachment.

Another vital ingredient of loving relationships is intimacy. A strong friendship or marriage offers **self-disclosure**, the revealing of intimate details about ourselves—our likes and dislikes, our dreams and worries, our proud and shameful moments. "When I am with my friend," noted the Roman statesman Seneca, "me thinks I am alone, and as much at liberty to speak anything as to think it." Self-disclosure breeds liking, and liking breeds self-disclosure (Collins & Miller, 1994). As one person reveals a little, the other reciprocates, the first then reveals more, and on and on, as friends or lovers move to deeper intimacy.

One experiment marched pairs of volunteer students through 45 minutes of increasingly self-disclosing conversation—from "When did you last sing to yourself" to "When did you last cry in front of another person? By yourself?" By the experiment's end, those experiencing the escalating intimacy felt remarkably close to their conversation partner, much closer than those who spent the time with small-talk questions such as "What was your high school like?" (Aron & others, 1997). Given self-disclosing intimacy plus mutually supportive equality, the odds favor enduring companionate love.

Altruism

Preview Questions: Why do we help others? When are we most likely to help?

As American Airlines Flight 1420 landed in the midst of a June 1999 thunderstorm in Little Rock, Arkansas, it skidded off the runway, struck a light tower, broke apart, and burst into flames. Inside, as panic and fire spread down the aisle, one calm presence was Ouachita Baptist University student James Harrison, who was returning from Europe with two dozen fellow members of his choir. As others fled the inferno, Harrison stayed behind, helping organize the exodus and assisting passengers to safety. "I heard him giving orders, shouting out for people to go one way or the other, taking charge," recalled one survivor. When his choir leader, standing on the wing to assist the survivors' escape, yelled into the plane asking if anyone was still there, Harrison yelled back, "That's the last of them." But rather than leave, the young man did a final search for victims, and himself became the crash's ninth casualty as he succumbed to the smoke and died in the aisle. He died as he had lived—as "someone who delighted in helping others" (Bensman, 1999; Root, 1999).

James Harrison provides a supreme example of **altruism**—the unselfish regard for the welfare of others. Altruism became a major concern of social psychologists after an especially vile act of sexual violence. On March 13, 1964, a stalker repeatedly stabbed Kitty Genovese, then raped her as she lay dying outside her Queens, New

■ **passionate love** an aroused state of intense positive absorption in another, usually present at the beginning of a love relationship.

■ **companionate love** the deep affectionate attachment we feel for those with whom our lives are intertwined.

■ **equity** a condition in which people receive from a relationship in proportion to what they give to it.

■ **self-disclosure** revealing intimate aspects of oneself to others.

■ **altruism** unselfish regard for the welfare of others.

York, apartment at 3:30 A.M. "Oh, my God, he stabbed me!" Genovese screamed into the early morning stillness. "Please help me!" Windows opened and lights went on as 38 of her neighbors heard her screams. Her attacker fled and then returned to stab her eight more times and rape her again. Not until he fled for good did anyone so much as call the police, at 3:50 A.M.

Bystander Intervention

Reflecting on the Genovese murder and other such tragedies, most commentators were outraged by the bystanders' "apathy" and "indifference." Rather than blaming the onlookers, social psychologists John Darley and Bibb Latané (1968b) attributed their inaction to an important situational factor—the presence of others. Given certain circumstances, they suspected, most of us might behave similarly.

After staging emergencies under various conditions, Darley and Latané assembled their findings into a decision scheme: We will help only if the situation enables us first to *notice* the incident, then to *interpret* it as an emergency, and finally to *assume responsibility* for helping (**FIGURE 55.7**).

At each step, the presence of other bystanders turns people away from the path that leads to helping. In the laboratory and on the street, people in a group of strangers are more likely than solitary individuals to keep their eyes focused on what they themselves are doing or where they are going. If they notice an unusual situation, they may infer from the blasé reactions of the other passersby that the situation is not an emergency. "The person lying on the sidewalk must be drunk," they think, and move on.

But sometimes, as with the Genovese murder, the emergency is unambiguous and people still fail to help. The witnesses looking out through their windows noticed the incident, correctly interpreted the emergency, and yet they still failed to assume responsibility. Why? To find out, Darley and Latané (1968a) simulated a physical emergency in their laboratory. University students participated in a discussion over an intercom. Each student was in a separate cubicle, and only the person whose microphone was switched on could be heard. One of the students was an accomplice of the experimenters. When his turn came, he made sounds as though he were having an epileptic seizure and called for help.

How did the other students react? As **FIGURE 55.8** shows, those who believed they were the only person who could hear the victim—and therefore thought they bore total responsibility for helping him—usually went to his aid. Those who thought others also could hear were more likely to react as did Kitty Genovese's neighbors. When more people shared responsibility for helping, any single listener was less likely to help.

In hundreds of additional experiments, psychologists have studied the factors that influence bystanders' willingness to relay an emergency phone call, aid a

FIGURE 55.7 The decision-making process for bystander intervention
Before helping, one must first notice an emergency, then correctly interpret it, and then feel responsible. (From Darley & Latané, 1968b.)

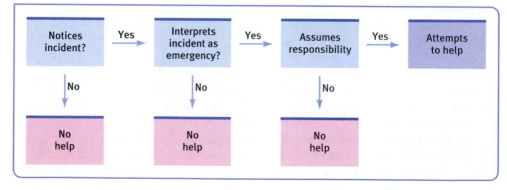

stranded motorist, donate blood, pick up dropped books, contribute money, and give time. For example, Latané, James Dabbs (1975), and 145 collaborators took 1497 elevator rides in three cities and "accidentally" dropped coins or pencils in front of 4813 fellow passengers. The women coin droppers were more likely to receive help than were the men—a gender difference often reported by other researchers (Eagly & Crowley, 1986). But the major finding was the **bystander effect**—any particular bystander was less likely to give aid with other bystanders present. When one other person was on the elevator, those who dropped the coins were helped 40 percent of the time. When there were six passengers, help came less than 20 percent of the time.

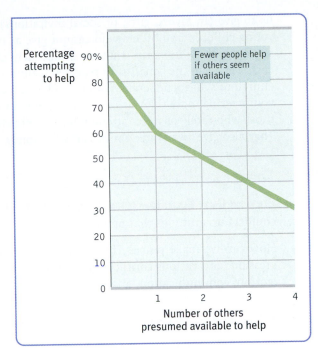

Percentage attempting to help

Fewer people help if others seem available

Number of others presumed available to help

FIGURE **55.8**
Responses to a simulated physical emergency
When people thought they alone heard the calls for help from a person they believed to be having an epileptic seizure, they usually helped. But when they thought four others were also hearing the calls, fewer than a third responded. (From Darley & Latané, 1968a.)

From their observations of behavior in tens of thousands of such "emergencies," altruism researchers have discerned some additional patterns. The *best* odds of our helping someone occur when

+ we have just observed someone else being helpful.
+ we are not in a hurry.
+ the victim appears to need and deserve help.
+ the victim is in some way similar to us.
+ we are in a small town or rural area.
+ we are feeling guilty.
+ we are focused on others and not preoccupied.
+ we are in a good mood.

This last result, that happy people are helpful people, is one of the most consistent findings in all of psychology. No matter how people are cheered—whether by being made to feel successful and intelligent, by thinking happy thoughts, by finding money, or even by receiving a posthypnotic suggestion—they become more generous and more eager to help (Carlson & others, 1988).

"Oh, make us happy and you make us good!"

Robert Browning, *The Ring and the Book*, 1868

The Psychology of Helping

So then *why* do we help? One widely held view is that self-interest underlies all human interactions: Our constant goal is to maximize rewards and minimize costs. Accountants call it cost-benefit analysis. Philosophers call it utilitarianism. Social psychologists call it **social exchange theory**. If you are pondering whether to donate blood, you may weigh the costs of doing so (time, discomfort, and anxiety) against the benefits (reduced guilt, social approval, good feelings). If you anticipate rewards from helping that exceed the costs, you help.

But why do we leave tips for people we will never see again and give directions to strangers? Social expectations also influence helping. They prescribe how we ought to behave, often to our mutual benefit. Through socialization, we learn the *reciprocity norm*, the expectation that we should return help, not harm, to those who have helped us. In our relations with others of similar status, the reciprocity norm compels

■ **bystander effect** the tendency for any given bystander to be less likely to give aid if other bystanders are present.

■ **social exchange theory** the theory that our social behavior is an exchange process, the aim of which is to maximize benefits and minimize costs.

us to give (in favors, gifts, or social invitations) about as much as we receive. With young children and others who cannot give as much as they receive, we also learn a *social responsibility norm*—that we should help those who need our help, even if the costs outweigh the benefits. In repeated Gallup surveys, people who each week attend church or synagogue services often exhibit the social responsibility norm: They report volunteering more than twice as many hours in helping the poor and infirm than do those who rarely or never attend religious services (Hodgkinson & Weitzman, 1992). They also give away three times as much money.

Peacemaking

Preview Question: How can we transform feelings of prejudice, aggression, and conflict into attitudes that promote peace?

How can we make peace? The transformation of antagonisms fed by prejudice, aggression, and various conflicts into attitudes that promote peace is enabled by cooperation, communication, and conciliation.

Cooperation

Does it help to put two conflicting parties into close contact? It depends. When such contact is noncompetitive and between parties with equal status, such as fellow store clerks, it may help. Initially prejudiced co-workers of different races have, in such circumstances, usually come to accept one another. Among Europeans, friendly contact with ethnic minorities has led to less prejudice (Pettigrew, 1969, 1997). However, mere contact is sometimes not enough. In most desegregated middle and junior high schools in the United States, white and black students resegregate themselves in the lunchrooms and on the school grounds (Schofield, 1986).

Contact alone was not enough to defuse intense conflicts instigated by researcher Muzafer Sherif (1966). He placed 22 Oklahoma City boys in two separate areas of a Boy Scout camp. He then put the two groups through a series of competitive activities, with prizes going to the victors. Before long, each group became intensely proud of itself and hostile to the other group's "sneaky," "smart-alecky stinkers." Food wars broke out during meals. Cabins were ransacked. Fistfights had to be broken up by members of the camp staff. When Sherif brought the two groups together, they avoided one another, except to taunt and threaten.

Nevertheless, within a few days Sherif transformed these young enemies into jovial comrades. He gave them **superordinate goals**—shared goals that overrode their differences and that could be achieved only through cooperation. A planned disruption of the camp water supply necessitated that all 22 boys work together to restore water. Renting a movie in those pre-VCR days required their pooled resources. A truck stalled until all the boys pulled and pushed together to get it moving. Having used isolation and competition to make strangers into enemies, Sherif used shared predicaments and goals to reconcile the enemies and make them friends. What reduced conflict was not mere contact, but *cooperative* contact.

Extending these findings, John Dovidio and Samuel Gaertner (1999) report that cooperation has especially positive effects when it leads people to define a new, inclusive group that dissolves their former subgroups. Seat the members of two groups not on opposite sides, but alternately around the table. Give them a new, shared name. Have them work together. Such experiences change "us and them" into "we." Those once perceived as being in another group now are seen as part of one's own group.

During the 1970s, several teams of educational researchers simultaneously wondered: If cooperative contacts between members of rival groups encourage posi-

"You cannot shake hands with a clenched fist."

Indira Gandhi, 1971

■ **superordinate goals** shared goals that override differences among people and require their cooperation.

Superordinate goals override differences
Cooperative efforts to achieve shared goals are an effective way to break down social barriers.

tive attitudes, could we apply this principle in multicultural schools? Could we promote interracial friendships by replacing competitive classroom situations with cooperative ones? And could cooperative learning maintain or even enhance student achievement? Many experiments confirm that in all three cases, the answer is yes (Johnson & Johnson, 1989, 1994; Slavin, 1989). Members of interracial groups who work together on projects and play together on athletic teams typically come to feel friendly toward those of the other race. So do those who engage in cooperative classroom learning. So encouraging are these results that more than 25,000 teachers have introduced interracial cooperative learning into their classrooms (Kohn, 1987). Working with fellow students in all their diversity sets the stage, declared the Carnegie Council on Adolescent Development (1989), for "adult work life and for citizenship in a multicultural society."

The power of cooperative activity to make friends of former enemies has led psychologists to urge increased international exchange and cooperation (Klineberg, 1984). As we engage in mutually beneficial trade, as we work to protect our common destiny on this fragile planet, and as we become more aware that our hopes and fears are shared, we can change misperceptions that lead to fragmentation and conflict into a solidarity based on common interests. Although we will never love all our differences or be friends with everyone, we can, as we work toward shared goals, grow to accept and value human diversity.

Communication

In the social trap game that we considered earlier, people are usually distrustful and pursue their individual interests as a defense against exploitation. But when they are allowed to discuss the dilemma and negotiate, cooperation increases (Jorgenson & Papciak, 1981).

When conflicts do become intense, a third-party mediator—a marriage counselor, labor mediator, diplomat, community volunteer—may facilitate much-needed communication (Rubin & others, 1994). Mediators help each party to voice its viewpoint and to understand the other's. By leading each side to think about the other's underlying needs and goals, the mediator aims to replace a competitive *win-lose* orientation with a cooperative *win-win* orientation that aims at a mutually beneficial resolution. A classic example: Two friends, after quarreling over an orange, agreed to split it. One squeezed his half for juice. The other used the peel from her half to make a cake. If only the two had understood each other's motives, they could have hit on the win-win solution of one having all the juice, the other all the peel.

Such understanding and cooperative resolution is most needed, yet least likely, in times of anger or crisis (Bodenhausen & others, 1994; Tetlock, 1988). When conflicts

"I am prepared this day to declare myself a citizen of the world, and to invite everyone everywhere to embrace this broader vision of our interdependent world, our common quest for justice, and ultimately for Peace on Earth."

Father Theodore Hesburgh, *The Human Imperative*, 1974

■ GRIT Graduated and Reciprocated Initiatives in Tension-Reduction—a strategy designed to decrease international tensions.

intensify, images become more stereotyped, communication more difficult, and judgments more rigid. Iraq's President Saddam Hussein, America's friend while attacking Iran in the 1980s, became to U.S. President George Bush "another Hitler" after attacking oil-producing Kuwait in 1990. To Hussein, Bush became "Satan in the White House."

Neutral third parties may also suggest proposals that would be dismissed if either side offered them. People often "reactively devalue" a concession offered by an adversary ("if they're willing to give that up, they must not value it"); the very same concession may seem less like a token gesture when suggested by a third party. Lee Ross and Constance Stillinger (1991) showed how this works. They found that a nuclear disarmament proposal that Americans dismissed when attributed to the Soviet Union seemed more acceptable when attributed to a neutral third party.

Conciliation

When tension and suspicion peak, cooperation and communication may become impossible. Each party is likely to threaten, coerce, or retaliate. In the weeks before the Persian Gulf War, President Bush threatened, in the full glare of publicity, to "kick Saddam's ass." Saddam Hussein communicated in kind, threatening to make Americans "swim in their own blood."

Under such conditions, is there an alternative to war or surrender? Social psychologist Charles Osgood (1962, 1980) has advocated a strategy of "Graduated and Reciprocated Initiatives in Tension-Reduction," nicknamed **GRIT**. In applying GRIT, one side first announces its recognition of mutual interests and its intent to reduce tensions. It then initiates one or more small, conciliatory acts. Without weakening one's retaliatory capability, this modest beginning opens the door for reciprocation by the other party. Should the enemy respond with hostility, one reciprocates in kind. But so, too, with any conciliatory response. Thus, President Kennedy's gesture of stopping atmospheric nuclear tests began a series of reciprocated conciliatory acts that culminated in the 1993 atmospheric test-ban treaty.

"To begin with, I would like to express my sincere thanks and deep appreciation for the opportunity to meet with you. While there are still profound differences between us, I think the very fact of my presence here today is a major breakthrough."

In laboratory experiments, GRIT has been the most effective strategy known for increasing trust and cooperation (Lindskold & others, 1978–1988). Even during intense personal conflict, when communication has been nonexistent, a small conciliatory gesture—a smile, a touch, a word of apology—may work wonders. Conciliations allow both parties to begin edging down the tension ladder to a safer rung where communication and mutual understanding can begin.

And how good that such can happen, for civilization advances not by cultural isolation—maintaining walls around ethnic enclaves—but by tapping the knowledge, the skills, and the arts that are each culture's legacy to the whole human race. Thomas Sowell (1991) notes that, thanks to cultural sharing, every modern society is enriched by a cultural mix. We have China to thank for paper and printing, and for the magnetic compass that opened the great explorations. We have Egypt to thank for trigonometry. We have the Islamic world and India's Hindus to thank for our Arabic numerals. While celebrating and claiming these cultural legacies, we can also welcome the enrichment of today's social diversity. We can view ourselves as individual instruments in a human orchestra. And we can therefore affirm our own culture's heritage while building bridges of communication, understanding, and cooperation across cultural traditions.

REVIEW AND REFLECT:

Social Relations

What are the social, emotional, and cognitive roots of prejudice?

Prejudice often arises as those who enjoy social and economic superiority attempt to justify the status quo. Even the temporary assignment of people to groups can cause an ingroup bias. Once established, the inertia of social influence often helps maintain prejudice. Prejudice may also focus the anger caused by frustration on a scapegoat.

Newer research reveals how our ways of processing information—for example, by overestimating similarities when we categorize people or by noticing and remembering vivid cases—work to create stereotypes. In addition, favored social groups will often rationalize their higher status with the just-world phenomenon.

What biological and psychological factors make us more prone to harm one another?

Aggressive behavior, like all behavior, is a product of nature and nurture. Although psychologists dismiss the idea that aggression is instinctual, aggressiveness is genetically influenced. Moreover, certain areas of the brain, when stimulated, activate or inhibit aggression, and these neural areas are biochemically influenced.

A variety of psychological factors also fuel aggression's fire. Aversive events heighten people's hostility. Such stimuli are especially likely to trigger aggression in those rewarded for their own aggression or those who have learned aggression from role models or observed violent media portrayals of aggressive models. Such factors desensitize people to cruelty and prime them to behave aggressively when provoked.

What social processes fuel conflict?

Conflicts between individuals and cultures often arise from malignant social processes. These include social traps, in which each party, by protecting and pursuing its self-interest, creates an outcome that no one wants. The spiral of conflict also feeds and is fed by distorted mirror-image perceptions, in which each party views itself as moral and the other as untrustworthy and evil-intentioned.

Why do we become friends with some people but not with others? Does our love for a partner remain the same as time passes?

Three factors are known to affect our liking for one another. Proximity—geographical nearness—is conducive to attraction, partly because mere exposure to novel stimuli enhances liking. Physical attractiveness influences social opportunities and the way one is perceived. As acquaintanceship moves toward friendship, similarity of attitudes and interests greatly increases liking.

We can view passionate love as an aroused state that we cognitively label as love. The strong affection of companionate love, which often emerges as a relationship matures, is enhanced by an equitable relationship and by intimate self-disclosure.

Why do we help others? When are we most likely to help?

In response to incidents where bystanders did not intervene in emergencies, social psychologists undertook experiments that revealed a bystander effect: Any given bystander is less likely to help if others are present. The bystander effect is especially apparent in situations where the presence of others inhibits one's noticing the event, interpreting it as an emergency, or assuming responsibility for offering help. Many factors, including mood, also influence one's willingness to help someone in distress.

Social exchange theory proposes that our social behaviors—even our helpful acts—maximize our benefits (which may include our own good feelings) and minimize our costs. Our desire to help is also affected by social norms, which prescribe reciprocating the help we have received and being socially responsible toward those in need.

How can we transform feelings of prejudice, aggression, and conflict into attitudes that promote peace?

Enemies sometimes become friends, especially when the circumstances favor cooperation to achieve superordinate goals, understanding through communication, and reciprocated conciliatory gestures.

Terms and Concepts to Remember

prejudice, p. 694	social trap, p. 708
stereotype, p. 694	mere exposure effect, p. 710
ingroup, p. 696	passionate love, p. 714
outgroup, p. 696	companionate love, p. 714
ingroup bias, p. 696	equity, p. 714
scapegoat theory, p. 697	self-disclosure, p. 715
just-world phenomenon, p. 698	altruism, p. 715
aggression, p. 698	bystander effect, p. 717
frustration-aggression principle, p. 701	social exchange theory, p. 717
	superordinate goals, p. 718
conflict, p. 708	GRIT, p. 720

Test Yourself

55.1. Experiments show that when people are temporarily frustrated, they express more intense prejudice. When things go wrong, prejudice provides an outlet for our anger—and gives us someone to blame. This effect is best described by

a. ingroup bias.

b. scapegoat theory.

c. Freud's theory on the death instinct.

d. the just-world phenomenon.

55.2. Stereotypes are a natural by-product of our usual ways of thinking. For example, we tend to judge the frequency of events in terms of cases that come readily to memory. Thus, if several well-publicized murders are committed by members of a particular group, we tend to react with fear and suspicion toward all members of the group. In other words, we

a. blame the victim.

b. overgeneralize from vivid, memorable cases.

c. create a scapegoat.

d. categorize people incorrectly.

Continued

55.3. Aggression is physical or verbal behavior that is intended to hurt someone. We find biological influences on aggression at three levels: the genetic, the neural, and the biochemical. Evidence of a biochemical influence on aggression is the finding that
a. aggressive behavior varies widely from culture to culture.
b. animals can be bred for aggressiveness.
c. stimulation of an area of the brain's limbic system produces aggressive behavior.
d. a higher-than-average level of the hormone testosterone is associated with violent behavior in males.

55.4. Studies show that delinquent young people tend to have parents who relied on beatings to enforce discipline. This demonstrates that aggression can be
a. learned through direct rewards.
b. triggered by exposure to violent media.
c. learned through observation of aggressive models.
d. caused by hormone changes at puberty.

55.5. A 1986 conference of social scientists who studied the effects of pornography on ordinary adult men generally agreed that violent pornography
a. has little effect on most viewers.
b. is the primary cause of reported and unreported rapes.
c. leads viewers to be more accepting of coercion in sexual relations.
d. has no short-term effects, other than arousal and entertainment.

55.6. Conflicts often arise from destructive social processes. In many situations, individuals, in rationally pursuing their self-interests, get caught up in behavior that harms both themselves and others. This destructive social process is called
a. gameplaying.
b. mirror-image perception.
c. a social trap.
d. the fundamental attribution error.

55.7. Repeated exposure to a stimulus—including a new human face—increases our liking of the stimulus. This *mere exposure effect* helps explain why proximity is a powerful predictor of friendship and marriage, and why, for example, people tend to marry someone
a. about as attractive as themselves.
b. who lives or works nearby.
c. of similar religious or ethnic background.
d. who has similar attitudes and habits.

55.8. Male subjects who are aroused by various stimuli and then introduced to an attractive woman tend to attribute their arousal to the woman, and to report positive feelings toward her. This supports the two-factor theory of emotion, which assumes that emotions such as passionate love consist of physical arousal plus
a. a reward.
b. proximity.
c. companionate love.
d. our interpretation of that arousal.

55.9. Companionate love is described as a deep, affectionate attachment. Vital to the maintenance of such loving relationships is (are)
a. equity and self-disclosure.
b. physical attraction.
c. intense positive absorption.
d. proximity and similarity.

55.10. Psychologists have studied the factors that determine whether a bystander will come to the aid of a stranger in an "emergency." They have found that people who are in a good mood are most likely to extend their help. Perhaps the most important finding, though, is the bystander effect, which states that a particular bystander is less likely to give aid if
a. the victim is similar to him or her in appearance.
b. there is no one else present.
c. other bystanders are present.
d. the incident occurs in a deserted or rural area.

55.11. Social psychologists have attempted to define the circumstances that facilitate conflict resolution. One way of fostering cooperation is by providing contentious groups with superordinate goals, which are
a. the goals of friendly competition.
b. shared goals that override differences.
c. goals for winning at negotiations.
d. goals for reducing conflict through increased contact.

Review: Why didn't anybody help Kitty Genovese? What social relations principle did this incident illustrate?

Reflect: Are there friends or family members with whom you do not get along but would like to? How might you go about reconciling these relationships?

Answers to the Test Yourself and Review questions can be found in the green appendix at the end of the book.

APPENDIX

Answers to Test Yourself and Review Questions

module 1 **The History and Scope of Psychology**

Test Yourself

1.1., c.; 1.2., b.; 1.3, a.; 1.4., d.; 1.5., c.

Review

What is behavior, and what are mental processes?

Behavior is anything an organism does—any action we can observe and record. *Mental processes* are internal, subjective experiences about which we make inferences by observing behavior.

module 2 **Research Strategies: How Psychologists Ask and Answer Questions**

Test Yourself

2.1., d.; 2.2., c.; 2.3., a.; 2.4., c.; 2.5., c.; 2.6., d.; 2.7., b.; 2.8., c.; 2.9., a.; 2.10., c.; 2.11., c.; 2.12., b.; 2.13., c.; 2.14., b.; 2.15., a.

Review

What are the strengths and weaknesses of the three different methods psychologists use to describe behavior—case studies, surveys, and naturalistic observation?

<u>Case studies</u> offer in-depth insights that may offer clues to what's true of others—or may, if the case is atypical, mislead. <u>Surveys</u> can accurately reveal the tendencies of large populations. But if the questions are leading, or if nonrandom samples are queried, the results can again mislead us. <u>Naturalistic observation</u> enables study of behavior undisturbed by researchers. But the lack of control may leave cause and effect ambiguous.

Here are some recently reported correlations, with interpretations drawn by journalists.

a. Alcohol use is associated with violence. (Interpretation: Drinking triggers or unleashes aggressive behavior.)

b. Educated people live longer, on average, than less-educated people. (Interpretation: Education lengthens life and enhances health.)

c. People who spend long hours on the Internet are somewhat less engaged with family and are lonelier and more depressed. (Interpretation: By isolating people from face-to-face contact, Internet absorption can be depressing.)

Consider a question posed by Christopher Jepson, David Krantz, and Richard Nisbett (1983) to University of Michigan introductory psychology students:

The registrar's office at the University of Michigan has found that usually about 100 students in Arts and Sciences have perfect marks at the end of their first term at the University. However, only about 10 to 15 students graduate with perfect marks. What do you think is the most likely explanation for the fact that there are more perfect marks after one term than at graduation?

Most students in the study came up with plausible causes for the drop in marks, such as, "Students tend to work harder at the beginning of their college careers than toward the end." Fewer than a third recognized the statistical phenomenon clearly at work: Averages based on fewer courses are more variable, which guarantees a greater number of extremely low and high marks at the end of the first term.

module 3   Neural and Hormonal Systems

Test Yourself

3.1., b.; 3.2., a.; 3.3., c.; 3.4., d.; 3.5., c.; 3.6., b.; 3.7., d.; 3.8., c.; 3.9., a.; 3.10., b.; 3.11., a.; 3.12., a.

Review

How does information flow through your nervous system as you pick up a fork? Summarize this process.

Your central nervous system's hungry brain activates and guides the muscles of your arm and hand via your peripheral nervous system's motor neurons. As you pick up the fork, your brain processes the information from your sensory nervous system, enabling it to continue to guide the fork to your mouth. The functional circle starts with sensory input, continues with interneuron processing by the central nervous system, and finishes with motor output.

module 4   The Brain

Test Yourself

4.1., b.; 4.2., c.; 4.3., d.; 4.4., a.; 4.5., b.; 4.6., d.; 4.7., b.; 4.8., d.; 4.9., d.; 4.10., c.; 4.11., c.; 4.12., b.; 4.13., c.; 4.14., d.; 4.15., a.; 4.16., b.

Review

Within what brain region would damage be most likely to disrupt your ability to skip rope? Your ability to sense tastes or sounds? In what brain region would damage perhaps leave you in a coma? Without the very breath and heartbeat of life?

These regions are respectively, the cerebellum, the thalamus, the reticular formation, and the medulla. These questions assess your understanding of the essential functions of lower-level brain areas.

module 5 Genetic Influences on Behavior

Test Yourself

5.1., c.; 5.2., b.; 5.3., c.; 5.4., c.; 5.5., b.; 5.6., b.; 5.7., c.; 5.8., b.

Review

Explain the relationships among chromosomes, DNA, genes, genome, and nucleotides.

The nucleotide "letters" are ordered to create the gene "words" that make up the chromosome "books." Chromosomes are made of giant DNA molecules that are organized as a two-stranded "double helix" held together by bonds between pairs of nucleotides. Genes are DNA segments capable of synthesizing a protein. All told, the human genome (the complete genetic instructions for making a human) contains 46 chromosomes, roughly 100,000 genes, and some 3 billion pairs of nucleotides.

What is heritability?

Heritability is the proportion of variation among individuals that we can attribute to genes. Note: Heritability is *not* the extent to which an *individual's* traits are genetically determined. Rather it is the extent to which variation *among* individuals is due to their differing genes. For any trait, heritability can vary, depending on the population and range of environments studied.

module 6 Environmental Influences on Behavior

Test Yourself

6.1., b.; 6.2., a.; 6.3., c.; 6.4., b.; 6.5., b.; 6.6., d.; 6.7., b.; 6.8., c.

Review

Many researchers have recently concluded that the shared home environment has less effect on children's development than is often supposed, and that peer influences matter more than we realized. What evidence supports that conclusion?

Despite sharing the same home, adopted siblings vary nearly as widely in personalities and abilities as do children paired at random. Although children may pick up manners and values from their home environments, peer influences often seem to matter more. For example, when parents speak with one accent and peers with another, children will inevitably adopt the accent of their peers.

What are gender roles, and what do their variations tell us about our human capacity for learning and adaptation?

Gender roles are social rules or norms for accepted and expected behavior for females and males. The norms associated with various roles, including gender roles, vary widely in different cultural contexts, which is proof that we are very capable of learning and adapting to the social demands of different environments.

module 7 Prenatal Development and the Newborn

Test Yourself

7.1., c.; 7.2., a.; 7.3., a.; 7.4., d.

Review

Your friend—a heavy smoker—hopes to become pregnant soon. She says she will stop smoking as soon as she learns she is pregnant. What can you tell her to convince her that the time to stop smoking is before she is pregnant?

The most harmful effects of teratogens, such as cigarette smoke, occur during the first trimester of pregnancy—often before a woman even knows she is pregnant. So, the time to quit smoking is before there is a chance that the pregnancy has begun.

module 8 Infancy and Childhood

Test Yourself

8.1., b.; 8.2., c.; 8.3., b.; 8.4., b.; 8.5., d.; 8.6., d.; 8.7., a.; 8.8., b.; 8.9., b.; 8.10., c.

Review

Researchers have presumed that Ugandan babies' earlier walking was a product of their nurture. Others might wonder if credit should instead go to their genetically predisposed nature. How might we test these alternative ideas?

As Chapter 3 suggested, we can evaluate nature's and nurture's relative contributions by allowing one to vary while the other remains constant. In the absence of twin studies one might, for example, compare the age of walking of Ugandans raised in traditional or Western contexts. Or, with Uganda, one might compare the walking age of similarly reared infants of European, Asian, and Ugandan ancestry.

Use Piaget's first three stages of cognitive development to explain why young children are not just miniature adults in the way they think.

Infants in the <u>sensorimotor stage</u> tend to be focused only on their own perceptions of the world and may, for example, be unaware that objects continue to exist when unseen. A <u>preoperational</u> child is still egocentric and incapable of appreciating simple logic, such as the reversibility of operations. A preteen in the <u>concrete operational stage</u> is beginning to think logically about concrete events but not about abstract concepts.

Parents who spank tend to have more physically aggressive children. What might explain this correlation?

Perhaps spanking causes aggressiveness (by creating frustration and pain and by modeling aggression). Perhaps aggressiveness causes spanking (naughty children elicit more swats from exasperated parents). Or perhaps parents' and children's shared genes predispose their being similarly aggressive.

module 9 Adolescence

Test Yourself

9.1., b.; 9.2., d.; 9.3., c.; 9.4., d.; 9.5., b.; 9.6., b.; 9.7., a.

Review

To predict whether a teenager smokes marijuana, ask how many of the teen's friends smoke it. One explanation for this correlation is peer influence. What is another?

There may also be a <u>selection effect</u>. Adolescents tend to sort themselves into like-minded groups—the jocks, the geeks, the druggies, and so forth. Those who smoke pot may similarly seek out other teenagers who also smoke it.

module 10 Adulthood

Test Yourself

10.1., c.; 10.2., a.; 10.3., d.; 10.4., c.; 10.5., d.; 10.6., c.

Review

Research has shown that living together before marriage predicts increased likelihood of future divorce. Can you imagine two possible explanations for this correlation?

William Axinn and Arland Thornton (1992) report data that support two explanations.

First, cohabitation attracts people who are more open to terminating unsatisfying relationships. The very idea of cohabitation presumes that intimate relationships need not be permanent: If either partner becomes dissatisfied, he or she can seek bliss elsewhere. So, love is conditional rather than committed. People who cohabit bring a more individualistic ethic to marriage, are more likely to see close relationships as temporary and fragile, are more accepting of divorce, and are about three times more likely after marriage to have an affair (Forste & Tanfer, 1996). This is another example of a <u>selection effect</u>.

A second explanation is the <u>causal effect</u> of cohabitation. The experience of cohabitation increases one's acceptance of divorce. Over time, those who cohabit tend to become more approving of dissolving an unfulfilling union. This divorce-accepting attitude increases the odds of later divorce.

module 11 Introduction to Sensation and Perception

Test Yourself

11.1., d.; 11.2., b.; 11.3., b.; 11.4., d.; 11.5., b.; 11.6., c.; 11.7., d.; 11.8., c.

Review

What is the rough distinction between sensation and perception?

Sensation refers to the bottom-up process by which the physical sensory system receives and represents stimuli. Perception refers to the mental process of organizing and interpreting the sensory input.

Your friend insists that he *did* call you to dinner as you intently watched TV. Was your not perceiving him a likely instance of subliminal stimulation?

Not if his voice was above your absolute threshold for hearing if you had been paying attention. Your not perceiving the voice probably reflects your selectively focusing your attention on the TV.

module 12 Vision

Test Yourself

12.1., b.; 12.2., c.; 12.3., c.; 12.4., b.; 12.5., a.; 12.6., d.; 12.7., b.

Review

Retrace the rapid sequence of events involved in seeing and recognizing someone you know.

Light waves reflect off the person and travel into your eye, where the rods and cones convert the light waves' energy into neural impulses sent to your brain. Your brain then processes the subdimensions of this visual input—including color, depth, movement, and form—separately but simultaneously, and then integrates this information (along with previously stored information) into a conscious perception of the person you know.

module 13 Hearing

Test Yourself

13.1., a.; 13.2., b.; 13.3., c.; 13.4., d.; 13.5., b.

Review

In a nutshell, how do we transform sound waves into perceived sound?

A simple figure offers a synopsis:

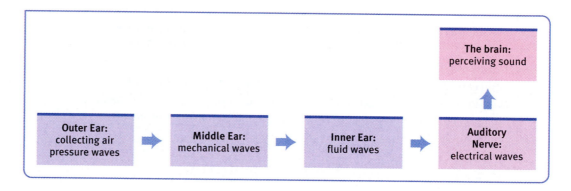

module 14 The Other Senses

Test Yourself

14.1., a.; 14.2., c.; 14.3., d.; 14.4., c.

Review

How does our system for sensing smell differ from our sensory systems for vision, touch, and taste?

We have three types of color receptors, four basic touch senses, and four basic taste sensations. But we have no basic smell receptors. Instead, 1000 odor receptors, individually and in combination, recognize some 10,000 discernible odors.

module 15 Perceptual Organization

Test Yourself

15.1., a.; 15.2., d.; 15.3., b.; 15.4., c.; 15.5., c.; 15.6., c.; 15.7., a.

Review

How does the study of illusions inform our understanding of normal perceptions?

Perceptual illusions reveal the ways we organize and interpret sensory information. Our occasional misperceptions demonstrate the workings of our normally effective perceptual processes. For example, the perceived relationship between distance and size is generally valid, but under special circumstances it can lead us astray—as when it helps create the moon illusion.

module 16 Perceptual Interpretation

Test Yourself

16.1., c.; 16.2., b.; 16.3., d.; 16.4., a.; 16.5., c.; 16.6., c.

Review

What type of evidence shows that, indeed, "there is more to perception than meets the senses"?

We construct our perceptions based on both sensory input and—experiments show—on our assumptions, expectations, schemas, and perceptual sets, often influenced by the surrounding context.

What psychic ability is being claimed by the sports channel in the nearby cartoon?

The psychic sports channel claims precognition—the ability to foresee future events.

module 17 Waking and Sleeping Rhythms

Test Yourself

17.1., b.; 17.2., a.; 17.3., b.; 17.4., b.; 17.5., d.; 17.6., c.; 17.7., d.; 17.8., d.; 17.9., a.; 17.10., c.

Review

During psychology's history, what were the ups and downs of "consciousness"?

Psychology began as the study of consciousness, but during the behaviorists era (for much of the first half of the twentieth century) psychologists focused on observations of *behavior*. During the last 40 years, consciousness—our awareness of ourselves and our environment—has reemerged as a major topic in psychology.

Are you getting enough sleep? What might you ask yourself to answer this question?

You could start with the true/false questions in James Maas' sleep deprivation quiz on page 254. Also, William Dement (1999, p. 73) invites you to consider these questions: "How often do you think about taking a quick snooze? How often do you rub your eyes and yawn during the day? How often do you feel like you really need some coffee?" Dement concludes that "each of these is a warning of a sleep debt that you ignore at your peril."

module 18 Hypnosis

Test Yourself

18.1., a.; 18.2., c.; 18.3., c.

Review

When is the use of hypnosis potentially harmful, and when can hypnosis be used to help?

Hypnosis is potentially harmful when therapists, seeking to "hypnotically refresh" memories, plant false memories. But posthypnotic suggestions have helped alleviate some ailments, and hypnosis can also help control pain.

module 19   Drugs and Consciousness

Test Yourself

19.1., c.; 19.2., a.; 19.3., d.; 19.4., c.; 19.5., c.; 19.6., a.; 19.7., b.

Review

A U.S. government survey of 27,616 current or former alcohol drinkers found that 40 percent of those who began drinking before age 15 become alcohol-dependent. The same was true of only 10 percent of those who first imbibed at ages 21 or 22 (Grant & Dawson, 1998). What possible explanations might there be for this correlation between early use and later abuse?

Possible explanations include (1) a biological predisposition to both early use and later abuse, (2) brain changes and taste preferences induced by early use, and (3) enduring habits, attitudes, activities, and/or peer relationships that are conducive to alcohol use.

module 20   Classical Conditioning

Test Yourself

20.1., c.; 20.2., c.; 20.3., a.; 20.4., b.; 20.5., d.; 20.6., b.; 20.7., b.

Review

In slasher movies, sexually arousing images of women are sometimes paired with violence against women. Based on classical conditioning principles, what might be an effect of this pairing?

If viewing an attractive nude or semi-nude woman (a UCS) elicits sexual arousal (a UCR), then pairing the UCS with a new stimulus (violence) could turn the violence into a conditioned stimulus (CS) that also becomes sexually arousing, a conditioned response (CR).

module 21   Operant Conditioning

Test Yourself

21.1., d.; 21.2., c.; 21.3., a.; 21.4., b.; 21.5., b.; 21.6., c.; 21.7., b.; 21.8., d.; 21.9., d.

Review

Positive reinforcement, negative reinforcement, and punishment are tricky concepts for many students. Can you fit the right term in the four boxes in this table? (The first one was done for you on page 316.)

Type of Stimulus	Give It	Take It Away
Desired (for example, a compliment):	Positive reinforcement	Punishment (e.g., time-out)
Undesired/aversive (for example, an insult):	Punishment	Negative reinforcement

module 22   Learning by Observation

Test Yourself

22.1., a.; 22.2., a.; 22.3., c.

Review

Juan's parents and older friends all smoke, but they advise him not to. Jason's parents and friends don't smoke, but they say nothing to deter him from doing so. Will Juan or Jason be more likely to start smoking?

Although both saying and doing can influence people, experiments suggest that children more often do as others do and say as they say. Generalizing this finding to smoking, we can expect that Juan will be more likely to start smoking.

module 23   Introduction to Memory

Test Yourself

23.1., b.; 23.2. a.

Review

Memory includes (in alphabetical order) long-term memory, sensory memory, short-term memory. What's the correct order of these three memory stores?

Sensory memory, short-term memory, long-term memory.

module 24   Encoding: Getting Information In

Test Yourself

24.1., c.; 24.2., b.; 24.3., a.; 24.4., d.; 24.5., c.

Review

What would be the most effective strategy to learn and retain a list of historical names of key figures for a week? For a year?

For a week: Make the names personally meaningful. For a year: Overlearn the list and space out rehearsals over the course of several weeks.

module 25   Storage: Retaining Information

Test Yourself

25.1., b.; 25.2., c.; 25.3., d.; 25.4., c.; 25.5., b.; 25.6., a.

Review

Your friend tells you that her father is suffering from the early signs of Alzheimer's. She wonders if psychology can explain why he can still play checkers very well but has a hard time holding a sensible conversation. What can you tell her?

Our explicit (declarable) memories differ from our implicit memories of skills and procedures, such as checkers. Our implicit memories are processed by more ancient brain areas, which are usually unaffected in the early stages of Alzheimer's disease.

module 26   Retrieval: Getting Information Out

Test Yourself

26.1., a.; 26.2., b.; 26.3., d.; 26.4., a.; 26.5., d.

Review

What is priming?

Priming is the activation (often without our awareness) of associations. Imagine that seeing a gun predisposed you shortly thereafter to interpret an ambiguous face as threatening or to recall your boss as nasty. Although you might not consciously remember the gun, it may "prime" how you interpret or recall events.

module 27 Forgetting and Memory Construction

Test Yourself

27.1., d.; 27.2., d.; 27.3., c.; 27.4., a.; 27.5., b.; 27.6., c.; 27.7., d.

Review

Can you offer an example of proactive interference?

Proactive (forward-acting) interference occurs when earlier learning disrupts your recall of a later experience. Proactive interference has occurred if learning names of new classmates in your first class makes it more difficult to learn the new names in your second class.

What—given the commonality of source amnesia—might life be like if we remembered all our waking experiences and all our dreams?

Real experiences would be confused with those dreamed. When meeting someone, we might therefore be unsure whether we were reacting to something they previously did or to something we dreamed they did. William Dement (1999, p. 298) thinks this "would put a great burden on your sanity. . . . I truly believe that the wall of memory is a blessed protection."

module 28 Thinking

Test Yourself

28.1., a.; 28.2., b.; 28.3., c.; 28.4., d.; 28.5., b.; 28.6., d.; 28.7., c.; 28.8., a.

Review

The availability heuristic is a quick-and-easy but sometimes misleading guide to judging reality. What is the availability heuristic?

The availability heuristic is our tendency to judge the likeliness of an event by how easily we can recall instances of it. Like all heuristics, this guide is efficient. But it can mislead, as it does when we attempt to judge various risks (for example, of plane travel).

module 29 Language and Thought

Test Yourself

29.1., c.; 29.2., c.; 29.3., d.; 29.4., b.; 29.5., a.; 29.6., a.

Review

If children are not yet speaking, is there any reason to think they would benefit from parents and other caregivers reading to them?

Indeed there is, because well before age 1 children are learning to detect words among the stream of spoken sounds and to discern grammatical rules. Before age

1 they also are babbling with the phonemes of their own language. More than many parents realize, their infants are soaking up language. As researcher Peter Jusczyk reminds us, "Little ears are listening."

To say that "words are the mother of ideas" assumes the truth of what concept?

This phrase supports the linguistic relativity hypothesis, which asserts that language determines (more accurately, influences) thought.

If your dog barks at a stranger at the front door, does this qualify as language? What if the dog yips in a telltale way to let you know she needs to go out?

These are definitely communications. But if language is words and how we combine them grammatically to communicate meaning, few scientists would label a dog's barking and yipping as language.

module 30 Introduction to Intelligence

Test Yourself

30.1., c.; 30.2., a.; 30.3., c.; 30.4., c.; 30.5., d.; 30.6., d.

Review

For the second time in a week, José and Miguel encountered a barking dog on their walk to class. Miguel picked up a stick and was about to yell at the dog when José began talking gently to the dog, and the dog began wagging its tail. Why was José's response more "intelligent" according to the definition in this section?

Intelligence is the ability to learn, solve problems, and adapt to new situations. José displayed a knack for doing just that in this challenging situation.

module 31 Assessing Intelligence

Test Yourself

31.1., d.; 31.2., c.; 31.3., a.; 31.4., c.; 31.5., b.; 31.6., d.; 31.7., b.

Review

How did Terman's motives for creating tests of mental abilities differ from Binet's?

Binet wanted to devise a test that would predict children's future progress in the French school system. Terman wanted to design a test to measure inherited intelligence, and to assess "vocational fitness."

Does leg strength predict *running* speed? To find out, Fiona correlates the muscular strength of the 10 fastest youths in her school with their 100-meter times—and finds only a weak correlation. But even if strong muscles do enable speed we could have expected this result. Why?

Because Fiona tested only those within a narrow range of speeds. Perhaps if her tests had included a wider range—from the slowest to the fastest—the correlation would have been stronger. Aptitude tests likewise are more predictive of school success in diverse samples of students.

The Smiths have enrolled their 2-year-old son, who they believe is gifted, in a special program that claims to "give your child a superior mind." Why is this endeavor of questionable value?

Two years is too young an age for reliably predicting future intelligence. Moreover, programs for raising young children's intelligence seem to have no substantial long-term effects.

module 32   Genetic and Environmental Influences on Intelligence

Test Yourself

32.1., a.; 32.2., c.; 32.3., c.; 32.4., d.; 32.5., b.

Review

As society succeeds in creating equality of opportunity, it will also increase the heritability of ability. The heritability of intelligence scores will be greater in a society marked by equal opportunity than in a society of peasants and aristocrats. Why?

Perfect environmental equality would create 100 percent heritability—because genes alone would account for any remaining human differences.

module 33   Introduction to Motivation

Test Yourself

33.1., b.; 33.2., a.; 33.3., d.; 33.4., c.; 33.5., c.; 33.6., a.

Review

While on a long road trip, your stomach is growling with hunger. So you pull off to eat at the nearest restaurant. What motivational perspective would most easily explain this behavior and why?

Drive-reduction theory—the idea that physical needs create an aroused state that drives us to reduce the need—helps explain your behavior.

module 34   Hunger

Test Yourself

34.1., b.; 34.2., a.; 34.3., c.; 34.4., b.

Review

You are traveling and have not eaten anything in eight hours. As your long-awaited favorite dish is placed in front of you, your mouth waters. Even imagining this may set your mouth to watering. What triggers this anticipatory drooling?

You, like Pavlov's dogs, have learned through <u>classical conditioning</u> to respond to the cues—the sight and aroma—that signal the food about to enter your mouth. Both <u>physiological cues</u> (eight hours of deprivation have left you with low blood sugar) and <u>psychological cues</u> (the anticipation of the tasty meal) have heightened your experienced hunger.

module 35   Sexual Motivation

Test Yourself

35.1., d.; 35.2., b.; 35.3., b.; 35.4., c.; 35.5., d.; 35.6., d.; 35.7., b.

Review

Research on sexual attitudes and behaviors has relied extensively on volunteers. How might this factor bias the results of such studies?

Volunteers responding to popular sex surveys often comprise a non-random sample. Their self-reported attitudes and behaviors may therefore not be representative of the whole population.

module 36   Achievement Motivation

Test Yourself

36.1., c.; 36.2., a.; 36.3., c.; 36.4., d.

Review

If a couple asked you, "What is the best way to motivate achievement in my child?" what two tips could you give them after reading this section?

In addition to allowing the child to experience the rewards of independent initiative, they might guide the child in ways that foster intrinsic motivation (rather than extrinsic motivation).

module 37   Theories of Emotion

Test Yourself

37.1., b.; 37.2., b.; 37.3., b.; 37.4., c.; 37.5., a.

Review

Christine is holding her 8-month-old baby when a fierce dog appears out of nowhere and, with teeth bared, leaps for the baby's face. Christine immediately ducks for cover to protect the baby, screams at the dog, then notices that her heart is banging in her chest and she's broken out in a cold sweat. How would the James-Lange, Cannon-Bard, and two-factor theories explain Christine's emotional reaction?

The James-Lange theory would say that Christine's emotional reaction consists of her awareness of her physiological responses to the dog attack. The Cannon-Bard theory would say that her fear experience happened simultaneously with her physiological arousal. Schacter's two-factor theory would presume that her emotional reaction stemmed from her interpreting and labeling the arousal.

module 38   Experiencing and Expressing Emotion

Test Yourself

38.1., b.; 38.2., d.; 38.3., d.; 38.4., a.; 38.5., b.; 38.6., b.; 38.7., a.; 38.8., d.; 38.9., c.

Review

How would an evolutionary psychologist explain our autonomic nervous system's reaction (increased heart rate and respiration, tense muscles, slowed digestion, and so on) to an alarming situation?

An evolutionary psychologist would presume that all such reactions prepare the organism to cope and survive. Those among our ancestors who didn't respond adaptively would have been less likely to leave descendants than those who did. Evolutionary psychologists would consider the adaptive value of each of these mechanisms. For example, slowed digestion allows the body to direct all its resources to a fight-or-flight response.

Who tends to express more emotion—men or women? How do we know the answer to that question?

Women tend to surpass men not only as emotion detectors but also at expressing certain emotions (though men have slightly surpassed women in conveying anger). Researchers discovered this by showing people brief, silent clips of men's and women's faces expressing various emotions and by observing who is most skilled at reading and sending emotions.

What things do (and don't) predict self-reported happiness?

People's age, sex, and income give only modest clues to their happiness. Their personality traits, close relationships, "flow" in work and leisure, and religious faith do provide clues.

module 39 The Psychoanalytic Perspective

Test Yourself

39.1., b.; 39.2., c.; 39.3., b.; 39.4., b.; 39.5., b.; 39.6., d.; 39.7., d.; 39.8., a.

Review

What, according to Freud, were some of the important defense mechanisms, and what do they defend against?

Freud believed repression to be the basic defense mechanism. Others include regression, projection, rationalization, and displacement. All supposedly serve to reduce anxiety.

module 40 The Trait Perspective

Test Yourself

40.1., c.; 40.2., b.; 40.3., c.; 40.4., c.; 40.5., b.

Review

How many trait dimensions are typically used to describe personality, and what are those dimensions?

"The Big Five" trait dimensions—emotional stability, extraversion, openness, agreeableness, and conscientiousness—provide a reasonably complete personality description.

module 41 The Humanistic Perspective

Test Yourself

41.1., d.; 41.2., b.; 41.3., b.; 41.4., c.; 41.5., d.; 41.6., d.

Review

In a 1997 Gallup poll, white Americans estimated 44 percent of their fellow white Americans to be high in prejudice (scoring them 5 or higher on a 10-point scale). How many rated themselves similarly high in prejudice? Just 14 percent. What phenomenon does this illustrate?

This illustrates the general tendency to see oneself as superior to the average other, which is one example of the self-serving bias.

module 42 The Social-Cognitive Perspective

Test Yourself

42.1., a.; 42.2., c.; 42.3., b.; 42.4., a.; 42.5., d.

Review

How do learned helplessness and optimism influence behavior?

Learned helplessness produces passive resignation after organisms find themselves unable to avoid aversive events. Concentration camps, prisons, and autocratic companies and countries have all been observed to produce symptoms of learned helplessness. Optimism has the opposite effect, leading to better moods, more persistence, and better health.

module 43 Introduction to Psychological Disorders

Test Yourself

43.1., a.; 43.2., c.; 43.3., c.; 43.4., c.; 43.5., c.; 43.6., d.; 43.7., c.

Review

What is the bio-psycho-social perspective, and why is it important?

This contemporary perspective assumes that biological, psychological, and sociocultural factors combine to produce psychological disorders. Genes matter. The brain matters. Inner thoughts and feelings matter. Social and cultural influences matter. To get the whole integrated picture, a bio-psycho-social perspective helps.

Does poverty cause psychological disorders? Explain.

Poverty-related stresses can indeed help trigger disorders. But disabling disorders can also contribute to poverty. Thus, poverty and disorder are often a chicken-and-egg situation, and it's hard to know which came first.

module 44 Anxiety Disorders

Test Yourself

44.1., a.; 44.2., c.; 44.3., a.; 44.4., d.; 44.5., c.

Review

Can you distinguish generalized anxiety disorders, phobias, and obsessive-compulsive disorders?

Generalized anxiety is unfocused tension, apprehension, and arousal. Phobias focus anxiety on specific feared objects or situations. Obsessive-compulsive disorders express anxiety through unwanted repetitive thoughts (obsessions) or actions (compulsions).

module 45 Dissociative and Personality Disorders

Test Yourself

45.1., b.; 45.2., c.; 45.3., c.

Review

Does a full moon trigger "madness" in some people? How could you test that question?

Here's how James Rotton and I. W. Kelly (1985) did it. They examined data from 37 studies that related lunar phase to crime, homicides, crisis calls, and mental hospital admissions. Their conclusion: There is virtually no evidence of "moon madness." Nor does lunar phase correlate with suicides, assaults, emergency room visits, or traffic disasters (Byrnes & Kelly, 1992; Kelly & others, 1990; Martin & others, 1992).

module 46   Mood Disorders

Test Yourself

46.1., c.; 46.2., a.; 46.3., d.; 46.4., b.; 46.5., d.

Review

When you show your depressed friend Figure 15.9 on p. 550, he responds, "You see? Depression is a vicious cycle and there's no way out!" What hope could you offer?

There are actually several points at which the vicious cycle may be broken: (1) seeking a less stressful environment, (2) reversing self-blaming explanations, (3) turning self-focused attention to other tasks, and (4) engaging in more positive, helpful behavior.

module 47   Schizophrenia

Test Yourself

47.1., d.; 47.2., a.; 47.3., b.; 47.4., a.; 47.5., b.

Review

What are the five subtypes of schizophrenia?

They are paranoid (marked by delusions or hallucinations), disorganized (disorganized speech, flat emotion), catatonic (immobility or repetitive purposeless movements), undifferentiated (varied symptoms), and residual (withdrawal, after hallucinations and delusions have disappeared).

module 48   The Psychological Therapies

Test Yourself

48.1., a.; 48.2., a.; 48.3., a.; 48.4., c.; 48.5., d.; 48.6., c.; 48.7., c.; 48.8., b.; 48.9., a.; 48.10., d.; 48.11., d.; 48.12., b.

Review

What is the major distinction between psychoanalytic therapies and behavior therapies?

Psychoanalytic therapies seek to provide insight into the presumed childhood origins of problems. Behavior therapists treat the problem behavior directly, paying less attention to its origins.

module 49   Evaluating Psychotherapies

Test Yourself

49.1., c.; 49.2., d.; 49.3., a.; 49.4., b.; 49.5., b.; 49.6., d.

Review

What is the placebo effect? Include an example in your answer.

A placebo is an inert substance or experience that may be administered instead of a presumed active agent, such as a drug, to see if the placebo triggers healing effects. The placebo effect, therefore, is the healing power of *belief* in a treatment. Expect a treatment to be effective, and it just may be.

module 50 The Biomedical Therapies

Test Yourself

50.1., c.; 50.2., b.; 50.3., c.; 50.4., b.

Review

How do psychologists evaluate the effectiveness of the multitude of treatment options available?

Ideally, researchers assign people to treatment and no-treatment conditions to see if those who receive therapy improve more than those who don't. In many studies, the no-treatment comparison includes a placebo condition, which allows a double-blind controlled study. If neither the therapist nor the client knows for sure whether the client has received the experimental treatment (for example, a drug), then any difference between the treated and untreated groups will reflect the treatment's actual effect.

module 51 Stress and Health

Test Yourself

51.1., b.; 51.2., b.; 51.3., c.; 51.4., c.; 51.5., d.; 51.6., b.; 51.7., c.; 51.8., b.

Review

Describe our stress response system.

When alerted to a threat (to negative, uncontrollable events), our sympathetic nervous system arouses us. Heart rate and respiration increase. Blood is diverted from digestion to the skeletal muscles. The body releases sugar and fat to prepare for fight or flight. Simultaneously, the brain (via the hypothalamus and adjacent pituitary gland) orders the adrenal glands to secrete the stress hormone cortisol. The system is wonderfully adaptive. But if stress is continuous, health consequences and exhaustion may result.

module 52 Promoting Health

Test Yourself

52.1., b.; 52.2., a.; 52.3., d.; 52.4., c.; 52.5., b.

Review

Nonsmokers, the text reports, are less likely to become depressed and get divorced. What type of research finding is this, and what explanations might it have?

This is a correlation finding. Like other correlational findings, it can be interpreted in several ways:

- Not smoking may be just one part of a generally healthy life-style that includes healthy emotions and relationships.

- Depressed people and those with troubled relationships may be drawn to smoking.

- Smoking, depression, and divorce may share common roots. Perhaps certain genes predispose a temperament that is prone to smoking, depression, and divorce. Or perhaps a certain upbringing or peer environment are conducive to smoking, depression, and divorce.

module 53 Social Thinking

Test Yourself

53.1., a.; 53.2., d.; 53.3., b.; 53.4., a.

Review

Driving to school one wintry day, Marco narrowly misses a car that slides through a red light. "Slow down! What a terrible driver," he thinks to himself. Moments later, Marco himself slips through an intersection and yelps, "Wow! These roads are awful. The city snow plows need to get out here." What social psychology principle has Marco just demonstrated? Explain.

By attributing the other person's behavior to the person ("he's a terrible driver") and his own to the situation ("the roads are awful"), Marco exhibits the fundamental attribution error.

module 54 Social Influence

Test Yourself

54.1., c.; 54.2., a.; 54.3., c.; 54.4., c.; 54.5., b.; 54.6., c.; 54.7., b.

Review

You are organizing a Town Hall–style meeting of fiercely competitive political candidates. To add to the fun, friends have suggested handing out masks of the candidates' faces for supporters to wear. What phenomenon might these masks engage?

The anonymity provided by the masks, combined with the arousal of the contentious setting, might create deindividuation (lessened self-awareness and self-restraint).

module 55 Social Relations

Test Yourself

55.1., b.; 55.2., b.; 55.3., d.; 55.4., c.; 55.5., c.; 55.6., c.; 55.7., b.; 55.8., d.; 55.9., a.; 55.10., c.; 55.11., b.

Review

Why didn't anybody help Kitty Genovese? What social relations principle did this incident illustrate?

The incident illustrated the bystander effect. This occurs because in the presence of others an individual is less likely to notice, correctly interpret, and take responsibility for an emergency.

Glossary

absolute threshold the minimum stimulation needed to detect a particular stimulus 50 percent of the time. (p. 171)

accommodation adapting one's current understandings (schemas) to incorporate new information. (p. 126)

accommodation the process by which the eye's lens changes shape to focus the image of near objects on the retina. (p. 180)

acetylcholine [ah-seat-el-KO-leen] **(ACh)** a neurotransmitter that, among its functions, triggers muscle contraction. (p. 51)

achievement motivation a desire for significant accomplishment: for mastery of things, people, or ideas; for attaining a high standard. (p. 464)

achievement test a test designed to assess what a person has learned. (p. 411)

acoustic encoding the encoding of sound, especially the sound of words. (p. 328)

acquisition the initial stage in classical conditioning; the phase associating a neutral stimulus with an unconditioned stimulus so that the neutral stimulus comes to elicit a conditioned response. In operant conditioning, the strengthening of a reinforced response. (p. 292)

action potential a neural impulse; a brief electrical charge that travels down an axon. The action potential is generated by the movement of positively charged atoms in and out of channels in the axon's membrane. (p. 46)

active listening empathic listening in which the listener echoes, restates, and clarifies. A feature of Rogers client-centered therapy. (p. 594)

acuity the sharpness of vision. (p. 180)

adaptation-level phenomenon our tendency to form judgments (of sounds, of lights, of income) relative to a "neutral" level defined by our prior experience. (p. 497)

adolescence the transition period from childhood to adulthood, extending from puberty to independence. (p. 141)

adrenal [ah-DREEN-el] **glands** a pair of endocrine glands just above the kidneys. The adrenals secrete the hormones epinephrine (adrenaline) and norepinephrine (noradrenaline), which help to arouse the body in times of stress. (p. 56)

aerobic exercise sustained exercise that increases heart and lung fitness; may also alleviate depression and anxiety. (p. 644)

aggression any physical or verbal behavior intended to hurt or destroy. (p. 698)

algorithm a methodical, logical rule or procedure that guarantees solving a particular problem. Contrasts with the usually speedier—but also more error-prone—use of *heuristics*. (p. 367)

alpha waves the relatively slow brain waves of a relaxed, awake state. (p. 246)

altruism unselfish regard for the welfare of others. (p. 715)

Alzheimer's disease a progressive and irreversible brain disorder characterized by gradual deterioration of memory, reasoning, language, and, finally, physical functioning. (p. 156)

amnesia the loss of memory. (p. 338)

amphetamines drugs that stimulate neural activity, causing speeded-up body functions and associated energy and mood changes. (p. 274)

amygdala [ah-MIG-dah-la] two almond-shaped neural clusters that are components of the limbic system and are linked to emotion. (p. 62)

anorexia nervosa an eating disorder in which a normal-weight person (usually an adolescent female) diets and becomes significantly (15 percent or more) underweight, yet, still feeling fat, continues to starve. (p. 444)

antisocial personality disorder a personality disorder in which the person (usually a man) exhibits a lack of conscience for wrongdoing, even toward friends and family members. May be aggressive and ruthless or a clever con artist. (p. 566)

anxiety disorders psychological disorders characterized by distressing, persistent anxiety or maladaptive behaviors that reduce anxiety. (p. 557)

aphasia impairment of language, usually caused by left hemisphere damage either to Broca's area (impairing speaking) or to Wernicke's area (impairing understanding). (p. 71)

applied research scientific study that aims to solve practical problems. (p. 9)

aptitude test a test designed to predict a person's future performance; *aptitude* is the capacity to learn. (p. 410)

artificial intelligence (AI) the science of designing and programming computer systems to do intelligent things and to simulate human thought processes such as intuitive reasoning, learning, and understanding language. Includes practical applications (chess playing, industrial robots, expert systems) and efforts to model human thinking inspired by our current understanding of how the brain works. (p. 378)

assimilation interpreting one's new experience in terms of one's existing schemas. (p. 126)

association areas areas of the cerebral cortex that are not involved in primary motor or sensory functions; rather, they are involved in higher mental functions such as learning, remembering, thinking, and speaking. (p. 68)

associative learning learning that certain events occur together. The events may be two stimuli (as in classical conditioning) or a response and its consequences (as in operant conditioning). (p. 290, 302)

attachment an emotional tie with another person; shown in young children by their seeking closeness to the caregiver and showing distress on separation. (p. 131)

attitude a belief and feeling that predisposes one to respond in a particular way to objects, people, and events. (p. 676)

attribution theory the theory that we tend to give a causal explanation for someone's behavior, often by crediting either the situation or the person's disposition. (p. 674)

audition   the sense of hearing. (p. 190)

automatic processing   unconscious encoding of incidental information, such as space, time, and frequency, and of well-learned information, such as word meanings. (p. 326)

autonomic [aw-tuh-NAHM-ik] **nervous system**   the part of the peripheral nervous system that controls the glands and the muscles of the internal organs (such as the heart). Its sympathetic division arouses; its parasympathetic division calms. (p. 53)

availability heuristic   estimating the likelihood of events based on their availability in memory; if instances come readily to mind (perhaps because of their vividness), we presume such events are common. (p. 371)

aversive conditioning   a type of counterconditioning that associates an unpleasant state (such as nausea) with an unwanted behavior (such as drinking alcohol). (p. 598)

axon   the extension of a neuron, ending in branching terminal fibers, through which messages are sent to other neurons or to muscles or glands. (p. 46)

babbling stage   beginning at 3 to 4 months, the stage of speech development in which the infant spontaneously utters various sounds at first unrelated to the household language. (p. 385)

barbiturates   drugs that depress the activity of the central nervous system, reducing anxiety but impairing memory and judgment. (p. 274)

basal metabolic rate   the body's resting rate of energy expenditure. (p. 442)

basic research   pure science that aims to increase the scientific knowledge base. (p. 7)

basic trust   according to Erik Erikson, a sense that the world is predictable and trustworthy; said to be formed during infancy by appropriate experiences with responsive caregivers. (p. 134)

behavior genetics   the study of the relative power and limits of genetic and environmental influences on behavior. (p. 92)

behavior therapy   therapy that applies learning principles to the elimination of unwanted behaviors. (p. 595)

behavioral medicine   an interdisciplinary field that integrates behavioral and medical knowledge and applies that knowledge to health and disease. (p. 631)

behaviorism   the view that psychology (1) should be an objective science that (2) studies behavior without reference to mental processes. Most research psychologists today agree with (1) but not with (2). (p. 298)

belief bias   the tendency for one's preexisting beliefs to distort logical reasoning, sometimes by making invalid conclusions seem valid, or valid conclusions seem invalid. (p. 376)

belief perseverance   clinging to one's initial conceptions after the basis on which they were formed has been discredited. (p. 376)

binocular cues   depth cues, such as retinal disparity and convergence, that depend on the use of two eyes. (p. 214)

bio-psycho-social perspective   a contemporary perspective which assumes that biological, psychological, and sociocultural factors combine and interact to produce psychological disorders. (p. 550)

biofeedback   a system for electronically recording, amplifying, and feeding back information regarding a subtle physiological state, such as blood pressure or muscle tension. (p. 646)

biological psychology   a branch of psychology concerned with the links between biology and behavior. (Some biological psychologists call themselves *behavioral neuroscientists, neuropsychologists, behavior geneticists, physiological psychologists,* or *biopsychologists.*) (p. 46)

biological rhythms   periodic physiological fluctuations. (p. 243)

bipolar disorder   a mood disorder in which the person alternates between the hopelessness and lethargy of depression and the overexcited state of mania. (p. 570)

blind spot   the point at which the optic nerve leaves the eye, creating a "blind" spot because no receptor cells are located there. (p. 181)

bottom-up processing   analysis that begins with the sense receptors and works up to the brain's integration of sensory information. (p. 170)

brainstem   the oldest part and central core of the brain, beginning where the spinal cord swells as it enters the skull; the brainstem is responsible for automatic survival functions. (p. 62)

Broca's area   an area of the frontal lobe, usually in the left hemisphere, that directs the muscle movements involved in speech. (p. 71)

bulimia nervosa   an eating disorder characterized by private, "binge-purge" episodes of overeating, usually of highly caloric foods, followed by vomiting or laxative use. (p. 445)

burnout   physical, emotional, and mental exhaustion brought on by persistent job-related stress. (p. 633)

bystander effect   the tendency for any given bystander to be less likely to give aid if other bystanders are present. (p. 717)

Cannon-Bard theory   the theory that an emotion-arousing stimulus simultaneously triggers (1) physiological responses and (2) the subjective experience of emotion. (p. 474)

case study   an observation technique in which one person is studied in depth in the hope of revealing universal principles. (p. 19)

catharsis   emotional release. In psychology, the catharsis hypothesis maintains that "releasing" aggressive energy (through action or fantasy) relieves aggressive urges. (p. 492)

central nervous system (CNS)   the brain and spinal cord. (p. 52)

cerebellum [sehr-uh-BELL-um]   the "little brain" attached to the rear of the brainstem; it helps coordinate voluntary movement and balance. (p. 62)

cerebral [seh-REE-bruhl] **cortex**   the intricate fabric of interconnected neural cells that covers the cerebral hemispheres; the body's ultimate control and information-processing center. (p. 65)

chromosomes   threadlike structures made of DNA molecules that contain the genes. (p. 87)

chunking   organizing items into familiar, manageable units; often occurs automatically. (p. 331)

circadian [ser-KAY-dee-an] **rhythm**   the biological clock; regular bodily rhythms (for example, of temperature and wakefulness) that occur on a 24-hour cycle. (p. 243)

classical conditioning   a type of learning in which an organism comes to associate stimuli. A neutral stimulus that signals an unconditioned stimulus (UCS) begins to produce a response that anticipates and prepares for the unconditioned stimulus. (Also called *Pavlovian conditioning.*) (p. 290)

client-centered therapy   a humanistic therapy, developed by Carl Rogers, in which the therapist uses techniques such as active listening within a genuine, accepting, empathic environment to facilitate clients' growth. (Also called *person-centered therapy*.) (p. 593)

clinical psychology a branch of psychology that studies, assesses, and treats people with psychological disorders. (p. 9)

cochlea [KOHK-lee-uh] a coiled, bony, fluid-filled tube in the inner ear through which sound waves trigger nerve impulses. (p. 191)

cognition all the mental activities associated with thinking, knowing, and remembering. (p. 126, 366)

cognitive-behavior therapy a popular integrated therapy that combines cognitive therapy (changing self-defeating thinking) with behavior therapy (changing behavior). (p. 602)

cognitive dissonance theory the theory that we act to reduce the discomfort (dissonance) we feel when two of our thoughts (cognitions) are inconsistent. For example, when our awareness of our attitudes and of our actions clash, we can reduce the resulting dissonance by changing our attitudes. (p. 679)

cognitive map a mental representation of the layout of one's environment. For example, after exploring a maze, rats act as if they have learned a cognitive map of it. (p. 309)

cognitive therapy therapy that teaches people new, more adaptive ways of thinking and acting; based on the assumption that thoughts intervene between events and our emotional reactions. (p. 600)

collective unconscious Carl Jung's concept of a shared, inherited reservoir of memory traces from our species' history. (p. 511)

collectivism giving priority to the goals of one's group (often one's extended family or work group) and defining one's identity accordingly. (p. 533)

color constancy perceiving familiar objects as having consistent color, even if changing illumination alters the wavelengths reflected by the object. (p. 188)

companionate love the deep affectionate attachment we feel for those with whom our lives are intertwined. (p. 714)

complementary and alternative medicine Unproven health care treatments not taught widely in medical schools, not used in hospitals, and not usually reimbursed by insurance companies. (p. 652)

computer neural networks computer circuits that mimic the brain's interconnected neural cells, performing tasks such as learning to recognize visual patterns and smells. (p. 380)

concept a mental grouping of similar objects, events, ideas, or people. (p. 366)

concrete operational stage in Piaget's theory, the stage of cognitive development (from about 6 or 7 to 11 years of age) during which children gain the mental operations that enable them to think logically about concrete events. (p. 131)

conditioned reinforcer a stimulus that gains its reinforcing power through its association with a primary reinforcer. (Also called *secondary reinforcer*.)(p. 305)

conditioned response (CR) in classical conditioning, the learned response to a previously neutral conditioned stimulus (CS). (p. 291)

conditioned stimulus (CS) in classical conditioning, an originally irrelevant stimulus that, after association with an unconditioned stimulus (UCS), comes to trigger a conditioned response. (p. 291)

conduction hearing loss hearing loss caused by damage to the mechanical system that conducts sound waves to the cochlea. (p. 195)

cones receptor cells that are concentrated near the center of the retina and that function in daylight or in well-lit conditions. The cones detect fine detail and give rise to color sensations. (p. 181)

confirmation bias a tendency to search for information that confirms one's preconceptions. (p. 368)

conflict a perceived incompatibility of actions, goals, or ideas. (p. 708)

conformity adjusting one's behavior or thinking to coincide with a group standard. (p. 682)

consciousness our awareness of ourselves and our environments. (p. 240)

conservation the principle (which Piaget believed to be a part of concrete operational reasoning) that properties such as mass, volume, and number remain the same despite changes in the forms of objects. (p. 128)

content validity the extent to which a test samples the behavior that is of interest (such as a driving test that samples driving tasks). (p. 414)

continuous reinforcement reinforcing the desired response every time it occurs. (p. 306)

control condition the condition of an experiment that contrasts with the experimental condition and serves as a comparison for evaluating the effect of the treatment. (p. 28)

convergence a binocular cue for perceiving depth; the extent to which the eyes converge inward when looking at an object. (p. 215)

coronary heart disease the clogging of the vessels that nourish the heart muscle; the leading cause of death in the United States. (p. 636)

corpus callosum [KOR-pus kah-LOW-sum] the large band of neural fibers connecting the two brain hemispheres and carrying messages between them. (p. 72)

correlation coefficient a statistical measure of the extent to which two factors vary together, and thus of how well either factor predicts the other. (p. 21)

counterconditioning a behavior therapy procedure that conditions new responses to stimuli that trigger unwanted behaviors; based on classical conditioning. Includes *systematic desensitization* and *aversive conditioning*. (p. 595)

creativity the ability to produce novel and valuable ideas. (p. 418)

criterion the behavior (such as college grades) that a test (such as the SAT) is designed to predict; thus, the measure used in defining whether the test has predictive validity. (p. 414)

critical period an optimal period shortly after birth when an organism's exposure to certain stimuli or experiences produces proper development. (p. 132)

critical thinking thinking that does not blindly accept arguments and conclusions. Rather, it examines assumptions, discerns hidden values, evaluates evidence, and assesses conclusions. (p. 16)

cross-sectional study a study in which people of different ages are compared with one another. (p. 159)

crystallized intelligence one's accumulated knowledge and verbal skills; tends to increase with age. (p. 161)

CT (computed tomography) scan a series of x-ray photographs taken from different angles and combined by computer into a composite representation of a slice through the body. (Also called *CAT scan*.) (p. 61)

culture the enduring behaviors, ideas, attitudes, and traditions shared by a large group of people and transmitted from one generation to the next. (p. 107)

defense mechanisms in psychoanalytic theory, the ego's protective methods of reducing anxiety by unconsciously distorting reality. (p. 508)

deindividuation the loss of self-awareness and self-restraint occurring in group situations that foster arousal and anonymity. (p. 689)

déjà vu that eerie sense that "I've experienced this before." Cues from the current situation may subconsciously trigger retrieval of an earlier experience. (p. 344)

delta waves the large, slow brain waves associated with deep sleep. (p. 247)

delusions false beliefs, often of persecution or grandeur, that may accompany psychotic disorders. (p. 580)

dendrite the bushy, branching extensions of a neuron that receive messages and conduct impulses toward the cell body. (p. 46)

dependent variable the experimental factor—in psychology, the behavior or mental process—that is being measured; the variable that may change in response to manipulations of the independent variable. (p. 28)

depressants drugs (such as alcohol, barbiturates, and opiates) that reduce neural activity and slow body functions. (p. 272)

depth perception the ability to see objects in three dimensions although the images that strike the retina are two-dimensional; allows us to judge distance. (p. 213)

developmental psychology a branch of psychology that studies physical, cognitive, and social change throughout the life span. (p. 118)

difference threshold the minimum difference that a person can detect between two stimuli. We experience the difference threshold as a just noticeable difference. (Also called *just noticeable difference* or *jnd*.) (p. 173)

discrimination in classical conditioning, the learned ability to distinguish between a conditioned stimulus and other stimuli that do not signal an unconditioned stimulus. (p. 294)

displacement defense mechanism that shifts sexual or aggressive impulses toward a more acceptable or less threatening object or person, as when redirecting anger toward a safer outlet. (p. 508)

dissociation a split in consciousness, which allows some thoughts and behaviors to occur simultaneously with others. (p. 265)

dissociative disorders disorders in which conscious awareness becomes separated (dissociated) from previous memories, thoughts, and feelings. (p. 564)

dissociative identity disorder a rare dissociative disorder in which a person exhibits two or more distinct and alternating personalities. (Also called *multiple personality disorder*.) (p. 564)

DNA (deoxyribonucleic acid) a complex molecule containing the genetic information that makes up the chromosomes. (A DNA molecule has two strands—forming a "double helix"—held together by bonds between pairs of nucleotides.) (p. 87)

double-blind procedure an experimental procedure in which both the research participants and the research staff are ignorant (blind) about whether the research participants have received the treatment or a placebo. Commonly used in drug evaluation studies. (p. 28)

Down syndrome a condition of retardation and associated physical disorders caused by an extra chromosome in one's genetic makeup. (p. 416)

dream a sequence of images, emotions, and thoughts passing through a sleeping person's mind. Dreams are notable for their hallucinatory imagery, discontinuities, and incongruities, and for the dreamer's delusional acceptance of the content and later difficulties remembering it. (p. 255)

drive-reduction theory the idea that a physiological need creates an aroused tension state (a drive) that motivates an organism to satisfy the need. (p. 437)

DSM-IV the American Psychiatric Association's *Diagnostic and Statistical Manual of Mental Disorders* (Fourth Edition), a widely used system for classifying psychological disorders. (p. 551)

dualism the presumption that mind and body are two distinct entities that interact. (p. 279)

echoic memory a momentary sensory memory of auditory stimuli; if attention is elsewhere, sounds and words can still be recalled within 3 or 4 seconds. (p. 335)

eclectic approach an approach to psychotherapy that, depending on the client's problems, uses techniques from various forms of therapy. (p. 590)

effortful processing encoding that requires attention and conscious effort. (p. 326)

ego the largely conscious, "executive" part of personality that, according to Freud, mediates among the demands of the id, superego, and reality. The ego operates on the *reality principle*, satisfying the id's desires in ways that will realistically bring pleasure rather than pain. (p. 506)

egocentrism in Piaget's theory, the inability of the preoperational child to take another's point of view. (p. 128)

electroconvulsive therapy (ECT) a biomedical therapy for severely depressed patients in which a brief electric current is sent through the brain of an anesthetized patient. (p. 622)

electroencephalogram (EEG) an amplified recording of the waves of electrical activity that sweep across the brain's surface. These waves are measured by electrodes placed on the scalp. (p. 61)

embryo the developing human organism from about 2 weeks after fertilization through the second month. (p. 118)

emotion a response of the whole organism, involving (1) physiological arousal, (2) expressive behaviors, and (3) conscious experience. (p. 474)

emotional intelligence the ability to perceive, express, understand, and regulate emotions. (p. 404)

empirically derived test a test (such as the MMPI) developed by testing a pool of items and then selecting those that discriminate between groups. (p. 521)

encoding the processing of information into the memory system—for example, by extracting meaning. (p. 323)

endocrine [EN-duh-krin] **system** the body's "slow" chemical communication system; a set of glands that secrete hormones into the bloodstream. (p. 55)

endorphins [en-DOR-fins] "morphine within"—natural, opiate-like neurotransmitters linked to pain control and to pleasure. (p. 51)

environment every nongenetic influence, from prenatal nutrition to the people and things around us. (p. 92)

equity a condition in which people receive from a relationship in proportion to what they give to it. (p. 714)

estrogen a sex hormone, secreted in greater amounts by females than by males. In nonhuman female mammals, estrogen levels peak during ovulation, promoting sexual receptivity. (p. 450)

evolutionary psychology the study of the evolution of behavior and the mind, using principles of natural selection. Natural selection is presumed to have favored genes that predisposed behavior and information-processing systems that solved adaptive problems faced by our ancestors, thus contributing to the survival and spread of their genes. (p. 89)

experiment a research method in which an investigator manipulates one or more factors (independent variables) to observe the effect on some behavior or mental process (the dependent variable). By random assignment of participants, the experiment controls other relevant factors. (p. 26)

experimental condition the condition of an experiment that exposes participants to the treatment, that is, to one version of the independent variable. (p. 28)

explicit memory memory of facts and experiences that one can consciously know and "declare." (Also called *declarative memory*.) (p. 339)

external locus of control the perception that chance or outside forces beyond one's personal control determine one's fate. (p. 539)

extinction the diminishing of a conditioned response; occurs in classical conditioning when an unconditioned stimulus (UCS) does not follow a conditioned stimulus (CS); occurs in operant conditioning when a response is no longer reinforced. (p. 293)

extrasensory perception (ESP) the controversial claim that perception can occur apart from sensory input. Said to include *telepathy, clairvoyance,* and *precognition.* (p. 231)

extrinsic motivation a desire to perform a behavior due to promised rewards or threats of punishment. (p. 466)

factor analysis a statistical procedure that identifies clusters of related items (called *factors*) on a test; used to identify different dimensions of performance that underlie one's total score. (p. 401)

false consensus effect the tendency to overestimate the extent to which others share our beliefs and behaviors. (p. 19)

family therapy therapy that treats the family as a system. Views an individual's unwanted behaviors as influenced by or directed at other family members; attempts to guide family members toward positive relationships and improved communication. (p. 603)

fantasy-prone personality someone who imagines and recalls experiences with lifelike vividness and who spends considerable time fantasizing. (p. 242)

farsightedness a condition in which faraway objects are seen more clearly than near objects because the image of near objects is focused behind the retina. (p. 180)

feature detectors nerve cells in the brain that respond to specific features of the stimulus, such as shape, angle, or movement. (p. 183)

feel-good, do-good phenomenon people's tendency to be helpful when already in a good mood. (p. 494)

fetal alcohol syndrome (FAS) physical and cognitive abnormalities in children caused by a pregnant woman's heavy drinking. In severe cases, symptoms include noticeable facial misproportions. (p. 120)

fetus the developing human organism from 9 weeks after conception to birth. (p. 118)

figure-ground the organization of the visual field into objects (the *figures*) that stand out from their surroundings (the *ground*). (p. 211)

fixation according to Freud, a lingering focus of pleasure-seeking energies at an earlier psychosexual stage, where conflicts were unresolved. (p. 507)

fixation the inability to see a problem from a new perspective; an impediment to problem solving. (p. 369)

fixed-interval schedule in operant conditioning, a schedule of reinforcement that reinforces a response only after a specified time has elapsed. (p. 307)

fixed-ratio schedule in operant conditioning, a schedule of reinforcement that reinforces a response only after a specified number of responses. (p. 306)

flashbulb memory a clear memory of an emotionally significant moment or event. (p. 323)

fluid intelligence one's ability to reason speedily and abstractly; tends to decrease during late adulthood. (p. 161)

foot-in-the-door phenomenon the tendency for people who have first agreed to a small request to comply later with a larger request. (p. 677)

formal operational stage in Piaget's theory, the stage of cognitive development (normally beginning about age 12) during which people begin to think logically about abstract concepts. (p. 131)

fovea the central focal point in the retina, around which the eye's cones cluster. (p. 181)

framing the way an issue is posed; how an issue is framed can significantly affect decisions and judgments. (p. 375)

fraternal twins twins who develop from separate eggs. They are genetically no closer than brothers and sisters, but they share a fetal environment. (p. 92)

free association in psychoanalysis, a method of exploring the unconscious in which the person relaxes and says whatever comes to mind, no matter how trivial or embarrassing. (p. 504)

frequency the number of complete wavelengths that pass a point in a given time (for example, per second). (p. 190)

frequency theory in hearing, the theory that the rate of nerve impulses traveling up the auditory nerve matches the frequency of a tone, thus enabling us to sense its pitch. (p. 194)

frontal lobes the portion of the cerebral cortex lying just behind the forehead; involved in speaking and muscle movements and in making plans and judgments. (p. 66)

frustration-aggression principle the principle that frustration—the blocking of an attempt to achieve some goal—creates anger, which can generate aggression. (p. 701)

functional fixedness the tendency to think of things only in terms of their usual functions; an impediment to problem solving. (p. 370)

fundamental attribution error the tendency for observers, when analyzing another's behavior, to underestimate the impact of the situation and to overestimate the impact of personal disposition. (p. 674)

gate-control theory theory that the spinal cord contains a neurological "gate" that blocks pain signals or allows them to pass on to the brain. The "gate" is opened by the activity of pain signals traveling up small nerve fibers and is closed by activity in larger fibers or by information coming from the brain. (p. 201)

gender in psychology, the characteristics, whether biologically or socially influenced, by which people define male and female. (p. 89)

gender identity one's sense of being male or female. (p. 112)

gender role a set of expected behaviors for males and for females. (p. 110)

gender schema theory the theory that children learn from their cultures a concept of what it means to be male and female and that they adjust their behavior accordingly. (p. 112)

gender-typing the acquisition of a traditional masculine or feminine role. (p. 112)

general adaptation syndrome (GAS) Selye's concept of the body's adaptive response to stress in three stages—alarm, resistance, exhaustion. (p. 631)

general intelligence (g) a general intelligence factor that Spearman and others believed underlies specific mental abilities and is therefore measured by every task on an intelligence test. (p. 401)

generalization the tendency, once a response has been conditioned, for stimuli similar to the conditioned stimulus to elicit similar responses. (p. 294)

generalized anxiety disorder an anxiety disorder in which a person is continually tense, apprehensive, and in a state of autonomic nervous system arousal. (p. 557)

genes the biochemical units of heredity that make up the chromosomes; a segment of DNA capable of synthesizing a protein. (p. 87)

genome the complete instructions for making an organism, consisting of all the genetic material in its chromosomes. The human genome has 3 billion weakly bonded pairs of nucleotides organized as coiled chains of DNA. (p. 87)

gestalt an organized whole. Gestalt psychologists emphasize our tendency to integrate pieces of information into meaningful wholes. (p. 210)

glial cells cells in the nervous system that are not neurons but that support, nourish, and protect neurons. (p. 65)

glucose the form of sugar that circulates in the blood and provides the major source of energy for body tissues. When its level is low, we feel hunger. (p. 441)

grammar a system of rules in a language that enables us to communicate with and understand others. (p. 383)

GRIT Graduated and Reciprocated Initiatives in Tension-Reduction—a strategy designed to decrease international tensions. (p. 720)

group polarization the enhancement of a group's prevailing attitudes through discussion within the group. (p. 690)

grouping the perceptual tendency to organize stimuli into coherent groups. (p. 212)

groupthink the mode of thinking that occurs when the desire for harmony in a decision-making group overrides a realistic appraisal of alternatives. (p. 690)

habituation decreasing responsiveness with repeated stimulation. As infants gain familiarity with repeated exposure to a visual stimulus, their interest wanes and they look away sooner. (p. 121)

hallucinations false sensory experiences, such as seeing something in the absence of an external visual stimulus. (p. 247)

hallucinogens psychedelic ("mind-manifesting") drugs, such as LSD, that distort perceptions and evoke sensory images in the absence of sensory input. (p. 272)

health psychology a subfield of psychology that provides psychology's contribution to behavioral medicine. (p. 631)

heritability the proportion of variation among individuals that we can attribute to genes. The heritability of a trait may vary, depending on the range of populations and environments studied. (p. 97)

heuristic a rule-of-thumb strategy that often allows us to make judgments and solve problems efficiently; usually speedier but also more error-prone than *algorithms*. (p. 367)

hidden observer Hilgard's term describing a hypnotized subject's awareness of experiences, such as pain, that go unreported during hypnosis. (p. 268)

hierarchy of needs Maslow's pyramid of human needs, beginning at the base with physiological needs that must first be satisfied before higher-level safety needs and then psychological needs become active. (p. 438)

hindsight bias the tendency to believe, after learning an outcome, that one would have foreseen it. (Also known as the *I-knew-it-all-along phenomenon*.) (p. 13)

hippocampus a neural center located in the limbic system that helps process explicit memories for storage. (p. 340)

homeostasis a tendency to maintain a balanced or constant internal state; the regulation of any aspect of body chemistry, such as blood glucose, around a particular level. (p. 437)

hormones chemical messengers, mostly those manufactured by the endocrine glands, that are produced in one tissue and affect another. (p. 55)

hue the dimension of color that is determined by the wavelength of light; what we know as the color names *blue, green,* and so forth. (p. 178)

hypnosis a social interaction in which one person (the hypnotist) suggests to another (the subject) that certain perceptions, feelings, thoughts, or behaviors will spontaneously occur. (p. 260)

hypothalamus [hi-po-THAL-uh-muss] a neural structure lying below (*hypo*) the thalamus; it directs several maintenance activities (eating, drinking, body temperature), helps govern the endocrine system via the pituitary gland, and is linked to emotion. (p. 65)

hypothesis a testable prediction, often implied by a theory. (p. 17)

iconic memory a momentary sensory memory of visual stimuli; a photographic or picture-image memory lasting no more than a few tenths of a second. (p. 334)

id contains a reservoir of unconscious psychic energy that, according to Freud, strives to satisfy basic sexual and aggressive drives. The id operates on the pleasure principle, demanding immediate gratification. (p. 506)

identical twins twins who develop from a single fertilized egg that splits in two, creating two genetically identical organisms. (p. 92)

identification the process by which, according to Freud, children incorporate their parents' values into their developing superegos. (p. 507)

identity one's sense of self; according to Erikson, the adolescent's task is to solidify a sense of self by testing and integrating various roles. (p. 146)

illusory correlation the perception of a relationship where none exists. (p. 22)

imagery mental pictures; a powerful aid to effortful processing, especially when combined with semantic encoding. (p. 330)

implicit memory retention without conscious recollection (of skills and dispositions). (Also called *procedural memory*.) (p. 339)

imprinting the process by which certain animals form attachments during a critical period very early in life. (p. 132)

incentive a positive or negative environmental stimulus that motivates behavior. (p. 437)

independent variable the experimental factor that is manipulated; the variable whose effect is being studied. (p. 28)

individualism giving priority to one's own goals over group goals, and defining one's identity in terms of personal attributes rather than group identifications. (p. 533)

industrial/organizational psychology a subfield of psychology that studies and advises on workplace behavior. Industrial/organizational (I/O) psychologists help organizations select and train employees, boost morale and productivity, and design products and assess responses to them. (p. 467)

informational social influence influence resulting from one's willingness to accept others' opinions about reality. (p. 683)

ingroup "Us"—people with whom one shares a common identity. (p. 696)

ingroup bias The tendency to favor one's own group. (p. 694)

inner ear the innermost part of the ear, containing the cochlea, semicircular canals, and vestibular sacs. (p. 191)

insight a sudden and often novel realization of the solution to a problem; it contrasts with strategy-based solutions. (p. 367)

insomnia recurring problems in falling or staying asleep. (p. 253)

instinct a complex behavior that is rigidly patterned throughout a species and is unlearned. (p. 436)

intelligence mental quality consisting of the ability to learn from experience, solve problems, and use knowledge to adapt to new situations. (p. 400)

intelligence quotient (IQ) defined originally as the ratio of mental age (*ma*) to chronological age (*ca*) multiplied by 100 (thus, IQ = $ma/ca \times 100$). On contemporary intelligence tests, the average performance for a given age is assigned a score of 100. (p. 409)

intelligence test a method for assessing an individual's mental aptitudes and comparing them with those of others, using numerical scores. (p. 400)

intensity the amount of energy in a light or sound wave, which we perceive as brightness or loudness, as determined by the wave's amplitude. (p. 178)

interaction the effect of one factor (such as environment) depends on another factor (such as heredity). (p. 99)

internal locus of control the perception that one controls one's own fate. (p. 539)

interneurons central nervous system neurons that internally communicate and intervene between the sensory inputs and motor outputs. (p. 52)

interpretation in psychoanalysis, the analyst's noting supposed dream meanings, resistances, and other significant behaviors in order to promote insight. (p. 591)

intimacy in Erikson's theory, the ability to form close, loving relationships; a primary developmental task in late adolescence and early adulthood. (p. 148)

intrinsic motivation a desire to perform a behavior for its own sake and to be effective. (p. 466)

iris a ring of muscle tissue that forms the colored portion of the eye around the pupil and controls the size of the pupil opening. (p. 178)

James-Lange theory the theory that our experience of emotion is our awareness of our physiological responses to emotion-arousing stimuli. (p. 474)

just-world phenomenon the tendency of people to believe the world is just and that people therefore get what they deserve and deserve what they get. (p. 698)

kinesthesis [kin-ehs-THEE-sehs] the system for sensing the position and movement of individual body parts. (p. 206)

language our spoken, written, or gestured words and the ways we combine them to communicate meaning. (p. 383)

latent content according to Freud, the underlying meaning of a dream (as distinct from its manifest content). Freud believed that a dream's latent content functions as a safety valve. (p. 256)

latent learning learning that occurs but is not apparent until there is an incentive to demonstrate it. (p. 310)

law of effect Thorndike's principle that behaviors followed by favorable consequences become more likely, and that behaviors followed by unfavorable consequences become less likely. (p. 303)

learned helplessness the hopelessness and passive resignation an animal or human learns when unable to avoid repeated aversive events. (p. 540)

learning a relatively permanent change in an organism's behavior due to experience. (p. 290, 303, 317)

lens the transparent structure behind the pupil that changes shape to focus images on the retina. (p. 180)

lesion [LEE-zhuhn] tissue destruction. A brain lesion is a naturally or experimentally caused destruction of brain tissue. (p. 61)

limbic system a doughnut-shaped system of neural structures at the border of the brainstem and cerebral hemispheres; associated with emotions such as fear and aggression and drives such as those for food and sex. Includes the hippocampus, amygdala, and hypothalamus. (p. 62)

linguistic relativity Whorf's hypothesis that language determines the way we think. (p. 390)

lithium a chemical that provides an effective drug therapy for the mood swings of bipolar (manic-depressive) disorders. (p. 622)

lobotomy a now-rare psychosurgical procedure once used to calm uncontrollably emotional or violent patients. The procedure cut the nerves that connect the frontal lobes to the emotion-controlling centers of the inner brain. (p. 624)

long-term memory the relatively permanent and limitless storehouse of the memory system. (p. 324)

long-term potentiation (LTP) an increase in a synapse's firing potential after brief, rapid stimulation. Believed to be a neural basis for learning and memory. (p. 337)

longitudinal study research in which the same people are restudied and retested over a long period. (p. 159)

LSD a powerful hallucinogenic drug; also known as acid (*lysergic acid diethylamide*). (p. 276)

lymphocytes the two types of white blood cells that are part of the body's immune system: *B lymphocytes* form in the *bone marrow* and release antibodies that fight bacterial infections; *T lymphocytes* form in the *thymus* and, among other duties, attack cancer cells, viruses, and foreign substances. (p. 638)

major depressive disorder a mood disorder in which a person, for no apparent reason, experiences two or more weeks of depressed moods, feelings of worthlessness, and diminished interest or pleasure in most activities. (p. 570)

manic episode a mood disorder marked by a hyperactive, wildly optimistic state. (p. 570)

manifest content according to Freud, the remembered story line of a dream (as distinct from its latent content). (p. 255)

maturation biological growth processes that enable orderly changes in behavior, relatively uninfluenced by experience. (p. 123)

mean the arithmetic average of a distribution, obtained by adding the scores and then dividing by the number of scores. (p. 31)

median the middle score in a distribution; half the scores are above it and half are below it. (p. 31)

medical model the concept that diseases have physical causes that can be diagnosed, treated, and, in most cases, cured. When applied to psychological disorders, the medical model assumes that these "mental" illnesses can be diagnosed on the basis of their symptoms and cured through therapy, which may include treatment in a psychiatric hospital. (p. 549)

medulla [muh-DUL-uh] the base of the brainstem; controls heartbeat and breathing. (p. 62)

memes self-replicating ideas, fashions, and innovations passed from person to person. (p. 108)

memory the persistence of learning over time through the storage and retrieval of information. (p. 322)

menarche [meh-NAR-key] the first menstrual period. (p. 143)

menopause the time of natural cessation of menstruation; also refers to the biological changes a woman experiences as her ability to reproduce declines. (p. 153)

mental age a measure of intelligence test performance devised by Binet; the chronological age that most typically corresponds to a given level of performance. Thus, a child who does as well as the average 8-year-old is said to have a mental age of 8. (p. 409)

mental retardation a condition of limited mental ability, indicated by an intelligence score below 70, and difficulty in adapting to the demands of life; varies from mild to profound. (p. 416)

mental set a tendency to approach a problem in a particular way, especially a way that has been successful in the past but may or may not be helpful in solving a new problem. (p. 369)

mere exposure effect the phenomenon that repeated exposure to novel stimuli increases liking of them. (p. 710)

meta-analysis a procedure for statistically combining the results of many different research studies. (p. 609)

middle ear the chamber between the eardrum and cochlea containing three tiny bones (hammer, anvil, and stirrup) that concentrate the vibrations of the eardrum on the cochlea's oval window. (p. 191)

Minnesota Multiphasic Personality Inventory (MMPI) the most widely researched and clinically used of all personality tests. Originally developed to identify emotional disorders (still considered its most appropriate use), this test is now used for many other screening purposes. (p. 520)

misinformation effect incorporating misleading information into one's memory of an event. (p. 353)

mnemonics [nih-MON-iks] memory aids, especially those techniques that use vivid imagery and organizational devices. (p. 330)

mode the most frequently occurring score in a distribution. (p. 31)

modeling the process of observing and imitating a specific behavior. (p. 317)

molecular genetics The subfield of biology that studies the molecular structure and function of genes. (p. 99)

monism the presumption that mind and body are different aspects of the same thing. (p. 279)

monocular cues distance cues, such as linear perspective and overlap, available to either eye alone. (p. 214)

mood-congruent memory the tendency to recall experiences that are consistent with one's current good or bad mood. (p. 344)

mood disorders psychological disorders characterized by emotional extremes. See *major depressive disorder*, *bipolar disorder*, and *manic episode*. (p. 569)

morpheme in a language, the smallest unit that carries meaning; may be a word or a part of a word (such as a prefix). (p. 383)

motivation a need or desire that energizes and directs behavior. (p. 437)

motor cortex an area at the rear of the frontal lobes that controls voluntary movements. (p. 67)

motor neurons the neurons that carry outgoing information from the central nervous system to the muscles and glands. (p. 52)

MRI (magnetic resonance imaging) a technique that uses magnetic fields and radio waves to produce computer-generated images that distinguish among different types of soft tissue; allows us to see structures within the brain. (p. 61)

mutation random errors in gene replication that lead to a change in the sequence of *nucleotides*; the source of all genetic diversity. (p. 89)

myelin [MY-uh-lin] **sheath** a layer of fatty tissue segmentally encasing the fibers of many neurons; enables vastly greater transmission speed of neural impulses as the impulse hops from one node to the next. (p. 46)

narcolepsy a sleep disorder characterized by uncontrollable sleep attacks. The sufferer may lapse directly into REM sleep, often at inopportune times. (p. 253)

natural selection the principle that, among the range of inherited trait variations, those contributing to reproduction and survival will most likely be passed on to succeeding generations. (pp. 5, 89)

naturalistic observation observing and recording behavior in naturally occurring situations without trying to manipulate and control the situation. (p. 21)

nature-nurture issue the longstanding controversy over the relative contributions that genes and experience make to the development of psychological traits and behaviors. (p. 5)

near-death experience an altered state of consciousness reported after a close brush with death (such as through cardiac arrest); often similar to drug-induced hallucinations. (p. 278)

nearsightedness a condition in which nearby objects are seen more clearly than distant objects because the lens focuses the image of distant objects in front of the retina. (p. 180)

nerves neural "cables" containing many axons. These bundled axons, which are part of the peripheral nervous system, connect the central nervous system with muscles, glands, and sense organs. (p. 52)

nervous system the body's speedy, electrochemical communication system, consisting of all the nerve cells of the peripheral and central nervous systems. (p. 52)

neural networks interconnected neural cells. With experience, networks can learn, as feedback strengthens or inhibits connections that produce certain results. Computer simulations of neural networks show analogous learning. (p. 55)

neuron a nerve cell; the basic building block of the nervous system. (p. 46)

neurotic disorder a psychological disorder that is usually distressing but that allows one to think rationally and function socially. Freud saw the neurotic disorders as ways of dealing with anxiety. (p. 551)

neurotransmitters chemical messengers that traverse the synaptic gaps between neurons. When released by the sending neuron, neurotransmitters travel across the synapse and bind to receptor sites on the receiving neuron, thereby influencing whether it will generate a neural impulse. (p. 48)

night terrors a sleep disorder characterized by high arousal and an appearance of being terrified; unlike nightmares, night terrors occur during Stage 4 sleep, within 2 or 3 hours of falling asleep, and are seldom remembered. (p. 254)

norm an understood rule for accepted and expected behavior. Norms prescribe "proper" behavior. (p. 107)

normal curve the symmetrical bell-shaped curve that describes the distribution of many physical and psychological attributes. Most scores fall near the average, and fewer and fewer scores lie near the extremes. (p. 412)

normative social influence influence resulting from a person's desire to gain approval or avoid disapproval. (p. 683)

object permanence the awareness that things continue to exist even when not perceived. (p. 126)

observational learning learning by observing others. (p. 317)

obsessive-compulsive disorder an anxiety disorder characterized by unwanted repetitive thoughts (obsessions) and/or actions (compulsions). (p. 557)

occipital [ahk-SIP-uh-tuhl] **lobes** the portion of the cerebral cortex lying at the back of the head; includes the visual areas, which receive visual information from the opposite visual field. (p. 66)

Oedipus [Ed-uh-puss] **complex** according to Freud, a boy's sexual desires toward his mother and feelings of jealousy and hatred for the rival father. (p. 507)

one-word stage the stage in speech development, from about age 1 to 2, during which a child speaks mostly in single words. (p. 385)

operant behavior behavior that operates on the environment, producing consequences. (p. 302)

operant chamber ("Skinner box") a chamber containing a bar or key that an animal can manipulate to obtain a food or water reinforcer, with attached devices to record the animal's rate of bar pressing or key pecking. Used in operant conditioning research. (p. 303)

operant conditioning a type of learning in which behavior is strengthened if followed by reinforcement or diminished if followed by punishment. (p. 302)

operational definition a statement of the procedures (operations) used to define research variables. For example, *intelligence* may be operationally defined as what an intelligence test measures. (p. 17)

opiates opium and its derivatives, such as morphine and heroin; they depress neural activity, temporarily lessening pain and anxiety. (p. 274)

opponent-process theory the theory that opposing retinal processes (red-green, yellow-blue, white-black) enable color vision. For example, some cells are stimulated by green and inhibited by red; others are stimulated by red and inhibited by green. (p. 188)

optic nerve the nerve that carries neural impulses from the eye to the brain. (p. 181)

outgroup "Them"—those perceived as different or apart from one's ingroup. (p. 696)

overconfidence the tendency to be more confident than correct—to overestimate the accuracy of one's beliefs and judgments. (p. 373)

overjustification effect the effect of promising a reward for doing what one already likes to do. The person may now see the reward, rather than intrinsic interest, as the motivation for performing the task. (p. 310)

panic disorder an anxiety disorder marked by a minutes-long episode of intense dread in which a person experiences terror and accompanying chest pain, choking, or other frightening sensations. (p. 557)

parallel processing the processing of several aspects of a problem simultaneously; the brain's natural mode of information processing for many functions, including vision. Contrasts with the step-by-step (serial) processing of most computers and of conscious problem solving. (p. 184)

parapsychology the study of paranormal phenomena, including ESP and psychokinesis. (p. 231)

parasympathetic nervous system the division of the autonomic nervous system that calms the body, conserving its energy. (p. 53)

parietal [puh-RYE-uh-tuhl] **lobes** the portion of the cerebral cortex lying at the top of the head and toward the rear; includes the sensory cortex. (p. 66)

partial (intermittent) reinforcement reinforcing a response only part of the time; results in slower acquisition of a response but much greater resistance to extinction than does continuous reinforcement. (p. 306)

passionate love An aroused state of intense positive absorption in another, usually present at the beginning of a love relationship. (p. 714)

perception the process of organizing and interpreting sensory information, enabling us to recognize meaningful objects and events. (p. 170)

perceptual adaptation in vision, the ability to adjust to an artificially displaced or even inverted visual field. (p. 226)

perceptual constancy perceiving objects as unchanging (having consistent lightness, color, shape, and size) even as illumination and retinal images change. (p. 218)

perceptual set a mental predisposition to perceive one thing and not another. (p. 227)

peripheral nervous system (PNS) the sensory and motor neurons that connect the central nervous system (CNS) to the rest of the body. (p. 52)

personal control our sense of controlling our environment rather than feeling helpless. (p. 539)

personal space the buffer zone we like to maintain around our bodies. (p. 107)

personality an individual's characteristic pattern of thinking, feeling, and acting. (p. 504)

personality disorders psychological disorders characterized by inflexible and enduring behavior patterns that impair social functioning. (p. 566)

personality inventory a questionnaire (often with true-false or agree-disagree items) on which people respond to items designed to gauge a wide range of feelings and behaviors; used to assess selected personality traits. (p. 520)

PET (positron emission tomography) scan a visual display of brain activity that detects where a radioactive form of glucose goes while the brain performs a given task. (p. 61)

phi phenomenon an illusion of movement created when two or more adjacent lights blink on and off in succession. (p. 218)

phobia an anxiety disorder marked by a persistent, irrational fear and avoidance of a specific object or situation. (p. 557)

phoneme in a spoken language, the smallest distinctive sound unit. (p. 383)

physical dependence a physiological need for a drug, marked by unpleasant withdrawal symptoms when the drug is discontinued. (p. 270)

pitch a tone's highness or lowness; depends on frequency. (p. 190)

pituitary gland the endocrine system's most influential gland. Under the influence of the hypothalamus, the pituitary regulates growth and controls other endocrine glands. (p. 56)

place theory in hearing, the theory that links the pitch we hear with the place where the cochlea's membrane is stimulated. (p. 194)

placebo [pluh-SEE-bo; Latin for "I shall please"] an inert substance or condition that may be administered instead of a presumed active agent, such as a drug, to see if it triggers the effects believed to characterize the active agent. (p. 26)

placebo effect any effect on behavior caused by a placebo. (p. 28)

plasticity the brain's capacity for modification, as evident in brain reorganization following damage (especially in children) and in experiments on the effects of experience on brain development. (p. 71)

polygraph a machine, commonly used in attempts to detect lies, that measures several of the physiological responses accompanying emotion (such as perspiration, heart rate, blood pressure, and breathing changes). (p. 485)

population all the cases in a group, from which samples may be drawn for a study. (p. 19)

positive psychology the scientific study of optimal human functioning; aims to discover and promote conditions that enable individuals and communities to thrive. (p. 541)

posthypnotic amnesia supposed inability to recall what one experienced during hypnosis; induced by the hypnotist's suggestion. (p. 260)

posthypnotic suggestion a suggestion, made during a hypnosis session, to be carried out after the subject is no longer hypnotized; used by some clinicians to help control undesired symptoms and behaviors. (p. 265)

preconscious information that is not conscious but is retrievable into conscious awareness. (p. 505)

predictive validity the success with which a test predicts the behavior it is designed to predict; it is assessed by computing the correlation between test scores and the criterion behavior. (Also called *criterion-related validity*.) (p. 414)

prejudice an unjustifiable (and usually negative) attitude toward a group and its members. Prejudice generally involves stereotyped beliefs, negative feelings, and a predisposition to discriminatory action. (p. 694)

preoperational stage in Piaget's theory, the stage (from about 2 to 6 or 7 years of age) during which a child learns to use language but does not yet comprehend the mental operations of concrete logic. (p. 128)

primary reinforcer an innately reinforcing stimulus, such as one that satisfies a biological need. (p. 305)

primary sex characteristics the body structures (ovaries, testes, and external genitalia) that make sexual reproduction possible. (p. 143)

priming the activation, often unconsciously, of particular associations in memory. (p. 342)

proactive interference the disruptive effect of prior learning on the recall of new information. (p. 349)

projection the defense mechanism by which people disguise their own threatening impulses by attributing them to others. (p. 508)

projective test a personality test, such as the Rorschach or TAT, that provides ambiguous stimuli designed to trigger projection of one's inner dynamics. (p. 509)

prosocial behavior positive, constructive, helpful behavior. The opposite of antisocial behavior. (p. 318)

prototype a mental image or best example of a category. Matching new items to the prototype provides a quick and easy method for including items in a category (as when comparing feathered creatures to a prototypical bird, such as a robin). (p. 366)

psychiatry a branch of medicine dealing with psychological disorders; practiced by physicians who sometimes provide medical (for example, drug) treatments as well as psychological therapy. (p. 9)

psychoactive drug a chemical substance that alters perceptions and mood. (p. 270)

psychoanalysis Freud's theory of personality and therapeutic technique that attributes our thoughts and actions to unconscious motives and conflicts. Freud believed the patient's free associations, resistances, dreams, and transferences—and the therapist's interpretations of them—released previously repressed feelings, allowing the patient to gain self-insight. (pp. 505, 590)

psychological dependence a psychological need to use a drug, such as to relieve negative emotions. (p. 270)

psychological disorder a "harmful dysfunction" in which behavior is judged to be atypical, disturbing, maladaptive, and unjustifiable. (p. 548)

psychology the science of behavior and mental processes. (p. 4)

psychopharmacology the study of the effects of drugs on mind and behavior. (p. 619)

psychophysics the study of relationships between the physical characteristics of stimuli, such as their intensity, and our psychological experience of them. (p. 170)

psychophysiological illness literally, "mind-body" illness; any stress-related physical illness, such as hypertension and some headaches. *Note:* This is distinct from *hypochondriasis*— misinterpreting normal physical sensations as symptoms of a disease. (p. 638)

psychosexual stages the childhood stages of development (oral, anal, phallic, latency, genital) during which, according to Freud, the id's pleasure-seeking energies focus on distinct erogenous zones. (p. 506)

psychosurgery surgery that removes or destroys brain tissue in an effort to change behavior. (p. 624)

psychotherapy an emotionally charged, confiding interaction between a trained therapist and someone who suffers from psychological difficulties. (p. 590)

psychotic disorder a psychological disorder in which a person loses contact with reality, experiencing irrational ideas and distorted perceptions. (p. 551)

puberty the period of sexual maturation, during which a person becomes capable of reproducing. (p. 143)

punishment an event that *decreases* the behavior that it follows. (p. 307)

pupil the adjustable opening in the center of the eye through which light enters. (p. 178)

random assignment assigning participants to experimental and control conditions by chance, thus minimizing preexisting differences between those assigned to the different groups. (p. 28)

random sample a sample that fairly represents a population because each member has an equal chance of inclusion. (p. 19)

range the difference between the highest and lowest scores in a distribution. (p. 31)

rationalization defense mechanism that offers self-justifying explanations in place of the real, more threatening, unconscious reasons for one's actions. (p. 508)

reaction formation defense mechanism by which the ego unconsciously switches unacceptable impulses into their opposites. Thus, people may express feelings that are the opposite of their anxiety-arousing unconscious feelings. (p. 508)

recall a measure of memory in which the person must retrieve information learned earlier, as on a fill-in-the-blank test. (p. 342)

reciprocal determinism the interacting influences between personality and environmental factors. (p. 538)

recognition a measure of memory in which the person need only identify items previously learned, as on a multiple-choice test. (p. 342)

reflex a simple, automatic, inborn response to a sensory stimulus, such as the knee-jerk response. (p. 55)

refractory period a resting period after orgasm, during which a man cannot achieve another orgasm. (p. 450)

regression defense mechanism in which an individual faced with anxiety retreats to a more infantile psychosexual stage, where some psychic energy remains fixated. (p. 508)

regression toward the mean the tendency for extremes of unusual scores to fall back (regress) toward the average. (p. 608)

rehearsal the conscious repetition of information, either to maintain it in consciousness or to encode it for storage. (p. 326)

reinforcer in operant conditioning, any event that *strengthens* the behavior it follows. (p. 305)

relative deprivation the perception that one is worse off relative to those with whom one compares oneself. (p. 497)

relearning a memory measure that assesses the amount of time saved when learning material for a second time. (p. 342)

reliability the extent to which a test yields consistent results, as assessed by the consistency of scores on two halves of the test, on alternate forms of the test, or on retesting. (p. 413)

REM rebound the tendency for REM sleep to increase following REM sleep deprivation (created by repeated awakenings during REM sleep). (p. 257)

REM sleep rapid eye movement sleep, a recurring sleep stage during which vivid dreams commonly occur. Also known as *paradoxical sleep* because the muscles are relaxed (except for minor twitches) but other body systems are active. (p. 246)

replication repeating the essence of a research study, usually with different subjects in different situations, to see whether the basic finding generalizes to other participants and circumstances. (p. 17)

representativeness heuristic a rule of thumb for judging the likelihood of things in terms of how well they seem to represent, or match, particular prototypes; may lead one to ignore other relevant information. (p. 371)

repression in psychoanalytic theory, the basic defense mechanism that banishes anxiety-arousing thoughts, feelings, and memories from consciousness. (pp. 351, 508)

resistance in psychoanalysis, the blocking from consciousness of anxiety-laden material. (p. 591)

respondent behavior behavior that occurs as an automatic response to some stimulus; Skinner's term for behavior learned through classical conditioning. (p. 302)

reticular formation a nerve network in the brainstem that plays an important role in controlling arousal. (p. 62)

retina   the light-sensitive inner surface of the eye, containing the receptor rods and cones plus layers of neurons that begin the processing of visual information. (p. 180)

retinal disparity   a binocular cue for perceiving depth: The greater the disparity (difference) between the two images the retina receives of an object, the closer the object is to the viewer. (p. 214)

retrieval   the process of getting information out of memory storage. (p. 323)

retroactive interference   the disruptive effect of new learning on the recall of old information. (p. 350)

rods   retinal receptors that detect black, white, and gray; necessary for peripheral and twilight vision, when cones don't respond. (p. 181)

role   a set of expectations (norms) about a social position, defining how those in the position ought to behave. (p. 110)

rooting reflex   a baby's tendency, when touched on the cheek, to open the mouth and search for the nipple. (p. 120)

Rorschach inkblot test   the most widely used projective test, a set of 10 inkblots, designed by Hermann Rorschach; seeks to identify people's inner feelings by analyzing their interpretations of the blots. (p. 509)

savant syndrome   a condition in which a person otherwise limited in mental ability has an exceptional specific skill, such as in computation or drawing. (p. 401)

scapegoat theory   The theory that prejudice provides an outlet for anger by providing someone to blame. (p. 697)

scatterplot   a graphed cluster of dots, each of which represents the values of two variables. The slope of the points suggests the direction of the relationship between the two variables. The amount of scatter suggests the strength of the correlation (little scatter indicates high correlation). (Also called a *scattergram* or *scatter diagram*.) (p. 21)

schema   a concept or framework that organizes and interprets information. (p. 125)

schizophrenia   a group of severe disorders characterized by disorganized and delusional thinking, disturbed perceptions, and inappropriate emotions and actions. (p. 580)

secondary sex characteristics   nonreproductive sexual characteristics, such as female breasts and hips, male voice quality, and body hair. (p. 143)

selective attention   the focusing of conscious awareness on a particular stimulus, as in the cocktail party effect. (p. 175)

self-actualization   according to Maslow, the ultimate psychological need that arises after basic physical and psychological needs are met and self-esteem is achieved; the motivation to fulfill one's potential. (p. 527)

self-concept   (1) a sense of one's identity and personal worth (p. 513); (2) all our thoughts and feelings about ourselves, in answer to the question, "Who am I?" (p. 137)

self-disclosure   revealing intimate aspects of oneself to others. (p. 715)

self-esteem   one's feelings of high or low self-worth. (p. 529)

self-fulfilling prophecy   occurs when one person's belief about others leads one to act in ways that induce the others to appear to confirm the belief. (p. 690)

self-serving bias   a readiness to perceive oneself favorably. (p. 531)

semantic encoding   the encoding of meaning, including the meaning of words. (p. 328)

semantics   the set of rules by which we derive meaning from morphemes, words, and sentences in a given language; also, the study of meaning. (p. 383)

sensation   the process by which our sensory receptors and nervous system receive and represent stimulus energies from our environment. (p. 170)

sensorimotor stage   in Piaget's theory, the stage (from birth to about 2 years of age) during which infants know the world mostly in terms of their sensory impressions and motor activities. (p. 126)

sensorineural hearing loss   hearing loss caused by damage to the cochlea's receptor cells or to the auditory nerves. (Also called *nerve deafness*) (p. 195)

sensory adaptation   diminished sensitivity as a consequence of constant stimulation. (p. 174)

sensory cortex   the area at the front of the parietal lobes that registers and processes body sensations. (p. 68)

sensory interaction   the principle that one sense may influence another, as when the smell of food influences its taste. (p. 204)

sensory memory   the immediate, initial recording of sensory information in the memory system. (p. 324)

sensory neurons   neurons that carry incoming information from the sense receptors to the central nervous system. (p. 52)

serial position effect   our tendency to recall best the last and first items in a list. (p. 328)

set point   the point at which an individual's "weight thermostat" is supposedly set. When the body falls below this weight, an increase in hunger and a lowered metabolic rate may act to restore the lost weight. (p. 442)

sexual disorder   a problem that consistently impairs sexual arousal or functioning. (p. 452)

sexual orientation   an enduring sexual attraction toward members of either one's own gender (homosexual orientation) or the other gender (heterosexual orientation). (p. 455)

sexual response cycle   the four stages of sexual responding described by Masters and Johnson—excitement, plateau, orgasm, and resolution. (p. 449)

shaping   an operant conditioning procedure in which reinforcers guide behavior toward closer and closer approximations of a desired goal. (p. 303)

short-term memory   activated memory that holds a few items briefly, such as the seven digits of a phone number while dialing, before the information is stored or forgotten. (p. 324)

signal detection theory   predicts how and when we detect the presence of a faint stimulus ("signal") amid background stimulation ("noise"). Assumes that there is no single absolute threshold and that detection depends partly on a person's experience, expectations, motivation, and level of fatigue. (p. 171)

sleep   periodic, natural, reversible loss of consciousness—as distinct from unconsciousness resulting from a coma, general anesthesia, or hibernation (after Dement, 1999). (p. 246)

sleep apnea   a sleep disorder characterized by temporary cessations of breathing during sleep and consequent momentary reawakenings. (p. 254)

social clock   the culturally preferred timing of social events such as marriage, parenthood, and retirement. (p. 161)

social exchange theory the theory that our social behavior is an exchange process, the aim of which is to maximize benefits and minimize costs. (p. 717)

social facilitation improved performance of tasks in the presence of others; occurs with simple or well-learned tasks but not with tasks that are difficult or not yet mastered. (p. 687)

social leadership group-oriented leadership that builds teamwork, mediates conflict, and offers support. (p. 469)

social learning theory the theory that we learn social behavior by observing and imitating and by being rewarded or punished. (p. 112)

social loafing the tendency for people in a group to exert less effort when pooling their efforts toward attaining a common goal than when individually accountable. (p. 689)

social psychology the scientific study of how we think about, influence, and relate to one another. (p. 674)

social trap a situation in which the conflicting parties, by each rationally pursuing their self-interest, become caught in mutually destructive behavior. (p. 708)

somatic nervous system the division of the peripheral nervous system that controls the body's skeletal muscles. (Also called the *skeletal nervous system.*) (p. 53)

source amnesia attributing to the wrong source an event that we have experienced, heard about, read about, or imagined. Source amnesia, along with the misinformation effect, is at the heart of many false memories. (Also called *source misattribution.*) (p. 354)

spacing effect the tendency for distributed study or practice to yield better long-term retention than is achieved through massed study or practice. (p. 327)

split brain a condition in which the two hemispheres of the brain are isolated by cutting the connecting fibers (mainly those of the corpus callosum) between them. (p. 72)

spontaneous recovery the reappearance, after a rest period, of an extinguished conditioned response. (p. 293)

standard deviation a computed measure of how much scores vary around the mean score. (p. 31)

standardization defining meaningful scores by comparison with the performance of a pretested "standardization group." (p. 412)

Stanford-Binet the widely used American revision (by Terman at Stanford University) of Binet's original intelligence test. (p. 409)

statistical significance a statistical statement of how likely it is that an obtained result occurred by chance. (p. 32)

stereotype a generalized (sometimes accurate but often overgeneralized) belief about a group of people. (p. 694)

stimulants drugs (such as caffeine, nicotine, and the more powerful amphetamines and cocaine) that excite neural activity and speed up body functions. (p. 272)

storage the retention of encoded information over time. (p. 323)

stranger anxiety the fear of strangers that infants commonly display, beginning by about 8 months of age. (p. 131)

stress the process by which we perceive and respond to certain events, called *stressors,* that we appraise as threatening or challenging. (p. 628)

subjective well-being self-perceived happiness or satisfaction with life. Used along with measures of objective well-being (for example, physical and economic indicators) to evaluate people's quality of life. (p. 494)

sublimation in psychoanalytic theory, the defense mechanism by which people rechannel their unacceptable impulses into socially approved activities. (p. 508)

subliminal below one's absolute threshold for conscious awareness. (p. 172)

superego the part of personality that, according to Freud, represents internalized ideals and provides standards for judgment (the conscience) and for future aspirations. (p. 506)

superordinate goals shared goals that override differences among people and require their cooperation. (p. 718)

survey a technique for ascertaining the self-reported attitudes or behaviors of people, usually by questioning a representative, random sample of them. (p. 19)

sympathetic nervous system the division of the autonomic nervous system that arouses the body, mobilizing its energy in stressful situations. (p. 53)

synapse [SIN-aps] the junction between the axon tip of the sending neuron and the dendrite or cell body of the receiving neuron. The tiny gap at this junction is called the *synaptic gap* or *cleft.* (p. 48)

syntax the rules for combining words into grammatically sensible sentences in a given language. (p. 383)

systematic desensitization a type of counterconditioning that associates a pleasant relaxed state with gradually increasing anxiety-triggering stimuli. Commonly used to treat phobias. (p. 596)

task leadership goal-oriented leadership that sets standards, organizes work, and focuses attention on goals. (p. 469)

telegraphic speech early speech stage in which the child speaks like a telegram—"go car"—using mostly nouns and verbs and omitting "auxiliary" words. (p. 386)

temperament a person's characteristic emotional reactivity and intensity. (p. 97)

temporal lobes the portion of the cerebral cortex lying roughly above the ears; includes the auditory areas, each of which receives auditory information primarily from the opposite ear. (p. 66)

teratogens agents, such as chemicals and viruses, that can reach the embryo or fetus during prenatal development and cause harm. (p. 118)

testosterone the most important of the male sex hormones. Both males and females have it, but the additional testosterone in males stimulates the growth of the male sex organs in the fetus and the development of the male sex characteristics during puberty. (p. 110, 450)

thalamus [THAL-uh-muss] the brain's sensory switchboard, located on top of the brainstem; it directs messages to the sensory receiving areas in the cortex and transmits replies to the cerebellum and medulla. (p. 62)

THC the major active ingredient in marijuana; triggers a variety of effects, including mild hallucinations. (p. 277)

Thematic Apperception Test (TAT) a projective test in which people express their inner feelings and interests through the stories they make up about ambiguous scenes. (p. 509)

theory an explanation using an integrated set of principles that organizes and predicts observations. (p. 17)

theory of mind people's ideas about their own and others' mental states—about their feelings, perceptions, and thoughts and the behavior these might predict. (p. 129)

Theory X   assumes that workers are basically lazy, error-prone, and extrinsically motivated by money and, thus, should be directed from above. (p. 470)

Theory Y   assumes that, given challenge and freedom, workers are motivated to achieve self-esteem and to demonstrate their competence and creativity. (p. 470)

threshold   the level of stimulation required to trigger a neural impulse. (p. 48)

token economy   an operant conditioning procedure that rewards desired behavior. A patient exchanges a token of some sort, earned for exhibiting the desired behavior, for various privileges or treats. (p. 599)

tolerance   the diminishing effect with regular use of the same dose of a drug, requiring the user to take larger and larger doses before experiencing the drug's effect. (p. 270)

top-down processing   information processing guided by higher-level mental processes, as when we construct perceptions drawing on our experience and expectations. (p. 170)

trait   a characteristic pattern of behavior or a disposition to feel and act, as assessed by self-report inventories and peer reports. (p. 517)

transduction   conversion of one form of energy into another. In sensation, the transforming of stimulus energies into neural impulses. (p. 178)

transference   in psychoanalysis, the patient's transfer to the analyst of emotions linked with other relationships (such as love or hatred for a parent). (p. 592)

two-factor theory   Schachter's theory that to experience emotion one must (1) be physically aroused and (2) cognitively label the arousal. (p. 476)

two-word stage   beginning about age 2, the stage in speech development during which a child speaks mostly two-word statements. (p. 386)

Type A   Friedman and Rosenman's term for competitive, hard-driving, impatient, verbally aggressive, and anger-prone people. (p. 636)

Type B   Friedman and Rosenman's term for easygoing, relaxed people. (p. 636)

unconditional positive regard   according to Rogers, an attitude of total acceptance toward another person. (p. 528)

unconditioned response (UCR)   in classical conditioning, the unlearned, naturally occurring response to the unconditioned stimulus (UCS), such as salivation when food is in the mouth. (p. 291)

unconditioned stimulus (UCS)   in classical conditioning, a stimulus that unconditionally—naturally and automatically—triggers a response. (p. 291)

unconscious   according to Freud, a reservoir of mostly unacceptable thoughts, wishes, feelings, and memories. According to contemporary psychologists, information processing of which we are unaware. (p. 505)

validity   the extent to which a test measures or predicts what it is supposed to. See also content *validity* and *predictive validity*. (p. 414)

variable-interval schedule   in operant conditioning, a schedule of reinforcement that reinforces a response at unpredictable time intervals. (p. 307)

variable-ratio schedule   in operant conditioning, a schedule of reinforcement that reinforces a response after an unpredictable number of responses. (p. 306)

vestibular sense   the sense of body movement and position, including the sense of balance. (p. 207)

visual capture   the tendency for vision to dominate the other senses. (p. 210)

visual cliff   a laboratory device for testing depth perception in infants and young animals. (p. 213)

visual encoding   the encoding of picture images. (p. 328)

wavelength   the distance from the peak of one light or sound wave to the peak of the next. Electromagnetic wavelengths vary from the short blips of cosmic rays to the long pulses of radio transmission. (p. 178)

Weber's law   the principle that, to perceive their difference, two stimuli must differ by a constant minimum percentage (rather than a constant amount). (p. 174)

Wechsler Adult Intelligence Scale (WAIS)   the WAIS is the most widely used intelligence test; contains verbal and performance (nonverbal) subtests. (p. 410)

Wernicke's area   a brain area involved in language comprehension and expression; usually in the left temporal lobe. (p. 71)

withdrawal   the discomfort and distress that follow discontinuing the use of an addictive drug. (p. 270)

working memory   (p. 324)

X chromosome   the sex chromosome found in both men and women. Females have two X chromosomes; males have one. An X chromosome from each parent produces a female. (p. 110)

Y chromosome   the sex chromosome found only in males. When paired with an X sex chromosome from the mother, it produces a male child. (p. 110)

Young-Helmholtz trichromatic (three-color) theory   the theory that the retina contains three different color receptors—one most sensitive to red, one to green, one to blue—which when stimulated in combination can produce the perception of any color. (p. 187)

zygote   the fertilized egg; it enters a 2-week period of rapid cell division and develops into an embryo. (p. 118)

References

Aas, H., & Klepp, K-I. (1992). Adolescents' alcohol use related to perceived norms. *Scandinavian Journal of Psychology, 33*, 315–325.

Abbey, A. (1987). Misperceptions of friendly behavior as sexual interest: A survey of naturally occurring incidents. *Psychology of Women Quarterly, 11*, 173–194.

Abbey, A. (1991). Acquaintance rape and alcohol consumption on college campuses: How are they linked? *Journal of American College Health, 39*, 165–169.

Abrams, D. (1991). AIDS: What young people believe and what they do. Paper presented at the British Association for the Advancement of Science conference.

Abrams, D. B., & Wilson, G. T. (1983). Alcohol, sexual arousal, and self-control. *Journal of Personality and Social Psychology, 45*, 188–198.

Abramson, L. Y., Metalsky, G. I., & Alloy, L. B. (1989). Hopelessness depression: A theory-based subtype. *Psychological Review, 96*, 358–372.

Acitelli, L. K., & Antonucci, T. C. (1994). Gender differences in the link between marital support and satisfaction in older couples. *Journal of Personality and Social Psychology, 67*, 688–698.

Acock, A. C., & Demo, D. H. (1994). *Family diversity and well-being.* Thousand Oaks, CA: Sage.

Adair, J. G., Paivio, A., & Ritchie, P. (1996). Psychology in Canada. *Annual Review of Psychology, 47*, 341–370.

Adelmann, P. K., Antonucci, T. C., Crohan, S. F., & Coleman, L. M. (1989). Empty nest, cohort, and employment in the well-being of midlife women. *Sex Roles, 20*, 173–189.

Ader, R., & Cohen, N. (1985). CNS-immune system interactions: Conditioning phenomena. *Behavioral and Brain Sciences, 8*, 379–394.

Adler, T. (1989, March). FAA establishes unit to study human error. *APA Monitor*, p. 4.

Adolphs, R., Tranel, D., & Damasio, A. R. (1998). The human amygdala in social judgment. *Nature, 393*, 470–474.

Adolphs, R., Tranel, D., Damasio, H., & Damasio, A. (1994). Impaired recognition of emotion in facial expressions following bilateral damage to the human amygdala. *Nature, 372*, 669–672.

Advertising Age. (1958, February 10). "Phone now," said CBC subliminally—but nobody did. P. 8.

Affleck, G., Tennen, H., Urrows, S., & Higgins, P. (1994). Person and contextual features of daily stress reactivity: Individual differences in relations of undesirable daily events with mood disturbance and chronic pain intensity. *Journal of Personality and Social Psychology, 66*, 329–340.

Aggleton, J. P., Kentridge, R. W., & Neave, N. J. (1993). Evidence for longevity differences between left handed and right handed men: An archival study of cricketers. *Journal of Epidemiology and Community Health, 47*, 206–209.

Agid, O., Shapira, B., Zislin, J., Ritsner, M., Hanin, B., Murad, H., Troudart, T., Bloch, M., Heresco-Levy, U., & Lerer, B. (1999). Environment and vulnerability to major psychiatric illness: A case control study of early parental loss in major depression, bipolar disorder and schizophrenia. *Molecular Psychiatry, 4*, 163–172.

Agnati, L. F., Bjelke, B., & Fuxe, K. (1992). Volume transmission in the brain. *American Scientist, 80*, 362–373.

Aiello, J. R., Thompson, D. D., & Brodzinsky, D. M. (1983). How funny is crowding anyway? Effects of room size, group size, and the introduction of humor. *Basic and Applied Social Psychology, 4*, 193–207.

Ainsworth, M. D. S. (1973). The development of infant-mother attachment. In B. Caldwell & H. Ricciuti (Eds.), *Review of child development research* (Vol. 3). Chicago: University of Chicago Press.

Ainsworth, M. D. S. (1979). Infant-mother attachment. *American Psychologist, 34*, 932–937.

Ainsworth, M. D. S. (1989). Attachments beyond infancy. *American Psychologist, 44*, 709–716.

Albee, G. W. (1986). Toward a just society: Lessons from observations on the primary prevention of psychopathology. *American Psychologist, 41*, 891–898.

Alcock, J. E. (1981). *Parapsychology: Science or magic?* Oxford: Pergamon.

Alcock, J. E. (1985, Spring). Parapsychology: The "spiritual" science. *Free Inquiry*, pp. 25–35.

Aldrich, M. S. (1989). Automobile accidents in patients with sleep disorders. *Sleep, 12*, 487–494.

Aldridge-Morris, R. (1989). *Multiple personality: An exercise in deception.* Hillsdale, NJ: Erlbaum.

Alexander, C. N., Langer, E. J., Newman, R. I., Chandler, H. M., & Davies, J. L. (1989). Transcendental meditation, mindfulness, and longevity: An experimental study with the elderly. *Journal of Personality and Social Psychology, 57*, 950–964.

Alkon, D. L., Amaral, D. G., Baer, M. F., Black, J., Carew, T. J., Cohen, N. J., Disterhoft, J. F., Eichenbaum, H., Golski, S., Gorman, L. K., Lynch, G., McNaughton, B. L., Mishkin, M., Moyer, J. R., Jr., Olds, J. L., Olton, D. S., Otto, T., Squire, L. R., Staubli, U., Thompson, L. T., & Wible, C. (1991). Learning and memory. *Brain Research Reviews, 16*, 193–220.

Allard, F., & Burnett, N. (1985). Skill in sport. *Canadian Journal of Psychology, 39*, 294–312.

Allen, J. B., Repinski, D. J., Ballard, J. C., & Griffin, B. W. (1996). Beliefs about the etiology of homosexuality may influence attitudes toward homosexuals. Paper presented to the American Psychological Society convention.

Allen, L. S., & Gorski, R. A. (1992). Sexual orientation and the size of the anterior commisure in the human brain. *Proceedings of the National Academy of Sciences, 89*, 7199–7202.

Allman, A. L. (1989). Subjective well-being of students with and without disabilities. Paper presented at the Midwestern Psychological Association convention.

Alloy, L. B., Abramson, L. Y., Whitehouse, W. G., Hogan, M. E., Tashman, N. A., Steinberg, D. L., Rose, D. T., & Donovan, P. (1999). Depressogenic cognitive styles: Predictive validity, information processing and personality characteristics, and developmental origins. *Behaviour Research and Therapy, 37,* 503–531.

Allport, G. W. (1967). Gordon W. Allport. In E. G. Boring & G. Lindzey (Eds.), *A history of psychology in autobiography* (Vol. V). New York: Appleton-Century-Crofts.

Allport, G. W., & Odbert, H. S. (1936). Trait-names: A psycholexical study. *Psychological Monographs, 47*(1).

Altman, D. G., Levine, D. W., Howard, G., & Hamilton, H. (1997). Tobacco farming and public health: Attitudes of the general public and farmers. *Journal of Social Issues, 53,* 113–128.

Altman, L. K. (1999, June 28). Study says gay men reducing levels of risky sexual behavior. *New York Times* (www.nytimes.com).

Alwin, D. F. (1990). Historical changes in parental orientations to children. In N. Mandell (Ed.), *Sociological studies of child development* (Vol. 3). Greenwich, CT: JAI Press.

Amabile, T. M. (1983). *The social psychology of creativity.* New York: Springer-Verlag.

Amabile, T. M. (1987). The motivation to be creative. In S. Isaksen (Ed.), *Frontiers in creativity: Beyond the basics.* Buffalo, NY: Bearly Limited.

Amabile, T. M. (1988). From individual creativity to organizational innovation. In K. Gronhaug & G. Kaufmann (Eds.), *Innovation: A crossdisciplinary perspective.* Oslo: Norwegian University Press.

Amabile, T. M., & Hennessey, B. A. (1992). The motivation for creativity in children. In A. K. Boggiano & T. S. Pittman (Eds.), *Achievement and motivation: A social-developmental perspective.* New York: Cambridge University Press.

Ambady, N., Hallahan, M., & Rosenthal, R. (1995). On judging and being judged accurately in zero-acquaintance situations. *Journal of Personality and Social Psychology, 69,* 518–529.

Ambady, N., & Rosenthal, R. (1992). Thin slices of expressive behavior as predictors of interpersonal consequences: A meta-analysis. *Psychological Bulletin, 111,* 256–274.

Ambady, N., & Rosenthal, R. (1993). Half a minute: Predicting teacher evaluations from thin slices of nonverbal behavior and physical attractiveness. *Journal of Personality and Social Psychology, 64,* 431–441.

American Enterprise. (1992, January/February). Women, men, marriages & ministers. P. 106.

American Psychiatric Association. (1990). *The practice of ECT: Recommendations for treatment, training, and privileging.* Washington, DC: American Psychiatric Press.

American Psychiatric Association. (1994). *Diagnostic and statistical manual of mental disorders (Fourth Edition).* Washington, DC: American Psychiatric Press.

American Psychological Association. (1991). Medical cost offset. Washington, DC: American Psychological Association Practice Directorate.

American Psychological Association. (1992). Ethical principles of psychologists and code of conduct. *American Psychologist, 47,* 1597–1611.

Anda, R., Williamson, D., Jones, D., Macera, C., Eaker, E., Glassman, A., & Marks, J. (1993). Depressed affect, hopelessness, and the risk of ischemic heart disease in a cohort of U.S. adults. *Epidemiology, 4,* 285–294.

Andersen, B. L. (1983). Primary orgasmic dysfunction: Diagnostic considerations and review of treatment. *Psychological Bulletin, 93,* 105–136.

Andersen, B. L. (1989). Health psychology's contribution to addressing the cancer problem: Update on accomplishments. *Health Psychology, 8,* 683–703.

Andersen, B. L., & Cyranowski, J. M. (1995). Women's sexuality: Behaviors, responses, and individual differences. *Journal of Consulting and Clinical Psychology, 63,* 891–906.

Andersen, R. E., Crespo, C. J., Bartlett, S. J., Cheskin, L. J., & Pratt, M. (1998). Relationship of physical activity and television watching with body weight and level of fatness among children. *Journal of the American Medical Association, 279,* 938–942.

Anderson, C. A., & Anderson, D. C. (1984). Ambient temperature and violent crime: Tests of the linear and curvilinear hypotheses. *Journal of Personality and Social Psychology, 46,* 91–97.

Anderson, C. A., Anderson, K. B., Dorr, N., DeNeve, K. M., & Flanagan, M. (2000). Temperature and aggression. *Advances in Experimental Social Psychology, 32,* 63–133.

Anderson, C. A., & Dill, K. E. (2000). Video games and aggressive thoughts, feelings, and behavior in the laboratory and in life. *Journal of Personality and Social Psychology, 78,* 772–790.

Anderson, C. A., Lepper, M. R., & Ross, L. (1980). Perseverance of social theories: The role of explanation in the persistence of discredited information. *Journal of Personality and Social Psychology, 39,* 1037–1049.

Anderson, C. A., Lindsay, J. J., & Bushman, B. J. (1999). Research in the psychological laboratory: Truth or triviality? *Current Directions in Psychological Science, 8,* 3–9.

Anderson, D. R., & Jose, W. S., II (1987, December). Employee lifestyle and the bottom line: Results from the StayWell evaluation. *Fitness in Business,* pp. 86–91.

Anderson, J. R., & Schooler, L. J. (1991). Reflections of the environment in memory. *Psychological Science, 2,* 396–408.

Anderson, R. C., Pichert, J. W., Goetz, E. T., Schallert, D. L., Stevens, K. V., & Trollip, S. R. (1976). Instantiation of general terms. *Journal of Verbal Learning and Verbal Behavior, 15,* 667–679.

Anderson, S. W., Bechara, A., Damasio, H., Tranel, D., & Damasio, A. R. (1999). Impairment of social and moral behavior related to early damage in human prefrontal cortex. *Nature Neuroscience, 2,* 1032–1037.

Andersson, B. E. (1989). Effects of public daycare: A longitudinal study. *Child Development, 60,* 857–866.

Andreasen, N. C. (1997). Linking mind and brain in the study of mental illnesses: A project for a scientific psychopathology. *Science, 275,* 1586–1593.

Andreasen, N. C., Arndt, S., Swayze, V., II, Cizadlo, T., & Flaum, M. (1994). Thalamic abnormalities in schizophrenia visualized through magnetic resonance image averaging. *Science, 266,* 294–298.

Angell, M., & Kassirer, J. P. (1998). Alternative medicine: The risks of untested and unregulated remedies. *New England Journal of Medicine, 17,* 839–841.

Angier, N. (1999, February 21). Men, women, sex and Darwin. *New York Times Magazine* (web.lexis-nexis.com).

Angoff, W. H. (1987). The nature-nurture debate, aptitudes, and group differences. Presidential address to American Psychological Association Division 5.

Angoff, W. H. (1988, Winter). A philosophical discussion: The issues of test and item bias. *ETS Developments*, pp. 10–11.

Antony, M. M., Brown, T. A., & Barlow, D. H. (1992). Current perspectives on panic and panic disorder. *Current Directions in Psychological Science, 1,* 79–82.

Antrobus, J. (1991). Dreaming: Cognitive processes during cortical activation and high afferent thresholds. *Psychological Review, 98,* 96–121.

Archer, J. (1996). Sex differences in social behavior: Are the social role and evolutionary explanations compatible? *American Psychologist, 51,* 909–917.

Arendt, H. (1963). *Eichmann in Jerusalem: A report on the banality of evil.* New York: Viking Press.

Arenson, K. W. (1997, May 4). Romanian woman breaks male grip on top math prize. *New York Times* News Service (in *Grand Rapids Press*, p. A7).

Aries, E. (1987). Gender and communication. In P. Shaver & C. Henrick (Eds.), *Review of Personality and Social Psychology, 7,* 177–200.

Armony, J. L., Quirk, G. J., & LeDoux, J. E. (1998). Differential effects of amygdala lesions on early and late plastic components of auditory cortex spike trains during fear conditioning. *Journal of Neuroscience, 18,* 2592–2601.

Arnett, J. J. (1999). Adolescent storm and stress, reconsidered. *American Psychologist, 54,* 317–326.

Aron, A., Melinat, E., Aron, E. N., Vallone, R. D., & Bator, R. J. (1997). The experimental generation of interpersonal closeness: A procedure and some preliminary findings. *Personality and Social Psychology Bulletin, 23,* 363–377.

Arrigo, J. M., & Pezdek, K. (1997). Lessons from the study of psychogenic amnesia. *Current Directions in Psychology, 6,* 148–152.

Asch, S. E. (1955). Opinions and social pressure. *Scientific American, 193,* 31–35.

Aserinsky, E. (1988, January 17). Personal communication.

Assanand, S., Pinel, J. P. J., & Lehman, D. R. (1998). Personal theories of hunger and eating. *Journal of Applied Social Psychology, 28,* 998–1015.

Associated Press (1999, April 26). Airline passengers mistakenly told plane would crash. *Grand Rapids Press*, p. A3.

Astin, A. W., Parrott, S. A., Korn, W. S., & Sax, L. J. (1997). *The American freshman: Thirty year trends, 1966–1996.* Los Angeles, CA: Higher Education Research Institute, UCLA.

Atkinson, R. (1988). *The teenage world: Adolescent self-image in ten countries.* New York: Plenum Press.

Atkinson, R. C., & Schiffrin, R. M. (1968). Human memory: A control system and its control processes. In K. Spence (Ed.), *The psychology of learning and motivation* (Vol. 2). New York: Academic Press.

Atwell, R. H. (1986, July 28). Drugs on campus: A perspective. *Higher Education & National Affairs*, p. 5.

August, D., & Hakuta, K. (Ed.). *Educating language-minority children.* Washington, DC: National Academy of Sciences.

Australian Bureau of Statistics (1999). *Australia now—A statistical profile: Health—overweight and obesity* (www.abs.gov.au).

Australian Bureau of Statistics (1999). *Australian social trends 1999.* Canberra: Australian Bureau of Statistics.

Averill, J. R. (1983). Studies on anger and aggression: Implications for theories of emotion. *American Psychologist, 38,* 1145–1160.

Averill, J. R. (1993). William James's other theory of emotion. In M. E. Donnelly (Ed.), *Reinterpreting the legacy of William James.* Washington, DC: American Psychological Association.

Ax, A. F. (1953). The physiological differentiation of fear and anger in humans. *Psychosomatic Medicine, 15,* 433–442.

Axel, R. (1995, October). The molecular logic of smell. *Scientific American*, pp. 154–159.

Azar, B. (1995, May). Several genetic traits linked to alcoholism. *APA Monitor*, pp. 21–22.

Azar, B. (1998, June). Why can't this man feel whether or not he's standing up? *APA Monitor* (www.apa.org/monitor/jun98/touch.html).

Azar, B. (1999, March). Classical conditioning could link disorders and brain dysfunction, researchers suggest. *APA Monitor*, p. 17.

Baars, B. J., & McGovern, K. (1994). Consciousness. In V. Ramachandran (Ed.), *Encyclopedia of human behavior.* Orlando, FL: Academic Press.

Babad, E., Bernieri, F., & Rosenthal, R. (1991). Students as judges of teachers' verbal and nonverbal behavior. *American Educational Research Journal, 28,* 211–234.

Bachman, J. G., Johnston, L. D., & O'Malley, P. M. (1998). Explaining recent increases in students' marijuana use: Impacts of perceived risks and disapproval, 1976 through 1996. *American Journal of Public Health, 88,* 887–892.

Bachman, J., Wadsworth, K., O'Malley, P., Johnston, L., & Schulenberg, J. (1997). *Smoking, drinking, and drug use in young adulthood: The impact of new freedoms and new responsibilities.* Mahwah, NJ: Erlbaum.

Backman, L., & Dixon, R. A. (1992). Psychological compensation: A theoretical framework. *Psychological Bulletin, 112,* 259–283.

Backus, J. (1977). *The acoustical foundations of music* (2nd ed.). New York: Norton.

Baddeley, A. D. (1982). *Your memory: A user's guide.* New York: Macmillan.

Baddeley, A. (1992). Working memory. *Science, 255,* 556–569.

Badenhoop, M. S., & Johansen, M. K. (1980). Do reentry women have special needs? *Psychology of Women Quarterly, 4,* 591–595.

Bahrick, H. P. (1984). Semantic memory content in permastore: 50 years of memory for Spanish learned in school. *Journal of Experimental Psychology: General, 111,* 1–29.

Bahrick, H. P., Bahrick, L. E., Bahrick, A. S., & Bahrick, P. E. (1993). Maintenance of foreign language vocabulary and the spacing effect. *Psychological Science, 4,* 316–321.

Bailey, J. M., Gaulin, S., Agyei, Y., & Gladue, B. A. (1994). Effects of gender and sexual orientation on evolutionary relevant aspects of human mating psychology. *Journal of Personality and Social Psychology, 66,* 1081–1093.

Bailey, J. M., Bobrow, D., Wolfe, M., & Mikach, S. (1995). Sexual orientation of adult sons of gay fathers. *Developmental Psychology, 31,* 124–129.

Bailey, J. M., Dunne, M. P., & Martin, N. G. (1997). Sex differences in the distribution and determinants of sexual orientation in a national twin sample. Unpublished manuscript, Northwestern University, Evanston, IL.

Bailey, J. M., & Pillard, R. C. (1991). A genetic study of male sexual orientation. *Archives of General Psychiatry, 48,* 1089–1096.

Bailey, J. M., & Pillard, R. C. (1994, January). The innateness of homosexuality. *Harvard Mental Health Letter,* pp. 4–6.

Bailey, J. M., & Pillard, R. C. (1995). Genetics of human sexual orientation. *Annual Review of Sex Research, 6,* 126–150.

Bailey, J. M., Pillard, R. C., Neale, M. C., & Agyei, Y. (1993). Heritable factors influence sexual orientation in women. *Archives of General Psychiatry, 50,* 217–223.

Bailey, J. M., & Zucker, K. J. (1995). Childhood sex-typed behavior and sexual orientation: A conceptual analysis and quantitative review. *Developmental Psychology, 31,* 43–55.

Baillargeon, R. (1995). A model of physical reasoning in infancy. In C. Rovee-Collier & L. P. Lipsitt (Eds.), *Advances in infancy research* (Vol. 9). Stamford, CT: Ablex.

Baillargeon, R. (1998). Infants' understanding of the physical world. In M. Sabourin, F. I. M. Craik, & M. Roberts (Eds.), *Advances in psychological science: Vol. 2. Biological and cognitive aspects.* Hove, England: Psychology Press.

Bairagi, R. (1987). Food crises and female children in rural Bangladesh. *Social Science, 72,* 48–51.

Baker, E. L. (1987). The state of the art of clinical hypnosis. *International Journal of Clinical and Experimental Hypnosis, 35,* 203–214.

Baker-Ward, L., Gordon, B. N., Ornstein, P. A., Larus, D. M., & Clubb, P. A. (1993). Young children's long-term retention of a pediatric examination. *Child Development, 64,* 1519–1533.

Baldwin, E. (1993). The case for animal research in psychology. *Journal of Social Issues, 49*(1), 121–131.

Baldwin, M. W., Carell, S. E., & Lopez, D. F. (1991). Priming relationship schemas: My advisor and the pope are watching me from the back of my mind. *Journal of Experimental Social Psychology, 26,* 435–454.

Ball, W., & Tronick, E. (1971). Infant responses to impending collision: Optical and real. *Science, 171,* 818–820.

Ballard, M. E., & Wiest, J. R. (1998). Mortal Kombat: The effects of violent videogame play on males' hostility and cardiovascular responding. *Journal of Applied Social Psychology, 26,* 717–730.

Balter, M. (1999). AIDS now world's fourth biggest killer. *Science, 284,* 1101.

Baltes, P. B. (1993). The aging mind: Potential and limits. *The Gerontologist, 33,* 580–594.

Baltes, P. B. (1994). Life-span developmental psychology: On the overall landscape of human development. Invited address, American Psychological Association convention.

Baltes, P. B., & Baltes, M. M. (1999, September-October). Harvesting the fruits of age: Growing older, growing wise. *Science and the Spirit,* pp. 11–14.

Bandura, A. (1982). The psychology of chance encounters and life paths. *American Psychologist, 37,* 747–755.

Bandura, A. (1986). *Social foundations of thought and action: A social-cognitive theory.* Englewood Cliffs, NJ: Prentice-Hall.

Bandura, A., Blanchard, E. B., & Ritter, B. (1969). Relative efficacy of desensitization and modeling approaches for inducing behavioral, affective, and attitudinal changes. *Journal of Personality and Social Psychology, 13,* 173–199.

Bandura, A., Ross, D., & Ross, S. A. (1961). Transmission of aggression through imitation of aggressive models. *Journal of Abnormal and Social Psychology, 63,* 575–582.

Bannon, L. (1995, October 25). Beastly gossip. *Grand Rapids Press,* pp. A1, A4 (reprinted from *Wall Street Journal*).

Bar, M., & Biederman, I. (1998). Subliminal visual priming. *Psychological Science, 9,* 464–469.

Bargh, J. A. (1997). The automaticity of everyday life. In R. S. Wyer, Jr. (Ed.), *Advances in social cognition* (Vol. 10). Mahwah, NJ: Erlbaum.

Barinaga, M. (1991). How long is the human life-span? *Science, 254,* 936–938.

Barinaga, M. (1992). How scary things get that way. *Science, 258,* 887–888.

Barinaga, M. (1992). The brain remaps its own contours. *Science, 258,* 216–218.

Barinaga, M. (1997). Visual system provides clues to how the brain perceives. *Science, 275,* 1583–1585.

Barinaga, M. B. (1997). How exercise works its magic. *Science, 276,* 1325.

Barinaga, M. (1999). Salmon follow watery odors home. *Science, 286,* 705–706.

Barker, S. L., Funk, S. C., & Houston, B. K. (1988). Psychological treatment versus nonspecific factors: A meta-analysis of conditions that engender comparable expectations for improvement. *Clinical Psychology Review, 8,* 579–594.

Barlow, D. H. (1988). *Anxiety and its disorders: The nature and treatment of anxiety and panic.* New York: Guilford.

Barnett, A. (1990). Air safety: End of the golden age? *Chance, 1*(2), 8–12.

Barnett, A. (1996, June 9). Quoted in Adam Bryan, Fly me; Why no airline brags: "We're the safest." *New York Times,* Section 4, p. 1.

Barnett, P. A., & Gotlib, I. H. (1988). Psychosocial functioning and depression: Distinguishing among antecedents, concomitants, and consequences. *Psychological Bulletin, 104,* 97–126.

Barnier, A. J., & McConkey, K. M. (1992). Reports of real and false memories: The relevance of hypnosis, hypnotizability, and context of memory test. *Journal of Abnormal Psychology, 101,* 521–527.

Barnier, A. J., & McConkey, K. M. (1998). Posthypnotic responding away from the hypnotic setting. *Psychological Science, 9,* 256–262.

Baron, R. A. (1987). Interviewer's mood and reaction to job applicants: The influence of affective states on applied social judgments. *Journal of Applied Social Psychology, 17,* 911–926.

Baron, R. A. (1988). Negative effects of destructive criticism: Impact on conflict, self-efficacy, and task performance. *Journal of Applied Psychology, 73,* 199–207.

Baron, R. A. (1990). Environmentally induced positive affect: Its impact on self-efficacy, task performance, negotiation, and conflict. *Journal of Applied Social Psychology, 20,* 368–384.

Baron, R. S., Cutrona, C. E., Hicklin, D., Russell, D. W., & Lubaroff, D. M. (1990). Social support and immune function among spouses of cancer patients. *Journal of Personality and Social Psychology, 59,* 344–352.

Baron, R. S., Vandello, J. A., & Brunsman, B. (1996). The forgotten variable in conformity research: Impact of task importance on social influence. *Journal of Personality and Social Psychology, 71,* 915–927.

Baron-Cohen, S., Leslie, A. M., & Frith, U. (1985). Does the autistic child have a "theory of mind"? *Cognition, 21,* 37–46.

Barry, D. (1995, September 17). Teen smokers, too, get cool, toxic, waste-blackened lungs. *Asbury Park Press,* p. D3.

Barry, D. (1996, August 11). Syndicated column.

Bartlett, M. S., Hager, J. C., Ekman, P., & Sejnowski, T. J. (1999). Measuring facial expressions by computer image analysis. *Psychophysiology, 36,* 253–263.

Barton, J., Chassin, L., Presson, C. C., & Sherman, S. J. (1982). Social image factors as motivators of smoking initiation in early and middle adolescence. *Child Development, 53,* 1499–1511.

Bartoshuk, L. M. (1993). The wisdom of the body: Using case studies to teach sensation and perception. Paper presented to the National Institute on the Teaching of Psychology, St. Petersburg Beach, FL.

Baruch, G. K., & Barnett, R. (1986). Role quality, multiple role involvement, and psychological well-being in midlife women. *Journal of Personality and Social Psychology, 51,* 578–585.

Bashore, T. R., Ridderinkhof, K. R., & van der Molen, M. W. (1997). The decline of cognitive processing speed in old age. *Current Directions in Psychological Science, 6,* 163–169.

Baskind, D. E. (1997, December 14). Personal communication, from Delta College.

Bass, E., & Davis, L. (1988). *The courage to heal.* New York: Harper & Row.

Bass, L. E., & Kane-Williams, E. (1993). Stereotype or reality: Another look at alcohol and drug use among African American children. U.S. Department of Health and Human Services, *Public Health Reports, 108* (Supplement 1), 78–84.

Bat-Chava, Y. (1993). Antecedents of self-esteem in deaf people: A meta-analytic review. *Rehabilitation Psychology, 38*(4), 221–234.

Bat-Chava, Y. (1994). Group identification and self-esteem of deaf adults. *Personality and Social Psychology Bulletin, 20,* 494–502.

Baum, A., & Fleming, I. (1993). Implications of psychological research on stress and technological accidents. *American Psychologist, 48,* 665–672.

Baum, A., & Posluszny, D. M. (1999). Health psychology: Mapping biobehavioral contributions to health and illness. *Annual Review of Psychology, 50,* 137–163.

Baumeister, R. F. (1989). The optimal margin of illusion. *Journal of Social and Clinical Psychology, 8,* 176–189.

Baumeister, R. F. (1993). Understanding the inner nature of low self-esteem: Uncertain, fragile, protective, and conflicted. In R. F. Baumeister (Ed.), *Self-esteem: The puzzle of low self-regard.* New York: Plenum.

Baumeister, R. F. (1996). Should schools try to boost self-esteem? Beware the dark side. *American Educator, 20,* 14019, 43.

Baumeister, R. F. (2000). Gender differences in erotic plasticity: The female sex drive as socially flexible and responsive. *Psychological Bulletin,* in press.

Baumeister, R. F., Dale, K., & Sommer, K. L. (1998). Freudian defense mechanisms and empirical findings in modern personality and social psychology: Reaction formation, projection, displacement, undoing, isolation, sublimation, and denial. *Journal of Personality, 66,* 1081–1124.

Baumeister, R. F., Heatherton, T. F., & Tice, C. M. (1993). When ego threats lead to self-regulation failure: The negative consequences of high self-esteem. *Journal of Personality and Social Psychology, 64,* 141–156.

Baumeister, R. F., & Leary, M. R. (1995). The need to belong: Desire for interpersonal attachments as a fundamental human motivation. *Psychological Bulletin, 117,* 497–529.

Baumeister, R. F., Stillwell, A., & Wotman, S. R. (1990). Victim and perpetrator accounts of interpersonal conflict: Autobiographical narratives about anger. *Journal of Personality and Social Psychology, 59,* 994–1005.

Baumeister, R. F., & Tice, D. M. (1986). How adolescence became the struggle for self: A historical transformation of psychological development. In J. Suls & A. G. Greenwald (Eds.), *Psychological perspectives on the self* (Vol. 3). Hillsdale, NJ: Erlbaum.

Baumgardner, A. H. (1990). To know oneself is to like oneself: Self-certainty and self-affect. *Journal of Personality and Social Psychology, 58,* 1062–1072.

Baumgardner, A. H., Kaufman, C. M., & Levy, P. E. (1989). Regulating affect interpersonally: When low esteem leads to greater enhancement. *Journal of Personality and Social Psychology, 56,* 907–921.

Baumrind, D. (1982). Adolescent sexuality: Comment on Williams' and Silka's comments on Baumrind. *American Psychologist, 37,* 1402–1403.

Baumrind, D. (1983). Rejoinder to Lewis's reinterpretation of parental firm control effects: Are authoritative families really harmonious? *Psychological Bulletin, 94,* 132–142.

Baumrind, D. (1991). Parenting styles and adolescent development. In J. Brooks-Gunn, R. Lerner, & A. C. Petersen (Eds.), *The encyclopedia of adolescence.* New York: Garland.

Baumrind, D. (1996). The discipline controversy revisited. *Family Relations, 45,* 405–414.

Bayley, N. (1949). Consistency and variability in the growth of intelligence from birth to eighteen years. *Journal of Genetic Psychology, 75,* 165–196.

Beaman, A. L., & Klentz, B. (1983). The supposed physical attractiveness bias against supporters of the women's movement: A meta-analysis. *Personality and Social Psychology Bulletin, 9,* 544–550.

Beardsley, L. M. (1994). Medical diagnosis and treatment across cultures. In W. J. Lonner & R. Malpass (Eds.), *Psychology and culture.* Boston: Allyn & Bacon.

Beardsley, T. (1996, July). Waking up. *Scientific American,* pp. 14, 18.

Beauchamp, G. K. (1987). The human preference for excess salt. *American Scientist, 75,* 27–33.

Beck, A. J., Kline, S. A., & Greenfeld, L. A. (1988). Survey of youth in custody, 1987. U.S. Department of Justice, Bureau of Justice Statistics Special Report.

Beck, A. T., Rush, A. J., Shaw, B. F., & Emery, G. (1979). *Cognitive therapy of depression.* New York: Guilford Press.

Beck, A. T., & Steer, R. A. (1989). Clinical predictors of eventual suicide: A 5- to 10-year prospective study of suicide attempters. *Journal of Affective Disorders, 17,* 203–209.

Beck, A. T., & Young, J. E. (1978, September). College blues. *Psychology Today,* pp. 80–92.

Becklen, R., & Cervone, D. (1983). Selective looking and the noticing of unexpected events. *Memory and Cognition, 11,* 601–608.

Beeman, M. J., & Chiarello, C. (1998). Complementary right- and left-hemisphere language comprehension. *Current Directions in Psychological Science, 7,* 2–8.

Beeman, M., Friedman, R. B., Grafman, J., Perez, E., Diamond, S., & Lindsay, M. B. (1994). Summation priming and coarse semantic coding in the right hemisphere. *Journal of Cognitive Neuroscience, 6*, 26–45.

Beilin, H. (1992). Piaget's enduring contribution to developmental psychology. *Developmental Psychology, 28*, 191–204.

Beitman, B. D., Goldfried, M. R., & Norcross, J. C. (1989). The movement toward integrating the psychotherapies: An overview. *American Journal of Psychiatry, 146*, 138–147.

Bell, A. P. (1982, November/December). Sexual preference: A postscript (SIECUS Report, 11, No. 2). *Church and Society*, pp. 34–37.

Bell, A. P., Weinberg, M. S., & Hammersmith, S. K. (1981). *Sexual preference: Its development in men and women*. Bloomington: Indiana University Press.

Bell, R. Q., & Waldrop, M. F. (1989). Achievement and cognitive correlates of minor physical anomalies in early development. In M. G. Bornstein & N. A. Krasnegor (Eds.), *Stability and continuity in mental development: Behavioral and biological perspectives*. Hillsdale, NJ: Erlbaum.

Bellugi, U. (1994, August). Quoted in P. Radetsky, Silence, signs, and wonder. *Discover*, pp. 60–68.

Beloff, J. (1985, Spring). Science, religion and the paranormal. *Free Inquiry*, pp. 36–41

Belsher, G., & Costello, C. G. (1988). Relapse after recovery from unipolar depression: A critical review. *Psychological Bulletin, 104*, 84–96.

Belsky, J. (1988). The "effects" of infant day care reconsidered. *Early Childhood Research Quarterly* (Vol. III), 235–272.

Belsky, J. (1990). Parental and nonparental child care and children's socioemotional development: A decade in review. *Journal of Marriage and the Family, 52*, 885–903.

Belsky, J. (1994). Effects of infant day care: 1986–1994. Invited address to the British Psychological Society Section on Developmental Psychology.

Belsky, J., Lang, M., & Huston, T. L. (1986). Sex typing and division of labor as determinants of marital change across the transition to parenthood. *Journal of Personality and Social Psychology, 50*, 517–522.

Bem, D. J. (1996). Exotic becomes erotic: A developmental theory of sexual orientation. *Psychological Review, 103*, 320–335.

Bem, D. J. (1998). Is EBE theory supported by the evidence? Is it androcentric? A reply to Peplau et al. (1998). *Psychological Review, 105*, 395–398.

Bem, D. J., & Honorton, C. (1994). Does psi exist? Replicable evidence for an anomalous process of information transfer. *Psychological Bulletin, 115*, 4–18.

Bem, S. L. (1987). Masculinity and femininity exist only in the mind of the perceiver. In J. M. Reinisch, L. A. Rosenblum, & S. A. Sanders (Eds.), *Masculinity/femininity: Basic perspectives*. New York: Oxford University Press.

Bem, S. L. (1993). *The lenses of gender*. New Haven: Yale University Press.

Benbow, C. P., & Stanley, J. C. (1996). Inequity in equity: How "equity" can lead to inequity for high-potential students. *Psychology, Public Policy, and Law, 2*, 249–292.

Bennett, R. (1991, February). Pornography and extrafamilial child sexual abuse: Examining the relationship. Unpublished manuscript, Los Angeles Police Department Sexually Exploited Child Unit.

Bennett, W., & DiIulio, J. (1996). *Body count*. New York: Simon & Schuster.

Bennett, W. I. (1995). Beyond overeating. *New England Journal of Medicine, 332*, 673–674.

Bensman, T. (1999, June 5). Witnesses remember man's bravery. *Dallas Morning News*.

Benson, H. (1996). *Timeless healing: The power and biology of belief*. New York: Scribner.

Benson, J. A., Jr., & Watson, S. J., Jr. (1999). *Marijuana and medicine: Assessing the science base*. Washington, DC: National Academy Press.

Benson, P. L. (1992, Spring). Patterns of religious development in adolescence and adulthood. *PIRI Newsletter*, 2–9.

Benson, P. L., Sharma, A. R., & Roehlkepartain, E. C. (1994). *Growing up adopted: A portrait of adolescents and their families*. Minneapolis: Search Institute.

Berenbaum, S. A., & Hines, M. (1992). Early androgens are related to childhood sex-typed toy preferences. *Psychological Science, 3*, 203–206.

Berenbaum, S. A., Korman, K., & Leveroni, C. (1995). Early hormones and sex differences in cognitive abilities. *Learning and Individual Differences, 7*, 303–321.

Bergin, A. E. (1980). Psychotherapy and religious values. *Journal of Consulting and Clinical Psychology, 48*, 95–105.

Bergin, A. E. (1991). Values and religious issues in psychotherapy and mental health. *American Psychologist, 46*, 394–403.

Bergsholm, P., Larsen, J. L., Rosendahl, K., & Holsten, F. (1989). Electroconvulsive therapy and cerebral computed tomography. *Acta Psychiatrica Scandinavia, 80*, 566–572.

Berk, L. E. (1994, November). Why children talk to themselves. *Scientific American*, pp. 78–83.

Berkel, J., & de Waard, F. (1983). Mortality pattern and life expectancy of Seventh Day Adventists in the Netherlands. *International Journal of Epidemiology, 12*, 455–459.

Berkowitz, L. (1983). Aversively stimulated aggression: Some parallels and differences in research with animals and humans. *American Psychologist, 38*, 1135–1144.

Berkowitz, L. (1989). Frustration-aggression hypothesis: Examination and reformulation. *Psychological Bulletin, 106*, 59–73.

Berkowitz, L. (1990). On the formation and regulation of anger and aggression: A cognitive-neoassociationistic analysis. *American Psychologist, 45*, 494–503.

Berman, M., Gladue, B., & Taylor, S. (1993). The effects of hormones, Type A behavior pattern, and provocation on aggression in men. *Motivation and Emotion, 17*, 125–138.

Berndt, T. J. (1992). Friendship and friends' influence in adolescence. *Current Directions in Psychological Science, 1*, 156–159.

Bernhardt, P. C., Dabbs, J. M., Jr., Fielden, J. A., & Lutter, C. D. (1998). Testosterone changes during vicarious experiences of winning and losing among fans at sporting events. *Physiology and Behavior, 65*, 59–62.

Berry, D. S., & McArthur, L. Z. (1986). Perceiving character in faces: The impact of age-related craniofacial changes on social perception. *Psychological Bulletin, 100*, 3–18.

Berscheid, E. (1981). An overview of the psychological effects of physical attractiveness and some comments upon the psychological effects of knowledge of the effects of physical attractiveness. In

G. W. Lucker, K. Ribbens, & J. A. McNamara (Eds.), *Psychological aspects of facial form* (Craniofacial growth series). Ann Arbor: Center for Human Growth and Development, University of Michigan.

Berscheid, E. (1985). Interpersonal attraction. In G. Lindzey & E. Aronson (Eds.), *The handbook of social psychology*. New York: Random House.

Berscheid, E., Gangestad, S. W., & Kulakowski, D. (1984). Emotion in close relationships: Implications for relationship counseling. In S. D. Brown & R. W. Lent (Eds.), *Handbook of counseling psychology*. New York: Wiley.

Besson, M., Faita, F., Peretz, I., Bonnel, A.-M., & Requin, J. (1998). Singing in the brain: Independence of lyrics and tunes. *Psychological Science, 9*, 494–498.

Best, C. T., & Avery, R. A. (1999). Left-hemisphere advantage for click consonants is determined by linguistic significance and experience. *Psychological Science, 10*, 65–70.

Best, J. A., & Suedfeld, P. (1982). Restricted environmental stimulation therapy and behavioral self-management in smoking cessation. *Journal of Applied Social Psychology, 12*, 408–419.

Bettencourt, R. A., & Dorr, N. (1997). Collective self-esteem as a mediator of the relationship between allocentrism and subjective well-being. *Personality and Social Psychology Bulletin, 23*, 955–964.

Beyerstein, B., & Beyerstein, D. (Eds.). (1992). *The write stuff: Evaluations of graphology*. Buffalo, NY: Prometheus Books.

Bhatt, R. S., Wasserman, E. A., Reynolds, W. F., Jr., & Knauss, K. S. (1988). Conceptual behavior in pigeons: Categorization of both familiar and novel examples from four classes of natural and artificial stimuli. *Journal of Experimental Psychology: Animal Behavior Processes, 14*, 219–234.

Bickman, L. (1999). Practice makes perfect and other myths about mental health services. *American Psychologist, 54*, 965–978.

Bigler, E. D., Johnson, S. C., Jackson, C., & Blatter, D. D. (1995). Aging, brain size, and IQ. *Intelligence, 21*, 109–119.

Binet, A., & Simon, T. (1905; reprinted 1916). New methods for the diagnosis of the intellectual level of subnormals. In A. Binet & T. Simon, *The development of intelligence in children*. Baltimore: Williams & Wilkins.

Binson, D., Michaels, S., Stall, R., Coates, T. J., Gagnon, J. H., & Catania, J. A. (1995). Prevalence and social distribution of men who have sex with men: United States and its urban centers. *Journal of Sex Research, 32*, 245–254.

Bishop, G. D. (1991). Understanding the understanding of illness: Lay disease representations. In J. A. Skelton & R. T. Croyle (Eds.), *Mental representation in health and illness*. New York: Springer-Verlag.

Bjork, R. A. (1978). The updating of human memory. In G. H. Bower (Ed.), *The psychology of learning and motivation* (Vol. 12). New York: Academic Press.

Bjorklund, D. F., & Green, B. L. (1992). The adaptive nature of cognitive immaturity. *American Psychologist, 47*, 46–54.

Blackmore, S. (1991, Fall). Near-death experiences: In or out of the body? *Skeptical Inquirer*, pp. 34–45.

Blackmore, S. (1993). *Dying to live*. Amherst, NY: Prometheus Books.

Blackmore, S. J. (1997). Probability misjudgment and belief in the paranormal: A newspaper survey. *British Journal of Psychology, 88*, 683–689.

Blackmore, S. (1999). *The meme machine*. Oxford: Oxford University Press.

Blakemore, C., & Cooper, G. F. (1970). Development of the brain depends on the visual environment. *Nature, 228*, 477–478.

Blakemore, S-J., Wolpert, D. M., & Frith, C. D. (1998). Central cancellation of self-produced tickle sensation. *Nature Neuroscience, 1*, 635–640.

Blanchard, R. (1997). Birth order and sibling sex ratio in homosexual versus heterosexual males and females. *Annual Review of Sex Research, 8*, 27–67.

Blass, T. (1996). Stanley Milgram: A life of inventiveness and controversy. In G. A. Kimble, C. A. Boneau, & M. Wertheimer (eds.), *Portraits of pioneers in psychology* (Vol. II). Washington, DC, and Mahwah, NJ: American Psychological Association and Lawrence Erlbaum Publishers.

Blass, T. (1999). The Milgram paradigm after 35 years: Some things we now know about obedience to authority. *Journal of Applied Social Psychology, 29*, 955–978.

Blatt, S. J., Sanislow, C. A., III, Zuroff, D. C., & Pilkonis, P. (1996). Characteristics of effective therapists: Further analyses of data from the National Institute of Mental Health Treatment of Depression Collaborative Research Program. *Journal of Consulting and Clinical Psychology, 64*, 1276–1284.

Blom, J. M. C., Tamarkin, L., Shiber, J. R., & Nelson, R. J. (1995). Learned immunosuppression is associated with an increased risk of chemically-induced tumors. *Neuroimmunomodulation, 2*, 92–99.

Bloom, B. J. (1964). *Stability and change in human characteristics*. New York: Wiley.

Bloom, B. S. (Ed.). (1985). *Developing talent in young people*. New York: Ballantine.

Bloom, F. E. (1993, January/February). What's new in neurotransmitters. *BrainWork*, pp. 7–9.

Blum, K., Cull, J. G., Braverman, E. R., & Comings, D. E. (1996). Reward deficiency syndrome. *American Scientist, 84*, 132–145.

Bock, B. C., Marcus, B. H., King. T. E., Borrelli, B., & Roberts, M. R. (1999). Exercise effects on withdrawal and mood among women attempting smoking cessation. *Addictive Behavior, 24*, 399–410.

Bodenhausen, G. V., Sheppard, L. A., & Kramer, G. P. (1994). Negative affect and social judgment: The differential impact of anger and sadness. *European Journal of Social Psychology, 24*, 45–62.

Boesch-Achermann, H., & Boesch, C. (1993). Tool use in wild chimpanzees: New light from dark forests. *Current Directions in Psychological Science, 2*, 18–21.

Boggiano, A. K., Barrett, M., Weiher, A. W., McClelland, G. H., & Lusk, C. M. (1987). Use of the maximal-operant principle to motivate children's intrinsic interest. *Journal of Personality and Social Psychology, 53*, 866–879.

Boggiano, A. K., Harackiewicz, J. M., Bessette, M. M., & Main, D. S. (1985). Increasing children's interest through performance-contingent reward. *Social Cognition, 3*, 400–411.

Bohman, M., & Sigvardsson, S. (1990). Outcome in adoption: Lessons from longitudinal studies. In D. Brodzinsky & M. Schechter (Eds.), *The psychology of adoption*. New York: Oxford University Press.

Bolger, N., DeLongis, A., Kessler, R. C., & Schilling, E. A. (1989). Effects of daily stress on negative mood. *Journal of Personality and Social Psychology, 57*, 808–818.

Bond, C. F., Jr., Pitre, U., & Van Leeuwen, M. D. (1991). Encoding operations and the next-in-line effect. *Personality and Social Psychology Bulletin, 17,* 435–441.

Bond, M. H. (1988). Finding universal dimensions of individual variation in multi-cultural studies of values: The Rokeach and Chinese values surveys. *Journal of Personality and Social Psychology, 55,* 1009–1015.

Bond, R., & Smith, P. B. (1996). Culture and conformity: A meta-analysis of studies using Asch's (1952b, 1956) line judgment task. *Psychological Bulletin, 119,* 111–137.

Boneva, B., Frieze, I. H., Ferligoj, A., Jarosova, E., Pauknerova, D., & Orgocka, A. (1998). Achievement, power, and affiliation motives as clues to (e)migration desires: A four-countries comparison. *European Psychologist, 3,* 247–254.

Bonke, B., Schmitz, P. I. M., Verhage, F., & Zwaverling, A. (1986). Clinical study of so-called unconscious perception during general anaesthesia. *British Journal of Anaesthesia, 58,* 957–964.

Boring, E. G. (1930). A new ambiguous figure. *American Journal of Psychology, 42,* 444–445.

Borkenau, P., & Liebler, A. (1993). Convergence of stranger ratings of personality and intelligence with self-ratings, partner ratings, and measured intelligence. *Journal of Personality and Social Psychology, 65,* 546–553.

Bornstein, M. H. (1989). Stability in early mental development: From attention and information processing in infancy to language and cognition in childhood. In M. G. Bornstein & N. A. Krasnegor (Eds.), *Stability and continuity in mental development: Behavioral and biological perspectives.* Hillsdale, NJ: Erlbaum.

Bornstein, M. H., Tal, J., Rahn, C., Galperin, C. Z., Pecheux, M-G., Lamour, M., Toda, S., Azuma, H., Ogino, M., & Tamis-LeMonda, C. S. (1992). Functional analysis of the contents of maternal speech to infants of 5 and 13 months in four cultures: Argentina, France, Japan, and the United States. *Developmental Psychology, 28,* 593–603.

Bornstein, M. H., Tamis-LeMonda, C. S., Tal, J., Ludemann, P., Toda, S., Rahn, C. W., Pecheux, M-G., Azuma, H., & Vardi, D. (1992). Maternal responsiveness to infants in three societies: The United States, France, and Japan. *Child Development, 63,* 808–821.

Bornstein, R. F. (1989). Exposure and affect: Overview and meta-analysis of research, 1968–1987. *Psychological Bulletin, 106,* 265–289.

Bornstein, R. F. (1999). Source amnesia, misattribution, and the power of unconscious perceptions and memories. *Psychoanalytic Psychology, 16,* 155–178.

Bornstein, R. F., Galley, D. J., Leone, D. R., & Kale, A. R. (1991). The temporal stability of ratings of parents: Test-retest reliability and influence of parental contact. *Journal of Social Behavior and Personality, 6,* 641–649.

Bornstein, R. F., & Pittman, T. S. (Eds.). (1992). *Perception without awareness: Cognitive, clinical, and social perspectives.* New York: Guilford.

Boroditsky, R., Fisher, W., & Sand, M. (1995, July). Teenagers and contraception. Section of The Canadian Contraception Study. *Journal of the Society of Obstetricians and Gynaecologists of Canada,* Special Supplement, pp. 22–25.

Boscarino, J. A. (1997). Diseases among men 20 years after exposure to severe stress: Implications for clinical research and medical care. *Psychosomatic Medicine, 59,* 605–614.

Bosma, H., Marmot, M. G., Hemingway, H., Nicolson, A. C., Brunner, E., & Stansfeld, S. A. (1997). Low job control and risk of coronary heart disease in Whitehall II (prospective cohort) study. *British Medical Journal, 314,* 558–565.

Bosma, H., Peter, R., Siegrist, J., & Marmot, M. (1998). Two alternative job stress models and the risk of coronary heart disease. *American Journal of Public Health, 88,* 68–74.

Bothwell, R. K., Brigham, J. C., & Malpass, R. S. (1989). Cross-racial identification. *Personality and Social Psychology Bulletin, 15,* 19–25.

Bothwell, R. K., Deffenbacher, K. A., & Brigham, J. C. (1987). Correlation of eyewitness accuracy and confidence: Optimality hypothesis revised. *Journal of Applied Psychology, 72,* 691–695.

Botwin, M. D., Buss, D. M., & Shackelford, T. K. (1997). Personality and mate preferences: Five factors in mate selection and marital satisfaction. *Journal of Personality, 65,* 107–136.

Bouchard, T. J., Jr. (1981, December 6). Interview on *Nova: Twins* [program broadcast by the Public Broadcasting Service].

Bouchard, T. J., Jr. (1995). Longitudinal studies of personality and intelligence: A behavior genetic and evolutionary psychology perspective. In D. H. Saklofske & M. Zeidner (Eds.), *International handbook of personality and intelligence.* New York: Plenum.

Bouchard, T. J., Jr. (1996a). IQ similarity in twins reared apart: Finding and responses to critics. In R. Sternberg & C. Grigorenko (Eds.), *Intelligence: Heredity and environment.* New York: Cambridge University Press.

Bouchard, T. J., Jr. (1996b). Behavior genetic studies of intelligence, yesterday and today: The long journey from plausibility to proof. *Journal of Biosocial Science, 28,* 527–555.

Bowden, E. M., & Beeman, M. J. (1998). Getting the right idea: Semantic activation in the right hemisphere may help solve insight problems. *Psychological Science, 9,* 435–440.

Bower, B. (1999, September 25). Slumber's unexplored landscape: People in traditional societies sleep in eye-opening ways. *Science News, 156,* 205–207.

Bower, G. H. (1983). Affect and cognition. *Philosophical Transaction: Royal Society of London, Series B, 302,* 387–402.

Bower, G. H. (1986). Prime time in cognitive psychology. In P. Eelen (Ed.), *Cognitive research and behavior therapy: Beyond the conditioning paradigm.* Amsterdam: North Holland Publishers.

Bower, G. H., & Clark, M. C. (1969). Narrative stories as mediators for serial learning. *Psychonomic Science, 14,* 181–182.

Bower, G. H., Clark, M. C., Lesgold, A. M., & Winzenz, D. (1969). Hierarchical retrieval schemes in recall of categorized word lists. *Journal of Verbal Learning and Verbal Behavior, 8,* 323–343.

Bower, G. H., & Morrow, D. G. (1990). Mental models in narrative comprehension. *Science, 247,* 44–48.

Bower, J. E., Kemeny, M. E., Taylor, S. E., & Fahey, J. L. (1998). Cognitive processing, discovery of meaning, CD4 decline, and AIDS-related mortality among bereaved HIV-seropositive men. *Journal of Consulting and Clinical Psychology, 66,* 979–986.

Bowers, K. S. (1984). Hypnosis. In N. Endler & J. M. Hunt (Eds.), *Personality and behavioral disorders* (2nd ed.). New York: Wiley.

Bowers, K. S. (1987, July). Personal communication.

Bowers, K. S. (1990). Unconscious influences and hypnosis. In J. E. Singer (Ed.), *Repression and dissociation: Implications for personality theory, psychopathology, and health.* Chicago: University of Chicago Press.

Bowers, K. S., & LeBaron, S. (1986). Hypnosis and hypnotizability: Implications for clinical intervention. *Hospital and Community Psychiatry, 37*, 457–467.

Bowers, T. G., & Clum, G. A. (1988). Relative contribution of specific and nonspecific treatment effects: Meta-analysis of placebo-controlled behavior therapy research. *Psychological Bulletin, 103*, 315–323.

Bowlby, J. (1973). *Separation: Anxiety and anger.* New York: Basic Books.

Bowlby, J. (1979). *The making and breaking of affectional bonds.* London: Tavistock.

Bowne, D. W., Russell, M. L., Morgan, M. A., Optenberg, S., & Clarke, A. (1984). Reduced disability and health care costs in an industrial fitness program. *Journal of Occupational Medicine, 26*, 809–816.

Boyatzis, C. J., Matillo, G. M., & Nesbitt, K. M. (1995). Effects of the "Mighty Morphin Power Rangers" on children's aggression with peers. *Child Study Journal, 25*, 45–55.

Boynton, R. M. (1979). *Human color vision.* New York: Holt, Rinehart & Winston.

Braden, J. P. (1994). *Deafness, deprivation, and IQ.* New York: Plenum.

Bradley, D. R., Dumais, S. T., & Petry, H. M. (1976). Reply to Cavonius. *Nature, 261*, 78.

Bradshaw, J. (1990). *Homecoming: Reclaiming and championing your inner child.* New York: Bantam Books.

Brady, N. (1997). Intelligence, schooling, and society. *American Psychologist, 52*, 1046–1050.

Brainerd, C. J. (1996). Piaget: A centennial celebration. *Psychological Science, 7*, 191–195.

Brainerd, C. J., & Poole, D. A. (1997). Long-term survival of children's memories: A review. *Learning and Individual Differences, 9*, 125–151.

Brainerd, C. J., & Reyna, V. F. (1998). When things that were never experienced are easier to "remember" than things that were. *Psychological Science, 9*, 484–489.

Brainerd, C. J., Reyna, V. F., & Brandse, E. (1995). Are children's false memories more persistent than their true memories? *Psychological Science, 6*, 359–364.

Brandon, S., Boakes, J., Glaser, & Green, R. (1998). Recovered memories of childhood sexual abuse: Implications for clinical practice. *British Journal of Psychiatry, 172*, 294–307.

Brannon, E. M., & Terrace, H. S. (1998). Ordering of the numerosities 1 to 9 by monkeys. *Science, 282*, 746–749.

Brannon, L. A., & Brock, T. C. (1994). Perilous underestimation of sex partners' sexual histories in calculating personal AIDS risk. Paper presented to the American Psychological Society convention.

Bransford, J. D., & Johnson, M. K. (1972). Contextual prerequisites for understanding: Some investigations of comprehension and recall. *Journal of Verbal Learning and Verbal Behavior, 11*, 717–726.

Braskamp, L. A. (1987). Spectrum: Utility for educational selection and organizational development. Paper presented at the American Psychological Association convention.

Braun, S. (1996). New experiments underscore warnings on maternal drinking. *Science, 273*, 738–739.

Bray, D. W., & Byham, W. C. (1991, Winter). Assessment centers and their derivatives. *Journal of Continuing Higher Education,* pp. 8–11.)

Bray, D. W., Byham, W., interviewed by Mayes, B. T. (1997). Insights into the history and future of assessment centers: An interview with Dr. Douglas W. Bray and Dr. William Byham. *Journal of Social Behavior and Personality, 12*, 3–12.

Bray, G. A. (1969). Effect of caloric restriction on energy expenditure in obese patients. *Lancet, 2*, 397–398.

Brayne, C., Spiegelhalter, D. J., Dufouil, C., Chi, L.-Y., Dening, T. R., Paykel, E. S., O'Connor, D. W., Ahmed, A., McGee, M. A., & Huppert, F. A. (1999). Estimating the true extent of cognitive decline in the old old. *Journal of the American Geriatrics Society, 47*, 1283–1288.

Breedlove, S. M. (1997). Sex on the brain. *Nature, 389*, 801.

Brehm, S., & Brehm, J. W. (1981). *Psychological reactance: A theory of freedom and control.* New York: Academic Press.

Breland, K., & Breland, M. (1961). The misbehavior of organisms. *American Psychologist, 16*, 661–664.

Brennan, P. A., Grekin, E. R., & Mednick, S. A. (1999). Maternal smoking during pregnancy and adult male criminal outcomes. *Archives of General Psychiatry, 56*, 215–219.

Brennan, P. A., & Mednick, S. A. (1993). Genetic perspectives on crime. *Acta Psychiatrica Scandinavia, Suppl. 370*, 19–26.

Brenner, M. (1973). The next-in-line effect. *Journal of Verbal Learning and Verbal Behavior, 12*, 320–323.

Breslau, N., & Klein, D. F. (1999). Smoking and panic attacks: An epidemiologic investigation. *Archives of General Psychiatry, 56*, 1141–1147.

Bretz, R. D. (1989). College grade point average as a predictor of adult success: A meta-analytic review and some additional evidence. *Public Personnel Management, 18*, 11–22.

Brewer, C. L. (1990). Personal correspondence.

Brewer, C. L. (1996). Personal communication.

Brewer, W. F. (1977). Memory for the pragmatic implications of sentences. *Memory & Cognition, 5*, 673–678.

Brewin, C. R., Andrews, B., Rose, S., & Kirk, M. (1999). Acute stress disorder and posttraumatic stress disorder in victims of violent crime. *American Journal of Psychiatry, 156*, 360–366.

Brickman, P., Coates, D., & Janoff-Bulman, R. J. (1978). Lottery winners and accident victims: Is happiness relative? *Journal of Personality and Social Psychology, 36*, 917–927.

Bril, B. (1986). Motor development and cultural attitudes. In H. T. A. Whiting & M. G. Wade (Eds.), *Themes in motor development.* Dordrecht, Netherlands: Martinus Nijhoff.

Brinson, S. L. (1992). The use and opposition of rape myths in prime-time television dramas. *Sex Roles, 27*, 359–375.

Briscoe, D. (1997, February 16). Women lawmakers still not in charge. Associated Press (in *Grand Rapids Press*, p. A23).

Brislin, R. (1993). *Understanding culture's influence on behavior.* Fort Worth, TX: Harcourt Brace.

British Psychological Society. (1993). Ethical principles for conducting research with human participants. *The Psychologist: Bulletin of the British Psychological Society, 6*, 33–36.

Broadbent, D. E. (1978). The current state of noise research: Reply to Poulton. *Psychological Bulletin, 85*, 1052–1067.

Brody, J. E. (1998, August 11). Study finds more fraternal twins in lands of plenty. *New York Times* (www.nytimes.com).

Brody, J. E. (1999, September 21). Increasingly, America's sweet tooth is tied to sour health. *New York Times* (www.nytimes.com).

Brody, J. E. (1999, November 30). Yesterday's precocious puberty is norm today. *New York Times* (www.nytimes.com).

Brody, N. (1992). *Intelligence*, 2nd ed. San Diego: Academic Press.

Brodzinsky, D. M., & Schechter, M. D. (Eds.). (1990). *The psychology of adoption*. New York: Oxford University Press.

Broman, S. H. (1989). Infant physical status and later cognitive development. In M. G. Bornstein & N. A. Krasnegor (Eds.), *Stability and continuity in mental development: Behavioral and biological perspectives*. Hillsdale, NJ: Erlbaum.

Bronner, E. (1998, February 25). U.S. high school seniors among worst in math and science. *New York Times* (www.nytimes.com).

Brooke, J. (2000, January 20). Canada proposes scaring smokers with pictures on the pack. *New York Times* (www.nytimes.com)

Brooks-Gunn, J. (1989). Adolescents as daughters and as mothers: A developmental perspective. In I. Sigel & G. Brody (Eds.), *Family research*. Hillsdale, NJ: Erlbaum.

Brooks-Gunn, J., & Furstenberg, F. F., Jr. (1989). Adolescent sexual behavior. *American Psychologist, 44,* 249–257.

Brothers, J. (1990, February 18). Why wives have affairs. *Parade,* pp. 4–7.

Brown, E. L., & Deffenbacher, K. (1979). *Perception and the senses.* New York: Oxford University Press.

Brown, J. D. (1991). Accuracy and bias in self-knowledge. In C. R. Snyder & D. F. Forsyth (Eds.), *Handbook of social and clinical psychology: The health perspective.* New York: Pergamon Press.

Brown, J. D. (1991). Staying fit and staying well: Physical fitness as a moderator of life stress. *Journal of Personality and Social Psychology, 60,* 555–561.

Brown, J. L., & Pollitt, E. (1996, February). Malnutrition, poverty and intellectual development. *Scientific American,* pp. 38–43.

Brown, L. R., Kane, H., & Ayres, E. (1993). *Vital signs 1993: The trends that are shaping our future.* New York: Norton.

Brown, P. J. (1993). Cultural perspectives on the etiology and treatment of obesity. In A. J. Stunkard & T. A. Wadden (Eds.), *Obesity: Theory and therapy,* 2nd ed. New York: Raven Press.

Brown, R. (1965). *Social psychology.* New York: Free Press.

Brown, R. (1973). *A first language: The early stages.* Cambridge, MA: Harvard University Press.

Brown, R. (1986). Linguistic relativity. In S. H. Hulse & B. F. Green, Jr. (Eds.), *One hundred years of psychological research in America.* Baltimore: Johns Hopkins University Press.

Brown, R., & Kulik, J. (1982). Flashbulb memories. In U. Neisser (Ed.), *Memory observed.* San Francisco: Freeman.

Brown, S. W., Garry, M., Loftus, E., Silver, B., DuBois, K., & DuBreuil, S. (1996). People's beliefs about memory: Why don't we have better memories? Paper presented at the American Psychological Society convention.

Brownell, K. D. (1991). Dieting and the search for the perfect body: Where physiology and culture collide. *Behavior Therapy, 22,* 1–12.

Brownell, K. D. (1997, March). We must be more militant about food. *APA Monitor,* p. 48.

Brownell, K. D., & Jeffery, R. W. (1987). Improving long-term weight loss: Pushing the limits of treatment. *Behavior Therapy, 18,* 353–374.

Brownell, K. D., & Wadden, T. A. (1992). Etiology and treatment of obesity: Understanding a serious, prevalent, and refractory disorder. *Journal of Consulting and Clinical Psychology, 60,* 505–517.

Browning, C. (1992). *Ordinary men: Reserve police battalion 101 and the final solution in Poland.* New York: HarperCollins.

Brownmiller, S. (1975). *Against our will: Men, women, and rape.* New York: Simon & Schuster.

Bruck, M., & Ceci, S. J. (1997). The suggestibility of young children. *Current Directions in Psychological Science, 6,* 75–79.

Bruck, M., & Ceci, S. J. (1999). The suggestibility of children's memory. *Annual Review of Psychology, 50,* 419–439.

Bruck, M., Ceci, S. J., & Hembrooke, H. (1998, February). Reliability and credibility of young children's reports: From research to policy and practice. *American Psychologist, 53*(2), 136–151.

Bruer, J. T. (1999). *The myth of the first three years: A new understanding of early brain development and lifelong learning.* New York: Free Press.

Buchel, C., Morris, J., Dolan, R. J., & Friston, K. J. (1998). Brain systems mediating aversive conditioning: An event-related fMRI study. *Neuron, 20,* 947–957.

Buehler, R., Griffin, D., & Ross, M. (1994). Exploring the "planning fallacy": Why people underestimate their task completion times. *Journal of Personality and Social Psychology, 67,* 366–381.

Bugelski, B. R., Kidd, E., & Segmen, J. (1968). Image as a mediator in one-trial paired-associate learning. *Journal of Experimental Psychology, 76,* 69–73.

Bugental, D. B. (1986). Unmasking the "polite smile": Situational and personal determinants of managed affect in adult-child interaction. *Personality and Social Psychology Bulletin, 12,* 7–16.

Buka, S. L., Goldstein, J. M., Seidman, L. J., Zornberg, G., Donatelli, J-A. A., Denny, L. R., & Tsuang, M. T. (1999). Prenatal complications, genetic vulnerability, and schizophrenia: The New England longitudinal studies of schizophrenia. *Psychiatric Annals, 29,* 151–156.

Bullard, T. E. (1987). *UFO abductions: The measure of a mystery: Vol. 2. Catalogue of cases.* Mount Ranier, MD: Fund for UFO Research. Cited by L. S. Newman & R. F. Baumeister (1996). Toward an explanation of the UFO abduction phenomenon: Hypnotic, elaboration, extraterrestrial sadomasochism, and spurious memories. *Psychological Inquiry, 7,* 99–126.

Bullough, V. (1990). The Kinsey scale in historical perspective. In D. P. McWhirter, S. A. Sanders, & J. M. Reinisch (Eds.), *Homosexuality/heterosexuality: Concepts of sexual orientation.* New York: Oxford University Press.

Buquet, R. (1988). Le reve et les deficients visuels (Dreams and the visually impaired). *Psychanalyse-a-l'Universite, 13,* 319–327.

Bureau of the Census. (1996). *Statistical abstract of the United States 1996.* Washington, DC: U.S. Government Printing Office.

Bureau of the Census. (1998). *Statistical abstract of the United States 1998.* Washington, DC: U.S. Government Printing Office.

Bureau of the Census. (1999). *Statistical abstract of the United States 1999.* Washington, DC: U.S. Government Printing Office.

Burger, J. M. (1987). Increased performance with increased personal control: A self-presentation interpretation. *Journal of Experimental Social Psychology, 23,* 350–360.

Burger, J. M., & Burns, L. (1988). The illusion of unique invulnerability and the use of effective contraception. *Personality and Social Psychology Bulletin, 14,* 264–270.

Burgess, C. A., Kirsch, I., Shane, H., Niederauer, K. L., Graham, S. M., & Bacon, A. (1998). Facilitated communication as an ideomotor response. *Psychological Science, 9,* 71–74.

Buri, J. R., Louiselle, P. A., Misukanis, T. M., & Mueller, R. A. (1988). Effects of parental authoritarianism and authoritativeness on self-esteem. *Personality and Social Psychology Bulletin, 14,* 271–282.

Burish, T. G., & Carey, M. P. (1986). Conditioned aversive responses in cancer chemotherapy patients: Theoretical and developmental analysis. *Journal of Counseling and Clinical Psychology, 54,* 593–600.

Busch, C. M., Zonderman, A. B., & Costa, P. T. (1994). Menopausal transition and psychological distress in a nationally representative sample: Is menopause associated with psychological distress? *Journal of Aging and Health, 6,* 209–228.

Bushman, B. J. (1993). Human aggression while under the influence of alcohol and other drugs: An integrative research review. *Current Directions in Psychological Science, 2,* 148–152.

Bushman, B. J., & Baumeister, R. F. (1998). Threatened egotism, narcissism, self-esteem, and direct and displaced aggression: Does self-love or self-hate lead to violence? *Journal of Personality and Social Psychology, 75,* 219–229.

Bushman, B. J., Baumeister, R. F., & Stack, A. D. (1999). Catharsis, aggression, and persuasive influence: Self-fulfilling or self-defeating prophecies? *Journal of Personality and Social Psychology, 76,* 367–376.

Busnel, M. C., Granier-Deferre, C., & Lecanuet, J. P. (1992, October). Fetal audition. *New York Academy of Sciences, 662,* 118–134.

Buss, A. H. (1989). Personality as traits. *American Psychologist, 44,* 1378–1388.

Buss, D. M. (1991). Evolutionary personality psychology. *Annual Review of Psychology, 42,* 459–491.

Buss, D. M. (1995). Evolutionary psychology: A new paradigm for psychological science. *Psychological Inquiry, 6,* 1–30.

Butcher, J. N. (1990). *The MMPI-2 in psychological treatment.* New York: Oxford University Press.

Butler, A. C., Hokanson, J. E., & Flynn, H. A. (1994). A comparison of self-esteem lability and low trait self-esteem as vulnerability factors for depression. *Journal of Personality and Social Psychology, 66,* 166–177.

Butler, J., & Rovee-Collier, C. (1989). Contextual gating of memory retrieval. *Developmental Psychobiology, 22,* 533–552.

Butler, R. A. (1954, February). Curiosity in monkeys. *Scientific American,* pp. 70–75.

Butterfield, F. (1999, July 12). Experts say study confirms prison's new role as mental hospital. *New York Times* (www.nytimes.com).

Butterworth, G. (1992). Origins of self-perception in infancy. *Psychological Inquiry, 3,* 103–111.

Byne, W., & Parsons, B. (1993). Human sexual orientation: The biologic theories reappraised. *Archives of General Psychiatry, 50,* 228–239.

Byrne, D. (1971). *The attraction paradigm.* New York: Academic Press.

Byrne, D. (1982). Predicting human sexual behavior. In A. G. Kraut (Ed.), *The G. Stanley Hall Lecture Series* (Vol. 2). Washington, DC: American Psychological Association.

Byrne, R. W. (1991, May/June). Brute intellect. *The Sciences,* pp. 42–47.

Cacioppo, J. T., Berntson, G. G., Klein, D. J., & Poehlmann, K. M. (1997). The psychophysiology of emotion across the lifespan. *Annual Review of Gerontology and Geriatrics, 17,* 27.

Cacioppo, J. T., Priester, J. R., & Berntson, G. G. (1993). Rudimentary determinants of attitudes. II: Arm flexion and extension have differential effects on attitudes. *Journal of Personality and Social Psychology, 65,* 5–17.

Cahill, L. (1994). (Beta)-adrenergic activation and memory for emotional events. *Nature, 371,* 702–704.

Cahill, S. P., Carrigan, M. H., & Frueh, B. C. (1999). Does EMDR work? And if so, why? A critical review of controlled outcome and dismantling research. *Journal of Anxiety Disorders, 13,* 5–33.

Calle, E. E., Thun, M. J., Petrelli, J. M., Rodriguez, C., & Health, C. W., Jr. (1999). Body-mass index and mortality in a prospective cohort of U.S. adults. *New England Journal of Medicine, 341,* 1097–1105.

Cameron, P., & Biber, H. (1973). Sexual thought throughout the life-span. *Gerontologist, 13,* 144–147.

Campbell, D. T. (1975). On the conflicts between biological and social evolution and between psychology and moral tradition. *American Psychologist, 30,* 1103–1126.

Campbell, D. T., & Specht, J. C. (1985). Altruism: Biology, culture, and religion. *Journal of Social and Clinical Psychology, 3*(1), 33–42.

Campbell, S. (1986). *The Loch Ness Monster: The evidence.* Willingborough, Northamptonshire, UK: Acquarian Press.

Campbell, S. S., & Murphy, P. J. (1998). Extraocular circadian phototransduction in humans. *Science, 279,* 396–399.

Camper, J. (1990, February 7). Drop pompom squad, U. of I. rape study says. *Chicago Tribune,* p. 1.

Campos, J. J., Bertenthal, B. I., & Kermoian, R. (1992). Early experience and emotional development: The emergence of wariness and heights. *Psychological Science, 3,* 61–64.

Cannon, T. D., & Marco, E. (1994). Structural brain abnormalities as indicators of vulnerability to schizophrenia. *Schizophrenia Bulletin, 20,* 89–102.

Cannon, W. B. (1929). *Bodily changes in pain, hunger, fear, and rage.* New York: Branford.

Cannon, W. B., & Washburn, A. (1912). An explanation of hunger. *American Journal of Physiology, 29,* 441–454.

Cantor, D. W. (1995, December). Summary of *Report of the Task Force on the Changing Gender Composition of Psychology* (Washington, DC: American Psychological Association Women's Programs Office), *APA Monitor,* p. 15.

Cantor, N., & Kihlstrom, J. F. (1987). *Personality and social intelligence.* Englewood Cliffs, NJ: Prentice-Hall.

Cantor, N., & Norem, J. K. (1989). Defensive pessimism and stress and coping. *Social Cognition, 7,* 92–112.

Cantril, H., & Bumstead, C. H. (1960). *Reflections on the human venture.* New York: New York University Press.

Caplan, N., Choy, M. H., & Whitmore, J. K. (1992, February). Indochinese refugee families and academic achievement. *Scientific American*, pp. 36–42.

Carducci, B. J., Cosby, P. C., & Ward, D. D. (1978). Sexual arousal and interpersonal evaluations. *Journal of Experimental Social Psychology, 14*, 449–457.

Carey, G. (1990). Genes, fears, phobias, and phobic disorders. *Journal of Counseling and Development, 68*, 628–632.

Carli, L. L., & Leonard, J. B. (1989). The effect of hindsight on victim derogation. *Journal of Social and Clinical Psychology, 8*, 331–343.

Carlson, M. (1995, August 29). Quoted in S. Blakeslee, In brain's early growth, timetable may be crucial. *New York Times*, pp. C1, C3.

Carlson, M., Charlin, V., & Miller, N. (1988). Positive mood and helping behavior: A test of six hypotheses. *Journal of Personality and Social Psychology, 55*, 211–229.

Carlson, R. (1984). What's social about social psychology? Where's the person in personality research? *Journal of Personality and Social Psychology, 47*, 1304–1309.

Carlson, S. (1985). A double-blind test of astrology. *Nature, 318*, 419–425.

Carnegie Council on Adolescent Development. (1989, June). *Turning points: Preparing American youth for the 21st century* (The report of the Task Force on Education of Young Adolescents). New York: Carnegie Corporation.

Carr, T. H., Kontowicz, A., & Dagenbach, D. (1987). Subthreshold priming and the cognitive unconscious. Invited paper presented to the Midwestern Psychological Association convention.

Carroll, D., Davey Smith, G., & Bennett, P. (1994, March). Health and socio-economic status. *The Psychologist*, pp. 122–125.

Carroll, J. M., & Russell, J. A. (1996). Do facial expressions signal specific emotions? Judging emotion from the face in context. *Journal of Personality and Social Psychology, 70*, 205–218.

Carskadon, T. G., & McCarley, N. G. (1997). Three hundred studies in psychological type: A grand synopsis. *Journal of Psychological Type, 42*, 6–58.

Carstensen, L. L., & Charles, S. T. (1999). Emotion in the second half of life. *Current Directions in Psychology, 7*, 144–149.

Carter, R. (1998). *Mapping the mind.* Berkeley: University of California Press.

Cartwright, R. D. (1978). *A primer on sleep and dreaming.* Reading, MA: Addison-Wesley.

Caryl, P. G. (1994). Early event-related potentials correlate with inspection time and intelligence. *Intelligence, 18*, 15–46.

Case, R. B., Moss, A. J., Case, N., McDermott, M., & Eberly, S. (1992). Living alone after myocardial infarction: Impact on prognosis. *Journal of the American Medical Association, 267*, 515–519.

Cash, T. F., & Deagle, E. A. III, (1997). The nature and extent of body-image disturbances in anorexia nervosa and bulimia nervosa: A meta-analysis. *International Journal of Eating Disorders, 22*, 107–125.

Cash, T. F., & Henry, P. E. (1995). Women's body images: The results of a national survey in the U.S.A. *Sex Roles, 33*, 19–28.

Cash, T., & Janda, L. H. (1984, December). The eye of the beholder. *Psychology Today*, pp. 46–52.

Caspi, A., & Moffitt, T. E. (1991). Individual differences are accentuated during periods of social change: The sample case of girls at puberty. *Journal of Personality and Social Psychology, 61*, 157–168.

Caspi, A., Moffitt, T. E., Newman, D. L., & Silva, P. A. (1996). Behavioral observations at age 3 years predict adult psychiatric disorders: Longitudinal evidence from a birth cohort. *Archives of General Psychiatry, 53*, 1033–1039.

Cassidy, J., & Shaver, P. R. (1999). *Handbook of attachment.* New York: Guilford.

Castillo, R. J. (1997). *Culture and mental illness: A client-centered approach.* Pacific Grove, CA: Brooks/Cole.

Castonguay, L. G., & Goldfried, M. R. (1994). Psychotherapy integration: An idea whose time has come. *Applied & Preventive Psychology, 3*, 159–172.

Cattell, R. B. (1963). Theory of fluid and crystallized intelligence: A critical experiment. *Journal of Educational Psychology, 54*, 1–22.

Cavalli-Sforza, L., Menozzi, P., & Piazza, A. (1994). *The history and geography of human genes.* Princeton, NJ: Princeton University Press.

Ceci, S. J. (1993). Cognitive and social factors in children's testimony. Master Lecture, American Psychological Association convention.

Ceci, S. J., & Bruck, M. (1993). Child witnesses: Translating research into policy. *Social Policy Report* (Society for Research in Child Development), *7*(3), 1–30.

Ceci, S. J., & Bruck, M. (1995). *Jeopardy in the courtroom: A scientific analysis of children's testimony.* Washington, DC: American Psychological Association.

Ceci, S. J., Huffman, M. L. C., Smith, E., & Loftus, E. F. (1994). Repeatedly thinking about a non-event: Source misattributions among preschoolers. *Consciousness and Cognition, 3*, 388–407.

Ceci, S. J., & Liker, J. K. (1986). A day at the races: A study of IQ, expertise, and cognitive complexity. *Journal of Experimental Psychology: General, 115*, 255–266.

Ceci, S. J., & Williams, W. M. (1997). Schooling, intelligence, and income. *American Psychologist, 52*, 1051–1058.

Centers for Disease Control. (1991). Body-weight perceptions and selected weight-management goals and practices of high school students—United States, 1990. *Morbidity and Mortality Weekly Report, 40*, 741, 747–750.

Centers for Disease Control. (1992, September 16). Serious mental illness and disability in the adult household population: United States, 1989. *Advance Data No. 218 from Vital and Health Statistics*, National Center for Health Statistics.

Centers for Disease Control Vietnam Experience Study. (1988). Health status of Vietnam veterans. *Journal of the American Medical Association, 259*, 2701–2709.

Centerwall, B. S. (1989). Exposure to television as a risk factor for violence. *American Journal of Epidemiology, 129*, 643–652.

Cerella, J. (1985). Information processing rates in the elderly. *Psychological Bulletin, 98*, 67–83.

Chalmers, R. (1995, September 19). Sizing sizzle of mutuals. *Edmonton Journal*, p. E1.

Chambless, D. L., Baker, M. J., Baucom, D. H., Beutler, L. E., Calhoun, K. S., Crits-Christoph, P., Daiuto, A., DeRubeis, R., Detweiler, J., Haaga, D. A. F., Johnson, S. B., McCurry, S., Mueser, K. T., Pope, K. S., Sanderson, W. C., Shoham, V., Stickle, T., Williams, D. A., & Woody, S. R. (1997). Update on empirically validated therapies, II. *The Clinical Psychologist, 51*(1), 3–16.

Chamove, A. S. (1980). Nongenetic induction of acquired levels of aggression. *Journal of Abnormal Psychology, 89*, 469–488.

Chance News. (1997, 25 November). More on the frequency of letters in texts. Dart.Chance@Dartmouth.edu

Chance News. (1997, 30 December). Gender and mortality statistics. Dart.Chance@Dartmouth.edu

Chance News. (1999, July 15). National lottery and death rates. From *Daily Express*, 13 August 1998.

Chang, E. C. (1996). Cultural differences in optimism, pessimism, and coping: Preditors of subsequent adjustment in Asian American and Caucasian American college students. *Journal of Counseling Psychology, 43,* 113–123.

Chartrand, T. L., & Bargh, J. A. (1999). The chameleon effect: The perception-behavior link and social interaction. *Journal of Personality and Social Psychology, 76,* 893–910.

Chase, M. H., & Morales, F. R. (1983). Subthreshold excitatory activity and motor neuron discharge during REM periods of active sleep. *Science, 221,* 1195–1198.

Chase, W. G., & Simon, H. A. (1973). Perception in chess. *Cognitive Psychology, 4,* 55–81.

Chassin, L., Presson, C. C., Sherman, S. J., & McGrew, J. (1987). The changing smoking environment for middle and high school students: 1980–1983. *Journal of Behavioral Medicine, 10,* 581–593.

Chaves, J. F. (1989). Hypnotic control of clinical pain. In N. P. Spanos & J. F. Chaves (Eds.), *Hypnosis: The cognitive-behavioral perspective.* Buffalo, NY: Prometheus Books.

Cheek, J. M., & Melchior, L. A. (1990). Shyness, self-esteem, and self-consciousness. In H. Leitenberg (Ed.), *Handbook of social and evaluation anxiety.* New York: Plenum.

Cheit, R. E. (1998). Consider this, skeptics of recovered memory. *Ethics & Behavior, 8,* 141–160.

Cherfas, J. (1990). Two bomb attacks on scientists in the U.K. *Science, 248,* 1485.

Chess, S., & Thomas, A. (1987). *Know your child: An authoritative guide for today's parents.* New York: Basic Books.

Chiles, J. A., Lambert, M. J., & Hatch, A. L. (1999). The impact of psychological interventions on medical cost offset: A meta-analytic review. *Clinical Psychology: Science and Practice, 6,* 204–220.

Chisholm, K. (in press). A three year follow-up of attachment and indiscriminate friendliness in children adopted from Romanian orphanages. *Child Development.*

Choi, P. (1999). Why I study the menstrual cycle. *The Psychologist, 12,* 388–399.

Chomsky, N. (1959). Review of B. F. Skinner's *Verbal behavior. Language, 35,* 26–58.

Chomsky, N. (1972). *Language and mind.* New York: Harcourt Brace Jovanovich.

Chomsky, N. (1987). Language in a psychological setting. Sophia Linguistic Working Papers in Linguistics, No. 22, Sophia University, Tokyo.

Chorney, M. J., Chorney, K., Seese, N., Owen, M. J., Daniels, J., McGuffin, P., Thompson, L. A., Detterman, D. K., Benbow, C., Lubinski, D., Eley, T., & Plomin, R. (1998). A quantitative trait locus associated with cognitive ability in children. *Psychological Science, 9,* 159–166.

Chorpita, B. F., & Barlow, D. H. (1998). The development of anxiety: The role of control in the early environment. *Psychological Bulletin, 124,* 3–21.

Christensen, A., & Jacobson, N. S. (1994). Who (or what) can do psychotherapy: The status and challenge of nonprofessional therapies. *Psychological Science, 5,* 8–14.

Christensen, L. (1993). Effects of eating behavior on mood: A review of the literature. *International Journal of Eating Disorders, 14,* 171–183.

Christensen, L. (1996). *Diet-behavior relationships: Focus on depression.* Washington, DC: American Psychological Association.

Christianson, S. A. (1992). Emotional stress and eyewitness memory: A critical review. *Psychological Bulletin, 112,* 284–309.

Christophersen, E. R., & Edwards, K. J. (1992). Treatment of elimination disorders: State of the art 1991. *Applied & Preventive Psychology, 1,* 15–22.

Chugani, H. T., & Phelps, M. E. (1986). Maturational changes in cerebral function in infants determined by [18]FDG Positron Emission Tomography. *Science, 231,* 840–843.

Chwalisz, K., Diener, E., & Gallagher, D. (1988). Autonomic arousal feedback and emotional experience: Evidence from the spinal cord injured. *Journal of Personality and Social Psychology, 54,* 820–828.

Cialdini, R. B. (1993). *Influence: Science and practice* (3rd ed.). New York: HarperCollins.

Cialdini, R. B., & Carpenter, K. (1981). The availability heuristic: Does imagining make it so? In P. H. Reingen & A. G. Woodside (Eds.), *Buyer-seller interactions: Empirical issues and normative issues.* Chicago: American Marketing Association.

Cialdini, R. B., Eisenberg, N., Green, B. L., Rhoads, K., & Bator, R. (1998). Undermining the undermining effect of reward on sustained interest. *Journal of Applied Social Psychology, 28,* 249–263.

Cialdini, R. B., & Richardson, K. D. (1980). Two indirect tactics of image management: Basking and blasting. *Journal of Personality and Social Psychology, 39,* 406–415.

Citrome, L., & Volavka, J. (1999). Schizophrenia: Violence and comorbidity. *Current Opinion in Psychiatry, 12,* 47–51.

Clark, R., Anderson, N. B., Clark, V. R., & Williams, D. R. (1999). Racism as a stressor for African Americans: A biopsychosocial model. *American Psychologist, 54,* 805–816.

Clark, R. D., III, & Hatfield, E. (1989). Gender differences in willingness to engage in casual sex. *Journal of Psychology and Human Sexuality, 2,* 39–55.

Clarke, A., & Clarke, A. (1998, September). Early experience and the life path. *Psychologist, 11*(9), 433–436.

Clarke-Stewart, A., Gruber, C. P., & Fitzgerald, L. M. (1994). *Children at home and in day care.* Hillsdale, NJ: Erlbaum.

Coats, E. J., & Feldman, R. S. (1996). Gender differences in nonverbal correlates of social status. *Personality and Social Psychology Bulletin, 22,* 1014–1022.

Coe, W. C. (1989a). Posthypnotic amnesia: Theory and research. In N. P. Spanos & J. F. Chaves (Eds.), *Hypnosis: The cognitive-behavioral perspective.* Buffalo, NY: Prometheus Books.

Coe, W. C. (1989b). Hypnosis: The role of sociopolitical factors in a paradigm clash. In N. P. Spanos & J. F. Chaves (Eds.), *Hypnosis: The cognitive-behavioral perspective.* Buffalo, NY: Prometheus Books.

Coffey, C. E. (Ed.). (1993). *Clinical science of electroconvulsive therapy.* Washington, DC: American Psychiatric Press.

Coffey, C. E., Lucke, J. F., Saxton, J. A., Ratcliff, G., Unitas, L. J., Billig, B., & Bryan, R. N. (1998). Sex differences in brain aging: A quantitative magnetic resonance imagine study. *Archives of Neurology, 55,* 169–179.

Coffey, C. E., Wilkinson, W. E., Weiner, R. D., Parashos, I. A., Djang, W. T., Webb, M. C., Figiel, G. S., & Spritzer, C. E. (1993). Quantitative cerebral anatomy in depression: A controlled magnetic resonance imaging study. *Archives of General Psychiatry, 50,* 7–16.

Cogan, J. C., Bhalla, S. K., Sefa-Dedeh, A., & Rothblum, E. D. (1996). A comparison study of United States and African students on perceptions of obesity and thinness. *Journal of Cross-Cultural Psychology, 27,* 98–113.

Cogan, J. C., & Ernsberger, P. (1999). Dieting, weight, and health: Reconceptualizing research and policy. *Journal of Social Issues, 55,* 187–205.

Cohen, D. (1995, June 17). Now we are one, or two, or three. *New Scientist,* pp. 14–15.

Cohen, G., Conway, M. A., & Maylor, E. A. (1994, September). Flashbulb memories in older adults. *Psychology & Aging, 9*(3), 454–463.

Cohen, S. (1988). Psychosocial models of the role of social support in the etiology of physical disease. *Health Psychology, 7,* 269–297.

Cohen, S., Doyle, W. J., & Skoner, D. P. (1999). Psychological stress, cytokine production, and severity of upper respiratory illness. *Psychosomatic Medicine, 61,* 175–180.

Cohen, S., Doyle, W. J., Skoner, D. P., Fireman, P., Gwaltney, J. M., Jr., & Newson, J. T. (1995). State and trait negative affect as predictors of objective and subjective symptoms of respiratory viral infections. *Journal of Personality and Social Psychology, 68,* 159–169.

Cohen, S., Doyle, W. J., Skoner, D. P., Rabin, B. S., & Gwaltney, J. M., Jr. (1997). Social ties and susceptibility to the common cold. *Journal of the American Medical Association, 277,* 1940–1944.

Cohen, S., Frank, E., Doyle, W. J., Skoner, D. P., Rabin, B. S., & Gwaltney, J. M., Jr. (1998). Types of stressors that increase susceptibility to the common cold in healthy adults. *Health Psychology, 17,* 214–223.

Cohen, S., Kaplan, J. R., Cunnick, J. E., Manuck, S. B., & Rabin, B. S. (1992). Chronic social stress, affiliation, and cellular immune response in nonhuman primates. *Psychological Science, 3,* 301–304.

Cohen, S., Line, S., Manuck, S. B., Rabin, B. S., Heise, E. R., & Kaplan, J. R. (1997). Chronic social stress, social status, and susceptibility to upper respiratory infections in nonhuman primates. *Psychosomatic Medicine, 59,* 213–221.

Cohen, S., & Rodriguez, M. S. (1995). Pathways linking affective disturbances and physical disorders. *Health Psychology, 14,* 374–380.

Cohen, S., Tyrrell, D. A. J., & Smith, A. P. (1991). Psychological stress and susceptibility to the common cold. *New England Journal of Medicine, 325,* 606–612.

Cohen, S., Tyrrell, D. A. J., & Smith, A. P. (1993). Negative life events, perceived stress, negative affect, and susceptibility to the common cold. *Journal of Personality and Social Psychology, 64,* 131–140.

Coile, D. C., & Miller, N. E. (1984). How radical animal activists try to mislead humane people. *American Psychologist, 39,* 700–701.

Cole, K. C. (1998). *The universe and the teacup: The mathematics of truth and beauty.* New York: Harcourt Brace.

Coleman, J. (1997, June 30). Cigarette industry thriving in Japan. Associated Press (in *Grand Rapids Press,* p. A14).

Coleman, J. C. (1980). *The nature of adolescence.* London: Methuen.

Coleman, P. D., & Flood, D. G. (1986). Dendritic proliferation in the aging brain as a compensatory repair mechanism. In D. F. Swaab, E. Fliers, M. Mirmiram, W. A. Van Gool, & F. Van Haaren (Eds.), *Progress in brain research* (Vol. 20). New York: Elsevier.

Colley, A. (1995, August). Psychology, science and women. *The Psychologist,* pp. 346–352.

Collins, D. W., & Kimura, D. (1997). A large sex difference on a two-dimensional mental rotation task. *Behavioral Neuroscience, 111,* 845–849.

Collins, N. L., & Miller, L. C. (1994). Self-disclosure and liking: A meta-analytic review. *Psychological Bulletin, 116,* 457–475.

Colombo, J. (1982). The critical period concept: Research, methodology, and theoretical issues. *Psychological Bulletin, 91,* 260–275.

Colon, E. A., Callies, A. L., Popkin, M. K., & McGlave, P. B. (1991). Depressed mood and other variables related to bone marrow transplantation survival in acute leukemia. *Psychosomatics, 32,* 420–425.

Commissioner of Official Languages. (1999). *Annual Report 1998.* Minister of Public Works and Government Services Canada, Cat. No. SF1–1998.

Comstock, G. W., & Partridge, K. B. (1972). Church attendance and health. *Journal of Chronic Disease, 25,* 665–672.

Conner, M., & McMillan, B. (1999). Interaction effects in the theory of planned behaviour: Studying cannabis use. *British Journal of Social Psychology, 38,* 195–222.

Consensus Conference. (1985). Electroconvulsive therapy. *Journal of the American Medical Association, 254,* 2103–2108.

Considine, R. V., Sinha, Madhur, K., Heiman, M. L., & Kriauciunas (1996). Serum immunoreactive-leptin concentrations in normal-weight and obese humans. *New England Journal of Medicine, 334,* 292–295.

Consumer Reports. (1995, November). Does therapy help? Pp. 734–739.

Conway, M., & Ross, M. (1984). Getting what you want by revising what you had. *Journal of Personality and Social Psychology, 47,* 738–748.

Cook, E. W., III, Hodes, R. L., & Lang, P. J. (1986). Preparedness and phobia: Effects of stimulus content on human visceral conditioning. *Journal of Abnormal Psychology, 95,* 195–207.

Cook, M., & Mineka, S. (1991). Selective associations in the origins of phobic fears and their implications for behavior therapy. In P. Martin (Ed.), *Handbook of behavior therapy and psychological science: An integrative approach.* New York: Pergamon Press.

Cooper, G. D., Adams, H. B., & Scott, J. C. (1988). Studies in REST: I. Reduced environmental stimulation therapy (REST) and reduced alcohol consumption. *Journal of Substance Abuse Treatment, 5,* 61–68.

Cooper, K. J. (1999, May 1). This time, copycat wave is broader. *Washington Post* (www.washingtonpost.com).

Cooper, W. H. (1983). An achievement motivation nomological network. *Journal of Personality and Social Psychology, 44,* 841–861.

Coopersmith, S. (1967). *The antecedents of self-esteem.* San Francisco: Freeman.

Corballis, M. C. (1989). Laterality and human evolution. *Psychological Review, 96,* 492–505.

Corballis, M. C. (1999, March-April). The gestural origins of language. *American Scientist,* pp. 138–145.

Coren, S. (1993a). Failure to find statistical significance in left-handedness and pathology studies: A forgotten consideration. *Bulletin of the Psychonomic Society, 31,* 443–446.

Coren, S. (1993b). *The left-hander syndrome: The causes and consequences of left-handedness.* New York: Vintage Books.

Coren, S. (1996). *Sleep thieves: An eye-opening exploration into the science and mysteries of sleep.* New York: Free Press.

Corina, D. P. (1998). The processing of sign language: Evidence from aphasia. In B. Stemmer & H. A. Whittaker (Eds.), *Handbook of neurolinguistics.* San Diego: Academic Press.

Corina, D. P., Vaid, J., & Bellugi, U. (1992). The linguistic basis of left hemisphere specialization. *Science, 255,* 1258–1260.

Costa, P. T., Jr., & McCrae, R. R. (1989). Personality continuity and the changes of adult life. In M. Storandt & G. R. VandenBos (Eds.), *The adult years: Continuity and change.* Washington, DC: American Psychological Association.

Costa, P. T., Jr., Zonderman, A. B., McCrae, R. R., Cornoni-Huntley, J., Locke, B. Z., & Barbano, H. E. (1987). Longitudinal analyses of psychological well-being in a national sample: Stability of mean levels. *Journal of Gerontology, 42,* 50–55.

Costanzo, M. (1997). *Just revenge: Costs and consequences of the death penalty.* New York: St. Martin's.

Courneya, K. S., & Carron, A. V. (1992). The home advantage in sports competitions: A literature review. *Journal of Sport and Exercise Psychology, 14,* 13–27.

Courtney, J. G., Longnecker, M. P., Theorell, T., & de Verdier, M. G. (1993). Stressful life events and the risk of colorectal cancer. *Epidemiology, 4,* 407–414.

Cousins, N. (1989). *Head first: The biology of hope.* New York: Dutton.

Covington, M. V., & Omelich, C. L. (1988). I can resist anything but temptation: Adolescent expectations for smoking cigarettes. *Journal of Applied Social Psychology, 18,* 203–227.

Cowan, G., Lee, C., Levy, D., & Snyder, D. (1988). Dominance and inequality in X-rated videocassettes. *Psychology of Women Quarterly, 12,* 299–311.

Cowan, N. (1988). Evolving conceptions of memory storage, selective attention, and their mutual constraints within the human information-processing system. *Psychological Bulletin, 104,* 163–191.

Cowan, N. (1994). Mechanisms of verbal short-term memory. *Current Directions in Psychological Science, 3,* 185–189.

Cowart, B. J. (1981). Development of taste perception in humans: Sensitivity and preference throughout the life span. *Psychological Bulletin, 90,* 43–73.

Craft, L. L., & Landers, D. M. (1998). The effect of exercise on clinical depression and depression resulting from mental illness: A meta-analysis. *Journal of Sport and Exercise Psychology, 20,* 339–357.

Craig, M. E., Kalichman, S. C., & Follingstad, D. R. (1989). Verbal coercive sexual behavior among college students. *Archives of Sexual Behavior, 18,* 421–434.

Craig, O., & Shields, J. (1996, July 14). For pity's sake. *New York Times,* Section 3, pp 1–2.

Craik, F. I. M. (1986). A functional account of age differences in memory. In F. Klix & H. Hagendorf (Eds.), *Human memory and cognitive capabilities.* Amsterdam: Elsevier.

Craik, F. I. M., & Tulving, E. (1975). Depth of processing and the retention of words in episodic memory. *Journal of Experimental Psychology: General, 104,* 268–294.

Craik, F. I. M., & Watkins, M. J. (1973). The role of rehearsal in short-term memory. *Journal of Verbal Learning and Verbal Behavior, 12,* 599–607.

Crain-Thoreson, C., & Dale, P. S. (1992). Do early talkers become early readers? Linguistic precocity, preschool language, and emergent literacy. *Developmental Psychology, 28,* 421–429.

Crandall, C. S. (1988). Social contagion of binge eating. *Journal of Personality and Social Psychology, 55,* 588–598.

Crandall, C. S. (1994). Prejudice against fat people: Ideology and self-interest. *Journal of Personality and Social Psychology, 66,* 882–894.

Crandall, J. E. (1984). Social interest as a moderator of life stress. *Journal of Personality and Social Psychology, 47,* 164–174.

Crawford, M., Chaffin, R., & Fitton, L. (1995). *Learning and Individual Differences, 7,* 341–362.

Crews, F. (1996). The verdict on Freud. *Psychological Science, 7,* 63–68.

Crews, F. (Ed.). (1998). *Unauthorized Freud: Doubters confront a legend.* New York: Viking.

Crocker, J., & Major, B. (1989). Social stigma and self-esteem: The self-protective properties of stigma, *Psychological Review, 89,* 608–630.

Crocker, J., Thompson, L. L., McGraw, K. M., & Ingerman, C. (1987). Downward comparison, prejudice, and evaluation of others: Effects of self-esteem and threat. *Journal of Personality and Social Psychology, 52,* 907–916.

Crocker, J., & Wolfe, C. (1999). Rescuing self-esteem: A contingencies of worth perspective. Unpublished manuscript, University of Michigan.

Crombie, A. C. (1964, May). Early concepts of the senses and the mind. *Scientific American,* pp. 108–116.

Crook, T. H., & West, R. L. (1990). Name recall performance across the adult life-span. *British Journal of Psychology, 81,* 335–340.

Cross-National Collaborative Group. (1992). The changing rate of major depression. *Journal of the American Medical Association, 268,* 3098–3105.

Crossen, C. (1994). *Tainted truth: The manipulation of fact in America.* New York: Simon & Schuster.

Crowell, J. A., & Waters, E. (1994). Bowlby's theory grown up: The role of attachment in adult love relationships. *Psychological Inquiry, 5,* 1–22.

Croyle, R. T., & Ditto, P. H. (1990). Illness cognition and behavior: An experimental approach. *Journal of Behavioral Medicine, 13,* 31–52.

Csikszentmihalyi, M. (1990). *Flow: The psychology of optimal experience.* New York: Harper & Row.

Csikszentmihalyi, M., & Larson, R. (1984). *Being adolescent: Conflict and growth in the teenage years.* New York: Basic Books.

Curtis, R. C., & Miller, K. (1986). Believing another likes or dislikes you: Behaviors making the beliefs come true. *Journal of Personality and Social Psychology, 51,* 284–290.

Curtiss, S. (1977). *Genie: A psycholinguistic study of a modern-day "wild child."* New York: Academic Press.

Cutler, B. L., & Penrod, S. D. (1989). Forensically relevant moderators of the relation between eyewitness identification accuracy and confidence. *Journal of Applied Psychology, 74,* 650–652.

Czeisler, C. A., Allan, J. S., Strogatz, S. H., Ronda, J. M., Sanchez, R., Rios, C. D., Freitag, W. O., Richardson, G. S., & Kronauer, R. E. (1986). Bright light resets the human circadian pacemaker independent of the timing of the sleep-wake cycle. *Science, 233,* 667–671.

Czeisler, C. A., Kronauer, R. E., Allan, J. S., & Duffy, J. F. (1989). Bright light induction of strong (type O) resetting of the human circadian pacemaker. *Science, 244,* 1328–1333.

Dabbs, J. M., Jr. (1992). Testosterone measurements in social and clinical psychology. *Journal of Social and Clinical Psychology, 11,* 302–321.

Dabbs, J. M., Jr., & Morris, R. (1990). Testosterone, social class, and antisocial behavior in a sample of 4,462 men. *Psychological Science, 1,* 209–211.

Dabbs, J. M., Jr., Ruback, R. B., & Besch, N. F. (1987). Male saliva testosterone following conversations with male and female partners. Paper presented at the American Psychological Association convention.

Damasio, A. R. (1994). *Descartes error: Emotion, reason, and the human brain.* New York: Grossett/Putnam & Sons.

Damasio, H., Grabowski, T., Frank, R., Galaburda, A. M., & Damasio, A. R. (1994). The return of Phineas Gage: Clues about the brain from the skull of a famous patient. *Science, 264,* 1102–1105.

Damon, W. (1995). *Greater expectations: Overcoming the culture of indulgence in America's homes and schools.* New York: Free Press.

Damon, W., & Hart, D. (1982). The development of self-understanding from infancy through adolescence. *Child Development, 53,* 841–864.

Damon, W., & Hart, D. (1988). *Self-understanding in childhood and adolescence.* Cambridge: Cambridge University Press.

Darley, J. M., & Latané, B. (1968a). Bystander intervention in emergencies: Diffusion of responsibility. *Journal of Personality and Social Psychology, 8,* 377–383.

Darley, J. M., & Latané, B. (1968b, December). When will people help in a crisis? *Psychology Today,* pp. 54–57, 70–71.

Darley, J. M., Seligman, C., & Becker, L. J. (1979, April). The lesson of twin rivers: Feedback works. *Psychology Today,* pp. 16, 23–24.

Darrach, B., & Norris, J. (1984, August). An American tragedy. *Life,* pp. 58–74.

Daum, I., & Schugens, M. M. (1996). On the cerebellum and classical conditioning. *Psychological Science, 5,* 58–61.

Davey, G. C. L. (1992). Classical conditioning and the acquisition of human fears and phobias: A review and synthesis of the literature. *Advances in Behavior Research and Therapy, 14,* 29–66.

Davey, G. C. L. (1995). Preparedness and phobias: Specific evolved associations or a generalized expectancy bias? *Behavioral and Brain Sciences, 18,* 289–297.

Davidoff, J., Davies, I., & Roberson, D. (1999). Colour categories in a Stone-Age tribe. *Nature, 398,* 203–204.

Davidson, M., Reichenberg, A., Rabinowitz, J., Weiser, M., Kaplan, Z., & Mark, M. (1999). Behavioral and intellectual markers for schizophrenia in apparently healthy male adolescents. *American Journal of Psychiatry, 156,* 1328–1335.

Davidson, N. E. (1996, September). Is hormone replacement therapy a risk? *Scientific American,* p. 101.

Davidson, R. J. (1999). Biological bases of personality. In V. J. Darlega, B. A. Winstead, & W. H. Jones. (Eds.), *Personality: Contemporary theory and research.* Chicago: Nelson-Hall.

Davies, D. R., Matthews, G., & Wong, C. S. K. (1991). Aging and work. *International Review of Industrial and Organizational Psychology, 6,* 149–211.

Davies, M. F. (1997). Positive test strategies and confirmatory retrieval processes in the evaluation of personality feedback. *Journal of Personality and Social Psychology, 73,* 574–583.

Davies, M., Stankov, L., & Roberts, R. D. (1998). Emotional intelligence: In search of an elusive construct. *Journal of Personality and Social Psychology, 75,* 989–1015.

Davies, P. (1992). *The mind of God: The scientific basis for a rational world.* New York: Simon & Schuster.

Davies, P. (1999). *The fifth miracle: The search for the origin and meaning of life.* New York: Simon & Schuster.

Davis, J. O., & Phelps, J. A. (1995). Twins with schizophrenia: Genes or germs? *Schizophrenia Bulletin, 21,* 13–18.

Davis, J. O., Phelps, J. A., & Bracha, H. S. (1995). Prenatal development of monozygotic twins and concordance for schizophrenia. *Schizophrenia Bulletin, 21,* 357–366.

Dawes, R. M. (1980). Social dilemmas. *Annual Review of Psychology, 31,* 169–193.

Dawes, R. M. (1994). *House of cards: Psychology and psychotherapy built on myth.* New York: Free Press.

Dawkins, R. (1998). *Unweaving the rainbow.* Boston: Houghton Mifflin.

Dawkins, R. (1999, April 8). Is science killing the soul (a discussion with Richard Dawkins and Steven Pinker). www.edge.org

Dawson, N. V., Arkes, H. R., Siciliano, C., Blinkhorn, R., Lakshmanan, M., & Petrelli, M. (1988). Hindsight bias: An impediment to accurate probability estimation in clinico-pathologic conferences. *Medical Decision Making, 8,* 259–264.

Dean, G. A., Kelly, I. W., Saklofske, D. H., & Furnham, A. (1992). Graphology and human judgment. In B. Beyerstein & D. Beyerstein (Eds.), *The write stuff: Evaluations of graphology.* Buffalo, NY: Prometheus Books.

DeAngelis, T. (1993, September). Controversial diagnosis is voted into latest DSM. *APA Monitor,* pp. 32–33.

Deardorff, J. (1994, July 28). "It feels like there's a beast inside me." *Chicago Tribune,* p. 1.

Deary, I. J., & Caryl, P. G. (1993). Intelligence, EEG and evoked potentials. In P. A. Vernon (Ed.), *Biological approaches to the study of human intelligence.* Norwood, NJ: Ablex.

Deary, I. J., & Matthews, G. (1993). Personality traits are alive and well. *The Psychologist: Bulletin of the British Psychological Society, 6,* 299–311.

Deary, I. J., & Stough, C. (1996). Intelligence and inspection time: Achievements, prospects, and problems. *American Psychologist, 51,* 599–608.

Deary, I. J., & Stough, C. (1997). Looking down on human intelligence. *American Psychologist, 52,* 1148–1149.

de Boysson-Bardies, B., Halle, P., Sagart, L., & Durand, C. (1989). A cross linguistic investigation of vowel formats in babbling. *Journal of Child Language, 16,* 1–17.

DeCasper, A. J., Lecanuet, J-P, Busnel, M-C, Granier-Deferre, C., et al. (1994). Fetal reactions to recurrent maternal speech. *Infant Behavior and Development, 17,* 159–164.

DeCasper, A. J., & Prescott, P. A. (1984). Human newborns' perception of male voices: Preference, discrimination and reinforcing value. *Developmental Psychobiology, 17,* 481–491.

DeCasper, A. J., & Spence, M. J. (1986). Prenatal maternal speech influences newborns' perception of speech sounds. *Infant Behavior and Development, 9,* 133–150.

Deci, E. L., Connell, J. P., & Ryan, R. M. (1989). Self-determination in a work organization. *Journal of Applied Psychology, 74,* 580–590.

Deci, E. L., Koestner, R., & Ryan, R. M. (1999, November). A meta-analytic review of experiments examining the effects of extrinsic rewards on intrinsic motivation. *Psychological Bulletin, 125*(6), 627–668.

Deci, E. L., & Ryan, R. M. (1985). *Intrinsic motivation and self-determination in human behavior.* New York: Plenum Press.

Deci, E. L., & Ryan, R. M. (1987). The support of autonomy and the control of behavior. *Journal of Personality and Social Psychology, 53,* 1024–1037.

Deci, E. L., & Ryan, R. M. (1992). The initiation and regulation of intrinsically motivated learning and achievement. In A. K. Boggiano & T. S. Pittman (Eds.), *Achievement and motivation: A social-developmental perspective.* New York: Cambridge University Press.

de Cuevas, J. (1990, September-October). "No, she holded them loosely." *Harvard Magazine,* pp. 60–67.

de Jong-Gierveld, J. (1987). Developing and testing a model of loneliness. *Journal of Personality and Social Psychology, 53,* 119–128.

Delaney, P. F., Ericsson, K. A., Weaver, G. E., & Mahadevan, S. (1999). Accounts of the memorist Rajan's exceptional performance: Comparing three theoretical proposals. Paper presented to the American Psychological Society convention.

Delgado, J. M. R. (1969). *Physical control of the mind: Toward a psychocivilized society.* New York: Harper & Row.

DeLisi, L. E. (1999). A critical overview of recent investigations into the genetics of schizophrenia. *Current Opinion in Psychiatry, 12,* 29–39.

DeLoache, J. S. (1995). Early understanding and use of symbols: The model model. *Current Directions in Psychological Science, 4,* 109–113.

DeLoache, J. S., & Brown, A. L. (1987, October-December). Differences in the memory-based searching of delayed and normally developing young children. *Intelligence, 11*(4), 277–289.

Dement, W. (1997, September). What all undergraduates should know about how their sleeping lives affect their waking lives. Stanford University: www-leland.stanford.edu/~dement/sleepless.html

Dement, W. C. (1978). *Some must watch while some must sleep.* New York: Norton.

Dement, W. C. (1999). *The promise of sleep.* New York: Delacorte Press.

Dement, W. C., & Wolpert, E. A. (1958). The relation of eye movements, body mobility, and external stimuli to dream content. *Journal of Experimental Psychology, 55,* 543–553.

Dempster, F. N. (1988). The spacing effect: A case study in the failure to apply the results of psychological research. *American Psychologist, 43,* 627–634.

Denes-Raj, V., Epstein, S., & Cole, J. (1995). The generality of the ratio-bias phenomenon. *Personality and Social Psychology Bulletin, 21,* 1083–1092.

DeNeve, K. M., & Cooper, H. (1998). The happy personality: A meta-analysis of 137 personality traits and subjective well-being. *Psychological Bulletin, 124,* 197–229.

Dennett, D. (1996, September 9). Quoted in Ian Parker, Richard Dawkins' evolution. *The New Yorker,* pp. 41–45.

Denton, K., & Krebs, D. (1990). From the scene to the crime: The effect of alcohol and social context on moral judgment. *Journal of Personality and Social Psychology, 59,* 242–248.

D'Eon, J. L. (1989). Hypnosis in the control of labor pain. In N. P. Spanos & J. F. Chaves (Eds.), *Hypnosis: The cognitive-behavioral perspective.* Buffalo, NY: Prometheus Books.

DePaulo, B. M., Blank, A. L., Swaim, G. W., & Hairfield, J. G. (1992). Expressiveness and expressive control. *Personality and Social Psychology Bulletin, 18,* 276–285.

DePaulo, B. M., Charlton, K., Cooper, H., Lindsay, J. J., & Muhlenbruck, L. (1997). The accuracy-confidence correlation in the detection of deception. *Personality and Social Psychology Review, 1,* 346–357.

De Pree, M. (1987). *Leadership is an art.* East Lansing: Michigan State University Press.

De Quervain, D. J.-F., Roozendaal, B., & McGaugh, J. L. (1998). Stress and glucocorticoids impair retrieval of long-term spatial memory. *Nature, 394,* 787–790.

Deregowski, J. B. (1989). Real space and represented space: Cross-cultural perspectives. *Behavioral and Brain Sciences, 12,* 51–119.

Dermer, M., Cohen, S. J., Jacobsen, E., & Anderson, E. A. (1979). Evaluative judgments of aspects of life as a function of vicarious exposure to hedonic extremes. *Journal of Personality and Social Psychology, 37,* 247–260.

Dermer, M., & Pyszczynski, T. A. (1978). Effects of erotica upon men's loving and liking responses for women they love. *Journal of Personality and Social Psychology, 36,* 1302–1309.

DeRubeis, R. J., & Crits-Christoph, P. (1998). Empirically supported individual and group psychological treatments for adult mental disorders. *Journal of Consulting and Clinical Psychology, 66,* 37–52.

Descartes, R. (1641/1948). *The meditations and selections from the principles of Rene Descartes.* Lasalle, IL: Open Court Publishing.

Deutsch, J. A. (1972, July). Brain reward: ESP and ecstasy. *Psychology Today,* pp. 46–48.

Deutsch, M. (1991). Egalitarianism in the laboratory and at work. In R. Vermunt & H. Steensma (Eds.), *Social justice in human relations.* New York: Plenum.

DeValois, R. L., & DeValois, K. K. (1975). Neural coding of color. In E. C. Carterette & M. P. Friedman (Eds.), *Handbook of perception: Vol. V. Seeing.* New York: Academic Press.

Devine, P. G. (1995). Prejudice and outgroup perception. In A. Tesser (Ed.), *Advanced social psychology.* New York: McGraw-Hill.

Devlin, B., Daniels, M., & Roeder, K. (1997). The heritability of IQ. *Nature, 388,* 468–471.

de Waal, F. B. M., & Johanowicz, D. L. (1993). Modification of reconciliation behavior through social experience: An experiment with two macaque species. *Child Development, 64,* 897–908.

De Wolff, M. S., & van Ijzendoorn, M. H. (1997). Sensitivity and attachment: A meta-analysis on parental antecedents of infant attachment. *Child Development, 68,* 571–591.

Dey, E. L., Astin, A. W., & Korn, W. S. (1991). *The American freshman: Twenty-five year trends.* Los Angeles: Higher Education Research Institute, UCLA.

Dhawan, N., Roseman, I. J., Naidu, R. K., Thapa, K., & Rettek, S. I. (1995). Self-concepts across two cultures: India and the United States. *Journal of Cross-Cultural Psychology, 26,* 606–621.

Diaconis, P., & Mosteller, F. (1989). Methods for studying coincidences. *Journal of the American Statistical Association, 84,* 853–861.

Diamond, J. (1986). Variation in human testis size. *Nature, 320,* 488–489.

Diamond, J. (1989, May). The great leap forward. *Discover,* pp. 50–60.

Diamond, R. (1993). Genetics and male sexual orientation (letter). *Science, 261,* p. 1258.

Diener, E. (1993). Most Americans are happy. Unpublished manuscript, University of Illinois.

Diener, E., Diener, M., & Diener, C. (1995). Factors predicting the subjective well-being of nations. *Journal of Personality and Social Psychology, 69,* 851–864.

Diener, E., Emmons, R. A., & Sandvik, E. (1986). The dual nature of happiness: Independence of positive and negative moods. Unpublished manuscript, University of Illinois.

Diener, E., & Oishi, S. (2000). Money and happiness: Income and subjective well-being across nations. In E. Diener & E. M. Suh (Eds.), *Subjective well-being across cultures.* Cambridge, MA: MIT Press.

Diener, E., Wolsic, B., & Fujita, F. (1995). Physical attractiveness and subjective well-being. *Journal of Personality and Social Psychology, 69,* 120–129.

Dietz, W. H., Jr., & Gortmaker, S. L. (1985). Do we fatten our children at the television set? Obesity and television viewing in children and adolescents. *Pediatrics, 75,* 807–812.

DiLalla, D. L., Carey, G., Gottesman, I. I., & Bouchard, T. J., Jr. (1996). Heritability of MMPI personality indicators of psychopathology in twins reared apart. *Journal of Abnormal Psychology, 105,* 491–499.

Dill, J. C., & Anderson, C.A. (1999). Loneliness, shyness, and depression: The etiology and interrelationships of everyday problems in living. In T. Joiner & J.C. Coyne (Eds.), *The interactional nature of depression: Advances in interpersonal approaches.* Washington, DC: American Psychological Association.

Dindia, K., & Allen, M. (1992). Sex differences in self-disclosure: A meta-analysis. *Psychological Bulletin, 112,* 106–124.

Dinges, N. G., & Hull, P. (1992). Personality, culture, and international studies. In D. Lieberman (Ed.), *Revealing the world: An interdisciplinary reader for international studies.* Dubuque, IA: Kendall-Hunt.

Dion, K. K., & Dion, K. L. (1993). Individualistic and collectivistic perspectives on gender and the cultural context of love and intimacy. *Journal of Social Issues, 49,* 53–69.

Discover (1996, May). A fistful of risks. Pp. 82–83.

Dishion, T. J., McCord, J., & Poulin, F. (1999). When interventions harm: Peer groups and problem behavior. *American Psychologist, 54,* 755–764.

Dodd, M. (1996, September 19). $500,000 ball raises skepticism. *USA Today,* p. 9C.

Doherty, E. W., & Doherty, W. J. (1998). Smoke gets in your eyes: Cigarette smoking and divorce in a national sample of American adults. *Families, Systems, and Health, 16,* 393–400.

Dohrenwend, B. P., Levav, I., Shrout, P. E., Schwartz, S., Naveh, G., Link, B. G., Skodol, A. E., & Stueve, A. (1992). Socioeconomic status and psychiatric disorders: The causation-selection issue. *Science, 255,* 946–952.

Dohrenwend, B., Pearlin, L., Clayton, P., Hamburg, B., Dohrenwend, B. P., Riley, M., & Rose, R. (1982). Report on stress and life events. In G. R. Elliott & C. Eisdorfer (Eds.), *Stress and human health: Analysis and implications of research* (A study by the Institute of Medicine/National Academy of Sciences). New York: Springer.

Dolan, B. (1991). Cross-cultural aspects of anorexia nervosa and bulimia: A review. *International Journal of Eating Disorders, 10,* 67–78.

Dolan, R. J. (1999). On the neurology of morals. *Nature Neuroscience, 2,* 927–929.

Dole, R. (1996, April 20). Quoted in M. Duffy, Look who's talking. *Time,* p. 48.

Dolezal, H. (1982). *Living in a world transformed.* New York: Academic Press.

Domhoff, G. W. (1996). *Finding meaning in dreams: A quantitative approach.* New York: Plenum.

Domhoff, G. W. (1999). New directions in the study of dream content using the Hall and Van de Castle coding system. *Dreaming, 9,* 115–137.

Domjan, M. (1992). Adult learning and mate choice: Possibilities and experimental evidence. *American Zoologist, 32,* 48–61.

Domjan, M. (1994). Formulation of a behavior system for sexual conditioning. *Psychonomic Bulletin & Review, 1,* 421–428.

Domjan, M. (1997). Behavior systems and the demise of equipotentiality: Historical antecedents and evidence from sexual conditioning. In M. E. Bouton & M. S. Fanselow (Eds.), *Learning, motivation, and cognition: The functional behaviorism of Robert C. Bolles.* Washington, DC: American Psychological Association.

Domjan, M., Blesbois, E., & Williams, J. (1998). The adaptive significance of sexual conditioning: Pavlovian control of sperm release. *Psychological Science, 9,* 411–415.

Donnerstein, E. (1998). Why do we have those new ratings on television? Invited address to the National Institute on the Teaching of Psychology.

Donnerstein, E., Linz, D., & Penrod, S. (1987). *The question of pornography.* New York: Free Press.

Dorner, G. (1976). *Hormones and brain differentiation.* Amsterdam: Elsevier Scientific.

Dorozyaski, A. (1993, January/February). Maternal alcoholism: Grapes of wrath. *Psychology Today,* p. 18.

Dorris, M. (1989). *The broken cord.* New York: HarperCollins.

Doty, R. L., Shaman, P., Applebaum, S. L., Giberson, R., Siksorski, L., & Rosenberg, L. (1984). Smell identification ability: Changes with age. *Science, 226,* 1441–1443.

Doty, R. W. (1998). The five mysteries of the mind, and their consequences. *Neuropsychologia, 36,* 1069–1076.

Dovidio, J. F., & Gaertner, S. L. (1999). Reducing prejudice: Combating intergroup biases. *Current Directions in Psychological Science, 8,* 101–105.

Draguns, J. G. (1990a). Normal and abnormal behavior in cross-cultural perspective: Specifying the nature of their relationship. *Nebraska Symposium on Motivation 1989, 37,* 235–277.

Draguns, J. G. (1990b). Applications of cross-cultural psychology in the field of mental health. In R. W. Brislin (Ed.), *Applied cross-cultural psychology.* Newbury Park, CA: Sage.

Draguns, J. G. (1997). Abnormal behavior patterns across cultures: Implications for counseling and psychotherapy. *International Journal of Intercultural Relations, 21*, 213–248.

Druckman, D., & Bjork, R. A. (1991). *In the mind's eye: Enhancing human performance.* National Academy Press: Washington, DC.

Druckman, D., & Bjork, R. A. (Eds.). (1994). *Learning, remembering, believing: Enhancing human performance.* Washington, DC: National Academy Press.

Druckman, D., & Swets, J. A. (Eds.). (1988). *Enhancing human performance: Issues, theories, and techniques.* Washington, DC: National Academy Press.

Drummey, A. B., & Newcombe, N. (1995). Remembering versus knowing the past: Children's explicit and implicit memories for pictures. *Journal of Experimental Child Psychology, 59*, 549–565.

Duclos, S. E., Laird, J. D., Sexter, M., Stern, L., & Van Lighten, O. (1989). Emotion-specific effects of facial expressions and postures on emotional experience. *Journal of Personality and Social Psychology, 57*, 100–108.

Duggan, J. P., & Booth, D. A. (1986). Obesity, overeating, and rapid gastric emptying in rats with ventromedial hypothalamic lesions. *Science, 231*, 609–611.

Duncan, B. L. (1976). Differential social perception and attribution of intergroup violence: Testing the lower limits of stereotyping of blacks. *Journal of Personality and Social Psychology, 34*, 590–598.

Duncan, G. J., Hill, M. S., & Hoffman, S. D. (1988). Welfare dependence within and across generations. *Science, 239*, 467–471.

Duncker, K. (1945). On problem solving. *Psychological Monographs, 58* (Whole no. 270).

Dunn, J., & Plomin, R. (1990). *Separate lives: Why siblings are so different.* New York: Basic Books.

Dunning, D., Griffin, D. W., Milojkovic, J. D., & Ross, L. (1990). *Journal of Personality and Social Psychology, 58*, 568–581.

DuPree, D. (1998, 26 February). Jordan's $33.14M tops NBA. *USA Today*, p. C1.

Dutton, D. G., & Aron, A. P. (1974). Some evidence for heightened sexual attraction under conditions of high anxiety. *Journal of Personality and Social Psychology, 30*, 510–517.

Dutton, D. G., & Aron, A. (1989). Romantic attraction and generalized liking for others who are sources of conflict-based arousal. *Canadian Journal of Behavioural Sciences, 21*, 246–257.

Dweck, C. S., & Elliott, E. S. (1983). Achievement motivation. In P. Mussen & E. M. Hetherington (Eds.), *Handbook of child psychology* (Vol. IV). New York: Wiley.

Dye, D. A., & Reck, M. (1989). College grade point average as a predictor of adult success: A reply. *Public Personnel Management, 18*, 235–241.

Eagles, J. M. (1991). Is schizophrenia disappearing? *British Journal of Psychiatry, 158*, 834–835.

Eagly, A. (1994). Are people prejudiced against women? Donald Campbell Award invited address, American Psychological Association convention.

Eagly, A. H., Ashmore, R. D., Makhijani, M. G., & Kennedy, L. C. (1991). What is beautiful is good, but . . .: A meta-analytic review of research on the physical attractiveness stereotype. *Psychological Bulletin, 110*, 109–128.

Eagly, A. H., & Crowley, M. (1986). Gender and helping behavior: A meta-analytic review of the social psychological literature. *Psychological Bulletin, 100*, 283–308.

Eagly, A. H., & Johnson, B. T. (1990). Gender and leadership style: A meta-analysis. *Psychological Bulletin, 108*, 233–256.

Eagly, A. H., & Karau, S. J. (1991). Gender and the emergence of leaders: A meta-analysis. *Journal of Personality and Social Psychology, 60*, 685–710.

Eagly, A. H., & Wood, W. (1999). The origins of sex differences in human behavior: Evolved dispositions versus social roles. *American Psychologist, 54*, 408–423.

Eastman, C. L., Boulos, Z., Terman, M., Campbell, S. S., Dijk, D.-J., & Lewy, A. J. (1995). Light treatment for sleep disorders: Consensus report. VI. Shift work. *Journal of Biological Rhythms, 10*, 157–164.

Eastman, C. L., Young, M. A., Fogg, L. F., Liu, L., & Meaden, P. M. (1998). Bright light treatment of winter depression: A placebo-controlled trial. *Archives of General Psychiatry, 55*, 883–889.

Ebbesen, E. B., Duncan, B., & Konecni, V. J. (1975). Effects of content of verbal aggression on future verbal aggression: A field experiment. *Journal of Experimental Social Psychology, 11*, 192–204.

Ebbinghaus, H. (1885). *Über das Gedachtnis.* Leipzig: Duncker & Humblot. Cited in R. Klatzky (1980), *Human memory: Structures and processes.* San Francisco: Freeman.

Ebstein, R. P., Levine, J., Geller, V., Auerbach, J., Gritsenko, I., & Belmaker, R. H. (1998). Dopamine D4 receptor and serotonin transporter promoter in the determination of neonatal temperament. *Molecular Psychiatry, 3*, 238–246.

Eccles, J. S., Jacobs, J. E., & Harold, R. D. (1990). Gender role stereotypes, expectancy effects, and parents' socialization of gender differences. *Journal of Social Issues, 46*, 183–201.

Eckensberger, L. H. (1994). Moral development and its measurement across cultures. In W. J. Lonner & R. Malpass (Eds.), *Psychology and culture.* Boston: Allyn and Bacon.

Eckert, E. D., Heston, L. L., & Bouchard, T. J., Jr. (1981). MZ twins reared apart: Preliminary findings of psychiatric disturbances and traits. In L. Gedda, P. Paris, & W. D. Nance (Eds.), *Twin research: Vol. 3. Pt. B. Intelligence, personality, and development.* New York: Alan Liss.

Ecklund-Flores, L. (1992). The infant as a model for the teaching of introductory psychology. Paper presented to the American Psychological Association annual convention.

Edelman, S., & Kidman, A. D. (1997). Mind and cancer: Is there a relationship? A review of the evidence. *Australian Psychologist, 32*, 1–7.

Edison, T. A. (1948). *The diary and sundry observations of Thomas Alva Edison*, edited by D. D. Runes. New York: Philosophical Library. Cited by S. Coren (1996). *Sleep thieves.* New York: Free Press.

Edwards, C. P. (1981). The comparative study of the development of moral judgment and reasoning. In R. H. Munroe, R. L. Munroe, & B. B. Whiting (Eds.), *Handbook of cross-cultural human development.* New York: Garland Press.

Edwards, C. P. (1982). Moral development in comparative cultural perspective. In D. A. Wagner & H. W. Stevenson (Eds.), *Cultural perspectives on child development.* San Francisco: Freeman.

Edwards, R., Peet, M., Shay, J., & Horrobin, D. (1998). Omega-3 polyunsaturated fatty acid levels in the diet and in red blood cell membranes of depressed patients. *Journal of Affective Disorders, 48*, 149–155.

Ehrhardt, A. A. (1987). A transactional perspective on the development of gender differences. In J. M. Reinisch, L. A. Rosenblum, & S. A. Sanders (Eds.), *Masculinity/femininity: Basic perspectives.* New York: Oxford University Press.

Ehrlichman, H., & Halpern, J. N. (1988). Affect and memory: Effects of pleasant and unpleasant odors on retrieval of happy and unhappy memories. *Journal of Personality and Social Psychology, 55,* 769–779.

Eibl-Eibesfeldt, I. (1971). *Love and hate: The natural history of behavior patterns.* New York: Holt, Rinehart & Winston.

Eich, E. (1990). Learning during sleep. In R. B. Bootzin, J. F. Kihlstrom, & D. L. Schacter (Eds.), *Sleep and cognition.* Washington, DC: American Psychological Association.

Eich, E. (1995). Searching for mood dependent memory. *Psychological Science, 6,* 67–75.

Eich, E., Macaulay, D., Loewenstein, R. J., & Dihle, P. H. (1997). Memory, amnesia, and dissociative identity disorder. *Psychological Science, 8,* 417–422.

Eich, J. E. (1980). The cue-dependent nature of state-dependent retrieval. *Memory and Cognition, 8,* 157–173.

Einstein, G. O., & McDaniel, M. A. (1990). Normal aging and prospective memory. *Journal of Experimental Psychology: Learning, Memory, and Cognition, 16,* 717–726.

Einstein, G. O., McDaniel, M. A., Richardson, S. L., Guynn, M. J., & Cunfer, A. R. (1995). Aging and prospective memory: Examining the influences of self-initiated retrieval processes. *Journal of Experimental Psychology: Learning, Memory, and Cognition, 21,* 996–1007.

Einstein, G. O., McDaniel, M. A., Smith, R. E., & Shaw, P. (1998). Habitual prospective memory and aging: Remembering intentions and forgetting actions. *Psychological Science, 9,* 284–288.

Eisenberg, N., Cumberland A., & Spinrad, T. L. (1998a). Parental socialization of emotion. *Psychological Inquiry, 9,* 241–271.

Eisenberg, N., & Lennon, R. (1983). Sex differences in empathy and related capacities. *Psychological Bulletin, 94,* 100–131.

Eisenberg, N., Spinrad, T. L., & Cumberland, A. (1998b). The socialization of emotion: Reply to commentaries. *Psychological Inquiry, 9,* 317–333.

Eisenberger, R., & Cameron, J. (1996). Detrimental effects of reward: Reality or myth? *American Psychologist, 51,* 1153–1166.

Eisenberger, R., Rhoades, L., & Cameron, J. (1999). Does pay for performance increase or decrease perceived self-determination and intrinsic motivation? *Journal of Personality and Social Psychology, 77,* 1026–1040.

Eiser, J. R. (1985). Smoking: The social learning of an addiction. *Journal of Social and Clinical Psychology, 3,* 446–457.

Ekman, P. (1994). Strong evidence for universals in facial expressions: A reply to Russell's mistaken critique. *Psychological Bulletin, 115,* 268–287.

Ekman, P., Davidson, R. J., & Friesen, W. V. (1990). The Duchenne smile: Emotional expression and brain physiology II. *Journal of Personality and Social Psychology, 58,* 342–353.

Ekman, P., & Friesen, W. V. (1975). *Unmasking the face.* Englewood Cliffs, NJ: Prentice-Hall.

Ekman, P., Friesen, W. V., O'Sullivan, M., Chan, A., Diacoyanni-Tarlatzis, I., Heider, K., Krause, R., LeCompte, W. A., Pitcairn, T., Ricci-Bitti, P. E., Scherer, K., Tomita, M., & Tzavaras, A. (1987). Universals and cultural differences in the judgments of facial expressions of emotion. *Journal of Personality and Social Psychology, 53,* 712–717.

Ekman, P., & O'Sullivan, M. (1991). Who can catch a liar? *American Psychologist, 46,* 913–920.

Ekman, P., O'Sullivan, M. O., & Frank, M. G. (1999). A few can catch a liar. *Psychological Science, 10,* 263–266.

Elbert, T., Pantev, C., Wienbruch, C., Rockstroh, B., & Taub, E. (1995). Increased cortical representation of the fingers of the left hand in string players. *Science, 270,* 305–307.

Elfenbein, H. A., & Ambady, N. (1999). Does it take one to know one? A meta-analysis of the universality and cultural specificity of emotion recognition. Unpublished manuscript, Harvard University.

Elkin, I., Shea, T., Watkins, J. T., Imber, S. D., Sotsky, S. M., Collins, J. F., Glass, D. R., Pilkonis, P. A., Leber, W. R., Docherty, J. P., Fiester, S. J., & Parloff, M. B. (1989). National Institute of Mental Health treatment of depression collaborative research program. *Archives of General Psychiatry, 46,* 971–983.

Elkind, D. (1970). The origins of religion in the child. *Review of Religious Research, 12,* 35–42.

Elkind, D. (1978). *The child's reality: Three developmental themes.* Hillsdale, NJ: Erlbaum.

Elkis, H., Friedman, L., Wise, A., & Meltzer, H. Y. (1995). Meta-analyses of studies of ventricular enlargement and cortical sulcal prominence in mood disorders: Comparisons with controls or patients with schizophrenia. *Archives of General Psychiatry, 52,* 735–746.

Elliot, A. (1996, January 18). Personal communication with Nielsen Media Research Director of Communications via e-mail (Anne_Elliot@tvratings.com).

Ellis, A. (1980). Psychotherapy and atheistic values: A response to A. E. Bergin's "Psychotherapy and religious values." *Journal of Consulting and Clinical Psychology, 48,* 635–639.

Ellis, A., & Becker, I. M. (1982). *A guide to personal happiness.* North Hollywood, CA: Wilshire Book Co.

Ellis, B. J., McFadyen-Ketchum, S., Dodge, K. A., Pettit, G. S., & Bates, J. E. (1999). Quality of early family relationships and individual differences in the timing of pubertal maturation in girls: A longitudinal test of an evolutionary model. *Journal of Personality and Social Psychology, 77,* 387–401.

Ellis, H. C., & Ashbrook, P. W. (1989). The "state" of mood and memory research: A selective review. *Journal of Social Behavior and Personality, 4,* 1–21.

Ellis, L., & Ames, M. A. (1987). Neurohormonal functioning and sexual orientation: A theory of homosexuality-heterosexuality. *Psychological Bulletin, 101,* 233–258.

Emde, R. N., Plomin, R., Robinson, J., Corley, R., DeFries, J., Fulker, D. W., Reznick, J. S., Campos, J., Kagan, J., & Zahn-Waxler, C. (1992). Temperament, emotion, and cognition at fourteen months: The MacArthur Longitudinal Twin Study. *Child Development, 63,* 1437–1455.

Emerging Trends. (1997, September). Teens turn more to parents than friends on whether to attend church. Princeton, NJ: Princeton Religion Research Center, p. 5.

Emmons, S., Geisler, C., Kaplan, K. J., & Harrow, M. (1997). *Living with schizophrenia.* Muncie, IN: Taylor and Francis (Accelerated Development).

Empson, J. A. C., & Clarke, P. R. F. (1970). Rapid eye movements and remembering. *Nature, 227,* 287–288.

Endler, N. S. (1982). *Holiday of darkness: A psychologist's personal journey out of his depression.* New York: Wiley.

Endler, N. S., & Speer, R. L. (1998). Personality psychology: Research trends for 1993–1995. *Journal of Personality, 66,* 621–669.

Engen, T. (1987). Remembering odors and their names. *American Scientist, 75,* 497–503.

Epstein, S. (1983a). Aggregation and beyond: Some basic issues on the prediction of behavior. *Journal of Personality, 51,* 360–392.

Epstein, S. (1983b). The stability of behavior across time and situations. In R. Zucker, J. Aronoff, & A. I. Rabin (Eds.), *Personality and the prediction of behavior.* San Diego: Academic Press.

Epstein, S., & Meier, P. (1989). Constructive thinking: A broad coping variable with specific components. *Journal of Personality and Social Psychology, 57,* 332–350.

Erber, R., & Tesser, A. (1992). Task effort and the regulation of mood: The absorption hypothesis. *Journal of Experimental Social Psychology, 28,* 339–359.

Erdberg, P. (1990). Rorschach assessment. In G. Goldstein & M. Hersen (Eds.), *Handbook of psychological assessment,* 2nd ed. New York: Pergamon.

Erdelyi, M. H. (1985). *Psychoanalysis: Freud's cognitive psychology.* New York: Freeman.

Erdelyi, M. H. (1988). Repression, reconstruction, and defense: History and integration of the psychoanalytic and experimental frameworks. In J. Singer (Ed.), *Repression: Defense mechanism and cognitive style.* Chicago: University of Chicago Press.

Erel, O., & Burman, B. (1995). Interrelatedness of marital relations and parent-child relations: A meta-analytic review. *Psychological Bulletin, 118,* 108–132.

Ericksen, J. A. (1998). With enough cases, why do you need statistics? Revisiting Kinsey's methodology. *Journal of Sex Research, 35,* 132–140.

Ericsson, K. A., & Chase, W. G. (1982). Exceptional memory. *American Scientist, 70,* 607–615.

Ericsson, K. A., Krampe, R. T., & Heizman, S. (1993). Can we create gifted people? In G. R. Bock & K. Ackrill (Eds.), *Ciba Foundation Symposium 178: The origins and development of high ability.* New York: Wiley. Cited by M. J. A. Howe, J. W. Davison, & J. A. Sioboda (1998). Innate talents: Reality or myth? *Behavioral and Brain Sciences, 21,* 399–442.

Erikson, E. H. (1963). *Childhood and society.* New York: Norton.

Erikson, E. H. (1983, June). A conversation with Erikson (by E. Hall). *Psychology Today,* pp. 22–30.

Ernsberger, P., & Koletsky, R. J. (1999). Biomedical rationale for a wellness approach to obesity: An alternative to a focus on weight loss. *Journal of Social Issues, 55,* 221–260.

Ernst, E. (1998). The rise and fall of complementary medicine. *Journal of the Royal Society of Medicine, 91,* 235–236.

Eron, L. D. (1987). The development of aggressive behavior from the perspective of a developing behaviorism. *American Psychologist, 42,* 435–442.

Espinosa, M. P., Sigman, M. D., Neumann, C. G., Bwibo, N. O., & McDonald, M. A. (1992). Playground behaviors of school-age children in relation to nutrition, schooling, and family characteristics. *Developmental Psychology, 28,* 1188–1195.

Esser, J. K., & Lindoerfer, J. S. (1989). Groupthink and the space shuttle *Challenger* accident: Toward a quantitative case analysis. *Journal of Behavioral Decision Making, 2,* 167–177.

Etcoff, N. (1999). *Survival of the prettiest: The science of beauty.* New York: Doubleday.

Etnier, J. L., Salazar, W., Landers, D. M., Petruzzello, S. J., Han, M., & Nowell, P. (1997). The influence of physical fitness and exercise upon cognitive functioning: A meta-analysis. *Journal of Sport & Exercise Psychology, 19,* 249–277.

ETS. (1992). Three reports shed new light on gender differences in testing. *ETS Developments, 37*(3), 4–7.

Evans, C. R., & Dion, K. L. (1991). Group cohesion and performance: A meta-analysis. *Small Group Research, 22,* 175–186.

Evans, G. W., Hygge, S., & Bullinger, M. (1995). Chronic noise and psychological stress. *Psychological Science, 6,* 333–338.

Evans, G. W., Palsane, M. N., & Carrere, S. (1987). Type A behavior and occupational stress: A cross-cultural study of blue-collar workers. *Journal of Personality and Social Psychology, 52,* 1002–1007.

Evans, G. W., Palsane, M. N., Lepore, S. J., & Martin, J. (1989). Residential density and psychological health: The mediating effects of social support. *Journal of Personality and Social Psychology, 57,* 994–999.

Evans, R. I., Dratt, L. M., Raines, B. E., & Rosenberg, S. S. (1988). Social influences on smoking initiation: Importance of distinguishing descriptive versus mediating process variables. *Journal of Applied Social Psychology, 18,* 925–943.

Evans, R. I., Raines, B. E., & Hanselka, L. (1984). Developing data-based communications in social psychological research: Adolescent smoking prevention. *Journal of Applied Social Psychology, 14,* 289–295.

Everson, S. A., Goldberg, D. E., Kaplan, G. A., Cohen, R. D., Pukkala, E., Tuomilehto, J., & Salonen, J. T. (1996). Hopelessness and risk of mortality and incidence of myocardial infarction and cancer. *Psychosomatic Medicine, 58,* 113–121.

Exner, J. E. (1993). *The Rorschach: A comprehensive system: Vol. 1. Basic foundations* (3rd ed.). New York: Wiley.

Eyer, D. E. (1992). *Mother-infant bonding: A scientific fiction.* New Haven: Yale University Press.

Eysenck, H. J. (1952). The effects of psychotherapy: An evaluation. *Journal of Consulting Psychology, 16,* 319–324.

Eysenck, H. J. (1990, April 30). An improvement on personality inventory. *Current Contents: Social and Behavioral Sciences, 22*(18), 20.

Eysenck, H. J. (1992). Four ways five factors are *not* basic. *Personality and Individual Differences, 13,* 667–673.

Eysenck, H. J., & Grossarth-Maticek, R. (1991). Creative novation behaviour therapy as a prophylactic treatment for cancer and coronary heart disease: Part II—Effects of treatment. *Behaviour Research and Therapy, 29,* 17–31.

Eysenck, H. J., Wakefield, J. A., Jr., & Friedman, A. F. (1983). Diagnosis and clinical assessment: The DSM-III. *Annual Review of Psychology, 34,* 167–193.

Eysenck, M. W., MacLeod, C., & Mathews, A. (1987). Cognitive functioning and anxiety. *Psychological Research, 49,* 189–195.

Eysenck, S. B. G., & Eysenck, H. J. (1963). The validity of questionnaire and rating assessments of extraversion and neuroticism, and their factorial stability. *British Journal of Psychology, 54,* 51–62.

Faber, N. (1987, July). Personal glimpse. *Reader's Digest,* p. 34.

Fagan, J. F., III (1992). Intelligence: A theoretical viewpoint. *Current Directions in Psychological Science, 1,* 82–86.

Fallon, A. (1990). Culture in the mirror: Sociocultural determinants of body image. In T. F. Cash & T. Pruzinsky (Eds.), *Body images: Development, deviance, and change.* New York: Guilford Press.

Fallon, A. E., & Rozin, P. (1985). Sex differences in perceptions of desirable body shape. *Journal of Abnormal Psychology, 94,* 102–105.

Fantz, R. L. (1961, May). The origin of form perception. *Scientific American,* pp. 66–72.

Farina, A. (1982). The stigma of mental disorders. In A. G. Miller (Ed.), *In the eye of the beholder.* New York: Praeger.

Farina, A., & Fisher, J. D. (1982). Beliefs about mental disorders: Findings and implications. In G. Weary & H. L. Mirels (Eds.), *Integrations of clinical and social psychology.* New York: Oxford University Press.

Farley, M, Baral, I., Kiremire, M., & Sezgin, U. (1998). Prostitution in five countries: Violence and post-traumatic stress disorder. *Feminism and Psychology, 8,* 405–426.

Farrell, P. A., Gates, W. K., Maksud, M. G., & Morgan, W. P. (1982). Increases in plasma beta-endorphin/beta-lipotropin immunoreactivity after treadmill running in humans. *Journal of Applied Physiology, 52,* 1245–1249.

Farrington, D. P. (1991). Antisocial personality from childhood to adulthood. *The Psychologist: Bulletin of the British Psychological Society, 4,* 389–394.

Fathalla, M. (1999). The missing millions. *People & the Planet.* www.oneworld.org/patp

Fava, M., Copeland, P. M., Schweiger, U., & Herzog, D. B. (1989). Neurochemical abnormalities of anorexia nervosa and bulimia nervosa. *American Journal of Psychiatry, 146,* 963–971.

Fazio, R. H. (1990). Multiple processes by which attitudes guide behavior: The MODE model as an integrative framework. In M. P. Zanna (Ed.), *Advances in experimental social psychology* (Vol. 23). San Diego: Academic Press.

Feder, H. H. (1984). Hormones and sexual behavior. *Annual Review of Psychology, 35,* 165–200.

Feeney, D. M. (1987). Human rights and animal welfare. *American Psychologist, 42,* 593–599.

Feeney, J. A., & Noller, P. (1990). Attachment style as a predictor of adult romantic relationships. *Journal of Personality and Social Psychology, 58,* 281–291.

Fehr, B., & Russell, J. A. (1991). The concept of love viewed from a prototype perspective. *Journal of Personality and Social Psychology, 60,* 425–438.

Feingold, A. (1990). Gender differences in effects of physical attractiveness on romantic attraction: A comparison across five research paradigms. *Journal of Personality and Social Psychology, 59,* 981–993.

Feingold, A. (1992). Good-looking people are not what we think. *Psychological Bulletin, 111,* 304–341.

Feingold, A., & Mazzella, R. (1996). Gender differences in body image are increasing. *The General Psychologist, 32,* 84–92.

Feingold, A., & Mazzella, R. (1998). Gender differences in body image are increasing. *Psychological Science, 9,* 190–195.

Feinleib, M., Lenfant, C., & Miller, S. A. (1984). Hypertension and calcium. *Science, 226,* 384–385.

Fenton, W. S., & McGlashan, T. H. (1994). Antecedents, symptom progression, and long-term outcome of the deficit syndrome in schizophrenia. *American Journal of Psychiatry, 151,* 351–356.

Ferguson, E. D. (1989). Adler's motivational theory: An historical perspective on belonging and the fundamental human striving. *Individual Psychology, 45,* 354–361.

Fernandez, E., & Turk, D. C. (1989). The utility of cognitive coping strategies for altering pain perception: A meta-analysis. *Pain, 38,* 123–135.

Fernandez-Dols, J-M., & Ruiz-Belda, M-A. (1995). Are smiles a sign of happiness? Gold medal winners at the Olympic Games. *Journal of Personality and Social Psychology, 69,* 1113–1119.

Ferris, C. F. (1996, March). The rage of innocents. *The Sciences,* pp. 22–26.

Fichter, M. M., Koniarczyk, M., Greifenhagen, A., & Koegel, P. (1996). Mental illness in a representative sample of homeless men in Munich, Germany. *European Archives of Psychiatry and Clinical Neuroscience, 246,* 185–196.

Fichter, M. M., & Noegel, R. (1990). Concordance for bulimia nervosa in twins. *International Journal of Eating Disorders, 9,* 255–263.

Fiedler, F. E. (1981). Leadership effectiveness. *American Behavioral Scientist, 24,* 619–632.

Fiedler, F. E. (1987, September). When to lead, when to stand back. *Psychology Today,* pp. 26–27.

Field, T. (1991). Quality infant daycare and grade school behavior and performance. *Child Development, 62,* 863–870.

Field, T. (1996). Attachment and separation in young children. *Annual Review of Psychology, 47,* 541–561.

Field, T. M. (1998). Massage therapy effects. *American Psychologist, 53,* 1270–1281.

Fincham, F. D., & Bradbury, T. N. (1993). Marital satisfaction, depression, and attributions: A longitudinal analysis. *Journal of Personality and Social Psychology, 64,* 442–452.

Fink, G. R., Markowitsch, H. J., Reinkemeier, M., Bruckbauer, T., Kessler, J., & Heiss, W-D. (1996). Cerebral representation of one's own past: Neural networks involved in autobiographical memory. *Journal of Neuroscience, 16,* 4275–4282.

Fink, M. (1998). ECT and managed care. *Journal Watch Psychiatry, 4,* pp. 73, 76.

Fink, M. (1999). *Electroshock: Restoring the mind.* New York: Oxford University Press.

Finkel, L. H., & Sajda, P. (1994). Constructing visual perception. *American Scientist, 82,* 224–237.

Finucci, J. M., & Childs, B. (1981). Are there really more dyslexic boys than girls? In A. Ansara, N. Geschwind, A. Galaburda, M. Albert, & N. Gartrell (Eds.), *Sex differences in dyslexia.* Towson, MD: The Orton Dyslexia Society.

Fiore, E. (1989). *Encounters: A psychologist reveals case studies of abductions by extraterrestrials.* New York: Doubleday. Cited by L. S. Newman & R. F. Baumeister (1994). Toward an explanation of the UFO abduction phenomenon: Hypnotic, elaboration, extraterrestrial sadomasochism, and spurious memories. Unpublished manuscript, University of Illinois at Chicago.

Fischer, P. J., & Breakey, W. R. (1991). The epidemiology of alcohol, drug, and mental disorders among homeless persons. *American Psychologist, 46,* 1115–1128.

Fischhoff, B. (1982). Debiasing. In D. Kahneman, P. Slovic, & A. Tversky (Eds.), *Judgment under uncertainty: Heuristics and biases.* New York: Cambridge University Press.

Fischhoff, B., Slovic, P., & Lichtenstein, S. (1977). Knowing with certainty: The appropriateness of extreme confidence. *Journal of Experimental Psychology: Human Perception and Performance, 3,* 552–564.

Fisher, H. E. (1993, March/April). After all, maybe it's biology. *Psychology Today,* pp. 40–45.

Fisher, H. T. (1984). Little Albert and Little Peter. *Bulletin of the British Psychological Society, 37,* 269.

Fisher, R. P., & Geiselman, R. E. (1992). *Memory-enhancing techniques for investigative interviewing: The cognitive interview.* Springfield, IL: Charles C. Thomas.

Fisher, R. P., Geiselman, R. E., & Raymond, D. S. (1987). Critical analysis of police interview techniques. *Journal of Police Science and Administration, 15,* 177–185.

Fisher, S., & Greenberg, R. (Eds.) (1997). *From placebo to panacea: Putting psychiatric drugs to the test.* New York: Wiley.

Fitch, R. H., & Denenberg, V. H. (1998). A role for ovarian hormones in sexual differentiation of the brain. *Behavioral and Brain Sciences, 21,* 311–352.

Flegal, K. M., Carroll, M. D., Kuczmarski, R. J., & Johnson, C. L. (1998). Overweight and obesity in the United States: Prevalence and trends, 1960–1994. *International Journal of Obesity, 22,* 39–47.

Fleming, I., Baum, A., & Weiss, L. (1987). Social density and perceived control as mediator of crowding stress in high-density residential neighborhoods. *Journal of Personality and Social Psychology, 52,* 899–906.

Fleming, J. H., & Scott, B. A. (1991). The costs of confession: The Persian Gulf War POW tapes in historical and theoretical perspective. *Contemporary Social Psychology, 15,* 127–138.

Fletcher, G. J. O., Fitness, J., & Blampied, N. M. (1990). The link between attributions and happiness in close relationships: The roles of depression and explanatory style. *Journal of Social and Clinical Psychology, 9,* 243–255.

Flynn, J. R. (1987). Massive IQ gains in 14 nations: What IQ tests really measure. *Psychological Bulletin, 101,* 171–191.

Flynn, J. R. (1999). Searching for justice: The discovery of IQ gains over time. *American Psychologist, 54,* 5–20.

Foa, E. B., & Kozak, M. J. (1986). Emotional processing of fear: Exposure to corrective information. *Psychological Bulletin, 99,* 20–35.

Folkman, S., Chesney, M., Collette, L., Boccellari, A., & Cooke, M. (1996). Postbereavement depressive mood and its prebereavement predictors in HIV+ and HIV- gay men. *Journal of Personality and Social Psychology, 70,* 336–348.

Foltved, P. (1996). The psychological profession in Denmark. In A. Schorr & S. Saari (Eds.), *Psychology in Europe: Facts, figures, realities.* Gottingen: Hogrefe & Huber.

Fong, G. T., Frantz, D. H., & Nisbett, R. E. (1986). The effects of statistical training on thinking about everyday problems. *Cognitive Psychology, 18,* 253–292.

Fontana, A., Rosenheck, R., & Brett, E. (1992). War zone traumas and posttraumatic stress disorder symptomatology. *Journal of Nervous and Mental Disease, 180,* 748–755.

Foree, D. D., & LoLordo, V. M. (1973). Attention in the pigeon: Differential effects of food-getting versus shock-avoidance procedures. *Journal of Comparative and Physiological Psychology, 85,* 551–558.

Forer, B. R. (1949). The fallacy of personal validation: A classroom demonstration of gullibility. *Journal of Abnormal and Social Psychology, 44,* 118–123.

Foreyt, J. P., Walker, S., Poston, C., II, & Goodrick, G. K. (1996). Future directions in obesity and eating disorders. *Addictive Behaviors, 21,* 767–778.

Forgas, J. P. (1998). On feeling good and getting your way: Mood effects on negotiator cognition and bargaining strategies. *Journal of Personality and Social Psychology, 74,* 565–577.

Forgas, J. P., Bower, G. H., & Krantz, S. E. (1984). The influence of mood on perceptions of social interactions. *Journal of Experimental Social Psychology, 20,* 497–513.

Forgatch, M. S. (1995, March). Reported in W. W. Gibbs, Seeking the criminal element. *Scientific American,* pp. 100–107.

Forge, A., Li, L., Corwin, J. T., & Nevill, G. (1993). Ultrastructural evidence for hair cell regeneration in the mammalian inner ear. *Science, 259,* 1616–1619.

Foss, D. J., & Hakes, D. T. (1978). *Psycholinguistics: An introduction to the psychology of language.* Englewood Cliffs, NJ: Prentice-Hall.

Foulkes, D. (1999). *Children's dreaming and the development of consciousness.* Cambridge, MA: Harvard University Press.

Fouts, R. (1997). *Next of kin: What chimpanzees have taught me about who we are.* New York: Morrow.

Fouts, R. S. (1992). Transmission of a human gestural language in a chimpanzee mother-infant relationship. *Friends of Washoe, 12/13,* 2–8.

Fouts, R. S., & Bodamer, M. (1987). Preliminary report to the National Geographic Society on: "Chimpanzee intrapersonal signing." *Friends of Washoe, 7*(1), 4–12.

Fowler, M. J., Sullivan, M. J., & Ekstrand, B. R. (1973). Sleep and memory. *Science, 179,* 302–304.

Fowler, R. C., Rich, C. L., & Young, D. (1986). San Diego suicide study: II. Substance abuse in young cases. *Archives of General Psychiatry, 43,* 962–965.

Fowler, R. D. (1986, May). Howard Hughes: A psychological autopsy. *Psychology Today,* pp. 22–33.

Fowles, D. C. (1992). Schizophrenia: Diathesis-stress revisited. *Annual Review of Psychology, 43,* 303–336.

Fox, B. H. (1998). Psychosocial factors in cancer incidence and prognosis. In P. M. Cinciripini & others (Eds.), *Psychological and behavioral factors in cancer risk.* New York: Oxford University Press.

Fox, J. L. (1984). The brain's dynamic way of keeping in touch. *Science, 225,* 820–821.

Fozard, J. L., & Popkin, S. J. (1978). Optimizing adult development: Ends and means of an applied psychology of aging. *American Psychologist, 33,* 975–989.

France-Presse, A. (1999, May 10). U.N. official says AIDS in Southern Africa "exceeds worst nightmares." *New York Times* (www.nytimes.com).

Francis, D., Diorio, J., Liu, D., & Meaney, M. J. (1999). Nongenomic transmission across generations of maternal behavior and stress responses in the rat. *Science, 286,* 1155–1158.

Frank, J. D. (1982). Therapeutic components shared by all psychotherapies. In J. H. Harvey & M. M. Parks (Eds.), *The Master Lecture Series: Vol. 1. Psychotherapy research and behavior change.* Washington, DC: American Psychological Association.

Frank, R. (1999). *Luxury fever: Why money fails to satisfy in an era of excess.* New York: Free Press.

Frank, S. J. (1988). Young adults' perceptions of their relationships with their parents: Individual differences in connectedness, competence, and emotional autonomy. *Developmental Psychology, 24,* 729–737.

Frankel, A., & Prentice-Dunn, S. (1990). Loneliness and the processing of self-relevant information. *Journal of Social and Clinical Psychology, 9,* 303–315.

Frankel, A., Strange, D. R., & Schoonover, R. (1983). CRAP: Consumer rated assessment procedure. In G. H. Scherr & R. Liebmann-Smith (Eds.), *The best of* The Journal of Irreproducible Results. New York: Workman Publishing.

Frankenburg, W., Dodds, J., Archer, P., Shapiro, H., & Bresnick, B. (1992). The Denver II: A major revision and restandardization of the Denver Developmental Screening Test. *Pediatrics, 89,* 91–97.

Frasure-Smith, N., Lesperance, F., Juneau, M., Talajic, M., & Bourassa, M. G. (1999). Gender, depression, and one-year prognosis after myocardial infarction. *Psychosomatic Medicine, 61,* 26–37.

Frasure-Smith, N., Lesperance, F., & Talajic, M. (1995). The impact of negative emotions on prognosis following myocardial infarction: Is it more than depression? *Health Psychology, 14,* 388–398.

Fredrickson, B. L. (1998). *Review of General Psychology, 2,* 300–319.

Fredrickson, B. L. (2000). Cultivating positive emotions to optimize health and well-being. *Prevention and Treatment, 3* (journal.apa.org. prevention).

Fredrickson, B. L., & Kahneman, D. (1993). Duration neglect in retrospective evaluations of affective episodes. *Journal of Personality and Social Psychology, 65,* 45–55.

Fredrickson, B. L., Roberts, T.-A., Noll, S. M., Quinn, D. M., & Twenge, J. M. (1998). That swimsuit becomes you: Sex differences in self-objectification, restrained eating, and math performance. *Journal of Personality and Social Psychology, 75,* 269–284.

Freedman, D. G. (1979). *Human sociobiology: A holistic approach.* New York: Free Press.

Freedman, J. L. (1978). *Happy people.* San Diego: Harcourt Brace Jovanovich.

Freedman, J. L. (1988). Television violence and aggression: What the evidence shows. In S. Oskamp (Ed.), *Television as a social issue.* Newbury Park, CA: Sage.

Freedman, J. L., & Fraser, S. C. (1966). Compliance without pressure: The foot-in-the-door technique. *Journal of Personality and Social Psychology, 4,* 195–202.

Freedman, J. L., & Perlick, D. (1979). Crowding, contagion, and laughter. *Journal of Experimental Social Psychology, 15,* 295–303.

Freedman, L. R., Rock, D., Roberts, S. A., Cornblatt, B. A., & Erlenmeyer-Kimling, L. (1998). The New York high-risk project: Attention, anhedonia and social outcome. *Schizophrenia Research, 30,* 1–9.

Freeman, W. J. (1991, February). The physiology of perception. *Scientific American,* pp. 78–85.

Freud, S. (1931; reprinted 1961). Female sexuality. In J. Strachey (Trans.), *The standard edition of the complete psychological works of Sigmund Freud.* London: Hogarth Press.

Freud, S. (1933). *New introductory lectures on psychoanalysis.* New York: Carlton House.

Freud, S. (1935; reprinted 1960). *A general introduction to psychoanalysis.* New York: Washington Square Press.

Freyd, J. J. (1996). *Betrayal trauma: The logic of forgetting childhood abuse.* Cambridge, MA: Harvard University Press.

Freyd, J. J. (1998). Science in the memory debate. *Ethics and Behavior, 8,* 101–113.

Freyd, J. J. (1999, June). Blind to betrayal: New perspectives on memory for trauma. *Harvard Mental Health Letter,* pp. 4–6.

Freyd, P. (1999, December 27). False Memory Syndrome Foundation lawsuits update. Personal correspondence from FMSF executive director.

Friedman, M. A., & Brownell, K. D. (1995). Psychological correlates of obesity: Moving to the next research generation. *Psychological Bulletin, 117,* 3–20.

Friedman, M., & Ulmer, D. (1984). *Treating Type A behavior—and your heart.* New York: Knopf.

Friedrich, O. (1987, December 7). New age harmonies. *Time,* pp. 62–72.

Friend, B. (1998, Fall). Quoted in Kay S. Hymowitz, Tweens: Ten going on sixteen." *City Journal* (www.city-journal.org/html/8_4_a1.htm).

Frieze, I. H., Parsons, J. E., Johnson, P. B., Ruble, D. N., & Zellman, G. L. (1978). *Women and sex roles: A social psychological perspective.* New York: Norton.

Frijda, N. H. (1988). The laws of emotion. *American Psychologist, 43,* 349–358.

Fritsch, G., & Hitzig, E. (1870; reprinted 1960). On the electrical excitability of the cerebrum. In G. Von Bonin (Trans.), *Some papers on the cerebral cortex.* Springfield, IL: Charles C. Thomas.

Fritsch, J. (1999, May 25). 95% regain lost weight, or do they? *New York Times* (www.nytimes.com).

Fromkin, V., & Rodman, R. (1983). *An introduction to language* (3rd ed.). New York: Holt, Rinehart & Winston.

Fry, A. F., & Hale, S. (1996). Processing speed, working memory, and fluid intelligence: Evidence for a developmental cascade. *Psychological Science, 7,* 237–241.

Fryauf-Bertschy, H., & Gantz, B. J. (1994, November/December). Cochlear implants for children: Candidacy and performance results to date. *SHHH Journal,* pp. 20–23.

Fuhriman, A., & Burlingame, G. M. (1994). Group psychotherapy: Research and practice. In A. Fuhriman & G. M. Burlingame (Eds.), *Handbook of group psychotherapy.* New York: Wiley.

Fuller, M. J., & Downs, A. C. (1990). Spermarche is a salient biological marker in men's development. Poster presented at the American Psychological Society convention.

Funder, D. C. (1987). Errors and mistakes: Evaluating the accuracy of social judgment. *Psychological Bulletin, 101,* 75–90.

Funder, D. C. (1991). Global traits: A neo-Allportian approach to personality. *Psychological Science, 2,* 31–39.

Funder, D. C. (1995). On the accuracy of personality judgment: A realistic approach. *Psychological Review, 102,* 652–670.

Funder, D. C., & Block, J. (1989). The role of ego-control, ego-resiliency, and IQ in delay of gratification in adolescence. *Journal of Personality and Social Psychology, 57,* 1041–1050.

Furlow, F. B., & Thornhill, R. (1996, January/February). The orgasm wars. *Psychology Today,* pp. 42–46.

Furnham, A. (1982). Explanations for unemployment in Britain. *European Journal of Social Psychology, 12,* 335–352.

Furnham, A. (1993). A comparison between psychology and nonpsychology students' misperceptions of the subject. *Journal of Social Behavior and Personality, 8,* 311–322.

Furnham, A., & Baguma, P. (1994). Cross-cultural differences in the evaluation of male and female body shapes. *International Journal of Eating Disorders, 15,* 81–89.

Furnham, A., & Gasson, L. (1998). Sex differences in parental estimates of their children's intelligence. *Sex Roles, 38,* 151–162.

Furnham, A., & Rawles, R. (1995). Sex differences in the estimation of intelligence. *Journal of Social Behavior and Personality, 10,* 741–748.

Furnham, A., & Taylor, L. (1990). Lay theories of homosexuality: Aetiology, behaviours, and 'cures.' *British Journal of Social Psychology, 29,* 135–147.

Furr, R. M., & Funder, D. C. (1998). A multimodal analysis of personal negativity. *Journal of Personality and Social Psychology, 74,* 1580–1591.

Furstenberg, F. F., Jr., Moore, K. A., & Peterson, J. L. (1985). Sex education and sexual experience among adolescents. *American Journal of Public Health, 75,* 1331–1332.

Gabbay, F. H. (1992). Behavior-genetic strategies in the study of emotion. *Psychological Science, 3,* 50–55.

Gabrieli, J. D. E., Desmond, J. E., Demb, J. E., Wagner, A. D., Stone, M. V., Vaidya, C. J., & Glover, G. H. (1996). Functional magnetic resonance imaging of semantic memory processes in the frontal lobes. *Psychological Science, 7,* 278–283.

Galambos, N. L. (1992). Parent-adolescent relations. *Current Directions in Psychological Science, 1,* 146–149.

Galati, D., Scherer, K. R., & Ricci-Bitti, P. E. (1997). Voluntary facial expression of emotion: Comparing congenitally blind with normally sighted encoders. *Journal of Personality and Social Psychology, 73,* 1363–1379.

Gallagher, M. (1990). Functional consequences of brain aging: The good news and the bad news. Address to the American Psychological Society convention.

Gallant, S. J., Popiel, D. A., Hoffman, D. M., Chakraborty, P. K., and Hamilton, J. A. (1992). Using daily ratings to confirm premenstrual syndrome/late luteal phase dysphoric disorder. Part II. What makes a "real" difference? *Psychosomatic Medicine, 54,* 167–181.

Gallup, G. G., Jr., & Suarez, S. D. (1985). Alternatives to the use of animals in psychological research. *American Psychologist, 40,* 1104–1111.

Gallup, G. G., Jr., & Suarez, S. D. (1986). Self-awareness and the emergence of mind in humans and other primates. In J. Suls & A. G. Greenwald (Eds.), *Psychological perspectives on the self* (Vol. 3.). Hillsdale, NJ: Erlbaum.

Gallup, G. H. (1972). *The Gallup poll: Public opinion 1935-1971* (Vol. 3). New York: Random House.

Gallup, G. H., Jr. (1994, October). Millions finding care and support in small groups. *Emerging Trends,* pp. 2–5.

Gallup, G. H., Jr. (1994, December). A nation in recovery. *PRRC Emerging Trends,* pp. 1–2.

Gallup, G. H., Jr., & Newport, F. (1991, Winter). Belief in paranormal phenomena among adult Americans. *Skeptical Inquirer,* pp. 137–146.

Gallup, G. H., Jr., & O'Connell, G. (1986). *Who do Americans say that I am?* Philadelphia, PA: Westminster Press.

Gallup, G., Jr. (1998). Can animals empathize? *Scientific American, 4,* 66.

Gallup International Institute (1996, February). Parents, grandparents OK with teens. *Youthviews,* p. 3.

Gallup Organization. (1993). Other hemispheres may think our religion is alien and exotic. *PRRC Emerging Trends, 15,* 1–3.

Gallup Organization. (1996, April). Majority disapprove of homosexual marriages. *Emerging Trends* (Princeton Religion Research Center), p. 2.

Gallup Poll (1997). Family values differ sharply around the world. Princeton, NJ: Gallup Organization (www.gallup.com/poll/releases/pr971107.asp).

Gallup Polls (1999, December 31). Reported in American opinion in the 20th century, *USA Today,* p. 11A.

Gallup Report. (1989, March/April). Commercial aviation. Pp. 32–33.

Gangestad, S. W., & Simpson, J. A. (2000). The evolution of human mating: Trade-offs and strategic pluralism. *Behavioral and Brain Sciences, 23.*

Garbarino, J., Dubrow, N., & Kostelny, K. (1992). *Children in danger: Coping with the consequences of community violence.* San Francisco: Jossey-Bass.

Garbarino, J., Kostelny, K., & Dubrow, N. (1991). What children can tell us about living in danger. *American Psychologist, 46,* 376–383.

Garcia, J., & Gustavson, A. R. (1997, January). Carl R. Gustavson (1946–1996): Pioneering wildlife psychologist. *APS Observer,* pp. 34–35.

Garcia, J., & Koelling, R. A. (1966). Relation of cue to consequence in avoidance learning. *Psychonomic Science, 4,* 123–124.

Gardner, H. (1983). *Frames of mind: The theory of multiple intelligences.* New York: Basic Books.

Gardner, H. (1993). *Creating minds.* New York: Basic Books.

Gardner, H. (1995). Perennial antinomies and perpetual redrawings: Is there progress in the study of mind? In R. L. Solso & D. W. Massaro (Eds.), *The science of the mind: 2001 and beyond.* New York: Oxford University Press.

Gardner, H. (1998, March 19). An intelligent way to progress. *The Independent* (London), p. E4.

Gardner, H. (1998, November 5). Do parents count? *New York Review of Books* (www.nybooks.com).

Gardner, H. (1999, February). Who owns intelligence? *Atlantic Monthly,* pp. 67–76.

Gardner, J. W. (1984). *Excellence: Can we be equal and excellent too?* New York: Norton.

Gardner, R. A., & Gardner, B. I. (1969). Teaching sign language to a chimpanzee. *Science, 165,* 664–672.

Gardner, R. M., & Tockerman, Y. R. (1994). A computer-TV video methodology for investigating the influence of somatotype on perceived personality traits. *Journal of Social Behavior and Personality, 9,* 555–563.

Garfield, C. (1986). *Peak performers: The new heroes of American business.* New York: Morrow.

Garner, D. M., & Wooley, S. C. (1991). Confronting the failure of behavioral and dietary treatments for obesity. *Clinical Psychology Review, 11,* 729–780.

Garnets, L., & Kimmel, D. (1990). Lesbian and gay dimensions in the psychological study of human diversity. Master lecture, American Psychological Association convention.

Garry, M., Loftus, E. F., & Brown, S. W. (1994). Memory: A river runs through it. *Consciousness and Cognition, 3,* 438–451.

Garry, M., Manning, C. G., Loftus, E. F., & Sherman, S. J. (1996). Imagination inflation: Imagining a childhood event inflates confidence that it occurred. *Psychonomic Bulletin & Review, 3,* 208–214.

Garza, D. L., & Feltz, D. L. (1998). Effects of selected mental practice on performance, self-efficacy, and competition confidence of figure skaters. *The Sports Psychologist, 12,* 1–15.

Gates, W. (1998, July 20). Charity begins when I'm ready (interview). *Fortune* (www.pathfinder.com/fortune/1998/980720/bil7.html).

Gawande, A. (1998, September 21). The pain perplex. *The New Yorker,* pp. 86–94.

Gawin, F. H. (1991). Cocaine addiction: Psychology and neurophysiology. *Science, 251,* 1580–1586.

Gazzaniga, M. S. (1967, August). The split brain in man. *Scientific American,* pp. 24–29.

Gazzaniga, M. S. (1983). Right hemisphere language following brain bisection: A 20-year perspective. *American Psychologist, 38,* 525–537.

Gazzaniga, M. S. (1988). *Mind matters: How mind and brain interact to create our conscious lives.* Boston: Houghton Mifflin.

Gazzaniga, M. S. (1988). Organization of the human brain. *Science, 245,* 947–952.

Gazzaniga, M. S. (1992). *Nature's mind: The biological roots of thinking, emotions, sexuality, language, and intelligence.* New York: Basic Books.

Gazzaniga, M. S. (1997). Brain, drugs, and society. *Science, 275,* 459.

Geary, D. C. (1995). Sexual selection and sex differences in spatial cognition. *Learning and Individual Differences, 7,* 289–301.

Geary, D. C. (1996). Sexual selection and sex differences in mathematical abilities. *Behavioral and Brain Sciences, 19,* 229–247.

Geary, D. C. (1998). *Male, female: The evolution of human sex differences.* Washington, DC: American Psychological Association.

Geary, D. C., Salthouse, T. A., Chen, G-P., & Fan, L. (1996). Are East Asian versus American differences in arithmetical ability a recent phenomenon? *Developmental Psychology, 32,* 254–262.

Geen, R. G. (1984). Human motivation: New perspectives on old problems. In A. M. Rogers & C. J. Scheirer (Eds.), *The G. Stanley Hall Lecture Series* (Vol. 4). Washington, DC: American Psychological Association.

Geen, R. G., & Quanty, M. B. (1977). The catharsis of aggression: An evaluation of a hypothesis. In L. Berkowitz (Ed.), *Advances in experimental social psychology* (Vol. 10). New York: Academic Press.

Geen, R. G., & Thomas, S. L. (1986). The immediate effects of media violence on behavior. *Journal of Social Issues, 42*(3), 7–28.

Geldard, F. A. (1972). *The human senses* (2nd ed.). New York: Wiley.

Gelman, D. (1989, May 15). Voyages to the unknown. *Newsweek,* pp. 66–69.

George. (1996, December). What does America believe? P. 117.

Gerald, C., Walker, M. W., Criscione, L., & Gustafson, E. L. (1996). A receptor subtype involved in neuropeptide-Y-induced food intake. *Nature, 382,* 168–171.

Gerard, R. W. (1953, September). What is memory? *Scientific American,* pp. 118–126.

Gerbner, G. (1985). Dreams that hurt: Mental illness in the mass media. Keynote address to the First Rosalynn Carter Symposium on Mental Health Policy, Emory University School of Medicine, Atlanta.

Gerbner, G. (1990). Stories that hurt: Tobacco, alcohol, and other drugs in the mass media. In H. Resnik (Ed.), *Youth and drugs: Society's mixed messages.* Rockville, MD: Office for Substance Abuse Prevention, U.S. Department of Health and Human Services.

Gerbner, G. (1993, June). Women and minorities on television: A study in casting and fate. A report to the Screen Actors Guild and the American Federation of Radio and Television Artists.

Gerbner, G., Gross, L., Morgan, M., & Signorielli, N. (1994). Growing up with television: The cultivation perspective. In J. Bryant & D. Zillman (Eds.), *Media effects: Advances in theory and research.* Hillsdale, NJ: Lawrence Erlbaum Associates, Inc., 17–41.

Gerbner, G., Morgan, M., & Signorielli, N. (1993). Television violence profile No. 16: The turning point from research to action. Annenberg School for Communication, University of Pennsylvania.

Gerhart, K. A., Koziol-McLain, J., Lowenstein, S. R., & Whiteneck, G. G. (1994). Quality of life following spinal cord injury: Knowledge and attitudes of emergency care providers. *Annals of Emergency Medicine, 23,* 807–812.

Gerrard, M., & Luus, C. A. E. (1995). Judgments of vulnerability to pregnancy: The role of risk factors and individual differences. *Personality and Social Psychology Bulletin, 21,* 160–171.

Geschwind, N. (1979, September). Specializations of the human brain. *Scientific American,* pp. 180–199.

Geschwind, N., & Behan, P. O. (1984). Laterality, hormones, and immunity. In N. Geschwind & A. M. Galaburda (Eds.), *Cerebral dominance: The biological foundations.* Cambridge, MA: Harvard University Press.

Gfeller, J. D., Lynn, S. J., & Pribble, W. E. (1987). Enhancing hypnotic susceptibility: Interpersonal and rapport factors. *Journal of Personality and Social Psychology, 52,* 586–595.

Giambra, L. M. (1974). Daydreaming across the life span: Late adolescent to senior citizen. *Aging and Human Development, 5,* 115–140.

Gibbons, A. (1992). Chimps: More diverse than a barrel of monkeys. *Science, 255,* 287–288.

Gibbons, F. X. (1986). Social comparison and depression: Company's effect on misery. *Journal of Personality and Social Psychology, 51,* 140–148.

Gibbs, W. W. (1996, June). Mind readings. *Scientific American,* pp. 34–36.

Gibson, E. J., & Walk, R. D. (1960, April). The "visual cliff." *Scientific American,* pp. 64–71.

Gibson, H. B. (1995, April). Recovered memories. *The Psychologist,* pp. 153–154.

Gilbert, D. T., Pinel, E. C., Wilson, T. D., Blumberg, S. J., & Wheatley, T. P. (1998). Immune neglect: A source of durability bias in affective forecasting. *Journal of Personality and Social Psychology, 75,* 617–638.

Giles, D. E., Dahl, R. E., & Coble, P. A. (1994). Childbearing, developmental, and familial aspects of sleep. In J. M. Oldham & M. B. Riba (Eds.), *Review of Psychiatry* (Vol. 13). Washington, DC: American Psychiatric Press.

Giles, T. R. (1983). Probable superiority of behavioral interventions—II: Empirical status of the equivalence of therapies hypothesis. *Journal of Behavior Therapy and Experimental Psychiatry, 14,* 189–196.

Gillham, J. E., & Reivich, K. J. (1999). Prevention of depressive symptoms in schoolchildren: A research update. *Psychological Science, 10,* 461–462.

Gilligan, C. (1982). *In a different voice: Psychological theory and women's development.* Cambridge, MA: Harvard University Press.

Gilligan, C., Lyons, N. P., & Hanmer, T. J. (Eds.). (1990). *Making connections: The relational worlds of adolescent girls at Emma Willard School.* Cambridge, MA: Harvard University Press.

Gilovich, T. (1991). *How we know what isn't so: The fallibility of human reason in everyday life.* New York: Free Press.

Gilovich, T. D. (1996). The spotlight effect: Exaggerated impressions of the self as a social stimulus. Unpublished manuscript, Cornell University.

Gilovich, T., & Medvec, V. H. (1995). The experience of regret: What, when, and why. *Psychological Review, 102,* 379–395.

Gilovich, T., & Savitsky, K. (1999). The spotlight effect and the illusion of transparency: Egocentric assessments of how we are seen by others. *Current Directions in Psychological Science, 8,* 165–168.

Gingerich, O. (1999, February 6). Is there a role for natural theology today? *The Real Issue* (www.origins.org/real/n9501/natural.html).

Giros, B., Jaber, M., Jones, S. R., Wrightman, R. M., & Caron, M. G. (1996). Hyperlocomotion and indifference to cocaine and amphetamine in mice lacking the dopamine transporter. *Nature, 379,* 606–612.

Gist, R., Lubin, B., & Redburn, B. G. (1998). Psychological, ecological, and community perspectives on disaster response. *Journal of Personal and Interpersonal Loss, 3,* 25–51.

Gist, R., & Welch, Q. B. (1989). Certification change versus actual behavior change in teenage suicide rates, 1955–1979. *Suicide and Life Threatening Behavior, 19,* 277–288.

Gist, R., & Woodall, S. J. (1999). Occupational stress in contemporary fire service: Systems approaches to assessment and intervention. In R. Gist & B. Lubin (Eds.), *Responses to disaster: Psychosocial, ecological, and community approaches.* Washington, DC: Taylor & Francis.

Giuliano, T. A., Barnes, L. C., Fiala, S. E., & Davis D. M. (1998a). An empirical investigation of male answer syndrome. Paper presented at the Southwestern Psychological Association convention.

Giuliano, T. A., Fiala, S. E., Davis, D. M., Barnes, L. C., & Patrick, E. C. (1998b). The reluctance to admit "I don't know": Exploring "male answer syndrome." Paper presented to the American Psychological Society convention.

Gjerde, P. F. (1983). Attentional capacity dysfunction and arousal in schizophrenia. *Psychological Bulletin, 93,* 57–72.

Gladue, B. A. (1990). Hormones and neuroendocrine factors in atypical human sexual behavior. In J. R. Feierman (Ed.), *Pedophilia: Biosocial dimensions.* New York: Springer-Verlag.

Gladue, B. A. (1994). The biopsychology of sexual orientation. *Current Directions in Psychological Science, 3,* 150–154.

Glass, D. C., & Singer, J. E. (1972). *Urban stress.* New York: Academic Press.

Gleaves, D. H. (1996). The sociocognitive model of dissociative identity disorder: A reexamination of the evidence. *Psychological Bulletin, 120,* 42–59.

Glenn, N. D. (1975). Psychological well-being in the postparental stage: Some evidence from national surveys. *Journal of Marriage and the Family, 37,* 105–110.

Glick, P., Gottesman, D., & Jolton, J. (1989). The fault is not in the stars: Susceptibility of skeptics and believers in astrology to the Barnum effect. *Personality and Social Psychology Bulletin, 15,* 572–583.

Gluhoski, V. L., & Wortman, C. B. (1996). The impact of trauma on world views. *Journal of Social and Clinical Psychology, 15,* 417–429.

Godden, D. R., & Baddeley, A. D. (1975). Context-dependent memory in two natural environments: On land and underwater. *British Journal of Psychology, 66,* 325–331.

Goff, D. C. (1993). Reply to Dr. Armstrong. *Journal of Nervous and Mental Disease, 181,* 604–605.

Goff, D. C., & Simms, C. A. (1993). Has multiple personality disorder remained consistent over time? *Journal of Nervous and Mental Disease, 181,* 595–600.

Goff, L. M., & Roediger, H. L. III, (1998). Imagination inflation for action events: Repeated imaginings lead to illusory recollections. *Memory and Cognition, 26,* 20–33.

Gold, M., & Yanof, D. S. (1985). Mothers, daughters, and girlfriends. *Journal of Personality and Social Psychology, 49,* 654–659.

Gold, P. E. (1987). Sweet memories. *American Scientist, 75,* 151–155.

Gold, P. E. (1992). A proposed neurobiological basis for regulating memory storage for significant events. In E. Winograd & U. Neisser (Eds.), *Affect and accuracy in recall: Studies of "flashbulb" memories.* New York: Cambridge University Press.

Goldberg, J., True, W. R., Eisen, S. A., & Henderson, W. G. (1990). A twin study of the effects of the Vietnam War on posttraumatic stress disorder. *Journal of the American Medical Association, 263,* 1227–1232.

Goldberg, L. R. (1993). The structure of phenotypic personality traits. *American Psychologist, 48,* 26–34.

Goldfried, M. R., & Padawer, W. (1982). Current status and future directions in psychotherapy. In M. R. Goldfried (Ed.), *Converging themes in psychotherapy: Trends in psychodynamic, humanistic, and behavioral practice.* New York: Springer.

Goldfried, M. R., Raue, P. J., & Castonguay, L. G. (1998). The therapeutic focus in significant sessions of master therapists: A comparison of cognitive-behavioral and psychodynamic-interpersonal interventions. *Journal of Consulting and Clinical Psychology, 66,* 803–810.

Goldin-Meadow, S., & Mylander, C. (1998). Spontaneous sign systems created by deaf children in two cultures. *Nature, 391,* 279–281.

Golding, J. M. (1996). Sexual assault history and women's reproductive and sexual health. *Psychology of Women Quarterly, 20,* 101–121.

Goldman, D. (1996). Why mice drink. *Nature Genetics, 13,* 137–138.

Goldstein, I., Lue, T. F., Padma-Nathan, H., Rosen, R. C., Steers, W. D., & Wicker, P. A. (1998). Oral sildenafil in the treatment of erectile dysfunction. *New England Journal of Medicine, 338,* 1397–1404.

Goleman, D. (1980, February). 1,528 little geniuses and how they grew. *Psychology Today,* pp. 28–53.

Goleman, D. (1995). *Emotional intelligence.* New York: Bantam.

Goleman, D. (1996, November 19). Research on brain leads to pursuit of designer drugs. *New York Times,* pp. C1, C3.

Golombok, S., & Tasker, F. (1996). Do parents influence the sexual orientation of their children? Findings from a longitudinal study of lesbian families. *Developmental Psychology, 32,* 3–11.

Golub, S. (1983). *Menarche: The transition from girl to woman.* Lexington, MA: Lexington Books.

Gonsiorek, J. C. (1982). Summary and conclusions. In W. Paul, J. D. Weinrich, J. C. Gonsiorek, & M. E. Hotvedt (Eds.), *Homosexuality: Social, psychological, and biological issues.* Beverly Hills, CA: Sage.

Goodall, J. (1968). The behaviour of free-living chimpanzees in the Gombe Stream Reserve. *Animal Behaviour Monographs, 1,* 161–311.

Goodall, J. (1986). *The chimpanzees of Gombe: Patterns of behavior.* Cambridge, MA: Harvard University Press.

Goodall, J. (1998). Learning from the chimpanzees: A message humans can understand. *Science, 282,* 2184–2185.

Goodchilds, J. (1987, September 27). Quoted in Carol Tavris, Old age is not what it used to be. *New York Times Magazine: Good Health Magazine,* pp. 24–25, 91–92.

Goode, E. (1999, February 16). Tales of midlife crisis found greatly exaggerated. *New York Times* (www.nytimes.com).

Goode, E. (1999, April 13). If things taste bad, "phantoms" may be at work. *New York Times* (www.nytimes.com).

Goode, E. (1999, May 20). Study finds TV trims Fijian girls' body image and eating habits. *New York Times* (www.nytimes.com).

Goodhart, D. E. (1986). The effects of positive and negative thinking on performance in an achievement situation. *Journal of Personality and Social Psychology, 51,* 117–124.

Goodman, L. A., Koss, M. P., & Russo, N. F. (1993). Violence against women: Mental health effects. Part II. Conceptualizations of posttraumatic stress. *Applied & Preventive Psychology, 2,* 123–130.

Goodwin, C. J. (1991). Misportraying Pavlov's apparatus. *American Journal of Psychology, 104,* 135–141.

Gopnik, A., & Meltzoff, A. N. (1986). Relations between semantic and cognitive development in the one-word stage: The specificity hypothesis. *Child Development, 57,* 1040–1053.

Goranson, R. E. (1978). The hindsight effect in problem solving. Unpublished manuscript. Cited by G. Wood (1984). Research methodology: A decision-making perspective. In A. M. Rogers & C. J. Scheirer (Eds.), *The G. Stanley Hall Lecture Series* (Vol. 4). Washington, DC: American Psychological Association.

Gore, A., Jr. (1992). *Earth in the balance: Ecology and the human spirit.* Boston: Houghton Mifflin.

Gore, T. (1999, September/October). Tipper Gore and Rosalynn Carter on America's mental health crisis. *Psychology Today,* pp. 31–32.

Gore, T., (1994, September 11). I know there is help (interviewed by C. Greer). *Parade,* pp. 4–7.

Gorsuch, R. L. (1988). Psychology of religion. *Annual Review of Psychology, 39,* 201–222.

Gortmaker, S. L., Must, A., Perrin, J. M., Sobol, A. M., & Dietz, W. H. (1993). Social and economic consequences of overweight in adolescence and young adulthood. *New England Journal of Medicine, 329,* 1008–1012.

Gotlib, I. H. (1992). Interpersonal and cognitive aspects of depression. *Current Directions in Psychological Science, 1,* 149–154.

Gotlib, I. H., & Hammen, C. L. (1992). *Psychological aspects of depression: Toward a cognitive-interpersonal integration.* New York: Wiley.

Gottesman, I. I. (1991). *Schizophrenia genesis: The origins of madness.* New York: Freeman.

Gottesman, I. I. (1993). The origins of schizophrenia: Past as prologue. In R. Plomin & G. E. McClearn (Eds.), *Nature, nurture, and psychology.* Washington, DC: American Psychological Association.

Gottman, J., with Silver, N. (1994). *Why marriages succeed or fail.* New York: Simon & Schuster.

Gould, E., Reeves, A. J., Graziano, M. S. A., & Gross, C. G. (1999). Neurogenesis in the neocortex of adult primates. *Science, 286,* 548–552.

Gould, S. J. (1981). *The mismeasure of man.* New York: Norton.

Grady, C. L., McIntosh, A. R., Horwitz, B., Maisog, J. M., Ungeleider, L. G., Mentis, M. J., Pietrini, P., Schapiro, M. B., & Haxby, J. V. (1995). Age-related reductions in human recognition memory due to impaired encoding. *Science, 269,* 218–221.

Graf, P. (1990). Life-span changes in implicit and explicit memory. *Bulletin of the Psychonomic Society, 28,* 353–358.

Graham, J. W., Marks, G., & Hansen, W. B. (1991). Social influence processes affecting adolescent substance use. *Journal of Applied Psychology, 76,* 291–298.

Grant, B. F., & Dawson, D. A. (1998). Age of onset of drug use and its association with DSM-IV drug abuse and dependence: Results from the national Longitudinal Alcohol Epidemiologic Survey. *Journal of Substance Abuse, 10,* 163–173.

Gray-Little, B., & Burks, N. (1983). Power and satisfaction in marriage: A review and critique. *Psychological Bulletin, 93,* 513–538.

Gray-Little, B., & Hafdahl, A. R. (2000). Factors influencing racial comparisons of self-esteem: A quantitative review. *Psychological Bulletin, 126,* 26–54.

Greeley, A. M. (1991). *Faithful attraction.* New York: Tor Books.

Greenberg, J., Solomon, S., & Pyszczynski, T. (1997). Terror management theory of self-esteem and cultural worldviews: Empirical assessments and conceptual refinements. *Advances in Social Psychology, 29,* 61–142.

Greene, R. L. (1987). Effects of maintenance rehearsal on human memory. *Psychological Bulletin, 102,* 403–413.

Greenfeld, L. A. (1998). *Alcohol and crime: An analysis of national data on the prevalence of alcohol involvement in crime.* Washington, DC: Document NCJ-168632, Bureau of Justice Statistics (www.ojp.usdoj.gov/bjs).

Greenough, W. T., Black, J. E., & Wallace, C. S. (1987). Experience and brain development. *Child Development, 58,* 539–559.

Greenwald, A. G. (1992). New look 3: Unconscious cognition reclaimed. *American Psychologist, 47,* 766–779.

Greenwald, A. G. (1992). Subliminal semantic activation and subliminal snake oil. Paper presented to the American Psychological Association Convention, Washington, DC.

Greenwald, A. G., McGhee, D. E., & Schwartz, J. L. K. (1998). Measuring individual differences in implicit cognition: The implicit association test. *Journal of Personality and Social Psychology, 74,* 1464–1480.

Greenwald, A. G., Spangenberg, E. R., Pratkanis, A. R., & Eskenazi, J. (1991). Double-blind tests of subliminal self-help audiotapes. *Psychological Science, 2,* 119–122.

Greenwood, M. R. C. (1989). Sexual dimorphism and obesity. In A. J. Stunkard & A. Baum (Eds.). *Perspectives in behavioral medicine: Eating, sleeping, and sex.* Hillsdale, NJ: Erlbaum.

Greer, G. (1984, April). The uses of chastity and other paths to sexual pleasures. *MS*, pp. 53–60, 96.

Gregory, R. L. (November, 1968). Visual illusions. *Scientific American, 219*(5), 66–76.

Gregory, R. L. (1978). *Eye and brain: The psychology of seeing* (3rd ed.). New York: McGraw-Hill.

Gregory, R. L., & Gombrich, E. H. (Eds.). (1973). *Illusion in nature and art.* New York: Charles Scribner's Sons.

Greif, E. B., & Ulman, K. J. (1982). The psychological impact of menarche on early adolescent females: A review of the literature. *Child Development, 53,* 1413–1430.

Greist, J. H., Jefferson, J. W., & Marks, I. M. (1986). *Anxiety and its treatment: Help is available.* Washington, DC: American Psychiatric Press.

Grenier, G., & Byers, E. S. (1995). Rapid ejaculation: A review of conceptual, etiological, and treatment issues. *Archives of Sexual Behavior, 24,* 447–472.

Griffin, D. R. (1984). Animal thinking. *American Scientist, 72,* 456–464.

Grilo, C. M., & Pogue-Geile, M. F. (1991). The nature of environmental influences on weight and obesity: A behavior genetic analysis. *Psychological Bulletin, 110,* 520–537.

Grobstein, C. (1979, June). External human fertilization. *Scientific American,* pp. 57–67.

Grolnick, W. S., & Ryan, R. M. (1987). Autonomy in children's learning: An experimental and individual difference investigation. *Journal of Personality and Social Psychology, 52,* 890–898.

Grosof, D. H., Shapley, R. M., & Hawken, M. J. (1993). Macaque V1 neurons can signal 'illusory' contours. *Nature, 365,* 550–552.

Gross, A. E., & Crofton, C. (1977). What is good is beautiful. *Sociometry, 40,* 85–90.

Grossberg, S. (1995). The attentive brain. *American Scientist, 83,* 438–449.

Grossman, M., & Wood, W. (1993). Sex differences in intensity of emotional experience: A social role interpretation. *Journal of Personality and Social Psychology, 65,* 1010–1022.

Gruder, C. L. (1977). Choice of comparison persons in evaluating oneself. In J. M. Suls & R. L. Miller (Eds.), *Social comparison processes.* New York: Hemisphere.

Guerin, B. (1986). Mere presence effects in humans: A review. *Journal of Personality and Social Psychology, 22,* 38–77.

Guion, R. M. (1992). Science, pseudoscience, and silly science in applied psychology. Paper presented to the American Psychological Association convention.

Gura, T. (1997). Obesity sheds its secrets. *Science, 275,* 751–753.

Gustavson, C. R., Garcia, J., Hankins, W. G., & Rusiniak, K. W. (1974). Coyote predation control by aversive conditioning. *Science, 184,* 581–583.

Gustavson, C. R., Kelly, D. J., & Sweeney, M. (1976). Prey-lithium aversions I: Coyotes and wolves. *Behavioral Biology, 17,* 61–72.

Gutmann, D. (1977). The cross-cultural perspective: Notes toward a comparative psychology of aging. In J. E. Birren & K. Warner Schaie (Eds.), *Handbook of the psychology of aging.* New York: Van Nostrand Reinhold.

Guttmacher Institute. (1993). *Facts in brief.* New York: Alan Guttmacher Institute.

Guttmacher Institute. (1994). *Sex and America's teenagers.* New York: Alan Guttmacher Institute.

Guttmacher Institute. (2000). *Fulfilling the promise: Public policy and U.S. family planning clinics.* New York: Alan Guttmacher Institute.

Haber, R. N. (1970, May). How we remember what we see. *Scientific American,* pp. 104–112.

Hackel, L. S., & Ruble, D. N. (1992). Changes in the marital relationship after the first baby is born: Predicting the impact of expectancy disconfirmation. *Journal of Personality and Social Psychology, 62,* 944–957.

Haddock, G., & Zanna, M. P. (1994). Preferring "housewives" to "feminists." *Psychology of Women Quarterly, 18,* 25–52.

Haier, R. J. (1993). Cerebral glucose metabolism and intelligence. In P. A. Vernon (Ed.), *Biologic approaches to the study of human intelligence.* Norwood, NJ: Ablex.

Halaas, J. L., Gajiwala, K. S., Maffei, M., Cohen, S. L., Chait, B. T., Rabinowitz, D., Lallone, R. L., Burley, S. K., & Friedman, J. M. (1995). Weight-reducing effects of the plasma protein encoded by the *obese* gene. *Science, 269,* 543–546.

Halberstadt, J. B., Niedenthal, P. M., & Kushner, J. (1995). Resolution of lexical ambiguity by emotional state. *Psychological Science, 6,* 278–281.

Haldeman, D. C. (1994). The practice and ethics of sexual orientation conversion therapy. *Journal of Consulting and Clinical Psychology, 62,* 221–227.

Hall, C. S. (1984). "A ubiquitous sex difference in dreams" revisited. *Journal of Personality and Social Psychology, 46,* 1109–1117.

Hall, C. S., Dornhoff, W., Blick, K. A., & Weesner, K. E. (1982). The dreams of college men and women in 1950 and 1980: A comparison of dream contents and sex differences. *Sleep, 5,* 188–194.

Hall, C. S., & Lindzey, G. (1978). *Theories of personality* (2nd ed.). New York: Wiley.

Hall, G. (1997). Context aversion, Pavlovian conditioning, and the psychological side effects of chemotherapy. *European Psychologist, 2,* 118–124.

Hall, G. S. (1904). *Adolescence: Its psychology and its relations to physiology, anthropology, sex, crime, religion and education* (Vol. I). New York: Appleton-Century-Crofts.

Hall, J. A. (1987). On explaining gender differences: The case of nonverbal communication. In P. Shaver & C. Hendrick (Eds.), *Review of Personality and Social Psychology, 7,* 177–200.

Hall, J. A. Y., & Kimura, D. (1994). Dermatoglyphic assymetry and sexual orientation in men. *Behavioral Neuroscience, 108,* 1203–1206.

Hall, N. R., & Goldstein, A. L. (1986, March/April). Thinking well: The chemical links between emotions and health. *The Sciences,* pp. 34–40.

Hallinan, J. T. (1997, January 14). State moves to end payments in repressed memory cases. Newhouse News Service (in *Grand Rapids Press*).

Halpern, D. F. (1991). Cognitive sex differences: Why diversity is a critical research issue. Paper presented to the American Psychological Association convention.

Halpern, D. F. (1997). Sex differences in intelligence: Implications for education. *American Psychologist, 52,* 1091–1102.

Halpern, D. F., & Coren, S. (1988). Do right-handers live longer? *Nature, 333,* 213.

Halpern, D. F., & Coren, S. (1990). Laterality and longevity: Is left-handedness associated with a younger age at death? In S. Coren (Ed.), *Left-handedness: Behavioral implications and anomalies.* Amsterdam: North-Holland.

Halpern, D. F., & Coren, S. (1991). Lateral preference and life span. *New England Journal of Medicine, 324,* 998.

Halpern, D. F., & Coren, S. (1993). Left-handedness and life span: A reply to Harris. *Psychological Bulletin, 114,* 235–241.

Halpern, D. F., Gilbert, R., & Coren, S. (1996). PC or not-PC? Contemporary challenges to unpopular research. *Journal of Social Distress and the Homeless, 5,* 251–271.

Hamida, S. B., Mineka, S., & Bailey, J. M. (1998). Sex differences in perceived controllability of mate value: An evolutionary perspective. *Journal of Personality and Social Psychology, 75,* 953–966.

Hamill, R., Wilson, T. D., & Nisbett, R. E. (1980). Insensitivity to sample bias: Generalizing from atypical cases. *Journal of Personality and Social Psychology, 39,* 578–589.

Hamilton, M. C. (1988). Using masculine generics: Does generic "he" increase male bias in the user's imagery? *Sex Roles, 19,* 785–799.

Hammersmith, S. K. (1982, August). *Sexual preference: An empirical study from the Alfred C. Kinsey Institute for Sex Research.* Paper presented at the meeting of the American Psychological Association, Washington, DC.

Haney, C., & Logan, D. D. (1994). Broken promise: The Supreme Court's response to social science research on capital punishment. *Journal of Social Issues, 50,* 75–101.

Hansen, C. H., & Hansen, R. D. (1988). Finding the face-in-the-crowd: An anger superiority effect. *Journal of Personality and Social Psychology, 54,* 917–924.

Harber, K. D. (1998). Feedback to minorities: Evidence of a positive bias. *Journal of Personality and Social Psychology, 74,* 622–628.

Hardin, C., & Banaji, M. R. (1993). The influence of language on thought. *Social Cognition, 11,* 277–308.

Hare, R. D. (1975). Psychophysiological studies of psychopathy. In D. C. Fowles (Ed.), *Clinical applications of psychophysiology.* New York: Columbia University Press.

Harkins, S. G., & Szymanski, K. (1989). Social loafing and group evaluation. *Journal of Personality and Social Psychology, 56,* 934–941.

Harlow, H. F., Harlow, M. K., & Suomi, S. J. (1971). From thought to therapy: Lessons from a primate laboratory. *American Scientist, 59,* 538–549.

Harlow, R. E., & Cantor, N. (1996). Still participating after all these years: A study of life task participation in later life. *Journal of Personality and Social Psychology.*

Harrington, D. M., Block, J. H., & Block, J. (1987). Testing aspects of Carl Rogers' theory of creative environments: Child-rearing antecedents of creative potential in young adolescents. *Journal of Personality and Social Psychology, 52,* 851–856.

Harris, B. (1979). Whatever happened to Little Albert? *American Psychologist, 34,* 151–160.

Harris, J. A. (1999). Review and methodological considerations in research on testosterone and aggression. *Aggression and Violent Behavior, 4,* 273–291.

Harris, J. R. (1998). *The nurture assumption.* New York: Free Press.

Harris, L. (1987). *Inside America.* New York: Random House.

Harris, L. J. (1993). Do left-handers die sooner than right-handers? Commentary on Coren and Halpern's (1991) "Left-handedness: A marker for decreased survival fitness." *Psychological Bulletin, 114,* 203–234.

Harris, R. (1999). Come up to beauty, come up to Ron's angels. www.ronsangels.com

Harris, R. J. (1994). The impact of sexually explicit media. In J. Brant & D. Zillmann (Eds.), *Media effects: Advances in theory and research.* Hillsdale, NJ: Erlbaum.

Harriston, K. A. (1993, December 24). 1 shakes, 1 snoozes; both win $45 million. *Washington Post* release (in *Tacoma News Tribune,* pp. A1, A2).

Hart, D. (1988). The development of personal identity in adolescence: A philosophical dilemma approach. *Merrill-Palmer Quarterly, 34,* 105–114.

Hartmann, E. (1981, April). The strangest sleep disorder. *Psychology Today,* pp. 14, 16, 18.

Hartmann, E. (1984). *The nightmare: The psychology and biology of terrifying dreams.* New York: Basic Books.

Hartshorne, H., & May, M. A. (1928). *Studies in deceit.* New York: Macmillan.

Harvey, S. M. (1987). Female sexual behavior: Fluctuations during the menstrual cycle. *Journal of Psychosomatic Research, 31,* 101–110.

Hasher, L., & Zacks, R. T. (1979). Automatic and effortful processes in memory. *Journal of Experimental Psychology: General, 108,* 356–388.

Haskins, R. (1989). Beyond metaphor: The efficacy of early childhood education. *American Psychologist, 44,* 274–282.

Hassan, R., & Carr, J. (1989). Changing patterns of suicide in Australia. *Australian and New Zealand Journal of Psychiatry, 23,* 226–234.

Hatfield, E. (1988). Passionate and companionate love. In R. J. Sternberg & M. L. Barnes (Eds.), *The psychology of love.* New Haven: Yale University Press.

Hatfield, E., & Sprecher, S. (1986). *Mirror, mirror . . . The importance of looks in everyday life.* Albany: State University of New York Press.

Hathaway, S. R. (1960). *An MMPI Handbook* (Vol. 1, Foreword). Minneapolis: University of Minnesota Press. (Revised edition, 1972).

Hauser, M. D. (1993). Right hemisphere dominance for the production of facial expression in monkeys. *Science, 261,* 475–477.

Hayes, J. R. (1981). *The complete problem solver.* Philadelphia: Franklin Institute Press.

Hazan, C., & Shaver, P. R. (1994). Attachment as an organizational framework for research on close relationships. *Psychological Inquiry, 5,* 1–22.

Hazelrigg, M. D., Cooper, H. M., & Borduin, C. M. (1987). Evaluating the effectiveness of family therapies: An integrative review and analysis. *Psychological Bulletin, 101,* 428–442.

Hearold, S. (1986). A synthesis of 1043 effects of television on social behavior. In G. Comstock (Ed.), *Public communication and behavior.* New York: Academic Press.

Heath, A. C. & Madden, P. A. F. (1995). Genetic influences on smoking behavior. In J. R. Turner & L. R. Cardon (Eds.), *Behavior genetic approaches in behavioral medicine.* New York: Plenum Press, 45–66.

Heath, L., & Petraitis, J. (1987). Television viewing and fear of crime: Where is the mean world? *Basic and Applied Social Psychology, 8,* 97–123.

Heatherton, T. F., & Baumeister, R. F. (1991). Binge eating as escape from self-awareness. *Psychological Bulletin, 110,* 86–108.

Hebb, D. O. (1980). *Essay on mind.* Hillsdale, NJ: Erlbaum.

Hebl, M. R., & Heatherton, T. F. (1998). The stigma of obesity in women: The difference is black and white. *Personality and Social Psychology Bulletin, 24.* 417–426.

Hedges, L. V., & Nowell, A. (1995). Sex differences in mental test scores, variability, and numbers of high-scoring individuals. *Science, 269,* 41–45.

Heider, F. (1958). *The psychology of interpersonal relations.* New York: Wiley.

Heiman, J. R. (1975, April). The physiology of erotica: Women's sexual arousal. *Psychology Today,* pp. 90–94.

Heishman, S. J., Kozlowski, L. T., & Henningfield, J. E. (1997). Nicotine addiction: Implications for public health policy. *Journal of Social Issues, 53,* 13–33.

Helgeson, V. S., Cohen, S., & Fritz, H. L. (1998). Social ties and cancer. In P. M. Cinciripini & others (eds.), *Psychological and behavioral factors in cancer risk.* New York: Oxford University Press.

Heller, W. (1990, May/June). Of one mind: Second thoughts about the brain's dual nature. *The Sciences,* pp. 38–44.

Heller, W., Nitschke, J. B., & Miller, G. A. (1998). Lateralization in emotion and emotion disorders. *Current Directions in Psychological Science, 7,* 26–32.

Hellige, J. B. (1993). Unity of thought and action: Varieties of interaction between the left and right cerebral hemispheres. *Current Directions in Psychological Science, 2,* 21–25.

Helmreich, W. B. (1992). *Against all odds: Holocaust survivors and the successful lives they made in America.* New York: Simon & Schuster.

Helmreich, W. B. (1994). Personal correspondence. Department of Sociology, City University of New York.

Helweg-Larsen, M. (1999). (The lack of) optimistic biases in response to the 1994 Northridge earthquake: The role of personal experience. *Basic and Applied Social Psychology, 21,* 119–129.

Hembree, R. (1988). Correlates, causes, effects, and treatment of test anxiety. *Review of Educational Research, 58,* 47–77.

Henley, N. M. (1989). Molehill or mountain? What we know and don't know about sex bias in language. In M. Crawford & M. Gentry (Eds.), *Gender and thought: Psychological perspectives.* New York: Springer-Verlag.

Henninger, P. (1992). Conditional handedness: Handedness changes in multiple personality disordered subject reflect shift in hemispheric dominance. *Consciousness and Cognition, 1,* 265–287.

Hepper, P. G., Shahidullah, S., & White, R. (1990). Origins of fetal handedness. *Nature, 347,* 431.

Herek, G. M., & Capitanio, J. P. (1996). "Some of my best friends": Intergroup contact, concealable stigma, and heterosexuals' attitudes toward gay men and lesbians. *Personality and Social Psychology Bulletin, 22,* 412–424.

Herman, C. P., & Polivy, J. (1980). Restrained eating. In A. J. Stunkard (Ed.), *Obesity.* Philadelphia: Saunders.

Heron, W. (1957, January). The pathology of boredom. *Scientific American,* pp. 52–56.

Herrmann, D. (1982). Know thy memory: The use of questionnaires to assess and study memory. *Psychological Bulletin, 92,* 434–452.

Herrnstein, R. J., & Loveland, D. H. (1964). Complex visual concept in the pigeon. *Science, 146,* 549–551.

Hershberger, S. L. (1997). A twin registry study of male and female sexual orientation. *Journal of Sex Research, 34,* 212–222.

Hershenson, M. (1989). *The moon illusion.* Hillsdale, NJ: Erlbaum.

Hess, E. H. (1956, July). Space perception in the chick. *Scientific American,* pp. 71–80.

Hetherington, E. M. (1979). Divorce: A child's perspective. *American Psychologist, 34,* 851–858.

Hetherington, E. M., Reiss, D., & Plomin, R. (1993). *The separate social worlds of siblings: The impact of nonshared environment on development.* Hillsdale, NJ: Erlbaum.

Hewlett, S. A., & West, C. (1998). *The war against parents.* Boston: Houghton Mifflin.

Heyes, C. M. (1998). Theory of mind in nonhuman primates. *Behavioral and Brain Sciences, 21,* 101–148.

Heymsfield, S. B., Greenberg, A. S., Fujioka, K., Dixon, R. M., Kushner, R., Hunt, T., Lubina, J. A., Patane, J., Self, B., Hunt, P., & McCamish, M. (1999). Recombinant leptin for weight loss in obese and lean adults. *Journal of the American Medical Association, 282,* 1568–1575.

Hibbeln, J. R. (1998). Fish consumption and major depression. *Lancet, 351,* 1213.

Hicks, R. A., Kilcourse, J., & Sinnott, M. A. (1983). Type A-B behavior and caffeine use in college students. *Psychological Reports, 52,* 338.

Hicks, R. A., & Pellegrini, R. J. (1982). Sleep problems and Type A-B behavior in college students. *Psychological Reports, 51,* 196.

Higgins, E. T. (1987). Self-discrepancy: A theory relating self and affect. *Psychological Review, 94,* 319–340.

Higgins, E. T., & Bargh, J. A. (1987). Social cognition and social perception. *Annual Review of Psychology, 38,* 369–425.

Hilgard, E. R. (1986). *Divided consciousness: Multiple controls in human thought and action.* New York: Wiley.

Hilgard, E. R. (1992). Dissociation and theories of hypnosis. In E. Fromm & M. R. Nash (Eds.), *Contemporary hypnosis research.* New York: Guilford.

Hines, M., & Green, R. (1991). Human hormonal and neural correlates of sex-typed behaviors. *Review of Psychiatry, 10,* 536–555.

Hintzman, D. L. (1978). *The psychology of learning and memory.* San Francisco: Freeman.

Hinz, L. D., & Williamson, D. A. (1987). Bulimia and depression: A review of the affective variant hypothesis. *Psychological Bulletin, 102,* 150–158.

Hirst, W., Neisser, U., & Spelke, E. (1978, June). Divided attention. *Human Nature,* pp. 54–61.

Hirt, E. R., Zillmann, D., Erickson, G. A., & Kennedy, C. (1992). Costs and benefits of allegiance: Changes in fans' self-ascribed competencies after team victory versus defeat. *Journal of Personality and Social Psychology, 63,* 724–738.

Hobfoll, S. E. (1989). Conservation of resources: A new attempt at conceptualizing stress. *American Psychologist, 44,* 513–524.

Hobfoll, S. E., Lomranz, J., Eyal, N., Bridges, A., & Tzemach, M. (1989). Pulse of a nation: Depressive mood reactions of Israelis to the Israel-Lebanon war. *Journal of Personality and Social Psychology, 56,* 1002–1012.

Hobson, J. A. (1988). *The dreaming brain.* New York: Basic Books.

Hobson, J. A. (1989). *Sleep.* New York: Scientific American Library.

Hobson, J. A. (1995, September). Quoted in C. H. Colt, The power of dreams. *Life,* pp. 36–49.

Hobson, J. A., & Silvestri, L. (1999, February). Parasomnias. *Harvard Mental Health Letter,* pp. 3–5.

Hodgkinson, V. A., & Weitzman, M. S. (1992). *Giving and volunteering in the United States.* Washington, DC: Independent Sector.

Hoebel, B. G., & Teitelbaum, P. (1966). Effects of forcefeeding and starvation on food intake and body weight in a rat with ventromedial hypothalamic lesions. *Journal of Comparative and Physiological Psychology, 61,* 189–193.

Hoffman, C., & Hurst, N. (1990). Gender stereotypes: Perception or rationalization? *Journal of Personality and Social Psychology, 58,* 197–208.

Hoffman, D. D. (1998). *Visual intelligence: How we create what we see.* New York: Norton.

Hoffman, L. W. (1989). Effects of maternal employment in the two-parent family. *American Psychologist, 44,* 283–292.

Hoffman, P. (1994, November). The science of race. *Discover,* p. 4.

Hofstede, G. (1980). *Culture's consequences: International differences in work-related values.* Beverly Hills: Sage.

Hogan, J. (1995, November). Get smart, take a test. *Scientific American,* pp. 12, 14.

Hogan, R. (1998). Reinventing personality. *Journal of Social and Clinical Psychology, 17,* 1–10.

Hogg, M. A. (1996). Intragroup processes, group structure and social identity. In W. P. Robinson (Ed.), *Social groups and identies: Developing the legacy of Henri Tajfel.* Oxford: Butterworth Heinemann.

Hohmann, G. W. (1966). Some effects of spinal cord lesions on experienced emotional feelings. *Psychophysiology, 3,* 143–156.

Hokanson, J. E., & Edelman, R. (1966). Effects of three social responses on vascular processes. *Journal of Personality and Social Psychology, 3,* 442–447.

Holahan, C. K., & Sears, R. R. (1995). *The gifted group in later maturity.* Stanford, CA: Stanford University Press.

Holden, C. (1980a). Identical twins reared apart. *Science, 207,* 1323–1325.

Holden, C. (1980b, November). Twins reunited. *Science, 80,* 55–59.

Holden, C. (1986a). Days may be numbered for polygraphs in the private sector. *Science, 232,* 705.

Holden, C. (1986b). Researchers grapple with problems of updating classic psychological test. *Science, 233,* 1249–1251.

Holden, C. (1991). Alcoholism gene: Coming or going? *Science, 254,* 200.

Holden, C. (1991). New center to study therapies and ethnicity. *Science, 251,* 748.

Holden, C. (1993). Wake-up call for sleep research. *Science, 259,* 305.

Holden, G. W., & Miller, P. C. (1999). Enduring and different: A meta-analysis of the similarity in parents' child rearing. *Psychological Bulletin, 125,* 223–254.

Holing, D. (1988, October). Dolphin defense. *Discover,* pp. 70–74.

Hollis, K. L. (1997). Contemporary research on Pavlovian conditioning: A "new" functional analysis. *American Psychologist, 52,* 956–965.

Holmes, A., & Conway, M. A. (1999). Generation identity and the reminiscence bump: Memory for public and private events. *Journal of Adult Development, 6,* 21–34.

Holmes, D. (1990). The evidence for repression: An examination of sixty years of research. In J. Singer (Ed.), *Repression and dissociation: Implications for personality theory, psychopathology, and health.* Chicago: University of Chicago Press.

Holmes, D. S. (1978). Projection as a defense mechanism. *Psychological Bulletin, 85,* 677–688.

Holmes, D. S. (1981). Existence of classical projection and the stress-reducing function of attributive projection: A reply to Sherwood. *Psychological Bulletin, 90,* 460–466.

Holmes, D. S. (1994). Is there evidence for repression? No. (Unexpurgated version on an article that was rewritten by the *Harvard Mental Health Letter* and published as "Is there evidence for repression? Doubtful," June, 1994, pp. 4–6.)

Holtgraves, T., & Skeel, J. (1992). Cognitive biases in playing the lottery: Estimating the odds and choosing the numbers. *Journal of Applied Social Psychology, 22,* 934–952.

Holzman, P. S., & Matthysse, S. (1990). The genetics of schizophrenia: A review. *Psychological Science, 1,* 279–286.

Hooper, J., & Teresi, D. (1986). *The three-pound universe.* New York: Macmillan.

Hooykaas, R. (1972). *Religion and the rise of modern science.* Grand Rapids, MI: Eerdmans.

Horgan, J. (1995, December). A sign is born. *Scientific American,* pp. 18–19.

Horn, J. L. (1982). The aging of human abilities. In J. Wolman (Ed.), *Handbook of developmental psychology.* Englewood Cliffs, NJ: Prentice-Hall.

Horne, J. A. (1989). Sleep loss and "divergent" thinking ability. *Sleep, 11,* 528–536.

House, J. S., Landis, K. R., & Umberson, D. (1988). Social relationships and health. *Science, 241,* 540–545.

House, R. J., & Singh, J. V. (1987). Organizational behavior: Some new directions for I/O psychology. *Annual Review of Psychology, 38,* 669–718.

Houts, A. C., Berman, J. S., & Abramson, H. (1994). Effectiveness of psychological and pharmacological treatments for nocturnal enuresis. *Journal of Consulting and Clinical Psychology, 62,* 737–745.

Howard Hughes Medical Institute (1997). *Seeing, hearing, and smelling the world.* Chevy Chase, MD: Howard Hughes Medical Institute. Also available at: www.hhmi.org/senses/

Howe, M. L. (1997). Children's memory for traumatic experiences. *Learning and Individual Differences, 9,* 153–174.

Howe, M. L. (1998). Individual differences in factors that modulate storage and retrieval of traumatic memories. *Development and Psychopathology, 10,* 681–698.

Howe, M. L., & Courage, M. L. (1993). On resolving the enigma of infantile amnesia. *Psychological Bulletin, 113,* 305–326.

Hoyer, G., & Lund, E. (1993). Suicide among women related to number of children in marriage. *Archives of General Psychiatry, 50,* 134–137.

Hubel, D. H. (1979, September). The brain. *Scientific American,* pp. 45–53.

Hubel, D. H., & Wiesel, T. N. (1979, September). Brian mechanisms of vision. *Scientific American,* pp. 150–162.

Hublin, C., Kaprio, J., Partinen, M., Heikkila, K., & Koskenvuo, M. (1997). Prevalence and genetics of sleepwalking—A population-based twin study. *Neurology, 48,* 177–181.

Hublin, C., Kaprio, J., Partinen, M., & Koskenvuo, M. (1998). Sleeptalking in twins: Epidemiology and psychiatric comorbidity. *Behavior Genetics, 28,* 289–298.

Hucker, S. J., & Bain, J. (1990). Androgenic hormones and sexual assault. In W. Marshall, R. Law, & H. Barbaree (Eds.), *The handbook on sexual assault.* New York: Plenum.

Hugick, L. (1989, July). Women play the leading role in keeping modern families close. *Gallup Report,* pp. 27–34.

Hull, J. G., & Bond, C. F., Jr. (1986). Social and behavioral consequences of alcohol consumption and expectancy: A meta-analysis. *Psychological Bulletin, 99,* 347–360.

Hull, J. G., Young, R. D., & Jouriles, E. (1986). Applications of the self-awareness model of alcohol consumption: Predicting patterns of use and abuse. *Journal of Personality and Social Psychology, 51,* 790–796.

Hull, J. M. (1990). *Touching the rock: An experience of blindness.* New York: Vintage Books.

Hulme, C., & Tordoff, V. (1989). Working memory development: The effects of speech rate, word length, and acoustic similarity on serial recall. *Journal of Experimental Child Psychology, 47,* 72–87.

Hummer, R. A., Rogers, R. G., Nam, C. B., & Ellison, C. G. (1999). Religious involvement and U.S. adult mortality. *Demography, 36,* 273–285.

Humphreys, L. G., & Davey, T. C. (1988). Continuity in intellectual growth from 12 months to 9 years. *Intelligence, 12,* 183–197.

Hunsley, J., & Bailey, J. M. (1999). The clinical utility of the Rorschach: Unfulfilled promises and an uncertain future. *Psychological Assessment, 11*(3), 266–277.

Hunt, E. (1983). On the nature of intelligence. *Science, 219,* 141–146.

Hunt, M. (1974). *Sexual behavior in the 1970s.* Chicago: Playboy Press.

Hunt, M. (1982). *The universe within.* New York: Simon & Schuster.

Hunt, M. (1990). *The compassionate beast: What science is discovering about the humane side of humankind.* New York: William Morrow.

Hunt, M. (1993). *The story of psychology.* New York: Doubleday.

Hunter, J. E. (1997). Needed: A ban on the significance test. *Psychological Science, 8,* 3–7.

Hunter, S., & Sundel, M. (Eds.). (1989). *Midlife myths: Issues, findings, and practice implications.* Newbury Park, CA: Sage.

Hurt, S. W., Schnurr, P. P., Severino, S. K., Freeman, E. W., Gise, L. H., Rivera-Tovar, A., & Steege, J. F. (1992). Late luteal phase dysphoric disorder in 670 women evaluated for premenstrual complaints. *American Journal of Psychiatry, 149,* 525–530.

Hurtado, S., Dey, E. L., & Trevino, J. G. (1994). Exclusion or self-segregation? Interaction across racial/ethnic groups on college campuses. Paper presented at the American Educational Research Association annual meeting.

Huston, A. C., Donnerstein, E., Fairchild, H., Feshbach, N. D., Katz, P. A., & Murray, J. P. (1992). *Big world, small screen: The role of television in American society.* Lincoln: University of Nebraska Press.

Hyde, J. S. (1983, November). Bem's gender schema theory. Paper presented at GLCA Women's Studies Conference, Rochester, IN.

Hyde, J. S. (1984, July). Children's understanding of sexist language. *Developmental Psychology, 20*(4), 697–706.

Hyde, J. S., Fennema, E., & Lamon, S. J. (1990). Gender differences in mathematics performance: A meta-analysis. *Psychological Bulletin, 107,* 139–155.

Hyler, S., Gabbard, G. O., & Schneider, I. (1991). Homicidal maniacs and narcissistic parasites: Stigmatization of mentally ill persons in the movies. *Hospital and Community Psychiatry, 42,* 1044–1048.

Hyman, I. E., Jr., Husband, T. H., & Billings, F. J. (1995). False memories of childhood experiences. *Applied Cognitive Psychology, 9,* 181–197.

Hyman, I. E., Jr., & Pentland, J. (1996). The role of mental imagery in the creation of false childhood memories. *Journal of Memory and Language, 35,* 101–117.

Hyman, R. (1981). Cold reading: How to convince strangers that you know all about them. In K. Frazier (Ed.), *Paranormal borderlands of science.* Buffalo, NY: Prometheus Books.

Hyman, R. (1994). Anomaly or artifact? Comments on Bem and Honorton. *Psychological Bulletin, 115,* 19–24.

Hyman, R. (1996, March/April). Evaluation of the military's twenty-year program on psychic spying. *The Skeptical Inquirer,* pp. 21–23, 27.

Hyman, R. (1996, March/April). The evidence for psychic functioning: Claims vs. reality. *The Skeptical Inquirer,* pp. 24–26.

Hyman, S. (1999). Quoted in M. Enserink, Can the placebo be the cure? *Science, 284,* 238–240.

Iacono, W. G., & Lykken, D. T. (1997). The validity of the lie detector: Two surveys of scientific opinion. *Journal of Applied Psychology, 82,* 426–433.

Ickes, W., Snyder, M., & Garcia, S. (1997). Personality influences on the choice of situations. In R. Hogan, J. Johnson, & S. Briggs (Eds.), *Handbook of Personality Psychology.* San Diego: Academic Press.

Immen, W. (1995, July 16). Canadians ignore 'safe sex' warning. *Toronto Globe and Mail* (in *Grand Rapids Press,* p. A22).

Ingham, A. G., Levinger, G., Graves, J., & Peckham, V. (1974). The Ringelmann effect: Studies of group size and group performance. *Journal of Experimental Social Psychology, 10,* 371–384.

Inglehart, M. R., Markus, H., & Brown, D. R. (1989). The effects of possible selves on academic achievement—A panel study. In J. P. Forgas & J. M. Innes (Eds.), *Recent advances in social psychology: An international perspective.* New York: Elsevier Science Publishers.

Inglehart, R. (1990). *Culture shift in advanced industrial society.* Princeton, NJ: Princeton University Press.

Inman, M. L., & Baron, R. S. (1996). Influence of prototypes on perceptions of prejudice. *Journal of Personality and Social Psychology, 70,* 727–739.

Irwin, M., Mascovich, A., Gillin, J. C., Willoughby, R., Pike, J., & Smith, T. L. (1994). Partial sleep deprivation reduces natural killer cell activity in humans. *Psychosomatic Medicine, 56,* 493–498.

Isen, A. M., & Means, B. (1983). The influence of positive affect on decision-making strategy. *Social Cognition, 2,* 28–31.

Isham, W. P., & Kamin, L. J. (1993). Blackness, deafness, IQ, and g. *Intelligence, 17,* 37–46.

Ito, T. A., Miller, N., & Pollock, V. E. (1996). Alcohol and aggression: A meta-analysis on the moderating effects of inhibitory cues, triggering events, and self-focused attention. *Psychological Bulletin, 120,* 60–82.

Iverson, J. M., & Goldin-Meadow, S. (1998). Why people gesture when they speak. *Nature, 396,* 228.

Izard, C. E. (1977). *Human emotions.* New York: Plenum Press.

Izard, C. E. (1994). Innate and universal facial expressions: Evidence from developmental and cross-cultural research. *Psychological Bulletin, 115,* 288–299.

Jablensky, A. (1999). Schizophrenia: Epidemiology. *Current Opinion in Psychiatry, 12,* 19–28.

Jackson, J. M., & Williams, K. D. (1988). Social loafing: A review and theoretical analysis. Unpublished manuscript, Fordham University.

Jackson, L. A., & Gerard, D. A. (1996). Diurnal types, the "Big Five" personality factors and other personal characteristics. *Journal of Social Behavior and Personality, 11,* 273–283.

Jackson, S. W. (1992). The listening healer in the history of psychological healing. *American Journal of Psychiatry, 149,* 1623–1632.

Jacobs, B. L. (1987). How hallucinogenic drugs work. *American Scientist, 75,* 386–392.

Jacobs, B. L. (1994). Serotonin, motor activity, and depression-related disorders. *American Scientist, 82,* 456–463.

Jacobs, W. J., & Nadel, L. (1985). Stress-induced recovery of fears and phobias. *Psychological Bulletin, 92,* 512–531.

Jacobson, J. W., Mulick, J. A., & Schwartz, A. A. (1995). A history of facilitated communication: Science, pseudoscience, and antiscience. Science working group on facilitated communication. *American Psychologist, 50,* 750–765.

Jakicic, J. M., Winters, C., Lang, W., & Wing R. R. (1999). Effects of intermittent exercise and use of home exercise equipment on adherence, weight loss, and fitness in overweight women. *Journal of the American Medical Association, 282,* 1554–1560.

James, K. (1986). Priming and social categorizational factors: Impact on awareness of emergency situations. *Personality and Social Psychology Bulletin, 12,* 462–467.

James, W. (1890). *The principles of psychology* (Vol. 2). New York: Holt.

James, W. (1902; reprinted 1958). *Varieties of religious experience.* New York: Mentor Books.

Jameson, D. (1985). Opponent-colors theory in light of physiological findings. In D. Ottoson & S. Zeki (Eds.), *Central and peripheral mechanisms of color vision.* New York: Macmillan.

Jamison, K. R. (1993). *Touched with fire: Manic-depressive illness and the artistic temperament.* New York: Free Press.

Jamison, K. R. (1995, February). Manic-depressive illness and creativity. *Scientific American,* pp. 62–67.

Janis, I. L. (1986). Problems of international crisis management in the nuclear age. *Journal of Social Issues, 42*(2), 201–220.

Janis, I. L. (1989). *Crucial decisions: Leadership in policymaking and crisis management.* New York: Free Press.

Janoff-Bulman, R., Timko, C., & Carli, L. L. (1985). Cognitive biases in blaming the victim. *Journal of Experimental Social Psychology, 21,* 161–177.

Jarvik, L. F. (1975). Thoughts on the psychobiology of aging. *American Psychologist, 30,* 576–583.

Jeffery, R. W., & Wing, R. R. (1983). Recidivism and self-cure of smoking and obesity: Data from population studies. *American Psychologist, 38,* 852.

Jelicic, M., De Roode, A., Bovill, J. G., & Bonke, B. (1992). Unconscious learning during anaesthesia. *Anaesthesia, 47,* 835–837.

Jemmott, J. B., III, & Magloire, K. (1988). Academic stress, social support, and secretory immunoglobulin A. *Journal of Personality and Social Psychology, 55,* 803–810.

Jenish, D. (1993, October 11). The king of porn. *Maclean's,* pp. 52–64.

Jenkins, J. G., & Dallenbach, K. M. (1924). Obliviscence during sleep and waking. *American Journal of Psychology, 35,* 605–612.

Jenkins, J. M., & Astington, J. W. (1996). Cognitive factors and family structure associated with theory of mind development in young children. *Developmental Psychology, 32,* 70–78.

Jensen, A. R. (1980). *Bias in mental testing.* New York: Free Press.

Jensen, A. R. (1983, August). The nature of the black-white difference on various psychometric tests: Spearman's hypothesis. Paper presented at the meeting of the American Psychological Association, Anaheim, CA.

Jensen, A. R. (1989). New findings on the intellectually gifted. *New Horizons, 30,* 73–80.

Jensen, A. R., & Johnson, F. W. (1994). Race and sex differences in head size and IQ. *Intelligence, 18.*

Jensen, J. P., & Bergin, A. E. (1988). Mental health values of professional therapists: A national interdisciplinary survey. *Professional Psychology: Research and Practice, 19,* 290–297.

Jepson, C., Krantz, D. H., & Nisbett, R. E. (1983). Inductive reasoning: Competence or skill. *The Behavioral and Brain Sciences, 3,* 494–501.

Jervis, R. (1985, April 2). Quoted in D. Goleman, Political forces come under new scrutiny of psychology. *New York Times,* pp. C1, C4.

Jing, H. (1999, Summer). China faces myriad psychological challenges of modernization. *Psychology International* (APA newsletter), p. 7.

John, O. P. (1990). The "Big Five" factor taxonomy: Dimensions of personality in the natural language and in questionnaires. In L. A. Pervin (Ed.), *Handbook of personality: Theory and research.* New York: Guilford Press.

Johnson, C. B., Stockdale, M. S., & Saal, F. E. (1991). Persistence of men's misperceptions of friendly cues across a variety of interpersonal encounters. *Psychology of Women Quarterly, 15,* 463–475.

Johnson, D. (1990). Animal rights and human lives: Time for scientists to right the balance. *Psychological Science, 1,* 213–214.

Johnson, D., & Drenick, E. J. (1977). Therapeutic fasting in morbid obesity. Long-term follow-up. *Archives of Internal Medicine, 137,* 1381–1382.

Johnson, D. L., Wiebe, J. S., Gold, S. M., Andreasen, N. C., Hichwa, R. D., Watkins, G. L., & Ponto, L. L. B. (1999). Cerebral blood flow and personality: A positron emission tomography study. *American Journal of Psychiatry, 156,* 252–257.

Johnson, D. W., & Johnson, R. T. (1989). *Cooperation and competition: Theory and research.* Edina, MN: Interaction Book.

Johnson, D. W., & Johnson, R. T. (1994). Constructive conflict in the schools. *Journal of Social Issues, 50*(1), 117–137.

Johnson, E. J., & Tversky, A. (1983). Affect, generalization, and the perception of risk. *Journal of Personality and Social Psychology, 45,* 20–31.

Johnson, J. S., & Newport, E. L. (1991). Critical period effects on universal properties of language: The status of subjacency in the acquisition of a second language. *Cognition, 39,* 215–258.

Johnson, M. H. (1992). Imprinting and the development of face recognition: From chick to man. *Current Directions in Psychological Science, 1,* 52–55.

Johnson-Laird, P. N. (1999). Deductive reasoning. *Annual Review of Psychology, 50,* 109–135.

Johnston, L. D. (1996, December 19). Monitoring the future study of drug use. Ann Arbor: News and Information Services, University of Michigan.

Johnston, L. D., Backman, J. G., & O'Malley, P. M. (1999, December 17). Drug trends in 1999 among American teens are mixed. Ann Arbor: News and Information Services, University of Michigan.

Johnston, L. D., O'Malley, P., & Bachman, J. (1994, January 27). Drug use rises among American teen-agers. Ann Arbor: News and Information Services, University of Michigan.

Joiner, T. E., Jr. (1999). The clustering and contagion of suicide. *Current Directions in Psychological Science, 8,* 89–92.

Jones, E. E., Cumming, J. D., & Horowitz, M. J. (1988). Another look at the nonspecific hypothesis of therapeutic effectiveness. *Journal of Consulting and Clinical Psychology, 56,* 48–55.

Jones, J. H. (1997a, August 25 and September 1). Dr. Yes. *The New Yorker,* pp. 98–113.

Jones, J. H. (1997b). *A public/private life.* New York: Norton.

Jones, M. C. (1924). A laboratory study of fear: The case of Peter. *Journal of Genetic Psychology, 31,* 308–315.

Jones, S. S., Collins, K., & Hong, H-W. (1991). An audience effect on smile production in 10-month-old infants. *Psychological Science, 2,* 45–49.

Jones, W. H., Carpenter, B. N., & Quintana, D. (1985). Personality and interpersonal predictors of loneliness in two cultures. *Journal of Personality and Social Psychology, 48,* 1503–1511.

Jorgenson, D. O., & Papciak, A. S. (1981). The effects of communication, resource feedback, and identifiability on behavior in a simulated commons. *Journal of Experimental Social Psychology, 17,* 373–385.

Jorm, A. F., Korten, A. E., & Henderson, A. S. (1987). The prevalence of dementia: A quantitative integration of the literature. *Acta Psychiatrica Scandinavica, 76,* 465–479.

Jose, W. S., II, & Anderson, D. R. (1991). Control data's StayWell program: A health cost management strategy. In S. M. Weiss, J. E. Fielding, & A. Baum (Eds.), *Health at work.* Hillsdale, NJ: Erlbaum.

Josey, E. S., & Tackett, R. L. (1999). St. John's wort: A new alternative for depression? *International Journal of Clinical Pharmacology and Therapeutics, 37,* 111–119.

Jusczyk, P. W. (1997). Finding and remembering words: Some beginnings by English-learning infants. *Current Directions in Psychological Science, 6,* 170–174.

Kagan, J. (1976). Emergent themes in human development. *American Scientist, 64,* 186–196.

Kagan, J. (1984). *The nature of the child.* New York: Basic Books.

Kagan, J. (1989). *Unstable ideas: Temperament, cognition, and self.* Cambridge, MA: Harvard University Press.

Kagan, J. (1990). Interview with M. V. Ellis & E. S. Robbins, In Celebration of nature: A dialogue with Jerome Kagan. *Journal of Counseling and Development, 68,* 623–627.

Kagan, J. (1995). On attachment. *Harvard Review of Psychiatry, 3,* 104–106.

Kagan, J. (1998). *Three seductive ideas.* Cambridge, MA: Harvard University Press.

Kagan, J., Arcus, D., Snidman, N., Feng, W. Y., Hendler, J., & Greene, S. (1994). Reactivity in infants: A cross-national comparison. *Developmental Psychology, 30,* 342–345.

Kagan, J., Lapidus, D. R., & Moore, M. (December, 1978). Infant antecedents of cognitive functioning: A longitudinal study. *Child Development, 49*(4), 1005–1023.

Kagan, J., Snidman, N., & Arcus, D. M. (1992). Initial reactions to unfamiliarity. *Current Directions in Psychological Science, 1,* 171–174.

Kahneman, D. (1985, June). Quoted in K. McKean, Decisions, decisions. *Discover,* pp. 22–31.

Kahneman, D. (1999). Assessments of individual well-being: A bottom-up approach. In D. Kahneman, E. Diener, & N. Schwartz (Eds.), *Well-being: The foundations of hedonic psychology.* New York: Russell Sage Foundation.

Kahneman, D. (1999). Assessments of objective happiness: A bottom-up approach. In D. Kahneman, E. Diener, & N. Schwartz (Eds.), *Understanding well-being: Scientific perspectives on enjoyment and suffering.* New York: Russell Sage Foundation.

Kahneman, D., Fredrickson, B. L., Schreiber, C. A., & Redelmeier, D. A. (1993). When more pain is preferred to less: Adding a better end. *Psychological Science, 4,* 401–405.

Kahneman, D., Knetsch, J. L., & Thaler, R. (1986). Fairness as a constraint on profit seeking: Entitlements in the market. *American Economic Review, 76,* 728–741.

Kahneman, D., & Tversky, A. (1972). Subjective probability: A judgment of representativeness. *Cognitive Psychology, 3,* 430–454.

Kahneman, D., & Tversky, A. (1979). Intuitive prediction: Biases and corrective procedures. *Management Science, 12,* 313–327.

Kail, R. (1991). Developmental change in speed of processing during childhood and adolescence. *Psychological Bulletin, 109,* 490–501.

Kalin, N. H. (1993, May). The neurobiology of fear. *Scientific American,* pp. 94–101.

Kamarck, T., & Jennings, J. R. (1991). Biobehavioral factors in sudden cardiac death. *Psychological Bulletin, 109,* 42–75.

Kamena, M. (1998). Repressed/false childhood sexual abuse memories: A survey of therapists. Paper presented to the Sexual Abuse memories Symposium at the American Psychological Association convention.

Kaminer, W. (1992). *I'm dysfunctional, you're dysfunctional: The recovery movement and other self-help fashions.* Reading, MA: Addison-Wesley.

Kandel, D. B., & Raveis, V. H. (1989). Cessation of illicit drug use in young adulthood. *Archives of General Psychiatry, 46*, 109–116.

Kandel, E. R., & Schwartz, J. H. (1982). Molecular biology of learning: Modulation of transmitter release. *Science, 218*, 433–443.

Kanekar, S., & Nazareth, A. (1988). Attributed rape victim's fault as a function of her attractiveness, physical hurt, and emotional disturbance. *Social Behaviour, 3*, 37–40.

Kann, L., Warren, W., Collins, J. L., Ross, J., Collins, B., & Kolbe, L. J. (1993). Results from the national school-based 1991 Youth Risk Behavior Survey and progress toward achieving related health objectives for the nation. U.S. Department of Health and Human Services, *Public Health Reports, 108* (Supplement 1), 47–55.

Kapitza, S. (1991, August). Antiscience trends in the U.S.S.R. *Scientific American*, pp. 32–38.

Kaplan, H. I., & Saddock, B. J. (Eds.). (1989). *Comprehensive textbook of psychiatry, V.* Baltimore, MD: Williams and Wilkins.

Kaprio, J., Koskenvuo, M., & Rita, H. (1987). Mortality after bereavement: A prospective study of 95,647 widowed persons. *American Journal of Public Health, 77*, 283–287.

Kapur, S., & Mann, J. J. (1993). Antidepressant action and the neurobiologic effects of ECT: Human studies. In C. E. Coffey (Ed.), *The clinical science of electroconvulsive therapy*. Washington, DC: American Psychiatric Press.

Karacan, I., Aslan, C., & Hirshkowitz, M. (1983). Erectile mechanisms in man. *Science, 220*, 1080–1082.

Karacan, I., Goodenough, D. R., Shapiro, A., & Starker, S. (1966). Erection cycle during sleep in relation to dream anxiety. *Archives of General Psychiatry, 15*, 183–189.

Karau, S. J., & Williams, K. D. (1993). Social loafing: A meta-analytic review and theoretical integration. *Journal of Personality and Social Psychology, 65*, 681–706.

Kark, J. D., Shemi, G., Friedlander, Y., Martin, O., Manor, O., & Blondheim, S. H. (1996). Does religious observance promote health? Mortality in secular vs. religious kibbutzim in Israel. *American Journal of Public Health, 86*, 341–346.

Karni, A., & Sagi, D. (1994). Dependence on REM sleep for overnight improvement of perceptual skills. *Science, 265*, 679–682.

Karno, M., Golding, J. M., Sorenson, S. B., & Burnam, A. (1988). The epidemiology of obsessive-compulsive disorder in five US communities. *Archives of General Psychiatry, 45*, 1094–1099.

Karon, P. B., & Widener, A. J. (1997). Repressed memories and World War II: Lest we forget. *Professional Psychology: Research and Practice, 28*, 338–340.

Karon, P. B., & Widener, A. (1998). Repressed memories: The real story. *Professional Psychology: Research and Practice, 29*, 482–487.

Kashima, Y., Siegal, M., Tanaka, K., & Kashima, E. S. (1992). Do people believe behaviours are consistent with attitudes? Towards a cultural psychology of attribution processes. *British Journal of Social Psychology, 31*, 111–124.

Kashima, Y., Yamaguchi, S., Kim, U., Choic, S-C., Gelfand, M. J., & Yuki, M. (1995). Culture, gender, and self: A perspective from individualism-collectivism research. *Journal of Personality and Social Psychology, 69*, 925–937.

Kasser, T. (in press). Two version of the American dream: Which goals and values make for a high quality of life? In E. Diener (ed.), *Advances in quality of life theory and research*. Dordrecth, Netherlands: Kluwer.

Kato, P. S., & Ruble, D. N. (1992). Toward an understanding of women's experience of menstrual cycle symptoms. In V. Adesso, D. Reddy, & R. Fleming (Eds.), *Psychological perspectives on women's health*. Washington, DC: Hemisphere.

Katon, W., & Sullivan, M. D. (1990). Depression and chronic medical illness. *Journal of Clinical Psychiatry, 51*, 3–11.

Kaufman, A. S., Reynolds, C. R., & McLean, J. E. (1989). Age and WAIS-R intelligence in a national sample of adults in the 20- to 74-year age range: A cross-sectional analysis with educational level controlled. *Intelligence, 13*, 235–253.

Kaufman, J., & Zigler, E. (1987). Do abused children become abusive parents? *American Journal of Orthopsychiatry, 57*, 186–192.

Kaufman, L., & Rock, I. (1962). The moon illusion I. *Science, 136*, 953–961.

Kawachi, I., Kennedy, B. P., Wilkinson, R. G., & Kawachi, K. W. (Eds.). (1999). *Society and population health reader: Income inequality and health*. New York: New Press.

Kawai, N., & Matsuzawa, T. (January, 2000). Numerical memory span in a chimpanzee. *Nature, 403*, 39–40.

Kaye, K. L., & Bower, T. G. R. (1994). Learning and intermodal transfer of information in newborns. *Psychological Science, 5*, 286–288.

Kaylor, J. A., King, D. W., & King, L. A. (1987). Psychological effects of military service in Vietnam: A meta-analysis. *Psychological Bulletin, 102*, 257–271.

Keesey, R. E., & Corbett, S. W. (1983). Metabolic defense of the body weight set-point. In A. J. Stunkard & E. Stellar (Eds.), *Eating and its disorders*. New York: Raven Press.

Kellehear, A. (1996). *Experiences near death: Beyond medicine and religion*. New York: Oxford University Press.

Kellerman, J., Lewis, J., & Laird, J. D. (1989). Looking and loving: The effects of mutual gaze on feelings of romantic love. *Journal of Research in Personality, 23*, 145–161.

Kellermann, A. L. (1997). Comment: Gunsmoke—changing public attitudes toward smoking and firearms. *American Journal of Public Health, 87*, 910–913.

Kellermann, A. L., Rivara, F. P., Rushforth, N. B., Banton, H. G., Feay, D. T., Francisco, J. T., Locci, A. B., Prodzinski, J., Hackman, B. B., & Somes, G. (1993). Gun ownership as a risk factor for homicide in the home. *New England Journal of Medicine, 329*, 1084–1091.

Kellermann, A. L., Somes, G., Rivara, F. P., Lee, R. K., & Banton, J. G. (1998). Injuries and deaths due to firearms in the home. *Journal of Trauma, 45*, 263-267.

Kelley, J., & De Graaf, N. D. (1997). National context, parental socialization, and religious belief: Results from 15 nations, *American Sociological Review, 62*, 639–659.

Kelling, S. T., & Halpern, B. P. (1983). Taste flashes: Reaction times, intensity, and quality. *Science, 219*, 412–414.

Kelly, I. W. (1997). Modern astrology: A critique. *Psychological Reports, 81*, 1035–1066.

Kelly, I. W. (1998). Why astrology doesn't work. *Psychological Reports, 82*, 527–546.

Kelly, T. A. (1990). The role of values in psychotherapy: A critical review of process and outcome effects. *Clinical Psychology Review, 10*, 171–186.

Kempe, R. S., & Kempe, C. C. (1978). *Child abuse*. Cambridge, MA: Harvard University Press.

Kempermann, G., & Gage, F. H. (1999, May). New nerve cells for the adult brain. *Scientific American,* pp. 48–53.

Kempermann, G., Kuhn, H. G., & Gage, F. H. (May, 1998). *Journal of Neuroscience, 18*(9), 3206–3212.

Kendall-Tackett, K. A., Williams, L. M., & Finkelhor, D. (1993). Impact of sexual abuse on children: A review and synthesis of recent empirical studies. *Psychological Bulletin, 113,* 164–180.

Kendler, K. S. (1983). Overview: A current perspective on twin studies of schizophrenia. *American Journal of Psychiatry 140,* 1413–1425.

Kendler, K. S. (1996). Parenting: A genetic-epidemiologic perspective. *The American Journal of Psychiatry, 153,* 11–20.

Kendler, K. S. (1997). Social support: A genetic-epidemiologic analysis. *American Journal of Psychiatry, 154,* 1398–1404.

Kendler, K. S. (January, 1998). Major depression and the environment: A psychiatric genetic perspective. *Pharmacopsychiatry, 31*(1), 5–9.

Kendler, K. S., Karkowski, L. M., & Prescott, C. A. (1999). Fears and phobias: Reliability and heritability. *Psychological Medicine, 29,* 539–553.

Kendler, K. S., Neale, M. C., Kessler, R. C., Heath, A. C., & Eaves, L. J. (1992). Generalized anxiety disorder in women: A population-based twin study. *Archives of General Psychiatry, 49,* 267–272.

Kendler, K. S., Neale, M., Kessler, R., Heath, A., & Eaves, L. (1993). A twin study of recent life events and difficulties. *Archives of General Psychiatry, 50,* 789–796.

Kennedy, S., & Over, R. (1990). Psychophysiological assessment of male sexual arousal following spinal cord injury. *Archives of Sexual Behavior, 19,* 15–27.

Kennell, J. N., & Klaus, M. (1982). *Parent-infant bonding.* St. Louis: C. V. Mosby.

Kenrick, D. T., & Funder, D. C. (1988). Profiting from controversy: Lessons from the person-situation debate. *American Psychologist, 43,* 23–34.

Kenrick, D. T., & Gutierres, S. E. (1980). Contrast effects and judgments of physical attractiveness: When beauty becomes a social problem. *Journal of Personality and Social Psychology, 38,* 131–140.

Kenrick, D. T., Gutierres, S. E., & Goldberg, L. L. (1989). Influence of popular erotica on judgments of strangers and mates. *Journal of Experimental Social Psychology, 25,* 159–167.

Kenrick, D. T., & Trost, M. R. (1987). A biosocial theory of heterosexual relationships. In K. Kelly (Ed.), *Females, males, and sexuality.* Albany: State University of New York Press.

Kerr, N. L., & Bruun, S. E. (1983). Dispensability of member effort and group motivation losses: Free-rider effects. *Journal of Personality and Social Psychology, 44,* 78–94.

Kessler, M., & Albee, G. (1975). Primary prevention. *Annual Review of Psychology, 26,* 557–591.

Kessler, R. C., Foster, C., Joseph, J., Ostrow, D., Wortman, C., Phair, J., & Chmiel, J. (1991). Stressful life events and symptom onset in HIV infection. *American Journal of Psychiatry, 148,* 733–738.

Kessler, R. C., McGonagle, K. A., Zhao, S., Nelson, C. B., Hughes, M., Eshleman, S., Wittchen, H-U., & Kendler, K. S. (1994). Lifetime and 12-month prevalence of DSM-III-R psychiatric disorders in the United States. *Archives of General Psychiatry, 51,* 8–19.

Keynes, M. (1980, December 20/27). Handel's illnesses. *The Lancet,* pp. 1354–1355.

Keys, A., Brozek, J., Henschel, A., Mickelsen, O., & Taylor, H. L. (1950). *The biology of human starvation.* Minneapolis: University of Minnesota Press.

Kiecolt-Glaser, J. K., & Glaser, R. (1995). Psychoneuoimmunology and health consequences: Data and shared mechanisms. *Psychosomatic Medicine, 57,* 269–274.

Kiecolt-Glaser, J. K., Malarkey, W. B., Chee, M., Newton, T., Cacioppo, J. T., Mao, H.-Y., & Glaser, R. (1993). Negative behavior during marital conflict is associated with immunological down-regulation. *Psychosomatic Medicine, 55,* 395–409.

Kiecolt-Glaser, J. K., Page, G. G., Marucha, P. T., MacCallum, R. C., & Glaser, R. (1998). Psychological influences on surgical recovery: Perspectives from psychoneuroimmunology. *American Psychologist, 53,* 1209–1218.

Kihlstrom, J. F. (1985). Hypnosis. *Annual Review of Psychology, 36,* 385–418.

Kihlstrom, J. F. (1990). Awareness, the psychological unconscious, and the self. Address to the American Psychological Association convention.

Kihlstrom, J. F. (1990). The psychological unconscious. In L. A. Pervin (Ed.), *Handbook of personality: Theory and research.* New York: Guilford Press.

Kihlstrom, J. F. (1994). The social construction of memory. Paper presented at the American Psychological Society convention.

Kihlstrom, J. F. (1996). Quoted in *Frequently asked questions about the False Memory Syndrome Foundation* (www.csicop.org/~fitz/fmsf/faq.html).

Kihlstrom, J. F. (1997, November 11). Freud as giant pioneer on whose shoulders we should stand. Social Psychology listserv posting (spsp@stolaf.edu).

Kihlstrom, J. F., & McConkey, K. M. (1990). William James and hypnosis: A centennial reflection. *Psychological Science, 1,* 174–177.

Kim, H. L., Streltzer, J., & Goebert, D. (1999). St. John's wort for depression: A meta-analysis of well-defined clinical trials. *Journal of Nervous and Mental Diseases, 187,* 532–538.

Kim, H., & Markus, H. R. (1999). Deviance or uniqueness, harmony or conformity? A cultural analysis. *Journal of Personality and Social Psychology, 77,* 785–800.

Kim, K. H. S., Relkin, N. R., Lee, K-M., & Hirsch, J. (1997). Distinct cortical areas associated with native and second languages. *Nature, 388,* 171–174.

Kim, Y., & Lee, S-H. (1994). The Confucian model of morality, justice, selfhood and society: Implications for modern society. In *The universal and particular natures of Confucianism.* The Academy of Korean Studies.

Kimball, M. M. (1989). A new perspective on women's math achievement. *Psychological Bulletin, 105,* 198–214.

Kimberg, D. Y., D'Esposito, M., & Farah, M. J. (1998). Cognitive functions in the prefrontal cortex—working memory and executive control. *Current Directions in Psychological Science, 6,* 185–192.

Kimura, D. (1995). Estrogen replacement therapy may protect against intellectual decline in postmenopausal women. *Hormones and Behavior, 29,* 312–321.

Kimzey, S. L. (1975). The effects of extended spaceflight on hematologic and immunologic systems. *Journal of the American Medical Women's Association, 30*(5), 218–232.

Kimzey, S. L., Johnson, P. C., Ritzman, S. E., & Mengel, C. E. (1976, April). Hematology and immunology studies: The second manned Skylab mission. *Aviation, Space, and Environmental Medicine,* pp. 383–390.

King, D. W., & King, L. A. (1991). Validity issues in research on Vietnam veteran adjustment. *Psychological Bulletin, 109,* 107–124.

King, N. J., & Montgomery, R. B. (1980). Biofeedback-induced control of human peripheral temperature: A critical review of the literature. *Psychological Bulletin, 88,* 738–752.

King, P. (1991, March 18). Bawl players. *Sports Illustrated,* pp. 14–17.

Kinnier, R. T., & Metha, A. T. (1989). Regrets and priorities at three stages of life. *Counseling and Values, 33,* 182–193.

Kinsey, A. C., Pomeroy, W., & Martin, C. (1948). *Sexual behavior in the human male.* Philadelphia: Saunders.

Kinsey, A. C., Pomeroy, W., Martin, C., & Gebhard, P. (1953). *Sexual behavior in the human female.* Philadelphia: Saunders.

Kinzl, J. F., Traweger, C., Guenther, V., & Biebl, W. (1994). Family background and sexual abuse associated with eating disorders. *American Journal of Psychiatry, 151,* 1127–1131.

Kirchner, W. H., & Towne, W. F. (1994, June). The sensory basis of the honeybee's dance language. *Scientific American,* pp. 74–80.

Kirk, S. A., & Gallagher, J. J. (1989). *Educating exceptional children.* Boston: Houghton Mifflin.

Kirkpatrick, L. (1999). Attachment and religious representations and behavior. In J. Cassidy & P. R. Shaver (1999), *Handbook of attachment.* New York: Guilford.

Kirsch, I. (1999). Clinical hypnosis as a nondeceptive placebo. In I. Kirsch, E. Cardena-Buelna, & A. Capafons (Eds.), *Clinical hypnosis and self-regulation: Cognitive-behavioral perspectives.* Washington, DC: American Psychological Association.

Kirsch, I., & Lynn, S. J. (1995). The altered state of hypnosis. *American Psychologist, 50,* 846–858.

Kirsch, I., & Lynn, S. J. (1998a). Dissociation theories of hypnosis. *Psychological Bulletin, 123,* 100–115.

Kirsch, I., & Lynn, S. J. (1998b). Social-cognitive alternatives to dissociation theories of hypnotic induction. *Review of General Psychology, 2,* 66–80.

Kirsch, I., & Lynn, S. J. (1999). Automaticity in clinical psychology. *American Psychologist, 54,* 504–515.

Kirsch, I., & Sapirstein, G. (1998). Listening to Prozac but hearing placebo: A meta-analysis of antidepressant medication. *Prevention and Treatment, 1* (journals.apa.org/prevention/volume1).

Kisor, H. (1990). *What's that pig outdoors.* New York: Hill and Wang.

Kitayama, S., & Markus, H. R. (2000). The pursuit of happiness and the realization of sympathy: Cultural patterns of self, social relations, and well-being. In E. Diener & E. M. Suh (Eds.), *Subjective well-being across cultures.* Cambridge, MA: MIT Press.

Kite, M. E., & Johnson, B. T. (1988). Attitudes toward older and younger adults: A meta-analysis. *Psychology and Aging, 3,* 233–244.

Kite, M. E., & Whitley, B. E., Jr. (1996). Sex differences in attitudes toward homosexual persons, behaviors, and civil rights: A meta-analysis. *Personality and Social Psychology Bulletin, 22,* 336–353.

Klasen, S. (1994). "Missing women" reconsidered. *World Development, 22.*

Klayman, J., & Ha, Y-W. (1987). Confirmation, disconfirmation, and information in hypothesis testing. *Psychological Review, 94,* 211–228.

Klein, E., Kreinin, I., Chistyakov, A., Koren, D., Mecz, L., Marmur, S., Ben-Shachar, D., & Feinsod, M. (1999). Therapeutic efficacy of right prefrontal slow repetitive transcranial magnetic stimulation in major depression. *Archives of General Psychiatry, 56,* 315–320.

Klein, S. B., & Kihlstrom, J. F. (1998). On bridging the gap between social-personality psychology and neuropsychology. *Personality and Social Psychology Review, 2,* 228–242.

Kleinfeld, J. (1998). The myth that schools shortchange girls: Social science in the service of deception. Washington, DC: Women's Freedom Network. Available from ERIC, Document ED423210, and at www.uaf.edu/northern/schools/myth.html

Kleinke, C. L. (1986). Gaze and eye contact: A research review. *Psychological Bulletin, 100,* 78–100.

Kleinke, C. L., Peterson, T. R., & Rutledge, T. R. (1998). Effects of self-generated facial expressions on mood. *Journal of Personality and Social Psychology, 74,* 272–279.

Kleinmuntz, B., & Szucko, J. J. (1984). A field study of the fallibility of polygraph lie detection. *Nature, 308,* 449–450.

Kleitman, N. (1960, November). Patterns of dreaming. *Scientific American,* pp. 82–88.

Klemm, W. R. (1990). Historical and introductory perspectives on brainstem-mediated behaviors. In W. R. Klemm & R. P. Vertes (Eds.), *Brainstem mechanisms of behavior.* New York: Wiley.

Kline, D., & Schieber, F. (1985). Vision and aging. In J. E. Birren & K. W. Schaie (Eds.), *Handbook of the psychology of aging.* New York: Van Nostrand Reinhold.

Kline, N. S. (1974). *From sad to glad.* New York: Ballantine Books.

Klineberg, O. (1938). Emotional expression in Chinese literature. *Journal of Abnormal and Social Psychology, 33,* 517–520.

Klineberg, O. (1984). Public opinion and nuclear war. *American Psychologist, 39,* 1245–1253.

Klinke, R., Kral, A., Heid, S., Tillein, J., & Hartmann, R. (1999). Recruitment of the auditory cortex in congenitally deaf cats by long-term cochlear electrostimulation. *Science, 285,* 1729–1733.

Klohnen, E. C., & Bera, S. (1998). Behavioral and experiential patterns of avoidantly and securely attached women across adulthood: A 31-year longitudinal perspective. *Journal of Personality and Social Psychology, 74,* 211–223.

Kluft, R. P. (1991). Multiple personality disorder. In A. Tasman & S. M. Goldfinger (Eds.), *Review of Psychiatry* (Vol. 10). Washington, DC: American Psychiatric Press.

Klüver, H., & Bucy, P. C. (1939). Preliminary analysis of functions of the temporal lobes in monkeys. *Archives of Neurology and Psychiatry, 42,* 979–1000.

Knudsen, E. L. (1998). Capacity for plasticity in the adult owl auditory system expanded by juvenile experience. *Science, 279,* 1531–1533.

Koenig, H. G., Cohen, H. J., George, L. K., Hays, J. C., Larson, D. B., & Blazer, D. G. (1997). Attendance at religious services, interleukin-6, and other biological indicators of immune function in older adults. *International Journal of Psychiatry in Medicine, 23,* 233–250.

Koenig, H. G., Hays, J. C., Larson, D. B., George, L. K., Cohen, H. J., McCullough, M. E., Meador, K. G., & Blazer, D. G. (1999). Does religious attendance prolong survival? A six-year follow-up study of 3,968 older adults. *Journal of Gerontology: Medical Sciences, 54A,* M370-M377.

Koenig, H. G., & Larson, D. B. (1998). Use of hospital services, religious attendance, and religious affiliation. *Southern Medical Journal, 91*, 925–932.

Kohlberg, L. (1981). *The philosophy of moral development: Essays on moral development* (Vol. I). San Francisco: Harper & Row.

Kohlberg, L. (1984). *The psychology of moral development: Essays on moral development* (Vol. II). San Francisco: Harper & Row.

Kohler, I. (1962, May). Experiments with goggles. *Scientific American*, pp. 62–72.

Kohn, A. (1987, October). It's hard to get left out of a pair. *Psychology Today*, pp. 53–57.

Kohn, P. M., & Macdonald, J. E. (1992). The survey of recent life experiences: A decontaminated hassles scale for adults. *Journal of Behavioral Medicine, 15*, 221–236.

Kolata, G. (1986). Youth suicide: New research focuses on a growing social problem. *Science, 233*, 839–841.

Kolata, G. (1987). Metabolic catch-22 of exercise regimens. *Science, 236*, 146–147.

Kolata, G. (1996, May 21). Could it be? Weather has nothing to do with your arthritis pain? *New York Times*, p. C13.

Kolata, G. (1996, December 10). With major math proof, brute computers show flash of reasoning power. *New York Times*, p. C1.

Kolb, B. (1989). Brain development, plasticity, and behavior. *American Psychologist, 44*, 1203–1212.

Kolb, B., & Whishaw, I. Q. (1998). Brain plasticity and behavior. *Annual Review of Psychology, 49*, 43–64.

Kolers, P. A. (1975). Specificity of operations in sentence recognition. *Cognitive Psychology, 7*, 289–306.

Kolodziej, M. E., & Johnson, B. T. (1996). Interpersonal contact and acceptance of persons with psychiatric disorders: A research synthesis. *Journal of Consulting and Clinical Psychology, 64*, 1387–1396.

Koltz, C. (1983, December). Scapegoating. *Psychology Today*, pp. 68–69.

Konishi, M. (1993, April). Listening with two ears. *Scientific American*, pp. 66–73.

Kopta, S. M., Lueger, R. J., Saunders, S. M., & Howard, K. I. (1999). Individual psychotherapy outcome and process research: Challenges leading to greater turmoil or a positive transition? *Annual Review of Psychology, 30*, 441–469.

Koslowsky, M., & Babkoff, H. (1992). Meta-analysis of the relationship between total sleep deprivation and performance. *Chronobiology International, 9*, 132–136.

Koss, M. P., Heise, L., & Russo, N. P. (1994). The global health burden of rape. *Psychology of Women Quarterly, 18*, 509–537.

Kosslyn, S. M., & Koenig, O. (1992). *Wet mind: The new cognitive neuroscience*. New York: Free Press.

Kotkin, M., Daviet, C., & Gurin, J. (1996). The *Consumer Reports* mental health survey. *American Psychologist, 51*, 1080–1082.

Kotva, H. J., & Schneider, H. G. (1990). Those "talks"—general and sexual communication between mothers and daughters. *Journal of Social Behavior and Personality, 5*, 603–613.

Kraft, C. (1978). A psychophysical approach to air safety: Simulator studies of visual illusions in night approaches. In H. L. Pick, H. W. Leibowitz, J. E. Singer, A. Steinschneider, & H. W. Stevenson (Eds.), *Psychology: From research to practice*. New York: Plenum Press.

Kraft, R. (1996, December 2, and 1994, July 20). Personal correspondence (from Otterbein College) regarding Holocaust memories.

Kramer, A. F., Hahn, S., Cohen, N. J., Banich, M. T., McAuley, E., Harrison, C. R., Chason, J., Vakil, E., Bardell, L., Boileau, R. A., & Colcombe, A. (1999). Ageing, fitness and neurocognitive function. *Nature, 400*, 418–419.

Kramer, M. S., Cutler, N., Feighner, J., Shrivastava, R., Carman, J., Sramek, J. J., Reines, S. A., Liu, G., Snavely, D., Wyatt-Knowles, E., Hale, J. J., Mills, S. G., MacCoss, M., Swain, C. J., Harrison, T., Hill, R. G., Hefti, F., Scolnick, E. M., Cascieri, M. A., Chicchi, G. G., Sadowski, S., Williams, A. R., Hewson, L., Smith, D., Carlson, E. J., Hargreaves, R. J., & Rupniak, N. M. J. (1998). Distinct mechanism for antidepressant activity by blockade of central substance P receptors. *Science, 281*, 1640–1645.

Kraus, S. J. (1991). Attitudes and the prediction of behavior. Doctoral dissertation, Harvard University.

Krauss, R. M. (1998). Why do we gesture when we speak? *Current Directions in Psychology, 7*, 54–60.

Kraut, R. E., & Johnston, R. E. (1979). Social and emotional messages of smiling: An ethological approach. *Journal of Personality and Social Psychology, 37*, 1539–1553.

Kraut, R., Patterson, M., Lundmark, V., Kiesler, S., Mukopadhyay, T., & Scherlis, W. (1998). Internet paradox: A social technology that reduces social involvement and psychological well-being? *American Psychologist, 53*, 1017–1031.

Krebs, D. L., & Van Hesteren, F. (1994). The development of altruism: Toward an integrative model. *Developmental Review, 14*, 103–158.

Kreiger, D. (1993). *Accepting your power to heal: The personal practice of therapeutic touch*. Santa Fe, NM: Bear.

Kreitner, R. (1992). *Management*, 5th ed. Boston: Houghton Mifflin.

Kring, A. M., & Gordon, A. H. (1998). Sex differences in emotion: Expression, experience, and physiology. *Journal of Personality and Social Psychology, 74*, 686–703.

Krosnick, J. A., & Alwin, D. F. (1989). Aging and susceptibility to attitude change. *Journal of Personality and Social Psychology, 57*, 416–425.

Krosnick, J. A., Betz, A. L., Jussim, L. J., & Lynn, A. R. (1992). Subliminal conditioning of attitudes. *Personality and Social Psychology Bulletin, 18*, 152–162.

Kruger, J., & Dunning, D. (1999). Unskilled and unaware of it: How difficulties in recognizing one's own incompetence lead to inflated self-assessments. *Journal of Personality and Social Psychology, 77*, 1121–1134.

Kruger, J., Epley, N., & Gilovich, T. (1999). Egocentrism over email. Paper presented to the American Psychological Society meeting.

Krupa, D. J., Thompson, J. K., & Thompson, R. F. (1993). Localization of a memory trace in the mammalian brain. *Science, 260*, 989–991.

Kuhl, P. K., & Meltzoff, A. N. (1982). The bimodal perception of speech in infancy. *Science, 218*, 1138–1141.

Kuhn, D., Weinstock, M., & Flaton, R. (1994). How well do jurors reason? Competence dimensions of individual variation in a juror reasoning task. *Psychological Science, 5*, 289–296.

Kujala, U. M., Kaprio, J., Sarna, S., & Koskenvuo, M. (1998). Relationship of leisure-time physical activity and mortality: The Finnish twin cohort. *Journal of the American Medical Association, 279*, 440–444.

Kurtz, P. (1983, Spring). Stars, planets, and people. *The Skeptical Inquirer*, pp. 65–68.

Kutas, M. (1990). Event-related brain potential (ERP) studies of cognition during sleep: Is it more than a dream? In R. R. Bootzin, J. F. Kihlstrom, & D. Schacter (Eds.), *Sleep and cognition.* Washington, DC: American Psychological Association.

Labouvie-Vief, G., & Schell, D. A. (1982). Learning and memory in later life. In B. B. Wolman (Ed.), *Handbook of developmental psychology.* Englewood Cliffs, NJ: Prentice-Hall.

Lacayo, R. (1995, June 12). Violent reaction. *Time,* pp. 25–39.

Lachman, M. E., & Weaver, S. L. (1998). The sense of control as a moderator of social class differences in health and well-being. *Journal of Personality and Social Psychology, 74,* 763–773.

Ladd, E. C. (1998, August/September). The tobacco bill and American public opinion. *The Public Perspective,* pp. 5–19.

Ladd, G. T. (1887). *Elements of physiological psychology.* New York: Scribner's.

Lagerweij, E., Nelis, P. C., van Ree, J. M., & Wiegant, V. M. (1984). The twitch in horses: A variant of acupuncture. *Science, 225,* 1172–1174.

Laird, J. D. (1974). Self-attribution of emotion: The effects of expressive behavior on the quality of emotional experience. *Journal of Personality and Social Psychology, 29,* 475–486.

Laird, J. D. (1984). The real role of facial response in the experience of emotion: A reply to Tourangeau and Ellsworth, and others. *Journal of Personality and Social Psychology, 47,* 909–917.

Laird, J. D., Cuniff, M., Sheehan, K., Shulman, D., & Strum, G. (1989). Emotion specific effects of facial expressions on memory for life events. *Journal of Social Behavior and Personality, 4,* 87–98.

Lambert, W. E. (1992). Challenging established views on social issues: The power and limitations of research. *American Psychologist, 47,* 533–542.

Lambert, W. E., Genesee, F., Holobow, N., & Chartrand, L. (1993). Bilingual education for majority English-speaking children. *European Journal of Psychology of Education, 8,* 3–22.

Lamberth, J. (1998, August 6). Driving while black: A statistician proves that prejudice still rules the road. *Washington Post,* p. C1.

Lancioni, G. (1980). Infant operant conditioning and its implications for early intervention. *Psychological Bulletin, 88,* 516–534.

Landauer, T. K. (1986). How much do people remember? Some estimates of the quantity of learned information in long-term memory. *Cognitive Science, 10,* 477–493.

Landauer, T. K. (1998). Learning and representing verbal meaning: The latent semantic analysis theory. *Current Directions in Psychological Science, 7,* 161–164.

Landauer, T. K., & Dumais, S. T. (April, 1997). A solution to Plato's problem: The latent semantic analysis theory of acquisition, induction, and representation of knowledge. *Psychological Review, 104(2),* 211–240.

Landauer, T. K., & Whiting, J. W. M. (1979). Correlates and consequences of stress in infancy. In R. Munroe, B. Munroe & B. Whiting (eds.), *Handbook of Cross-Cultural Human Development.* New York: Garland.

Landers, A. (1969, April 8). Cited in L. Berkowitz, The case for bottling up rage. *Psychology Today,* September, 1973, pp. 24–31.

Landfield, P., Cadwallader, L. B., & Vinsant, S. (1988). Quantitative changes in hippocampal structure following long-term exposure to delta-9-tetrahydrocannabinol: Possible mediation by glucocorticoid systems. *Brain Research, 443,* 47–62.

Landry, D. W. (1997, February). Immunotherapy for cocaine addiction. *Scientific American,* pp. 42–45.

Langer, E. J. (1983). *The psychology of control.* Beverly Hills, CA: Sage.

Langer, E. J., & Abelson, R. P. (1974). A patient by any other name . . . : Clinician group differences in labeling bias. *Journal of Consulting and Clinical Psychology, 42,* 4–9.

Langer, E. J., & Imber, L. (1980). The role of mindlessness in the perception of deviance. *Journal of Personality and Social Psychology, 39,* 360–367.

Langlois, J. H., & Roggman, L. A. (1990). Attractive faces are only average. *Psychological Science, 1,* 115–121.

Langlois, J. H., Roggman, L. A., Casey, R. J., Ritter, J. M., Rieser-Danner, L. A., & Jenkins, V. Y. (1987). Infant preferences for attractive faces: Rudiments of a stereotype? *Developmental Psychology, 23,* 363–369.

Larrance, D. T., & Twentyman, C. T. (1983). Maternal attributions and child abuse. *Journal of Abnormal Psychology, 92,* 449–457.

Larsen, R. J., & Diener, E. (1987). Affect intensity as an individual difference characteristic: A review. *Journal of Research in Personality, 21,* 1–39.

Larsen, R. J., Diener, E., & Cropanzano, R. S. (1987). Cognitive operations associated with individual differences in affect intensity. *Journal of Personality and Social Psychology, 53,* 767–774.

Larsen, R. J., Kasimatis, M., & Frey, K. (1992). Facilitating the furrowed brow: An unobtrusive test of the facial feedback hypothesis applied to unpleasant affect. *Cognition and Emotion, 6,* 321–338.

Larson, R. W., & Verma, S. (1999). How children and adolescents spend time across the world: Work, play, and developmental opportunities. *Psychological Bulletin, 125,* 701–736.

Larzelere, R. E. (1996). A review of the outcomes of parental use of nonabusive or customary physical punishment. *Pediatrics, 78,* 824–828.

Larzelere, R. E. (1998). Affidavit No. 98–CV–158948, Ontario Court (General Division).

Larzelere, R. E. (1999). The intervention selection bias. Unpublished manuscript. Boys Town, NE: Boys Town.

Lashley, K. S. (1950). In search of the engram. In *Symposium of the Society for Experimental Biology* (Vol. 4). New York: Cambridge University Press.

Lassiter, G. D., & Irvine, A. A. (1986). Video-taped confessions: The impact of camera point of view on judgments of coercion. *Journal of Personality and Social Psychology, 16,* 268–276.

Latané, B. (1981). The psychology of social impact. *American Psychologist, 36,* 343–356.

Latané, B., & Dabbs, J. M., Jr. (1975). Sex, group size and helping in three cities. *Sociometry, 38,* 180–194.

Lau, S., & Gruen, G. E. (1992). The social stigma of loneliness: Effect of target person's and perceiver's sex. *Personality and Social Psychology Bulletin, 18,* 182–189.

Laudenslager, M. L., & Reite, M. L. (1984). Losses and separations: Immunological consequences and health implications. *Review of Personality and Social Psychology, 5,* 285–312.

Laumann, E. O., Gagnon, J. H., Michael, R. T., & Michaels, S. (1994). *The social organization of sexuality: Sexual practices in the United States.* Chicago: University of Chicago Press.

Laumann, E. O., Paik, A., & Rosen R. C. (1999). Sexual dysfunction in the United States: Prevalence and predictors. *Journal of the American Medical Association, 281,* 537–544.

Laurence, J.-R., & Perry, C. (1988). *Hypnosis, will and memory: A psycho-legal history.* New York: Guilford.

Laursen, B., Coy, K. C., & Collins, W. A. (1998). Reconsidering changes in parent-child conflict across adolescence: A meta-analysis. *Child Development, 69,* 817–832.

Lazarus, R. S. (1990). Theory-based stress measurement. *Psychological Inquiry, 1,* 3–13.

Lazarus, R. S. (1991). Progress on a cognitive-motivational-relational theory of emotion. *American Psychologist, 46,* 352–367.

Lazarus. R. S. (1998). *Fifty years of the research and theory of R. S. Lazarus: An analysis of historical and perennial issues.* Mahwah, NJ: Erlbaum.

Leach, P. (1993). Should parents hit their children? *The Psychologist: Bulletin of the British Psychological Society, 6,* 216–220.

Leach, P. (1994). *Children first.* New York: Knopf.

Leary, M. R. (1999). The social and psychological importance of self-esteem. In R. M. Kowalski & M. R. Leary (Eds.), *The social psychology of emotional and behavioral problems.* Washington, DC: APA Books.

Leary, M. R., Haupt, A. L., Strausser, K. S., & Chokel, J. T. (1998). Calibrating the sociometer: The relationship between interpersonal appraisals and state self-esteem. *Journal of Personality and Social Psychology, 74,* 1290–1299.

Leary, M. R., Schreindorfer, L. S., & Haupt, A. L. (1995). The role of low self-esteem in emotional and behavioral problems: Why is low self-esteem dysfunctional? *Journal of Social and Clinical Psychology, 14,* 297–314.

Leary, W. E. (1998, September 28). Older people enjoy sex, survey says. *New York Times* (www.nytimes.com).

Lebow, J. (1982). Consumer satisfaction with mental health treatment. *Psychological Bulletin, 91,* 244–259.

LeDoux, J., & Armony, J. (1999). Can neurobiology tell us anything about human feelings? In D. Dahneman, E. Diener, & N. Schwartz (Eds.), *Well-being: The foundations of hedonic psychology.* New York: Sage.

Lefcourt, H. M. (1982). *Locus of control: Current trends in theory and research.* Hillsdale, NJ: Erlbaum.

Lefcourt, H. M., & Davidson-Katz, K. (1991). The role of humor and the self. In C. R. Snyder & D. R. Forsyth (Eds.), *Handbook of social and clinical psychology: The health perspective.* New York: Pergamon Press.

Lehman, A. F., Steinwachs, D. M., Dixon, L. B., Goldman, H. H., Osher, F., Postrado, L., Scott, J. E., Thompson, J. W., Fahey, M., Fischer, P., Kasper, J. A., Lyles, A., Skinner, E. A., Buchanan, R., Carpenter, W. T., Jr., Levine, J., McGlynn, E. A., Rosenheck, R., & Zito, J. (1998). Translating research into practice: The schizophrenia patient outcomes research team (PORT) treatment recommendations. *Schizophrenia Bulletin, 24,* 1–10.

Lehman, D. R., Lempert, R. O., & Nisbett, R. E. (1988). The effects of graduate training on reasoning: Formal discipline and thinking about everyday-life events. *American Psychologist, 43,* 431–442.

Lehman, D. R., & Nisbett, R. E. (1985). Effects of higher education on inductive reasoning. Unpublished manuscript, University of Michigan.

Lehman, D. R., Wortman, C. B., & Williams, A. F. (1987). Long-term effects of losing a spouse or child in a motor vehicle crash. *Journal of Personality and Social Psychology, 52,* 218–231.

Leibowitz, H. W. (1985). Grade crossing accidents and human factors engineering. *American Scientist, 73,* 558–562.

Leigh, B. C. (1989). In search of the seven dwarves: Issues of measurement and meaning in alcohol expectancy research. *Psychological Bulletin, 105,* 361–373.

Leikind, B., & McCarthy, W. J. (1985). An investigation of firewalking. *The Skeptical Inquirer, 10,* 23–34.

Leikind, B., & McCarthy, W. J. (1988). Firewalking. *Experientia, 44,* 310–315.

Leitenberg, H., & Henning, K. (1995). Sexual fantasy. *Psychological Bulletin, 117,* 469–496.

Lenat, D. B. (1995, September). Artificial intelligence. *Scientific American,* pp. 80–82.

Lennox, B. R., Bert, S., Park, G., Jones, P. B., & Morris, P. G. (1999). Spatial and temporal mapping of neural activity associated with auditory hallucinations. *Lancet, 353,* 644.

Lenzenweger, M. F., Dworkin, R. H., & Wethington, E. (1989). Models of positive and negative symptoms in schizophrenia: An empirical evaluation of latent structures. *Journal of Abnormal Psychology, 98,* 62–70.

Leo, J. (1991, August 19). No-fault syntax. *U.S. News & World Report,* p. 17.

Lepper, M. R., Anderson, C. A., & Ross, L. (December, 1980). Perseverance of social theories: The role of explanation in the persistence of discredited information. *Journal of Personality & Social Psychology, 39,* 1037–1049.

Lepper, M. R., Ross, L., & Lau, R. R. (1986). Persistence of inaccurate beliefs about the self: Perseverance effects in the classroom. *Journal of Personality and Social Psychology, 50,* 482–491.

Lerman, C., Caporaso, N. E., Audrain, J., Main, D., Bowman, E. D., Lockshin, B., Boyd, N. R., & Shields, P. G. (1999). Evidence suggesting the role of specific genetic factors in cigarette smoking. *Health Psychology, 18,* 14–20.

Lerner, M. J. (1980). *The belief in a just world: A fundamental delusion.* New York: Plenum Press.

Leserman, J., Jackson, E. D., Petitto, J. M., Golden, R. N., Silva, S. G., Perkins, D. O., Cai, J., Folds, J. D., & Evans, D. L. (1999). Progression to AIDS: The effects of stress, depressive symptoms, and social support. *Psychosomatic Medicine, 61,* 397–406.

Leshner, A. I. (1992). *Outcasts on main street: Report of the federal task force on homelessness and severe mental illness.* Washington, DC: Interagency Council on the Homeless, Office of the Programs for the Homeless Mentally Ill, National Institute of Mental Health.

Lessard, N., Pare, M., Lepore, F., & Lassonde, M. (1998). Early-blind human subjects localize sound sources better than sighted subjects. *Nature, 395,* 278–280.

Levanen, S., Jousmak, V., & Hari, R. (1998). Vibration-induced auditory-cortex activation in a congenitally deaf adult. *Current Biology, 8,* 869–872.

LeVay, S. (1991). A difference in hypothalamic structure between heterosexual and homosexual men. *Science, 253,* 1034–1037.

LeVay, S. (1994, March). Quoted in D. Nimmons, Sex and the brain. *Discover,* pp. 64–71.

Levenson, R. W., Ekman, P., Heider, K., & Friesen, W. V. (1991). Emotion and autonomic nervous system activity in an Indonesian culture. Unpublished manuscript, University of California, Berkeley.

Levenson, R. W., Ekman, P., Heider, K., & Friesen, W. V. (1992). Emotion and autonomic nervous system activity in the Minangkabau of West Sumatra. *Journal of Personality and Social Psychology, 62*, 972–988.

Levesque, M. J., & Kenny, D. A. (1993). Accuracy of behavioral predictions at zero acquaintance: A social relations analysis. *Journal of Personality and Social Psychology, 65*, 1178–1187.

Levin, I. P., & Gaeth, G. J. (1988). How consumers are affected by the framing of attribute information before and after consuming the product. *Journal of Consumer Research, 15*, 374–378.

Levin, I. P., Schnittjer, S. K., & Thee, S. L. (1988). Information framing effects in social and personal decisions. *Journal of Experimental Social Psychology, 24*, 520–529.

Levin, J. S., Larson, D. B., & Puchalski, C. M. (1997). Religion and spirituality in medicine: Research and education. *Journal of the American Medical Association, 278*, 792–793.

Levine, I. S., & Rog, D. J. (1990). Mental health services for homeless mentally ill persons: Federal initiatives and current service trends. *American Psychologist, 45*, 963–968.

Levine, J. A., Eberhardt, N. L., & Jensen, M. D. (1999). Role of nonexercise activity thermogenesis in resistance to fat gain in humans. *Science, 283*, 212–214.

Levine, R. V., & Norenzayan, A. (1999). The pace of life in 31 countries. *Journal of Cross-Cultural Psychology, 30*, 178–205.

Levine, R., Sato, S., Hashimoto, T., & Verma, J. (1995). Love and marriage in eleven cultures. *Journal of Cross-Cultural Psychology, 26*, 554–571.

Levitt, E. E. (1986). Coercion, voluntariness, compliance and resistance: The essence of hypnosis twenty-seven years after Orne. Invited address to the American Psychological Association convention.

Levy, B., & Langer, E. (1992). Avoidance of the memory loss stereotype: Enhanced memory among the elderly deaf. Paper presented at the American Psychological Association convention, Washington, DC.

Levy, J. (1985, May). Right brain, left brain: Fact and fiction. *Psychology Today*, pp. 38–44.

Lewicki, P., Hill, T., & Czyzewska, M. (1992). Nonconscious acquisition of information. *American Psychologist, 47*, 796–801.

Lewinsohn, P. M., Hoberman, H., Teri, L., & Hautziner, M. (1985). An integrative theory of depression. In S. Reiss & R. Bootzin (Eds.), *Theoretical issues in behavior therapy*. Orlando, FL: Academic Press.

Lewinsohn, P. M., Rohde, P., & Seeley, J. R. (1998). Major depressive disorder in older adolescents: Prevalence, risk factors, and clinical implications. *Clinical Psychology Review, 18*, 765–794.

Lewis, C. C. (1981). The effects of parental firm control: A reinterpretation of findings. *Psychological Bulletin, 90*, 547–563.

Lewis, C. S. (1967). *Christian reflections*. Grand Rapids, MI: Eerdmans.

Lewis, D. O., Pincus, J. H., Bard, B., Richardson, E., Prichep, L. S., Feldman, M., & Yeager, C. (1988). Neuropsychiatric, psychoeducational, and family characteristics of 14 juveniles condemned to death in the United States. *American Journal of Psychiatry, 145*, 584–589.

Lewis, D. O., Pincus, J. H., Feldman, M., Jackson, L., & Bard, B. (1986). Psychiatric, neurological, and psychoeducational characteristics of 15 death row inmates in the United States. *American Journal of Psychiatry, 143*, 838–845.

Lewis, D. O., Yeager, C. A., Swica, Y., Pincus, J. H., & Lewis, M. (1997). Objective documentation of child abuse and dissociation in 12 murderers with dissociative identity disorder. *American Journal of Psychiatry, 154*, 1703–1710.

Lewis, M. (1992). Commentary. *Human Development, 35*, 44–51.

Lewontin, R. (1976). Race and intelligence. In N. J. Block & G. Dworkin (Eds.), *The IQ controversy: Critical readings*. New York: Pantheon.

Lewontin, R. (1982). *Human diversity*. New York: Scientific American Library.

Lewy, A. J., Bauer, V. K., Cutler, N, L., Sack, R. L., Ahmed, S., Thomas, K. H., Blood, M. L., & Jackson, J. M. L. (1998). Morning vs evening light treatment of patients with winter depression. *Archives of General Psychiatry, 55*, 890–896.

Li, J. C., Dunning, D., & Malpass, R. L. (1996). Cross-racial identification among European-Americans' basketball fandom and the contact hypothesis. Unpublished manuscript, Cornell University.

Libet, B. (1985). Unconscious cerebral initiative and the role of conscious will in voluntary action. *Behavioral and Brain Sciences, 12*, 181–187.

Licata, A., Taylor, S., Berman, M., & Cranston, J. (1993). Effects of cocaine on human aggression. *Pharmacology Biochemistry and Behavior, 45*, 549–552.

Lichtman, S. W., Pisarska, K., Berman, E. R., Pestone, M., Dowling, H., Offenbacher, E., Weisel, H., Heshka, S., Matthews, D. E., & Heymsfield, S. B. (1992). Discrepancy between self-reported and actual caloric intake and exercise in obese subjects. *New England Journal of Medicine, 327*, 1893–1898.

Light, K. C., Koepke, J. P., Obrist, P. A., & Willis, P. W., Jr. (1983). Psychological stress induces sodium and fluid retention in men at high risk for hypertension. *Science, 220*, 429–431.

Lilienfeld, S. O. (1998). Pseudoscience in contemporary clinical psychology: What it is and what we can do about it. *The Clinical Psychologist, 51*(4), 3–5.

Lilienfeld, S. O., Lynn, S. J., Kirsch, I., Chaves, J. F., Sarbin, T. R., Ganaway, G. K., & Powell, R. A. (1999). Dissociative identity disorder and the sociocognitive model: Recalling the lessons of the past. *Psychological Bulletin, 125*, 507–523.

Lin, L., Faraco, J., Li, R., Kadotani, H., Rogers, W., Lin, X., Qiu, X., de Jong, P. J., Nishino, S., & Mignot E. (1999). The sleep disorder canine narcolepsy is caused by a mutation in the hypocretin (orexin) receptor 2 gene. *Cell, 98*, 365–376.

Linder, D. (1982). Social trap analogs: The tragedy of the commons in the laboratory. In V. J. Derlega & J. Grzelak (Eds.), *Cooperative and helping behavior: Theories and research*. New York: Academic Press.

Lindsay, D. S. (1995). Psychotherapy and memories of childhood sexual abuse. Invited address to the American Psychological Association convention.

Lindskold, S. (1978). Trust development, the GRIT proposal, and the effects of conciliatory acts on conflict and cooperation. *Psychological Bulletin, 85*, 772–793.

Lindskold, S. (1986). GRIT: Reducing distrust through carefully introduced conciliation. In S. Worchel & W. G. Austin (Eds.), *Psychology of intergroup relations* (2nd ed.). Chicago: Nelson-Hall.

Lindskold, S., & Han, G. (1988). GRIT as a foundation for integrative bargaining. *Personality and Social Psychology Bulletin, 14,* 335–345.

Lindskold, S., Han, G., & Betz, B. (1986). Repeated persuasion in interpersonal conflict. *Journal of Personality and Social Psychology, 51,* 1183–1188.

Lindskold, S., Walters, P. S., & Koutsourais, H. (1983). Cooperators, competitors, and response to GRIT. *Journal of Conflict Resolution, 27,* 521–532.

Linville, P. W., Fischer, G. W., & Fischhoff, B. (1992). AIDS risk perceptions and decision biases. In J. B. Pryor & G. D. Reeder (Eds.), *The social psychology of HIV infection.* Hillsdale, NJ: Erlbaum.

Lippman, J. (1992, October 25). Global village is characterized by a television in every home. *Los Angeles Times* Syndicate (in *Grand Rapids Press,* p. F9).

Lipps, H. M. (1999). *A new psychology of women: Gender, culture, and ethnicity.* Mountain View, CA: Mayfield Publishing.

Lipsey, M. W., & Wilson, D. B. (1993). The efficacy of psychological, educational, and behavioral treatment: Confirmation from meta-analyses. *American Psychologist, 48,* 1181–1209.

Livingstone, M., & Hubel, D. (1988). Segregation of form, color, movement, and depth: Anatomy, physiology, and perception. *Science, 240,* 740–749.

Lock, M. (1998). Menopause: Lessons from anthropology. *Psychosomatic Medicine, 60,* 410–419.

Locke, E. A., & Latham, G. P. (1990). Work motivation and satisfaction: Light at the end of the tunnel. *Psychological Science, 1,* 240–246.

Loehlin, J. C., McCrae, R. R., & Costa, P. T., Jr. (1998). Heritabilities of common and measure-specific components of the Big Five personality factors. *Journal of Research in Personality, 32,* 431–453.

Loehlin, J. C., & Nichols, R. C. (1976). *Heredity, environment, and personality.* Austin: University of Texas Press.

Loewenstein, G., & Furstenberg, F. (1991). Is teenage sexual behavior rational? *Journal of Applied Social Psychology, 21,* 957–986.

Loftus, E. F. (1979). The malleability of human memory. *American Scientist, 67,* 313–320.

Loftus, E. F. (1980). *Memory: Surprising new insights into how we remember and why we forget.* Reading, MA: Addison-Wesley.

Loftus, E. F. (1993). The reality of repressed memories. *American Psychologist, 48,* 518–537.

Loftus, E. (1995, March/April). Remembering dangerously. *Skeptical Inquirer,* pp. 20–29.

Loftus, E. F., Coan, J., & Pickrell, J. E. (1996). Manufacturing false memories using bits of reality. In L. Reder (Ed.), *Implicit memory and metacognition.* Mahway, NJ: Erlbaum.

Loftus, E. F., & Kaufman, L. (1992). Why do traumatic experiences sometimes produce good memory (flashbulbs) and sometimes no memory (repression)? In E. Winograd & U. Neisser (Eds.), *Affect and accuracy in recall: Studies of "flashbulb" memories.* New York: Cambridge University Press.

Loftus, E., & Ketcham, K. (1994). *The myth of repressed memory.* New York: St. Martin's Press.

Loftus, E. F., Levidow, B., & Duensing, S. (1992). Who remembers best? Individual differences in memory for events that occurred in a science museum. *Applied Cognitive Psychology, 6,* 93–107.

Loftus, E. F., & Loftus, G. R. (1980). On the permanence of stored information in the human brain. *American Psychologist, 35,* 409–420.

Loftus, E. F., Milo, E. M., & Paddock, J. R. (1995). The accidental executioner: Why psychotherapy must be informed by science. *The Counseling Psychologist, 23,* 300–309.

Loftus, E. F., & Palmer, J. C. (October, 1974). Reconstruction of automobile destruction: An example of the interaction between language and memory. *Journal of Verbal Learning & Verbal Behavior, 13*(5), 585–589.

Loftus, G. R. (1992). When a lie becomes memory's truth: Memory distortion after exposure to misinformation. *Current Directions in Psychological Science, 1,* 121–123.

Logothetis, N. K., & Schall, J. D. (1989). Neuronal correlates of subjective visual perception. *Science, 245,* 761–763.

Logue, A. W. (1998a). Laboratory research on self-control: Applications to administration. *Review of General Psychology, 2,* 221–238.

Logue, A. W. (1998b). Self-control. In W. T. O'Donohue (Eds.), *Learning and behavior therapy.* Boston, MA: Allyn & Bacon.

Logue, M. B., Sher, K. J., & Frensch, P. A. (1992). Purported characteristics of adult children of alcoholics: A possible "Barnum effect." *Professional Psychology: Research and Practice, 23,* 226–232.

Lohr, J. M., Lilienfeld, S. O., Tolin, D. F., & Herbert, J. D. (1999). Eye movement desensitization and reprocessing: An analysis of specific versus nonspecific treatment factors. *Journal of Anxiety Disorders, 13,* 185–207.

London, P. (1970). The rescuers: Motivational hypotheses about Christians who saved Jews from the Nazis. In J. Macaulay & L. Berkowitz (Eds.), *Altruism and helping behavior.* New York: Academic Press.

Long, B. C., & van Stavel, R. (1995). Effects of exercise training on anxiety: A meta-analysis. *Journal of Applied Sport Psychology, 7,* 167–189.

Long, R., Bernhardt, P., & Evans, W. (1999). Perception of conventional sensory cues as an alternative to the postulated "human energy field" of therapeutic touch. *Scientific Review of Alternative Medicine, 3*(2), in press.

Lopez, A. D. (1999). Measuring the health hazards of tobacco: Commentary. *Bulletin of the World Health Organization, 77*(1), 82–83.

LoPiccolo, J. L., & Stock, W. E. (1986). Treatment of sexual dysfunction. *Journal of Consulting and Clinical Psychology, 54,* 158–167.

Lord, C. G., Lepper, M. R., & Preston, E. (1984). Considering the opposite: A corrective strategy for social judgment. *Journal of Personality and Social Psychology, 47,* 1231–1247.

Lord, C. G., Ross, L., & Lepper, M. (1979). Biased assimilation and attitude polarization: The effects of prior theories on subsequently considered evidence. *Journal of Personality and Social Psychology, 37,* 2098–2109.

Lorenz, K. (1937). The companion in the bird's world. *Auk, 54,* 245–273.

Los Angeles Times. (1998, 14 March). Daughters give birth on same day. P. A15.

Lourenco, O., & Machado, A. (1996). In defense of Piaget's theory: A reply to 10 common criticisms. *Psychological Review, 103,* 143–164.

Lovaas, O. I. (1987). Behavioral treatment and normal educational and intellectual functioning in young autistic children. *Journal of Consulting and Clinical Psychology, 55,* 3–9.

Lowry, P. E. (1997). The assessment center process: New directions. *Journal of Social Behavior and Personality, 12,* 53–62.

Lozoff, B. (1989). Nutrition and behavior. *American Psychologist, 44,* 231–236.

Lu, Z.-L., Williamson, S. J., & Kaufman, L. (1992). Behavioral lifetime of human auditory sensory memory predicted by physiological measures. *Science, 258,* 1668–1670.

Lubart, T. I. (1990). Creativity and cross-cultural variation. *International Journal of Psychology, 25,* 39–59.

Lubinski, D., & Benbow, C. P. (1992). Gender differences in abilities and preferences among the gifted: Implications for the math-science pipeline. *Current Directions in Psychological Science, 1,* 61–66.

Lubinski, D., & Benbow, C. P. (2000). States of excellence. *American Psychologist,* 137–150.

Luchins, A. S. (1946). Classroom experiments on mental set. *American Journal of Psychology, 59,* 295–298.

Ludwig, A. M. (1995). *The price of greatness: Resolving the creativity and madness controversy.* New York: Guilford Press.

Lukoff, D., Lu, F., & Turner, R. (1992). Toward a more culturally sensitive DSM-IV: Psychoreligious and psychospiritual problems. *Journal of Nervous and Mental Disease, 180,* 673–682.

Lull, J. (Ed.). (1988). *World families watch television.* Newbury Park, CA: Sage.

Lumsden, C. J., & Wilson, E. O. (1983). *Promethean fire: Reflections on the origin of mind.* Cambridge, MA: Harvard University Press.

Luria, A. M. (1968). In L. Solotaroff (Trans.), *The mind of a mnemonist.* New York: Basic Books.

Lykken, D. T. (1982, September). Fearlessness: Its carefree charm and deadly risks. *Psychology Today,* pp. 20–28.

Lykken, D. T. (1983, April). Polygraph prejudice. *APA Monitor,* p. 4.

Lykken, D. T. (1992). Science, lies, and controversy: An epitaph for the polygraph. Invited address upon receipt of the Senior Career award for Distinguished Contribution to Psychology in the Public Interest, American Psychological Association convention.

Lykken, D. T. (1995). *The antisocial personalities.* Hillsdale, NJ: Erlbaum.

Lykken, D. T. (1998). The genetics of genius. In Steptoe, A. (Ed.), *Genius and mind: Studies of creativity and temperament.* New York: Oxford University Press, 15–37.

Lykken, D. (1999). *Happiness.* New York: Golden Books.

Lykken, D. T., McGue, M., Tellegen, A., & Bouchard, T. J., Jr. (1992). Emergenesis: Genetic traits that may not run in families. *American Psychologist, 47,* 1565–1577.

Lykken, D. T., & Tellegen, A. (1993) Is human mating adventitious or the result of lawful choice? A twin study of mate selection. *Journal of Personality and Social Psychology, 65,* 56–68.

Lykken, D., & Tellegen, A. (1996). Happiness is a stochastic phenomenon. *Psychological Science, 7,* 186–189.

Lyman, D. R. (1996). Early identification of chronic offenders: Who is the fledgling psychopath? *Psychological Bulletin, 120,* 209–234.

Lynch, G., & Staubli, U. (1991). Possible contributions of long-term potentiation to the encoding and organization of memory. *Brain Research Reviews, 16,* 204–206.

Lynch, J. W., Kaplan, G. A., Pamuk, E. R., Cohen, R. D., Heck, K. E., Balfour, J. L., & Yen, I. H. (1998). Income inequality and mortality in metropolitan areas of the United States. *American Journal of Public Health, 88,* 1074–1080.

Lynch, J. W., Smith, G. D., Kaplan, G. A., & House, J. S. (2000). Income inequality and health: A neo-material interpretation. *British Medical Journal,* in press.

Lyness, S. A. (1993). Predictors of differences between Type A and B individuals in heart rate and blood pressure reactivity. *Psychological Bulletin, 114,* 266–295.

Lynn, M. (1988). The effects of alcohol consumption on restaurant tipping. *Personality and Social Psychology Bulletin, 14,* 87–91.

Lynn, R. (1987). Japan: Land of the rising IQ. A reply to Flynn. *Bulletin of the British Psychological Society, 40,* 464–468.

Lynn, R. (1991, Fall/Winter). The evolution of racial differences in intelligence. *The Mankind Quarterly, 32,* 99–145.

Lynn, R. (1997). *Dysgenics.* London: Praeger Publishers.

Lynn, S. J., & Rhue, J. W. (1986). The fantasy-prone person: Hypnosis, imagination, and creativity. *Journal of Personality and Social Psychology, 51,* 404–408.

Lynn, S. J., Rhue, J. W., & Weekes, J. R. (1990). Hypnotic involuntariness: A social cognitive analysis. *Psychological Review, 97,* 169–184.

Lyon, D., & Greenberg, J. (1991). Evidence of codependency in women with an alcoholic parent: Helping out Mr. Wrong. *Journal of Personality and Social Psychology, 61,* 435–439.

Lyons, M. J., True, W. R., Eisen, S. A., Goldberg, J., Meyer, J. M., Faraone, S. V., Eaves, L. J., & Tsuang, M. T. (1995). Differential heritability of adult and juvenile antisocial traits. *Archives of General Psychiatry, 52,* 906–915.

Lytton, H., & Romney, D. M. (1991). Parents' differential socialization of boys and girls: A meta-analysis. *Psychological Bulletin, 109,* 267–296.

Lyubomirsky, S., & Nolen-Hoeksema, S. (1994). The effects of depressive rumination on thinking and problem solving. Unpublished manuscript, Stanford University.

Ma, L. (1997, September). On the origin of Darwin's ills. *Discover,* p. 27.

Maas, J. B. (1999). *Power sleep. The revolutionary program that prepares your mind for peak performance.* New York: HarperCollins.

Macaskill, P., Pierce, J. P., Simpson, J. M., & Lyle, D. M. (1992). Mass media-led antismoking campaign can remove the education gap in quitting behavior. *American Journal of Public Health, 82,* 96–98.

Maccoby, E. (1980). *Social development: Psychological growth and the parent-child relationship.* New York: Harcourt Brace Jovanovich.

Maccoby, E. E. (1990). Gender and relationships: A developmental account. *American Psychologist, 45,* 513–520.

Maccoby, E. E. (1995). Divorce and custody: The rights, needs, and obligations of mothers, fathers, and children. *Nebraska Symposium on Motivation, 42,* 135–172.

Maccoby, E. E. (1998). *The paradox of gender.* Cambridge, MA: Harvard University Press.

MacDonald, N. (1960). Living with schizophrenia. *Canadian Medical Association Journal, 82,* 218–221.

MacDonald, T. K., Zanna, M. P., & Fong, G. T. (1995). Decision making in altered states: Effects of alcohol on attitudes toward drinking and driving. *Journal of Personality and Social Psychology, 68,* 973–985.

MacDonald, T. K., Zanna, M. P., & Fong, G. T. (1996). Why common sense goes out the window: The effects of alcohol on intentions to use condoms. *Personality and Social Psychology Bulletin, 22,* 763–775.

MacDonald, T. K., Zanna, M. P., & Fong, G. T. (1998). Alcohol and intentions to engage in risky health-related behaviors: Experimental evidence for a causal relationship. In J. Adair & F. Craik (Eds.), *Advances in psychological science: Vol. 2. Developmental, personal, and social aspects.* East Sussex, UK: Psychology Press.

MacFarlane, A. (1978, February). What a baby knows. *Human Nature,* pp. 74–81.

Macfarlane, J. W. (1964). Perspectives on personality consistency and change from the guidance study. *Vita Humana, 7,* 115–126.

MacKay, D. G. (1983). Prescriptive grammar and the pronoun problem. In B. Thorne, C. Kramarae, & N. Henley (Eds.), *Language, gender and society.* Rowley, MA: Newbury House.

MacKinnon, D. W., & Hall, W. B. (1972). Intelligence and creativity. In *Proceedings, XVIIth International Congress of Applied Psychology* (Vol. 2). Brussels: Editest.

MacLeod, C., & Campbell, L. (1992). Memory accessibility and probability judgments: An experimental evaluation of the availability heuristic. *Journal of Personality and Social Psychology, 63,* 890–902.

Maehr, M. L., & Braskamp, L. A. (1986). *The motivation factor: A theory of personal investment.* Lexington, MA: Lexington Books.

Maes, H. H. M., Neale, M. C., & Eaves, L. J. (1997). Genetic and environmental factors in relative body weight and human adiposity. *Behavior Genetics, 27,* 325–351.

Maes, M. C. A., Delanghe, J., Altamura, C., Neels, H., & Meltzer, H. Y. (1999). Lowered omega3 polyunsaturated fatty acids in serum phospholipids and cholesteryl esters of depressed patients. *Psychiatry Residency, 85,* 275–291.

Maestripieri, D., & Carroll, K. A. (1998). Child abuse and neglect: Usefulness of the animal data. *Psychological Bulletin, 123,* 211–223.

Magnusson, D. (1990). Personality research—Challenges for the future. *European Journal of Personality, 4,* 1–17.

Mahowald, M. W., & Ettinger, M. G. (1990). Things that go bump in the night: The parsomias revisted. *Journal of Clinical Neurophysiology, 7,* 119–143.

Maier, S. F., Watkins, L. R., & Fleshner, M. (1994). Psychoneuroimmunology: The interface between behavior, brain, and immunity. *American Psychologist, 49,* 1004–1017.

Major, B., Carrington, P. I., & Carnevale, P. J. D. (1984). Physical attractiveness and self-esteem: Attribution for praise from an other-sex evaluator. *Personality and Social Psychology Bulletin, 10,* 43–50.

Major, B., Cozzarelli, C., Sciacchitano, A. M., Cooper, M. L., Testa, M., & Mueller, P. M. (1990). Perceived social support, self-efficacy, and adjustment to abortion. *Journal of Personality and Social Psychology, 58,* 634–643.

Malamuth, N. M. (1996). Sexually explicit media, gender differences, and evolutionary theory. *Journal of Communication, 46,* 8–31.

Malamuth, N. M., & Check, J. V. P. (1981). The effects of media exposure on acceptance of violence against women: A field experiment. *Journal of Research in Personality, 15,* 436–446.

Malamuth, N. M., Linz, D., Heavey, C. L., Barnes, G., & Acker, M. (1995). Using the confluence model of sexual aggression to predict men's conflict with women: A 10-year follow-up study. *Journal of Personality and Social Psychology, 69,* 353–369.

Malamuth, N. M., Sockloskie, R. J., Koss, M. P., & Tanaka, J. S. (1991). Characteristics of aggressors against women: Testing a model using a national sample of college students. *Journal of Consulting and Clinical Psychology, 59,* 670–681.

Malan, D. H. (1978). "The case of the secretary with the violent father." In H. Davanloo (Ed.), *Basic principles and techniques in short-term dynamic psychotherapy.* New York: Spectrum.

Malinosky-Rummell, R., & Hansen, D. J. (1993). Long-term consequences of childhood physical abuse. *Psychological Bulletin, 114,* 68–79.

Malkiel, B. (1985). *A random walk down Wall Street* (4th ed.). New York: Norton.

Malkiel, B. G. (1989). Is the stock market efficient? *Science, 243,* 1313–1318.

Malkiel, B. G. (1995, June). Returns from investing in equity mutual funds 1971 to 1991. *Journal of Finance,* pp. 549–572.

Malmquist, C. P. (1986). Children who witness parental murder: Post-traumatic aspects. *Journal of the American Academy of Child Psychiatry, 25,* 320–325.

Malnic, B., Hirono, J., Sato, T., & Buck, L. B. (1999). Combinatorial receptor codes for odors. *Cell, 96,* 713–723.

Malone, T. W., & Lepper, M. R. (1986). Making learning fun: A taxonomy of intrinsic motivations for learning. In R. E. Snow & M. J. Farr (Eds.), *Aptitude, learning, and instruction: III. Cognitive and affective process analysis.* Hillsdale, NJ: Erlbaum.

Manber, R., Bootzin, R. R., Acebo, C., & Carskadon, M. A. (1996). The effects of regularizing sleep-wake schedules on daytime sleepiness. *Sleep, 19,* 432–441.

Mandel, D. (1983, March 13). One man's Holocaust: Part II. The story of David Mandel's journey through hell as told to David Kagan. *Wonderland Magazine (Grand Rapids Press),* pp. 2–7.

Mandler, J. M., & McDonough, L. (1995). Long-term recall of event sequences in infancy. *Journal of Experimental Child Psychology, 59,* 457–474.

Manning, W. G., Keefer, E. B., Newhouse, J. P., Sloss, E. M., & Wasserman, J. (1989). The taxes of sin: Do smokers and drinkers pay their way? *Journal of the American Medical Association, 261,* 1604–1609.

Mansnerus, L. (1992, October 4). Smoking: Is it a habit or is it genetic? *New York Times Magazine,* Part 2.

Maquet, P., Peters, J.-M., Aerts, J., Delfiore, G., Degueldre, C., Luxen, A., & Franck, G. (1996). Functional neuroanatomy of human rapid-eye-movement sleep and dreaming. *Nature, 383,* 163–166.

Marano, H. E. (1998, August 4). Debunking the marriage myth: It works for women, too. *New York Times* (www.nytimes.com).

Marcel, A. (1983). Conscious and unconscious perception: Experiments on visual masking and word recognition. *Cognitive Psychology, 15,* 197–237.

Marcus, G. F., Vijayan, S., Rao, S. B., & Vishton, P. M. (1999). Rule learning by seven-month-old infants. *Science, 283,* 77–80.

Marino, L. A., Reiss, D., & Gallup, G. G., Jr. (1994). Mirror self-recognition in bottlenose dolphins: Implications for comparative investigations of highly dissimilar species. In S. P. Parker, R.

Mitchell, & M. Boccia (Eds.), *Self-awareness in animals and humans: Developmental perspectives*. New York: Cambridge University Press.

Mark, V., & Ervin, F. (1970). *Violence and the brain*. New York: Harper & Row.

Markowitsch, H. J. (1995). Which brain regions are critically involved in the retrieval of old episodic memory? *Brain Research Reviews, 21*, 117–127.

Markowitz, J. C., Svartberg, M., & Swartz, H. A. (1998). Is IPT time-limited psychodynamic psychotherapy? *Journal of Psychotherapy Practice and Research, 7*, 185–195.

Markus, G. B. (1986). Stability and change in political attitudes: Observe, recall, and "explain." *Political Behavior, 8*, 21–44.

Markus, H., & Kitayama, S. (1991). Culture and the self: Implications for cognition, emotion, and motivation. *Psychological Review, 98*, 224–253.

Markus, H., & Nurius, P. (1986). Possible selves. *American Psychologist, 41*, 954–969.

Marlatt, G. A. (1991). Substance abuse: Etiology, prevention, and treatment issues. Master Lecture, American Psychological Association convention.

Marmot, M. G., Bosma, H., Hemingway, H., Brunner, E., & Stansfeld, S. (1997). Contribution of job control and other risk factors to social variations in coronary heart disease incidents. *Lancet, 350*, 235–239.

Marmot, M. G., & Wilkinson, R. G. (Eds.). (1999). *Social determinants of health*. Oxford: Oxford University Press.

Marr, D. (1982). *Vision*. San Francisco: W. H. Freeman.

Marschark, M., Richman, C. L., Yuille, J. C., & Hunt, R. R. (1987). The role of imagery in memory: On shared and distinctive information. *Psychological Bulletin, 102*, 28–41.

Marsh, H. W., & Parker, J. W. (1984). Determinants of student self-concept: Is it better to be a relatively large fish in a small pond even if you don't learn to swim as well? *Journal of Personality and Social Psychology, 47*, 213–231.

Marshall, J. C., & Halligan, P. W. (1988). Blindsight and insight in visuo-spatial neglect. *Nature, 336*, 766–767.

Marshall, W. L. (1989). Pornography and sex offenders. In D. Zillmann & J. Bryant (Eds.), *Pornography: Research advances and policy considerations*. Hillsdale, NJ: Erlbaum.

Marteau, T. M. (1989). Framing of information: Its influences upon decisions of doctors and patients. *British Journal of Social Psychology, 28*, 89–94.

Martin, A., Wiggs, C. L., Ungerleider, L. G., & Haxby, J. V. (1996). Neural correlates of category-specific knowledge. *Nature, 379*, 649–652.

Martin, R. J., White, B. D., & Hulsey, M. G. (1991). The regulation of body weight. *American Scientist, 79*, 528–541.

Martinez, J. L., Jr., Schulteis, G., & Weinberger, S. B. (1991). How to increase and decrease the strength of memory traces. In J. L. Martinez, Jr. & R. P. Kesner (Eds.), *Learning and memory* (2nd ed.) San Diego: Academic Press.

Martyna, W. (1978). What does "he" mean? Use of generic masculine. *Journal of Communication, 28*(1), 131–138.

Marx, J. (1998). New gene tied to common form of Alzheimer's. *Science, 281*, 507–509.

Maslach, C. (1982). *Burnout: The cost of caring*. Englewood Cliffs, NJ: Prentice-Hall.

Maslow, A. H. (1970). *Motivation and personality* (2nd ed.). New York: Harper & Row.

Maslow, A. H. (1971). *The farther reaches of human nature*. New York: Viking Press.

Masse, L. C., & Tremblay, R. E. (1997). Behavior of boys in kindergarten and the onset of substance use during adolescence. *Archives of General Psychiatry, 54*, 62–68.

Masters, M. S., & Sanders, B. (1993). Is the gender difference in mental rotation disappearing? *Behavior Genetics, 23*, 337–341.

Masters, W. H., & Johnson, V. E. (1966). *Human sexual response*. Boston: Little, Brown.

Matarazzo, J. D. (1983). Computerized psychological testing. *Science, 221*, 323.

Matsumoto, D. (1994). *People: Psychology from a cultural perspective*. Pacific Grove, CA: Brooks/Cole.

Matsumoto, D., & Ekman, P. (1989). American-Japanese cultural differences in intensity ratings of facial expressions of emotion. *Motivation and Emotion, 13*, 143–157.

Matsumoto, D., Kudoh, T., Scherer, K., & Wallbott, H. (1988). Antecedents of and reactions to emotions in the United States and Japan. *Journal of Cross-Cultural Psychology, 19*, 267–286.

Matt, G. E., Vazquez, C., & Campbell, W. K. (1992). Mood-congruent recall of affectively toned stimuli: A meta-analytic review. *Clinical Psychology Review, 12*, 227–255.

Matthews, D. A., & Larson, D. B. (1997). *The faith factor: An annotated bibliography of clinical research on spiritual subjects* Vol. I–IV. Rockville, MD: National Institute for Healthcare Research and Georgetown University Press.

Matthews, K. A. (1992). Myths and realities of the menopause. *Psychosomatic Medicine, 54*, 1–9.

Mauer, D., Lewis, T. L., Brent, H. P., & Levin, A. V. (1999). Rapid improvement in the acuity of infants after visual input. *Science, 286*, 108–110.

Maunsell, J. H. (1995). The brain's visual world: Representation of visual targets in cerebral cortex. *Science, 270*, 764–769.

Maurer, D., & Maurer, C. (1988). *The world of the newborn*. New York: Basic Books.

May, C. P., Hasher, L., & Stoltzfus, E. R. (1993). Optimal time of day and the magnitude of age differences in memory. *Psychological Science, 4*, 326–330.

May, C., Yoon, C., & Hasker, L. (1999). Aging, circadian arousal patterns, and cognition. In N. Schwartz, D. C. Park, and others (Eds.), *Cognition, aging, and self-reports*. Hove, UK: Psychology Press/Erlbaum (UK) and Taylor & Frances.

May, R. (1982). The problem of evil: An open letter to Carl Rogers. *Journal of Humanistic Psychology, 22*, 10–21.

Mayer, J. D., & Salovey, P. (1993). The intelligence of emotional intelligence. *Intelligence, 17*, 433–442.

Mayne, T. J., Norcross, J. C., & Sayette, M. A. (1994). Admission requirements, acceptance rates, and financial assistance in clinical psychology programs. *American Psychologist, 49*, 806–811.

Mazur, A., & Booth, A. (1998). Testosterone and dominance in men. *Behavioral and Brain Sciences, 21*, 353–363.

McAlister, A., Perry, C., Killen, J., Slinkard, L. A., & Maccoby, N. (1980). Pilot study of smoking, alcohol and drug abuse prevention. *American Journal of Public Health, 70*, 719–721.

McAneny, L. (1996, September). Large majority think government conceals information about UFO's. *Gallup Poll Monthly*, pp. 23–26.

McBeath, M. K., Shaffer, D. M., & Kaiser, M. K. (1995). How baseball outfielders determine where to run to catch fly balls. *Science, 268*, 569–572.

McBurney, D. H. (1996). *How to think like a psychologist: Critical thinking in psychology*. Upper Saddle River, NJ: Prentice-Hall.

McBurney, D. H., & Collings, V. B. (1984). *Introduction to sensation and perception* (2nd ed.). Englewood Cliffs, NJ: Prentice-Hall.

McBurney, D. H., & Gent, J. F. (1979). On the nature of taste qualities. *Psychological Bulletin, 86*, 151–167.

McCall, R. B. (1994). Academic underachievers. *Current Directions in Psychological Science, 3*, 15–19.

McCall, R. B., & Carriger, M. S. (1993). A meta-analysis of infant habituation and recognition memory performance as predictors of later IQ. *Child Development, 64*, 57–79.

McCall, R. B., Evahn, C., & Kratzer, L. (1992). *High school underachievers*. Newbury Park, CA: Sage.

McCann, I. L., & Holmes, D. S. (1984). Influence of aerobic exercise on depression. *Journal of Personality and Social Psychology, 46*, 1142–1147.

McCarron, D. A., Morris, C. D., Henry, H. J., & Stanton, J. L. (1984). Blood pressure and nutrient intake in the United States. *Science, 225*, 1392–1398.

McCarthy, P. (1986, July). Scent: The tie that binds? *Psychology Today*, pp. 6, 10.

McCarty, D., Argeriou, M., Huebner, R. B., & Lubran, B. (1991). Alcoholism, drug abuse, and the homeless. *American Psychologist, 46*, 1139–1148.

McCaul, K. D., & Malott, J. M. (1984). Distraction and coping with pain. *Psychological Bulletin, 95*, 516–533.

McCauley, C. R., & Segal, M. E. (1987). Social psychology of terrorist groups. In C. Hendrick (Ed.), *Group processes and intergroup relations*. Beverly Hills, CA: Sage.

McClearn, G. E., Johansson, B., Berg, S., Pedersen, N. L., Ahern, F., Petrill, S. A., & Plomin, R. (1997). Substantial genetic influence on cognitive abilities in twins 80 or more years old. *Science, 276*, 1560–1563.

McClintock, M. K., & Herdt, G. (December, 1996). Rethinking puberty: The development of sexual attraction. *Current Directions in Psychological Science, 5*(6), 178–183.

McCloskey, M., Wible, C. G., & Cohen, N. J. (1988). Is there a special flashbulb-memory mechanism? *Journal of Experimental Psychology: General, 117*, 171–181.

McConkey, K. M. (1992). The effects of hypnotic procedures on remembering: The experimental findings and their implications for forensic hypnosis. In E. Fromm & M. R. Nash (Eds.), *Contemporary hypnosis research*. New York: Guilford Press.

McConkey, K. M. (1995). Hypnosis, memory, and the ethics of uncertainty. *Australian Psychologist, 30*, 1–10.

McConnell, A., & Fazio, R. H. (1996). Women as men and people: Effects of gender-marked language. *Personality and Social Psychology Bulletin, 22*, 1004–1013.

McConnell, R. A. (1991). National Academy of Sciences opinion on parapsychology. *Journal of the American Society for Psychical Research, 85*, 333–365.

McCool, G. (1999, October 26). Mirror-gazing Venezuelans top of vanity stakes. *Toronto Star* (web.lexis-nexis.com).

McCord, J. (1978). A thirty-year follow-up on treatment effects. *American Psychologist, 33*, 284–289.

McCord, J. (1979). Following up on Cambridge-Somerville. *American Psychologist, 34*, 727.

McCormick, C. M., & Witelson, S. F. (1991). A cognitive profile of homosexual men compared to heterosexual men and women. *Psychoneuroendocrinology, 16*, 459–473.

McCrae, R. R., & Costa, P. T., Jr. (1986). Clinical assessment can benefit from recent advances in personality psychology. *American Psychologist, 41*, 1001–1003.

McCrae, R. R., & Costa, P. T., Jr. (1990). *Personality in adulthood*. New York: Guilford.

McCrae, R. R., & Costa, P. T., Jr. (1994). The stability of personality: Observations and evaluations. *Current Directions in Psychological Science, 3*, 173–175.

McCrae, R. R., Costa, P. T., Jr., de Lirna, M. P., Simoes, A., Ostendorf, F., Angleitner, A., Marusic, I., Bratko, D., Caprara, G. V., Barbaranelli, C., Chae, J-H., & Piedmont, R. L. (1999). Age differences in personality across the adult life span: Parallels in five cultures. *Developmental Psychology, 35*, 466–477.

McCrae, R. R., Costa, P. T., Jr., del Pilar, G. H., Rolland, J. P., & Parker, W. D. (1998). Cross-cultural assessment of the five-factor Model: The revised NEO personality inventory. *Journal of Cross-Cultural Psychology, 29*, 171–188.

McCullough, M. E., Hoyt, W. T., Larson, D. B., Koenig, H. G., & Thoresen, C. (2000). Religious involvement and mortality: A meta-analytic review. *Health Psychology*, in press.

McDonald, J. (1997, August 24). Butt out: China split over popular, hazardous habit: smoking. Associated Press (in *Grand Rapids Press*, p. A21).

McEwen, B. S. (1998). Protective and damaging effects of stress mediators. *Seminars in Medicine of the Beth Israel Deaconess Medical Center, 338*, 171–179.

McFadden, D., & Pasanen, E. G. (1998). Comparison of the auditory systems of heterosexuals and homosexuals: Click-evoked otoacoustic emissions. *Proceedings of the National Academcy of Sciences, 95*, 2709–2913.

McFadden, D., & Pasanen, E. G. (1999). Spontaneous otoacoustic emissions in heterosexuals, homosexuals, and bisexuals. *Journal of the Acoustical Society of America, 105*, 2403–2413.

McFarland, C., & Ross, M. (1987). The relation between current impressions and memories of self and dating partners. *Psychological Bulletin, 13*, 228–238.

McFarland, C., Ross, M., & DeVourville, N. (1989). Women's theories of menstruation and biases in recall of menstrual symptoms. *Journal of Personality and Social Psychology, 57*, 522–531.

McGarry-Roberts, P. A., Stelmack, R. M., & Campbell, K. B. (1992). Intelligence, reaction time, and event-related potentials. *Intelligence, 16*, 289–313.

McGaugh, J. L. (1994). Quoted in B. Bower, Stress hormones hike emotional memories. *Science News, 146*, p. 262.

McGhee, P. E. (June, 1976). Children's appreciation of humor: A test of the cognitive congruency principle. *Child Development, 47(2)*, 420–426.

McGrath, J. J., & Welham, J. L. (1999). Season of birth and schizophrenia: A systematic review and meta-analysis of data from the Southern hemisphere. *Schizophrenia Research, 35*, 237–242.

McGrath, J., Welham, J., & Pemberton, M. (1995). Month of birth, hemisphere of birth and schizophrenia. *British Journal of Psychiatry, 167*, 783–785.

McGrath, M. J., & Cohen, D. G. (1978). REM sleep facilitation of adaptive waking behavior: A review of the literature. *Psychological Bulletin, 85*, 24–57.

McGregor, D. (1960). *The human side of enterprise*. New York: McGraw-Hill.

McGue, M. (1999). The behavioral genetics of alcoholism. *Current Directions in Psychological Science, 8*, 111–115.

McGue, M., & Bouchard, T. J., Jr. (1998). Genetic and environmental influences on human behavioral differences. *Annual Review of Neuroscience, 21*, 1–24.

McGue, M., Bouchard, T. J., Jr., Iacono, W. G., & Lykken, D. T. (1993). Behavioral genetics of cognitive ability: A life-span perspective. In R. Plomin & G. E. McClearn (Eds.), *Nature, nurture and psychology*. Washington, DC: American Psychological Association.

McGue, M., & Lykken, D. T. (1992). Genetic influence on risk of divorce. *Psychological Science, 3*, 368–373.

McGuire, M. T., Wing, R. R., Klem, M. L., Lang, W., & Hill, J. O. (1999). What predicts weight regain in a group of successful weight losers? *Journal of Consulting and Clinical Psychology, 67*, 177–185.

McGuire, W. J. (1986). The myth of massive media impact: Savings and salvagings. In G. Comstock (Ed.), *Public communication and behavior*. Orlando, FL: Academic Press.

McHugh, P. R. (1995a). Witches, multiple personalities, and other psychiatric artifacts. *Nature Medicine, 1(2)*, 110–114.

McHugh, P. R. (1995b). Resolved: Multiple personality disorder is an individually and socially created artifact. *Journal of the American Academy of Child and Adolescent Psychiatry, 34*, 957–959.

McHugh, P. R., & Moran, T. H. (1978). Accuracy of the regulation of caloric ingestion in the rhesus monkey. *American Journal of Physiology, 235*, R29–R34.

Mckelvie, S. (1999, November 4). Personal communication, based on Bishop's University accident and report in *The Record*, Sherbrooke, Ontario, October 25, 1999.

McKenna, K. Y. A., & Bargh, J. A. (1998). Coming out in the age of the Internet: Identity "demarginalization" through virtual group participation. *Journal of Personality and Social Psychology, 75*, 681–694.

McKenna, M. C., Zevon, M. A., Corn, B., & Rounds, J. (1999). Psychosocial factors and the development of breast cancer: A meta-analysis. *Health Psychology, 18*, 520–531.

McKinlay, J. B., McKinlay, S. M., & Brambilla, D. J. (1987a). Health status and utilization behavior associated with menopause. *American Journal of Epidemiology, 125*, 110–121.

McKinlay, J. B., McKinlay, S. M., & Brambilla, D. (1987b). The relative contributions of endocrine changes and social circumstances to depression in mid-aged women. *Journal of Health and Social Behavior, 28*, 345–363.

McLaughlin, C. S., Chen, C., Greenberger, E., & Biermeier, C. (1997). Family, peer, and individual correlates of sexual experience among Caucasian and Asian American late adolescents. *Journal of Research on Adolescence, 7*, 33–53.

McMillen, D. L., Smith, S. M., & Wells-Parker, E. (1989). The effects of alcohol, expectancy, and sensation seeking on driving risk taking. *Addictive Behaviors, 14*, 477–483.

McNally, R. J. (1987). Preparedness and phobias: A review. *Psychological Bulletin, 101*, 283–303.

McNally, R. J. (1999). EMDR and Mesmerism: A comparative historical analysis. *Journal of Anxiety Disorders, 13*, 225–236.

McVeigh, C. (1999, October 1). Medical schools offering spirituality and medicine courses. Table and personal correspondence from National Institute for Healthcare Research (www.nihr.org).

Meador, B. D., & Rogers, C. R. (1984). Person-centered therapy. In R. J. Corsini (Ed.), *Current psychotherapies* (3rd ed.). Itasca, IL: Peacock.

Meaney, M. J., Aitken, D. H., Van Berkel, C., Bhatnagar, S., & Sapolsky, R. M. (1988). Effect of neonatal handling on age-related impairments associated with the hippocampus. *Science, 239*, 766–768.

Mediascope. (1995). *National television violence study: Executive Summary, 1994–1995*. Studio City, CA: Mediascope, Inc.

Medical Institute for Sexual Health. (1994, April). Condoms ineffective against human papilloma virus. *Sexual Health Update, 2*.

Mednick, S. A., Huttunen, M. O., & Machon, R. A. (1994). Prenatal influenza infections and adult schizophrenia. *Schizophrenia Bulletin, 20*, 263–267.

Meichenbaum, D. (1977). *Cognitive-behavior modification: An integrative approach*. New York: Plenum Press.

Meichenbaum, D. (1985). *Stress inoculation training*. New York: Pergamon.

Meier, R. P. (1991). Language acquisition by deaf children. *American Scientist, 79*, 60–70.

Meltzoff, A. N. (1988). Infant imitation after a 1-week delay: Long-term memory for novel acts and multiple stimuli. *Developmental Psychology, 24*, 470–476.

Meltzoff, A. N., & Borton, R. W. (1979). Intermodal matching by human neonates. *Nature, 282*, 403–404.

Meltzoff, A. N., & Moore, M. K. (1989). Imitation in newborn infants: Exploring the range of gestures imitated and the underlying mechanisms. *Developmental Psychology, 25*, 954–962.

Meltzoff, A. N., & Moore, M. K. (1997). Explaining facial imitation: A theoretical model. *Early Development and Parenting, 6*, 179–192.

Melzack, R. (1984). The myth of painless childbirth. *Pain, 19*, 321–337.

Melzack, R. (1990, February). The tragedy of needless pain. *Scientific American*, pp. 27–33.

Melzack, R. (1992, April). Phantom limbs. *Scientific American*, pp. 120–126.

Melzack, R. (1993). Distinguished contribution series. *Canadian Journal of Experimental Psychology, 47*, 615–629.

Melzack, R. (1998, February). Quoted in Phantom limbs. *Discover*, p. 20.

Melzack, R. (1999). Pain and stress: A new perspective. In R. J. Gatchel & D. C. Turk (Eds.), *Psychosocial factors in pain: Critical perspectives*. New York: Guilford Press.

Mendolia, M., & Kleck, R. E. (1993). Effects of talking about a stressful event on arousal: Does what we talk about make a difference? *Journal of Personality and Social Psychology, 64,* 283–292.

Menon, T., Morris, M. W., Chiu, C-Y., & Hong, Y-Y. (1999). Culture and the construal of agency: Attribution to individual versus group dispositions. *Journal of Personality and Social Psychology, 76,* 701–717.

Mento, A. J., Steel, R. P., & Karren, R. J. (1987). A meta-analytic study of the effects of goal setting on task performance: 1966-1984. *Organizational Behavior and Human Decision Processes, 39,* 52–83.

Merikle, P. M., & Daneman, M. (1996). Memory for unconsciously perceived events: Evidence from anesthetized patients. *Consciousness and Cognition, 5,* 525–541.

Merriman, J. (1999, May 13). These pounds aren't sterling. Reuters (www.abcnews.go.com).

Merskey, H. (1992). The manufacture of personalities: The production of multiple personality disorder. *British Journal of Psychiatry, 160,* 327–340.

Merton, R. K. (1938; reprinted 1970). *Science, technology and society in seventeenth-century England.* New York: Fertig.

Merton, R. K., & Kitt, A. S. (1950). Contributions to the theory of reference group behavior. In R. K. Merton & P. F. Lazarsfeld (Eds.), *Continuities in social research: Studies in the scope and method of the American soldier.* Glencoe, IL: Free Press.

Mesquita, B., & Frijda, N. H. (1992). Cultural variations in emotions: A review. *Psychological Bulletin, 112,* 179–204.

Messer, W. S., & Griggs, R. A. (1989). Student belief and involvement in the paranormal and performance in introductory psychology. *Teaching of Psychology, 16,* 187–191.

Mestel, R. (1997, April 26). Get real, Siggi. *New Scientist* (www.newscientist.com/ns/970426/siggi.html)

Meston, C. M., Trapnell, P. D., & Gorzalka, B. B. (1996). Ethnic and gender differences in sexuality: Variations in sexual behavior between Asian and non-Asian university students. *Archives of Sexual Behavior, 25,* 33–72.

Metalsky, G. I., Joiner, T. E., Jr., Hardin, T. S., & Abramson, L. Y. (1993). Depressive reactions to failure in a naturalistic setting: A test of the hopelessness and self-esteem theories of depression. *Journal of Abnormal Psychology, 102,* 101–109.

Metcalfe, J. (1998). Cognitive optimism: Self-deception or memory-based processing heuristics. *Personality and Social Psychology Review, 2,* 100–110.

Metcalfe, J., Funnell, M., & Gazzaniga, M. S. (1995). Right-hemisphere memory superiority: Studies of a split-brain patient. *Psychological Science, 6,* 157–164.

Meuwissen, I., & Over, R. (1992). Sexual arousal across phases of the human menstrual cycle. *Archives of Sexual Behavior, 21,* 101–119.

Meyer-Bahlburg, H. F. L. (1995). Psychoneuroendocrinology and sexual pleasure: The aspect of sexual orientation. In P. R. Abramson & S. D. Pinkerton (Eds.), *Sexual nature/sexual culture.* Chicago: University of Chicago Press.

Michaels, J. W., Bloomel, J. M., Brocato, R. M., Linkous, R. A., & Rowe, J. S. (1982). Social facilitation and inhibition in a natural setting. *Replications in Social Psychology, 2,* 21–24.

Michel, G. F. (1981). Right-handedness: A consequence of infant supine head-orientation preference? *Science, 212,* 685–687.

Middlebrooks, J. C., & Green, D. M. (1991). Sound localization by human listeners. *Annual Review of Psychology, 42,* 135–159.

Mikulincer, M., Babkoff, H., Caspy, T., & Sing, H. (1989). The effects of 72 hours of sleep loss on psychological variables. *British Journal of Psychology, 80,* 145–162.

Milan, R. J., Jr., & Kilmann, P. R. (1987). Interpersonal factors in premarital contraception. *Journal of Sex Research, 23,* 289–321.

Miles, D. R., & Carey, G. (1997). Genetic and environmental architecture of human aggression. *Journal of Personality and Social Psychology, 72,* 207–217.

Milgram, S. (1963). Behavioral study of obedience. *Journal of Abnormal & Social Psychology, 67*(4), 371–378.

Milgram, S. (1974). *Obedience to authority.* New York: Harper & Row.

Miller, C. T., & Downey, K. T. (1999). A meta-analysis of heavyweight and self-esteem. *Personality and Social Psychology Review, 3,* 68–84.

Miller, G. A. (1956). The magical number seven, plus or minus two: Some limits on our capacity for processing information. *Psychological Review, 63,* 81–97.

Miller, G. A. (1962). *Psychology: The science of mental life.* New York: Harper & Row.

Miller, G. A., & Gildea, P. M. (1987, September). How children learn words. *Scientific American,* pp. 94–99.

Miller, J. D., & Pifer, L. (1996). *Science and engineering indicators.* Washington, DC: National Science Foundation.

Miller, K. I., & Monge, P. R. (1986). Participation, satisfaction, and productivity: A meta-analytic review. *Academy of Management Journal, 29,* 727–753.

Miller, L. K. (1999). The savant syndrome: Intellectual impairment and exceptional skill. *Psychological Bulletin, 125,* 31–46.

Miller, N. E. (1985, February). Rx: Biofeedback. *Psychology Today,* pp. 54–59.

Miller, N. E. (1995). Clinical-experimental interactions in the development of neuroscience: A primer for nonspecialists and lessons for young scientists. *American Psychologist, 50,* 901–911.

Miller, N. E., & Brucker, B. S. (1979). A learned visceral response apparently independent of skeletal ones in patients paralyzed by spinal lesions. In N. Birbaumer & H. D. Kimmel (Eds.), *Biofeedback and self-regulation.* Hillsdale, NJ: Erlbaum.

Miller, P. A., Eisenberg, N., Fabes, R. A., & Shell, R. (1996). Relations of moral reasoning and vicarious emotion to young children's prosocial behavior toward peers and adults. *Developmental Psychology, 32,* 210–219.

Miller, P. C., Lefcourt, H. M., Holmes, J. G., Ware, E. E., & Saleh, W. E. (1986). Marital locus of control and marital problem solving. *Journal of Personality and Social Psychology, 51,* 161–169.

Miller, S. D., Blackburn, T., Scholes, G., White, G. L., & Mamalis, N. (1991). Optical differences in multiple personality disorder: A second look. *Journal of Nervous and Mental Disease, 179,* 132–135.

Miller, T. Q., Smith, T. W., Turner, C. W., Guijarro, M. L., & Hallet, A. J. (1996). A meta-analytic review of research on hostility and physical health. *Psychological Bulletin, 119,* 322–348.

Miller, W. C. (1999). Fitness and fatness in relation to health: Implications for a paradigm shift. *Journal of Social Issues, 55,* 207–220.

Millers, J. G., & Bersoff, D. M. (1995). Development in the context of everyday family relationships: Culture, interpersonal morality and adaptation. In M. Killen & D. Hart (Eds.), *Morality in everyday life: A developmental perspective.* New York: Cambridge University Press.

Mills, M., & Melhuish, E. (1974). Recognition of mother's voice in early infancy. *Nature, 252,* 123–124.

Milner, A. D. (1995). Cerebral correlates of visual awareness. *Neuropsychologia, 33,* 1117–1130.

Milton, J. (1999). Should ganzfeld research continue to be crucial in the search for a replicable psi effect? Part I. Discussion paper and introduction to an electronic-mail discussion. *Journal of Parapsychology, 63,* 309–334.

Milton, J., & Wiseman, R. (1999). Does psi exist? Lack of replication of an anomalous process of information transfer. *Psychological Bulletin, 125,* 387–391.

Mineka, S. (1985). The frightful complexity of the origins of fears. In F. R. Brush & J. B. Overmier (Eds.), *Affect, conditioning and cognition: Essays on the determinants of behavior.* Hillsdale, NJ: Erlbaum.

Mineka, S., & Suomi, S. J. (1978). Social separation in monkeys. *Psychological Bulletin, 85,* 1376–1400.

Mineka, S., & Sutton, S. K. (1992). Cognitive biases and the emotional disorders. *Psychological Science, 3,* 65–69.

Mineka, S., & Zinbarg, R. (1996). Conditioning and ethological models of anxiety disorders: Stress-in-dynamic-context anxiety models. In D. Hope (Ed.), *Perspectives on anxiety, panic, and fear. Nebraska symposium on motivation.* Lincoln: University of Nebraska Press.

Mintz, L. B., & Betz, N. E. (1986). Sex differences in the nature, realism, and correlates of body image. *Sex Roles, 15,* 185–195.

Mirin, S. M., & Weiss, R. D. (1989). Genetic factors in the development of alcoholism. *Psychiatric Annals, 19,* 239–242.

Mischel, W. (1968). *Personality and assessment.* New York: Wiley.

Mischel, W. (1981). Current issues and challenges in personality. In L. T. Benjamin, Jr. (Ed.), *The G. Stanley Hall Lecture Series* (Vol. 1). Washington, DC: American Psychological Association.

Mischel, W. (1984). Convergences and challenges in the search for consistency. *American Psychologist, 39,* 351–364.

Mischel, W., Shoda, Y., & Peake, P. K. (1988). The nature of adolescent competencies predicted by preschool delay of gratification. *Journal of Personality and Social Psychology, 54,* 687–696.

Mischel, W., Shoda, Y., & Rodriguez, M. L. (1989). Delay of gratification in children. *Science, 244,* 933–938.

Mita, T. H., Dermer, M., & Knight, J. (1977). Reversed facial images and the mere-exposure hypothesis. *Journal of Personality and Social Psychology, 35,* 597–601.

Mitchell, T. R., Thompson, L., Peterson, E., & Cronk, R. (1997). Temporal adjustments in the evaluation of events: The "rosy view." *Journal of Experimental Social Psychology, 33,* 421–448.

Miyamoto, Y., & Sancar, A. (1998). Vitamin B2-based blue-light photoreceptors in the retinohypothalamic tract as the photoactive pigments for setting the circadian clock in mammals. *Proceedings of the National Academy of Sciences, 95,* 6097–6102.

MMWR. (1999, April 2). Tobacco use among middle and high school students—Florida, 1998 and 1999. *Morbility and Mortality Weekly Report, 48,* 248–253.

Mollica, R. F., McInnes, K., Pham, T., Fawzi, M. C. S., Murphy, E., & Lin, L. (1998). The dose-effect relationships between torture and psychiatric symptoms in Vietnamese ex-political detainees and a comparison group. *Journal of Nervous and Mental Diseases, 186,* 543–553.

Monaghan, P. (1992, September 23). Professor of psychology stokes a controversy on the reliability and repression of memory. *Chronicle of Higher Education,* pp. A9–A10.

Mondloch, C. J., Lewis, T. L., Budreau, D. R., Maurer, D., Dannemiller, J. L., Stephens, B. R., & Kleiner-Gathercoal, K. A. (1999). Face perception during early infancy. *Psychological Science, 10,* 419–422.

Money, J. (1987). Sin, sickness, or status? Homosexual gender identity and psychoneuroendocrinology. *American Psychologist, 42,* 384–399.

Money, J. (1988). *Gay, straight, and in-between.* New York: Oxford University Press.

Money, J., Berlin, F. S., Falck, A., & Stein, M. (1983). *Antiandrogenic and counseling treatment of sex offenders.* Baltimore: Department of Psychiatry and Behavioral Sciences, Johns Hopkins University School of Medicine.

Moody, R. (1976). *Life after life.* Harrisburg, PA: Stackpole Books.

Mook, D. G. (1983). In defense of external invalidity. *American Psychologist, 38,* 379–387.

Moorcroft, W. (1993). *Sleep, dreaming, and sleep disorders: An introduction* (2nd ed.). Landam, MD: University Press of America.

Moore, D. W. (1993, April). Public polarized on gay issue. *Gallup Poll Monthly,* pp. 30–34.

Moore, T. E. (1988). The case against subliminal manipulation. *Psychology and Marketing, 5,* 297–316.

Moravec, H. (1999, December). Rise of the robots. *Scientific American,* pp. 124–135.

Moreland, R. L., & Beach, S. R. (1992). Exposure effects in the classroom: The development of affinity among students. *Journal of Experimental Social Psychology, 28,* 255–276.

Moreland, R. L., & Zajonc, R. B. (1982). Exposure effects in person perception: Familiarity, similarity, and attraction. *Journal of Experimental Social Psychology, 18,* 395–415.

Morell, V. (1995). Attacking the causes of "silent" infertility. *Science, 269,* 775–776.

Morell, V. (1995). Zeroing in on how hormones affect the immune system. *Science, 269,* 773–775.

Morelli, G. A., Rogoff, B., Oppenheim, D., & Goldsmith, D. (1992). Cultural variation in infants' sleeping arrangements: Questions of independence. *Developmental Psychology, 26,* 604–613.

Morin, R., & Brossard, M. A. (1997, March 4). Communication breakdown on drugs. *Washington Post,* pp. A1, A6.

Morris, J. S., Ohman, A., & Dolan, R. (1998). Conscious and unconscious emotional learning in the human amygdala. *Nature, 393,* 467–470.

Morrison, D. C. (1988). Marine mammals join the Navy. *Science, 242,* 1503–1504.

Morrison, D. M. (1985). Adolescent contraceptive behavior: A review. *Psychological Bulletin, 98,* 538–568.

Mortensen, P. B. (1999). Effects of family history and place and season of birth on the risk of schizophrenia. *New England Journal of Medicine, 340,* 603–608.

Morton, J., & Johnson, M. H. (April, 1991). CONSPEC and CONLERN: A two-process theory of infant face recognition. *Psychological Review, 98*(2), 164–181.

Moruzzi, G., & Magoun, H. W. (1949). Brain stem reticular formation and activation of the EEG. *Electroencephalography and Clinical Neurophysiology, 1,* 455–473.

Moscovici, S. (1985). Social influence and conformity. In G. Lindzey & E. Aronson (Eds.), *The handbook of social psychology* (3rd ed.). Hillsdale, NJ: Erlbaum.

Moser, P. W. (1987, May). Are cats smart? Yes, at being cats. *Discover*, pp. 77–88.

Mosher, D. L., & Anderson, R. D. (1986). Macho personality, sexual aggression, and reactions to guided imagery of realistic rape. *Journal of Research in Personality, 20,* 77–94.

Moss, A. J., Allen, K. F., Giovino, G. A., & Mills, S. L. (1992, December 2). Recent trends in adolescent smoking, smoking-update correlates, and expectations about the future. *Advance Data* No. 221 (from Vital and Health Statistics of the Centers for Disease Control and Prevention).

Moss, H. A., & Susman, E. J. (1980). Longitudinal study of personality development. In O. G. Brim, Jr. & J. Kagan (Eds.), *Constancy and change in human development.* Cambridge, MA: Harvard University Press.

Mott, F. L. (1991). Developmental effects of infant care: The mediating role of gender and health. *Journal of Social Issues, 47*(2), 139–158.

Moyer, K. E. (1983). The physiology of motivation: Aggression as a model. In C. J. Scheier & A. M. Rogers (Eds.), *G. Stanley Hall Lecture Series* (Vol. 3). Washington, DC: American Psychological Association.

Mroczek, D. K., & Kolarz, D. M. (1998). The effect of age on positive and negative affect: A developmental perspective on happiness. *Journal of Personality and Social Psychology, 75,* 1333–1349.

Muehlenhard, C. L. (1988). Misinterpreted dating behaviors and the risk of date rape. *Journal of Social and Clinical Psychology, 6,* 20–37.

Mueller, C. M., & Dweck, C. S. (1998). Praise for intelligence can undermine children's motivation and performance. *Journal of Personality and Social Psychology, 75,* 33–52.

Muhlnickel, W. (1998). Tinnitus processing in the brain. *Proceedings of the National Academy of Sciences, 95,* 10340–10343.

Mukerjee, M. (1997, January). Trends in animal research. *Scientific American*, pp. 86–93.

Muller, J. E., Mittleman, M. A., Maclure, M., Sherwood, J. B., & Tofler, G. H. (1996). Triggering myocardial infarction by sexual activity. *Journal of the American Medical Association, 275,* 1405–1409.

Muller, J. E., & Verrier, R. L. (1996). Triggering of sudden death—Lessons from an earthquake. *New England Journal of Medicine, 334,* 460–461.

Mullin, C. R., & Linz, D. (1995). Desensitization and resensitization to violence against women: Effects of exposure to sexually violent films on judgments of domestic violence victims. *Journal of Personality and Social Psychology, 69,* 449–459.

Murnen, S. K., & Stockton, M. (1997). Gender and self-reported sexual arousal in response to sexual stimuli: A meta-analytic review. *Sex Roles, 37,* 135–153.

Murphy, G. E., & Wetzel, R. D. (1990). The lifetime risk of suicide in alcoholism. *Archives of General Psychiatry, 47,* 383–392.

Murphy, S. T., Monahan, J. L., & Miller, L. C. (1998). Inference under the influence: The impact of alcohol and inhibition conflict on women's sexual decision making. *Personality and Social Psychology Bulletin, 24,* 517–528.

Murphy, S. T., Monahan, J. L., & Zajonc, R. B. (1995). Additivity of nonconscious affect: Combined effects of priming and exposure. *Journal of Personality and Social Psychology, 69,* 589–602.

Murphy, S. T., & Zajonc, R. B. (1993). Affect, cognition, and awareness: Affective priming with optimal and suboptimal stimulus exposures. *Journal of Personality and Social Psychology, 64,* 723–739.

Murphy, T. N. (1982). Pain: Its assessment and management. In R. J. Gatchel, A. Baum, & J. E. Singer (Eds.), *Handbook of psychology and health: Vol. I. Clinical psychology and behavioral medicine: Overlapping disciplines.* Hillsdale, NJ: Erlbaum.

Murray, B. (1998, May). Psychology is key to airline safety at Boeing. *APA Monitor*, p. 36.

Murray, C., & Herrnstein, R. J. (1994, October 31). Race, genes and I.Q.—An apologia. *New Republic*, pp. 27–37.

Murray, C. J., & Lopez, A. D. (Eds.). (1996). *The global burden of disease: A comprehensive assessment of mortality and disability from diseases, injuries, and risk factors in 1990 and projected to 2020.* Cambridge, MA: Harvard University Press.

Murray, D. M., Johnson, C. A., Luepker, R. V., & Mittelmark, M. B. (1984). The prevention of cigarette smoking in children: A comparison of four strategies. *Journal of Applied Social Psychology, 14,* 274–288.

Murray, D. M., Pirie, P., Luepker, R. V., & Pallonen, U. (1989). Five- and six-year follow-up results from four seventh-grade smoking prevention strategies. *Journal of Behavioral Medicine, 12,* 207–218.

Murray, H. (1938). *Explorations in personality.* New York: Oxford University Press.

Murray, H. A. (1933). The effect of fear upon estimates of the maliciousness of other personalities. *Journal of Social Psychology, 4,* 310–329.

Murray, H. A., & Wheeler, D. R. (1937). A note on the possible clairvoyance of dreams. *Journal of Psychology, 3,* 309–313.

Murray, R., Jones, P., O'Callaghan, E., Takei, N., & Sham, P. (1992). Genes, viruses, and neurodevelopmental schizophrenia. *Journal of Psychiatric Research, 26,* 225–235.

Murray, S. L., & Holmes, J. G. (2000). The (mental) ties that bind: Cognitive structures that predict relationship resilience. *Journal of Personality and Social Psychology*, in press.

Murray, S. L., Holmes, J. G., & Griffin, D. (1996). The benefits of positive illusions: Idealization and the construction of satisfaction in close relationships. *Journal of Personality and Social Psychology, 70,* 79–98.

Mutiso, C. (1998, April 13). Raising hope. *Time*, pp. 200–201.

Myers, D. G. (1993). *The pursuit of happiness.* New York: Avon Books.

Myers, D. G. (1999). *Social psychology.* Boston: McGraw-Hill.

Myers, D. G. (2000). *The American paradox: Spiritual hunger in an age of plenty.* New Haven: Yale University Press.

Myers, D. G., & Bishop, G. D. (1970). Discussion effects on racial attitudes. *Science, 169,* 778–779.

Myers, D. G., & Diener, E. (1995). Who is happy? *Psychological Science, 6,* 10–19.

Myers, I. B. (1987). *Introduction to type: A description of the theory and applications of the Myers-Briggs Type Indicator.* Palo Alto, CA: Consulting Psychologists Press.

Myerson, J., Rank, M. R., Raines, F. Q., & Schnitzler, M. A. (1998). Race and general cognitive ability: The myth of diminishing returns to education. *Psychological Science, 9,* 139–142.

Nadel, L., & Jacobs, W. J. (1998). Traumatic memory is special. *Current Directions in Psychology, 7,* 154–157.

Nando Times. (1999, January 7). Chinca reportedly has 20 percent more males than females. www.nandotimes.com

Napolitan, D. A., & Goethals, G. R. (1979). The attribution of friendliness. *Journal of Experimental Social Psychology, 15,* 105–113.

Nash, M. (1987). What, if anything, is regressed about hypnotic age regression? A review of the empirical literature. *Psychological Bulletin, 102,* 42–52.

National Academy of Science. (1984). *Bereavement: Reactions, consequences, and cure.* Washington, DC: National Academy Press.

National Academy of Sciences. (1991). *Science, medicine, and animals.* Washington, DC: National Academy Press.

National Academy of Sciences. (1999). *Marijuana and medicine: Assessing the science base* (by J. A. Benson, Jr., and S. J. Watson, Jr.). Washington, DC: National Academy Press.

National Academy of Sciences, Institute of Medicine. (1982). *Marijuana and health.* Washington, DC: National Academy Press.

National Center for Health Statistics. (1990). *Health, United States, 1989.* Washington, DC: U.S. Department of Health and Human Services.

National Center for Health Statistics. (1991). Family structure and children's health: United States, 1988. *Vital and Health Statistics, Series 10, No. 178,* DHHS Publication No. PHS 91-1506 by Deborah A. Dawson.

National Center for Health Statistics. (1992, May). *Health United States 1991.* Hyattsville, MD: Department of Health and Human Services Pub. No. PHS 92-1232, Table 27.

National Council on the Aging. (1976). *The myth and reality of aging in America.* Washington, DC.

National Institutes of Health. (1998). Clinical guidelines on the identification, evaluation, and treatment of overweight and obesity in adults. Executive summary, Obesity Education Initiative, National heart, Lung, and Blood Institute.

National Research Council. (1987). *Risking the future: Adolescent sexuality, pregnancy, and childbearing.* Washington, DC: National Academy Press.

National Research Council. (1990). *Human factors research needs for an aging population.* Washington, DC: National Academy Press.

National Safety Council. (1991). *Accident facts.* Chicago: National Safety Council.

Naylor, T. H. (1990). Redefining corporate motivation, Swedish style. *Christian Century, 107,* 566–570.

NCTV News. (1987, July-August). More research links harmful effects to non-violent porn. P. 12.

Needles, D. J., & Abramson, L. Y. (1990). Positive life events, attributional style, and hopefulness: Testing a model of recovery from depression. *Journal of Abnormal Psychology, 99,* 156–165.

Neeleman, J., & Persaud, R. (1995). Why do psychiatrists neglect religion? *British Journal of Medical Psychology, 68,* 169–178.

Neese, R. M. (1991, November/December). What good is feeling bad? The evolutionary benefits of psychic pain. *The Sciences,* pp. 30–37.

Neisser, U. (1979). The control of information pickup in selective looking. In A. D. Pick (Ed.), *Perception and its development: A tribute to Eleanor J. Gibson.* Hillsdale, NJ: Erlbaum.

Neisser, U. (1982). Snapshots or benchmarks? In U. Neiser (Ed.), *Memory observed: Remembering in natural settings.* San Francisco: W. H. Freeman.

Neisser, U. (1997). The ecological study of memory. *Philosophical Transactions of the Royal Society of London, 352,* 1697–1701.

Neisser, U. (1997). Rising scores on intelligence tests. *American Scientist, 85,* 440–447.

Neisser, U. (1998). *The rising curve: Long-term gains in IQ and related measures.* Washington, DC: American Psychological Association.

Neisser, U., Boodoo, G., Bouchard, T. J., Jr., Boykin, A. W., Brody, N., Ceci, S. J., Halpern, D. F., Loehlin, J. C., Perloff, R., Sternberg, R. J., & Urbina, S. (1996). Intelligence: Knowns and unknowns. *American Psychologist, 51,* 77–101.

Neisser, U., & Harsch, N. (1992). Phantom flashbulbs: False recollections of hearing the news about *Challenger.* In E. Winograd & U. Neisser (Eds.), *Affect and accuracy in recall: Studies of "flashbulb" memories.* New York: Cambridge University Press.

Neisser, U., Winograd, E., & Weldon, M. S. (1991). Remembering the earthquake: "What I experienced" vs. "How I heard the news." Paper presented to the Psychonomic Society convention.

Neitz, J., Geist, T., & Jacobs, G. H. (1989). Color vision in the dog. *Visual Neuroscience, 3,* 119–125.

Nelson, K. (1993). The psychological and social origins of autobiographical memory. *Psychological Science, 4,* 7–13.

Nelson, M. D., Saykin, A. J., Flashman, L. A., & Riordan, H. J. (1998). Hippocampal volume reduction in schizophrenia as assessed by magnetic resonance imaging. *Archives of General Psychiatry, 55,* 433–440.

Nelson, N. (1988). A meta-analysis of the life-event/health paradigm: The influence of social support. Doctoral dissertation, Temple University, Philadelphia, PA.

Neubauer, P. B., & Neubauer, A. (1990). *Nature's thumbprint: The new genetics of personality.* Reading, MA: Addison-Wesley.

Neugarten, B. L., Wood, V., Kraines, R. J., & Loomis, B. (1963). Women's attitudes toward the menopause. *Vita Humana, 6,* 140–151.

Nevin, J. A. (1988). Behavioral momentum and the partial reinforcement effect. *Psychological Bulletin, 103,* 44–56.

New York Times. (1999, December 5). AIDS, the worsening catastrophe. www.nytimes.com

Newcomb, M. D., & Bentler, P. M. (1988). Impact of adolescent drug use and social support on problems of young adults: A longitudinal study. *Journal of Abnormal Psychology, 97,* 64–75.

Newcomb, M. D., & Harlow, L. L. (1986). Life events and substance use among adolescents: Mediating effects of perceived loss of control and meaninglessness in life. *Journal of Personality and Social Psychology, 51,* 564–577.

Newcombe, N., & Fox, N. A. (1994). Infantile amnesia: Through a glass darkly. *Child Development, 65,* 31–40.

Newman, D. L., Caspi, A., Moffit, T. E., & Silva, P. A. (1997). Antecedents of adult interpersonal functioning: Effects of individual differences in age-3 temperament. *Developmental Psychology, 33,* 206–217.

Newman, L. S., & Baumeister, R. F. (1996). Toward an explanation of the UFO abduction phenomenon: Hypnotic, elaboration, extraterrestrial sadomasochism, and spurious memories. *Psychological Inquiry, 7,* 99–126.

Newman, L. S., Duff, K. J., & Baumeister, R. F. (1997). A new look at defensive projection: Thought suppression, accessibility, and biased person perception. *Journal of Personality and Social Psychology, 72*, 980–1001.

Newman, L. S., & Ruble, D. N. (1988). Stability and change in self-understanding: The early elementary school years. *Early Child Development and Care, 40*, 77–99.

Newport, E. L. (1990). Maturational constraints on language learning. *Cognitive Science, 14*, 11–28.

Newport, F. (1998, July). Americans remain more likely to believe sexual orientation due to environment, not genetics. *Gallup Poll Monthly*, pp. 14–16.

Nezu, A. M., Nezu, C. M., & Blissett, S. E. (1988). Sense of humor as a moderator of the relation between stressful events and psychological distress: A prospective analysis. *Journal of Personality and Social Psychology, 54*, 520–525.

NFFRE. (1996). Family facts. *Family Matters, 1*(1), 8. Published by National Foundation for Family Research and Education, Calgary, AB T2P 3H5.

Ng, S. H. (1990). Androcentric coding of *man* and *his* in memory by language users. *Journal of Experimental Social Psychology, 26*, 455–464.

Niccols, G. A. (1994). Fetal alcohol syndrome: Implications for psychologists. *Clinical Psychology Review, 14*, 91–111.

NICHD Early Child Care Research Network. (1997a). Mother-child interaction and cognitive outcomes associated with early childhood: Results of the NICHD study. Presented at the Society for Research in Child Development convention.

NICHD Early Child Care Research Network. (1997b). The effects of infant child care on infant-mother attachment security: Results of the NICHD study of early child care. *Child Development, 68*, 860–897.

NICHD Early Child Care Research Network. (1999). Child care and mother-child interaction in the first 3 years of life. *Developmental Psychology, 35*, 1399–1413.

Nicholson, N. (1998, July-August). How hardwired is human behavior? *Harvard Business Review*, pp., 135–147.

Nickell, J. (1996, May/June). A study of fantasy proneness in the thirteen cases of alleged encounters in John Mack's *Abduction. Skeptical Inquirer*, pp. 18–20, 54.

Nicol, S. E., & Gottesman, I. I. (1983). Clues to the genetics and neurobiology of schizophrenia. *American Scientist, 71*, 398–404.

Nicolaus, L. K., Cassel, J. F., Carlson, R. B., & Gustavson, C. R. (1983). Taste-aversion conditioning of crows to control predation on eggs. *Science, 220*, 212–214.

Niemi, R. G., Mueller, J., & Smith, T. W. (1989). *Trends in public opinion: A compendium of survey data.* New York: Greenwood Press.

Nigro, G. (1984). Cited in U. Neisser, The role of invariant structures in the control of movement. In M. Frese & J. Sabini (Eds.), *Goal directed behavior: The concept of action in psychology.* Hillsdale, NJ: Erlbaum.

NIH. (1998, June 17). First federal obesity clinical guidelines released. National Heart, Lunch, and Blood Institute, National Institutes of Health (www.nhlbi.nih.gov).

Nisbet, M. (1998, May/June). Psychic telephone networks profit on yearning, gullibility. *Skeptical Inquirer*, pp. 5–6.

Nisbett, R. E., & Borgida, E. (1975). Attribution and the psychology of prediction. *Journal of Personality and Social Psychology, 32*, 932–943.

Nisbett, R. E., & Cohen, D. (1996). *Culture of honor: The psychology of violence in the South.* Boulder, CO: Westview Press.

Nisbett, R. E., & Ross, L. (1980). *Human inference: Strategies and shortcomings of social judgment.* Englewood Cliffs, NJ: Prentice-Hall.

Nisbett, R., & Ross, L. (1991). *The person and the situation.* New York: McGraw-Hill.

Nishizawa, S. (1996). The religiousness and subjective well-being of Japanese students. Paper presented at the XXVI International Congress of Psychology.

Noble, E. P. (1993). The D2 dopamine receptor gene: A review of association studies in alcoholism. *Behavior Genetics, 23*, 119–129.

Noel, J. G., Forsyth, D. R., & Kelley, K. N. (1987). Improving the performance of failing students by overcoming their self-serving attributional biases. *Basic and Applied Social Psychology, 8*, 151–162.

Nolen-Hoeksema, S. (1990). *Sex differences in depression.* Stanford, CA: Stanford University Press.

Nolen-Hoeksema, S., & Larson, J. (1999). *Coping with loss.* Mahwah, NJ: Erlbaum.

Nolen-Hoeksema, S., Larson, J., & Grayson, C. (2000). Explaining the gender difference in depressive symptoms. *Journal of Personality and Social Psychology*, in press.

Nolen-Hoeksema, S., & Morrow, J. (1991). A prospective study of depression and post-traumatic stress symptoms following a natural disaster: The 1989 Loma Prieta earthquake. *Journal of Personality and Social Psychology, 61*, 115–121.

NORC (National Opinion Research Center). (1985, October/November). Images of the world. *Public Opinion*, p. 38.

Norman, D. A. (1988). *The psychology of everyday things.* New York: Basic Books.

Norris, P. A. (1986). On the status of biofeedback and clinical practice. *American Psychologist, 41*, 1009–1010.

North, M. M., North, S. M., & Coble, J. R. (1998). Virtual reality therapy: An effective treatment for phobias. In G. Riva & B. K. Wiederhold (Eds.), *Virtual environments in clinical psychology and neuroscience: Methods and techniques in advanced patient-therapist interaction.* Amsterdam: IOS Press.

Norton, K. L., Olds, T. S., Olive, S., & Dank, S. (1996). Ken and Barbie at life size. *Sex Roles, 34*, 287–294.

Notarius, C., & Markman, H. (1993). *We can work it out.* New York: Putnam.

Nowak, R. (1994). Nicotine scrutinized as FDA seeks to regulate cigarettes. *Science, 263*, 1555–1556.

Nowell, A., & Hedges, L. V. (1998). Trends in gender differences in academic achievement from 1960 to 1994: An analysis of differences in mean, variance, and extreme scores. *Sex Roles, 39*, 21–43.

Nuttin, J. M., Jr. (1987). Affective consequences of mere ownership: The name letter effect in twelve European languages. *European Journal of Social Psychology, 17*, 381–402.

Oakhill, J., Garnham, A., & Johnson-Laird, P. N. (1990). Belief bias effects in syllogistic reasoning. In D. J. Gilhooly, M. T. G. Keane, R. H. Logie, & G. Erdos (Eds.), *Lines of thinking* (Vol. 1). Chichester, UK: Wiley.

Oakhill, J. V., Johnson-Laird, P. N., & Garnham, A. (1989). Believability and syllogistic reasoning. *Cognition, 31*, 117–140.

O'Connor, P., & Brown, G. W. (1984). Supportive relationships: Fact or fancy? *Journal of Social and Personal Relationships, 1,* 159–175.

Oetting, E. R., & Beauvais, F. (1987). Peer cluster theory, socialization characteristics, and adolescent drug use: A path analysis. *Journal of Counseling Psychology, 34,* 205–213.

Oetting, E. R., & Beauvais, F. (1990). Adolescent drug use: Findings of national and local surveys. *Journal of Social and Personal Relationships, 1,* 159–319.

Oettingen, G., & Seligman, M. E. P. (1990). Pessimism and behavioural signs of depression in East versus West Berlin. *European Journal of Social Psychology, 20,* 207–220.

Offer, D., Ostrov, E., Howard, K. I., & Atkinson, R. (1988). *The teenage world: Adolescents' self-image in ten countries.* New York: Plenum.

Ohman, A. (1986). Face the beast and fear the face: Animal and social fears as prototypes for evolutionary analyses of emotion. *Psychophysiology, 23,* 123–145.

Oishi, S., Diener, E. F., Lucas, R. E., & Suh, E. M. (1999). Cross-cultural variations in predictors of life satisfaction: Perspectives from needs and values. *Personality and Social Psychology Bulletin, 25,* 980–990.

Olds, J. (1958). Self-stimulation of the brain. *Science, 127,* 315–324.

Olds, J. (1975). Mapping the mind onto the brain. In F. G. Worden, J. P. Swazey, & G. Adelman (Eds.), *The neurosciences: Paths of discovery.* Cambridge, MA: MIT Press.

Olds, J., & Milner, P. (1954). Positive reinforcement produced by electrical stimulation of the septal area and other regions of rat brain. *Journal of Comparative and Physiological Psychology, 47,* 419–427.

O'Leary, A. (1990). Stress, emotion, and human immune function. *Psychological Bulletin, 108,* 363–382.

O'Leary, V. E., & Ickovics, J. R. (1995). Resilience and thriving in response to challenge: An opportunity for a paradigm shift in women's health. *Women's Health: Research on Gender, Behavior, and Policy, 1,* 121–142.

Olin, S. S., & Mednick, S. A. (1996). Risk factors of psychosis: Identifying vulnerable populations premorbidly. *Schizophrenia Bulletin, 22,* 223–240.

Oliner, S. P., & Oliner, P. M. (1988). *The altruistic personality: Rescuers of Jews in Nazi Europe.* New York: Free Press.

Oliver, M. B., & Hyde, J. S. (1993). Gender differences in sexuality: A meta-analysis. *Psychological Bulletin, 114,* 29–51.

Olney, B. (1998, July 9). As baseball's second-half begins, Mark McGwire leads the Maris chase. *New York Times* (www.nytimes.com).

Olshansky, S. J., Carnes, B. A., & Cassel, C. K. (1993, April). The aging of the human species. *Scientific American,* pp. 46–52.

Olweus, D., Mattsson, A., Schalling, D., & Low, H. (1988). Circulating testosterone levels and aggression in adolescent males: A causal analysis. *Psychosomatic Medicine, 50,* 261–272.

O'Malley, P. M., & Bachman, J. G. (1983). Self-esteem: Change and stability between ages 13 and 23. *Developmental Psychology, 19,* 257–268.

O'Neill, M. J. (1993). The relationship between privacy, control, and stress responses in office workers. Paper presented to the Human Factors and Ergonomics Society convention.

Oren, D. A., & Terman, M. (1998). Tweaking the human circadian clock with light. *Science, 279,* 333–334.

Orne, M. T., & Evans, F. J. (1965). Social control in the psychological experiment: Antisocial behavior and hypnosis. *Journal of Personality and Social Psychology, 1,* 189–200.

Ornstein, R. E. (1991). *The evolution of consciousness: Of Darwin, Freud, and cranial fire.* New York: Prentice-Hall.

Osborne, J. W. (1997). Race and academic disidentification. *Journal of Educational Psychology, 89,* 728–735.

Osborne, L. (1999, October 27). A linguistic big bang. *New York Times Magazine* (www.nytimes.com).

Osgood, C. E. (1962). *An alternative to war or surrender.* Urbana: University of Illinois Press.

Osgood, C. E. (1980). GRIT: A strategy for survival in mankind's nuclear age? Paper presented at the Pugwash Conference on New Directions in Disarmament.

OSS Assessment Staff. (1948). *The assessment of men.* New York: Rinehart.

Ost, L. G., & Hugdahl, K. (1981). Acquisition of phobias and anxiety response patterns in clinical patients. *Behaviour Research and Therapy, 16,* 439–447.

Ostfeld, A. M., Kasl, S. V., D'Atri, D. A., & Fitzgerald, E. F. (1987). *Stress, crowding, and blood pressure in prison.* Hillsdale, NJ: Erlbaum.

Ouellette, J. A., & Wood, W. (1998). Habit and intention in everyday life: The multiple processes by which past behavior predicts future behavior. *Psychological Bulletin, 124,* 54–74.

Overmier, J. B., & Murison, R. (1997). Animal models reveal the "psych" in the psychosomatics of peptic ulcers. *Current Directions in Psychological Science, 6,* 180–184.

Padgett, V. R. (1989). Predicting organizational violence: An application of 11 powerful principles of obedience. Paper presented to the American Psychological Association convention.

Padilla, R. V., & Benavides, A. H. (Eds.). (1992). *Critical perspectives on bilingual education research.* Tempe, AZ: Bilingual Press.

Paffenbarger, R. S., Jr., Hyde, R. T., Wing, A. L., & Hsieh, C.-C. (1986). Physical activity, all-cause mortality, and longevity of college alumni. *New England Journal of Medicine, 314,* 605–612.

Page, S. (1977). Effects of the mental illness label in attempts to obtain accommodation. *Canadian Journal of Behavioral Science, 9,* 84–90.

Paikoff, R. L., & Brooks-Gunn, J. (1991). Do parent-child relationships change during puberty? *Psychological Bulletin, 110,* 47–66.

Paivio, A. (1986). *Mental representations: A dual coding approach.* New York: Oxford University Press.

Palace, E. M. (1995). Modification of dysfunctional patterns of sexual response through autonomic arousal and false physiological feedback. *Journal of Consulting and Clinical Psychology, 63,* 604–615.

Palladino, J. J., & Carducci, B. J. (1983). "Things that go bump in the night": Students' knowledge of sleep and dreams. Paper presented at the meeting of the Southeastern Psychological Association.

Palmer, S., Schreiber, C., & Box, C. (1991). Remembering the earthquake: "Flashbulb" memory for experienced vs. reported events. Paper presented to the Psychonomic Society convention.

Palumbo, S. R. (1978). *Dreaming and memory: A new information-processing model.* New York: Basic Books.

Pandey, J., Sinha, Y., Prakash, A., & Tripathi, R. C. (1982). Right-left political ideologies and attribution of the causes of poverty. *European Journal of Social Psychology, 12,* 327–331.

Panksepp, J. (1982). Toward a general psychobiological theory of emotions. *Behavioral and Brain Sciences, 5,* 407–467.

Pantev, C., Oostenveld, R., Engelien, A., Ross, B., Roberts, L. R., & Hoke, M. (1998). Increased auditory cortical representation in musicians. *Nature, 392,* 811–814.

Parducci, A. (1995). *Happiness, pleasure, and judgment: The contextual theory and its applications.* Hillsdale, NJ: Erlbaum.

Park, R. L. (1999, July 12). Liars never break a sweat. *New York Times,* (www.nytimes.com).

Parker, G., Roy, K., Hadzi, P. D., Pedic, F. (1992). Psychotic (delusional) depression: A meta-analyis of physical treatments. *Journal of Affective Disorders, 24,* 17–24.

Parker, S., Nichter, M., Nichter, M., & Vuckovic, N. (1995). Body image and weight concerns among African American and white adolescent females: Differences that make a difference. *Human Organization, 54,* 103–114.

Parks, R. W., Loewenstein, D. A., Dodrill, K. L., Barker, W. W., Yoshi, F., Chang, J. Y., Emran, A., Apicella, A., Shermata, W. A., & Duara, R. (1988). Cerebral metabolic effects of a verbal fluency test: A PET scan study. *Journal of Clinical and Experimental Neuropsychology, 10,* 565–575.

Parloff, M. B. (1987, February). Psychotherapy: An import from Japan. *Psychology Today,* pp. 74–75.

Parrott, A. C. (1999). Does cigarette smoking *cause* stress? *American Psychologist, 54,* 817–820.

Passell, P. (1993, March 9). Like a new drug, social programs are put to the test. *New York Times,* pp. C1, C10.

Pate, J. E., Pumariega, A. J., Hester, C., & Garner, D. M. (1992). Cross-cultural patterns in eating disorders: A review. *Journal of the American Academy of Child and Adolescent Psychiatry, 31,* 802–809.

Paton, D. (1992). Disaster research: The Scottish dimension. *The Psychologist: Bulletin of the British Psychological Society, 5,* 535–538.

Patterson, F. (1978, October). Conversations with a gorilla. *National Geographic,* pp. 438–465.

Patterson, G. R., Chamberlain, P., & Reid, J. B. (1982). A comparative evaluation of parent training procedures. *Behavior Therapy, 13,* 638–650.

Patterson, G. R., Reid, J. B., & Dishion, T. J. (1992). *Antisocial boys.* Eugene, OR: Castalia.

Patterson, R. (1951). *The riddle of Emily Dickinson.* Boston: Houghton Mifflin.

Patton, W., & Mannison, M. (1995). Sexual coercion in dating situations among university students: Preliminary Australian data. *Australian Journal of Psychology, 47,* 66–72.

Paulos, J. A. (1995). *A mathematician reads the newspaper.* New York: Basic Books.

Pauls, D. L., Morton, L. A., & Egeland, J. A. (1992). Risks of affective illness among first-degree relatives of bipolar I old-order Amish probands. *Archives of General Psychiatry, 49,* 703–708.

Paus, T., Zijdenbos, A., Worsley, K., Collins, D. L., Blumenthal, J., Giedd, J. N., Rapoport, J. L., & Evans, A. C. (1999). Structural maturation of neural pathways in children and adolescents: In vivo study. *Science, 283,* 1908–1911.

Pedersen, N. L., Plomin, R., McClearn, G. E., & Friberg, L. (1988). Neuroticism, extraversion, and related traits in adult twins reared apart and reared together. *Journal of Personality and Social Psychology, 55,* 950–957.

Pekkanen, J. (1982, June). Why do we sleep? *Science, 82,* p. 86.

Pelham, B. W. (1993). On the highly positive thoughts of the highly depressed. In R. F. Baumeister (Ed.), *Self-esteem: The puzzle of low self-regard.* New York: Plenum.

Pendergrast, M. (1996, May). False memory—forget it. *The Psychologist,* p. 200.

Pendick, D. (1994, January/February). The mind of violence. *Brain Work: The Neuroscience Newsletter,* pp. 1–3, 5.

Penfield, W. (1969). Consciousness, memory, and man's conditioned reflexes. In K. Pigram (Ed.), *On the biology of learning.* New York: Harcourt, Brace & World.

Penfield, W. (1975). *The mystery of the mind.* Princeton, NJ: Princeton University Press.

Pennebaker, J. (1990). *Opening up: The healing power of confiding in others.* New York: William Morrow.

Pennebaker, J. W., Barger, S. D., & Tiebout, J. (1989). Disclosure of traumas and health among Holocaust survivors. *Psychosomatic Medicine, 51,* 577–589.

Pennebaker, J. W., & Harber, K. D. (1993). A social stage model of collective coping: The Loma Prieta earthquake and the Persian Gulf war. *Journal of Social Issues, 49,* 125–145.

Pennebaker, J. W., & O'Heeron, R. C. (1984). Confiding in others and illness rate among spouses of suicide and accidental death victims. *Journal of Abnormal Psychology, 93,* 473–476.

Pennington, N., & Hastie, R. (1993). The story model for juror decision making. In R. Hastie (Ed.), *Inside the juror: The psychology of juror decision making.* New York: Cambridge University Press.

Peplau, L. A. (1982). Research on homosexual couples: An overview. *Journal of Homosexuality, 8*(2), 3–8.

Pepperberg, I. M. (1994). Numerical competence in an African gray parrot (*Psittacus erithacus*). *Journal of Comparative Psychology, 108,* 36–44.

Pepperberg, I. (2000). *The Alex studies : Cognitive and communicative abilities of grey parrots.* Cambridge, MA: Harvard University Press.

Perkins, H. W. (1991). Religious commitment, Yuppie values, and well-being in post-collegiate life. *Review of Religious Research, 32,* 244–251.

Perkins, K. A., Dubbert, P. M., Martin, J. E., Faulstich, M. E., & Harris, J. K. (1986). Cardiovascular reactivity to psychological stress in aerobically trained versus untrained mild hypertensives and normotensives. *Health Psychology, 5,* 407–421.

Perlmutter, M. (1983). Learning and memory through adulthood. In M. W. Riley, B. B. Hess, & K. Bond (Eds.), *Aging in society: Selected reviews of recent research.* Hillsdale, NJ: Erlbaum.

Perls, T., & Silver, M. H., with Lauerman, J. F. (1999). *Living to 100: Lessons in living to your maximum potential.* Thorndike, ME: Thorndike Press.

Perrett, D. I., Harries, M., Misflin, A. J., & Chitty, A. J. (1988). Three stages in the classification of body movements by visual neurons. In H. B. Barlow, C. Blakemore, & M. Weston Smith (Eds.), *Images and understanding.* Cambridge, UK: Cambridge University Press.

Perrett, D. I., Hietanen, J. K., Oram, M. W., & Benson, P. J. (1992). Organization and functions of cells responsive to faces in the temporal cortex. *Philosophical Transactions of the Royal Society of London: Series B, 335,* 23–30.

Perrett, D. I., Lee, K. J., Penton-Voak, I., Rowland, D., Yoshikawa, S., Burt, D. M., Henzi, S. P., Castles, D. L., & Akamatsu, S. (1998). Effects of sexual dimorphism on facial attractiveness. *Nature, 394,* 884–887.

Perrett, D. I., May, K. A., & Yoshikawa, S. (1994). Facial shape and judgments of female attractiveness. *Nature, 368,* 239–242.

Persky, V. W., Kempthorne-Rawson, J., & Shekelle, R. B. (1987). Personality and risk of cancer: 20-year follow-up of the Western Electric study. *Psychosomatic Medicine, 49,* 435–449.

Persons, J. B. (1986). The advantages of studying psychological phenomena rather than psychiatric diagnoses. *American Psychologist, 41,* 1252–1260.

Pert, C. (1986). Quoted in J. Hooper & D. Teresi, *The three-pound universe.* New York: Macmillan.

Pert, C. B. (1986, Summer). The wisdom of the receptors: Neuropeptides, the emotions, and bodymind. *Advances* (Institute for the Advancement of Health), *3,* 8–16.

Pert, C. B., & Snyder, S. H. (1973). Opiate receptor: Demonstration in nervous tissue. *Science, 179,* 1011–1014.

Perugini, E. M., Kirsch, I., Allen, S. T., Coldwell, E., Meredith, J., Montgomery, G. H., & Sheehan, J. (1998). Surreptitious observation of responses to hypnotically suggested hallucinations: A test of the compliance hypothesis. *International Journal of Clinical and Experimental Hypnosis, 46,* 191–203.

Peschel, E. R., & Peschel, R. E. (1987). Medical insights into the castrati in opera. *American Scientist, 75,* 578–583.

Peters, T. J., & Waterman, R. H., Jr. (1982). *In search of excellence: Lessons from America's best-run companies.* New York: Harper & Row.

Peterson, C., & Barrett, L. C. (1987). Explanatory style and academic performance among university freshmen. *Journal of Personality and Social Psychology, 53,* 603–607.

Peterson, C., Peterson, J., & Skevington, S. (1986). Heated argument and adolescent development. *Journal of Social and Personal Relationships, 3,* 229–240.

Peterson, C. C., & Siegal, M. (1999). Representing inner worlds: Theory of mind in autistic, deaf, and normal hearing children. *Psychological Science, 10,* 126–129.

Peterson, L. R., & Peterson, M. J. (1959). Short-term retention of individual verbal items. *Journal of Experimental Psychology, 58,* 193–198.

Petitto, L. A., & Marentette, P. F. (1991). Babbling in the manual mode: Evidence for the ontogeny of language. *Science, 251,* 1493–1496.

Peto, R. (1994). *Mortality from smoking in developed countries, 1950-2000: Indirect estimates from national vital statistics.* New York: Oxford University Press.

Pettegrew, J. W., Keshavan, M. S., & Minshew, N. J. (1993). 31P nuclear magnetic resonance spectroscopy: Neurodevelopment and schizophrenia. *Schizophrenia Bulletin, 19,* 35–53.

Petticrew, M., Fraser, J. M., & Regan, M. F. (1999). Adverse life events and risk of breast cancer: A meta-analysis. *British Journal of Health Psychology, 4,* 1–17.

Pettigrew, T. F. (1969). Racially separate or together? *Journal of Social Issues, 25,* 43–69.

Pettigrew, T. F. (1997). Generalized intergroup contact effects on prejudice. *Personality and Social Psychology Bulletin, 23,* 173–185.

Pettigrew, T. F. (1998). Reactions toward the new minorities of Western Europe. *Annual Review of Sociology, 24,* 77–103.

Pfeffer, J., Cialdini, R. B., Hanna, B., & Knopoff, K. (1998). Faith in supervision and the self-enhancement bias: Two psychological reasons why managers don't empower workers. *Basic and Applied Social Psychology, 20,* 313–321.

Pfeiffer, E. (1977). Sexual behavior in old age. In E. W. Busse & E. Pfeiffer (Eds.), *Behavior and adaptation in late life* (2nd ed.). Boston: Little, Brown.

Phelps, J. A., Davis J. O., & Schartz, K. M. (1997). Nature, nurture, and twin research strategies. *Current Directions in Psychological Science 6,* 117–120.

Phillips, D. P. (1985). Natural experiments on the effects of mass media violence on fatal aggression: Strengths and weaknesses of a new approach. In L. Berkowitz (Ed.), *Advances in experimental social psychology* (Vol. 19). Orlando, FL: Academic Press.

Phillips, D. P., Carstensen, L. L., & Paight, D. J. (1989). Effects of mass media news stories on suicide, with new evidence on the role of story content. In D. R. Pfeffer (Ed.), *Suicide among youth: Perspectives on risk and prevention.* Washington, DC: American Psychiatric Press.

Phillips, J. L. (1969). *Origins of intellect: Piaget's theory.* San Francisco: Freeman.

Piaget, J. (1930). *The child's conception of physical causality.* London: Routledge & Kegan Paul.

Piaget, J. (1932). *The moral judgment of the child.* New York: Harcourt, Brace & World.

Piccione, C., Hilgard, E. R., & Zimbardo, P. G. (1989). On the degree of stability of measured hypnotizability over a 25-year period. *Journal of Personality and Social Psychology, 56,* 289–295.

Pickar, D., Labarca, R., Linnoila, M., Roy, A., Hommer, D., Everett, D., & Payl, S. M. (1984). Neuroleptic-induced decrease in plasma homovanillic acid and antipsychotic activity in schizophrenic patients. *Science, 225,* 954–957.

Pigott, T. A., & Seay, S. (1997). Pharmacotherapy of obsessive-compulsive disorder. *International Review of Psychiatry, 9,* 133–147.

Pike, K. M., & Rodin, J. (1991). Mothers, daughters, and disordered eating. *Journal of Abnormal Psychology, 100,* 198–204.

Pillemer, D. G. (1995). What is remembered about early childhood events? Invited paper presented at the American Psychological Society convention.

Pillemer, D. (1998). *Momentous events, vivid memories.* Cambridge, MA: Harvard University Press, 1998.

Pincus, H. A. (1997) Commentary: Spirituality, religion, and health: Expanding and using the knowledge base. *Mind/Body Medicine, 2,* 49.

Pinel, J. P. J. (1993). *Biopsychology* (2nd ed.). Boston: Allyn & Bacon.

Pingitore, R., Dugoni, B. L., Tindale, R. S., & Spring, B. (1994). Bias against overweight job applicants in a simulated employment interview. *Journal of Applied Psychology, 79,* 909–917.

Pinker, S. (1990, September-October). Quoted in J. de Cuevas, "No, she holded them loosely." *Harvard Magazine,* pp. 60–67.

Pinker, S. (1995). The language instinct. *The General Psychologist, 31,* 63–65.

Pinker, S. (1999, June 24). His brain measured up. *New York Times* (www.nytimes.com).

Pinkerton, S. D., & Abramson, P. R. (1997). Condoms and the prevention of AIDS. *American Scientist, 85,* 364–373.

Pipe, M-E. (1996). Children's eyewitness memory. *New Zealand Journal of Psychology, 25,* 36–43.

Piper, A., Jr. (1998, Winter). Multiple personality disorder: Witchcraft survives in the twentieth century. *Skeptical Inquirer,* pp. 44–50.

Pittenger, D. J. (1993). The utility of the Myers-Briggs Type Indicator. *Review of Educational Research, 63,* 467–488.

Pittman, T. S., Davey, M. E., Alafat, K. A., Vetherill, K. V., & Kramer, N. A. (1980). Informational versus controlling verbal rewards. *Personality and Social Psychology Bulletin, 6,* 228–233.

Planned Parenthood Federation of America. (December 15, 1986). Sex education for parents. *USA Today,* p. 11A.

Pleck, J. H., Sonenstein, F. L., & Ku, L. C. (1993). Masculinity ideology: Its impact on adolescent males' heterosexual relationships. *Journal of Social Issues, 49,* 11–29.

Pliner, P. (1982). The effects of mere exposure on liking for edible substances. *Appetite: Journal for Intake Research, 3,* 283–290.

Pliner, P., & Pelchat, M. L. (1991). Neophobia in humans and the special status of foods of animal origin. *Appetite, 16,* 205–218.

Pliner, P., Pelchat, M., & Grabski, M. (1993). Reduction of neophobia in humans by exposure to novel foods. *Appetite, 20,* 111–123.

Plomin, R. (1999). Genetics and general cognitive ability. *Nature, 402* (Suppl), C25–C29.

Plomin, R., & Bergeman, C. S. (1991). The nature of nurture: Genetic influence on "environmental" measures. *Behavioral and Brain Sciences, 14,* 373–427.

Plomin, R., & Crabbe, J. (2000). DNA. *Psychological Bulletin,* in press.

Plomin, R., & Dale, P. S. (2000). Genetics and early language development: A UK study of twins. In D. V. M. Bishop & L. B. Leonard (Eds.), *Speech and language impairments in children: Causes, characteristics, intervention and outcome.* Oxford: Oxford University Press.

Plomin, R., & Daniels, D. (1987). Why are children in the same family so different from one another? *Behavioral and Brain Sciences, 10,* 1–60.

Plomin, R., & DeFries, J. C. (1998, May). The genetics of cognitive abilities and disabilities. *Scientific American,* pp. 62–69.

Plomin, R., DeFries, J. C., McClearn, G. E., & Rutter, M. (1997). *Behavioral genetics.* New York: Freeman.

Plomin, R., Fulker, D. W., Corley, R., & DeFries, J. C. (1997). Nature, nurture and cognitive development from 1 to 16 years: A parent-offspring adoption study. *Psychological Science, 8,* 442–447.

Plomin, R., McClearn, G. E., Pedersen, N. L., Nesselroade, J. R., & Bergeman, C. S. (1988). Genetic influence on childhood family environment perceived retrospectively from the last half of the life span. *Developmental Psychology, 24,* 37–45.

Plomin, R., Reiss, D., Hetherington, E. M., & Howe, G. W. (January, 1994). Nature and nurture: Genetic contributions to measures of the family environment. *Developmental Psychology, 30(1),* 32–43.

Plous, S. (1993). Psychological mechanisms in the human use of animals. *Journal of Social Issues, 49(1),* 11–52.

Plous, S. (1993). The nuclear arms race: Prisoner's dilemma or perceptual dilemma? *Journal of Peace Research, 30,* 163–179.

Plous, S. (1996). A comparison of strategies for reducing interval overconfidence in group judgments. *Journal of Applied Psychology.*

Polich, J., Pollock, V. E., & Bloom, F. E. (1994). Meta-analysis of P300 amplitude from males at risk for alcoholism. *Psychological Bulletin, 115,* 55–73.

Polivy, J., & Herman, C. P. (1985). Dieting and binging: A causal analysis. *American Psychologist, 40,* 193–201.

Polivy, J., & Herman, C. P. (1987). Diagnosis and treatment of normal eating. *Journal of Personality and Social Psychology, 55,* 635–644.

Pollak, S., Cicchetti, D., & Klorman, R. (1998). Stress, memory, and emotion: Developmental considerations from the study of child maltreatment. *Developmental Psychopathology, 10,* 811–828.

Pollard, R. (1992). 100 years in psychology and deafness: A centennial retrospective. Invited address to the American Psychological Association convention, Washington, DC.

Polusny, M. A., & Follette, V. M. (1995). Long-term correlates of child sexual abuse: Theory and review of the empirical literature. *Applied and Preventive Psychology, 4,* 143–166.

Pomerleau, O. F., Collins, A. C., Shiffman, S., & Pomerleau, C. S. (1993). Why some people smoke and others do not: New perspectives. *Journal of Consulting and Clinical Psychology, 61,* 723–731.

Pomeroy, W. B. (1972). *Dr. Kinsey and the Institute for Sex Research.* New York: Harper & Row.

Pons, T. P., Garraghty, P. E., Ommaya, A. K., Kaas, J. H., Taub, E., & Mishkin, M. (1991). Massive cortical reorganization after sensory deafferentation in adult macaques. *Science, 252,* 1857–1860.

Poole, D. A., & Lindsay, D. S. (1995). Interviewing preschoolers: Effects of nonsuggestive techniques, parental coaching and leading questions on reports of nonexperienced events. *Journal of Experimental Child Psychology, 60,* 129–154.

Poole, D. A., Lindsay, D. S., Memon, A., & Bull, R. (1995). Psychotherapy and the recovery of memories of childhood sexual abuse: U.S. and British practitioners' opinions, practices, and experiences. *Journal of Consulting and Clinical Psychology, 63,* 426–437.

Poon, L. W. (1987). Myths and truisms: Beyond extant analyses of speed of behavior and age. Address to the Eastern Psychological Association convention.

Pope, H. G., Jr., & Hudson, J. I. (1992). Is childhood sexual abuse a risk factor for bulimia nervosa? *American Journal of Psychiatry, 149,* 455–463.

Pope, H. G., Jr., & Hudson, J. I. (1995). Can memories of childhood sexual abuse be repressed? *Psychological Medicine, 25,* 121–126.

Pope, H. G., Mangweth, B., Negrao, A. B., Hudson, J. I., & Cordias, T. A. (1994). Childhood sexual abuse and bulimia nervosa: A comparison of American, Austrian, and Brazilian women. *American Journal of Psychiatry, 151,* 732–737.

Pope, H. G., & Yurgelun-Todd, D. (1996). The residual cognitive effects of heavy marijuana use in college students. *Journal of the American Medical Association, 275,* 521–527.

Pope John Paul II (1996, October 22). Magisterium is concerned with question of evolution for it involves conception of man. Message to Pontifical Academy of Sciences (www.cin.org/jp2evolu.html).

Popenoe, D. (1993). The evolution of marriage and the problem of stepfamilies: A biosocial perspective. Paper presented at the National Symposium on Stepfamilies, Pennsylvania State University.

Porac, C., Coren, S., & Duncan, P. (1980). Life-span age trends in laterality. *Journal of Gerontology, 35,* 715–721.

Porkka-Heiskanen, T., Strecker, R. E., Thakkar, M., Bjorkum, A. A., Greene, R. W., & McCarley, R. W. (1997). Adenosine: A mediator of the sleep-inducing effects of prolonged wakefulness. *Science, 276*, 1265–1268.

Porter, D., & Neuringer, A. (1984). Music discriminations by pigeons. *Journal of Experimental Psychology: Animal Behavior Processes, 10*, 138–148.

Porter, R. P. (1998). Twisted tongues: The failure of bilingual education. The Communitarian Network (www.gwu.edu/~ccps/pop_biling.html).

Posavac, H. D., Posavac, S. S., & Posavac, E. J. (1998). Exposure to media images of female attractiveness and concern with body weight among young women. *Sex Roles, 38*, 187–201.

Posner, M. I., & Carr, T. H. (1992). Lexical access and the brain: Anatomical constraints on cognitive models of word recognition. *American Journal of Psychology, 105*, 1–26.

Posner, M. I., & Raichle, M. E. (1998). The neuroimaging of human brain function. *Proceedings of the National Academy of Sciences, 95*, 763–764.

Povinelli, D. J. (1999). Social understanding in chimpanzees: New evidence from a longitudinal approach. In P. D. Zelazo, J. W. Astington, & D. R. Olson (Eds.), *Developing theories of intention: Social understanding and self-control.* Mahwah, NJ: Erlbaum.

Powell, J. (1989). *Happiness is an inside job.* Valencia, CA: Tabor.

Powell, K. E., Thompson, P. D., Caspersen, C. J., & Kendrick, J. S. (1987). Physical activity and the incidence of coronary heart disease. *Annual Review of Public Health, 8*, 253–287.

Powell, M. C., & Fazio, R. H. (1984). Attitude accessibility as a function of repeated attitudinal expression. *Personality and Social Psychology Bulletin, 10*, 139–148.

Powell, R. A., & Boer, D. P. (1994). Did Freud mislead patients to confabulate memories of abuse? *Psychological Reports, 74*, 1283–1298.

Prairie Home Companion. (1999). *The Prairie Home Companion's Pretty Good Joke Book* (Vol. 4). St. Paul, MN: Prairie Home Companion.

Pratkanis, A. R. (1992). The cargo-cult science of subliminal persuasion. *Skeptical Inquirer, 16*, 260–272.

Pratkanis, A. R., Eskenazi, J., & Greenwald, A. G. (1994). What you expect is what you believe (but not necessarily what you get): A test of the effectiveness of subliminal self-help audiotapes. *Basic and Applied Social Psychology, 15*, 251–276.

Pratkanis, A. R., & Greenwald, A. G. (1988). Recent perspectives on unconscious processing: Still no marketing applications. *Psychology and Marketing, 5*, 337–353.

Pratt, L. A., Ford, D. E., Crum, R. M., Armenian, H. K., Gallo, J. J., & Eaton, W. W. (December 15, 1994). Depression, psychotropic medication, and risk of myocardial infarction. Prospective data from the Baltimore ECA follow-up. *Circulation (DAW), 94*(12), 3123–3129.

Pratto, F. (1996). Sexual politics: The gender gap in the bedroom, the cupboard, and the cabinet. In D. M. Buss & N. M. Malamuth (Eds.), *Sex, power, conflict: Evolutionary and feminist perspectives.* New York: Oxford University Press.

PRB. (1998). *Women of our world, 1998.* Population Reference Bureau (www.prb.org/pubs/women98.htm).

Prentice, D. A., & Miller, D. T. (1993). Pluralistic ignorance and alcohol use on campus: Some consequences of misperceiving the social norm. *Journal of Personality and Social Psychology, 64*, 243–256.

Prescott, C. A., Hewitt, J. K., Truett, K. R., Heath, A. C., Neale, M. C., & Eaves, L. J. (1994, March). Genetic and environmental influences on lifetime alcohol-related problems in a volunteer sample of older twins. *Journal of Studies on Alcohol,* pp. 184–202.

Presley, C. A., Meilman, P. W., & Lyerla, R. (1997). *Alcohol and drugs on American college campuses: Issues of violence and harrassment.* Carbondale, IL: Core Institute, Southern Illinois University.

Presson, P. K., & Benassi, V. A. (1996). Locus of control orientation and depressive symptomatology: A meta-analysis. *Journal of Social Behavior and Personality, 11*, 201–212.

Prevention. (1995, March 6). Prevention index survey by *Prevention* magazine, summarized by Associated Press (in *Grand Rapids Press,* p. A1).

Prioleau, L., Murdock, M., & Brody, N. (1983). An analysis of psychotherapy versus placebo studies. *The Behavioral and Brain Sciences, 6*, 275–310.

Pritchard, R. M. (1961, June). Stabilized images on the retina. *Scientific American,* pp. 72–78.

Project Match Research Group. (1997). Matching alcoholism treatments to client heterogeneity: Project MATCH posttreatment drinking outcomes. *Journal of Studies on Alcohol, 58*, 7–29.

Project on Redefining the Meaning and Purpose of Baccalaureate Degrees. (1985). *Integrity in the college curriculum.* Washington, DC: Association of American Colleges.

Public Opinion. (1984, August/September). Phears and phobias. P. 32.

Public Opinion. (1987, May/June). Teen angels (report of University of Michigan survey). P. 32.

Pugh, G. E. (1977). *The biological origin of human values.* New York: Basic Books.

Putnam, F. W. (1991). Recent research on multiple personality disorder. *Psychiatric Clinics of North America, 14*, 489–502.

Putnam, F. W. (1995). Rebuttal of Paul McHugh. *Journal of the American Academy of Child and Adolescent Psychiatry, 34*, 963.

Putnam, R. (2000). *Bowling alone.* New York: Simon & Schuster.

Pyszczynski, T., Hamilton, J. C., Greenberg, J., & Becker, S. E. (1991). Self-awareness and psychological dysfunction. In C. R. Snyder & D. O. Forsyth (Eds.), *Handbook of social and clinical psychology: The health perspective.* New York: Pergamon.

Qualls, P. J., & Sheehan, P. W. (1981). Electromyograph biofeedback as a relaxation technique: A critical appraisal and reassessment. *Psychological Bulletin, 90*, 21–42.

Quasha, S. (1980). *Albert Einstein: An intimate portrait.* New York: Forest.

Quinn, G. E., Shin, C. H., Maguire, M. G., & Stone, R. A. (1999). Myopia and ambient lighting at night. *Nature, 399*, 113.

Quittner, A. L., Smith, L. B., Osberger, M. J., Mitchell, T. V., & Katz, D. B. (1994). The impact of audition on the development of visual attention. *Psychological Science, 5*, 347–353.

Rabin, A. S., Kaslow, N. J., & Rehm, L. P. (1986). Aggregate outcome and follow-up results following self-control therapy for depression. Paper presented at the American Psychological Association convention.

Radford, B. (1999, March/April). The ten-percent myth. *Skeptical Inquirer,* pp. 52–54.

Raglin, J. S. (1992). Anxiety and sport performance. In J. O. Holloszy (Ed.), *Exercise and sports sciences reviews* (Vol. 20). Baltimore: Williams & Wilkins.

Raine, A. (1999). Murderous minds: Can we see the mark of Cain? *Cerebrum: The Dana Forum on Brain Science 1*(1), 15–29.

Raine, A., Brennan, P., Mednick, B., & Mednick, S. A. (1996). High rates of violence, crime, academic problems, and behavioral problems in males with both early neuromotor deficits and unstable family environments. *Archives of General Psychiatry, 53,* 544–549.

Rajecki, D. W., Bledsoe, S. B., & Rasmussen, J. L. (1991). Successful personal ads: Gender differences and similarities in offers, stipulations, and outcomes. *Basic and Applied Social Psychology, 12,* 457–469.

Ramey, C. T., & Ramey, S. L. (1998). Early intervention and early experience. *American Psychologist, 53,* 109–120.

Ramey, S. L., & Ramey, C. T. (1992). Early educational intervention with disadvantaged children—To what effect? *Applied and Preventive Psychology, 1,* 131–140.

Rand, C. S. W., & Macgregor, A. M. C. (1990). Morbidly obese patients' perceptions of social discrimination before and after surgery for obesity. *Southern Medical Journal, 83,* 1390–1395.

Randi, J. (1999, February 4). 2000 Club mailing list e-mail letter.

Rapoport, J. L. (1989, March). The biology of obsessions and compulsions. *Scientific American,* pp. 83–89.

Raskin, D. C. (1982). University of Utah, as shown in *Science '82,* June, 24–27.

Rauch, S. L., & Jenike, M. A. (1993). Neurobiological models of obsessive-compulsive disorder. *Psychomatics, 34,* 20–32.

Ray, O., & Ksir, C. (1990). *Drugs, society, and human behavior* (5th ed.). St. Louis: Times Mirror/Mosby.

Reason, J. (1987). The Chernobyl errors. *Bulletin of the British Psychological Society, 40,* 201–206.

Reason, J., & Mycielska, K. (1982). *Absent-minded? The psychology of mental lapses and everyday errors.* Englewood Cliffs, NJ: Prentice-Hall.

Redburn, B. G., Gensheimer, L. K., & Gist, R. (1993). Disaster aftermath: Social support among resilient rescue workers. Paper presented at the Fourth Biennial Conference on Community Research and Action, Division 27, American Psychological Association, Williamsburg, VA.

Redelmeier, D. A., & Tversky, D. A. (1996). On the belief that arthritis pain is related to the weather. *Proceedings of the National Academy of Sciences, 93,* 2895–2896.

Reed, T. E., & Jensen, A. R. (1992). Conduction velocity in a brain nerve pathway of normal adults correlates with intelligence level. *Intelligence, 16,* 259–272.

Reeve, C. (1995). ABC *20/20,* October 6, 1995, and Associated Press report, October 17, 1995 (in *Holland Sentinel,* p. A12).

Regeth, R., & Lewis, M. (1995). Sex differences in depression: A meta-analysis. Paper presented at the American Psychological Society convention.

Regier, D. A., Kaelber, C. T., Rae, D. S., Farmer, M. E., Knauper, B., Kessler, R. C., & Norquist, G. S. (1998). Limitations of diagnostic criteria and assessment instruments for mental disorders: Implications for research and policy. *Archives of General Psychiatry, 55,* 109–115.

Regier, D. A., Narrow, W. E., Rae, D. S., Manderscheid, R. W., Locke, B. Z., & Goodwin, F. K. (1993). The de facto U.S. mental and addictive disorders service system: Epidemiologic catchment area prospective 1-year prevalence rates of disorders and services. *Archives of General Psychiatry, 50,* 85–94.

Reichman, J. (1998). *I'm not in the mood: What every woman should know about improving her libido.* New York: Morrow.

Reisenzein, R. (1983). The Schachter theory of emotion: Two decades later. *Psychological Bulletin, 94,* 239–264.

Reiser, M. (1982). *Police psychology.* Los Angeles: LEHI.

Relman, A. S. (1998, December 14). A trip to stonesville. *New Republic* (www.thenewrepublic.com).

Remafedi, G. (1999). Suicide and sexual orientation: Nearing the end of controversy? *Archives of General Psychiatry, 56,* 885–886.

Remley, A. (1988, October). From obedience to independence. *Psychology Today,* pp. 56–59.

Renner, M. J. (1992). Curiosity and exploration. In L. R. Squire (Ed.), *Encyclopedia of learning and memory.* New York: Macmillan.

Renner, M. J., & Renner, C. H. (1993). Expert and novice intuitive judgments about animal behavior. *Bulletin of the Psychonomic Society, 31,* 551–552.

Renner, M. J., & Rosenzweig, M. R. (1987). *Enriched and impoverished environments: Effects on brain and behavior.* New York: Springer-Verlag.

Rescorla, R. A., & Wagner, A. R. (1972). A theory of Pavlovian conditioning: Variations in the effectiveness of reinforcement and nonreinforcement. In A. H. Black & W. F. Perokasy (Eds.), *Classical conditioning II: Current theory.* New York: Appleton-Century-Crofts.

Resnick, M. D., Bearman, P. S., Blum, R. W., Bauman, K. E., Harris, K. M., Jones, J., Tabor, J., Beuhring, T., Sieving, R., Shew, M., Bearinger, L. H., & Udry, J. R. (1997). Protecting adolescents from harm: Findings from the National Longitudinal Study on Adolescent Health. *Journal of the American Medical Association, 278,* 823–832.

Resnick, S. M. (1992). Positron emission tomography in psychiatric illness. *Current Directions in Psychological Science, 1,* 92–98.

Resnick, S. M., Metter, E. J., & Zonderman, A. B. (1997). Estrogen replacement therapy and longitudinal decline in visual memory: A possible protective effect? *Neurology, 49,* 1491–1497.

Responsive Community. (1996, Fall). Age vs. weight (reported from a *Wall Street Journal* survey). Page 83.

Ressler, R. K., Burgess, A. W., & Douglas, J. E. (1988). *Sexual homicide patterns.* Boston: Lexington Books.

Retterstol, N. (1993). *Suicide: A European perspective.* New York: Cambridge University Press.

Reveen, P. J. (1987–88). Fantasizing under hypnosis: Some experimental evidence. *The Skeptical Inquirer, 12,* 181–183.

Reynolds, D. K. (1982). *The quiet therapies.* Honolulu: University of Hawaii Press.

Reynolds, D. K. (1986). *Even in summer the ice doesn't melt: Japan's Morita therapy.* New York: Morrow.

Rhodes, G., Sumich, A., & Byatt, G. (1999). Are average facial configurations attractive only because of their symmetry? *Psychological Science, 10,* 52–58.

Rhodes, S. R. (1983). Age-related differences in work attitudes and behavior: A review and conceptual analysis. *Psychological Bulletin, 93,* 328–367.

Rice, B. (1985, September). Performance review: The job nobody likes. *Psychology Today,* pp. 30–36.

Rice, M. E., & Grusec, J. E. (1975). Saying and doing: Effects on observer performance. *Journal of Personality and Social Psychology, 32,* 584–593.

Richardson, J. (1993). The curious case of coins: Remembering the appearance of familiar objects. *The Psychologist: Bulletin of the British Psychological Society, 6,* 360–366.

Richardson, J. T. E. (1990). Questionnaire studies of paramenstrual symptoms. *Psychology of Women Quarterly, 14,* 15–42.

Richardson, J. T. E. (1993). The premenstrual syndrome: A brief history. Paper presented to the Annual Conference of the British Psychological Society.

Richardson, J. T. E., & Zucco, G. M. (1989). Cognition and olfaction: A review. *Psychological Bulletin, 105,* 352–360.

Ridge, R. D., & Reber, J. S. (1998). *Women's responses to men's flirtations in a professional setting: Implications for sexual harassment.* Paper presented at the annual meeting of the American Psychological Society, Washington, DC.

Rieff, P. (1979). *Freud: The mind of a moralist* (3rd ed.). Chicago: University of Chicago Press.

Ring, K. (1980). *Life at death: A scientific investigation of the near-death experience.* New York: Coward, McCann & Geoghegan.

Ripple, C. H., Gilliam, W. S., Chanana, N., & Zigler, E. (1999). Will fifty cooks spoil the broth? The debate over entrusting Head Start to the states. *American Psychologist, 54,* 327–343.

Riskind, J. H., Beck, A. T., Berchick, R. J., Brown, G., & Steer, R. A. (1987). Reliability of DSM-III diagnoses for major depression and generalized anxiety disorder using the structured clinical interview for DSM-III. *Archives of General Psychiatry, 44,* 817–820.

Roberts, A. H., Kewman, D. G., Mercier, L., & Hovell, M. (1993). The power of nonspecific effects in healing: Implications for psychosocial and biological treatments. *Clinical Psychology Review, 13,* 375–391.

Roberts, B. W. (1997). Plaster or plasticity: Are adult work experiences associated with personality change in women? *Journal of Personality, 65,* 205–232.

Roberts, B. W., & DelVecchio, W. F. (2000). The rank-order consistency of personality traits from childhood to old age: A quantitative review of longitudinal studies. *Psychological Bulletin, 126,* 3–25.

Roberts, L. (1988). Beyond Noah's ark: What do we need to know? *Science, 242,* 1247.

Roberts, T-A. (1991). Determinants of gender differences in responsiveness to others' evaluations. *Dissertation Abstracts International, 51*(8-B).

Robins, L., & Regier, D. (Eds.). (1991). *Psychiatric disorders in America.* New York: Free Press.

Robins, L. N., Davis, D. H., & Goodwin, D. W. (1974). Drug use by U.S. Army enlisted men in Vietnam: A follow-up on their return home. *American Journal of Epidemiology, 99,* 235–249.

Robins, R. W., Gosling, S. D., & Craik, K. H. (1999). An empirical analysis of trends in psychology. *American Psychologist, 54,* 117–128.

Robinson, J. L., Kagan, J., Reznick, J. S., & Corley, R. (1992). The heritability of inhibited and uninhibited behavior: A twin study. *Developmental Psychology, 28,* 1030–1037.

Robinson, T. N. (1999). Reducing children's television viewing to prevent obesity. *Journal of the American Medical Association, 282,* 1561–1567.

Robinson, V. M. (1983). Humor and health. In P. E. McGhee & J. H. Goldstein (Eds.), *Handbook of humor research: Vol. II. Applied studies.* New York: Springer-Verlag.

Robison, L. (1999). Why our MENTALLY ILL son is on DEATH ROW. www.swuuc.org/fjuuc/Courier/robison.htm. See also www.larryrobison.org

Rochat, F. (1993). How did they resist authority? Protecting refugees in Le Chambon during World War II. Paper presented at the American Psychological Association convention.

Rock, I., Hall, S., & Davis, J. (1994). Why do ambiguous figures reverse? *Acta Psychologica, 87,* 33–57.

Rock, I., & Palmer, S. (1990, December). The legacy of Gestalt psychology. *Scientific American,* pp. 84–90.

Rodin, J. (1979). *Obesity theory and behavior therapy: An uneasy couple?* Paper presented at the meeting of the Association for the Advancement of Behavior Therapy.

Rodin, J. (1984, December). A sense of control [interview]. *Psychology Today,* pp. 38–45.

Rodin, J. (1985). Insulin levels, hunger and food intake: An example of feedback loops in body weight regulation. *Health Psychology, 4,* 1–18.

Rodin, J. (1986). Aging and health: Effects of the sense of control. *Science, 233,* 1271–1276.

Rodin, J., & Slochower, J. (1976). Externality in the non-obese: Effects of environmental responsiveness on weight. *Journal of Personality and Social Psychology, 33,* 338–344.

Rodin, M. (1992). The social construction of premenstrual syndrome. *Social Science and Medicine, 35,* 49–56.

Rodriguez, E., George, N., Lachaux, J-P., Martinerie, J., Renault, B., & Varela, F. J. (1999). Perception's shadow: Long-distance synchronization of human brain activity. *Nature, 297,* 430–433.

Roediger, H. L., III, & McDermott, K. B. (1995). Creating false memories: Remembering words not presented in lists. *Journal of Experimental Psychology: Learning, Memory, and Cognition, 21,* 803–814.

Roediger, H. L., III, Wheeler, M. A., & Rajaram, S. (1993). Remembering, knowing, and reconstructing the past. In D. L. Medin (Ed.), *The psychology of learning and motivation: Advances in research and theory* (Vol. 30). Orlando, FL: Academic Press.

Roehling, M. V. (2000). Weight-based discrimination in employment: Psychological and legal aspects. *Personnel Psychology, 52* (4), 969–1016.

Roesser, R. (1998). What you should know about hearing conservation. Better Hearing Institute (www.betterhearing.org).

Rogers, C. R. (1958). Reinhold Niebuhr's *The self and the dramas of history:* A criticism. *Pastoral Psychology, 9,* 15–17.

Rogers, C. R. (1961). *On becoming a person: A therapist's view of psychotherapy.* Boston: Houghton Mifflin.

Rogers, C. R. (1980). *A way of being.* Boston: Houghton Mifflin.

Rogers, C. R. (1981). Notes on Rollo May. *Perspectives, 2*(1), 16.

Rogers, S. (1992–1993, Winter). How a publicity blitz created the myth of subliminal advertising. *Public Relations Quarterly,* pp. 12–17.

Rogers, S. (1994). Subliminal advertising: Grand scam of the 20th century. Paper presented to the American Academy of Advertising convention.

Rogerson, P. A. (1994). On the relationship between handedness and longevity. *Social Biology, 40,* 283–287.

Rohan, M. J., & Zanna, M. P. (1996). Value transmission in families." In C. Seligman, J. M. Olson, & M. P. Zanna (Eds.), *The psychology of values: The Ontario Symposium* (Vol. 8). Malwah, NJ: Erlbaum.

Rohner, R. P. (1986). *The warmth dimension: Foundations of parental acceptance-rejection theory.* Newbury Park, CA: Sage.

Rohner, R. P. (1994). Patterns of parenting: The warmth dimension in worldwide perspective. In W. J. Lonner & R. Malpass (Eds.), *Psychology and culture.* Boston: Allyn & Bacon.

Rook, K. S. (1984). Promoting social bonding: Strategies for helping the lonely and socially isolated. *American Psychologist, 39,* 1389–1407.

Rook, K. S. (1987). Social support versus companionship: Effects on life stress, loneliness, and evaluations by others. *Journal of Personality and Social Psychology, 52,* 1132–1147.

Root, J. (1999). Focused on faith. *Ouachita Circle* (alumni magazine of Ouachita Baptist University), *2,* 2–7.

Rorty, M., Yager, J., & Rossotto, E. (1994). Childhood sexual, physical, and psychological abuse in bulimia nervosa. *American Journal of Psychiatry, 151,* 1122–1126.

Rosa, L., Rosa, E., Sarner, L., & Barrett, S. (1998). A close look at therapeutic touch. *Journal of the American Medical Association, 279,* 1005–1010.

Rosch, E. (1974). Linguistic relativity. In A. Silverstein (Ed.), *Human communication: Theoretical perspectives.* New York: Halsted Press.

Rosch, E. (1978). Principles of categorization. In E. Rosch & B. L. Lloyd (Eds.), *Cognition and categorization.* Hillsdale, NJ: Erlbaum.

Rose, J. S., Chassin, L., Presson, C. C., & Sherman, S. J. (1999). Peer influences on adolescent cigarette smoking: A prospective sibling analysis. *Merrill-Palmer Quarterly, 45,* 62–84.

Rose, S. A., & Feldman, J. F. (1997). Memory and speed: Their role in the relation of infant information processing to later IQ. *Child Development, 68,* 630–641.

Rosen, G. M., & Lohr, J. (1997, March). Can eye movements cure mental ailments? *Skeptical Briefs,* p. 12.

Rosen, R. C., & Leiblum, S. R. (1995). Treatment of sexual disorders in the 1990s: An integrated approach. *Journal of Consulting and Clinical Psychology, 63,* 877–890.

Rosenbaum, M. (1986). The repulsion hypothesis: On the nondevelopment of relationships. *Journal of Personality and Social Psychology, 51,* 1156–1166.

Rosenhan, D. L. (1973). On being sane in insane places. *Science, 179,* 250–258.

Rosenthal, E. (1999, January 24). Suicides reveal bitter roots of China's rural life. *New York Times* (www.nytimes.com).

Rosenthal, R., Hall, J. A., Archer, D., DiMatteo, M. R., & Rogers, P. L. (1979). The PONS test: Measuring sensitivity to nonverbal cues. In S. Weitz (Ed.), *Nonverbal communication* (2nd ed.). New York: Oxford University Press.

Rosenzweig, M. R. (1984). Experience, memory, and the brain. *American Psychologist, 39,* 365–376.

Rosenzweig, M. R. (1992). Psychological science around the world. *American Psychologist, 47,* 718–722.

Rosenzweig, M. R. (1999). Continuity and change in the development of psychology around the world. *American Psychologist, 54,* 252–259.

Ross, H. (1975, June 19). Mist, murk, and visual perception. *New Scientist,* pp. 658–660.

Ross, L., Greene, D., & House, P. (1977). The false consensus effect: An egocentric bias in social perception and attribution process. *Journal of Experimental Social Psychology, 13,* 279–301.

Ross, L., & Stillinger, C. (1991). Barriers to conflict resolution. *Negotiation Journal, 7,* 389–404.

Ross, M. (1996). Validating memories. In N. L. Stein, P. A. Ornstein, B. Tversky, & C. Brainerd (Eds.), *Memory for everyday and emotional events.* Hillsdale, NJ: Erlbaum.

Ross, M., McFarland, C., & Fletcher, G. J. O. (1981). The effect of attitude on the recall of personal histories. *Journal of Personality and Social Psychology, 40,* 627–634.

Rossi, A. S., & Rossi, P. H. (1993). *Of human bonding: Parentchild relations across the life course.* Hawthorne, NY: Aldine de Gruyter.

Rossi, P. J. (1968). Adaptation and negative aftereffect to lateral optical displacement in newly hatched chicks. *Science, 160,* 430–432.

Roth, T., Roehrs, T., Zwyghuizen-Doorenbos, A., Stpeanski, E., & Witting, R. (1988). Sleep and memory. In I. Hindmarch & H. Ott (Eds.), *Benzodiazepine receptor ligans, memory and information processing.* New York: Springer-Verlag.

Rothbart, M., Fulero, S., Jensen, C., Howard, J., & Birrell, P. (1978). From individual to group impressions: Availability heuristics in stereotype formation. *Journal of Experimental Social Psychology, 14,* 237–255.

Rothbaum, B. O., Hodges, L. F., Kooper, R., Opdyke, D., Williford, J., & North, M. M. (1995). Effectiveness of computer-generated (virtual reality) graded exposure in the treatment of acrophobia. *American Journal of Psychiatry, 152,* 626–628.

Rothbaum, B. O., Hodges, L., & Kooper, R. (1997). Virtual reality exposure therapy. *Journal of Psychotherapy Practice and Research, 6,* 219–226.

Rothbaum, F., & Tsang, B. Y-P. (1998). Love songs in the United States and China: On the nature of romantic love. *Journal of Cross-Cultural Psychology, 29,* 306–319.

Rothbaum, F., & Xu, X. (1995). The theme of giving back to parents in Chinese and American songs. *Journal of Cross-Cultural Psychology, 26,* 698–713.

Rothblum, E. D. (1990). Women and weight: Fad and fiction. *Journal of Psychology, 124,* 5–24.

Rothman, A. J., & Salovey, P. (1997). Shaping perceptions to motivate healthy behavior: The role of message framing. *Psychological Bulletin, 121,* 3–19.

Rothstein, W. G. (1980). The significance of occupations in work careers: An empirical and theoretical review. *Journal of Vocational Behavior, 17,* 328–343.

Rovee-Collier, C. (1989). The joy of kicking: Memories, motives, and mobiles. In P. R. Solomon, G. R. Goethals, C. M. Kelley, & B. R. Stephens (Eds.), *Memory: Interdisciplinary approaches.* New York: Springer-Verlag.

Rovee-Collier, C. (1993). The capacity for long-term memory in infancy. *Current Directions in Psychological Science, 2,* 130–135.

Rovee-Collier, C. (1997). Dissociations in infant memory: Rethinking the development of implicit and explicit memory. *Psychological Review, 104,* 467–498.

Roviaro, S., Holmes, D. S., & Holmsten, R. D. (1984). Influence of a cardiac rehabilitation program on the cardiovascular, psychological, and social functioning of cardiac patients. *Journal of Behavioral Medicine, 7*, 61–81.

Rowe, D. C. (1990). As the twig is bent? The myth of child-rearing influences on personality development. *Journal of Counseling and Development, 68*, 606–611.

Rowe, D. C. (1997). A place at the policy table? Behavior genetics and estimates of family environmental effects on IQ. *Intelligence, 24*, 133–158.

Rowe, D. C., Almeida, D. M., & Jacobson, K. C. (1999). School context and genetic influences on aggression in adolescence. *Psychological Science, 10*, 277–280.

Rowe, D. C., Jacobson, K. C., & Van den Oord, E. J. C. G. (1999). Genetic and environmental influences on vocabulary IQ: Parental education level as moderator. *Child Development, 70*(5), 1151–1162.

Rowe, D. C., Vazsonyi, A. T., & Flannery, D. J. (1994). No more than skin deep: Ethnic and racial similarity in developmental process. *Psychological Review, 101*(3), 396.

Rowe, D. C., Vazsonyi, A. T., & Flannery, D. J. (1995). Ethnic and racial similarity in developmental process: A study of academic achievement. *Psychological Science, 6*, 33–38.

Roy, M-A., Neale, M. C., Pedersen, N. L., Mathe, A. A., & Kendler, K. S. (1995). A twin study of generalized anxiety disorder and major depression. *Psychological Medicine, 25*, 1037–1049.

Rozin, P. (1976). The selection of food by rats, humans and other animals. In J. Rosenblatt, R. A. Hinde, C. Beer, & E. Shaw (Eds.), *Advances in the study of behavior* (Vol. 6). New York: Academic Press.

Rozin, P., Dow, S., Mosovitch, M., & Rajaram, S. (1998). What causes humans to begin and end a meal? A role for memory for what has been eaten, as evidenced by a study of multiple meal eating in amnesic patients. *Psychological Science, 9*, 392–396.

Rozin, P., Millman, L., & Nemeroff, C. (1986). Operation of the laws of sympathetic magic in disgust and other domains. *Journal of Personality and Social Psychology, 50*, 703–712.

Ruback, R. B., Carr, T. S., & Hopper, C. H. (1986). Perceived control in prison: Its relation to reported crowding, stress, and symptoms. *Journal of Applied Social Psychology, 16*, 375–386.

Rubin, D. C., Rahhal, T. A., & Poon, L. W. (1998). Things learned in early adulthood are remembered best. *Memory and Cognition, 26*, 3–19.

Rubin, J. Z., Pruitt, D. G., & Kim, S. H. (1994). *Social conflict: Escalation, stalemate, and settlement.* New York: McGraw-Hill.

Rubin, L. B. (1985). *Just friends: The role of friendship in our lives.* New York: Harper & Row.

Rubin, Z. (1970). Measurement of romantic love. *Journal of Personality and Social Psychology, 16*, 265–273.

Rubonis, A. V., & Bickman, L. (1991). Psychological impairment in the wake of disaster: The disaster-psychopathology relationship. *Psychological Bulletin, 109*, 384–399.

Ruchlis, H. (1990). *Clear thinking: A practical introduction.* Buffalo, NY: Prometheus Books.

Ruffin, C. L. (1993). Stress and health—little hassles vs. major life events. *Australian Psychologist, 28*, 201–208.

Rule, B. G., & Ferguson, T. J. (1986). The effects of media violence on attitudes, emotions, and cognitions. *Journal of Social Issues, 42*(3), 29–50.

Rumbaugh, D. M. (1977). *Language learning by a chimpanzee: The Lana project.* New York: Academic Press.

Rumbaugh, D. M. (1994, February 15). Remarks on *Nova: Can chimps talk?* PBS Television.

Rumbaugh, D. M., & Savage-Rumbaugh, S. (1978). Chimpanzee language research: Status and potential. *Behavior Research Methods & Instrumentation, 10*, 119–131.

Rumbaugh, D. M., & Savage-Rumbaugh, S. (1994, January/February). Language and apes. *Psychology Teacher Network,* pp. 2–5, 9.

Rumelhart, D. E. (1989). The architecture of mind: A connectionist approach. In M. Posner (Ed.), *Foundations of cognitive science.* Cambridge, MA: MIT Press.

Rupp, R. (1998). *How we remember and why we forget.* New York: Three Rivers Press.

Rushton, J. P. (1975). Generosity in children: Immediate and long-term effects of modeling, preaching, and moral judgment. *Journal of Personality and Social Psychology, 31*, 459–466.

Rushton, J. P. (1990). Race differences, r/K theory, and a reply to Flynn. *The Psychologist: Bulletin of the British Psychological Society, 5*, 195–198.

Rushton, J. P., & Ankney, C. D. (1996). Brain size and cognitive ability: Correlations with age, sex, social class, and race. *Psychonomic Bulletin & Review, 3*, 21–36.

Russell, B. (1930/1985). *The conquest of happiness.* London: Unwin Paperbacks.

Russell, J. A., & Carroll, J. M. (January, 1999). On the bipolarity of positive and negative affect. *Psychological Bulletin 125*(1), 3–30.

Russell, J. A., & Carroll, J. M. (1999). The phoenix of bipolarity: Reply to Watson and Tellegan (1999). *Psychological Bulletin, 125*, 611–617.

Russell, J. A., Lewicka, M., & Niit, T. (1989). A cross-cultural study of a circumplex model of affect. *Journal of Personality and Social Psychology, 57*, 848–856.

Russian scientists. (1999). Science needs to combat pseudoscience: A statement by 32 Russian scientists and philosophers. *Skeptical Inquirer,* pp. 37–38. Reprinted from *Izvestiya,* July 17, 1998.

Rusting, C. L., & Nolen-Hoeksema, S. (1998). Regulating responses to anger: Effects of rumination and distraction on angry mood. *Journal of Personality and Social Psychology, 74*, 790–803.

Rutter, M., and the English and Romanian Adoptees (ERA) study team. (1998). Developmental catch-up, and deficit, following adoption after severe global early privation. *Journal of Child Psychology and Psychiatry, 39*, 465–476.

Rutter, M. L. (1997). Nature-nurture integration: The example of antisocial behavior. *American Psychologist, 52*, 390–398.

Ryan, E. D. (1980). Attribution, intrinsic motivation, and athletics: A replication and extension. In C. H. Nadeau, W. R. Halliwell, K. M. Newell, & G. C. Roberts (Eds.), *Psychology of motor behavior and sport—1979.* Champaign, IL: Human Kinetics Press.

Ryan, R. (1999, February 2). Quoted in Alfie Kohn, In pursuit of affluence, at a high price. *New York Times* (www.nytimes.com).

Ryckman, R. M., Robbins, M. A., Kaczor, L. M., & Gold J. A. (1989). Male and female raters' stereotyping of male and female physiques. *Personality and Social Psychology Bulletin, 15*, 244–251.

Rymer, R. (1993). *Genie: An abused child's flight from silence.* New York: HarperCollins.

Rzewnicki, R., & Forgays, D. G. (1987). Recidivism and self-cure of smoking and obesity: An attempt to replicate. *American Psychologist, 42,* 97–100.

Sabini, J. (1986). Stanley Milgram (1933–1984). *American Psychologist, 41,* 1378–1379.

Sabol, S. Z., Nelson, M. L., Fisher, C., Gunzerath, L., Brody, C. L., Hu, S., Sirota, L. A., Marcus, S. E., Greenberg, B. D., Lucas, F. R., IV, Benjamin, J., Murphy, D. L., & Hamer, D. H. (1999). A genetic association for cigarette smoking behavior. *Health Psychology, 18,* 7–13.

Sachdev, P., & Sachdev, J. (1997). Sixty years of psychosurgery: Its present status and its future. *Australian and New Zealand Journal of Psychiatry, 31,* 457–464.

Sacks, O. (1985). *The man who mistook his wife for a hat.* New York: Summit Books.

Sacks, O. (1990). *Seeing voices: A journey into the world of the deaf.* New York: HarperCollins.

Sacks, O. (1995, January 9). Prodigies. *New Yorker,* pp. 44–65.

Sadato, N., Pascual-Leone, A., Grafman, J., Ibanez, V., Deiber, M-P., Dold, G., & Hallett, M. (1996). Activation of the primary visual cortex by Braille reading in blind subjects. *Nature, 380,* 526–528.

Saffran, J. R., Aslin, R. N., & Newport, E. L. (1996). Statistical learning by 8-month-old infants. *Science, 274,* 1926–1928.

Sagan, C. (1979). *Broca's brain.* New York: Random House.

Sagan, C. (1987, February 1). The fine art of baloney detection. *Parade.*

Sagan, C., & Druyan, A. (1992). *Shadows of forgotten ancestors: A search for who we are.* New York: Random House.

Sakurai, T., Amemiya, A., Ishii, M., Matsuzaki, I., Chemelli, R. M., Tanaka, H., Williams, S. C., Richardson, J. A., Kozlowski, G. P., Wilson, S., Arch, J. R. S., Buckingham, R. E., Haynes, A. C., Carr, S. A., Annan, R. S., McNulty, D. E., Liu, W-S., Terrett, J. A., Elshourbagy, N. A., Bergsma, D. J., & Yanagisawa, M. (1998). Orexins and orexin receptors: A family of hypothalamic neuropeptides and G protein-coupled receptors that regulate feeding behavior. *Cell, 92,* 573–585.

Salive, M. E., Guralnik, J. M., & Glynn, R. J. (1993). Left-handedness and mortality. *American Journal of Public Health, 83,* 265–267.

Salovey, P. (1990, January/February). Interview. *American Scientist,* pp. 25–29.

Salovey, P., & Birnbaum, D. (1989). Influence of mood on health-relevant cognitions. *Journal of Personality and Social Psychology, 57,* 539–551.

Samuels, J., & Nestadt, G. (1997). Epidemiology and genetics of obsessive-compulsive disorder. *International Review of Psychiatry, 9,* 61–71.

Samuels, S., & McCabe, G. (1989). Quoted in P. Diaconis & F. Mosteller, Methods for studying coincidences. *Journal of the American Statistical Association, 84,* 853–861.

Sanchez, R. D., Contri, G. B., & Pardo, I. Q. (1996). Spanish psychologists on the labor market. In A. Schorr & S. Saari (Eds.), *Psychology in Europe: Facts, figures, realities.* Gottingen: Hogrefe & Huber.

Sandberg, G. G., Jackson, T. L., & Petretic-Jackson, P. (1985). Sexual aggression and courtship violence in dating relationships.

Paper presented at the meeting of the Midwestern Psychological Association.

Sanders, G., & Wright, M. (1997). Sexual orientation differences in cerebral asymmetry and in the performance of sexually dimorphic cognitive and motor tasks. *Archives of Sexual Behavior, 26,* 463–479.

Sanes, J., Donoghue, J., Thangaraj, V., Edelman, R. R., & Warach, S. (1995). Shared neural substrates controlling hand movements in human motor cortex. *Science, 269,* 1775–1777.

Sanz, C., Blicher, A., Dalke, K., Gratton-Fabri, L., McClure-Richards, T., & Fouts, R. (1998, Winter-Spring). Enrichment object use: Five chimpanzees' use of temporary and semi-permanent enrichment objects. *Friends of Washoe, 19*(1,2), 9–14.

Sapadin, L. A. (1988). Friendship and gender: Perspectives of professional men and women. *Journal of Social and Personal Relationships, 5,* 387–403.

Sapolsky, B. S., & Tabarlet, J. O. (1991). Sex in primetime television: 1979 versus 1989. *Journal of Broadcasting and Electronic Media, 35,* 505–516.

Sapolsky, R. (1999, March). Stress and your shrinking brain. *Discover,* pp. 116–120.

Sapolsky, R. M., & Finch, C. E. (1991, March/April). On growing old. *The Sciences,* pp. 30–38.

Sartorius, N. R. (1994). Description of WHO's mental health programme. In W. J. Lonner & R. Malpass (Eds.), *Psychology and culture.* Boston: Allyn & Bacon.

Sato, K. (1987). Distribution of the cost of maintaining common resources. *Journal of Experimental Social Psychology, 23,* 19–31.

Savage-Rumbaugh, E. S., Murphy, J., Sevcik, R. A., Brakke, K. E., Williams, S. L., & Rumbaugh, D. M., with commentary by Bates, E. (1993). Language comprehension in ape and child. *Monographs of the Society for Research in Child Development, 58* (no. 233), 1–254.

Savoy, C., & Beitel, P. (1996). Mental imagery for basketball. *International Journal of Sport Psychology, 27,* 454–462.

Sax, L. J., Astin, A. W., Korn, W. S., & Mahoney, K. M. (1996). *The American freshman: National norms for fall 1996.* Los Angeles: Higher Education Research Institute, UCLA.

Sax, L. J., Astin, A. W., Korn, W. S., & Mahoney, K. M. (1999). *The American freshman: National norms for fall 1999.* Los Angeles: Higher Education Research Institute, UCLA.

Saxe, L. (1994). Detection of deception: Polygraph and integrity tests. *Current Directions in Psychological Science, 3,* 69–73.

Sayre, R. F. (1979). The parents' last lessons. In D. D. Van Tassel (Ed.), *Aging, death, and the completion of being.* Philadelphia: University of Pennsylvania Press.

Scarr, S. (1986). *Mother care/other care.* New York: Basic Books.

Scarr, S. (1989). Protecting general intelligence: Constructs and consequences for interventions. In R. J. Linn (Ed.), *Intelligence: Measurement, theory, and public policy.* Champaign: University of Illinois Press.

Scarr, S. (1990). Back cover comments on J. Dunn & R. Plomin, *Separate lives: Why siblings are so different.* New York: Basic Books.

Scarr, S. (1993, May/June). Quoted in *Psychology Today,* Nature's thumbprint: So long, superparents. P. 16.

Scarr, S. (1997). Why child care has little impact on most children's development. *Current Directions in Psychological Science, 6,* 143–148.

Scarr, S. (1998). American child care today. *American Psychologist, 53,* 95–108.

Scarr, S., Phillips, D., & McCartney, K. (1990). Facts, fantasies and the future of child care in the United States. *Psychological Science, 1,* 26–35.

Schab, F. R. (1991). Odor memory: Taking stock. *Psychological Bulletin, 109,* 242–251.

Schachter, S. (1982). Recidivism and self-cure of smoking and obesity. *American Psychologist, 37,* 436–444.

Schachter, S., & Singer, J. E. (1962). Cognitive, social and physiological determinants of emotional state. *Psychological Review, 69,* 379–399.

Schacter, D. L. (1992). Understanding implicit memory: A cognitive neuroscience approach. *American Psychologist, 47,* 559–569.

Schacter, D. L. (1996). *Searching for memory: The brain, the mind, and the past.* New York: Basic Books.

Schacter, D. L. (1999). The seven sins of memory: Insights from psychology and cognitive neuroscience. *American Psychologist, 54,* 182–201.

Schafran, L. H. (1995, August 26). Rape is still underreported. *New York Times,* p. I19.

Schaie, K. W. (1987). Old dogs can learn new tricks: Intellectual decline and its remediation in later adulthood. Address to the Eastern Psychological Association convention.

Schaie, K. W. (1994). The life course of adult intellectual abilities. *American Psychologist, 49,* 304–313.

Schaie, K. W., & Geiwitz, J. (1982). *Adult development and aging.* Boston: Little, Brown.

Scheerer, M. (1963, April). Problem solving. *Scientific American,* pp. 118–128.

Scheiber, B., & Selby, C. (1997, May-June). UAB final report of therapeutic touch—An appraisal. *Skeptical Inquirer, 21,* 53–54.

Scheier, M. F., & Carver, C. S. (1992). Effects of optimism on psychological and physical well-being: Theoretical overview and empirical update. *Cognitive Therapy and Research, 16,* 201–228.

Schein, E. H. (1956). The Chinese indoctrination program for prisoners of war: A study of attempted brainwashing. *Psychiatry, 19,* 149–172.

Schelling, T. C. (1992). Addictive drugs: The cigarette experience. *Science, 255,* 430–433.

Schiavi, R. C., & Schreiner-Engel, P. (1988). Nocturnal penile tumescence in healthy aging men. *Journal of Gerontology: Medical Sciences, 43,* M146–M150.

Schiffenbauer, A., & Schiavo, R. S. (1976). Physical distance and attraction: An intensification effect. *Journal of Experimental Social Psychology, 12,* 274–282.

Schkade, D. A., & Kahneman, D. (1998). Does living in California make people happy? A focusing illusion in judgments of life satisfaction. *Psychological Science, 9,* 340–346.

Schlaug, G., Jancke, L., Huang, Y., & Steinmetz, H. (1995). In vivo evidence of structural brain asymmetry in musicians. *Science, 267,* 699–701.

Schleifer, S. J., Keller, S. E., McKegney, F. P., & Stein, M. (1979). The influence of stress and other psychosocial factors on human immunity. Paper presented at the 36th Annual Meeting of the American Psychosomatic Society.

Schlesinger, A. M., Jr. (1965). *A thousand days.* Boston: Houghton Mifflin.

Schmidt, F. L., & Hunter, J. E. (1998). The validity and utility of selection methods in personnel psychology: Practical and theoretical implications of 85 years of research findings. *Psychological Bulletin, 124,* 262–274.

Schmidt, G., Klusmann, D., Zeitzschel, U., & Lange, C. (1994). Changes in adolescents' sexuality between 1970 and 1990 in West-Germany. *Archives of Sexual Behavior, 23,* 489–513.

Schmidtke, A. (1997). Perspective: Suicide in Europe. *Suicide and Life-Threatening Behavior, 27,* 127–136.

Schnaper, N. (1980). Comments germane to the paper entitled "The reality of death experiences" by Ernst Rodin. *Journal of Nervous and Mental Disease, 168,* 268–270.

Schneiderman, N. (1999). Behavioral medicine and the management of HIV/AIDS. *International Journal of Behavioral Medicine, 6,* 3–12.

Schneiderman, N., Chesney, M. A., & Krantz, D. S. (1989). Biobehavioral aspects of cardiovascular disease: Progress and prospects. *Health Psychology, 8,* 649–676.

Schnitzer, B. (1984, May). Repunctuated message. *Games,* pp. 57, 62.

Schoeneman, T. J. (1994). *Individualism.* In V. S. Ramachandran (Ed.), *Encyclopedia of human behavior.* San Diego: Academic Press.

Schoenfeld, B. (1995, May 14). The loneliness of being white. *New York Times Magazine,* 34–37. .

Schofield, J. W. (1986). Black-white contact in desegregated schools. In M. Hewstone & R. Brown (Eds.), *Contact and conflict in intergroup encounters.* Oxford: Basil Blackwell.

Schonfield, D., & Robertson, B. A. (1966). Memory storage and aging. *Canadian Journal of Psychology, 20,* 228–236.

Schooler, C., Neumann, E., Caplan, L. J., & Roberts, B. R. (1997). A time course analysis of Stroop interference and facilitation: Comparing normal individuals and individuals with schizophrenia. *Journal of Experimental Psychology: General, 126,* 19–36.

Schooler, J. W., Gerhard, D., & Loftus, E. F. (1986). Qualities of the unreal. *Journal of Experimental Psychology: Learning, Memory, and Cognition, 12,* 171–181.

Schuckit, M. A., & Smith, T. L. (1996, March). An 8-year follow-up of 450 sons of alcoholic and control subjects. *Archives of General Psychiatry, 53,* 202–210.

Schulenberg, J., Bachman, J. G., O'Malley, P. M., & Johnston, L. D. (March, 1994). High school educational success and subsequent substance use: A panel analysis following adolescents into young adulthood. *Journal of Health and Social Behavior, 35*(1), 45–62.

Schuman, H., & Scott, J. (June, 1989). Generations and collective memories. *American Sociological Review, 54*(3), 359–381.

Schwartz, B. (1984). *Psychology of learning and behavior* (2nd ed.). New York: Norton.

Schwartz, J., & Pomfret, J. (1998, November 20). Smoking-related deaths in China are up sharply. *Washington Post* (www.washingtonpost.com).

Schwartz, J. E., Friedman, H. S., Tucker, J. S., Tomlinson-Keasey, C., Wingard, D. L., & Criqui, M. H. (1995). Sociodemographic and psychosocial factors in childhood as predictors of adult mortality. *American Journal of Public Health, 85,* 1237–1245.

Schwartz, J. M., Stoessel, P. W., Baxter, L. R., Jr., Martin, K. M., & Phelps, M. E. (1996). Systematic changes in cerebral glucose metabolic rate after successful behavior modification treatment of obsessive-compulsive disorder. *Archives of General Psychiatry, 53,* 109–113.

Schwarz, N., & Clore, G. L. (1983). Mood, misattribution, and judgments of well-being: Informative and directive functions of affective states. *Journal of Personality and Social Psychology, 45,* 513–523.

Schwarz, N., Strack, F., Kommer, D., & Wagner, D. (1987). Soccer, rooms, and the quality of your life: Mood effects on judgments of satisfaction with life in general and with specific domains. *European Journal of Social Psychology, 17, 69–79.*

Sclafani, A. (1995). How food preferences are learned: Laboratory animal models. *Proceedings of the Nutrition Society, 54,* 419–427.

Scott, W. A., Scott, R., & McCabe, M. (1991). Family relationships and children's personality: A cross-cultural, cross-source comparison. *British Journal of Social Psychology, 30,* 1–20.

Sechrest, L., Stickle, T. R., & Stewart, M. (1998). The role of assessment in clinical psychology. In A. Bellack, M. Hersen (Series eds.), & C. R. Reynolds (Vol. ed.), *Comprehensive clinical psychology: Vol 4: Assessment.* New York: Pergamon.

Seeman, P., Guan, H-C., & Van Tol, H. H. M. (1993). Dopamine D4 receptors elevated in schizophrenia. *Nature, 365,* 441–445.

Segal, N. L. (1999). *Entwined lives: Twins and what they tell us about human behavior.* New York: Dutton.

Segall, M. H., Dasen, P. R., Berry, J. W., & Poortinga, Y. H. (1990). *Human behavior in global perspective: An introduction to cross-cultural psychology.* New York: Pergamon.

Segerstrom, S. C., McCarthy, W. J., Caskey, N. H., Gross, T. D., & Jarvik, M. E. (1993). Optimistic bias among cigarette smokers. *Journal of Applied Social Psychology, 23,* 1606–1618.

Segerstrom, S. C., Taylor, S. E., Kemeny, M. E., & Fahey, J. L. (1998). Optimism is associated with mood, coping, and immune change in response to stress. *Journal of Personality and Social Psychology, 74,* 1646–1655.

Seidenberg, M. S. (1997). Language acquisition and use: Learning and applying probabilistic constraints. *Science, 275,* 1599–1603.

Seidlitz, L., & Diener, E. (1998). Sex differences in the recall of affective experiences. *Journal of Personality and Social Psychology, 74,* 262–271.

Seiff, E. M., Dawes, R. M., Loewenstein, G. (1999, Summer). Anticipated versus actual reaction to HIV test results. *American Journal of Psychology, 112*(2), 297–311.

Seligman, M. E. P. (1974, May). Submissive death: Giving up on life. *Psychology Today,* pp. 80–85.

Seligman, M. E. P. (1975). *Helplessness: On depression, development and death.* San Francisco: Freeman.

Seligman, M. E. P. (1988, October). Boomer blues. *Psychology Today,* pp. 50–55.

Seligman, M. E. P. (1989). Explanatory style: Predicting depression, achievement, and health. In M. D. Yapko (Ed.), *Brief therapy approaches to treating anxiety and depression.* New York: Brunner/Mazel.

Seligman, M. E. P. (1991). *Learned optimism.* New York: Knopf.

Seligman, M. E. P. (1994). *What you can change and what you can't.* New York: Knopf.

Seligman, M. E. P. (1995). The effectiveness of psychotherapy: The *Consumer Reports* study. *American Psychologist, 50,* 965–974.

Seligman, M. E. P. (1998a, January). Building human strength: Psychology's forgotten mission. *APA Monitor* (www.apa.org).

Seligman, M. E. P. (1998b, April). Positive social science. *APA Monitor* (www.apa.org).

Seligman, M. E. P., & Schulman, P. (1986). Explanatory style as a predictor of productivity and quitting among life insurance sales agents. *Journal of Personality and Social Psychology, 50,* 832–838.

Seligman, M. E. P., & Yellen, A. (1987). What is a dream? *Behavior Research and Therapy, 25,* 1–24.

Selye, H. (1936). A syndrome produced by diverse nocuous agents. *Nature, 138,* 32.

Selye, H. (1976). *The stress of life.* New York: McGraw-Hill.

Serdula, M. K., Mokdad, A., Williamson, D. F., Galuska, D. A., Mendlein, J. M., & Heath, G. W. (1999). Prevalence of attempting weight loss and strategies for controlling weight. *Journal of the American Medical Association, 282,* 1353–1358.

Service, R. F. (1994). Will a new type of drug make memory-making easier? *Science, 266,* 218–219.

Seto, M. C., & Barbaree, H. E. (1995). The role of alcohol in sexual aggression. *Clinical Psychology Review, 15,* 545–566.

Shadish, W. R., Montgomery, L. M., Wilson, P., Wilson, M. R., Bright, I., & Okwumabua, T. (1993). Effects of family and marital psychotherapies: A meta-analysis. *Journal of Consulting and Clinical Psychology, 61,* 992–1002.

Shamir, B., House, R. J., & Arthur, M. B. (1993). The motivational effects of charismatic leadership: A self-concept based theory. *Organizational Science, 4*(4), 577–594.

Shanahan, T. L., Kronauer, R. E., Duffy, J. F., Williams, G. H., & Czeisler, C. A. (June, 1999). Melatonin rhythm observed throughout a three-cycle bright-light stimulus designed to reset the human circadian pacemaker. *Journal of Biological Rhythms, 14*(3), 237–253.

Shapiro, F. (1989). Efficacy of the eye movement desensitization procedure in the treatment of traumatic memories. *Journal of Traumatic Stress, 2,* 199–223.

Shapiro, F. (1995). *Eye movement desensitization and reprocessing: Basic principles, protocols, and procedures.* New York: Guilford.

Shapiro, F. (1999). Eye movement desensitization and reprocessing (EMDR) and the anxiety disorders: Clinical and research implications of an integrated psychotherapy treatment. *Journal of Anxiety Disorders, 13,* 35–67.

Sharley, J. (1999, July 2). Beholding beauty: Scholars nip and tuck at our quest for physical perfection. *Chronicle of Higher Education,* pp. A15–A16.

Sharma, A. R., McGue, M. K., & Benson, P. L. (1998). The psychological adjustment of United States adopted adolescents and their nonadopted siblings. *Child Development, 69,* 791–802.

Shaughnessy, J., & Zechmeister, E. (1992). Memory monitoring accuracy as influenced by the distribution of retrieval practice. *Bulletin of the Psychonomic Society, 30,* 125–128.

Shaver, P. R., & Hazan, C. (1993). Adult romantic attachment: Theory and evidence. In D. Perlman & W. Jones (Eds.), *Advances in personal relationships* (Vol. 4). Greenwich, CT: JAI.

Shaver, P. R., Morgan, H. J., & Wu, S. (1996). Is love a basic emotion? *Personal Relationships, 3,* 81–96.

Shaw, H. L. (1989–90). Comprehension of the spoken word and ASL translation by chimpanzees (Pan troglodytes). *Friends of Washoe, 9*(1/2), 8–19.

Shaywitz, B. A., Shaywitz, S. E., Pugh, K. R., Constable, R. T., & Skudlarski, P. (1995). Sex differences in the functional organization of the brain for language. *Nature, 373,* 607–609.

Shaywitz, S. E., Shaywitz, B. A., Pugh, K. R., Fulbright, R. K., Skudlarksi, P., Mencl, W. E., Constable, R. T., Naftolin, F., Palter, S. F., Marchione, K. E., Katz, L., Shankweiler, D. P., Fletcher, J. M., Lacadie, C., Keltz, M., & Gore, J. C. (1999). Effect of estrogen on brain activation patterns in postmenopausal women during working memory tasks. *Journal of the American Medical Association, 281,* 1197–1202.

Shea, M. T., Elkin, I., Imber, S. D., Sotsky, S. M., Watkins, J. T., Collins, J. F., Pilkonis, P. A., Beckham, E., Glass, D. R., Dolan, R. T., & Parloff, M. B. (1992). Course of depressive symptoms over follow-up: Findings from the National Institute of Mental Health Treatment of Depression Collaborative Research Program. *Archives of General Psychiatry, 49,* 782–787.

Sheehan, S. (1982). *Is there no place on earth for me?* Boston: Houghton Mifflin.

Sheldon, W. H. (1954). *Atlas of man: A guide for somatotyping the adult male of all ages.* New York: Harper & Row.

Shenon, P. (1994, May 15). The world: Asia's having one huge nicotine fit. *New York Times,* 4, p. 1.

Shenton, M. E. (1992). Abnormalities of the left temporal lobe and thought disorder in schizophrenia: A quantitative magnetic resonance imaging study. *New England Journal of Medicine, 327,* 604–612.

Shepard, R. N. (1981). Psychophysical complementarity. In M. Kubovy & J. R. Pomerantz (Eds.), *Perceptual organization.* Hillsdale, NJ: Erlbaum.

Shepard, R. N. (1990). *Mind sights.* New York: Freeman.

Shepherd, C. (1997, April). News of the weird. *Funny Times,* p. 15.

Shepherd, C. (1999, June). News of the wierd. *Funny Times,* p. 21.

Shepherd, C., Kohut, J. J., & Sweet, R. (1990). *More news of the weird.* New York: Penguin/Plume Books.

Sheridan, E. P. (1999). Psychology's future in medical schools and academic health care centers. *American Psychologist, 54,* 267–271.

Sherif, M. (1966). *In common predicament: Social psychology of intergroup conflict and cooperation.* Boston: Houghton Mifflin.

Sherry, D., & Vaccarino, A. L. (1989). Hippocampus and memory for food caches in black-capped chickadees. *Behavioral Neuroscience, 103,* 308–318.

Shettleworth, S. J. (1973). Food reinforcement and the organization of behavior in golden hamsters. In R. A. Hinde & J. Stevenson-Hinde (Eds.), *Constraints on learning.* London: Academic Press.

Shettleworth, S. J. (1993). Where is the comparison in comparative cognition? Alternative research programs. *Psychological Science, 4,* 179–184.

Shneidman, E. (1987, March). At the point of no return. *Psychology Today,* pp. 54–58.

Shobe, K. K., & Kihlstrom, J. F. (June, 1997). Is traumatic memory special? *Current Directions in Psychological Science, 6*(3), 70–74.

Shotland, R. L. (1984, March 12). Quoted in Maureen Dowd, 20 years after the murder of Kitty Genovese, the question remains: Why? *New York Times,* p. B1.

Shotland, R. L. (1989). A model of the causes of date rape in developing and close relationships. In C. Hendrick (Ed.), *Review of personality and social psychology* (Vol. 10). Newbury Park, CA: Sage.

Showers, C. (1992). The motivational and emotional consequences of considering positive or negative possibilities for an upcoming event. *Journal of Personality and Social Psychology, 63,* 474–484.

Siegel, J. M. (1990). Stressful life events and use of physician services among the elderly: The moderating role of pet ownership. *Journal of Personality and Social Psychology, 58,* 1081–1086.

Siegel, R. K. (1977, October). Hallucinations. *Scientific American,* pp. 132–140.

Siegel, R. K. (1980). The psychology of life after death. *American Psychologist, 35,* 911–931.

Siegel, R. K. (1984, March 15). Personal communication.

Siegel, R. K. (1990). *Intoxication.* New York: Pocket Books.

Siegel, R. K. (1982, October). Quoted in J. Hooper, Mind tripping. *Omni,* pp. 72–82, 159–160.

Siegler, R. S., & Ellis, S. (1996). Piaget on childhood. *Psychological Science, 7,* 211–215.

Silva, A. J., Stevens, C. F., Tonegawa, S., & Wang, Y. (1992). Deficient hippocampal long-term potentiation in alpha-calcium-calmodulin kinase II mutant mice. *Science, 257,* 201–206.

Silva, C. E., & Kirsch, I. (1992). Interpretive sets, expectancy, fantasy proneness, and dissociation as predictors of hypnotic response. *Journal of Personality and Social Psychology, 63,* 847–856.

Silver, M., & Geller, D. (1978). On the irrelevance of evil: The organization and individual action. *Journal of Social Issues, 34,* 125–136.

Silverman, I., & Eals, M. (1992). Sex differences in spatial abilities: Evolutionary theory and data. In J. H. Barkow, L. Cosmides, & J. Tooby (Eds.), *The adapted mind: Evolutionary psychology and the generation of culture.* New York: Oxford University Press.

Silverman, I., & Phillips, K. (1998). The evolutionary psychology of spatial sex differences. In C. Crawford & D. L. Krebs (Eds.), *Handbook of evolutionary psychology: Ideas, issues, and applications.* Mahwah, NJ: Erlbaum.

Silverman, K., Evans, S. M., Strain, E. C., & Griffiths, R. R. (1992). Withdrawal syndrome after the double-blind cessation of caffeine consumption. *New England Journal of Medicine, 327,* 1109–1114.

Silverman, P. S., & Retzlaff, P. D. (1986). Cognitive stage regression through hypnosis: Are earlier cognitive stages retrievable? *International Journal of Clinical and Experimental Hypnosis, 34,* 192–204.

Simek, T. C., & O'Brien, R. M. (1981). *Total golf: A behavioral approach to lowering your score and getting more out of your game.* Huntington, NY: B-MOD Associates.

Simek, T. C., & O'Brien, R. M. (1988). A chaining-mastery, discrimination training program to teach Little Leaguers to hit a baseball. *Human Performance, 1,* 73–84.

Simon, H. (1998, November 16). Flash of genius (interview with P. E. Ross). *Forbes,* pp. 98–104.

Simonton, D. K. (1988). Age and outstanding achievement: What do we know after a century of research? *Psychological Bulletin, 104,* 251–267.

Simonton, D. K. (1990). Creativity in the later years: Optimistic prospects for achievement. *The Gerontologist, 30,* 626–631.

Simonton, D. K. (1992). The social context of career success and course for 2,026 scientists and inventors. *Personality and Social Psychology Bulletin, 18,* 452–463.

Simonton, D. K. (1994). *Greatness: Who makes history and why.* New York: Guilford Press.

Simpson, J. A., Rholes, W. S., & Nelligan, J. S. (1992). Support seeking and support giving within couples in an anxiety-provoking situation: The role of attachment styles. *Journal of Personality and Social Psychology, 62,* 434–446.

Sinclair, R. C., Hoffman, C., Mark, M. M., Martin, L. L., & Pickering, T. L. (1994). Construct accessibility and the misattribution of arousal: Schachter and Singer revisited. *Psychological Science, 5,* 15–18.

Singelis, T. M., Bond, M. H., Sharkey, W. F., & Lai, C. S. Y. (1999). Unpackaging culture's influence on self-esteem and embarrassability: The role of self-construals. *Journal of Cross-Cultural Psychology, 30,* 315–341.

Singelis, T. M., & Sharkey, W. F. (1995). Culture, self-construal, and embarrassability. *Cross-Cultural Psychology, 26,* 622–644.

Singer, J. L. (1975). Navigating the stream of consciousness: Research in daydreaming and related inner experience. *American Psychologist, 30,* 727–738.

Singer, J. L. (1976, July). Fantasy: The foundation of serenity. *Psychology Today,* pp. 32–37.

Singer, J. L. (1981). Clinical intervention: New developments in methods and evaluation. In L. T. Benjamin, Jr. (Ed.), *The G. Stanley Hall Lecture Series* (Vol. 1). Washington, DC: American Psychological Association.

Singer, J. L. (1986). Is television bad for children? *Social Science, 71,* 178–182.

Singer, J. L., & Singer, D. G. (1986). Family experiences and television viewing as predictors of children's imagination, restlessness, and aggression. *Journal of Social Issues, 42(3),* 7–28.

Singh, D. (1993). Adaptive significance of female physical attractiveness: Role of waist-to-hip ratio. *Journal of Personality and Social Psychology, 65,* 293–307.

Singh, D. (1995). Female health, attractiveness, and desirability for relationships: Role of breast asymmetry and waist-to-hip ratio. *Ethology and Sociobiology, 16,* 465–481.

Singh, S. (1998). *Fermat's enigma: The epic quest to solve the world's greatest mathematical problem.* New York: Bantam Books.

Sipski, M. L., & Alexander, C. J. (1999). Sexual response in women with spinal cord injuries: Implications for our understanding of the able bodied. *Journal of Sex and Marital Therapy, 25,* 11–22.

Sireteanu, R. (1999). Switching on the infant brain. *Science, 286,* 59, 61.

Sivard, R. L. (1995). *Women . . . a world survey,* 2nd ed. Washington, DC: World Priorities.

Sivard, R. L. (1996). *World military and social expenditures 1996,* 16th edition. Washington, DC: World Priorities.

Sjostrom, L. (1980). Fat cells and body weight. In A. J. Stunkard (Ed.), *Obesity.* Philadelphia: Saunders.

Skevington, S. M., & White, A. (1998). Is laughter the best medicine? *Psychology and Health, 13(1),* 157.

Skinner, B. F. (1957). *Verbal behavior.* Englewood Cliffs, NJ: Prentice-Hall.

Skinner, B. F. (1983, September). Origins of a behaviorist. *Psychology Today,* pp. 22–33.

Skinner, B. F. (1985). *Cognitive science and behaviorism.* Unpublished manuscript, Harvard University.

Skinner, M., & Mullen, B. (1991). Facial asymmetry in emotional expression: A meta-analysis of research. *British Journal of Social Psychology, 30,* 113–124.

Sklar, L. S., & Anisman, H. (1981). Stress and cancer. *Psychological Bulletin, 89,* 369–406.

Skoog, G., & Skoog, I. (1999). A 40-year follow-up of patients with obsessive-compulsive disorder. *Archives of General Psychiatry, 56,* 121–127.

Skov, R. B., & Sherman, S. J. (1986). Information-gathering processes: Diagnosticity, hypothesis-confirmatory strategies, and perceived hypothesis confirmation. *Journal of Experimental Social Psychology, 22,* 93–121.

Slater, A. (1994, February 15). Personal correspondence.

Slater, A., Morison, V., & Somers, M. (1988). Orientation discrimination and cortical function in the human newborn. *Perception, 17,* 597–602.

Slavin, R. E. (1989). Cooperative learning and student achievement. In R. E. Slavin (Ed.), *School and classroom organization.* Hillsdale, NJ: Erlbaum.

Slavin, R. E., & Braddock, J. H., III (1993, Summer). Ability grouping: On the wrong track. *The College Board Review,* pp. 11–18.

Sloan, R. P., Bagiella, E., & Powell, T. (1999). Religion, spirituality, and medicine. *Lancet, 353,* 664–667.

Slovic, P. (1987). Perception of risk. *Science, 236,* 280–285.

Slovic, P., & Fischhoff, B. (1977). On the psychology of experimental surprises. *Journal of Experimental Psychology: Human Perception and Performance, 3,* 544–551.

Small, M. F. (1997). Making connections. *American Scientist, 85,* 502–504.

Small, M. F. (1999, March 30). Are we losers? Putting a mating theory to the test. *New York Times* (www.nytimes.com).

Smart, R. G., Adlaf, E. M., & Walsh, G. W. (1991). The Ontario student drug use survey: Trends between 1977 and 1991. Toronto: Addiction Research Foundation.

Smith, A. (1987). Personal communication.

Smith, A., & Sugar, O. (1975). Development of above normal language and intelligence 21 years after left hemispherectomy. *Neurology, 25,* 813–818.

Smith, K. H., & Rogers, M. (1994). Effectiveness of subliminal messages in television commercials: Two experiments. *Journal of Applied Psychology, 79,* 866–874.

Smith, M. B. (1978). Psychology and values. *Journal of Social Issues, 34,* 181–199.

Smith, M. L., & Glass, G. V. (1977). Meta-analysis of psychotherapy outcome studies. *American Psychologist, 32,* 752–760.

Smith, M. L., Glass, G. V., & Miller, R. L. (1980). *The benefits of psychotherapy.* Baltimore: Johns Hopkins University Press.

Smith, P. B., & Tayeb, M. (1989). Organizational structure and processes. In M. Bond (Ed.), *The cross-cultural challenge to social psychology.* Newbury Park, CA: Sage.

Smith, P. F. (1995). Cannabis and the brain. *New Zealand Journal of Psychology, 24,* 5–12.

Smith, S. B. (1999). *Diana in search of herself : Portrait of a troubled princess*. New York: Times Books.

Smith, S. M., McIntosh, W. D., & Bazzini, D. G. (1999). Are the beautiful good in Hollywood? An investigation of the beauty-and-goodness stereotype on film. *Basic and Applied Social Psychology, 21,* 69–80.

Smith, T. W. (1997). Personal correspondence. Data from the General Social Survey, National Opinion Research Center, University of Chicago.

Smith, T. W. (1998, December). American sexual behavior: Trends, socio-demographic differences, and risk behavior. National Opinion Research Center GSS Topical Report No. 25.

Smyth, J. M., Stone, A. A., Murewitz, A., & Kaell, A. (1999). Effects of writing about stressful experiences on symptom reduction in patients with asthma or rheumatoid arthritis: A randomized trial. *Journal of the American Medical Association, 281,* 1304–1309.

Snarey, J. (1987, June). A question of morality. *Psychology Today,* pp. 6–7.

Snarey, J. R. (1985). Cross-cultural universality of social-moral development: A critical review of Kohlbergian research. *Psychological Bulletin, 97,* 202–233.

Snodgrass, M. A. (1987). The relationships of differential loneliness, intimacy and characterological attributional style to duration of loneliness. *Journal of Social Behavior and Personality, 2,* 173–186.

Snodgrass, S. E., Higgins, J. G., & Todisco, L. (1986). The effects of walking behavior on mood. Paper presented at the American Psychological Association convention.

Snyder, C. R., & Lopez, S. J. (Eds.). (in press). *Handbook of positive psychology*. New York: Oxford University Press.

Snyder, F., & Scott, J. (1972). The psychophysiology of sleep. In N. S. Greenfield & R. A. Sterbach (Eds.), *Handbook of psychophysiology*. New York: Holt, Rinehart & Winston.

Snyder, M. (1984). When belief creates reality. In L. Berkowitz (Ed.), *Advances in experimental social psychology* (Vol. 18). New York: Academic Press.

Snyder, M., Tanke, E. D., & Berscheid, E. (1977). Social perception and interpersonal behavior: On the self-fulfilling nature of social stereotypes. *Journal of Personality and Social Psychology, 35,* 656–666.

Snyder, S. H. (1984). Neurosciences: An integrative discipline. *Science, 225,* 1255–1257.

Snyder, S. H. (1986). *Drugs and the brain*. New York: Scientific American Library.

Sobel, D. S. (1993). Mind matters, money matters. *Mental Medicine Update Special Report,* pp. 1–8.

Sokhadze, E. M., & Shtark, M. B. (1991). Scientific and clinical biofeedback in the USSR. *Biofeedback and Self-Regulation, 16,* 253–260.

Sokoll, G. R., & Mynatt, C. R. (1984). *Arousal and free throw shooting*. Paper presented at the meeting of the Midwestern Psychological Association.

Solomon, D. A., Keitner, G. I., Miller, I. W., Shea, M. T., & Keller, M. B. (1995). Course of illness and maintenance treatments for patients with bipolar disorder. *Journal of Clinical Psychiatry, 56,* 5–13.

Solomon, J. (1996, May 20). Breaking the silence. *Newsweek,* pp. 20–22.

Solomon, M. (1987, December). Standard issue. *Psychology Today,* pp. 30–31.

Solomon, R. L. (1980). The opponent-process theory of acquired motivation: The costs of pleasure and the benefits of pain. *American Psychologist, 35,* 691–712.

Solomon, Z. (1990). Does the war end when the shooting stops? The psychological toll of war. *Journal of Applied Social Psychology, 20,* 1733–1745.

Sommer, B. (1992). Cognitive performance and the menstrual cycle. In J. T. Richardson (Ed.), *Cognition and the menstrual cycle: Research, theory, and culture*. New York: Springer-Verlag.

Sommer, R. (1969). *Personal space*. Englewood Cliffs, NJ: Prentice-Hall.

Sonenstein, F. L. (1992). Condom use. *Science, 257,* 861.

Sontag, S. (1978). *Illness as metaphor*. New York: Farrar, Straus, & Giroux.

Sourcebook of Criminal Justice Statistics Online. (1998). Bureau of Justice Statistics (www.albany.edu/sourcebook).

Sowell, T. (1991, May/June). Cultural diversity: A world view. *American Enterprise,* pp. 44–55.

Spanos, N. P. (1982). A social psychological approach to hypnotic behavior. In G. Weary & H. L. Mirels (Eds.), *Integrations of clinical and social psychology*. New York: Oxford University Press.

Spanos, N. P. (1986). Hypnosis, nonvolitional responding, and multiple personality: A social psychological perspective. *Progress in Experimental Personality Research, 14,* 1–62.

Spanos, N. P. (1987–88). Past-life hypnotic regression: A critical view. *The Skeptical Inquirer, 12,* 174–180.

Spanos, N. P. (1991). Hypnosis, hypnotizability, and hypnotherapy. In C. R. Snyder & D. R. Forsyth (Eds.), *Handbook of social and clinical psychology: The health perspective*. New York: Pergamon Press.

Spanos, N. P. (1994). Multiple identity enactments and multiple personality disorder: A sociocognitive perspective. *Psychological Bulletin, 116,* 143–165.

Spanos, N. P. (1996). *Multiple identities and false memories: A sociocognitive perspective*. Washington, DC: American Psychological Association Books.

Spanos, N. P., Burgess, C. A., & Burgess, M. F. (1994). Past-life identities, UFO abductions, and Satanic ritual abuse: The social construction of memories. *International Journal of Clinical and Experimental Hypnosis, 42,* 433–446.

Spanos, N. P., & Coe, W. C. (1992). A social-psychological approach to hypnosis. In E. Fromm & M. R. Nash (Eds.), *Contemporary hypnosis research*. New York: Guilford.

Spanos, N. P., Radtke, L., & Bertrand, L. D. (1985). Hypnotic amnesia as a strategic enactment: Breaching amnesia in highly susceptible subjects. *Journal of Personality and Social Psychology, 47,* 1155–1169.

Spector, P. E. (1986). Perceived control by employees: A meta-analysis of studies concerning autonomy and participation at work. *Human Relations, 39,* 1005–1016.

Spencer, S. J., Steele, C. M., & Quinn, D. M. (1997). Stereotype threat and women's math performance. Unpublished manuscript, Hope College.

Sperling, G. (1960). The information available in brief visual presentations. *Psychological Monographs, 74* (Whole No. 498).

Sperry, R. W. (1956, May). The eye and the brain. *Scientific American,* pp. 48–52.

Sperry, R. W. (1964). Problems outstanding in the evolution of brain function. James Arthur Lecture, American Museum of Natural History, New York. Cited in R. Ornstein (1977), *The psychology of consciousness* (2nd ed.). New York: Harcourt Brace Jovanovich.

Sperry, R. W. (1982). Some effects of disconnecting the cerebral hemispheres. *Science, 217,* 1223–1226.

Sperry, R. W. (1985). Changed concepts of brain and consciousness: Some value implications. *Zygon, 20,* 41–57.

Sperry, R. W. (Summer, 1992). Turnabout on consciousness: A mentalist view. *Journal of Mind and Behavior, 13*(3), 259–280.

Spiegel, K., Leproult, R., & Van Cauter, E. (1999). Impact of sleep debt on metabolic and endrocrine function. *Lancet, 354,* 1435–1439.

Spielberger, C., & London, P. (1982). Rage boomerangs. *American Health, 1,* 52–56.

Spiess, W. F. J., Greer, J. H., & O'Donohue, W. T. (1984). Premature ejaculation: Investigation of factors in ejaculatory latency. *Journal of Abnormal Psychology, 93,* 242–245.

Spitzberg, B. H., & Hurt, H. T. (1987). The relationship of interpersonal competence and skill to reported loneliness across time. *Journal of Social Behavior and Personality, 2,* 157–172.

Spitzer, R. L. (1975). On pseudoscience in science, logic in remission, and psychiatric diagnosis: A critique of Rosenhan's "On being sane in insane places." *Journal of Abnormal Psychology, 84,* 442–452.

Spitzer, R. L. (1997). Brief comments from a psychiatric nosologist weary from his own attempts to define mental disorder: Why Ossorio's definition muddles and Wakefield's "harmful dysfunction" illuminates the issues. *Clinical Psychology Science and Practice, 4,* 259–266.

Spradley, J. P., & Phillips, M. (1972). Culture and stress: A quantitative analysis. *American Anthropologist, 74,* 518–529.

Sprecher, S. (1989). The importance to males and females of physical attractiveness, earning potential, and expressiveness in initial attraction. *Sex Roles, 21,* 591–607.

Sprecher, S., & Sedikides, C. (1993). Gender differences in perceptions of emotionality: The case of close heterosexual relationships. *Sex Roles, 28,* 511–530.

Spring, B., Chiodo, J., & Bowen, D. J. (1987). Carbohydrates, tryptophan, and behavior: A methodological review. *Psychological Bulletin, 102,* 234–256.

Spring, B., Pingitore, R., Bourgeois, M., Kessler, K. H., & Bruckner, E. (1992). The effects and non-effects of skipping breakfast: Results of three studies. Paper presented at the American Psychological Association convention.

Springer, S. P., & Deutsch, G. (1985). *Left brain, right brain.* San Francisco: Freeman.

Squire, L. R. (1987). *Memory and brain.* New York: Oxford University Press.

Squire, L. R. (1992). Memory and the hippocampus: A synthesis from findings with rats, monkeys, and humans. *Psychological Review, 99,* 195–231.

Squire, L., & Zola-Morgan, S. (1991). The medial temporal lobe memory system. *Science, 253,* 1380–1386.

Sroufe, L. A., Fox, N. E., & Pancake, V. R. (1983). Attachment and dependency in developmental perspective. *Child Development, 54,* 1615–1627.

Stack, S. (1992). Marriage, family, religion, and suicide. In R. Maris, A. Berman, J. Maltsberger, & R. Yufit (Eds.), *Assessment and prediction of suicide.* New York: Guilford Press.

Stanley, J. C. (1997). Varieties of intellectual talent. *Journal of Creative Behavior, 31,* 93–119.

Stanovich, K. (1996). *How to think straight about psychology.* New York: HarperCollins.

Staples, B. (1999a, May 2). When the "paranoids" turn out to be right. *New York Times* (www.nytimes.com).

Staples, B. (1999b, May 24). Why "racial profiling" will be tough to fight. *New York Times* (www.nytimes.com).

Statistics Canada. (1996). Control and sale of alcoholic beverages 1993/1994. www.statcan.ca/documents/English/MediaRel/Newprod/alcohol.htm.

Statistics Canada. (1999). *Statistical report on the health of Canadians.* Prepared by the Federal, Provincial and Territorial Advisory Committee on Population Health for the Meeting of Ministers of Health, Charlottetown, PEI, September 16–17, 1999.

Stattin, H., & Magnusson, D. (1990). *Pubertal maturation in female development.* Hillsdale, NJ: Erlbaum.

Staub, E. (1989). *The roots of evil: The psychological and cultural sources of genocide.* New York: Cambridge University Press.

Steadman, H. J., Mulvey, E. P., Monahan, J., Robbins, P. C., Appelbaum, P. S., Grisso, T., Roth, L. H., & Silver, E. (1998). Violence by people discharged from acute psychiatric inpatient facilities and by others in the same neighborhoods. *Archives of General Psychiatry, 55,* 393–401.

Steele, C. (1990a, May). A conversation with Claude Steele. *APS Observer,* pp. 11–17.

Steele, C. M. (1995, August 31). Black students live down to expectations. *New York Times.*

Steele, C. M. (1997). A threat in the air: How stereotypes shape intellectual identity and performance. *American Psychologist, 52,* 613–629.

Steele, C. M., & Aronson, J. (1996). Stereotype threat and the intellectual test performance of African Americans. *Journal of Personality and Social Psychology, 69,* 797–811.

Steele, C. M., & Josephs, R. A. (1990). Alcohol myopia: Its prized and dangerous effects. *American Psychologist, 45,* 921–933.

Stein, J. A., Newcomb, M. D., & Bentler, P. M. (1986). Stability and change in personality: A longitudinal study from early adolescence to young adulthood. *Journal of Research In Personality, 20,* 276–291.

Steinberg, L. (1987, September). Bound to bicker. *Psychology Today,* pp. 36–39.

Steinberg, N. (1993, February). Astonishing love stories (from an earlier United Press International report). *Games,* p. 47.

Steinem, G. (1988). Six great ideas that television is missing. In G. Comstock (Ed.), *Public communication and behavior.* New York: Academic Press.

Steinmetz, J. E. (1999). The localization of a simple type of learning and memory: The cerebellum and classical eyeblink conditioning. *Contemporary Psychology, 7,* 72–77.

Stellar, E. (1985). Hunger in animals and humans. Distinguished lecture to the Eastern Psychological Association convention.

Stengel, E. (1981). Suicide. In *The new encyclopaedia britannica, macropaedia* (Vol. 17, pp. 777–782). Chicago: Encyclopaedia Britannica.

Stephens, T. (1988). Physical activity and mental health in the United States and Canada: Evidence from four population surveys. *Preventive Medicine, 17,* 35–47.

Stepp, L. S. (1996, July 2). Universal goals: Family, achievement and dreams. *International Herald Tribune,* p. 2.

Stern, M., & Karraker, K. H. (1989). Sex stereotyping of infants: A review of gender labeling studies. *Sex Roles, 20,* 501–522.

Sternbach, H. (1998). Age-associated testosterone decline in men: Clinical issues for psychiatry. *American Journal of Psychiatry, 155,* 1310–1318.

Sternberg, R. J. (1988). Applying cognitive theory to the testing and teaching of intelligence. *Applied Cognitive Psychology, 2,* 231–255.

Sternberg, R. J. (1997). *Successful intelligence.* New York: Plume.

Sternberg, R. J. (1998). Principles of teaching for successful intelligence. *Educational Psychologist, 33,* 65–72.

Sternberg, R. J. (1999). The theory of successful intelligence. *Review of General Psychology, 3,* 292–316.

Sternberg, R. J., & Grajek, S. (1984). The nature of love. *Journal of Personality and Social Psychology, 47,* 312–329.

Sternberg, R. J., & Kaufman, J. C. (1998). Human abilities. *Annual Review of Psychology, 49,* 479–502.

Sternberg, R. J., & Lubart, T. I. (1991). An investment theory of creativity and its development. *Human Development,* 1–31.

Sternberg, R. J., & Lubart, T. I. (1992). Buy low and sell high: An investment approach to creativity. *Psychological Science, 1,* 1–5.

Sternberg, R. J., & Wagner, R. K. (1993). The g-ocentric view of intelligence and job performance is wrong. *Current Directions in Psychological Science, 2,* 1–5.

Sternberg, R. J., Wagner, R. K., Williams, W. M., & Horvath, J. A. (1995). Testing common sense. *American Psychologist, 50,* 912–927.

Stevenson, H. W. (1992, December). Learning from Asian schools. *Scientific American,* pp. 70–76.

Stevenson, H. W., & Lee, S-Y. (1990). Contexts of achievement: A study of American, Chinese, and Japanese children. *Monographs of the Society for Research in Child Development, 55* (Serial No. 221, Nos. 1–2).

Stice, E., & Shaw, H. E. (1994). Adverse effects of the media portrayed thin-ideal on women and linkages to bulimic symptomatology. *Journal of Social and Clinical Psychology, 13,* 288–308.

Stipek, D. (1992). The child at school. In M. H. Bornstein & M. E. Lamb (Eds.), *Developmental psychology: An advanced textbook.* Hillsdale, NJ: Erlbaum.

Stock, R. W. (1995, July 13). Reducing the risk for older drivers. *New York Times,* p. C1.

Stockton, M. C., & Murnen, S. K. (1992). Gender and sexual arousal in response to sexual stimuli: A meta-analytic review. Paper presented at the American Psychological Society convention.

Stone, A. A., Cox, D. S., Valdimarsdottir, H., Jandor, L., & Neale, J. M. (1987). Evidence that secretory IgA antibody is associated with daily mood. *Journal of Personality and Social Psychology, 52,* 988–993.

Stone, A. A., & Neale, J. M. (1984). Effects of severe daily events on mood. *Journal of Personality and Social Psychology, 46,* 137–144.

Stone, J., Perry, Z. W., & Darley, J. M. (1997). "White men can't jump": Evidence for the perceptual confirmation of racial stereotypes following a basketball game. *Basic and Applied Social Psychology, 19*(3), 291–306.

Stoolmiller, M. (1999). Implications of the restricted range of family environments for estimates of heritability and nonshared environment in behavior-genetic adoption studies. *Psychological Bulletin, 125,* 392–409.

Stoppard, J. M., & Gruchy, C. D. G. (1993). Gender, context, and expression of positive emotion. *Personality and Social Psychology Bulletin, 19,* 143–150.

Storms, M. D. (1973). Videotape and the attribution process: Reversing actors' and observers' points of view. *Journal of Personality and Social Psychology, 27,* 165–175.

Storms, M. D. (1981). A theory of erotic orientation development. *Psychological Review, 88,* 340–353.

Storms, M. D. (1983). *Development of sexual orientation.* Washington, DC: Office of Social and Ethical Responsibility, American Psychological Association.

Storms, M. D., & Thomas, G. C. (1977). Reactions to physical closeness. *Journal of Personality and Social Psychology, 35,* 412–418.

Strack, F., Martin, L., & Stepper, S. (1988). Inhibiting and facilitating conditions of the human smile: A nonobtrusive test of the facial feedback hypothesis. *Journal of Personality and Social Psychology, 54,* 768–777.

Strack, S., & Coyne, J. C. (1983). Social confirmation of dysphoria: Shared and private reactions to depression. *Journal of Personality and Social Behavior, 44,* 798–806.

Strange, S. L., & Forsyth, D. R. (1993). Long-term benefits of adolescent peer groups. Paper presented at the Eastern Psychological Association convention.

Stratton, G. M. (1986). Some preliminary experiments on vision without inversion of the retinal image. *Psychological Review, 3,* 611–617.

Straub, R. O., Seidenberg, M. S., Bever, T. G., & Terrace, H. S. (1979). Serial learning in the pigeon. *Journal of the Experimental Analysis of Behavior, 32,* 137–148.

Strauman, T. J., Vookles, J., Berenstein, V., Chaiken, S., & Higgins, E. T. (1991). Self-discrepancies and vulnerability to body dissatisfaction and disordered eating. *Journal of Personality and Social Psychology, 61,* 946–956.

Straus, M. A., & Gelles, R. J. (1980). *Behind closed doors: Violence in the American family.* New York: Anchor/Doubleday.

Straus, M. A., Sugarman, D. B., & Giles-Sims, J. (1997). Spanking by parents and subsequent antisocial behavior of children. *Archives of Pediatric Adolescent Medicine, 151,* 761–767.

Strawbridge, W. J. (1999). Mortality and religious involvement: A review and critique of the results, the methods, and the measures. Paper presented at a Harvard University conference on religion and health, sponsored by the National Instititue for Healthcare Research and the John Templeton Foundation.

Strawbridge, W. J., Cohen, R. D., & Shema, S. J. (1997). Frequent attendance at religious services and mortality over 28 years. *American Journal of Public Health, 87,* 957–961.

Streissguth, A. P. (1993). Fetal alcohol fact sheet. Fetal Alcohol & Drug Unit, University of Washington, School of Medicine.

Streissguth, A. P., Aase, J. M., Clarren, S. K., Randels, S. P., LaDue, R. A., & Smith, D. F. (1991). Fetal alcohol syndrome in adolescents and adults. *Journal of the American Medical Association, 265,* 1961–1967.

Strentz, H. (1986, January 1). Become a psychic and amaze your friends! *Atlanta Journal*, p. 15A.

Strickland, B. (1992, February 20). Gender differences in health and illness. Sigma Xi national lecture delivered at Hope College.

Striegel-Moore, R. H., Silberstein, L. R., & Rodin, J. (1986). Toward an understanding of risk factors for bulimia. *American Psychologist, 41*, 246–263.

Striegel-Moore, R. H., Silberstein, L. R., & Rodin, J. (1993). The social self in bulimia nervosa: Public self-consciousness, social anxiety, and perceived fraudulence. *Journal of Abnormal Psychology, 102*, 297–303.

Strunsky, S. (1999, September 2). DNA evidence secures release of man convicted of '82 rape. *New York Times* (www.nytimes.com).

Strupp, H. H. (1982). The outcome problem in psychotherapy: Contemporary perspectives. In J. H. Harvey & M. M. Parks (Eds.), *The master lecture series: Vol. 1. Psychotherapy research and behavior change.* Washington, DC: American Psychological Association.

Strupp, H. H. (1986). Psychotherapy: Research, practice, and public policy (How to avoid dead ends). *American Psychologist, 41*, 120–130.

Stuart, G. W., Day, R. H., & Dickinson, R. G. (November, 1984). Mueller-Lyer: Illusion of size or position? *Quarterly Journal of Experimental Psychology: Human Experimental Psychology, 36A*(4), 663–672.

Stumpf, H., & Jackson, D. N. (1994). Gender-related differences in cognitive abilities: Evidence from a medical school admissions testing program. *Personality and Individual Differences, 17*, 335–344.

Stumpf, H., & Stanley, J. C. (1998). Stability and change in gender-related differences on the College Board advanced placement and achievement tests. *Current Directions in Psychology, 7*, 192–196.

Stunkard, A. J., Harris, J. R., Pedersen, N. L., & McClearn, G. E. (1990). A separated twin study of the body mass index. *New England Journal of Medicine, 322*, 1483–1487.

Suddath, R. L., Christison, G. W., Torrey, E. F., Casanova, M. F., & Weinberger, D. R. (1990). Anatomical abnormalities in the brains of monozygotic twins discordant for schizophrenia. *New England Journal of Medicine, 322*, 789–794.

Sue, D. W. (1990). Culture-specific strategies in counseling: A conceptual framework. *Professional Psychology: Research and Practice, 21*, 424–433.

Suedfeld, P. (1980). *Restricted environmental stimulation: Research and clinical applications.* New York: Wiley.

Suedfeld, P., & Kristeller, J. L. (1982). Stimulus reduction as a technique in health psychology. *Health Psychology, 1*, 337–357.

Suedfeld, P., & Mocellin, J. S. P. (1987). The "sensed presence" in unusual environments. *Environment and Behavior, 19*, 33–52.

Suinn, R. M. (1997). Mental practice in sports psychology: Where have we been, Where do we go? *Clinical Psychology: Science and Practice.*

Suls, J. M., & Tesch, F. (1978). Students' preferences for information about their test performance: A social comparison study. *Journal of Experimental Social Psychology, 8*, 189–197.

Summers, M. (1996, December 9). Mister clean. *People Weekly*, pp. 139–142.

Sundstrom, E., De Meuse, K. P., & Futrell, D. (1990). Work teams: Applications and effectiveness. *American Psychologist, 45*, 120–133.

Suomi, S. J. (1986). Anxiety-like disorders in young nonhuman primates. In R. Gettleman (Ed.), *Anxiety disorders of childhood.* New York: Guilford Press.

Suomi, S. J. (1987). Genetic and maternal contributions to individual differences in rhesus monkey biobehavioral development. In N. A. Krasnegor & others (Eds.), *Perinatal development: A psychobiological perspective.* Orlando, FL: Academic Press.

Suppes, P. (1982). Quoted in R. H. Ennis, Children's ability to handle Piaget's propositional logic: A conceptual critique. In S. Modgil & C. Modgil (Eds.), *Jean Piaget: Consensus and controversy.* New York: Praeger.

Surgeon General. (1986). *The Surgeon General's workshop on pornography and public health,* June 22–24. Report prepared by E. P. Mulvey & J. L. Haugaard and released by Office of the Surgeon General on August 4, 1986.

Surgeon General. (1999). *Mental health: A report of the Surgeon General.* Rockville, MD: U.S. Department of Health and Human Services.

Susser, E. (1999). Life course cohort studies of schizophrenia. *Psychiatric Annals, 29*, 161–165.

Susser, E., Neugenbauer, R., Hoek, H. W., Brown, A. S., Lin, S., Labovitz, D., & Gorman, J. M. (1996). Schizophrenia after prenatal famine. *Archives of General Psychiatry, 53*(1), 25–31

Sweat, J. A., & Durm, M. W. (1993). Psychics: Do police departments really use them? *Skeptical Inquirer, 17*, 148–158.

Swerdlow, N. R., & Koob, G. F. (1987). Dopamine, schizophrenia, mania, and depression: Toward a unified hypothesis of corticostiato-pallido-thalamic function (with commentary). *Behavioral and Brain Sciences, 10*, 197–246.

Swim, J. K. (1994). Perceived versus meta-analytic effect sizes: An assessment of the accuracy of gender stereotypes. *Journal of Personality and Social Psychology, 66*, 21–36.

Symbaluk, D. G., Heth, C. D., Cameron, J., & Pierce, W. D. (1997). Social modeling, monetary incentives, and pain endurance: The role of self-efficacy and pain perception. *Personality and Social Psychology Bulletin, 23*, 258–269.

Symons, C. S., & Johnson, B. T. (1997). The self-reference effect in memory: A meta-analysis. *Psychological Bulletin, 121*(3), 371–394.

Tafarodi, R. W., & Vu, C. (1997). Two-dimensional self-esteem and reactions to success and failure. *Personality and Social Psychology Bulletin, 23*, 626–635.

Taha, F. A. (1972). A comparative study of how sighted and blind perceive the manifest content of dreams. *National Review of Social Sciences, 9*(3), 28.

Tajfel, H. (Ed.). (1982). *Social identity and intergroup relations.* New York: Cambridge University Press.

Talal, N. (1995). Quoted in V. Morell, Zeroing in on how hormones affect the immune system. *Science, 269*, 773–775.

Talbot, M. (1999, October 31). The Rorschach chronicles. *New York Times* (www.nytimes.com).

Tanda, G., Pontieri, F. E., & Di Chiara, G. (1997). Cannabinoid and heroin activation of mesolimbic dopamine transmission by a common mu-1 opioid receptor mechanism. *Science, 276*, 2048–2050.

Tang, S-H., & Hall, V. C. (1995). The overjustification effect: A meta-analysis. *Applied Cognitive Psychology, 9*, 365–404.

Tannen, D. (1990). *You just don't understand: Women and men in conversation.* New York: Morrow.

Tanner, J. M. (1978). *Fetus into man: Physical growth from conception to maturity.* Cambridge, MA: Harvard University Press.

Tassinary, L. G., & Cacioppo, J. T. (1992). Unobservable facial actions and emotion. *Psychological Science, 3,* 28–33.

Tatarkiewicz, W. (1976). *Analysis of happiness.* The Hague: Martinus Nijhoff, 1976.

Taubes, G. (1994). Will new dopamine receptors offer a key to schizophrenia? *Science, 265,* 1034–1035.

Tavris, C. (1982, November). Anger defused. *Psychology Today,* pp. 25–35.

Tavris, C. (1992). *The mismeasure of woman.* New York: Simon & Schuster.

Tavris, C. (1993, January 3). Beware the incest-survivor machine. *New York Times Book Review,* pp. 1, 16–18.

Taylor, K. M., & Shepperd, J. A. (1998). Bracing for the worst: Severity, testing, and feedback timing as moderators of the optimistic bias. *Personality and Social Psychology Bulletin, 24,* 915–926.

Taylor, S. E. (1989). *Positive illusions.* New York: Basic Books.

Taylor, S. E., Pham, L. B., Rivkin, I. D., & Armor, D. A. (1998). Harnessing the imagination: Mental simulation, self-regulation, and coping. *American Psychologist, 53,* 429–439.

Taylor, S., Kuch, K., Koch, W. J., Crockett, D. J., & Passey, G. (1998). The structure of posttraumatic stress symptoms. *Journal of Abnormal Psychology, 107,* 154–160.

Taylor, S. P., & Chermack, S. T. (1993). Alcohol, drugs and human physical aggression. *Journal of Studies on Alcohol,* Supplement No. 11, 78–88.

Teevan, R. C., & McGhee, P. E. (1972). Childhood development of fear of failure motivation. *Journal of Personality and Social Psychology, 21,* 345–348.

Teghtsoonian, R. (1971). On the exponents in Stevens' law and the constant in Ekinan's law. *Psychological Review, 78,* 71–80. p. 175)

Temoshok, L. (1992). *The Type C connection: The behavioral links to cancer and your health.* New York: Random House.

Teran-Santos, J., Jimenez-Gomez, A., & Cordero-Guevara, J. (1999). The association between sleep apnea and the risk of traffic accidents. *New England Journal of Medicine, 340,* 847–851.

Terman, L. M. (1916). *The measurement of intelligence.* Boston: Houghton Mifflin.

Terman, M., Terman, J. S., & Ross, D. C. (1998). A controlled trial of timed bright light and negative air ionization for treatment of winter depression. *Archives of General Psychiatry, 55,* 875–882.

Terrace, H. S. (1979, November). How Nim Chimpsky changed my mind. *Psychology Today,* pp. 65–76.

Tesser, A., Forehand, R., Brody, G., & Long, N. (1989). Conflict: The role of calm and angry parent-child discussion in adolescent development. *Journal of Social and Clinical Psychology, 8,* 317–330.

Tetlock, P. E. (1988). Monitoring the integrative complexity of American and Soviet policy rhetoric: What can be learned? *Journal of Social Issues, 44,* 101–131.

Tetlock, P. E. (1998). Close-call counterfactuals and belief-system defenses: I was not almost wrong but I was almost right. *Journal of Personality and Social Psychology, 75,* 639–652.

Thatcher, R. W., Walker, R. A., & Giudice, S. (1987). Human cerebral hemispheres develop at different rates and ages. *Science, 236,* 1110–1113.

Thayer, R. E. (1987). Energy, tiredness, and tension effects of a sugar snack versus moderate exercise. *Journal of Personality and Social Psychology, 52,* 119–125.

Thayer, R. E. (1993). Mood and behavior (smoking and sugar snacking) following moderate exercise: A partial test of self-regulation theory. *Personality and Individual Differences, 14,* 97–104.

Thelen, E. (1994). Three-month-old infants can learn task-specific patterns of interlimb coordination. *Psychological Science, 5,* 280–285.

Thelen, E. (1995). Motor development: A new synthesis. *American Psychologist, 50,* 79–95.

Thiele, T. E., Marsh, D. J., Ste. Marie, L., Bernstein, I. L., & Palmiter, R. D. (1998). Ethanol consumption and resistance are inversely related to neuropeptide Y levels. *Nature, 396,* 366–369.

Thomas, A., & Chess, S. (1986). The New York Longitudinal Study: From infancy to early adult life. In R. Plomin & J. Dunn (Eds.), *The study of temperament: Changes, continuities, and challenges.* Hillsdale, NJ: Erlbaum.

Thomas, G. V., & Blackman, D. (1991). Are animal experiments on the way out? *The Psychologist, 14,* 208–212.

Thomas, L. (1974). *The lives of a cell.* New York: Viking Press.

Thomas, L. (1983). *The youngest science: Notes of a medicine watcher.* New York: Viking Press.

Thomas, L. (1992). *The fragile species.* New York : Scribner's.

Thomas, W. P., & Collier, V. P. (1998). Two languages are better than one. *Educational Leadership, 55,* 23–36.

Thompson, C. P., Frieman, J., & Cowan, T. (1993). Rajan's memory. Paper presented to the American Psychological Society convention.

Thompson, C. P., Vogl, R. J., Walker, W. R., & Wooten, L. (1996). Involuntary memories in depressed and nondepressed individuals. Paper presented to the Psychonomic Society convention.

Thompson, G. (1998, December 14). As obesity in children increases, so do cases of adult-onset diabetes. *New York Times* (www.nytimes.com).

Thompson, J. K. (1986, April). Larger than life. *Psychology Today,* pp. 38–44.

Thompson, J. K., Jarvie, G. J., Lahey, B. B., & Cureton, K. J. (1982). Exercise and obesity: Etiology, physiology, and intervention. *Psychological Bulletin, 91,* 55–79.

Thompson, P. (1980). Margaret Thatcher: A new illusion. *Perception, 9,* 483–484.

Thorndike, A. L., & Hagen, E. P. (1977). Measurement and evaluation in psychology and education. New York: Macmillan.

Thorne, J., with Rothstein, L. (1993). *You are not alone: Words of experience and hope for the journey through depression.* New York: HarperPerennial.

Thornhill, R., & Gangestad, G. W. (1994). Human fluctuating asymmetry and sexual behavior. *Psychological Science, 5,* 297–302.

Thornton, B., & Moore, S. (1993). Physical attractiveness contrast effect: Implications for self-esteem and evaluations of the social self. *Personality and Social Psychology Bulletin, 19,* 474–480.

Thorpe, W. H. (1974). *Animal nature and human nature.* London: Metheun.

Tiggemann, M., & Rothblum, E. D. (1988). Gender differences in social consequences of perceived overweight in the United States and Australia. *Sex Roles, 18,* 75–86.

Tiihonen, J., Isohanni, M., Rasanen, P, Koiranen, M., & Moring, J. (1997). Specific major mental disorders and criminality: A 26-year prospective study of the 1966 northern Finland birth cohort. *American Journal of Psychiatry, 154,* 840–845.

Time. (1997, December 22). Greeting card association data. p. 19.

Tinbergen, N. (1951). *The study of instinct.* Oxford: Clarendon.

Tincoff, R., & Jusczyk, P. W. (1999). Some beginnings of word comprehension in 6-month-olds. *Psychological Science, 10,* 172–175.

Tirrell, M. E. (1990). Personal communication.

Todes, D. P. (1997). From the machine to the ghost within: Pavlov's transition from digestive physiology to conditional reflexes. *American Psychologist, 52,* 947–955.

Tolchin, M. (1994, April 17). Major airlines go two years without a fatality. *New York Times* report (in *Grand Rapids Press,* p. A10).

Tollefson, G. D., Fawcett, J., Winokur, G., Beasley, C. M., and others. (1993). Evaluation of suicidality during pharmacologic treatment of mood and nonmood disorders. *Annals of Clinical Psychiatry, 5*(4), 209–224.

Tollefson, G. D., Rampey, A. H., Beasley, C. M., & Enas, G. G. (1994). Absence of a relationship between adverse events and suicidality during pharmacotherapy for depression. *Journal of Clinical Psychopharmacology, 14,* 163–169.

Tolman, E. C., & Honzik, C. H. (1930). Introduction and removal of reward, and maze performance in rats. *University of California Publications in Psychology, 4,* 257–275.

Tolstoy, L. (1904). *My confessions.* Boston: Dana Estes.

Tondo, L., Jamison, K. R., & Baldessarini, R. J. (1997). Effect of lithium maintenance on suicidal behavior in major mood disorders. In D. M. Stoff & J. J. Mann (Eds.), *The neurobiology of suicide: From the bench to the clinic.* New York: New York Academy of Sciences.

Toni, N., Buchs, P.-A., Nikonenko, I., Bron, C. R., & Muller, D. (1999). LTP promotes formation of multiple spine synapses between a single axon terminal and a dendrite. *Nature, 402,* 421–442.

Torrey, E. F. (1986). *Witchdoctors and psychiatrists.* New York: Harper & Row.

Torrey, E. F. (1998, February 22). Quoted in M. Winerip, Schizophrenia's most zealous foe. *New York Times Magazine,* pp. 26–28.

Torrey, E. F., Miller, J., Rawlings, R., & Yolken, R. H. (1997). Seasonality of births in schizophrenia and bipolar disorder: A review of the literature. *Schizophrenia Research, 28,* 1–38.

Totterdell, P., Kellett, S., Briner, R. B., & Teuchmann, K. (1998). Evidence of mood linkage in work groups. *Journal of Personality and Social Psychology, 74,* 1504–1515.

Tovee, M. J., Mason, S. M., Emery, J. L., McCluskey, S. E., & Cohen-Tovee, E. M. (1997). Supermodels: Stick insects or hourglasses? *The Lancet, 350,* 1474–1475.

Towler, G. (1986). From zero to one hundred: Coaction in a natural setting. *Perceptual and Motor Skills, 62,* 377–378.

Tramontana, M. G., Hooper, S. R., & Selzer, S. C. (1988). Research on the preschool prediction of later academic achievement: A review. *Developmental Review, 8,* 89–146.

Travis, J. (1994). Glia: The brain's other cells. *Science, 266,* 970–972.

Treisman, A. (1987). Properties, parts, and objects. In K. R. Boff, L. Kaufman, & J. P. Thomas (Eds.), *Handbook of perception and human performance.* New York: Wiley.

Tremblay, R. E., Pihl, R. O., Vitaro, F., & Dobkin, P. L. (1994). Predicting early onset of male antisocial behavior from preschool behavior. *Archives of General Psychiatry, 51,* 732–739.

Triandis, H. C. (1981). Some dimensions of intercultural variation and their implications for interpersonal behavior. Paper presented at the American Psychological Association convention.

Triandis, H. C. (1989a). The self and social behavior in differing cultural contexts. *Psychological Review, 96,* 506–520.

Triandis, H. C. (1989b). Cross-cultural studies of individualism and collectivism. In J. J. Berman (Ed.), *Nebraska symposium on motivation 1989* (Vol. 37). Lincoln: University of Nebraska Press.

Triandis, H. C. (1994). *Culture and social behavior.* New York: McGraw-Hill.

Triandis, H. C., Bontempo, R., Villareal, M. J., Asai, M., & Lucca, N. (1988). Individualism and collectivism: Cross-cultural perspectives on self-ingroup relationships. *Journal of Personality and Social Psychology, 54,* 323–338.

Trickett, P. K., & McBride-Chang, C. (1995). The developmental impact of different forms of child abuse and neglect. *Developmental Review, 15,* 311–337.

Triplett, N. (1898). The dynamogenic factors in pacemaking and competition. *American Journal of Psychology, 9,* 507–533.

Trolier, T. K., & Hamilton, D. L. (1986). Variables influencing judgments of correlational relations. *Journal of Personality and Social Psychology, 50,* 879–888.

Trut, L. N. (1999). Early canid domestication: The farm-fox experiment. *American Scientist, 87,* 160–169.

Tsang, Y. C. (1938). Hunger motivation in gastrectomized rats. *Journal of Comparative Psychology, 26,* 1–17.

Tsien, J. Z. (April, 2000). Building a brainier mouse. *Scientific American,* pp. 62–68.

Tsuang, M. T., & Faraone, S. V. (1990). *The genetics of mood disorders.* Baltimore, MD: Johns Hopkins University Press.

Tubbs, M. E. (1986). Goal setting: A meta-analytic examination of the empirical evidence. *Journal of Applied Psychology, 71,* 474–483.

Tucker, L. A. (1983). Muscular strength and mental health. *Journal of Personality and Social Psychology, 45,* 1355–1360.

Tulving, E. (1996, August 18). Quoted in J. Gatehouse, Technology revealing brain's secrets. *Montreal Gazette,* p. A3.

Turk, D. C., Meichenbaum, D. H., & Berman, W. H. (1979). Application of biofeedback for the regulation of pain: A critical review. *Psychological Bulletin, 86,* 1322–1338.

Turnbull, C. (1961). *The forest people.* New York: Simon & Schuster.

Turner, C. W., Hesse, B. W., & Peterson-Lewis, S. (1986). Naturalistic studies of the long-term effects of television violence. *Journal of Social Issues, 42*(3), 7–28.

Turner, J. C. (1987). *Rediscovering the social group: A self-categorization theory.* New York: Basil Blackwell.

Tversky, A. (1985, June). Quoted in K. McKean, Decisions, decisions. *Discover,* pp. 22–31.

Tversky, A., & Kahneman, D. (1974). Judgment under uncertainty: Heuristics and biases. *Science, 185,* 1124–1131.

Twiss, C., Tabb, S., & Crosby, F. (1989). Affirmative action and aggregate data: The importance of patterns in the perception of discrimination. In F. Blanchard & F. Crosby (Eds.), *Affirmative action: Social psychological perspectives.* New York: Springer-Verlag.

Tyler, C. (1998). An eye-placement principle in 500 years of portraits. Smith-Kettlewell Eye Reseach Institute (http://www.ski.org/CWTyler_lab/ARVO/cwtarvo.html).

Uchino, B. N., Cacioppo, J. T., & Kiecolt-Glaser, J. K. (1996). The relationship between social support and physiological processes: A review with emphasis on underlying mechanisms and implications for health. *Psychological Bulletin, 119,* 488–531.

Uchino, B. N., Uno, D., & Holt-Lunstad, J. (1999). Social support, physiological processes, and health. *Current Directions in Psychological Science, 8,* 145–148.

Uehling, M. C. (1998, August). A brief history of Stephen Hawking. *Biography Magazine,* pp. 61–65, 116–117.

Ulrich, R. E. (1991). Animal rights, animal wrongs and the question of balance. *Psychological Science, 2,* 197–201.

Ulrich, R. S. (1984). View through a window may influence recovery from surgery. *Science, 224,* 420–421.

Underwood, B. J. (1957). Interference and forgetting. *Psychological Review, 64,* 49–60.

United Nations (1991). *The world's women 1970-1990: Trends and statistics.* New York: United Nations.

United Nations (1992). *1991 demographic yearbook.* New York: United Nations.

United Nations (1997). Infonation. United Nations Statistic Division (srch.un.org).

University of California (1993, December). The new American body. *University of California at Berkeley Wellness Letter,* pp. 1–2.

Urbany, J. E., Bearden, W. O., & Weilbaker, D. C. (1988). The effect of plausible and exaggerated reference prices on consumer perceptions and price search. *Journal of Consumer Research, 15,* 95–110.

U.S. News & World Report. (1997, March 31). Oprah: A heavenly body? Survey finds talk-show host a celestial shoo-in. P. 18.

Usher, J. M. (1992). Research and theory related to female reproduction: Implications for clinical psychology. *British Journal of Clinical Psychology, 31,* 129–151.

Valenstein, E. (1998). *Blaming the brain: The truth about drugs and mental health.* Glencoe, IL: Free Press.

Valenstein, E. S. (1986). *Great and desperate cures: The rise and decline of psychosurgery.* New York: Basic Books.

Vallerand, R. J., Fortier, M. S., & Guay, F. (1997). Self-determination and persistence in a real-life setting: Toward a motivational model of high school dropout. *Journal of Personality and Social Psychology, 72,* 1161–1176.

Vallone, R. P., Griffin, D. W., Lin, S., & Ross, L. (1990). Overconfident prediction of future actions and outcomes by self and others. *Journal of Personality and Social Psychology, 58,* 582–592.

Vance, E. B., & Wagner, N. N. (1976). Written descriptions of orgasm: A study of sex differences. *Archives of Sexual Behavior, 5,* 87–98.

Vandello, J. A., & Cohen, D. (1999). Patterns of individualism and collectivism across the United States. *Journal of Personality and Social Psychology, 77,* 279–292.

Vandenberg, S. G., & Kuse, A. R. (1978). Mental rotations: A group test of three-dimensional spatial visualization. *Perceptual and Motor Skills, 47,* 599–604.

van den Boom, D. (1990). Preventive intervention and the quality of mother-infant interaction and infant exploration in irritable infants. In W. Koops, H. J. G. Soppe, J. L. van der Linden, P. C. M. Molenaar, & J. J. F. Schroots (Eds.), *Developmental psychology behind the dikes: An outline of developmental psychology research in The Netherlands.* The Netherlands: Uitgeverij Eburon. Cited in C. Hazan & P. R. Shaver (1994). Deeper into attachment theory. *Psychological Inquiry, 5,* 68–79.

van der Meer, A. L. H., van der Weel, F. R., & Lee, D. N. (1995). The functional significance of arm movements in neonates. *Science, 267,* 693–695.

VanderStoep, S. W., & Shaughnessy, J. J. (1997). Taking a course in research methods improves reasoning about real-life events. *Teaching of Psychology, 24,* 122–124.

van Drunen, P. (1996). Professional psychology in the Netherlands: History and recent trends. In A. Schorr & S. Saari (Eds.), *Psychology in Europe: Facts, figures, realities.* Gottingen: Hogrefe & Huber.

Van Dyke, C., & Byck, R. (1982, March). Cocaine. *Scientific American,* pp. 128–141.

van IJzendoorn, M. H. (1997). In search of the absent father—Meta-analyses of infant-father attachment: A rejoinder to our discussants. *Child Development, 68,* 604–609.

van IJzendoorn, M. H., & Kroonenberg, P. M. (1988). Cross-cultural patterns of attachment: A meta-analysis of the strange situation. *Child Development, 59,* 147–156.

Van Leeuwen, M. S. (1982). IQism and the just society: Historical background. *Journal of the American Scientific Affiliation, 34,* 193–201.

VanTassel-Baska, J. (1983). Profiles of precocity: The 1982 Midwest Talent Search finalists. *Gifted Child Quarterly, 27,* 139–145.

Van Yperen, N. W., & Buunk, B. P. (1990). A longitudinal study of equity and satisfaction in intimate relationships. *European Journal of Social Psychology, 20,* 287–309.

Vaughn, K. B., & Lanzetta, J. T. (1981). The effect of modification of expressive displays on vicarious emotional arousal. *Journal of Experimental Social Psychology, 17,* 16–30.

Vaux, A. (1988). Social and personal factors in loneliness. *Journal of Social and Clinical Psychology, 6,* 462–471.

Veggeberg, S. K. (1996, March-April). Manic depression: Gene-hunters' hopes rise. *Brain Work,* pp. 1–2.

Vekassy, L. (1977). Dreams of the blind. *Magyar Pszichologiai Szemle, 34,* 478–491.

Vemer, E., Coleman, M., Ganong, L. H., & Cooper, H. (1989). Marital satisfaction in remarriage: A meta-analysis. *Journal of Marriage and the Family, 51,* 713–725.

Venn, J. (1986). Hypnosis and the Lamaze method: A reply to Wideman and Singer. *American Psychologist, 41,* 475–476.

Verhaeghen, P., & Salthouse, T. A. (1997). Meta-analyses of age-cognition relations in adulthood: Estimates of linear and nonlinear age effects and structural models. *Psychological Bulletin, 122,* 231–249.

Vernon, P. A. (1983). Speed of information processing and general intelligence. *Intelligence, 7,* 53–70.

Vincelli, F., & Molinari. E. (1998). Virtual reality and imaginative techniques in clinical psychology. In G. Riva, B. K. Wiederhold, & E.

Molinari (Eds.), *Virtual environments in clinical psychology and neuroscience: Methods and techniques in advanced patient-therapist interaction*. Amsterdam: IOS Press.

Vines, G. (1995, July 8). Genes in black and white. *New Scientist*, pp. 34–37.

Vines, G. (1995, July 22). Fight fat with feeling. *New Scientist*, pp. 14–15.

Vining, E. P. G., Freeman, J. M., Pillas, D. J., Uematsu, S., Carson, B. S., Brandt, J., Boatman, D., Pulsifer, M. B., & Zukerberg, A. (1997). Why would you remove half a brain? The outcome of 58 children after hemispherectomy—The Johns Hopkins Experience: 1968 to 1996. *Pediatrics, 100*, 163–171.

Vita, A. J., Terry, R. B., Hubert, H. B., & Fries, J. F. (1998). Aging, health risks, and cumulative disability. *New England Journal of Medicine, 338*, 1035–1041.

Vogel, S. (1999). *The skinny on fat: Our obsession with weight control*. New York: W. H. Freeman.

Vokey, J. R., & Read, J. D. (1985). Subliminal messages: Between the devil and the media. *American Psychologist, 40*, 1231–1239.

von Békésy, G. (1957, August). The ear. *Scientific American*, pp. 66–78.

von Frisch, K. (1950). *Bees: Their vision, chemical senses, and language*. Ithaca, NY: Cornell University Press.

von Frisch, K. (1974). Decoding the language of the bee. *Science, 185*, 663–668.

von Senden, M. (1932; reprinted 1960). In P. Heath (Trans.), *Space and sight: The perception of space and shape in the congenitally blind before and after operation*. Glencoe, IL: Free Press.

Voyer, D., Voyer, S., & Bryden, M. P. (1995). Magnitude of sex differences in spatial abilities: A meta-analysis and consideration of critical variables. *Psychological Bulletin, 117*, 250–270.

Vreeland, C. N., Gallagher, B. J., III, & McFalls, J. A., Jr. (1995). The beliefs of members of the American Psychiatric Association on the etiology of male homosexuality: A national survey. *Journal of Psychology, 129*, 507–517.

Vygotsky, L. S. (1932; reprinted 1962). *Thought and language* (E. Haufmann & G. Vaker, Eds. & Trans.). Cambridge, MA: MIT Press.

Wadden, T. A., Vogt, R. A., Foster, G. D., & Anderson, D. A. (1998). Exercise and the maintenance of weight loss: 1-year follow-up of a controlled clinical trial. *Journal of Consulting and Clinical Psychology, 66*, 429–433.

Waddington, J. L. (1993). Neurodynamics of abnormalities in cerebral metabolism and structure in schizophrenia. *Schizophrenia Bulletin, 19*, 55–69.

Wade, N. (1999, September 23). Number of human genes is put at 140,000, a significant gain. *New York Times* (www.nytimes.com).

Wagner, A. D., Schacter, D. L., Rotte, M., Koutstaal, W., Maril, A., Dale, A. M., Rosen, B. R., & Buckner, R. L. (1998). Building memories: Remembering and forgetting of verbal experiences as predicted by brain activity. *Science, 281*, 1188–1191.

Wagstaff, G. (1982). Attitudes to rape: The "just world" strikes again? *Bulletin of the British Psychological Society, 13*, 275–283.

Wahl, O. F. (1992). Mass media images of mental illness: A review of the literature. *Journal of Community Psychology, 20*, 343–352.

Wahlbeck, K., Cheine, M., Essali, A., & Adams, C. (1999). Evidence of clozapine's effectiveness in schizophrenia: A systematic review and meta-analysis of randomized trials. *American Journal of Psychiatry, 156*, 990–999.

Wakefield, J. C. (1987). The semantics of success: Do masturbation exercises lead to partner orgasm? *Journal of Sex and Marital Therapy, 13*, 3–14.

Wakefield, J. C. (1992). The concept of mental disorder: On the boundary between biological facts and social values. *American Psychologist, 47*, 373–388.

Wakefield, J. C. (1997). Normal inability versus pathological disability: Why Ossorio's definition of mental disorder is not sufficient. *Clinical Psychology Science and Practice, 4*, 249–258.

Waldrop, M. M. (1987). The workings of working memory. *Science, 237*, 1564–1567.

Walker, E. F., & Diforio, D. (1997). Schizophrenia: A neural diathesis-stress model. *Psychological Bulletin, 104*, 667–685.

Walker-Andrews, A. S. (1997). Infants' perception of expressive behaviors: Differentiation of multimodal information. *Psychological Bulletin, 121*, 437–456.

Wall Street Journal. (1999, December 17). Money and misery. Editorial, p. A14.

Wallace, D. S., Lord, C. G., & Bond, C. F., Jr. (1996). Which behaviors do attitudes predict? Review and meta-analysis of 60 years' research. Unpublished manuscript, Ohio University.

Wallach, M. A., & Wallach, L. (1983). *Psychology's sanction for selfishness: The error of egoism in theory and therapy*. New York: Freeman.

Wallach, M. A., & Wallach, L. (1985, February). How psychology sanctions the cult of the self. *Washington Monthly*, pp. 46–56.

Wallbott, H. G. (1988). In and out of context: Influences of facial expression and context information on emotion attributions. *British Journal of Social Psychology, 27*, 357–369.

Waller, D. (1995, December 11). The vision thing. *Time*, p. 48.

Wallis, C. (1983, June 6). Stress: Can we cope? *Time*, pp. 48–54.

Wallis, C. (1987, October 12). Back off, buddy: A new Hite report stirs up a furor over sex and love in the '80s. *Time*, pp. 68–73.

Walster (Hatfield), E., Aronson, V., Abrahams, D., & Rottman, L. (1966). Importance of physical attractiveness in dating behavior. *Journal of Personality and Social Psychology, 4*, 508–516.

Wampold, B. E., Mondin, G. W., Moody, M., & Ahn, H. (1997). The flat earth as a metaphor for the evidence for uniform efficacy of bona fide psychotherapies: Reply to Crits-Christoph (1997) and Howard et al. (1997). *Psychological Bulletin, 122*, 226–230.

Warchol, M. E., Lambert, P. R., Goldstein, B. J., Forge, A., & Corwin, J. T. (1993). Regenerative proliferation in inner ear sensory epithelia from adult guinea pigs and humans. *Science, 259*, 1619–1622.

Ward, C. (1994). Culture and altered states of consciousness. In W. J. Lonner & R. Malpass (Eds.), *Psychology and culture*. Boston: Allyn & Bacon.

Ward, K. D., Klesges, R. C., & Halpern, M. T. (1997). Predictors of smoking cessation and state-of-the-art smoking interventions. *Journal of Social Issues, 53*, 129–145.

Warm, J. S., & Dember, W. N. (1986, April). Awake at the switch. *Psychology Today*, pp. 46–53.

Warr, P., & Payne, R. (1982). Experiences of strain and pleasure among British adults. *Social Science and Medicine, 16*, 1691–1697.

Wason, P. C. (1960). On the failure to eliminate hypotheses in a conceptual task. *Quarterly Journal of Experimental Psychology, 12,* 129–140.

Wason, P. C. (1981). The importance of cognitive illusions. *The Behavioral and Brain Sciences, 4,* 356.

Wasserman, E. A. (1993). Comparative cognition: Toward a general understanding of cognition in behavior. *Psychological Science, 4,* 156–161.

Wasserman, E. A. (1995). The conceptual abilities of pigeons. *American Scientist, 83,* 246–255.

Waterhouse, R. (1993, July 19). Income for 62 percent is below average pay. *The Independent,* p. 4.

Waterman, A. S. (1988). Identity status theory and Erikson's theory: Commonalities and differences. *Developmental Review, 8,* 185–208.

Watkins, J. G. (1984). The Bianchi (L. A. Hillside Strangler) case: Sociopath or multiple personality? *International Journal of Clinical and Experimental Hypnosis, 32,* 67–101.

Watson, D., Wiese, D., Vaidya, J., & Tellegen, A. (1999). The two general activation systems of affect: Structured findings, evolutionary considerations, and psychobiological evidence. *Journal of Personality and Social Psychology, 76,* 820–838.

Watson, J. B. (1913). Psychology as the behaviorist views it. *Psychological Review, 20,* 158–177.

Watson, J. B., & Rayner, R. (1920). Conditioned emotional reactions. *Journal of Experimental Psychology, 3,* 1–14.

Watson, R. I., Jr. (1973). Investigation into deindividuation using a cross-cultural survey technique. *Journal of Personality and Social Psychology, 25,* 342–345.

Wayment, H. A., & Peplau, L. A. (1995). Social support and well-being among lesbian and heterosexual women: A structural modeling approach. *Personality and Social Psychology Bulletin, 21,* 1189–1199.

Weaver, J. B., Masland, J. L., & Zillmann, D. (1984). Effect of erotica on young men's aesthetic perception of their female sexual partners. *Perceptual and Motor Skills, 58,* 929–930.

Webb, W. B. (1992). *Sleep: The gentle tyrant.* Bolton, MA: Anker Publishing.

Webb, W. B., & Campbell, S. S. (1983). Relationships in sleep characteristics of identical and fraternal twins. *Archives of General Psychiatry, 40,* 1093–1095.

Wechsler, D. (1972). "Hold" and "don't hold" tests. In S. M. Chown (Ed.), *Human aging.* New York: Penguin.

Wechsler, H., Davenport, A., Dowdall, G., Moeykens, B., & Castillo, S. (1994). Health and behavioral consequences of binge drinking in college. *Journal of the American Medical Association, 272,* 1672–1677.

Wegner, D. M. (1990). *White bears and other unwanted thoughts: Suppression, obsession, and the psychology of mental control.* New York: Penguin Books.

Weinberg, M. S., & Williams, C. (1974). *Male homosexuals: Their problems and adaptations.* New York: Oxford University Press.

Weiner, B. (1985). An attributional theory of achievement motivation and emotion. *Psychological Review, 92,* 548–573.

Weingartner, H., Rudorfer, M. V., Buchsbaum, M. S., & Linnoila, M. (1983). Effects of serotonin on memory impairments produced by ethanol. *Science, 221,* 472–473.

Weinstein, N. D. (1980). Unrealistic optimism about future life events. *Journal of Personality and Social Psychology, 39,* 806–820.

Weinstein, N. D. (1982). Unrealistic optimism about susceptibility to health problems. *Journal of Behavioral Medicine, 5,* 441–460.

Weinstein, N. D. (1987). Unrealistic optimism about susceptibility to health problems: Conclusions from a community-wide sample. *Journal of Behavioral Medicine, 10,* 481–500.

Weinstein, N. D. (1996, October 4). 1996 optimistic bias bibliography (weinstein_c@aesop.rutgers.edu).

Weiss, A., King, J. E., & Enns, R. M. (1999). Can we breed a happier ape? The heritability of subjective well-being in zoo chimpanzees (*Pan troglodytes*). Paper presented at the Behavior Genetics Association meeting.

Weiss, J. M. (1977). Psychological and behavioral influences on gastrointestinal lesions in animal models. In J. D. Maser & M. E. P. Seligman (Eds.), *Psychopathology: Experimental models.* San Francisco: Freeman.

Weissman, M. M. (1999). Interpersonal psychotherapy and the health care scene. In D. S. Janowsky (Ed.), *Psychotherapy indications and outcomes.* Washington, DC: American Psychiatric Press.

Weissman, M. M., Bland, R. C., Canino, G. J., Faravelli, C., Greenwald, S., Hwu, H-G., Joyce, P. R., Karam, E. G., Lee, C-K., Lellouch, J., Lepine, J-P., Newman, S. C., Rubio-Stepic, M., Wells, J. E., Wickramaratne, P. J., Wittchen, H-U., & Yeh, E-K. (1996). Cross-national epidemiology of major depression and bipolar disorder. *Journal of the American Medical Association, 276,* 293–299.

Weissman, M. M., Merikangas, K. R., Wickramaratne, P., Kidd, K. K., Prusoff, B. A., Leckman, J. F., & Pauls, D. L. (1986). Understanding the clinical heterogeneity of major depression using family data. *Archives of General Psychiatry, 43,* 430–434.

Wellman, H. M., & Gelman, S. A. (1992). Cognitive development: Foundational theories of core domains. *Annual Review of Psychology, 43,* 337–375.

Wells, B. L. (1986). Predictors of female nocturnal orgasms: A multivariate analysis. *Journal of Sex Research, 22,* 421–437.

Wells, G. L. (1981). Lay analyses of causal forces on behavior. In J. Harvey (Ed.), *Cognition, social behavior and the environment.* Hillsdale, NJ: Erlbaum.

Wells, G. L., & Bradfield, A. L. (1998). "Good, you identified the suspect": Feedback to eyewitnesses distorts their reports of the witnessing experience. *Journal of Applied Psychology, 83,* 360–376.

Wells, G., & Murray, D. M. (1984). Eyewitness confidence. In G. L. Wells & E. F. Loftus (Eds.), *Eyewitness testimony: Psychological perspectives.* New York: Cambridge University Press.

Wender, P. H., Kety, S. S., Rosenthal, D., Schulsinger, F., Ortmann, J., & Lunde, I. (1986). Psychiatric disorders in the biological and adoptive families of adopted individuals with affective disorders. *Archives of General Psychiatry, 43,* 923–929.

Wenderoth, P. (1992). Perceptual illusions. *Australian Journal of Psychology, 44,* 147–151.

Wener, R., Frazier, W., & Farbstein, J. (1987, June). Building better jails. *Psychology Today,* pp. 40–49.

Werker, J. F. (1989). Becoming a native listener. *American Scientist, 77,* 54–59.

West, P. D. B., & Evans, E. F. (1990). Early detection of hearing damage in young listeners resulting from exposure to amplified music. *British Journal of Audiology, 24,* 89–103.

Westen, D. (1996). Is Freud really dead? Teaching psychodynamic theory to introductory psychology. Presentation to the Annual Institute on the Teaching of Psychology, St. Petersburg Beach, Florida.

Westen, D. (1998). The scientific legacy of Sigmund Freud: Toward a psychodynamically informed psychological science. *Psychological Bulletin, 124,* 333–371.

Wetter, D. W., Fiore, M. C., Gritz, E. R., Lando, H. A., Stitzer, M. L., Hasselblad, V., & Baker, T. B. (1998). The Agency for Health Care Policy and Research. Smoking cessation clinical practice guideline: Findings and implications for psychologists. *American Psychologist, 53,* 657–669.

Wever, E. G. (1949). *Theory of hearing.* New York: Wiley.

Wheeler, D. L., Jacobson, D. L., Paglieri, R. A., & Schwartz, A. A. (1993). An experimental assessment of facilitated communication. *Mental Retardation, 31,* 49–60.

Whitam, F. L., Diamond, M., & Martin, J. (1993). Homosexual orientation in twins: A report on 61 pairs and three triplet sets. *Archives of Sexual Behavior, 22,* 187–206.

White, G. L., & Kight, T. D. (1984). Misattribution of arousal and attraction: Effects of salience of explanations for arousal. *Journal of Experimental Social Psychology, 20,* 55–64.

White, H. R., Brick, J., & Hansell, S. (1993). A longitudinal investigation of alcohol use and aggression in adolescence. *Journal of Studies on Alcohol,* Supplement No. 11, 62–77.

White, K. M. (1983). Young adults and their parents: Individuation to mutuality. *New Directions for Child Development, 22,* 61–76.

White, L., & Edwards, J. (1990). Emptying the nest and parental well-being: An analysis of national panel data. *American Sociological Review, 55,* 235–242.

White, P. H., Kjelgaard, M. M., & Harkins, S. G. (1995). Testing the contribution of self-evaluation to goal-setting effects. *Journal of Personality and Social Psychology, 69,* 69–79.

White House. (1999, June 7). White House fact sheet on myths and facts about mental illness. Washington, DC: White House Press Office.

Whiten, A., & Byrne, R. W. (1988). Tactical deception in primates. *Behavioral and Brain Sciences, 11,* 233–244, 267–273.

Whiten, A., Goodall, J., McGrew, W. C., Nishida, T., Reynolds, V., Sugiyama, Y., Tutin, C. E. G., Wrangham, R. W., & Boesch, C. (1999). Cultures in chimpanzees. *Nature, 399,* 682–685.

Whiting, B. B., & Edwards, C. P. (1988). *Children of different worlds: The formation of social behavior.* Cambridge, MA: Harvard University Press.

Whitley, B. E., Jr. (1990). The relationships of heterosexuals' attributions for the causes of homosexuality to attitudes toward lesbians and gay men. *Personality and Social Psychology Bulletin, 16,* 369–377.

Whitley, B. E., Jr. (1999). Right-wing authoritarianism, social dominance orientation, and prejudice. *Journal of Personality and Social Psychology, 77,* 126–134.

Whooley, M. A., & Browner, W. S. (1998). Association between depressive symptoms and mortality in older women. *Archives of Internal Medicine, 158,* 2129–2135.

Whorf, B. L. (1956). Science and linguistics. In J. B. Carroll (Ed.), *Language, thought, and reality: Selected writings of Benjamin Lee Whorf.* Cambridge, MA: MIT Press.

Wickelgren, W. A. (1977). *Learning and memory.* Englewood Cliffs, NJ: Prentice-Hall.

Wicker, A. W. (1971). An examination of the "other variables" explanation of attitude-behavior inconsistency. *Journal of Personality and Social Psychology, 19,* 18–30.

Wickless, C., & Kirsch, I. (1989). Effects of verbal and experiential expectancy manipulations on hypnotic susceptibility. *Journal of Personality and Social Psychology, 57,* 762–768.

Widom, C. S. (1989a). Does violence beget violence? A critical examination of the literature. *Psychological Bulletin, 106,* 3–28.

Widom, C. S. (1989b). The cycle of violence. *Science, 244,* 160–166.

Wiederman, M. W. (1997). The truth must be in here somewhere: Examining the gender discrepancy in self-reported lifetime number of sex partners. *Journal of Sex Research, 34,* 375–386.

Wiens, A. N., & Menustik, C. E. (1983). Treatment outcome and patient characteristics in an aversion therapy program for alcoholism. *American Psychologist, 38,* 1089–1096.

Wierson, M., & Forehand, R. (1994). Parent behavioral training for child noncompliance: Rationale, concepts, and effectiveness. *Current Directions in Psychological Science, 3,* 146–149.

Wierzbicki, M. (1993). Psychological adjustment of adoptees: A meta-analysis. *Journal of Clinical Child Psychology, 22,* 447–454.

Wiesel, T. N. (1982). Postnatal development of the visual cortex and the influence of environment. *Nature, 299,* 583–591.

Wigdor, A. K., & Garner, W. R. (1982). *Ability testing: Uses, consequences, and controversies.* Washington, DC: National Academy Press.

Wilder, D. A. (1981). Perceiving persons as a group: Categorization and intergroup relations. In D. L. Hamilton (Ed.), *Cognitive processes in stereotyping and intergroup behavior.* Hillsdale, NJ: Erlbaum.

Wilford, J. N. (1999, February 9). New findings help balance the cosmological books. *New York Times* (www.nytimes.com).

Wilkinson, C. B. (1983). Aftermath of a disaster: The collapse of the Hyatt Regency Hotel skywalks. *American Journal of Psychiatry, 140,* 1134–1139.

Williams, C. L., & Berry, J. W. (1991). Primary prevention of acculturative stress among refugees. *American Psychologist, 46,* 632–641.

Williams, J. E., & Best, D. L. (1990). *Measuring sex stereotypes: A multination study.* Newbury Park, CA: Sage.

Williams, K. D., & Zadro, L. (in press). Ostracism: On being ignored, excluded and rejected. In M. Leary (Ed.), *Rejection.* New York: Oxford University Press.

Williams, L. M. (June, 1995). Recall of childhood trauma: A prospective study of women's memories of child sexual abuse: Correction. *Journal of Consulting and Clinical Psychology, 63*(3).

Williams, R. (1989). *The trusting heart: Great news about Type A behavior.* New York: Random House.

Williams, R. (1993). *Anger kills.* New York: Times Books.

Williams, R. B., Barefoot, J. C., Califf, R. M., Haney, T. L., Saunders, W. B., Pryor, D. B., Hlatky, M. A., Siegler, I. C., & Mark, D. B. (1992). Prognostic importance of social and economic resources among medically treated patients with angiographically documented coronary artery disease. *Journal of the American Medical Association, 267,* 520–524.

Williams, S., & Kohut, J. L. (1999). Psychologists in medical schools in 1997: Research brief. *American Psychologist, 54,* 272–276.

Williams, S. L. (1987). Self-efficacy and mastery-oriented treatment for severe phobias. Paper presented to the American Psychological Association convention.

Willingham, W. W., Lewis, C., Morgan, R., & Ramist, L. (1990). *Predicting college grades: An analysis of institutional trends over two decades.* Princeton, NJ: Educational Testing Service.

Willmuth, M. E. (1987). Sexuality after spinal cord injury: A critical review. *Clinical Psychology Review, 7,* 389–412.

Wilson, J. G. (1993). *The moral sense.* New York: Free Press.

Wilson, J. P., Harel, Z., & Kahana, B. (1988). *Human adaptation to extreme stress: From the Holocaust to Vietnam.* New York: Plenum Press.

Wilson, R. C., Gaft, J. G., Dienst, E. R., Wood, L., & Bavry, J. L. (1975). *College professors and their impact on students.* New York: Wiley.

Wilson, R. S. (1979). Analysis of longitudinal twin data: Basic model and applications to physical growth measures. *Acta Geneticae medicae et Gemellologiae, 28,* 93–105.

Wilson, R. S., & Matheny, A. P., Jr. (1986). Behavior-genetics research in infant temperament: The Louisville twin study. In R. Plomin & J. Dunn (Eds.), *The study of temperament: Changes, continuities, and challenges.* Hillsdale, NJ: Erlbaum.

Wilson, S. C., & Barber, T. X. (1983). The fantasy-prone personality: Implications for understanding imagery, hypnosis, and parapsychological phenomena. In A. A. Sheikh (Ed.), *Imagery: Current theory, research, and applications.* New York: Wiley.

Wilson, W. R. (1979). Feeling more than we can know: Exposure effects without learning. *Journal of Personality and Social Psychology, 37,* 811–821.

Winckelgren, I. (1992). How the brain "sees" borders where there are none. *Science, 256,* 1520–1521.

Windholz, G. (1989, April-June). The discovery of the principles of reinforcement, extinction, generalization, and differentiation of conditional reflexes in Pavlov's laboratories. *Pavlovian Journal of Biological Science, 26,* 64–74.

Windholz, G. (1997). Ivan P. Pavlov: An overview of his life and psychological work. *American Psychologist, 52,* 941–946.

Wing, R. R., & Jeffrey, R. W. (1979). Outpatient treatments of obesity: A comparison of methodology and clinical results. *International Journal of Obesity, 3,* 261–279.

Wingo, P. A., Ries, L. A. G., Giovino, G. A., Miller, D. S., Rosenberg, H. M., Shopland, D. R., Thun, M. J., & Edwards, B. K. (1999) The annual report to the nation on the status of cancer, 1973–1996, with a special section on lung cancer and tobacco smoking. *Journal of the National Cancer Institute, 91,* 675–690.

Winn, P. (1995). The lateral hypothalamus and motivated behavior: An old syndrome reassessed and a new perspective gained. *Current Directions in Psychological Science, 4,* 182–187.

Wintemute, G. J., Parham, C. A., Beaumont, J. J., Wright, M., & Drake, C. (1999). Mortality among recent purchasers of handguns. *New England Journal of Medicine, 341,* 1583–1589.

Wiseman, R., Jeffreys, C., Smith, M., & Nyman, A. (1999). The psychology of the seance. *The Skeptical Inquirer, 23*(2), 30–33.

Witelson, S. F., Kigar, D. L., & Harvey, T. (1999). The exceptional brain of Albert Einstein. *The Lancet, 353,* 2149–2153.

Witelson, S. F., & McCulloch, P. B. (1991). Premortem and postmortem measurement to study structure with function: A human brain collection. *Schizophrenia Bulletin, 17,* 583–591.

Witvliet, C. V. O., & Vrana, S. R. (1995). Psychophysiological responses as indices of affective dimensions. *Psychophysiology, 32,* 436–443.

Wixted, J. T., & Ebbesen, E. B. (1991). On the form of forgetting. *Psychological Science, 2,* 409–415.

Woehr, D. J., & Cavell, T. A. (1993). Self-report measures of ability, effort, and nonacademic activity as predictors of introductory psychology test scores. *Teaching of Psychology, 20,* 156–160.

Wolf, R. (1996, May/June). Believing what we see, hear, and touch: The delights and dangers of sensory illusions. *Skeptical Inquirer,* pp. 23–30.

Woll, S. (1986). So many to choose from: Decision strategies in videodating. *Journal of Social and Personal Relationships, 3,* 43–52.

Wolpe, J. (1958). *Psychotherapy by reciprocal inhibition.* Stanford, CA: Stanford University Press.

Wolpe, J., & Plaud, J. J. (1997). Pavlov's contributions to behavior therapy: The obvious and the not so obvious. *American Psychologist, 52,* 966–972.

Wong, D. F., Wagner, H. N., Tune, L. E., Dannals, R. F., et al. (1986). Positron emission tomography reveals elevated D_2 dopamine receptors in drug-naive schizophrenics. *Science, 234,* 1588–1593.

Wong, M. M., & Csikszentmihalyi, M. (1991). Affiliation motivation and daily experience: Some issues on gender differences. *Journal of Personality and Social Psychology, 60,* 154–164.

Wood, C. J, & Aggleton, J. P. (1989). Handedness in 'fast ball' sports: Do left-handers have an innate advantage? *British Journal of Psychology, 80,* 227–240.

Wood, G. (1979). The knew-it-all-along effect. *Journal of Experimental Psychology: Human Perception and Performance, 4,* 345–353.

Wood, J. M., Bootzin, R. R., Kihlstrom, J. F., & Schacter, D. L. (1992). Implicit and explicit memory for verbal information presented during sleep. *Psychological Science, 3,* 236–239.

Wood, J. M., Bootzin, R. R., Rosenhan, D., Nolen-Hoeksema, S., & Jourden, F. (1992). Effects of the 1989 San Francisco earthquake on frequency and content of nightmares. *Journal of Abnormal Psychology, 101,* 219–224.

Wood, J. V., Saltzberg, J. A., & Goldsamt, L. A. (1990a). Does affect induce self-focused attention? *Journal of Personality and Social Psychology, 58,* 899–908.

Wood, J. V., Saltzberg, J. A., Neale, J. M., Stone, A. A., & Rachmiel, T. B. (1990b). Self-focused attention, coping responses, and distressed mood in everyday life. *Journal of Personality and Social Psychology, 58,* 1027–1036.

Wood, W. (1987). Meta-analytic review of sex differences in group performance. *Psychological Bulletin, 102,* 53–71.

Wood, W., Lundgren, S., Ouellette, J. A., Busceme, S., & Blackstone, T. (1994). Minority influence: A meta-analytic review of social influence processes. *Psychological Bulletin, 115,* 323–345.

Wood, W., Wong, F. Y., & Chachere, J. G. (1991). Effects of media violence on viewers' aggression in unconstrained social interaction. *Psychological Bulletin, 109,* 371–383.

Woodruff-Pak, D. S. (1989). Aging and intelligence: Changing perspectives in the twentieth century. *Journal of Aging Studies, 3,* 91–118.

Woodruff-Pak, D. S., & Papka, M. (1999). Theories of neuropsychology and aging. In V. L. Bengtson & K. W. Schaie (Eds.), *Handbook of theories of aging.* New York: Springer.

Woods, N. F., Dery, G. K., & Most, A. (1983). Recollections of menarche, current menstrual attitudes, and premenstrual symptoms. In S. Golub (Ed.), *Menarche: The transition from girl to woman.* Lexington, MA: Lexington Books.

Woody, E. Z., & Bowers, K. S. (1994). A frontal assault on dissociated control. In S. J. Lynn & J. W. Rhue (Eds.), *Dissociation: Clinical, theoretical and research perspectives.* New York: Guilford.

Wooley, S., & Wooley, O. (1983). Should obesity be treated at all? *Psychiatric Annals, 13*(11), 884–885, 888.

World Health Organization.(1979). *Schizophrenia: An international follow-up study.* Chicester, UK: Wiley.

Worobey, J., & Blajda, V. M. (1989). Temperament ratings at 2 weeks, 2 months, and 1 year: Differential stability of activity and emotionality. *Developmental Psychology, 25,* 257–263.

Worthington, E. L., Jr. (1989). Religious faith across the life span: Implications for counseling and research. *The Counseling Psychologist, 17,* 555–612.

Worthington, E. L., Jr., Kurusu, T. A., McCullogh, M. E., & Sandage, S. J. (1996). Empirical research on religion and psychotherapeutic processes and outcomes: A 10-year review and research prospectus. *Psychological Bulletin, 119,* 448–487.

Worthington, E. L., Jr., Martin, G. A., Shumate, M., & Carpenter, J. (1983). The effect of brief Lamaze training and social encouragement on pain endurance in a cold pressor tank. *Journal of Applied Social Psychology, 13,* 223–233.

Wortman, C. B., & Silver, R. C. (1989). The myths of coping with loss. *Journal of Consulting and Clinical Psychology, 57,* 349–357.

Wren, C. S. (1999, April 8). Drug survey of children finds middle school a pivotal time. *New York Times* (www.nytimes.com).

Wright, K. (November, 1996). The Tarzan syndrome. *Discover, 17*(11), 88–94, 96, 98.

Wright, P., Takei, N., Rifkin, L., & Murray, R. M. (1995). Maternal influenza, obstetric complications, and schizophrenia. *American Journal of Psychiatry, 152,* 1714–1720.

Wright, R. (1999, January11). Who gets the good genes? *Time,* p. 67.

Wright, W. (1998). *Born that way: Genes, behavior, personality.* New York: Knopf.

Wu, T-C., Tashkin, D. P., Djahed, B., & Rose, J. E. (1988). Pulmonary hazards of smoking marijuana as compared with tobacco. *New England Journal of Medicine, 318,* 347–351.

Wulff, D. (1991). *The psychology of religion.* New York: Wiley.

Wulsin, L. R., Vaillant, G. E., & Wells, V. E. (1999). A systematic review of the mortality of depression. *Psychosomatic Medicine, 61,* 6–17.

Wyatt, J. K., & Bootzin, R. R. (1994). Cognitive processing and sleep: Implications for enhancing job performance. *Human Performance, 7,* 119–139.

Wynn, K. (1992). Addition and subtraction by human infants. *Nature, 358,* 749–759.

Wynn, K. (1998). Psychological foundations of number: Numerical competence in human infants. *Trends in Cognitive Science, 2,* 296–303.

Wynn, V., & Gilhooly, K. (1999). The veracity of memories for what you were doing and who you were with when you heard of the death of Diana. *British Psychological Society 1999 Proceedings, 71,* p. 47.

Wysocki, C. J., & Gilbert, A. N. (1989). *National Geographic* survey: Effects of age are heterogeneous. *Annals of the New York Academy of Sciences, 561,* 12–28.

Yalom, I. D. (1985). *The theory and practice of group psychotherapy* (3rd ed.). New York: Basic Books.

Yang, N., & Linz, D. (1990). Movie ratings and the content of adult videos: The sex-violence ratio. *Journal of Communication, 40*(2), 28–42.

Yankelovich Partners. (1993). *Inside affluent America.* Westport, CT: Yankelovich Partners.

Yankelovich Partners. (1995, May/June). Growing old. *American Enterprise,* p. 108.

Yankelovich Partners. (1997, December 15). Ability of spirituality to help people who are sick. (Press release.)

Yankelovich Partners. (1998, September). Reported in New poll points to increase in paranormal belief. *Skeptical Inquirer,* pp. 9–10.

Yapko, M. D. (1994). Suggestibility and repressed memories of abuse: A survey of psychotherapists' beliefs. *American Journal of Clinical Hypnosis, 36,* 163–171.

Yarmey, A. D. (1991). Voice identification over the telephone. *Journal of Applied Social Psychology, 21,* 1868–1876.

Yarnell, P. R., & Lynch, S. (1970, April 25). Retrograde memory immediately after concussion. *Lancet,* pp. 863–865.

Yarrow, L. J., Goodwin, M. S., Manheimer, H., & Milowe, I. D. (1973). Infancy experience and cognitive and personality development at ten years. In L. J. Stone, H. T. Smith, & L. B. Murphy (Eds.), *The competent infant.* New York: Basic Books.

Yates, A. (1989). Current perspectives on the eating disorders: I. History, psychological and biological aspects. *Journal of the American Academy of Child and Adolescent Psychiatry, 28,* 813–828.

Yates, A. (1990). Current perspectives on the eating disorders: II. Treatment, outcome, and research directions. *Journal of the American Academy of Child and Adolescent Psychiatry, 29,* 1–9.

Ybarra, O. (1999). Misanthropic person memory when the need to self-enhance is absent. *Personality and Social Psychology Bulletin, 25,* 261–269.

Yip, P. S. F. (1998). Age, sex, marital status and suicide: An empirical study of east and west. *Psychological Reports, 82,* 311–322.

Yirmiya, N., Erel, O., Shaken, M., & Solomonica-Levi, D. (1998). Meta-analyses comparing theory of mind abilities of individuals with autism, individuals with mental retardation, and normally developing individuals. *Psychological Bulletin, 124,* 283–307.

Youn, G. (1996). Sexual activities and attitudes of adolescent Koreans. *Archives of Sexual Behavior, 25,* 629–643.

Young, A. (1996). *The harmony of illusions: Inventing post-traumatic stress disorder.* Princeton, NJ: Princeton University Press.

Zajonc, R. B. (1965). Social facilitation. *Science, 149,* 269–274.

Zajonc, R. B. (1980). Feeling and thinking: Preferences need no inferences. *American Psychologist, 35,* 151–175.

Zajonc, R. B. (1984a). On the primacy of affect. *American Psychologist, 39,* 117–123.

Zajonc, R. B. (1984b, July 22). Quoted in D. Goleman, Rethinking IQ tests and their value. *The New York Times,* p. D22.

Zajonc, R. B. (1998). Emotions. In D. Gilbert, S. T. Fiske, & G. Lindzey (Eds.), *Handbook of social psychology* (4th ed). New York: McGraw-Hill.

Zajonc, R. B., & Markus, G. B. (1975). Birth order and intellectual development. *Psychological Review, 82,* 74–88.

Zajonc, R. B., Murphy, S. T., & Inglehart, M. (1989). Feeling and facial efference: Implications of the vascular theory of emotions. *Psychological Review, 96,* 395–416.

Zaslow, M. J. (1991). Variation in child care quality and its implications for children. *Journal of Social Issues, 47*(2), 125–138.

Zeidner, M. (1990). Perceptions of ethnic group modal intelligence: Reflections of cultural stereotypes or intelligence test scores? *Journal of Cross-Cultural Psychology, 21,* 214–231.

Zelnick, M., & Kim, Y. J. (1982). Sex education and its association with teenage sexual activity, pregnancy, and contraceptive use. *Family Planning Perspectives, 14*(3), 117–126.

Zhang, S. D., & Odenwald, W. F. (1995). Misexpression of the white (w) gene triggers male-male courtship in Drosophila. *Proceedings of the National Academy of Sciences of the United States of America, 92,* 5525–5529.

Zigler, E. F. (1986, February). Quoted in D. Meredith, Day care: The nine-to-five dilemma. *Psychology Today,* pp. 36–39, 42–44.

Zigler, E. F. (1987). Formal schooling for four-year-olds? No. *American Psychologist, 42,* 254–260.

Zigler, E. F., & Muenchow, S. (1992). *Head Start: The inside story of a great American experiment.* New York: Basic Books.

Zilbergeld, B. (1983). *The shrinking of America: Myths of psychological change.* Boston: Little, Brown.

Zillmann, D. (1986). Effects of prolonged consumption of pornography. Background paper for The Surgeon General's Workshop on Pornography and Public Health, June 22–24. Report prepared by E. P. Mulvey & J. L. Haugaard and released by Office of the Surgeon General on August 4, 1986.

Zillmann, D. (1989). Effects of prolonged consumption of pornography. In D. Zillmann & J. Bryant (Eds.), *Pornography: Research advances and policy considerations.* Hillsdale, NJ: Erlbaum.

Zillmann, D., & Bryant, J. (1984). Effects of massive exposure to pornography. In N. Malamuth & E. Donnerstein (Eds.), *Pornography and sexual aggression.* Orlando, FL: Academic Press.

Zimbardo, P. G. (1970). The human choice: Individuation, reason, and order versus deindividuation, impulse, and chaos. In W. J. Arnold & D. Levine (Eds.), *Nebraska Symposium on Motivation, 1969.* Lincoln: University of Nebraska Press.

Zimbardo, P. G. (1972, April). Pathology of imprisonment. *Transaction/Society,* pp. 4–8.

Zucker, G. S., & Weiner, B. (1993). Conservatism and perceptions of poverty: An attributional analysis. *Journal of Applied Social Psychology, 23,* 925–943.

Zuckerman, M. (1979). *Sensation seeking: Beyond the optimal level of arousal.* Hillsdale, NJ: Erlbaum.

Credits

Photographs

MODULE 1

p. 2 (*top*) Sally Cassidy/The Picture Cube; **p. 2** (*center*) Joe Carini/The Image Works; **p. 2** (*bottom*) Robert Caputo/Stock, Boston; **p. 3** Ebbinghaus, The Bettmann Archive; **p. 3** Binet, Wundt, Thorndike, Hall, Freud, Watson, James, Brown Brothers; **p. 3** Washburn, National Library of Medicine; **p. 3** Calkins, Wellesley College Archives; **p. 3** Pavlov, Sovfoto; **p. 5** Rob Nelson/Black Star; **p. 6** Robert Brenner/Photo Edit; **p. 8** (*right*) Laura Dwight/Photo Edit; **p. 8** (*center*) Treë; **p. 8** (*top*) Treë; **p. 8** (*bottom*) Laura Dwight;

MODULE 2

p. 12 Jim Pickerell/Stock Boston; **p. 15** Rob Kinmonth; **p. 18** Susan Kuklin/Photo Researchers; **p. 20** Courtesy of Richard Byrne and David Myers; **p. 23** Michael Newman Jr./Photo Edit; **p. 25** UPI/Corbis-Bettmann; **p. 26** R. Sidney/The Image Works; **p. 38** Mark S. Wexler/Woodfin Camp & Associates; **p. 40** Jim Amos/Science Source/Photo Researchers;

MODULE 3

p. 49 From: Mapping the Mind by Rita Carter © 1998 University of California Press; **p. 50** Bob Daemmrich/Stock, Boston;

MODULE 4

p. 59 Courtesy of Haroon Ashraf, Lancet; **p. 60** (*top*) Alexander Tsiaras/Stock, Boston; **p. 61** (*bottom*) Hank Morgan/Rainbow; **p. 61** Daniel R. Weinberger, M.D. CBDB, NIMH; **p. 63** John Gress/AP Photo; **p. 64** Frank Siteman/Stock, Boston; **p. 64** Pix*ELATION from Fran Heyl Associates; **p. 67** (*top*) Courtesy of Drs. Jack Belliveau and Bruce Rosen, Massachusetts General hospital, NMR Center; **p. 69** Hanna Damasio, M.D. University of Iowa and Science; **p. 67** (*bottom*) Courtesy of V.P. Clark, K. Keill, J. Ma. Maisog, S. Courtney, L.G. Ungerleider, and J.V. Haxby, National Institute of Health; **p. 72** Joe McNally; **p. 73** (*right*) Martin M. Rotker; **p. 73** (*left*) Courtesy of Terence Williams, University of Iowa; **p. 76** (*bottom left*) The Platt Collection/Archive Photos; **p. 76** (*bottom right*) Chris Trotman/Duomo; **p. 76** (*top*) Reuters/The Bettmann Archive; **p. 78** Robert Brenner/Photo Edit;

MODULE 5

p. 92 Jeffrey W. Myers/Stock, Boston; **p. 87** Charles Bennett/AP Photo; **p. 87** From: L.N. Trut, American Scientist, (1999)87: 160-169; **p. 94** Bob Sacha; **p. 95** Kathleen Marie Menke/Crystal Images/Monkmeyer; **p. 96** Michele-Salmieri/FPG International/Picture Quest; **p. 97** Doris Pinney; **p. 99** (*left*) Jeff Christensen/Gamma Liaison; **p. 99** (*right*) Janne Makinen/AP Photo;

MODULE 6

p. 103 Miguel L. Fairbanks; **p. 104** Courtsey of C. Brune; **p. 105** (*top left and right*) Courtesy of Avi Karni & Leslie Ungerleider, National Institute of Mental Health; **p. 105** (*bottom*) Sybil Shackman/Monkmeyer; **p. 106** Kevin R. Morris/Corbis; **p. 107** Robert Azzi/Woodfin Camp & Associates; **p. 108** Sybil Shackman/Monkmeyer; **p. 111** Monkmeyer; **p. 112** (*top*) Mitchell Gerber/Corbis; **p. 112** (*bottom*) Siteman/Monkmeyer;

MODULE 7

p. 118 (*left*) Francis Leroy, Biocosmos/Science Photo Library/Photo Researchers; **p. 118** (*right*) Lennart Nilsson/Bonnier Fakta Bokforlag; **p. 119** (*from right*) Petit Format/Science Source/Photo Researchers; **p. 119** (*far left*) Donald Yeager/Camera MD Studios;

MODULE 8

p. 124 (*top*) Courtesy of Carolyn Rovee-Collier, Rugers University; **p. 124** (*left*) Felicia Martinez/Photo Edit; **p. 124** (*center right*) Shackman/Monkmeyer; **p. 124** (*bottom left*) Alan Carruthers/Photo Researchers; **p. 124** (*bottom right*) Bob Daemmrich/Stock, Boston; **p. 126** (*top*) Bill Anderson/Monkmeyer; **p. 126** (*bottom*) Patti Putnam/The Stock Market; **p. 127** Doug Goodman/Monkmeyer; **p. 128** (*left and right*) Ontario Science Center; **p. 131** Elizabeth Crews/The Image Works; **pp. 132 & 133** Harlow Primate Laboratory, University of Wisconsin; **p. 136** Susan Greenwood/The Gamma Liason Network; **p. 137** Sybil Shackman/Monkmeyer;

MODULE 9

p. 141 Michael Newman/Photo Edit; **p. 142** (*top*) Owen Franken/Stock, Boston; **p. 142** (*bottom*) J. Gerard Smith/Monkmeyer; **p. 144** (*left*) Bob Daemmrich/The Image Works; **p. 144** (*right*) Charles Harbutt/Actuality; **p. 147** (*top*) John Eastcott/YVA Momatiuk/The Image Works; **p. 147** (*center*) Esbin-Anderson/The Image Works; **p. 147** (*bottom left*) David Vance/The Image Bank; **p. 147** (*bottom right*) David Delossy/The Image Bank;

MODULE 10

p. 154 (*top*) Georges Gobet/AP Photo; **p. 154** (*bottom*) Michael Newman/Photo Edit; **p. 155** David Wells/The Image Bank; **p. 158** David Myers; **p. 162** (*top*) Henley & Savage/Stock, Boston; **p. 162** (*bottom*) Tom & DeAnn McCarthy/Rainbow; **p. 164** (*left*) Joe McNally; **p. 164** (*center*) Bob Daemmrich/The Image Works; **p. 164** (*right*) Charles Harbutt/Actuality;

MODULE 11

p. 170 Detail "The Forest has Eyes" by Bev Doolittle © The Greenwich Workshops, Inc. Trumbull, CT; **p. 171** Carol Lee/Tony Stone Images; **p. 172** Marvin Lyons/The Image Bank;

MODULE 12

p. 178 (*left & right*) Thomas Eisner; **p. 181** E.R. Lewis, Y.Y. Zeevi, F.S. Werblin, 1969; **p. 183** (*top*) Ross Kinnaird/Allsport; **p. 183** Fritz Goro, LIFE Magazine, ©1971 Time Warner, Inc.; **p. 186** Tim Bieber/The Image Bank; **p. 187** Frtiz Goro, LIFE Magazine ©1971 Time Warner, Inc.; **p. 188** From Albers, J. (1975). The Interaction of Color (revised pocket edition) (Plate VI-3). New Haven, CT: Yale University Press. Photo courtesy of the Josef Albers Foundation;

MODULE 29

p. 384 M & E. Bernheim/Woodfin Camp & Associates; **p. 385** *(top & bottom)* Adapted from Werker, J.F. (1989). "Becoming 54: A Native Listener. American Scientist", 77-59. Reprinted with permission of American Scientist, Journal of Sygma Xi, The Scientific Research Society. Photos Courtesy of Peter McLeod, Acadia University; **p. 386** David Young-Wolff/Photo Edit; **p. 388** *(bottom)* Susan Meiselas, Magnum Photos; **p. 389** Shackman/Monkmeyer; **p. 390** *(top)* Courtesy of Kathryn Brownson/Hope College; **p. 390** *(bottom)* George Ancona in Ancona, G. & Beth, M. (1989) The Handtalk Zoo. New York: Macmillan Publishing Company; **p. 391** Stephen Dunn/Allsport; **p. 393** *(top)* Matthew Stockman/Allsport; **p. 393** *(bottom)* Goodwin/ Monkmeyer; **p. 394** *(top)* Elizabeth Crews/The Image Works; **p. 394** *(bottom)* Courtesy of Jennifer Byrne, c/o Richard Byrne, Department of Psychology, University of St. Andrews, Scotland; **p. 395** William Munoz; **p. 396** Paul Fusco/Magnum Photos; **p. 397** Language Research Center, Yerkes Regional Primate Research Center; **p. 409** National Library of Medicine; **p. 409** *(bottom)* New Service, Stanford University;

MODULE 30

p. 401 Courtesy of Tom Renner, Hope College; **p. 402** Courtesy of Cameras on Wheels; **p. 404** Lee Celano/Liaison;

MODULE 31

p. 410 Lew Merrim/Monkmeyer; **p. 413** *(top)* Archives of the History of American Psychology/University of Akron; **p. 413** *(bottom)* Ray Scott/The Image Works; **p. 414** Jim W. Grace/Photo Researchers; **p. 415** Courtesy Dr. Joseph Fagan, Infantest Corp.; **p. 416** Greenlar/The Image Works; **p. 417** Michael O'Neill;

MODULE 32

p. 423 *(top)* Mark Richards/Photo Edit; **p. 425** *(top)* Jacques Chenet/Woodfin Camp & Associates; **p. 425** *(bottom)* Susan Lapides/Design Conceptions; **p. 427** Jason Goltz; **p. 429** Courtesy Robert Allen Strawn; **p. 430** Maria Melin/ABC; **p. 431** J. Griffin/The Image Works;

MODULE 33

p. 461 AP/Wide World Photos, Inc.; **p. 436** *(left)* Bob Daemmrich/The Image Works; **p. 424** *(right)* Tony Brandenburg/Bruce Coleman, Inc.; **p. 437** *(left)* Harlow Primate Laboratory, University of Wisconsin; **p. 437** *(right)* George Ancona/International Stock; **p. 438** *(top right)* Michael Dwyer/Stock, Boston; **p. 438** *(bottom right)* Dale Spartas/Liaison International; **p. 438** *(left)* Wesley Hitt/Liaison International;

MODULE 34

p. 441 *(top)* Pix*ELATION from Fran Heyl Associates; **p. 442** *(bottom)* Richard Howard; **p. 444** Richard Olsenius/Black Star; **p. 445** Kansas City Star/Sipa Press;

MODULE 35

p. 449 Photo by Dellenback reprinted by permission of the Kinsey Institute for Research in Sex, Gender, and Reproduction, Inc.; **p. 452** Sotographs/The Gamma-Liason Network; **p. 457** Cynthia Johnson/Time Magazine; **p. 460** Nathaniel Antman/The Image Works;

MODULE 36

p. 464 McClelland, D. C. , et al (1953). The achievement motive. New York: Appleton-Centuy Crofts. Reprinted by permission of Irv-ington Publishers, New York; **p. 465** Stephen Jaffe/The Gamma Liaison Network; **p. 466** Jack Smith/Associated Press Photo; **p. 468** *(top)* Fujifotos/The Image Works; **p. 468** *(bottom)* Michael S. Green/AP Photo. **p. 470** Courtesy of Herman Miller Inc.;

MODULE 37

p. 476 Bob Thomas/Gamma-Liaison;

MODULE 38

p. 482 M. Grecco/Stock, Boston; **p. 484** Bernard Gottfryd/Woodfin Camp & Associates; **p. 483** Dr. Paul Ekman, University of California at San Francisco; **p. 486** Culver Pictures; **p. 487** Ekman & Matsumoto, Japanese and Caucasian Facial Expressions of Emotions; **p. 489** *(four images)* Courtesy of Louis Schakel/Michael Kausman/The New York Times Pictures; **p. 490** *(top left)* Tom McCarthy/Rainbow; **p. 490** *(top center)* Patrick Donehue/Photo Researchers; **p. 490** *(top left)* Bob Daemmrich/The Image Works; **p. 490** *(bottom, center left)* Nancy Brown/The Image Bank; **p. 490** *(bottom, center right)* Marc Grimberg/The Image Bank; **p. 490** *(bottom right)* Michael Newman/Photo Edit; **p. 490** *(bottom left)* Merrim/Monkmeyer; **p. 491** Alan L. Detrick/Photo Researchers; **p. 493** *(top)* Wolfgang Kaehler; **p. 493** *(bottom)* Mark Lennihan/AP/Wide World Photos, Inc.;

MODULE 39

p. 504 Culver Pictures; **p. 505** Edmund Engelman; **p. 507** Grant-pix/Monkmeyer; **p. 508** *(left)* Rick Friedman/Black Star; **p. 508** *(right)* Harlow Primate Laboratory, University of Wisconsin; **p. 509** Merrim/Monkmeyer; **p. 510** *(top)* Merrim/Monkmeyer; **p. 510** *(bottom)* National Library of Medicine; **p. 511** *(left)* The Bettmann Archive; **p. 511** *(right)* Archives of the History of American Psychology;

MODULE 40

p. 518 AP/Wide World Photos, Inc.; **p. 519** *(top)* Joel Gordon; **p. 519** *(bottom)* Wolf/Monkmeyer;

MODULE 41

p. 527 Ted Polumbaum/Life Magazine © 1968 Time Warner, Inc.; **p. 528** Mark Antman/The Image Works; **p. 529** Sybil Shackman/Monkmeyer; **p. 533** B. & C. Alexander/Photo Researchers; **p. 538** Stephen Wade/Allsport USA; **p. 540** Joe McNally; **p. 541** Courtesy of Dr. Martin Seligman, University of Pennsylvania.;

MODULE 43

p. 548 Tony Ray Jones/Magnum Photos; **p. 552** B. Markel/Liaison; **p. 554** Elaine Thompson/AP Photo;

MODULE 44

p. 558 Tom Russo/AP Photo; **p. 562** *(top)* John Coletti/Stock, Boston; **p. 562** *(bottom)* Baxter, L. R., et al. (1987). Local cerebral glucose metabolic rates in obsessive-compulsive disorder. Archives of General Psychology, 44(3), 211-218. Copyright © 1987 American Medical Association;

MODULE 45

p. 565 AP/Wide World Photos, Inc; **p. 567** Courtesy of Adrian Raine, University of Southern California;

MODULE 46

p. 570 Walt Whitman: Bettmann/Corbis; Virginia Woolf: George C. Beresford/Hulton Getty Picture Library; Edgar Allen Poe: Hulton

Text and Illustrations

MODULE 2

Fig. 2.7 Adapted with permission of The Free Press, a division of Simon & Schuster from *How We Know What Isn't So: The Fallibility of Human Reason in Everyday Life* by Thomas Gilovich. Copyright © 1991 Thomas Gilovich. **Fig. 2.9** Adapted from Ross, B. (Jan. 1987). In K. McKean, "The orderly pursuit of pure disorder." *Discover*, pp. 72-81. Barry Ross/Copyright © 1987 Discover Magazine **Fig. 1** From *Mind Sights* by Shepard. Copyright © 1990 Roger N. Shepard. Used with permission of W.H. Freeman and Company.

MODULE 4

Fig. 4.8 From *Scientific American*, Oct. 1994, p. 102. Left side © Dana Bums-Pizer. Right side © Judith Glick. **Fig. 4.18** Gazzaniga, M.S. (1983). Right hemisphere language following brain bisection: A 20-year perspective. *American Psychologist, 38*, 525-537. **Fig. 4.19 and illustration** Adapted with the permission of The Free Press, a division of Simon & Schuster from *The left-hander syndrome: The causes and consequences of left-handedness* by Stanley Coren. Copyright © 1993 by Stanley Coren.

MODULE 5

Fig. 5.2 Buss, D. (1994). *The evolution of desire.* New York: Basic Books. Copyright © 1994 by David M. Buss. Reprinted by permission of BasicBooks, a division of HarperCollins Publishers, Inc.

MODULE 6

Fig. 6.3 Adapted from figure in "Brain changes in response to experience" by M. R. Rosenzweig, E. L. Bennett, and M. C. Diamond. Copyright © Ikuyo Tagawa Garber for Bunji Tagawa. **Fig. 6.4** Dey, E. L. et al. (1991). *The American freshman: Twenty-five year trends.* Los Angeles: Higher Education Research Institute, UCLA. Sax, L. J. eta al. (1999). *The American freshman: National norms for fall 1999.* Los Angeles: Higher Education Research Institute, UCLA.

MODULE 7

Fig. 7.3 Johnson & Morton (1991). *Psychological Review, 98*, 164-181. Copyright © 1991 by the American Psychological Association. Reprinted with permission.

MODULE 8

Fig. 8.1 Conel, J.L. (1939-1963). *The postnatal development of the human cerebral cortex (Vols. I-VI).* Reprinted by permission of Harvard University Press. **Fig. 8.4** Wynn, K. (1992). Addition and subtraction by human infants. *Nature, 358*, 749-759. Reprinted by permission of Nature. Copyright © 1992 Macmillan Magazines Limited. **Page 129** Adapted from Baron-Cohen, S., Leslie, A. M., & Frith, U. (1985). Does the autistic child have a "theory of mind"? *Cognition, 21*, 37–46. **Fig. 8.7** Kagan, J. (1976). Emergent themes in human development. *American Scientist, 64*, 186-196. Reprinted by permission of *American Scientist*, Journal of Sigma XI, The Scientific Research Society.

MODULE 9

Fig. 9.1 Reproduced with the permission of the Alan Guttmacher Institute from *Sex and America's teenagers.* Alan Guttmacher Institute, New York, 1994, 2000. **Fig. 9.2** Tanner, J.M. (1978). *Fetus into man: Physical growth from conception to maturity.* Cambridge, MA: Harvard University Press. Reprinted by permission. **Table 9.1** From *Childhood and Society* by Erik H. Erikson. Copyright 1950, © 1963 by W.W. Norton & Company, Inc., renewed © 1978, 1991 by Erik H. Erikson.

MODULE 10

Fig. 10.1 Adapted with permission from Doty, R.L., et al. (1984). Smell identification ability: Changes with age. *Science, 226*, 1441-1443. Copyright © 1984 by the American Association for the Advancement of Science. **Fig. 10.2** Stock, R.W. (1995, July 13). Reducing the risk for older drivers. *New York Times*, p. C1. Copyright © 1995 by The New York Times Co. **Fig. 10.3** Jorm A.F., Korten, A.E., & Henderson, A.S. (1987). The prevalence of dementia: A quantitative integration of the literature. *Acta Psychiatrica Scandinivica, 76*, 465-479. Copyright © 1987 Munksgaard International Publishers, Ltd., Copenhagen, Denmark. **Fig. 10.4** Data from Crook, P.H. & West, R.L. (1990). Name and recall performance across the adult lifespan. *British Journal of Psychology, 81*, 335-349. **Fig. 10.5** Schonfield, D. & Robertson, B.A. (1966). Memory Storage and Aging. *Canadian Journal of Psychology, 20*, 228-236. Copyright © 1966. Canadian Psychological Association. Reprinted with permission. **Fig 10.6** Adapted from Schail, K.W. (1994). The life course of adult intellectual abilities. *American Psychologist, 49*, 304–313. Copyright © 1994 American Psychological Association. Adapted by permission. **Fig. 10.7** Adapted from Kaufman, A.S., Reynolds, C.R., & McLean, J.E. (1989). Age and WAIS-R intelligence in a national sample of adults in the 20 to 74 year age range: A cross-sectional analysis with educational level controlled. *Intelligence, 13*, 235-253. Reprinted with permission from Ablex Publishing Corporation. **Fig. 10.8** McCrae, R.R. & Costa, P.T. Jr. (1990). *Personality in adulthood.* New York: Guilford Press, p. 149. Copyright © 1990 Guilford Press. **Fig. 10.9** Data from Inglehart, R. (1990). *Culture shift in advanced industrial society.* Princeton, NJ: Princeton University Press.

MODULE 11

Fig. 11.3 Copyright © Eric Mose, Jr. *Scientific American*, June 1961, p. 75.

MODULE 12

p. 184 Edward S. Gazsi © National Geographic Society. **Fig. 12.11** Reprinted by permission from *Nature*: Rodriguez, E., George, N., Lachaux, J-P., Martinerie, J., Renault, B., & Varela, F. (1999). Perception's shadow: Long-distance synchronization of human brain activity. *Nature, 397*, 430–433. Reprinted from Macmillan Magazines, Ltd.

MODULE 13

Fig. 13.5 Data from Bunch and Raiford. From Boring, Langfeld, and Weld *Introduction to Psychology*, 1939, p. 571.

MODULE 14

Fig. 14.3 Wysocki, C.J. & Gilbert, A.N. (1989). In C. Murphy & W.S. Cain (Eds.), *Proceedings of the conference on nutrition and the chemical senses in aging* (Annals of the New York Academy of Sciences), Vol. 561. New York: New York Academy of Sciences.

MODULE 15

Fig. 15.1 Bradley, D.R., Dumais, & Petry (1976). Reply to Cavonius. *Nature, 261*, 78. Reprinted with permission from Nature. Copyright © 1976 Macmillan Magazines Limited. **page 209,** (*bottom*) Reprinted from Redies, C., & Spillmann, L. (1981). The neon color effect in the Ehrenstein illusion. *Perception, 10*, 667–681 (fig. 5d). © 1981 by permission of Christoph Redies and Lothar Spillmann and Pion Limited, London. **Page 210** Adapted from Hoffman, D., & Richards, W. (1984). Parts of recognition. *Cognition, 63*, 29–78. Reprinted with kind permission from Elsevier Science—NL, Sara Burgerhartstraat 25, 1055 KV Amsterdam, The Netherlands. **Page 212,** (*bottom*) Adapted

MODULE 29

Fig. 29.1 Adapted from Werker, J.F. (1989). Becoming a native listener. *American Scientist, 77,* 54-59. Reprinted by permission of *American Scientist,* Journal of Sigma Xi, The Scientific Research Society. **Fig. 29.3** Johnson, J.S. & Newport, E.L. (1989). Critical period effects in second language learning: The influence of maturational state on the acquisition of English as a second language. *Cognitive Psychology, 21,* 60-99. Reprinted by permission of Academic Press, Inc. **Fig. 29.4** von Frisch, K. (1974). Decoding the language of the bee. *Science, 185,* 663-668. Copyright © 1974 American Association for the Advancement of Science.

MODULE 30

Fig. 30.1 From *Floating cities* by Stephen Wiltshire (Michael Joseph, 1991, p. 27) copyright © Stephen Wiltshire, 1991. **Fig. 30.2** Deary, I.J., & Stough, C. (1996). Intelligence and inspection time: Achievements, prospects, and problems. *American Psychologist, 51,* 599-608. Copyright © 1996 by the American Psychological Association. Reprinted by permission.

MODULE 31

Fig. 31.1 Thorndike et al. *Measurement and evaluation in psychology and education, 5/e,* © 1990, p. 364. Reprinted by permission of Prentice Hall, Upper Saddle River, New Jersey. **Fig. 31.3** Copyright © Dimitry Schidlovsky. In "Get Smart, Take a Test" by J. Hogan (Nov. 1995). *Scientific American,* p. 14. **Table 31.1** American Psychiatric Association (1994). *Diagnostic and statistical manual of mental disorders, Fourth Edition,* Washington, DC: American Psychiatric Association, 1994.

MODULE 32

Fig. 32.3 From Neisser, U. (1997). Rising scores on intelligence tests. *American Scientist, 85,* 440-447. **Fig. 32.4** Lewontin, R. (1976). Race and intelligence. In N.J. Block & G. Dworken (Eds.), *The IQ controversy: Critical readings,* New York: Pantheon. Copyright © 1976 N.J. Block & G. Dworken. Reprinted by permission. **Fig. 32.5** Reprinted with permission of authors and publishers from Vandenberg, S.G. & Kuse, A.R. Mental rotations, a group test of three-dimensional spatial visualization. *Perceptual and Motor Skills, 47,* 1978, pp. 599-604. Copyright © Perceptual and Motor Skills, 1978.

MODULE 33

Fig. 33.1 Maslow's hierarchy of needs from *Motivation and Personality (3rd edition)* by Abraham H. Maslow, revised by Robert Frager et al. Copyright © 1954, 1987. by Harper & Row Publishers, Inc. Copyright © 1970 by Abraham H. Maslow. Reprinted by permission of Addison-Wesley Educational Publishers, Inc.

MODULE 34

Fig. 34.1 Adapted from Cannon, W.B. (1929). *Bodily changes in pain, hunger, fear, and rage.* New York: Branford. **Fig. 34.3** Scale adapted from "Use of the Danish Adoption Register for the Study of Obesity and Thinness" by A. Stunkard, T. Sorensen, and F. Schulsinger in *The Genetics of Neurological and Psychiatric Disorders,* edited by S. Kety, 1980, p. 119. Copyright 1983 by Raven Press. Adapted by permission of Lippincott-Raven Publishers, Philadelphia, PA.

MODULE 35

Fig. 35.1 Byrne, D. (1982). Predicting human sexual behavior. In A.G. Kraut, *The G. Stanley Hall Lecture Series (Vol. 2).* Copyright © 1982 by the American Psychological Association. Reprinted by permission of the author and publisher.

MODULE 38

Fig. 38.3 Kring, A., M., & Gordon, A. H. (1998). Sex differences in emotion: Expression, experience, and physiology. *Journal of Personality and Social Psychology, 74,* 686–703. **Fig. 38.5** Courtesy of David Raskin, University of Utah, as shown in *Science,* June 1982, pp. 24–27. **Fig. 38.6** Kleinmuntz, B. & Szucko, J.J. (1984). A field study of the fallibility of polygraph lie detection. *Nature, 308,* 449-450. Reprinted by permission of Nature. Copyright © 1984 Macmillan Journals Limited. **Fig. 38.11** Sax, L. J. et al. (1999). *The American freshman: National norms for fall 1999.* Los Angeles: Higher Education Research Institute, UCLA. **Fig. 38.13** Diener, E., & Oishi, A. (2000). Money and happiness: Income and subjective well-being across nations. In E. Diener & E. M. Suh (Eds.). *Subjective well-being across cultures.* Cambridge MA: MIT Press.

MODULE 40

Fig. 40.1 Eysenck, S.B.G. & Eysenck, H.J. (1963). The validity of questionnaire and rating assessments of extraversion and neuroticism, and their factorial stability. *British Journal of Psychology, 54,* 51-62. Fig. 1. **Table 40.1** Adapted from McCrae, R. & Costa, P.T. Jr. (1986). Clinical assessment can benefit from recent advances in personality psychology. *American Psychologist, 41,* 1002. Copyright © 1986 American Psychological Association. Adapted by permission. **Fig. 40.2** Adapted from *The MMPI-2 in psychological treatment* by J. N. Butcher. Copyright © 1990 Oxford University Press, Inc. Used with permission of Oxford University Press, Inc.

MODULE 44

Fig. 44.1 Roper report 84-3, February 11-25, 1984. *Public Opinion,* August/September, 25. Reprinted with permission of the American Enterprise Institute for Public Policy Research, Washington, D.C. **Table 44.1** Adapted from Rapoport (1989). The biology of obsessions and compulsions. *Scientific American,* pp. 83-89.

MODULE 45

Fig. 45.1 Adapted from Magnusson, D. (1990). Personality research—challenges for the future. *European Journal of Personality, 4,* 1-17. Copyright © 1990, reprinted by permission of John Wiley & Sons, Ltd. **Fig. 45.3** Adapted from Raine & others, 1996. *Archives of General Psychiatry, 53,* p. 548.

MODULE 46

Fig. 46.7 Forgas, J.P., et al. (1984). The influence of mood on perceptions of social interactions. *Journal of Experimental and Social Psychology, 20,* 497-513. Orlando, FL: Academic Press, Journals Division. **Fig. 46.8** Adapted from Lewinsohn, P.M., et al. (1985). An integrative theory of depression. In S. Reiss and R. Bootzin (Eds.), *Theoretical issues in behavior therapy.* Orlando, FL: Academic Press.

MODULE 47

Fig. 47.1 Data from *Schizophrenia genesis: The origins of madness* by I.I. Gottesman. Copyright © 1991 by W.H. Freeman and Company. Used with permission.

MODULE 48

Fig. 48.1 Gilling, D. & Brightwell, R. (1982). *The human brain*. New York: Facts on File. Reprinted by permission of Little, Brown & Co. (UK). **Fig. 48.5** Rabin, A.S. et al. (1986). Aggregate outcome and follow-up results following self-control therapy for depression. Paper presented at the American Psychological Association convention.

MODULE 49

Fig. 49.2 Adapted from Smith, M.L. et al. (1980). *The benefits of psychotherapy* (p. 88) Baltimore, MD: Johns Hopkins University Press. Reprinted by permission.

MODULE 51

Fig. 51.5 Weiss, J.M. (1977). Psychological and behavioral influences on gastrointestinal lesions in animal models. In *Psychopathology: Experimental models* by Maser and Seligman. Copyright © 1977 by Martin E.P. Seligman and Jack Maser. Used with permission of W.H. Freeman and Company.

MODULE 52

Fig. 52.1 Adapted from McCann, I.L., & Holmes, D.S. (1984). Influence of aerobic exercise on depression. *Journal of Personality and Social Psychology, 46*, 1142-1147. Copyright © 1984 by the American Psychological Association. Adapted by permission of the authors. **Fig. 52.3** From *Treating Type A Behavior and Your Heart* by Meyer Friedman, M.D. and Diane Ulmer, R.N., M.S. Copyright © 1984 by Meyer Friedman. Reprinted by permission of Alfred A. Knopf, Inc. **Fig. 52.6** From Strawbridge, W. J. (1999). Mortality and religious involvement: A review and critique of the results, the methods, and the measures. Paper presented at a Harvard University conference on religion and health, sponsored by the National Institute for Healthcare Research and the John Templeton Foundation; and from Strawbridge, W. J., Cohen, R. D., & Shema, S. J. (1997). Frequent attendance at religious services and mortality over 28 years. *American Journal of Public Health, 87*, 957–961. **Fig. 52.12** Johnston, L. D., Backman, J. G., & O'Malley, P. M. (1999, December 17). Drug trends in 1999 among American teens are mixed. Ann Arbor: News and Information Services, University of Michigan. **Fig. 52.14** From Calle, E.E., Thun, M. J., Petrelli, J. M., Rodriguez, C., & Health, C. W., Jr. (1999). Body-mass index and mortality in a prospective cohort of U.S. Adults. *New England Journal of Medicine, 341*, 1097–1105. **Fig. 52.16** Bray, G.A. (1969). Effect of caloric restriction on energy expenditure in obese patients. *Lancet, 2*, 397-398. Copyright © 1969 by the Lancet Ltd. **Fig. 52.17** Adapted from Brownell, K.D. & Jeffrey, R.W. (1987). Improving long-term weight loss: Pushing the limits of treatment. *Behavior Therapy, 18*, 353-374. Copyright © 1987 by the Association for Advancement of Behavior Therapy. Reprinted by permission of the publisher. **Fig. 52.18** From Andersen, R. E., Crespo, C. J., Bartlett, S.J., Cheskin. L.J., & Pratt, M. (1998). Relationship of physical activity and television watching with body weight and level of fatness among children. *Journal of the American Medical Association, 279*, 938–942; and from Deitz, W. H., Jr., & Gortmaker, S. L. (1985). Do we fatten our children at the television set? Obesity and television viewing in children and adolescents. *Pediatrics, 75*, 807–812.

MODULE 55

Fig. 55.1 Niemi, R. G., Moeller, J., & Smith T. W. (1989). *Trends in public opinion: A compendium of survey data*. New York: Greenwood Press. Reprinted with permission of Greenwood Publishing Group, Inc., Westport CT; Smith, T. W. (1994). Personal communication., Data from General Social Survey, National Opinion Research Center, University of Chicago. **Fig. 55.3** Anderson, C. A., & Anderson D. C. (1984). Ambient temperature and violent crime: Tests on the linear and curvilinear hypotheses. *Journal of Personality and Social Psychology, 46*, 91–97. Copyright © 1984 American Psychological Association. Reprinted by permission of the authors. **Fig. 55.7** Darley, J.M., & Latane, B. (1968, December). When will people help in a crisis? *Psychology Today*, pp. 54–57, 70–71. Copyright © 1968 Sussex Publishers, Inc. Reprinted by permission of *Psychology Today*. **Fig. 55.8** Darley, J. M., & Latane, B. (1968). Bystander intervention in emergencies: Diffusion of responsibility. *Journal of Personality and Social Psychology, 8*, 377–383. Copyright © 1968 American Psychological Association. Reprinted by permission of the authors.

Name Index

Subject Index